FIFTH EDITION

Programming iOS 8

Matt Neuburg

Beijing · Cambridge · Farnham · Köln · Sebastopol · Tokyo

Programming iOS 8, Fifth Edition

by Matt Neuburg

Printed in the United States of America.

Published by O'Reilly Media, Inc., 1005 Gravenstein Highway North, Sebastopol, CA 95472.

O'Reilly books may be purchased for educational, business, or sales promotional use. Online editions are also available for most titles (*http://safaribooksonline.com*). For more information, contact our corporate/institutional sales department: (800) 998-9938 or *corporate@oreilly.com*.

Editor: Rachel Roumeliotis	**Cover Designer:** Randy Comer
Production Editor: Kristen Brown	**Interior Designer:** David Futato
Proofreader: O'Reilly Production Services	**Illustrator:** Matt Neuburg
Indexer: Matt Neuburg	

May 2011:	First Edition
March 2012:	Second Edition
March 2013:	Third Edition
December 2013:	Fourth Edition
December 2014:	Fifth Edition

Revision History for the Fifth Edition:

2014-11-21:   First release

2015-05-01:   Second release

See *http://oreilly.com/catalog/errata.csp?isbn=9781491908730* for release details.

The O'Reilly logo is a registered trademark of O'Reilly Media, Inc. *Programming iOS 8*, the image of a kingbird, and related trade dress are trademarks of O'Reilly Media, Inc.

Many of the designations used by manufacturers and sellers to distinguish their products are claimed as trademarks. Where those designations appear in this book, and O'Reilly Media, Inc., was aware of a trademark claim, the designations have been printed in caps or initial caps.

While the publisher and the author have used good faith efforts to ensure that the information and instructions contained in this work are accurate, the publisher and the author disclaim all responsibility for errors or omissions, including without limitation responsibility for damages resulting from the use of or reliance on this work. Use of the information and instructions contained in this work is at your own risk. If any code samples or other technology this work contains or describes is subject to open source licenses or the intellectual property rights of others, it is your responsibility to ensure that your use thereof complies with such licenses and/or rights.

ISBN: 978-1-491-90873-0

[LSI]

Table of Contents

Part II. Interface

Part IV. Final Topics

Preface

Aut lego vel scribo; doceo scrutorve sophian.

—Sedulius Scottus

On June 2, 2014, Apple's WWDC keynote address ended with a shocking announcement: "We have a new programming language." This was surprising in several ways:

- Apple buried the lede (or, looking at it another way, they saved the biggest until last).
- Like the weather, everyone had long talked about the need for a new language to replace Objective-C, but no one believed Apple would ever actually *do* anything about it.
- How on earth had Apple done all the groundwork needed to design, prepare, and implement a whole new programming language without the least rumor leaking out?

Having picked themselves up off the floor, developers immediately began to examine this new language — Swift — studying it, critiquing it, and deciding whether to adopt it. My own first move was to translate all my existing iOS apps into Swift; this was enough to convince me that, for all its faults, Swift deserved to be adopted by new students of iOS programming, and that my books, therefore, should henceforth assume that readers are using Swift.

Therefore, Swift is the programming language used throughout this book. Nevertheless, the reader will also need some awareness of Objective-C (including C). There are two chief reasons for this:

- The Foundation and Cocoa APIs, the built-in commands with which your code must interact in order to make anything happen on an iOS device, are still written in C and Objective-C. In order to interact with them, you have to know what those languages would expect. For example, in order to pass a Swift array where an

NSArray is expected, you need to know what consitutes an object acceptable as an element of an Objective-C NSArray.

- Swift can't do everything that C and Objective-C can do. Apple likes to claim that Swift can "access all of the Cocoa Touch frameworks" and that it constitutes "a complete replacement for both the C and Objective-C languages" — I'm quoting from the Xcode 6 release notes — but the truth is that Swift can't interface directly with every facet of the Cocoa Touch APIs. Swift can't form a C function or obtain the address of such a function; Swift can't declare a property `@dynamic` in the Objective-C sense; in certain situations, Swift can be prohibitively slow in comparison to equivalent Objective-C code; and so on. Thus, I occasionally show some Objective-C code in this edition, in order to do things that Swift alone can't accomplish.

Because Swift is new, I have had to settle on my own conventions for presenting and describing code. The most important question has been how to state the name of a method. My solution is to give *the method's Objective-C name*. As an example, what is the name of the method that you call when you set a value using key–value coding? The actual call, in Swift, would be something like this:

```
someObject.setValue(someValue, forKey:"someKey")
```

But when I *give the name* of the method being called here, that name is `setValue:forKey:`. This choice has several advantages:

- It is clear, compact, and predictable, being formed according to perfectly consistent and well-established rules.

- For those who have been programming in Objective-C all these years, it's what we're used to. The way Objective-C methods are named is a thoroughly entrenched convention; even Swift programmers must accommodate themselves to seeing Objective-C method names plastered all over the Internet and Apple's own documentation.

- That name *is* in fact its name as far as Objective-C and the Cocoa APIs are concerned, and even in Swift you would need to know this. For example, if you wanted to specify this method when providing its name as a selector parameter (or as a string representing a selector), it is the Objective-C name that you would have to provide.

- The translation from the Objective-C name into practical Swift syntax is mechanical and unambiguous — the first colon is replaced by parentheses embracing the first parameter plus the names and values of any remaining parameters — and is something that every Swift programmer needs to know how to do.

Similarly, I will speak of the `setValue:` parameter, even though, in an actual Swift method call, the name of that parameter appears before the parentheses, with no colon.

The grand exception to this rule is my treatment of initializers. Here, the difference between Objective-C and Swift is greater than a simple shorthand can readily encompass, so I give the initializer's name *as you would implement it*. For example, in Objective-C, the default initializer for a UIView is `initWithFrame:`. In this book, I will call that initializer `init(frame:)`. The same thing applies to what in Objective-C would be class factory methods with a corresponding initializer: when I want to mention what in Objective-C would be the UIImage class factory method `imageNamed:`, I'll call it `init(named:)`.

This treatment of initializer names has the great virtue that the name clarifies instantly that such a method *is* an initializer. Swift effectively abolishes class factory methods and brings such methods into the fold of formal initializers; my treatment of their names is a way of supporting and adopting that innovation.

Again, this convention requires some mental translation on the reader's part, because in Swift the way you would name an initializer when you *implement* it is not the same as the way you would name it when you *call* it. If you were to override this method in a UIView subclass, you'd override `init(frame:)`; but if you were to *call* it to create a new UIView, you'd say `UIView(frame:)`. This mental translation, however, is hardly objectionable, as it is a practical fact to which every Swift user is already habituated.

So much for Swift. A new language is big news, but Swift is not the only big news connected with iOS 8. Nor is it the only welcome news. I've been arguing for years that Apple needs to check the rampant growth and evolution of the basic Cocoa Touch APIs and concentrate, for one release at least, on *rationalizing* the changes that have accumulated, often seemingly by random accretion, over the years. iOS 8 appears to do exactly that. To give just a couple of obvious examples:

- An app, when it rotates to compensate for a change in the orientation of the device, no longer does so by applying a transform to the root view. Instead, in iOS 8, rotation is a feature of the app *as a whole* — the window itself, and indeed the screen, is resized.

- A popover, in iOS 8, is just a variety of presented view controller. Not only does this vastly simplify popover management (whose wretchedness I've been complaining about since the first edition of this book), but also it eliminates the need, in a universal app, for large chunks of conditional code depending on what type of device the app runs on: a presented view controller is legal everywhere. Similarly, alerts and action sheets are now forms of presented view controller.

Such rationalization permeates iOS 8, and I have eagerly adopted it, even where the prior approach is not yet deprecated. You *could* still create popovers and alerts the way we created them in iOS 7 and before; and obviously if you wanted your code to run on iOS 7 as well as iOS 8, you'd have to. But in this edition I behave, in effect, as if the old way didn't exist. It's the business of this edition to teach iOS 8, not to help you write backwards-compatible code; if you want to know how to deal with popovers (or anything else) in iOS 7 or before, consult an earlier edition of the book.

This book retains the structure of the previous edition. Like Homer's *Iliad*, it begins in the middle of the story, with the reader jumping with all four feet into views and view controllers, and with a knowledge of the language and the Xcode IDE already presupposed. As in *Programming iOS 7*, discussion of the programming language, the Xcode IDE (including the nature of nibs, outlets, and actions, and the mechanics of nib loading), and the fundamental conventions, classes, and architectures of the Cocoa Touch framework (including delegation, the responder chain, key–value coding, memory management, and so on), has been expunged and relegated to a different book. This is material that constituted Chapters 1–13 of earlier editions, before *Programming iOS 7*, but whose presence was deemed to be making this book unwieldy in size and scope.

Here's a summary of this book's major sections:

- Part I describes *views*, the fundamental units of an iOS app's interface. Views are what the user can see and touch in an iOS app. To make something appear before the user's eyes, you need a view. To let the user interact with your app, you need a view. This part of the book explains how views are created, arranged, drawn, layered, animated, and touched.

- Part II starts by discussing *view controllers*. Perhaps the most remarkable and important feature of iOS programming, view controllers enable views to come and go coherently within the interface, thus allowing a single-windowed app running on what may be a tiny screen to contain multiple screens of material. This part of the book talks about all the ways in which view controllers can be manipulated in order to make their views appear. It also describes *every kind of view* provided by the Cocoa framework — the built-in building blocks with which you'll construct an app's interface.

- Part III surveys the most important secondary *frameworks* provided by iOS. These are clumps of code, sometimes with built-in interface, that are not part of your app by default, but are there for the asking if you need them, allowing you to work with such things as sound, video, user libraries, mail, maps, and the device's sensors.

- Part IV wraps up the book with some miscellaneous but important topics: files, networking, threading, and how to implement Undo.

- Appendix A summarizes the most important lifetime event messages sent to your app delegate.

- Appendix B, new in this edition, appends some useful Swift utility functions. You should keep an eye on this appendix, consulting it whenever a mysterious method name appears. For instance, my example code frequently uses my `delay` function, which embraces `dispatch_after` with a convenient shorthand; when I use `delay` and you don't know what it is, consult this appendix.

Someone who has read this book will, I believe, be capable of writing a real-life iOS app, and to do so with a clear understanding of what he or she is doing and where the app is going as it grows and develops. The book itself doesn't show how to write any particularly interesting iOS apps (though it is backed by dozens of example projects that you can download from my GitHub site, *http://github.com/mattneub/Programming-iOS-Book-Examples*), but it does constantly use my own real apps and real programming situations to illustrate and motivate its explanations.

Just as important, this book is intended to prepare you for your own further explorations. In the case of some topics, especially in Parts III and IV, I guide you past the initial barrier of no knowledge into an understanding of the topic, its concepts, its capabilities, and its documentation, along with some code examples; but the topic itself may be so huge that there is room only to introduce it here. Your feet, nevertheless, will now be set firmly on the path, and you will know enough that you can now proceed further down that path on your own whenever the need or interest arises.

Indeed, there is *always* more to learn about iOS. iOS is vast! It is all too easy to find areas of iOS that have had to be ruled outside the scope of this book. In Part IV, for example, I peek at Core Data, and demonstrate its use in code, but a true study of Core Data would require an entire book of its own (and such books exist); so, having opened the door, I quickly close it again, lest this book suddenly double in size. By the same token, many areas of iOS are not treated at all in this book:

OpenGL
> An open source C library for drawing, including 3D drawing, that takes full advantage of graphics hardware. This is often the most efficient way to draw, especially when animation is involved. iOS incorporates a simplified version of OpenGL called OpenGL ES. See Apple's *OpenGL Programming Guide for iOS*. Open GL interface configuration, texture loading, shading, and calculation are simplified by the GLKit framework; see the *GLKit Framework Reference*. New in iOS 8 are the Metal classes, which you'll also want to investigate.

Sprite Kit
> Sprite Kit provides a built-in framework for designing 2D animated games.

Scene Kit
> New in iOS 8, Scene Kit is ported from OS X, making it much easier to create 3D games and interactive graphics.

Accelerate
> Certain computation-intensive processes will benefit from the vector-based Accelerate framework. See the *vDSP Programming Guide*.

Game Kit
> The Game Kit framework covers three areas that can enhance your user's game experience: Wireless or Bluetooth communication directly between devices (peer-

to-peer); voice communication across an existing network connection; and Game Center, which facilitates these and many other aspects of interplayer communication, such as posting and viewing high scores and setting up competitions. See the *Game Kit Programming Guide*.

Advertising

The iAD framework lets your free app attempt to make money by displaying advertisements provided by Apple. See the *iAD Programming Guide*.

Newsstand

Your app may represent a subscription to something like a newspaper or magazine. See the *Newsstand Kit Framework Reference*.

Printing

See the "Printing" chapter of the *Drawing and Printing Guide for iOS*.

Security

This book does not discuss security topics such as keychains, certificates, and encryption. See the *Security Overview* and the Security framework.

Accessibility

VoiceOver assists visually impaired users by describing the interface aloud. To participate, views must be configured to describe themselves usefully. Built-in views already do this to a large extent, and you can extend this functionality. See the *Accessibility Programming Guide for iOS*.

Telephone

The Core Telephony framework lets your app get information about a particular cellular carrier and call.

Pass Kit

The Pass Kit framework allows creation of downloadable passes to go into the user's Passbook app. See the *Passbook Programming Guide*.

Health Kit

New in iOS 8, the Health Kit framework lets your app obtain, store, share, and present data and statistics related to body activity and exercise. See the *HealthKit Framework Reference*.

External accessories

The user can attach an external accessory to the device, either directly via USB or wirelessly via Bluetooth. Your app can communicate with such an accessory. See *External Accessory Programming Topics*. New in iOS 8, the Home Kit framework lets the user communicate with devices in the physical world, such as light switches and door locks. See the *HomeKit Framework Reference*.

Handoff

New in iOS 8, Handoff permits your app to post to the user's iCloud account a record of what the user is doing, so that the user can switch to another copy of your app on another device and resume doing the same thing. See the *Handoff Programming Guide.*

Versions

This book was originally geared to iOS 8.1 and Xcode 6.1, both of which became publicly available in October, 2014. Subsequently, it was updated for iOS 8.3 and Swift 1.2, which is part of Xcode 6.3, released in April, 2015. Because of changes in the Swift language and in the Swift version of the Cocoa APIs, most of the code now will *not* compile in any version of Xcode earlier than 6.3!

In general, only very minimal attention is given to earlier versions of iOS and Xcode. As I've already said, it is not my intention to embrace in this book any detailed knowledge about earlier versions of the software, which is, after all, readily and compendiously available in my earlier books. The book does contain, nevertheless, a few words of advice about backward compatibility, and now and then I will call out a particularly noteworthy change from earlier system versions, especially where your existing iOS 7 code is likely to break or behave differently when compiled against iOS 8.

Xcode 6 has eliminated some of the templates that you choose from when creating a new project. The loss of the Utility Application template is a pity, because it embodied and illustrated the standard techniques for passing data to and from a presented view controller; but it hasn't affected this book, because the template itself had become so ugly and crufty that in the previous edition I didn't mention it in any case. The loss of the Empty Application template, on the other hand, is severe; it is, after all, perfectly reasonable to write an app without a storyboard (several of my own apps are structured in that way). Accordingly, near the start of the first chapter, I have given instructions for turning a Single View Application–based template into something similar to what the Empty Application template would have given you. Also, although I treat storyboards as the primary Interface Builder design milieu, I still do also assume that you know how to make and work with a *.xib* file when that is what you need or prefer.

At the time of this writing, Apple was still making frequent adjustments to the Swift language and to the way the Objective-C APIs are bridged to it. I have tried to keep my code up-to-date, but please make allowances, and be prepared to compensate, for the possibility that my examples may contain slight occasional impedance mismatches, such as the lack of a needed Optional unwrap or the presence of a superfluous one.

Screenshots of Xcode were originally taken using Xcode 6.1 under OS X 10.9 Mavericks, and have *not* been updated to Xcode 6.3, which runs only under OS X 10.10 and later. This means that your interface will naturally look slightly different from the screenshots, but this difference will be minimal and shouldn't cause any confusion.

Acknowledgments

My thanks go first and foremost to the people at O'Reilly Media who have made writing a book so delightfully easy: Rachel Roumeliotis, Sarah Schneider, Kristen Brown, Dan Fauxsmith, and Adam Witwer come particularly to mind. And let's not forget my first and long-standing editor, Brian Jepson, who had nothing whatever to do with this edition, but whose influence is present throughout.

As in the past, I have been greatly aided by some fantastic software, whose excellences I have appreciated at every moment of the process of writing this book. I should like to mention, in particular:

- git (*http://git-scm.com*)
- SourceTree (*http://www.sourcetreeapp.com*)
- TextMate (*http://macromates.com*)
- AsciiDoc (*http://www.methods.co.nz/asciidoc*)
- BBEdit (*http://barebones.com/products/bbedit/*)
- Snapz Pro X (*http://www.ambrosiasw.com*)
- GraphicConverter (*http://www.lemkesoft.com*)
- OmniGraffle (*http://www.omnigroup.com*)

The book was typed and edited entirely on my faithful Unicomp Model M keyboard (*http://pckeyboard.com*), without which I could never have done so much writing over so long a period so painlessly. For more about my physical work environment, see *http://matt.neuburg.usesthis.com*.

From the Programming iOS 4 Preface

A programming framework has a kind of personality, an overall flavor that provides an insight into the goals and mindset of those who created it. When I first encountered Cocoa Touch, my assessment of its personality was: "Wow, the people who wrote this are really clever!" On the one hand, the number of built-in interface objects was severely and deliberately limited; on the other hand, the power and flexibility of some of those objects, especially such things as UITableView, was greatly enhanced over their OS X counterparts. Even more important, Apple created a particularly brilliant way (UIViewController) to help the programmer make entire blocks of interface come and go and supplant one another in a controlled, hierarchical manner, thus allowing that tiny iPhone display to unfold virtually into multiple interface worlds within a single app without the user becoming lost or confused.

The popularity of the iPhone, with its largely free or very inexpensive apps, and the subsequent popularity of the iPad, have brought and will continue to bring into the fold many new programmers who see programming for these devices as worthwhile and doable, even though they may not have felt the same way about OS X. Apple's own annual WWDC developer conventions have reflected this trend, with their emphasis shifted from OS X to iOS instruction.

The widespread eagerness to program iOS, however, though delightful on the one hand, has also fostered a certain tendency to try to run without first learning to walk. iOS gives the programmer mighty powers that can seem as limitless as imagination itself, but it also has fundamentals. I often see questions online from programmers who are evidently deep into the creation of some interesting app, but who are stymied in a way that reveals quite clearly that they are unfamiliar with the basics of the very world in which they are so happily cavorting.

It is this state of affairs that has motivated me to write this book, which is intended to ground the reader in the fundamentals of iOS. I love Cocoa and have long wished to write about it, but it is iOS and its popularity that has given me a proximate excuse to do so. Here I have attempted to marshal and expound, in what I hope is a pedagogically helpful and instructive yet ruthlessly Euclidean and logical order, the principles and elements on which sound iOS programming rests. My hope, as with my previous books, is that you will both read this book cover to cover (learning something new often enough to keep you turning the pages) and keep it by you as a handy reference.

This book is not intended to disparage Apple's own documentation and example projects. They are wonderful resources and have become more wonderful as time goes on. I have depended heavily on them in the preparation of this book. But I also find that they don't fulfill the same function as a reasoned, ordered presentation of the facts. The online documentation must make assumptions as to how much you already know; it can't guarantee that you'll approach it in a given order. And online documentation is more suitable to reference than to instruction. A fully written example, no matter how well commented, is difficult to follow; it demonstrates, but it does not teach.

A book, on the other hand, has numbered chapters and sequential pages; I can assume you know views before you know view controllers for the simple reason that Part I precedes Part II. And along with facts, I also bring to the table a degree of experience, which I try to communicate to you. Throughout this book you'll find me referring to "common beginner mistakes"; in most cases, these are mistakes that I have made myself, in addition to seeing others make them. I try to tell you what the pitfalls are because I assume that, in the course of things, you will otherwise fall into them just as naturally as I did as I was learning. You'll also see me construct many examples piece by piece or extract and explain just one tiny portion of a larger app. It is not a massive finished program that teaches programming, but an exposition of the thought process that developed that program. It is this thought process, more than anything else, that I hope you will gain from reading this book.

Conventions Used in This Book

The following typographical conventions are used in this book:

Italic
> Indicates new terms, URLs, email addresses, filenames, and file extensions.

`Constant width`
> Used for program listings, as well as within paragraphs to refer to program elements such as variable or function names, databases, data types, environment variables, statements, and keywords.

`Constant width bold`
> Shows commands or other text that should be typed literally by the user.

`Constant width italic`
> Shows text that should be replaced with user-supplied values or by values determined by context.

 This element signifies a tip or suggestion.

 This element signifies a general note.

 This element indicates a warning or caution.

Using Code Examples

Supplemental material (code examples, exercises, etc.) is available for download at *https://github.com/mattneub/Programming-iOS-Book-Examples*.

This book is here to help you get your job done. In general, if example code is offered with this book, you may use it in your programs and documentation. You do not need to contact us for permission unless you're reproducing a significant portion of the code. For example, writing a program that uses several chunks of code from this book does not require permission. Selling or distributing a CD-ROM of examples from O'Reilly books does require permission. Answering a question by citing this book and quoting example code does not require permission. Incorporating a significant amount of example code from this book into your product's documentation does require permission.

We appreciate, but do not require, attribution. An attribution usually includes the title, author, publisher, and ISBN. For example: "*Programming iOS 8* by Matt Neuburg (O'Reilly). Copyright 2015 Matt Neuburg, 978-1-491-90873-0."

If you feel your use of code examples falls outside fair use or the permission given above, feel free to contact us at *permissions@oreilly.com*.

Safari® Books Online

 Safari Books Online is an on-demand digital library that delivers expert content in both book and video form from the world's leading authors in technology and business.

Technology professionals, software developers, web designers, and business and creative professionals use Safari Books Online as their primary resource for research, problem solving, learning, and certification training.

Safari Books Online offers a range of plans and pricing for enterprise, government, education, and individuals.

Members have access to thousands of books, training videos, and prepublication manuscripts in one fully searchable database from publishers like O'Reilly Media, Prentice Hall Professional, Addison-Wesley Professional, Microsoft Press, Sams, Que, Peachpit Press, Focal Press, Cisco Press, John Wiley & Sons, Syngress, Morgan Kaufmann, IBM Redbooks, Packt, Adobe Press, FT Press, Apress, Manning, New Riders, McGraw-Hill, Jones & Bartlett, Course Technology, and hundreds more. For more information about Safari Books Online, please visit us online.

How to Contact Us

Please address comments and questions concerning this book to the publisher:

O'Reilly Media, Inc.
1005 Gravenstein Highway North
Sebastopol, CA 95472
800-998-9938 (in the United States or Canada)
707-829-0515 (international or local)
707-829-0104 (fax)

We have a web page for this book, where we list errata, examples, and any additional information. You can access this page at *http://bit.ly/programmingiOS8_5E*.

To comment or ask technical questions about this book, send email to *bookquestions@oreilly.com*.

For more information about our books, courses, conferences, and news, see our website at *http://www.oreilly.com*.

Find us on Facebook: *http://facebook.com/oreilly*

Follow us on Twitter: *http://twitter.com/oreillymedia*

Watch us on YouTube: *http://www.youtube.com/oreillymedia*

PART I

Views

The things that appear in your app's interface are, ultimately, *views*. A view is a unit of your app that knows how to draw itself. A view also knows how to sense that the user has touched it. Views are what your user sees on the screen, and what your user interacts with by touching the screen. Thus, views are the primary constituent of an app's visible, touchable manifestation. They *are* your app's interface. So it's going to be crucial to know how views work.

- Chapter 1 discusses views in their most general aspect — their hierarchy, visibility, and position, including an explanation of autolayout.

- Chapter 2 is about drawing. A view knows how to draw itself; this chapter explains how to tell a view what you want it to draw, from displaying an existing image to constructing a drawing in code.

- Chapter 3 explains about layers. The drawing power of a view comes ultimately from its layer. To put it another way, a layer is effectively the aspect of a view that knows how to draw — with even more power.

- Chapter 4 tells about animation. An iOS app's interface isn't generally static; it's lively. Much of that liveliness comes from animation. iOS gives you great power to animate your interface with remarkable ease; that power, it turns out, resides ultimately in layers.

- Chapter 5 is about touches. A view knows how to sense that the user is touching it. This chapter explains the iOS view-based mechanisms for sensing and responding to touches, with details on how touches are routed to the appropriate view and how you can customize that routing.

CHAPTER 1

Views

A *view* (an object whose class is UIView or a subclass of UIView) knows how to draw itself into a rectangular area of the interface. Your app has a visible interface thanks to views. Creating and configuring a view can be extremely simple: "Set it and forget it." For example, you can drag an interface object, such as a UIButton, into a view in the nib editor; when the app runs, the button appears, and works properly. But you can also manipulate views in powerful ways, in real time. Your code can do some or all of the view's drawing of itself (Chapter 2); it can make the view appear and disappear, move, resize itself, and display many other physical changes, possibly with animation (Chapter 4).

A view is also a responder (UIView is a subclass of UIResponder). This means that a view is subject to user interactions, such as taps and swipes. Thus, views are the basis not only of the interface that the user sees, but also of the interface that the user touches (Chapter 5). Organizing your views so that the correct view reacts to a given touch allows you to allocate your code neatly and efficiently.

The *view hierarchy* is the chief mode of view organization. A view can have subviews; a subview has exactly one immediate superview. Thus there is a tree of views. This hierarchy allows views to come and go together. If a view is removed from the interface, its subviews are removed; if a view is hidden (made invisible), its subviews are hidden; if a view is moved, its subviews move with it; and other changes in a view are likewise shared with its subviews. The view hierarchy is also the basis of, though it is not identical to, the responder chain.

A view may come from a nib, or you can create it in code. On balance, neither approach is to be preferred over the other; it depends on your needs and inclinations and on the overall architecture of your app.

The Window

The top of the view hierarchy is the app's window. It is an instance of UIWindow (or your own subclass thereof), which is a UIView subclass. Your app should have *exactly one main window*. It is created at launch time and is never destroyed or replaced. It occupies the entire screen and forms the background to, and is the ultimate superview of, all your other visible views. Other views are visible by virtue of being subviews, at some depth, of your app's window.

 If your app can display views on an external screen, you'll create an additional UIWindow to contain those views; but in this chapter I'll behave as if there were just one screen, the device's own screen, and just one window. I repeat: if there is just one screen, your app should create just one UIWindow. You may encounter online tutorials that advise explicit creation of a second UIWindow as a way of making content appear in front of the app's main interface; *such statements are wrong* and should be disregarded. To make content appear in front of the interface, add a view, not another entire window.

The window must fill the device's screen. Therefore, its size and position must be identical to the size and position of the screen. This is done by setting the window's frame to the screen's bounds as the window is instantiated. (I'll explain later in this chapter what "frame" and "bounds" are.) If you're using a main storyboard, that's taken care of for you automatically behind the scenes by the UIApplicationMain function as the app launches; but an app without a main storyboard is possible, and in that case you'd need to set the window's frame yourself, very early in the app's lifetime, like this:

```
let w = UIWindow(frame: UIScreen.mainScreen().bounds)
```

The window must also persist for the lifetime of the app. To make this happen, the app delegate class has a window property with a strong retain policy. As the app launches, the UIApplicationMain function instantiates the app delegate class and retains the resulting instance. This is the app delegate instance; it is never released, so it persists for the lifetime of the app. The window instance is then assigned to the app delegate instance's window property; therefore it, too, persists for the lifetime of the app.

You will typically not put any view content manually and directly inside your main window. Instead, you'll obtain a view controller and assign it to the main window's rootViewController property. Once again, if you're using a main storyboard, this is done automatically behind the scenes; the view controller in question will be your storyboard's initial view controller.

When a view controller becomes the main window's rootViewController, its main view (its view) is made the one and only immediate subview of your main window — the main window's *root view*. All other views in your main window will be subviews of the root view. Thus, the root view is the highest object in the view hierarchy that the user will usually see. There might be just a chance, under certain circumstances, that the user will catch a glimpse of the window, behind the root view; for this reason, you may want to assign the main window a reasonable backgroundColor. But this seems unlikely, and in general you'll have no reason to change anything about the window itself.

Your app's interface is not visible until the window, which contains it, is made the app's key window. This is done by calling the UIWindow instance method makeKeyAnd-Visible.

Let's summarize how all the initial creation, configuration, and showing of the main window happens. There are two cases to consider:

App with a main storyboard
> If your app has a main storyboard, as specified by its *Info.plist* key "Main storyboard file base name" (UIMainStoryboardFile) — the default for all Xcode 6 app templates — then UIApplicationMain instantiates UIWindow, sets its frame correctly, and assigns that instance to the app delegate's window property. It also instantiates the storyboard's initial view controller and assigns that instance to the window's rootViewController property. All of that happens *before* the app delegate's application:didFinishLaunchingWithOptions: is called (Appendix A).
>
> Finally, UIApplicationMain calls makeKeyAndVisible to display your app's interface. This in turn automatically causes the root view controller to obtain its main view (typically by loading it from a nib), which the window adds as its own root view. That happens *after* application:didFinishLaunchingWithOptions: is called.

App without a main storyboard
> If your app has no main storyboard, then creation and configuration of the window must be done in some other way. Typically, it is done in code. No Xcode 6 app template lacks a main storyboard, but if you start with, say, the Single View Application template, you can experiment as follows:
>
> 1. Edit the target. In the General pane, select "Main" in the Main Interface field and delete it (and press Tab to set this change).
> 2. Delete *Main.storyboard* and *ViewController.swift* from the project.
> 3. Delete the entire content of *AppDelegate.swift*.

You now have a project with an app target but no storyboard and no code. To make a minimal working app, you need to edit *AppDelegate.swift* in such a way as to recreate the AppDelegate class with just enough code to create and show the window, as shown in Example 1-1. The result is a minimal working app with an empty white window; you can prove to yourself that your code is creating the window by changing its `backgroundColor` to something else (such as `UIColor.redColor()`) and running the app again. We didn't set a root view controller, so you will also see a warning about that in the console ("Application windows are expected to have a root view controller at the end of application launch"); I'll explain in a moment what to do about that.

Example 1-1. An App Delegate class with no storyboard

```
import UIKit
@UIApplicationMain
class AppDelegate : UIResponder, UIApplicationDelegate {
    var window : UIWindow?
    func application(application: UIApplication,
        didFinishLaunchingWithOptions launchOptions: [NSObject: AnyObject]?)
        -> Bool {
            self.window = UIWindow(frame:UIScreen.mainScreen().bounds)
            self.window!.backgroundColor = UIColor.whiteColor()
            self.window!.makeKeyAndVisible()
            return true
    }
}
```

It is extremely improbable that you would ever need to subclass UIWindow. If, however, you wanted to create a UIWindow subclass and make an instance of that subclass your app's main window, then how you proceed depends on how the window is instantiated in the first place:

App with a main storyboard

As the app launches, after `UIApplicationMain` has instantiated the app delegate, it asks the app delegate instance for the value of its `window` property. If that value is nil, `UIApplicationMain` instantiates UIWindow and assigns that instance to the app delegate's `window` property. If that value is *not* nil, `UIApplicationMain` leaves it alone and uses it as the app's main window. Therefore, to make your app's main window be an instance of your UIWindow subclass, you'll make that instance the default value for the app delegate's `window` property, like this:

```
lazy var window : UIWindow? = {
    return MyWindow(frame: UIScreen.mainScreen().bounds)
}()
```

App without a main storyboard

You're already instantiating UIWindow and assigning that instance to the app delegate's `self.window` property, in code (Example 1-1). So instantiate your UIWindow subclass instead:

```
// ...
self.window = MyWindow(frame:UIScreen.mainScreen().bounds)
// ...
```

Once the app is running, there are various ways to refer to the window:

- If a UIView is in the interface, it automatically has a reference to the window through its own `window` property.

  You can also use a UIView's `window` property as a way of asking whether it is ultimately embedded in the window; if it isn't, its `window` property is nil. A UIView whose `window` property is nil cannot be visible to the user.

- The app delegate instance maintains a reference to the window through its `window` property. You can get a reference to the app delegate from elsewhere through the shared application's `delegate` property, and through it you can refer to the window:

  ```
  let w = UIApplication.sharedApplication().delegate!.window!!
  ```

  If you prefer something less generic (and requiring less extreme unwrapping of Optionals), cast the `delegate` explicitly to your app delegate class:

  ```
  let w = (UIApplication.sharedApplication().delegate as! AppDelegate).window!
  ```

- The shared application maintains a reference to the window through its `keyWindow` property:

  ```
  let w = UIApplication.sharedApplication().keyWindow!
  ```

  That reference, however, is slightly volatile, because the system can create temporary windows and interpose them as the application's key window.

Experimenting With Views

In the course of this and subsequent chapters, you may want to experiment with views in a project of your own. Since view controllers aren't formally explained until Chapter 6, I'll just outline two simple approaches.

One way is to start your project with the Single View Application template. It gives you a main storyboard containing one scene containing one view controller instance containing its own main view; when the app runs, that view controller will become the app's main window's `rootViewController`, and its main view will become the window's root view. You can drag a view from the Object library into the main view as a subview, and it will be instantiated in the interface when the app runs. Alternatively, you can create views and add them to the interface in code; the simplest place to do this, for now, is the view controller's `viewDidLoad` method, which has a reference to the view controller's main view as `self.view`. For example:

```
override func viewDidLoad() {
    super.viewDidLoad()
    let mainview = self.view
    let v = UIView(frame:CGRectMake(100,100,50,50))
    v.backgroundColor = UIColor.redColor() // small red square
    mainview.addSubview(v) // add it to main view
}
```

Alternatively, you can start with the empty application without a storyboard that I described in Example 1-1. It has no *.xib* or *.storyboard* file, so your views will have to be created entirely in code. As I mentioned a moment ago, we did not assign any view controller to the window's `rootViewController` property, which causes the runtime to complain when the application is launched. A simple solution is to add a line of code in the app delegate's `application:didFinishLaunchingWithOptions:`, creating a minimal root view controller. We can then access its main view through its `view` property. For example:

```
func application(application: UIApplication,
    didFinishLaunchingWithOptions launchOptions: [NSObject: AnyObject]?)
    -> Bool {
        self.window = UIWindow(frame:UIScreen.mainScreen().bounds)
        self.window!.rootViewController = UIViewController() // *
        // and now we can add subviews
        let mainview = self.window!.rootViewController!.view
        let v = UIView(frame:CGRectMake(100,100,50,50))
        v.backgroundColor = UIColor.redColor() // small red square
        mainview.addSubview(v) // add it to main view
        // and the rest is as before...
        self.window!.backgroundColor = UIColor.whiteColor()
        self.window!.makeKeyAndVisible()
        return true
}
```

Subview and Superview

Once upon a time, and not so very long ago, a view owned precisely its rectangular area. No part of any view that was not a subview of this view could appear inside it, because when this view redrew its rectangle, it would erase the overlapping portion of the other view. No part of any subview of this view could appear outside it, because the view took responsibility for its own rectangle and no more.

Those rules, however, were gradually relaxed, and starting in OS X 10.5, Apple introduced an entirely new architecture for view drawing that lifted those restrictions completely. iOS view drawing is based on this revised architecture. In iOS, some or all of a subview can appear outside its superview, and a view can overlap another view and can be drawn partially or totally in front of it without being its subview.

Figure 1-1. Overlapping views

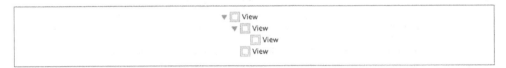

Figure 1-2. A view hierarchy as displayed in the nib editor

For example, Figure 1-1 shows three overlapping views. All three views have a background color, so each is completely represented by a colored rectangle. You have no way of knowing, from this visual representation, exactly how the views are related within the view hierarchy. In actual fact, the view in the middle (horizontally) is a sibling view of the view on the left (they are both direct subviews of the root view), and the view on the right is a subview of the middle view.

When views are created in the nib, you can examine the view hierarchy in the nib editor's document outline to learn their actual relationship (Figure 1-2). When views are created in code, you know their hierarchical relationship because you created that hierarchy. But the visible interface doesn't tell you, because view overlapping is so flexible.

 To study your app's view hierarchy at runtime while paused in the debugger, choose Debug → View Debugging → Capture View Hierarchy (new in Xcode 6). I'll talk more about this feature later in this chapter.

Nevertheless, a view's position within the view hierarchy is extremely significant. For one thing, the view hierarchy dictates the *order* in which views are drawn. Sibling subviews of the same superview have a definite order: one is drawn before the other, so if they overlap, it will appear to be behind its sibling. Similarly, a superview is drawn before its subviews, so if they overlap it, it will appear to be behind them.

You can see this illustrated in Figure 1-1. The view on the right is a subview of the view in the middle and is drawn on top of it. The view on the left is a sibling of the view in the middle, but it is a later sibling, so it is drawn on top of the view in the middle and on top of the view on the right. The view on the left *cannot* appear behind the view on the right but in front of the view in the middle, because those two views are subview and superview and are drawn together — both are drawn either before or after the view on the left, depending on the ordering of the siblings.

This layering order can be governed in the nib editor by arranging the views in the document outline. (If you click in the canvas, you may be able to use the menu items of the Editor → Arrange menu instead — Send to Front, Send to Back, Send Forward, Send Backward.) In code, there are methods for arranging the sibling order of views, which we'll come to in a moment.

Here are some other effects of the view hierarchy:

- If a view is removed from or moved within its superview, its subviews go with it.
- A view's degree of transparency is inherited by its subviews.
- A view can optionally limit the drawing of its subviews so that any parts of them outside the view are not shown. This is called *clipping* and is set with the view's `clipsToBounds` property.
- A superview *owns* its subviews, in the memory-management sense, much as an array owns its elements; it retains them and is responsible for releasing a subview when that subview ceases to be its subview (it is removed from the collection of this view's subviews) or when it itself goes out of existence.
- If a view's size is changed, its subviews can be resized automatically (and I'll have much more to say about that later in this chapter).

A UIView has a `superview` property (a UIView) and a `subviews` property (an array of UIView objects, in back-to-front order), allowing you to trace the view hierarchy in code. There is also a method `isDescendantOfView:` letting you check whether one view is a subview of another at any depth. If you need a reference to a particular view, you will probably arrange this beforehand as a property, perhaps through an outlet. Alternatively, a view can have a numeric tag (its `tag` property), and can then be referred to by sending any view higher up the view hierarchy the `viewWithTag:` message. Seeing that all tags of interest are unique within their region of the hierarchy is up to you.

Manipulating the view hierarchy in code is easy. This is part of what gives iOS apps their dynamic quality, and it compensates for the fact that there is basically just a single window. It is perfectly reasonable for your code to rip an entire hierarchy of views out of the superview and substitute another! You can do this directly; you can combine it with animation (Chapter 4); you can govern it through view controllers (Chapter 6).

The method `addSubview:` makes one view a subview of another; `removeFrom-Superview` takes a subview out of its superview's view hierarchy. In both cases, if the superview is part of the visible interface, the subview will appear or disappear; and of course this view may itself have subviews that accompany it. Just remember that removing a subview from its superview releases it; if you intend to reuse that subview later on, you will wish to retain it first. This is often taken care of by assignment to a property.

Events inform a view of these dynamic changes. To respond to these events requires subclassing. Then you'll be able to override any of these methods:

- `didAddSubview:`, `willRemoveSubview:`
- `didMoveToSuperview`, `willMoveToSuperview:`
- `didMoveToWindow`, `willMoveToWindow:`

When `addSubview:` is called, the view is placed last among its superview's subviews; thus it is drawn last, meaning that it appears frontmost. A view's subviews are indexed, starting at 0, which is rearmost. There are additional methods for inserting a subview at a given index, or below (behind) or above (in front of) a specific view; for swapping two sibling views by index; and for moving a subview all the way to the front or back among its siblings:

- `insertSubview:atIndex:`
- `insertSubview:belowSubview:`, `insertSubview:aboveSubview:`
- `exchangeSubviewAtIndex:withSubviewAtIndex:`
- `bringSubviewToFront:`, `sendSubviewToBack:`

Oddly, there is no command for removing all of a view's subviews at once. However, a view's `subviews` array is an immutable copy of the internal list of subviews, so it is legal to cycle through it and remove each subview one at a time:

```
for v in myView.subviews as! [UIView] {
    v.removeFromSuperview()
}
```

Or, more compactly (deliberately misusing `map`):

```
(myView.subviews as! [UIView]).map{$0.removeFromSuperview()}
```

Visibility and Opacity

A view can be made invisible by setting its hidden property to true, and visible again by setting it to false. This takes it (and its subviews, of course) out of the visible interface without the overhead of actually removing it from the view hierarchy. A hidden view does not (normally) receive touch events, so to the user it really is as if the view weren't there. But it is there, so it can still be manipulated in code.

A view can be assigned a background color through its backgroundColor property. A color is a UIColor; this is not a difficult class to use, and I'm not going to go into details. A view whose background color is nil (the default) has a transparent background. It is perfectly reasonable for a view to have a transparent background and to do no additional drawing of its own, just so that it can act as a convenient superview to other views, making them behave together.

A view can be made partially or completely transparent through its alpha property: 1.0 means opaque, 0.0 means transparent, and a value may be anywhere between them, inclusive. This affects subviews: if a superview has an alpha of 0.5, none of its subviews can have an *apparent* opacity of more than 0.5, because whatever alpha value they have will be drawn relative to 0.5. (Just to make matters more complicated, colors have an alpha value as well. So, for example, a view can have an alpha of 1.0 but still have a transparent background because its backgroundColor has an alpha less than 1.0.) A view that is completely transparent (or very close to it) is like a view whose hidden is true: it is invisible, along with its subviews, and cannot (normally) be touched.

A view's alpha property value affects both the apparent transparency of its background color and the apparent transparency of its contents. For example, if a view displays an image and has a background color and its alpha is less than 1, the background color will seep through the image (and whatever is behind the view will seep through both).

A view's opaque property, on the other hand, is a horse of a different color; changing it has no effect on the view's appearance. Rather, this property is a hint to the drawing system. If a view completely fills its bounds with ultimately opaque material and its alpha is 1.0, so that the view has no effective transparency, then it can be drawn more efficiently (with less drag on performance) if you inform the drawing system of this fact by setting its opaque to true. Otherwise, you should set its opaque to false. The opaque value is *not* changed for you when you set a view's backgroundColor or alpha! Setting it correctly is entirely up to you; the default, perhaps surprisingly, is true.

Frame

A view's frame property, a CGRect, is the position of its rectangle within its superview, *in the superview's coordinate system*. By default, the superview's coordinate system will have the origin at its top left, with the x-coordinate growing positively rightward and the y-coordinate growing positively downward.

Setting a view's frame to a different CGRect value repositions the view, or resizes it, or both. If the view is visible, this change will be visibly reflected in the interface. On the other hand, you can also set a view's frame when the view is not visible — for example, when you create the view in code. In that case, the frame describes where the view *will* be positioned within its superview when it is given a superview. UIView's designated initializer is init(frame:), and you'll often assign a frame this way, especially because the default frame might otherwise be (0.0,0.0,0.0,0.0), which is rarely what you want.

 Forgetting to assign a view a frame when creating it in code, and then wondering why it isn't appearing when added to a superview, is a common beginner mistake. A view with a zero-size frame is effectively invisible. If a view has a standard size that you want it to adopt, especially in relation to its contents (like a UIButton in relation to its title), an alternative is to call its sizeToFit method.

We are now in a position to generate programmatically the interface displayed in Figure 1-1:

```
let v1 = UIView(frame:CGRectMake(113, 111, 132, 194))
v1.backgroundColor = UIColor(red: 1, green: 0.4, blue: 1, alpha: 1)
let v2 = UIView(frame:CGRectMake(41, 56, 132, 194))
v2.backgroundColor = UIColor(red: 0.5, green: 1, blue: 0, alpha: 1)
let v3 = UIView(frame:CGRectMake(43, 197, 160, 230))
v3.backgroundColor = UIColor(red: 1, green: 0, blue: 0, alpha: 1)
mainview.addSubview(v1)
v1.addSubview(v2)
mainview.addSubview(v3)
```

In that code, we determined the layering order of v1 and v3 (the middle and left views, which are siblings) by the order in which we inserted them into the view hierarchy with addSubview:.

Bounds and Center

Suppose we have a superview and a subview, and the subview is to appear inset by 10 points, as in Figure 1-3. The Foundation utility function CGRectInset and the Swift CGRect method rectByInsetting make it easy to derive one rectangle as an inset from another, so we'll use one of them to determine the subview's frame. But *what* rectangle should this be inset from? Not the superview's frame; the frame represents a view's position within *its* superview, and in that superview's coordinates. What we're after is a CGRect describing our superview's rectangle in its *own* coordinates, because those are

Figure 1-3. A subview inset from its superview

the coordinates in which the subview's frame is to be expressed. The CGRect that describes a view's rectangle in its own coordinates is the view's bounds property.

So, the code to generate Figure 1-3 looks like this:

```
let v1 = UIView(frame:CGRectMake(113, 111, 132, 194))
v1.backgroundColor = UIColor(red: 1, green: 0.4, blue: 1, alpha: 1)
let v2 = UIView(frame:v1.bounds.rectByInsetting(dx: 10, dy: 10))
v2.backgroundColor = UIColor(red: 0.5, green: 1, blue: 0, alpha: 1)
mainview.addSubview(v1)
v1.addSubview(v2)
```

You'll very often use a view's bounds in this way. When you need coordinates for drawing inside a view, whether drawing manually or placing a subview, you'll often refer to the view's bounds.

Interesting things happen when you set a view's bounds. If you change a view's bounds *size*, you change its *frame*. The change in the view's frame takes place around its *center*, which remains unchanged. So, for example:

```
let v1 = UIView(frame:CGRectMake(113, 111, 132, 194))
v1.backgroundColor = UIColor(red: 1, green: 0.4, blue: 1, alpha: 1)
let v2 = UIView(frame:v1.bounds.rectByInsetting(dx: 10, dy: 10))
v2.backgroundColor = UIColor(red: 0.5, green: 1, blue: 0, alpha: 1)
mainview.addSubview(v1)
v1.addSubview(v2)
v2.bounds.size.height += 20
v2.bounds.size.width += 20
```

What appears is a single rectangle; the subview completely and exactly covers its superview, its frame being the same as the superview's bounds. The call to `rectByInsetting` started with the superview's bounds and shaved 10 points off the left, right, top, and bottom to set the subview's frame (Figure 1-3). But then we added 20 points to the subview's bounds height and width, and thus added 20 points to the subview's frame

Figure 1-4. A subview exactly covering its superview

height and width as well (Figure 1-4). The center didn't move, so we effectively put the 10 points back onto the left, right, top, and bottom of the subview's frame.

When you create a UIView, its bounds coordinate system's zero point (0.0,0.0) is at its top left. If you change a view's bounds *origin*, you move the *origin of its internal coordinate system*. Because a subview is positioned in its superview with respect to its superview's coordinate system, a change in the bounds origin of the superview will change the apparent position of a subview. To illustrate, we start once again with our subview inset evenly within its superview, and then change the bounds origin of the superview:

```
let v1 = UIView(frame:CGRectMake(113, 111, 132, 194))
v1.backgroundColor = UIColor(red: 1, green: 0.4, blue: 1, alpha: 1)
let v2 = UIView(frame:v1.bounds.rectByInsetting(dx: 10, dy: 10))
v2.backgroundColor = UIColor(red: 0.5, green: 1, blue: 0, alpha: 1)
mainview.addSubview(v1)
v1.addSubview(v2)
v1.bounds.origin.x += 10
v1.bounds.origin.y += 10
```

Nothing happens to the superview's size or position. But the subview has moved up and to the left so that it is flush with its superview's top-left corner (Figure 1-5). Basically, what we've done is to say to the superview, "Instead of calling the point at your upper left (0.0,0.0), call that point (10.0,10.0)." Because the subview's frame origin is itself at (10.0,10.0), the subview now touches the superview's top-left corner. The effect of changing a view's bounds origin may seem directionally backward — we increased the superview's origin in the positive direction, but the subview moved in the negative direction — but think of it this way: a view's bounds origin point coincides with its frame's top left.

We have seen that changing a view's bounds size affects its frame size. The converse is also true: changing a view's frame size affects its bounds size. What is *not* affected by changing a view's bounds size is the view's center. This property, like the frame property,

Figure 1-5. The superview's bounds origin has been shifted

represents the view's position within its superview, in the superview's coordinates, but it is the position of the bounds center, the point derived from the bounds like this:

```
let c = CGPointMake(theView.bounds.midX, theView.bounds.midY)
```

A view's center is thus a single point establishing the positional relationship between a view's bounds and its superview's bounds. Changing a view's bounds does not change its center; changing a view's center does not change its bounds.

Thus, a view's bounds and center are orthogonal (independent), and describe (among other things) both the view's size and its position within its superview. The view's frame is therefore superfluous! In fact, the frame property is merely a convenient expression of the center and bounds values. In most cases, this won't matter to you; you'll use the frame property anyway. When you first create a view from scratch, the designated initializer is init(frame:). You can change the frame, and the bounds size and center will change to match. You can change the bounds size or the center, and the frame will change to match. Nevertheless, the proper and most reliable way to position and size a view within its superview is to use its bounds and center, not its frame; there are some situations in which the frame is meaningless (or will at least behave very oddly), but the bounds and center will always work.

We have seen that every view has its own coordinate system, expressed by its bounds, and that a view's coordinate system has a clear relationship to its superview's coordinate system, expressed by its center. This is true of every view in a window, so it is possible to convert between the coordinates of any two views in the same window. Convenience methods are supplied to perform this conversion both for a CGPoint and for a CGRect:

- convertPoint:fromView:, convertPoint:toView:
- convertRect:fromView:, convertRect:toView:

If the second parameter is nil, it is taken to be the window.

For example, if v2 is a subview of v1, then to center v2 within v1 you could say:

```
v2.center = v1.convertPoint(v1.center, fromView:v1.superview)
```

 When setting a view's position by setting its center, if the height or width of the view is not an integer (or, on a single-resolution screen, not an even integer), the view can end up *misaligned*: its point values in one or both dimensions are located between the screen pixels. This can cause the view to be displayed incorrectly; for example, if the view contains text, the text may be blurry. You can detect this situation in the Simulator by checking Debug → Color Misaligned Images. A simple solution is to set the view's frame, after positioning it, to the CGRectIntegral of its frame, or (in Swift) to call integerize on the view's frame.

Window Coordinates and Screen Coordinates

The device screen has no frame, but it has bounds. The main window has no superview, but its frame is set with respect to the screen's bounds, as I showed earlier:

```
let w = UIWindow(frame: UIScreen.mainScreen().bounds)
```

Thus, *window coordinates are screen coordinates.*

In iOS 7 and before, the screen's coordinates were invariant, regardless of the orientation of the device and of the rotation of the app to compensate. iOS 8 makes a major change in this coordinate system: when the app rotates to compensate for the rotation of the device, the screen (and therefore the window) is what rotates. This change is expressed in part as a reversal of the size components of the bounds of the screen and window (and the frame of the window): in portrait orientation, the size is taller than wide, but in landscape orientation, the size is wider than tall.

This change may break your existing code, but once you've made the necessary adjustments, you'll find it extremely convenient. For example, as you'll discover in Chapter 10, you no longer have to compensate for the device's rotation when calculating how the onscreen keyboard overlaps your interface.

For those occasions where you need device coordinates, independent of the rotation of the app, iOS 8 introduces the UICoordinateSpace protocol, which provides a bounds property. UIView adopts the UICoordinateSpace protocol, and so do two additional objects:

UIScreen's coordinateSpace *property*
This coordinate space rotates, so that its height and width are reversed when the app rotates to compensate for a change in the orientation of the device; its (0.0,0.0) point is at the app's top left.

UIScreen's `fixedCoordinateSpace` *property*

This coordinate space is invariant, meaning that its top left represents the physical top left of the device *qua* physical device; its (`0.0,0.0`) point thus might be in any corner (from the user's perspective).

To help you convert between coordinate spaces, UICoordinateSpace also provides four methods parallel to the coordinate-conversion methods I listed in the previous section:

- `convertPoint:fromCoordinateSpace:`, `convertPoint:toCoordinateSpace:`
- `convertRect:fromCoordinateSpace:`, `convertRect:toCoordinateSpace:`

So, for example, suppose we have a UIView `v` in our interface, and we wish to learn its position in fixed device coordinates. We could do it like this:

```
let r = v.convertRect(
    v.frame, toCoordinateSpace: UIScreen.mainScreen().fixedCoordinateSpace)
```

It doesn't actually matter to what view or coordinate space we send the `convertRect:to-CoordinateSpace:` message; the result will be the same.

Occasions where you need such information, however, will be rare. Everything takes place within your root view controller's main view, and the bounds of that view, which are adjusted for you automatically when the app rotates to compensate for a change in device orientation, are the highest coordinate system that will normally interest you.

Transform

A view's `transform` property alters how the view is drawn — it may, for example, change the view's perceived size and orientation — without affecting its bounds and center. A transformed view continues to behave correctly: a rotated button, for example, is still a button, and can be tapped in its apparent location and orientation.

A transform value is a CGAffineTransform, which is a struct representing six of the nine values of a 3×3 transformation matrix (the other three values are constants, so there's no need to represent them in the struct). You may have forgotten your high-school linear algebra, so you may not recall what a transformation matrix is. For the details, which are quite simple really, see the "Transforms" chapter of Apple's *Quartz 2D Programming Guide*, especially the section called "The Math Behind the Matrices." But you don't really need to know those details, because convenience functions, whose names start with `CGAffineTransformMake...`, are provided for creating three of the basic types of transform: rotation, scaling, and translation (i.e., changing the view's apparent position). A fourth basic transform type, skewing or shearing, has no convenience function.

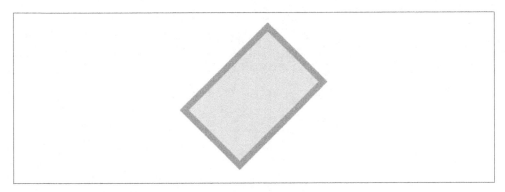

Figure 1-6. A rotation transform

By default, a view's transformation matrix is `CGAffineTransformIdentity`, the identity transform. It has no visible effect, so you're unaware of it. Any transform that you do apply takes place around the view's center, which is held constant.

Here's some code to illustrate use of a transform:

```
let v1 = UIView(frame:CGRectMake(113, 111, 132, 194))
v1.backgroundColor = UIColor(red: 1, green: 0.4, blue: 1, alpha: 1)
let v2 = UIView(frame:v1.bounds.rectByInsetting(dx: 10, dy: 10))
v2.backgroundColor = UIColor(red: 0.5, green: 1, blue: 0, alpha: 1)
mainview.addSubview(v1)
v1.addSubview(v2)
v1.transform = CGAffineTransformMakeRotation(45 * CGFloat(M_PI)/180.0)
```

The `transform` property of the view `v1` is set to a rotation transform. The result (Figure 1-6) is that the view appears to be rocked 45 degrees clockwise. (I think in degrees, but Core Graphics thinks in radians, so my code has to convert.) Observe that the view's `center` property is unaffected, so that the rotation seems to have occurred around the view's center. Moreover, the view's `bounds` property is unaffected; the internal coordinate system is unchanged, so the subview is drawn in the same place relative to its superview. The view's `frame`, however, is now useless, as no mere rectangle can describe the region of the superview apparently occupied by the view; the frame's actual value, roughly `(63.7,92.7,230.5,230.5)`, describes the minimal bounding rectangle surrounding the view's apparent position. The rule is that if a view's `transform` is not the identity transform, you should not set its `frame`; also, automatic resizing of a subview, discussed later in this chapter, requires that the superview's transform be the identity transform.

Suppose, instead of `CGAffineTransformMakeRotation`, we call `CGAffineTransform-MakeScale`, like this:

```
v1.transform = CGAffineTransformMakeScale(1.8, 1)
```

Figure 1-7. A scale transform

The bounds property of the view v1 is still unaffected, so the subview is still drawn in the same place relative to its superview; this means that the two views seem to have stretched horizontally together (Figure 1-7). No bounds or centers were harmed by the application of this transform!

Transformation matrices can be chained. There are convenience functions for applying one transform to another. Their names do *not* contain "Make." These functions are not commutative; that is, order matters. (That high school math is starting to come back to you now, isn't it?) If you start with a transform that translates a view to the right and then apply a rotation of 45 degrees, the rotated view appears to the right of its original position; on the other hand, if you start with a transform that rotates a view 45 degrees and then apply a translation to the right, the meaning of "right" has changed, so the rotated view appears 45 degrees down from its original position. To demonstrate the difference, I'll start with a subview that exactly overlaps its superview:

```
let v1 = UIView(frame:CGRectMake(20, 111, 132, 194))
v1.backgroundColor = UIColor(red: 1, green: 0.4, blue: 1, alpha: 1)
let v2 = UIView(frame:v1.bounds)
v2.backgroundColor = UIColor(red: 0.5, green: 1, blue: 0, alpha: 1)
mainview.addSubview(v1)
v1.addSubview(v2)
```

Then I'll apply two successive transforms to the subview, leaving the superview to show where the subview was originally. In this example, I translate and then rotate (Figure 1-8):

```
v2.transform = CGAffineTransformMakeTranslation(100, 0)
v2.transform = CGAffineTransformRotate(v2.transform, 45 * CGFloat(M_PI)/180.0)
```

In this example, I rotate and then translate (Figure 1-9):

```
v2.transform = CGAffineTransformMakeRotation(45 * CGFloat(M_PI)/180.0)
v2.transform = CGAffineTransformTranslate(v2.transform, 100, 0)
```

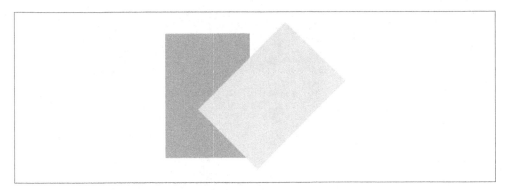

Figure 1-8. Translation, then rotation

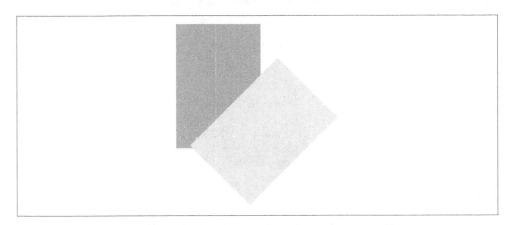

Figure 1-9. Rotation, then translation

The function `CGAffineTransformConcat` concatenates two transform matrices using matrix multiplication. Again, this operation is not commutative. The order is the *opposite* of the order when using convenience functions for applying one transform to another. For example, this gives the same result as Figure 1-9:

```
let r = CGAffineTransformMakeRotation(45 * CGFloat(M_PI)/180.0)
let t = CGAffineTransformMakeTranslation(100, 0)
v2.transform = CGAffineTransformConcat(t,r) // not r,t
```

To remove a transform from a combination of transforms, apply its inverse. A convenience function lets you obtain the inverse of a given affine transform. Again, order matters. In this example, I rotate the subview and shift it to its "right," and then remove the rotation (Figure 1-10):

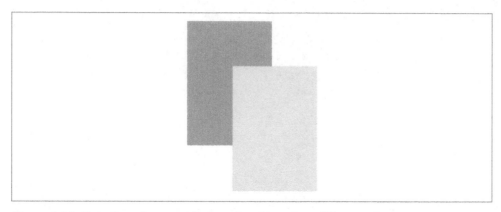

Figure 1-10. Rotation, then translation, then inversion of the rotation

Figure 1-11. Skew (shear)

```
let r = CGAffineTransformMakeRotation(45 * CGFloat(M_PI)/180.0)
let t = CGAffineTransformMakeTranslation(100, 0)
v2.transform = CGAffineTransformConcat(t,r)
v2.transform = CGAffineTransformConcat(
    CGAffineTransformInvert(r), v2.transform)
```

Finally, as there are no convenience methods for creating a skew (shear) transform, I'll illustrate by creating one manually, without further explanation (Figure 1-11):

```
v1.transform = CGAffineTransformMake(1, 0, -0.2, 1, 0, 0)
```

Transforms are useful particularly as temporary visual indicators. For example, you might call attention to a view by applying a transform that scales it up slightly, and then applying the identity transform to restore it to its original size, and animating those changes (Chapter 4).

In iOS 7 and before, the transform property lay at the heart of an iOS app's ability to rotate its interface: the window's frame and bounds were invariant, locked to the screen, and an app's interface rotated to compensate for a change in device orientation by applying a rotation transform to the root view, so that its (0.0,0.0) point moved to what the user now saw as the top left of the view.

In iOS 8, however, as I've already mentioned, this is no longer the case. The screen's coordinate space is effectively rotated, but a coordinate space doesn't have a transform property, so the rotation transform applied to that coordinate space is fictitious: you can work out what has happened, if you really want to, by comparing the screen's coordinateSpace with its fixedCoordinateSpace, but none of the views in the story — neither the window, nor the root view, nor any of its subviews — receives a rotation transform when the app's interface rotates. If you had code, inherited from iOS 7 or before, that relied on the assumption that a rotated app's root view had a rotation transform, *that code will break* when compiled and run against iOS 8.

Instead, iOS 8 expects you to concentrate on the *dimensions* of the window, the root view, and so forth. And this doesn't mean their absolute dimensions (though you might have reason to consider these), but their dimensions relative to an iPad. This dimensional relationship is embodied in a set of *size classes* which are vended by a view's trait-Collection property as a UITraitCollection object. I'll discuss trait collections and size classes further in the next section.

One purpose of this innovation in iOS 8 is so that you can treat app rotation as effectively nothing more than a change in the interface's *proportions*: when the app rotates, the long dimension (of the root view, the window, and the screen's coordinate space bounds) becomes its short dimension and *vice versa*. This, after all, is what your interface needs to take into account in order to keep working when the app rotates.

Consider, for example, a subview of the root view, located at the bottom right of the screen when the device is in portrait orientation. If the root view's bounds width and bounds height are effectively swapped, then that poor old subview will now be outside the bounds height, and therefore off the screen — unless your app responds in some way to this change to reposition it. Such a response is called *layout*, a subject that will occupy most of the rest of this chapter. The point, however, is that what you're responding *to*, in iOS 8, is just a change in the window's proportions; the fact that this change stems from rotation of the app's interface is virtually irrelevant.

Trait Collections and Size Classes

Trait collections are a major iOS 8 innovation. Every view in the interface, from the window on down, as well as any view controller whose view is part of the interface, inherits from the environment the value of its traitCollection property, which it has by virtue of implementing the UITraitEnvironment protocol. The traitCollection is a UITraitCollection, a value class consisting of four properties:

displayScale

> The scale inherited from the current screen, typically 1 or 2 for a single- or double-resolution screen respectively — or 3 for the iPhone 6 Plus. (This will be the same, by default, as the UIScreen `scale` property.)

userInterfaceIdiom

> A UserInterfaceIdiom value, either `.Phone` or `.Pad`, stating generically what kind of device we're running on. (This will be the same, by default, as the UIDevice `userInterfaceIdiom` property.)

horizontalSizeClass, verticalSizeClass

> A UIUserInterfaceSizeClass value, either `.Regular` or `.Compact`. These are called *size classes*. The size classes, in combination, have the following meanings:

> *Both the vertical and horizontal size classes are* `.Regular`
>> We're running on an iPad.

> *The vertical size class is* `.Regular`, *but the horizontal size class is* `.Compact`
>> We're running on an iPhone with the app in portrait orientation.

> *Both the vertical and horizontal size classes are* `.Compact`
>> We're running on an iPhone (except an iPhone 6 Plus) with the app in landscape orientation.

> *The vertical size class is* `.Compact`, *but the horizontal size class is* `.Regular`
>> We're running on an iPhone 6 Plus with the app in landscape orientation.

 To be iPhone 6 Plus–native, your app must either designate a *.xib* or *.storyboard* file as its launch screen or contain a Retina HD 5.5 launch image in the asset catalog. Otherwise, the size classes on an iPhone 6 Plus will be the same as for any other iPhone (and your app will be displayed scaled up).

The trait collection properties might not change during the lifetime of an app, but they still might differ, and thus be of interest to your code, from one run of an app to another. In particular, if you write a universal app, one that runs natively on different device types (iPhone and iPad), you will probably want your interface to differ depending on which device type we're running on; trait collections are the iOS 8 way to detect that.

Moreover, some trait collection properties *can* change during the lifetime of an app. In particular, the size classes, on an iPhone, reflect the orientation of the app — which can change as the app rotates in response to a change in the orientation of the device.

Thus, the environment's trait collection is considered to have changed on two main occasions:

- The interface is assembled initially.
- The app rotates on an iPhone.

At such moments, the `traitCollectionDidChange:` message is propagated down the hierarchy of UITraitEnvironments (meaning primarily, for our purposes, view controllers and views); the old trait collection is provided as the parameter, and the new trait collection can be retrieved as `self.traitCollection`.

 Perhaps you are now saying to yourself: "Wait, there aren't enough size classes!" You're absolutely right. Apple has decided that size classes should not differentiate between an iPad in portrait orientation and an iPad in landscape orientation. This seems an odd design decision (especially since iPad apps whose interface changes radically between landscape and portrait are standard, as I'll illustrate when discussing split views in Chapter 9); I can't explain it.

It is also possible to create a trait collection yourself. (It may not be immediately obvious why this would be a useful thing to do; I'll give an example in the next chapter.) Oddly, however, you can't set any trait collection properties directly; instead, you form a trait collection through an initializer that determines just *one* property, and if you want to add further property settings, you have to combine trait collections by calling `init(traitsFromCollections:)`. For example:

```
let tcdisp = UITraitCollection(displayScale: 2.0)
let tcphone = UITraitCollection(userInterfaceIdiom: .Phone)
let tcreg = UITraitCollection(verticalSizeClass: .Regular)
let tc = UITraitCollection(traitsFromCollections: [tcdisp, tcphone, tcreg])
```

When combining trait collections with `init(traitsFromCollections:)`, an *ordered intersection* is performed. If two trait collections are combined, and one sets a property and the other doesn't (the property isn't set or its value isn't yet known), the one that sets the property wins; if they both set the property, the winner is the trait collection that appears later in the array.

Similarly, if you create a trait collection and you don't specify a property, this means that the value for that property is to be inherited if the trait collection finds itself in the inheritance hierarchy.

(You cannot, however, insert a trait collection directly into the inheritance hierarchy simply by setting a view's trait collection; `traitCollection` isn't a settable property. Instead, you'll use a UIViewController method, `setOverrideTraitCollection:for-ChildViewController:`; view controllers are the subject of Chapter 6.)

To compare trait collections, call `containsTraitsInCollection:`. This returns `true` if the value of every *specified* property of the second trait collection (the argument) matches that of the first trait collection (the target of the message).

Layout

We have seen that a subview moves when its superview's bounds *origin* is changed. But what happens to a subview when its superview's bounds (or frame) *size* is changed?

Of its own accord, nothing happens. The subview's bounds and center haven't changed, and the superview's bounds origin hasn't moved, so the subview stays in the same position relative to the top left of its superview. In real life, however, that often won't be what you want. You'll want subviews to be resized and repositioned when their superview's bounds size is changed. This is called *layout*.

The need for layout is obvious in a context such as OS X, where the user can freely resize a window, potentially disturbing your interface. For example, you'd want an OK button near the lower-right corner to stay in the lower-right corner as the window grows, while a text field at the top of the window should stay at the top of the window, but perhaps should widen as the window widens.

There are no user-resizable windows on an iOS device, but still, a superview might be resized dynamically. For example:

- Your app might compensate for the user rotating the device 90 degrees by rotating itself so that its top moves to the new top of the screen, matching its new orientation — and, as a consequence, swapping its bounds width and height values.

- An iPhone app might launch on screens with different aspect ratios: for example, the screen of the iPhone 4s is relatively shorter than the screen of later iPhone models, and the app's interface may need to adapt to this difference.

- A universal app might launch on an iPad or on an iPhone. The app's interface may need to adapt to the size of the screen on which it finds itself running.

- A view instantiated from a nib, such as a view controller's main view or a table view cell, might be resized to fit into the interface into which it is placed.

- A view might grow or shrink in response to a change in its surrounding views. For example, in iOS 8, a navigation controller's navigation bar and toolbar may be shown or hidden dynamically, as the user pleases.

Layout is performed in three primary ways:

Manual layout
> The superview is sent the `layoutSubviews` message whenever it is resized; so, to lay out subviews manually, provide your own subclass and override `layout-`

`Subviews`. Clearly this could turn out to be a lot of work, but it means you can do anything you like.

Autoresizing

Autoresizing is the pre-iOS 6 way of performing layout automatically. A subview will respond to its superview's being resized, in accordance with the rules prescribed by the subview's `autoresizingMask` property value.

Autolayout

Autolayout, introduced in iOS 6, depends on the *constraints* of views. A constraint (an instance of NSLayoutConstraint) is a full-fledged object with numeric values describing some aspect of the size or position of a view, often in terms of some other view; it is much more sophisticated, descriptive, and powerful than the `autoresizingMask`. Multiple constraints can apply to an individual view, and they can describe a relationship between *any* two views (not just a subview and its superview). Autolayout is implemented behind the scenes in `layoutSubviews`; in effect, constraints allow you to write sophisticated `layoutSubviews` functionality without code.

Your layout strategy can involve any combination of these. The need for manual layout is rare, but it's there if you need it. Autoresizing is used automatically unless you deliberately turn it off by setting a superview's `autoresizesSubviews` property to `false`, or unless a view uses autolayout instead. Autolayout is an opt-in technology, and can be used for whatever areas of your interface you find appropriate; a view that uses autolayout can live side by side with a view that uses autoresizing.

One of the chief places where you opt in to autolayout is the nib file, and in Xcode 5 and 6 all new *.storyboard* and *.xib* files do opt in — they have autolayout turned on, by default. To see this, select the file in the Project navigator, show the File inspector, and examine the "Use Auto Layout" checkbox. On the other hand, a view that your code creates and adds to the interface, by default, uses autoresizing, not autolayout.

Autoresizing

Autoresizing is a matter of conceptually assigning a subview "springs and struts." A spring can stretch; a strut can't. Springs and struts can be assigned internally or externally, horizontally or vertically. Thus you can specify (using internal springs and struts) whether and how the view can be resized, and (using external springs and struts) whether and how the view can be repositioned. For example:

- Imagine a subview that is centered in its superview and is to stay centered, but is to resize itself as the superview is resized. It would have struts externally and springs internally.

- Imagine a subview that is centered in its superview and is to stay centered, and is *not* to resize itself as the superview is resized. It would have springs externally and struts internally.

- Imagine an OK button that is to stay in the lower right of its superview. It would have struts internally, struts externally to its right and bottom, and springs externally to its top and left.

- Imagine a text field that is to stay at the top of its superview. It is to widen as the superview widens. It would have struts externally, but a spring to its bottom; internally it would have a vertical strut and a horizontal spring.

In code, a combination of springs and struts is set through a view's `autoresizing-Mask` property. It's a bitmask, so you use bitwise-or to combine options. The options, members of the `UIViewAutoresizing` struct, represent springs; whatever isn't specified is a strut. The default is `.None`, apparently meaning all struts — but of course it can't really be *all* struts, because if the superview is resized, *something* needs to change; in reality, `.None` is the same as `.FlexibleRightMargin` together with `.FlexibleBottom-Margin`.

 In debugging, when you log a UIView to the console, its `autoresizingMask` is reported using the word "autoresize" and a list of the springs. The margins are LM, RM, TM, and BM; the internal dimensions are W and H. For example, `autoresize = LM+TM` means that what's flexible is the left and top margins; `autoresize = W+BM` means that what's flexible is the width and the bottom margin.

To demonstrate autoresizing, I'll start with a view and two subviews, one stretched across the top, the other confined to the lower right (Figure 1-12):

```
let v1 = UIView(frame:CGRectMake(100, 111, 132, 194))
v1.backgroundColor = UIColor(red: 1, green: 0.4, blue: 1, alpha: 1)
let v2 = UIView(frame:CGRectMake(0, 0, 132, 10))
v2.backgroundColor = UIColor(red: 0.5, green: 1, blue: 0, alpha: 1)
let v3 = UIView(frame:CGRectMake(
    v1.bounds.width-20, v1.bounds.height-20, 20, 20))
v3.backgroundColor = UIColor(red: 1, green: 0, blue: 0, alpha: 1)
mainview.addSubview(v1)
v1.addSubview(v2)
v1.addSubview(v3)
```

To that example, I'll add code applying springs and struts to the two subviews to make them behave like the text field and the OK button I was hypothesizing earlier:

```
v2.autoresizingMask = .FlexibleWidth
v3.autoresizingMask = .FlexibleTopMargin | .FlexibleLeftMargin
```

Figure 1-12. Before autoresizing

Figure 1-13. After autoresizing

Now I'll resize the superview, thus bringing autoresizing into play; as you can see (Figure 1-13), the subviews remain pinned in their correct relative positions:

```
v1.bounds.size.width += 40
v1.bounds.size.height -= 50
```

That example shows exactly what autoresizing is about, but it's a little artificial; in real life, the superview is more likely to be resized, not because you resize it in code, but because of automatic behavior, such as compensatory resizing of the interface when the device is rotated. To see this, you might modify the previous example to pin the size of v1 to the size of the root view, and then run the app and rotate the device. Thus you might initially configure v1 like this:

```
v1.frame = mainview.bounds
v1.autoresizingMask = .FlexibleHeight | .FlexibleWidth
```

Now run the app and rotate the device (in the Simulator, repeatedly choose Hardware → Rotate Left). The view v1 now fills the screen as the interface rotates, and its subviews stay pinned in their correct relative positions.

Autoresizing is effective but simple — sometimes too simple. The only relationship it describes is between a subview and its superview; it can't help you do such things as space a row of views evenly across the screen relative to one another. Before autolayout, the way to achieve more sophisticated goals of that sort was to combine autoresizing with manual layout in `layoutSubviews`. Autoresizing happens before `layout-Subviews` is called, so your `layoutSubviews` code is free to come marching in and tidy up whatever autoresizing didn't get quite right.

Autolayout

Autolayout is an opt-in technology, at the level of each individual view. A view may opt in to autolayout in any of three ways:

- Your code adds an autolayout constraint to a view. The views involved in this constraint use autolayout.
- Your app loads a nib for which "Use Auto Layout" is checked. *Every* view instantiated from that nib uses autolayout.
- A view in the interface, which would be an instance of a custom UIView subclass of yours, returns `true` from the class method `requiresConstraintBasedLayout`. That view uses autolayout.

  The reason for this third approach to opting in to autolayout is that you might need autolayout to be switched on in order to add autolayout constraints in code. A common place to create constraints in code is in a view's `updateConstraints` implementation (discussed later in this chapter). However, if autolayout isn't switched on, `updateConstraints` won't be called. So `requiresConstraintBasedLayout` provides a way of switching it on.

One sibling view can use autolayout while another sibling view does not, and a superview can use autolayout while one or indeed all of its subviews do not. However, autolayout is implemented through the superview chain, so if a view uses autolayout, then automatically so do all its superviews; and if (as will almost certainly be the case) one of those views is the main view of a view controller, that view controller receives autolayout-related events that it would not have received otherwise.

 You can't turn off autolayout for just part of a nib. Either all views instantiated from a nib use autolayout or they all use autoresizing. To generate different parts of your interface from nibs, one part with autoresizing, another part with autolayout, separate those parts into different nibs (different *.storyboard* or *.xib* files) and then load and combine them at runtime.

Constraints

An autolayout constraint, or simply *constraint*, is an NSLayoutConstraint instance, and describes either the absolute width or height of a view or a relationship between an attribute of one view and an attribute of another view. In the latter case, the attributes don't have to be the same attribute, and the two views don't have to be siblings (subviews of the same superview) or parent and child (superview and subview) — the only requirement is that they share a common ancestor (a superview somewhere up the view hierarchy).

Here are the chief properties of an NSLayoutConstraint:

`firstItem`, `firstAttribute`, `secondItem`, `secondAttribute`
> The two views and their respective attributes (NSLayoutAttribute) involved in this constraint. If the constraint is describing a view's absolute height or width, the second view will be nil and the second attribute will be `.NotAnAttribute`. Additional NSLayoutAttribute values are:
>
> - `.Left`, `.Right`
> - `.Top`, `.Bottom`
> - `.Leading`, `.Trailing`
> - `.Width`, `.Height`
> - `.CenterX`, `.CenterY`
> - `.Baseline`, `.FirstBaseline`
>
> `.FirstBaseline`, new in iOS 8, applies primarily to multiline labels (Chapter 10); `.Baseline` is the *last* baseline, which is some distance up from the bottom of the label, whereas the first baseline is some distance down from the top of the label. The meanings of the other attributes are intuitively obvious, except that you might wonder what "leading" and "trailing" mean: they are the international equivalent of "left" and "right," automatically reversing their meaning on systems whose language is written right-to-left (making it easy, say, to align the beginnings of several labels of different lengths, irrespective of localization).
>
> (iOS 8 also introduces the notion of alignment with respect to a view's *margins;* I'll discuss that in a moment.)

`multiplier`, `constant`
> These numbers will be applied to the second attribute's value to determine the first attribute's value. The `multiplier` is multiplied by the second attribute's value; the `constant` is added to that product. The first attribute is set to the result. (The name *constant* is a very poor choice, as this value isn't constant; have the Apple folks never heard the term *addend*?) Basically, you're writing an equation of the form $a_1 = ma_2 + c$, where a_1 and a_2 are the two attributes, and m and c are the multiplier and the constant. Thus, in the degenerate case where the first attribute's value is to equal the second attribute's value, the multiplier will be 1 and the constant will be 0. If you're describing a view's width or height absolutely, the multiplier will be 1 and the constant will be the width or height value.

relation
> An NSLayoutRelation stating how the two attribute values are to be related to one another, as modified by the `multiplier` and the `constant`. This is the operator that goes in the spot where I put the equal sign in the equation in the preceding paragraph. It might be an equal sign (`.Equal`), but inequalities are also permitted (`.LessThanOrEqual`, `.GreaterThanOrEqual`).

priority
> Priority values range from 1000 (required) down to 1, and certain standard behaviors have standard priorities. Constraints can have different priorities, determining the order in which they are applied. Constraints are permitted to conflict with one another provided they have different priorities.

A constraint belongs to a view. A view can have many constraints: a UIView has a `constraints` property, along with these instance methods:

- `addConstraint:`, `addConstraints:`
- `removeConstraint:`, `removeConstraints:`

The question then is *which* view a given constraint should belong to. The answer is: the view that is closest up the view hierarchy from both views involved in the constraint. If possible, it should *be* one of those views. Thus, for example, if the constraint dictates a view's absolute width, it belongs to that view; if it sets the top of a view in relation to the top of its superview, it belongs to that superview; if it aligns the tops of two sibling views, it belongs to their common superview. (The runtime may permit you to cheat and add a constraint at too high a level.) Adding a constraint that refers to a view outside the subview hierarchy of the view to which you add it will cause a crash (with a helpful error message). Both views involved in a constraint must be present in the view hierarchy before the constraint can be added.

New in iOS 8, a constraint has a Bool `active` property, and constraints can be activated or deactivated together with NSLayoutConstraint class methods `activateConstraints:` and `deactivateConstraints:`. Unfortunately, these features are currently undocumented; but it appears that activating a constraint is equivalent to adding it automatically to the correct view, and thus these are ways to add and remove constraints with the focus of attention on the *constraint* rather than on the *view*.

NSLayoutConstraint properties are read-only, except for `priority` and `constant`. In Chapter 4, it will turn out that changing a constraint's `constant` in real time is a good way to animate a view. If you want to change anything else about an existing constraint, you must remove the constraint and add a new one.

Autoresizing constraints

The mechanism whereby individual views can opt in to autolayout can suddenly involve other views in autolayout, even though those other views were not using autolayout previously. Therefore, there needs to be a way, when such a view becomes involved in autolayout, to determine that view's position and layout through constraints in the same way they were previously being determined through its frame and its `autoresizing-Mask`. The runtime takes care of this for you: it translates the view's frame and `autoresizingMask` settings into constraints. The result is a set of implicit constraints, of class NSAutoresizingMaskLayoutConstraint, affecting this view (though they may be attached to its superview). Thanks to these implicit constraints, the layout dictated by the view's `autoresizingMask` continues to work, even though the view is no longer obeying its `autoresizingMask` but rather is using autolayout and constraints.

For example, suppose I have a UILabel whose frame is (`20.0,20.0,42.0,22.0`), and whose `autoresizingMask` is `.None`. If this label were suddenly to come under autolayout, then its superview would acquire four implicit constraints setting its width and height at 42 and 22 and its center X and center Y at 41 and 31.

This conversion is performed only if the view in question has its `translates-AutoresizingMaskIntoConstraints` property set to `true`. That is, in fact, the default if the view came into existence either in code or by instantiation from a nib where "Use Auto Layout" is not checked. The assumption is that if a view came into existence in either of those ways, you want its frame and `autoresizingMask` to act as its constraints if it becomes involved in autolayout.

That's a sensible rule, but it means that if you intend to apply any explicit constraints of your own to such a view, you'll probably want to remember to turn off this automatic behavior by setting the view's `translatesAutoresizingMaskIntoConstraints` property to `false`. If you don't, you're going to end up with both implicit constraints and explicit constraints affecting this view, and it's unlikely that you would want that. Typically, that sort of situation will result in a conflict between constraints, as I'll explain a little later; indeed, what usually happens to me is that I *don't* remember to set the view's `translatesAutoresizingMaskIntoConstraints` property to `false`, and am reminded to do so only when I *do* get a conflict between constraints.

 For some obscure reason, `translatesAutoresizingMaskIntoConstraints` is not a directly settable property in Swift; to set it, you have to call a view's `setTranslates-AutoresizingMaskIntoConstraints:` method.

Creating constraints in code

We are now ready to write some code involving constraints! I'll generate the same views and subviews and layout behavior as in Figures 1-12 and 1-13, but using constraints.

Observe that I don't bother to assign the subviews v2 and v3 explicit frames as I create them, because constraints will take care of positioning them, and that I remember (for once) to set their translatesAutoresizingMaskIntoConstraints properties to false:

```
let v1 = UIView(frame:CGRectMake(100, 111, 132, 194))
v1.backgroundColor = UIColor(red: 1, green: 0.4, blue: 1, alpha: 1)
let v2 = UIView()
v2.backgroundColor = UIColor(red: 0.5, green: 1, blue: 0, alpha: 1)
let v3 = UIView()
v3.backgroundColor = UIColor(red: 1, green: 0, blue: 0, alpha: 1)
mainview.addSubview(v1)
v1.addSubview(v2)
v1.addSubview(v3)
v2.setTranslatesAutoresizingMaskIntoConstraints(false)
v3.setTranslatesAutoresizingMaskIntoConstraints(false)
v1.addConstraint(
    NSLayoutConstraint(item: v2,
        attribute: .Left,
        relatedBy: .Equal,
        toItem: v1,
        attribute: .Left,
        multiplier: 1, constant: 0)
)
v1.addConstraint(
    NSLayoutConstraint(item: v2,
        attribute: .Right,
        relatedBy: .Equal,
        toItem: v1,
        attribute: .Right,
        multiplier: 1, constant: 0)
)
v1.addConstraint(
    NSLayoutConstraint(item: v2,
        attribute: .Top,
        relatedBy: .Equal,
        toItem: v1,
        attribute: .Top,
        multiplier: 1, constant: 0)
)
v2.addConstraint(
    NSLayoutConstraint(item: v2,
        attribute: .Height,
        relatedBy: .Equal,
        toItem: nil,
        attribute: .NotAnAttribute,
        multiplier: 1, constant: 10)
)
v3.addConstraint(
    NSLayoutConstraint(item: v3,
        attribute: .Width,
        relatedBy: .Equal,
        toItem: nil,
```

```
            attribute: .NotAnAttribute,
            multiplier: 1, constant: 20)
    )
    v3.addConstraint(
        NSLayoutConstraint(item: v3,
            attribute: .Height,
            relatedBy: .Equal,
            toItem: nil,
            attribute: .NotAnAttribute,
            multiplier: 1, constant: 20)
    )
    v1.addConstraint(
        NSLayoutConstraint(item: v3,
            attribute: .Right,
            relatedBy: .Equal,
            toItem: v1,
            attribute: .Right,
            multiplier: 1, constant: 0)
    )
    v1.addConstraint(
        NSLayoutConstraint(item: v3,
            attribute: .Bottom,
            relatedBy: .Equal,
            toItem: v1,
            attribute: .Bottom,
            multiplier: 1, constant: 0)
    )
```

Now, I know what you're thinking. You're thinking: "What are you, nuts? That is a boatload of code!" (Except that you probably used another four-letter word instead of "boat.") But that's something of an illusion. I'd argue that what we're doing here is actually *simpler* than the code with which we created Figure 1-12 using explicit frames and autoresizing.

After all, we merely create eight constraints in eight simple commands. (I've broken each command into multiple lines, but that's just a matter of formatting.) They're verbose, but they are the same command repeated with different parameters, so creating them is just a matter of copy-and-paste. Moreover, our eight constraints determine the *position, size, and layout behavior* of our two subviews, so we're getting a lot of bang for our buck.

Even more telling, constraints are a far clearer expression of what's supposed to happen than setting a frame and `autoresizingMask`. The position of our subviews is described once and for all, both as they will initially appear and as they will appear if their superview is resized. And it is described meaningfully; we don't have to use arbitrary math. Recall what we had to say before:

```
let v3 = UIView(frame:CGRectMake(
    v1.bounds.width-20, v1.bounds.height-20, 20, 20))
```

That business of subtracting the view's height and width from its superview's bounds height and width in order to position the view is confusing and error-prone. With constraints, we can speak the truth directly; our constraints say, plainly and simply, "v3 is 20 points wide and 20 points high and flush with the bottom-right corner of v1."

In addition, of course, constraints can express things that autoresizing can't. For example, instead of applying an absolute height to v2, we could require that its height be exactly one-tenth of v1's height, regardless of how v1 is resized. To do that without constraints, you'd have to implement layoutSubviews and enforce it manually, in code.

 Once you are using explicit constraints to position and size a view, *do not set its frame* (or bounds and center) subsequently; use constraints alone. Otherwise, when layoutSubviews is called, the view will jump back to where its constraints position it. (The exception is that you *may* set a view's frame if you are *in* layoutSubviews, as I'll explain later.)

Visual format

If you find constraint-creation code too verbose, it may be possible to condense it somewhat. Instead of creating each constraint individually, it is sometimes possible to describe multiple constraints simultaneously through a sort of text-based shorthand, called a *visual format*. The shorthand is best understood by example:

```
"V:|[v2(10)]"
```

In that expression, V: means that the vertical dimension is under discussion; the alternative is H:, which is also the default (so it is permitted to specify no dimension). A view's name appears in square brackets, and a pipe (|) signifies the superview, so here we're portraying v2's top edge as butting up against its superview's top edge. Numeric dimensions appear in parentheses, and a numeric dimension accompanying a view's name sets that dimension of that view, so here we're also setting v2's height to 10.

To use a visual format, you have to provide a dictionary mapping the string name of each view mentioned to the actual view. For example, the dictionary accompanying the preceding expression might be ["v2":v2]. So here's another way of expressing of the preceding code example, using the visual format shorthand throughout:

```
let d = ["v2":v2,"v3":v3]
v1.addConstraints(
    NSLayoutConstraint.constraintsWithVisualFormat(
        "H:|[v2]|", options: nil, metrics: nil, views: d)
)
v1.addConstraints(
    NSLayoutConstraint.constraintsWithVisualFormat(
        "V:|[v2(10)]", options: nil, metrics: nil, views: d)
)
```

```
v1.addConstraints(
    NSLayoutConstraint.constraintsWithVisualFormat(
        "H:[v3(20)]|", options: nil, metrics: nil, views: d)
)
v1.addConstraints(
    NSLayoutConstraint.constraintsWithVisualFormat(
        "V:[v3(20)]|", options: nil, metrics: nil, views: d)
)
```

That example creates the same constraints as the previous example, but in four commands instead of eight.

The visual format syntax shows itself to best advantage when multiple views are laid out in relation to one another along the same dimension; in that situation, you get a lot of bang for your buck (many constraints generated by one visual format string). The syntax, however, is severely limited in what constraints it can express (you can't even use it to center things); it conceals the number and exact nature of the constraints that it produces; and personally I find it easier to make a mistake with the visual format syntax than with the complete expression of each constraint. Still, you'll want to become familiar with the visual format syntax, not least because console messages describing a constraint sometimes use it.

Here are some further things to know when generating constraints with the visual format syntax:

- The `metrics:` parameter is a dictionary with numeric values. This lets you use a name in the visual format string where a numeric value needs to go.

- The `options:` parameter is a bitmask (NSLayoutFormatOptions) chiefly letting you do things like add alignments. The alignments you specify are applied to all the views mentioned in the visual format string.

- To specify the distance between two successive views, use hyphens surrounding the numeric value, like this: `"[v1]-20-[v2]"`. The numeric value may optionally be surrounded by parentheses. A single hyphen means that a default distance should be used. (New in iOS 8, that default distance is the *margin*; I'll talk more about margins in a moment.)

- A numeric value in parentheses may be preceded by an equality or inequality operator, and may be followed by an at sign with a priority. Multiple numeric values, separated by comma, may appear in parentheses together. For example: `"[v1(>=20@400,<=30)]"`.

For formal details of the visual format syntax, see the "Visual Format Syntax" chapter of Apple's *Auto Layout Guide*.

In Objective-C, you can form a dictionary for mapping view names to view references more or less automatically, thanks to the NSDictionaryOfVariableBindings macro; for example, NSDictionaryOfVariableBindings(v2,v3) yields the Objective-C equivalent of the dictionary ["v2":v2,"v3":v3] that we formed manually in the preceding code. But Swift lacks macros; there's no preprocessor, so the textual transformation needed to generate a literal dictionary from a literal list of view variable names is impossible. For an alternative, see the dictionaryOfNames utility function in Appendix B.

Constraints as objects

Although the examples so far have involved creating constraints and adding them directly to the interface — and then forgetting about them — it is frequently useful to form constraints and keep them on hand for future use (typically in a property). A common use case is where you intend, at some future time, to change the interface in some radical way, such as by inserting or removing a view; you'll probably find it convenient to keep multiple sets of constraints on hand, each set being appropriate to a particular configuration of the interface. It is then trivial to swap constraints out of and into the interface along with views that they affect.

In this example, we have prepared two properties, constraintsWith and constraintsWithout, initialized as empty arrays of NSLayoutConstraint:

```
var constraintsWith = [NSLayoutConstraint]()
var constraintsWithout = [NSLayoutConstraint]()
```

We create within our main view (mainview) three views, v1, v2, and v3, which are red, yellow, and blue rectangles respectively. We keep strong references (as properties) to all three views. For some reason, we will later want to remove and insert the yellow view (v2) dynamically as the app runs, moving the blue view to where the yellow view was when the yellow view is absent (Figure 1-14). So we create *two* sets of constraints, one describing the positions of v1, v2, and v3 when all three are present, the other describing the positions of v1 and v3 when v2 is absent. We start with v2 present, so it is the first set of constraints that we initially hand over to our main view:

```
let v1 = UIView()
v1.backgroundColor = UIColor.redColor()
v1.setTranslatesAutoresizingMaskIntoConstraints(false)
let v2 = UIView()
v2.backgroundColor = UIColor.yellowColor()
v2.setTranslatesAutoresizingMaskIntoConstraints(false)
let v3 = UIView()
v3.backgroundColor = UIColor.blueColor()
v3.setTranslatesAutoresizingMaskIntoConstraints(false)
mainview.addSubview(v1)
mainview.addSubview(v2)
mainview.addSubview(v3)
```

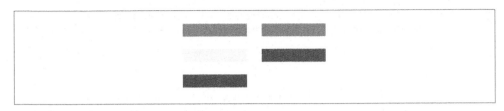

Figure 1-14. Alternate sets of views and constraints

```
self.v1 = v1
self.v2 = v2
self.v3 = v3
// construct constraints
let c1 = NSLayoutConstraint.constraintsWithVisualFormat("H:|-(20)-[v(100)]",
    options: nil, metrics: nil, views: ["v":v1]) as! [NSLayoutConstraint]
let c2 = NSLayoutConstraint.constraintsWithVisualFormat("H:|-(20)-[v(100)]",
    options: nil, metrics: nil, views: ["v":v2]) as! [NSLayoutConstraint]
let c3 = NSLayoutConstraint.constraintsWithVisualFormat("H:|-(20)-[v(100)]",
    options: nil, metrics: nil, views: ["v":v3]) as! [NSLayoutConstraint]
let c4 = NSLayoutConstraint.constraintsWithVisualFormat("V:|-(100)-[v(20)]",
    options: nil, metrics: nil, views: ["v":v1]) as! [NSLayoutConstraint]
let c5with = NSLayoutConstraint.constraintsWithVisualFormat(
    "V:[v1]-(20)-[v2(20)]-(20)-[v3(20)]", options: nil, metrics: nil,
    views: ["v1":v1, "v2":v2, "v3":v3]) as! [NSLayoutConstraint]
let c5without = NSLayoutConstraint.constraintsWithVisualFormat(
    "V:[v1]-(20)-[v3(20)]", options: nil, metrics: nil,
    views: ["v1":v1, "v3":v3]) as! [NSLayoutConstraint]
// first set of constraints
self.constraintsWith.extend(c1)
self.constraintsWith.extend(c2)
self.constraintsWith.extend(c3)
self.constraintsWith.extend(c4)
self.constraintsWith.extend(c5with)
// second set of constraints
self.constraintsWithout.extend(c1)
self.constraintsWithout.extend(c3)
self.constraintsWithout.extend(c4)
self.constraintsWithout.extend(c5without)
// apply first set
NSLayoutConstraint.activateConstraints(self.constraintsWith)
```

All that preparation may seem extraordinarily elaborate, but the result is that when the time comes to swap v2 out of or into the interface, swapping the appropriate constraints is trivial:

```
if self.v2.superview != nil {
    self.v2.removeFromSuperview()
    NSLayoutConstraint.deactivateConstraints(self.constraintsWith)
    NSLayoutConstraint.activateConstraints(self.constraintsWithout)
} else {
```

```
mainview.addSubview(v2)
NSLayoutConstraint.deactivateConstraints(self.constraintsWithout)
NSLayoutConstraint.activateConstraints(self.constraintsWith)
}
```

Guides and margins

In iOS, the top and bottom of the interface are often occupied by a bar (status bar, navigation bar, toolbar, tab bar — see Chapter 12). Your layout will typically occupy the region *between* these bars. On iOS 6 and before, this was trivial, because a view controller would automatically resize its view to fit into that region. But in iOS 7 and iOS 8, a view can extend vertically to the edges of the screen *behind* those bars. Moreover, such bars can come and go dynamically, and can change their heights; for example, in iOS 8 the default behavior is for the status bar to vanish when an iPhone app is in landscape orientation, and a navigation bar is taller when an iPhone app is in portrait orientation than it is when the same app is in landscape orientation.

Therefore, you need something else to anchor your vertical constraints to — something that will move vertically to reflect the location of the bars. Otherwise, an interface that looks right under some circumstances will look wrong in others. For example, consider a view whose top is constrained to the top of the view controller's main view, which is its superview:

```
mainview.addConstraints(
    NSLayoutConstraint.constraintsWithVisualFormat(
        "V:|-0-[v]", options: nil, metrics: nil, views: ["v":v])
)
```

When the app is in landscape orientation, with the status bar removed by default, this view will be right up against the top of the screen, which is fine. But in portrait orientation, this view will *still* be right up against the top the screen, which looks bad because the status bar reappears and overlaps it.

Therefore, UIViewController supplies and maintains two invisible views, the *top layout guide* and the *bottom layout guide*, which it injects as subviews into the view hierarchy of its main view. Your topmost and bottommost vertical constraints will usually not be between a subview and the top or bottom of the main view, but between a subview and the bottom of the top layout guide, or a subview and the top of the bottom layout guide. The bottom of the top layout guide matches the bottom of the lowest top bar, or the top of the main view if there is no top bar; the top of bottom layout guide matches the top of the bottom bar, or the bottom of the main view if there is no bottom bar.

You can access these layout guides programmatically through the UIViewController properties topLayoutGuide and bottomLayoutGuide. For example (this code is in a view controller, so the top layout guide is self.topLayoutGuide):

```
mainview.addConstraints(
    NSLayoutConstraint.constraintsWithVisualFormat(
        "V:[tlg]-0-[v]", options: nil, metrics: nil,
        views: ["tlg":self.topLayoutGuide, "v":v])
)
```

And here's the same thing without a visual format string:

```
mainview.addConstraint(
    NSLayoutConstraint(item: v,
        attribute: .Top,
        relatedBy: .Equal,
        toItem: self.topLayoutGuide,
        attribute: .Bottom,
        multiplier: 1, constant: 0)
)
```

New in iOS 8, views also have *margins*. A view's layoutMargins property is a UIEdge-Insets expressing the minimum standard distance of subviews from the edge of this view as superview. A visual format string that pins a subview's edge to its superview's edge, expressed as a pipe character (|) and a hyphen with no explicit distance value, will cause the subview to butt up against the superview's margin. In iOS 7 and before, this standard minimum spacing was fixed at 20; in iOS 8, it is up to the individual superview. The default for a view controller's main view is a top and bottom margin of 0 and a right and left margin of 16 (which means that the position of your subviews might be different between iOS 7 and iOS 8 if you use the same visual format string and don't change the superview's margins); for any other view, it's 8 on all four margins.

Thus, for example, here's a view that's butting up against its superview's left margin:

```
mainview.addConstraints(
    NSLayoutConstraint.constraintsWithVisualFormat(
        "H:|-[v]", options: nil, metrics: nil, views: ["v":v])
)
```

When using the full constraint-creation syntax, you pin a view with respect to another view's margins using an additional set of NSLayoutAttribute values that's new in iOS 8:

- .LeftMargin, .RightMargin
- .TopMargin, .BottomMargin
- .LeadingMargin, .TrailingMargin
- .CenterXWithinMargins, .CenterYWithinMargins

So here's the same view placed against its superview's left margin, without using a visual format string:

```
mainview.addConstraint(
    NSLayoutConstraint(item: v,
        attribute: .Left,
        relatedBy: .Equal,
        toItem: mainview,
        attribute: .LeftMargin,
        multiplier: 1, constant: 0)
)
```

An additional UIView property, preservesSuperviewLayoutMargins, if true, causes a
view to adopt as its layoutMargins the intersection of its own and its superview's layout-
Margins. For example, consider the following:

```
let v = UIView()
v.backgroundColor = UIColor.redColor()
v.setTranslatesAutoresizingMaskIntoConstraints(false)
mainview.addSubview(v)
mainview.addConstraints(NSLayoutConstraint.constraintsWithVisualFormat(
    "H:|-(0)-[v]-(0)-|", options: nil, metrics: nil, views: ["v":v]))
mainview.addConstraints(NSLayoutConstraint.constraintsWithVisualFormat(
    "V:|-(0)-[v]-(0)-|", options: nil, metrics: nil, views: ["v":v]))
v.preservesSuperviewLayoutMargins = true
```

The view v has, by default, layout margins {8, 8, 8, 8}. Its superview, mainview, is
the view controller's main view, and has, by default, layout margins {0, 16, 0, 16}.
The subview v exactly covers its superview mainview: their edges match. Normally this
would have no effect on v's layout margins, but because we have set its preserves-
SuperviewLayoutMargins to true, the part of mainview's layout margins that extends
further inwards than v's layout margins is adopted by v as its own, so that v's layout
margins are now actually {8, 16, 8, 16}. We can see the effect of this if we subsequently
give v a subview pinned to its layout margins:

```
let v1 = UIView()
v1.backgroundColor = UIColor.greenColor()
v1.setTranslatesAutoresizingMaskIntoConstraints(false)
v.addSubview(v1)
v.addConstraints(NSLayoutConstraint.constraintsWithVisualFormat(
    "H:|-[v1]-|", options: nil, metrics: nil, views: ["v1":v1]))
v.addConstraints(NSLayoutConstraint.constraintsWithVisualFormat(
    "V:|-[v1]-|", options: nil, metrics: nil, views: ["v1":v1]))
```

The green subview v1 is inset 16 points at the left and right from its red superview v,
and 8 points at the top and bottom.

Mistakes with constraints

Creating constraints manually, as I've been doing so far in this chapter, is an invitation
to make a mistake. Your totality of constraints constitute instructions for view layout,
and it is all too easy, as soon as more than one or two views are involved, to generate
faulty instructions. You can (and will) make two major kinds of mistake with constraints:

Conflict

You can apply constraints that can't be satisfied simultaneously. This will be reported in the console (at great length). Only required constraints (priority 1000) can contribute to a conflict, as the runtime is free to ignore lower-priority constraints that it can't satisfy.

Underdetermination (ambiguity)

A view uses autolayout, but you haven't supplied sufficient information to determine its size and position. This is a far more insidious problem, because nothing bad may seem to happen, so you might not discover it until much later. If you're lucky, the view will at least fail to appear, or will appear in an undesirable place, alerting you to the problem.

Let's start by generating a conflict. In this example, we return to our small red square in the lower right corner of a big purple square (Figure 1-12) and append a contradictory constraint:

```
v1.addConstraints(
    NSLayoutConstraint.constraintsWithVisualFormat(
        "H:[v3(20)]|", options: nil, metrics: nil, views: d)
)
v1.addConstraints(
    NSLayoutConstraint.constraintsWithVisualFormat(
        "V:[v3(20)]|", options: nil, metrics: nil, views: d)
)
v1.addConstraints(
    NSLayoutConstraint.constraintsWithVisualFormat(
        "V:[v3(10)]|", options: nil, metrics: nil, views: d)
)
```

The height of v3 can't be both 10 and 20. The runtime reports the conflict, and tells you which constraints are causing it:

```
Unable to simultaneously satisfy constraints. Probably at least one of the
constraints in the following list is one you don't want...

    "<NSLayoutConstraint:0x7f7fabc10750 V:[UIView:0x7f7fabc059d0(20)]>",
    "<NSLayoutConstraint:0x7f7fabc10d10 V:[UIView:0x7f7fabc059d0(10)]>"
```

Now we'll generate an ambiguity. Here, we neglect to give our small red square a height:

```
v1.addConstraints(
    NSLayoutConstraint.constraintsWithVisualFormat(
        "H:[v3(20)]|", options: nil, metrics: nil, views: d)
)
```

No console message alerts us to our mistake. Fortunately, however, v3 fails to appear in the interface, so we know something's wrong. *If your views fail to appear, suspect ambiguity.*

Figure 1-15. View debugging

Suspecting ambiguity is one thing; tracking it down and proving it is another. UIView's `hasAmbiguousLayout` method will help; be sure to remove that call before submitting your app to the App Store. I find it useful to set up a utility method that lets me check a view and all its subviews at any depth for ambiguity (see Appendix B).

To get a full list of the constraints responsible for positioning a particular view within its superview, log the results of calling the UIView instance method `constraints-AffectingLayoutForAxis:`; again, be sure to remove that call before finalizing your app. These constraints do not necessarily belong to this view (and the output doesn't tell you what view they do belong to). Your choices of axis (UILayoutConstraintAxis) are `.Horizontal` and `.Vertical`. If a view doesn't participate in autolayout, the result will be an empty array. Again, a utility method can come in handy (see Appendix B).

Also, use Xcode 6's new view debugging feature (Figure 1-15). With the app running, choose Debug → View Debugging → Capture View Hierarchy, or click the Debug View Hierarchy button in the debug toolbar. At the left, the Debug navigator lists your window and all its views hierarchically, along with their constraints. (Interpreting the constraints here is something of an art, because a constraint involving two views is listed twice.) What's more, when a view is selected in this list or in the canvas, the Size inspector at the right lists its bounds and all the constraints that determine those bounds. This, along with the layered graphical display of your views and constraints in the canvas, is very likely to help you penetrate to the cause of any constraint-related difficulties.

New in Xcode 6, Instruments includes the Cocoa Layout template, which tracks changes to your constraints over time and can help you work out how and when things went awry.

Given the notions of conflict and ambiguity, we can understand what priorities are for. Imagine that all constraints have been placed in boxes, where each box is a priority value, in descending order. The first box (1000) contains all the required constraints, so all required constraints are obeyed first. (If they conflict, that's bad, and a report appears in the log; meanwhile, the system implicitly lowers the priority of one of the conflicting constraints, so that it doesn't have to obey it and can continue with layout by satisfying the remaining required constraints.) If there still isn't enough information to perform unambiguous layout given the required priorities alone, we pull the constraints out of the next box and try to obey them. If we can, consistently with what we've already done, fine; if we can't, or if ambiguity remains, we look in the *next* box — and so on. For a box after the first, we don't care about obeying exactly the constraints it contains; if an ambiguity remains, we can use a lower-priority constraint value to give us something to aim at, resolving the ambiguity, without fully obeying the lower-priority constraint's desires. For example, an inequality is an ambiguity, because an infinite number of values will satisfy it; a lower-priority equality can tell us what value to prefer, resolving the ambiguity, but there's no conflict even if we can't fully achieve that preferred value.

Intrinsic content size

Some built-in interface objects, when using autolayout, have an inherent size in one or both dimensions, so they are not ambiguously laid out even if no explicit NSLayout-Constraint dictates their size. Rather, the inherent size is used to generate constraints implicitly, of class NSContentSizeLayoutConstraint. For example, a button has a standard height, and its width is determined by its title. This inherent size is the object's *intrinsic content size.*

 A change in the font size or text content of a built-in interface object may cause its intrinsic size to change. (I'll give examples in Chapter 10.) You will want to configure your autolayout constraints so that your interface responds to such changes gracefully.

The tendency of an interface object to size itself to its intrinsic content size must not be allowed to conflict with its tendency to obey explicit constraints. Assigning a UILabel an explicit, absolute width constraint should not cause a conflict with its intrinsic content size; and we wouldn't want a UILabel with a lot of text to be compelled by its intrinsic content size to extend outside of its superview. Therefore these tendencies have a lowered priority, and come into force only if no constraint of a higher priority prevents them. Methods taking a UILayoutConstraintAxis parameter (.Horizontal or .Vertical) allow you to access these priorities:

contentHuggingPriorityForAxis:
A view's resistance to growing larger than its intrinsic size in this dimension. In effect, there is an inequality constraint saying that the view's size in this dimension should be less than or equal to its intrinsic size. The default priority for a UILabel is 251; for a UIButton it's 250 (the same as UILayoutPriorityDefaultLow).

contentCompressionResistancePriorityForAxis:
A view's resistance to shrinking smaller than its intrinsic size in this dimension. In effect, there is an inequality constraint saying that the view's size in this dimension should be greater than or equal to its intrinsic size. The default priority is 750 (the same as UILayoutPriorityDefaultHigh).

Those methods are getters; there are corresponding setters. Situations where you would need to change the priorities of these tendencies are few, but they do exist. For example, here are the visual formats configuring two adjacent labels pinned to the superview and to one another:

```
"V:|-20-[_lab1]"
"V:|-20-[_lab2]"
"H:|-20-[_lab1]"
"H:[_lab2]-20-|"
"H:[_lab1]-(>=20)-[_lab2]"
```

There may be no ambiguity initially, but as the superview becomes narrower or the text of the labels becomes longer, an ambiguity arises: which label should be truncated? To dictate the answer, it suffices to raise the compression resistance priority of one of the labels by a single point:

```
let p = self.lab2.contentCompressionResistancePriorityForAxis(.Horizontal)
self.lab1.setContentCompressionResistancePriority(p+1, forAxis: .Horizontal)
```

Alternatively, you may want to lower the priority of some other constraint, to allow intrinsic content size to predominate. An example that Apple gives is a label to the left of a centered button and not permitted to overlap with it. As the text of the label becomes longer, at first, the label grows leftward. But the label should not stretch leftward past the left side of its superview, so it has an inequality constraint pinning its left at a guaranteed minimum distance from the superview's left. When it hits that limit, the label's text should not then be truncated if it doesn't have to be, so the priority with which the button is horizontally centered is set lower than the label's compression resistance priority; in effect, the label is able to force the button to move to the right:

```
self.button.setTranslatesAutoresizingMaskIntoConstraints(false)
self.label.setTranslatesAutoresizingMaskIntoConstraints(false)
let d = dictionaryOfNames(button, label)
self.view.addConstraints(
    NSLayoutConstraint.constraintsWithVisualFormat(
```

```
            "V:[v1]-(112)-|", options: nil, metrics: nil, views: d)
    )
    self.view.addConstraints(
        NSLayoutConstraint.constraintsWithVisualFormat(
            "H:|-(>=10)-[v2]-[v1]-(>=10)-|",
            options: NSLayoutFormatOptions.AlignAllBaseline,
            metrics: nil, views: d)
    )
    let con = NSLayoutConstraint(item: button,
        attribute: .CenterX,
        relatedBy: .Equal,
        toItem: self.view,
        attribute: .CenterX,
        multiplier: 1, constant: 0)
    con.priority = 700
    self.view.addConstraint(con)
```

You can supply an intrinsic size in your own custom UIView subclass by implementing `intrinsicContentSize`. Obviously you should do this only if your view's size depends on its contents. If you need the runtime to call `intrinsicContentSize` again, because that size has changed and the view needs to be laid out afresh, call your view's `invalidate-IntrinsicContentSize` method.

By the same token, you may want to be able to align your custom UIView with another view by their baselines. If your view's baseline is its own bottom, there's nothing to do; but it may be that your view has content that gives a different meaning to the notion of a baseline. To dictate where your custom view's baseline should be, you do not provide a numeric value. Rather, your custom view must contain a subview whose bottom will function as the baseline, and whose top (in iOS 8) will function as the first baseline, and you return that subview in your UIView subclass's `viewForBaselineLayout`.

 The intrinsic size of a UILabel has some additional complications connected with its text wrapping behavior. I'll discuss the matter in detail in Chapter 10.

Configuring Layout in the Nib

The focus of the discussion so far has been on configuring layout in code. This, however, will often be unnecessary; instead, you'll set up your layout (autoresizing or autolayout) in the nib, using the nib editor (Interface Builder). It would not be true to say that you can do absolutely anything in the nib that you could do in code, but the nib editor is certainly a remarkably powerful way of configuring layout (and where it falls short, you can always supplement it with some code in addition).

Autoresizing in the nib

To configure autoresizing in the nib editor, you'll need to ensure that autolayout is turned off for the *.storyboard* or *.xib* file you're editing. To do so, select that file in the Project navigator and show the File inspector: uncheck "Use Auto Layout."

When editing a nib file with autolayout turned off, you can assign a view springs and struts in the Size inspector. A solid line externally represents a strut; a solid line internally represents a spring. A helpful animation shows you the effect on your view's position as its superview is resized.

Constraints in the nib

In a *.xib* or *.storyboard* file where "Use Auto Layout" is checked, a vast array of tools springs to life in the nib editor to help you create constraints that will be instantiated from the nib along with the views. What's more, the nib editor will help prevent you from ending up with conflicting or ambiguous constraints.

Even in a nib with "Use Auto Layout" checked, the nib editor *doesn't generate any constraints* unless you ask it to. However, it doesn't want the app to run with ambiguous layout, because then you might not see any views at all; you wouldn't be able to test your app until you'd fully worked out all the constraints throughout the interface. Therefore, if your views lack needed constraints, the nib supplies them implicitly behind the scenes so that they are present at runtime:

No constraints
> If a view is affected by no constraints at all, it is given constraints tagged in the debugger as "IB auto generated at build time for view with fixed frame."

Ambiguous constraints
> If a view is affected by some constraints but not enough to disambiguate fully, it is given additional constraints tagged in the debugger as "IB auto generated at build time for view with ambiguity."

The nib editor also *doesn't change any constraints* unless you ask it to. If you create constraints and then move or resize a view affected by those constraints, the constraints are *not* automatically changed. This means that the constraints no longer match the way the view is portrayed; if the constraints were to position the view, they wouldn't put it where you've put it. The nib editor will alert you to this situation (a Misplaced Views issue), and can readily resolve it for you, but it won't do so unless you explicitly ask it to.

Creating a constraint

The nib editor provides two primary ways to create a constraint:

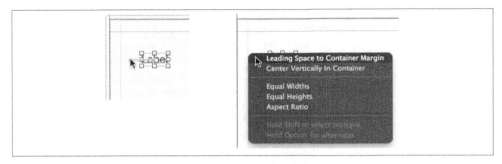

Figure 1-16. Creating a constraint by control-dragging

- Control-drag from one view to another. A HUD appears, listing constraints that you can create (Figure 1-16). Either view can be in the canvas or in the document outline. To create an internal width or height constraint, control-drag from a view to itself! When you control-drag within the canvas, the direction of the drag is used to winnow the options presented in the HUD; for example, if you control-drag horizontally within a view in the canvas, the HUD lists Width but not Height.

- Choose from the Editor → Align or Editor → Pin hierarchical menus, or click the first ("Align") or second ("Pin") buttons at the right end of the layout bar below the canvas.

The buttons in the layout bar are very powerful! They present little popover dialogs where you can choose multiple constraints to create (possibly for multiple views, if that's what you've selected beforehand) and provide them with numeric values (Figure 1-17). Constraints are not actually added until you click Add Constraints at the bottom. Before clicking Add Constraints, think about the Update Frames pop-up menu; if you don't update frames, the views may end up being drawn in the canvas differently from how the constraints describe them (a Misplaced Views issue).

As I mentioned earlier in this chapter, a view controller generates a Top Layout Guide and a Bottom Layout Guide. In the nib editor, these guides are listed in the document outline and elsewhere. An attempt to create a vertical constraint to a view controller's main view from a subview by Control-dragging will *automatically* make a constraint to the corresponding guide rather than to the absolute top or bottom of the main view.

The Xcode 6 nib editor must work with iOS 8, so it also takes account of layout margins (discussed earlier in this chapter). Layout margins are physically shown as faint lines in the canvas. (The faint vertical line at the left of Figure 1-16 is a margin.) By default, when you Control-drag to form a constraint from a view to its superview, the constraint may connect to the superview's layout margin rather than to the superview's absolute edge; if that isn't what you want, hold Option when the HUD is visible to view and choose the nonmargin alternative. Similarly, the popover dialog from the Pin button in the layout

Figure 1-17. Creating constraints from the layout bar

Figure 1-18. A view's constraints displayed in the nib

bar has a "Constrain to margins" checkbox (Figure 1-17). Finally, when editing a constraint (as I describe in the next section), the First Item and Second Item pop-up menus have a "Relative to margin" option.

Viewing and editing constraints

Constraints in the nib are full-fledged objects. They can be selected, edited, and deleted. Moreover, you can create an outlet to a constraint (and there are reasons why you might want to do so).

Constraints in the nib are visible in three places (Figure 1-18):

In the document outline
> Constraints are listed in a special category, "Constraints," under the view to which they belong. (You'll have a much easier time distinguishing these constraints if you give your views meaningful labels!)

In the canvas
> Constraints appear graphically as dimension lines when you select a view that they affect.

In the Size inspector
> When a view affected by constraints is selected, the Size inspector lists those constraints. New in Xcode 6, a Constraints grid also displays the view's constraints graphically.

When you select a constraint in the document outline or the canvas, you can view and edit its values in the Attributes or Size inspector. Alternatively, for simple editing of a constraint's constant, relation, and priority, double-click the constraint in the canvas to summon a little popover dialog. Similarly, when a constraint is listed in a view's Size inspector, double-click it to edit it in its Size inspector, or click its Edit button to summon the little popover dialog.

A view's Size inspector also provides access to its content hugging and content compression resistance priority settings. Beneath these, there's an Intrinsic Size pop-up menu. The idea here is that your custom view might have an intrinsic size, but the nib editor doesn't know this, so it will report an ambiguity when you fail to provide (say) a width constraint that you know isn't actually needed; choose Placeholder to supply an intrinsic size and relieve the nib editor's worries (and to prevent the missing constraints from being generated automatically at runtime).

There is also a Placeholder checkbox in the Attributes inspector when you've selected a constraint ("Remove at build time"). If you check this checkbox, the constraint you're editing *won't* be instantiated when the nib is loaded, and it will *not* be replaced by an automatically generated constraint: in effect, you are deliberately generating ambiguous layout when the views and constraints are instantiated from the nib.

Why might you want to do such a thing? One typical reason is in order to take a view out of the influence of autolayout altogether. Suppose you intend to reposition this view dynamically while the app is running, and the easiest way to do this will be to keep changing its frame or center. As I mentioned earlier, you can't do that to a view that's governed by autolayout, because when layout comes along it will put your view back where it was. On the other hand, you want the convenience of being able design this view in the nib along with the rest of the interface. So you give it constraints in the nib editor and designate them as placeholders. In code, when the app launches, you set this view's `translatesAutoresizingMaskIntoConstraints` to `true` (you can't do that in the

Even Distribution

A common problem is how to distribute views equally within their superview. This is easy to arrange initially, but it is not obvious how to design evenly spaced views that will remain evenly spaced when their superview is resized. The problem is that constraints describe relationships between *views*, not between *constraints*; there is no way to constrain the spacing constraints between views to remain equal to one another automatically as the superview is resized.

You can, on the other hand, constrain the heights or widths of *views* to remain equal to one another. The simplest solution, therefore, is to resort to spacer views with their `hidden` set to `true`.

For example, suppose (in the nib editor) that I have four views that are to remain equally distributed vertically. I constrain their left and right edges, their heights, and the top of the first view and the bottom of the last view, but I do nothing about the vertical position of the two middle views.

Now I introduce three spacer views *between* my real views. I constrain their left edges and widths. I now pin each spacer view, with a constant of 0, to the bottom of the view above it and the top of the view below it. Finally, I select all the spacer views and choose Editor → Pin → Heights Equally. This resolves all ambiguities, fixing the heights of the spacer views and the positions of the two middle real views. The spacer views are hidden, so the user never sees them, but they are responsible for the vertical positioning of the views that the user does see. (Figure 1-18 in fact shows me setting up exactly such a configuration.)

nib editor, unfortunately). Now that view is an autoresizing view, not an autolayout view, and subsequently changing its frame is fine.

Problems with constraints

I've already said that generating constraints manually, in code, is error-prone. The nib editor, however, knows whether it contains problematic constraints. If a view is affected by any constraints, the Xcode nib editor will permit them to be ambiguous or conflicting, but it will also complain helpfully. You should pay attention to such complaints! The nib editor will bring the situation to your attention in various places:

Canvas
> Constraints drawn in the canvas when you select a view that they affect use color coding to express their status:

> *Conflicting constraints*
>> Drawn in red.

Insufficient constraints
> Drawn in orange. These are ambiguous constraints: they don't conflict, but they aren't sufficient to describe a view completely.

Satisfactory constraints
> Drawn in blue.

Document outline
> If there are layout issues, the document outline displays a right arrow in a red or orange circle. Click it to see a detailed list of the issues (Figure 1-19). Hover the mouse over a title to see an Info button which you can click to learn more about the nature of this issue. The icons at the right are buttons: click one for a list of things the nib editor is offering to do to fix the issue for you. The chief issues are:

Conflicting Constraints
> A conflict between constraints.

Missing Constraints
> Ambiguous layout.

Misplaced Views
> If you manually change the frame of a view that is affected by constraints (including its intrinsic size), then the nib editor canvas may be displaying that view differently from how it would really appear if the current constraints were obeyed. A Misplaced Views situation is also reflected in the canvas:
>
> • The constraints in the canvas display the numeric *difference* between their values and the view's frame. They are drawn in orange even if they are not insufficient.
>
> • A dotted outline in the canvas may show where the view would be drawn if the existing constraints were obeyed.

A hierarchical menu, Editor → Resolve Auto Layout Issues, also available from the third button at the bottom right of the layout bar ("Resolve Auto Layout Issues"), proposes five large-scale moves involving *all* the constraints affecting selected views or all views:

Update Frames
> Changes the way the view is drawn in the canvas, to show how it would really appear in the running app under the constraints as they stand. Be careful: if constraints are ambiguous, *this can cause a view to disappear.*
>
> Alternatively, if you have resized a view with intrinsic size constraints, such as a button or a label, and you want it to resume the size it would have according to those intrinsic size constraints, select the view and choose Editor → Size to Fit Content.

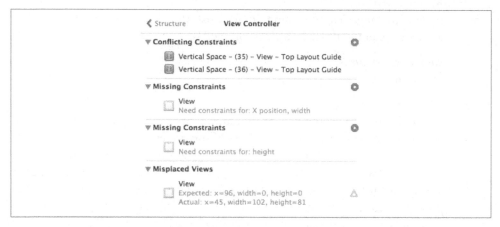

Figure 1-19. Layout issues in the document outline

Update Constraints
> Choose this menu item to change numerically all the existing constraints affecting a view to match the way the canvas is currently drawing the view's frame.

Add Missing Constraints
> Create new constraints so that the view has sufficient constraints to describe its frame unambiguously. The added constraints correspond to the way the canvas is currently drawing the view's frame.
>
> Not everything that this command does may be what you ultimately want; you should regard it as a starting point. For example, the nib editor doesn't know whether you think a certain view's width should be determined by an internal width constraint or by pinning it to the left and right of its superview; and it may generate alignment constraints with other views that you never intended.

Reset to Suggested Constraints
> This is as if you chose Clear Constraints followed by Add Missing Constraints: it removes all constraints affecting the view, and replaces them with a complete set of automatically generated constraints describing the way the canvas is currently drawing the view's frame.

Clear Constraints
> Removes all constraints affecting the view.

Conditional constraints

New in Xcode 6, constraints and views can be made conditional in the nib editor. The conditions on which they depend are the iOS 8 size classes that I discussed earlier. This means that you can design your interface's constraints, and even the presence or absence of views, to depend on the size of the screen. In effect, the interface detects `trait-CollectionDidChange:` and responds to it. Thus:

- You can design directly into your interface a complex rearrangement of that interface when an iPhone app rotates to compensate for a change in device orientation.
- A single *.storyboard* or *.xib* file can be used to design the interface of a universal app, even though the iPad interface and the iPhone interface may be quite different from one another.

Use of conditional constraints is an opt-in feature of the nib editor. You have opted in if "Use Size Classes" is checked in the File inspector for this *.storyboard* or *.xib*. In that case, the following nib editor interface features are present:

- The main view in the canvas, by default, is portrayed as a square, to suggest the dimension-agnostic nature of the design process.
- The center of the layout bar, below the canvas, acquires a pop-up menu where you can choose any combination of size classes. Your choices are Compact, Regular, and (between them) Any, so the choice is represented as a 3×3 grid.

The idea is that you design your interface initially for the general case (Any width, Any height, which is the default). You then use the pop-up grid to switch to a specific case — the layout bar turns blue to indicate that you're in specific-case mode — and modify the design for that case. Do *not* impulsively start moving interface items around! Instead, use the inspectors:

- Use a view's Attributes inspector to determine whether that view is present for a particular size class combination. Note the Installed checkbox! Initially, it applies to the general case. Click the Plus button, at its left, to add *another* Installed checkbox applicable to a particular set of size classes. Now you can check or uncheck Installed checkboxes so that this view is present for some size class combinations but removed for others.
- Use a constraint's Attributes or Size inspector to determine:
  - Whether that constraint is present for a particular size class combination. There is an Installed checkbox, which works just like the Installed checkbox for a view.
  - The value of that constraint's constant for a particular size class combination. The Constant field has a Plus button, at its left, just like the Installed checkbox; click it to add *another* Constant field applicable to a particular set of size classes.

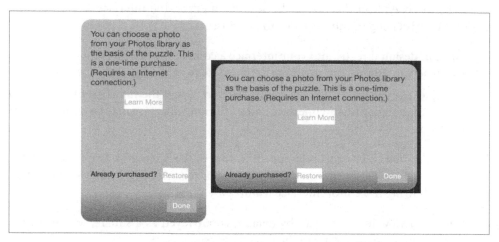

Figure 1-20. A view with differing layout for portrait and landscape

 A constraint or view that is not installed for the set of size classes you're looking at is listed in gray in the document outline.

Here's a simple example from one of my own apps. The view that informs the user of an available in-app purchase appears on the iPad in portrait in a popover, but on the iPhone it appears in landscape completely covering the screen (Figure 1-20). Simple constraints can handle differences such as the width of the descriptive label at the top, but the rearrangement of interface elements at the bottom requires conditional constraints:

- The Restore button is 88 pixels from the bottom in the base case, but is 14 pixels from the bottom in the Compact height case (iPhone in landscape). That's one constraint with two Constant values.

- The Done button is at the lower left in the base case, but is vertically aligned with the Restore button in the Compact height case. That's two constraints — a vertical space constraint between the Done button and the bottom of its superview that's installed only in the general case, and a baseline alignment constraint between the two buttons that's installed only in the Compact height case (Figure 1-21).

View Debugging, Previewing, and Designing

Xcode 6 has several features for helping you visualize and understand your view hierarchy and the effect of your constraints. This section calls attention to some of these.

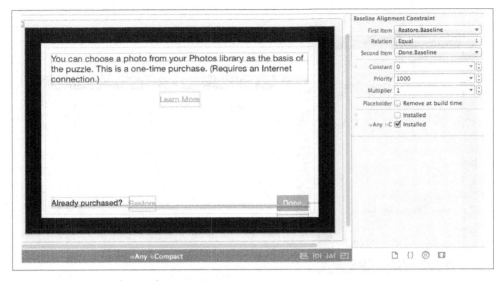

Figure 1-21. A conditional constraint

View debugger

I have already mentioned the view debugger earlier in this chapter. You pause your running app in the debugger and choose Debug → View Debugging → Capture View Hierarchy. Alternatively, click the Debug View Hierarchy button in the debug bar. (You don't actually have to pause the running app in advance; if it isn't paused, either of these commands will pause it.)

The result is that your app's current view hierarchy is analyzed and displayed in two ways (Figure 1-15):

- On the left, in the Debug navigator, the views and their constraints are listed hierarchically.

- At the top, the jump bar shows you the same hierarchy in a different way, and helps you navigate it.

- In the center, in the canvas, the views and their constraints are displayed graphically. The window starts out facing front, much as if you were looking at the screen with the app running; but if you swipe sideways a little in the canvas, the window rotates and its subviews are displayed in front of it, in layers. The slider at the lower left changes the distance between these layers. The double-slider at the lower right lets you eliminate the display of views from the front or back of the layering order (or both). You can switch to wireframe mode. You can display constraints for the currently selected view.

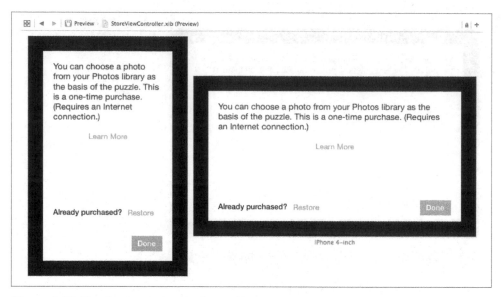

Figure 1-22. Previewing a view in the assistant pane

- On the right, the Object inspector and the Size inspector tell you details about the currently selected object (view or constraint).

 Apple did *not* simply steal, copy, or otherwise infringe upon the idea or interface of existing view hierarchy inspection utilities such as Reveal (*http://revealapp.com*). No.

Previewing your interface

When you're displaying the nib editor in Xcode, the assistant pane's Tracking menu (the first component in its jump bar, Control-4) includes the Preview option. Choose it to see a preview of the currently selected view controller's view (or, in a *.xib* file, the top-level view). The Plus button at the lower left lets you add previews for different devices and device sizes; thus, for example, you can view your interface on iPad and iPhone simultaneously. At the bottom of each preview, a Rotate button lets you switch this preview to the other orientation (Figure 1-22).

In Xcode 6, these previews take account of conditional constraints. Thus, this feature is a very good way to view the effects of your conditional constraints immediately and simultaneously for different combinations of size class.

At the lower right, a language pop-up menu lets you switch your app's text (buttons and labels) to another language for which you have localized your app, or to an artificial "double-length" version of your base language. Again, this is intended as a way of letting you preview the results of your constraints, which need to accomodate possible changes in the width of labels and buttons caused by running the app in a different language.

Resizable simulator

Another new Xcode 6 feature is the resizable simulator. When you choose Resizable iPhone or Resizable iPad as your destination and run your app in the simulator, you get a window where you can change the horizontal and vertical dimensions — either by setting size classes (Compact or Regular) or by providing an arbitrary absolute numerical value. Once again, this is intended as a way to let you test the robustness of your constraints under different runtime conditions.

Observe that if you want your app to respond to a change in size classes while running within a resizable simulator, then either your nib editor must use conditional constraints or your code must implement `traitCollectionDidChange:`.

Designable views and inspectable properties

Also new in Xcode 6, even if your view configures itself and its subviews in code, you can make it appear more or less correctly in the nib editor canvas and preview. To take advantage of this feature, you need a UIView subclass declared `@IBDesignable`:

```
@IBDesignable class MyView: UIView {
    // ... your code goes here ...
}
```

If an instance of this UIView subclass appears in the nib, then whatever code your app runs to prepare the subclass in methods such as `init(coder:)` or `willMoveToSuperview:` will be run also as the nib editor prepares to portray your view. For example, if your `init(coder:)` method adds a UILabel as a subview of this view, then that label will appear not only in the running app but also in the nib editor's drawing of an instance of this view.

In addition, your view can implement `prepareForInterfaceBuilder` to perform visual configurations aimed specifically at how it will be portrayed in the nib editor. For example, if your view contains a UILabel that comes into existence empty but whose purpose is to portray some kind of data at runtime, you could implement `prepareForInterfaceBuilder` to set the label's text to some actual sample data, so that its appearance in the nib editor will be more realistic.

In Figure 1-23, the nib editor displays a MyView instance; the green and red subviews come from MyView's initializer, and the purple background is added in `prepareForInterfaceBuilder`.

Xcode 6's nib editor also has a new interface for setting runtime attributes. (This is unrelated to designable views, but is often mentioned in the same breath.) If your UI-

Figure 1-23. A designable view with an inspectable property

View subclass has a property whose value type is understood by the nib editor, and if this property is declared `@IBInspectable`, then if an instance of this UIView subclass appears in the nib, that property will get a field of its own at the top of the view's Attributes inspector. Thus, when a custom UIView subclass is to be instantiated from the nib, its custom properties can be set in the nib editor rather than having to be set in code. (This feature isn't really new; it's equivalent to setting a nib object's User Defined Runtime Attributes in the Identity inspector, which has been possible for years. But it's a convenient new interface, which Apple presumably hopes will make it more discoverable and useful.)

Inspectable property types are: Bool, number, String, CGRect, CGPoint, CGSize, UI-Color, or UIImage — or an Optional wrapping any of these. You can assign a default value in code; Interface Builder won't portray this value as the default, but you can tell Interface Builder to use the default by leaving the field empty (or, if you've entered a value, by deleting that value).

In Figure 1-23, the nib editor displays MyView's custom `name` property.

Events Related to Layout

I've talked about *how* you configure layout, but I haven't said very much about *when* you configure layout. The simple answer, in many cases, will be: when your interface loads. For instance, our code setting up three colored rectangles with autoresizing or

Autolayout and View Transforms

Ever since autolayout was introduced, back in iOS 6, every edition of this book has contained at this point a rant about the conflict between autolayout and view transforms. The problem was twofold:

- Autolayout was incorrectly implemented. What happened at `layoutSubviews` time was that autolayout used a view's constraints to set its *frame*. But setting the frame of a view whose transform is not the identity transform is exactly what you must *not* do! Doing that, in effect, can undo the transform.

- Merely applying a transform to a view was triggering layout immediately. Thus, autolayout wasn't merely lying in wait to wreck your view transform at some future layout time (such as when the app was rotated); it was wrecking your view transform *immediately*.

In iOS 8, both bugs are gone; autolayout now behaves as it should have done all along. Not only does applying a transform to a view no longer trigger immediate layout, but when layout does come along, autolayout sets your view's bounds and center, not its frame — thus leaving any applied view transforms intact. The workarounds that I suggested in earlier editions of this book are no longer necessary.

autolayout could appropriately go into a view controller's `viewDidLoad` or some similar event early in the lifetime of a view controller (I'll talk much more about view controller lifetime events in Chapter 6). If your interface's autoresizing or autolayout is configured in the nib, the early event in question will be the loading of the nib, and the nib-loading process may well take care of the entire thing, with no code being involved.

Nevertheless, it will be useful to be aware of the chief UIView events related to layout. These are events that you can receive and respond to by overriding them in your UIView subclass. You might want to do this in situations where layout is complex — for example, when you need to supplement autoresizing or autolayout with manual layout in code, or when your autoresizing or autolayout configuration itself needs to change in response to changing conditions.

In iOS 8, the earliest possible layout-related event is the `traitCollectionDidChange:` message, which, as I've already said, is propagated *down* the hierarchy of UITrait-Environments. Thus, if your interface needs to respond to a change in the trait collection — by changing constraints, adding or removing subviews, or what have you — an override of `traitCollectionDidChange:` is the place to do it.

For example, earlier in this chapter I showed some code for swapping a view into or out of the interface together with the entire set of constraints laying out that interface. But I left open the matter of the conditions under which we wanted such swapping to occur.

If we wanted to do this swapping in response to rotation of the app on iPhone, trait-
CollectionDidChange: would be an appropriate event to use as a trigger.

If your interface involves autolayout and constraints, then after traitCollectionDid-
Change: is propagated *down* the hierarchy, the updateConstraints event is propagated
up the hierarchy, starting at the bottom of the hierarchy (the deepest subview) and
working up to the top (typically the root view). This event may be omitted for a view if
its constraints have not changed, but it will certainly be called for the view at the top of
the hierarchy.

You might override updateConstraints in a UIView subclass if your subclass is capable
of altering its own constraints and you need a signal that now is the time to do so. You
must call super or the app will crash (with a helpful error message).

You should never call updateConstraints directly. To trigger an immediate call to
updateConstraints, send a view the updateConstraintsIfNeeded message. But
updateConstraints may still not be sent unless constraints have changed or the view
is at the top of the hierarchy. To force updateConstraints to be sent to a view, send it
the setNeedsUpdateConstraints message.

After the (possible) propagation of traitCollectionDidChange: and (if appropriate)
updateConstraints, a view and its subviews are sent layoutSubviews, starting at the
top of the hierarchy (typically the root view) and working down to the bottom (the
deepest subview).

You can override layoutSubviews in a subclass in order to take a hand in the layout
process. If you're not using autolayout, layoutSubviews does nothing by default; layout-
Subviews is your opportunity to perform manual layout after autoresizing has taken
place. If you are using autolayout, you must call super or the app will crash (with a
helpful error message).

You should never call layoutSubviews directly; to trigger an immediate call to layout-
Subviews, send a view the layoutIfNeeded message (which may cause layout of the
entire view tree, not only below but also above this view), or send setNeedsLayout to
trigger a call to layoutSubviews later on, after your code finishes running, when layout
would normally take place.

When you're using autolayout, what happens in layoutSubviews? The runtime exam-
ines all the constraints affecting this view's subviews, works out values for their center
and bounds, and assigns those views those center and bounds values. In other words,
layoutSubviews performs manual layout! The constraints are merely instructions attached to the views; layoutSubviews reads them and responds accordingly, sizing and
positioning views in the good old-fashioned way. (Thus, layoutSubviews is a place
where it is legal — and indeed necessary — to set the size and position of a view governed
by explicit constraints.)

Knowing this, you might override `layoutSubviews` when you're using autolayout, in order to tweak the outcome. First you call `super`, causing all the subviews to adopt their new frames. Then you examine those frames. If you don't like the outcome, you can change the situation, removing subviews, adding or removing constraints, and so on — and then you call `super` again, to get a new layout outcome.

Unless you explicitly demand immediate layout, layout isn't performed until your code finishes running (and then only if needed). Moreover, ambiguous layout isn't ambiguous until layout actually takes place. Thus, for example, it's perfectly reasonable to cause an ambiguous layout temporarily, provided you resolve the ambiguity before `layout-Subviews` is called. On the other hand, a conflicting constraint conflicts the instant it is added.

It is also possible to *simulate* layout of a view in accordance with its constraints and those of its subviews. This is useful for discovering ahead of time what a view's size would be if layout were performed at this moment. Send the view the `systemLayout-SizeFittingSize:` message. The system will attempt to reach or at least approach the size you specify, at a very low priority; mostly likely you'll specify either `UILayout-FittingCompressedSize` or `UILayoutFittingExpandedSize`, depending on whether what you're after is the smallest or largest size the view can legally attain. New in iOS 8, you can dictate the individual axis priorities explicitly (`systemLayoutSizeFitting-Size:withHorizontalFittingPriority:verticalFittingPriority:`).

CHAPTER 2

Drawing

Many UIView subclasses, such as a UIButton or a UILabel, know how to draw themselves; sooner or later, though, you're going to want to do some drawing of your own. You can draw an image in code, and then display it in your interface in a class that knows how to show an image, such as a UIImageView or a UIButton. A pure UIView is all about drawing, and it leaves that drawing largely up to you; your code determines what the view draws, and hence what it looks like in your interface.

This chapter discusses the mechanics of drawing. Don't be afraid to write drawing code of your own! It isn't difficult, and it's often the best way to make your app look the way you want it to.

(For how to draw text, see Chapter 12.)

UIImage

The basic general UIKit image class is UIImage. UIImage can read a file from disk, so if an image does not need to be created dynamically, but has already been created before your app runs, then drawing may be as simple as providing an image file as a resource in your app's bundle. The system knows how to work with many standard image file types, such as TIFF, JPEG, GIF, and PNG; when an image file is to be included in your app bundle, iOS has a special affinity for PNG files, and you should prefer them whenever possible. You can also obtain image data in some other way, such as by downloading it, and transform this into a UIImage. Conversely, you can construct your own UIImage for display in your interface or for saving to disk (image file output is discussed in Chapter 23).

A pre-existing image file in your app's bundle can be obtained through the UIImage initializer `init(named:)`. This method looks in two places for the image:

Asset catalog

> We look in the asset catalog for an image set with the supplied name. The name is case-sensitive.

Top level of app bundle

> We look at the top level of the app's bundle for an image file with the supplied name. The name is case-sensitive and should include the file extension; if it doesn't include a file extension, *.png* is assumed.

When calling `init(named:)`, an asset catalog is searched before the top level of the app's bundle. If there are multiple asset catalogs, they are all searched, but the search order is indeterminate and cannot be specified, so avoid image sets with the same name.

A nice thing about `init(named:)` is that the image data may be cached in memory, and if you ask for the same image by calling `init(named:)` again later, the cached data may be supplied immediately. Alternatively, you can read an image file from anywhere in your app's bundle directly and without caching, using `init(contentsOfFile:)`, which expects a pathname string; you can get a reference to your app's bundle with `NSBundle.mainBundle()`, and NSBundle then provides instance methods for getting the pathname of a file within the bundle, such as `pathForResource:ofType:`.

Methods that specify a resource in the app bundle, such as `init(named:)` and `pathForResource:ofType:`, respond to suffixes in the name of an actual resource file. On a device with a double-resolution screen, when an image is obtained by name from the app bundle, a file with the same name extended by `@2x`, if there is one, will be used automatically, with the resulting UIImage marked as double-resolution by assigning it a `scale` property value of `2.0`. New in iOS 8, if there is a file with the same name extended by `@3x`, it will be used on the triple-resolution screen of the iPhone 6 Plus, with a `scale` property value of `3.0`.

In this way, your app can contain multiple versions of an image file at different resolutions. Thanks to the `scale` property, a high-resolution version of an image is drawn at the same size as the single-resolution image. Thus, on a high-resolution screen, your code continues to work without change, but your images look sharper.

 iOS 8 doesn't run on any single-resolution iPhone-sized devices, so an iPhone-only app doesn't need any single-resolution image variants. But iOS 8 does run on a single-resolution iPad.

Similarly, a file with the same name extended by `~ipad` will automatically be used if the app is running on an iPad. You can use this in a universal app to supply different images automatically depending on whether the app runs on an iPhone or iPod touch, on the one hand, or on an iPad, on the other. (This is true not just for images but for *any* resource obtained by name from the bundle. See Apple's *Resource Programming Guide*.)

One of the great benefits of an asset catalog, though, is that you can forget all about those name suffix conventions. An asset catalog knows when to use an alternate image within an image set, not from its name, but from its place in the catalog. Put the single-, double-, and triple-resolution alternatives into the slots marked "1x," "2x," and "3x" respectively. For a distinct iPad version of an image, switch the Devices pop-up menu in the image set's Attributes inspector from Universal to Device Specific and check the boxes for the cases you want to distinguish; separate slots for those device types will appear in the asset catalog.

New in iOS 8, an asset catalog can also distinguish between versions of an image intended for different size class situations. (See the discussion of size classes and trait collections in Chapter 1.) In the Attributes inspector for your image set, use the Width and Height pop-up menus to specify which size class possibilities you want to distinguish. Thus, for example, if we're on an iPhone with the app rotated to landscape orientation, and if there's both an Any height and a Compact height alternative in the image set, the Compact height version is used. Moreover, these features are live; for example, if the app rotates from landscape to portrait, and there's both an Any height and a Compact height alternative in the image set, the Compact height version is replaced with the Any height version in your interface, automatically.

The way an asset catalog performs all this magic, in iOS 8, is through trait collections and the UIImageAsset class. When an image is extracted from an asset catalog through `init(named:)` and the name of its image set, its `imageAsset` property is a UIImageAsset. All the images in that image set are available through the UIImageAsset; each image has a trait collection associated with it (its `traitCollection`), and you can ask the UIImageAsset for the image appropriate to a particular trait collection by calling `imageWithTraitCollection:`. A built-in interface object that displays an image is automatically trait collection–aware in iOS 8; it receives the `traitCollectionDidChange:` message and responds accordingly. We can imagine how this works under the hood by building a UIView with an `image` property that does the same thing:

```
class MyView: UIView {
    var image : UIImage!
    override func traitCollectionDidChange(previous: UITraitCollection?) {
        if self.traitCollection != previous {
            self.setNeedsDisplay()
        }
    }
    override func drawRect(rect: CGRect) {
        if var im = self.image {
            if let asset = self.image.imageAsset {
                let tc = self.traitCollection
                im = asset.imageWithTraitCollection(tc)
            }
```

```
            im.drawAtPoint(CGPointZero)
        }
    }
}
```

Moreover, your code can combine images into a UIImageAsset — the code equivalent of an image set in an asset catalog, but *without* an asset catalog. Thus you could, for example, create images in real time (as I'll describe later in this chapter), or fetch images out of your app bundle, and configure them so that one is used when an iPhone app is in portrait orientation and the other is used when the app is in landscape orientation, automatically, like this:

```
let tcdisp = UITraitCollection(displayScale: UIScreen.mainScreen().scale)
let tcphone = UITraitCollection(userInterfaceIdiom: .Phone)
let tcreg = UITraitCollection(verticalSizeClass: .Regular)
let tc1 = UITraitCollection(traitsFromCollections: [tcdisp, tcphone, tcreg])
let tccom = UITraitCollection(verticalSizeClass: .Compact)
let tc2 = UITraitCollection(traitsFromCollections: [tcdisp, tcphone, tccom])
let moods = UIImageAsset()
let frowney = UIImage(named:"frowney")!
let smiley = UIImage(named:"smiley")!
moods.registerImage(frowney, withTraitCollection: tc1)
moods.registerImage(smiley, withTraitCollection: tc2)
```

After that, if `frowney` is placed into the interface — for example, by handing it over to a UIImageView as its image, as I'll explain in a moment — it automatically alternates with `smiley` when the app changes orientation. The remarkable thing is that this works even though there is no persistent reference to `frowney`, `smiley`, or the UIImageAsset (`moods`). The reason is that `frowney` and `smiley` are cached by the system (because of the call to `init(named:)`), and they each maintain a strong reference to the UIImage-Asset with which they are registered.

 New in iOS 8, you can also specify a target trait collection while fetching an image from the asset catalog or from your app bundle, by calling `init(named:in-Bundle:compatibleWithTraitCollection:)`. The bundle specified will usually be nil, meaning the app's main bundle.

UIImageView

Many built-in Cocoa interface objects will accept a UIImage as part of how they draw themselves; for example, a UIButton can display an image, and a UINavigationBar or a UITabBar can have a background image. I'll discuss those in Chapter 12. But when you simply want an image to appear in your interface, you'll probably hand it to a UIImage-View, which has the most knowledge and flexibility with regard to displaying images and is intended for this purpose.

The nib editor supplies some shortcuts in this regard: the Attributes inspector of an interface object that can have an image will have a pop-up menu listing known images in your project, and such images are also listed in the Media library (Command-Option-Control-4). Media library images can often be dragged onto an interface object in the canvas to assign them, and if you drag a Media library image into a plain view, it is transformed into a UIImageView displaying that image.

A UIImageView can actually have *two* images, one assigned to its `image` property and the other assigned to its `highlightedImage` property; the value of the UIImageView's `highlighted` property dictates which of the two is displayed at any given moment. A UIImageView does not automatically highlight itself merely because the user taps it, the way a button does. However, there are certain situations where a UIImageView will respond to the highlighting of its surroundings; for example, within a table view cell, a UIImageView will show its highlighted image when the cell is highlighted (Chapter 8).

A UIImageView is a UIView, so it can have a background color in addition to its image, it can have an alpha (transparency) value, and so forth (see Chapter 1). An image may have areas that are transparent, and a UIImageView will respect this; thus an image of any shape can appear. A UIImageView without a background color is invisible except for its image, so the image simply appears in the interface, without the user being aware that it resides in a rectangular host. A UIImageView without an image and without a background color is invisible, so you could start with an empty UIImageView in the place where you will later need an image and subsequently assign the image in code. You can assign a new image to substitute one image for another, or set the image view's `image` property to nil to remove it.

How a UIImageView draws its image depends upon the setting of its `contentMode` property (UIViewContentMode). (The `contentMode` property is inherited from UI-View; I'll discuss its more general purpose later in this chapter.) For example, `.ScaleToFill` means the image's width and height are set to the width and height of the view, thus filling the view completely even if this alters the image's aspect ratio; `.Center` means the image is drawn centered in the view without altering its size. The best way to get a feel for the meanings of the various `contentMode` settings is to assign a UIImageView a small image in a nib and then, in the Attributes inspector, change the Mode pop-up menu, and see where and how the image draws itself.

You should also pay attention to a UIImageView's `clipsToBounds` property; if it is `false`, its image, even if it is larger than the image view and even if it is not scaled down by the `contentMode`, may be displayed in its entirety, extending beyond the image view itself.

When creating a UIImageView in code, you can take advantage of a convenience initializer, `init(image:)` (or `init(image:highlightedImage:)`). The default `contentMode` is `.ScaleToFill`, but the image is not initially scaled; rather, *the view itself is sized*

Figure 2-1. Mars appears in my interface

to match the image. You will still probably need to position the UIImageView correctly in its superview. In this example, I'll put a picture of the planet Mars in the center of the app's interface (Figure 2-1; for the CGRect `center` property, see Appendix B):

```
let iv = UIImageView(image:UIImage(named:"Mars")) // asset catalog
mainview.addSubview(iv)
iv.center = iv.superview!.bounds.center
iv.frame.integerize()
```

What happens to the size of an existing UIImageView when you assign an image to it depends on whether the image view is using autolayout. If it isn't, or if its size is constrained absolutely, the image view's size doesn't change. But under autolayout, the size of the new image becomes the image view's new `intrinsicContentSize`, so the image view will adopt the image's size unless other constraints prevent.

Resizable Images

A UIImage can generate a *resizable image*, by calling its `resizableImageWithCap-Insets:resizingMode:` method. The `capInsets:` argument is a UIEdgeInsets, a struct consisting of four floats representing inset values starting at the top and proceeding counterclockwise — top, left, bottom, right. They represent distances inward from the edges of the image. In a context larger than the image, a resizable image can behave in one of two ways, depending on the `resizingMode:` value (UIImageResizingMode):

`.Tile`

The interior rectangle of the inset area is tiled (repeated) in the interior; each edge is formed by tiling the corresponding edge rectangle outside the inset area. The four corner rectangles outside the inset area are drawn unchanged.

`.Stretch`

The interior rectangle of the inset area is stretched *once* to fill the interior; each edge is formed by stretching the corresponding edge rectangle outside the inset area *once*. The four corner rectangles outside the inset area are drawn unchanged.

Certain places in the interface require a resizable image; for example, a custom image that serves as the track of a slider or progress view (Chapter 12) must be resizable, so

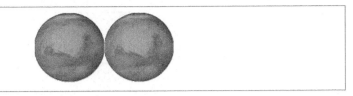

Figure 2-2. Tiling the entire image of Mars

Figure 2-3. Tiling the interior of Mars

that it can fill a space of any length. And there can frequently be other situations where you want to fill a background by tiling or stretching an existing image.

In these examples, assume that `self.iv` is a UIImageView with absolute height and width (so that it won't adopt the size of its image) and with a `contentMode` of `.ScaleTo-Fill` (so that the image will exhibit resizing behavior). First, I'll illustrate tiling an entire image (Figure 2-2); note that the `capInsets:` is `UIEdgeInsetsZero`:

```
let mars = UIImage(named:"Mars")!
let marsTiled = mars.resizableImageWithCapInsets(
    UIEdgeInsetsZero, resizingMode: .Tile)
self.iv.image = marsTiled
```

Now we'll tile the interior of the image, changing the `capInsets:` argument from the previous code (Figure 2-3):

```
let marsTiled = mars.resizableImageWithCapInsets(
    UIEdgeInsetsMake(
        mars.size.height / 4.0,
        mars.size.width / 4.0,
        mars.size.height / 4.0,
        mars.size.width / 4.0
    ), resizingMode: .Tile)
```

Next, I'll illustrate stretching. We'll start by changing just the `resizingMode:` from the previous code (Figure 2-4):

Figure 2-4. Stretching the interior of Mars

Figure 2-5. Stretching a few pixels at the interior of Mars

```
let marsTiled = mars.resizableImageWithCapInsets(
    UIEdgeInsetsMake(
        mars.size.height / 4.0,
        mars.size.width / 4.0,
        mars.size.height / 4.0,
        mars.size.width / 4.0
    ), resizingMode: .Stretch)
```

A common stretching strategy is to make almost half the original image serve as a cap inset, leaving just a pixel or two in the center to fill the entire interior of the resulting image (Figure 2-5):

```
let marsTiled = mars.resizableImageWithCapInsets(
    UIEdgeInsetsMake(
        mars.size.height / 2.0 - 1,
        mars.size.width / 2.0 - 1,
        mars.size.height / 2.0 - 1,
        mars.size.width / 2.0 - 1
    ), resizingMode: .Stretch)
```

You should also experiment with different scaling `contentMode` settings. In the preceding example, if the image view's `contentMode` is `.ScaleAspectFill`, and if the image view's `clipsToBounds` is `true`, we get a sort of gradient effect, because the top and bottom of the stretched image are outside the image view and aren't drawn (Figure 2-6).

Alternatively, you can configure a resizable image without code, in the project's asset catalog. It is often the case that a particular image will be used in your app chiefly as a resizable image, and always with the same `capInsets:` and `resizingMode:`, so it makes sense to configure this image once rather than having to repeat the same code. And even if an image is configured in the asset catalog to be resizable, it can appear in your interface

Figure 2-6. Mars, stretched and clipped

Figure 2-7. Mars, sliced in the asset catalog

as a normal image as well — for example, if you use it to initialize an image view, or assign it to an image view under autolayout, or if the image view doesn't scale its image (it has a contentMode of .Center, for example).

To configure an image in an asset catalog as a resizable image, select the image and, in the Slicing section of the Attributes inspector, change the Slices pop-up menu to Horizontal, Vertical, or Horizontal and Vertical. When you do this, additional interface appears. You can specify the resizingMode with another pop-up menu. You can work numerically, or click Show Slicing at the lower right of the canvas and work graphically. The graphical editor is zoomable, so zoom in to work comfortably.

The reason this feature is called Slicing and not Resizing is that it can do more than resizableImageWithCapInsets:resizingMode: can do: it lets you specify the end caps *separately* from the tiled or stretched region, with the rest of the image being sliced out. The meaning of your settings is intuitively clear from the graphical slicing editor. In Figure 2-7, for example, the dark areas at the top left, top right, bottom left, and bottom right will be drawn as is. The narrow bands will be stretched, and the small rectangle at the top center will be stretched to fill most of the interior. But the rest of the image, the large central area covered by a sort of gauze curtain, will be omitted entirely. The result is shown in Figure 2-8.

Figure 2-8. Mars, sliced and stretched

Image Rendering Mode

Several places in an iOS app's interface automatically treat an image as a *transparency mask*, also known as a *template*. This means that the image color values are ignored, and only the transparency (alpha) values of each pixel matter. The image shown on the screen is formed by combining the image's transparency values with a single tint color. Such, for example, is the behavior of a tab bar item's image.

The way an image will be treated is a property of the image, its `renderingMode`. This property is read-only; to change it, generate a new image with a different rendering mode, by calling `imageWithRenderingMode:`. The rendering mode values (UIImage-RenderingMode) are:

- `.Automatic`
- `.AlwaysOriginal`
- `.AlwaysTemplate`

The default is `.Automatic`, which means that the image is drawn normally everywhere except in certain limited contexts, where it is used as a transparency mask.

With the `renderingMode` property, you can *force* an image to be drawn normally, even in a context that would usually treat it as a transparency mask. You can also do the opposite: you can *force* an image to be treated as a transparency mask, even in a context that would otherwise treat it normally.

To accompany this feature, iOS gives every UIView a `tintColor`, which will be used to tint any template images it contains. Moreover, this `tintColor` by default is inherited down the view hierarchy, and indeed throughout the entire app, starting with the UI-Window (Chapter 1). Thus, assigning your app's main window a tint color is probably one of the few changes you'll make to the window; otherwise, your app adopts the system's blue tint color. (Alternatively, if you're using a main storyboard, set the Global Tint color in its File inspector.) Individual views can be assigned their own tint color, which is inherited by their subviews. Figure 2-9 shows two buttons displaying the same background image, one in normal rendering mode, the other in template rendering

Figure 2-9. One image in two rendering modes

mode, in an app whose window tint color is red. (I'll say more about template images and `tintColor` in Chapter 12.)

New in Xcode 6, an asset catalog can assign an image a rendering mode. Select the image set in the asset catalog, and use the Render As pop-up menu in the Attributes inspector to set the rendering mode to Default (`.Automatic`), Original Image (`.Always-Original`), or Template Image (`.AlwaysTemplate`). This is an excellent approach whenever you have an image that you will primarily use in a specific rendering mode, because it saves you from having to remember to set that rendering mode in code every time you fetch the image. Instead, any time you call `init(named:)`, this image arrives with the rendering mode already set.

Graphics Contexts

A UIImageView draws an existing image for you and takes care of all the details; in many cases, it will be all you'll need. Eventually, though, you may want to create some drawing yourself, directly, in code. To do so, you will always need a *graphics context*.

A graphics context is basically a place you can draw. Conversely, you can't draw in code unless you've got a graphics context. There are several ways in which you might obtain a graphics context; in this chapter I will concentrate on two, which have proven in my experience to be far and away the most common:

You create an image context
> The function `UIGraphicsBeginImageContextWithOptions` creates a graphics context suitable for use as an image. You then draw into this context to generate the image. When you've done that, you call `UIGraphicsGetImageFromCurrentImageContext` to turn the context into a UIImage, and then `UIGraphicsEndImageContext` to dismiss the context. Now you have a UIImage that you can display in your interface or draw into some other graphics context or save as a file.

Cocoa hands you a graphics context
> You subclass UIView and implement `drawRect:`. At the time your `drawRect:` implementation is called, Cocoa has already created a graphics context and is asking you to draw into it, right now; whatever you draw is what the UIView will display.

A slight variant of this situation is that you subclass CALayer and implement `draw-InContext:`, or make some object the delegate of a layer and implement `draw-Layer:inContext:`; layers are discussed in Chapter 3.

Moreover, at any given moment there either is or is not a *current graphics context*:

- `UIGraphicsBeginImageContextWithOptions` not only creates an image context, it also makes that context the current graphics context.
- When `drawRect:` is called, the UIView's drawing context is already the current graphics context.
- Callbacks with a `context:` argument have *not* made any context the current graphics context; rather, that argument is a reference to a graphics context.

What beginners find most confusing about drawing is that there are two separate sets of tools for drawing. These tool sets take different attitudes toward the context in which they will draw:

UIKit

Various Cocoa classes know how to draw themselves; these include UIImage, NSString (for drawing text), UIBezierPath (for drawing shapes), and UIColor. Some of these classes provide convenience methods with limited abilities; others are extremely powerful. In many cases, UIKit will be all you'll need.

With UIKit, you can draw *only into the current context*. So if you're in a `UIGraphics-BeginImageContextWithOptions` or `drawRect:` situation, you can use the UIKit convenience methods directly; there is a current context and it's the one you want to draw into. If you've been handed a `context:` argument, on the other hand, then if you want to use the UIKit convenience methods, you'll have to make that context the current context; you do this by calling `UIGraphicsPushContext` (and be sure to restore things with `UIGraphicsPopContext` later).

Core Graphics

This is the full drawing API. Core Graphics, often referred to as Quartz, or Quartz 2D, is the drawing system that underlies all iOS drawing — UIKit drawing is built on top of it — so it is low-level and consists of C functions. There are a lot of them! This chapter will familiarize you with the fundamentals; for complete information, you'll want to study Apple's *Quartz 2D Programming Guide*.

With Core Graphics, you must *specify a graphics context* (a CGContext) to draw into, explicitly, in every function call. If you've been handed a `context:` argument, then that's probably the graphics context you want to draw into. But in a `UIGraphics-BeginImageContextWithOptions` or `drawRect:` situation, you have no reference to a context; to use Core Graphics, you need to get such a reference. Since the context you want to draw into is the current graphics context, you call `UIGraphicsGet-CurrentContext` to get the needed reference.

So we have two sets of tools and three ways in which a context might be supplied; that makes six ways of drawing. To clarify, I'll now demonstrate all six of them! Without worrying just yet about the actual drawing commands, focus your attention on how the context is specified and on whether we're using UIKit or Core Graphics. First, I'll draw a blue circle by implementing a UIView subclass's `drawRect:`, using UIKit to draw into the current context, which Cocoa has already prepared for me:

```
override func drawRect(rect: CGRect) {
    let p = UIBezierPath(ovalInRect: CGRectMake(0,0,100,100))
    UIColor.blueColor().setFill()
    p.fill()
}
```

Now I'll do the same thing with Core Graphics; this will require that I first get a reference to the current context:

```
override func drawRect(rect: CGRect) {
    let con = UIGraphicsGetCurrentContext()
    CGContextAddEllipseInRect(con, CGRectMake(0,0,100,100))
    CGContextSetFillColorWithColor(con, UIColor.blueColor().CGColor)
    CGContextFillPath(con)
}
```

Next, I'll implement a UIView subclass's `drawLayer:inContext:`. In this case, we're handed a reference to a context, but it isn't the current context. So I have to make it the current context in order to use UIKit:

```
override func drawLayer(layer: CALayer, inContext con: CGContext) {
    UIGraphicsPushContext(con)
    let p = UIBezierPath(ovalInRect: CGRectMake(0,0,100,100))
    UIColor.blueColor().setFill()
    p.fill()
    UIGraphicsPopContext()
}
```

To use Core Graphics in `drawLayer:inContext:`, I simply keep referring to the context I was handed:

```
override func drawLayer(layer: CALayer, inContext con: CGContext) {
    CGContextAddEllipseInRect(con, CGRectMake(0,0,100,100))
    CGContextSetFillColorWithColor(con, UIColor.blueColor().CGColor)
    CGContextFillPath(con)
}
```

Finally, for the sake of completeness, let's make a UIImage of a blue circle. We can do this at any time (we don't need to wait for some particular method to be called) and in any class (we don't need to be in a UIView subclass). The resulting UIImage (here called `im`) is suitable anywhere you would use a UIImage. For instance, you could hand it over to a visible UIImageView as its `image`, thus causing the image to appear onscreen. Or you could save it as a file. Or, as I'll explain in the next section, you could use it in another drawing.

First, I'll draw my image using UIKit:

```
UIGraphicsBeginImageContextWithOptions(CGSizeMake(100,100), false, 0)
let p = UIBezierPath(ovalInRect: CGRectMake(0,0,100,100))
UIColor.blueColor().setFill()
p.fill()
let im = UIGraphicsGetImageFromCurrentImageContext()
UIGraphicsEndImageContext()
// im is the blue circle image, do something with it here ...
```

Here's the same thing using Core Graphics:

```
UIGraphicsBeginImageContextWithOptions(CGSizeMake(100,100), false, 0)
let con = UIGraphicsGetCurrentContext()
CGContextAddEllipseInRect(con, CGRectMake(0,0,100,100))
CGContextSetFillColorWithColor(con, UIColor.blueColor().CGColor)
CGContextFillPath(con)
let im = UIGraphicsGetImageFromCurrentImageContext()
UIGraphicsEndImageContext()
// im is the blue circle image, do something with it here ...
```

You may be wondering about the arguments to `UIGraphicsBeginImageContextWith-Options`. The first argument is obviously the size of the image to be created. The second argument declares whether the image should be opaque; if I had passed `true` instead of `false` here, my image would have a black background, which I don't want. The third argument specifies the image scale, corresponding to the UIImage `scale` property I discussed earlier; by passing 0, I'm telling the system to set the scale for me in accordance with the main screen resolution, so my image will look good on both single-resolution and high-resolution devices.

You don't have to use UIKit or Core Graphics exclusively; on the contrary, you can intermingle UIKit calls and Core Graphics calls to operate on the same graphics context. They merely represent two different ways of telling a graphics context what to do.

 You may find that the dance required to begin an image context, draw into it, extract the image, and end the context, is a bit tedious and error-prone. If so, you might like to consider a utility function that I provide in Appendix B. It has the advantage that you provide the drawing instructions in a closure and an image is returned directly.

Figure 2-10. Two images of Mars combined side by side

UIImage Drawing

A UIImage provides methods for drawing itself into the current context. We know how to obtain a UIImage, and we know how to obtain an image context and make it the current context, so we can experiment with these methods. Here, I'll make a UIImage consisting of two pictures of Mars side by side (Figure 2-10):

```
var mars = UIImage(named:"Mars")!
var sz = mars.size
UIGraphicsBeginImageContextWithOptions(
    CGSizeMake(sz.width*2, sz.height), false, 0)
mars.drawAtPoint(CGPointMake(0,0))
mars.drawAtPoint(CGPointMake(sz.width,0))
var im = UIGraphicsGetImageFromCurrentImageContext()
UIGraphicsEndImageContext()
```

Observe that image scaling works perfectly in that example. If we have multiple resolution versions of our original Mars image, the correct one for the current device is used, and is assigned the correct `scale` value. Our call to `UIGraphicsBeginImageContextWithOptions` has a third argument of 0, so the image context that we are drawing into also has the correct `scale`. And the image that results from calling `UIGraphicsGetImageFromCurrentImageContext` has the correct `scale` as well. Thus, this same code produces an image that looks correct on the current device, whatever its screen resolution may be.

Additional UIImage methods let you scale an image into a desired rectangle as you draw, and specify the compositing (blend) mode whereby the image should combine with whatever is already present. To illustrate, I'll create an image showing Mars centered in another image of Mars that's twice as large, using the Multiply blend mode (Figure 2-11):

```
mars = UIImage(named:"Mars")!
sz = mars.size
UIGraphicsBeginImageContextWithOptions(
    CGSizeMake(sz.width*2, sz.height*2), false, 0)
mars.drawInRect(CGRectMake(0,0,sz.width*2, sz.height*2))
mars.drawInRect(
```

Figure 2-11. Two images of Mars in different sizes, composited

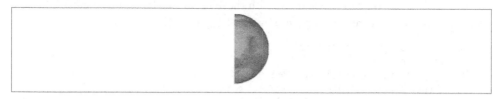

Figure 2-12. Half the original image of Mars

```
        CGRectMake(sz.width/2.0, sz.height/2.0, sz.width, sz.height),
        blendMode: kCGBlendModeMultiply, alpha: 1.0)
    im = UIGraphicsGetImageFromCurrentImageContext()
    UIGraphicsEndImageContext()
```

There is no UIImage drawing method for specifying the source rectangle — that is, for times when you want to extract a smaller region of the original image. You can work around this by creating a smaller graphics context and positioning the image drawing so that the desired region falls into it. For example, to obtain an image of the right half of Mars, you'd make a graphics context half the width of the `mars` image, and then draw `mars` shifted left, so that only its right half intersects the graphics context. There is no harm in doing this, and it's a perfectly standard strategy; the left half of `mars` simply isn't drawn (Figure 2-12):

```
mars = UIImage(named:"Mars")!
sz = mars.size
UIGraphicsBeginImageContextWithOptions(
    CGSizeMake(sz.width/2.0, sz.height), false, 0)
mars.drawAtPoint(CGPointMake(-sz.width/2.0,0))
im = UIGraphicsGetImageFromCurrentImageContext()
UIGraphicsEndImageContext()
```

Figure 2-13. Image of Mars split in half (and flipped)

CGImage Drawing

The Core Graphics version of UIImage is CGImage. They are easily converted to one another: a UIImage has a `CGImage` property that accesses its Quartz image data, and you can make a UIImage from a CGImage using `init(CGImage:)` or its more configurable sibling, `init(CGImage:scale:orientation:)`.

A CGImage lets you create a new image directly from a rectangular region of the original image, which you can't do with UIImage. (A CGImage has other powers a UIImage doesn't have; for example, you can apply an image mask to a CGImage.) I'll demonstrate by splitting the image of Mars in half and drawing the two halves separately (Figure 2-13):

```
mars = UIImage(named:"Mars")!
// extract each half as CGImage
sz = mars.size
var marsLeft = CGImageCreateWithImageInRect(
    mars.CGImage,
    CGRectMake(0,0,sz.width/2.0,sz.height))
var marsRight = CGImageCreateWithImageInRect(
    mars.CGImage,
    CGRectMake(sz.width/2.0,0,sz.width/2.0,sz.height))
// draw each CGImage
UIGraphicsBeginImageContextWithOptions(
    CGSizeMake(sz.width*1.5, sz.height), false, 0)
var con = UIGraphicsGetCurrentContext()
CGContextDrawImage(con,
    CGRectMake(0,0,sz.width/2.0,sz.height), marsLeft)
CGContextDrawImage(con,
    CGRectMake(sz.width,0,sz.width/2.0,sz.height), marsRight)
im = UIGraphicsGetImageFromCurrentImageContext()
UIGraphicsEndImageContext()
```

But there's a problem with that example: the drawing is upside-down! It isn't rotated; it's mirrored top to bottom, or, to use the technical term, *flipped*. This phenomenon can arise when you create a CGImage and then draw it with `CGContextDrawImage`, and is due to a mismatch in the native coordinate systems of the source and target contexts.

There are various ways of compensating for this mismatch between the coordinate systems. One is to draw the CGImage into an intermediate UIImage and extract *another* CGImage from that. Example 2-1 presents a utility function for doing this.

Example 2-1. Utility for flipping an image drawing

```
func flip (im: CGImage) -> CGImage {
    let sz = CGSizeMake(
        CGFloat(CGImageGetWidth(im)), CGFloat(CGImageGetHeight(im)))
    UIGraphicsBeginImageContextWithOptions(sz, false, 0)
    CGContextDrawImage(UIGraphicsGetCurrentContext(),
        CGRectMake(0, 0, sz.width, sz.height), im)
    let result = UIGraphicsGetImageFromCurrentImageContext().CGImage
    UIGraphicsEndImageContext()
    return result;
}
```

Armed with the utility function from Example 2-1, we can fix our calls to `CGContext-DrawImage` in the previous example so that they draw the halves of Mars the right way up:

```
CGContextDrawImage(con,
    CGRectMake(0,0,sz.width/2.0,sz.height), flip(marsLeft))
CGContextDrawImage(con,
    CGRectMake(sz.width,0,sz.width/2.0,sz.height), flip(marsRight))
```

However, we've *still* got a problem: on a high-resolution device, if there is a high-resolution variant of our image file, the drawing comes out all wrong. The reason is that we are obtaining our initial Mars image using UIImage's `init(named:)`, which returns a UIImage that compensates for the increased size of a high-resolution image by setting its own `scale` property to match. But a CGImage doesn't have a `scale` property, and knows nothing of the fact that the image dimensions are increased! Therefore, on a high-resolution device, the CGImage that we extract from our Mars UIImage as `mars.CGImage` is larger (in each dimension) than `mars.size`, and all our calculations after that are wrong.

The best solution for dealing a CGImage, therefore, is to wrap it in a UIImage and draw the UIImage instead of the CGImage. The UIImage can be formed in such a way as to compensate for scale: call `init(CGImage:scale:orientation:)` as you form the UI-Image from the CGImage. Moreover, by drawing a UIImage instead of a CGImage, we avoid the flipping problem! So here's an approach that deals with both flipping and scale, with no need for the `flip` utility:

```
mars = UIImage(named:"Mars")!
sz = mars.size
// derive CGImage first, use its dimensions to extract its halves
marsCG = mars.CGImage
szCG = CGSizeMake(
    CGFloat(CGImageGetWidth(marsCG)), CGFloat(CGImageGetHeight(marsCG)))
```

```
marsLeft =
    CGImageCreateWithImageInRect(
        marsCG, CGRectMake(0,0,szCG.width/2.0,szCG.height))
marsRight =
    CGImageCreateWithImageInRect(
        marsCG, CGRectMake(szCG.width/2.0,0,szCG.width/2.0,szCG.height))
UIGraphicsBeginImageContextWithOptions(
    CGSizeMake(sz.width*1.5, sz.height), false, 0)
// instead of calling flip, pass through UIImage
UIImage(CGImage: marsLeft, scale: mars.scale,
    orientation: mars.imageOrientation)!
    .drawAtPoint(CGPointMake(0,0))
UIImage(CGImage: marsRight, scale: mars.scale,
    orientation: mars.imageOrientation)!
    .drawAtPoint(CGPointMake(sz.width,0))
im = UIGraphicsGetImageFromCurrentImageContext()
UIGraphicsEndImageContext()
```

Yet another solution to flipping is to apply a transform to the graphics context before drawing the CGImage, effectively flipping the context's internal coordinate system. This is elegant, but can be confusing if there are other transforms in play. I'll talk more about graphics context transforms later in this chapter.

Snapshots

An entire view — anything from a single button to your whole interface, complete with its contained hierarchy of views — can be drawn into the current graphics context by calling the UIView instance method drawViewHierarchyInRect:afterScreen-Updates:. (This method is much faster than the CALayer method renderInContext:; nevertheless, renderInContext: does still come in handy, as I'll show in Chapter 5.) The result is a *snapshot* of the original view: it looks like the original view, but it's basically just a bitmap image of it, a lightweight visual duplicate.

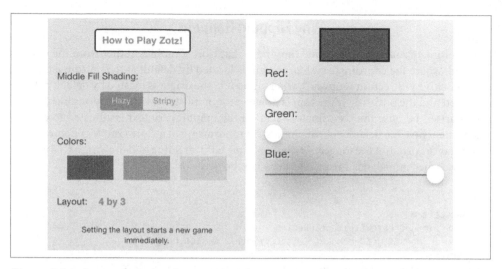

Figure 2-14. A snapshot view in an animation

An even faster way to obtain a snapshot of a view is to use the UIView (or UIScreen) instance method `snapshotViewAfterScreenUpdates:`. The result is a UIView, not a UIImage; it's rather like a UIImageView that knows how to draw only one image, namely the snapshot. Such a snapshot view will typically be used as is, but you can enlarge its bounds and the snapshot image will stretch. If you want the stretched snapshot to behave like a resizable image, call `resizableSnapshotViewFromRect:afterScreen-Updates:withCapInsets:` instead. It is perfectly reasonable to make a snapshot view from a snapshot view.

Snapshots are useful because of the dynamic nature of the iOS interface. For example, you might place a snapshot of a view in your interface in front of the real view to hide what's happening, or use it during an animation to present the illusion of a view moving when in fact it's just a snapshot.

Here's an example from one of my apps. Figure 2-14 shows the "before" and "after" state of a custom transition between view controller views. The user taps one of the three colored rectangles in the first view (left), and the second view rises up from the bottom of the screen to let the user edit, with sliders, the colors of that rectangle (right); in this case, the user has tapped the blue rectangle. What you can't see in the illustration is the animation: as the second view rises, so does the blue rectangle, passing from its position in the first view to its position in the second view, growing as it does so, to emphasize that what the user is about to edit is the same color swatch that was just tapped.

Or so it seems! In reality, it would make no sense to move the literal color swatch rectangle from the first view to the second view. What rises and grows during the animation is just a snapshot of the color swatch rectangle. Here's the relevant part of the code; it won't mean much to you until you've read about animations (Chapter 4) and custom view transitions (Chapter 6), but you can readily see why this would be a typical situation for using a snapshot:

```
// take snapshot of swatch
let cpc = (vc1 as! UINavigationController).viewControllers[0]
    as! ColorPickerController
let snapshot = cpc.swatch.snapshotViewAfterScreenUpdates(false)
// work out initial and final positions for snapshot
let r1 = con.convertRect(cpc.swatch.frame, fromView:cpc.swatch.superview)
let r2 = self.tappedColor.superview!.convertRect(
    self.tappedColor.frame, toView:vc2.view)
// add snapshot to interface in place of original swatch
snapshot.frame = r1
con.addSubview(snapshot)
cpc.swatch.hidden = true
// animate!
UIView.animateWithDuration(0.8, animations:{
    snapshot.frame = r2
    // ...
}
```

CIFilter and CIImage

The "CI" in CIFilter and CIImage stands for Core Image, a technology for transforming images through mathematical filters. About 130 such filters are available in iOS 8. Core Image started life on the desktop (OS X); some of the filters available on the desktop aren't available in iOS (presumably because they are too intensive mathematically for a mobile device).

A filter is a CIFilter. The available filters fall naturally into several categories:

Patterns and gradients
These filters create CIImages that can then be combined with other CIImages, such as a single color, a checkerboard, stripes, or a gradient.

Compositing
These filters combine one image with another, using compositing blend modes familiar from image processing programs such as Photoshop.

Color
These filters adjust or otherwise modify the colors of an image. Thus you can alter an image's saturation, hue, brightness, contrast, gamma and white point, exposure, shadows and highlights, and so on.

Geometric
These filters perform basic geometric transformations on an image, such as scaling, rotation, and cropping.

Transformation

These filters distort, blur, or stylize an image. Relatively few of them are available on iOS.

Transition

These filters provide a frame of a transition between one image and another; by asking for frames in sequence, you can animate the transition (I'll demonstrate in Chapter 4).

Special purpose

These filters perform highly specialized operations such as face detection and generation of QR codes.

The basic use of a CIFilter is quite simple:

- You specify what filter you want by supplying its string name; to learn what these names are, consult Apple's *Core Image Filter Reference*, or call the CIFilter class method `filterNamesInCategories:` with a nil argument.

- Each filter has a small number of keys and values that determine its behavior (as if a filter were a kind of dictionary). You can learn about these keys entirely in code, but typically you'll consult the documentation. For each key that you're interested in, you supply a key–value pair. In supplying values, a number must be wrapped up as an NSNumber (Swift will take care of this for you), and there are a few supporting classes such as CIVector (like CGPoint and CGRect combined) and CIColor, whose use is easy to grasp.

Among a CIFilter's keys are the input image or images on which the filter is to operate; such an image must be a CIImage. You can obtain this CIImage from a CGImage with `init(CGImage:)` or from a UIImage with `init(image:)`.

 Do not attempt, as a shortcut, to obtain a CIImage directly from a UIImage by calling the UIImage instance method `CIImage`. This method does *not* transform a UIImage into a CIImage! It merely points to the CIImage that already backs the UIImage, and your images are not backed by a CIImage, but rather by a CGImage. I'll explain where a CIImage-backed UIImage comes from in just a moment.

Alternatively, you can obtain a CIImage as the output of a filter — which means that *filters can be chained together*.

There are three ways to describe and use a filter:

- Create the filter with CIFilter's `init(name:)`. Now append the keys and values by calling `setValue:forKey:` repeatedly. Obtain the output CIImage as the filter's `outputImage`.

- Create the filter and supply the keys and values in a single move, by calling CIFilter's `init(name:withInputParameters:)`. Obtain the output CIImage as the filter's `outputImage`.

- New in iOS 8, if a CIFilter requires an input image and you already have a CIImage to fulfill this role, specify the filter and supply the keys and values (as a dictionary), *and receive the output CIImage as a result*, all in a single move, by calling the CIImage instance method `imageByApplyingFilter:withInputParameters:`.

As you build a chain of filters, nothing actually happens. The only calculation-intensive move comes at the very end, when you transform the final CIImage in the chain into a bitmap drawing. There are two ways to do this:

- Create a CIContext (by calling `init(options:)`) and then call `createCGImage:fromRect:`, handing it the final CIImage as the first argument. The only mildly tricky thing here is that a CIImage doesn't have a frame or bounds; it has an `extent`. You will often use this as the second argument to `createCGImage:fromRect:`. The final output CGImage is ready for any purpose, such as for display in your app, for transformation into a UIImage, or for use in further drawing.

- Create a UIImage directly from the final CIImage by calling `init(CIImage:)` or `init(CIImage:scale:orientation:)`. You must then *draw the UIImage* into some graphics context. That last step is essential; the CIImage is not transformed into a bitmap until you do it. Thus, a UIImage generated from `imageWithCIImage:` is *not* suitable for display directly in a UIImageView. It is useful for drawing, not for display.

 Okay, I lied. There's a third way to render visibly the CIImage that comes out of a CIFilter: you can call a CIContext's `drawImage:inRect:fromRect:` to draw into an GLKView. This book doesn't talk about GLKView — it involves GLKit and Open-GLES, which are outside its purview.

To illustrate, I'll start with an ordinary photo of myself (it's true I'm wearing a motorcycle helmet, but it's still ordinary) and create a circular vignette effect (Figure 2-15). We derive from the image of me (`moi`) a CIImage (`moici`). We use a CIFilter (`grad`) to form a radial gradient between the default colors of white and black. Then we use a second CIFilter that treats the radial gradient as a mask for blending between the photo of me and a default clear background: where the radial gradient is white (everything inside the gradient's inner radius) we see just me, and where the radial gradient is black (everything outside the gradient's outer radius) we see just the clear color, with a gradation in between, so that the image fades away in the circular band between the gradient's radii:

Figure 2-15. A photo of me, vignetted

```
let moi = UIImage(named:"Moi")!
let moici = CIImage(image:moi)
let moiextent = moici.extent()
let center = CIVector(x: moiextent.width/2.0, y: moiextent.height/2.0)
let smallerDimension = min(moiextent.width, moiextent.height)
let largerDimension = max(moiextent.width, moiextent.height)
// first filter, old way: form filter, set values, get output
let grad = CIFilter(name: "CIRadialGradient")
grad.setValue(center, forKey:"inputCenter")
grad.setValue(smallerDimension/2.0 * 0.85, forKey:"inputRadius0")
grad.setValue(largerDimension/2.0, forKey:"inputRadius1")
let gradimage = grad.outputImage
// second filter, new iOS 8 way: turn one CIImage into another
let blendimage = moici.imageByApplyingFilter(
    "CIBlendWithMask", withInputParameters: [
        "inputMaskImage":gradimage
    ])
```

We now have the final CIImage in the chain (`blendimage`); remember, the processor has not yet performed any drawing. Now, however, we want to generate the final bitmap and display it. Let's say we're going to display it as the `image` of a UIImageView. We can create a CGImage by passing the CIImage through a CIContext:

```
let moicg = CIContext(options: nil)
    .createCGImage(blendimage, fromRect: moiextent)
self.iv.image = UIImage(CGImage: moicg)
```

Alternatively, we could capture our final CIImage as a UIImage directly — but then we must draw with it in order to generate the bitmap output of the filter chain. For example, we could draw it into an image context:

```
UIGraphicsBeginImageContextWithOptions(moiextent.size, false, 0)
UIImage(CIImage: blendimage)!.drawInRect(moiextent)
let im = UIGraphicsGetImageFromCurrentImageContext()
UIGraphicsEndImageContext()
self.iv.image = im
```

A filter chain can be encapsulated into a single custom filter by subclassing CIFilter. Your subclass just needs to override the `outputImage` property (and possibly other methods such as `setDefaults`), with additional properties to make it key–value coding compliant for any input keys. Here's our vignette filter as a simple CIFilter subclass, where the input keys are the input image and a percentage that adjusts the gradient's smaller radius:

```
class MyVignetteFilter : CIFilter {
    var inputImage : CIImage!
    var inputPercentage = NSNumber(double:1.0)
    override var outputImage : CIImage! {
        get {
            return self.makeOutputImage()
        }
    }
    private func makeOutputImage () -> CIImage {
        let moiextent = self.inputImage.extent()
        let grad = CIFilter(name: "CIRadialGradient")
        let center = CIVector(x: moiextent.width/2.0, y: moiextent.height/2.0)
        let smallerDimension = min(moiextent.width, moiextent.height)
        let largerDimension = max(moiextent.width, moiextent.height)
        grad.setValue(center, forKey:"inputCenter")
        grad.setValue(
            smallerDimension/2.0 * CGFloat(self.inputPercentage.doubleValue),
            forKey:"inputRadius0")
        grad.setValue(largerDimension/2.0, forKey:"inputRadius1")
        let gradimage = grad.outputImage
        let blend = CIFilter(name: "CIBlendWithMask")
        blend.setValue(self.inputImage, forKey: "inputImage")
        blend.setValue(gradimage, forKey: "inputMaskImage")
        return blend.outputImage
    }
}
```

And here's how to use our CIFilter subclass and display its output:

```
let vig = MyVignetteFilter()
let moici = CIImage(image: UIImage(named:"Moi"))
vig.setValue(moici, forKey: "inputImage")
vig.setValue(NSNumber(double:0.7), forKey: "inputPercentage")
let outim = vig.outputImage
let outimcg = CIContext(options: nil).createCGImage(
    outim, fromRect: outim.extent())
self.iv.image = UIImage(CGImage: outimcg)
```

New in iOS 8, you can create your own CIFilter from scratch — not by combining existing filters, but by coding the actual mathematics of the filter. The details are outside the scope of this book; you'll want to look at the CIKernel class.

Blur and Vibrancy Views

iOS 7 introduced a convention where certain views, such as navigation bars and the control center, are translucent and display a blurred rendition of what's behind them. Apple encouraged developers to imitate this convention, as a way of subliminally suggesting that the current view is temporary and secondary, but neglected to supply any standard way of doing so; there was no access to whatever trickery Apple itself was using to perform this blurring rapidly and efficiently. Typically, your code would snapshot the view to be covered, as I described earlier in this chapter, and then blur it; but how? There's a blurring CIFilter, but it's much too slow. A better approach was to add the UIImageEffects class from Apple's Blurring and Tinting an Image sample code, but then why hadn't Apple made this class part of iOS itself? In addition, Apple's blurred views can show views moving behind them, but a snapshot, obviously, is frozen and can't do that.

iOS 8 corrects this omission by introducing the UIVisualEffectView class. To use a UIVisualEffectView, create it with `init(effect:)`; the `effect:` argument will be an instance of a UIVisualEffect subclass, either a UIBlurEffect or a UIVibrancyEffect. You can place other views in front of the UIVisualEffectView, but don't give it any direct subviews; subviews must go inside its `contentView`. To tint what's seen through the UIVisualEffectView, set the `backgroundColor` of its `contentView`.

UIBlurEffect

> To initialize a UIBlurEffect, call `init(style:)`; the styles (UIBlurEffectStyle) are `.Dark`, `.Light`, and `.ExtraLight`. (`.ExtraLight` is suitable particularly for pieces of interface that function like a navigation bar or toolbar.) Here's a complete example from my own code (this is, in fact, the background view that appears on the right side of Figure 2-14):
>
> ```
> let fuzzy = UIVisualEffectView(effect:(UIBlurEffect(style:.Light)))
> ```

UIVibrancyEffect

> To initialize a UIVibrancyEffect, call `init(forBlurEffect:)`. Vibrancy tints a view so as to make it harmonize with the blurred colors underneath it. The intention here is that the vibrancy effect view should sit in front of a blur effect view, typically in its `contentView`, adding vibrancy to a single UIView that's inside its *own* `contentView`; you tell the vibrancy effect what the underlying blur effect is, so that they harmonize. You can fetch a visual effect view's blur effect as its `effect` property, but that's a UIVisualEffect — the superclass — so you'll have to cast to a UIBlurEffect in order to hand it to `init(forBlurEffect:)`.

Here's an example of a blur effect view covering the interface, blurring what's behind it, and containing a UILabel wrapped in a vibrancy effect view (Figure 2-16):

Figure 2-16. A blurred background and a vibrant label

```
let blur = UIVisualEffectView(effect: UIBlurEffect(style: .Light))
blur.frame = mainview.bounds
blur.autoresizingMask = .FlexibleWidth | .FlexibleHeight
let vib = UIVisualEffectView(effect: UIVibrancyEffect(
    forBlurEffect: blur.effect as! UIBlurEffect))
let lab = UILabel()
lab.text = "Hello, world!"
lab.sizeToFit()
vib.frame = lab.frame
vib.contentView.addSubview(lab)
vib.center = CGPointMake(blur.bounds.midX, blur.bounds.midY)
vib.autoresizingMask = .FlexibleTopMargin | .FlexibleBottomMargin |
    .FlexibleLeftMargin | .FlexibleRightMargin
blur.contentView.addSubview(vib)
mainview.addSubview(blur)
```

Apple seems to think that vibrancy makes a view more legible in conjunction with the underlying blur, but I'm not persuaded. The vibrant view's color is made to harmonize with the blurred color behind it, but harmony implies similarity, which can make the vibrant view *less* legible. You'll have to experiment. With the particular interface I'm blurring, the vibrant label in Figure 2-16 looks okay with a .Dark or .ExtraLight blur effect view, but is very hard to see with a .Light blur effect view.

There are a lot of useful additional notes, well worth consulting, in the *UIVisualEffect-View.h* header. Observe that both a blur effect view and a blur effect with an embedded vibrancy view are available as built-in objects in the nib editor.

Drawing a UIView

The examples of drawing so far in this chapter have mostly produced UIImage objects, chiefly by calling `UIGraphicsBeginImageContextWithOptions` to obtain a graphics context, suitable for display by a UIImageView or any other interface object that knows how to display an image. But, as I've already explained, a UIView provides a graphics context; whatever you draw into that graphics context will appear in that view. The technique here is to subclass UIView and implement the subclass's `drawRect:` method. At the time that `drawRect:` is called, the current graphics context has already been set to the view's own graphics context. You can use Core Graphics functions or UIKit convenience methods to draw into that context.

So, for example, let's say we have a UIView subclass called MyView. You would then instantiate this class and get the instance into the view hierarchy. One way to do this would be to drag a UIView into a view in the nib editor and set its class to MyView in the Identity inspector; another would be to create the MyView instance and put it into the interface in code. The result is that, from time to time, MyView's `drawRect:` will be called. This is your subclass, so you get to write the code that runs at that moment. Whatever you draw will appear inside the MyView instance. There will usually be no need to call `super`, since UIView's own implementation of `drawRect:` does nothing.

 You should *never* call `drawRect:` yourself! If a view needs updating and you want its `drawRect:` called, send the view the `setNeedsDisplay` message. This will cause `drawRect:` to be called at the next proper moment. Also, don't override `drawRect:` unless you are assured that this is legal. For example, it is not legal to override `drawRect:` in a subclass of UIImageView; you cannot combine your drawing with that of the UIImageView.

The need to draw in real time, on demand, surprises some beginners, who worry that drawing may be a time-consuming operation. This can indeed be a reasonable consideration, and where the same drawing will be used in many places in your interface, it may well make sense to draw a UIImage instead, once, and then reuse that UIImage. In general, however, you should not optimize prematurely. The code for a drawing operation may appear verbose and yet be extremely fast. Moreover, the iOS drawing system is efficient; it doesn't call `drawRect:` unless it has to (or is told to, through a call to `setNeedsDisplay`), and once a view has drawn itself, the result is cached so that the cached drawing can be reused instead of repeating the drawing operation from scratch. (Apple refers to this cached drawing as the view's *bitmap backing store*.) You can readily satisfy yourself of this fact with some caveman debugging, logging in your `drawRect:` implementation; you may be amazed to discover that your custom UIView's `drawRect:` code is called only once in the entire lifetime of the app! In fact, moving code to `drawRect:` is commonly a way to *increase* efficiency. This is because it is more efficient for the drawing engine to render directly onto the screen than for it to render offscreen and then copy those pixels onto the screen.

Where drawing is extensive and can be compartmentalized into sections, you may be able to gain some additional efficiency by paying attention to the rect parameter passed into drawRect:. It designates the region of the view's bounds that needs refreshing. Normally, this is the view's entire bounds; but if you call setNeedsDisplayInRect:, it will be the CGRect that you passed in as argument. You could respond by drawing only what goes into those bounds; but even if you don't, your drawing will be clipped to those bounds, so, while you may not spend less time drawing, the system will draw more efficiently.

When creating a custom UIView subclass instance in code, you may be surprised and annoyed to find that the view has a black background:

```
let mv = MyView(frame:CGRectMake(20,20,150,100))
self.view.addSubview(mv)
```

This can be frustrating if what you expected and wanted was a transparent background, and it's a source of considerable confusion among beginners. The black background arises when two things are true:

- The view's backgroundColor is nil.
- The view's opaque is true.

Unfortunately, when creating a UIView in code, both those things *are* true by default! So if you don't want the black background, you must do something about one or the other of them (or both). If a view isn't going to be opaque, its opaque should be set to false anyway, so that's probably the cleanest solution:

```
let mv = MyView(frame:CGRectMake(20,20,150,100))
self.view.addSubview(mv)
mv.opaque = false
```

Alternatively, this being your own UIView subclass, you could implement its init(frame:) (the designated initializer) to have the view set its *own* opaque to false:

```
override init(frame: CGRect) {
    super.init(frame:frame)
    self.opaque = false
}
```

With a UIView created in the nib, on the other hand, the black background problem doesn't arise. This is because such a UIView's backgroundColor is not nil. The nib assigns it *some* actual background color, even if that color is UIColor.clearColor().

Of course, if a view fills its rectangle with opaque drawing or has an opaque background color, you can leave opaque set to true and gain some drawing efficiency (see Chapter 1).

Graphics Context Settings

As you draw in a graphics context, the drawing obeys the context's current settings. Thus, the procedure is always to configure the context's settings first, and then draw. For example, to draw a red line followed by a blue line, you would first set the context's line color to red, and then draw the first line; then you'd set the context's line color to blue, and then draw the second line. To the eye, it appears that the redness and blueness are properties of the individual lines, but in fact, at the time you draw each line, line color is a feature of the entire graphics context. This is true regardless of whether you use UIKit methods or Core Graphics functions.

A graphics context thus has, at every moment, a *state*, which is the sum total of all its settings; the way a piece of drawing looks is the result of what the graphics context's state was at the moment that piece of drawing was performed. To help you manipulate entire states, the graphics context provides a *stack* for holding states. Every time you call CGContextSaveGState, the context pushes the entire current state onto the stack; every time you call CGContextRestoreGState, the context retrieves the state from the top of the stack (the state that was most recently pushed) and sets itself to that state.

Thus, a common pattern is: call CGContextSaveGState; manipulate the context's settings, thus changing its state; draw; call CGContextRestoreGState to restore the state and the settings to what they were before you manipulated them. You do not have to do this before *every* manipulation of a context's settings, however, because settings don't necessarily conflict with one another or with past settings. You can set the context's line color to red and then later to blue without any difficulty. But in certain situations you do want your manipulation of settings to be undoable, and I'll point out several such situations later in this chapter.

Many of the settings that constitute a graphics context's state, and that determine the behavior and appearance of drawing performed at that moment, are similar to those of any drawing application. Here are some of them, along with some of the commands that determine them. I list Core Graphics functions, followed by some UIKit convenience methods that call them:

Line thickness and dash style
> CGContextSetLineWidth, CGContextSetLineDash (and UIBezierPath lineWidth, setLineDash:count:phase:)

Line end-cap style and join style
> CGContextSetLineCap, CGContextSetLineJoin, CGContextSetMiterLimit (and UIBezierPath lineCapStyle, lineJoinStyle, miterLimit)

Line color or pattern
CGContextSetRGBStrokeColor, CGContextSetGrayStrokeColor, CGContextSet-StrokeColorWithColor, CGContextSetStrokePattern (and UIColor setStroke)

Fill color or pattern
CGContextSetRGBFillColor, CGContextSetGrayFillColor, CGContextSetFill-ColorWithColor, CGContextSetFillPattern (and UIColor setFill)

Shadow
CGContextSetShadow, CGContextSetShadowWithColor

Overall transparency and compositing
CGContextSetAlpha, CGContextSetBlendMode

Anti-aliasing
CGContextSetShouldAntialias

Additional settings include:

Clipping area
Drawing outside the clipping area is not physically drawn.

Transform (or "CTM," for "current transform matrix")
Changes how points that you specify in subsequent drawing commands are mapped onto the physical space of the canvas.

Many of these settings will be illustrated by examples later in this chapter.

Paths and Shapes

By issuing a series of instructions for moving an imaginary pen, you trace out a *path*. The path is constructed by tracing it out from point to point. You must first tell the pen where to position itself, setting the current point; after that, you issue a series of commands telling it how to trace out each subsequent piece of the path. Each additional piece of the path starts at the current point; its end becomes the new current point.

Note that a path, in and of itself, does *not* constitute drawing! First you provide a path; *then* you draw. Drawing can mean stroking the path or filling the path, or both. Again, this should be a familiar notion from certain drawing applications.

Here are some path-drawing commands you're likely to give:

Position the current point
CGContextMoveToPoint

Trace a line
CGContextAddLineToPoint, CGContextAddLines

Trace a rectangle
CGContextAddRect, CGContextAddRects

Trace an ellipse or circle
CGContextAddEllipseInRect

Trace an arc
CGContextAddArcToPoint, CGContextAddArc

Trace a Bezier curve with one or two control points
CGContextAddQuadCurveToPoint, CGContextAddCurveToPoint

Close the current path
CGContextClosePath. This appends a line from the last point of the path to the first point. There's no need to do this if you're about to fill the path, since it's done for you.

Stroke or fill the current path
CGContextStrokePath, CGContextFillPath, CGContextEOFillPath, CGContext-DrawPath. Stroking or filling the current path *clears the path*. Use CGContextDraw-Path if you want both to fill and to stroke the path in a single command, because if you merely stroke it first with CGContextStrokePath, the path is cleared and you can no longer fill it. There are also a lot of convenience functions that create a path and stroke or fill it all in a single move:

- CGContextStrokeLineSegments
- CGContextStrokeRect
- CGContextStrokeRectWithWidth
- CGContextFillRect
- CGContextFillRects
- CGContextStrokeEllipseInRect
- CGContextFillEllipseInRect

A path can be compound, meaning that it consists of multiple independent pieces. For example, a single path might consist of two separate closed shapes: a rectangle and a circle. When you call CGContextMoveToPoint in the middle of constructing a path (that is, after tracing out a path and without clearing it by filling, stroking, or calling CGContextBeginPath), you pick up the imaginary pen and move it to a new location without tracing a segment, thus preparing to start an independent piece of the same path. If you're worried, as you begin to trace out a path, that there might be an existing path and that your new path might be seen as a compound part of that existing path,

Figure 2-17. A simple path drawing

you can call `CGContextBeginPath` to specify that this is a different path; many of Apple's examples do this, but in practice I usually do not find it necessary.

To illustrate the typical use of path-drawing commands, I'll generate the up-pointing arrow shown in Figure 2-17. This might not be the best way to create the arrow, and I'm deliberately avoiding use of the convenience functions, but it's clear and shows a nice basic variety of typical commands:

```
// obtain the current graphics context
let con = UIGraphicsGetCurrentContext()
// draw a black (by default) vertical line, the shaft of the arrow
CGContextMoveToPoint(con, 100, 100)
CGContextAddLineToPoint(con, 100, 19)
CGContextSetLineWidth(con, 20)
CGContextStrokePath(con)
// draw a red triangle, the point of the arrow
CGContextSetFillColorWithColor(con, UIColor.redColor().CGColor)
CGContextMoveToPoint(con, 80, 25)
CGContextAddLineToPoint(con, 100, 0)
CGContextAddLineToPoint(con, 120, 25)
CGContextFillPath(con)
// snip a triangle out of the shaft by drawing in Clear blend mode
CGContextMoveToPoint(con, 90, 101)
CGContextAddLineToPoint(con, 100, 90)
CGContextAddLineToPoint(con, 110, 101)
CGContextSetBlendMode(con, kCGBlendModeClear)
CGContextFillPath(con)
```

If a path needs to be reused or shared, you can encapsulate it as a CGPath. You can copy the graphics context's current path using `CGContextCopyPath`. Even without a graphics context, you can create a new CGMutablePath and construct the path using various CGPath functions that parallel the CGContext path-construction functions. Also, there are a number of CGPath functions for creating a path based on simple geometry or based on an existing path:

- `CGPathCreateWithRect`
- `CGPathCreateWithEllipseInRect`

- `CGPathCreateCopyByStrokingPath`
- `CGPathCreateCopyByDashingPath`
- `CGPathCreateCopyByTransformingPath`

The UIKit class UIBezierPath wraps CGPath (in its `CGPath` property); it, too, provides methods parallel to the CGContext path-construction functions, such as:

- `init(rect:)`
- `init(ovalInRect:)`
- `moveToPoint:`
- `addLineToPoint:`
- `addArcWithCenter:radius:startAngle:endAngle:clockwise:`
- `addQuadCurveToPoint:controlPoint:`
- `addCurveToPoint:controlPoint1:controlPoint2:`
- `closePath`

Also, UIBezierPath offers one extremely useful convenience constructor, `init(rounded-Rect:cornerRadius:)` — drawing a rectangle with rounded corners using only Core Graphics functions is rather tedious.

When you call the UIBezierPath instance method `fill` or `stroke` (or `fillWithBlend-Mode:alpha:` or `strokeWithBlendMode:alpha:`), the current graphics context is saved, the wrapped CGPath is made the current graphics context's path and stroked or filled, and the current graphics context is restored.

Thus, using UIBezierPath together with UIColor, we could rewrite our arrow-drawing routine entirely with UIKit methods:

```
let p = UIBezierPath()
// shaft
p.moveToPoint(CGPointMake(100,100))
p.addLineToPoint(CGPointMake(100, 19))
p.lineWidth = 20
p.stroke()
// point
UIColor.redColor().set()
p.removeAllPoints()
p.moveToPoint(CGPointMake(80,25))
p.addLineToPoint(CGPointMake(100, 0))
p.addLineToPoint(CGPointMake(120, 25))
p.fill()
// snip
p.removeAllPoints()
```

```
p.moveToPoint(CGPointMake(90,101))
p.addLineToPoint(CGPointMake(100, 90))
p.addLineToPoint(CGPointMake(110, 101))
p.fillWithBlendMode(kCGBlendModeClear, alpha:1.0)
```

There's no savings of code here over calling Core Graphics functions, so your choice of Core Graphics or UIKit is a matter of taste. UIBezierPath is particularly useful when you want to capture a CGPath and pass it around as an object; an example appears in Chapter 21. See also the discussion in Chapter 3 of CAShapeLayer, which takes a CGPath that you've constructed and draws it for you within its own bounds on the screen.

Clipping

Another use of a path is to mask out areas, protecting them from future drawing. This is called *clipping*. By default, a graphics context's clipping region is the entire graphics context: you can draw anywhere within the context.

The clipping area is a feature of the context as a whole, and any new clipping area is applied by intersecting it with the existing clipping area; so if you apply your own clipping region, the way to remove it from the graphics context later is to plan ahead and wrap things with calls to `CGContextSaveGState` and `CGContextRestoreGState`.

To illustrate, I'll rewrite the code that generated our original arrow (Figure 2-17) to use clipping instead of a blend mode to "punch out" the triangular notch in the tail of the arrow. This is a little tricky, because what we want to clip to is not the region inside the triangle but the region outside it. To express this, we'll use a compound path consisting of more than one closed area — the triangle, and the drawing area as a whole (which we can obtain with `CGContextGetClipBoundingBox`).

Both when filling a compound path and when using it to express a clipping region, the system follows one of two rules:

Winding rule
> The fill or clipping area is denoted by an alternation in the direction (clockwise or counterclockwise) of the path demarcating each region.

Even-odd rule (EO)
> The fill or clipping area is denoted by a simple count of the paths demarcating each region.

Our situation is extremely simple, so it's easier to use the even-odd rule. So we set up the clipping area using `CGContextEOClip` and then draw the arrow:

```
// obtain the current graphics context
let con = UIGraphicsGetCurrentContext()
// punch triangular hole in context clipping region
CGContextMoveToPoint(con, 90, 100)
CGContextAddLineToPoint(con, 100, 90)
```

```
CGContextAddLineToPoint(con, 110, 100)
CGContextClosePath(con)
CGContextAddRect(con, CGContextGetClipBoundingBox(con))
CGContextEOClip(con)
// draw the vertical line
CGContextMoveToPoint(con, 100, 100)
CGContextAddLineToPoint(con, 100, 19)
CGContextSetLineWidth(con, 20)
CGContextStrokePath(con)
// draw the red triangle, the point of the arrow
CGContextSetFillColorWithColor(con, UIColor.redColor().CGColor)
CGContextMoveToPoint(con, 80, 25)
CGContextAddLineToPoint(con, 100, 0)
CGContextAddLineToPoint(con, 120, 25)
CGContextFillPath(con)
```

The UIBezierPath clipping commands are `usesEvenOddFillRule` and `addClip`.

Gradients

Gradients can range from the simple to the complex. A simple gradient (which is all I'll describe here) is determined by a color at one endpoint along with a color at the other endpoint, plus (optionally) colors at intermediate points; the gradient is then painted either linearly between two points in the context or radially between two circles in the context.

You can't use a gradient as a path's fill color, but you can restrict a gradient to a path's shape by clipping, which amounts to the same thing.

To illustrate, I'll redraw our arrow, using a linear gradient as the "shaft" of the arrow (Figure 2-18):

```
// obtain the current graphics context
let con = UIGraphicsGetCurrentContext()
CGContextSaveGState(con)
// punch triangular hole in context clipping region
CGContextMoveToPoint(con, 90, 100)
CGContextAddLineToPoint(con, 100, 90)
```

Figure 2-18. Drawing with a gradient

```
CGContextAddLineToPoint(con, 110, 100)
CGContextClosePath(con)
CGContextAddRect(con, CGContextGetClipBoundingBox(con))
CGContextEOClip(con)
// draw the vertical line, add its shape to the clipping region
CGContextMoveToPoint(con, 100, 100)
CGContextAddLineToPoint(con, 100, 19)
CGContextSetLineWidth(con, 20)
CGContextReplacePathWithStrokedPath(con)
CGContextClip(con)
// draw the gradient
let locs : [CGFloat] = [ 0.0, 0.5, 1.0 ]
let colors : [CGFloat] = [
    0.3,0.3,0.3,0.8, // starting color, transparent gray
    0.0,0.0,0.0,1.0, // intermediate color, black
    0.3,0.3,0.3,0.8 // ending color, transparent gray
]
let sp = CGColorSpaceCreateDeviceGray()
let grad =
    CGGradientCreateWithColorComponents (sp, colors, locs, 3)
CGContextDrawLinearGradient (
    con, grad, CGPointMake(89,0), CGPointMake(111,0), 0)
// done clipping
CGContextRestoreGState(con)
// draw the red triangle, the point of the arrow
CGContextSetFillColorWithColor(con, UIColor.redColor().CGColor)
CGContextMoveToPoint(con, 80, 25)
CGContextAddLineToPoint(con, 100, 0)
CGContextAddLineToPoint(con, 120, 25)
CGContextFillPath(con)
```

The call to `CGContextReplacePathWithStrokedPath` pretends to stroke the current path, using the current line width and other line-related context state settings, but then creates a new path representing the outside of that stroked path. Thus, instead of a thick line we have a rectangular region that we can use as the clip region.

We then create the gradient and paint it. The procedure is verbose but simple; everything is boilerplate. We describe the gradient as an array of locations on the continuum between one endpoint (`0.0`) and the other endpoint (`1.0`), along with the RGB components of the colors corresponding to each location; in this case, I want the gradient to

Figure 2-19. A patterned fill

be lighter at the edges and darker in the middle, so I use three locations, with the dark one at 0.5. We must also supply a color space in order to create the gradient. Finally, we create the gradient and paint it into place.

There are also gradient CIFilters, as I demonstrated earlier in this chapter; for yet another way to create a simple gradient, see the discussion of CAGradientLayer in the next chapter.

Colors and Patterns

A color is a CGColor. CGColor is not difficult to work with, and can be converted to and from a UIColor through UIColor's init(CGColor:) and CGColor methods.

A pattern is also a kind of color. You can create a pattern color and stroke or fill with it. The simplest way is to draw a minimal tile of the pattern into a UIImage and create the color by calling UIColor's init(patternImage:). To illustrate, I'll create a pattern of horizontal stripes and use it to paint the point of the arrow instead of a solid red color (Figure 2-19):

```
// CGContextSetFillColorWithColor(con, UIColor.redColor().CGColor)
// not any more, we're going to paint with a pattern instead of red!
// create the pattern image tile
UIGraphicsBeginImageContextWithOptions(CGSizeMake(4,4), false, 0)
let imcon = UIGraphicsGetCurrentContext()
CGContextSetFillColorWithColor(imcon, UIColor.redColor().CGColor)
CGContextFillRect(imcon, CGRectMake(0,0,4,4))
CGContextSetFillColorWithColor(imcon, UIColor.blueColor().CGColor)
CGContextFillRect(imcon, CGRectMake(0,0,4,2))
let stripes = UIGraphicsGetImageFromCurrentImageContext()
UIGraphicsEndImageContext()
// paint the point of the arrow with it
let stripesPattern = UIColor(patternImage:stripes)
stripesPattern.setFill()
let p = UIBezierPath()
p.moveToPoint(CGPointMake(80,25))
p.addLineToPoint(CGPointMake(100,0))
p.addLineToPoint(CGPointMake(120,25))
p.fill()
```

The Core Graphics equivalent, CGPattern, is considerably more powerful, but also much more elaborate. As of this writing, it can't be constructed in pure Swift, because the C API expects you to form a C function and pass a pointer to it, neither of which can be done in Swift. So the heart of the code, the formation of the CGPattern itself, must be done in C. I'll use a utility class, PatternHelper, written in Objective-C:

```
void drawStripes (void *info, CGContextRef con) {
    // assume 4 x 4 cell
    CGContextSetFillColorWithColor(con, [[UIColor redColor] CGColor]);
    CGContextFillRect(con, CGRectMake(0,0,4,4));
    CGContextSetFillColorWithColor(con, [[UIColor blueColor] CGColor]);
    CGContextFillRect(con, CGRectMake(0,0,4,2));
}
- (CGPatternRef) patternMaker {
    CGPatternCallbacks callback = {
        0, drawStripes, nil
    };
    CGAffineTransform tr = CGAffineTransformIdentity;
    CGPatternRef patt = CGPatternCreate(nil,
        CGRectMake(0,0,4,4),
        tr,
        4, 4,
        kCGPatternTilingConstantSpacingMinimalDistortion,
        true,
        &callback);
    return patt;
}
```

Everything in the above code revolves around the call to CGPatternCreate. A pattern is a drawing in a rectangular "cell"; we have to state both the size of the cell (the second argument) and the spacing between origin points of cells (the fourth and fifth arguments). In this case, the cell is 4×4, and every cell exactly touches its neighbors both horizontally and vertically. We have to supply a transform to be applied to the cell (the third argument); in this case, we're not doing anything with this transform, so we supply the identity transform. We supply a tiling rule (the sixth argument). We have to state whether this is a color pattern or a stencil pattern; it's a color pattern, so the seventh argument is true. And we have to supply a pointer to a callback function that actually draws the pattern into its cell (the eighth argument).

Except that that's *not* what we have to supply as the eighth argument. To make matters more complicated, what we actually have to supply here is a pointer to a CGPattern-Callbacks struct. This struct consists of the number 0 and pointers to *two* functions, one called to draw the pattern into its cell, the other called when the pattern is released. We're not specifying the second function, however; it is for memory management, and we don't need it in this simple example.

As you can see, the actual pattern-drawing code (drawStripes) is very simple. The only tricky issue is that the call to CGPatternCreate must be in agreement with the pattern-drawing function as to the size of a cell, or the pattern won't come out the way you expect. We know in this case that the cell is 4×4. So we fill it with red, and then fill its lower half with blue. When these cells are tiled touching each other horizontally and vertically, we get the stripes that you see in Figure 2-19.

Now back to Swift. Here's how to use PatternHelper's `patternMaker` method to generate the CGPattern and paint the point of the arrow with it:

```
// draw the red triangle, the point of the arrow
let sp2 = CGColorSpaceCreatePattern(nil)
CGContextSetFillColorSpace(con, sp2)
let patt = PatternHelper().patternMaker().takeRetainedValue()
var alph : CGFloat = 1.0
CGContextSetFillPattern(con, patt, &alph)
CGContextMoveToPoint(con, 80, 25)
CGContextAddLineToPoint(con, 100, 0)
CGContextAddLineToPoint(con, 120, 25)
CGContextFillPath(con)
```

The important thing here is the call to `CGContextSetFillPattern`; instead of setting a fill color, we're setting a fill pattern, to be used the next time we fill a path (in this case, the triangular arrowhead). The third parameter to `CGContextSetFillPattern` is a pointer to a CGFloat, so we have to set up the CGFloat itself beforehand. The second parameter to `CGContextSetFillPattern` is a CGPattern — the CGPattern that our Objective-C code generates for us.

The only thing left to explain is the first two lines of that code. It turns out that before you can call `CGContextSetFillPattern` with a colored pattern, you have to set the context's fill color space to a pattern color space. If you neglect to do this, you'll get an error when you call `CGContextSetFillPattern`. This means that the code as presented has left the graphics context in an undesirable state, with its fill color space set to a pattern color space. This would cause trouble if we were later to try to set the fill color to a normal color. The solution, as usual, is to wrap the code in calls to `CGContextSave-GState` and `CGContextRestoreGState`.

You may have observed in Figure 2-19 that the stripes do not fit neatly inside the triangle of the arrowhead: the bottommost stripe is something like half a blue stripe. This is because a pattern is positioned not with respect to the shape you are filling (or stroking), but with respect to the graphics context as a whole. We could shift the pattern position by calling `CGContextSetPatternPhase` before drawing.

Graphics Context Transforms

Just as a UIView can have a transform, so can a graphics context. However, applying a transform to a graphics context has no effect on the drawing that's already in it; it affects only the drawing that takes place after it is applied, altering the way the coordinates you provide are mapped onto the graphics context's area. A graphics context's transform is called its CTM, for "current transform matrix."

It is quite usual to take full advantage of a graphics context's CTM to save yourself from performing even simple calculations. You can multiply the current transform by any CGAffineTransform using `CGContextConcatCTM`; there are also convenience functions for applying a translate, scale, or rotate transform to the current transform.

The base transform for a graphics context is already set for you when you obtain the context; this is how the system is able to map context drawing coordinates onto screen coordinates. Whatever transforms you apply are applied to the current transform, so the base transform remains in effect and drawing continues to work. You can return to the base transform after applying your own transforms by wrapping your code in calls to `CGContextSaveGState` and `CGContextRestoreGState`.

For example, we have hitherto been drawing our upward-pointing arrow with code that knows how to place that arrow at only one location: the top left of its rectangle is hard-coded at (80,0). This is silly. It makes the code hard to understand, as well as inflexible and difficult to reuse. Surely the sensible thing would be to draw the arrow at (0,0), by subtracting 80 from all the x-values in our existing code. Now it is easy to draw the arrow at *any* position, simply by applying a translate transform beforehand, mapping (0,0) to the desired top-left corner of the arrow. So, to draw it at (80,0), we would say:

```
CGContextTranslateCTM(con, 80, 0)
// now draw the arrow at (0,0)
```

A rotate transform is particularly useful, allowing you to draw in a rotated orientation without any nasty trigonometry. However, it's a bit tricky because the point around which the rotation takes place is the origin. This is rarely what you want, so you have to apply a translate transform first, to map the origin to the point around which you really want to rotate. But then, after rotating, in order to figure out where to draw you will probably have to reverse your translate transform.

To illustrate, here's code to draw our arrow repeatedly at several angles, pivoting around the end of its tail (Figure 2-20). Since the arrow will be drawn multiple times, I'll start by encapsulating the drawing of the arrow as a UIImage. This is not merely to reduce repetition and make drawing more efficient; it's also because we want the entire arrow to pivot, including the pattern stripes, and this is the simplest way to achieve that:

```
func arrowImage () -> UIImage {
    UIGraphicsBeginImageContextWithOptions(CGSizeMake(40,100), false, 0.0)
    // obtain the current graphics context
    let con = UIGraphicsGetCurrentContext()
    // draw the arrow into the image context
    // draw it at (0,0)! adjust all x-values by subtracting 80
    // ... actual code omitted ...
```

Figure 2-20. Drawing rotated with a CTM

```
    let im = UIGraphicsGetImageFromCurrentImageContext()
    UIGraphicsEndImageContext()
    return im
}
```

We produce the arrow image once and store it somewhere — I'll use a property accessed as `self.arrow`. In our `drawRect:` implementation, we draw the arrow image multiple times:

```
override func drawRect(rect: CGRect) {
    let con = UIGraphicsGetCurrentContext()
    self.arrow.drawAtPoint(CGPointMake(0,0))
    for _ in 0..<3 {
        CGContextTranslateCTM(con, 20, 100)
        CGContextRotateCTM(con, 30 * CGFloat(M_PI)/180.0)
        CGContextTranslateCTM(con, -20, -100)
        self.arrow.drawAtPoint(CGPointMake(0,0))
    }
}
```

A transform is also one more solution for the "flip" problem we encountered earlier with `CGContextDrawImage`. Instead of reversing the drawing, we can reverse the context into which we draw it. Essentially, we apply a "flip" transform to the context's coordinate system. You move the context's top downward, and then reverse the direction of the y-coordinate by applying a scale transform whose y-multiplier is -1:

```
CGContextTranslateCTM(con, 0, theHeight)
CGContextScaleCTM(con, 1.0, -1.0)
```

How far down you move the context's top (`theHeight`) depends on how you intend to draw the image.

Shadows

To add a shadow to a drawing, give the context a shadow value before drawing. The shadow position is expressed as a CGSize, where the positive direction for both values indicates down and to the right. The blur value is an open-ended positive number; Apple

Figure 2-21. Drawing with a shadow

doesn't explain how the scale works, but experimentation shows that 12 is nice and blurry, 99 is so blurry as to be shapeless, and higher values become problematic.

Figure 2-21 shows the result of the same code that generated Figure 2-20, except that before we start drawing the arrow repeatedly, we give the context a shadow:

```
let con = UIGraphicsGetCurrentContext()
CGContextSetShadow(con, CGSizeMake(7, 7), 12)
[self.arrow drawAtPoint:CGPointMake(0,0)]; // ... and so on
```

It may not be evident from Figure 2-21, but we are adding a shadow each time we draw. Thus the arrows are able to cast shadows on one another. Suppose, however, that we want all the arrows to cast a single shadow collectively. The way to achieve this is with a *transparency layer*; this is basically a subcontext that accumulates all drawing and then adds the shadow. Our code for drawing the shadowed arrows now looks like this:

```
let con = UIGraphicsGetCurrentContext()
CGContextSetShadow(con, CGSizeMake(7, 7), 12)
CGContextBeginTransparencyLayer(con, nil)
self.arrow.drawAtPoint(CGPointMake(0,0))
for _ in 0..<3 {
    CGContextTranslateCTM(con, 20, 100)
    CGContextRotateCTM(con, 30 * CGFloat(M_PI)/180.0)
    CGContextTranslateCTM(con, -20, -100)
    self.arrow.drawAtPoint(CGPointMake(0,0))
}
CGContextEndTransparencyLayer(con)
```

Erasing

The function CGContextClearRect erases all existing drawing in a rectangle; combined with clipping, it can erase an area of any shape. The result can "punch a hole" through all existing drawing.

The behavior of CGContextClearRect depends on whether the context is transparent or opaque. This is particularly obvious and intuitive when drawing into an image context. If the image context is transparent — the second argument to UIGraphicsBegin-

Figure 2-22. The very strange behavior of CGContextClearRect

ImageContextWithOptions is false — CGContextClearRect erases to transparent; otherwise it erases to black.

When drawing directly into a view (as with drawRect: or drawLayer:inContext:), if the view's background color is nil or a color with even a tiny bit of transparency, the result of CGContextClearRect will appear to be transparent, punching a hole right through the view including its background color; if the background color is completely opaque, the result of CGContextClearRect will be black. This is because the view's background color determines whether the view's graphics context is transparent or opaque; thus, this is essentially the same behavior that I described in the preceding paragraph.

Figure 2-22 illustrates; the blue square on the left has been partly cut away to black, while the blue square on the right has been partly cut away to transparency. Yet these are instances of the same UIView subclass, drawn with exactly the same code! The difference between the views is that the backgroundColor of the first view is solid red with an alpha of 1, while the backgroundColor of the second view is solid red with an alpha of 0.99. This difference is utterly imperceptible to the eye (not to mention that the red color never appears, as it is covered with a blue fill), but it completely changes the effect of CGContextClearRect. The UIView subclass's drawRect: looks like this:

```
let con = UIGraphicsGetCurrentContext()
CGContextSetFillColorWithColor(con, UIColor.blueColor().CGColor)
CGContextFillRect(con, rect)
CGContextClearRect(con, CGRectMake(0,0,30,30))
```

Points and Pixels

A point is a dimensionless location described by an x-coordinate and a y-coordinate. When you draw in a graphics context, you specify the points at which to draw, and this works regardless of the device's resolution, because Core Graphics maps your drawing nicely onto the physical output using the base CTM and anti-aliasing. Therefore, throughout this chapter I've concerned myself with graphics context points, disregarding their relationship to screen pixels.

However, pixels do exist. A pixel is a physical, integral, dimensioned unit of display in the real world. Whole-numbered points effectively lie between pixels, and this can matter if you're fussy, especially on a single-resolution device. For example, if a vertical path with whole-number coordinates is stroked with a line width of 1, half the line falls on each side of the path, and the drawn line on the screen of a single-resolution device will seem to be 2 pixels wide (because the device can't illuminate half a pixel).

You will sometimes encounter advice suggesting that if this effect is objectionable, you should try shifting the line's position by 0.5, to center it in its pixels. This advice may appear to work, but it makes some simpleminded assumptions. A more sophisticated approach is to obtain the UIView's contentScaleFactor property. You can divide by this value to convert from pixels to points. Consider also that the most accurate way to draw a vertical or horizontal line is not to stroke a path but to fill a rectangle. So this UIView subclass code will draw a perfect 1-pixel-wide vertical line on any device (con is the current graphics context):

```
CGContextFillRect(con, CGRectMake(100,0,1.0/self.contentScaleFactor,100))
```

Content Mode

A view that draws something within itself, as opposed to merely having a background color and subviews (as in the previous chapter), has *content*. This means that its content-Mode property becomes important whenever the view is resized. As I mentioned earlier, the drawing system will avoid asking a view to redraw itself from scratch if possible; instead, it will use the cached result of the previous drawing operation (the bitmap backing store). So, if the view is resized, the system may simply stretch or shrink or reposition the cached drawing, if your contentMode setting instructs it to do so.

It's a little tricky to illustrate this point when the view's content is coming from draw-Rect:, because I have to arrange for the view to obtain its content (from drawRect:) and then cause it to be resized without also causing it to be redrawn (that is, without drawRect: being called *again*). Here's how I'll do that. As the app starts up, I'll create an instance of a UIView subclass, MyView, that knows how to draw our arrow. Then I'll use delayed performance to resize the instance after the window has shown and the interface has been initially displayed (for the delay utility function, see Appendix B):

```
delay(0.1) {
    mv.bounds.size.height *= 2 // mv is the MyView instance
}
```

We double the height of the view without causing drawRect: to be called. The result is that the view's drawing appears at double its correct height. For example, if our view's drawRect: code is the same as the code that generated Figure 2-18, we get Figure 2-23.

Figure 2-23. Automatic stretching of content

Sooner or later, however, `drawRect:` will be called, and the drawing will be refreshed in accordance with our code. Our code doesn't say to draw the arrow at a height that is relative to the height of the view's bounds; it draws the arrow at a fixed height. Thus, the arrow will snap back to its original size.

A view's `contentMode` property should therefore usually be in agreement with how the view draws itself. Our `drawRect:` code dictates the size and position of the arrow relative to the view's bounds origin, its top left; so we could set its `contentMode` to `.TopLeft`. Alternatively, we could set it to `.Redraw`; this will cause automatic scaling of the cached content to be turned off — instead, when the view is resized, its `setNeedsDisplay` method will be called, ultimately triggering `drawRect:` to redraw the content.

CHAPTER 3

Layers

The tale told in Chapters 1 and 2 of how a UIView works and how it draws itself is only half the story. A UIView has a partner called its *layer*, a CALayer. A UIView does not actually draw itself onto the screen; it draws itself into its layer, and it is the layer that is portrayed on the screen. As I've already mentioned, a view is not redrawn frequently; instead, its drawing is cached, and the cached version of the drawing (the bitmap backing store) is used where possible. The cached version is, in fact, the layer. What I spoke of in Chapter 2 as the view's graphics context is actually the layer's graphics context.

This might seem like a mere implementation detail, but layers are important and interesting. To understand layers is to understand views more deeply; layers extend the power of views. In particular:

Layers have properties that affect drawing.
> Layers have drawing-related properties beyond those of a UIView. Because a layer is the recipient and presenter of a view's drawing, you can modify how a view is drawn on the screen by accessing the layer's properties. In other words, by reaching down to the level of its layer, you can make a view do things you can't do through UIView methods alone.

Layers can be combined within a single view.
> A UIView's partner layer can contain additional layers. Since the purpose of layers is to draw, portraying visible material on the screen, this allows a UIView's drawing to be composited of multiple distinct pieces. This can make drawing easier, with the constituents of a drawing being treated as objects.

Layers are the basis of animation.
> Animation allows you to add clarity, emphasis, and just plain coolness to your interface. Layers are made to be animated; the "CA" in "CALayer" stands for "Core Animation." Animation is the subject of Chapter 4.

Figure 3-1. A compass, composed of layers

For example, suppose we want to add a compass indicator to our app's interface. Figure 3-1 portrays a simple version of such a compass. It takes advantage of the arrow that we figured out how to draw in Chapter 2; the arrow is drawn into a layer of its own. The other parts of the compass are layers too: the circle is a layer, and each of the cardinal point letters is a layer. The drawing is thus easy to composite in code (and later in this chapter, that's exactly what we'll do); even more intriguing, the pieces can be repositioned and animated separately, so it's easy to rotate the arrow without moving the circle (and in Chapter 4, that's exactly what we'll do).

The documentation discusses layers chiefly in connection with animation (in particular, in the *Core Animation Programming Guide*). This categorization gives the impression that layers are of interest only if you intend to animate. That's misleading. Layers are the basis of animation, but they are also the basis of view drawing, and are useful and important even if you don't use them for animation.

View and Layer

A UIView instance has an accompanying CALayer instance, accessible as the view's `layer` property. This layer has a special status: it is partnered with this view to embody all of the view's drawing. The layer has no corresponding `view` property, but the view is the layer's `delegate`. The documentation sometimes speaks of this layer as the view's "underlying layer."

By default, when a UIView is instantiated, its layer is an instance of CALayer. But if you subclass UIView and you want your subclass's underlying layer to be an instance of a CALayer subclass (built-in or your own), implement the UIView subclass's `layerClass` class method to return that CALayer subclass.

That, for example, is how the compass in Figure 3-1 is created. We have a UIView subclass, CompassView, and a CALayer subclass, CompassLayer. Here is Compass-View's implementation:

```
class CompassView : UIView {
    override class func layerClass() -> AnyClass {
        return CompassLayer.self
    }
}
```

Thus, when CompassView is instantiated, its underlying layer is a CompassLayer. In this example, there is no drawing in CompassView; its job — in this case, its *only* job — is to give CompassLayer a place in the visible interface, because a layer cannot appear without a view.

Because every view has an underlying layer, there is a tight integration between the two. The layer portrays all the view's drawing; if the view draws, it does so by contributing to the layer's drawing. The view is the layer's delegate. And the view's properties are often merely a convenience for accessing the layer's properties. For example, when you set the view's backgroundColor, you are really setting the layer's backgroundColor, and if you set the layer's backgroundColor directly, the view's backgroundColor is set to match. Similarly, the view's frame is really the layer's frame and *vice versa*.

 A CALayer's delegate property is settable, but you must never set the delegate property of a UIView's underlying layer. To do so would be to break the integration between them, thereby causing drawing to stop working correctly. A UIView *must* be the delegate of its underlying layer; moreover, it must *not* be the delegate of any *other* layer. *Don't do anything to mess this up.*

The view draws into its layer, and the layer caches that drawing; the layer can then be manipulated, changing the view's appearance, without necessarily asking the view to redraw itself. This is a source of great efficiency in the drawing system. It also explains such phenomena as the content stretching that we encountered in the last section of Chapter 2: when the view's bounds size changes, the drawing system, by default, simply stretches or repositions the cached layer image, until such time as the view is told to draw freshly (drawRect:), replacing the layer's content.

Layers and Sublayers

A layer can have sublayers, and a layer has at most one superlayer. Thus there is a tree of layers. This is similar and parallel to the tree of views (Chapter 1). In fact, so tight is the integration between a view and its underlying layer that these hierarchies are effectively the same hierarchy. Given a view and its underlying layer, that layer's superlayer is the view's superview's underlying layer, and that layer has as sublayers all the under-

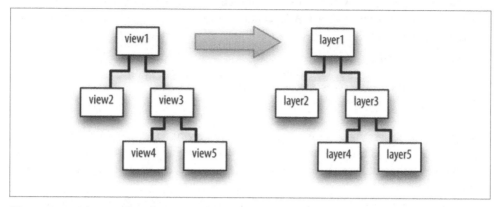

Figure 3-2. A hierarchy of views and the hierarchy of layers underlying it

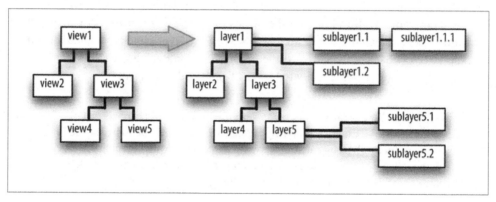

Figure 3-3. Layers that have sublayers of their own

lying layers of all the view's subviews. Indeed, because the layers are how the views actually get drawn, one might say that the view hierarchy really *is* a layer hierarchy (Figure 3-2).

At the same time, the layer hierarchy can go beyond the view hierarchy. A view has exactly one underlying layer, but a layer can have sublayers that are not the underlying layers of any view. So the hierarchy of layers that underlie views exactly matches the hierarchy of views, but the total layer tree may be a superset of that hierarchy. In Figure 3-3, we see the same view-and-layer hierarchy as in Figure 3-2, but two of the layers have additional sublayers that are theirs alone (that is, sublayers that are not any view's underlying layers).

From a visual standpoint, there may be nothing to distinguish a hierarchy of views from a hierarchy of layers. For example, in Chapter 1 we drew three overlapping rectangles

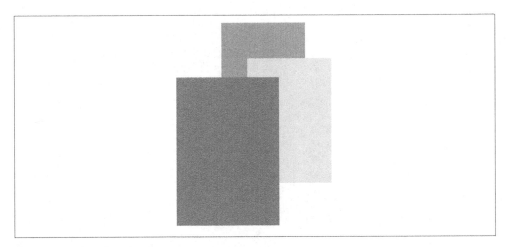

Figure 3-4. Overlapping layers

using a hierarchy of views (Figure 1-1). This code gives exactly the same visible display by manipulating layers (Figure 3-4):

```
let lay1 = CALayer()
lay1.backgroundColor = UIColor(red: 1, green: 0.4, blue: 1, alpha: 1).CGColor
lay1.frame = CGRectMake(113, 111, 132, 194)
mainview.layer.addSublayer(lay1)
let lay2 = CALayer()
lay2.backgroundColor = UIColor(red: 0.5, green: 1, blue: 0, alpha: 1).CGColor
lay2.frame = CGRectMake(41, 56, 132, 194)
lay1.addSublayer(lay2)
let lay3 = CALayer()
lay3.backgroundColor = UIColor(red: 1, green: 0, blue: 0, alpha: 1).CGColor
lay3.frame = CGRectMake(43, 197, 160, 230)
mainview.layer.addSublayer(lay3)
```

A view's subview's underlying layer is a sublayer of that view's underlaying layer, just like any other sublayers of that view's underlying layer. Therefore, it can be positioned anywhere among them in the drawing order. The fact that a view can be interspersed among the sublayers of its superview's underlying layer is surprising to beginners. For example, let's construct Figure 3-4 again, but between adding lay2 and lay3 to the interface, we'll add a subview:

```
// ...
lay1.addSublayer(lay2)
let iv = UIImageView(image:UIImage(named:"smiley"))
mainview.addSubview(iv)
iv.frame.origin = CGPointMake(180,180)
let lay3 = CALayer() // the red rectangle
// ...
```

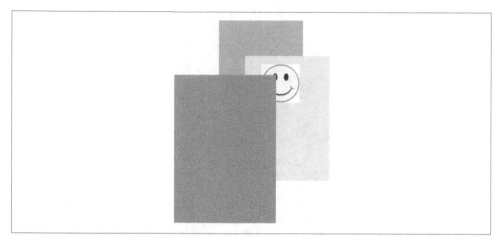

Figure 3-5. Overlapping layers and a view

The result is Figure 3-5. The smiley face was added to the interface before the red (left) rectangle, so it appears behind that rectangle. By reversing the order in which the red rectangle (`lay3`) and the smiley face (`iv`) are added to the interface, the smiley face can be made to appear in front of that rectangle. The smiley face is a *view*, whereas the rectangle is just a *layer*; so they are not siblings as views, since the rectangle is not a view. But the smiley face is both a view and its layer; as layers, the smiley face and the rectangle *are* siblings, since they have the same superlayer, so either one can be made to appear in front of the other.

Whether a layer displays regions of its sublayers that lie outside that layer's own bounds depends upon the value of its `masksToBounds` property. This is parallel to a view's `clipsToBounds` property, and indeed, for a layer that is its view's underlying layer, they are the same thing. In Figures 3-4 and 3-5, the layers all have `clipsToBounds` set to `false` (the default); that's why the right layer is visible beyond the bounds of the middle layer, which is its superlayer.

Like a UIView, a CALayer has a `hidden` property that can be set to take it and its sublayers out of the visible interface without actually removing it from its superlayer.

Manipulating the Layer Hierarchy

Layers come with a full set of methods for reading and manipulating the layer hierarchy, parallel to the methods for reading and manipulating the view hierarchy. A layer has a `superlayer` property and a `sublayers` property, and these methods:

- `addSublayer:`
- `insertSublayer:atIndex:`

- `insertSublayer:below:`, `insertSublayer:above:`
- `replaceSublayer:with:`
- `removeFromSuperlayer`

Unlike a view's `subviews` property, a layer's `sublayers` property is writable; thus, you can give a layer multiple sublayers in a single move, by assigning to its `sublayers` property. To remove all of a layer's sublayers, set its `sublayers` property to nil.

Although a layer's sublayers have an order, reflected in the `sublayers` order and regulated with the methods I've just mentioned, this is not necessarily the same as their back-to-front drawing order. By default, it is, but a layer also has a `zPosition` property, a CGFloat, and this also determines drawing order. The rule is that all sublayers with the same `zPosition` are drawn in the order they are listed among their `sublayers` siblings, but lower `zPosition` siblings are drawn before higher `zPosition` siblings. (The default `zPosition` is `0.0`.)

Sometimes, the `zPosition` property is a more convenient way of dictating drawing order than sibling order is. For example, if layers represent playing cards laid out in a solitaire game, it will likely be a lot easier and more flexible to determine how the cards overlap by setting their `zPosition` than by rearranging their sibling order. Moreover, a subview's layer is itself just a layer, so you can rearrange the drawing order of subviews by setting the `zPosition` of their underlying layers. In our code constructing Figure 3-5, if we assign the image view's underlying layer a `zPosition` of 1, it is drawn in front of the red (left) rectangle:

```
mainview.addSubview(iv)
iv.layer.zPosition = 1
```

Methods are also provided for converting between the coordinate systems of layers within the same layer hierarchy:

- `convertPoint:fromLayer:`, `convertPoint:toLayer:`
- `convertRect:fromLayer:`, `convertRect:toLayer:`

Positioning a Sublayer

Layer coordinate systems and positioning are similar to those of views. A layer's own internal coordinate system is expressed by its bounds, just like a view; its size is its bounds size, and its bounds origin is the internal coordinate at its top left.

However, a sublayer's position within its superlayer is not described by its `center`, like a view; a layer does not have a `center`. Instead, a sublayer's position within its superlayer is defined by a combination of two properties, its `position` and its `anchorPoint`. Think of the sublayer as pinned to its superlayer; then you have to say both where the pin passes through the sublayer and where it passes through the superlayer. (I didn't make up that analogy, but it's pretty apt.)

position

A point expressed in the superlayer's coordinate system.

anchorPoint

Where the position point is located, with respect to the layer's own bounds. It is a pair of floating-point numbers (a CGPoint) describing a fraction (or multiple) of the layer's own bounds width and bounds height. Thus, for example, (0.0,0.0) is the top left of the layer's bounds, and (1.0,1.0) is the bottom right of the layer's bounds.

If the anchorPoint is (0.5,0.5) (the default), the position property works like a view's center property. A view's center is thus a special case of a layer's position. This is quite typical of the relationship between view properties and layer properties; the view properties are often a simpler, more convenient, and less powerful version of the layer properties.

A layer's position and anchorPoint are orthogonal (independent); changing one does not change the other. Therefore, changing either of them without changing the other changes where the layer is drawn within its superlayer.

For example, in Figure 3-1, the most important point in the circle is its center; all the other objects need to be positioned with respect to it. Therefore they all have the same position: the center of the circle. But they differ in their anchorPoint. For example, the arrow's anchorPoint is (0.5,0.8), the middle of the shaft, near the tail. On the other hand, the anchorPoint of a cardinal point letter is (0.5,3.0), well outside the letter's bounds, so as to place the letter near the edge of the circle.

A layer's frame is a purely derived property. When you get the frame, it is calculated from the bounds size along with the position and anchorPoint. When you set the frame, you set the bounds size and position. In general, you should regard the frame as a convenient façade and no more. Nevertheless, it is convenient! For example, to position a sublayer so that it exactly overlaps its superlayer, you can just set the sublayer's frame to the superlayer's bounds.

 A layer created in code (as opposed to a view's underlying layer) has a frame and bounds of (0.0,0.0,0.0,0.0) and will not be visible on the screen even when you add it to a superlayer that is on the screen. Be sure to give your layer a nonzero width and height if you want to be able to see it. Creating a layer and adding it to a superlayer and then wondering why it isn't appearing in the interface is a common beginner error.

CAScrollLayer

If you're going to be moving a layer's bounds origin as a way of repositioning its sublayers *en masse*, you might like to make the layer a CAScrollLayer, a CALayer subclass that provides convenience methods for this sort of thing. (Despite the name, a CAScrollLayer provides no scrolling interface; the user can't scroll it by dragging, for example.) By default, a CAScrollLayer's masksToBounds property is true; thus, the CAScrollLayer acts like a window through which you see can only what is within its bounds. (You can set its masksToBounds to false, but this would be an odd thing to do, as it somewhat defeats the purpose.)

To move the CAScrollLayer's bounds, you can talk either to it or to a sublayer (at any depth):

Talking to the CAScrollLayer

scrollToPoint:
> Changes the CAScrollLayer's bounds origin to that point.

scrollToRect:
> Changes the CAScrollLayer's bounds origin minimally so that the given portion of the bounds rect is visible.

Talking to a sublayer

scrollPoint:
> Changes the CAScrollLayer's bounds origin so that the given point *of the sublayer* is at the top left of the CAScrollLayer.

scrollRectToVisible:
> Changes the CAScrollLayer's bounds origin so that the given rect *of the sublayer's bounds* is within the CAScrollLayer's bounds area. You can also ask the sublayer for its visibleRect, the part of this sublayer now within the CAScrollLayer's bounds.

Layout of Sublayers

The view hierarchy is actually a layer hierarchy (Figure 3-2). The positioning of a view within its superview is actually the positioning of its layer within its superlayer (the superview's layer). A view can be repositioned and resized automatically in accordance with its autoresizingMask or through autolayout based on its constraints. Thus, there is automatic layout for layers *if they are the underlying layers of views*. Otherwise, there is *no* automatic layout for layers in iOS. The only option for layout of sublayers that are not the underlying layers of views is manual layout that you perform in code.

When a layer needs layout, either because its bounds have changed or because you called setNeedsLayout, you can respond in either of two ways:

- The layer's `layoutSublayers` method is called; to respond, override `layout-Sublayers` in your CALayer subclass.

- Alternatively, implement `layoutSublayersOfLayer:` in the layer's delegate. (Remember, if the layer is a view's underlying layer, the view is its delegate.)

To do effective manual layout of sublayers, you'll probably need a way to identify or refer to the sublayers. There is no layer equivalent of `viewWithTag:`, so such identification and reference is entirely up to you. Key–value coding can be helpful here; layers implement key–value coding in a special way, discussed at the end of this chapter.

For a view's underlying layer, `layoutSublayers` or `layoutSublayersOfLayer:` is called after the view's `layoutSubviews`. Under autolayout, you must call `super` or else autolayout will break. Moreover, these methods may be called more than once during the course of autolayout; if you're looking for an automatically generated signal that it's time to do manual layout of sublayers, a view layout event might be a better choice (see "Events Related to Layout" on page 60).

Drawing in a Layer

A view draws into its underlying layer if its `drawRect:` is implemented (Chapter 2). Now let's talk about how to draw into *other* layers.

The simplest way to make something appear in a layer is through its `contents` property. This is parallel to the `image` in a UIImageView (Chapter 2). It is expected to be a CGImage (or nil, signifying no image). So, for example, here's how we might modify the code that generated Figure 3-5 in such a way as to generate the smiley face as a layer rather than a view:

```
let lay4 = CALayer()
let im = UIImage(named:"smiley")!
lay4.frame = CGRect(origin:CGPointMake(180,180), size:im.size)
lay4.contents = im.CGImage
mainview.layer.addSublayer(lay4)
```

 Setting a layer's `contents` to a UIImage, rather than a CGImage, will fail silently — the image doesn't appear, but there is no error either. This is absolutely maddening, and I wish I had a nickel for every time I've done it and then wasted hours figuring out why my layer isn't appearing.

There are also four methods that can be implemented to provide or draw a layer's content on demand, similar to a UIView's `drawRect:`. A layer is very conservative about calling these methods (and you must not call any of them directly). When a layer *does* call these methods, I will say that the layer *redisplays itself*. Here is how a layer can be caused to redisplay itself:

- If the layer's `needsDisplayOnBoundsChange` property is `false` (the default), then the only way to cause the layer to redisplay itself is by calling `setNeedsDisplay` (or `setNeedsDisplayInRect:`). Even this might not cause the layer to redisplay itself right away; if that's crucial, then you will also call `displayIfNeeded`.
- If the layer's `needsDisplayOnBoundsChange` property is `true`, then the layer will also redisplay itself when the layer's bounds change (rather like a UIView's `UIView-ContentMode.Redraw`).

Here are the four methods that can be called when a layer redisplays itself; pick one to implement (don't try to combine them, you'll just confuse things):

`display` *in a subclass*

> Your CALayer subclass can override `display`. There's no graphics context at this point, so `display` is pretty much limited to setting the `contents` image.

`displayLayer:` *in the delegate*

> You can set the CALayer's `delegate` property and implement `displayLayer:` in the delegate. As with `display`, there's no graphics context, so you'll just be setting the `contents` image.

`drawInContext:` *in a subclass*

> Your CALayer subclass can override `drawInContext:`. The parameter is a graphics context into which you can draw directly; it is *not* automatically made the current context.

`drawLayer:inContext:` *in the delegate*

> You can set the CALayer's `delegate` property and implement `drawLayer:in-Context:`. The second parameter is a graphics context into which you can draw directly; it is *not* automatically made the current context.

Remember, you must not set the `delegate` property of a view's underlying layer! The view is its delegate and must remain its delegate. A useful architecture for drawing into a layer through a delegate of your choosing is to treat a view as a *layer-hosting* view: the view and its underlying layer do nothing except to serve as a host to a sublayer of the view's underlying layer, which is where the drawing occurs (Figure 3-6).

Assigning a layer a `contents` image and drawing directly into the layer are, in effect, mutually exclusive. So:

- If a layer's `contents` is assigned an image, this image is shown immediately and replaces whatever drawing may have been displayed in the layer.

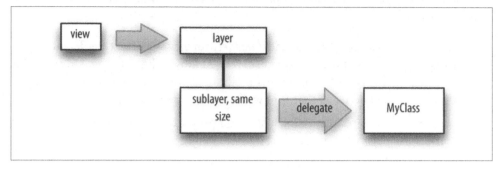

Figure 3-6. A view and a layer delegate that draws into it

- If a layer redisplays itself and `drawInContext:` or `drawLayer:inContext:` draws into the layer, the drawing replaces whatever image may have been displayed in the layer.

- If a layer redisplays itself and none of the four methods provides any content, the layer will be empty.

A layer has a scale, its `contentsScale`, which maps point distances in the layer's graphics context to pixel distances on the device. A layer that's managed by Cocoa, if it has contents, will adjust its `contentsScale` automatically as needed; for example, if a UI-View implements `drawRect:`, then on a device with a double-resolution screen its underlying layer is assigned a `contentsScale` of 2. A layer that you are creating and managing yourself, however, has no such automatic behavior; it's up to you, if you plan to draw into the layer, to set its `contentsScale` appropriately. Content drawn into a layer with a `contentsScale` of 1 may appear pixellated or fuzzy on a high-resolution screen. And when you're starting with a UIImage and assigning its CGImage as a layer's `contents`, if there's a mismatch between the UIImage's `scale` and the layer's `contentsScale`, then the image may be displayed at the wrong size.

Three layer properties strongly affect what the layer displays, in ways that can be baffling to beginners:

`backgroundColor`

Equivalent to a view's `backgroundColor` (and if this layer is a view's underlying layer, it *is* the view's `backgroundColor`). Changing the `backgroundColor` takes effect immediately. Think of the `backgroundColor` as separate from the layer's own drawing, and as painted *behind* the layer's own drawing.

`opacity`

Affects the overall apparent transparency of the layer. It is equivalent to a view's `alpha` (and if this layer is a view's underlying layer, it *is* the view's `alpha`). It affects the apparent transparency of the layer's sublayers as well. It affects the apparent transparency of the background color and the apparent transparency of the layer's content separately (just as with a view's alpha). Changing the opacity property takes effect immediately.

opaque

Determines whether the layer's graphics context is opaque. An opaque graphics context is black; you can draw on top of that blackness, but the blackness is still there. A non-opaque graphics context is clear; where no drawing is, it is completely transparent. Changing the opaque property has no effect until the layer redisplays itself. A view's underlying layer's opaque property is independent of the view's opaque property; they are unrelated and do entirely different things.

 If a layer is the underlying layer of a view that implements drawRect:, then setting the view's backgroundColor changes the layer's opaque — setting it to true if the new background color is opaque (alpha component of 1), to false otherwise. This is the reason behind the strange behavior of CGContextClearRect described in Chapter 2.

Also, when drawing directly into a *layer*, the behavior of CGContextClearRect differs from what was described in Chapter 2 for drawing into a *view*: instead of punching a hole through the background color, it effectively paints with the layer's background color. (This can have curious side effects.)

I regard all this as deeply weird.

Content Resizing and Positioning

A layer's content is stored (cached) as a bitmap which is then treated like an image and drawn in relation to the layer's bounds in accordance with various layer properties:

- If the content came from setting the layer's `contents` property to an image, the cached content is that image; its size is the point size of the CGImage we started with.

- If the content came from drawing directly into the layer's graphics context (`drawInContext:`, `drawLayer:inContext:`), the cached content is the layer's entire graphics context; its size is the point size of the layer itself at the time the drawing was performed.

The layer properties in question cause the cached content to be resized, repositioned, cropped, and so on, as it is displayed. The properties are:

contentsGravity

    This property, a string, is parallel to a UIView's `contentMode` property, and describes how the content should be positioned or stretched in relation to the bounds. For example, `kCAGravityCenter` means the content is centered in the bounds without resizing; `kCAGravityResize` (the default) means the content is sized to fit the bounds, even if this means distorting its aspect; and so forth.

 For historical reasons, the terms "bottom" and "top" in the names of the `contentsGravity` settings have the opposite of their expected meanings.

contentsRect

    A CGRect expressing the proportion of the content that is to be displayed. The default is `(0.0,0.0,1.0,1.0)`, meaning the entire content is displayed. The specified part of the content is sized and positioned in relation to the bounds in accordance with the `contentsGravity`. Thus, for example, by setting the `contentsRect`, you can scale up part of the content to fill the bounds, or slide part of a larger image into view without redrawing or changing the `contents` image.

    You can also use the `contentsRect` to scale down the content, by specifying a larger `contentsRect` such as `(-0.5,-0.5,1.5,1.5)`; but any content pixels that touch the edge of the `contentsRect` will then be extended outward to the edge of the layer (to prevent this, make sure that the outermost pixels of the content are all empty).

contentsCenter

    A CGRect, structured like `contentsRect`, expressing the central region of nine rectangular regions of the `contentsRect` that are variously allowed to stretch if the `contentsGravity` calls for stretching. The central region (the actual value of the `contentsCenter`) stretches in both directions. Of the other eight regions (inferred from the value you provide), the four corner regions don't stretch, and the four side regions stretch in one direction. (This should remind you of how a resizable image stretches! See Chapter 2.)

If a layer's content comes from drawing directly into its graphics context, then the layer's contentsGravity, of itself, has no effect, because the size of the graphics context, by definition, fits the size of the layer exactly; there is nothing to stretch or reposition. But the contentsGravity *will* have an effect on such a layer if its contentsRect is not (0.0,0.0,1.0,1.0), because now we're specifying a rectangle of some *other* size; the contentsGravity describes how to fit that rectangle into the layer.

Again, if a layer's content comes from drawing directly into its graphics context, then when the layer is resized, if the layer is asked to display itself again, the drawing is performed again, and once more the layer's content fits the size of the layer exactly. But if the layer's bounds are resized when needsDisplayOnBoundsChange is false, then the layer does *not* redisplay itself, so its cached content no longer fits the layer, and the contentsGravity matters.

By a judicious combination of settings, you can get the layer to perform some clever drawing for you that might be difficult to perform directly. For example, Figure 3-7 shows the result of the following settings:

```
arrow.needsDisplayOnBoundsChange = false
arrow.contentsCenter = CGRectMake(0.0, 0.4, 1.0, 0.6)
arrow.contentsGravity = kCAGravityResizeAspect
arrow.bounds.inset(dx: -20, dy: -20)
```

Because needsDisplayOnBoundsChange is false, the content is not redisplayed when the arrow's bounds are increased; instead, the cached content is used. The contents-Gravity setting tells us to resize proportionally; therefore, the arrow is both longer and wider than in Figure 3-1, but not in such a way as to distort its proportions. However, notice that although the triangular arrowhead is wider, it is not longer; the increase in length is due entirely to the stretching of the arrow's shaft. That's because the contents-Center region is within the shaft.

A layer's masksToBounds property has the same effect on its content that it has on its sublayers. If it is false, the whole content is displayed, even if that content (after taking account of the contentsGravity and contentsRect) is larger then the layer. If it is true, only the part of the content within the layer's bounds will be displayed.

 The value of a layer's bounds origin does not affect where its content is drawn. It affects only where its sublayers are drawn.

Figure 3-7. One way of resizing the compass arrow

Layers that Draw Themselves

A few built-in CALayer subclasses provide some basic but extremely helpful self-drawing ability:

CATextLayer

A CATextLayer has a `string` property, which can be an NSString or NSAttributed-String, along with other text formatting properties, somewhat like a simplified UI-Label; it draws its `string`. The default text color, the `foregroundColor` property, is white, which is unlikely to be what you want. The text is different from the `contents` and is mutually exclusive with it: either the contents image or the text will be drawn, but not both, so in general you should not give a CATextLayer any contents image. In Figures 3-1 and 3-7, the cardinal point letters are CATextLayer instances.

CAShapeLayer

A CAShapeLayer has a `path` property, which is a CGPath. It fills or strokes this path, or both, depending on its `fillColor` and `strokeColor` values, and displays the result; the default is a `fillColor` of black and no `strokeColor`. It has properties for line thickness, dash style, end-cap style, and join style, similar to a graphics context; it also has the remarkable ability to draw only part of its path (`strokeStart` and `strokeEnd`), making it very easy, for example, to draw an arc of an ellipse. A CAShapeLayer may also have `contents`; the shape is displayed on top of the contents image, but there is no property permitting you to specify a compositing mode. In Figures 3-1 and 3-7, the background circle is a CAShapeLayer instance, stroked with gray and filled with a lighter, slightly transparent gray.

Figure 3-8. A gradient drawn behind the compass

 An Apple WWDC 2014 video points out that CAShapeLayer, while convenient, may entail some drawing inefficiency, because the shape must be rasterized into an image every time you change it. See also the discussion of layer drawing efficiency later in this chapter.

CAGradientLayer

A CAGradientLayer covers its background with a simple linear gradient; thus, it's an easy way to draw a gradient in your interface (and if you need something more elaborate you can always draw with Core Graphics instead). The gradient is defined much as in the Core Graphics gradient example in Chapter 2, an array of locations and an array of corresponding colors, along with a start and end point. To clip the gradient's shape, you can add a mask to the CAGradientLayer (masks are discussed later in this chapter). A CAGradientLayer's `contents` are not displayed.

The `colors` array requires CGColors, not UIColors. That's legal in a Swift array, but NSArray expects objects (CGColor is not an object type), so you'll need to typecast each color to `AnyObject` or you'll crash at runtime.

Figure 3-8 shows our compass drawn with an extra CAGradientLayer behind it.

Transforms

The way a layer is drawn on the screen can be modified though a transform. This is not surprising, because a view can have a transform (see Chapter 1), and a view is drawn on the screen by its layer. But a layer's transform is more powerful than a view's transform; you can use it to accomplish things that you can't accomplish with a view's transform alone.

In the simplest case, when a transform is two-dimensional, you can access a layer's transform through the `affineTransform` method (and the corresponding setter, `set-`

AffineTransform:). The value is a CGAffineTransform, familiar from Chapters 1 and 2. The transform is applied around the anchorPoint. (Thus, the anchorPoint has a second purpose that I didn't tell you about when discussing it earlier.)

You now know everything needed to understand the code that generated Figure 3-8, so here it is. In this code, self is the CompassLayer; it does no drawing of its own, but merely assembles and configures its sublayers. The four cardinal point letters are each drawn by a CATextLayer and placed using a transform. They are drawn at the same coordinates, but they have different rotation transforms, and are anchored so that their rotation is centered at the center of the circle. To generate the arrow, we make ourselves the arrow layer's delegate and call setNeedsDisplay; this causes drawLayer:inContext: to be called in CompassLayer (that code is just the same code we developed for drawing the arrow in Chapter 2, and is not repeated here). The arrow layer is positioned by an anchorPoint pinning its tail to the center of the circle, and rotated around that pin by a transform:

```
// the gradient
let g = CAGradientLayer()
g.contentsScale = UIScreen.mainScreen().scale
g.frame = self.bounds
g.colors = [
    UIColor.blackColor().CGColor as AnyObject,
    UIColor.redColor().CGColor as AnyObject
    ]
g.locations = [0.0,1.0]
self.addSublayer(g)
// the circle
let circle = CAShapeLayer()
circle.contentsScale = UIScreen.mainScreen().scale
circle.lineWidth = 2.0
circle.fillColor = UIColor(red:0.9, green:0.95, blue:0.93, alpha:0.9).CGColor
circle.strokeColor = UIColor.grayColor().CGColor
let p = CGPathCreateMutable()
CGPathAddEllipseInRect(p, nil, CGRectInset(self.bounds, 3, 3))
circle.path = p
self.addSublayer(circle)
circle.bounds = self.bounds
circle.position = self.bounds.center
// the four cardinal points
let pts = "NESW"
for (ix,c) in enumerate(pts) {
    let t = CATextLayer()
    t.contentsScale = UIScreen.mainScreen().scale
    t.string = String(c)
    t.bounds = CGRectMake(0,0,40,40)
    t.position = circle.bounds.center
    let vert = circle.bounds.midY / t.bounds.height
    t.anchorPoint = CGPointMake(0.5, vert)
    // println(t.anchorPoint)
    t.alignmentMode = kCAAlignmentCenter
```

```
        t.foregroundColor = UIColor.blackColor().CGColor
        t.setAffineTransform(
            CGAffineTransformMakeRotation(CGFloat(ix)*CGFloat(M_PI)/2.0))
        circle.addSublayer(t)
    }
    // the arrow
    let arrow = CALayer()
    arrow.contentsScale = UIScreen.mainScreen().scale
    arrow.bounds = CGRectMake(0, 0, 40, 100)
    arrow.position = self.bounds.center
    arrow.anchorPoint = CGPointMake(0.5, 0.8)
    arrow.delegate = self // we will draw the arrow in the delegate method
    arrow.setAffineTransform(CGAffineTransformMakeRotation(CGFloat(M_PI)/5.0))
    self.addSublayer(arrow)
    arrow.setNeedsDisplay() // draw, please
```

A full-fledged layer transform, the value of the transform property, takes place in three-dimensional space; its description includes a z-axis, perpendicular to both the x-axis and y-axis. (By default, the positive z-axis points out of the screen, toward the viewer's face.) Layers do not magically give you realistic three-dimensional rendering — for that you would use OpenGL, which is beyond the scope of this discussion. Layers are two-dimensional objects, and they are designed for speed and simplicity. Nevertheless, they do operate in three dimensions, quite sufficiently to give a cartoonish but effective sense of reality, especially when performing an animation. We've all seen the screen image flip like turning over a piece of paper to reveal what's on the back; that's a rotation in three dimensions.

A three-dimensional transform takes place around a three-dimensional extension of the anchorPoint, whose z-component is supplied by the anchorPointZ property. Thus, in the reduced default case where anchorPointZ is 0.0, the anchorPoint is sufficient, as we've already seen in using CGAffineTransform.

The transform itself is described mathematically by a struct called a CATransform3D. The *Core Animation Function Reference* lists the functions for working with these transforms. They are a lot like the CGAffineTransform functions, except they've got a third dimension. For example, the function for making a 2D scale transform, CGAffineTransformMakeScale, takes two parameters; the function for making a 3D scale transform, CATransform3DMakeScale, takes three parameters.

The rotation 3D transform is a little more complicated. In addition to the angle, you also have to supply three coordinates describing the vector around which the rotation takes place. Perhaps you've forgotten from your high-school math what a vector is, or perhaps trying to visualize three dimensions boggles your mind, so think of it this way.

Pretend for purposes of discussion that the anchor point is the origin, (0.0,0.0,0.0). Now imagine an arrow emanating from the anchor point; its other end, the pointy end, is described by the three coordinates you provide. Now imagine a plane that intersects

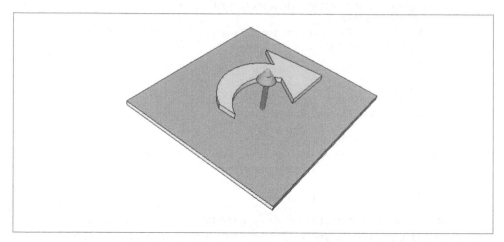

Figure 3-9. An anchor point plus a vector defines a rotation plane

the anchor point, perpendicular to the arrow. That is the plane in which the rotation will take place; a positive angle is a clockwise rotation, as seen from the side of the plane with the arrow (Figure 3-9). In effect, the three coordinates you supply describe (relative to the anchor point) where your eye would have to be to see this rotation as an old-fashioned two-dimensional rotation.

A vector specifies a direction, not a point. Thus it makes no difference on what scale you give the coordinates: `(1.0,1.0,1.0)` means the same thing as `(10.0,10.0,10.0)`. If the three values are `(0.0,0.0,1.0)`, with all other things being equal, the case is collapsed to a simple CGAffineTransform, because the rotational plane is the screen. If the three values are `(0.0,0.0,-1.0)`, it's a backward CGAffineTransform, so that a positive angle looks counterclockwise (because we are looking at the "back side" of the rotational plane).

A layer can itself be rotated in such a way that its "back" is showing. For example, the following rotation flips a layer around its y-axis:

```
someLayer.transform = CATransform3DMakeRotation(CGFloat(M_PI), 0, 1, 0)
```

By default, the layer is considered double-sided, so when it is flipped to show its "back," what's drawn is an appropriately reversed version of the content of the layer (along with its sublayers, which by default are still drawn in front of the layer, but reversed and positioned in accordance with the layer's transformed coordinate system). But if the layer's `doubleSided` property is `false`, then when it is flipped to show its "back," the layer disappears (along with its sublayers); its "back" is transparent and empty.

Depth

There are two ways to place layers at different nominal depths with respect to their siblings. One is through the z-component of their `position`, which is the `zPosition` property. (Thus the `zPosition`, too, has a second purpose that I didn't tell you about earlier.) The other is to apply a transform that translates the layer's position in the z-direction. These two values, the z-component of a layer's position and the z-component of its translation transform, are related; in some sense, the `zPosition` is a shorthand for a translation transform in the z-direction. (If you provide both a `zPosition` and a z-direction translation, you can rapidly confuse yourself.)

In the real world, changing an object's `zPosition` would make it appear larger or smaller, as it is positioned closer or further away; but this, by default, is not the case in the world of layer drawing. There is no attempt to portray perspective; the layer planes are drawn at their actual size and flattened onto one another, with no illusion of distance. (This is called *orthographic projection*, and is the way blueprints are often drawn to display an object from one side.)

However, there's a widely used trick for introducing a quality of perspective into the way layers are drawn: make them sublayers of a layer whose `sublayerTransform` property maps all points onto a "distant" plane. (This is probably just about the only thing the `sublayerTransform` property is ever used for.) Combined with orthographic projection, the effect is to apply one-point perspective to the drawing, so that things do get perceptibly smaller in the negative z-direction.

For example, let's try applying a sort of "page-turn" rotation to our compass: we'll anchor it at its right side and then rotate it around the y-axis. Here, the sublayer we're rotating (accessed through a property, `rotationLayer`) is the gradient layer, and the circle and arrow are its sublayers so that they rotate with it:

```
self.rotationLayer.anchorPoint = CGPointMake(1,0.5)
self.rotationLayer.position = CGPointMake(
    self.bounds.maxX, self.bounds.midY)
self.rotationLayer.transform = CATransform3DMakeRotation(
    CGFloat(M_PI)/4.0, 0, 1, 0)
```

The results are disappointing (Figure 3-10); the compass looks more squashed than rotated. Now, however, we'll also apply the distance-mapping transform. The superlayer here is `self`:

```
var transform = CATransform3DIdentity
transform.m34 = -1.0/1000.0
self.sublayerTransform = transform
```

The results (shown in Figure 3-11) are better, and you can experiment with values to replace `1000.0`; for example, `500.0` gives an even more exaggerated effect. Also, the `zPosition` of the `rotationLayer` will now affect how large it is.

Figure 3-10. A disappointing page-turn rotation

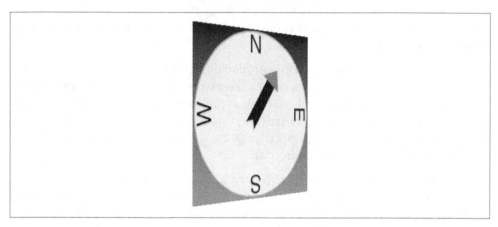

Figure 3-11. A dramatic page-turn rotation

Another way to draw layers with depth is to use CATransformLayer. This CALayer subclass doesn't do any drawing of its own; it is intended solely as a host for other layers. It has the remarkable feature that you can apply a transform to it and it will maintain the depth relationships among its own sublayers. For example:

```
// lay1 is a layer, f is a CGRect
let lay2 = CALayer()
lay2.frame = f
lay2.backgroundColor = UIColor.blueColor().CGColor
lay1.addSublayer(lay2)
let lay3 = CALayer()
lay3.frame = f.rectByOffsetting(dx: 20, dy: 30)
lay3.backgroundColor = UIColor.greenColor().CGColor
lay3.zPosition = 10
lay1.addSublayer(lay3)
lay1.transform = CATransform3DMakeRotation(CGFloat(M_PI), 0, 1, 0)
```

In that code, the superlayer lay1 has two sublayers, lay2 and lay3. The sublayers are added in that order, so lay3 is drawn in front of lay2. Then lay1 is flipped like a page being turned by setting its transform. If lay1 is a normal CALayer, the sublayer drawing order doesn't change; lay3 is *still* drawn in front of lay2, even after the transform is applied. But if lay1 is a CATransformLayer, lay3 is drawn *behind* lay2 after the transform; they are both sublayers of lay1, so their depth relationship is maintained.

Figure 3-12 shows our page-turn rotation yet again, still with the sublayerTransform applied to self, but this time the only sublayer of self is a CATransformLayer:

```
var transform = CATransform3DIdentity
transform.m34 = -1.0/1000.0
self.sublayerTransform = transform
let master = CATransformLayer()
master.frame = self.bounds
self.addSublayer(master)
self.rotationLayer = master
```

The CATransformLayer, to which the page-turn transform is applied, holds the gradient layer, the circle layer, and the arrow layer. Those three layers are at different depths (using different zPosition settings), and I've tried to emphasize the arrow's separation from the circle by adding a shadow (discussed in the next section):

```
circle.zPosition = 10
arrow.shadowOpacity = 1.0
arrow.shadowRadius = 10
arrow.zPosition = 20
```

You can see from its apparent offset that the circle layer floats in front of the gradient layer, but I wish you could see this page-turn as an animation, which makes the circle jump right out from the gradient as the rotation proceeds.

Even more remarkable, I've added a little white peg sticking through the arrow and running into the circle! It is a CAShapeLayer, rotated to be perpendicular to the CATransformLayer (I'll explain the rotation code later in this chapter):

```
let peg = CAShapeLayer()
peg.contentsScale = UIScreen.mainScreen().scale
peg.bounds = CGRectMake(0,0,3.5,50)
let p2 = CGPathCreateMutable()
CGPathAddRect(p2, nil, peg.bounds)
peg.path = p2
peg.fillColor = UIColor(red:1.0, green:0.95, blue:1.0, alpha:0.95).CGColor
peg.anchorPoint = CGPointMake(0.5,0.5)
peg.position = master.bounds.center
master.addSublayer(peg)
peg.setValue(M_PI/2, forKeyPath:"transform.rotation.x")
peg.setValue(M_PI/2, forKeyPath:"transform.rotation.z")
peg.zPosition = 15
```

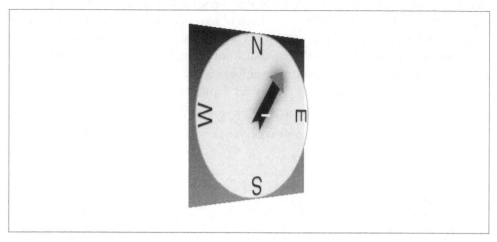

Figure 3-12. Page-turn rotation applied to a CATransformLayer

In that code, the peg runs straight out of the circle toward the viewer, so it is seen end-on, and because a layer has no thickness, it is invisible. But as the CATransformLayer pivots forward in our page-turn rotation, the peg maintains its orientation relative to the circle, and comes into view. In effect, the drawing portrays a 3D model constructed entirely out of layers.

There is, I think, a slight additional gain in realism if the same `sublayerTransform` is applied also to the CATransformLayer, but I have not done so here.

Shadows, Borders, and Masks

A CALayer has many additional properties that affect details of how it is drawn. Since these drawing details can be applied to a UIView's underlying layer, they are effectively view features as well.

A CALayer can have a shadow, defined by its `shadowColor`, `shadowOpacity`, `shadowRadius`, and `shadowOffset` properties. To make the layer draw a shadow, set the `shadowOpacity` to a nonzero value. The shadow is normally based on the shape of the layer's nontransparent region, but deriving this shape can be calculation-intensive (so much so that in early versions of iOS, layer shadows weren't implemented). You can vastly improve performance by defining the shape yourself and assigning this shape as a CGPath to the `shadowPath` property.

Figure 3-13. A layer with a mask

 If a layer's maskToBounds is true, no part of its shadow lying outside its bounds is drawn. (This includes the underlying layer of a view whose clipsToBounds is true.) Wondering why the shadow isn't appearing for a layer that masks to its bounds is a common beginner quandary.

A CALayer can have a border (borderWidth, borderColor); the borderWidth is drawn inward from the bounds, potentially covering some of the content unless you compensate.

A CALayer can be bounded by a rounded rectangle, by giving it a cornerRadius greater than zero. If the layer has a border, the border has rounded corners too. If the layer has a backgroundColor, that background is clipped to the shape of the rounded rectangle. If the layer's maskToBounds is true, the layer's content and its sublayers are clipped by the rounded corners.

A CALayer can have a mask. This is itself a layer, whose content must be provided somehow. The transparency of the mask's content in a particular spot becomes (all other things being equal) the transparency of the layer at that spot. The mask's colors (hues) are irrelevant; only transparency matters. To position the mask, pretend it's a sublayer.

For example, Figure 3-13 shows our arrow layer, with the gray circle layer behind it, and a mask applied to the arrow layer. The mask is silly, but it illustrates very well how masks work: it's an ellipse, with an opaque fill and a thick, semitransparent stroke. Here's the code that generates and applies the mask:

```
let mask = CAShapeLayer()
mask.frame = arrow.bounds
let p2 = CGPathCreateMutable()
CGPathAddEllipseInRect(p2, nil, CGRectInset(mask.bounds, 10, 10))
mask.strokeColor = UIColor(white:0.0, alpha:0.5).CGColor
mask.lineWidth = 20
mask.path = p2
arrow.mask = mask
```

Using a mask, we can do manually and in a more general way what the cornerRadius and maskToBounds properties do. For example, here's a utility method that generates a CALayer suitable for use as a rounded rectangle mask:

```
func maskOfSize(sz:CGSize, roundingCorners rad:CGFloat) -> CALayer {
    let r = CGRect(origin:CGPointZero, size:sz)
    UIGraphicsBeginImageContextWithOptions(r.size, false, 0)
    let con = UIGraphicsGetCurrentContext()
    CGContextSetFillColorWithColor(
        con, UIColor(white:0, alpha:0).CGColor)
    CGContextFillRect(con, r)
    CGContextSetFillColorWithColor(
        con, UIColor(white:0, alpha:1).CGColor)
    let p = UIBezierPath(roundedRect:r, cornerRadius:rad)
    p.fill()
    let im = UIGraphicsGetImageFromCurrentImageContext()
    UIGraphicsEndImageContext()
    let mask = CALayer()
    mask.frame = r
    mask.contents = im.CGImage
    return mask
}
```

The CALayer returned from that method can be placed as a mask anywhere in a layer by adjusting its frame origin and assigning it as the layer's mask. The result is that all of that layer's content drawing and its sublayers (including, if this layer is a view's underlying layer, the view's subviews) are clipped to the rounded rectangle shape; everything outside that shape is not drawn. That's just one example of the sort of thing you can do with a mask. A mask can have values between opaque and transparent, and it can be any shape. And the transparent region doesn't have to be on the outside of the mask; you can use a mask that's opaque on the outside and transparent on the inside to punch a hole in a layer (or a view).

New in iOS 8, you can apply a mask as a view directly to another view through its mask-View property, rather than having to drop down to the level of layers. This may be a notational convenience, but it is not functionally distinct from applying the mask view's layer to the view's layer; under the hood, in fact, it *is* applying the mask view's layer to the view's layer. Thus, for example, it does nothing to solve the problem that the mask is not automatically resized along with the view.

Layer Efficiency

By now, you're probably envisioning all sorts of compositing fun, with layers masking sublayers and laid semitransparently over other layers. There's nothing wrong with that, but when an iOS device is asked to shift its drawing from place to place, the movement may stutter because the device lacks the necessary computing power to composite repeatedly and rapidly. This sort of issue is likely to emerge particularly when your code performs an animation (Chapter 4) or when the user is able to animate drawing through touch, as when scrolling a table view (Chapter 8). You may be able to detect these problems by eye, and you can quantify them on a device by using the Core Animation template in Instruments, which shows the frame rate achieved during animation. Also, both the Core Animation template and the Simulator's Debug menu let you summon colored overlays that provide clues as to possible sources of inefficient drawing which can lead to such problems.

In general, opaque drawing is most efficient. (Nonopaque drawing is what Instruments marks in red as "blended layers.") If a layer will always be shown over a background consisting of a single color, you can give the layer its own background of that same color; when additional layer content is supplied, the visual effect will be the same as if that additional layer content were composited over a transparent background. For example, instead of an image masked to a rounded rectangle (with a layer's `cornerRadius` or `mask` property), you could use Core Graphics to clip the drawing of that image to a rounded rectangle shape within the graphics context of a layer whose background color is the same as that of the destination in front of which the drawing will be shown.

Another way to gain some efficiency is by "freezing" the entirety of the layer's drawing as a bitmap. In effect, you're drawing everything in the layer to a secondary cache and using the cache to draw to the screen. Copying from a cache is less efficient than drawing directly to the screen, but this inefficiency may be compensated for, if there's a deep or complex layer tree, by not having to composite that tree every time we render. To do this, set the layer's `shouldRasterize` to `true` and its `rasterizationScale` to some sensible value (probably `UIScreen.mainScreen().scale`). You can always turn rasterization off again by setting `shouldRasterize` to `false`, so it's easy to rasterize just before some massive or sluggish rearrangement of the screen and then unrasterize afterward.

In addition, there's a layer property `drawsAsynchronously`. The default is `false`. If set to `true`, the layer's graphics context accumulates drawing commands and obeys them later on a background thread. Thus, your drawing commands run very quickly, because they are not in fact being obeyed at the time you issue them. I haven't had occasion to use this, but presumably there could be situations where it keeps your app responsive when drawing would otherwise be time-consuming.

Layers and Key–Value Coding

All of a layer's properties are accessible through key–value coding by way of keys with the same name as the property. Thus, to apply a mask to a layer, instead of saying this:

```
layer.mask = mask
```

we could have said:

```
layer.setValue(mask, forKey: "mask")
```

In addition, CATransform3D and CGAffineTransform values can be expressed through key–value coding and key paths. For example, instead of writing this:

```
self.rotationLayer.transform = CATransform3DMakeRotation(
    CGFloat(M_PI)/4.0, 0, 1, 0)
```

we can write this:

```
self.rotationLayer.setValue(M_PI/4, forKeyPath:"transform.rotation.y")
```

This notation is possible because CATransform3D is key–value coding compliant for a repertoire of keys and key paths. These are not properties, however; a CATransform3D doesn't have a rotation property. It doesn't have *any* properties, because it isn't even an object. You cannot say:

```
self.rotationLayer.transform.rotation.y = //... No, sorry
```

The transform key paths you'll use most often are:

- `"rotation.x"`, `"rotation.y"`, `"rotation.z"`
- `"rotation"` (same as `"rotation.z"`)
- `"scale.x"`, `"scale.y"`, `"scale.z"`
- `"translation.x"`, `"translation.y"`, `"translation.z"`
- `"translation"` (two-dimensional, a CGSize)

The Quartz Core framework also injects KVC compliance into CGPoint, CGSize, and CGRect, allowing you to use keys and key paths matching their struct component names. For a complete list of KVC compliant classes related to CALayer, along with the keys and key paths they implement, plus rules for how to wrap nonobject values as objects, see "Core Animation Extensions to Key-Value Coding" in Apple's *Core Animation Programming Guide.*

Moreover, you can treat a CALayer as a kind of NSDictionary, and get and set the value for *any* key. This means you can attach arbitrary information to an individual layer instance and retrieve it later. For example, earlier I mentioned that to apply manual layout to a layer's sublayers, you will need a way of identifying those sublayers. This feature could provide a way of doing that. For example:

```
myLayer1.setValue("Manny", forKey:"name")
myLayer2.setValue("Moe", forKey:"name")
```

A layer doesn't have a name property; the `"name"` key is something I'm attaching to these layers arbitrarily. Now I can identify these layers later by getting the value of their respective `"name"` keys.

Also, CALayer has a `defaultValueForKey:` class method; to implement it, you'll need to subclass and override. In the case of keys whose value you want to provide a default for, return that value; otherwise, return the value that comes from calling `super`. Thus, even if a value for a particular key has never been explicitly provided, it can have a non-nil value.

The truth is that this feature, though delightful (and I often wish that all classes behaved like this), is not put there for your convenience and enjoyment. It's there to serve as the basis for animation, which is the subject of the next chapter.

CHAPTER 4

Animation

Animation is the visible change of an attribute over time. The changing attribute might be positional: something moves or changes size. But other kinds of attribute can animate as well. For example, a view's background color might change from red to green, not instantly, but perceptibly fading from one to the other. Or a view might change from opaque to transparent, not instantly, but perceptibly fading away.

Without help, most of us would find animation beyond our reach. There are just too many complications — complications of calculation, of timing, of screen refresh, of threading, and many more. Fortunately, help is provided. You don't perform an animation yourself; you describe it, you order it, and it is performed for you. You get *animation on demand*.

Asking for an animation can be as simple as setting a property value; under some circumstances, a single line of code will result in animation:

```
myLayer.backgroundColor = UIColor.redColor().CGColor // animate to red
```

And this is no coincidence. Apple wants to facilitate your use of animation. Animation is crucial to the character of the iOS interface. It isn't just cool and fun; it clarifies that something is changing or responding. For example, one of my first apps was based on an OS X game in which the user clicks cards to select them. In the OS X version, a card was highlighted to show it was selected, and the computer would beep to indicate a click on an ineligible card. On iOS, these indications were insufficient: the highlighting felt weak, and you can't use a sound warning in an environment where the user might have the volume turned off or be listening to music. So in the iOS version, animation is the indicator for card selection (a selected card waggles eagerly) and for tapping on an ineligible card (the whole interface shudders, as if to shrug off the tap).

(If you're looking to create a complete constantly running animated world, as for certain types of game, look into Sprite Kit. This book doesn't discuss Sprite Kit, but an understanding of the concepts in this chapter will prepare you very well for Sprite Kit.)

The Simulator's Debug → Toggle Slow Animations menu item helps you inspect animations by making them run more slowly.

Drawing, Animation, and Threading

When you change a visible view property, even *without* animation, that change does *not* visibly take place there and then. Rather, the system records that this is a change you would like to make, and marks the view as needing to be redrawn. You can change many visible view properties, but these changes merely constitute an accumulated set of instructions. Later, when all your code has run to completion and the system has, as it were, a free moment, then it redraws all views that need redrawing, applying their new visible property features. Let's call this the *redraw moment*. (I'll explain what the redraw moment really is later in this chapter.)

You can see that this is true simply by changing some visible aspect of a view and changing it back again, in the same code: on the screen, nothing happens. For example, suppose a view's background color is green. Suppose your code changes it to red, and then later changes it back to green:

```
// view starts out green
view.backgroundColor = UIColor.redColor()
// ... time-consuming code goes here ...
view.backgroundColor = UIColor.greenColor()
// code ends, redraw moment arrives
```

The system accumulates all the desired changes until the redraw moment happens, and the redraw moment doesn't happen until after your code has finished, so when the redraw moment does happen, the last accumulated change in the view's color is to green — which is its color already. Thus, no matter how much time-consuming code lies between the change from green to red and the change from red to green, the user won't see any color change at all.

That's why you don't order a view to be redrawn; rather, you tell it that it *needs* redrawing — setNeedsDisplay — at the next redraw moment. It's also why I used delayed performance in the contentMode example in Chapter 2: it was to allow the redraw moment a chance to happen, thus giving the view some content, *before* resizing the view. This use of delayed performance to let a redraw moment happen is quite common; later in this chapter I'll suggest another way of accomplishing the same goal.

Similarly, when you ask for an animation to be performed, the animation doesn't start happening on the screen until the next redraw moment. (You can force an animation to be performed immediately, but this is unusual.)

Now let's talk about the mechanism by which animation is performed. It's all a kind of ingenious illusion. Think of the animation as a kind of movie, a cartoon, interposed between the user and the "real" screen. While the animation lasts, this movie is super-imposed onto the screen. When the animation is finished, the movie is removed, revealing the state of the "real" screen behind it. The user is unaware of all this, because (if you've done things correctly) at the time that it starts, the movie's first frame looks just like the state of the "real" screen at that moment, and at the time that it ends, the movie's last frame looks just like the state of the "real" screen at *that* moment.

So, when you reposition a view from position 1 to position 2 with animation, you can envision a typical sequence of events like this:

1. The view is set to position 2, but there has been no redraw moment, so it is still portrayed at position 1.

2. The rest of your code runs to completion.

3. The redraw moment arrives. If there were no animation, the view would now suddenly be portrayed at position 2. But there *is* an animation, and it (the "animation movie") starts with the view portrayed at position 1, so that is still what the user sees.

4. The animation proceeds, portraying the view at intermediate positions between position 1 and position 2. The documentation describes the animation as now *in-flight*.

5. The animation ends, portraying the view ending up at position 2.

6. The "animation movie" is removed, revealing the view indeed at position 2.

Realizing that the "animation movie" is different from what happens to the *real* view is key to configuring an animation correctly. A frequent complaint of beginners is that a position animation is performed as expected, but then, at the end, the view "jumps" to some other position. This happens because you set up the animation but failed to move the view to match its final position in the "animation movie"; the "jump" happens because, when the "movie" is whipped away at the end of the animation, the real situation that's revealed doesn't match the last frame of the "movie."

There isn't really an "animation movie" in front of the screen — but it's a good analogy, and the effect is much the same. In reality, it is not a layer itself that is portrayed on the screen; it's a derived layer called the *presentation layer*. Thus, when you animate the change of a view's position or a layer's position from position 1 to position 2, its nominal position changes immediately; meanwhile, the presentation layer's position remains unchanged until the redraw moment, and then changes over time, and because that's what's actually drawn on the screen, that's what the user sees.

(A layer's presentation layer can be accessed through its `presentationLayer` method — and the layer itself may be accessed through the presentation layer's `modelLayer` method. I'll give examples later in this chapter and in the next chapter of situations where accessing the presentation layer is a useful thing to do.)

The existence of the presentation layer can be confusing, because it means that every animated layer is *copied*. You may need to be aware of this fact when designing a custom CALayer subclass. For example, you might use logging or breakpoints to test when certain events take place in an instance of your custom CALayer; you may think there is only such instance, but if this layer is animated, there are two such instances, and your console messages or pauses may take place in the presentation layer rather than in your "real" layer.

The "animation movie" analogy is an apt one, because, like a movie (especially an old-fashioned animated cartoon), there are "frames." An animating layer does not change smoothly and continuously; it changes in small, individual increments that give the *illusion* of smooth, continuous change. This illusion works because the device itself undergoes a periodic, rapid, more or less regular screen refresh, and the incremental changes are made to fall between these refreshes. Apple calls the system component responsible for this the *animation server*.

Animation (meaning the animation server) operates on an independent thread. You don't have to worry about the details (thank heavens, because multithreading is generally rather tricky and complicated), but you can't ignore it either. Your code runs independently of and possibly simultaneously with the animation — that's what multithreading means — so communication between the animation and your code can require some planning.

Arranging for your code to be notified when an animation ends is a common need. Most of the animation APIs provide a way to set up such a notification. One use of an "animation ended" notification might be to chain animations together: one animation ends and then another begins, in sequence. Another use is to perform some sort of cleanup. A very frequent kind of cleanup has to do with handling of touches: while an animation is in-flight, if your code is not running, the interface by default is responsive to the user's touches, which might cause all kinds of havoc as your views try to respond while the animation is still happening and the screen presentation doesn't match reality. To take care of this, it's common practice to turn off your app's responsiveness to touches as you set up an animation and then turn it back on when you're notified that the animation is over; locking down all the relevant situations so that this toggling of the app's responsiveness is performed coherently can be challenging.

Since your code can run even after you've set up an animation, or might start running while an animation is in-flight, you need to be careful about setting up conflicting animations. Multiple animations can be set up (and performed) simultaneously, but trying to animate or change a property that's already in the middle of being animated is an incoherency that can kill the animation there and then. You may sometimes do this intentionally as a way of interrupting an animation, but just as often you'll want to take care not to let your animations step on each other's feet.

New in iOS 8, conflicting view animations may automatically be combined additively, rather than the second one superseding the first. I'll talk more about that later in this chapter.

Outside forces can interrupt your animations as well. The user might click the Home button to send your app to the background, or an incoming phone call might arrive while an animation is in-flight. The system deals coherently with this situation by simply canceling all in-flight animations when an app is backgrounded; you've already arranged *before* the animation for your views to assume the final states they will have *after* the animation, so no harm is done — when your app resumes, everything is in that final state you arranged beforehand. But if you wanted your app to resume an animation in the middle, where it left off when it was interrupted, that would require some canny coding on your part.

UIImageView and UIImage Animation

UIImageView provides a form of animation so simple as to be scarcely deserving of the name; still, sometimes it might be all you need. You supply the UIImageView with an array of UIImages, as the value of its `animationImages` or `highlightedAnimation-Images` property. This array represents the "frames" of a simple cartoon; when you send the `startAnimating` message, the images are displayed in turn, at a frame rate determined by the `animationDuration` property, repeating as many times as specified by the `animationRepeatCount` property (the default is 0, meaning to repeat forever), or until the `stopAnimating` message is received. Before and after the animation, the image view continues displaying its `image` (or `highlightedImage`).

For example, suppose we want an image of Mars to appear out of nowhere and flash three times on the screen. This might seem to require some sort of NSTimer-based solution, but it's far simpler to use an animating UIImageView:

```
let mars = UIImage(named: "Mars")!
UIGraphicsBeginImageContextWithOptions(mars.size, false, 0)
let empty = UIGraphicsGetImageFromCurrentImageContext()
UIGraphicsEndImageContext()
let arr = [mars, empty, mars, empty, mars]
let iv = UIImageView(image:empty)
iv.frame.origin = CGPointMake(100,100)
self.view.addSubview(iv)
iv.animationImages = arr
iv.animationDuration = 2
iv.animationRepeatCount = 1
iv.startAnimating()
```

You can combine UIImageView animation with other kinds of animation. For example, you could flash the image of Mars while at the same time sliding the UIImageView rightward, using view animation as described in the next section.

UIImage supplies a form of animation parallel to that of UIImageView: an image can itself be an *animated image*. Just as with UIImageView, this really means that you've prepared multiple images that form a sequence serving as the "frames" of a simple cartoon. You can create an animated image with one of these UIImage class methods:

animatedImageWithImages:duration:
As with UIImageView's animationImages, you supply an array of UIImages. You also supply the duration for the whole animation.

animatedImageNamed:duration:
You supply the name of a single image file, as with init(named:), with no file extension. The runtime appends "0" (or, if that fails, "1") to the name you supply and makes *that* image file the first image in the animation sequence. Then it increments the appended number, gathering images and adding them to the sequence (until there are no more, or we reach "1024").

animatedResizableImageNamed:capInsets:resizingMode:duration:
Combines an animated image with a resizable image (Chapter 2).

You do not tell an animated image to start animating, nor are you able to tell it how long you want the animation to repeat. Rather, an animated image is *always animating*, repeating its sequence once every duration seconds, so long as it appears in your interface; to control the animation, add the image to your interface or remove it from the interface, possibly exchanging it for a similar image that isn't animated. Moreover, an animated image can appear in the interface *anywhere a UIImage can appear* as a property of some interface object.

In this example, I construct a sequence of red circles of different sizes, in code, and build an animated image which I then display in a UIButton:

```
var arr = [UIImage]()
let w : CGFloat = 18
for i in 0 ..< 6 {
    UIGraphicsBeginImageContextWithOptions(CGSizeMake(w,w), false, 0)
    let con = UIGraphicsGetCurrentContext()
    CGContextSetFillColorWithColor(con, UIColor.redColor().CGColor)
    let ii = CGFloat(i)
    CGContextAddEllipseInRect(con, CGRectMake(0+ii,0+ii,w-ii*2,w-ii*2))
    CGContextFillPath(con)
    let im = UIGraphicsGetImageFromCurrentImageContext()
    UIGraphicsEndImageContext()
    arr += [im]
}
let im = UIImage.animatedImageWithImages(arr, duration:0.5)
b.setImage(im, forState:.Normal) // b is a button in the interface
```

View Animation

All animation is ultimately layer animation. However, for a limited range of properties, you can animate a UIView directly: these are its `alpha`, `backgroundColor`, `bounds`, `center`, `frame`, and `transform`. You can also animate a UIView's change of contents. This list of animatable features, despite its brevity, will often prove quite sufficient. (If it doesn't, you can drop down to a lower level and animate a layer, as described later in this chapter.)

The syntax for animating a UIView involves calling a UIView class method and expressing the desired animation in a closure. Such a closure corresponds to an Objective-C *block*, so the documentation refers to this as *block-based animation*, and I will use phrases such as "animation block" or "`animations:` block" even though "block" is not the official Swift term for such a construct.

For example, suppose we have a UIView `self.v` in the interface, with a yellow background color, and we want to animate that view's change of background color to red. This will do it:

```
UIView.animateWithDuration(0.4, animations: {
    self.v.backgroundColor = UIColor.redColor()
})
```

Any animatable change made within an `animations:` block will be animated, so we can animate a change both to the view's color and to its position simultaneously:

```
UIView.animateWithDuration(0.4, animations: {
    self.v.backgroundColor = UIColor.redColor()
    self.v.center.y += 100
})
```

We can also animate changes to multiple views within the same `animations:` block. For example, suppose we want to make one view dissolve into another. We start with the second view present in the view hierarchy, but with an `alpha` of 0, so that it is invisible. Then we animate the change of the first view's `alpha` to 0 and the second view's `alpha` to 1.

In that case, we might like to place the second view in the view hierarchy just before the animation starts (invisibly, because its `alpha` starts at 0) and remove the first view just after the animation ends (invisibly, because its `alpha` ends at 0). An additional parameter, `completion:`, lets us specify what should happen after the animation ends:

```
let v2 = // ... create and configure new view here ...
v2.alpha = 0
self.v.superview!.addSubview(v2)
UIView.animateWithDuration(0.4, animations: {
    self.v.alpha = 0
    v2.alpha = 1
```

```
    }, completion: {
        _ in
        self.v.removeFromSuperview()
})
```

Code that isn't about animatable view properties can appear in an `animations:` block with no problem, but we must be careful to keep any changes to animatable properties that we do *not* want animated out of the `animations:` block. In the preceding example, in setting `v2.alpha` to 0, I just want to set it right now, instantly; I don't want that change to be animated. So I've put that line before the `animations:` block.

Sometimes, though, that's not so easy; perhaps, within the `animations:` block, we must call a method that might perform animatable changes. The `performWithoutAnimation:` method solves the problem; it goes inside an `animations:` block, but whatever happens in *its* block is *not* animated. In this rather artificial example, the view jumps to its new position and then slowly turns red:

```
UIView.animateWithDuration(0.4, animations: {
    self.v.backgroundColor = UIColor.redColor()
    UIView.performWithoutAnimation {
        self.v.center.y += 100
    }
})
```

The material inside an `animations:` block (but not inside a `performWithoutAnimation:` block) *orders* the animation — that is, it gives instructions for what the animation will be when the redraw moment comes. If you change an animatable view property as part of the animation, you should not change that property again afterward; the results can be confusing. This code, for example, is essentially incoherent:

```
UIView.animateWithDuration(2, animations: {
    self.v.center.y = 100
})
self.v.center.y = 300
```

What actually happens is that the view *jumps* to a center y position of 100, even though that setting is *inside* the animation block, and then *animates* to a center y position of 300, even though that setting is *outside* the animation block. What has happened, in effect, is that the second setting of `self.v.center.y` has cancelled the first animation and replaced it with another. I could try to explain why this is, but I'm not even sure I understand it completely; what I do know is that you should try not to do that sort of thing. After you've ordered an animatable view property to be animated inside an `animations:` block, *don't change that view property's value again* until after the animation is over.

On the other hand, this code jumps and then animates on iOS 7 and before, but on iOS 8 it does a smooth single animation from its original position to a center y position of 300:

```
UIView.animateWithDuration(2, animations: {
    self.v.center.y = 100
    self.v.center.y = 300
})
```

This is an important change in iOS 8 animation behavior, and I do know the reason for it (because Apple explains it in a WWDC 2014 video): it's because basic positional view animations are *additive* by default in iOS 8. This means, in effect, that although there are two animations of the same view attribute in that code, the second one does not cancel or conflict with the first, as it did in iOS 7 and before; instead, both animations are allowed to stand, and the second one is run simultaneously with the first, and is blended with it.

 In that example, it's particularly obvious what such blending entails. Sometimes, however, this new iOS 8 blending of animations can give results that may initially surprise you. If your existing iOS 7 animation code results in new behavior when your app is compiled for iOS 8, additive animations may be the reason.

View Animation Options

The UIView class methods animateWithDuration: and animateWith-Duration:completion: are both reduced forms. The full form of this method, which you should use whenever you need the maximum in flexibility and power, is animate-WithDuration:delay:options:animations:completion:. The parameters are:

duration
:   The duration of the animation: how long it takes (in seconds) to run from start to finish. You can also think of this as the animation's speed. Obviously, if two views are told to move different distances in the same time, the one that must move further must move faster.

delay
:   The delay before the animation starts. The default is no delay. A delay is *not* the same as applying the animation using delayed performance; the animation is applied immediately, but when it starts running it spins its wheels, with no visible change, until the delay time has elapsed.

options
:   A bitmask combining additional options (using the bitwise-or operator).

animations
:   The block containing view property changes to be animated.

completion

> The block to run when the animation ends (or nil). It takes one Bool parameter indicating whether the animation ran to completion. The block is called, with a parameter indicating `true`, even if nothing in the `animations:` block triggers any animations. It's fine for this block to order a further animation, thus chaining animations.

Here are some of the chief `options:` values (UIViewAnimationOptions) that you might wish to use:

Animation curve

> An animation curve describes how the animation changes speed during its course. The term "ease" means that there is a gradual acceleration or deceleration between the animation's central speed and the zero speed at its start or end. Specify one at most:
>
> - `.CurveEaseInOut` (the default)
> - `.CurveEaseIn`
> - `.CurveEaseOut`
> - `.CurveLinear` (constant speed throughout)

`.Repeat`

> If included, the animation will repeat indefinitely. There is no way to specify a certain number of repetitions; you either repeat forever or not at all. This feels like an oversight (a serious oversight); I'll suggest a workaround in a moment.

`.Autoreverse`

> If included, the animation will run from start to finish (in the given duration time), and will then run from finish to start (also in the given duration time). The documentation's claim that you can autoreverse only if you also repeat is incorrect; you can use either or both (or neither).

When using `.Autoreverse`, you will want to clean up at the end so that the view is back in its original position when the animation is over. To see what I mean, consider this code:

```
let opts = UIViewAnimationOptions.Autoreverse
UIView.animateWithDuration(1, delay: 0, options: opts, animations: {
    self.v.center.x += 100
    }, completion: nil)
```

The view animates 100 points to the right and then animates 100 points back to its original position — and then jumps 100 points to the right again. The reason for the jump is that the last actual value we assigned to the view's center x is 100 points to the right, so when the animation is over and the "animation movie" is whipped away, the view is revealed still sitting 100 points to the right. The solution is to move the view back to its original position in the `completion:` handler:

```
let opts = UIViewAnimationOptions.Autoreverse
let xorig = self.v.center.x
UIView.animateWithDuration(1, delay: 0, options: opts, animations: {
    self.v.center.x += 100
    }, completion: {
        _ in
        self.v.center.x = xorig
})
```

Working around the inability to specify a finite number of repetitions is not easy. Let's say you want to repeat the above animation exactly three times. A simple counting loop won't work, because animations are asynchronous and time-consuming. One clear solution is to append a tail-recursion to the `completion:` handler:

```
func animate(count:Int) {
    let opts = UIViewAnimationOptions.Autoreverse
    let xorig = self.v.center.x
    UIView.animateWithDuration(1, delay: 0, options: opts, animations: {
        self.v.center.x += 100
        }, completion: {
            _ in
            self.v.center.x = xorig
            if count > 1 {
                self.animate(count-1)
            }
    })
}
```

If we call the `animate:` method with an argument of 3, our animation takes place three times and stops. There is always a danger, with recursion, of filling up the stack and running out of memory, but I think we're safe if we start with a small `count` value. (That example, of course, suffers from lack of generality; for a general utility function that can do a finite count repetition of *any* animation, see Appendix B.)

There are also some options saying what should happen if another animation is already ordered or in-flight:

`.BeginFromCurrentState`
If this animation animates a property already being animated by an animation that is previously ordered or in-flight, then instead of canceling the previous animation (completing the requested change instantly), if that is what would normally happen, this animation will use the presentation layer to decide where to start, and, if possible, will "blend" its animation with the previous animation.

`.OverrideInheritedDuration`
Prevents inheriting the duration from a surrounding or in-flight animation (the default is to inherit it).

`.OverrideInheritedCurve`

> Prevents inheriting the animation curve from a surrounding or in-flight animation (the default is to inherit it).

To illustrate `.BeginFromCurrentState` is not as easy as it was in iOS 7 and before, because simple view animations, as I've already said, are additive by default in iOS 8. Consider the following:

```
UIView.animateWithDuration(1, animations: {
    self.v.center.x += 100
})
UIView.animateWithDuration(1, delay: 0, options: nil,
    animations: {
    self.v.center.y += 100
}, completion: nil)
```

In iOS 7, that code would cause the view to jump 100 points rightward and then animate 100 points downward. That's because both animations have to do with the position of the view, and they conflict; the second animation therefore caused the first animation to be thrown away. Setting `options:` to `.BeginFromCurrentState`, on the other hand, caused the two animations to combine: the view animates diagonally down and to the right.

In iOS 8, however, additive animation is the default, so the view animates diagonally down and to the right *even if `options:` is nil.*

Thus, `.BeginFromCurrentState` is unlikely to be useful in iOS 8 — though it does no harm to use it. Observe, however, that the effect of additive animations in iOS 8 is not identical to the effect of `.BeginFromCurrentState` in iOS 7. To see the difference, experiment with code such as this:

```
UIView.animateWithDuration(2, animations: {
    self.v.center.x += 100
})
delay(1) {
    let opts = UIViewAnimationOptions.BeginFromCurrentState
    UIView.animateWithDuration(1, delay: 0, options: opts,
        animations: {
            self.v.center.y += 100
        }, completion: nil)
}
```

The second animation launches under delayed performance halfway through the first animation. In iOS 7, this stops the first animation dead in its tracks; the animation does resume from that stopping point, but the view turns a sharp corner and makes a beeline for its final position (down and to the right). In iOS 8, on the other hand, the view never stops moving, because the first animation is never cancelled; when the second animation starts, the view turns the corner gently, with some residual horizontal motion from the first animation.

Canceling a View Animation

Once a view animation is in-flight, how can you cancel it? This has always been a tricky problem, and the change in iOS 8 to additive view animations actually makes it even trickier.

The simple answer, which is not tricky at all, is to reach down to the CALayer level and call `removeAllAnimations`. (If the layer has more than one animation and you only want to cancel one of them, you can call `removeAnimationForKey:`; I'll talk later in this chapter about how to distinguish layer animations by key.) This has the advantage of simplicity, but the disadvantage that it simply stops the animation dead: the "animation movie" is whipped away instantly, leaving the view at its final position.

To illustrate, I'll start with a simple unidirectional positional animation, with a long duration so that we can interrupt it in mid-flight (by tapping a button, for example). To facilitate the explanation, I'll conserve both the view's original position and its final position in properties:

```
self.pOrig = self.v.center
self.pFinal = self.v.center
self.pFinal.x += 100
UIView.animateWithDuration(4, animations: {
    self.v.center = self.pFinal
})
```

We can certainly stop that animation abruptly by mindlessly removing all animations from the layer; this is effectively the same as what the system does automatically when the app goes into the background:

```
self.v.layer.removeAllAnimations()
```

That code, obviously, jumps the view to its final position — because that's where it really is, and that fact is revealed when the "animation movie" is removed. Now let's try to devise a more subtle form of cancellation: the view should hurry to its final position. In iOS 7 and before, the way to do this was to order another animation that brings the animated view rapidly to its final state. But the second animation must not assign the animated property exactly the same value that the first animation assigned it, or nothing will happen; we must generate a *conflict* between the two animations. The solution was to order a very slightly different, conflicting animation and use its `completion:` handler to assign the view property its true final value:

```
let opts = UIViewAnimationOptions.BeginFromCurrentState
UIView.animateWithDuration(0.1, delay:0.1, options:opts,
    animations: {
        var p = self.pFinal!
        p.x += 1
        self.v.center = p
```

```
    }, completion: {
        _ in
        self.v.center = self.pFinal
    })
```

That doesn't work in iOS 8, however, because the two animations *don't conflict*; they are additive. The second animation thus doesn't remove the first animation, which is what we're trying to accomplish. Therefore we must remove the first animation manually. We already know how to do that: call removeAllAnimations. But we also know that if we do that, the view will jump to its final position; we want it to remain, for the moment, at its current position — meaning *the animation's* current position. That position is where the presentation layer currently is. Therefore we reposition the view at the location of its presentation layer, and *then* remove the animation, and *then* perform the final "hurry home" animation:

```
self.v.layer.position = self.v.layer.presentationLayer().position
self.v.layer.removeAllAnimations()
UIView.animateWithDuration(0.1, animations: {
    self.v.center = self.pFinal
})
```

One nice thing about our solution is that if we decide that cancellation means returning the view to its original position, we have only to set the view's center to self.pOrig instead of self.pFinal.

Now let's suppose that the animation we want to cancel is an infinitely repeating autoreversing animation:

```
self.pOrig = self.v.center
let opts : UIViewAnimationOptions = .Autoreverse | .Repeat
UIView.animateWithDuration(1, delay: 0, options: opts,
    animations: {
        self.v.center.x += 100
    }, completion: nil)
```

In that case, the iOS 7 technique of imposing a conflicting animation *does* work in iOS 8, because the new animation is *not* additive with the first one. The reason is that, as I've said already, only *simple* view animations are additive in iOS 8; I have not elaborated on what "simple" means, but one thing it means is "not repeating." So here's how to cancel that animation by returning it rapidly to its original position:

```
UIView.animateWithDuration(0.1, delay:0,
    options:.BeginFromCurrentState,
    animations: {
        self.v.center = self.pOrig
    }, completion:nil)
```

The .BeginFromCurrentState option is necessary to prevent the view from jumping momentarily to the "final" position, 100 points to the right, to which we set it to initiate the repeating animation.

(If you object that storage of the view's original or final position as a view controller property is not a very encapsulated solution, then consider storing it instead in the view's layer using key–value coding. The implementation is left as an exercise for the reader. Hint: a CGPoint will need to be wrapped in an NSValue.)

Custom Animatable View Properties

Even though the view attributes that are animatable through block-based view animation are officially limited to its `alpha`, `backgroundColor`, `bounds`, `center`, `frame`, and `transform`, you can define your own custom view properties that respond by animating when they themselves are changed in an animation block.

Here's an example of what I mean. Imagine a UIView subclass, MyView, which has a Bool `swing` property. All this does is reposition the view: when `swing` is set to `true`, the view's center x value is increased by 100; when `swing` is set to `false`, the view's center x value is decreased by 100. A view's `center` is animatable, so we can make it be the case that when a MyView's `swing` is set in an animation block, the position change is animated.

The trick is a simple one (though I personally had never thought of it until an Apple WWDC 2014 video suggested it): implement MyView's `swing` setter with a zero-duration animation block. This basically means that there is no animation by default, but if we happen to be inside an animation block already when the `swing` property is set, the setter's animation block inherits the duration of the surrounding animation block — because such inheritance is, as I mentioned earlier, the default:

```
class MyView : UIView {
    var swing : Bool = false {
        didSet {
            var p = self.center
            p.x = self.swing ? p.x + 100 : p.x - 100
            UIView.animateWithDuration(0, animations: {
                self.center = p
                })
        }
    }
}
```

The result is exactly as I've already said. If, in code elsewhere, we change a MyView's `swing` directly, the view jumps to its new position. But now suppose we change it in an animation block:

```
UIView.animateWithDuration(1, animations: {
    self.v.swing = !self.v.swing // "animatable" Bool property
})
```

In that case, the change in position is animated, with the specified duration of 1.

Springing View Animation

A springing view animation is an animation curve with a very fast ease-in and a very slow ease-out; the animation can even oscillate for a while around its final value, as if it were being snapped into place by a spring. To use it, call `animateWithDuration:delay:usingSpring....` For example:

```
UIView.animateWithDuration(0.8, delay: 0,
    usingSpringWithDamping: 0.7,
    initialSpringVelocity: 20,
    options: nil,
    animations: {
        self.v.center.y += 100
    }, completion: nil)
```

The `damping:` and `initialSpringVelocity:` parameters modify the behavior of the animation curve. If the damping is less than 1, there's a waggle as the animated view assumes its final position; this waggle becomes quite pronounced at values less than about `0.7`, and at values like `0.3` there are several waggles before the view settles into place.

The initial spring velocity gives the view an initial "kick," speeding up the initial ease-in and increasing the tendency of the view to overshoot its final position on its first approach. Depending on the duration and damping amount, it may need to be quite large to make an appreciable difference. You can have a lot of waggly fun with smaller damping values and larger initial spring velocity values. Conversely, a small initial spring value (about `10` or less) and a high damping value (`1.0` or close to it) gives a normal animation that wouldn't particularly remind anyone of a spring, but that does have a pleasingly rapid beginning and slow ending; many of Apple's own system animations are actually spring animations of that type (consider, for example, the way folders open in the springboard).

Keyframe View Animation

A view animation can be ordered as a set of keyframes. This means that, instead of a simple beginning and end point, you specify multiple stages in the animation and those stages are joined together for you. You call `animateKeyframesWithDuration:...;` it has an `animations:` block, and inside that block you call `addKeyframe...` multiple times to specify each stage. Each keyframe's start time and duration is between 0 and 1, *relative to the animation as a whole*. (Giving the start time and duration in seconds is a common beginner mistake.)

For example, here I'll waggle a view back and forth horizontally while moving it down the screen vertically:

```
var p = self.v.center
let dur = 0.25
var start = 0.0
let dx : CGFloat = 100
let dy : CGFloat = 50
var dir : CGFloat = 1
UIView.animateKeyframesWithDuration(4,
    delay: 0, options: nil,
    animations: {
        UIView.addKeyframeWithRelativeStartTime(start,
            relativeDuration: dur,
            animations: {
                p.x += dx*dir; p.y += dy
                self.v.center = p
        })
        start += dur; dir *= -1
        UIView.addKeyframeWithRelativeStartTime(start,
            relativeDuration: dur,
            animations: {
                p.x += dx*dir; p.y += dy
                self.v.center = p
        })
        start += dur; dir *= -1
        UIView.addKeyframeWithRelativeStartTime(start,
            relativeDuration: dur,
            animations: {
                p.x += dx*dir; p.y += dy
                self.v.center = p
        })
        start += dur; dir *= -1
        UIView.addKeyframeWithRelativeStartTime(start,
            relativeDuration: dur,
            animations: {
                p.x += dx*dir; p.y += dy
                self.v.center = p
        })
}, completion: nil)
```

In that code, there are four keyframes, evenly spaced: each is .25 in duration (one-fourth of the whole animation) and each starts .25 later than the previous one (as soon as the previous one ends). In each keyframe, the view's center x value increases or decreases by 100, alternately, while its center y value keeps increasing by 50.

The keyframe values are points in space and time; the actual animation interpolates between them. How this interpolation is done depends upon the options:, which are UIKeyframeAnimationOptions values whose names start with "CalculationMode." The default is .CalculationModeLinear. In our example, this means that the path followed by the view is a sharp zig-zag, the view seeming to bounce off invisible walls at the right and left. But if the setting is .CalculationModeCubic, our view describes a smooth S-curve, starting at the view's initial position and ending at the last keyframe point, and passing through the three other keyframe points like the maxima and minima of a sine wave.

Because my keyframes are perfectly even, I could achieve the same effects by using `.CalculationModePaced` (same effect as `.CalculationModeLinear`) and `.CalculationModeCubicPaced` (same effect as `.CalculationModeCubic`). The `Paced` options simply ignore the relative start time and relative duration values of the keyframes; you might as well pass `0` for all of them. Instead, they divide up the times and durations evenly, exactly as my code has done.

Finally, `.CalculationModeDiscrete` means that the changed animatable properties don't animate: the animation jumps to each keyframe.

The outer `animations:` block can contain other changes to animatable view properties, as long as they don't conflict with the keyframe `animations:`; these are animated over the total duration. For example:

```
UIView.animateKeyframesWithDuration(4,
    delay: 0, options: nil,
    animations: {
        self.v.alpha = 0
        // ...
```

The result is that as the view zigzags back and forth down the screen, it also gradually fades away.

It is also legal and meaningful to supply an animation curve as part of the `options:` argument. Unfortunately, the documentation fails to make this clear; and Swift's obsessive-compulsive attitude towards data types resists folding a UIViewAnimation-Options animation curve directly into a value typed as a UIViewKeyframeAnimation-Options. Yet if you don't do it, the default is `.CurveEaseInOut`, which may not be what you want. Here's how to combine `.CalculationModeLinear` with `.CurveLinear`:

```
let opt1 : UIViewKeyframeAnimationOptions = .CalculationModeLinear
let opt2 : UIViewAnimationOptions = .CurveLinear
let opts = opt1 | UIViewKeyframeAnimationOptions(opt2.rawValue)
```

That's two different senses of "Linear." The first means that the path described by the moving view is a sequence of straight lines. The second means that the moving view's speed along that path is steady.

Transitions

A transition is an animation that emphasizes a view's change of content. Transitions are ordered using one of two UIView class methods:

- `transitionWithView:duration:options:animations:completion:`
- `transitionFromView:toView:duration:options:completion:`

The transition animation types are expressed as part of the `options:` bitmask:

- `.TransitionFlipFromLeft`, `.TransitionFlipFromRight`
- `.TransitionCurlUp`, `.TransitionCurlDown`
- `.TransitionFlipFromBottom`, `.TransitionFlipFromTop`
- `.TransitionCrossDissolve`

In this example, a UIImageView containing an image of Mars flips over as its image changes to a smiley face; it looks as if the image view were two-sided, with Mars on one side and the smiley face on the other:

```
let opts : UIViewAnimationOptions = .TransitionFlipFromLeft
UIView.transitionWithView(self.iv, duration: 0.8, options: opts,
    animations: {
        self.iv.image = UIImage(named:"Smiley")
    }, completion: nil)
```

In that example, I've put the content change inside the `animations:` block. That's conventional but misleading; the truth is that if all that's changing is the content, *nothing* needs to go into the `animations:` block. The change of content can be anywhere, before or even after this entire line of code. It's the flip that's being animated. You might use the `animations:` block here to order additional animations, such as a change in a view's center.

You can do the same sort of thing with a custom view that does its own drawing. Let's say that I have a UIView subclass, MyView, that draws either a rectangle or an ellipse depending on the value of its Bool `reverse` property:

```
class MyView : UIView {
    var reverse = false
    override func drawRect(rect: CGRect)  {
        let f = self.bounds.rectByInsetting(dx: 10, dy: 10)
        let con = UIGraphicsGetCurrentContext()
        if self.reverse {
            CGContextStrokeEllipseInRect(con, f)
        }
        else {
            CGContextStrokeRect(con, f)
        }
    }
}
```

This code flips a MyView instance while changing its drawing from a rectangle to an ellipse or *vice versa*:

```
let opts : UIViewAnimationOptions = .TransitionFlipFromLeft
self.v.reverse = !self.v.reverse
UIView.transitionWithView(self.v, duration: 1, options: opts,
    animations: {
        self.v.setNeedsDisplay()
    }, completion: nil)
```

During a transition, by default, the view's appearance changes directly to its final appearance; in effect, a snapshot of the view's final appearance has been taken beforehand. If that isn't what you want — that is, if you want to display a subview of the transitioning view being animated as it assumes its final state — use .AllowAnimatedContent in the options bitmask.

transitionFromView:toView:... names two views; the first is replaced by the second, while their superview undergoes the transition animation. There are two possible configurations, depending on the options you provide:

Remove one subview, add the other
> If .ShowHideTransitionViews is *not* one of the options, then the second subview is not in the view hierarchy when we start; the transition removes the first subview from its superview and adds the second subview to that same superview.

Hide one subview, show the other
> If .ShowHideTransitionViews *is* one of the options, then both subviews are in the view hierarchy when we start; the hidden of the first is false, the hidden of the second is true, and the transition reverses these values.

In this example, a label self.lab is already in the interface. The animation causes the superview of self.lab to flip over, while at the same time a different label, lab2, is substituted for it:

```
let lab2 = UILabel(frame:self.lab.frame)
lab2.text = self.lab.text == "Hello" ? "Howdy" : "Hello"
lab2.sizeToFit()
UIView.transitionFromView(self.lab, toView: lab2,
    duration: 0.8, options: .TransitionFlipFromLeft,
    completion: {
        _ in
        self.lab = lab2
    })
```

It's up to you to make sure beforehand that the second view (toView:) has the desired position, so that it will appear in the right place in its superview.

Implicit Layer Animation

If a layer is already present in the interface and is not a view's underlying layer, animating it can be as simple as setting a property. A change in what the documentation calls an *animatable property* is *automatically* interpreted as a request to animate that change. In other words, animation of layer property changes is the default! Multiple property changes are considered part of the same animation. This mechanism is called *implicit animation*.

 You cannot use implicit animation on a UIView's underlying layer. You can animate a UIView's underlying layer directly, but you must use explicit layer animation (discussed later in this chapter).

For example, in Chapter 3 we constructed a compass out of layers. The compass itself is a CompassView that does no drawing of its own; its underlying layer is a Compass-Layer that also does no drawing, serving only as a superlayer for the layers that constitute the drawing. None of the layers that constitute the actual drawing is the underlying layer of a view, so a property change to any of them, once they are established in the interface, is animated automatically.

So, presume that we have a reference to the arrow layer (arrow). If we rotate the arrow by changing its transform property, that rotation is animated:

```
// an implicit animation
arrow.transform = CATransform3DRotate(
    arrow.transform, CGFloat(M_PI)/4.0, 0, 0, 1)
```

CALayer properties listed in the documentation as animatable in this way are anchor-Point and anchorPointZ, backgroundColor, borderColor, borderWidth, bounds, contents, contentsCenter, contentsRect, cornerRadius, doubleSided, hidden, masksToBounds, opacity, position and zPosition, rasterizationScale and should-Rasterize, shadowColor, shadowOffset, shadowOpacity, shadowRadius, and sublayerTransform and transform.

In addition, a CAShapeLayer's path, strokeStart, strokeEnd, fillColor, stroke-Color, lineWidth, lineDashPhase, and miterLimit are animatable; so are a CAText-Layer's fontSize and foregroundColor, and a CAGradientLayer's colors, locations, and endPoint. (See Chapter 3 for discussion of those classes; the fact that a CAShape-Layer's path can be animated is particularly intriguing, and I'll give an example later in this chapter.)

Basically, a property is animatable because there's some sensible way to interpolate the intermediate values between one value and another. The nature of the animation attached to each property is therefore generally just what you would intuitively expect. When you change a layer's hidden property, it fades out of view (or into view). When you change a layer's contents, the old contents are dissolved into the new contents. And so forth.

Implicit layer animation doesn't affect a layer as it is being created, configured, and added to the interface. Implicit animation comes into play when you change an animatable property of a layer that is *already* present in the interface.

Animation Transactions

Implicit animation operates with respect to a *transaction* (a CATransaction), which collects all animation requests and hands them over to the animation server in a single batch. Every animation request takes place in the context of some transaction. You can make this explicit by wrapping your animation requests in calls to the CATransaction class methods begin and commit; the result is a *transaction block*. Additionally, there is always an *implicit transaction* surrounding your code, and you can operate on this implicit transaction without any begin and commit.

To modify the characteristics of an implicit animation, you modify the transaction that surrounds it. Typically, you'll use these CATransaction class methods:

setAnimationDuration:
> The duration of the animation.

setAnimationTimingFunction:
> A CAMediaTimingFunction; timing functions are discussed in the next section.

setCompletionBlock:
> A block to be called when the animation ends. The block takes no parameters. The block is called even if no animation is triggered during this transaction.

By nesting transaction blocks, you can apply different animation characteristics to different elements of an animation. But you can also use transaction commands outside of any transaction block to modify the implicit transaction. So, in our previous example, we could slow down the animation of the arrow like this:

```
CATransaction.setAnimationDuration(0.8)
arrow.transform = CATransform3DRotate(
    arrow.transform, CGFloat(M_PI)/4.0, 0, 0, 1)
```

An important use of transactions is to turn implicit animation *off*. This is valuable because implicit animation is the default, and can be unwanted (and a performance drag). To turn off implicit animation, call the CATransaction class method setDisable-Actions: with argument true. There are other ways to turn off implicit animation (discussed later in this chapter), but this is the simplest.

setCompletionBlock: is an extraordinarily useful and probably underutilized tool. The transaction's completion block signals the end, not only of the implicit layer property animations you yourself have ordered as part of this transaction, but of *all* animations ordered during this transaction, including Cocoa's own animations. Thus, it's a way to be notified when any and all animations come to an end.

CATransaction implements KVC to allow you to set and retrieve a value for an arbitrary key, similar to CALayer.

 An explicit transaction block that orders an animation to a layer, if the block is *not preceded by any other changes to the layer*, can cause animation to begin immediately when the CATransaction class method commit is called, without waiting for the redraw moment, while your code continues running. In my experience, this can cause trouble (animation delegate messages cannot arrive, and the presentation layer can't be queried properly) and should be avoided.

Media Timing Functions

The CATransaction class method setAnimationTimingFunction: takes as its parameter a media timing function (CAMediaTimingFunction). This class is the general expression of the animation curves we have already met (ease-in-out, ease-in, ease-out, and linear), and you can use it with those very same predefined curves, by calling the CAMediaTimingFunction initializer init(name:) with one of these parameters:

- kCAMediaTimingFunctionLinear
- kCAMediaTimingFunctionEaseIn
- kCAMediaTimingFunctionEaseOut
- kCAMediaTimingFunctionEaseInEaseOut
- kCAMediaTimingFunctionDefault

Figure 4-1. An ease-in-out Bézier curve

A media timing function is a Bézier curve defined by two points. The curve graphs the fraction of the animation's time that has elapsed (the x-axis) against the fraction of the animation's change that has occurred (the y-axis); its endpoints are therefore at (0.0,0.0) and (1.0,1.0), because at the beginning of the animation there has been no elapsed time and no change, and at the end of the animation all the time has elapsed and all the change has occurred.

The curve's defining points are its endpoints, and each endpoint needs only one Bézier control point to define the tangent to the curve. And because the curve's endpoints are known, defining the two control points is sufficient to describe the entire curve. And because a point is a pair of floating-point values, a media timing function can be expressed as four floating-point values. That is, in fact, how it is expressed.

So, for example, the ease-in-out timing function is expressed as the four values 0.42, 0.0, 0.58, 1.0. That defines a Bézier curve with one endpoint at (0.0,0.0), whose control point is (0.42,0.0), and the other endpoint at (1.0,1.0), whose control point is (0.58,1.0) (Figure 4-1).

To define your own media timing function, supply the coordinates of the two control points by calling init(controlPoints:). (It helps to design the curve in a standard drawing program first so that you can visualize how the placement of the control points shapes the curve.) For example, here's a media timing function that starts out quite slowly and then whips quickly into place after about two-thirds of the time has elapsed. I call this the "clunk" timing function, and it looks great with the compass arrow:

```
let clunk = CAMediaTimingFunction(controlPoints: 0.9, 0.1, 0.7, 0.9)
CATransaction.setAnimationTimingFunction(clunk)
arrow.transform = CATransform3DRotate(
    arrow.transform, CGFloat(M_PI)/4.0, 0, 0, 1)
```

Core Animation

Core Animation is the fundamental underlying iOS animation technology. View animation and implicit layer animation are merely convenient façades for Core Animation. Core Animation is *explicit layer animation*, and revolves primarily around the CAAnimation class and its subclasses, which allow you to create far more elaborate specifications of an animation than anything we've encountered so far.

You may never program at the level of Core Animation, but you should read this section anyway, if only to learn how animation really works and to get a sense of its mighty powers. In particular, Core Animation:

- Works even on a view's underlying layer. Thus, Core Animation is the *only* way to apply full-on layer property animation to a view.
- Provides fine control over the intermediate values and timing of an animation.
- Allows animations to be grouped into complex combinations.
- Adds transition animation effects that aren't available otherwise, such as new content "pushing" the previous content out of a layer.

 Animating a view's underlying layer with Core Animation is layer animation, not view animation — so you don't get any automatic layout of that view's subviews. This can be a reason for preferring view animation.

CABasicAnimation and Its Inheritance

The simplest way to animate a property with Core Animation is with a CABasicAnimation object. CABasicAnimation derives much of its power through its inheritance, so I'll describe that inheritance along with CABasicAnimation itself. You will readily see that all the property animation features we have met so far are embodied in a CABasicAnimation instance.

CAAnimation
> CAAnimation is an abstract class, meaning that you'll only ever use a subclass of it. Some of CAAnimation's powers come from its implementation of the CAMediaTiming protocol.

delegate
> The delegate messages are `animationDidStart:` and `animationDidStop:finished:`.
>
> A CAAnimation instance *retains its delegate*; this is very unusual behavior and can cause trouble if you're not conscious of it (I'm speaking from experience). Alternatively, don't set a delegate; to make your code run after the animation

ends, call the CATransaction class method `setCompletionBlock:` before configuring the animation.

duration, timingFunction

The length of the animation, and its timing function (a CAMediaTiming-Function). A duration of `0` (the default) means `.25` seconds unless overridden by the transaction.

autoreverses, repeatCount, repeatDuration, cumulative

For an infinite `repeatCount` (in Swift), use `Float.infinity`. The `repeat-Duration` property is a different way to govern repetition, specifying how long the repetition should continue rather than how many repetitions should occur; don't specify both a `repeatCount` and a `repeatDuration`. If `cumulative` is `true`, a repeating animation starts each repetition where the previous repetition ended (rather than jumping back to the start value).

beginTime

The delay before the animation starts. To delay an animation with respect to now, call `CACurrentMediaTime` and add the desired delay in seconds. The delay does not eat into the animation's duration.

timeOffset

A shift in the animation's overall timing; looked at another way, specifies the starting frame of the "animation movie," which is treated as a loop. For example, an animation with a duration of 8 and a time offset of 4 plays its second half followed by its first half.

CAAnimation, along with all its subclasses, implements KVC to allow you to set and retrieve a value for an arbitrary key, similar to CALayer (Chapter 3) and CA-Transaction.

CAPropertyAnimation

CAPropertyAnimation is a subclass of CAAnimation. It too is abstract, and adds the following:

keyPath

The all-important string specifying the CALayer key that is to be animated. Recall from Chapter 3 that CALayer properties are accessible through KVC keys; now we are using those keys! The convenience initializer `init(keyPath:)` creates the instance and assigns it a `keyPath`.

additive

If `true`, the values supplied by the animation are added to the current presentation layer value.

valueFunction
> Converts a simple scalar value that you supply into a transform.

 There is no animatable CALayer key called "frame". To animate a layer's frame using explicit layer animation, if both its position and bounds are to change, you must animate both. Similarly, you cannot use explicit layer animation to animate a layer's affineTransform property, because affineTransform is not a property (it's a pair of convenience methods); you must animate its transform instead. Attempting to form an animation with a key path of "frame" or "affineTransform" is a common beginner error.

CABasicAnimation
> CABasicAnimation is a subclass (not abstract!) of CAPropertyAnimation. It adds the following:

fromValue, toValue
> The starting and ending values for the animation. These values must be Objective-C objects, so numbers and structs will have to be wrapped accordingly, using NSNumber and NSValue (Swift will automatically take care of the former but not the latter). If neither fromValue nor toValue is provided, the former and current values of the property are used. If just one of fromValue or toValue is provided, the other uses the current value of the property.

byValue
> Expresses one of the endpoint values as a *difference* from the other rather than in absolute terms. So you would supply a byValue instead of a fromValue or instead of a toValue, and the actual fromValue or toValue would be calculated for you by subtraction or addition with respect to the other value. If you supply *only* a byValue, the fromValue is the property's current value.

Using a CABasicAnimation

Having constructed and configured a CABasicAnimation, the way you order it to be performed is to *add it to a layer*. This is done with the CALayer instance method add-Animation:forKey:. (I'll discuss the purpose of the forKey: parameter later; it's fine to ignore it and use nil, as I do in the examples that follow.)

However, there's a slight twist. A CAAnimation is *merely* an animation; all it does is describe the hoops that the presentation layer is to jump through, the "animation movie" that is to be presented. It has no effect on the layer *itself*. Thus, if you naively create a CABasicAnimation and add it to a layer with addAnimation:forKey:, the animation happens and then the "animation movie" is whipped away to reveal the layer sitting there in exactly the same state as before. It is up to *you* to change the layer to match what the animation will ultimately portray.

This requirement may seem odd, but keep in mind that we are now in a much more fundamental, flexible world than the automatic, convenient worlds of view animation and implicit layer animation. Using explicit animation is more work, but you get more power. The converse, of course, is that you *don't* have to change the layer if it *doesn't* change as a result of the animation.

To assure good results, start by taking a plodding, formulaic approach to the use of CABasicAnimation, like this:

1. Capture the start and end values for the layer property you're going to change, because you're likely to need these values in what follows.

2. Change the layer property to its end value, first calling `setDisableActions:` if necessary to prevent implicit animation.

3. Construct the explicit animation, using the start and end values you captured earlier, and with its `keyPath` corresponding to the layer property you just changed.

4. Add the explicit animation to the layer.

 The explicit animation is *copied* when it is added to the layer. Therefore the animation must be configured first and added to the layer later. Configuring an animation after it has been added to a layer will have no effect on how that layer is animated, because the animation that has been added to the layer is no longer the animation you are configuring.

Here's how you'd use this approach to animate our compass arrow rotation:

```
// capture the start and end values
let startValue = arrow.transform
let endValue = CATransform3DRotate(
    startValue, CGFloat(M_PI)/4.0, 0, 0, 1)
// change the layer, without implicit animation
CATransaction.setDisableActions(true)
arrow.transform = endValue
// construct the explicit animation
let anim = CABasicAnimation(keyPath:"transform")
anim.duration = 0.8
let clunk = CAMediaTimingFunction(controlPoints:0.9, 0.1, 0.7, 0.9)
anim.timingFunction = clunk
anim.fromValue = NSValue(CATransform3D:startValue)
anim.toValue = NSValue(CATransform3D:endValue)
// ask for the explicit animation
arrow.addAnimation(anim, forKey:nil)
```

Once you're comfortable with the full form, you will find that in many cases it can be condensed. For example, when the `fromValue` and `toValue` are not set, the former and current values of the property are used automatically. (This magic is possible because, at the time the CABasicAnimation is added to the layer, the presentation layer still has the former value of the property, while the layer itself has the new value; thus, the CABasicAnimation is able to retrieve them.) In our example, therefore, there is no need to set the `fromValue` and `toValue`, and no need to capture the start and end values beforehand. Here's the condensed version:

```
CATransaction.setDisableActions(true)
arrow.transform = CATransform3DRotate(
    arrow.transform, CGFloat(M_PI)/4.0, 0, 0, 1)
let anim = CABasicAnimation(keyPath:"transform")
anim.duration = 0.8
let clunk = CAMediaTimingFunction(controlPoints:0.9, 0.1, 0.7, 0.9)
anim.timingFunction = clunk
arrow.addAnimation(anim, forKey:nil)
```

As I mentioned earlier, you will omit changing the layer if it doesn't change as a result of the animation. For example, let's make the compass arrow appear to vibrate rapidly, without ultimately changing its current orientation. To do this, we'll waggle it back and forth, using a repeated animation, between slightly clockwise from its current position and slightly counterclockwise from its current position. The "animation movie" neither starts nor stops at the current position of the arrow, but for this animation it doesn't matter, because it all happens so quickly as to appear perfectly natural:

```
// capture the start and end values
let nowValue = arrow.transform
let startValue = CATransform3DRotate(
    nowValue, CGFloat(M_PI)/40.0, 0, 0, 1)
let endValue = CATransform3DRotate(
    nowValue, CGFloat(-M_PI)/40.0, 0, 0, 1)
// construct the explicit animation
let anim = CABasicAnimation(keyPath:"transform")
anim.duration = 0.05
anim.timingFunction = CAMediaTimingFunction(
    name:kCAMediaTimingFunctionLinear)
anim.repeatCount = 3
anim.autoreverses = true
anim.fromValue = NSValue(CATransform3D:startValue)
anim.toValue = NSValue(CATransform3D:endValue)
// ask for the explicit animation
arrow.addAnimation(anim, forKey:nil)
```

That code, too, can be shortened considerably from its full form. We can eliminate the need to calculate the new rotation values based on the arrow's current transform by setting our animation's `additive` property to `true`; this means that the animation's property values are added to the existing property value for us, so that they are relative, not absolute. For a transform, "added" means "matrix-multiplied," so we can describe the waggle without any reference to the arrow's current rotation. Moreover, because our rotation is so simple (around a cardinal axis), we can take advantage of CAProperty-Animation's `valueFunction`; the animation's property values can then be simple scalars (in this case, angles), because the `valueFunction` tells the animation to interpret these as rotations around the z-axis:

```
let anim = CABasicAnimation(keyPath:"transform")
anim.duration = 0.05
anim.timingFunction = CAMediaTimingFunction(
    name:kCAMediaTimingFunctionLinear)
anim.repeatCount = 3
anim.autoreverses = true
anim.additive = true
anim.valueFunction = CAValueFunction(
    name:kCAValueFunctionRotateZ)
anim.fromValue = M_PI/40
anim.toValue = -M_PI/40
arrow.addAnimation(anim, forKey:nil)
```

 Instead of using a `valueFunction`, we could have set the animation's key path to `"transform.rotation.z"` to achieve the same effect. However, Apple advises against this, as it can result in mathematical trouble when there is more than one rotation.

Let's return once more to our arrow "clunk" rotation for one final alternative implementation using the `additive` and `valueFunction` properties. We set the arrow layer to its final transform at the outset, so when the time comes to configure the animation, its `toValue`, in `additive` terms, will be 0; the `fromValue` will be its current value expressed *negatively*, like this:

```
let rot = CGFloat(M_PI)/4.0
CATransaction.setDisableActions(true)
arrow.transform = CATransform3DRotate(arrow.transform, rot, 0, 0, 1)
// construct animation additively
let anim = CABasicAnimation(keyPath:"transform")
anim.duration = 0.8
let clunk = CAMediaTimingFunction(controlPoints:0.9, 0.1, 0.7, 0.9)
anim.timingFunction = clunk
anim.fromValue = -rot
anim.toValue = 0
anim.additive = true
anim.valueFunction = CAValueFunction(name:kCAValueFunctionRotateZ)
arrow.addAnimation(anim, forKey:nil)
```

This is an interesting way of describing the animation; in effect, it expresses the animation in reverse, regarding the final position as correct and the current position as an aberration to be corrected. It also happens to be the way iOS 8 additive view animations are rewritten behind the scenes, and explains their behavior.

Keyframe Animation

Keyframe animation (CAKeyframeAnimation) is an alternative to basic animation (CABasicAnimation); they are both subclasses of CAPropertyAnimation and they are used in identical ways. The difference is that a keyframe animation, in addition to specifying a starting and ending value, also specifies multiple values through which the animation should pass on the way, the stages (*frames*) of the animation. This can be as simple as setting the animation's `values` array.

Here's a more sophisticated version of our animation for waggling the compass arrow: the animation includes both the start and end states, and the degree of waggle gets progressively smaller:

```
var values = [0.0]
for (var i = 20, direction = 1.0; i < 60; i += 5, direction *= -1) {
    values.append( direction * M_PI / Double(i) )
}
values.append(0.0)
let anim = CAKeyframeAnimation(keyPath:"transform")
anim.values = values
anim.additive = true
anim.valueFunction = CAValueFunction(name: kCAValueFunctionRotateZ)
arrow.addAnimation(anim, forKey:nil)
```

Here are some CAKeyframeAnimation properties:

values

> The array of values the animation is to adopt, including the starting and ending value.

timingFunctions

> An array of timing functions, one for each stage of the animation (so that this array will be one element shorter than the `values` array).

keyTimes

> An array of times to accompany the array of values, defining when each value should be reached. The times start at 0 and are expressed as increasing fractions of 1, ending at 1.

calculationMode

> Describes how the `values` are treated to create *all* the values through which the animation must pass.
>
> - The default is kCAAnimationLinear, a simple straight-line interpolation from value to value.
>
> - kCAAnimationCubic constructs a single smooth curve passing through all the values (and additional advanced properties, tensionValues, continuity-Values, and biasValues, allow you to refine the curve).

- kCAAnimationPaced and kCAAnimationCubicPaced means the timing functions and key times are ignored, and the velocity is made constant through the whole animation.

- kCAAnimationDiscrete means no interpolation: we jump directly to each value at the corresponding key time.

path

> When you're animating a property whose values are pairs of floats (CGPoints), this is an alternative way of describing the values; instead of a values array, which must be interpolated to arrive at the intermediate values along the way, you supply the entire interpolation as a single CGPath. The points used to draw the path are the keyframe values, so you can still apply timing functions and key times. If you're animating a position, the rotationMode property lets you ask the animated object to rotate so as to remain perpendicular to the path.

In this example, the values array is a sequence of five images to be presented successively and repeatedly in a layer's contents, like the frames in a movie; the effect is similar to UIImageView and UIImage animation, discussed earlier in this chapter:

```
let anim = CAKeyframeAnimation(keyPath:"contents")
// self.images is an array of UIImage
anim.values = self.images.map {$0.CGImage as AnyObject}
anim.keyTimes = [0.0, 0.25, 0.5, 0.75, 1.0]
anim.calculationMode = kCAAnimationDiscrete
anim.duration = 1.5
anim.repeatCount = Float.infinity
// self.sprite is a CALayer
self.sprite.addAnimation(anim, forKey:nil)
```

Making a Property Animatable

So far, we've been animating built-in animatable properties. If you define your own property on a CALayer subclass, you can easily make that property animatable through a CAPropertyAnimation (a CABasicAnimation or a CAKeyframeAnimation). For example, here we animate the increase or decrease in a CALayer subclass property called thickness, using essentially the pattern for explicit animation that we've already developed:

```
let lay = self.v.layer as! MyLayer
let cur = lay.thickness
let val : CGFloat = cur == 10 ? 0 : 10
lay.thickness = val
let ba = CABasicAnimation(keyPath:"thickness")
ba.fromValue = cur
lay.addAnimation(ba, forKey:nil)
```

To make our layer responsive to such a command, it needs a `thickness` property (obviously) and it must return `true` from the class method `needsDisplayForKey:`, where the key is the string name of the property:

```
class MyLayer : CALayer {
    var thickness : CGFloat = 0
    override class func needsDisplayForKey(key: String) -> Bool {
        if key == "thickness" {
            return true
        }
        return super.needsDisplayForKey(key)
    }
}
```

Returning `true` from `needsDisplayForKey:` causes this layer to be redisplayed repeatedly as the `thickness` property changes. So if we want to *see* the animation, this layer also needs to draw itself in some way that depends on the `thickness` property. Here, I'll implement the layer's `drawInContext:` to make `thickness` the thickness of the black border around a red rectangle:

```
override func drawInContext(con: CGContext) {
    let r = self.bounds.rectByInsetting(dx:20, dy:20)
    CGContextSetFillColorWithColor(con, UIColor.redColor().CGColor)
    CGContextFillRect(con, r)
    CGContextSetLineWidth(con, self.thickness)
    CGContextStrokeRect(con, r)
}
```

At every frame of the animation, `drawInContext:` is called, and because the `thickness` value differs at each step, it appears animated.

We have made MyLayer's `thickness` property animatable when using explicit layer animation, but it would be even cooler to make it animatable when using implicit layer animation (that is, when setting `lay.thickness` directly). Later in this chapter, I'll show how to do that.

Grouped Animations

A grouped animation (CAAnimationGroup) combines multiple animations into one, by means of its `animations` property (an array of animations). By delaying and timing the various component animations, complex effects can be achieved.

A CAAnimationGroup is itself an animation; it is a CAAnimation subclass, so it has a `duration` and other animation features. Think of the CAAnimationGroup as the parent, and its `animations` as its children. Then *the children inherit default property values from their parent*. Thus, for example, if you don't set a child's duration explicitly, it will inherit the parent's duration.

Let's use a grouped animation to construct a sequence where the compass arrow rotates and then waggles. This requires very little modification of code we've already written. We express the first animation in its full form, with explicit fromValue and toValue. We postpone the second animation using its beginTime property; notice that we express this in relative terms, as a number of seconds into the parent's duration, not with respect to CACurrentMediaTime. Finally, we set the overall parent duration to the sum of the child durations, so that it can embrace both of them (failing to do this, and then wondering why some child animations never occur, is a common beginner error):

```
// capture current value, set final value
let rot = M_PI/4.0
CATransaction.setDisableActions(true)
let current = arrow.valueForKeyPath("transform.rotation.z")!.doubleValue
arrow.setValue(current + rot, forKeyPath:"transform.rotation.z")
// first animation (rotate and clunk)
let anim1 = CABasicAnimation(keyPath:"transform")
anim1.duration = 0.8
let clunk = CAMediaTimingFunction(controlPoints:0.9, 0.1, 0.7, 0.9)
anim1.timingFunction = clunk
anim1.fromValue = current
anim1.toValue = current + rot
anim1.valueFunction = CAValueFunction(name:kCAValueFunctionRotateZ)
// second animation (waggle)
var values = [0.0]
for (var i = 20, direction = 1.0; i < 60; i += 5, direction *= -1) {
    values.append( direction * M_PI / Double(i) )
}
values.append(0.0)
let anim2 = CAKeyframeAnimation(keyPath:"transform")
anim2.values = values
anim2.duration = 0.25
anim2.additive = true
anim2.beginTime = anim1.duration - 0.1
anim2.valueFunction = CAValueFunction(name: kCAValueFunctionRotateZ)
// group
let group = CAAnimationGroup()
group.animations = [anim1, anim2]
group.duration = anim1.duration + anim2.duration
arrow.addAnimation(group, forKey:nil)
```

In that example, I grouped two animations that animated the same property sequentially. Now let's go to the other extreme and group some animations that animate different properties simultaneously. I have a small view (self.v), located near the top-right corner of the screen, whose layer contents are a picture of a sailboat facing to the left. I'll "sail" the boat in a curving path, both down the screen and left and right across the screen, like an extended letter "S" (Figure 4-2). Each time the boat comes to a vertex of the curve, changing direction across the screen, I'll turn the boat picture so that it faces the way it's about to move. At the same time, I'll constantly rock the boat, so that it always appears to be pitching a little on the waves.

Figure 4-2. A boat and the course she'll sail

Here's the first animation, the movement of the boat along its curving path. It illustrates the use of a CAKeyframeAnimation with a CGPath; the calculationMode of kCAAnimationPaced ensures an even speed over the whole path. We don't set an explicit duration because we want to adopt the duration of the group:

```
let h : CGFloat = 200
let v : CGFloat = 75
let path = CGPathCreateMutable()
var leftright : CGFloat = 1
var next : CGPoint = self.v.layer.position
var pos : CGPoint
CGPathMoveToPoint(path, nil, next.x, next.y)
for i in 0 ..< 4 {
    pos = next
    leftright *= -1
    next = CGPointMake(pos.x+h*leftright, pos.y+v)
    CGPathAddCurveToPoint(path, nil,
        pos.x, pos.y+30,
        next.x, next.y-30,
        next.x, next.y)
}
let anim1 = CAKeyframeAnimation(keyPath:"position")
anim1.path = path
anim1.calculationMode = kCAAnimationPaced
```

Here's the second animation, the reversal of the direction the boat is facing. This is simply a rotation around the y-axis. It's another CAKeyframeAnimation, but we make no attempt at visually animating this reversal: the calculationMode is kCAAnimation-Discrete, so that the boat image reversal is a sudden change, as in our earlier "sprite" example. There is one less value than the number of points in our first animation's path, and the first animation has an even speed, so the reversals take place at each curve apex with no further effort on our part. (If the pacing were more complicated, we could give both the first and the second animation identical keyTimes arrays, to coordinate them.) Once again, we don't set an explicit duration:

```
let revs = [0.0, M_PI, 0.0, M_PI]
let anim2 = CAKeyframeAnimation(keyPath:"transform")
anim2.values = revs
anim2.valueFunction = CAValueFunction(name:kCAValueFunctionRotateY)
anim2.calculationMode = kCAAnimationDiscrete
```

Here's the third animation, the rocking of the boat. It has a short duration, and repeats indefinitely:

```
let pitches = [0.0, M_PI/60.0, 0.0, -M_PI/60.0, 0.0]
let anim3 = CAKeyframeAnimation(keyPath:"transform")
anim3.values = pitches
anim3.repeatCount = Float.infinity
anim3.duration = 0.5
anim3.additive = true
anim3.valueFunction = CAValueFunction(name:kCAValueFunctionRotateZ)
```

Finally, we combine the three animations, assigning the group an explicit duration that will be adopted by the first two animations. As we hand the animation over to the layer displaying the boat, we also change the layer's position to match the final position from the first animation, so that the boat won't jump back to its original position afterward:

```
let group = CAAnimationGroup()
group.animations = [anim1, anim2, anim3]
group.duration = 8
self.v.layer.addAnimation(group, forKey:nil)
CATransaction.setDisableActions(true)
self.v.layer.position = next
```

Here are some further CAAnimation properties (from the CAMediaTiming protocol) that come into play especially when animations are grouped:

speed
    The ratio between a child's timescale and the parent's timescale. For example, if a parent and child have the same duration, but the child's speed is 1.5, its animation runs one-and-a-half times as fast as the parent.

fillMode
    Suppose the child animation begins after the parent animation, or ends before the parent animation, or both. What should happen to the appearance of the property being animated, outside the child animation's boundaries? The answer depends on the child's fillMode:

- kCAFillModeRemoved means the child animation is removed, revealing the layer property at its actual current value whenever the child is not running.
- kCAFillModeForwards means the final presentation layer value of the child animation remains afterward.
- kCAFillModeBackwards means the initial presentation layer value of the child animation appears right from the start.
- kCAFillModeBoth combines the previous two.

Freezing an Animation

CALayer adopts the CAMediaTiming protocol. Thus, a layer can have a speed. This will affect any animation attached to it. A CALayer with a speed of 2 will play a 10-second animation in 5 seconds. A layer can also have a timeOffset.

One remarkably powerful way to take advantage of this feature of CALayer is to assign a layer a speed of 0. This effectively "freezes" any animation attached to the layer. You can then change the layer's timeOffset to display any single frame of the animation. In effect, the frozen animation has given you a whole slew of interpolated states "for free," any of which you can select by setting the layer's timeOffset.

To illustrate, let's explore the animatable path property of a CAShapeLayer. Consider a layer that can display a rectangle or an ellipse *or any of the intermediate shapes between them*. I can't imagine what the notion of an intermediate shape between a rectangle or an ellipse may mean, let alone how to draw such an intermediate shape; but thanks to frozen animations, I don't have to. Here, I'll construct the CAShapeLayer, add it to the interface, give it an animation from a rectangle to an ellipse, and keep a reference to it as a property:

```
let shape = CAShapeLayer()
shape.frame = v.bounds
v.layer.addSublayer(shape)
shape.fillColor = UIColor.clearColor().CGColor
shape.strokeColor = UIColor.redColor().CGColor
let path = CGPathCreateWithRect(shape.bounds, nil)
shape.path = path
let path2 = CGPathCreateWithEllipseInRect(shape.bounds, nil)
let ba = CABasicAnimation(keyPath: "path")
ba.duration = 1
ba.fromValue = path
ba.toValue = path2
shape.speed = 0
shape.timeOffset = 0
shape.addAnimation(ba, forKey: nil)
self.shape = shape
```

I've added the animation to the layer, but because the layer's `speed` is 0, no animation takes place; the rectangle is displayed and that's all. There's also a UISlider in the interface. I'll respond to the user changing the value of the slider by setting the frame of the animation:

```
@IBAction func doSlider(sender: AnyObject) { // slider action
    let slider = sender as! UISlider
    self.shape.timeOffset = Double(slider.value)
}
```

This astonishing feature of layers and animations can be used in many powerful ways. It lies at the heart of interactive view controller transition animations (Chapter 6), and is probably used in unsuspected places throughout the iPhone and iPad interface.

Transitions

A layer transition is an animation involving two "copies" of a single layer, in which the second "copy" appears to replace the first. It is described by an instance of CATransition (a CAAnimation subclass), which has these chief properties describing the animation:

type
> Your choices are:
>
> - kCATransitionFade
> - kCATransitionMoveIn
> - kCATransitionPush
> - kCATransitionReveal

subtype
> If the type is not kCATransitionFade, your choices are:
>
> - kCATransitionFromRight
> - kCATransitionFromLeft
> - kCATransitionFromTop
> - kCATransitionFromBottom

 For historical reasons, the terms "bottom" and "top" in the names of the subtype settings have the opposite of their expected meanings.

To understand a layer transition, first implement one without changing anything else about the layer:

Figure 4-3. A push transition

```
let t = CATransition()
t.type = kCATransitionPush
t.subtype = kCATransitionFromBottom
t.duration = 2
lay.addAnimation(t, forKey: nil)
```

The entire layer exits moving down from its original place while fading away, and another copy of the very same layer enters moving down from above while fading in. If, at the same time, we change something about the layer's contents, then the old contents will appear to exit downward while the new contents appear to enter from above:

```
// ... configure the transition as before ...
CATransaction.setDisableActions(true)
lay.contents = UIImage(named: "Smiley")!.CGImage
lay.addAnimation(t, forKey: nil)
```

A common device is for the layer that is to be transitioned to be inside a superlayer that is exactly the same size and whose `masksToBounds` is `true`. This confines the visible transition to the bounds of the layer itself. Otherwise, the entering and exiting versions of the layer are visible outside the layer. In Figure 4-3, which shows a smiley face pushing an image of Mars out of the layer, I've emphasized this arrangement by giving the superlayer a border as well.

A transition on a superlayer can happen simultaneously with animation of a sublayer. The animation will be seen to occur on the second "copy" of the layer as it moves into position. This is analogous to the `.AllowAnimatedContent` option for view animation.

Animations List

The method that asks for an explicit animation to happen is CALayer's `add-Animation:forKey:`. To understand how this method actually works (and what the "key" is), you need to know about a layer's *animations list*.

An animation is an object (a CAAnimation) that modifies how a layer is drawn. It does this merely by being attached to the layer; the layer's drawing mechanism does the rest. A layer maintains a list of animations that are currently in force. To add an animation to this list, you call `addAnimation:forKey:`. When the time comes to draw itself, the layer looks through its animations list and draws itself in accordance with any animations it finds there. (The list of things the layer must do in order to draw itself is sometimes referred to by the documentation as the *render tree*.) The order in which animations were added to the list is the order in which they are applied.

The animations list is maintained in a curious way. The list is not exactly a dictionary, but it behaves somewhat like a dictionary. An animation has a key — the forKey: parameter in addAnimation:forKey:. If an animation with a certain key is added to the list, and an animation with that key is already in the list, the one that is already in the list is removed. Thus a rule is maintained that *only one animation with a given key* can be in the list at a time (the *exclusivity rule*). This explains why sometimes ordering an animation can cancel an animation already ordered or in-flight: the two animations had the same key, so the first one was removed. In iOS 8, additive view animations affecting the same property work around this limitation simply by giving the additional animations a different key name (for example, "position" and "position-2").

It is also possible to add an animation with *no key* (the key is nil); it is then *not* subject to the exclusivity rule (that is, there can be more than one animation in the list with no key).

The forKey: parameter in addAnimation:forKey: is thus *not a property name*. It *could* be a property name, but it can be any arbitrary value. Its purpose is to enforce the exclusivity rule. It does *not* have any meaning with regard to what property a CAPropertyAnimation animates; that is the job of the animation's keyPath. (Apple's use of the term "key" in addAnimation:forKey: is thus unfortunate and misleading; I wish they had named this method addAnimation:withIdentifier: or something like that.)

 Actually, there *is* a relationship between the "key" in addAnimation:forKey: and a CAPropertyAnimation's keyPath — if a CAPropertyAnimation's keyPath is nil at the time that it is added to a layer with addAnimation:forKey:, *that keyPath is set to the forKey: value*. Thus, you can *misuse* the forKey: parameter in addAnimation:forKey: as a way of specifying what keyPath an animation animates. (This fact is not documented, so far as I know, but it's easily verified experimentally, and it should remain reliably true, as implicit layer animation crucially depends on it.) I have seen many prominent but misleading examples that use this technique, apparently in the mistaken belief that the "key" in addAnimation:forKey: is the way you are *supposed* to specify what property to animate. *This is wrong.* Set the CAPropertyAnimation's keyPath explicitly (as do all my examples); that's what it's for.

You can use the exclusivity rule to your own advantage, to keep your code from stepping on its own feet. Some code of yours might add an animation to the list using a certain key; then later, some other code might come along and correct this, removing that animation and replacing it with another. By using the same key, the second code is easily able to override the first: "You may have been given some other animation with this key, but throw it away; play this one instead."

In some cases, the key you supply is ignored and a different key is substituted. In particular, the key with which a CATransition is added to the list is always kCATransition (which happens to be "transition"); thus there can be only one transition animation in the list.

You can think of an animation in a layer's animations list as being the "animation movie" I spoke of at the start of this chapter. As long as an animation is in the list, the movie is present, either waiting to be played or actually playing. An animation that has finished playing is, in general, pointless; the animation should now be removed from the list. Therefore, an animation has a removedOnCompletion property, which defaults to true: when the "movie" is over, the animation removes itself from the list.

You can, if desired, set removedOnCompletion to false. However, even the presence in the list of an animation that has already played might make no difference to the layer's appearance, because an animation's fillMode is kCAFillModeRemoved, which removes the animation from the layer's drawing when the movie is over. Thus, it can usually do no harm to leave an animation in the list after it has played, but it's not a great idea either, because this is just one more thing for the drawing system to worry about. Typically, you'll leave removedOnCompletion set at true.

 You may encounter examples that set removedOnCompletion to false and set the animation's fillMode to kCAFillModeForwards or kCAFillModeBoth, as a way of causing the layer to keep the appearance of the last frame of the "animation movie" even after the animation is over, and preventing a property from apparently jumping back to its initial value when the animation ends. *This is wrong.* The correct approach, as I have explained, is to change the property value to match the final frame of the animation. The proper use of kCAFillModeForwards is in connection with a child animation within a grouped animation.

You can't access the entire animations list directly. You can access the key names of the animations in the list, with animationKeys; and you can obtain or remove an animation with a certain key, with animationForKey: and removeAnimationForKey:; but animations with a nil key are inaccessible. You can, however, remove all animations, including animations with a nil key, using removeAllAnimations. When your app is suspended, removeAllAnimations is called on all layers for you; that is why it is possible to suspend an app coherently in the middle of an animation.

If an animation is in-flight when you remove it from the animations list manually, by calling removeAllAnimations or removeAnimationForKey:, it will stop; however, that doesn't happen until the next redraw moment. You might be able to work around this, if you need an animation to be removed immediately, by wrapping the `remove...` call in an explicit transaction block.

Actions

For the sake of completeness, I will now explain how implicit animation really works — that is, how implicit animation is turned into explicit animation behind the scenes. The basis of implicit animation is the *action mechanism*. Feel free to skip this section if you don't want to get into the under-the-hood nitty-gritty of implicit animation.

What an Action Is

An *action* is an object that adopts the CAAction protocol. This means simply that it implements `runActionForKey:object:arguments:`. The action object could do *anything* in response to this message. The notion of an action is completely general. The only class that adopts the CAAction protocol is CAAnimation, but in fact the action object doesn't have to be an animation — it doesn't even have to perform an animation.

You would never send `runActionForKey:object:arguments:` to an animation directly. Rather, this message is sent to an action object for you, as the basis of implicit animation. The `key` is the property that was set, and the `object` is the layer whose property was set.

What an animation does when it receives `runActionForKey:object:arguments:` is to assume that the second parameter, the `object:`, is a layer, and to add itself to that layer's animations list. Thus, for an animation, receiving the `runActionForKey:object:arguments:` message is like being told: "Play yourself!"

This is where the rule comes into play, which I mentioned earlier, that if an animation's `keyPath` is nil, the key by which the animation is assigned to a layer's animations list is used as the `keyPath`. When an animation is sent `runActionForKey:object:arguments:`, it calls `addAnimation:forKey:` to add itself to the layer's animation's list, *using the name of the property as the key*. The animation's `keyPath` for an implicit layer animation is usually nil, so the animation's `keyPath` winds up being set to the same key! That is how the property that you set ends up being the property that is animated.

Action Search

When you set a property of a layer and trigger an implicit animation, you are actually triggering the *action search*: the layer *searches* for an action object (a CAAction) to which it can send the `runActionForKey:object:arguments:` message. The procedure by which the layer searches for this animation is quite elaborate.

The search for an action object begins when something causes the layer to be sent the actionForKey: message. Three sorts of event can cause this to happen:

- A specially marked CALayer property is set — by calling the setter method explicitly, by setting the property itself, or by means of setValue:forKey:. All animatable properties, and indeed most (or all) other CALayer properties, are marked in this special way. (You can mark a custom property in this same way by designating it as @dynamic in Objective-C, as I'll demonstrate later in this chapter.)

  Setting a layer's frame property sets its position and bounds and calls actionFor-Key: for the "position" and "bounds" keys. Calling a layer's setAffineTransform: sets its transform and calls actionForKey: for the "transform" key.

- The layer is sent setValue:forKey: with a key that is *not* a property. This is because CALayer's setValue:forUndefinedKey:, by default, calls actionForKey:.

- Various other miscellaneous types of event take place, such as the layer being added to the interface. I'll give some examples later in this chapter.

 CATransaction's setDisableActions:, with an argument of true, prevents the actionForKey: message from being sent. That's how it actually works behind the scenes.

At each stage of the action search, the following rules are obeyed regarding what is returned from that stage of the search:

An action object
 If an action object is produced, that is the end of the search. The action mechanism sends that action object the runActionForKey:object:arguments: message; if this an animation, the animation responds by adding itself to the layer's animations list.

NSNull()
 If NSNull() is produced, that is the end of the search. There will be no implicit animation; NSNull() means, "Do nothing and stop searching."

nil
 If nil is produced, the search continues to the next stage.

The action search proceeds by stages, as follows:

1. The layer's actionForKey: might terminate the search before it even starts. For example, the layer will do this if it is the underlying layer of a view, or if a property is set to the same value it already has. In such a case, there should be no implicit animation, so the whole mechanism is nipped in the bud. (This stage is special in that a returned value of nil ends the search and no animation takes place.)

2. If the layer has a delegate that implements `actionForLayer:forKey:`, that message is sent to the delegate, with this layer as the layer and the property name as the key. If an action object or `NSNull()` is returned, the search ends.

3. The layer has a property called `actions`, which is a dictionary. If there is an entry in this dictionary with the given key, that value is used, and the search ends.

4. The layer has a property called `style`, which is a dictionary. If there is an entry in this dictionary with the key `actions`, it is assumed to be a dictionary; if this `actions` dictionary has an entry with the given key, that value is used, and the search ends. Otherwise, if there is an entry in the `style` dictionary called `style`, the same search is performed within it, and so on recursively until either an `actions` entry with the given key is found (the search ends) or there are no more `style` entries (the search continues).

   (If the `style` dictionary sounds profoundly weird, that's because it is profoundly weird. It is actually a special case of a larger, separate mechanism, which is also profoundly weird, having to do not with actions, but with a CALayer's implementation of KVC. When you call `valueForKey:` on a layer, if the key is undefined by the layer itself, the `style` dictionary is consulted. I have never written or seen code that uses this mechanism for anything, and I'll say no more about it.)

5. The layer's class is sent `defaultActionForKey:`, with the property name as the key. If an action object or `NSNull()` is returned, the search ends.

6. If the search reaches this last stage, a default animation is supplied, as appropriate. For a property animation, this is a plain vanilla CABasicAnimation.

Hooking Into the Action Search

You can affect the action search at any of its various stages to modify what happens when the search is triggered.

For example, you can turn off implicit animation for some particular property. One way would be to return nil from `actionForKey:` itself, in a CALayer subclass. Here's the code from a CALayer subclass that doesn't animate its `position` property (but does animate its other properties normally):

```swift
override func actionForKey(key: String!) -> CAAction! {
    if key == "position" {
            return nil
        }
    return super.actionForKey(key)
}
```

For more flexibility, we can take advantage of the fact that a CALayer acts like a dictionary (allowing us to set an arbitrary key's value) — we'll embed a switch in our CALayer subclass that we can use to turn implicit `position` animation on and off at will:

```
override func actionForKey(key: String!) -> CAAction! {
    if key == "position" {
        if self.valueForKey("suppressPositionAnimation") != nil {
            return nil
        }
    }
    return super.actionForKey(key)
}
```

To turn off implicit `position` animation for an instance of this layer, we set its `"suppress-PositionAnimation"` key to a non-nil value:

```
layer.setValue(true, forKey:"suppressPositionAnimation")
```

Another possibility is to cause some stage of the search to produce an action object of your own. You would then be affecting how implicit animation behaves.

Let's say we want a certain layer's duration for an implicit `position` animation to be 5 seconds. We can achieve this with a minimally configured animation, like this:

```
let ba = CABasicAnimation()
ba.duration = 5
```

The idea now is to situate this animation where it will be produced by the action search for the `"position"` key. We could, for instance, put it into the layer's `actions` dictionary:

```
layer.actions = ["position": ba]
```

The only property of this animation that we have set is its duration; that setting, however, is final. Although animation properties that you don't set can be set through CATransaction, in the usual manner for implicit property animation, animation properties that you *do* set can *not* be overridden through CATransaction. Thus, when we set this layer's `position`, if an implicit animation results, its duration is 5 seconds, even if we try to change it through CATransaction:

```
CATransaction.setAnimationDuration(1.5) // won't work
layer.position = CGPointMake(100,100)
```

Storing an animation in the `actions` dictionary, however, is a somewhat inflexible way to hook into the action search. If we have to write our animation beforehand, we know nothing about the layer's starting and ending values for the changed property. A much more powerful approach is to make our action object a custom CAAction object — because in that case, it will be sent `runActionForKey:...`, and we can construct and run an animation *now*, when we are in direct contact with the layer to be animated. Here's a barebones version of such an object:

```
class MyAction : NSObject, CAAction {
    func runActionForKey(event: String!, object anObject: AnyObject!,
        arguments dict: [NSObject : AnyObject]!) {
            let anim = CABasicAnimation(keyPath: event)
            anim.duration = 5
            let lay = anObject as! CALayer
            let newP : AnyObject? = lay.valueForKey(event)
            let oldP : AnyObject? = lay.presentationLayer()!.valueForKey(event)
            lay.addAnimation(anim, forKey:nil)
    }
}
```

The idea is that this would then be the action object that we store in the actions dictionary:

```
layer.actions = ["position": MyAction()]
```

Our custom CAAction object, MyAction, doesn't do anything very interesting — but it could. That's the point. As the code demonstrates, we have access to the name of the animated property (event), the old value of that property (from the layer's presentation layer), and the new value of that property (from the layer itself). We are thus free to configure the animation in all sorts of ways. In fact, we can add more than one animation to the layer, or a group animation. We don't have to add an animation to the layer! We are free to interpret the setting of this property in any way we like.

Here's a modification of our MyAction object that creates and runs a keyframe animation that "waggles" as it goes from the start value to the end value:

```
class MyAction : NSObject, CAAction {
    func runActionForKey(event: String!, object anObject: AnyObject!,
        arguments dict: [NSObject : AnyObject]!) {
            let lay = anObject as! CALayer
            let newP = (lay.valueForKey(event) as! NSValue).CGPointValue()
            let oldP =
                (lay.presentationLayer()!.valueForKey(event) as! NSValue)
                    .CGPointValue()
            let d = sqrt(pow(oldP.x - newP.x, 2) + pow(oldP.y - newP.y, 2))
            let r = Double(d/3.0)
            let theta = Double(atan2(newP.y - oldP.y, newP.x - oldP.x))
            let wag = 10*M_PI/180.0
            let p1 = CGPointMake(
                oldP.x + CGFloat(r*cos(theta+wag)),
                oldP.y + CGFloat(r*sin(theta+wag)))
            let p2 = CGPointMake(
                oldP.x + CGFloat(r*2*cos(theta-wag)),
                oldP.y + CGFloat(r*2*sin(theta-wag)))
            let anim = CAKeyframeAnimation(keyPath: event)
            anim.values = [oldP,p1,p2,newP].map{NSValue(CGPoint:$0)}
            anim.calculationMode = kCAAnimationCubic
            lay.addAnimation(anim, forKey:nil)
    }
}
```

By adding this CAAction object to a layer's `actions` dictionary under the `"position"` key, we have created a CALayer that waggles when its position is set. The power of this mechanism is simply staggering. We can modify *any* layer in this way — even one that doesn't belong to us.

Instead of modifying the layer's `actions` dictionary, we could hook into the action search by setting the layer's delegate to an instance that responds to `actionForLayer:forKey:`. This has the advantage of serving as a single locus that can do different things depending on what the layer is and what the key is. Here's an implementation that does exactly what the `actions` dictionary did — it returns an instance of our custom CAAction object, so that setting the layer's position waggles it into place:

```
override func actionForLayer(layer: CALayer!,
    forKey key: String!) -> CAAction! {
        if key == "position" {
            return MyAction()
        }
        return nil
}
```

Finally, I'll demonstrate overriding `defaultActionForKey:`. This code would go into a CALayer subclass; setting this layer's `contents` will automatically trigger a push transition from the left:

```
override class func defaultActionForKey(key: String!) -> CAAction! {
    if key == "contents" {
        let tr = CATransition()
        tr.type = kCATransitionPush
        tr.subtype = kCATransitionFromLeft
        return tr
    }
    return super.defaultActionForKey(key)
}
```

 Both the delegate's `actionForLayer:forKey:` and the subclass's `defaultActionForKey:` are declared as returning a CAAction. Therefore, to return `NSNull()` from your implemention of one of these methods, you'll need to typecast it to CAAction to quiet the compiler; you're lying (NSNull does not adopt the CAAction protocol), but it doesn't matter.

Making a Custom Property Implicitly Animatable

Earlier in this chapter, we made a custom layer's `thickness` property animatable through explicit layer animation. Now that we know how implicit layer animation works, we can make our layer's `thickness` property animatable through implicit animation as well. Thus, we will be able to animate our layer's thickness with code like this:

```
let lay = self.v.layer as! MyLayer
let cur = lay.thickness
let val : CGFloat = cur == 10 ? 0 : 10
lay.thickness = val // implicit animation
```

We have already implemented `needsDisplayForKey:` to return `true` for the
"thickness" key, and we have provided an appropriate `drawInContext:` implementation. Now we'll add two further pieces of the puzzle. As we now know, to make our
MyLayer class respond to direct setting of a property, we need to hook into the action
search and return a CAAction. The obvious place to do this is in the layer itself, at the
very start of the action search, in an `actionForKey:` implementation:

```
override func actionForKey(key: String!) -> CAAction! {
    if key == "thickness" {
        let ba = CABasicAnimation(keyPath: key)
        ba.fromValue = (self.presentationLayer() as! CALayer).valueForKey(key)
        return ba
    }
    return super.actionForKey(key)
}
```

Finally, we must declare our `thickness` property `@dynamic` in the Objective-C sense —
in fact, we must make this declaration in Objective-C (Swift's `dynamic` is not the same
thing). Otherwise, `actionForKey:` won't be called in the first place (the action search
will never happen). Thus, the MyLayer class is now declared in Objective-C:

```
// MyLayer.h:
@interface MyLayer : CALayer
@property CGFloat thickness;
@end
// MyLayer.m:
#import "MyLayer.h"
@implementation MyLayer
@dynamic thickness;
@end
```

The Swift code must import "MyLayer.h" in the bridging header, and is now an extension of the Objective-C class:

```
public extension MyLayer {
    // ... code goes here ...
}
```

Nonproperty Actions

An action search is also triggered when a layer is added to a superlayer (key `kCAOnOrder-
In`) and when a layer's sublayers are changed by adding or removing a sublayer (key
"sublayers").

These triggers and their keys are incorrectly described in Apple's documentation (and headers).

In this example, we use our layer's delegate so that when our layer is added to a superlayer, it will "pop" into view:

```
let layer = CALayer()
// ... configure layer here ...
layer.delegate = self
self.view.layer.addSublayer(layer)
```

In the layer's delegate (`self`), we implement the actual animation as a group animation, fading the layer quickly in from an opacity of 0 and at the same time scaling its transform to make it momentarily appear a little larger:

```
override func actionForLayer(layer: CALayer!,
    forKey key: String!) -> CAAction! {
        if key == kCAOnOrderIn {
            let anim1 = CABasicAnimation(keyPath:"opacity")
            anim1.fromValue = 0.0
            anim1.toValue = layer.opacity
            let anim2 = CABasicAnimation(keyPath:"transform")
            anim2.toValue = NSValue(CATransform3D:
                CATransform3DScale(layer.transform, 1.2, 1.2, 1.0))
            anim2.autoreverses = true
            anim2.duration = 0.1
            let group = CAAnimationGroup()
            group.animations = [anim1, anim2]
            group.duration = 0.2
            return group
        }
}
```

The documentation says that when a layer is removed from a superlayer, an action is sought under the key kCAOnOrderOut. This is true but useless, because by the time the action is sought, the layer has already been removed from the superlayer, so returning an animation has no visible effect. Similarly, an animation returned as an action when a layer's hidden is set to true is never played. A possible workaround is to trigger the animation in some other way (and remove the layer afterward, if desired).

Recall, for example, that an action search is triggered when an arbitrary key is set on a layer. Let's implement the key "farewell" so that it shrinks and fades the layer and then removes it from its superlayer:

```
layer.delegate = self
layer.setValue("", forKey:"farewell")
```

The supplier of the action object — in this case, the layer's delegate — returns the shrink-and-fade animation; it also sets itself as that animation's delegate, and removes the layer when the animation ends:

```swift
override func actionForLayer(layer: CALayer!,
    forKey key: String!) -> CAAction! {
        if key == "farewell" {
            let anim1 = CABasicAnimation(keyPath:"opacity")
            anim1.fromValue = layer.opacity
            anim1.toValue = 0.0
            let anim2 = CABasicAnimation(keyPath:"transform")
            anim2.toValue = NSValue(CATransform3D:
                CATransform3DScale(layer.transform, 0.1, 0.1, 1.0))
            let group = CAAnimationGroup()
            group.animations = [anim1, anim2]
            group.duration = 0.2
            group.delegate = self // animationDidStop will be called
            group.setValue(layer, forKey:"remove") // identifier
            layer.opacity = 0
            return group
        }
    }
override func animationDidStop(anim: CAAnimation!, finished flag: Bool) {
    if let layer = anim.valueForKey("remove") as? CALayer {
        layer.removeFromSuperlayer()
    }
}
```

Emitter Layers

Emitter layers (CAEmitterLayer) are, to some extent, on a par with animated images: once you've set up an emitter layer, it just sits there animating all by itself. The nature of this animation is rather narrow: an emitter layer emits particles, which are CAEmitterCell instances. However, by clever setting of the properties of an emitter layer and its emitter cells, you can achieve some astonishing effects. Moreover, the animation is itself animatable using Core Animation.

Here are some useful basic properties of a CAEmitterCell:

contents, contentsRect
> These are modeled after the eponymous CALayer properties, although CAEmitterLayer is not a CALayer subclass; so, respectively, an image (a CGImage) and a CGRect specifying a region of that image. They define the image that a cell will portray.

birthrate, lifetime
> How many cells per second should be emitted, and how many seconds each cell should live before vanishing, respectively.

velocity

> The speed at which a cell moves. The unit of measurement is not documented; perhaps it's points per second.

emissionLatitude, emissionLongitude

> The angle at which the cell is emitted from the emitter, as a variation from the perpendicular. Longitude is an angle within the plane; latitude is an angle out of the plane.

So, here's code to create a very elementary emitter cell:

```
// make a gray circle image
UIGraphicsBeginImageContextWithOptions(CGSizeMake(10,10), false, 1)
let con = UIGraphicsGetCurrentContext()
CGContextAddEllipseInRect(con, CGRectMake(0,0,10,10))
CGContextSetFillColorWithColor(con, UIColor.grayColor().CGColor)
CGContextFillPath(con)
let im = UIGraphicsGetImageFromCurrentImageContext()
UIGraphicsEndImageContext()
// make a cell with that image
let cell = CAEmitterCell()
cell.birthRate = 5
cell.lifetime = 1
cell.velocity = 100
cell.contents = im.CGImage
```

(In the first line, we deliberately keep the scale at 1, even on a high-resolution screen, because a CAEmitterLayer has no contentsScale, as a CALayer does; we're going to derive a CGImage from this image, and we don't want its size doubled.)

The result is that little gray circles should be emitted slowly and steadily, five per second, each one vanishing in one second. Now we need an emitter layer from which these circles are to be emitted. Here are some basic CAEmitterLayer properties (beyond those it inherits from CALayer); these define an imaginary object, an emitter, that will be producing the emitter cells:

emitterPosition

> The point at which the emitter should located, in superlayer coordinates. You can optionally add a third dimension to this point, emitterZPosition.

emitterSize

> The size of the emitter.

emitterShape

> The shape of the emitter. The dimensions of the shape depend on the emitter's size; the cuboid shape depends also on a third size dimension, emitterDepth. Your choices are:

> - kCAEmitterLayerPoint

Figure 4-4. A really boring emitter layer

- kCAEmitterLayerLine
- kCAEmitterLayerRectangle
- kCAEmitterLayerCuboid
- kCAEmitterLayerCircle
- kCAEmitterLayerSphere

emitterMode

The region of the shape from which cells should be emitted. Your choices are:

- kCAEmitterLayerPoints
- kCAEmitterLayerOutline
- kCAEmitterLayerSurface
- kCAEmitterLayerVolume

Let's start with the simplest possible case, a single point emitter:

```
let emit = CAEmitterLayer()
emit.emitterPosition = CGPointMake(30,100)
emit.emitterShape = kCAEmitterLayerPoint
emit.emitterMode = kCAEmitterLayerPoints
```

We tell the emitter what types of cell to emit by assigning those cells to its `emitter-Cells` property (an array of CAEmitterCell). We then add the emitter to our interface, and presto, it starts emitting:

```
emit.emitterCells = [cell]
self.view.layer.addSublayer(emit)
```

The result is a constant stream of gray circles emitted from the point (30.0,100.0), each circle marching steadily to the right and vanishing after one second (Figure 4-4).

Now that we've succeeded in creating a boring emitter layer, we can start to vary some parameters. The `emissionRange` defines a cone in which cells will be emitted; if we increase the `birthRate` and widen the `emissionRange`, we get something that looks like a stream shooting from a water hose:

```
cell.birthRate = 100
cell.lifetime = 1.5
cell.velocity = 100
cell.emissionRange = CGFloat(M_PI)/5.0
```

In addition, as the cell moves, it can be made to accelerate (or decelerate) in each dimension, using its xAcceleration, yAcceleration, and zAcceleration properties. Here, we turn the stream into a falling cascade, like a waterfall coming from the left:

```
cell.xAcceleration = -40
cell.yAcceleration = 200
```

All aspects of cell behavior can be made to vary randomly, using the following CAEmitterCell properties:

lifetimeRange, velocityRange

How much the lifetime and velocity values are allowed to vary randomly for different cells.

scale

scaleRange, scaleSpeed

The scale alters the size of the cell; the range and speed determine how far and how rapidly this size alteration is allowed to change over the lifetime of each cell.

color

redRange, greenRange, blueRange, alphaRange

redSpeed, greenSpeed, blueSpeed, alphaSpeed

The color is painted in accordance with the opacity of the cell's contents image; it combines with the image's color, so if we want the color stated here to appear in full purity, our contents image should use only white. The range and speed determine how far and how rapidly each color component is to change.

spin, spinRange

The spin is a rotational speed (in radians per second); its range determines how far this speed is allowed to change over the lifetime of each cell.

Here we add some variation so that the circles behave a little more independently of one another. Some live longer than others, some come out of the emitter faster than others. And they all start out a shade of blue, but change to a shade of green about half-way through the stream (Figure 4-5):

```
cell.lifetimeRange = 0.4
cell.velocityRange = 20
cell.scaleRange = 0.2
cell.scaleSpeed = 0.2
cell.color = UIColor.blueColor().CGColor
cell.greenRange = 0.5
cell.greenSpeed = 0.75
```

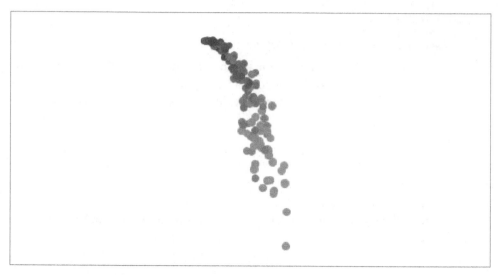

Figure 4-5. An emitter layer that makes a sort of waterfall

Once the emitter layer is in place and animating, you can change its parameters and the parameters of its emitter cells through key–value coding on the emitter layer. You can access the emitter cells through the emitter layer's `"emitterCells"` key path; to specify a cell type, use its `name` property (which you'll have to have assigned earlier) as the next piece of the key path. For example, suppose we've set `cell.name` to `"circle"`; now we'll change the cell's `greenSpeed` so that each cell changes from blue to green much earlier in its lifetime:

```
emit.setValue(3.0, forKeyPath:"emitterCells.circle.greenSpeed")
```

The significance of this is that such changes can themselves be animated! Here, we'll attach to the emitter layer a repeating animation that causes our cell's `greenSpeed` to move back and forth between two values. The result is that the stream varies, over time, between being mostly blue and mostly green:

```
let key = "emitterCells.circle.greenSpeed"
let ba = CABasicAnimation(keyPath:key)
ba.fromValue = -1.0
ba.toValue = 3.0
ba.duration = 4
ba.autoreverses = true
ba.repeatCount = Float.infinity
emit.addAnimation(ba, forKey:nil)
```

A CAEmitterCell can itself function as an emitter — that is, it can have cells of its own. Both CAEmitterLayer and CAEmitterCell conform to the CAMediaTiming protocol, and their `beginTime` and `duration` properties can be used to govern their times of

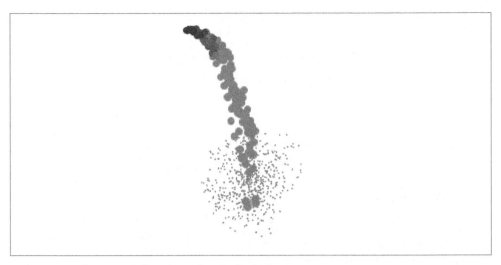

Figure 4-6. The waterfall makes a kind of splash

operation, much as in a grouped animation. For example, this code causes our existing waterfall to spray tiny droplets in the region of the "nozzle" (the emitter):

```
let cell2 = CAEmitterCell()
cell.emitterCells = [cell2]
cell2.contents = im.CGImage
cell2.emissionRange = CGFloat(M_PI)
cell2.birthRate = 200
cell2.lifetime = 0.4
cell2.velocity = 200
cell2.scale = 0.2
cell2.beginTime = 0.04
cell2.duration = 0.2
```

But if we change the `beginTime` to be larger (hence later), the tiny droplets happen near the bottom of the cascade. We must also increase the `duration`, or stop setting it altogether, since if the `duration` is less than the `beginTime`, no emission takes place at all (Figure 4-6):

```
cell2.beginTime = 1.4
cell2.duration = 0.4
```

We can also alter the picture by changing the behavior of the emitter itself. This change turns the emitter into a line, so that our cascade becomes broader (more like Niagara Falls):

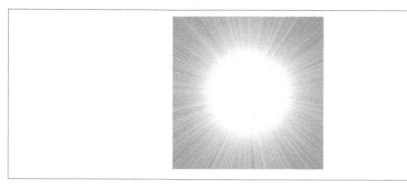

Figure 4-7. Midway through a starburst transition

```
emit.emitterPosition = CGPointMake(100,25)
emit.emitterSize = CGSizeMake(100,100)
emit.emitterShape = kCAEmitterLayerLine
emit.emitterMode = kCAEmitterLayerOutline
cell.emissionLongitude = 3*CGFloat(M_PI)/4
```

There's more to know about emitter layers and emitter cells, but at this point you know enough to understand Apple's sample code simulating such things as fire and smoke and pyrotechnics, and you can explore further on your own.

CIFilter Transitions

Core Image filters (Chapter 2) include transitions. You supply two images and a frame time between 0 and 1; the filter supplies the corresponding frame of a one-second animation transitioning from the first image to the second. For example, Figure 4-7 shows the frame at frame time .75 for a starburst transition from a solid red image to a photo of me. (You don't see the photo of me, because this transition, by default, "explodes" the first image to white first, and then quickly fades to the second image.)

Animating a Core Image transition filter is up to you. Thus we need a way of rapidly calling the same method repeatedly; in that method, we'll request and draw each frame of the transition. This could be a job for an NSTimer, but a better way is to use a *display link* (CADisplayLink), a form of timer that's highly efficient, especially when repeated drawing is involved, because it is linked directly to the refreshing of the display (hence the name). The display refresh rate is typically about one-sixtieth of a second; the actual value is given as the display link's `duration`, and will undergo slight fluctuations. Like a timer, the display link calls a designated method of ours every time it fires. We can slow the rate of calls by an integral amount by setting the display link's `frame-Interval`; for example, a display link with a `frameInterval` of 2 will call us about every one-thirtieth of a second. We can learn the exact time when the display link last fired by querying its `timestamp`.

In this example, I'll display the animation in a view's layer. We start by initializing and storing ahead of time, in properties, everything we'll need later to obtain an output image for a given frame of the transition — the CIFilter, the image's extent, and the CIContext used for rendering. We also have a timestamp property, which we initialize as well:

```
let moi = CIImage(image:UIImage(named:"moi"))
self.moiextent = moi.extent()
let col = CIFilter(name:"CIConstantColorGenerator")
let cicol = CIColor(color:UIColor.redColor())
col.setValue(cicol, forKey:"inputColor")
let colorimage = col.valueForKey("outputImage") as! CIImage
let tran = CIFilter(name:"CIFlashTransition")
tran.setValue(colorimage, forKey:"inputImage")
tran.setValue(moi, forKey:"inputTargetImage")
let center = CIVector(x:self.moiextent.width/2.0, y:self.moiextent.height/2.0)
tran.setValue(center, forKey:"inputCenter")
self.con = CIContext(options:nil)
self.tran = tran
self.timestamp = 0.0
```

We create the display link, setting it to call into our nextFrame: method, and set it going by adding it to the run loop, which retains it:

```
let link = CADisplayLink(target:self, selector:"nextFrame:")
link.addToRunLoop(NSRunLoop.mainRunLoop(), forMode:NSDefaultRunLoopMode)
```

Our nextFrame: method is called with the display link as parameter (sender). We store the initial timestamp in a property, and use the difference between that and each successive timestamp value to calculate our desired frame. We ask the filter for the corresponding image and display it. When the frame value exceeds 1, the animation is over and we invalidate the display link (just like a repeating timer), which releases it from the run loop:

```
func nextFrame(sender:CADisplayLink) {
    if self.timestamp < 0.01 { // pick up and store first timestamp
        self.timestamp = sender.timestamp
        self.frame = 0.0
    } else { // calculate frame
        self.frame = (sender.timestamp - self.timestamp) // * SCALE
    }
    sender.paused = true // defend against frame loss
    self.tran.setValue(self.frame, forKey:"inputTime")
    let moi = self.con.createCGImage(
        tran.outputImage, fromRect:self.moiextent)
    CATransaction.setDisableActions(true)
    self.v.layer.contents = moi
    if self.frame > 1.0 {
```

```
            sender.invalidate()
        }
        sender.paused = false
    }
```

I have surrounded the time-consuming calculation and drawing of the image with calls to the display link's `paused` property, in case the calculation time exceeds the time between screen refreshes; perhaps this isn't necessary, but it can't hurt. Our animation occupies one second; changing that value is merely a matter of multiplying by a scale value when we set our `frame` property (as I have shown in a comment). If you experiment with this code, run on the device, as display links do not work well in the Simulator.

UIKit Dynamics

The term *UIKit dynamics* refers to a suite of classes that supplies a convenient API for animating views in a manner reminiscent of real-world physical behavior. For example, views can be subjected to gravity, collisions, bouncing, and momentary forces, with effects that would otherwise be difficult to achieve.

UIKit dynamics should not be treated as a game engine. It is deliberately quite cartoony and simple, treating views as rectangular blocks and animating only their position (`center`) and rotation transform within a flat two-dimensional space. Like CIFilter animated transitions, UIKit dynamics relies on CADisplayLink, and the calculation of each frame takes place on the main thread (not on the animation server's background thread). There's no "animation movie" and no distinct presentation layer; the views really are being repositioned in real time. Thus, UIKit Dynamics is not intended for extended use; it is a way of momentarily emphasizing or clarifying functional transformations of your interface.

Implementing UIKit dynamics involves configuring a "stack" of three things:

A dynamic animator
> A dynamic animator, a UIDynamicAnimator instance, is the ruler of the physics world you are creating. It has a reference view, which is the superview of the views to be animated, and which defines the coordinate system of its world. Retaining the animator is up to you; a strong property will do. It's fine for an animator to sit empty until you need it; an animator whose world is empty (or at rest) is not running, and occupies no processor time.

A behavior
> A UIDynamicBehavior is a rule describing how a view should behave. You'll typically use a built-in subclass, such as UIGravityBehavior or UICollisionBehavior. You configure the behavior and add it to the animator; an animator has methods and properties for managing its behaviors, such as `addBehavior:`, `behaviors`, `removeBehavior:`, and `removeAllBehaviors`. A behavior's configuration can be

changed, and behaviors can be added to and removed from an animator, even while an animation is in progress.

An item

An item is any object that implements the UIDynamicItem protocol. A UIView is such an object! You add a UIView (one that's a subview of your animator's reference view) to a behavior (one that belongs to that animator) — and at that moment, the view comes under the influence of that behavior. If this behavior is one that causes motion, and if no other behaviors prevent, the view will now move (the animator is running).

Some behaviors can accept multiple items, and have methods and properties such as `addItem:`, `items`, and `removeItem:`. Others can have just one or two items and must be initialized with these from the outset.

That's sufficient to get started, so let's try it! I'll start by creating my animator and storing it in a property:

```
self.anim = UIDynamicAnimator(referenceView: self.view)
```

Now I'll cause an existing subview of `self.view` (a UIImageView, `self.iv`) to drop off the screen, under the influence of gravity. I create a UIGravityBehavior, add it to the animator, and add `self.iv` to it:

```
let grav = UIGravityBehavior()
self.anim.addBehavior(grav)
grav.addItem(self.iv)
```

As a result, `self.iv` comes under the influence of gravity and is now animated downward off the screen. (A UIGravityBehavior object has properties configuring the strength and direction of gravity, but I've left them here at their defaults.)

An immediate concern is that our view falls forever. This is a serious waste of memory and processing power. If we no longer need the view after it has left the screen, we should take it out of the influence of UIKit dynamics by removing it from any behaviors to which it belongs (and we can also remove it from its superview). One way to do this is by removing from the animator any behaviors that are no longer needed. In our simple example, where the animator's entire world contains just this one item, it will be sufficient to call `removeAllBehaviors`.

But how will we know when the view is off the screen? A UIDynamicBehavior can have an `action` block (a closure), which is called repeatedly as the animator drives the animation. I'll configure our gravity behavior's `action` block to check whether `self.iv` is still within the bounds of the reference view, by calling the animator's `itemsInRect:` method. Here's my first attempt:

```
grav.action = {
    let items = self.anim.itemsInRect(self.view.bounds) as! [UIView]
    let ix = find(items, self.iv)
    if ix == nil {
        self.anim.removeAllBehaviors()
        self.iv.removeFromSuperview()
    }
}
```

This works in the sense that, after the image view leaves the screen, the image view is removed from the window and the animation stops. Unfortunately, there is also a memory leak: neither the image view nor the gravity behavior has been released. One solution is, in `grav.action`, to set `self.anim` (the animator property) to nil, thus breaking the retain cycle. This is a perfectly appropriate solution if, as here, we no longer need the animator for anything; a UIDynamicAnimator is a lightweight object and can very reasonably come into existence only for as long as we need to run an animation. Another possibility is to use delayed performance; even a delay of 0 solves the problem, presumably because the behavior's `action` closure is no longer running at the time we remove the behavior:

```
grav.action = {
    let items = self.anim.itemsInRect(self.view.bounds) as! [UIView]
    let ix = find(items, self.iv)
    if ix == nil {
        delay(0) {
            self.anim.removeAllBehaviors()
            self.iv.removeFromSuperview()
        }
    }
}
```

Now let's add some further behaviors. If falling straight down is too boring, we can add a UIPushBehavior to create a slight rightward impulse to be applied to the view as it begins to fall:

```
let push = UIPushBehavior(items:[self.iv], mode:.Instantaneous)
push.pushDirection = CGVectorMake(2, 0)
self.anim.addBehavior(push)
```

The view now falls in a parabola to the right. Next, let's add a UICollisionBehavior to make our view strike the "floor" of the screen:

```
let coll = UICollisionBehavior()
coll.collisionMode = .Boundaries
coll.addBoundaryWithIdentifier("floor",
    fromPoint:CGPointMake(0, self.view.bounds.height),
    toPoint:CGPointMake(self.view.bounds.width,
        self.view.bounds.height))
self.anim.addBehavior(coll)
coll.addItem(self.iv)
```

The view now falls in a parabola onto the floor of the screen, bounces a tiny bit, and comes to rest. It would be nice if the view bounced a bit more. Characteristics internal to a dynamic item's physics, such as bounciness (`elasticity`), are configured by assigning it to a UIDynamicItemBehavior:

```
let bounce = UIDynamicItemBehavior()
bounce.elasticity = 0.4
self.anim.addBehavior(bounce)
bounce.addItem(self.iv)
```

Our view now bounces higher; nevertheless, when it hits the floor, it stops moving to the right, so it ends up at rest on the floor. I'd prefer that, after it bounces, it should start spinning to the right, so that it eventually leaves the screen. A UICollisionBehavior has a delegate to which it sends messages when a collision occurs. I'll make `self` the collision behavior's delegate, and when the delegate message arrives, I'll add rotational velocity to the existing dynamic item behavior `bounce`, so that our view starts spinning clockwise:

```
func collisionBehavior(behavior: UICollisionBehavior,
    beganContactForItem item: UIDynamicItem,
    withBoundaryIdentifier identifier: NSCopying,
    atPoint p: CGPoint) {
        // look for the dynamic item behavior
        for b in self.anim.behaviors as! [UIDynamicBehavior] {
            if let bounce = b as? UIDynamicItemBehavior {
                let v = bounce.angularVelocityForItem(self.iv)
                if v <= 0.1 {
                    bounce.addAngularVelocity(30, forItem:self.iv)
                }
                break;
            }
        }
}
```

The view now falls in a parabola to the right, strikes the floor, spins clockwise, and bounces off the floor and out the right side of the screen!

We have now developed a complex behavior by a combination of several built-in UI-DynamicBehavior subclass instances. For neatness, clarity, maintainability, and reusability, it might make sense to express that combination as a single custom UIDynamicBehavior subclass. Let's call it MyDropBounceAndRollBehavior. Now we can apply this behavior to our view, `self.iv`, very simply:

```
self.anim.addBehavior(MyDropBounceAndRollBehavior(view:self.iv))
```

All the work is now done by the MyDropBounceAndRollBehavior instance. I've designed it to affect just one view, so its initializer looks like this:

```
init(view v:UIView) {
    self.v = v
    super.init()
}
```

A UIDynamicBehavior receives a reference to its dynamic animator just before being added to it, by implementing willMoveToAnimator:, and can refer to it subsequently as self.dynamicAnimator. To incorporate actual behaviors into itself, our custom UI-DynamicBehavior subclass creates and configures them, and calls addChild-Behavior:; it can refer to the array of its child behaviors as self.childBehaviors. When our custom behavior is added to or removed from the dynamic animator, the effect is the same as if its child behaviors themselves were added or removed.

Here is the rest of MyDropBounceAndRollBehavior. Our precautions in the gravity behavior's action block not to cause a retain cycle are simpler than before; it suffices to designate self as an unowned reference and remove self from the animator explicitly:

```
override func willMoveToAnimator(anim: UIDynamicAnimator!) {
    if anim == nil { return }
    let sup = self.v.superview!
    let grav = UIGravityBehavior()
    grav.action = {
        [unowned self] in
        let items = anim.itemsInRect(sup.bounds) as! [UIView]
        if find(items, self.v) == nil {
            anim.removeBehavior(self)
            self.v.removeFromSuperview()
        }
    }
    self.addChildBehavior(grav)
    grav.addItem(self.v)
    let push = UIPushBehavior(items:[self.v], mode:.Instantaneous)
    push.pushDirection = CGVectorMake(2, 0)
    self.addChildBehavior(push)
    let coll = UICollisionBehavior()
    coll.collisionMode = .Boundaries
    coll.collisionDelegate = self
    coll.addBoundaryWithIdentifier("floor",
        fromPoint:CGPointMake(0, sup.bounds.size.height),
        toPoint:CGPointMake(sup.bounds.size.width,
            sup.bounds.size.height))
    self.addChildBehavior(coll)
    coll.addItem(self.v)
    let bounce = UIDynamicItemBehavior()
    bounce.elasticity = 0.4
    self.addChildBehavior(bounce)
    bounce.addItem(self.v)
}
func collisionBehavior(behavior: UICollisionBehavior,
    beganContactForItem item: UIDynamicItem,
    withBoundaryIdentifier identifier: NSCopying,
    atPoint p: CGPoint) {
        // look for the dynamic item behavior
        for b in self.childBehaviors as! [UIDynamicBehavior] {
            if let bounce = b as? UIDynamicItemBehavior {
```

```
                    let v = bounce.angularVelocityForItem(item)
                    if v <= 0.1 {
                        bounce.addAngularVelocity(30, forItem:item)
                    }
                    break;
            }
        }
    }
```

Here are some further UIDynamicAnimator methods and properties:

delegate

The delegate (UIDynamicAnimatorDelegate) is sent messages dynamicAnimator-DidPause: and dynamicAnimatorWillResume:. The animator is paused when it has nothing to do: it has no dynamic items, or all its dynamic items are at rest.

running

If true, the animator is not paused; some dynamic item is being animated.

elapsedTime

The total time during which this animator has been running since it first started running. The elapsedTime does not increase while the animator is paused, nor is it reset. You might use this in a delegate method or action method to decide that the animation is over.

updateItemUsingCurrentState:

Once a dynamic item has come under the influence of the animator, the animator is responsible for positioning that dynamic item. If your code subsequently manually changes the dynamic item's position or other relevant attributes, call this method so that the animator can take account of those changes.

Here is some more about the various built-in UIDynamicBehavior subclasses:

UIGravityBehavior

Imposes an acceleration on its dynamic items. By default, this acceleration is downward with a magnitude of 1 (arbitrarily defined as 1000 points per second per second).

UIPushBehavior

Applies a force either instantaneously or continuously (mode), the latter constituting an acceleration. How this force affects an object depends in part upon the object's "mass," which is based on its size combined with its density (the latter can be set through a UIDynamicItemBehavior); thus, by default, a smaller view is easier to push. The effect of a push behavior can be toggled with the active property; an instantaneous push is repeated each time the active property is set to true.

In addition to a direction and a magnitude, a push may be given an offset from the center of an item. This will apply an additional angular acceleration. Thus, I could have started the image view spinning clockwise by means of its initial push, like this:

```
push.setTargetOffsetFromCenter(UIOffsetMake(0, -200), forItem:self.v)
```

UICollisionBehavior

Watches for collisions either amongst items belonging to this same behavior or between an item and a boundary (mode). One collision behavior can have many boundaries. A boundary may be described as a line between two points or as a UIBezierPath, or you can turn the reference view's bounds into boundaries (set-TranslatesReferenceBoundsIntoBoundaryWithInsets:). Boundaries that you create can have an identifier. The collisionDelegate (UICollisionBehavior-Delegate) is called when a collision begins and again when it ends.

How a given collision affects the item(s) involved depends on the physical characteristics of the item(s), which may be configured through a UIDynamicItem-Behavior.

UISnapBehavior

Causes one item to snap to one point as if pulled by a spring. Its damping describes how much the item should oscillate as its settles into that point. This is a very simple behavior: the snap occurs once, immediately (when the behavior is added to the animator), and there's no notification when it's over.

UIAttachmentBehavior

Attaches an item by a bar or a spring to another item or to a point in the reference view, depending on how you initialize it:

- init(item:attachedToItem:)
- init(item:attachedToAnchor:)

The attachment point is, by default, the item's center; to change that, there's a different pair of initializers:

- init(item:offsetFromCenter:attachedToItem:offsetFromCenter:)
- init(item:offsetFromCenter:attachedToAnchor:)

The physics of the attaching medium is governed by the behavior's length, frequency, and damping. They are set for you when you initialize the behavior, but you can modify them, and the anchorPoint (if the attachment is to an anchor), over the behavior's lifetime.

As the other item or the anchorPoint moves, this item moves with it, in accordance with the physics of the attaching medium. An anchorPoint is particularly useful for implementing a draggable view within an animator world, as I'll demonstrate in the next chapter.

UIDynamicItemBehavior

Endows its items with internal physical characteristics such as `density` (changes the impulse-resisting mass in relation to size), `elasticity` (bounce on collision), `friction`, and `resistance` (tendency to come to rest unless forces are actively applied), as well as injecting linear velocity or angular velocity.

Motion Effects

A view can respond in real time to the way the user tilts the device. Typically, the view's response will be to shift its position slightly. This is used, for example, in various parts of the interface, to give a sense of the interface's being layered (parallax). When an alert is present, for example, if the user tilts the device, the alert shifts its position; the effect is subtle, but sufficient to suggest subconsciously that the alert is floating slightly in front of everything else on the screen.

Your own views can behave in the same way. A view will respond to shifts in the position of the device if it has one or more motion effects (UIMotionEffect). Motion effects are added to a view with `addMotionEffect:`, listed with `motionEffects`, and removed with `removeMotionEffect:`.

The UIMotionEffect class is abstract: its job is to be subclassed. The chief subclass provided is UIInterpolatingMotionEffect. Every UIInterpolatingMotionEffect has a single key path, which uses key–value coding to specify the property of its view that it affects. It also has a type, specifying which axis of the device's tilting (horizontal tilt or vertical tilt) is to affect this property. Finally, it has a maximum and minimum relative value, the furthest distance that the affected property of the view is to be permitted to wander from its actual value as the user tilts the device. Related motion effects should be combined into a UIMotionEffectGroup (a UIMotionEffect subclass), and the group added to the view.

So, for example:

```
let m1 = UIInterpolatingMotionEffect(
    keyPath:"center.x", type:.TiltAlongHorizontalAxis)
m1.maximumRelativeValue = 10.0
m1.minimumRelativeValue = -10.0
let m2 = UIInterpolatingMotionEffect(
    keyPath:"center.y", type:.TiltAlongVerticalAxis)
m2.maximumRelativeValue = 10.0
m2.minimumRelativeValue = -10.0
let g = UIMotionEffectGroup()
g.motionEffects = [m1,m2]
v.addMotionEffect(g)
```

You can write your own UIMotionEffect subclass by implementing a single method, `keyPathsAndRelativeValuesForViewerOffset:`, but this will rarely be necessary.

The user can turn off motion effects in the Settings app (under General → Accessibility → Reduce Motion).

Animation and Autolayout

The interplay between animation and autolayout can be tricky. As part of an animation, you may be changing a view's frame (or bounds, or center). You're really not supposed to do that when you're using autolayout. If you do, an animation may not work correctly. Or, it may appear to work perfectly, because no layout has happened; however, it is entirely possible that layout *will* happen, and that it will be accompanied by undesirable effects.

As I explained in Chapter 1, when layout takes place under autolayout, what matters are a view's constraints. If the constraints affecting a view don't resolve to the size and position that the view has at the moment of layout, the view will jump as the constraints are obeyed. This is almost certainly not what you want.

To persuade yourself that this can be a problem, just animate a view's position and then ask for immediate layout by calling `layoutIfNeeded`, like this:

```
UIView.animateWithDuration(1, animations:{
    self.v.center.x += 100
    }, completion: {
        _ in
        self.v.layoutIfNeeded() // this is what will happen at layout time
    })
```

If we're using autolayout, the view slides to the right and then jumps back to the left. This is bad. It's up to us to keep the constraints synchronized with the reality, so that when layout comes along in the natural course of things, our views don't jump into undesirable states.

One option is to revise the violated constraints to match the new reality. If we've planned far ahead, we may have armed ourselves in advance with a reference to those constraints; in that case, our code can now remove and replace them — or, if the only thing that needs changing is the `constant` value of a constraint, we can change that value in place (recall that the `constant` is the *only* writable property of an existing constraint). Otherwise, discovering what constraints are now violated, and getting a reference to them, is not at all easy.

Alternatively, instead of performing the animation first and then revising the constraints, we can change the constraints first and then *animate the act of layout*. Again, this assumes that we have a reference to the constraints in question. For example, if we are animating a view 100 points rightward, and if we have a reference to the constraint whose `constant` positions that view horizontally, we would say this:

```
let con = self.v_horizontalPositionConstraint
con.constant += 100
UIView.animateWithDuration(1, animations:{
    self.v.layoutIfNeeded()
})
```

This technique is not limited to a simple change of `constant`. You can overhaul the constraints quite dramatically and still animate the resulting change of layout. In this example, I animate a subview from one side of the screen to the other by removing its left constraint and replacing it with a right constraint:

```
let c = self.oldConstraint.constant
NSLayoutConstraint.deactivateConstraints([self.oldConstraint])
let newConstraint = NSLayoutConstraint(
    item: self.v, attribute: .Trailing, relatedBy: .Equal,
    toItem: self.view, attribute: .TrailingMargin,
    multiplier: 1, constant: -c)
NSLayoutConstraint.activateConstraints([newConstraint])
UIView.animateWithDuration(0.4) {
    self.v.layoutIfNeeded()
}
```

Another possibility is to use a snapshot of the original view (Chapter 1). Add the snapshot temporarily to the interface — without using autolayout, and perhaps hiding the original view — and animate the snapshot:

```
let snap = self.v.snapshotViewAfterScreenUpdates(false)
snap.frame = self.v.frame
self.v.superview!.addSubview(snap)
self.v.hidden = true
UIView.animateWithDuration(1, animations:{
    snap.center.x += 100
})
```

That works because the snapshot view is not under the influence of autolayout, so it stays where we put it even if layout takes place. If, however, we need to remove the snapshot view and reveal the real view, and if the nature of the animation is such that the real view ultimately needs to be shifted to a new permanent position, then its constraints will still have to be revised. Still another possibility, obviously, is to remove the animated view *itself* from the influence of autolayout (remove its constraints and set its `translatesAutoresizingMaskIntoConstraints` to true).

It is unfortunate that such elaborate tactics are needed. Autolayout was introduced into iOS 6 with a seeming disregard for its fundamental incompatibility with animation; that incompatibility is a serious flaw in iOS, and Apple, far from grappling with it, has studiously glossed over it ever since.

CHAPTER 5

Touches

[Winifred the Woebegone illustrates hit-testing:]
Hey nonny nonny, is it you? — Hey nonny nonny
nonny no! — Hey nonny nonny, is it you? — Hey
nonny nonny nonny no!

—Marshall Barer, *Once Upon a Mattress*

A *touch* is an instance of the user putting a finger on the screen. The system and the hardware, working together, know *when* a finger contacts the screen and *where* it is. A finger is fat, but its location is cleverly reduced to a single appropriate point.

A UIView, by virtue of being a UIResponder, is the visible locus of touches. There are other UIResponder subclasses, but none of them is visible on the screen. What the user sees are views; what the user is touching are views. (The user actually sees layers, but a layer is not a UIResponder and is not involved with touches.)

It would make sense, therefore, if every touch were reported directly to the view in which it occurred. However, what the system "sees" is not particular views but an app as a whole. So a touch is represented as an object (a UITouch instance) which is bundled up in an envelope (a UIEvent) which the system delivers to your app. It is then up to your app to deliver the envelope to an appropriate UIView. In the vast majority of cases, this will happen automatically the way you expect, and you will respond to a touch by way of the view in which the touch occurred.

In fact, usually you won't concern yourself with UIEvents and UITouches at all. Most built-in interface views deal with these low-level touch reports themselves, and notify your code at a higher level — you hear about functionality and intention rather than raw touches. When a UIButton emits an action message to report a control event such as Touch Up Inside, it has already performed a reduction of a complex sequence of touches ("the user put a finger down inside me and then, possibly with some dragging hither and yon, raised it when it was still reasonably close to me"). A UITextField reports touches on the keyboard as changes in its own text. A UITableView reports that the user selected a cell. A UIScrollView, when dragged, reports that it scrolled; when pinched outward, it reports that it zoomed.

Nevertheless, it is useful to know how to respond to touches directly, so that you can implement your own touchable views, and so that you understand what Cocoa's built-in views are actually doing. This chapter discusses touch detection and response by views (and other UIResponders) at their lowest level, along with a higher-level, more practical mechanism, gesture recognizers, that categorizes touches into gesture types for you; then it deconstructs the touch-delivery architecture by which touches are reported to your views in the first place.

Touch Events and Views

Imagine a screen that the user is not touching at all: the screen is "finger-free." Now the user touches the screen with one or more fingers. From that moment until the time the screen is once again finger-free, all touches and finger movements together constitute what Apple calls a single *multitouch sequence*.

The system reports to your app, during a given multitouch sequence, every change in finger configuration, so that your app can figure out what the user is doing. Every such report is a UIEvent. In fact, every report having to do with the same multitouch sequence is *the same UIEvent instance*, arriving repeatedly, each time there's a change in finger configuration.

Every UIEvent reporting a change in the user's finger configuration contains one or more UITouch objects. Each UITouch object corresponds to a single finger; conversely, every finger touching the screen is represented in the UIEvent by a UITouch object. Once a UITouch instance has been created to represent a finger that has touched the screen, *the same UITouch instance* is used to represent that finger throughout this multitouch sequence until the finger leaves the screen.

Now, it might sound as if the system has to bombard the app with huge numbers of reports constantly during a multitouch sequence. But that's not really true. The system needs to report only *changes* in the finger configuration. For a given UITouch object (representing, remember, a specific finger), only four things can happen. These are called *touch phases*, and are described by a UITouch instance's phase property (UI-TouchPhase):

.Began
> The finger touched the screen for the first time; this UITouch instance has just been created. This is always the first phase, and arrives only once.

.Moved
> The finger moved upon the screen.

`.Stationary`

> The finger remained on the screen without moving. Why is it necessary to report this? Well, remember, once a UITouch instance has been created, it must be present every time the UIEvent arrives. So if the UIEvent arrives because something *else* happened (e.g., a new finger touched the screen), we must report what *this* finger has been doing, even if it has been doing nothing.

`.Ended`

> The finger left the screen. Like `.Began`, this phase arrives only once. The UITouch instance will now be destroyed and will no longer appear in UIEvents for this multitouch sequence.

Those four phases are sufficient to describe everything that a finger can do. Actually, there is one more possible phase:

`.Cancelled`

> The system has aborted this multitouch sequence because something interrupted it. What might interrupt a multitouch sequence? There are many possibilities. Perhaps the user clicked the Home button or the screen lock button in the middle of the sequence. A local notification alert may have appeared (Chapter 13); on an iPhone, a call might have come in. And as we shall see, a gesture recognizer recognizing its gesture may also trigger touch cancellation. The point is, if you're dealing with touches yourself, you cannot afford to ignore touch cancellation; they are your opportunity to get things into a coherent state when the sequence is interrupted.

When a UITouch first appears (`.Began`), your app works out which UIView it is associated with. (I'll give full details, later in this chapter, as to how it does that.) This view is then set as the touch's `view` property, and *remains* so; from then on, this UITouch is *always* associated with this view (until that finger leaves the screen).

The same UIEvent containing the same UITouches can be sent to multiple views. Accordingly, a UIEvent is distributed to *all the views of all the UITouches it contains*. Conversely, if a view is sent a UIEvent, it's because that UIEvent contains at least one UITouch whose `view` is this view.

If every UITouch in a UIEvent associated with a certain UIView has the phase `.Stationary`, that UIEvent is *not* sent to that UIView. There's no point, because as far as that view is concerned, nothing happened.

Receiving Touches

A UIResponder, and therefore a UIView, has four methods corresponding to the four UITouch phases that require UIEvent delivery. A UIEvent is delivered to a view by calling one of these four methods (the *touches... methods*):

`touchesBegan:withEvent:`

A finger touched the screen, creating a UITouch.

`touchesMoved:withEvent:`

A finger previously reported to this view with `touchesBegan:withEvent:` has moved.

`touchesEnded:withEvent:`

A finger previously reported to this view with `touchesBegan:withEvent:` has left the screen.

`touchesCancelled:withEvent:`

We are bailing out on a finger previously reported to this view with `touches-Began:withEvent:`.

The parameters of these methods are:

The relevant touches

These are the event's touches whose phase corresponds to the name of the method and (normally) whose view is this view. They arrive as an NSSet — a Swift `Set<NSObject>`. If there is only one touch in the set, or if any touch in the set will do, you can retrieve it with `first` (a set is unordered, so *which* element is `first` is arbitrary).

The event

This is the UIEvent instance. It contains its touches as a Set, which you can retrieve with the `allTouches` message. This means *all* the event's touches, including but not necessarily limited to those in the first parameter; there might be touches in a different phase or intended for some other view. You can call `touchesForView:` or `touchesForWindow:` to ask for the set of touches associated with a particular view or window.

A UITouch has some useful methods and properties:

`locationInView:, previousLocationInView:`

The current and previous location of this touch with respect to the coordinate system of a given view. The view you'll be interested in will often be `self` or `self.superview`; supply nil to get the location with respect to the window. The previous location will be of interest only if the phase is `.Moved`.

 Recall (from Chapter 1) that the coordinate system of the window works differently in iOS 8 from previous systems: in a rotated app, the window rotates in iOS 8, whereas in iOS 7 and before it didn't. If your code was relying on the location of a touch with respect to the window in iOS 7, it may break in iOS 8.

timestamp
> When the touch last changed. A touch is timestamped when it is created (`.Began`) and each time it moves (`.Moved`). There can be a delay between the occurrence of a physical touch and the delivery of the corresponding UITouch, so to learn about the timing of touches, consult the timestamp, not the clock.

tapCount
> If two touches are in roughly the same place in quick succession, and the first one is brief, the second one may be characterized as a repeat of the first. They are different touch objects, but the second will be assigned a `tapCount` one larger than the previous one. The default is 1, so if (for example) a touch's `tapCount` is 3, then this is the third tap in quick succession in roughly the same spot.

view
> The view with which this touch is associated.

majorRadius, majorRadiusTolerance
> New in iOS 8, the radius of the touch (approximately half its size) and the uncertainty of that measurement, in points.

Here are some additional UIEvent properties:

type
> This will be `UIEventType.Touches`. There are other event types, but you're not going to receive any of them this way.

timestamp
> When the event occurred.

So, when we say that a certain view *is receiving a touch*, that is a shorthand expression meaning that it is being sent a UIEvent containing this UITouch, over and over, by calling one of its `touches...` methods, corresponding to the phase this touch is in, from the time the touch is created until the time it is destroyed.

Restricting Touches

Touch events can be turned off entirely at the application level with UIApplication's `beginIgnoringInteractionEvents`. It is quite common to do this during animations and other lengthy operations during which responding to a touch could cause undesirable results. This call should be balanced by `endIgnoringInteractionEvents`. Pairs can be nested, in which case interactivity won't be restored until the outermost `endIgnoringInteractionEvents` has been reached.

A number of UIView properties also restrict the delivery of touches to particular views:

`userInteractionEnabled`

If set to `false`, this view (along with its subviews) is excluded from receiving touches. Touches on this view or one of its subviews "fall through" to a view behind it.

`alpha`

If set to `0.0` (or extremely close to it), this view (along with its subviews) is excluded from receiving touches. Touches on this view or one of its subviews "fall through" to a view behind it.

`hidden`

If set to `true`, this view (along with its subviews) is excluded from receiving touches. This makes sense, since from the user's standpoint, the view and its subviews are not even present.

`multipleTouchEnabled`

If set to `false`, this view never receives more than one touch simultaneously; once it receives a touch, it doesn't receive any other touches until that first touch has ended.

`exclusiveTouch`

This is the only one of these properties that can't be set in the nib editor. An `exclusiveTouch` view receives a touch only if no other views in the same window have touches associated with them; once an `exclusiveTouch` view has received a touch, then while that touch exists no other view in the same window receives any touches.

Interpreting Touches

Thanks to gesture recognizers (discussed later in this chapter), in most cases you won't have to interpret touches at all; you'll let a gesture recognizer do most of that work. Even so, it is beneficial to be conversant with the nature of touch interpretation; this will help you interact with a gesture recognizer, write your own gesture recognizer, or subclass an existing one. Furthermore, not every touch sequence can be codified through a gesture recognizer; sometimes, directly interpreting touches is the best approach.

To figure out what's going on as touches are received by a view, your code must essentially function as a kind of state machine. You'll receive various `touches...` method calls, and your response will partly depend upon what happened previously, so you'll have to record somehow, such as in properties, the information that you'll need in order to decide what to do when the next `touches...` method is called. Such an architecture can make writing and maintaining touch-analysis code quite tricky. Moreover, although you can distinguish a particular UITouch or UIEvent object over time by keeping a reference to it, you mustn't retain that reference; it doesn't belong to you.

To illustrate the business of interpreting touches, we'll start with a view that can be dragged with the user's finger. For simplicity, I'll assume that this view receives only a single touch at a time. (This assumption is easy to enforce by setting the view's multiple-TouchEnabled to false, which is the default.)

The trick to making a view follow the user's finger is to realize that a view is positioned by its center, which is in superview coordinates, but the user's finger might not be at the center of the view. So at every stage of the drag we must change the view's center by the change in the user's finger position in superview coordinates:

```
override func touchesMoved(touches: Set<NSObject>, withEvent e: UIEvent) {
    let t = touches.first as! UITouch
    let loc = t.locationInView(self.superview)
    let oldP = t.previousLocationInView(self.superview)
    let deltaX = loc.x - oldP.x
    let deltaY = loc.y - oldP.y
    var c = self.center
    c.x += deltaX
    c.y += deltaY
    self.center = c
}
```

Next, let's add a restriction that the view can be dragged only vertically or horizontally. All we have to do is hold one coordinate steady; but which coordinate? Everything seems to depend on what the user does initially. So we'll do a one-time test the first time we receive touchesMoved:withEvent:. Now we're maintaining two Bool state properties, decided and horiz:

```
override func touchesBegan(touches: Set<NSObject>, withEvent e: UIEvent) {
    self.decided = false
}
override func touchesMoved(touches: Set<NSObject>, withEvent e: UIEvent) {
    let t = touches.first as! UITouch
    if !self.decided {
        self.decided = true
        let then = t.previousLocationInView(self)
        let now = t.locationInView(self)
        let deltaX = fabs(then.x - now.x)
        let deltaY = fabs(then.y - now.y)
        self.horiz = deltaX >= deltaY
    }
    let loc = t.locationInView(self.superview)
    let oldP = t.previousLocationInView(self.superview)
    let deltaX = loc.x - oldP.x
    let deltaY = loc.y - oldP.y
    var c = self.center
    if self.horiz {
        c.x += deltaX
    } else {
```

```
        c.y += deltaY
    }
    self.center = c
}
```

Look at how things are trending. We are maintaining multiple state properties, which we are managing across multiple methods, and we are subdividing a touches... method implementation into tests depending on the state of our state machine. Our state machine is very simple, but already our code is becoming difficult to read and to maintain — and things will only become more messy as we try to make our view's behavior more sophisticated.

Another area in which manual touch handling can rapidly prove overwhelming is when it comes to distinguishing between different gestures that the user is to be permitted to perform on a view. Imagine, for example, a view that distinguishes between a finger tapping briefly and a finger remaining down for a longer time. We can't know how long a tap is until it's over, so we must wait until then before deciding; once again, this requires maintaining state in a property (time):

```
override func touchesBegan(touches: Set<NSObject>, withEvent e: UIEvent) {
    self.time = (touches.first as! UITouch).timestamp
}
override func touchesEnded(touches: Set<NSObject>, withEvent e: UIEvent) {
    let diff = event.timestamp - self.time
    if (diff < 0.4) {
        println("short")
    } else {
        println("long")
    }
}
```

A similar challenge is distinguishing between a single tap and a double tap. The UITouch tapCount property already makes this distinction, but that, by itself, is not enough to help us react differently to the two. What we must do, having received a tap whose tap-Count is 1, is to use delayed performance in responding to it, so that we wait long enough to give a second tap a chance to arrive. This is unfortunate, because it means that if the user intends a single tap, some time will elapse before anything happens in response to it; however, there's nothing we can readily do about that.

Distributing our various tasks correctly is tricky. We *know* when we have a double tap as early as touchesBegan:withEvent:, but we *respond* to the double tap in touches-Ended:withEvent:. Therefore we use a property (single) to communicate between the two. We don't start our delayed response to a single tap until touchesEnded:with-Event:, because what matters is the time between the taps as a whole, not between the starts of the taps:

```
override func touchesBegan(touches: Set<NSObject>, withEvent e: UIEvent) {
    let ct = (touches.first as! UITouch).tapCount
    switch ct {
    case 2:
        self.single = false
    default: break
    }
}
override func touchesEnded(touches: Set<NSObject>, withEvent e: UIEvent) {
    let ct = (touches.first as! UITouch).tapCount
    switch ct {
    case 1:
        self.single = true
        delay(0.3) {
            if self.single { // no second tap intervened
                println("single tap")
            }
        }
    case 2:
        println("double tap")
    default: break
    }
}
```

As that code weren't confusing enough, let's now consider combining our detection for
a single or double tap with our earlier code for dragging a view horizontally or vertically.
This is to be a view that can detect four kinds of gesture: a single tap, a double tap, a
horizontal drag, and a vertical drag. We must include the code for all possibilities and
make sure they don't interfere with each other. The result is horrifying — a forced join
between two already complicated sets of code, along with an additional pair of state
properties (drag, decidedTapOrDrag) to track the decision between the tap gestures on
the one hand and the drag gestures on the other:

```
override func touchesBegan(touches: Set<NSObject>, withEvent e: UIEvent) {
    // be undecided
    self.decidedTapOrDrag = false
    // prepare for a tap
    let ct = (touches.first as! UITouch).tapCount
    switch ct {
    case 2:
        self.single = false
        self.decidedTapOrDrag = true
        self.drag = false
        return
    default: break
    }
    // prepare for a drag
    self.decidedDirection = false
}
override func touchesMoved(touches: Set<NSObject>, withEvent e: UIEvent) {
    if self.decidedTapOrDrag && !self.drag {return}
```

```
        let t = touches.first as! UITouch
        self.decidedTapOrDrag = true
        self.drag = true
        if !self.decidedDirection {
            self.decidedDirection = true
            let then = t.previousLocationInView(self)
            let now = t.locationInView(self)
            let deltaX = fabs(then.x - now.x)
            let deltaY = fabs(then.y - now.y)
            self.horiz = deltaX >= deltaY
        }
        let loc = t.locationInView(self.superview)
        let oldP = t.previousLocationInView(self.superview)
        let deltaX = loc.x - oldP.x
        let deltaY = loc.y - oldP.y
        var c = self.center
        if self.horiz {
            c.x += deltaX
        } else {
            c.y += deltaY
        }
        self.center = c
    }
    override func touchesEnded(touches: Set<NSObject>, withEvent e: UIEvent) {
        if !self.decidedTapOrDrag || !self.drag {
            // end for a tap
            let ct = (touches.first as! UITouch).tapCount
            switch ct {
            case 1:
                self.single = true
                delay(0.3) {
                    if self.single {
                        println("single tap")
                    }
                }
            case 2:
                println("double tap")
            default: break
            }
        }
    }
}
```

That code seems to work, but it's hard to say whether it covers all possibilities coherently; it's barely legible and the logic borders on the mysterious. This is the kind of situation for which gesture recognizers were devised.

Gesture Recognizers

Writing and maintaining a state machine that interprets touches across a combination of three or four touches... methods is hard enough when a view confines itself to expecting only one kind of gesture, such as dragging. It becomes even more involved when a view wants to accept and respond differently to different kinds of gesture. Furthermore, many types of gesture are conventional and standard; it seems insane to require developers to implement independently the elements that constitute what is, in effect, a universal vocabulary.

The solution is gesture recognizers, which standardize common gestures and allow the code for different gestures to be separated and encapsulated into different objects. Thanks to gesture recognizers, it is unnecessary to subclass UIView merely in order to implement touch analysis.

Gesture Recognizer Classes

A *gesture recognizer* (a subclass of UIGestureRecognizer) is an object whose job is to detect that a multitouch sequence equates to *one particular type of gesture*. It is attached to a UIView, which has for this purpose methods `addGestureRecognizer:` and `removeGestureRecognizer:`, and a `gestureRecognizers` property. A UIGestureRecognizer implements the four `touches...` handlers, but it is not a responder (a UIResponder), so it does not participate in the responder chain.

If a new touch is going to be delivered to a view, it is also associated with and delivered to that view's gesture recognizers if it has any, and that view's superview's gesture recognizers if it has any, and so on up the view hierarchy. Thus, the place of a gesture recognizer in the view hierarchy matters, even though it isn't part of the responder chain.

UITouch and UIEvent provide complementary ways of learning how touches and gesture recognizers are associated. UITouch's `gestureRecognizers` lists the gesture recognizers that are currently handling this touch. UIEvent's `touchesForGestureRecognizer:` lists the touches that are currently being handled by a particular gesture recognizer.

Each gesture recognizer maintains its own state as touch events arrive, building up evidence as to what kind of gesture this is. When one of them decides that it has recognized *its own particular type of gesture*, it emits either a single message (to indicate, for example, that a finger has tapped) or a series of messages (to indicate, for example, that a finger is moving); the distinction here is between a *discrete* and a *continuous* gesture.

What message a gesture recognizer emits, and to what object it sends it, is set through a target–action dispatch table attached to the gesture recognizer; a gesture recognizer is rather like a UIControl in this regard. Indeed, one might say that a gesture recognizer simplifies the touch handling of *any* view to be like that of a control. The difference is that one control may report several different control events, whereas each gesture recognizer reports only one gesture type, with different gestures being reported by different gesture recognizers.

UIGestureRecognizer itself is abstract, providing methods and properties to its sub-classes. Among these are:

init(target:action:)
> The designated initializer. Each message emitted by a UIGestureRecognizer is a matter of sending the action message to the target. Further target–action pairs may be added with addTarget:action: and removed with removeTarget:action:.

> Two forms of action: selector are possible: either there is no parameter, or there is a single parameter which will be the gesture recognizer. Most commonly, you'll use the second form, so that the target can identify and query the gesture recognizer; moreover, using the second form also gives the target a reference to the view, through the gesture recognizer's view property.

locationOfTouch:inView:
> The touch is specified by an index number. The numberOfTouches property provides a count of current touches; the touches themselves are inaccessible by way of the gesture recognizer.

enabled
> A convenient way to turn a gesture recognizer off without having to remove it from its view.

state, view
> I'll discuss state later on. The view is the view to which this gesture recognizer is attached.

Built-in UIGestureRecognizer subclasses are provided for six common gesture types: tap, pinch (inward or outward), pan (drag), swipe, rotate, and long press. Each embodies properties and methods likely to be needed for each type of gesture, either in order to configure the gesture recognizer beforehand or in order to query it as to the state of an ongoing gesture:

UITapGestureRecognizer (discrete)
> Configuration: numberOfTapsRequired, numberOfTouchesRequired ("touches" means simultaneous fingers).

UIPinchGestureRecognizer (continuous)
> Two fingers moving toward or away from each other. State: scale, velocity.

UIRotationGestureRecognizer (continuous)
> Two fingers moving round a common center. State: rotation, velocity.

UISwipeGestureRecognizer (discrete)
> A straight-line movement in one of the four cardinal directions. Configuration: direction (meaning permitted directions, a bitmask), numberOfTouchesRequired.

UIPanGestureRecognizer (continuous)
> Dragging. Configuration: `minimumNumberOfTouches`, `maximumNumberOfTouches`. State: `translationInView:`, `setTranslation:inView:`, and `velocityInView:`; the coordinate system of the specified view is used.

UIScreenEdgePanGestureRecognizer
> A UIPanGestureRecognizer subclass. It recognizes a pan gesture that starts at an edge of the screen. It adds a configuration property, `edges`, a UIRectEdge; despite the name (and the documentation), this must be set to a single edge.

UILongPressGestureRecognizer (continuous)
> Configuration: `numberOfTapsRequired`, `numberOfTouchesRequired`, `minimum-PressDuration`, `allowableMovement`. The `numberOfTapsRequired` is the count of taps *before* the tap that stays down; so it can be 0 (the default). The `allowable-Movement` setting lets you compensate for the fact that the user's finger is unlikely to remain steady during an extended press; thus we need to provide some limit before deciding that this gesture is, say, a drag, and not a long press after all. On the other hand, once the long press is recognized, the finger is permitted to drag.

UIGestureRecognizer also provides a `locationInView:` method. This is a single point, even if there are multiple touches. The subclasses implement this variously. For example, for UIPanGestureRecognizer, the location is where the touch is if there's a single touch, but it's a sort of midpoint ("centroid") if there are multiple touches.

We already know enough to implement, using a gesture recognizer, a view that responds to a single tap, or a view that responds to a double tap. We don't yet know quite enough to implement a view that lets itself be dragged around, or a view that can respond to more than one gesture; we'll come to that. Meanwhile, here's code that implements a view (v) that responds to a single tap:

```
let t1 = UITapGestureRecognizer(target:self, action:"singleTap")
self.v.addGestureRecognizer(t1)
// ...
func singleTap () {
    println("single tap")
}
```

And here's code that implements a view (v) that responds to a double tap:

```
let t2 = UITapGestureRecognizer(target:self, action:"doubleTap")
t2.numberOfTapsRequired = 2
self.v.addGestureRecognizer(t2)
// ...
func doubleTap () {
    println("double tap")
}
```

For a continuous gesture like dragging, we need to know both when the gesture is in progress and when the gesture ends. This brings us to the subject of a gesture recognizer's state.

A gesture recognizer implements a notion of *states* (the state property, UIGesture-RecognizerState); it passes through these states in a definite progression. The gesture recognizer remains in the .Possible state until it can make a decision one way or the other as to whether this is in fact the correct gesture. The documentation neatly lays out the possible progressions:

Wrong gesture
> .Possible → .Failed. No action message is sent.

Discrete gesture (like a tap), recognized
> .Possible → .Ended. One action message is sent, when the state changes to .Ended.

Continuous gesture (like a drag), recognized
> .Possible → .Began → .Changed (repeatedly) → .Ended. Action messages are sent once for .Began, as many times as necessary for .Changed, and once for .Ended.

Continuous gesture, recognized but later cancelled
> .Possible → .Began → .Changed (repeatedly) → .Cancelled. Action messages are sent once for .Began, as many times as necessary for .Changed, and once for .Cancelled.

The same action message arrives at the same target every time, so the handler must differentiate by asking about the gesture recognizer's state. To illustrate, we will implement, using a gesture recognizer, a view (v) that lets itself be dragged around in any direction by a single finger. Our maintenance of state is greatly simplified, because a UIPanGestureRecognizer maintains a delta (translation) for us. This delta, available using translationInView:, is reckoned from the touch's initial position. We don't even need to record the view's original center, because we are allowed to reset the UIPan-GestureRecognizer's delta, using setTranslation:inView:. So:

```
func dragging(p : UIPanGestureRecognizer) {
    let vv = p.view!
    switch p.state {
    case .Began, .Changed:
        let delta = p.translationInView(vv.superview!)
        var c = vv.center
        c.x += delta.x; c.y += delta.y
        vv.center = c
        p.setTranslation(CGPointZero, inView: vv.superview)
    default: break
    }
}
```

A pan gesture recognizer can be used also to make a view draggable under the influence of a UIDynamicAnimator (Chapter 4). The strategy here is that the view is attached to one or more anchor points through a UIAttachmentBehavior; as the user drags, we move the anchor point(s), and the view follows. In this example, I set up the whole UIKit dynamics "stack" of objects as the gesture begins, anchoring the view at the point where the touch is; then I move the anchor point to stay with the touch. Instance variables anim and att store the UIDynamicAnimator and the UIAttachmentBehavior, respectively; self.view is our view's superview, and is the animator's reference view:

```
@IBAction func dragging(g: UIPanGestureRecognizer) {
    switch g.state {
    case .Began:
        self.anim = UIDynamicAnimator(referenceView:self.view)
        let loc = g.locationOfTouch(0, inView:g.view)
        let cen = CGPointMake(g.view!.bounds.midX, g.view!.bounds.midY)
        let off = UIOffsetMake(loc.x-cen.x, loc.y-cen.y)
        let anchor = g.locationOfTouch(0, inView:self.view)
        let att = UIAttachmentBehavior(item:g.view!,
            offsetFromCenter:off, attachedToAnchor:anchor)
        self.anim.addBehavior(att)
        self.att = att
    case .Changed:
        self.att.anchorPoint = g.locationOfTouch(0, inView: self.view)
    default:
        self.anim = nil
    }
}
```

The outcome is that the view both moves and rotates in response to dragging, like a plate being pulled about on a table by a single finger. Another implementation, suggested in a WWDC 2013 video, is to attach the view by springs to four anchor points at some distance outside its corners and move all four anchor points; the view then jiggles while being dragged.

Gesture Recognizer Conflicts

The question naturally arises of what happens when multiple gesture recognizers are in play. This isn't a matter merely of multiple recognizers attached to a single view; as I have said, if a view is touched, not only its own gesture recognizers but also any gesture recognizers attached to views further up the view hierarchy are in play simultaneously. I like to think of a view as surrounded by a *swarm* of gesture recognizers — its own, and those of its superview, and so on. (In reality, it is a touch that has a swarm of gesture recognizers; that's why a UITouch has a gestureRecognizers property, in the plural.)

The superview gesture recognizer swarm comes as a surprise to beginners, but it makes sense, because without it, certain gestures would be impossible. Imagine, for example, a pair of views, each of which the user can tap individually, but which the user can also touch simultaneously (one finger on each view) to rotate them together around their mutual centroid. Neither view can detect the rotation *qua* rotation, because neither view receives both touches; only the superview can detect it, so the fact that the views themselves respond to touches must not prevent the superview's gesture recognizer from operating.

In general, once a gesture recognizer succeeds in recognizing its gesture, any *other* gesture recognizers associated with its touches are *forced into the* .Failed *state*, and whatever touches were associated with those gesture recognizers are no longer sent to them; in effect, the first gesture recognizer in a swarm that recognizes its gesture owns the gesture (and its touches) from then on.

In many cases, this "first past the post" behavior, on its own, will correctly eliminate conflicts. If it doesn't, you can modify it.

For example, we can add *both* our UITapGestureRecognizer for a single tap *and* our UIPanGestureRecognizer to a view and everything will just work; "first past the post" is exactly the desired behavior. What happens, though, if we also add the UITapGesture-Recognizer for a double tap? Dragging works, and single tap works; double tap works too, but without preventing the single tap from working. So, on a double tap, both the single tap action handler and the double tap action handler are called.

If that isn't what we want, we don't have to use delayed performance, as we did earlier. Instead, we can create a *dependency* between one gesture recognizer and another, telling the first to suspend judgement until the second has decided whether this is its gesture. We can do this by sending the first gesture recognizer the requireGestureRecognizer-ToFail: message. (This message is rather badly named; it doesn't mean "force this other recognizer to fail," but rather, "you can't succeed unless this other recognizer has failed.")

So our view v is now configured as follows:

```
let t2 = UITapGestureRecognizer(target:self, action:"doubleTap")
t2.numberOfTapsRequired = 2
self.v.addGestureRecognizer(t2)
let t1 = UITapGestureRecognizer(target:self, action:"singleTap")
t1.requireGestureRecognizerToFail(t2) // *
self.v.addGestureRecognizer(t1)
let p = UIPanGestureRecognizer(target: self, action: "dragging:")
self.v.addGestureRecognizer(p)
```

 Apple would prefer, if you're going to have a view respond both to a single tap and to a double tap, that you *not* make the former wait upon the latter (because this delays your response after the single tap). Rather, they would like you to arrange things so that it doesn't matter if you respond to a single tap that is the first tap of a double tap. This isn't always feasible, however; Apple's own Mobile Safari is a clear counterexample.

Another conflict that can arise is between a gesture recognizer and a view that already knows how to respond to the same gesture, such as a UIControl. This problem pops up particularly when the gesture recognizer belongs to the UIControl's superview. The UIControl's mere presence does not "block" the superview's gesture recognizer from recognizing a gesture on the UIControl, even if it is a UIControl that responds autonomously to touches. For example, your window's root view might have a UITapGestureRecognizer attached to it (perhaps because you want to be able to recognize taps on the background), but there is also a UIButton within it. How is that gesture recognizer to ignore a tap on the button?

The UIView instance method `gestureRecognizerShouldBegin:` solves the problem. It is called automatically; to modify its behavior, use a custom UIView subclass and override it. Its parameter is a gesture recognizer belonging to this view or to a view further up the view hierarchy. That gesture recognizer has recognized its gesture as taking place in this view; but by returning `false`, the view can tell the gesture recognizer to bow out and do nothing, not sending any action messages, and permitting this view to respond to the touch as if the gesture recognizer weren't there.

Thus, for example, a UIButton could return `false` for a single tap UITapGestureRecognizer; a single tap on the button would then trigger the button's action message, not the gesture recognizer's action message. And in fact a UIButton, by default, *does* return `false` for a single tap UITapGestureRecognizer whose view is not the UIButton itself. (If the gesture recognizer is for some gesture other than a tap, then the problem never arises, because a tap on the button won't cause the gesture recognizer to recognize in the first place.) Other built-in controls may also implement `gestureRecognizer-ShouldBegin:` in such a way as to prevent accidental interaction with a gesture recognizer; the documentation says that a UISlider implements it in such a way that a UISwipeGestureRecognizer won't prevent the user from sliding the "thumb," and there may be other cases that aren't documented explicitly. Naturally, you can take advantage of this feature in your own UIView subclasses.

Another way of resolving possible gesture recognizer conflicts is through the gesture recognizer's delegate, or with a gesture recognizer subclass. I'll discuss these in a moment.

Subclassing Gesture Recognizers

To subclass UIGestureRecognizer or a built-in gesture recognizer subclass, you must do the following things:

- In the bridging header, import `<UIKit/UIGestureRecognizerSubclass.h>`. This file contains a category on UIGestureRecognizer that allows you to set the gesture recognizer's state (which is otherwise read-only), along with declarations for the methods you may need to override.

- Override any `touches...` methods you need to (as if the gesture recognizer were a UIResponder); if you're subclassing a built-in gesture recognizer subclass, you will almost certainly call `super` so as to take advantage of the built-in behavior. In overriding a `touches...` method, you need to think like a gesture recognizer. As these methods are called, a gesture recognizer is setting its state; you must interact with that process.

To illustrate, we will subclass UIPanGestureRecognizer so as to implement a view that can be moved only horizontally or vertically. Our strategy will be to make *two* UIPan-GestureRecognizer subclasses — one that allows only horizontal movement, and another that allows only vertical movement. They will make their recognition decisions in a mutually exclusive manner, so we can attach an instance of each to our view. This separates the decision-making logic in a gorgeously encapsulated object-oriented manner — a far cry from the spaghetti code we wrote earlier to do this same task.

I will show only the code for the horizontal drag gesture recognizer, because the vertical recognizer is symmetrically identical. We maintain just one property, `origLoc`, which we will use once to determine whether the user's initial movement is horizontal. We override `touchesBegan:withEvent:` to set our property with the first touch's location:

```
override func touchesBegan(touches: Set<NSObject>, withEvent e: UIEvent) {
    self.origLoc =
        (touches.first as! UITouch).locationInView(self.view!.superview)
    super.touchesBegan(touches, withEvent:e)
}
```

We then override `touchesMoved:withEvent:`; all the recognition logic is here. This method will be called for the first time with the state still at `.Possible`. At that moment, we look to see if the user's movement is more horizontal than vertical. If it isn't, we set the state to `.Failed`. But if it is, we just step back and let the superclass do its thing:

```
override func touchesMoved(touches: Set<NSObject>, withEvent e: UIEvent) {
    if self.state == .Possible {
        let loc = (touches.first as! UITouch)
            .locationInView(self.view!.superview)
        let deltaX = fabs(loc.x - self.origLoc.x)
        let deltaY = fabs(loc.y - self.origLoc.y)
        if deltaY >= deltaX {
            self.state = .Failed
        }
    }
    super.touchesMoved(touches, withEvent:e)
}
```

We now have a view that moves only if the user's initial gesture is horizontal. But that isn't the entirety of what we want; we want a view that, itself, moves horizontally only. To implement this, we'll simply lie to our client about where the user's finger is, by overriding `translationInView::`

```
override func translationInView(view: UIView) -> CGPoint {
    var proposedTranslation = super.translationInView(view)
    proposedTranslation.y = 0
    return proposedTranslation
}
```

That example was simple, because we subclassed a fully functional built-in UIGesture-Recognizer subclass. If you were to write your own UIGestureRecognizer subclass entirely from scratch, there would be more work to do:

- You should definitely implement all four `touches...` handlers. Their job, at a minimum, is to advance the gesture recognizer through the canonical progression of its states. When the first touch arrives at a gesture recognizer, its state will be `.Possible`; you never explicitly set the recognizer's state to `.Possible` yourself. As soon as you know this can't be our gesture, you set the state to `.Failed` (Apple says that a gesture recognizer should "fail early, fail often"). If the gesture gets past all the failure tests, you set the state instead either to `.Ended` (for a discrete gesture) or to `.Began` (for a continuous gesture); if `.Began`, then you might set it to `.Changed`, and ultimately you must set it to `.Ended`. Action messages will be sent automatically at the appropriate moments.

- You should probably implement `reset`. This is called after you reach the end of the progression of states to notify you that the gesture recognizer's state is about to be set back to `.Possible`; it is your chance to return your state machine to its starting configuration (resetting properties, for example).

Keep in mind that your gesture recognizer might stop receiving touches without notice. Just because it gets a `touchesBegan:withEvent:` call for a particular touch doesn't mean it will ever get `touchesEnded:withEvent:` for that touch. If your gesture recognizer fails to recognize its gesture, either because it declares failure or because it is still in the `.Possible` state when another gesture recognizer recognizes, it won't get any more `touches...` calls for any of the touches that were being sent to it. This is why `reset` is so important; it's the one reliable signal that it's time to clean up and get ready to receive the beginning of another possible gesture.

Gesture Recognizer Delegate

A gesture recognizer can have a delegate (UIGestureRecognizerDelegate), which can perform two types of task.

These delegate methods can *block a gesture recognizer's operation*:

`gestureRecognizerShouldBegin:`
    Sent to the delegate before the gesture recognizer passes out of the `.Possible` state; return `false` to force the gesture recognizer to proceed to the `.Failed` state. (This happens *after* `gestureRecognizerShouldBegin:` has been sent to the view in which

the touch took place. That view must not have returned `false`, or we wouldn't have reached this stage.)

`gestureRecognizer:shouldReceiveTouch:`
> Sent to the delegate before a touch is sent to the gesture recognizer's `touches-Began:...` method; return `false` to prevent that touch from ever being sent to the gesture recognizer.

These delegate methods can *mediate gesture recognition conflict*:

`gestureRecognizer:shouldRecognizeSimultaneouslyWithGestureRecognizer:`
> Sent when a gesture recognizer recognizes its gesture, if this will force the failure of another gesture recognizer, to the delegates of *both* gesture recognizers. Return `true` to prevent that failure, thus allowing both gesture recognizers to operate simultaneously. For example, a view could respond to both a two-fingered pinch and a two-fingered pan, the one applying a scale transform, the other changing the view's center.

`gestureRecognizer:shouldRequireFailureOfGestureRecognizer:`
`gestureRecognizer:shouldBeRequiredToFailByGestureRecognizer:`
> Sent very early in the life of a gesture, when all gesture recognizers in a view's swarm are still in the `.Possible` state, to the delegates of *all* of them, pairing the gesture recognizer whose delegate this is with every other gesture recognizer in the swarm. Return `true` to prioritize between a pair, saying that one gesture recognizer cannot succeed until another has first failed. In essence, these delegate methods turn the decision made once and permanently in `requireGestureRecognizerToFail:` into a live decision that can be made freshly every time a gesture occurs.

As an example, we will use delegate messages to combine a UILongPressGesture-Recognizer and a UIPanGestureRecognizer, as follows: the user must perform a tap-and-a-half (tap and hold) to "get the view's attention," which we will indicate by a pulsing animation on the view; then (and only then) the user can drag the view.

The UIPanGestureRecognizer's handler will take care of the drag, as shown earlier in this chapter. The UILongPressGestureRecognizer's handler will take care of starting and stopping the animation:

```
func longPress(lp:UILongPressGestureRecognizer) {
    switch lp.state {
    case .Began:
        let anim = CABasicAnimation(keyPath: "transform")
        anim.toValue = NSValue(
            CATransform3D:CATransform3DMakeScale(1.1, 1.1, 1))
        anim.fromValue = NSValue(CATransform3D:CATransform3DIdentity)
        anim.repeatCount = Float.infinity
        anim.autoreverses = true
        lp.view!.layer.addAnimation(anim, forKey:nil)
    case .Ended, .Cancelled:
```

```
            lp.view!.layer.removeAllAnimations()
        default: break
        }
    }
```

As we created our gesture recognizers, we kept a reference to the UILongPressGesture-Recognizer (`self.longPresser`), and we made ourself the UIPanGestureRecognizer's delegate. So we will receive delegate messages. If the UIPanGestureRecognizer tries to declare success while the UILongPressGestureRecognizer's state is `.Failed` or still at `.Possible`, we prevent it. If the UILongPressGestureRecognizer succeeds, we permit the UIPanGestureRecognizer to operate as well:

```
func gestureRecognizerShouldBegin(g: UIGestureRecognizer) -> Bool {
    // g is the pan gesture recognizer
    var result = true
    switch self.longPresser.state {
    case .Possible, .Failed:
        result = false
    default: break
    }
    return result
}
func gestureRecognizer(g: UIGestureRecognizer,
    shouldRecognizeSimultaneouslyWithGestureRecognizer
    g2: UIGestureRecognizer) -> Bool {
        println("sim")
        return true
}
```

The result is that the view can be dragged only while it is pulsing; in effect, what we've done is to compensate, using delegate methods, for the fact that UIGestureRecognizer has no `requireGestureRecognizerToSucceed:` method.

If you are subclassing a gesture recognizer class, you can incorporate delegate-like behavior into the subclass, by overriding the following methods:

- `canPreventGestureRecognizer:`
- `canBePreventedByGestureRecognizer:`
- `shouldRequireFailureOfGestureRecognizer:`
- `shouldBeRequiredToFailByGestureRecognizer:`

The "Prevent" methods are similar to the delegate `shouldBegin:` method, and the "Fail" methods are similar to the delegate "Fail" methods. In this way, you can mediate gesture recognizer conflict at the class level. The built-in gesture recognizer subclasses already do this; that is why, for example, a single tap UITapGestureRecognizer does not, by recognizing its gesture, cause the failure of a double tap UITapGestureRecognizer.

You can also, in a gesture recognizer subclass, send `ignoreTouch:forEvent:` directly to a gesture recognizer (typically, to `self`). This has the same effect as the delegate method `gestureRecognizer:shouldReceiveTouch:` returning `false`, blocking all future delivery of that touch to the gesture recognizer. For example, if you're in the middle of an already recognized gesture and a new touch arrives, you might well elect to ignore it.

Gesture Recognizers in the Nib

Instead of instantiating a gesture recognizer in code, you can create and configure it in a *.xib* or *.storyboard* file. In the nib editor, drag a gesture recognizer from the Object library into a view; the gesture recognizer becomes a top-level nib object, and the view's `gestureRecognizers` outlet is connected to the gesture recognizer. (You can add more than one gesture recognizer to a view in the nib: the view's `gestureRecognizers` property is an array, and its `gestureRecognizers` outlet is an outlet collection.) The gesture recognizer's properties are configurable in the Attributes inspector, and the gesture recognizer has a `delegate` outlet. The gesture recognizer is a full-fledged nib object, so you can make an outlet to it.

To configure a gesture recognizer's target–action pair in the nib, treat it like a UIControl's control event. The action method's signature should be marked `@IBAction`, and it should take a single parameter, which will be a reference to the gesture recognizer. You will then be able to form the Sent Action connection in the usual way.

 A gesture recognizer can have multiple target–action pairs, but only one target–action pair can be configured for a gesture recognizer using the nib editor.

A view retains its gesture recognizers, so there will usually be no need for additional memory management on a gesture recognizer instantiated from a nib.

Touch Delivery

Here's the full standard procedure by which a touch is delivered to views and gesture recognizers:

- Whenever a new touch appears, the application uses hit-testing (see the next section) to determine the view that was touched. This view will be permanently associated with this touch, and is called, appropriately, the *hit-test view*. The logic of ignoring a view (denying it the ability to become the hit-test view) in response to its `userInteractionEnabled`, `hidden`, and `alpha` is implemented at this stage.

- Each time the touch situation changes, the application calls its own sendEvent:, which in turn calls the window's sendEvent:. The window delivers each of an event's touches by calling the appropriate touches... method(s), as follows:

  - As a touch first appears, the logic of obedience to multipleTouchEnabled and exclusiveTouch is considered. If permitted by that logic (which I'll discuss in detail later):

    - The touch is delivered to the hit-test view's swarm of gesture recognizers.

    - The touch is delivered to the hit-test view itself.

  - If a gesture is recognized by a gesture recognizer, then for any touch associated with this gesture recognizer:

    - touchesCancelled:forEvent: is sent to the touch's view, and the touch is no longer delivered to its view.

    - If that touch was associated with any other gesture recognizer, that gesture recognizer is forced to fail.

  - If a gesture recognizer fails, either because it declares failure or because it is forced to fail, its touches are no longer delivered to it, but (except as already specified) they continue to be delivered to their view.

  - If a touch would be delivered to a view, but that view does not respond to the appropriate touches... method, a responder further up the responder chain is sought that does respond to it, and the touch is delivered there.

The rest of this chapter discusses the details. As you'll see, nearly every bit of that standard procedure can be customized to some extent.

Hit-Testing

Hit-testing is the determination of what view the user touched. View hit-testing uses the UIView instance method hitTest:withEvent:, which returns either a view (the hit-test view) or nil. The idea is to find the frontmost view containing the touch point. This method uses an elegant recursive algorithm, as follows:

1. A view's hitTest:withEvent: first calls the same method on its own subviews, if it has any, because a subview is considered to be in front of its superview. The subviews are queried in reverse order, because that's front-to-back order (Chapter 1): thus, if two sibling views overlap, the one in front reports the hit first.

2. If, as a view hit-tests its subviews, any of those subviews responds by returning a view, it stops querying its subviews and immediately returns the view that was returned to it. Thus, the very first view to declare itself the hit-test view immediately percolates all the way to the top of the call chain and *is* the hit-test view.

3. If, on the other hand, a view has no subviews, or if all of its subviews return nil (indicating that neither they nor their subviews was hit), then the view calls `point-Inside:withEvent:` on itself. If this call reveals that the touch was inside this view, the view returns itself, declaring itself the hit-test view; otherwise it returns nil.

   No problem arises if a view has a transform, because `pointInside:withEvent:` takes the transform into account. That's why a rotated button continues to work correctly.

It is also up to `hitTest:withEvent:` to implement the logic of touch restrictions exclusive to a view. If a view's `userInteractionEnabled` is `false`, or its `hidden` is `true`, or its `alpha` is close to `0.0`, it returns nil without hit-testing any of its subviews and without calling `pointInside:withEvent:`. Thus these restrictions do not, of themselves, exclude a view from being hit-tested; on the contrary, they operate precisely by modifying a view's hit-test result.

However, hit-testing knows nothing about `multipleTouchEnabled` (which involves multiple touches) or `exclusiveTouch` (which involves multiple views). The logic of obedience to these properties is implemented at a later stage of the story.

You can use hit-testing yourself at any moment where it might prove useful. In calling `hitTest:withEvent:`, supply a point *in the coordinates of the view to which the message is sent*. The second parameter can be nil if you have no event.

For example, suppose we have a UIView with two UIImageView subviews. We want to detect a tap in either UIImageView, but we want to handle this at the level of the UIView. We can attach a UITapGestureRecognizer to the UIView, but then the gesture recognizer's `view` is the UIView, so how will we know which subview, if any, the tap was in?

First, verify that `userInteractionEnabled` is `true` for both UIImageViews. UIImageView is one of the few built-in view classes where this is `false` by default, and a view whose `userInteractionEnabled` is `false` won't normally be the result of a call to `hitTest:withEvent:`. Then, when our gesture recognizer's action handler is called, we can use hit-testing to determine where the tap was:

```
// g is the gesture recognizer
let p = g.locationOfTouch(0, inView: g.view)
let v = g.view!.hitTest(p, withEvent: nil)
if let v = v as? UIImageView { // ...
```

You can also override `hitTest:withEvent:` in a view subclass, to alter its results during touch delivery, thus customizing the touch delivery mechanism. I call this *hit-test munging*. Hit-test munging can be used selectively as a way of turning user interaction on or off in an area of the interface. In this way, some unusual effects can be produced.

An important use of hit-test munging is to permit the touching of parts of subviews outside the bounds of their superview. If a view's `clipsToBounds` is `false`, a paradox arises: the user can *see* the regions of its subviews that are outside its bounds, but can't *touch* them. This can be confusing and seems wrong. The solution is for the view to override `hitTest:withEvent:` as follows:

```
override func hitTest(point: CGPoint, withEvent e: UIEvent?) -> UIView? {
    if let result = super.hitTest(point, withEvent:e) {
        return result
    }
    for sub in self.subviews.reverse() as! [UIView] {
        let pt = self.convertPoint(point, toView:sub)
        if let result = sub.hitTest(pt, withEvent:e) {
            return result
        }
    }
    return nil
}
```

Hit-testing for layers

There is also hit-testing for layers. It doesn't happen automatically, as part of `sendEvent:` or anything else; it's up to you. It's just a convenient way of finding out which layer would receive a touch at a point, if layers received touches. To hit-test layers, call `hitTest:` on a layer, with a point *in superlayer coordinates*.

Keep in mind, though, that layers do *not* receive touches. A touch is reported to a view, not a layer. A layer, except insofar as it is a view's underlying layer and gets touch reporting because of its view, is completely untouchable; from the point of view of touches and touch reporting, it's as if the layer weren't on the screen at all. No matter where a layer may appear to be, a touch falls through the layer, to whatever view is behind it.

In the case of the layer that is a view's underlying layer, you don't need hit-testing. It is the view's drawing; where it appears is where the view is. So a touch in that layer is equivalent to a touch in its view. Indeed, one might say (and it is often said) that this is what views are actually for: to provide layers with touchability.

The only layers on which you'd need special hit-testing, then, would presumably be layers that are not themselves any view's underlying layer, because those are the only ones you don't find out about by normal view hit-testing. However, all layers, including a layer that is its view's underlying layer, are part of the layer hierarchy, and can participate in layer hit-testing. So the most comprehensive way to hit-test layers is to start with the topmost layer, the window's layer. In this example, we subclass UIWindow (see Chapter 1) and override its `hitTest:withEvent:` so as to get layer hit-testing every time there is view hit-testing:

```
override func hitTest(point: CGPoint, withEvent e: UIEvent?) -> UIView? {
    let lay = self.layer.hitTest(point)
    // ... possibly do something with that information
    return super.hitTest(point, withEvent:e)
}
```

In that example, the view hit-test point works as the layer hit-test point; window bounds are screen bounds (Chapter 1). But usually you'll have to convert to superlayer coordinates. In this next example, we return to the CompassView developed in Chapter 3, in which all the parts of the compass are layers; we want to know whether the user tapped on the arrow layer. For simplicity, we've given the CompassView a UITapGesture-Recognizer, and this is its action handler, in the CompassView itself. We convert to our superview's coordinates, because these are also our layer's superlayer coordinates:

```
@IBAction func tapped(t:UITapGestureRecognizer) {
    let p = t.locationOfTouch(0, inView: self.superview)
    let hitLayer = self.layer.hitTest(p)
    let arrow = (self.layer as! CompassLayer).arrow
    if hitLayer !== nil && hitLayer == arrow { // respond to touch
        arrow.transform = CATransform3DRotate(
            arrow.transform, CGFloat(M_PI)/4.0, 0, 0, 1)
    }
}
```

Layer hit-testing knows nothing of the restrictions on touch delivery; it just reports on every sublayer, even one whose view (for example) has userInteractionEnabled set to false.

 The documentation warns that hitTest: must not be called on a CATransform-Layer.

Hit-testing for drawings

The preceding example (letting the user tap on the compass arrow) worked, but we might complain that it is reporting a hit on the arrow even if the hit misses the *drawing* of the arrow. That's true for view hit-testing as well. A hit is reported if we are within the view or layer as a whole; hit-testing knows nothing of drawing, transparent areas, and so forth.

If you know how the region is drawn and can reproduce the edge of that drawing as a CGPath, you can test whether a point is inside it with CGPathContainsPoint. So, in our compass layer, we could override hitTest along these lines:

```
override func hitTest(p: CGPoint) -> CALayer! {
    var lay = super.hitTest(p)
    if lay == self.arrow {
        // artificially restrict touchability to roughly the arrow area
        let pt = self.arrow.convertPoint(p, fromLayer:self.superlayer)
        let path = CGPathCreateMutable()
        CGPathAddRect(path, nil, CGRectMake(10,20,20,80))
        CGPathMoveToPoint(path, nil, 0, 25)
        CGPathAddLineToPoint(path, nil, 20, 0)
        CGPathAddLineToPoint(path, nil, 40, 25)
        CGPathCloseSubpath(path)
```

```
            if !CGPathContainsPoint(path, nil, pt, false) {
                lay = nil;
            }
        }
        return lay
    }
```

(Layer hit-testing works by calling containsPoint:. However, containsPoint: takes a point in the layer's coordinates, so to hand it a point that arrives through hitTest: we must first convert from superlayer coordinates.)

Alternatively, it might be the case that if a pixel of the drawing is transparent, it's outside the drawn region, so that it suffices to detect whether the pixel tapped is transparent. Unfortunately, there's no way to ask a drawing (or a view, or a layer) for the color of a pixel; you have to make a bitmap and copy the drawing into it, and then ask the bitmap for the color of a pixel. If you can reproduce the content as an image, and all you care about is transparency, you can make a one-pixel alpha-only bitmap, draw the image in such a way that the pixel you want to test is the pixel drawn into the bitmap, and examine the transparency of the resulting pixel:

```
// assume im is a UIImage, point is the CGPoint to test
let info - CGBitmapInfo(CGImageAlphaInfo.Only.rawValue)
let pixel = UnsafeMutablePointer<CUnsignedChar>.alloc(1)
pixel[0] = 0
let context = CGBitmapContextCreate(pixel,
    1, 1, 8, 1, nil, info)
UIGraphicsPushContext(context)
im.drawAtPoint(CGPointMake(-point.x, -point.y))
UIGraphicsPopContext()
let p = pixel[0]
let alpha = Double(p)/255.0
let transparent = alpha < 0.01
```

However, there may not be a one-to-one relationship between the pixels of the underlying drawing and the points of the drawing as portrayed on the screen — because the drawing is stretched, for example. In many cases, the CALayer method renderIn-Context: can be helpful here. This method allows you to copy a layer's actual drawing into a context of your choice. If that context is, say, an image context created with UIGraphicsBeginImageContextWithOptions, you can now use the resulting image as im in the code above:

```
UIGraphicsBeginImageContextWithOptions(self.bounds.size, false, 0)
let lay = // ... the layer whose drawing we're interested in
lay.renderInContext(UIGraphicsGetCurrentContext())
let im = UIGraphicsGetImageFromCurrentImageContext()
UIGraphicsEndImageContext()
```

Hit-testing during animation

The simplest solution to the problem of touch during animation is to disallow it entirely. By default, view animation turns off touchability of a view while it's being animated (though you can prevent that with `.AllowUserInteraction` in the `options:` argument), and you can temporarily turn off touchability altogether with UIApplication's `begin-IgnoringInteractionEvents`, as I mentioned earlier in this chapter.

If user interaction is allowed during an animation that moves a view from one place to another, then if the user taps on the animated view, the tap might mysteriously fail because the view (the model layer) is elsewhere; conversely, the user might accidentally tap where the view actually is, and the tap will hit the animated view even though it appears to be elsewhere. If the position of a view or layer is being animated and you want the user to be able to tap on it, therefore, you'll need to *hit-test the presentation layer*.

In this simple example, we have a superview containing a subview. To allow the user to tap on the subview even when it is being animated, we implement hit-test munging in the subview:

```
override func hitTest(point: CGPoint, withEvent e: UIEvent?) -> UIView? {
    let pres = self.layer.presentationLayer() as! CALayer
    let suppt = self.convertPoint(point, toView: self.superview!)
    let prespt = self.superview!.layer.convertPoint(suppt, toLayer: pres)
    return super.hitTest(prespt, withEvent: e)
}
```

However, as Apple puts it in the WWDC 2011 videos, the animated view "swallows the touch." For example, suppose the view in motion is a button. Although our hit-test munging makes it possible for the user to tap the button as it is being animated, and although the user sees the button highlight in response, the button's action message is not sent in response to this highlighting if the animation is in-flight when the tap takes place. This behavior seems unfortunate, but it's generally possible to work around it (for instance, with a gesture recognizer).

Initial Touch Event Delivery

When the touch situation changes, an event containing all touches is handed to the UIApplication instance by calling its `sendEvent:`, and the UIApplication in turn hands it to the relevant UIWindow by calling *its* `sendEvent:`. The UIWindow then performs the complicated logic of examining, for every touch, the hit-test view and its superviews and their gesture recognizers and deciding which of them should be sent a `touches...` message, and does so.

You can override `sendEvent:` in a subclass of UIWindow or UIApplication (this is, indeed, just about the *only* reason you might have for subclassing UIApplication). These are delicate and crucial maneuvers, however, and you wouldn't want to lame your application by interfering with them. Moreover, it is unlikely, nowadays, that you would need to resort to such measures. A typical case before the advent of gesture recognizers was that you needed to detect touches directed to an object of some built-in interface class in a way that subclassing it wouldn't permit. For example, you want to know when the user swipes a UIWebView; you're not allowed to subclass UIWebView, and in any case it eats the touch. The solution used to be to subclass UIWindow and override `send-Event:`; you would then work out whether this was a swipe on the UIWebView and respond accordingly, or else call `super`. Now, however, you can attach a UISwipeGestureRecognizer to the UIWebView.

Gesture Recognizer and View

When a touch first appears and is delivered to a gesture recognizer, it is also delivered to its hit-test view, the same `touches...` method being called on both. Later, if a gesture recognizer in a view's swarm recognizes its gesture, that view is sent `touchesCancelled:withEvent:` for any touches that went to that gesture recognizer and were hit-tested to that view, and subsequently the view no longer receives those touches.

This comes as a surprise to beginners, but it is the most reasonable approach, as it means that touch interpretation by a view isn't jettisoned just because gesture recognizers are in the picture. Later on in the multitouch sequence, if all the gesture recognizers in a view's swarm declare failure to recognize their gesture, that view's internal touch interpretation just proceeds as if gesture recognizers had never been invented.

Moreover, touches and gestures are two different things; sometimes you want to respond to both. In one of my apps, where the user can tap cards, each card has a single tap gesture recognizer and a double tap gesture recognizer, but it also responds directly to `touchesBegan:withEvent:` by reducing its own opacity (and restores its opacity on `touchesEnded:withEvent:` and `touchesCancelled:withEvent:`). The result is that the user always sees feedback when touching a card, *instantly*, regardless of what the gesture turns out to be.

This behavior can be changed by setting a gesture recognizer's `cancelsTouchesInView` property to `false`. If this is the case for every gesture recognizer in a view's swarm, the view will receive touch events more or less as if no gesture recognizers were in the picture.

If a gesture recognizer happens to be ignoring a touch (because, for example, it was told to do so by `ignoreTouch:forEvent:`), then `touchesCancelled:withEvent:` *won't* be sent to the view for that touch when that gesture recognizer recognizes its gesture. Thus, a gesture recognizer's ignoring a touch is the same as simply letting it fall through to the view, as if the gesture recognizer weren't there.

Gesture recognizers can also *delay* the delivery of touches to a view, and by default they do. The UIGestureRecognizer property `delaysTouchesEnded` is `true` by default, meaning that when a touch reaches `.Ended` and the gesture recognizer's `touchesEnded:with-Event:` is called, if the gesture recognizer is still allowing touches to be delivered to the view because its state is still `.Possible`, it doesn't deliver this touch until it has resolved the gesture. When it does, either it will recognize the gesture, in which case the view will have `touchesCancelled:withEvent:` called instead (as already explained), or it will declare failure and *now* the view will have `touchesEnded:withEvent:` called.

The reason for this behavior is most obvious with a gesture where multiple taps are required. The first tap ends, but this is insufficient for the gesture recognizer to declare success or failure, so it withholds that touch from the view. In this way, the gesture recognizer gets the proper priority. In particular, if there is a second tap, the gesture recognizer should succeed and send `touchesCancelled:withEvent:` to the view — but it can't do that if the view has already been sent `touchesEnded:withEvent:`.

It is also possible to delay the entire suite of `touches...` methods from being called on a view, by setting a gesture recognizer's `delaysTouchesBegan` property to `true`. Again, this delay would be until the gesture recognizer can resolve the gesture: either it will recognize it, in which case the view will have `touchesCancelled:withEvent:` called, or it will declare failure, in which case the view will receive `touchesBegan:withEvent:` plus any further `touches...` calls that were withheld — except that it will receive *at most* one `touchesMoved:withEvent:` call, the last one, because if a lot of these were withheld, to queue them all up and send them all at once now would be simply insane.

It is unlikely that you'll change a gesture recognizer's `delaysTouchesBegan` property to `true`, however. You might do so, for example, if you have an elaborate touch analysis within a view that simply cannot operate simultaneously with a gesture recognizer, but this is improbable, and the latency involved may look strange to your user.

When touches are delayed and then delivered, what's delivered is the original touch with the original event, which still have their original timestamps. Because of the delay, these timestamps may differ significantly from now. For this reason (and many others), Apple warns that touch analysis that is concerned with timing should always look at the timestamp, not the clock.

Touch Exclusion Logic

It is up to the UIWindow's `sendEvent:` to implement the logic of `multipleTouch-Enabled` and `exclusiveTouch`.

If a new touch is hit-tested to a view whose `multipleTouchEnabled` is `false` and which already has an existing touch hit-tested to it, then `sendEvent:` never delivers the new touch to that view. However, that touch *is* delivered to the view's swarm of gesture recognizers.

Similarly, if there's an `exclusiveTouch` view in the window, then `sendEvent:` must decide whether a particular touch should be delivered, in accordance with the meaning of `exclusiveTouch`, which I described earlier. If a touch is not delivered to a view because of `exclusiveTouch` restrictions, it is *not* delivered to its swarm of gesture recognizers either.

The logic of touch delivery to gesture recognizers in response to `exclusiveTouch` has changed in a confusing and possibly buggy way from system to system, but I believe I'm describing it correctly for the current system. The statement in Apple's Simple Gesture Recognizers sample code that "recognizers ignore the exclusive touch setting for views" probably dates back to an earlier implementation; it appears to be flat-out false nowadays. Apple's comment continues: "This is so that they can consistently recognize gestures even if they cross other views. For example, suppose you had two buttons, each marked exclusive touch, and you added a pinch gesture recognizer to their superview. That a finger came down in one of the buttons shouldn't prevent you from pinching in the general case." That's a good argument for how things *should* work, but it isn't how things *actually* work: a test project implementing that thought-experiment proves that if the buttons are "marked exclusive touch," that *does* "prevent you from pinching."

Gesture Recognition Logic

When a gesture recognizer recognizes its gesture, everything changes. As we've already seen, the touches for this gesture recognizer are sent to their hit-test views as a `touchesCancelled:forEvent:` message, and then no longer arrive at those views (unless the gesture recognizer's `cancelsTouchesInView` is `false`). Moreover, all other gesture recognizers pending with regard to these touches are made to fail, and then are no longer sent the touches they were receiving either.

If the very same event would cause more than one gesture recognizer to recognize, there's an algorithm for picking the one that will succeed and make the others fail: a gesture recognizer lower down the view hierarchy (closer to the hit-test view) prevails over one higher up the hierarchy, and a gesture recognizer more recently added to its view prevails over one less recently added.

There are various means for modifying this "first past the post" behavior:

Dependency order

Certain methods institute a dependency order, causing a gesture recognizer to be put on hold when it tries to transition from the `.Possible` state to the `.Began` (continuous) or `.Ended` (discrete) state; only if a certain other gesture recognizer fails is this one permitted to perform that transition. Apple says that in a dependency like this, the gesture recognizer that fails first is not sent `reset` (and won't receive any touches) until the second finishes its state sequence and is sent `reset`, so that they resume recognizing together. The methods are:

- `requireGestureRecognizerToFail:` (sent to a gesture recognizer)
- `shouldRequireFailureOfGestureRecognizer:` (overridden in a subclass)
- `shouldBeRequiredToFailByGestureRecognizer:` (overridden in a subclass)
- `gestureRecognizer:shouldRequireFailureOfGestureRecognizer:` (implemented by the delegate)
- `gestureRecognizer:shouldBeRequiredToFailByGestureRecognizer:` (implemented by the delegate)

The first of those methods sets up a permanent relationship between two gesture recognizers, and cannot be undone; but the others are sent every time a gesture starts in a view whose swarm includes both gesture recognizers, and each applies only on this occasion.

The delegate methods work together as follows. For each pair of gesture recognizers in the hit-test view's swarm, the members of that pair are arranged in a fixed order (as I've already described). The first of the pair is sent `shouldRequire` and then `shouldBeRequired`, and then the second of the pair is sent `shouldRequire` and then `shouldBeRequired`. But if any of those four methods returns `true`, the relationship between that pair is settled; the sequence stops (and we proceed to the next pair).

Success into failure

Certain methods, by returning `false`, turn success into failure; at the moment when the gesture recognizer is about to declare that it recognizes its gesture, transitioning from the `.Possible` state to the `.Began` (continuous) or `.Ended` (discrete) state, it is forced to fail instead:

- UIView's `gestureRecognizerShouldBegin:`
- The delegate's `gestureRecognizerShouldBegin:`

Simultaneous recognition

A gesture recognizer succeeds, but some other gesture recognizer is *not* forced to fail, in accordance with these methods:

- `gestureRecognizer:shouldRecognizeSimultaneouslyWithGestureRecognizer:` (implemented by the delegate)
- `canPreventGestureRecognizer:` (overridden in a subclass)
- `canBePreventedByGestureRecognizer:` (overridden in a subclass)

In the subclass methods, "prevent" means "by succeeding, you force failure upon this other," and "be prevented" means "by succeeding, this other forces failure on you." They work together as follows. `canPreventGestureRecognizer:` is called first; if it returns `false`, that's the end of the story for that gesture recognizer, and `canPreventGestureRecognizer:` is called on the other gesture recognizer. But if `canPreventGestureRecognizer:` returns `true` when it is first called, the other gesture recognizer is sent `canBePreventedByGestureRecognizer:`. If it returns `true`, that's the end of the story; if it returns `false`, the process starts over the other way around, sending `canPreventGestureRecognizer:` to the second gesture recognizer, and so forth. In this way, conflicting answers are resolved without the device exploding: prevention is regarded as exceptional (even though it is in fact the norm) and will happen only if it is acquiesced to by everyone involved.

Touches and the Responder Chain

A UIView is a responder, and participates in the responder chain. In particular, if a touch is to be delivered to a UIView (because, for example, it's the hit-test view) and that view doesn't implement the relevant `touches...` method, a walk up the responder chain is performed, looking for a responder that *does* implement it; if such a responder is found, the touch is delivered to that responder. Moreover, the default implementation of the `touches...` methods — the behavior that you get if you call `super` — is to perform the same walk up the responder chain, starting with the next responder in the chain.

The relationship between touch delivery and the responder chain can be useful, but you must be careful not to allow it to develop into an incoherency. For example, if `touchesBegan:withEvent:` is implemented in a superview but not in a subview, then a touch to the subview will result in the superview's `touchesBegan:withEvent:` being called, with the first parameter (the touches) containing a touch whose `view` is the subview. But most UIView implementations of the `touches...` methods rely upon the assumption that the first parameter consists of all and only touches whose `view` is `self`; built-in UIView subclasses certainly assume this.

Again, if `touchesBegan:withEvent:` is implemented in both a superview and a subview, and you call `super` in the subview's implementation, passing along the same arguments that came in, then the same touch delivered to the subview will trigger both the subview's `touchesBegan:withEvent:` and the superview's `touchesBegan:withEvent:` (and once again the first parameter to the superview's `touchesBegan:withEvent:` will contain a touch whose `view` is the subview).

The solution is to behave rationally, as follows:

- If all the responders in the affected part of the responder chain are instances of your own subclass of UIView itself or of your own subclass of UIViewController, you will generally want to follow the simplest possible rule: implement *all* the `touches...` events together in one class, so that touches arrive at an instance either because it was the hit-test view or because it is up the responder chain from the hit-test view, and do *not* call `super` in any of them. In this way, "the buck stops here"

— the touch handling for this object or for objects below it in the responder chain is bottlenecked into one well-defined place.

- If you subclass a built-in UIView subclass and you override its touch handling, you don't have to override every single touches... event, but you *do* need to call super so that the built-in touch handling can occur.

- Don't allow touches to arrive from lower down the responder chain at an instance of a built-in UIView subclass that implements built-in touch handling, because such a class is completely unprepared for the first parameter of a touches... method containing a touch not intended for itself. Judicious use of userInteraction-Enabled or hit-test munging can be a big help here.

I'm not saying, however, that you have to block all touches from percolating up the responder chain; it's normal for unhandled touches to arrive at the UIWindow or UIApplication, for example, because these classes do not (by default) do any touch handling — so those touches will remain unhandled and will percolate right off the end of the responder chain, which is perfectly fine.

- Never call a touches... method directly (except to call super).

 Apple's documentation has some discussion of a technique called *event forwarding* where you *do* call touches... methods directly. But you are far less likely to need this now that gesture recognizers exist, and it can be extremely tricky and even downright dangerous to implement, so I won't give an example, and I suggest that you not use it.

PART II

Interface

This part of the book is about view controllers, and about all the various kinds of view provided by the Cocoa framework — the built-in building blocks with which you'll construct an app's interface.

- Chapter 6 is about view controllers, the fundamental iOS mechanism for allowing an entire interface to be replaced by another. Every app you write will have its interface managed by at least one view controller.

- Chapter 7 is about scroll views, the iOS mechanism for letting the user scroll and zoom the interface.

- Chapter 8 explains table views, a type of scroll view that lets the user navigate through any amount of data, along with collection views, a generalization of table views.

- Chapter 9 is about two forms of interface especially characteristic of the iPad — popovers and split views.

- Chapter 10 describes several ways of presenting text (including styled text) in an app's interface — labels, text fields, text views, and text drawn directly.

- Chapter 11 discusses web views. A web view is an easy-to-use interface object backed by the power of a full-fledged web browser.

- Chapter 12 describes all the remaining built-in iOS (UIKit) interface objects.

- Chapter 13 is about the forms of modal dialog that can appear in front of an app's interface.

CHAPTER 6

View Controllers

An iOS app's interface is dynamic, and with good reason. On the desktop, an application's windows can be big, and there can be more than one of them, so there's room for lots of interface. With iOS, everything needs to fit on a single display consisting of a single window, which in the case of the iPhone can be almost forbiddingly tiny. The iOS solution is to introduce, at will, completely new interface — a new view, possibly with an elaborate hierarchy of subviews — replacing or covering the previous interface.

For this to work, regions of interface material — often the entire contents of the screen — must come and go in an agile fashion that is understandable to the user. There will typically be a logical, structural, and functional relationship between the view that was present and the view that replaces or covers it, and this relationship will need to be maintained behind the scenes, in your code, as well as being indicated to the user: multiple views may be pure alternatives or siblings of one another, or one view may be a temporary replacement for another, or views may be like successive pages of a book. Animation is often used to emphasize and clarify these relationships as one view is superseded by another. Navigational interface and a vivid, suggestive gestural vocabulary give the user an ability to control what's seen and an understanding of the possible options: a tab bar whose buttons summon alternate views, a back button or a swipe gesture for returning to a previously visited view, a tap on an interface element to dive deeper into a conceptual world, a Done or Cancel button to escape from a settings screen, and so forth.

In iOS, the management of this dynamic interface is performed through view controllers. A *view controller* is an instance of UIViewController. Actually, a view controller is most likely to be an instance of a UIViewController subclass; the UIViewController class is designed to be subclassed, and you are very unlikely to use a plain vanilla UIViewController object without subclassing it. You might write your own UIViewController subclass; you might use a built-in UIViewController subclass such as

UINavigationController or UITabBarController; or you might subclass a built-in UIViewController subclass such as UITableViewController (Chapter 8).

A view controller manages a single view (which can, of course, have subviews); its `view` property points to the view it manages. This is the view controller's *main view*, or simply its view. A view controller's main view has no explicit pointer to the view controller that manages it, but a view controller is a UIResponder and is in the responder chain just above its view, so it is the view's `nextResponder`.

View Controller Responsibilities

A view controller's most important responsibility is its view. A view controller must have a view (it is useless without one). If that view is to be useful, it must somehow *get into the interface*, and hence onto the screen; a view controller is usually responsible for seeing to that, too, but typically *not* the view controller whose view this is; rather, this will be taken care of by some view controller whose view is *already* in the interface. In many cases, this will happen automatically (I'll talk more about that in the next section), but you can participate in the process, and for some view controllers you may have to do the work yourself. The reverse is also true: a view that comes may also eventually go, and the view controller responsible for putting a view into the interface will also be responsible for removing it.

A view controller will also typically provide *animation* of the interface as a view comes or goes. Built-in view controller subclasses and built-in ways of summoning or removing a view controller and its view come with built-in animations. We are all familiar, for example, with tapping something to make new interface slide in from the right, and then tapping a back button to make that interface slide back out to the right. In cases where you are responsible for getting a view controller's view onto the screen, you are also responsible for providing the animation. And you can take complete charge of the animation even for built-in view controllers.

View controllers, working together, can *save and restore state* automatically. This feature helps you ensure that if your app is terminated in the background and subsequently relaunched, it will quickly resume displaying the same interface that was showing when the user last saw it.

The most powerful view controller is the *root view controller*. This is the view controller managing the view that sits at the top of the view hierarchy, as the one and only direct subview of the main window, acting as the superview for all other interface (the *root view*). I described in Chapter 1 how this view controller attains its lofty position: it is assigned to the window's `rootViewController` property. The window then takes that view controller's main view, gives it the correct frame (resizing it if necessary), and makes it its own subview. The root view controller bears ultimate responsibility for two important decisions about the behavior of your app:

Rotation of the interface

The user can rotate the device, and you might like the interface to rotate in response, to compensate. This decision is made, in large part, by the root view controller.

Manipulation of the status bar

The status bar is actually a secondary window belonging to the runtime, but the runtime consults the root view controller as to whether the status bar should be present and, if so, whether its text should be light or dark.

Finally, above and beyond all this, view controllers are typically the heart of any app, by virtue of their role in the model–view–controller architecture: view controllers are *controllers* (hence the name). Views give the user something to tap, and display data for the user to see; they are *view*. The data itself is *model*. But the logic of determining, at any given moment, *what* views are shown, *what* data those views display, and *what* the response to the user's gestures should be, is *controller* logic. Typically, that means view controller logic. In any app, view controllers will be the most important controllers — frequently, in fact, the only controllers. View controllers are where you'll put the bulk of the code that actually makes your app do what your app does.

View Controller Hierarchy

As I said in the previous section, there is always one root view controller, along with its view, the root view. There may also be other view controllers, each of which has its own main view. Such view controllers are *subordinate* to the root view controller. In iOS, there are two subordination relationships between view controllers:

Parentage (containment)

A view controller can *contain* another view controller. The containing view controller is the *parent* of the contained view controller; the contained view controller is a *child* of the containing view controller. A containment relationship between two view controllers is reflected in their views: the child view controller's view, if it is in the interface at all, is a *subview* of the parent view controller's view. ("Subview" here means "subview at some depth.")

Replacement of one view with another often involves a parent view controller managing its children and their views. The parent view controller is responsible for getting a child view controller's view into the interface, by making it a subview of its own view, and (if necessary) for removing it later.

A familiar example is the navigation interface: the user taps something and new interface slides in from the right, replacing the current interface. Figure 6-1 shows the TidBITS News app displaying a typical iPhone interface, consisting of a list of story headlines and summaries. This interface is managed by a parent view controller (a UINavigationController) with a child view controller whose view is the list of headlines and summaries. If the user taps an entry in the list, the whole list

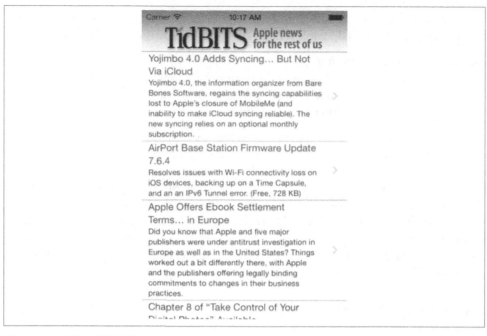

Figure 6-1. The TidBITS News app

will slide away to the left and the text of that story will slide in from the right; the parent view controller has added a new child view controller, and has manipulated the views of its children to bring about this animated change of the interface. The parent view controller itself, meanwhile, stays put — and so does its own view. (In this example, the UINavigationController is the root view controller, and its view is the root view.)

Presentation (modal views)

A view controller can *present* another view controller. The first view controller is the *presenting* view controller (not the parent) of the second; the second view controller is the *presented* view controller (not a child) of the first. The second view controller's view replaces or covers, completely or partially, the first view controller's view.

The name of this mechanism, and of the relationship between the view controllers involved, has changed over time. In iOS 4 and before, the presented view controller was called a *modal view controller*, and its view was a *modal view*; there is an analogy here to the desktop, where a window is modal if it sits in front of, and denies the user access to, the rest of the interface until it is explicitly dismissed. The terms *presented view controller* and *presented view* are more recent and more general, but the historical term "modal" still appears in the documentation and in the API.

A presented view controller's view does indeed sometimes look rather like a desktop modal view; for example, it might have a button such as Done or Save for dismissing the view, the implication being that this is a place where the user must make a decision and can do nothing else until the decision is made. However, as I'll explain later, that isn't the only use of a presented view controller.

There is thus a *hierarchy of view controllers*. In a properly constructed iOS app, there should be exactly one root view controller, and it is the *only* nonsubordinate view controller — it has neither a parent view controller nor a presenting view controller. Any other view controller, if its view appears in the interface, *must* be a child view controller of some parent view controller or a presented view controller of some presenting view controller — and that view controller's *view* must be a subview of that parent or presenting view controller's view. In this way, the actual views of the interface form a hierarchy dictated by *and parallel to* some portion of the view controller hierarchy: *every* view visible in the interface owes its presence to a view controller's view, either it because it *is* a view controller's view, or because it's a subview of a view controller's view.

The place of a view controller's view in the view hierarchy will often be automatic. You might never need to put a UIViewController's view into the view hierarchy manually. You'll manipulate view controllers; their hierarchy and their built-in functionality will construct and manage the view hierarchy for you.

For example, in Figure 6-1, we see two interface elements:

- The navigation bar, containing the TidBITS logo.
- The list of stories, which is actually a UITableView.

I will describe how all of this comes to appear on the screen through the view controller hierarchy and the view hierarchy (Figure 6-2):

- The app's root view controller is a UINavigationController; the UINavigationController's view is the window's sole immediate subview (the root view). The navigation bar is a subview of that view.
- The UINavigationController contains a second UIViewController — a parent–child relationship. The child is a custom UIViewController subclass; *its* view is what occupies the rest of the window, as another subview of the UINavigationController's view. That view is the UITableView. This architecture means that when the user taps a story listing in the UITableView, the whole table will slide out, to be replaced by the view of a different UIViewController, while the navigation bar stays.

In Figure 6-2, notice the word "automatic" in the two large right-pointing arrows associating a view controller with its view. This is intended to tell you how the view controller's view became part of the view hierarchy. The UINavigationController's view became the window's subview automatically, by virtue of the UINavigationController

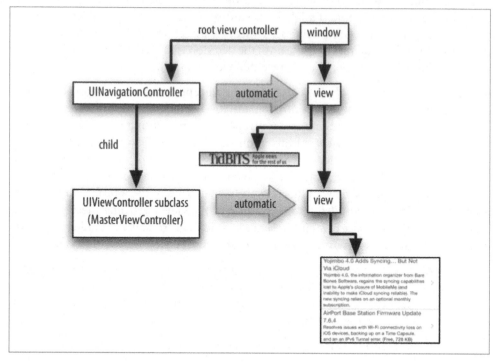

Figure 6-2. The TidBITS News app's initial view controller and view hierarchy

being the window's `rootViewController`. The custom UIViewController's view became the UINavigationController's view's subview automatically, by virtue of the UIView-Controller being the UINavigationController's child.

Sometimes, you'll write your own parent view controller class. In that case, *you* will be doing the kind of work that the UINavigationController was doing in that example, so you will need to put a child view controller's view into the interface *manually*, as a subview (at some depth) of the parent view controller's view.

I'll illustrate with another app of mine (Figure 6-3). The interface displays a flashcard containing information about a Latin word, along with a toolbar (the dark area at the bottom) where the user can tap an icon to choose additional functionality.

Again, I will describe how the interface shown in Figure 6-3 comes to appear on the screen through the view controller hierarchy and the view hierarchy (Figure 6-4). The app actually contains over a thousand of these Latin words, and I want the user to be able to navigate between flashcards to see the next or previous word; there is an excellent built-in view controller for this purpose, the UIPageViewController. However, that's just for the card; the toolbar at the bottom stays there, so the toolbar can't be inside the UIPageViewController's view. Therefore:

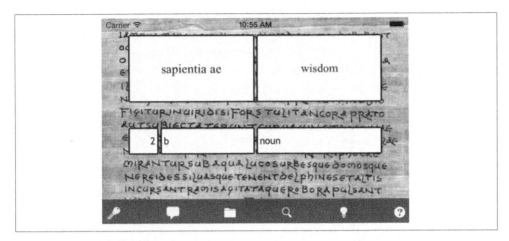

Figure 6-3. A Latin flashcard app

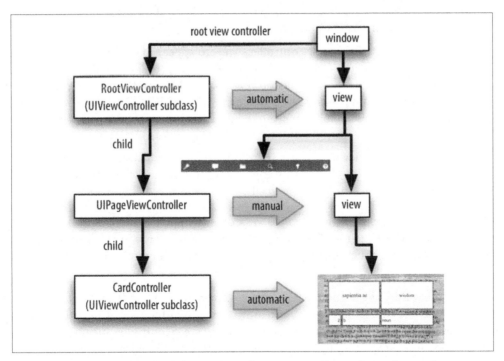

Figure 6-4. The Latin flashcard app's initial view controller and view hierarchy

- The app's root view controller is my own UIViewController subclass, which I call RootViewController; its view contains the toolbar, and is also to contain the UIPageViewController's view. My RootViewController's view becomes the win-

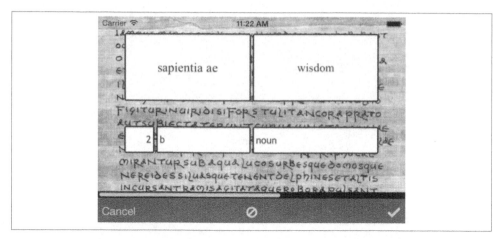

Figure 6-5. The Latin flashcard app, in drill mode

dow's subview (the root view) automatically, by virtue of the RootViewController's being the window's `rootViewController`.

- In order for the UIPageViewController's view to appear in the interface, since it is not the root view controller, it *must* be some view controller's child. There is only one possible parent — my RootViewController. My RootViewController must function as a custom parent view controller, with the UIPageViewController as its child. So I have made that happen, and I have therefore also had to put the UIPage-ViewController's view *manually* into my RootViewController's view.

- I hand the UIPageViewController an instance of my CardController class (another UIViewController subclass) as its child, and the UIPageViewController displays the CardController's view automatically.

Finally, here's an example of a presented view controller. My Latin flashcard app has a second mode, where the user is drilled on a subset of the cards in random order; the interface looks very much like the first mode's interface (Figure 6-5), but it behaves completely differently.

To implement this, I have another UIViewController subclass, DrillViewController; it is structured very much like RootViewController. When the user is in drill mode, a DrillViewController is being *presented* by the RootViewController, meaning that the DrillViewController's interface takes over the screen automatically: the DrillView-Controller's view, with its whole subview hierarchy, including the views of the Drill-ViewController's children in the view controller hierarchy, replaces the RootView-Controller's view and *its* whole subview hierarchy (Figure 6-6). The RootViewController and its hierarchy of child view controllers remains in place, but the corresponding view hierarchy is not in the interface; it will be returned to the interface automatically when

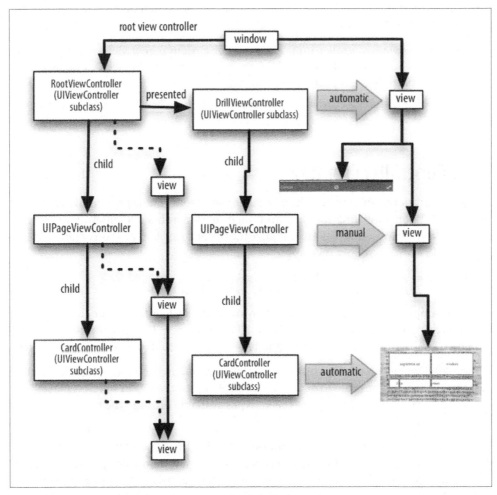

Figure 6-6. The Latin flashcard app's drill mode view controller and view hierarchy

we leave drill mode (because the presented DrillViewController is dismissed), and the situation will look like Figure 6-4 once again.

For any app that you write, you should be able to construct a diagram showing the hierarchy of view controllers and charting how each view controller's view fits into the view hierarchy. The diagram should be similar to mine! The view hierarchy should run neatly parallel with the view controller hierarchy; there should be no crossed wires or orphan views. And every view controller's view should be placed automatically into the view hierarchy, unless you have written your own parent view controller.

Do *not* put a view controller's view into the interface manually, unless one of the following is the case:

- The view controller is the child of your custom parent view controller. There is a complicated parent–child dance you have to do. See "Container View Controllers" on page 337.

- You're doing a custom transition animation. See "Custom Transition" on page 313.

View Controller Creation

A view controller is an instance like any other instance, and it is created like any other instance — by instantiating its class. You might perform this instantiation in code; in that case, you will of course have to initialize the instance properly as you create it. Here's an example from one of my own apps:

```
let llc = LessonListController(terms: self.data)
let nav = UINavigationController(rootViewController:llc)
```

In that example, LessonListController is my own UIViewController subclass, so I have called its designated initializer, which I myself have defined; UINavigationController is a built-in UIViewController subclass, and I have used one of its convenience initializers.

Alternatively, a view controller instance might come into existence through the loading of a nib. To make it possible to get a view controller into the nib in the first place, view controllers are included among the object types available through the Object library in the nib editor.

It is legal, though in practice not common, for a *.xib* file to contain a view controller. A *.storyboard* file, on the other hand, is chock full of view controllers; view controllers are the basis of a storyboard's structure, with each scene consisting of and corresponding to one view controller object. A view controller in a storyboard will go into a nib file in the built app, and that nib file will be loaded when the view controller instance is needed. Usually, that happens automatically. Nevertheless, a view controller in a storyboard is an ordinary nib object and, if it is to be used in the running app, will be instantiated through the loading of the nib just like any other nib object. I'll give full details on how and why a view controller is instantiated from a storyboard later in this chapter.

Once a view controller comes into existence, it must be retained so that it will persist. This will happen automatically when the view controller is assigned a place in the view controller hierarchy that I described in the previous section. A view controller assigned as a window's rootViewController is retained by the window. A view controller assigned as another view controller's child is retained by that other view controller (the parent). A presented view controller is retained by the presenting view controller. The parent view controller or presenting view controller then takes ownership, and will release the other view controller in good order when it is no longer needed.

Here's an example, from one of my apps, of view controllers being instantiated and then being retained by being placed into the view controller hierarchy:

```
let llc = LessonListController(terms: self.data) ❶
let nav = UINavigationController(rootViewController:llc) ❷
self.presentViewController(nav, animated:true, completion:nil) ❸
```

That's the same code I showed a moment ago, extended by one line. It comes from a view controller class called RootViewController. Here's how view controller creation and memory management works in those three lines:

❶ I instantiate LessonListController.

❷ I instantiate UINavigationController, and I assign the LessonListController instance to the UINavigationController instance as its child; the UINavigationController retains the LessonListController instance and takes ownership of it.

❸ I present the UINavigationController instance on `self`, a RootViewController instance; the RootViewController instance is the presenting view controller, and it retains and takes ownership of the UINavigationController instance as its presented view controller. The RootViewController instance itself is already the window's `rootViewController`, and is retained by the window — and so the view controller hierarchy is safely established.

All of this sounds straightforward, but it is worth dwelling on, because things can go wrong. It is quite possible, if things are mismanaged, for a view controller's view to get into the interface while the view controller itself is allowed to go out of existence. *This must not be permitted.* If such a thing happens, at the very least the view will apparently misbehave, failing to perform its intended functionality, because that functionality is embodied by the view controller, which no longer exists. (I've made this mistake, so I speak from experience here.) If you instantiate a view controller in code, you should immediately ask yourself who will be retaining this view controller.

If a view controller is instantiated automatically from a storyboard, on the other hand, it will be retained automatically. That isn't magic, however; it's done in exactly the same ways I just listed — by assigning it as the window's `rootViewController`, or by making it another view controller's child view controller or presented view controller.

How a View Controller Gets Its View

Initially, when it first comes into existence, a view controller has no view. A view controller is a small, lightweight object; a view is a relatively heavyweight object, involving interface elements that occupy memory. Therefore, a view controller postpones obtaining its view until it has to do so, namely, when it is asked for the value of its `view` property. At that moment, if its `view` property is nil, the view controller sets about obtaining its view. (We say that a view controller loads its view *lazily*.) Typically, this happens because it is time to put the view controller's view into the interface.

In working with a newly instantiated view controller, be careful not to refer to its `view` property if you don't need to, since this will trigger the view controller's obtaining its view prematurely. To learn whether a view controller has a view without causing it to load its view, call `isViewLoaded`. (As usual, I speak from experience here. I once made the mistake of mentioning a UIViewController's `view` in its `awakeFromNib` and caused the view to be loaded twice.)

As soon as a view controller has its view, its `viewDidLoad` method is called. If this view controller is an instance of your own UIViewController subclass, `viewDidLoad` is your opportunity to modify the contents of this view — to populate it with subviews, to tweak the subviews it already has, and so forth — as well as to perform other initializations of the view controller consonant with its acquisition of a view. The `view` property is now pointing to the view, so it is safe to refer to `self.view`. Bear in mind, however, that the view may not yet be part of the interface! In fact, it almost certainly is not; `self.view.window` will be nil. Thus, for example, you cannot necessarily rely on the *dimensions* of the view at this point to be the dimensions that the view will assume when it becomes visible in the interface. Performing certain customizations prematurely in `viewDidLoad` is a common beginner mistake. I'll have more to say about this later in the chapter.

Before `viewDidLoad` will be called, however, the view controller must obtain its view. The question of where and how the view controller will get its view is often crucial. In some cases, to be sure, you won't care about this; in particular, when a view controller is an instance of a built-in UIViewController subclass such as UINavigationController or UITabBarController, its view is out of your hands — you might never even have cause to refer to it over the entire course of your app's lifetime — and you simply trust that the view controller will somehow generate its view. But when the view controller is an instance of your own subclass of UIViewController, and when you yourself will design or modify its view, it becomes essential to understand the process whereby a view controller gets its view.

This process is not difficult to understand, but it is rather elaborate, because there are multiple possibilities. Most important, this process is *not magic*. Yet it quite possibly causes more confusion to beginners than any other matter connected with iOS programming. Therefore, I will explain it in detail. The more you know about the details of how a view controller gets its view, the deeper and clearer will be your understanding of the entire workings of your app, its view controllers, its *.storyboard* and *.xib* files, and so on.

The alternatives are as follows:

- The view may be created in the view controller's own code, manually.
- The view may be created as an empty generic view, automatically.
- The view may be created in its own separate nib.
- The view may be created in a nib, which is the same nib from which the view controller itself is instantiated.

Manual View

To supply a UIViewController's view manually, in code, implement its `loadView` method. Your job here is to obtain an instance of UIView (or a subclass of UIView) and *assign it to `self.view`*. You must *not* call `super` (for reasons that I'll make clear later on).

 Do not confuse `loadView` with `viewDidLoad`. Yes, I've made this mistake myself. I confess! `loadView` creates the view; `viewDidLoad` is called afterward.

Let's try it. We are going to do everything manually, so we don't need or want a storyboard; therefore, start with an app without a main storyboard (I explained how to make such an app at the start of Chapter 1), and modify it as follows:

1. We need a UIViewController subclass, so choose File → New → File; specify iOS → Source → Cocoa Touch Class. Click Next.
2. Name the class RootViewController, and specify that it is to be a UIViewController subclass. Uncheck "Also create XIB file" (if it happens to be checked). Click Next.
3. Confirm that we're saving into the appropriate folder and group, and that these files will be part of the app target. Click Create.

We now have a RootViewController class, and we proceed to edit its code. In *RootViewController.swift*, we'll implement `loadView`. To convince ourselves that the example is working correctly, we'll give the view an identifiable color, and we'll put some interface inside it, namely a "Hello, World" label:

```
override func loadView() {
    let v = UIView()
    v.backgroundColor = UIColor.greenColor()
    self.view = v
    let label = UILabel()
    v.addSubview(label)
    label.text = "Hello, World!"
    label.autoresizingMask =
        .FlexibleTopMargin |
```

```
            .FlexibleLeftMargin |
            .FlexibleBottomMargin |
            .FlexibleRightMargin
        label.sizeToFit()
        label.center = CGPointMake(v.bounds.midX, v.bounds.midY)
        label.frame.integerize()
    }
```

We have not yet given a RootViewController instance a place in our view controller
hierarchy — in fact, we have no RootViewController instance (and no view controller
hierarchy). Let's make one. To do so, we turn to *AppDelegate.swift*. (It's a little frustrating
having to set things up in two different places before our labors can bear any visible
fruit, but such is life.)

In *AppDelegate.swift*, modify the implementation of `application:didFinish-`
`LaunchingWithOptions:` (see Appendix A) to create a RootViewController instance
and make it the window's `rootViewController` (see Example 1-1). Observe that we
must do this *after* our `window` property actually has a UIWindow as its value:

```
import UIKit
@UIApplicationMain
class AppDelegate : UIResponder, UIApplicationDelegate {
    var window : UIWindow?
    func application(application: UIApplication,
        didFinishLaunchingWithOptions launchOptions: [NSObject: AnyObject]?)
        -> Bool {
            self.window = UIWindow(frame: UIScreen.mainScreen().bounds)
            let theRVC = RootViewController() // *
            self.window!.rootViewController = theRVC // *
            self.window!.backgroundColor = UIColor.whiteColor()
            self.window!.makeKeyAndVisible()
            return true
    }
}
```

Build and run the app. Sure enough, there's our green background and our "Hello,
world" label!

When we created our view controller's view (`self.view`), we never gave it a reasonable
frame. This is because we are relying on someone else to frame the view appropriately.
In this case, the "someone else" is the window, which responds to having its `rootView-`
`Controller` property set to a view controller by framing the view controller's view appropriately as the root view before putting it into the window as a subview. In general,
it is the responsibility of whoever puts a view controller's view into the interface to give
the view the correct frame — and this will never be the view controller itself (although
under some circumstances the view controller can express a preference in this regard).
Indeed, the size of a view controller's view may be changed as it is placed into the interface, and you must keep in mind, as you design your view controller's view and its
subviews, the possibility that this will happen.

Generic Automatic View

We should distinguish between creating a view and populating it. The preceding example fails to draw this distinction. The lines that create our RootViewController's view are merely these:

```
let v = UIView()
self.view = v
```

Everything else configures and populates the view, turning it green and putting a label into it. A more appropriate place to populate a view controller's view is in its viewDidLoad implementation, which, as I've already mentioned, is called after the view exists (so that it can be referred to as self.view). We could therefore rewrite the preceding example like this (just for fun, I'll use autolayout this time):

```
override func loadView() {
    let v = UIView()
    self.view = v
}
override func viewDidLoad() {
    super.viewDidLoad()
    let v = self.view
    v.backgroundColor = UIColor.greenColor()
    let label = UILabel()
    v.addSubview(label)
    label.text = "Hello, World!"
    label.setTranslatesAutoresizingMaskIntoConstraints(false)
    self.view.addConstraint(
        NSLayoutConstraint(item: label,
            attribute: .CenterX,
            relatedBy: .Equal,
            toItem: self.view,
            attribute: .CenterX,
            multiplier: 1, constant: 0))
    self.view.addConstraint(
        NSLayoutConstraint(item: label,
            attribute: .CenterY,
            relatedBy: .Equal,
            toItem: self.view,
            attribute: .CenterY,
            multiplier: 1, constant: 0))
}
```

But if we're going to do that, we can go even further and remove our implementation of loadView altogether! It turns out that if you don't implement loadView, and if no view is supplied in any other way, then UIViewController's default implementation of loadView will do exactly what we are already doing in code: it creates a generic UIView object and assigns it to self.view. If we needed our view controller's view to be a particular UIView subclass, that wouldn't be acceptable; but in this case, our view controller's view *is* a generic UIView object, so it *is* acceptable. Comment out or delete the entire `loadView` implementation from the preceding code, and build and run the app; our example still works!

View in a Separate Nib

A view controller's view can be supplied from a nib file. This approach gives you the convenience of configuring and populating the view by designing it graphically in the nib editor interface.

When the nib loads, the view controller instance will already have been created, and it will serve as the nib's owner. The view controller has a `view` property; the view controller's representative in the nib has a `view` outlet, which must point to the view object in the nib. Thus, when the nib loads, the view controller obtains its view through the nib-loading mechanism.

I'll illustrate by modifying the preceding example to use a *.xib* file. (I'll deal later with the use of a *.storyboard* file; knowing first how the process works for a *.xib* file will greatly enhance your understanding of how it works for a *.storyboard* file.)

In a *.xib* file, the owner's representative is the File's Owner proxy object. Therefore, a *.xib* file that is to serve as the source of a view controller's view must be a *.xib* file in which the following two things are true:

- The File's Owner class must be set to a UIViewController subclass (depending on the class of the view controller whose view this will be).
- The File's Owner proxy now has a `view` outlet, corresponding to a UIViewController's `view` property. This outlet must be connected to the view.

Let's try it. We begin with the example we've already developed, with our RootViewController class. Delete the implementation of `loadView` and `viewDidLoad` from *RootViewController.swift*, because we want the view to come from a nib and we're going to populate it in the nib. Then:

1. Choose File → New → File and specify an iOS → User Interface → View document. This will be a *.xib* file containing a UIView object. Click Next.
2. Name the file *MyNib* (or *MyNib.xib*). Confirm the appropriate folder and group, and make sure that the file will be part of the app target. Click Create.
3. Edit *MyNib.xib*. Prepare it in the way I described a moment ago:
   a. Set the File's Owner class to RootViewController (in the Identity inspector).
   b. Connect the File's Owner `view` outlet to the View object.
4. Design the view. To make it clear that this is not the same view we were creating previously, perhaps you should give the view a red background color (in the At-

tributes inspector). Drag a UILabel into the middle of the view and give it some text, such as "Hello, World!"

We have designed the nib, but we have done nothing as yet to associate this nib with our RootViewController instance. To do so, let's once again return to *App-Delegate.swift*, where we create our RootViewController instance:

```
let theRVC = RootViewController()
self.window!.rootViewController = theRVC
```

We're going to modify this code so that our RootViewController instance, theRVC, is aware of this nib file, *MyNib.xib*, as its own nib file. That way, when theRVC needs to acquire its view, it will load that nib file with itself as owner, thus ending up with the correct view as its own view property. A UIViewController has a nibName property for this purpose. However, we are not allowed to set its nibName property (it is read-only). Instead, as we instantiate the view controller, we use the designated initializer, init(nibName:bundle:), like this:

```
let theRVC = RootViewController(nibName:"MyNib", bundle:nil)
self.window!.rootViewController = theRVC
```

(The nil argument to the bundle: parameter specifies the main bundle, which is almost always what you want.)

To prove that this works, build and run. The red background appears! Our view is loading from the nib.

Now I'm going to describe a shortcut based on the name of the nib. It turns out that if the nib name passed to init(nibName:bundle:) is nil, a nib will be sought automatically *with the same name as the view controller's class*. Moreover, UIViewController's init() calls init(nibName:bundle:), passing nil for both arguments. This means, in effect, that we can return to using init() to initialize the view controller, provided that the nib file has a name that matches the name of the view controller class.

Let's try it. Rename *MyNib.xib* to *RootViewController.xib*, and change the code that instantiates and initializes our RootViewController back to what it was before, like this:

```
let theRVC = RootViewController()
self.window!.rootViewController = theRVC
```

Build and run, and... Oops, it doesn't work! The window is empty.

The reason is that the Swift language itself is getting in the way. Remember, I said that a nib will be sought with the same name as the view controller's class. Unfortunately, Swift has some funny ideas about the name of this class. You may think it's called Root-ViewController, but Swift's name for it prepends the name of the module, which by default is the name of the project and the app. For example, if this project is called

TestNib, then Swift thinks that this class is called `TestNib.RootViewController`. The nib-loading system doesn't find a nib file with that name, so the nib is not found.

Here are four ways to work around this problem:

- Make the RootViewController class an Objective-C class, not a Swift class. Objective-C's name for this class is still RootViewController, so the nib file's name matches. That's unacceptable and I'm not going to consider it further; this is a Swift class and it's going to stay a Swift class.

- Change the name of the *.xib* file to match Swift's idea of the class name. For example, if this project is called TestNib, the *.xib* file would have to be named *TestNib.RootViewController.xib*. That works, but it's dreadfully inconvenient in numerous ways.

- Force Swift's idea of the class name to match the Objective-C name. To do so, use the `@objc()` notation when the view controller is declared, like this:

    ```
    @objc(RootViewController) class RootViewController : UIViewController {
    ```

    That's a pretty good solution. It's portable, reliable, reasonably convenient, and presumably won't break if Apple ever changes this behavior.

- Give up and use an explicit nib name when you call `init(nibName:bundle:)`. There are two ways to do this: you can call `init(nibName:bundle:)` everywhere you instantiate this nib, or you can implement `init()` in your view controller subclass (in which case you'll also have to override `init(coder:)`), so that all other classes can call `init()`:

    ```
    required init(coder: NSCoder) {
        fatalError("NSCoding not supported")
    }
    init() {
        super.init(nibName:"RootViewController", bundle:nil)
    }
    ```

There's an additional aspect to this shortcut based on the name of the nib. It seems ridiculous that we should end up with a nib that has "Controller" in its name merely because our view controller, as is so often the case, has "Controller" in *its* name. A nib, after all, is not a controller. It turns out that the runtime, in looking for a view controller's corresponding nib, will in fact try stripping "Controller" off the end of the view controller class's name. Thus, we can name our nib file *RootView.xib* instead of *RootViewController.xib*, and it will *still* be properly associated with our RootViewController instance (once we've implemented one of the workarounds I've just listed).

Which of these is my favorite workaround? None of them! I prefer a fifth alternative:

- Override the getter for the UIViewController read-only `nibName` property, like this:

```
override var nibName : String {
    get {
        return "RootView"
    }
}
```

With that override in place, other code can instantiate this view controller with `init()` and it finds its nib correctly. Note this approach does *not* participate in the automatic stripping of "Controller" from the name. If the nib is named *RootView.xib* and you supply `"RootViewController"` as the value of the `nibName` property in its getter, your app will crash. The names must match exactly. (The documentation is misleading on this point.)

When you create a UIViewController subclass, the Xcode dialog has a checkbox (which we unchecked earlier) offering to create an eponymous *.xib* file at the same time. If you accept that option, the nib is created with the File's Owner's class already set to the view controller's class and with its `view` outlet already hooked up to the view. This automatically created *.xib* file does *not* have "Controller" stripped off the end of its name; you can rename it manually later (I generally do) if the default name bothers you.

Another convention involving the nib name has to do with the rules for loading resources by name generally. I mentioned in Chapter 2 that when an image file is sought by calling `init(named:)` or `pathForResource:ofType:`, an image file with the specified name but extended by the suffix `~ipad` will be used, if there is one, when the app runs on an iPad. The same rule applies to nib files. So, for example, a nib file named *RootViewController~ipad.xib* will be loaded on an iPad when a nib named `"RootView-Controller"` is sought, regardless of whether it is specified explicitly, as the first argument to `init(nibName:bundle:)`, or implicitly. This principle can greatly simplify your life when you're writing a universal app — though in Xcode and iOS 8, conditional constraints (see Chapter 1) may permit you to design an interface differing on iPad and iPhone in a single *.xib* file.

Finally, let's be explicit about the place of this way of obtaining a view controller's view among the other of ways of obtaining it:

1. When the view controller first decides that it needs its view, `loadView` is *always* called.

2. If we override `loadView`, we supply and set the `view` in code, and we do *not* call `super`. Therefore the process of seeking a view comes to an end.

3. If we *don't* override `loadView`, UIViewController's built-in default implementation of `loadView` is used. It is this default implementation of `loadView` that loads the view controller's associated nib (the one specified by its `nibName`, or, if that's nil, the one whose name matches the name of the view controller's class).

That, indeed, is why, if we do override `loadView`, we must *not* call `super` — that would cause us to get *both* behaviors!

4. If the previous steps all fail — we don't override `loadView`, and there is no associated nib — UIViewController's default implementation of `loadView` proceeds to create a generic UIView as discussed in the previous section.

 It follows from what I've just said that if a view controller's view is to come from a nib, you should *not* implement `loadView`. I've made this mistake. The results were not pretty.

Nib-Instantiated View Controller

As I mentioned earlier, a view controller can be a nib object, to be instantiated through the loading of the nib. In the nib editor, the Object library contains a View Controller (UIViewController) as well as several built-in UIViewController subclasses. Any of these can be dragged into the nib. This is the standard way of creating a scene in a *.storyboard* file; doing the same with a *.xib* file is rare but perfectly possible.

When a view controller has been instantiated from a nib, and when it comes eventually to obtain its view, all the ways I've already described whereby a view controller can obtain its view still apply. (There's also an additional way, which I'll discuss in a moment.)

If you'd like to try it, start over with an empty project without a storyboard, and give it a *.xib* file containing a view controller, as follows:

1. Choose File → New → File and specify an iOS → User Interface → Empty document. Press Next.

2. Name the new file *Main.xib*, make sure it's being saved into the right place and that it is part of the app target, and click Create.

3. Edit *Main.xib*. Drag a plain vanilla View Controller object into the canvas.

4. In the view controller you just dragged into the canvas, there's a View object serving as the main view. Select it and delete it! Don't worry, we'll discuss in a moment what it's for.

In *AppDelegate.swift*, we must now arrange to load *Main.xib* and extract the view controller instance created from the nib object we just put into the nib, making that view controller our app's root view controller. Here's one very simple way to do that:

```
let arr = UINib(nibName: "Main", bundle: nil)
    .instantiateWithOwner(nil, options: nil) as! [UIViewController]
self.window!.rootViewController = arr[0]
```

You can now proceed, if you like, to experiment with various ways of helping this view controller get its view. At the moment it is a plain UIViewController instance. Let's make it a class of our own:

1. Give the project a RootViewController class (a UIViewController subclass).

2. In *Main.xib*, select the view controller object and use its Identity inspector to set its class to RootViewController.

Now you can help RootViewController get its view, in any of the ways we've already explored:

- Implement `loadView` in RootViewController.

- Or, implement `viewDidLoad` but not `loadView` in RootViewController.

- Or, add another nib called *RootViewController.xib* (or *RootView.xib*) — and work around the Swift behavior involving the class name.

There is also a way to specify *in the nib editor* the name of the nib that this view controller should use to find its nib: select the view controller in its nib, and enter the name of the view's nib in the NIB Name field in its Attributes inspector. This is the equivalent of specifying a nib name when you call `init(nibName:bundle:)`.

When a nib contains a view controller, there is, as I hinted a moment ago, *an additional way* for it to obtain its view — and you've probably already guessed what it is. When you drag a View Controller into the canvas in the nib editor, it already contains a view, hooked up and ready to act as its main view! The view controller, in fact, is portrayed in the canvas more or less as if it *were* this view. Thus, using the nib editor we can design the view controller's main view's interface *in the view controller itself*. Let's try it:

1. If you've been experimenting with the code in *RootViewController.swift*, remove any implementation of `loadView` or `viewDidLoad`.

2. In *Main.xib*, find the plain vanilla View object in the Object library and drag it *into the view controller object* in the canvas. (This replaces the view that we deleted earlier.) This view object automatically becomes the view controller's view, and is drawn inside it in the canvas. Thus, you can now add further interface objects to this view.

Build and run. The interface you designed inside the view object inside the view controller object in *Main.xib* appears in the running app.

Like any other nib object, when a view controller is instantiated from a nib, its designated initializer in your code (init(nibName:bundle:)) is not called. If your nib-instantiated UIViewController subclass needs access to the view controller instance very early in its lifetime, override init(coder:) or awakeFromNib.

Storyboard-Instantiated View Controller

If you've ever used a storyboard, it will not have escaped your attention that what we just constructed in *Main.xib*, in the previous section — a view controller directly containing its view — looks a lot like a scene in a storyboard. That's because, by default, this *is* the structure of a scene in a storyboard. Indeed, we are now ready to appreciate and understand exactly how a storyboard works.

Each scene in a *.storyboard* file is rather like a *.xib* file containing a view controller nib object. A scene's view controller is instantiated only when needed; the underlying mechanism is that the scene's view controller is stored in a nib file in the built app, inside the *.storyboardc* bundle, and this nib file is loaded on demand and the view controller is instantiated from it, as we did in the previous section.

Moreover, by default, the view controller in a scene in a *.storyboard* file comes equipped with a view, which appears inside it in the canvas. You design the view and its subviews in the nib editor. When the app is built, each view controller's view goes into *a separate nib file*, inside the *.storyboardc* bundle, and the view controller, once instantiated, loads its view from that nib file lazily, exactly as we did earlier.

In this way, a storyboard embodies the very same mechanisms we've already explored through *.xib* files. Even though a storyboard may appear, in the nib editor, to contain many view controllers and their main views, each view controller and each main view is loaded from its own nib in the running app, on demand, when needed, just as if we had configured the project with multiple *.xib* files. Thus a storyboard combines the memory management advantages of *.xib* files, which are not loaded until they're needed, and can be loaded multiple times to give additional instances of the same nib objects, with the convenience to you of being able to see and edit a lot of your app's interface simultaneously in one place.

You don't *have* to use the default scene structure in a storyboard. The default is that a view controller in a storyboard contains its view — *but you can delete the view*. If you do, then that view controller will obtain its view in any of the *other* ways we've already discussed: by an implementation of loadView in the code of that view controller class, or by loading a nib file that comes from a *.xib* with the same name as this view controller's class — assuming you've worked around the Swift naming issue — or even (if all of that fails) by creating a generic UIView. However, there's no way in a *.storyboard* file to specify as the source of a view controller's view a *.xib* file with a different name from the view controller's class. The nib editor lacks the NIB Name field in a view controller's Attributes inspector when you're working in a storyboard.

The Xcode app templates start with a single main storyboard called *Main.storyboard*, which is designated the app's main storyboard by the *Info.plist* key "Main storyboard file base name" (UIMainStoryboardFile). Therefore, as the app launches, UIApplicationMain gets a reference to this storyboard (by calling the UIStoryboard initializer init(name:bundle:)), instantiates its initial view controller (by calling instantiateInitialViewController), and makes that instance the window's root-ViewController. If you edit the storyboard to contain segues, then when one of those segues is performed — which can be configured to happen automatically in response to the user tapping an interface object — the destination view controller is automatically instantiated. In this way it is perfectly possible for a single storyboard to be the source of every view controller that your app will ever instantiate, and for all of that instantiation to take place automatically.

That's convenient for beginners, but it can also be restrictive. You might have a feeling that your app *must* have a main storyboard, and that every view controller *must* be instantiated from it automatically. That's not the case. It is possible to use storyboards in a much more agile, intentional way, much as one would use *.xib* files. For example, your app can have multiple storyboards. Why might that be useful? Well, since auto-layout is configured at the file level — either an entire *.storyboard* file uses autolayout or none of it does — multiple storyboards constitute a very good way to use autolayout selectively in only certain areas of your interface. Or you might use an ancillary story-board as a source of just one view controller, a more convenient and memory-efficient way to do what we did with a view controller in a *.xib* file earlier.

I'll summarize the ways in which a view controller can be instantiated from a storyboard. You can get a reference to a storyboard either by calling the UIStoryboard initializer init(name:bundle:) or through the storyboard property of a view controller that has already been instantiated from that storyboard. With a storyboard instance in hand, a view controller can be instantiated from that storyboard in one of four ways:

- At most one view controller in the storyboard is designated the storyboard's *initial view controller*. To instantiate that view controller, call `instantiateInitialView-Controller`. The instance is returned.

- A view controller in a storyboard can be assigned an arbitrary string identifier; this is its Storyboard ID in the Identity inspector. To instantiate that view controller, call `instantiateViewControllerWithIdentifier:`. The instance is returned.

- A parent view controller in a storyboard may have immediate children, such as a UINavigationController and its initial child view controller. The nib editor will show a *relationship* connection between them. When the parent is instantiated (the source of the relationship), the initial children (the destination of the relationship) are instantiated automatically.

- A view controller in a storyboard may be (or contain) the source of a *segue* whose destination is a *future* child view controller or a *future* presented view controller. When the segue is triggered and performed, it instantiates the new view controller.

I'll go into much greater detail about storyboards and segues later in this chapter.

View Resizing

A view controller's view (meaning its main view) is likely to be resized. Other views can be resized as well, of course, but this is typically by virtue of being subviews of a view controller's main view, which has itself been resized. A view controller's view is resized when it is put into the interface. It is resized when the app rotates. It may be resized in response to interface changes, such as when a navigation bar gets taller or shorter, appears or disappears. On the iPhone 6, it may even be resized because a change in the Display Zoom setting changes the effective size of the screen. In iOS 8, Apple describes views and view controllers as *adaptive* to size changes.

Because a view controller is a controller, it is typically the locus of logic for helping the interface to cope with all this resizing. A view controller has properties and receives events connected to the resizing of its view, so that it can correctly dictate the arrangement of the interface.

View Size in the Nib Editor

When you design your interface in the nib editor, you can be misled into forgetting about view resizing. A view controller's view has to be displayed at some definite size, so you may design the interface for that size, as if what you see in the nib editor canvas is what you'll get when the app runs. That, however, is false. Suppose you design the interface with the view sized like an iPhone 4s; then when the app loads on an iPhone 5, the view is a different size, and the interface as designed isn't the interface you actually see — and of course with the advent of the two iPhone 6 models, the problem is compounded. It's crucial to remember that the size at which a view controller's main view is portrayed in the nib editor canvas has *no effect on the size it will assume at runtime*.

In the nib editor, you can display the view at the size of any actual device: for a storyboard, select the view controller (for a *.xib* file, select the top-level view) and choose a specific device from the Size pop-up menu under Simulated Metrics at the top of the Attributes inspector. You can also specify an orientation, as well as the presence or absence of interface elements that can affect layout (status bar, top bar, bottom bar). The Interface Builder Preview feature can also be a big help here, allowing you to view your interface laid out for multiple devices simultaneously. But don't forget that the specific size you see may not reflect runtime reality. From this point of view, Xcode 6's "Use Size Classes" option is a boon (see Chapter 1). By default, it shows a view controller's main view as a square — a neutral shape that will never be encountered in real life. This serves as a reminder that the interface you are designing must adapt to a variety of real sizes when the app runs.

Bars and Underlapping

A view controller's view will often have to adapt to the presence of bars at the top and bottom of the screen:

The status bar is underlapped
> The status bar is transparent, so that the region of a view behind it is visible through it. The root view, and any other fullscreen view, must occupy the *entire window*, including the status bar area, the top of the view being visible behind the transparent status bar. You'll want to design your view so that its top doesn't contain any interface objects that will be overlapped by the status bar.

Top and bottom bars may be underlapped
> The top and bottom bars displayed by a navigation controller (navigation bar, tool-bar) or tab bar controller (tab bar) can be translucent. When they are, your view controller's view displayed here is, by default, extended *behind* the translucent bar, underlapping it.

The status bar may be present or absent. Top and bottom bars may be present or absent, and, if present, their height can change. How will your interface cope with such changes? The primary coping mechanism is the view controller's *layout guides*.

Recall (from Chapter 1) that a view controller supplies two properties, its `topLayout-Guide` and its `bottomLayoutGuide`. The position of these guide objects moves automatically at runtime to reflect the view's environment:

`topLayoutGuide`
> The `topLayoutGuide` is positioned as follows:

- If there is a status bar and no top bar, the `topLayoutGuide` is positioned at the bottom of the status bar.

- If there is a top bar, the `topLayoutGuide` is positioned at the bottom of the top bar.

- If there is no top bar and no status bar, the `topLayoutGuide` is positioned at the top of the view.

`bottomLayoutGuide`

The `bottomLayoutGuide` is positioned as follows:

- If there is a bottom bar, the `bottomLayoutGuide` is positioned at the top of the bottom bar.

- If there is no bottom bar, the `bottomLayoutGuide` is positioned at the bottom of the view.

The easiest way to involve the layout guides in your view layout is through autolayout and constraints. By pinning a view by its top to the `topLayoutGuide`, or by its bottom to the `bottomLayoutGuide`, you guarantee that the view will move when the layout guide moves.

If you need actual numbers in order to perform layout-related calculations, a layout guide's distance from the corresponding edge of the view controller's main view is reported by its `length` property. Note that `viewDidLoad` is too early to obtain a meaningful value; the earliest coherent opportunity is probably `viewWillLayoutSubviews` (I'll discuss this event later).

Status bar visibility

The default behavior of the status bar is that it is present, except in landscape orientation on an iPhone, where it is absent (this behavior is new in iOS 8). The root view controller, as I mentioned at the start of this chapter, gets a say in this behavior; it also determines the look of the status bar when present. Your UIViewController subclass can override these methods:

`preferredStatusBarStyle`

Your choices (UIStatusBarStyle) are `.Default` and `.LightContent`, meaning dark text and light text, respectively. Use light text for legibility if the view content underlapping the status bar is dark.

`prefersStatusBarHidden`

Return `true` to make the status bar invisible; return `false` to make the status bar visible, even in landscape orientation on iPhone. (Return the result of a call to `super` to get the default behavior.)

`childViewControllerForStatusBarStyle`
`childViewControllerForStatusBarHidden`

> Used to delegate the decision on the status bar style or visibility to a child view controller's `preferredStatusBarStyle` or `prefersStatusBarHidden` instead of this view controller. For example, a navigation controller implements these methods to allow your view controller to decide the status bar style and visibility when your view controller's view occupies the navigation controller's view.

You never call any of those methods yourself; they are called automatically when the view controller situation changes (including, on iOS 8, when the interface rotates). If you want them to be called immediately, because they are not being called when you need them to be, or because the situation has changed and a call to one of them would now give a different answer, call `setNeedsStatusBarAppearanceUpdate` on your view controller. If this call is inside an animation block, the animation of the change in the look of the status bar will have the specified duration. The character of the animation from visible to invisible (and *vice versa*) is set by your view controller's implementation of `preferredStatusBarUpdateAnimation`; the value you return (UIStatusBar-Animation) can be `.Fade`, `.Slide`, or `.None`.

When you toggle the visibility of the status bar, the top layout guide will move up or down by 20 points. If your main view has subviews with constraints to the top layout guide, those subviews will move. If this happens when the main view is visible, the user will see this movement as a jump. That is probably not what you want. To prevent it, call `layoutIfNeeded` on your view in the same animation block in which you call `setNeedsStatusBarAppearanceUpdate`; your layout update will then be animated together with the change in status bar visibility.

Extended layout

If your UIViewController's parent is a navigation controller or tab bar controller, you can govern whether its view underlaps a top bar (navigation bar) or bottom bar (toolbar, tab bar) with these UIViewController properties:

`edgesForExtendedLayout`

> A UIRectEdge. The default is `.All`, meaning that this view controller's view will underlap a translucent top bar or a translucent bottom bar. The other extreme is `.None`, meaning that this view controller's view won't underlap top and bottom bars. Other possibilities are `.Top` (underlap top bars only) and `.Bottom` (underlap bottom bars only).

`extendedLayoutIncludesOpaqueBars`

> If `true`, then if `edgesForExtendedLayout` permits underlapping of bars, those bars will be underlapped *even if they are opaque*. The default is `false`, meaning that only translucent bars are underlapped.

Resizing Events

A UIViewController receives events that notify it of pending view size changes.

The following events, new in iOS 8, are associated primarily with rotation of the interface (for trait collections and size classes, as well as view layout events, see Chapter 1):

willTransitionToTraitCollection:withTransitionCoordinator:
Sent when the app is about to undergo rotation, if this involves a change in the trait collection (because the size classes will change). Rotation on an iPad does not change the trait collection, so this event will not arrive. Rotation of 180 degrees on an iPhone does not change the trait collection, so this event will not arrive. This event is *not* sent on launch or when your view controller's view is first embedded into the interface. If you override this method, call super.

UIViewController receives this event by virtue of adopting the UIContent-Container protocol.

viewWillTransitionToSize:withTransitionCoordinator:
Sent when the app is about undergo rotation; may be sent even if the view's size will not change (because we are rotating 180 degrees). The new size is the first parameter; the old size is available as self.view.bounds.size. This event is *not* sent on launch or when your view controller's view is first embedded into the interface. If you override this method, call super.

UIViewController receives this event by virtue of adopting the UIContent-Container protocol.

traitCollectionDidChange:
Sent after the trait collection changes. The parameter is the old trait collection; the new trait collection is available as self.traitCollection. Sent after the trait collection changes, *including* on launch or when the trait collection is set for the first time (in which case the parameter will be nil).

UIViewController receives this event by virtue of adopting the UITraitEnvironment protocol.

(I'll describe the use of the transitionCoordinator: parameter later in this chapter.)

In addition, a UIViewController receives these events related to the layout of its view (these are *not* new in iOS 8):

updateViewConstraints
The view is about to be told to update its constraints (updateConstraints), *including* at application launch. If you override this method, call super.

`viewWillLayoutSubviews`
`viewDidLayoutSubviews`
> These events surround the moment when the view is sent `layoutSubviews`, *including* at application launch.

In a situation where all these events are sent, the order is:

- `willTransitionToTraitCollection:withTransitionCoordinator:`
- `viewWillTransitionToSize:withTransitionCoordinator:`
- `updateViewConstraints`
- `traitCollectionDidChange:`
- `viewWillLayoutSubviews`
- `viewDidLayoutSubviews`

 It's a pity that the `viewWillTransitionToSize:...` event is confined primarily to rotation situations. Your view can be resized under many other circumstances, but to detect these, you'll have to fall back on layout events such as `viewWillLayout-Subviews`.

Rotation

Your app can rotate, moving its top to correspond to a different edge of the device's screen. In earlier versions of the system, this rotation was something of an illusion: the window remained pinned to the screen, and rotation was a matter of applying a rotate transform to the root view and changing the bounds size to match the new orientation. In iOS 8, however, the app really does rotate. Rotation expresses itself in two ways:

The status bar orientation changes
> You can hear about this (though this will rarely be necessary) by way of these app delegate events and notifications:
>
> - `application:willChangeStatusBarOrientation:duration:` (and the corresponding `UIApplicationWillChangeStatusBarOrientationNotification`)
> - `application:didChangeStatusBarOrientation:` (and the corresponding `UIApplicationDidChangeStatusBarOrientationNotification`)

The current orientation (which is also the app's current orientation) is available from the UIApplication as its `statusBarOrientation`; the app delegate methods also provide the other orientation (the one we are changing to or from, respectively) as the second parameter. Possible values (UIInterfaceOrientation) are:

- `.Portrait`

- `.PortraitUpsideDown`

- `.LandscapeLeft`

- `.LandscapeRight`

Global convenience functions `UIInterfaceOrientationIsLandscape` and `UIInterfaceOrientationIsPortrait` take a UIInterfaceOrientation and return a Bool.

The view controller's view is resized

There may also be an accompanying change in the trait collection. Thus, the view controller receives events related to resizing, as I described in the preceding section.

 In iOS 8, all UIViewController instance methods from iOS 7 and before with "Rotate," "Rotation," or "Rotating" in their names *are deprecated*. The events related to app rotation are the resizing events listed in the previous section. App rotation is to be regarded as an aspect of view resizing.

There are two complementary uses for rotation:

Compensatory rotation

The app rotates to compensate for the orientation of the device, so that the app appears right way up with respect to how the user is holding the device. The challenge of compensatory rotation stems, quite simply, from the fact that the screen is not square. This means that if the app rotates 90 degrees, the interface no longer fits the screen, and must be changed to compensate.

Forced rotation

The app rotates when a particular view appears in the interface, or when the app launches, to indicate that the user needs to rotate the device in order to view the app the right way up. This is typically because the interface has been specifically designed, in the face of the fact that the screen is not square, to appear in one particular mode (portrait or landscape).

In the case of the iPhone, no law says that your app has to perform compensatory rotation. Most of my iPhone apps do not do so; indeed, I have no compunction about doing just the opposite. My view controller views often look best in just one orientation (or one pair of opposed orientations, either just portrait or just landscape), and they stubbornly stay there regardless of how the user holds the device. A single app may contain view controller views that work best in different orientations; thus, my app forces the user to rotate the device differently depending on what view is being displayed. This is reasonable, because the iPhone is small and easily reoriented with a twist of the user's wrist, and it has a natural right way up, especially because it's a phone. (The iPod touch isn't a phone, but the same argument works by analogy.)

On the other hand, Apple would prefer iPad apps to rotate to at least two opposed orientations (such as landscape with the button on the right and landscape with the button on the left), and preferably to all four possible orientations, so that the user isn't restricted in how the device is held.

It's fairly trivial to let your app rotate to two opposed orientations, because once the app is set up to work in one of them, it can work with no change in the other. But allowing a single interface to rotate between two orientations that are 90 degrees apart is trickier, because its dimensions must change — roughly speaking, its height and width are swapped — and this may require a change of layout and might even call for more substantial alterations, such as removal or addition of part of the interface. A good example is the behavior of Apple's Mail app on the iPad: in landscape mode, the master pane and the detail pane appear side by side, but in portrait mode, the master pane is removed and must be summoned as a temporary overlay on top of the detail pane.

 The orientation of your view as displayed in the nib editor has *no* effect on the orientation of your app, any more than its size does. When the app runs, its runtime characteristics (as I'm about to describe) will determine its rotation, just as they will determine its size.

Permitting compensatory rotation

By default, when you create an Xcode project, the resulting app will perform compensatory rotation in response to the user's rotation of the device. For an iPhone app, this means that the app can appear with its top at the top of the device or either of the two sides of the device; having the app's top appear at the bottom of the device (because the device is held upside-down) is generally frowned on. For an iPad app, this means that the app can assume any orientation.

If this isn't what you want, it is up to you to prevent it. There are three levels at which you can make changes:

- The app itself, in its *Info.plist*, may declare once and for all every orientation the interface will ever be permitted to assume. It does this under the "Supported interface orientations" key, `UISupportedInterfaceOrientations` (supplemented, for a universal app, by "Supported interface orientations (iPad)," `UISupportedInterfaceOrientations~ipad`). These keys can also be set through checkboxes when you edit the app target, in the General tab.

- The app delegate may implement `application:supportedInterfaceOrientationsForWindow:`, returning a bitmask listing every orientation the interface is permitted to assume. This list *overrides* the *Info.plist* settings. Thus, the app delegate can do dynamically what the *Info.plist* can do only statically. `application:supportedInterfaceOrientationsForWindow:` is called at least once every time the device rotates.

- A view controller may implement `supportedInterfaceOrientations`, returning a bitmask listing a set of orientations that *intersects* the set of orientations permitted by the app or the app delegate. The resulting intersection will then be the set of orientations permitted at that moment. This intersection must not be empty; if it is, your app will crash (with a useful message: "Supported orientations has no common orientation with the application"). `supportedInterfaceOrientations` is called at least once every time the device rotates.

  The view controller has a second way to interfere with the app's permitted orientations: it can implement `shouldAutorotate`. This method returns a Bool, and the default is `true`. `shouldAutorotate` is called at least once every time the device rotates; if it returns `false`, the interface will not rotate to compensate at this moment. This can be a simpler way than `supportedInterfaceOrientations` to veto the app's rotation. If `shouldAutorotate` is implemented and returns `false`, `supportedInterfaceOrientations` is not called.

  Only the view controller at the top of the visible view controller hierarchy is consulted — that is, the root view controller, or a view controller presented fullscreen. Built-in view controllers do not consult their children in response. Thus, if your view controller is, say, a child view controller of a UINavigationController, it has no say in how the app rotates. (This was a major change from iOS 5 to iOS 6, and is still the cause of much confusion, not to mention gnashing of teeth.)

A UIViewController class method `attemptRotationToDeviceOrientation` prompts the runtime to do immediately what it would do if the user were to rotate the device, namely to walk the three levels I've just described and, if the results permit rotation of the interface to match the current device orientation, to rotate the interface. This would be useful if, say, your view controller had returned `false` from `shouldAutorotate`, so that the interface does not match the current device orientation, but is now for some reason prepared to return `true` and wants to be asked again, immediately.

The bitmask you return from `application:supportedInterfaceOrientationsForWindow:` or `supportedInterfaceOrientations` may be one of these values, or multiple values combined with bitwise-or:

- `UIInterfaceOrientationMask.Portrait`
- `UIInterfaceOrientationMask.LandscapeLeft`
- `UIInterfaceOrientationMask.LandscapeRight`

- `UIInterfaceOrientationMask.PortraitUpsideDown`

- `UIInterfaceOrientationMask.Landscape` (a convenient combination of `.Left` and `.Right`)

- `UIInterfaceOrientationMask.All` (a convenient combination of `.Portrait`, `.Upside-Down`, `.Left`, and `.Right`)

- `UIInterfaceOrientationMask.AllButUpsideDown` (a convenient combination of `.Portrait`, `.Left`, and `.Right`)

Unfortunately, the Swift notation is extremely clumsy, for two reasons:

- These methods expect you to return an Int, not a UIInterfaceOrientationMask.

- UIInterfaceOrientationMask is typed as a UInt, not an Int.

Therefore, in order to return a bitmask from these methods, you have to derive the underlying value with `rawValue` and cast the result to Int. For example:

```
override func supportedInterfaceOrientations() -> Int {
    return Int(UIInterfaceOrientationMask.Portrait.rawValue)
}
```

 In the preceding code, do not accidentally start with a different enum, such as UIInterfaceOrientation. A different enum has a different set of values, so if you implement `supportedInterfaceOrientations` to return, say, `UIInterface-Orientation.Portrait.rawValue`, you'll crash. Because `supportedInterface-Orientations` expects an Int result, not a UIInterfaceOrientationMask, Swift's strict typing doesn't prevent you from making this mistake!

If your code needs to know the current physical orientation of the device (as opposed to the current orientation of the app), it can ask the device:

```
let orientation = UIDevice.currentDevice().orientation
```

Possible results (UIDeviceOrientation) are `.Unknown`, `.Portrait`, and so on. Global convenience functions `UIDeviceOrientationIsPortrait` and `UIDeviceOrientation-IsLandscape` take a UIDeviceOrientation and return a Bool. By the time you get a rotation-related event, the device's orientation has already changed.

Initial orientation

I've talked about how to determine what orientations your app can support in the course of its lifetime; but what about its initial orientation, the very first orientation your app will assume when it launches?

On the iPad, an app has no fixed initial orientation. iPad apps are supposed to be more or less orientation-agnostic, so the app will launch into whatever permitted orientation is closest to the device's current orientation at launch time.

On the iPhone, however, things are different. The rule is that the app will attempt to launch into the *first* orientation listed in the app's *Info.plist* file in the "Supported interface orientations" array (`UISupportedInterfaceOrientations`). There is no graphical user interface for arranging the order of this array; you have to edit the *Info.plist* directly. You can do this either by selecting the *Info.plist* in the Project navigator or by editing the target and switching to the Info pane. From there, the editor lets you drag the elements of the array to reorder them.

It is *crucial* that the order of the "Supported interface orientations" array entries in the *Info.plist* should harmonize with the `supportedInterfaceOrientations` of the initial root view controller. To illustrate what I mean, I'll give an example of what you should *not* do. Suppose that your app, over its lifetime, needs to support portrait, landscape left, and landscape right, but your initial root view controller supports only landscape left and landscape right. Then, in the *Info.plist*, portrait orientation (`UIInterfaceOrientationPortrait`) must *not* come first.

The reason is that, by definition, at the time the app launches, the app is not yet running. Thus, there is not yet any root view controller, and so `supportedInterfaceOrientations` can't yet be called. The only information the system has, as it launches your app, is the *Info.plist* (it can read this by looking directly into the app bundle, and it does so). So if portrait orientation comes first in the *Info.plist*, the app will try to launch into portrait orientation, only to discover, as your code finally starts running and your root view controller's `supportedInterfaceOrientations` is called, that this was wrong. This will cause trouble for the visible interface (the user will see a sudden rotation at launch) and trouble for your code (you'll get an extra initial set of rotation-related events).

Initial layout

If you have code that performs or contributes to the initial construction and layout of your app's interface, where should that code go? If you've configured your permitted orientations and initial orientation correctly, in iOS 8 your root view controller will receive these events at launch:

- `viewDidLoad`
- `traitCollectionDidChange:`
- `viewWillLayoutSubviews`

There is a natural temptation to perform initial layout-related tasks in `viewDidLoad`, because, being called just once as early as possible in the life of the view controller's view,

Extra Rotation at Launch

In previous editions of this book, I warned that if your app's initial orientation was anything but portrait orientation, there would be an extra set of rotation events as the app launches. This was because, regardless of your initial orientation settings, all apps actually launched in portrait, even if the user never saw this. In iOS 8, though, that's no longer true! (This change is surely connected with the fact that in iOS 8, the app itself, including the window, is what rotates.) Thus, that warning is no longer necessary. This means that if your iOS 7 app's initial orientation is landscape orientation, and if your code was taking precautions to work around the extra initial rotation, those precautions are no longer needed when you recompile for iOS 8.

It is still perfectly possible that you'll get a rotation very early in the life of the app, but this, if you've configured your app's initial orientation correctly, will be a *real* rotation. For example, if your iPhone app's initial root view controller permits rotation to any orientation, and your *Info.plist* specifies portrait orientation as the initial orientation, and if the user is holding the device in landscape orientation as your app launches, then the app will launch normally, correctly, and fully into portrait orientation, and will then almost immediately afterward rotate to landscape. But this is essentially no different than if the user had been holding the device in portrait orientation while launching your app and then rotated it to landscape.

it is a conventional locus for preparation of the interface (as well as other view controller initializations). This can be a mistake. At the time `viewDidLoad` is called, the view has been loaded, but it has not yet been inserted into the interface! Thus it has not yet been fully resized for the first time. A layout-related task that depends upon the absolute dimensions of the view is therefore destined to generate erroneous results.

In iOS 8, however, this problem is not as severe as in previous versions of the system, because the view's size already matches the screen, regardless of initial orientation, by the time `viewDidLoad` is called. `viewDidLoad` is still too early, though, to make accurate decisions based on what the initial size of the view will be when the interface has settled down; for example, the view's height may subsequently be reduced by the presence of a top or bottom bar.

If your initial layout involves autolayout, therefore, `viewDidLoad` is a perfectly reasonable place to do it, as long as you aren't relying on a knowledge of the final absolute dimensions of your view. In this (completely artificial) example, I'll insert a small black square at the top center of the interface, using constraints:

```
override func viewDidLoad() {
    super.viewDidLoad()
    let square = UIView()
    square.backgroundColor = UIColor.blackColor()
    self.view.addSubview(square)
```

```
square.setTranslatesAutoresizingMaskIntoConstraints(false)
let side : CGFloat = 10
square.addConstraint(
    NSLayoutConstraint(item:square, attribute:.Width,
    relatedBy:.Equal,
    toItem:nil, attribute:.NotAnAttribute,
    multiplier:1, constant:side))
self.view.addConstraints(
    NSLayoutConstraint.constraintsWithVisualFormat("V:|[square(side)]",
    options:nil, metrics:["side":side],
    views:["square":square]))
self.view.addConstraint(
    NSLayoutConstraint(item:square, attribute:.CenterX,
    relatedBy:.Equal,
    toItem:self.view, attribute:.CenterX,
    multiplier:1, constant:0))
}
```

Our view (`self.view`) may proceed to be resized further as the interface settles down, but the small black square will still be positioned correctly, because the constraints determine that position relative to *whatever* the size of our view may be.

If we were to do the same thing without using autolayout, `viewDidLoad` would be an unwise choice; we should use `traitCollectionDidChange:` or `viewWillLayout-Subviews`. This leaves us in something of a quandary: such methods can be called multiple times over the lifetime of a view controller, so how can we perform initializations just once? The solution is to make use of a Bool property flag to ensure that our initialization code runs only the first time. For example:

```
override func viewWillLayoutSubviews() {
    if !self.viewInitializationDone {
        self.viewInitializationDone = true // ensure we do this just once
        let square = UIView(frame:CGRectMake(0,0,10,10))
        square.backgroundColor = UIColor.blackColor()
        square.center = CGPointMake(self.view.bounds.midX,5)
        self.view.addSubview(square)
    }
}
```

The correctness of our layout depends upon the value of `self.view.bounds`; by the time `viewWillLayoutSubviews` is called, initial view resizing is over and that value has settled down, so our code works.

Responding to rotation

When your app rotates 90 degrees, your view controller's main view may have its height and width bounds dimensions effectively swapped. This is an extraordinarily dramatic and extreme resizing, especially on an iPhone, where the typical aspect ratio is 16:9. In iOS 8, you get a little extra usable height in landscape orientation — for example, the status bar vanishes by default, and a navigation controller can be made to hide its top and bottom bars automatically — but your interface may still need to be rearranged, perhaps quite heavily, to cope with this change in size.

In many cases, autoresizing or (more likely) autolayout will handle the situation; in iOS 8, you can get a serious boost from conditional constraints and the ability to configure your nib in Xcode 6's nib editor so that views and constraints are removed and inserted *automatically* in response to a trait collection change (see Chapter 1).

Sometimes, however, code is needed to perform or supplement the rearrangement of your interface at rotation time. In iOS 8, you'll want to implement `willTransitionTo-TraitCollection...` or `viewWillTransitionToSize...` to respond to rotation. (Recall that the former event is *not* sent when an iPad rotates, because iPad rotation does not cause any change in the trait collection.)

Rotation is animated, and you'll probably want your layout changes to harmonize with and participate in that animation. This is where the `transitionCoordinator:` parameter comes in. It is (not surprisingly) a transition coordinator; in particular, it's an object adopting the UIViewControllerTransitionCoordinator protocol, which means that it is reponsible for governing a runtime animation (in this case, the rotation animation), and that it implements this method:

`animateAlongsideTransition:completion:`
> Takes an animation block and a completion block. The animation you supply is incorporated into the transition coordinator's animation. Returns a Bool, informing you in case your commands couldn't be animated.
>
> Both blocks receive as parameter a context object implementing the UIView-ControllerTransitionCoordinatorContext protocol. This object, among other things, has a `targetTransform` method that you can call to learn how far and in what direction the interface is rotating. The transition coordinator, too, is such a context object.
>
> In particular, if `rot` is the result of calling `targetTransform`, the rotation is 180 degrees — the thing you're most likely to want to know — if and only if both `rot.b` and `rot.c` are 0.

(Other methods implemented by the transition coordinator and context object are irrelevant to rotation; I'll discuss them later in this chapter, in connection with custom view controller transitions.)

In this (completely artificial) example, I'll specify that our interface should display a large black rectangle occupying the left side of the screen if the device is in landscape orientation, but not if the device is in portrait orientation. Let's say that this is an iPhone app. In that case, I can be notified of the rotation by implementing `willTransitionTo-TraitCollection:withTransitionCoordinator:`, and I can test which way we're about to rotate by examining the new trait collection's vertical size class. I'll animate the black rectangle on and off the screen in coordination with the rotation animation:

```
lazy var blackRect : UIView = self.makeBlackRect()
func makeBlackRect() -> UIView {
    var f = self.view.bounds
    if self.traitCollection.verticalSizeClass != .Compact {
        // probably will be called in portrait, swap dimensions
        (f.size.width, f.size.height) = (f.size.height, f.size.width)
    }
    f.size.width /= 3.0
    f.origin.x = -f.size.width
    let br = UIView(frame:f)
    br.backgroundColor = UIColor.blackColor()
    return br
}
override func willTransitionToTraitCollection(
    newCollection: UITraitCollection,
    withTransitionCoordinator coordinator:
    UIViewControllerTransitionCoordinator) {
        super.willTransitionToTraitCollection(
            newCollection, withTransitionCoordinator: coordinator)
        let v = self.blackRect
        var newFrameOriginX = v.frame.origin.x
        if newCollection.verticalSizeClass == .Compact { // landscape
            if v.superview == nil {
                self.view.addSubview(v)
                newFrameOriginX = 0
            }
        } else { // portrait
            if v.superview != nil {
                newFrameOriginX = -v.frame.size.width
            }
        }
        coordinator.animateAlongsideTransition({
            _ in
            v.frame.origin.x = newFrameOriginX // animate the change
        }, completion: {
            _ in
            if newCollection.verticalSizeClass != .Compact {
                self.blackRect.removeFromSuperview()
            }
        })
}
```

As usual, a constraint-based solution would be more robust. This is a good use of the technique I described in Chapter 1, where we prepare two sets of constraints and swap them in and out. I won't even bother to remove the black rectangle from the interface; I'll add it once and for all as I configure the view initially, and just slide it onscreen and offscreen as needed:

```swift
var blackRectConstraintsOnscreen : [NSLayoutConstraint]!
var blackRectConstraintsOffscreen : [NSLayoutConstraint]!
override func viewDidLoad() {
    let br = UIView()
    br.setTranslatesAutoresizingMaskIntoConstraints(false)
    br.backgroundColor = UIColor.blackColor()
    self.view.addSubview(br)
    // "b.r. is pinned to top and bottom of superview"
    self.view.addConstraints(
        NSLayoutConstraint.constraintsWithVisualFormat("V:|[br]|",
            options:nil, metrics:nil, views:["br":br]))
            // "b.r. is 1/3 the width of superview"
    self.view.addConstraint(
        NSLayoutConstraint(item:br, attribute:.Width,
            relatedBy:.Equal,
            toItem:self.view, attribute:.Width,
            multiplier:1.0/3.0, constant:0))
            // "onscreen, b.r.'s left is pinned to superview's left"
    let marrOn =
    NSLayoutConstraint.constraintsWithVisualFormat("H:|[br]",
        options:nil, metrics:nil, views:["br":br])
        // "offscreen, b.r.'s right is pinned to superview's left"
    let marrOff = [
        NSLayoutConstraint(item:br, attribute:.Right,
            relatedBy:.Equal,
            toItem:self.view, attribute:.Left,
            multiplier:1, constant:0)
    ]
    self.blackRectConstraintsOnscreen = marrOn as! [NSLayoutConstraint]
    self.blackRectConstraintsOffscreen = marrOff
    // start out offscreen!
    self.view.addConstraints(self.blackRectConstraintsOffscreen)
}
override func willTransitionToTraitCollection(
    newCollection: UITraitCollection,
    withTransitionCoordinator coordinator:
    UIViewControllerTransitionCoordinator) {
        super.willTransitionToTraitCollection(
            newCollection, withTransitionCoordinator: coordinator)
        self.view.removeConstraints(self.blackRectConstraintsOnscreen)
        self.view.removeConstraints(self.blackRectConstraintsOffscreen)
        if newCollection.verticalSizeClass == .Compact {
            self.view.addConstraints(self.blackRectConstraintsOnscreen)
        } else {
            self.view.addConstraints(self.blackRectConstraintsOffscreen)
        }
    }
}
```

The movement of the black rectangle is animated as the interface rotates, because *any* constraint-based layout performed as the interface rotates is animated.

For this particular example, an even more elegant solution is possible: the entire change of interface can be configured in the nib, using conditional constraints. The details are left as an exercise for the reader.

Presented View Controller

Back when the only iOS device was an iPhone, a presented view controller was called a *modal view controller*. The root view controller remained in place, but its view was taken out of the interface and the modal view controller's view was used instead. Thus, this was the simplest way to replace the entire interface with a different interface.

You can see why this configuration was characterized as "modal." The presented view controller's view has, in a sense, blocked access to the "real" view, the root view controller's view. The user is forced to work in the presented view controller's view, until that view is "dismissed" and the "real" view is visible again — similar to a modal dialog in a desktop application, where the user can't do anything else but work in the dialog as long as it is present. A presented view controller's view often reinforces this analogy with obvious dismissal buttons with titles like Save, Done, or Cancel.

The color picker view in my own Zotz! app is a good example (Figure 6-7); this is an interface that says, "You are now configuring a color, and that's all you can do; change the color or cancel, or you'll be stuck here forever." The user can't get out of this view without tapping Cancel or Done, and the view that the user was previously using is visible as a blur behind this view, waiting for the user to return to it.

Figure 6-5, from my Latin flashcard app, is another example of a presented view. It has a Cancel button, and the user is in a special "mode," performing a drill exercise rather than scrolling through flashcards.

Nevertheless, the "modal" characterization is not always apt. A presented view controller might be no more than a technique that you, the programmer, have used to alter the interface; the user needn't be conscious of this. A presented view controller's view may have a complex interface; it may have child view controllers; it may present yet *another* view controller; it may take over the interface *permanently*, with the user *never* returning to the interface that it replaced.

Furthermore, the range of ways in which a presented view controller's view can be displayed now goes far beyond merely replacing the root view controller's view. For example:

- Instead of replacing the entire interface, a presented view controller's view can replace a *subview* within the existing interface. (This ability was originally confined to the iPad alone; new in iOS 8, it is available on the iPhone as well.)

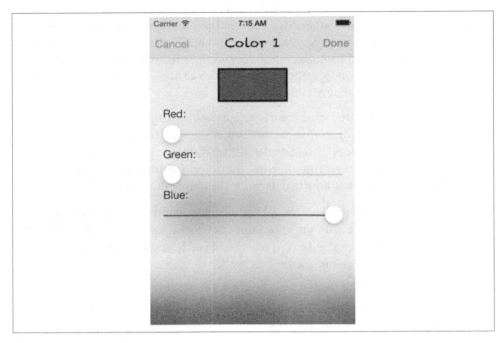

Figure 6-7. A modal view

- A presented view controller's view may cover the existing interface only *partially*; the existing interface is never removed. (This, too, was originally an iPad-only feature; it became possible on the iPhone starting in iOS 7.)

Presenting a View

The two key methods for presenting and dismissing a view are:

`presentViewController:animated:completion:`
> To make a view controller present another view controller, you send the first view controller this message, handing it the second view controller, which you will probably instantiate for this very purpose. (The first view controller is very typically `self`.)

> We now have two view controllers that stand in the relationship of `presentingView-Controller` and `presentedViewController`, and the latter is retained. The presented view controller's view effectively replaces or covers the presenting view controller's view in the interface (I'll talk later about ways to refine that arrangement).

`dismissViewControllerAnimated:completion:`
> The "presented" state of affairs described in the previous paragraph persists until the presenting view controller is sent this message. The presented view controller's view is then removed from the interface, and the presented view controller is released; it will thereupon typically go out of existence, together with its view, its child view controllers and *their* views, and so on.

As the view of the presented view controller appears, and again when it is dismissed, there's an option for animation to be performed as the transition takes place (the `animated:` argument, a Bool). The `completion:` parameter, which can be nil, lets you supply a block of code to be run after the transition (including the animation) has occurred. I'll talk later about how to determine the nature of the animation.

The presenting view controller (the presented view controller's `presentingViewController`) is not necessarily the view controller to which you sent `presentViewController:animated:completion:`. It will help if we distinguish *three* roles that view controllers can play in presenting a view controller:

Presented view controller
> The view controller specified as the first argument to `presentViewController:animated:completion:`.

Original presenter
> The view controller to which `presentViewController:animated:completion:` was sent. Apple sometimes refers to this view controller as the *source*; "original presenter" is my own term.
>
> The presented view controller is set as the original presenter's `presentedViewController`.

Presenting view controller
> The presented view controller's `presentingViewController`. This is the view controller whose view is replaced or covered by the presented view controller's view. By default, it is *the view controller whose view is the entire interface* — namely, either the root view controller or an already existing presented view controller. It might not be the same as the original presenter.
>
> The presented view controller is set as the presenting view controller's `presentedViewController`. Thus, the presented view controller might be the `presentedViewController` of two different view controllers.

The receiver of `dismissViewControllerAnimated:completion:` may be *any* of those three objects; the runtime will use the linkages between them to transmit the necessary messages up the chain on your behalf to the `presentingViewController`.

A view controller can have at most one `presentedViewController`. If you send `present-ViewController:animated:completion:` to a view controller whose `presentedViewController` isn't nil, nothing will happen (and you'll get a warning from the runtime). However, a presented view controller can itself present a view controller, so there can be a chain of presented view controllers.

Conversely, you can test for a nil `presentedViewController` or `presentingViewController` to learn whether view presentation is occurring. For example, a view controller whose `presentingViewController` is nil is not a presented view controller at this moment.

Let's make one view controller present another. We could do this simply by connecting one view controller to another in a storyboard with a modal segue, but I don't want you to do that: a modal segue calls `presentViewController:animated:completion:` for you, whereas I want you to call it yourself.

So start with an iPhone project made from the Single View Application template. This contains one view controller class, called ViewController. Our first move must be to add a second view controller class, an instance of which will function as the presented view controller:

1. Choose File → New → File and specify iOS → Source → Cocoa Touch Class. Click Next.

2. Name the class SecondViewController, make sure it is a subclass of UIViewController, and check the XIB checkbox so that we can design this view controller's view quickly and easily in a nib. Click Next.

3. Confirm the folder, group, and app target membership, and click Create.

4. Edit *SecondViewController.xib*, and do something there to make the view distinctive, so that you'll recognize it when it appears; for example, give it a red background color.

5. We need a way to trigger the presentation of SecondViewController. Edit *Main.storyboard* and add a button to the ViewController's view's interface. Connect that button to an action method in *ViewController.swift*; let's call it `doPresent:`.

6. In *ViewController.swift*, write the code for `doPresent:`, as follows:

```
@IBAction func doPresent(sender:AnyObject?) {
    let svc = SecondViewController(
        nibName: "SecondViewController", bundle: nil)
    self.presentViewController(svc, animated:true, completion:nil)
}
```

Run the project. In ViewController's view, tap the button. SecondViewController's view slides into place over ViewController's view.

In our lust for instant gratification, we have neglected to provide a way to dismiss the presented view controller. If you'd like to do that, edit *SecondViewController.xib*, put a button into SecondViewController's view, and connect it to an action method in *SecondViewController.swift*:

```
@IBAction func doDismiss(sender:AnyObject?) {
    self.presentingViewController!.dismissViewControllerAnimated(
        true, completion: nil)
}
```

Run the project. You can now alternate between ViewController's view and Second-ViewController's view, presenting and dismissing in turn.

Communication With a Presented View Controller

In real life, it is highly probable that the original presenter will have additional information to impart to the presented view controller as the latter is created and presented, and that the presented view controller will want to pass information back to the original presenter as it is dismissed. Knowing how to arrange this exchange of information is very important.

Passing information from the original presenter to the presented view controller is usually easy, because the original presenter typically has a reference to the presented view controller before the latter's view appears in the interface. For example, suppose the presented view controller has a public `data` property. Then the original presenter can easily set this property:

```
@IBAction func doPresent(sender:AnyObject?) {
    let svc = SecondViewController(
        nibName: "SecondViewController", bundle: nil)
    svc.data = "This is very important data!" // *
    self.presentViewController(svc, animated:true, completion:nil)
}
```

Indeed, if you're calling `presentViewController:animated:completion:` explicitly like this, you might even give your SecondViewController a designated initializer that accepts — and thus requires — this data. In my Latin vocabulary app, for example, I've given DrillViewController a designated initializer `init(data:)` precisely so that whoever creates it *must* pass it the data it will need to do its job while it exists.

Passing information back from the presented view controller to the original presenter is a more interesting problem. The presented view controller will need to know who the original presenter is, but it doesn't automatically have a reference to it (the original presenter, remember, is not necessarily the same as the `presentingViewController`). Moreover, the presented view controller will need to know the signature of some method, implemented by the original presenter, which it can call in order to hand over the information — and this needs to work regardless of the original presenter's class.

The standard solution is to use delegation, as follows:

- The presented view controller defines a *protocol* declaring a method that the presented view controller wants to call before it is dismissed.
- The original presenter conforms to this protocol: it declares adoption of the protocol, and it implements the required method.
- The presented view controller provides a means whereby it can be handed a reference to an object conforming to this protocol. Think of that reference as the presented view controller's *delegate*. Very often, this will be a property — perhaps called delegate! — typed as the protocol. (Such a property should be weak, since an object usually has no business retaining its delegate.)
- As the original presenter creates and configures the presented view controller, it hands the presented view controller a reference to itself, in its role as adopter of the protocol, by assigning itself as the presented view controller's delegate.

This sounds elaborate, but with practice you'll find yourself able to impement it very quickly. And you can see why it works: because its delegate is typed as the protocol, the presented view controller is guaranteed that, if it has a delegate, that delegate implements the method declared in the protocol. Thus, the desired communication from the presented view controller to whoever configured and created it is assured.

Let's modify our example to embody this architecture. First, edit *SecondView-Controller.swift* to look like this:

```
protocol SecondViewControllerDelegate : class {
    func acceptData(data:AnyObject!)
}
class SecondViewController : UIViewController {
    var data : AnyObject?
    weak var delegate : SecondViewControllerDelegate?
    @IBAction func doDismiss(sender:AnyObject?) {
        self.delegate?.acceptData("Even more important data!")
    }
}
```

It is now ViewController's job to adopt the SecondViewControllerDelegate protocol, and to set itself as the SecondViewController's delegate. When the delegate method is called, ViewController will be handed the data, and it should then dismiss the Second-ViewController:

```
class ViewController : UIViewController, SecondViewControllerDelegate {
    @IBAction func doPresent(sender:AnyObject?) {
        let svc = SecondViewController(
            nibName: "SecondViewController", bundle: nil)
        svc.data = "This is very important data!"
        svc.delegate = self // *
        self.presentViewController(svc, animated:true, completion:nil)
```

```
    }
    func acceptData(data:AnyObject!) {
        // do something with data here
        self.dismissViewControllerAnimated(true, completion: nil)
    }
}
```

That is a perfectly satisfactory implementation, and we could stop at this point. For completeness, I'll just show a possible variation. You might object that too much responsibility rests upon the original presenter (the delegate): it is sent the data and then it must also dismiss the presented view controller. Surely the presented view controller should hand back any data and should then dismiss itself (as in the preceding section). Even better, the presented view controller should hand back any data *automatically*, regardless of how it is dismissed.

We can arrange that by putting all the responsibility on the presented view controller. First, edit ViewController's `acceptData:` so that it accepts the data and no more (it no longer performs the dismissal). Second, back in SecondViewController, we will implement *both* the task of dismissal *and* the task of handing back the data, *separately*. To make the latter task automatic, SecondViewController will arrange to hear about its own dismissal by implementing `viewWillDisappear:` (discussed later in this chapter), which will then call `acceptData:` to ensure that the data is handed across. There is more than one reason why `viewWillDisappear:` might be called; we can ensure that this really is the moment of our own dismissal by calling `isBeingDismissed`. Here is what Second-ViewController looks like now:

```
protocol SecondViewControllerDelegate : class {
    func acceptData(data:AnyObject!)
}
class SecondViewController : UIViewController {
    var data : AnyObject?
    weak var delegate : SecondViewControllerDelegate?
    @IBAction func doDismiss(sender:AnyObject?) {
        self.presentingViewController!.dismissViewControllerAnimated(
            true, completion: nil)
    }
    override func viewWillDisappear(animated: Bool) {
        super.viewWillDisappear(animated)
        if self.isBeingDismissed() {
            self.delegate?.acceptData("Even more important data!")
        }
    }
}
```

 If you're using a storyboard, you may be able to make do without some of this architecture, by using an unwind segue instead. I'll discuss that later in this chapter.

Presented View Animation

When a view is presented and later when it is dismissed, a simple animation can be performed, according to whether the `animated:` parameter of the corresponding method is `true`. There are a few different built-in animation styles (*modal transition styles*) to choose from.

 Instead of choosing a simple built-in modal transition style, you can supply your own animation, as I'll explain later in the chapter.

Your choice of built-in animation style is not passed as a parameter when presenting or dismissing a view controller; rather, it is attached beforehand to a view controller as its `modalTransitionStyle` property. This value can be set in code or in the nib editor. Your choices (UIModalTransitionStyle) are:

`.CoverVertical` *(the default)*
    The presented view slides up from the bottom to cover the presenting view on presentation and down to reveal the presenting view on dismissal. "Bottom" is defined differently depending on the orientation of the device and the orientations the view controllers support.

`.FlipHorizontal`
    The view flips on the vertical axis as if the two views were the front and back of a piece of paper. The "vertical axis" is the device's long axis, regardless of the app's orientation.

    This animation style provides one of those rare occasions where the user may directly glimpse the window behind the transitioning views. You may want to set the window's background color appropriately.

`.CrossDissolve`
    The views remain stationary, and one fades into the other.

`.PartialCurl`
    The first view curls up like a page in a notepad to expose most of the second view, but remains covering the top-left region of the second view. Thus there must not be any important interface in that region, as the user will not be able to see it.

    If the user clicks on the curl, `dismissViewControllerAnimated:completion:` is called on the original presenter. That's convenient, but make sure it doesn't disrupt communication between your view controllers; this is another reason for factoring out any final handing back of information from the presented view controller into its `viewWillDisappear:`, as I did in the previous section.

In iOS 8, as of this writing, after the Partial Curl animation, the curled page is not present, but tapping where it would be dismisses the presented view controller. That's confusing, not to say incoherent, and is presumably a bug; this style should be avoided until it is fixed.

Presentation Styles

By default, the presented view controller's view occupies the entire screen, completely replacing that of the presenting view controller. But you can choose from a few other built-in options expressing how the presented view controller's view should cover the screen (*modal presentation styles*).

 Instead of choosing a simple built-in modal presentation style, you can place the presented view controller's view anywhere you like, as I'll explain later in this chapter.

To choose a presentation style, set the presented view controller's `modalPresentation-Style` property. This value can be set in code or in the nib editor. Your choices (UIModal-PresentationStyle) are:

`.FullScreen`
: The default. The presenting view controller is the root view controller or a fullscreen presented view controller, and its view — meaning the entire interface — is replaced.

`.OverFullScreen`
: New in iOS 8. Similar to `.FullScreen`, but the presenting view controller's view is *not* replaced; instead, it stays where it is, possibly being visible during the transition, and remaining visible behind the presented view controller's view if the latter has some transparency.

`.PageSheet`
: Similar to `.FullScreen`, but in landscape orientation the presented view is narrower, with the presenting view controller's view remaining partially visible (and dimmed) behind it. Treated as `.FullScreen` on the iPhone.

`.FormSheet`
: Similar to `.PageSheet`, but even smaller, allowing the user to see more of the presenting view controller's view behind it. As the name implies, this is intended to allow the user to fill out a form (Apple describes this as "gathering structured information from the user"). Treated as `.FullScreen` on the iPhone.

In iOS 8, "on the iPhone" (with respect to the .PageSheet and .FormSheet styles) means the iPhone *except for the iPhone 6 Plus in landscape orientation*, which is treated as an iPad for this purpose. This is, in part, the significance of the fact that the iPhone 6 Plus's horizontal size class in landscape orientation is .Regular.

.CurrentContext

> The presenting view controller can be *any* view controller, such as a child view controller. The presented view controller's view replaces the presenting view controller's view, both of which may occupy only a portion of the screen. New in iOS 8, this works on both iPhone and iPad (previously, it was confined to iPad only).

.OverCurrentContext

> New in iOS 8. Like .CurrentContext, but the presented view controller's view covers the presenting view controller's view rather than replacing it (parallel to the difference between .FullScreen and .OverFullScreen).

When the presented view controller's modalPresentationStyle is .CurrentContext or .OverCurrentContext, a decision has to be made by the runtime as to what view controller should be the presenting view controller. This will determine what view will be replaced or covered by the presented view controller's view. The decision involves another UIViewController property, definesPresentationContext (a Bool), and possibly still *another* UIViewController property, providesPresentationContextTransitionStyle. Here's how the decision operates:

1. Starting with the original presenter (the view controller to which presentViewController:animated:completion: was sent), we walk up the chain of parent view controllers, looking for one whose definesPresentationContext property is true. If we find one, that's the one; it will be the presentingViewController, and its view will be replaced or covered by the presented view controller's view.

   (If we *don't* find one, things work as if the presented view controller's modalPresentationStyle had been .FullScreen.)

2. If, during the search just described, we find a view controller whose definesPresentationContext property is true, we look to see if that view controller's providesPresentationContextTransitionStyle property is *also* true. If so, *that* view controller's modalTransitionStyle is used for this transition animation, instead of using the presented view controller's modalTransitionStyle.

To illustrate, I need a parent–child view controller arrangement to work with. This chapter hasn't yet discussed any parent view controllers in detail, but the simplest is UITabBarController, which I discuss in the next section, and it's easy to create a working app with a UITabBarController-based interface, so that's the example I'll use.

Start with the Tabbed Application project template. As in the previous example, I want us to create and present the presented view controller manually, rather than letting the storyboard do it automatically; so make a new view controller class with an accompanying *.xib* file, to use as a presented view controller — call it ExtraViewController. In *ExtraViewController.xib*, give the view a distinctive background color, so you'll recognize it when it appears.

In the storyboard, put a button in the First View Controller view, and connect it to an action method in *FirstViewController.swift* that summons the new view controller as a presented view controller:

```
@IBAction func doPresent(sender:AnyObject?) {
    let vc = ExtraViewController(nibName: "ExtraViewController", bundle: nil)
    self.presentViewController(vc, animated: true, completion: nil)
}
```

Run the project and tap the button. Observe that the presented view controller's view occupies the *entire* interface, covering even the tab bar; it replaces the root view, because the presentation style is `.FullScreen`. The presenting view controller is the root view controller, which is the UITabBarController.

Now change the code to look like this:

```
@IBAction func doPresent(sender:AnyObject?) {
    let vc = ExtraViewController(nibName: "ExtraViewController", bundle: nil)
    self.definesPresentationContext = true
    vc.modalPresentationStyle = .CurrentContext
    self.presentViewController(vc, animated: true, completion: nil)
}
```

Run the project and tap the button. The presented view controller's view replaces only the first view controller's view; the tab bar remains, and you can switch back and forth between the tab bar's first and second views even while the first view remains covered by the presented view. That's because the presented view controller's `modal-PresentationStyle` is `.CurrentContext`, and `definesPresentationContext` is `true` in FirstViewController, which is the original presenter. Thus the search for a context stops in FirstViewController, which thus becomes the presenting view controller — meaning that the presented view replaces FirstViewController's view instead of the root view.

We can also override the presented view controller's transition animation through the `modalTransitionStyle` property of the presenting view controller:

```
@IBAction func doPresent(sender:AnyObject?) {
    let vc = ExtraViewController(nibName: "ExtraViewController", bundle: nil)
    self.definesPresentationContext = true
    self.providesPresentationContextTransitionStyle = true
    self.modalTransitionStyle = .CoverVertical
```

```
        vc.modalPresentationStyle = .CurrentContext
        vc.modalTransitionStyle = .FlipHorizontal // this will be overridden
        self.presentViewController(vc, animated: true, completion: nil)
    }
```

Because the presenting view controller's `providesPresentationContextTransition-Style` is `true`, the transition uses the `.CoverVertical` animation belonging to the presenting view controller, rather than the `.FlipHorizontal` animation of the presented view controller.

 The example just given also elicits a tab bar controller bug: if you summon the presented view controller, switch to the Second tab, switch back to the First tab, and dismiss the presented view controller, the First view is black. Until this is fixed, this configuration should not be used in production code.

When a view controller is presented, if its presentation style is *not* `.FullScreen`, a question arises of whether its status bar methods (`prefersStatusBarHidden` and `preferredStatusBarStyle`) should be consulted. By default, the answer is no, because this view controller is not the top-level view controller. To make the answer be yes, set this view controller's `modalPresentationCapturesStatusBarAppearance` to `true`.

Adaptive Presentation

I have said that the `.PageSheet` and `.FormSheet` presentation styles are treated as `.FullScreen` on the iPhone, but in fact you get a little more flexibility than that: you can choose between `.FullScreen` and `.OverFullScreen`. To exercise this flexibility, you use *adaptive presentation*. This means that, in adaptive situations — meaning, in this case, that the horizontal size class is `.Compact` — your code is consulted in real time as to how you want this presentation treated.

Adaptive presentation gives you even more power than that; you can elect to present *a different view controller* from the one that was originally to be presented. Thus, you can design one view controller and its view for the iPad, and a different view controller and its view for the more limited screen space of the iPhone.

To implement adaptive presentation, iOS 8 introduces a new object, a view controller's *presentation controller* (`presentationController`, a UIPresentationController). Before presenting a view controller, you set its presentation controller's delegate (UIAdaptivePresentationControllerDelegate). Before the presented view controller's view appears, the delegate is sent these messages:

`adaptivePresentationStyleForPresentationController:`
     Asks for a presentation style. Return either `.FullScreen` or `.OverFullScreen`. (There is also a `.None` option, whose significance I'll discuss in Chapter 9.)

`presentationController:viewControllerForAdaptivePresentationStyle:`
    Called only if the previous method is implemented. Return a view controller to be presented, substituting it for the current presented view controller.

Here's how to present a view controller as a `.PageSheet` on iPad but as `.OverFull-Screen` on iPhone:

```
class ViewController : UIViewController,
    UIAdaptivePresentationControllerDelegate {
        @IBAction func doPresent(sender:AnyObject?) {
            let svc = SecondViewController(
                nibName: "SecondViewController", bundle: nil)
            svc.modalPresentationStyle = .FormSheet
            svc.presentationController!.delegate = self // *
            self.presentViewController(svc, animated:true, completion:nil)
        }
        func adaptivePresentationStyleForPresentationController(
            controller: UIPresentationController)
            -> UIModalPresentationStyle {
                return .OverFullScreen // *
        }
}
```

And here's an example of replacing the view controller presented on iPad with a different view controller to be presented on iPhone:

```
class ViewController : UIViewController,
    UIAdaptivePresentationControllerDelegate {
        @IBAction func doPresent(sender:AnyObject?) {
            let svc = SecondViewController(
                nibName: "SecondViewController", bundle: nil)
            svc.modalPresentationStyle = .FormSheet
            svc.presentationController!.delegate = self
            self.presentViewController(svc, animated:true, completion:nil)
        }
        func adaptivePresentationStyleForPresentationController(
            controller: UIPresentationController)
            -> UIModalPresentationStyle {
                return .OverFullScreen
        }
        func presentationController(controller: UIPresentationController,
            viewControllerForAdaptivePresentationStyle
            style: UIModalPresentationStyle) -> UIViewController? {
                let newvc = ThirdViewController(
                    nibName: "ThirdViewController", bundle: nil)
                return newvc
        }
}
```

In real life, of course, if you were really going to substitute a completely different view controller, you'd probably need to prepare it before returning it (for example, giving it data and setting its delegate). A more probable scenario is that you'd return a view controller which is actually the *same* view controller, but wrapped in a navigation controller; I'll illustrate in Chapter 9.

You might object that all of this could equally well be done with if-statements and run-time examination of the environment: if we're on an iPad, use `.FormSheet` and Second-ViewController; otherwise, use `.OverFullScreen` and ThirdViewController. The purpose of this mechanism, though, is partly so that you *don't* have to use if-statements; the presentation is itself adaptive, and adapts when that's appropriate. Besides, there's much more to the full power and purpose of the presentation controller, as I'll explain later in this chapter and in Chapter 9.

Rotation of a Presented View

When the presenting view controller is the top-level view controller — the root view controller, or a fullscreen presented view controller — the presented view controller becomes the new top-level view controller. This means that its `supportedInterfaceOrientations` is consulted and honored. If these `supportedInterfaceOrientations` do not intersect with the app's current orientation, the app's orientation will rotate, as the presented view appears, to an orientation that the presented view controller supports — and the same thing will be true in reverse when the presented view controller is dismissed.

Thus, a presented view controller allows you to *force* the interface to rotate. In fact, a presented view controller is the *only* officially sanctioned way to force the interface to rotate.

In iOS 5 and before, the interface could be forced to rotate by other kinds of view controller transition, such as pushing a view controller onto a navigation controller's stack, but this is no longer the case; attempts to circumvent this change and emulate the historic iOS 5 behavior are generally futile (and unnecessary).

Forced rotation is a perfectly reasonable thing to do, especially on the iPhone, where the user can easily rotate the device to compensate for the new orientation of the interface. Some views work better in portrait than landscape; some views work better in landscape than portrait (especially on the small screen). Forced rotation lets you ensure that each view appears only in the orientation in which it works best.

The presented view controller's `supportedInterfaceOrientations` may be a mask permitting multiple possible orientations. Such a view controller may wish to specify which of those orientations it would like to appear in *initially* when it is presented. To do so, override `preferredInterfaceOrientationForPresentation`; this method is called before `supportedInterfaceOrientations`, and should return a single UIInterfaceOrientation (*not* a mask). For example:

```
override func preferredInterfaceOrientationForPresentation()
    -> UIInterfaceOrientation {
        return .LandscapeLeft
}
```

Tab Bar Controller

A *tab bar* (UITabBar, see also Chapter 12) is a horizontal bar containing items. Each item is a UITabBarItem; it displays, by default, an image and a title. At all times, exactly one of these items is selected (highlighted); when the user taps an item, it becomes the selected item.

If there are too many items to fit on a tab bar, the excess items are automatically subsumed into a final More item. When the user taps the More item, a list of the excess items appears, and the user can select one; the user can also be permitted to edit the tab bar, determining which items appear in the tab bar itself and which ones spill over into the More list.

A tab bar is an independent interface object, but it is most commonly used in conjunction with a *tab bar controller* (UITabBarController, a subclass of UIViewController) to form a *tab bar interface*. The tab bar controller displays the tab bar at the bottom of its own view. From the user's standpoint, the tab bar items correspond to views; when the user selects a tab bar item, the corresponding view appears. The user is thus employing the tab bar to choose an entire area of your app's functionality. In reality, the UITabBarController is a parent view controller; you give it child view controllers, which the tab bar controller then contains, and the views summoned by tapping the tab bar items are the views of those child view controllers.

Familiar examples of a tab bar interface on the iPhone are Apple's Clock app, which has four tab bar items, and Apple's Music app, which has four tab bar items plus a More item that reveals a list of five more.

You can get a reference to the tab bar controller's tab bar through its `tabBar` property. In general, you won't need this. When using a tab bar interface by way of a UITabBarController, you do not interact (as a programmer) with the tab bar itself; you don't create it or set its delegate. You provide the UITabBarController with children, and it does the rest; when the UITabBarController's view is displayed, there's the tab bar along with the view of the selected item. You can, however, customize the *look* of the tab bar (see Chapter 12 for details).

If a tab bar controller is the top-level view controller, it determines your app's compensatory rotation behavior. To take a hand in that determination without having to subclass UITabBarController, make one of your objects the tab bar controller's delegate (UITabBarControllerDelegate) and implement these methods, as needed:

- `tabBarControllerSupportedInterfaceOrientations:`
- `tabBarControllerPreferredInterfaceOrientationForPresentation:`

A top-level tab bar controller also determines your app's status bar appearance. However, a tab bar controller implements `childViewControllerForStatusBarStyle` and `child-ViewControllerForStatusBarHidden` so that the actual decision is relegated to the child view controller whose view is currently being displayed. Thus, your `preferredStatus-BarStyle` and `prefersStatusBarHidden` are consulted and obeyed.

Tab Bar Items

For each view controller you assign as a tab bar controller's child, you're going to need a *tab bar item*, which will appear as its representative in the tab bar. This tab bar item will be your child view controller's `tabBarItem`. A tab bar item is a UITabBarItem; this is a subclass of UIBarItem, an abstract class that provides some of its most important properties, such as `title`, `image`, and `enabled`.

There are two ways to make a tab bar item:

By borrowing it from the system

Instantiate UITabBarItem using `init(tabBarSystemItem:tag:)`, and assign the instance to your child view controller's `tabBarItem`. Consult the documentation for the list of available system items. Unfortunately, you can't customize a system tab bar item's title; you must accept the title the system hands you. (You can't work around this restriction by somehow copying a system tab bar item's image.)

By making your own

Instantiate UITabBarItem using `init(title:image:tag:)` and assign the instance to your child view controller's `tabBarItem`. Alternatively, use the view controller's existing `tabBarItem` and set its `image` and `title`. Instead of setting the `title` of the `tabBarItem`, you can set the `title` property of the view controller itself; doing this automatically sets the `title` of its current `tabBarItem` (unless the tab bar item is a system tab bar item), though the converse is not true.

You can add a separate `selectedImage` (possibly by initializing with `init(title:image:selectedImage:)`). The `selectedImage` will be displayed in place of the normal `image` when this tab bar item is selected in the tab bar.

The `image` (and `selectedImage`) for a tab bar item should be a 30×30 PNG; if it is larger, it will be scaled down as needed. By default, it will be treated as a transparency mask (a template): the hue of its pixels will be ignored, and the transparency of its pixels will be combined with the tab bar's `tintColor`, which may be inherited from higher up the view hierarchy. However, you can instead display the image as is, and not as a transparency mask, by deriving and using an image whose rendering mode is `.Always-Original` (see Chapter 2 and the discussion of `imageWithRenderingMode:`).

You can also give a tab bar item a badge (see the documentation on the `badgeValue` property). Other ways in which you can customize the look of a tab bar item are discussed in Chapter 12. For example, you can control the font and style of the title, or you can give it an empty title and offset the image.

Configuring a Tab Bar Controller

Basic configuration of a tab bar controller is very simple: just hand it the view controllers that will be its children. To do so, collect those view controllers into an array and set the UITabBarController's `viewControllers` property to that array. The view controllers in the array are now the tab bar controller's child view controllers; the tab bar controller is the `parentViewController` of the view controllers in the array. The tab bar controller is also the `tabBarController` of the view controllers in the array and of all their children; thus a child view controller at any depth can learn that it is contained by a tab bar controller and can get a reference to that tab bar controller. The tab bar controller retains the array, and the array retains the child view controllers.

Here's a simple example from one of my apps, in which I construct and display a tab bar interface in code (in the app delegate's `application:didFinishLaunchingWith-Options:`):

```
let viewController1 = GameBoardController()
let viewController2 = UINavigationController(
    rootViewController:SettingsController())
self.tabBarController.viewControllers = [viewController1, viewController2]
self.tabBarController.selectedIndex = 0
self.tabBarController.delegate = self
self.window!.rootViewController = self.tabBarController
```

The tab bar controller's tab bar will automatically display the `tabBarItem` of each child view controller. The order of the tab bar items is the order of the view controllers in the tab bar controller's `viewControllers` array. Thus, a child view controller will probably want to configure its `tabBarItem` property early in its lifetime, so that the `tabBarItem` is ready by the time the view controller is handed as a child to the tab bar controller. Observe that `viewDidLoad` is *not* early enough! That's because the view controllers (other than the initially selected view controller) have no view when the tab bar controller initially appears. Thus it is common to implement an initializer for this purpose.

Here's an example from the same app as the previous code (in the GameBoardController class):

```
init() {
    super.init(nibName:nil, bundle:nil)
    // tab bar configuration
    self.tabBarItem.image = UIImage(named: "game.png")
    self.title = "Game"
}
```

In the tab bar, the image "game.png" is displayed as is, not as a template. I don't have to call imageWithRenderingMode: because the rendering mode is set directly in the asset catalog that holds the image.

If you change the tab bar controller's view controllers array later in its lifetime and you want the corresponding change in the tab bar's display of its items to be animated, call setViewControllers:animated:.

Initially, by default, the first child view controller's tab bar item is selected and its view is displayed. To tell the tab bar controller which tab bar item should be selected, you can couch your choice in terms of the contained view controller (selectedView-Controller) or by index number in the array (selectedIndex). The same properties also tell you what view controller's view the user has displayed by tapping in the tab bar.

 You can supply an animation when a tab bar controller's selected tab item changes and one child view controller's view is replaced by another. I'll discuss this topic later in the chapter.

You can also set the UITabBarController's delegate (adopting UITabBarController-Delegate). The delegate gets messages allowing it to prevent a given tab bar item from being selected, and notifying it when a tab bar item is selected and when the user is customizing the tab bar from the More item.

If the tab bar contains few enough items that it doesn't need a More item, there won't be one, and the tab bar won't be user-customizable. If there *is* a More item, you can exclude some tab bar items from being customizable by setting the customizableView-Controllers property to an array that lacks them; setting this property to nil means that the user can see the More list but can't rearrange the items. Setting the view-Controllers property sets the customizableViewControllers property to the same value, so if you're going to set the customizableViewControllers property, do it *after* setting the viewControllers property. The moreNavigationController property can be compared with the selectedViewController property to learn whether the user is currently viewing the More list; apart from this, the More interface is mostly out of your control, but I'll discuss some sneaky ways of customizing it in Chapter 12.

(If you allow the user to rearrange items, you would presumably want to save the new arrangement and restore it the next time the app runs. You might use NSUserDefaults for this; you could also take advantage of the built-in automatic state saving and restoration facilities, discussed later in this chapter.)

You can also configure a UITabBarController in a *.storyboard* or *.xib* file. The UITab-BarController's contained view controllers can be set directly — in a storyboard, there will be a "view controllers" relationship between the tab bar controller and each of its children — and the contained view controllers will be instantiated together with the tab bar controller. Moreover, each contained view controller has a Tab Bar Item; you can select this and set many aspects of the `tabBarItem`, such as its system item or its title, image, selected image, and tag, directly in the nib. (If a view controller in a nib doesn't have a Tab Bar Item and you want to configure this view controller for use in a tab bar interface, drag a Tab Bar Item from the Object library onto the view controller.)

To start a project with a main storyboard that has a UITabBarController as its root view controller, begin with the Tabbed Application template.

Navigation Controller

A *navigation bar* (UINavigationBar, see also Chapter 12) is a horizontal bar displaying a center title and a right button. When the user taps the right button, the navigation bar animates, sliding its interface out to the left and replacing it with a new interface that enters from the right. The new interface displays a back button at the left side, and a new center title — and possibly a new right button. The user can tap the back button to go back to the first interface, which slides in from the left; or, if there's a right button in the second interface, the user can tap it to go further forward to a third interface, which slides in from the right.

The successive interfaces of a navigation bar thus behave like a stack. In fact, a navigation bar does represent an actual stack — an internal stack of *navigation items* (UINavigationItem). It starts out with one navigation item: the *root* or *bottom item* of the stack. Since there is just one navigation item, this is also the *top item* of the stack (the navigation bar's `topItem`). It is the top item whose interface is always reflected in the navigation bar. When the user taps a right button, a new navigation item is pushed onto the stack; it becomes the top item, and its interface is seen. When the user taps a back button, the top item is popped off the stack, and what was previously the next item beneath it in the stack — the *back item* (the navigation bar's `backItem`) — becomes the top item, and its interface is seen.

The state of the stack is thus reflected in the navigation bar's interface. The navigation bar's center title comes automatically from the top item, and its back button comes from the back item. (See Chapter 12 for a complete description.) Thus, the title tells the user what item is current, and the left side is a button telling the user what item we would return to if the user were to tap that button. The animations reinforce this notion of directionality, giving the user a sense of position within a chain of items.

A navigation bar is an independent interface object, but it is most commonly used in conjunction with a *navigation controller* (UINavigationController, a subclass of UIViewController) to form a *navigation interface*. Just as there is a stack of navigation items in the navigation bar, there is a stack of view controllers in the navigation controller. These view controllers are the navigation controller's children, and each navigation item belongs to a view controller — it is a view controller's `navigationItem`.

The navigation controller performs automatic coordination of the navigation bar and the overall interface. Whenever a view controller comes to the top of the navigation controller's stack, its view is displayed in the interface. At the same time, its `navigation-Item` is automatically pushed onto the top of the navigation bar's stack — and thus is automatically displayed in the navigation bar. Moreover, the animation in the navigation bar is reinforced by animation of the interface as a whole: by default, a view controller's view slides into the main interface from the left or right just as its navigation item slides into the navigation bar from the left or right.

 You can supply a different animation when a view controller is pushed onto or popped off of a navigation controller's stack. I'll discuss this topic later in the chapter.

Your code can control the overall navigation, so in real life, the user may well navigate to the right, not by tapping the right button in the navigation bar, but by tapping something inside the main interface, such as a listing in a table view. (Figure 6-1 is a navigation interface that works this way.) In this situation, your code is deciding in real time what the next view should be; typically, you won't even create the next view controller until the user asks to navigate to it. The navigation interface thus becomes a *master–detail interface*.

Conversely, you might put a view controller inside a navigation controller just to get the convenience of the navigation bar, with its title and buttons, even when no actual push-and-pop navigation is going to take place.

You can get a reference to the navigation controller's navigation bar through its `navigationBar` property. In general, you won't need this. When using a navigation interface by way of a UINavigationController, you do not interact (as a programmer) with the navigation bar itself; you don't create it or set its delegate. You provide the UINavigationController with children, and it does the rest, handing each child view controller's `navigationItem` to the navigation bar for display and showing the child view controller's view each time navigation occurs. You can, however, customize the *look* of the navigation bar (see Chapter 12 for details).

A navigation interface may also optionally display a toolbar at the bottom. A toolbar (UIToolbar) is a horizontal view displaying a row of items, any of which the user can tap. Typically, the tapped item may highlight momentarily, but it is not selected; it represents the initiation of an action, like a button. You can get a reference to a UINavigationController's toolbar through its `toolbar` property. The look of the toolbar can be customized (Chapter 12). In a navigation interface, however, the *contents* of the toolbar are determined automatically by the view controller that is currently the top item in the stack: they are its `toolbarItems`.

 A UIToolbar can also be used independently, and often is. It then typically appears at the bottom on an iPhone — Figure 6-3 has a toolbar at the bottom — but often appears at the top on an iPad, where it plays something of the role that the menu bar plays on the desktop. When a toolbar is displayed by a navigation controller, though, it always appears at the bottom.

A familiar example of a navigation interface is Apple's Settings app on the iPhone. The Mail app on the iPhone is a navigation interface that includes a toolbar.

If a navigation controller is the top-level view controller, it determines your app's compensatory rotation behavior. To take a hand in that determination without having to subclass UINavigationController, make one of your objects the navigation controller's delegate (UINavigationControllerDelegate) and implement these methods, as needed:

- `navigationControllerSupportedInterfaceOrientations:`
- `navigationControllerPreferredInterfaceOrientationForPresentation:`

A top-level navigation controller also determines your app's status bar appearance. However, a navigation controller implements `childViewControllerForStatusBarStyle` and `childViewControllerForStatusBarHidden` so that the actual decision is relegated to the child view controller whose view is currently being displayed — with the following caveats:

- Your child view controllers can implement `prefersStatusBarHidden`, but showing and hiding the status bar during navigation causes the navigation bar to stop working in iOS 8 and should be avoided. (This is presumably a bug.)
- Your child view controllers can implement `preferredStatusBarStyle`, but the navigation controller respects this only if the navigation bar is hidden. If the navigation bar is showing, the navigation controller sets the status bar style based on the navigation bar's `barStyle` — to `.Default` if the bar style is `.Default`, and to `.LightContent` if the bar style is `.Black`. So, if the navigation bar is showing, the way to change the status bar style is to change the navigation bar style.

Bar Button Items

The buttons in a UIToolbar or a UINavigationBar are bar button items — UIBarButtonItem, a subclass of UIBarItem. A bar button item comes in one of two broadly different flavors:

Basic bar button item
> The bar button item behaves like a simple button.

Custom view
> The bar button item has no inherent behavior, but has (and displays) a `customView`.

UIBarItem is not a UIView subclass. A basic bar button item is button-like, but it has no frame, no UIView touch handling, and so forth. A UIBarButtonItem's `customView`, however, *is* a UIView — indeed, it can be *any* kind of UIView. Thus, a bar button item with a `customView` can display any sort of view in a toolbar or navigation bar, and that view can implement touch handling however it likes.

Let's start with the basic bar button item (no custom view). A bar button item, like a tab bar item, inherits from UIBarItem the `title`, `image`, and `enabled` properties. The title text color, by default, comes from the bar button item's `tintColor`, which may be inherited from the bar itself or from higher up the view hierarchy. Assigning an image removes the title. The image should usually be quite small; Apple recommends 22×22. By default, it will be treated as a transparency mask (a template): the hue of its pixels will be ignored, and the transparency of its pixels will be combined with the bar button item's `tintColor`. However, you can instead display the image as is, and not as a transparency mask, by deriving and using an image whose rendering mode is `.AlwaysOriginal` (see Chapter 2 and the discussion of `imageWithRenderingMode:`).

A basic bar button item has a `style` property (UIBarButtonItemStyle); this will usually be `.Plain`. The alternative, `.Done`, causes the title to be bold. You can further refine the title font and style. In addition, a bar button item can have a background image; this will typically be a small, resizable image, and can be used to provide a border. Full details appear in Chapter 12.

A bar button item also has `target` and `action` properties. These contribute to its button-like behavior: tapping a bar button item can trigger an action method elsewhere.

There are three ways to make a bar button item:

By borrowing it from the system
> Make a UIBarButtonItem with `init(barButtonSystemItem:target:action:)`. Consult the documentation for the list of available system items; they are not the same as for a tab bar item. You can't assign a title or change the image. (But you can change the tint color or assign a background image.)

By making your own basic bar button item

Make a UIBarButtonItem with `init(title:style:target:action:)` or with `init(image:style:target:action:)`.

An additional initializer, `init(image:landscapeImagePhone:style:target:action:)`, lets you supply two images, one for portrait orientation, the other for landscape orientation; this is because by default, the bar's height might change when the interface is rotated. In iOS 8, you are more likely to use size class–aware images to handle this situation (see Chapter 2).

By making a custom view bar button item

Make a UIBarButtonItem with `init(customView:)`, supplying a UIView that the bar button item is to display. The bar button item has no action and target; the UIView itself must somehow implement button behavior if that's what you want. For example, the `customView` might be a UISegmentedButton, but then it is the UISegmentedButton's target and action that give it button behavior.

Bar button items in a toolbar are horizontally positioned automatically by the system. You can provide hints to help with this positioning. If you know that you'll be changing an item's title dynamically, you'll probably want its width to accommodate the longest possible title right from the start; to arrange that, set the `possibleTitles` property to a Set of strings that includes the longest title. Alternatively, you can supply an absolute `width`. Also, you can incorporate spacers into the toolbar; these are created with `init(barButtonSystemItem:target:action:)`, but they have no visible appearance, and cannot be tapped. Place `.FlexibleSpace` system items between the visible items to distribute the visible items equally across the width of the toolbar. There is also a `.FixedSpace` system item whose `width` lets you insert a space of defined size.

Navigation Items and Toolbar Items

What appears in a navigation bar (UINavigationBar) depends upon the navigation items (UINavigationItem) in its stack. In a navigation interface, the navigation controller will manage the navigation bar's stack for you, but you must still configure each navigation item by setting properties of the `navigationItem` of each child view controller. The UINavigationItem properties are as follows (see also Chapter 12):

`title` *or* `titleView`

Determines what is to appear in the center of the navigation bar when this navigation item is at the top of the stack.

The `title` is a string. Setting the view controller's `title` property sets the `title` of the `navigationItem` automatically, and is usually the best approach.

The `titleView` can be any kind of UIView; if set, it will be displayed instead of the `title`. The `titleView` can implement further UIView functionality; for example,

Figure 6-8. A segmented control in the center of a navigation bar

it can be tappable. Even if you are using a `titleView`, you should still give your view controller a `title`, as it will be needed for the back button when a view controller is pushed onto the stack on top of this one.

Figure 6-1 shows the TidBITS News master view, with the navigation bar displaying a `titleView` which is a (tappable) image view; the master view controller's `title`, which is `"TidBITS"`, is therefore not displayed. In the TidBITS News detail view controller's navigation item, the `titleView` is a segmented control providing a Previous and Next button; when it is pushed onto the stack, the back button displays the master view controller's `title` (Figure 6-8).

prompt
:   An optional string to appear centered above everything else in the navigation bar. The navigation bar's height will be increased to accommodate it.

rightBarButtonItem *or* rightBarButtonItems
:   A bar button item or, respectively, an array of bar button items to appear at the right side of the navigation bar; the first item in the array will be rightmost.

    In Figure 6-8, the text size button is a right bar button item; it has nothing to do with navigation, but is placed here merely because space is at a premium on the small iPhone screen.

backBarButtonItem
:   When a view controller is pushed on top of this view controller, the navigation bar will display at its left a button pointing to the left, whose title is this view controller's `title`. That button is *this* view controller's navigation item's `backBarButtonItem`. That's right: the back button displayed in the navigation bar belongs, not to the top item (the `navigationItem` of the current view controller), but to the back item (the `navigationItem` of the view controller that is one level down in the stack). In Figure 6-8, the back button in the detail view is the master view controller's default back button, displaying its `title`.

    The vast majority of the time, the default behavior is the behavior you'll want, and you'll leave the back button alone. If you wish, though, you can customize the back button by setting a view controller's `navigationItem.backBarButtonItem` so that it contains an image, or a title differing from the view controller's `title`. The best technique is to provide a new UIBarButtonItem whose target and action are nil; the runtime will add a correct target and action, so as to create a working back button. Here's how to create a back button with a custom image instead of a title:

```
let b = UIBarButtonItem(
    image:UIImage(named:"files.png"), style:.Plain, target:nil, action:nil)
self.navigationItem.backBarButtonItem = b
```

A Bool property, hidesBackButton, allows the top navigation item to suppress display of the back item's back bar button item. If you set this to true, you'll probably want to provide some other means of letting the user navigate back.

The visible indication that the back button *is* a back button is a left-pointing chevron (the *back indicator*) that's separate from the button itself. This chevron can also be customized, but it's a feature of the navigation bar, not the bar button item: set the navigation bar's backIndicatorImage and backIndicatorTransitionMask. (I'll give an example in Chapter 12.) Alternatively, if the back button is assigned a background image, the back indicator is removed; it is up to the background image to point left, if desired.

leftBarButtonItem *or* leftBarButtonItems
> A bar button item or, respectively, an array of bar button items to appear at the left side of the navigation bar; the first item in the array will be leftmost. The leftItems-SupplementBackButton property, if set to true, allows both the back button and one or more left bar button items to appear.

A view controller's navigation item can have its properties set at any time while being displayed in the navigation bar. This (and not direct manipulation of the navigation bar) is the way to change the navigation bar's contents dynamically. For example, in one of my apps, the titleView is a progress view (UIProgressView, Chapter 12) that needs updating every second, and the right bar button should be either the system Play button or the system Pause button, depending on whether music from the library is playing, paused, or stopped. So I have a timer that periodically checks the state of the music player:

```
// change the progress bar
if let item = self.nowPlayingItem {
    let current = self.mp.currentPlaybackTime
    let total = item.valueForProperty(
        MPMediaItemPropertyPlaybackDuration).doubleValue
    self.prog.progress = Float(current) / Float(total)
} else {
    self.prog.progress = 0
}
// change the bar button
var whichButton : UIBarButtonSystemItem = .Cancel // placeholder
if self.mp.currentPlaybackRate > 0.1 {
    whichButton = .Pause
} else if self.mp.currentPlaybackRate <= 0.1 {
    whichButton = .Play
```

```
    }
    self.previousButton = whichButton
    if whichButton == .Cancel {
        self.navigationItem.rightBarButtonItem = nil
    } else {
        let bb = UIBarButtonItem(barButtonSystemItem: whichButton,
            target: self, action: "doPlayPause:")
        self.navigationItem.rightBarButtonItem = bb
    }
```

Each view controller to be pushed onto the navigation controller's stack is responsible for supplying the items to appear in the navigation interface's toolbar, if there is one. To configure this, set the view controller's `toolbarItems` property to an array of UIBarButtonItem instances. You can change the toolbar items even while the view controller's view and current `toolbarItems` are showing, optionally with animation, by sending `setToolbarItems:animated:` to the view controller.

A view controller has the power to specify that its ancestor's bottom bar (a navigation controller's toolbar, or a tab bar controller's tab bar) should be hidden as this view controller is pushed onto a navigation controller's stack. To do so, set the view controller's `hidesBottomBarWhenPushed` property to `true`. The trick is that you must do this very early, before the view loads; the view controller's initializer is a good place. The bottom bar remains hidden from the time this view controller is pushed to the time it is popped, even if other view controllers are pushed and popped on top of it in the meantime. You can also send `setToolbarHidden:animated:` to a UINavigationController at any time.

Configuring a Navigation Controller

You configure a navigation controller by manipulating its stack of view controllers. This stack is the navigation controller's `viewControllers` array property, though you will rarely need to manipulate that property directly.

The view controllers in a navigation controller's `viewControllers` array are the navigation controller's child view controllers; the navigation controller is the `parentViewController` of the view controllers in the array. The navigation controller is also the `navigationController` of the view controllers in the array and of all their children; thus a child view controller at any depth can learn that it is contained by a navigation controller and can get a reference to that navigation controller. The navigation controller retains the array, and the array retains the child view controllers.

The normal way to manipulate a navigation controller's stack is by pushing or popping one view controller at a time. When the navigation controller is instantiated, it is usually initialized with `init(rootViewController:)`; this is a convenience method that assigns the navigation controller a single initial child view controller, the root view controller that goes at the bottom of the stack:

```
let fvc = FirstViewController()
let nav = UINavigationController(rootViewController:fvc)
self.window!.rootViewController = nav
```

Instead of `init(rootViewController:)`, you might choose to create the navigation controller with `init(navigationBarClass:toolbarClass:)`, in order to set a custom subclass of UINavigationBar or UIToolbar. Typically, this will be in order to customize the appearance of the navigation bar and toolbar; sometimes you'll create, say, a UI-Toolbar subclass for no other reason than to mark this kind of toolbar as needing a certain appearance. I'll explain about that in Chapter 12. If you use this initializer, you'll have to set the navigation controller's root view controller separately.

You can also set the UINavigationController's delegate (adopting UINavigation-ControllerDelegate). The delegate receives messages before and after a child view controller's view is shown.

A navigation controller will typically appear on the screen initially containing just its root view controller, and displaying its root view controller's view. There will be no back button, because there is no back item; there is nowhere to go back to. Subsequently, when the user asks to navigate to a new view, you (typically meaning code in the current view controller) obtain the next view controller (typically by creating it) and push it onto the stack by calling `pushViewController:animated:` on the navigation controller. The navigation controller performs the animation, and displays the new view controller's view:

```
let svc = SecondViewController()
self.navigationController!.pushViewController(svc, animated: true)
```

There is usually no need to worry about going back; when the user taps the back button to navigate back, the runtime will call `popViewControllerAnimated:` for you. When a view controller is popped from the stack, the `viewControllers` array removes and releases the view controller, which is usually permitted to go out of existence at that point.

New in iOS 8, there's a second way to push a view controller onto the navigation controller's stack, without referring to the navigation controller: `showView-Controller:sender:`. This method lets the caller be agnostic about the current interface situation; for example, it pushes onto a navigation controller if the view controller to which it is sent is in a navigation interface, but generates a presented view controller if not. I'll talk more about this method in Chapter 9; meanwhile, I'll continue using `push-ViewController:animated:` in my examples.

Instead of tapping the back button, the user can go back by dragging a pushed view controller's view from the left edge of the screen. This is actually a way of calling `pop-ViewControllerAnimated:`, with the difference that the animation is interactive. (Interactive view controller transition animation is the subject of the next section.) The UINavigationController uses a UIScreenEdgePanGestureRecognizer to detect and track the user's gesture. You can obtain a reference to this gesture recognizer as the navigation controller's `interactivePopGestureRecognizer`; thus you can disable the gesture recognizer and prevent this way of going back, or you can mediate between your own gesture recognizers and this one (see Chapter 5).

You can manipulate the stack more directly if you wish. You can call `popViewController-Animated:` explicitly; to pop multiple items so as to leave a particular view controller at the top of the stack, call `popToViewController:animated:`, or to pop all the items down to the root view controller, call `popToRootViewControllerAnimated:`. All of these methods return the popped view controller (or view controllers, as an array), in case you want to do something with them.

To set the entire stack at once, call `setViewControllers:animated:`. You can access the stack through the `viewControllers` property. Manipulating the stack directly is the only way, for instance, to delete or insert a view controller in the middle of the stack.

The view controller at the top of the stack is the `topViewController`; the view controller whose view is displayed is the `visibleViewController`. Those will normally be the same, but they needn't be, as the `topViewController` might present a view controller, in which case the presented view controller will be the `visibleViewController`. Other view controllers can be accessed through the `viewControllers` array by index number. The root view controller is at index 0; if the array's `count` is c, the back view controller (the one whose `navigationItem.backBarButtonItem` is currently displayed in the navigation bar) is at index c-2.

The `topViewController` may need to communicate with the next view controller as the latter is pushed onto the stack, or with the back view controller as it itself is popped off the stack. The problem is parallel to that of communication between an original presenter and a presented view controller, which I discussed earlier in this chapter, so I won't say more about it here.

A child view controller will probably want to configure its `navigationItem` early in its lifetime, so as to be ready for display in the navigation bar by the time the view controller is handed as a child to the navigation controller. Apple warns (in the UIViewController class reference, under `navigationItem`) that `loadView` and `viewDidLoad` are not appropriate places to do this, because the circumstances under which the view is needed are not related to the circumstances under which the navigation item is needed. Apple's own code examples routinely violate this warning, but it is probably best to override `init(nibName:bundle:)` — or `init(coder:)` or `awakeFromNib`, if appropriate — for this purpose.

A navigation controller's navigation bar is accessible as its `navigationBar`, and can be hidden and shown with `setNavigationBarHidden:animated:`. (It is possible, though not common, to maintain and manipulate a navigation stack through a navigation controller whose navigation bar never appears.) Its toolbar is accessible as its `toolbar`, and can be hidden and shown with `setToolbarHidden:animated:`.

New in iOS 8, a navigation controller can perform automatic hiding and showing of its navigation bar (and, if normally shown, its toolbar) in response to various situations, as configured by properties:

When tapped
> If the navigation controller's `hidesBarsOnTap` is `true`, a tap that falls through the top view controller's view is taken as a signal to toggle bar visibility.

When swiped
> If the navigation controller's `hidesBarsOnSwipe` is `true`, an upward or downward swipe respectively hides or shows the bars.

In landscape
> If the navigation controller's `hidesBarsWhenVerticallyCompact` is `true`, bars are automatically hidden when the app rotates to landscape on the iPhone (and `hidesBarsOnTap` is treated as `true`, so the bars can be shown again by tapping).

When the user is typing
> If the navigation controller's `hidesBarsWhenKeyboardAppears` is `true`, bars are automatically hidden when the onscreen keyboard appears (see Chapter 10).

You can also configure a UINavigationController or any view controller that is to serve in a navigation interface in a *.storyboard* or *.xib* file. In the Attributes inspector, use a navigation controller's Bar Visibility and Hide Bars checkboxes to determine the presence of the navigation bar and toolbar. The navigation bar and toolbar are themselves subviews of the navigation controller, and you can configure them with the Attributes inspector as well. A navigation controller's root view controller can be specified; in a storyboard, there will be a "root view controller" relationship between the navigation controller and its root view controller.

A view controller in a *.storyboard* or *.xib* file has a Navigation Item where you can specify its title, its prompt, and the text of its back button. (If a view controller in a nib doesn't have a Navigation Item and you want to configure this view controller for use in a navigation interface, drag a Navigation Item from the Object library onto the view controller.) You can drag Bar Button Items into a view controller's navigation bar in the canvas to set the left button and right button of its `navigationItem`. Moreover, the Navigation Item has outlets, one of which permits you to set its `titleView`. (However, you can't assign a navigation item multiple `rightBarButtonItems` or `leftBarButtonItems` in the nib editor.) Similarly, you can give a view controller Bar Button Items that will appear in the toolbar.

To start an iPhone project with a main storyboard that has a UINavigationController as its root view controller, begin with the Master–Detail Application template. Alternatively, start with the Single View Application template, remove the existing view controller from the storyboard, and add a Navigation Controller in its place. Unfortunately, the nib editor assumes that the navigation controller's root view controller should be a UITableViewController. If that's not the case, here's a better way: start with the Single View Application template, select the existing view controller, and choose Editor → Embed In → Navigation Controller. A view controller to be subsequently pushed onto the navigation stack can be configured in the storyboard as the destination of a push segue; I'll talk more about that later in the chapter.

Custom Transition

You can customize the transition that occurs between view controller views, as follows:

- When a tab bar controller changes which of its child view controllers is selected, you can *animate* the change of views.

- When a navigation controller pushes or pops a child view controller, you can *customize* the animation of views.

- When a view controller is presented or dismissed, you can customize the animation of views *and the placement* of the presented view.

Given the extensive animation resources of iOS 8 (see Chapter 4), this is an excellent chance for you to provide your app with variety, interest, and distinctiveness. The view of a child view controller pushed onto a navigation controller's stack, for example, needn't arrive sliding from the right; it can expand by zooming from the middle of the screen, drop from above and fall into place with a bounce, snap into place like a spring, or whatever else you can dream up. A familiar example is Apple's Calendar app, which transitions from a year to a month, in a navigation controller, by zooming in.

A custom transition animation can optionally be *interactive* — meaning that it is driven in real time by the user's gesture. The user does not merely tap and cause an animation to take place; the user performs an extended gesture and gradually summons the new view to supersede the old one. The user can thus participate in the progress of the transition. An example is the way a navigation controller's view can be popped by dragging from the left edge of the screen. Another example is the iOS 8 Photos app, which lets the user pinch a photo, in a navigation controller, to pop to the album containing it.

In the case of a presented view controller, you also get to dictate the ultimate size and position of the presented view, and how the presenting view is seen behind it; you can also provide intermediate views that remain during the presentation. New in iOS 8, the presentation controller (introduced earlier in this chapter) participates in, and is crucial to, the transition.

I'll start by talking about how to add a custom animation to a tab bar controller transition, and work up to the more involved business of customizing a view controller presentation.

Noninteractive Custom Transition Animation

Let's start with the base case, where the custom animation is *not* interactive. Configuring your custom animation requires three steps:

1. The view controller in charge of the transition must have a delegate.

2. As the transition begins, the delegate will be asked for an *animation controller*, meaning any object adopting the UIViewControllerAnimatedTransitioning protocol. Return nil to specify that the default animation (if any) should be used.

3. The animation controller will be sent two messages:

    `transitionDuration:`
    > The animation controller must return the duration of the custom animation.

    `animateTransition:`
    > The animation controller should perform the animation.

The implementation of `animateTransition:` works, in general, as follows:

1. The parameter is an object called the *transition context* (adopting the UIViewControllerContextTransitioning protocol). By querying the transition context, you can obtain:

    - The *container view*, an already existing view within which all the action is to take place.
    - The outgoing and incoming view controllers.
    - The outgoing and incoming views. These are probably the main views of the outgoing and incoming view controllers, but (new in iOS 8) you should obtain the views directly from the transition context, just in case they aren't. The outgoing view is already inside the container view.
    - The initial frame of the outgoing view, and the ultimate frame of the incoming view.

2. Having gathered this information, your mission is to put the incoming view into the container view and animate it in such a way as to end up at its correct ultimate position. You may also animate the outgoing view if you wish.

3. When the animation ends, you *must* call the transition context's `complete-Transition:` to tell it that the animation is over. The outgoing view is then removed automatically.

To illustrate, consider the transition between two child view controllers of a tab bar controller. By default, this transition isn't animated; one view just replaces the other. Let's animate the transition.

One obvious custom animation is that the new view controller's view should slide in from one side while the old view controller's view should slide out the other side. The direction of the slide should depend on whether the index of the new view controller is greater or less than that of the old view controller.

Take the steps in order. First, configure a delegate for the tab bar controller. Assume that the tab bar controller is our app's root view controller. For simplicity, I'll set its delegate in code, in the app delegate's `application:didFinishLaunchingWith-Options:`, and I'll make that delegate be the app delegate itself:

```
(self.window!.rootViewController as! UITabBarController).delegate = self
```

On to the second step. The app delegate, in its role as UITabBarControllerDelegate, will now be sent a message whenever the tab bar controller is about to change view controllers. That message is:

- `tabBarController:animationControllerForTransitionFromView-Controller:toViewController:`

We must implement this method to return an animation controller, namely, some object implementing UIViewControllerAnimatedTransitioning. In this case, to keep things simple, I'll return `self`. Here we go:

```
func tabBarController(tabBarController: UITabBarController,
    animationControllerForTransitionFromViewController
    fromVC: UIViewController,
    toViewController toVC: UIViewController)
    -> UIViewControllerAnimatedTransitioning? {
        return self
}
```

(There is no particular reason why the animation controller should be `self`, or any existing object; it can be a dedicated lightweight object instantiated just to govern this transition. There is also no particular reason why the animation controller should be the same object every time this method is called. We know, in real time, what's about to happen, because we receive the tab bar controller and both child view controllers as parameters. Thus we could readily provide a different animation controller under different circumstances, or we could return nil to use the default transition — meaning, in this case, no animation.)

On to the third step! Here we are in the animation controller (UIViewController-AnimatedTransitioning). Our first job is to reveal in advance the duration of our animation:

```
func transitionDuration(
    transitionContext: UIViewControllerContextTransitioning)
    -> NSTimeInterval {
        return 0.4
}
```

(Again, the value returned needn't be the same every time this method is called. The transition context has arrived as parameter, and we could query it to identify the two view controllers involved and make a decision based on that. But make sure that the value you return here is indeed the duration of the animation you'll perform in animate-Transition:.)

Finally, we come to animateTransition: itself:

```
func animateTransition(
    transitionContext: UIViewControllerContextTransitioning) {
        // ...
}
```

Once more, simply perform the steps in order. First, query the transition context. This code is practically boilerplate for any custom view controller transition animation:

```
let vc1 = transitionContext.viewControllerForKey(
    UITransitionContextFromViewControllerKey)!
let vc2 = transitionContext.viewControllerForKey(
    UITransitionContextToViewControllerKey)!
let con = transitionContext.containerView()
let r1start = transitionContext.initialFrameForViewController(vc1)
let r2end = transitionContext.finalFrameForViewController(vc2)
let v1 = transitionContext.viewForKey(UITransitionContextFromViewKey)!
let v2 = transitionContext.viewForKey(UITransitionContextToViewKey)!
```

We have the view controllers and their views, and the initial frame of the outgoing view and the destination frame of the incoming view. Now, to prepare for our intended animation, we want to calculate the converse, namely the final frame of the outgoing view and the initial frame of the incoming view. We are sliding the views sideways, so those frames should be positioned sideways from the initial frame of the outgoing view and the final frame of the incoming view. *Which* side they go on depends upon the relative place of these view controllers among the children of the tab bar controller — is this to be a leftward slide or a rightward slide? Since the animation controller is the app delegate, we can get a reference to the tab bar controller the same way we did before:

```
let tbc = self.window!.rootViewController as! UITabBarController
let ix1 = find(tbc.viewControllers as! [UIViewController], vc1)
let ix2 = find(tbc.viewControllers as! [UIViewController], vc2)
let dir : CGFloat = ix1 < ix2 ? 1 : -1
```

```
var r1end = r1start
r1end.origin.x -= r1end.size.width * dir
var r2start = r2end
r2start.origin.x += r2start.size.width * dir
```

We are now ready for the second step: put the second view controller's view into the container view at its initial frame, and perform the animation. The end of the animation is also the moment to perform the all-important third step, namely to call complete-Transition: to signal that our part has been played and our hands are off the views:

```
v2.frame = r2start
con.addSubview(v2)
UIView.animateWithDuration(0.4, animations: {
    v1.frame = r1end
    v2.frame = r2end
    }, completion: {
        _ in
        transitionContext.completeTransition(true)
    })
```

That's all there is to it. Of course, that wasn't a very complex animation; but an animation needn't be complex to be interesting, significant, and helpful to the user. And even a more complex animation would be implemented along the same basic lines. One possibility that I didn't illustrate in my example is that you are free to introduce additional views temporarily into the container view during the course of the animation; you'll probably want to remove them in the completion handler.

A custom transition for a navigation controller is similar to a custom transition for a tab bar controller, so I don't need to give a separate example. The only slight difference lies in the name of the navigation controller delegate method that will be called to discover whether there's an animation controller:

- navigationController:animationControllerForOperation:fromView-
  Controller:toViewController:

The operation: parameter allows you to distinguish a push from a pop.

 Implementing a navigation controller custom push animation while returning nil for the pop animation controller will cause the built-in swipe-to-pop interactive transition to stop working.

Interactive Custom Transition Animation

With an interactive custom transition animation, the idea is that we track something the user is doing, typically by means of a gesture recognizer (see Chapter 5), and perform the "frames" of the transition in response. There are two ways to write an interactive custom transition animation. In both cases, we're going to need an *interaction control-*

ler, namely an object that conforms to the UIViewControllerInteractiveTransitioning protocol. The two ways of writing the code correspond to the two ways of supplying this object:

Create a UIPercentDrivenInteractiveTransition instance
We supply an instance of the built-in UIPercentDrivenInteractiveTransition class (let's call this the *percent driver*). This percent driver object performs the frames of the animation for us by calling our `animateTransition:` and "freezing" the animation. All we have to do is track the gesture and repeatedly call the percent driver's `updateInteractiveTransition:`, telling it how far the gesture has proceeded; the percent driver updates the interface, changing our animation's "frame" to match the extent of the gesture. At the end of the gesture, we decide whether to finish or cancel the transition; accordingly, we call the percent driver's `finishInteractive-Transition` or `cancelInteractiveTransition`. Finally, we call the transition context's `completeTransition:`.

Adopt UIViewControllerInteractiveTransitioning
We supply our own object with our own code. This object, conforming to the UIViewControllerInteractiveTransitioning protocol, will need to respond to `start-InteractiveTransition:`, whose parameter will be the transition context. Once we are told that the transition has started, we will set up the initial conditions for the animation and then constantly track the gesture, changing the interface and calling the transition context's `updateInteractiveTransition:`. When the interaction ends, we decide whether to finish or cancel the transition; accordingly, we animate into the final or initial conditions, and call the transition context's `finish-InteractiveTransition` or `cancelInteractiveTransition`. Finally, we call the transition context's `completeTransition:`.

Using a percent driver

If we have already written a noninteractive version of our transition animation, using the percent driver is going to be simplest, because we get to keep our existing `animate-Transition:` code. The steps build upon those of a noninteractive transition animation:

1. The view controller in charge of the transition must have a delegate.
2. We observe that the user is gesturing in a way that should trigger a change of view controller. We respond by triggering that change.
3. The delegate will be asked for an animation controller, as before. We return an object adopting the UIViewControllerAnimatedTransitioning protocol, as before.
4. The delegate is also asked for an *interaction controller*. (This happened before, but we didn't supply one, which is why our transition animation wasn't interactive.) We have elected to use a UIPercentDrivenInteractiveTransition object. So we return that object.

5. The animation controller is sent the same two messages as before:

transitionDuration:
> The duration of the custom animation.

animateTransition:
> The animation controller should perform the animation. But the animation will not in fact proceed at this moment; it will be "frozen" and its "frames" will be produced as the interaction proceeds.
>
> (To perform this magic, the percent driver takes advantage of the fact that a CALayer conforms to the CAMediaTiming protocol, as I explained in Chapter 4. It asks the transition context for the container view, obtains that view's layer, and sets the layer's speed to 0. Subsequently, as we call the percent driver's updateInteractiveTransition:, it adjusts that layer's timeOffset accordingly, thus displaying a different "frame" of the animation.)

6. We continue tracking the interaction, calling our percent driver's update-InteractiveTransition: to tell it how far the gesture has proceeded. The percent driver displays that frame of our animation for us.

7. Sooner or later the gesture will end. At this point, we must decide whether to declare the transition completed or cancelled. The usual approach is to say that if the user performed more than half the full gesture, that constitutes completion; otherwise, it constitutes cancellation. We call the percent driver's finishInteractive-Transition or cancelInteractiveTransition accordingly. The percent driver either completes the animation or (if we cancelled) *reverses the animation*.

8. The animation is now completed, and its completion block is called. We call completeTransition:, with the argument stating whether the transition was finished or cancelled.

As an example, I'll describe how to make an interactive version of the tab bar controller transition animation that we developed in the previous section, such that the user can drag the tab bar controller's adjacent view controller in from the right or from the left. All the code we've already written can be left more or less as is! To track the user's gesture, I'll put a pair of UIScreenEdgePanGestureRecognizers into the interface, and keep references to them so they can be identified later. The gesture recognizers are attached to the tab view controller's view (tbc.view), as this will remain constant while the views of its view controllers are sliding across the screen:

```
let sep = UIScreenEdgePanGestureRecognizer(target:self, action:"pan:")
sep.edges = UIRectEdge.Right
tbc.view.addGestureRecognizer(sep)
sep.delegate = self
self.rightEdger = sep
let sep2 = UIScreenEdgePanGestureRecognizer(target:self, action:"pan:")
```

```
sep2.edges = UIRectEdge.Left
tbc.view.addGestureRecognizer(sep2)
sep2.delegate = self
self.leftEdger = sep2
```

Acting as the delegate of the two gesture recognizers, we prevent either pan gesture recognizer from operating unless there is another child of the tab view controller available on that side of the current child:

```
func gestureRecognizerShouldBegin(g: UIGestureRecognizer) -> Bool {
    let tbc = self.window!.rootViewController as! UITabBarController
    var result = false
    if g == self.rightEdger {
        result = (tbc.selectedIndex < tbc.viewControllers!.count - 1)
    }
    else {
        result = (tbc.selectedIndex > 0)
    }
    return result
}
```

If the gesture recognizer action handler pan: is called, we now know that this means our interactive transition animation is to take place. I'll break down the discussion according to the gesture recognizer's stages. First, I collect some information that will be needed later:

```
func pan(g:UIScreenEdgePanGestureRecognizer) {
    let v = g.view!
    let tbc = self.window!.rootViewController as! UITabBarController
    let delta = g.translationInView(v)
    let percent = fabs(delta.x/v.bounds.size.width)
    switch g.state {
        // ... to be continued ...
    }
}
```

As the gesture begins, we create the UIPercentDrivenInteractiveTransition object and store it in a property (self.inter). We then set the tab bar controller's selectedIndex:

```
case .Began:
    self.inter = UIPercentDrivenInteractiveTransition()
    self.interacting = true
    if g == self.rightEdger {
        tbc.selectedIndex = tbc.selectedIndex + 1
    } else {
        tbc.selectedIndex = tbc.selectedIndex - 1
    }
```

Changing the tab bar controller's selectedIndex causes the runtime to turn to the tab bar controller's delegate to see whether there is an animation controller, and hence a custom animation; as before, we make ourselves the animation controller:

```
func tabBarController(tabBarController: UITabBarController,
    animationControllerForTransitionFromViewController
    fromVC: UIViewController,
    toViewController toVC: UIViewController)
    -> UIViewControllerAnimatedTransitioning? {
        return self
}
```

The runtime now asks if there is also an interaction controller. There wasn't one in our previous example, but now there is — the percent driver:

```
func tabBarController(tabBarController: UITabBarController,
    interactionControllerForAnimationController
    animationController: UIViewControllerAnimatedTransitioning)
    -> UIViewControllerInteractiveTransitioning? {
        let result : UIViewControllerInteractiveTransitioning? =
            self.interacting ? self.inter : nil
        return result
}
```

The runtime now calls our percent driver's startInteractiveTransition:, handing it a reference to the transition context. The percent driver immediately turns around and calls our animateTransition: method, *without performing the animation*. The percent driver "freezes" the animation instead. Our job now is to keep calling the percent driver, telling it what "frame" of the animation to display at every moment; the percent driver will also call the transition context on our behalf.

We are now back in the gesture recognizer's action handler. As the gesture proceeds, we keep sending updateInteractiveTransition: to the percent driver:

```
case .Changed:
    self.inter.updateInteractiveTransition(percent)
```

When the gesture ends, we decide whether this counts as finishing or canceling, and we report to the percent driver accordingly:

```
case .Ended:
    if percent > 0.5 {
        self.inter.finishInteractiveTransition()
    } else {
        self.inter.cancelInteractiveTransition()
    }
    self.interacting = false
```

If we call finishInteractiveTransition, the percent driver quickly plays the rest of the animation forward to completion. If we call cancelInteractiveTransition, the percent driver plays the animation backward to its beginning.

Finally, we find ourselves back inside animateTransition:, in the animation completion: handler. This is the only place where a change is needed in our previously existing code. As I've just said, the transition can complete in one of two ways. We must still call `completeTransition:` ourselves, but we must tell the transition context which way things turned out, so that the transition context can restore the previous state of things if the transition was cancelled. Luckily, the transition context already knows whether the transition was cancelled! So we simply ask it:

```
UIView.animateWithDuration(0.4, delay:0, options:opts, animations: {
    v1.frame = r1end
    v2.frame = r2end
    }, completion: {
        _ in
        let cancelled = transitionContext.transitionWasCancelled()
        transitionContext.completeTransition(!cancelled)
})
```

That's all there is to it, and in fact, as a bonus, I have sneakily added a bit of extra functionality to our code: not only does this work as an interactive transition, but I've also kept the noninteractive transition that we developed earlier. In other words, the user can tap a tab bar item to get the original sliding animation left or right, or the user can manually slide a view to get the interactive animation.

Without a percent driver

If we *don't* use a percent driver, then the entire interactive transition is up to us. We ourselves must repeatedly reposition the views at every stage of the gesture, and when the gesture ends, we ourselves must animate them either into their final position or back into their initial position. We will no longer need an `animateTransition:` method (it must be present, to satisfy the protocol requirements, but it can be empty); all the logic of initializing, positioning, and finalizing the moving views must be effectively deconstructed and folded into the various stages of our gesture recognizer action handler. At every stage, we must keep talking to the transition context itself.

The resulting code is verbose, and can be difficult to express in a compact or object-oriented way. However, it is more powerful, more flexible, and possibly more reliable than using a percent driver. We don't need to rely on the percent driver's trick of using a frozen animation; we can reposition the actual views (or their snapshots) as the gesture proceeds.

I'll just sketch out how to rewrite our tab bar controller interactive transition without a percent driver. We have our gesture recognizer(s) as before. When the gesture begins, the `.Began` section of the action handler triggers the transition as before. The delegate is asked for an animation controller and an interaction controller; the interaction controller is now not a percent driver, but some object that we will supply — let's say it's `self`.

The result is that, in our role as adopter of the UIViewControllerInteractive-Transitioning protocol, our `startInteractiveTransition:` is called. Here, we set up the initial conditions of the transition, putting the views into place, and storing a reference to the `transitionContext` in a property where our gesture recognizer action handler can access it:

```
func startInteractiveTransition(
    transitionContext: UIViewControllerContextTransitioning){
    // store transition context so the gesture recognizer can get at it
    self.context = transitionContext
    // ... set up initial conditions ...
    // ... store any additional instance variables ...
    self.r1end = r1end
    self.r2start = r2start
}
```

Our gesture recognizer action handler is called again, repeatedly, at the `.Changed` stage. We keep repositioning our views in accordance with the progress of the interactive gesture. At the same time, we keep informing the transition context of that progress:

```
case .Changed:
    // ... calculate progress (percent)
    // ... put views into position corresponding to current "frame" ...
    // ... and finally, notify the transition context
    v1.frame = // whatever
    v2.frame = // whatever
    tc.updateInteractiveTransition(percent)
```

(Why must we call `updateInteractiveTransition:` throughout the progress of the gesture? For a tab bar controller's transition, this call has little or no significance. But in the case, say, of a navigation controller, the animation has a component separate from what you're doing — the change in the appearance of the navigation bar, as the old title departs and the new title arrives and so forth. The transition context needs to coordinate that animation with the interactive gesture and with your animation. So you need to keep telling it where things are in the course of the interaction.)

Finally, our gesture recognizer action handler is called one last time, at the `.Ended` stage. We now animate our views the rest of the way, or else back to the start, and call either `finishInteractiveTransition` or `cancelInteractiveTransition` followed by `completeTransition:` with the appropriate argument:

```
case .Ended:
    if percent > 0.5 {
        UIView.animateWithDuration(0.2, animations:{
            v1.frame = self.r1end
            v2.frame = r2end
            }, completion: {
                _ in
            tc.finishInteractiveTransition()
            tc.completeTransition(true)
            })
    }
    else {
        UIView.animateWithDuration(0.2, animations:{
```

```
                    v1.frame = r1start
                    v2.frame = self.r2start
                    }, completion: {
                        _ in
                    tc.cancelInteractiveTransition()
                    tc.completeTransition(false)
                    })
        }
```

Custom Presented View Controller Transition

Customizing what happens when a view controller is presented is more complex, and more powerful, than customizing a tab bar controller or navigation controller transition. With a presented view controller, you can customize not only the *animation* but also the final *position* of the presented view. Moreover, you can introduce extra views which *remain in the scene* until dismissal; for example, if the presented view is smaller than the presenting view and covers it only partially, you might add a dimming view between them, to darken the presenting view (just as a .FormSheet presentation does).

What the runtime must do while a view is being presented in order to make the presentation customizable is also more complex. There is no existing view to serve as the container view; therefore, when the presentation starts, the runtime must construct the container view and insert it into the interface and leave it there for only as long as the view remains presented. In the case of a .FullScreen presentation, the runtime must also rip the presenting view out of the interface and insert it into the container view, because you might want the presenting view to participate in the animation. For other styles of presentation, the container view is *in front of* the presenting view, which can't be animated and is left in place as the presentation proceeds.

In iOS 7, all the work of customizing a presentation was done through an animation controller (or an interaction controller), parallel to customizing a tab bar controller animation or a navigation controller animation. New in iOS 8, the work is distributed between *two* objects: the animation controller (or interaction controller) on the one hand, and the presentation controller on the other. The idea is that the animation controller should be responsible for *only* the animation, the movement of the presented view into its final position. The *determination* of that final position is the job of the presentation controller. The presentation controller is also responsible for inserting any extra views, such as a dimming view, into the container view; Apple says that the animation controller animates the content, while the presentation controller animates the "chrome." This distribution of responsibilities may require some extra effort on your part, but in fact it also simplifies considerably the task of customizing the animation itself.

Customizing the animation

I'll start with a situation where we *don't* need to use the presentation controller: all we want to do is customize the animation part of a built-in presentation style. The steps are almost completely parallel to how we customized a tab bar controller animation:

1. Give the presented view controller a delegate. Here, we assign to the presented view controller's `transitioningDelegate` property an object adopting the UIViewControllerTransitioningDelegate protocol.

2. The delegate will be asked for an animation controller, and will return an object adopting the UIViewControllerAnimatedTransitioning protocol. Unlike a tab bar controller or navigation controller, a presented view controller's view undergoes *two* animations — the presentation and the dismissal — and therefore the delegate is asked *separately* for controllers:

   - `animationControllerForPresentedController:presenting-`
     `Controller:sourceController:`

   - `interactionControllerForPresentation:`

   - `animationControllerForDismissedController:`

   - `interactionControllerForDismissal:`

   You are free to customize just one animation, leaving the other at the default by not providing a controller for it.

3. The animation controller will implement `transitionDuration` and `animate-`
   `Transition:`.

To illustrate, let's say we're on iPad, and we want to present a view using the `.Form-`
`Sheet` presentation style. But instead of using any of the built-in animation styles, we'll have the presented view appear to grow from the middle of the screen. The only mildly tricky step is the first one. The problem is that the delegate must be assigned very early in the presented view controller's life — before the presentation begins. But the presented view controller doesn't *exist* before the presentation begins. The most reliable approach, therefore, is for the presented view controller to assign its own delegate in its own initializer:

```
required init(coder aDecoder: NSCoder) {
    super.init(coder:aDecoder)
    self.transitioningDelegate = self
}
```

On to step two. The transitioning delegate is asked for an animation controller; here, I'll have it supply `self` once again, and I'll do this only for the presentation, leaving the dismissal to use the default animation:

```
func animationControllerForPresentedController(
    presented: UIViewController,
    presentingController presenting: UIViewController,
    sourceController source: UIViewController)
    -> UIViewControllerAnimatedTransitioning? {
        return self
}
```

Finally, step three — the actual animation. This is extremely simple, especially because we don't care or inquire about the "From" view controller, which remains in place during the presentation (indeed, its view isn't even in the container view):

```
func transitionDuration(
    transitionContext: UIViewControllerContextTransitioning)
    -> NSTimeInterval {
        return 0.4
}
func animateTransition(
    transitionContext: UIViewControllerContextTransitioning) {
        let vc2 = transitionContext.viewControllerForKey(
            UITransitionContextToViewControllerKey)
        let con = transitionContext.containerView()
        let r2end = transitionContext.finalFrameForViewController(vc2!)
        let v2 = transitionContext.viewForKey(UITransitionContextToViewKey)!
        v2.frame = r2end
        v2.transform = CGAffineTransformMakeScale(0.1, 0.1)
        v2.alpha = 0
        con.addSubview(v2)
        UIView.animateWithDuration(0.4, animations: {
            v2.alpha = 1
            v2.transform = CGAffineTransformIdentity
            }, completion: {
                _ in
                transitionContext.completeTransition(true)
        })
}
```

There is just one complication when you animate a presented view controller's view. If you also animate the dismissal of that view, and if the animation controller is the same object so that the same animateTransition: implementation is called, the roles are reversed: on presentation, the presented view controller is the "To" view controller (UITransitionContextToViewControllerKey and UITransitionContextToViewKey), but on dismissal, it is the "From" view controller (UITransitionContextFromView-ControllerKey and UITransitionContextFromViewKey). For a presentation that isn't .FullScreen, the unused view is nil, so you can distinguish the cases by structuring your code like this:

```
let v1 = transitionContext.viewForKey(UITransitionContextFromViewKey)
let v2 = transitionContext.viewForKey(UITransitionContextToViewKey)
if let v2 = v2 { // presenting
    // ...
} else if let v1 = v1 {
    // ...
}
```

Customizing the presentation

Now let's involve the presentation controller. This will require some additional steps:

1. In addition to setting a `transitioningDelegate`, we set the presented view controller's `modalPresentationStyle` to `.Custom`.

2. The result of the preceding step is that the delegate is sent an additional message:

   - `presentationControllerForPresentedViewController:presentingView-Controller:sourceViewController:`

   (The `sourceViewController:` parameter is what I have termed the "original presenter.") Your mission is to return an instance of a *custom UIPresentationController subclass* which you have previously declared and implemented. This will then be the presented view controller's presentation controller during the course of this presentation, from the time presentation begins to the time dismissal ends. You must create this instance by calling (directly or indirectly) the designated initializer:

   - `init(presentedViewController:presentingViewController:)`

3. By overriding appropriate UIPresentationController methods in your UIPresentationController subclass, you participate in the presentation, setting the presented view controller's position and adding "chrome" to the presentation as desired.

The UIPresentationController has properties pointing to the `presentingView-Controller` as well the `presentedViewController` and the `presentedView`, plus the `presentationStyle` set by the presented view controller. It also obtains the `container-View`, which it subsequently communicates to the animation controller's transition context. It has some methods that you can override in your subclass, but you only need to override the ones that require customization for your particular implementation:

`frameOfPresentedViewInContainerView`
> Returns the final position of the presented view. The animation coordinator, if there is one, will obtain this frame through the transition context's `finalFrameForView-Controller:` method and must cause the presented view to end up there (as you already know).

It is perfectly legal for the transitioning delegate to supply a custom presentation controller and *no* animation controller! In that case, a default animation will be performed, but the presented view will end up at the position your custom presentation controller dictates. This is a good example of the delightful "separation of powers" of the presentation controller and the animation controller in iOS 8.

presentationTransitionWillBegin
presentationTransitionDidEnd
dismissalTransitionWillBegin
dismissalTransitionDidEnd
>   Use these events as signals to add or remove "chrome" (extra views) to the container view.

containerViewWillLayoutSubviews
containerViewDidLayoutSubviews
>   Use these layout events as signals to update the "chrome" views if needed.

shouldPresentInFullscreen
>   The default is to return `true`; returning `false` turns this presentation into a `.CurrentContext` presentation.

shouldRemovePresentersView
>   The default is to return `false`, except that of course it is `true` for a standard `.FullScreen` presentation, meaning that the presenting view is ripped out of the interface at the end of the presentation transition. You can return `true` for a custom presentation, but it would be rare to do this; even if the presented view completely covers the presenting view, there is no harm in leaving the presenting view in place.

A UIPresentationController is not a UIViewController, but it adopts some protocols that UIViewController adopts, and thus gets the same resizing-related messages that a UIViewController gets, as I described earlier in this chapter. It adopts UITraitEnvironment, meaning that it has a `traitCollection` and participates in the trait collection inheritance hierarchy, and receives the `traitCollectionDidChange:` message. It also adopts UIContentContainer, meaning that it receives `willTransitionToTraitCollection:withTransitionCoordinator:` and `viewWillTransitionToSize:withTransitionCoordinator:`.

In addition, a presentation controller functions as the *parent* of the presented view controller, and can override its inherited trait collection and respond to changes in its `preferredContentSize`, as I'll explain later.

To illustrate the use of a custom presentation controller, I'll expand the preceding example to implement a custom presentation style that looks like a `.FormSheet` *even on iPhone.* The first step is to set the presentation style to .Custom at the same time that we set the transitioning delegate:

```
required init(coder aDecoder: NSCoder) {
    super.init(coder:aDecoder)
    self.transitioningDelegate = self
    self.modalPresentationStyle = .Custom
}
```

The result (step two) is that the extra delegate method is called so that we can provide a custom presentation controller, and we do so:

```
func presentationControllerForPresentedViewController(
    presented: UIViewController,
    presentingViewController presenting: UIViewController!,
    sourceViewController source: UIViewController)
    -> UIPresentationController? {
        let pc = MyPresentationController(
            presentedViewController: presented,
            presentingViewController: presenting)
        return pc
}
```

Everything else happens in our implementation of MyPresentationController. To make the presentation look like a .FormSheet, we inset the presented view's frame:

```
override func frameOfPresentedViewInContainerView() -> CGRect {
    return super.frameOfPresentedViewInContainerView()
        .rectByInsetting(dx: 40, dy: 40)
}
```

We could actually stop at this point! The presented view now appears in the correct position. However, the presenting view is appearing undimmed behind it. Let's add dimming, by inserting a translucent dimming view into the container view. Note that we are careful to deal with the possibility of subsequent rotation:

```
override func presentationTransitionWillBegin() {
    let con = self.containerView
    let shadow = UIView(frame:con.bounds)
    shadow.backgroundColor = UIColor(white:0, alpha:0.4)
    con.insertSubview(shadow, atIndex: 0)
    shadow.autoresizingMask = .FlexibleWidth | .FlexibleHeight
}
```

Again, this works perfectly, but now I don't like what happens when the presented view is dismissed: the dimming view stays in place, and then vanishes suddenly at the end of the dismissal. I'd rather have the dimming view fade out, and I'd like it to fade out *in coordination with the dismissal animation.* The way to arrange that is through the object vended by the presented view controller's transitionCoordinator method. This object is just like the transition coordinator I've already discussed earlier in this chapter in connection with resizing events and rotation: in particular, we can call its `animate-AlongsideTransition:` method to add our own animation:

```
override func dismissalTransitionWillBegin() {
    let con = self.containerView
    let shadow = (con.subviews as! [UIView])[0]
    let tc = self.presentedViewController.transitionCoordinator()!
    tc.animateAlongsideTransition({
        _ in
        shadow.alpha = 0
        }, completion: nil)
}
```

Once again, we could stop at this point. But I'd like to add a further refinement. A `.Form-Sheet` view has rounded corners. I'd like to make our presented view look the same way:

```
override func presentedView() -> UIView! {
    let v = super.presentedView()
    v.layer.cornerRadius = 6
    v.layer.masksToBounds = true
    return v
}
```

Finally, for completeness, it would be nice, during presentation, to dim the appearance of any button titles and other tinted interface elements visible through the dimming view, to emphasize that they are disabled:

```
override func presentationTransitionDidEnd(completed: Bool) {
    let vc = self.presentingViewController
    let v = vc.view
    v.tintAdjustmentMode = .Dimmed
}
override func dismissalTransitionDidEnd(completed: Bool) {
    let vc = self.presentingViewController
    let v = vc.view
    v.tintAdjustmentMode = .Automatic
}
```

Transition Coordinator

I have already mentioned, in the previous section, the UIViewController `transition-Coordinator` method, which yields an object adopting the UIViewControllerTransition-Coordinator protocol. This object, the *transition coordinator*, is a kind of wrapper around the transition context, and also adopts the UIViewControllerTransition-CoordinatorContext protocol, just like the transition context. Thus, in effect, view controllers can find out about the transition they are involved in.

In addition to the methods that it implements by virtue of adopting the UIView-ControllerTransitionCoordinatorContext protocol, a transition coordinator implements the following methods:

`animateAlongsideTransition:completion:`
> Takes an animation block and a completion block. The animation you supply is incorporated into the transition coordinator's animation. Returns a Bool, informing you in case your commands couldn't be animated. Both blocks receive the transition context as a parameter. (See also "Responding to rotation" on page 280, where I discussed this method in connection with rotation.)

A view controller's use of this method will typically be to add animation of its view's internal interface as part of a transition animation. Observe that this works equally for a custom animation or a built-in animation; in fact, the point is that the view controller can behave agnostically with regard to how its own view is being animated. In this example, a presented view controller animates part of its interface into place as the animation proceeds (whatever that animation may be):

```
override func viewWillAppear(animated: Bool) {
    super.viewWillAppear(animated)
    if let tc = self.transitionCoordinator() {
        tc.animateAlongsideTransition({
            _ in
            self.button.frame.origin.y += 100
        }, completion: nil)
    }
}
```

`animateAlongsideTransitionInView:animation:completion:`
> Just like the previous method, except that the animated view can be outside the container view.

`notifyWhenInteractionEndsUsingBlock:`
> Called at the moment the user abandons an interactive gesture and the transition is about to be either completed or cancelled. This is useful particularly if the interactive transition is being cancelled, as it may well be that what your view controller wants to do will differ in this situation. The parameter to the block is the transition context.

In this example, a navigation controller has pushed a view controller, and now the user is popping it interactively (using the default drag-from-the-left-edge gesture). If the user cancels, the back view controller can hear about it, like this:

```
override func viewWillAppear(animated: Bool) {
    super.viewWillAppear(animated)
    if let tc = self.transitionCoordinator() {
        if tc.initiallyInteractive() {
            tc.notifyWhenInteractionEndsUsingBlock {
                context in
                if context.isCancelled() {
                    // ...
                }
```

```
                }
              }
            }
          }
```

 In iOS 8, I have not found any occasion when the child of a tab bar controller has a non-nil transition coordinator. This is different from iOS 7, and feels like a bug.

Page View Controller

A page view controller (UIPageViewController) displays its child view controller's view. The user, by a gesture, can navigate in one direction or the other to see the next or the previous child view controller's view, successively — like turning the pages of a book. In reality, the page view controller has only one child view controller at a time (or, if so configured, two at a time); it navigates by releasing its existing child view controller and replacing it with another.

Preparing a Page View Controller

To create a UIPageViewController, use its designated initializer:

- `init(transitionStyle:navigationOrientation:options:)`

Here's what the parameters mean:

`transitionStyle:`
  The animation style during navigation (UIPageViewControllerTransitionStyle). Your choices are:

  - `.PageCurl`
  - `.Scroll` (sliding)

`navigationOrientation:`
  The direction of navigation (UIPageViewControllerNavigationOrientation). Your choices are:

  - `.Horizontal`
  - `.Vertical`

`options:`
  A dictionary. Possible keys are:

UIPageViewControllerOptionSpineLocationKey
>   If you're using the page curl transition, this is the position of the pivot line
>   around which those page curl transitions rotate. The value (UIPageView-
>   ControllerSpineLocation) is one of the following:
>
>   - .Min (left or top)
>
>   - .Mid (middle; two pages are shown at once)
>
>   - .Max (right or bottom)

UIPageViewControllerOptionInterPageSpacingKey
>   If you're using the scroll transition, this is the spacing between successive pages,
>   visible as a gap during the transition (the default is 0).

You assign the page view controller a dataSource, which should conform to the UIPage-
ViewControllerDataSource protocol, and configure the page view controller's initial
content by handing it its initial child view controller(s). You do that by calling this
method:

- setViewControllers:direction:animated:completion:

Here's what the parameters mean:

viewControllers:
>   An array of one view controller, unless you're using the page curl transition and
>   the .Mid spine location, in which case it's an array of two view controllers.

direction:
>   The animation direction (UIPageViewControllerNavigationDirection). This prob-
>   ably won't matter when you're assigning the page view controller its initial content,
>   as you are not likely to want any animation. Possible values are:
>
>   - .Forward
>
>   - .Backward

animated:, completion:
>   A Bool and a completion handler.

Here's a minimal example. Each page in the page view controller is to portray an image
of a named Pep Boy. The first question is where the pages will come from. My data
model consists of an array (self.pep) of the string names of the three Pep Boys, along
with three eponymous image files in my app bundle portraying each Pep Boy. I've also
got a UIViewController subclass called Pep, capable of displaying a Pep Boy. I initialize
a Pep object with the designated initializer init(pepBoy:), supplying the name of a Pep
Boy from the array; the Pep object sets its own boy property:

```
init(pepBoy boy:String) {
    self.boy = boy
    super.init(nibName: "Pep", bundle: nil)
}
```

Pep's `viewDidLoad` then fetches the corresponding image and assigns it as the image of a UIImageView within its own view:

```
override func viewDidLoad() {
    super.viewDidLoad()
    self.pic.image = UIImage(named:"\(self.boy.lowercaseString).jpg")
}
```

Here's how I create the page view controller itself (in my app delegate):

```
// make a page view controller
let pvc = UIPageViewController(
    transitionStyle: .Scroll,
    navigationOrientation: .Horizontal, options: nil)
// give it an initial page
let page = Pep(pepBoy: self.pep[0])
pvc.setViewControllers(
    [page], direction: .Forward, animated: false, completion: nil)
// give it a data source
pvc.dataSource = self
// puts its view into the interface
self.window!.rootViewController = pvc
```

The page view controller is a UIViewController, and its view must get into the interface by standard means. You can make the page view controller the window's `rootView-Controller`, as I do here; you can make it a presented view controller; you can make it a child view controller of a tab bar controller or a navigation controller. If you want the page view controller's view to be a subview of a custom view controller's view, that view controller must be a custom container view controller, as I'll describe in the next section.

Page View Controller Navigation

We now have a page view controller's view in our interface, itself containing and displaying the view of a Pep view controller that is its child. In theory, we also have three pages, because we have three Pep Boys and their images — but the page view controller knows about only one of them. Just as with a navigation controller, you don't supply (or even create) a page *until the moment comes to navigate to it*. When that happens, one of these data source methods will be called:

- `pageViewController:viewControllerAfterViewController:`

- `pageViewController:viewControllerBeforeViewController:`

The job of those methods is to return the requested successive view controller. You'll need a strategy for doing that; the strategy you devise will depend on how your model maintains the data.

My data is an array of unique strings, so all I have to do is find the previous name or the next name in the array. Here's one of my data source methods:

```
func pageViewController(pageViewController: UIPageViewController,
    viewControllerAfterViewController viewController: UIViewController)
    -> UIViewController? {
        let boy = (viewController as! Pep).boy
        let ix = find(self.pep, boy)! + 1
        if ix >= self.pep.count {
            return nil
        }
        return Pep(pepBoy: self.pep[ix])
}
```

You can also, at any time, call `setViewControllers:...` to change programmatically what page is being displayed, possibly with animation.

Page indicator

If you're using the scroll style, the page view controller will optionally display a page indicator (a UIPageControl, see Chapter 12). The user can look at this to get a sense of what page we're on, and can tap to the left or right of it to navigate. To get the page indicator, you must implement two more data source methods; they are consulted in response to `setViewControllers:...`. We called that method initially to configure the page view controller; if we never call it again (because the user simply keeps navigating to the next or previous page), these data source methods won't be called again either, but they don't need to be: the page view controller will thenceforth keep track of the current index on its own. Here's my implementation for the Pep Boy example:

```
func presentationCountForPageViewController(
    pageViewController: UIPageViewController) -> Int {
        return self.pep.count
}
func presentationIndexForPageViewController(
    pvc: UIPageViewController) -> Int {
        let page = pvc.viewControllers[0] as! Pep
        let boy = page.boy
        return find(self.pep, boy)!
}
```

Unfortunately, the page view controller's page indicator by default has white dots and a clear background, so it is invisible in front of a white background. Moreover, there is no direct access to it. Use the appearance proxy (Chapter 12) to customize it. For example:

```
let proxy = UIPageControl.appearance()
proxy.pageIndicatorTintColor = UIColor.redColor().colorWithAlphaComponent(0.6)
proxy.currentPageIndicatorTintColor = UIColor.redColor()
proxy.backgroundColor = UIColor.yellowColor()
```

Navigation gestures

If you've assigned the page view controller the `.PageCurl` transition style, the user can ask for navigation by tapping at either edge of the view or by dragging across the view. These gestures are detected through two gesture recognizers, which you can access through the page view controller's `gestureRecognizers` property. The documentation suggests that you might change where the user can tap or drag by attaching them to a different view, and other customizations are possible as well. In this code, I change a `.PageCurl` page view controller's behavior so that the user must double tap to request navigation:

```
for g in pvc.gestureRecognizers as! [UIGestureRecognizer] {
    if let g = g as? UITapGestureRecognizer {
        g.numberOfTapsRequired = 2
    }
}
```

Of course you are also free to add to the user's stock of gestures for requesting navigation. You can supply any controls or gesture recognizers that make sense for your app, and respond by calling `setViewControllers:...`. For example, if you're using the `.Scroll` transition style, there's no tap gesture recognizer, so the user can't tap at either edge of the page view controller's view to request navigation. Let's change that. I've added invisible views at either edge of my Pep view controller's view, with tap gesture recognizers attached. When the user taps, the tap gesture recognizer fires, and the action handler posts a notification whose `object` is the tap gesture recognizer:

```
@IBAction func tap (sender: UIGestureRecognizer?) {
    NSNotificationCenter.defaultCenter().postNotificationName(
        "tap", object: sender)
}
```

I receive this notification and use the tap gesture recognizer's view's `tag` to learn which view it is; I then navigate accordingly (n is the notification, pvc is the page view controller):

```
let g = n.object as! UIGestureRecognizer
let which = g.view!.tag
let vc0 = pvc.viewControllers[0] as! UIViewController
let vc = (which == 0 ?
    self.pageViewController(pvc, viewControllerBeforeViewController: vc0) :
    self.pageViewController(pvc, viewControllerAfterViewController: vc0))
if vc == nil {
    return
```

```
    }
    let dir : UIPageViewControllerNavigationDirection =
        which == 0 ? .Reverse : .Forward
    pvc.setViewControllers([vc!], direction: dir, animated: true, completion: nil)
```

Other Page View Controller Configurations

It is possible to assign a page view controller a delegate (UIPageViewController-Delegate), which gets an event when the user starts turning the page and when the user finishes turning the page, and can change the spine location dynamically in response to a change in device orientation. As with a tab bar controller's delegate or a navigation controller's delegate, a page view controller's delegate also gets messages allowing it to specify the page view controller's rotation policy, so there's no need to subclass UIPage-ViewController solely for that purpose.

One further bit of configuration applicable to a .PageCurl page view controller is the doubleSided property. If it is true, the next page occupies the back of the previous page. The default is false, unless the spine is in the middle, in which case it's true and can't be changed. Your only option here, therefore, is to set it to true when the spine isn't in the middle, and in that case the back of each page would be a sort of throwaway page, glimpsed by the user during the page curl animation.

A page view controller in a storyboard lets you configure its transition style, navigation orientation, page spacing, spine location, and doubleSided property. (It also has delegate and data source outlets, but you're not allowed to connect them to other view controllers, because you can't draw an outlet from one scene to another in a storyboard.) It has no child view controller relationship, so you can't set the page view controller's initial child view controller in the storyboard; you'll have to complete the page view controller's initial configuration in code.

Container View Controllers

UITabBarController, UINavigationController, and UIPageViewController are built-in *parent view controllers*: you hand them a child view controller and they put that child view controller's view into the interface for you, inside their own view. What if you want your own view controller to do the same thing?

In iOS 3 and 4, that was illegal; the only way a view controller's view could get into the interface was if a built-in parent view controller put it there. You could put a view into the interface, of course — but not a view controller's view. (Naturally, developers ignored this restriction, and got themselves into all kinds of difficulties.) In iOS 5, Apple introduced a coherent way for you to create your own parent view controllers, which can legally manage child view controllers and put their views into the interface. A custom parent view controller of this sort is called a *container view controller*.

Container view controllers give you the flexibility and power to construct the kind of hierarchy shown in Figure 6-4 from your own view controllers and their views, nesting them in what whatever manner and degree you like. Your own view controller becomes like one of the built-in parent view controllers, except that *you* get to define what it does — what it means for a view controller to be a child of this kind of parent view controller, how many children it has, which of its children appear in the interface and where they appear, and so on.

In iOS 8, container view controllers are of increased importance, because when your UIViewController subclass acts as a container view controller, it participates actively in the business of trait collection inheritance and view resizing.

Adding and Removing Children

Your view controller has a `childViewControllers` array. You must not, however, just wantonly populate this array. A child view controller needs to receive certain definite events at particular moments:

- As it becomes a child view controller
- As its view is added to and removed from the interface
- As it ceases to be a child view controller

Therefore, to act as a parent view controller, your UIViewController subclass must fulfill certain responsibilities:

Adding a child
When a view controller is to *become your view controller's child*, your view controller must do these things, in this order:

1. Send `addChildViewController:` to itself, with the child as argument. The child is automatically added to your `childViewControllers` array and is retained.

2. Get the child view controller's view into the interface (as a subview of your view controller's view), if that's what adding a child view controller means.

3. Send `didMoveToParentViewController:` to the child with your view controller as its argument.

Removing a child
When a view controller is to *cease being your view controller's child*, your view controller must do these things, in this order:

1. Send `willMoveToParentViewController:` to the child with a nil argument.

2. Remove the child view controller's view from your interface.

3. Send `removeFromParentViewController` to the child. The child is automatically removed from your `childViewControllers` array and is released.

This is a clumsy and rather confusing dance. The underlying reason for it is that a child view controller must always receive `willMoveToParentViewController:` followed by `didMoveToParentViewController:` (and your own child view controllers can take advantage of these events however you like). But it turns out that you don't always send both these messages explicitly, because:

- `addChildViewController:` *automatically* sends `willMoveToParentViewController:` for you.

- `removeFromParentViewController` *automatically* sends `didMoveToParentViewController:` for you.

Thus, in each case you must send manually the *other* message, the one that adding or removing a child view controller *doesn't* send for you — and of course you must send it so that everything happens in the correct order, as dictated by the rules I just listed.

Example 6-1 provides a schematic approach for how to obtain an initial child view controller and put its view into the interface, where no child view controller's view was previously. (Alternatively, a storyboard can do this work for you, with no code, as I'll explain later in this chapter.)

Example 6-1. Adding an initial child view controller

```
let vc = // whatever; this is the initial child view controller
self.addChildViewController(vc) // "will" called for us
vc.view.frame = // whatever, or use constraints
// insert view into interface between "will" and "did"
self.view.addSubview(vc.view)
// when we call add, we must call "did" afterwards
vc.didMoveToParentViewController(self)
```

The next question is how to *replace* one child view controller's view in the interface with another (comparable to how UITabBarController behaves when a different tab bar item is selected). The simplest, most convenient way is for the parent view controller to send itself this message:

- `transitionFromViewController:toViewController:duration:options: animations:completion:`

That method manages the stages in good order, adding one child view controller's view to the interface before the transition and removing the other child view controller's view from the interface after the transition, and seeing to it that the child view controllers receive lifetime events (such as `viewWillAppear:`) at the right moment. Here's what the last three arguments are for:

`options:`

A bitmask (UIViewAnimationOptions) comprising the same possible options that apply to any block-based view transition (see "Transitions" on page 158).

`animations:`

A block that may be used for additional view animations, besides the transition animation specified in the `options:` argument. Alternatively, if none of the built-in transition animations is suitable, you can animate the views yourself here; they are both in the interface during this block.

`completion:`

This block will be important if the transition involves the removal or addition of a child view controller. At the time when `transitionFromViewController:toView-Controller:...` is called, both view controllers must be children of the parent view controller; so if you're going to remove one of the view controllers as a child, you'll do it in the `completion:` block. Similarly, if you owe a new child view controller a `didMoveToParentViewController:` call, you'll use the `completion:` block to fulfill that debt.

Here's an example. To keep things simple, suppose that our view controller has just one child view controller at a time, and displays the view of that child view controller within its own view. So let's say that when our view controller is handed a new child view controller, it substitutes that new child view controller for the old child view controller and replaces the old child view controller's view with the new child view controller's view. Here's code that does that correctly; the view controllers are `fromvc` and `tovc`:

```
// we have already been handed the new view controller
// set up the new view controller's view's frame
tovc.view.frame = // ... whatever
// must have both as children before we can transition between them
self.addChildViewController(tovc) // "will" called for us
// note: when we call remove, we must call "will" (with nil) beforehand
fromvc.willMoveToParentViewController(nil)
// then perform the transition
self.transitionFromViewController(fromvc,
    toViewController:tovc,
    duration:0.4,
    options:.TransitionFlipFromLeft,
    animations:nil,
    completion:{
        _ in
        // finally, finish up
```

```
        // note: when we call add, we must call "did" afterwards
        tovc.didMoveToParentViewController(self)
        fromvc.removeFromParentViewController() // "did" called for us
    })
```

If we're using constraints to position the new child view controller's view, where will we set up those constraints? Before `transitionFromViewController:...` is too soon, as the new child view controller's view is not yet in the interface. The `completion:` block is too late: if the view is added with no constraints, it will have no initial size or position, so the animation will be performed and then the view will suddenly seem to pop into existence as we provide its constraints. The `animations:` block turns out to be a very good place:

```
// must have both as children before we can transition between them
self.addChildViewController(tovc) // "will" called for us
// note: when we call remove, we must call "will" (with nil) beforehand
fromvc.willMoveToParentViewController(nil)
// then perform the transition
self.transitionFromViewController(fromvc,
    toViewController:tovc,
    duration:0.4,
    options:.TransitionFlipFromLeft,
    animations: {
        tovc.view.setTranslatesAutoresizingMaskIntoConstraints(false)
        // ... configure tovc.view constraints here ...
    },
    completion:{
        _ in
        // finally, finish up
        // note: when we call add, we must call "did" afterwards
        tovc.didMoveToParentViewController(self)
        fromvc.removeFromParentViewController() // "did" called for us
    })
```

Alternatively, you can use a layout-related event, such as `viewWillLayoutSubviews`; still, I prefer the `animations:` block, as it is called just once at exactly the right moment.

If the built-in transition animations are unsuitable, you can set the `options:` argument to `.None` and provide your own animation in the `animations:` block, at which time both views are in the interface. In this example, I animate a substitute view (an image view showing a snapshot of `tovc.view`) to grow from the top left corner; then I configure the real view's constraints and remove the substitute:

```
// tovc.view.frame is already set
UIGraphicsBeginImageContextWithOptions(tovc.view.bounds.size, true, 0)
tovc.view.layer.renderInContext(UIGraphicsGetCurrentContext())
let im = UIGraphicsGetImageFromCurrentImageContext()
UIGraphicsEndImageContext()
let iv = UIImageView(image:im)
iv.frame = CGRectZero
self.view.addSubview(iv)
```

```
    tovc.view.alpha = 0
    // must have both as children before we can transition between them
    self.addChildViewController(tovc) // "will" called for us
    // note: when we call remove, we must call "will" (with nil) beforehand
    fromvc.willMoveToParentViewController(nil)
    // then perform the transition
    self.transitionFromViewController(fromvc,
        toViewController:tovc,
        duration:0.4,
        options:.TransitionNone,
        animations: {
            iv.frame = tovc.view.frame // animate bounds change
            // ... configure tovc.view constraints here ...
        },
        completion:{
            _ in
            tovc.view.alpha = 1
            iv.removeFromSuperview()
            // finally, finish up
            // note: when we call add, we must call "did" afterwards
            tovc.didMoveToParentViewController(self)
            fromvc.removeFromParentViewController() // "did" called for us
            UIApplication.sharedApplication().endIgnoringInteractionEvents()
        })
```

If your parent view controller is going to be consulted about the status bar (whether it should be shown or hidden, and if shown, whether its text should be light or dark), it can elect to defer the decision to one of its children, by implementing these methods:

- childViewControllerForStatusBarStyle
- childViewControllerForStatusBarHidden

Container View Controllers, Traits, and Resizing

New in iOS 8, a container view controller participates in trait collection inheritance and view resizing. In fact, you may well insert a container view controller into your view controller hierarchy for no other purpose than to engage in such participation.

Thus far, I have treated trait collection inheritance as immutable; and for the most part, it is. A UITraitEnvironment (an object with a traitCollection property: UIScreen, UIView, UIViewController, or UIPresentationController) ultimately gets its trait collection from the environment, and the environment is simply a fact. Nevertheless, a parent view controller has the amazing ability to lie to a child view controller about the environment, thanks to this method:

- setOverrideTraitCollection:forChildViewController:

The first parameter is a UITraitCollection that will be combined with the inherited trait collection and communicated to the specified child.

This is a UIViewController instance method, so only view controllers have this mighty power. Moreover, you have to specify a child view controller, so only *parent* view controllers have this mighty power. However, UIPresentationController has a similar power, through its `overrideTraitCollection` property; setting this property combines the override trait collection with the inherited collection and communicates it to the presented view controller.

Why would you want to do such a thing as lie to a child view controller about its environment? Well, imagine that we're writing an iPad app, and we have a view controller whose view can appear either fullscreen or as a small subview of a parent view controller's main view. The view's interface might need to be different when it appears in the smaller size. You could configure that using size classes (conditional constraints) in the nib editor, with one interface for a `.Regular` horizontal size class (iPad) and another interface for a `.Compact` horizontal size class (iPhone). Then, when the view is to appear in its smaller size, we lie to its view controller and tell it that this *is* an iPhone:

```
let vc = // the view controller we're going to use as a child
self.addChildViewController(vc)
let tc = UITraitCollection(horizontalSizeClass: .Compact)
self.setOverrideTraitCollection(tc, forChildViewController: vc) // heh heh
vc.view.frame = // whatever
self.view.addSubview(vc.view)
vc.didMoveToParentViewController(self)
```

Apple's own motivating example involves UISplitViewController, a class that (new in iOS 8) behaves differently depending on its trait environment. For example, by lying to a split view controller and making it believe we're on an iPad, you can cause the split view controller to *look* like a split view controller (displaying two subviews, such as a master table view and a detail view) even on an iPhone. I'll talk more about that in Chapter 9.

A parent view controller sets the size of a child view controller's view. A child view controller, however, can express a preference as to what size it would like its view to be, by setting its own `preferredContentSize` property. The chief purpose of this property is to be consulted by a parent view controller when this view controller is its child. This property is a preference and no more; no law says that the parent must consult the child, or that the parent must obey the child's preference.

If a view controller's `preferredContentSize` is set while it is a child view controller, the runtime automatically communicates this fact to the parent view controller, by calling this UIContentContainer method:

- `preferredContentSizeDidChangeForChildContentContainer:`

The parent view controller may implement this method to consult the child's `preferred-ContentSize` and change the child's view's size in response. Again, no law requires the parent to do this. This method, and the `preferredContentSize` property, are ways of allowing a child view controller a voice in its view's size; it is the parent who dictates what that size will actually be.

A parent view controller, as an adopter of the UIContentContainer protocol (along with UIPresentationController), is also responsible for communicating to its children that their sizes are changing and what their new sizes will be. It is the parent view controller's duty to implement this method:

`sizeForChildContentContainer:withParentContainerSize:`
> Should be implemented to return each child view controller's correct size at any moment. Failure to implement this method will cause the child view controller to be handed the wrong size in its implementation of `viewWillTransitionTo-Size:withTransitionCoordinator:` — it will be given the *parent's* new size rather than its own new size!

If your parent view controller implements `viewWillTransitionToSize:with-TransitionCoordinator:`, calling `super` is sufficient to get the same message passed on to the children. This works even if your implementation explicitly changed the size of a child view controller at this time, provided that you implemented `sizeForChild-ContentContainer:withParentContainerSize:` to return the new size.

Storyboards

Throughout this chapter, I've been describing how to create a view controller and present it or make it another view controller's child *manually*, entirely in code. But if you're using a storyboard, you will often (or always) allow the storyboard to do those things for you *automatically*. A storyboard can be helpful and convenient in this regard, though not, perhaps, for the reasons one might expect. It doesn't necessarily reduce the amount of code you'll have to write; indeed, in some cases using a storyboard may compel you to write *more* code, and in a less readable and maintainable way, than if you were creating your view controllers manually. But a storyboard does clarify the relationships between your view controllers over the course of your app's lifetime. Instead of having to hunt around in each of your classes to see which class creates which view controller and when, you can view and manage the chain of view controller creation graphically in the nib editor (Figure 6-9).

A storyboard, as I've already explained, is basically a collection of view controller nibs (scenes) and view nibs. Each view controller is instantiated from its own nib, as needed, and will then obtain its view, as needed — typically from a view nib that you've configured in the same storyboard by editing the view controller's view. I described this process in detail, and listed the ways in which a view controller in a storyboard can be instan-

Figure 6-9. The storyboard of an actual app

tiated, in "Storyboard-Instantiated View Controller" on page 266. One of those ways is manual (calling `instantiateViewControllerWithIdentifier:`); the other three are, or can be, automatic:

Initial view controller

If your app has a main storyboard, as specified by its *Info.plist*, that storyboard's initial view controller will be instantiated and assigned as the window's `rootViewController` automatically as the app launches. To specify that a view controller is a storyboard's initial view controller, check the "Is Initial View Controller" checkbox in its Attributes inspector (or, if you're using Xcode 6.2 or later, drag the Storyboard Entry Point object from the Object library into a view controller). This will cause any existing initial view controller to lose its initial view controller status. The initial view controller is distinguished graphically in the canvas by an arrow pointing to it from the left.

Relationship

Two built-in parent view controllers can specify their children directly in the storyboard, setting their `viewControllers` array:

- UITabBarController can specify multiple children.
- UINavigationController can specify its single initial child (its root view controller).

To add a view controller as a `viewControllers` child to a parent view controller, Control-drag from the parent view controller to the child view controller; in the little HUD that appears, choose (under Relationship Segue) "view controllers" for a UITabBarController, or "root view controller" for a UINavigationController. The result is a *relationship* whose source is the parent and whose destination is the child. The destination view controller will be instantiated automatically when the source view controller is instantiated, and will be assigned into its `viewControllers` array, thus making it a child and retaining it.

Segue

A segue configures a *future* situation, when the segue will be *triggered*. At that time, one view controller that already exists will cause the instantiation of another, bringing the latter into existence. Two types of segue are particularly common; they have new names in Xcode 6 if your *.storyboard* or *.xib* file uses size classes:

Push (with size classes: "show")

The future view controller will be pushed onto the stack of the navigation controller of which the existing view controller is already a child.

The new name comes from the `showViewController:sender:` method, which pushes a view controller onto the parent navigation controller if there is one, but behaves adaptively if there is not (I'll talk more about that in Chapter 9).

Modal (with size classes: "present modally")

The future view controller will be a presented view controller (and the existing view controller will be its original presenter).

Unlike a relationship, a segue does not have to emanate from a view controller; it can emanate from certain kinds of gesture recognizer, or from an appropriate view (such as a button or a table view cell) in the first view controller's view. This is a graphical shorthand signifying that the segue should be triggered, bringing the second view controller into existence, when a tap or other gesture occurs.

To create a segue, Control-drag from the view in the first view controller, or from the first view controller itself, to the second view controller. In the little HUD that appears, choose the type of segue you want.

In the rest of this chapter, I'll continue to use the older terms "push segue" and "modal segue." The new official names associated with size classes, "show segue" and "present modally segue," are too cumbersome. (Even Apple seems unsettled by its own choice of names: in the Segue pop-up menu in the Attributes inspector, a push segue is called "Show (e.g. Push)" — a clear case of renamer's remorse.)

(The arrows to the left of the four view controllers in Figure 6-9 are, sequentially, the initial view controller indicator, a relationship, a push segue, and a modal segue.)

Segues

Xcode confusingly and misleadingly tries to characterise relationships as a kind of segue ("Relationship Segue"); but the segue that concerns us here is what Xcode terms a Manual Segue, such as a push segue or a modal segue. Such a segue is a full-fledged object, an instance of UIStoryboardSegue (or your custom subclass thereof). In a storyboard, however, it is not a nib object, in the sense that it is not instantiated by the loading of a nib, and it cannot be pointed to by an outlet. Rather, it will be instantiated when the segue is triggered, at which time its designated initializer will be called, namely `init(identifier:source:destination:)`. It can, however, be configured in the nib editor, through the Attributes inspector.

A segue's `source` and `destination` are the two view controllers between which it runs. The segue is directional, so the source and destination are clearly distinguished. The source view controller is the one that will exist at the time the segue is triggered; the destination view controller is the one that the segue itself will be responsible for instantiating.

A segue's `identifier` is a string. You can set this string for a segue in a storyboard through its Attributes inspector; this can be useful when you want to trigger the segue manually in code (you'll specify it by means of its identifier), or when you have code that can receive a segue as parameter and you need to distinguish which segue this is.

In the case of a push segue, the identifier is the only thing you can customize in the Attributes inspector. The segue is going to call `pushViewController:animated:` for you, and you can't change anything about that.

In the case of a modal segue, the Attributes inspector lets you specify the Presentation (equivalent to the view controller's `modalPresentationStyle`) and the Transition (equivalent to the view controller's `modalTransitionStyle`); if you change these settings from Default, the segue will set that property to your choice when it instantiates the destination view controller, overriding whatever setting the destination view controller already has. The Animates checkbox is effectively the same as the second argument in `presentViewController:animated:completion:`.

Custom transition animations work just fine with segues. A segue is calling `pushView-Controller:animated:` or `presentViewController:animated:completion:` just as you would do in code, so if the relevant view controller has a delegate which returns an animation controller, your custom transition animation will be performed as usual. Remember, though, to configure the view controller early enough; `viewDidLoad` will not do as a place for a view controller to assign itself, say, a `transitioningDelegate`. This view controller is being instantiated from a nib, so `awakeFromNib` or `init(coder:)` is appropriate.

You can also specify a segue as a Custom segue, either in the HUD when you Control-drag to create the segue, or in the Attributes inspector. The Attributes inspector for a custom segue lets you specify a segue class, which must be a UIStoryboardSegue sub-class. In that subclass, you must override `perform`, which will be called after the segue is triggered and instantiated. Your `perform` implementation can access the segue's `identifier`, `sourceViewController`, and `destinationViewController` properties.

The `destinationViewController` has already been instantiated, but that's all; doing something with this view controller so as to make it a child view controller or presented view controller, retaining it and causing its view to appear in the interface, is entirely up to your code.

Now let's talk about how a segue will be triggered:

- If a segue emanates from a gesture recognizer or from a tappable view, it will be triggered automatically when the tap or other gesture occurs. The source view controller can prevent this; if you don't want this segue triggered on this occasion, implement `shouldPerformSegueWithIdentifier:sender:` and return `false`.

- If a segue emanates from a view controller as a whole, then triggering it is up to your code. To do so, send `performSegueWithIdentifier:sender:` to the source view controller. (In this case, `shouldPerformSegueWithIdentifier:sender:` will not be called.)

When a segue is triggered, the destination view controller is instantiated automatically. This is nice in the sense that automatic behavior is convenient, but it raises a crucial question: how on earth are you going to communicate between the source view controller and the destination view controller? This, you'll remember, was the subject of an earlier section of this chapter ("Communication With a Presented View Controller" on page 288), where I used this code as an example:

```
let svc = SecondViewController(
    nibName: "SecondViewController", bundle: nil)
svc.data = "This is very important data!"
svc.delegate = self
self.presentViewController(svc, animated:true, completion:nil)
```

In that code, the first view controller created the second view controller, and therefore had an opportunity of passing along some data to it before presenting it. With a segue, however, the second view controller is instantiated for you, and the segue itself is going to call `presentViewController:animated:completion:`. So when and how will you be able to set `svc.data` and set yourself as `svc`'s delegate?

The answer is that, after the segue has instantiated the second view controller but before it is performed, the source view controller is sent `prepareForSegue:sender:`. (For a custom segue, this happens before the segue's own `perform` is called.) This is the moment when the source view controller and the destination view controller meet! The source view controller can thus perform configurations on the destination view controller, hand it data, and so forth. The source view controller can work out which segue is being triggered by examining the segue's `identifier` and `destinationViewController` properties, and the `sender` is the interface object that was tapped to trigger the segue (or, if `performSegueWithIdentifier:sender:` was called in code, whatever object was supplied as the `sender:` argument).

This solves the communication problem, though in a clumsy way; `prepareFor-Segue:sender:` feels like a blunt instrument. The `destinationViewController` arrives typed as a generic `AnyObject`, and it is up to your code to know its actual type, cast it, and configure it. Moreover, if more than one segue emanates from a view controller, they are all bottlenecked through the same `prepareForSegue:sender:` implementation, which thus devolves into an ugly collection of conditions to distinguish them.

Container Views

You can configure a UITabViewController's child view controllers or a UINavigationController's root view controller in a storyboard, because these are *built-in* parent view controllers and the nib editor understands how they work. But if you write your own *custom* container view controller, the nib editor doesn't even know that your view controller *is* a container view controller. Nevertheless, you can perform some initial parent–child configuration of your container view controller in a storyboard, if your situation conforms to these assumptions:

- Your parent view controller will have one initial child view controller.
- You want the child view controller's view placed somewhere in the parent view controller's view when the child view controller is instantiated.

Those are reasonable assumptions, and you can work around them if they don't quite give the desired effect. For example, if your parent view controller is to have additional children, you can always add them later, in code; and if the child view controller's view is not to be initially visible in the parent view controller's view, you can always hide it.

To configure your parent view controller in a storyboard, locate the Container View object in the Object library and drag it into the parent view controller's view in the canvas. The result is a view, together with a segue from it to an additional child view controller. You can then assign the child view controller its correct class in its Identity inspector.

The segue here is an *embed* segue. When it is triggered, the destination view controller is instantiated and made the source view controller's child, and its view is placed exactly inside the container view as its subview. Thus, the container view is not only a way of generating the embed segue, but also a way of specifying where you want the child view controller's view to go. The entire child-addition dance is performed correctly and automatically for you: `addChildViewController:` is called, the child's view is put into the interface, and `didMoveToParentViewController:` is called.

Despite its superficial resemblance to a relationship, an embed segue is a true segue. It can have an identifier, and the standard messages are sent to the source view controller when the segue is triggered. Nevertheless, it has this similarity to a relationship: when the source (parent) view controller is instantiated, the runtime wants to trigger the segue automatically, instantiating the child view controller and embedding its view in the container view *now*. If that isn't what you want, override `shouldPerformSegueWith-Identifier:sender:` in the parent view controller to return `false` for this segue, and call `performSegueWithIdentifier:sender:` later when you do want the child view controller instantiated.

The parent view controller is sent `prepareForSegue:sender:` before the child's view loads. At this time, the child has not yet been added to the parent's `childViewControllers` array. If you allow the segue to be triggered when the parent view controller is instantiated, then by the time the parent's `viewDidLoad` is called, the child has been added to the parent's `childViewControllers`, and the child's view is inside the parent's view.

Subsequently replacing one child view controller's view with another in the interface will require that you call `transitionFromViewController:...` just as you would have done if a storyboard weren't involved (as I described earlier in this chapter). Still, you can configure this through a storyboard by using a custom segue and a UIStoryboard-Segue subclass.

Unwind Segues

Storyboards and segues would appear to be useful only half the time, because segues are asymmetrical. There is a push segue but no pop segue. There is a modal segue that presents a view controller but no modal segue that dismisses it.

In a nutshell, you can't use a normal segue to mean "go back." A segue's destination is a *class*; triggering the segue *instantiates* that class. But when dismissing a presented view controller or popping a pushed view controller, we don't need any *new* view controller instances. We want to return, somehow, to an *existing instance* of a view controller.

 A common mistake among beginners is to make a manual segue from view controller A to view controller B, and then try to express the notion "go back" by making *another* manual segue from view controller B to view controller A. The result, of course, is not presentation and subsequent dismissal, but presentation piled on presentation, or push piled on push, one view controller instantiated on top of another on top of another. *Do not construct a cycle of segues.* (Unfortunately, the nib editor doesn't alert you to this mistake.)

Thus, when storyboards were introduced in iOS 5, the way to call `popViewController-Animated:` was to call it, in code (or let a back button call it for you), just as if there were no such thing as a storyboard. The way to call `dismissViewController-Animated:completion:` was to call it, in code, just as if there were no such thing as a storyboard.

Figure 6-10. Creating an unwind segue

To deal with this shortcoming, iOS 6 introduced the *unwind segue*. An unwind segue *does* let you express the notion "go back" in a storyboard. It works in an ingenious and rather elaborate way. It has to, because (as I've just shown) it can't possibly work like a normal segue! So how *does* it work?

Let's talk first about how you create an unwind segue in the first place. Before you can do that, you must implement an *unwind method* in the class of any view controller represented in the storyboard. This should be a method marked @IBAction as a hint to the storyboard editor, and taking a single parameter, a UIStoryboardSegue. You can call it unwind: if you like, but the name doesn't really matter:

```
@IBAction func unwind(seg:UIStoryboardSegue!) {
    // ...
}
```

Now you can create an unwind segue. Doing so involves the use of the Exit proxy object that appears in every scene of a storyboard. Control-drag from the view controller you want to go back *from*, connecting it to the Exit proxy object *in the same scene* (Figure 6-10). A little HUD appears, listing all the unwind methods known to this storyboard (similar to how action methods are listed in the HUD when you connect a button to its target). Click the name of the unwind method you want. You have now made an unwind segue, bound to that unwind method.

Even so, the name of the unwind method to which the unwind segue is bound is *only a name*. The unwind segue's source view controller is the view controller that contains it. But *its destination view controller is unknown*; it will not be determined until the app runs and the segue is triggered. At runtime, when the unwind segue is triggered, the runtime starts walking *up the view controller hierarchy* looking for a destination view controller. Put simply, the first view controller it finds that *implements the unwind method* will be the destination view controller. (I'll describe the actual details of this search in a moment.)

Once the destination view controller is found, the following steps are performed:

1. The source view controller's `shouldPerformSegueWithIdentifier:sender:` is called — just as for a normal segue. This is your chance to stop the whole process dead at this point by returning `false`.

2. The source view controller's `prepareForSegue:identifier:` is called — just as for a normal segue. The two view controllers are now in contact (because the other view controller is the segue's `destinationViewController`). This is an opportunity for the source view controller to hand information to the destination view controller before being destroyed! (Thus, an unwind segue is an alternative to a `delegate` property as a way of putting one view controller into communication with another: see "Communication With a Presented View Controller" on page 288.)

3. The destination view controller's unwind method is called. Its parameter is the segue; this segue can be identified through its `identifier` property. The two view controllers are now in contact *again* (because the other view controller is the segue's `sourceViewController`). It is perfectly reasonable, however, for the unwind method body to be empty; the unwind method's real purpose is to mark this view controller as the destination view controller.

4. The segue is performed, *destroying* the source controller and any intervening view controllers up to (but not including) the destination view controller, in good order.

Now I'll go back and explain in detail how the destination view controller is found and used to construct the actual segue. This is partly out of sheer interest (it's a devilishly clever procedure), and partly in case you need to customize the process.

When an unwind segue is triggered, the runtime starts walking up the view controller hierarchy from the source view controller instance toward the root view controller. This walk is well-defined: every view controller has either a `parentViewController` or a `presentingViewController`, so the next view controller up the hierarchy is that view controller. The runtime asks each view controller for the destination view controller, by calling this UIViewController method:

`viewControllerForUnwindSegueAction:fromViewController:withSender:`
    There are two possible responses:

    A view controller returns nil
        The runtime will proceed to the next view controller up the hierarchy.

    A view controller returns a view controller (possibly itself)
        The search ends: the destination view controller has been found.

The default UIViewController implementation of `viewControllerForUnwindSegueAction:...` is for a view controller to send *itself* this message:

`canPerformUnwindSegueAction:fromViewController:withSender:`
    There are two possible outcomes:

canPerformUnwindSegueAction:... *returns* false

> In that case, viewControllerForUnwindSegueAction:... returns nil, and the search continues.

canPerformUnwindSegueAction:... *returns* true

> In that case, viewControllerForUnwindSegueAction:... returns self, and the search ends here.

The default implementation of canPerformUnwindSegueAction:..., in turn, is for a view controller to send itself respondsToSelector: for the unwind method! Thus, the normal outcome is that if a view controller implements the unwind method, it will end up as the destination view controller, and otherwise, the search will continue on up the hierarchy.

(You can, however, override canPerformUnwindSegueAction:... to return false, to force the runtime search to continue on up the view controller hierarchy past this view controller.)

What I have said so far, however, does not explain how a push is reversible. After all, the next view controller that the runtime comes to as it walks up the hierarchy from a pushed view controller is the *parent* of the pushed view controller, namely *the UINavigationController itself.* But a push does not unwind to the navigation controller; it unwinds (usually) by popping to the next sibling down the navigation controller's stack. How does that happen?

The answer is that the runtime walk does indeed come to the UINavigationController itself, and does indeed ask the navigation controller for a destination by sending it view-ControllerForUnwindSegueAction:...; but UINavigationController has its own elaborate default implementation of viewControllerForUnwindSegueAction:.... It doesn't consider itself as a possible destination; that wouldn't make sense. Instead, it *consults its children*, starting at the top of the stack and polling them in reverse order, looking for the first one that returns true from canPerformUnwindSegueAction:...; if it finds one, it returns it (and otherwise it returns nil). Moreover, by default, can-PerformUnwindSegueAction:... returns false if the fromViewController: is self. This algorithm suffices to choose the correct view controller to pop to.

I have explained how the destination view controller is chosen, but not how the unwinding process itself is implemented. How does it come about that sometimes we dismiss (a presented view controller) and sometimes we pop (a pushed view controller) — and sometimes a combination of both?

The answer is that if a view controller supplies the runtime with a destination view controller (by returning one from its viewControllerForUnwindSegueAction:...), it is then also asked to supply the actual segue! This is done by sending it this message:

`segueForUnwindingToViewController:fromViewController:identifier:`

> Must return a segue whose `perform` method is tailor-made for the current situation, dictating the entire "go back" sequence that will release the source view controller and all intervening view controllers in good order, and performing an appropriate transition animation.
>
> The resulting segue's `identifier` will be the identifier, if any, that you specified for the original unwind segue in the storyboard; its `sourceViewController` will be the source view controller from the storyboard (the `fromViewController:`); and its `destinationViewController` will be the destination view controller we have at last settled on (the `toViewController:`).

How is such a segue constructed? By calling this UIStoryboardSegue class method:

`segueWithIdentifier:source:destination:performHandler:`

> Creates a segue on the fly. Its `perform` implementation will be the block (closure) supplied as the `performHandler:` parameter.

To illustrate, let's modify the segue performed by a navigation controller. Consider this sequence: a navigation controller, its root view controller, a pushed view controller, and a presented view controller. By default, if we unwind directly from the presented view controller all the way back to the root view controller, we get only the reverse of the presented view controller's original animation. That's not very clear to the user, since in fact we're going back two steps. Let's improve that so that there are two successive animations, a dismissal followed by a pop. We replace the UINavigationController with a custom subclass, and override `segueForUnwinding:...` as follows:

```
override func segueForUnwindingToViewController(
    toViewController: UIViewController,
    fromViewController: UIViewController,
    identifier: String?) -> UIStoryboardSegue {
        let vcs = self.viewControllers as! [UIViewController]
        if vcs.count == 2 && toViewController == vcs[0] {
            if fromViewController == self.presentedViewController {
                return UIStoryboardSegue(identifier: identifier,
                    source: fromViewController,
                    destination: toViewController) {
                        self.dismissViewControllerAnimated(true) { // anim 1
                            _ in
                            self.popToViewController(
                                toViewController, animated: true) // anim 2
                            return
                        }
                }
            }
        }
    }
```

```
       return super.segueForUnwindingToViewController(
           toViewController, fromViewController: fromViewController,
           identifier: identifier)
   }
```

New in iOS 8, if the runtime walk up the view controller hierarchy comes to a child view controller, it turns *immediately* to the parent. In other words, in iOS 8, `viewController-ForUnwindSegueAction:...` is *never* sent by the runtime to a child view controller. If a view controller has a parent, the parent is consulted, not the child.

This is different from iOS 7 and before. The difference is manifest particularly in the edge case where we unwind a presented view controller to a child view controller. Consider again the same sequence I posited a moment ago: a navigation controller, its root view controller, a pushed view controller, and a presented view controller, which unwinds. In iOS 7, the first view controller to be sent `viewControllerForUnwindSegue-Action:...` was the pushed view controller — although, if the pushed view controller nominated itself as the destination, it was the navigation controller that had to supply the segue. In iOS 8, the first view controller to be sent `viewControllerForUnwindSegue-Action:...` is the navigation controller.

The iOS 8 approach is more rational, but it can break your existing code, especially if you have a custom container view controller. If you want your custom container view controller to work with unwind segues, it must do the kind of thing UINavigation-Controller does. The implementation is not difficult, but if unwind segues were working with your existing parent view controller from iOS 7, they may appear to be broken when your app is recompiled for iOS 8 until you adjust to deal with this edge case.

View Controller Lifetime Events

As views come and go, driven by view controllers and the actions of the user, events arrive that give your view controller the opportunity to respond to the various stages of its own existence and the management of its view. By overriding these methods, your UIViewController subclass can perform appropriate tasks at appropriate moments. Here's a list:

`viewDidLoad`
> The view controller has obtained its view. See the discussion earlier in this chapter of how a view controller gets its view.

```
willTransitionToTraitCollection:withTransitionCoordinator:
viewWillTransitionToSize:withTransitionCoordinator:
traitCollectionDidChange:
```
The view controller's view is being resized or the trait environment is changing (or both). See the discussion of resizing events earlier in this chapter. Your implementation of the first two methods must call super.

```
updateViewConstraints
viewWillLayoutSubviews
viewDidLayoutSubviews
```
The view is receiving updateConstraints and layoutSubviews events. See Chapter 1, and the discussion of resizing events earlier in this chapter. Your implementation of updateViewConstraints must call super.

```
willMoveToParentViewController:
didMoveToParentViewController:
```
The view controller is being added or removed as a child of another view controller. See the discussion of container view controllers earlier in this chapter.

```
viewWillAppear:
viewDidAppear:
viewWillDisappear:
viewDidDisappear:
```
The view is being added to or removed from the interface. This includes being supplanted by another view controller's view or being restored by the removal of another view controller's view. A view that has appeared (or has not yet disappeared) is in the window; it is part of your app's active view hierarchy. A view that has disappeared (or has not yet appeared) is not in the window; its window is nil. *You must call super* in your override of any of these four methods; if you forget to do so, things may go wrong in subtle ways.

To distinguish more precisely *why* your view is appearing or disappearing, call any of these methods on self:

- isBeingPresented
- isBeingDismissed
- isMovingToParentViewController
- isMovingFromParentViewController

A good way to get a sense for when these events are useful is to track the sequence in which they normally occur. Take, for example, a UIViewController being pushed onto the stack of a navigation controller. It receives, in this order, the following messages:

- `viewWillAppear:`
- `traitCollectionDidChange:`
- `viewWillLayoutSubviews`
- `updateViewConstraints`
- `viewDidLayoutSubviews`
- `viewDidAppear:`
- `didMoveToParentViewController:`

(There is then a second round of layout messages.)

When this same UIViewController is popped off the stack of the navigation controller, it receives, in this order, the following messages:

- `willMoveToParentViewController:` (with parameter nil)
- `viewWillDisappear:`
- `viewWillLayoutSubviews`
- `updateViewConstraints`
- `viewDidLayoutSubviews`
- `viewDidDisappear:`
- `didMoveToParentViewController:` (with parameter nil)

Disappearance, as I mentioned a moment ago, can happen because another view controller's view supplants this view controller's view. For example, consider a UIViewController functioning as the top (and visible) view controller of a navigation controller. When another view controller is pushed on top of it, the first view controller gets these messages:

- `viewWillDisappear:`
- `viewWillLayoutSubviews`
- `updateViewConstraints`
- `viewDidLayoutSubviews`
- `viewDidDisappear:`
- `didMoveToParentViewController:`

The converse is also true. For example, when a view controller is popped from a navigation controller, the view controller that was below it in the stack (the back view controller) receives these events:

- `viewWillAppear:`

- `viewWillLayoutSubviews`

- `updateViewConstraints`

- `viewDidLayoutSubviews`

- `viewDidAppear`

- `didMoveToParentViewController:`

(There is then a second round of layout messages.)

Incoherencies in View Controller Events

Unfortunately, the exact sequence of events and the number of times they will be called for any given view controller transition situation sometimes seems nondeterministic or incoherent. The previous section contains a number of cases in point, and there are others. For example:

- Sometimes `didMoveToParentViewController:` arrives without a corresponding `willMoveToParentViewController:`.

- Sometimes `didMoveToParentViewController:` arrives even though this view controller was previously the child of this parent and remains the child of this parent.

- Sometimes the layout events (`updateViewConstraints`, `viewWillLayout-Subviews`, `viewDidLayoutSubviews`) arrive more than once for the same view controller for the same transition.

- Sometimes the layout events arrive needlessly, as when the view controller's view is about to leave the interface and the view controller is about to be destroyed.

- Sometimes `viewWillAppear:` or `viewWillDisappear:` arrives without the corresponding `viewDidAppear:` or `viewDidDisappear:`. For example, if an interactive transition animation begins and is cancelled, the cancelled view controller receives `viewWillAppear:` at the start, *without* `viewDidAppear:`, and receives `viewWill-Disappear:` and `viewDidDisappear:` at the end.

The best advice I can offer is that you should try to structure your code in such a way that incoherencies of this sort don't matter.

Appear and Disappear Events

The `appear`/`disappear` methods are particularly appropriate for making sure that a view reflects the model or some form of saved state whenever it appears. Changes to the interface performed in `viewDidAppear:` or `viewWillDisappear:` may be visible to the user as they occur! If that's not what you want, use the other member of the pair. For example, in a certain view containing a long scrollable text, I want the scroll position to be the same when the user returns to this view as it was when the user left it, so I save the scroll position in `viewWillDisappear:` and restore it in `viewWillAppear:` (not `viewDidAppear:`, where the user might see the scroll position jump).

Similarly, they are useful when something must be true exactly so long as a view is in the interface. For example, a timer that must be running while a view is present can be started in the view controller's `viewDidAppear:` and stopped in its `viewWillDisappear:`. (This architecture also allows you to avoid the retain cycle that could result if you waited to invalidate the timer in a `deinit` that might otherwise never arrive.)

A view does not disappear if a presented view controller's view merely covers it rather than supplanting it. For example, a view controller that presents another view controller using the `.FormSheet` presentation style gets no lifetime events during presentation and dismissal.

A view does not disappear merely because the app is backgrounded and suspended. Once suspended, your app might be killed. So you cannot rely on `viewWillDisappear:` and `viewDidDisappear:` alone for saving data that the app will need the next time it launches. If you are to cover every case, you may need to ensure that your data-saving code also runs in response to an application lifetime event such as `applicationWillResignActive:` or `applicationDidEnterBackground:` (and see Appendix A for a discussion of the application lifetime events).

Event Forwarding to a Child View Controller

A custom container (parent) view controller, as I explained earlier, must effectively send `willMoveToParentViewController:` and `didMoveToParentViewController:` to its children manually.

It must also forward resizing events to its children. This will happen automatically if you call `super` in your implementation of `willTransitionToTraitCollection:...` and `viewWillTransitionToSize:...`. By the same token, if you implement these methods, failure to call `super` may prevent them from being forwarded correctly to the child view controller.

The `appear` events are normally passed along automatically. However, you can take charge of calling these events manually, by implementing this method:

`shouldAutomaticallyForwardAppearanceMethods`
    If you override this method to return `false`, you are responsible for seeing that these methods on your view controller's children are called:

- `viewWillAppear:`
- `viewDidAppear:`

- viewWillDisappear:

- viewDidDisappear:

You do *not* do this by calling these methods directly. The reason is that you have no access to the correct moment for sending them. Instead, you call these two methods on your child view controller:

- beginAppearanceTransition:animated:; the first parameter is a Bool saying whether this view controller's view is about to appear (true) or disappear (false)

- endAppearanceTransition

Here's what to do if you've implemented shouldAutomaticallyForwardAppearance-Methods to return false. There are two main occasions on which your custom container view controller must forward appear events to a child.

First, what happens when your custom container view controller's own view itself appears or disappears? If it has a child view controller's view within its own view, it must implement and forward all four appear events to that child. You'll need an implementation along these lines, for each of the four appear events:

```
override func viewWillAppear(animated: Bool) {
    super.viewWillAppear(animated)
    let child = // whatever
    if child.isViewLoaded() && child.view.superview != nil {
        child.beginAppearanceTransition(true, animated: true)
    }
}
override func viewDidAppear(animated: Bool) {
    super.viewDidAppear(animated)
    let child = // whatever
    if child.isViewLoaded() && child.view.superview != nil {
        child.endAppearanceTransition()
    }
}
```

(The implementations for viewDidAppear: and viewDidDisappear: are similar, except that the first argument for beginAppearanceTransition: is false.)

Second, what happens when you swap one view controller's child for another in your interface? You must *not* call the UIViewController method transitionFromView-Controller:toViewController:...! It takes charge of sending the appear calls to the children itself, and it isn't going to do so correctly in this situation. Instead, you must perform the transition animation directly. A minimal correct implementation might involve the UIView class method transitionFromView:toView:... (see Chapter 4).

Here, you can and should call `beginAppearanceTransition:` and `endAppearance-Transition` yourself.

Here's an example of a parent view controller swapping one child view controller and its view for another, while taking charge of notifying the child view controllers of the appearance and disappearance of their views. I've put asterisks to call attention to the additional method calls that forward the appear events to the children:

```
self.addChildViewController(tovc)
fromvc.willMoveToParentViewController(nil)
fromvc.beginAppearanceTransition(false, animated:true) // *
tovc.beginAppearanceTransition(true, animated:true) // *
UIView.transitionFromView(fromvc.view,
    toView:tovc.view,
    duration:0.4,
    options:.TransitionFlipFromLeft,
    completion:{
        _ in
        tovc.endAppearanceTransition() // *
        fromvc.endAppearanceTransition() // *
        tovc.didMoveToParentViewController(self)
        fromvc.removeFromParentViewController()
})
```

View Controller Memory Management

Memory is at a premium on a mobile device. Thus you want to minimize your app's use of memory. Your motivations, in the multitasking world, are partly altruistic and partly selfish. You want to keep your memory usage as low as possible so that other apps can be launched and the user can switch between suspended apps. You also want to prevent your own app from being terminated! If your app is backgrounded and suspended while using a lot of memory, it may be terminated in the background when memory runs short. If your app uses an inordinate amount of memory while in the foreground, it may be summarily killed before the user's very eyes.

One strategy for avoiding using too much memory is to release any memory-hogging objects you're retaining if they are not needed at this moment. Because a view controller is the basis of so much of your application's architecture, it is likely to be a place where you'll concern yourself with releasing unneeded memory.

One of your view controller's most memory-intensive objects is its view. Fortunately, the iOS runtime manages a view controller's view's memory for you. If a view controller's view is not in the interface, it can be temporarily dispensed with. In such a situation, if memory is getting tight, then even though the view controller itself persists, and even though it retains its actual view, the runtime may release its view's backing store (the cached bitmap representing the view's drawn contents). The view will then be redrawn when and if it is to be shown again later.

In addition, if memory runs low, your view controller may be sent this message:

didReceiveMemoryWarning

> Sent to a view controller to advise it of a low-memory situation. It is preceded by a call to the app delegate's applicationDidReceiveMemoryWarning:, together with a UIApplicationDidReceiveMemoryWarningNotification posted to any registered objects. You are invited to respond by releasing any data that you can do without. Do not release data that you can't readily and quickly recreate! The documentation advises that you should call super.

If you're going to release data in didReceiveMemoryWarning, you must concern yourself with how you're going to get it back. A simple and reliable mechanism is *lazy loading* — a getter that reconstructs or fetches the data if it is nil.

For example, suppose we have a property myBigData which might be a big piece of data. We make this a calculated property, storing the real data in a private property (I'll call it myBigDataReal). Our calculated property's setter simply writes through to the private property. In didReceiveMemoryWarning we write myBigData out as a file to disk (Chapter 23) and set myBigData to nil — thus setting myBigDataReal to nil as well, and releasing the big data from memory. The getter for myBigData implements lazy loading: if we try to get myBigData when myBigDataReal is nil, we attempt to fetch the data from disk — and if we succeed, we delete it from disk (to prevent stale data):

```
private var myBigDataReal : NSData!
var myBigData : NSData! {
    set (newdata) {
        self.myBigDataReal = newdata
    }
    get {
        if myBigDataReal == nil {
            let fm = NSFileManager()
            let f = NSTemporaryDirectory()
                .stringByAppendingPathComponent("myBigData")
            if fm.fileExistsAtPath(f) {
                self.myBigDataReal = NSData(contentsOfFile: f)
                var err : NSError?
                let ok = fm.removeItemAtPath(f, error: &err)
                assert(ok, "Couldn't remove temp file")
            }
        }
        return self.myBigDataReal
    }
}
func saveAndReleaseMyBigData() {
    if let myBigData = self.myBigData {
        let f = NSTemporaryDirectory()
            .stringByAppendingPathComponent("myBigData")
        myBigData.writeToFile(f, atomically:false)
        self.myBigData = nil
```

```
        }
    }
    override func didReceiveMemoryWarning() {
        super.didReceiveMemoryWarning()
        self.saveAndReleaseMyBigData()
    }
```

To test low-memory circumstances artificially, run your app in the Simulator and choose Hardware → Simulate Memory Warning. I don't believe this has any actual effect on memory, but a memory warning of sufficient severity is sent to your app, so you can see the results of triggering your low-memory response code, including the app delegate's `applicationDidReceiveMemoryWarning:` and your view controller's `didReceive-MemoryWarning`.

On the device, the equivalent is to call an undocumented method (in Objective-C):

```
[[UIApplication sharedApplication]
    performSelector:@selector(_performMemoryWarning)];
```

(Be sure to remove that code when it is no longer needed for testing, as the App Store won't accept it.)

You will also wish to concern yourself with releasing memory when your app is about to be suspended. If your app has been backgrounded and suspended and the system later discovers it is running short of memory, it will go hunting through the suspended apps, looking for memory hogs that it can kill in order to free up that memory. If the system decides that your suspended app is a memory hog, it isn't politely going to wake your app and send it a memory warning; it's just going to terminate your app in its sleep. The time to be concerned about releasing memory, therefore, is *before* the app is suspended. You'll probably want your view controller to be registered with the shared application to receive `UIApplicationDidEnterBackgroundNotification`. The arrival of this notification is an opportunity to release any easily restored memory-hogging objects, such as `myBigData` in the previous example:

```
    override func viewDidLoad() {
        super.viewDidLoad()
        NSNotificationCenter.defaultCenter().addObserver(
            self, selector: "backgrounding:",
            name: UIApplicationDidEnterBackgroundNotification,
            object: nil)
    }
    func backgrounding(n:NSNotification) {
        self.saveAndReleaseMyBigData()
    }
```

Testing how your app's memory behaves in the background isn't easy. In a WWDC 2011 video, an interesting technique is demonstrated. The app is run under Instruments on the device, using the virtual memory instrument, and is then backgrounded by pressing the Home button, thus revealing how much memory it voluntarily relinquishes at that time. Then a special memory-hogging app is launched on the device: its interface loads and displays a very large image in a UIImageView. Even though your app is backgrounded and suspended, the virtual memory instrument continues to track its memory usage, and you can see whether further memory is reclaimed under pressure from the demands of the memory-hogging app in the foreground.

State Restoration

In the multitasking world, when the user leaves your app and then later returns to it, one of two things might have happened in the meantime:

Your app was suspended

Your app was suspended in the background, and remained suspended while the user did something else. When the user returns to your app, the system simply unfreezes your app, and there it is, looking just as it did when the user left it.

Your app was terminated

Your app was suspended in the background, and then, as the user worked with other apps, a moment came where the system decided it needed the resources (such as memory) being held by your suspended app. Therefore it terminated your app. When the user returns to your app, the app launches from scratch.

For most apps, a general goal should be to make those two situations more or less indistinguishable to the user. The user, after all, doesn't know the difference between those two things, so why should the app behave differently some of the time? Ideally, it should *always* feel to the user as if the app is being resumed from where it left off the last time it was in the foreground, even if in fact the app was terminated while suspended in the background. Otherwise, as the WWDC 2013 video on this topic puts it, the user will feel that the app has mysteriously and annoyingly "lost my place."

This goal is *state restoration*. Your app has a state at every moment: some view controller's view is occupying the screen, and views within it are displaying certain values (for example, a certain switch is set to On, or a certain table view is scrolled to a certain position). The idea of state restoration is to save that information when the app goes into the background, and use it to make all those things true again if the app is subsequently launched from scratch.

iOS provides a general solution to the problem of state restoration. This solution is centered around view controllers, which makes sense, since view controllers are the heart of the problem. What is the user's "place" in the app, which we don't want to "lose"? It's the chain of view controllers that got us to where we were when the app was backgrounded, along with the configuration of each one. The goal of state restoration must therefore be to *reconstruct all existing view controllers*, initializing each one into the state it previously had.

Note that state, in this sense, is neither user defaults nor data. If something is a preference, make it a preference and store it in NSUserDefaults. If something is data (for example, the underlying model on which your app's functionality is based), keep it in a file (Chapter 23). Don't misuse the state saving and restoration mechanism for such things. The reason for this is not only conceptual; it's also because *saved state can be lost*. You don't want to commit anything to the state restoration mechanism if it would be a disaster to have lost it the next time the app launches.

For example, suppose the user kills your app outright by double-clicking the Home button to show the app switcher interface and flicking your app's snapshot upward; the system will throw away its state. Similarly, if your app crashes, the system will throw away its state. In both cases, the system assumes that something went wrong, and doesn't want to launch your app into what might be a troublesome saved state. Instead, your app will launch cleanly, from the beginning. There's no problem for the user, barring a mild inconvenience — as long as the only thing that gets thrown away is state.

How to Test State Restoration

To test whether your app is saving and restoring state as you expect:

1. Run the app as usual, in the Simulator or on a device.
2. At some point, in the Simulator or on the device, click the Home button (Hardware → Home in the Simulator). This causes the app to be suspended in good order, and state is saved.
3. Now, back in Xcode, stop the running project (Product → Stop).
4. Run the project again. If there is saved state, it is restored.

(To test the app's behavior from a truly cold start, delete it from the Simulator or device. You might need to do this after changing something about the underlying save-and-restore model.)

Apple also provides (at *http://developer.apple.com/downloads*) a number of debugging tools:

restorationArchiveTool
> A command-line tool letting you examine a saved state archive in textual format. The archive is in a folder called Saved Application State in your app's sandboxed Library. See Chapter 23 for more about the app's sandbox, and how to copy it to your computer from a device.

StateRestorationDebugLogging.mobileconfig
> A configuration profile. When installed on a device (through the iPhone Configuration Utility, or by emailing it to yourself and opening it on the device), it causes the console to dump information as state saving and restoration proceeds.

StateRestorationDeveloperMode.mobileconfig

   A configuration profile. When installed on a device, it prevents the state archive from being jettisoned after unexpected termination of the app (a crash, or manual termination through the app switcher interface). This can allow you to test state restoration a bit more conveniently.

Participating in State Restoration

Built-in state restoration operates more or less automatically. All you have to do is tell the system that you want to participate in it. To do so, you take three basic steps:

Implement app delegate methods

   The app delegate must implement these methods to return `true`:

   - `application:shouldSaveApplicationState:`
   - `application:shouldRestoreApplicationState:`

   (Naturally, your code can instead return `false` to prevent state from being saved or restored on some particular occasion.)

Implement `application:willFinishLaunchingWithOptions:`

   Although it is very early, `application:didFinishLaunchingWithOptions:` is too late for state restoration. Your app needs its basic interface *before* state restoration begins. The solution is to use a different app delegate method, `application:will-FinishLaunchingWithOptions:`.

   Typically, you can just change "did" to "will" in the name of this method, keeping your existing code unchanged. However, your implementation *must* call `makeKey-AndVisible` explicitly on the window if the existing code doesn't already call it! Otherwise, the interface doesn't come into existence soon enough for restoration to happen during launch.

Provide restoration IDs

   Both UIViewController and UIView have a `restorationIdentifier` property, which is a string. Setting this string to a non-nil value is your signal to the system that you want this view controller (or view) to participate in state restoration. If a view controller's `restorationIdentifier` is nil, neither it nor any subsequent view controllers down the chain will be saved or restored. (A nice feature of this architecture is that it lets you participate *partially* in state restoration, omitting some view controllers by not assigning them a restoration identifier.)

   You can set the `restorationIdentifier` manually, in code; typically you'll do that early in a view controller's lifetime. If a view controller or view is instantiated from a nib, you'll want to set the restoration identifier in the nib editor; the Identity inspector has a Restoration ID field for this purpose. (If you're using a storyboard, it's a good idea, in general, to make a view controller's restoration ID in the storyboard the same as its storyboard ID, the string used to identify the view controller in a call to `instantiateViewControllerWithIdentifier:`; in fact, it's such a good idea that the storyboard editor provides a checkbox, "Use Storyboard ID," that makes the one value automatically the same as the other.)

In the case of a simple storyboard-based app, where each needed view controller instance can be reconstructed directly from the storyboard, those steps alone can be sufficient to bring state restoration to life, operating correctly at the view controller level. Let's test it. Start with a storyboard-based app with the following architecture (Figure 6-11):

- A navigation controller.
- Its root view controller, connected by a relationship from the navigation controller. Call its class RootViewController.
  - A presented view controller, connected by a modal segue from a Present button in the root view controller's view. Call its class PresentedViewController. Its view contains a Dismiss button.
- A second view controller, connected by a push segue from a Push bar button item in the root view controller's navigation item. Call its class SecondViewController.
  - The very same presented view controller (PresentedViewController), also connected by a modal segue from a Present button in the second view controller's view.

This storyboard-based app runs perfectly with just about no code at all; all we need is an empty implementation of an unwind method in RootViewController and SecondViewController so that we can create an unwind segue from the PresentedViewController Dismiss button.

We will now make this app implement state restoration:

1. Change the name of `application:didFinishLaunchingWithOptions:` in the app delegate to `application:willFinishLaunchingWithOptions:`, and insert this line of code if it isn't already present:

    ```
    self.window?.makeKeyAndVisible()
    ```

2. Implement `application:shouldSaveApplicationState:` and `application:shouldRestoreApplicationState:` in the app delegate to return `true`.

3. Give all four view controller instances in the storyboard restoration IDs: let's call them `"nav"`, `"root"`, `"second"`, and `"presented"`.

That's all! The app now saves and restores state.

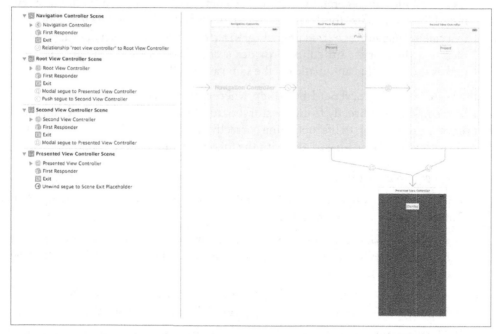

Figure 6-11. Architecture of an app for testing state restoration

 Before calling `makeKeyAndVisible`, it may also be useful to assign the window a restoration identifier: `self.window!.restorationIdentifier = "window"`. This might not make any detectable difference, but in some cases it can help restore size class information.

Restoration ID, Identifier Path, and Restoration Class

Having everything done for us by the storyboard reveals nothing about what's really happening. To learn more, let's rewrite the example without a storyboard. Throw away the storyboard (and delete the Main Storyboard entry from the *Info.plist*) and implement the same architecture using code alone:

```swift
// AppDelegate.swift:
func application(application: UIApplication,
    didFinishLaunchingWithOptions launchOptions: [NSObject: AnyObject]?)
    -> Bool {
        self.window = UIWindow(frame:UIScreen.mainScreen().bounds)
        let rvc = RootViewController()
        let nav = UINavigationController(rootViewController:rvc)
        self.window!.rootViewController = nav
        self.window!.backgroundColor = UIColor.whiteColor()
        self.window!.makeKeyAndVisible()
```

```
        return true
    }

    // RootViewController.swift:
    override func viewDidLoad() {
        super.viewDidLoad()
        // ... color view background, create buttons ...
    }
    func doPresent(sender:AnyObject?) {
        let pvc = self.dynamicType.makePresentedViewController()
        self.presentViewController(pvc, animated:true, completion:nil)
    }
    func doPush(sender:AnyObject?) {
        let pvc = self.dynamicType.makeSecondViewController()
        self.navigationController!.pushViewController(pvc, animated:true)
    }

    // SecondViewController.swift:
    override func viewDidLoad() {
        super.viewDidLoad()
        // ... color view background, create button ...
    }
    func doPresent(sender:AnyObject?) {
        let pvc = self.dynamicType.makePresentedViewController()
        self.presentViewController(pvc, animated:true, completion:nil)
    }

    // PresentedViewController.m:
    override func viewDidLoad() {
        super.viewDidLoad()
        // ... color view background, create button ...
    }
    func doDismiss(sender:AnyObject?) {
        self.dismissViewControllerAnimated(true, completion: nil)
    }
```

That's a working app. Now let's start adding state restoration, just as before:

1. Change the name of `application:didFinishLaunchingWithOptions:` in the app delegate to `application:willFinishLaunchingWithOptions:`.

2. Implement `application:shouldSaveApplicationState:` and `application:shouldRestoreApplicationState:` in the app delegate to return `true`.

3. Give all four view controller instances restoration IDs: let's call them `"nav"`, `"root"`, `"second"`, and `"presented"`. We'll have to do this in code. We're creating each view controller instance manually, so we may as well assign its `restoration-Identifier` in the next line, like this:

```
let rvc = RootViewController()
rvc.restorationIdentifier = "root"
let nav = UINavigationController(rootViewController:rvc)
nav.restorationIdentifier = "nav"
```

And so on.

Run the app. We are *not* getting state restoration. Why not?

The reason is that the restorationIdentifier alone is not sufficient to tell the state restoration mechanism what to do as the app launches. The restoration mechanism knows the chain of view controller *classes* that needs to be generated, but it is up to us to generate the *instances* of those classes. (Our storyboard-based example didn't exhibit this problem, because the storyboard itself was the source of the instances.) To do that, we need to know about the *identifier path* and the *restoration class*.

The restorationIdentifier serves as a guide during restoration as to what view controller is needed at each point in the view controller hierarchy. Any particular view controller instance, given its position in the view controller hierarchy, is uniquely identified by the sequence of restorationIdentifier values of *all* the view controllers (including itself) in the chain that leads to it. Those restorationIdentifier values, taken together and in sequence, constitute the *identifier path* for any given view controller instance.

Each identifier path is, in fact, merely an array of strings. In effect, the identifier paths are like a trail of breadcrumbs that you left behind as you created each view controller while the app was running, and that will now be used to identify each view controller *again* as the app launches.

For example, if we launch the app and press the Push button and then the Present button, then all four view controllers have been instantiated; those instances are identified as:

- ["nav"]
- ["nav", "root"]
- ["nav", "second"]
- ["nav", "presented"] (because the navigation controller is the actual presenting view controller)

Observe that a view controller's identifier path is not a record of the full story of how we got here. It's just an identifier! The state-saving mechanism also saves a relational tree of identifiers. For example, if the app is suspended in the current situation, then the state-saving mechanism will record the true state of affairs, namely that the root view controller has two children and a presented view controller, along with their identifiers.

Now consider what the state restoration mechanism needs to do when the app has been suspended and killed, and comes back to life, from the situation I just described. We need to restore four view controllers; we know their identifiers and mutual relationships. State restoration doesn't start until *after* `application:willFinishLaunchingWith-Options:`. So when the state restoration mechanism starts examining the situation, it discovers that the `["nav"]` and `["nav", "root"]` view controller instances have already been created! However, the view controller instances for `["nav", "second"]` and `["nav", "presented"]` must also be created now. The state restoration mechanism doesn't know how to do that — so it's going to ask your code for the instances.

But *what* code should it ask? One way of specifying this is for you to provide a *restoration class* for each view controller instance that is *not* restored by the time `application:will-FinishLaunchingWithOptions:` returns. Here's how you do that:

1. Give the view controller a `restorationClass`. Typically, this will be the view controller's own class, or the class of the view controller responsible for creating this view controller instance.

2. Implement the class method `viewControllerWithRestorationIdentifier-Path:coder:` on the class named by each view controller's `restorationClass` property, returning a view controller instance as specified by the identifier path. Very often, the implementation will be to instantiate the view controller directly and return that instance.

3. Specify formally that each class named as a `restorationClass` implements the UIViewControllerRestoration protocol.

 In the past, omitting that third step caused state restoration to fail silently and mysteriously. New in iOS 8, you'll get a delightful and helpful warning message at runtime: "Restoration class for view controller does not conform to UIView-ControllerRestoration protocol."

Let's make our PresentedViewController and SecondViewController instances restorable. I'll start with PresentedViewController. Our app can have *two* PresentedView-Controller instances (though not simultaneously) — the one created by RootView-Controller, and the one created by SecondViewController. Let's start with the one created by RootViewController.

Since RootViewController creates and configures a PresentedViewController instance, it can reasonably act also as the restoration class for that instance. In its implementation of `viewControllerWithRestorationIdentifierPath:coder:`, RootViewController should then create and configure a PresentedViewController instance *exactly* as it was doing before we added state restoration to our app — except for putting it into the view controller hierarchy! The state restoration mechanism itself, remember, is responsible for assembling the view controller hierarchy; our job is merely to supply any needed view controller instances.

So RootViewController now must adopt UIViewControllerRestoration, and will contain this code:

```
func doPresent(sender:AnyObject?) {
    let pvc = PresentedViewController()
    pvc.restorationIdentifier = "presented"
    pvc.restorationClass = self.dynamicType // *
    self.presentViewController(pvc, animated:true, completion:nil)
}
class func viewControllerWithRestorationIdentifierPath(ip: [AnyObject],
    coder: NSCoder) -> UIViewController? {
        var vc : UIViewController? = nil
        let last = ip.last as! String
        switch last {
        case "presented":
            let pvc = PresentedViewController()
            pvc.restorationIdentifier = "presented"
            pvc.restorationClass = self
            vc = pvc
        default: break
        }
        return vc
}
```

You can see what I mean when I say that the restoration class must do exactly what it was doing before state restoration was added. Clearly this situation has led to some annoying code duplication, so let's factor out the common code. In doing so, we must bear in mind that doPresent: is an instance method, whereas viewControllerWith-RestorationIdentifierPath:coder: is a class method; our factored-out code must therefore be a class method, so that they can both call it:

```
class func makePresentedViewController () -> UIViewController {
    let pvc = PresentedViewController()
    pvc.restorationIdentifier = "presented"
    pvc.restorationClass = self
    return pvc
}
func doPresent(sender:AnyObject?) {
    let pvc = self.dynamicType.makePresentedViewController()
    self.presentViewController(pvc, animated:true, completion:nil)
}
class func viewControllerWithRestorationIdentifierPath(ip: [AnyObject],
    coder: NSCoder) -> UIViewController? {
        var vc : UIViewController? = nil
        let last = ip.last as! String
        switch last {
        case "presented":
```

```
            vc = self.makePresentedViewController()
        default: break
        }
        return vc
    }
```

The structure of our `viewControllerWithRestorationIdentifierPath:coder:` is typical. We test the identifier path — usually, it's sufficient to examine its last element — and return the corresponding view controller; ultimately, we are also prepared to return nil, in case we are called with an identifier path we can't interpret. We can also return nil deliberately, to tell the restoration mechanism, "Go no further; don't restore the view controller you're asking for here, or any view controller further down the same path."

Continuing in the same vein, we expand RootViewController still further to make it also the restoration class for SecondViewController, and SecondViewController can make itself the restoration class for the PresentedViewController instance that it creates. There's no conflict in the notion that both RootViewController and SecondView-Controller can fulfill the role of PresentedViewController restoration class, as we're talking about two different PresentedViewController instances. The app now performs state saving and restoration correctly! (The details are left as an exercise for the reader.)

I said earlier that the state restoration mechanism can ask your code for needed instances in two ways. The second way is that you implement this method in your app delegate:

- `application:viewControllerWithRestorationIdentifierPath:coder:`

If you implement this method, it will be called for *every* view controller that doesn't have a restoration class. This works in a storyboard-based app, and thus is a chance for you to intervene and prevent the restoration of a particular view controller on a particular occasion (by returning nil). Be prepared to receive identifier paths for an existing view controller! If that happens, return the existing view controller — don't make a new one.

For example, if we were to implement `application:viewControllerWithRestoration-IdentifierPath:coder:` in the example app I've been describing, it would be called for `["nav"]` and for `["nav", "root"]`, because those view controllers have no restoration class. But we needn't, and we mustn't, create a new view controller; those view controller instances have already been created, and we must return those existing instances.

Restoring View Controller State

I have explained how the state restoration mechanism creates a view controller and places it into the view controller hierarchy. But at that point, the work of restoration is only half done. What about the *state* of that view controller?

A newly restored view controller probably won't yet have the data and property values it was holding at the time the app was terminated. The history of the creation and configuration of this view controller is *not* magically recapitulated during restoration. If the view controller comes from a storyboard, then any settings in its Attributes inspector are obeyed, but the segue that generated the view controller in the first place is never run, so the previous view controller's `prepareForSegue:sender:` is never called, and the previous view controller never gets to hand this view controller any data. If the view controller is created by a restoration class, it may have been given some initial configuration, but this very likely falls short of the full state that the view controller was holding when the app was terminated. Any additional communication between one view controller and another to hand it data will be missing from the process. Indeed, since the history of the app during its previous run is not recapitulated, there will be no data to hand over in the first place.

It is up to each view controller, therefore, to *restore its own state* when it itself is restored. And in order to do that, it must previously *save its own state* when the app is backgrounded. The state saving and restoration mechanism provides a way of helping your view controllers do this, through the use of a *coder* (an NSCoder object). Think of this coder as a box in which the view controller is invited to place its valuables for safekeeping, and from which it can retrieve them later. Each of these valuables needs to be identified, so it is tagged with a key (an arbitrary string) when it is placed into the box, and is then later retrieved by using the same key, much as in a dictionary.

Anyone who has anything to save at the time it is handed a coder can do so by sending the coder an appropriate encode message with a key, such as `encodeFloat:forKey:` or `encodeObject:forKey:`. If an object's class doesn't adopt the NSCoding protocol, you may have to archive it to an NSData object before you can encode it. However, views and view controllers can be handled by the coder directly, because they are treated as references. Whatever was saved in the coder can later be extracted by sending the coder the reverse operation using the same key, such as `decodeFloatForKey:` or `decodeObjectForKey:`.

The keys do not have to be unique across the entire app; they only need to be unique for a particular view controller. Each object that is handed a coder is handed *its own personal coder*. It is handed this coder at state saving time, and it is handed the same coder (that is, a coder with the same archived objects and keys) at state restoration time.

Here's the sequence of events involving coders:

When state is saved
>   When it's time to save state (as the app is about to be backgrounded), the state saving mechanism provides coders as follows:

>   1. The app delegate is sent `application:shouldSaveApplicationState:`. The coder is the second parameter.

2. The app delegate is sent `application:willEncodeRestorableStateWith-Coder:`. This is the same coder as in the previous step, because this is the same object (the app delegate).

3. Each view controller down the chain, starting at the root view controller, is sent `encodeRestorableStateWithCoder:` if it implements it. The implementation should call `super`. Each view controller gets its own coder.

When state is restored

When the app is launched, if state is to be restored, the state restoration mechanism provides coders as follows:

1. The app delegate is sent `application:shouldRestoreApplicationState:`. The coder (the one belonging to the app delegate) is the second parameter.

2. As each view controller down the chain is to be created, one of these methods is called (as I've already explained):

   - The restoration class's `viewControllerWithRestorationIdentifier-Path:coder:`, if the view controller has a restoration class.

   - The app delegate's `application:viewControllerWithRestoration-IdentifierPath:coder:`, if implemented.

   The coder is the one appropriate to the view controller that's to be created.

3. Each view controller down the chain, starting at the root view controller, is sent `decodeRestorableStateWithCoder:` if it implements it. The implementation should call `super`. The coder is the one appropriate to this view controller.

4. The app delegate is sent `application:didDecodeRestorableStateWith-Coder:`. The coder is the same one sent to `application:shouldRestore-ApplicationState:` (the one belonging to the app delegate).

The *UIStateRestoration.h* header file describes five built-in keys that are available from every coder during restoration:

`UIStateRestorationViewControllerStoryboardKey`
A reference to the storyboard from which this view controller came, if any.

`UIApplicationStateRestorationBundleVersionKey`
Your *Info.plist* `CFBundleVersion` string when state saving happened.

`UIApplicationStateRestorationUserInterfaceIdiomKey`
An NSNumber wrapping a UIUserInterfaceIdiom value, either `.Phone` or `.Pad`, telling what kind of device we were running on when state saving happened. You can extract this information as follows:

```
        if let idiomraw = coder.decodeObjectForKey(
            UIApplicationStateRestorationUserInterfaceIdiomKey) as? Int {
                if let idiom = UIUserInterfaceIdiom(rawValue:idiomraw) {
                    if idiom == .Phone {
                        // ...
                    }
                }
        }
```

UIApplicationStateRestorationTimestampKey

> An NSDate telling when state saving happened.

UIApplicationStateRestorationSystemVersionKey

> A NSString telling the system version from when state saving happened.

One purpose of these keys is to allow your app to opt out of state restoration, wholly or in part, because the archive is too old, was saved on the wrong kind of device (and presumably migrated to this one by backup and restore), and so forth.

A typical implementation of `encodeRestorableStateWithCoder:` and `decode-RestorableStateWithCoder:` will concern itself with properties and interface views. `decodeRestorableStateWithCoder:` is guaranteed to be called *after* `viewDidLoad`, so you know that `viewDidLoad` won't overwrite any direct changes to the interface performed in `decodeRestorableStateWithCoder:`.

To illustrate, I'll add state saving and restoration to my earlier UIPageViewController example, the one that displays a Pep Boy on each page. Recall how that example is architected. The project has no storyboard. The code defines just two classes, the app delegate and the Pep view controller. The app delegate creates a UIPageViewController and makes it the window's root view controller, and makes itself the page view controller's data source. The page view controller's data source methods create and supply an appropriate Pep instance whenever a page is needed for the page view controller, along these lines:

```
// ... work out index of new name ...
return Pep(pepBoy: self.pep[ix])
```

The challenge is to restore the Pep object displayed in the page view controller as the app launches. One solution involves recognizing that a Pep object is completely configured once created, and it is created just by handing it the name of a Pep Boy in its designated initializer, which becomes its boy property. Thus we can mediate between a Pep object and a mere string, and all we really need to save and restore is that string.

All the additional work, therefore, can be performed in the app delegate. As usual, we change "did" to "will" so that we are now implementing `application:willFinish-LaunchingWithOptions:`, and we implement `application:shouldSaveApplication-State:` and `application:shouldRestoreApplicationState:` to return `true`. Now we save and restore the current Pep Boy name in the app delegate's encode and decode methods:

```
func application(application: UIApplication,
    willEncodeRestorableStateWithCoder coder: NSCoder) {
        let pvc = self.window!.rootViewController as! UIPageViewController
        let boy = (pvc.viewControllers[0] as! Pep).boy
        coder.encodeObject(boy, forKey:"boy")
}
func application(application: UIApplication,
    didDecodeRestorableStateWithCoder coder: NSCoder) {
        let boy: AnyObject? = coder.decodeObjectForKey("boy")
        if let boy = boy as? String {
            let pvc = self.window!.rootViewController as! UIPageViewController
            let pep = Pep(pepBoy: boy)
            pvc.setViewControllers(
                [pep], direction: .Forward, animated: false, completion: nil)
        }
}
```

A second solution, which is more realistic, assumes that we want our Pep view controller class itself to be capable of saving and restoration. This means that every view controller down the chain from the root view controller to our Pep view controller must have a restoration identifier. In our simple app, there's just one such view controller, the UIPageViewController; the app delegate can assign it a restoration ID when it creates it:

```
let pvc = UIPageViewController(transitionStyle: .Scroll,
    navigationOrientation: .Horizontal, options: nil)
pvc.restorationIdentifier = "pvc" // *
```

We'll have a Pep object assign itself a restoration ID in its own designated initializer. The Pep object will also need a restoration class; as I mentioned earlier, this can perfectly well be the Pep class itself, and that seems most appropriate here:

```
required init(pepBoy boy:String) {
    self.boy = boy
    super.init(nibName: "Pep", bundle: nil)
    self.restorationIdentifier = "pep" // *
    self.restorationClass = self.dynamicType // *
}
```

The only state that a Pep object needs to save is its boy string. The coder in which that boy value is saved will come back to us in Pep's viewControllerWithRestoration-IdentifierPath:coder:, so we can use it to create the new Pep object by calling the designated initializer, thus avoiding code duplication:

```
override func encodeRestorableStateWithCoder(coder: NSCoder) {
    super.encodeRestorableStateWithCoder(coder)
    coder.encodeObject(self.boy, forKey:"boy")
}
```

```
class func viewControllerWithRestorationIdentifierPath(
    ip: [AnyObject], coder: NSCoder) -> UIViewController? {
        let boy = coder.decodeObjectForKey("boy") as! String
        return self(pepBoy: boy)
}
```

(Swift won't permit a class to instantiate itself through an initializer on self unless we guarantee that any subclass implements that initializer; our marking of init(pepBoy:) as required constitutes just such a guarantee.)

Now comes a surprise. We run the app and test it, and we find that we're *not* getting saving and restoration of our Pep object. It isn't being archived! Its encodeRestorable-StateWithCoder: isn't even being called! The reason is that the state saving mechanism doesn't work automatically for a UIPageViewController and its children (or for a custom container view controller and *its* children, for that matter). It is up to us to see to it that the current Pep object is archived.

To do so, we can archive and unarchive the current Pep object in an implementation of encodeRestorableStateWithCoder: and decodeRestorableStateWithCoder: that *is* being called. For our app, that would have to be in the app delegate. The code we've written so far has all been necessary to make the current Pep object archivable and restorable; now the app delegate will make sure that it *is* archived and restored:

```
func application(application: UIApplication,
    willEncodeRestorableStateWithCoder coder: NSCoder) {
        let pvc = self.window!.rootViewController as! UIPageViewController
        let pep = pvc.viewControllers[0] as! Pep
        coder.encodeObject(pep, forKey:"pep")
}
func application(application: UIApplication,
    didDecodeRestorableStateWithCoder coder: NSCoder) {
        let pep : AnyObject? = coder.decodeObjectForKey("pep")
        if let pep = pep as? Pep {
            let pvc = self.window!.rootViewController as! UIPageViewController
            pvc.setViewControllers(
                [pep], direction: .Forward, animated: false, completion: nil)
        }
}
```

This solution may seem rather heavyweight, but it isn't. We're not really archiving an entire Pep instance; it's just a reference. The actual Pep instance is the one created by viewControllerWithRestorationIdentifierPath:coder:.

Restoration Order of Operations

When you implement state saving and restoration for a view controller, the view controller ends up with two different ways of being configured. One way involves the lifetime events I discussed earlier in this chapter ("View Controller Lifetime Events" on page 355). The other involves the events I've been discussing in this section. You want your view controller to be correctly configured no matter whether this view controller is undergoing state restoration or not.

Before state saving and restoration, you were probably configuring your view controller, at least in part, in `viewWillAppear:` and `viewDidAppear:`. With state saving and restoration added to the picture, you may also be receiving `decodeRestorableStateWith-Coder:`. If you configure your view controller here, will you be overriding what happens in `viewWillAppear:` and `viewDidAppear:`, or will they come along later and override what you do in `decodeRestorableStateWithCoder:`?

The unfortunate fact is that you don't know. For `viewWillAppear:` and `viewDid-Appear:`, in particular, the only thing you *do* know during state restoration is that you'll get both of them for the top view controller (the one whose view actually appears). You don't know *when* they will arrive; it might be before or after `decodeRestorableState-WithCoder:`. For other view controllers, you don't even know *whether* `viewDidAppear:` will arrive: it might well *never* arrive, even if `viewWillAppear:` arrives. This is another of those view controller lifetime event incoherencies I complained about earlier in this chapter.

However, there's another event I haven't mentioned yet: `applicationFinished-RestoringState`. If you implement this method, it will be called if and only if we're doing state restoration, at a time when all view controllers have already been sent `decode-RestorableStateWithCoder:`.

Thus, the known order of events during state restoration is like this:

- `application:shouldRestoreApplicationState:`
- `application:viewControllerWithRestorationIdentifierPath:coder:`
- `viewControllerWithRestorationIdentifierPath:coder:`, in order down the chain
- `viewDidLoad`, in order down the chain; possibly interleaved with the foregoing
- `decodeRestorableStateWithCoder:`, in order down the chain
- `application:didDecodeRestorableStateWithCoder:`
- `applicationFinishedRestoringState`, in order down the chain

You still don't know when `viewWillAppear:` and `viewDidAppear:` will arrive, or whether `viewDidAppear:` will arrive at all. But in `applicationFinishedRestoringState` you can reliably finish configuring your view controller and your interface.

Thus, a typical situation is that you will want to update your interface after all properties have been set. So you'll factor out your interface-updating code into a single method. Now there are two possibilities, and they are both handled coherently:

We're not restoring state
> Properties will be set through initialization and configuration, and then `viewWill-Appear:` calls your interface-updating method.

We are restoring state
> Properties will be set by `decodeRestorableStateWithCoder:`, and then `applicationFinishedRestoringState` calls your interface-updating method.

There is still some indeterminacy as to what's going to happen, but the interface-updating method can mediate that indeterminacy by checking for two things that can go wrong:

It is called too soon
> The interface-updating method should check to see that the properties have in fact been set; if not, it should just return. It will be called again when the properties *have* been set.

It is called unnecessarily
> The interface-updating method might run twice in quick succession with the same set of properties. This is not a disaster, but if you don't like it, you can prevent it by comparing the properties to the interface and return if the interface has already been configured with these properties.

 If your app has additional state restoration work to do on a background thread (Chapter 25), the documentation says you should call UIApplication's `extendState-Restoration` as you begin and `completeStateRestoration` when you've finished. The idea is that if you *don't* call `completeStateRestoration`, the system can assume that something has gone very wrong (like, your app has crashed) and will throw away the saved state information in case it is faulty.

Restoration of Other Objects

A view will participate in automatic saving and restoration of state if its view controller does, and if it itself has a restoration identifier. Some built-in UIView subclasses also have built-in restoration abilities. For example, a scroll view that participates in state saving and restoration will automatically return to the point to which it was scrolled previously. You should consult the documentation on each UIView subclass to see whether it participates usefully in state saving and restoration, and I'll mention a few significant cases when we come to discuss those views in later chapters.

In addition an arbitrary object can be made to participate in automatic saving and restoration of state. There are three requirements for such an object:

- The object's class must adopt the UIStateRestoring protocol. This declares three optional methods:
  - `encodeRestorableStateWithCoder:`
  - `decodeRestorableStateWithCoder:`
  - `applicationFinishedRestoringState`
- When the object is created, someone must register it with the runtime by calling this UIApplication class method:
  - `registerObjectForStateRestoration:restorationIdentifier:`
- Someone who participates in state saving and restoration, such as a view controller, must make the archive aware of this object by storing a reference to it in the archive (typically in `encodeRestorableStateWithCoder:`) — much as we did with the Pep object earlier.

So, for example, here's an NSObject subclass Thing with a `word` property, that participates in state saving and restoration:

```
class Thing : NSObject, UIStateRestoring {
    func encodeRestorableStateWithCoder(coder: NSCoder) {
        coder.encodeObject(self.word, forKey:"word")
    }
    func decodeRestorableStateWithCoder(coder: NSCoder) {
        self.word = coder.decodeObjectForKey("word") as! String
    }
    func applicationFinishedRestoringState() {
        // not used
    }
}
```

And here's a view controller with a Thing property (`self.thing`):

```
class func makeThing () -> Thing {
    let thing = Thing()
    UIApplication.registerObjectForStateRestoration(
        thing, restorationIdentifier: "thing")
    return thing
}
override func awakeFromNib() {
    super.awakeFromNib()
    self.thing = self.dynamicType.makeThing()
}
override func encodeRestorableStateWithCoder(coder: NSCoder) {
    super.encodeRestorableStateWithCoder(coder)
    coder.encodeObject(self.thing, forKey: "mything") // important!
}
```

That last line is crucial; it introduces our Thing object to the archive and brings its UIStateRestoring methods to life.

There is an optional `objectRestorationClass` property of the restorable object, and an `objectWithRestorationIdentifierPath:coder:` method that the designated class must implement. But our object is restorable even without an `objectRestoration-Class`! Presumably, just calling `registerObjectForStateRestoration:restoration-Identifier:` sufficiently identifies this object to the runtime. If you do want to assign an `objectRestorationClass`, you'll have to declare it:

```
var objectRestorationClass: UIObjectRestoration.Type!
```

The class in question should adopt the UIObjectRestoration protocol; its `objectWith-RestorationIdentifierPath:coder:` will then be called, and can return the restorable object, by creating it or pointing to it. Alternatively, it can return nil to prevent restoration.

Another optional property of the restorable object is `restorationParent`. Again, if you want to assign to it, you'll have to declare it:

```
var restorationParent: UIStateRestoring!
```

The parent should adopt the UIStateRestoring protocol. The purpose of the parent is to give the restorable object an identifier path. For example, if we have a chain of view controllers with a path `["nav", "second"]`, then if that last view controller is the `restorationParent` of our Thing object, the Thing object's identifier path in `object-WithRestorationIdentifierPath:coder:` will be `["nav", "second", "thing"]`, rather than simply `["thing"]`. This is useful if we are worried that `["thing"]` alone will not uniquely identify this object.

Snapshot Suppression

When your app is backgrounded, the system takes a snapshot of your interface. It is used in the app switcher interface, and as a launch image when your app is resumed. But what happens if your app is killed in the background and relaunched?

If your app isn't participating in state restoration, then its default launch image is used. This makes sense, because your app is starting from scratch. But if your app *is* participating in state restoration, then the snapshot is used as a launch image. This makes sense, too, because the interface that was showing when the app was backgrounded is presumably the very interface your state restoration process is about to restore.

However, you might decide, while saving state, that there is reason not to use the system's snapshot when relaunching. (Perhaps there is something in your interface that would be inappropriate to display when the app is subsequently launched.) In that case, you can call the UIApplication instance method `ignoreSnapshotOnNextApplication-Launch`. When the app launches with state restoration, the user will see your app's default launch image, followed by a change to the restored interface. They may not match, but at least there is a nice cross-dissolve between them.

By the same token, if the view controller whose view was showing at state saving time is not restorable (it has no restoration ID), then if the app is killed in the background and subsequently launches with state restoration, the restoration mechanism knows that the snapshot taken at background time doesn't match the interface we're about to restore to, so the user will initially see your app's default launch image.

CHAPTER 7

Scroll Views

A scroll view (UIScrollView) is a view whose content is larger than its bounds. To reveal a desired area, the user can scroll the content by dragging, or you can reposition the content in code.

A scroll view isn't magic; it takes advantage of ordinary UIView features (Chapter 1). The content is simply the scroll view's subviews. When the scroll view scrolls, what's really changing is the scroll view's own bounds origin; the subviews are positioned with respect to the bounds origin, so they move with it. The scroll view's `clipsToBounds` is usually `true`, so any content positioned within the scroll view is visible and any content positioned outside it is not.

In addition, a scroll view brings to the table some nontrivial abilities:

- It knows how to shift its bounds origin in response to the user's gestures.
- It provides scroll indicators whose size and position give the user a clue as to the content's size and position.
- It can enforce paging, whereby the user can scroll only by a fixed amount.
- It supports zooming, so that the user can resize the content with a pinch gesture.
- It provides a plethora of delegate methods, so that your code knows exactly how the user is scrolling and zooming.

As I've just said, a scroll view's subviews, like those of any view, are positioned with respect to its bounds origin; to scroll is to change the bounds origin. The scroll view thus already knows how far it should be allowed to slide its subviews downward and rightward — the limit is reached when the scroll view's bounds origin is (0.0,0.0). What the scroll view *needs* to know is how far it should be allowed to slide its subviews upward and leftward. That is the scroll view's *content size* — its `contentSize` property. The scroll view uses its `contentSize`, in combination with its own bounds size, to set the limits on how large its bounds origin can become. It may also be helpful to think of the scroll view's scrollable *content* as the rectangle defined by `CGRect(origin:CGPoint-Zero, size:contentSize)`; this is the rectangle that the user can inspect by scrolling.

If a dimension of the `contentSize` isn't larger than the same dimension of the scroll view's own bounds, the content won't be scrollable in that dimension: there is nothing to scroll, as the entire scrollable content is already showing. The default is that the `contentSize` is (`0.0,0.0`) — meaning that the scroll view isn't scrollable.

To get a working scroll view, therefore, it will be crucial to set its `contentSize` correctly. You can do this directly, in code; or, if you're using autolayout (Chapter 1), the `content-Size` is calculated for you based on the constraints of the scroll view's subviews. I'll demonstrate both approaches.

Creating a Scroll View in Code

I'll start by creating a scroll view, providing it with subviews, and making those subviews viewable by scrolling, entirely in code.

Manual Content Size

In the first instance, let's not use autolayout. Our project is based on the Single View Application template, with a single view controller class, ViewController, and with the storyboard's "Use Auto Layout" unchecked. In the ViewController's `viewDidLoad`, I'll create the scroll view to fill the main view, and populate it with 30 UILabels whose text contains a sequential number so that we can see where we are when we scroll:

```
let sv = UIScrollView(frame: self.view.bounds)
sv.autoresizingMask = .FlexibleWidth | .FlexibleHeight
self.view.addSubview(sv)
sv.backgroundColor = UIColor.whiteColor()
var y : CGFloat = 10
for i in 0 ..< 30 {
    let lab = UILabel()
    lab.text = "This is label \(i+1)"
    lab.sizeToFit()
    lab.frame.origin = CGPointMake(10,y)
    sv.addSubview(lab)
    y += lab.bounds.size.height + 10
}
var sz = sv.bounds.size
sz.height = y
sv.contentSize = sz // *
```

The crucial move is the last line, where we tell the scroll view how large its content is to be. If we omit this step, the scroll view won't be scrollable; the window will appear to consist of a static column of labels.

There is no rule about the order in which you perform the two operations of setting the `contentSize` and populating the scroll view with subviews. In that example, we set the `contentSize` afterward because it is more convenient to track the heights of the subviews as we add them than to calculate their total height in advance. Similarly, you can alter a scroll view's content (subviews) or `contentSize`, or both, dynamically as the app runs.

Any direct subviews of the scroll view may need to have their autoresizing set appropriately in case the scroll view is resized, as would happen, for instance, if our app performs compensatory rotation. To see this, add these lines to the preceding example, inside the for loop:

```
lab.frame.width = self.view.bounds.width - 20
lab.backgroundColor = UIColor.redColor()
lab.autoresizingMask = .FlexibleWidth
```

Run the app, and rotate the device or the Simulator. The labels are wider in portrait orientation because the scroll view itself is wider.

This, however, has nothing to do with the `contentSize`! The `contentSize` does not change just because the scroll view's bounds change; if you want the `contentSize` to change in response to rotation, you will need to change it manually, in code. Conversely, resizing the `contentSize` has no effect on the size of the scroll view's subviews; it merely determines the scrolling limit.

Automatic Content Size With Autolayout

With autolayout, things are different. The difficult thing to understand — and it is certainly counterintuitive — is that a constraint between a scroll view and its direct subview is *not* a way of positioning the subview relative to the scroll view (as it would be if the superview were an ordinary UIView). Instead, it's a way of describing the scroll view's `contentSize`.

To see this, let's rewrite the preceding example to use autolayout. If the only change is that the storyboard's "Use Auto Layout" is checked, the example continues to work, because the scroll view and its subviews all have their `translatesAutoresizingMask-IntoConstraints` set to `true` by default; all constraints are implicit, as if we weren't using autolayout at all. But what if the scroll view and its subviews have their `translates-AutoresizingMaskIntoConstraints` set to `false`, and we're giving them explicit constraints? Let's try it:

```
let sv = UIScrollView()
sv.backgroundColor = UIColor.whiteColor()
sv.setTranslatesAutoresizingMaskIntoConstraints(false)
self.view.addSubview(sv)
self.view.addConstraints(
    NSLayoutConstraint.constraintsWithVisualFormat(
```

```
        "H:|[sv]|",
        options:nil, metrics:nil,
        views:["sv":sv]))
self.view.addConstraints(
    NSLayoutConstraint.constraintsWithVisualFormat(
        "V:|[sv]|",
        options:nil, metrics:nil,
        views:["sv":sv]))
var previousLab : UILabel? = nil
for i in 0 ..< 30 {
    let lab = UILabel()
    lab.setTranslatesAutoresizingMaskIntoConstraints(false)
    lab.text = "This is label \(i+1)"
    sv.addSubview(lab)
    sv.addConstraints(
        NSLayoutConstraint.constraintsWithVisualFormat(
            "H:|-(10)-[lab]",
            options:nil, metrics:nil,
            views:["lab":lab]))
    if previousLab == nil { // first one, pin to top
        sv.addConstraints(
            NSLayoutConstraint.constraintsWithVisualFormat(
                "V:|-(10)-[lab]",
                options:nil, metrics:nil,
                views:["lab":lab]))
    } else { // all others, pin to previous
        sv.addConstraints(
            NSLayoutConstraint.constraintsWithVisualFormat(
                "V:[prev]-(10)-[lab]",
                options:nil, metrics:nil,
                views:["lab":lab, "prev":previousLab!]))
    }
    previousLab = lab
}
```

The labels are correctly positioned relative to one another, but the scroll view isn't scrollable. Moreover, setting the contentSize manually doesn't help. The solution is to add one more constraint, showing the scroll view what the height of its contentSize should be:

```
// last one, pin to bottom, this dictates content size height!
sv.addConstraints(
    NSLayoutConstraint.constraintsWithVisualFormat(
        "V:[lab]-(10)-|",
        options:nil, metrics:nil,
        views:["lab":previousLab!]))
```

The constraints of the scroll view's subviews now describe the contentSize height: the top label is pinned to the top of the scroll view, the next one is pinned to the one above it, and so on — *and the bottom one is pinned to the bottom of the scroll view*. Consequently, the runtime calculates the contentSize height from the inside out, as it were, as the sum of all the vertical constraints (including the intrinsic heights of the labels), and the scroll view is vertically scrollable to show all the labels.

Using a Content View

Instead of putting all of our scroll view's content directly inside the scroll view as its immediate subviews, we can provide a generic UIView as the sole immediate subview of the scroll view; everything else inside the scroll view is to be a subview of this generic UIView, which we may term the *content view*. This is a commonly used arrangement.

Under autolayout, we then have two choices for setting the scroll view's `contentSize`:

- Set the content view's `translatesAutoresizingMaskIntoConstraints` to `true`, and set the scroll view's `contentSize` manually to the size of the content view.

- Set the content view's `translatesAutoresizingMaskIntoConstraints` to `false`, set its size with width and height constraints, and pin its edges to its superview (the scroll view) with a `constant` of `0`.

A convenient consequence of this arrangement is that it works independently of whether the content view's own subviews are positioned explicitly by their frames or using constraints. There are thus four possible combinations.

I'll illustrate by rewriting the previous example to use a content view. All four possible combinations start the same way:

```
let sv = UIScrollView()
sv.backgroundColor = UIColor.whiteColor()
sv.setTranslatesAutoresizingMaskIntoConstraints(false)
self.view.addSubview(sv)
self.view.addConstraints(
    NSLayoutConstraint.constraintsWithVisualFormat(
        "H:|[sv]|",
        options:nil, metrics:nil,
        views:["sv":sv]))
self.view.addConstraints(
    NSLayoutConstraint.constraintsWithVisualFormat(
        "V:|[sv]|",
        options:nil, metrics:nil,
        views:["sv":sv]))
let v = UIView() // content view
sv.addSubview(v)
```

The first combination is that no constraints are used. It's just like the first example in the chapter, except that the labels are added to the content view, not to the scroll view:

```
var y : CGFloat = 10
for i in 0 ..< 30 {
    let lab = UILabel()
    lab.text = "This is label \(i+1)"
```

```
        lab.sizeToFit()
        lab.frame.origin = CGPointMake(10,y)
        v.addSubview(lab) // *
        y += lab.bounds.size.height + 10
    }
    // set content view frame and content size explicitly
    v.frame = CGRectMake(0,0,0,y)
    sv.contentSize = v.frame.size
```

The second combination is that the content view uses explicit constraints, but its sub-views don't. It's just like the preceding code, except that we set the content view's constraints rather than the scroll view's content size:

```
    var y : CGFloat = 10
    for i in 0 ..< 30 {
        let lab = UILabel()
        lab.text = "This is label \(i+1)"
        lab.sizeToFit()
        lab.frame.origin = CGPointMake(10,y)
        v.addSubview(lab)
        y += lab.bounds.size.height + 10
    }
    // set content view width, height, and frame-to-superview constraints
    // content size is calculated for us
    v.setTranslatesAutoresizingMaskIntoConstraints(false)
    sv.addConstraints(
        NSLayoutConstraint.constraintsWithVisualFormat("V:|[v(y)]|",
            options:nil, metrics:["y":y], views:["v":v]))
    sv.addConstraints(
        NSLayoutConstraint.constraintsWithVisualFormat("H:|[v(0)]|",
            options:nil, metrics:nil, views:["v":v]))
```

The third combination is that explicit constraints are used throughout. This is just like the second example in the chapter (except that the labels are added to the content view), combined with the preceding code where we set the content view's constraints:

```
    var previousLab : UILabel? = nil
    for i in 0 ..< 30 {
        let lab = UILabel()
        // lab.backgroundColor = UIColor.redColor()
        lab.setTranslatesAutoresizingMaskIntoConstraints(false)
        lab.text = "This is label \(i+1)"
        v.addSubview(lab)
        v.addConstraints( // *
            NSLayoutConstraint.constraintsWithVisualFormat(
                "H:|-(10)-[lab]",
                options:nil, metrics:nil,
                views:["lab":lab]))
        if previousLab == nil { // first one, pin to top
            v.addConstraints( // *
                NSLayoutConstraint.constraintsWithVisualFormat(
                    "V:|-(10)-[lab]",
                    options:nil, metrics:nil,
```

```
                    views:["lab":lab]))
        } else { // all others, pin to previous
            v.addConstraints( // *
                NSLayoutConstraint.constraintsWithVisualFormat(
                    "V:[prev]-(10)-[lab]",
                    options:nil, metrics:nil,
                    views:["lab":lab, "prev":previousLab!]))
        }
        previousLab = lab
    }
    // last one, pin to bottom, this dictates content size height!
    v.addConstraints( // *
        NSLayoutConstraint.constraintsWithVisualFormat(
            "V:[lab]-(10)-|",
            options:nil, metrics:nil,
            views:["lab":previousLab!]))
    // set content view width and frame-to-superview constraints
    // (height comes from subview constraints)
    // content size is calculated for us
    v.setTranslatesAutoresizingMaskIntoConstraints(false)
    sv.addConstraints(
        NSLayoutConstraint.constraintsWithVisualFormat("V:|[v]|",
            options:nil, metrics:nil, views:["v":v])) // *
    sv.addConstraints(
        NSLayoutConstraint.constraintsWithVisualFormat("H:|[v]|",
            options:nil, metrics:nil, views:["v":v]))
```

The fourth combination is a curious hybrid: the content view's subviews are positioned using constraints, but we set the content view's frame and the scroll view's content size explicitly. There is no y to track as we position the subviews, so how can we find out the final content size height? Fortunately, `systemLayoutSizeFittingSize:` tells us:

```
    // ... starts the same as previous example ...
    // last one, pin to bottom, this dictates content size height!
    v.addConstraints( // *
        NSLayoutConstraint.constraintsWithVisualFormat(
            "V:[lab]-(10)-|",
            options:nil, metrics:nil,
            views:["lab":previousLab!]))
    // autolayout helps us learn the consequences of those constraints
    let minsz = v.systemLayoutSizeFittingSize(UILayoutFittingCompressedSize)
    // set content view frame and content size explicitly
    v.frame = CGRectMake(0,0,0,minsz.height)
    sv.contentSize = v.frame.size
```

Scroll View in a Nib

A UIScrollView is available in the nib editor in the Object library, so you can drag it into a view in the canvas and give it subviews. Alternatively, you can wrap existing views in the canvas in a UIScrollView as an afterthought: to do so, select the views and choose

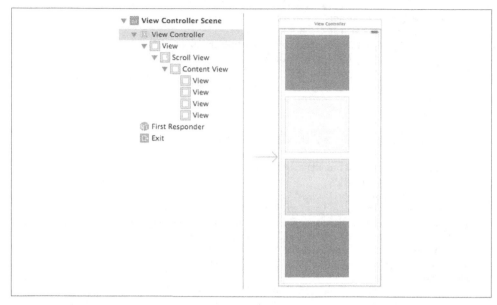

Figure 7-1. A scroll view in the nib editor

Editor → Embed In → Scroll View. The scroll view can't be scrolled in the nib editor, so to design its subviews, you make the scroll view large enough to accommodate them; if this makes the scroll view too large, you can resize the actual scroll view instance when the nib loads. If the scroll view is inside the view controller's main view, you may have to make *that* view too large, in order to see and work with the full scroll view and its contents (Figure 7-1). Set the view controller's Size pop-up menu in the Simulated Metrics section of its Attributes inspector to Freeform; now you can change the main view's size, and the view controller's size in the canvas will change with it.

If you're not using autolayout, judicious use of autoresizing settings in the nib editor can be a big help here. In Figure 7-1, the scroll view is the main view's subview; the scroll view's edges are pinned (struts) to its superview, and its width and height are flexible (springs). Thus, when the app runs and the main view is resized (as I discussed in Chapter 6), the scroll view will be resized too, to fit the main view. The content view, on the other hand, must not be resized, so its width and height are not flexible (they are struts, not springs), and only its top and left edges are pinned to its superview (struts).

But although everything is correctly sized at runtime, the scroll view doesn't scroll. That's because we have failed to set the scroll view's `contentSize`. Unfortunately, the nib editor provides no way to do that! Thus, we'll have to do it in code. This, in fact, is why I'm using a content view. The content view is the correct size in the nib, and it won't be resized through autoresizing, so at runtime, when the nib loads, its size will be the desired `contentSize`. I have an outlet to the scroll view, and I set its `contentSize` to the content view's size in `viewDidLayoutSubviews`. I don't need an outlet to the content view, because it is known to be the scroll view's first subview:

```
override func viewDidLayoutSubviews() {
    if !self.didSetup {
        self.didSetup = true
        self.sv.contentSize = (self.sv.subviews[0] as! UIView).bounds.size
    }
}
```

If you *are* using autolayout, constraints take care of everything; there is no need for any code to set the scroll view's `contentSize`. The scroll view's edges are pinned to those of its superview, the main view. The content view's edges are pinned to those of *its* superview, the scroll view. Be sure to set the `constant` of each constraint between the content view and the scroll view to 0! That tells the scroll view: "The `contentSize` is the size of the content view."

The only question now is how you'd like to dictate the content view's size. You have two choices, roughly corresponding to the second and third combinations in the preceding section: you can set the content view's width and height constraints explicitly, or you can let the content view's width and height be completely determined by the constraints of its subviews. Do whichever feels suitable. The nib editor understands this aspect of scroll view configuration, and will alert you with a warning (about the "scrollable content size") until you've provided enough constraints to determine unambiguously the scroll view's `contentSize`.

Scrolling

For the most part, the purpose of a scroll view will be to let the user scroll. A number of properties affect the user experience with regard to scrolling:

`scrollEnabled`
> If `false`, the user can't scroll, but you can still scroll in code (as explained later in this section). You could put a UIScrollView to various creative purposes other than letting the user scroll; for example, scrolling in code to a different region of the content might be a way of replacing one piece of interface by another, possibly with animation.

`scrollsToTop`
> If `true` (the default), and assuming scrolling is enabled, the user can tap on the status bar as a way of making the scroll view scroll its content to the top (that is, the content moves all the way down). You can also override this setting dynamically through the scroll view's delegate, discussed later in this chapter.

`bounces`

If `true` (the default), then when the user scrolls to a limit of the content, it is possible to scroll somewhat further (possibly revealing the scroll view's `backgroundColor` behind the content, if a subview was covering it); the content then snaps back into place when the user releases it. Otherwise, the user experiences the limit as a sudden inability to scroll further in that direction.

`alwaysBounceVertical`
`alwaysBounceHorizontal`

If `true`, and assuming that `bounces` is `true`, then even if the `contentSize` in the given dimension isn't larger than the scroll view (so that no scrolling is actually possible in that dimension), the user can nevertheless scroll somewhat and the content then snaps back into place when the user releases it; otherwise, the user experiences a simple inability to scroll in that dimension.

`directionalLockEnabled`

If `true`, and if scrolling is possible in both dimensions (even if only because the appropriate `alwaysBounce...` is `true`), then the user, having begun to scroll in one dimension, can't scroll in the other dimension without ending the gesture and starting over. In other words, the user is constrained to scroll vertically or horizontally but not both at once.

`decelerationRate`

The rate at which scrolling is damped out, and the content comes to a stop, after the user's gesture ends. As convenient examples, standard constants are provided:

- `UIScrollViewDecelerationRateNormal` (0.998)
- `UIScrollViewDecelerationRateFast` (0.99)

Lower values mean faster damping; experimentation suggests that values lower than 0.5 are viable but barely distinguishable from one another. You can also effectively override this value dynamically through the scroll view's delegate, discussed later in this chapter.

`showsHorizontalScrollIndicator`
`showsVerticalScrollIndicator`

The scroll indicators are bars that appear only while the user is scrolling in a scrollable dimension (where the content is larger than the scroll view), and serve to indicate both the size of the content in that dimension relative to the scroll view and where the user is within it. The default is `true` for both.

Because the user cannot see the scroll indicators except when actively scrolling, there is normally no indication that the view is scrollable. I regard this as somewhat unfortunate, because it makes the possibility of scrolling less discoverable; I'd prefer an option to make the scroll indicators constantly visible. Apple suggests that you call `flashScrollIndicators` when the scroll view appears, to make the scroll indicators visible momentarily.

 The scroll indicators are subviews of the scroll view (they are actually UIImage-Views). Do not assume that the subviews you add to a UIScrollView are its only subviews!

indicatorStyle
    The way the scroll indicators are drawn. Your choices (UIScrollViewIndicatorStyle) are .Black, .White, and .Default (black with a white border).

You can scroll in code even if the user can't scroll. The content simply moves to the position you specify, with no bouncing and no exposure of the scroll indicators. You can specify the new position in two ways:

contentOffset
    The point (CGPoint) of the content that is located at the scroll view's top left (effectively the same thing as the scroll view's bounds origin). You can get this property to learn the current scroll position, and set it to change the current scroll position. The values normally go up from (0.0,0.0) until the limit dictated by the content-Size and the scroll view's own bounds size is reached.

    To set the contentOffset with animation, call setContentOffset:animated:. The animation does not cause the scroll indicators to appear; it just slides the content to the desired position.

    If a scroll view participates in state restoration (Chapter 6), its contentOffset is saved and restored, so when the app is relaunched, the scroll view will reappear scrolled to the same position as before.

scrollRectToVisible:animated:
    Adjusts the content so that the specified CGRect of the content is within the scroll view's bounds. This is less precise than setting the contentOffset, because you're not saying exactly what the resulting scroll position will be, but sometimes guaranteeing the visibility of a certain portion of the content is exactly what you're after.

If you call a method to scroll with animation and you need to know when the animation ends, implement scrollViewDidEndScrollingAnimation: in the scroll view's delegate.

Finally, these properties affect the scroll view's structural dimensions:

contentInset
    A UIEdgeInsets struct (four CGFloats: top, left, bottom, right) specifying margin space around the content.

If a scroll view participates in state restoration (Chapter 6), its `contentInset` is saved and restored.

`scrollIndicatorInsets`
A UIEdgeInsets struct specifying a shift in the position of the scroll indicators.

A typical use for the `contentInset` would be that your scroll view underlaps an interface element, such as a status bar, navigation bar, or toolbar, and you want your content to be visible even when scrolled to its limit.

A good example is the app with 30 labels that we created at the start of this chapter. The scroll view occupies the entirety of the view controller's main view. But that means that the scroll view underlaps the status bar. And *that* means that at launch time, and whenever the scroll view's content is scrolled all the way down, the first label, which is as far down as it can go, is partly hidden by the text of the status bar. We can prevent this by setting the scroll view's `contentInset`:

```
sv.contentInset = UIEdgeInsetsMake(20, 0, 0, 0)
```

The scroll view still underlaps the status bar, and its scrolled content is still visible behind the status bar; what's changed is only that at the extreme scrolled-down position, where the content offset is (`0.0,0.0`), the scroll view's content is *not* behind the status bar.

When changing the `contentInset`, you will probably want to change the `scroll-IndicatorInsets` to match. Consider again the scroll view whose `contentInset` we have just set. When scrolled all the way down, it now has a nice gap between the bottom of the status bar and the top of the first label; but the top of the scroll indicator is still up behind the status bar. We can prevent this by setting the `scrollIndicatorInsets` to the same value as the `contentInset`:

```
sv.contentInset = UIEdgeInsetsMake(20, 0, 0, 0)
sv.scrollIndicatorInsets = sv.contentInset
```

As I mentioned in Chapter 6, top bars and bottom bars are likely to be translucent, and the runtime would like to make your view underlap them. With a scroll view, this looks cool, because the scroll view's contents are visible in a blurry way through the translucent bar; but the `contentInset` and `scrollIndicatorInsets` need to be adjusted so that the scrolling limits stay between the top bar and the bottom bar. Moreover, the height of the bars can change, depending on such factors as how the interface is rotated. (Recall, too, that this behavior is possible even if the bars are not translucent.)

Therefore, if a scroll view is going to underlap top and bottom bars, it would be nice, instead of hard-coding the top inset of 20 as in the preceding code, to make the scroll view's inset respond to its environment. A layout event seems the best place for such a response, and we can use the view controller's `topLayoutGuide` and `bottomLayout-Guide` to help us:

```
override func viewWillLayoutSubviews() {
    if let sv = self.sv {
        let top = self.topLayoutGuide.length
        let bot = self.bottomLayoutGuide.length
        sv.contentInset = UIEdgeInsetsMake(top, 0, bot, 0)
        sv.scrollIndicatorInsets = self.sv.contentInset
    }
}
```

Even better, if our view controller's main view contains one primary scroll view, and if it contains it sufficiently early — in the nib, for example — then if our view controller's automaticallyAdjustsScrollViewInsets property is true, the runtime will adjust our scroll view's contentInset and scrollIndicatorInsets with no code on our part. This property won't help us in the examples earlier in this chapter where we create the scroll view in code. But if the scroll view is created from the nib, as in Figure 7-1, this property applies and works. Moreover, a value of true is the default. In the nib editor, you can change it with the Adjust Scroll View Insets checkbox in the Attributes inspector. Be sure to set this property to false if you want to take charge of adjusting a scroll view's contentInset and scrollIndicatorInsets yourself.

Paging

If its pagingEnabled property is true, the scroll view doesn't let the user scroll freely; instead, the content is considered to consist of equal-sized sections. The user can scroll only in such a way as to move to a different section. The size of a section is set automatically to the size of the scroll view's bounds. The sections are the scroll view's *pages*.

When the user stops dragging, a paging scroll view gently snaps automatically to the nearest whole page. For example, let's say that the scroll view scrolls only horizontally, and that its subviews are image views showing photos, sized to match the scroll view's bounds. If the user drags horizontally to the left to a point where *less* than half of the next photo to the right is visible, and raises the dragging finger, the paging scroll view snaps its content back to the right until the entire first photo is visible again. If the user drags horizontally to the left to a point where *more* than half of the next photo to the right is visible, and raises the dragging finger, the paging scroll view snaps its content further to the left until the entire second photo is visible.

The usual arrangement is that a paging scroll view is at least as large, or nearly as large, in its scrollable dimension, as the screen. A moment's thought will reveal that, under this arrangement, it is impossible for the user to move the content more than a single page in any direction with a single gesture. The reason is that the size of the page is the size of the scroll view's bounds. Thus the user will run out of surface area to drag on before being able to move the content the distance of a page and a half, which is what would be needed to make the scroll view snap to a page not adjacent to the page we started on.

Sometimes, indeed, the paging scroll view will be slightly *larger* than the window in its scrollable dimension. This allows each page's content to fill the scroll view while also providing gaps between the pages, visible when the user starts to scroll. The user is still able to move from page to page, because it is still readily possible to drag more than half a new page into view (and the scroll view will then snap the rest of the way when the user raises the dragging finger).

When the user raises the dragging finger, the scroll view's action in adjusting its content is considered to be *decelerating*, and the scroll view's delegate (discussed in more detail later in this chapter) will receive `scrollViewWillBeginDecelerating:`, followed by `scrollViewDidEndDecelerating:` when the scroll view's content has stopped moving and a full page is showing. Thus, these messages can be used to detect efficiently that the page may have changed.

You can take advantage of this, for example, to coordinate a paging scroll view with a UIPageControl (Chapter 12). In this example, a page control (`pager`) is updated whenever the user causes a horizontally scrollable scroll view (`sv`) to display a different page:

```
func scrollViewDidEndDecelerating(scrollView: UIScrollView) {
    let x = self.sv.contentOffset.x
    let w = self.sv.bounds.size.width
    self.pager.currentPage = Int(x/w)
}
```

Conversely, we can scroll the scroll view to a new page manually when the user taps the page control; in this case we have to calculate the page boundaries ourselves:

```
@IBAction func userDidPage(sender:AnyObject?) {
    let p = self.pager.currentPage
    let w = self.sv.bounds.size.width
    self.sv.setContentOffset(CGPointMake(CGFloat(p)*w,0), animated:true)
}
```

A useful interface is a paging scroll view where you supply pages dynamically as the user scrolls. In this way, you can display a huge number of pages without having to put them all into the scroll view at once. A scrolling UIPageViewController (Chapter 6) provides exactly that interface. Its `UIPageViewControllerOptionInterPageSpacing-Key` even provides the gap between pages that I mentioned earlier.

 Prior to iOS 5, when UIPageViewController was introduced, I was using a paging scroll view that did the same thing. If you're curious about the technique I was using, watch the Advanced Scroll View Techniques video from WWDC 2011, which describes something very similar, calling it "infinite scrolling."

A compromise between a UIPageViewController and a completely preconfigured paging scroll view is a scroll view whose `contentSize` can accommodate all pages, but whose actual page content is supplied lazily. The only pages that have to be present at all times are the page visible to the user and the two pages adjacent to it on either side (so that there is no delay in displaying a new page's content when the user starts to scroll). This approach is exemplified by Apple's PageControl sample code. Unfortunately, that example does not also remove page content that is no longer needed, so there is ultimately no conservation of memory.

There are times when a scroll view, even one requiring a good deal of dynamic configuration, is better than a scrolling UIPageViewController, because the scroll view provides full information to its delegate about the user's scrolling activity (as described later in this chapter). For example, if you wanted to respond to the user's dragging one area of the interface by programmatically scrolling another area of the interface in a coordinated fashion, you might want what the user is dragging to be a scroll view, because it tells you what the user is up to at every moment.

Tiling

Suppose we have some finite but really big content that we want to display in a scroll view, such as a very large image that the user can inspect, piecemeal, by scrolling. To hold the entire image in memory may be onerous or impossible.

Tiling is one solution to this kind of problem. It takes advantage of the insight that there's really no need to hold the entire image in memory; all we need at any given moment is the part of the image visible to the user right now. Mentally, divide the content rectangle into a matrix of rectangles; these rectangles are the tiles. In reality, divide the huge image into corresponding rectangles. Then whenever the user scrolls, we look to see whether part of any empty tile has become visible, and if so, we supply its content. At the same time, we can release the content of all tiles that are completely offscreen. Thus, at any given moment, only the tiles that are showing have content. There is some latency associated with this approach (the user scrolls, then any empty newly visible tiles are filled in), but we will have to live with that.

There is actually a built-in CALayer subclass for helping us implement tiling — CATiledLayer. Its `tileSize` property sets the dimensions of a tile. Its `drawLayer:inContext:` is called when content for an empty tile is needed; calling `CGContextGetClipBoundingBox` on the context reveals the location of the desired tile, and now we can supply that tile's content.

The usual approach is to implement `drawRect:` in a UIView that hosts the CATiledLayer. Here, the CATiledLayer is the view's underlying layer; therefore the view is the CATiledLayer's delegate (see Chapter 3). This means that when the CATiledLayer's `drawLayer:inContext:` is called, the host view's `drawRect:` is called, and the `drawRect:` parameter is the same as the result of calling `CGContextGetClipBoundingBox` — namely, it's the rect of the tile we are to draw.

The `tileSize` may need to be adjusted for the screen resolution. On a double-resolution device, for example, the CATiledLayer's `contentsScale` will be doubled, and the tiles will be half the size that we ask for. If that isn't acceptable, we can double the `tile-Size` dimensions.

To illustrate, we'll use some tiles already created for us as part of Apple's own Photo-Scroller sample code. In particular, I'll use a few of the "CuriousFrog_500" images. These all have names of the form *CuriousFrog_500_x_y.png*, where *x* and *y* are integers corresponding to the picture's position within the matrix. The images are 256×256 pixels, except for the ones on the extreme right and bottom edges of the matrix, which are shorter in one dimension, but I won't be using those in this example; I've selected a square matrix of 9 square images.

We will give our scroll view (`sv`) one subview, a TiledView, a UIView subclass that exists purely to give our CATiledLayer a place to live. TILESIZE is defined as 256, to match the image dimensions:

```
override func viewDidLoad() {
    let f = CGRectMake(0,0,3*TILESIZE,3*TILESIZE)
    let content = TiledView(frame:f)
    let tsz = TILESIZE * content.layer.contentsScale
    (content.layer as! CATiledLayer).tileSize = CGSizeMake(tsz, tsz)
    self.sv.addSubview(content)
    self.sv.contentSize = f.size
    self.content = content
}
```

Here's the code for TiledView. As Apple's sample code points out, we must fetch images with `init(contentsOfFile:)` in order to avoid the automatic caching behavior of `init(named:)` — after all, we're going to all this trouble exactly to avoid using more memory than we have to:

```
override class func layerClass() -> AnyClass {
    return CATiledLayer.self
}
override func drawRect(r: CGRect) {
    let tile = r
    let x = Int(tile.origin.x/TILESIZE)
    let y = Int(tile.origin.y/TILESIZE)
    let tileName = String(format:"CuriousFrog_500_\(x+3)_\(y)")
    let path = NSBundle.mainBundle().pathForResource(tileName, ofType:"png")!
    let image = UIImage(contentsOfFile:path)!
    image.drawAtPoint(CGPointMake(CGFloat(x)*TILESIZE,CGFloat(y)*TILESIZE))
}
```

You may encounter a nasty issue where a CATiledLayer's `drawRect:` is called simultaneously on multiple threads. It isn't clear to me whether this problem is confined to the Simulator or whether it can also occur on a device. The workaround is to wrap the whole interior of `drawRect:` in a call to `dispatch_sync` on a serial queue (see Chapter 25).

There is no special call for invalidating an offscreen tile. You can call `setNeedsDisplay` or `setNeedsDisplayInRect:` on the TiledView, but this doesn't erase offscreen tiles. You're just supposed to trust that the CATiledLayer will eventually clear offscreen tiles if needed to conserve memory.

CATiledLayer has a class method `fadeDuration` that dictates the duration of the animation that fades a new tile into view. You can create a CATiledLayer subclass and override this method to return a value different from the default (`0.25`), but this is probably not worth doing, as the default value is a good one. Returning a smaller value won't make tiles appear faster; it just replaces the nice fade-in with an annoying flash.

Zooming

To implement zooming of a scroll view's content, you set the scroll view's `minimumZoomScale` and `maximumZoomScale` so that at least one of them isn't 1 (the default). You also implement `viewForZoomingInScrollView:` in the scroll view's delegate to tell the scroll view which of its subviews is to be the scalable view. The scroll view then zooms by applying a scale transform (Chapter 1) to this subview. The amount of that transform is the scroll view's `zoomScale` property. Typically, you'll want the scroll view's entire content to be scalable, so you'll have one direct subview of the scroll view that acts as the scalable view, and anything else inside the scroll view will be a subview of the scalable view, so as to be scaled together with it. This is another reason for arranging your scroll view's subviews inside a single content view, as I suggested earlier.

To illustrate, we can start with any of the four content view–based versions of our scroll view containing 30 labels. I called the content view v. Now we add these lines:

```
v.tag = 999
sv.minimumZoomScale = 1.0
sv.maximumZoomScale = 2.0
sv.delegate = self
```

We have assigned a tag to the view that is to be scaled, so that we can refer to it later. We have set the scale limits for the scroll view. And we have made ourselves the scroll view's delegate. Now all we have to do is implement `viewForZoomingInScrollView:` to return the scalable view:

```
func viewForZoomingInScrollView(scrollView: UIScrollView) -> UIView? {
    return scrollView.viewWithTag(999)
}
```

This works: the scroll view now responds to pinch gestures by scaling appropriately! But it doesn't look quite as good as I'd like when we zoom, and in particular I don't like the way the labels snap into place when we stop zooming. The reason is that, in my earlier examples, I gave the content view and the contentSize a zero width; that was sufficient to prevent the scroll view from scrolling horizontally, which was all that mattered. Now, however, these widths also affect how the content behaves as the user zooms it. This particular example, I think, looks best while zooming if the content view width is a bit wider than the widest label. (Implementing that is left as an exercise for the reader.)

The user can actually scale considerably beyond the limits we set in both directions; in that case, when the gesture ends, the scale snaps back to the limit value. If we wish to confine scaling strictly to our defined limits, we can set the scroll view's bouncesZoom to false; when the user reaches a limit, scaling will simply stop.

The actual amount of zoom is reflected as the scroll view's current zoomScale. If a scroll view participates in state restoration, its zoomScale is saved and restored, so when the app is relaunched, the scroll view will reappear zoomed by the same amount as before.

If the minimumZoomScale is less than 1, then when the scalable view becomes smaller than the scroll view, it is pinned to the scroll view's top left. If you don't like this, you can change it by subclassing UIScrollView and overriding layoutSubviews, or by implementing the scroll view delegate method scrollViewDidZoom:. Here's a simple example (drawn from a WWDC 2010 video) demonstrating an override of layout-Subviews that keeps the scalable view centered in either dimension whenever it is smaller than the scroll view in that dimension:

```
override func layoutSubviews() {
    super.layoutSubviews()
    if let v = self.delegate?.viewForZoomingInScrollView?(self) {
        let svw = self.bounds.width
        let svh = self.bounds.height
        let vw = v.frame.width
        let vh = v.frame.height
        var f = v.frame
        if vw < svw {
            f.origin.x = (svw - vw) / 2.0
        } else {
            f.origin.x = 0
        }
        if vh < svh {
            f.origin.y = (svh - vh) / 2.0
        } else {
            f.origin.y = 0
```

```
        }
        v.frame = f
    }
}
```

Zooming Programmatically

To zoom programmatically, you have two choices:

setZoomScale:animated:
> Zooms in terms of scale value. The contentOffset is automatically adjusted to keep the current center centered and the content occupying the entire scroll view.

zoomToRect:animated:
> Zooms so that the given rectangle of the content occupies as much as possible of the scroll view's bounds. The contentOffset is automatically adjusted to keep the content occupying the entire scroll view.

In this example, I implement double tapping as a zoom gesture. In my action handler for the double-tap UITapGestureRecognizer attached to the scalable view, a double tap means to zoom to maximum scale, minimum scale, or actual size, depending on the current scale value:

```
@IBAction func tapped(tap : UIGestureRecognizer) {
    let v = tap.view!
    let sv = v.superview as! UIScrollView
    if sv.zoomScale < 1 {
        sv.setZoomScale(1, animated:true)
    }
    else if sv.zoomScale < sv.maximumZoomScale {
        sv.setZoomScale(sv.maximumZoomScale, animated:true)
    }
    else {
        sv.setZoomScale(sv.minimumZoomScale, animated:true)
    }
}
```

Zooming with Detail

By default, when a scroll view zooms, it merely applies a scale transform to the scaled view. The scaled view's drawing is cached beforehand into its layer, so when we zoom in, the bits of the resulting bitmap are drawn larger. This means that a zoomed-in scroll view's content may be fuzzy (pixellated). In some cases this might be acceptable, but in others you might like the content to be redrawn more sharply at its new size.

(On a high-resolution device, this might not be such an issue. For example, if the user is allowed to zoom only up to double scale, you can draw at double scale right from the start; the results will look good at single scale, because the screen has high resolution, as well as at double scale, because that's the scale you drew at.)

One solution is to take advantage of a CATiledLayer feature that I didn't mention earlier. It turns out that CATiledLayer is aware not only of scrolling but also of scaling: you can configure it to ask for tiles to be drawn when the layer is scaled to a new order of magnitude. When your drawing routine is called, the graphics context itself has already been scaled appropriately by a transform.

In the case of an image into which the user is to be permitted to zoom deeply, you would be forearmed with multiple tile sets constituting the image, each set having double the tile size of the previous set (as in Apple's PhotoScroller example). In other cases, you may not need tiles at all; you'll just draw again, at the new resolution.

Besides its `tileSize`, you'll need to set two additional CATiledLayer properties:

`levelsOfDetail`

> The number of different resolutions at which you want to redraw, where each level has twice the resolution of the previous level. So, for example, with two levels of detail we can ask to redraw when zooming to double size (2x) and when zooming back to single size (1x).

`levelsOfDetailBias`

> The number of levels of detail that are *larger* than single size (1x). For example, if `levelsOfDetail` is 2, then if we want to redraw when zooming to 2x and when zooming back to 1x, the `levelsOfDetailBias` needs to be 1, because one of those levels is larger than 1x. (If we were to leave `levelsOfDetailBias` at 0, the default, we would be saying we want to redraw when zooming to 0.5x and back to 1x — we have two levels of detail but neither is larger than 1x, so one must be smaller than 1x.)

The CATiledLayer will ask for a redraw at a higher resolution as soon as the view's size becomes larger than the previous resolution. In other words, if there are two levels of detail with a bias of 1, the layer will be redrawn at 2x as soon as it is zoomed even a little bit larger than 1x. This is an excellent approach, because although a level of detail would look blurry if scaled up, it looks pretty good scaled down.

For example, let's say I have a TiledView that hosts a CATiledLayer, in which I intend to draw an image. I haven't broken the image into tiles, because the maximum size at which the user can view it isn't prohibitively large; the original image is 838×958, and can be held in memory easily. Rather, I'm using a CATiledLayer in order to take advantage of its ability to change resolutions automatically. The image will be displayed initially at 208×238, and if the user never zooms in to view it larger, we can save memory by drawing a quarter-size version of the image.

The CATiledLayer is configured as follows:

```
let scale = lay.contentsScale
lay.tileSize = CGSizeMake(208*scale,238*scale)
lay.levelsOfDetail = 3
lay.levelsOfDetailBias = 2
```

The tileSize has been adjusted for screen resolution, so the result is as follows:

- As originally displayed at 208×238, there is one tile and we can draw our image at quarter size.

- If the user zooms in, to show the image larger than its originally displayed size, there will be 4 tiles and we can draw our image at half size.

- If the user zooms in still further, to show the image larger than double its originally displayed size (416×476), there will be 16 tiles and we can draw our image at full size, which will continue to look good as the user zooms all the way in to the full size of the original image.

We do not, however, need to draw each tile individually. Each time we're called upon to draw a tile, we'll draw the entire image into the TiledView's bounds; whatever falls outside the requested tile will be clipped out and won't be drawn.

Here's my TiledView's drawRect: implementation. I have a UIImage property current-Image, initialized to nil, and a CGRect property currentSize initialized to CGSize-Zero. Each time drawRect: is called, I compare the tile size (the incoming rect parameter's size) to currentSize. If it's different, I know that we've changed by one level of detail and we need a new version of currentImage, so I create the new version of current-Image at a scale appropriate to this level of detail. Finally, I draw currentImage into the TiledView's bounds:

```
override func drawRect(rect: CGRect) {
    let oldSize = self.currentSize
    if !CGSizeEqualToSize(oldSize, rect.size) {
        // make a new size
        self.currentSize = rect.size
        // make a new image
        let lay = self.layer as! CATiledLayer
        let tr = CGContextGetCTM(UIGraphicsGetCurrentContext())
        let sc = tr.a/lay.contentsScale
        let scale = sc/4.0
        let path = NSBundle.mainBundle().pathForResource(
            "earthFromSaturn", ofType:"png")!
        let im = UIImage(contentsOfFile:path)!
        let sz = CGSizeMake(im.size.width * scale, im.size.height * scale)
        UIGraphicsBeginImageContextWithOptions(sz, true, 1)
        im.drawInRect(CGRectMake(0,0,sz.width,sz.height))
        self.currentImage = UIGraphicsGetImageFromCurrentImageContext()
        UIGraphicsEndImageContext()
    }
    self.currentImage.drawInRect(self.bounds)
}
```

An alternative and much simpler approach (from a WWDC 2011 video) is to make yourself the scroll view's delegate so that you get an event when the zoom ends, and then change the scalable view's `contentScaleFactor` to match the current zoom scale, compensating for the high-resolution screen at the same time:

```
func scrollViewDidEndZooming(scrollView: UIScrollView,
    withView view: UIView,
    atScale scale: CGFloat) {
        view.contentScaleFactor = scale * UIScreen.mainScreen().scale
}
```

In response, the scalable view's `drawRect:` will be called, and its `rect` parameter will be the CGRect to draw into. Thus, the view may appear fuzzy for a while as the user zooms in, but when the user stops zooming, the view is redrawn sharply. That approach comes with a caveat, however: you mustn't overdo it. If the zoom scale, screen resolution, and scalable view size are high, you will be asking for a very large graphics context to be maintained in memory, which could cause your app to run low on memory or even to be abruptly terminated by the system.

For more about displaying a large image in a zoomable scroll view, see Apple's Large Image Downsizing example.

Scroll View Delegate

The scroll view's delegate (adopting the UIScrollViewDelegate protocol) receives lots of messages that can help you track, in great detail, exactly what the scroll view is up to:

`scrollViewDidScroll:`
> If you scroll in code without animation, you will receive this message *once* afterward. If the user scrolls, either by dragging or with the scroll-to-top feature, or if you scroll in code with animation, you will receive this message *repeatedly* throughout the scroll, including during the time the scroll view is decelerating after the user's finger has lifted; there are other delegate messages that tell you, in those cases, when the scroll has finally ended.

`scrollViewDidEndScrollingAnimation:`
> If you scroll in code with animation, you will receive this message afterward, when the animation ends.

`scrollViewWillBeginDragging:`
`scrollViewWillEndDragging:withVelocity:targetContentOffset:`
`scrollViewDidEndDragging:willDecelerate:`
> If the user scrolls by dragging, you will receive these messages at the start and end of the user's finger movement. If the user brings the scroll view to a stop before lifting the finger, `willDecelerate` is `false` and the scroll is over. If the user lets go of the scroll view while the finger is moving, or when paging is turned on, `willDecelerate` is `true` and we proceed to the delegate messages reporting deceleration.
>
> The purpose of `scrollViewWillEndDragging:...` is to let you customize the outcome of the content's deceleration. The third argument is a pointer to a CGPoint; you can use it to set a different CGPoint, specifying the `contentOffset` value the scroll view should have when the deceleration is over.

`scrollViewWillBeginDecelerating:`
`scrollViewDidEndDecelerating:`
> Sent once each after `scrollViewDidEndDragging:willDecelerate:` arrives with a value of `true`. When `scrollViewDidEndDecelerating:` arrives, the scroll is over.

`scrollViewShouldScrollToTop:`
`scrollViewDidScrollToTop:`
> These have to do with the feature where the user can tap the status bar to scroll the scroll view's content to its top. You won't get either of them if `scrollsToTop` is `false`, because the scroll-to-top feature is turned off in that case. The first lets you prevent the user from scrolling to the top on this occasion even if `scrollsToTop` is `true`. The second tells you that the user has employed this feature and the scroll is over.

In addition, the scroll view has read-only properties reporting its state:

`tracking`
> The user has touched the scroll view, but the scroll view hasn't decided whether this is a scroll or some kind of tap.

dragging

The user is dragging to scroll.

decelerating

The user has scrolled and has lifted the finger, and the scroll is continuing.

So, if you wanted to do something after a scroll ends completely regardless of how the scroll was performed, you'd need to implement multiple delegate methods:

- `scrollViewDidEndDragging:willDecelerate:` in case the user drags and stops (`willDecelerate` is `false`).

- `scrollViewDidEndDecelerating:` in case the user drags and the scroll continues afterward.

- `scrollViewDidScrollToTop:` in case the user uses the scroll-to-top feature.

- `scrollViewDidEndScrollingAnimation:` in case you scroll with animation.

(You don't need a delegate method to tell you when the scroll is over after you scroll in code *without* animation: it's over immediately, so if you have work to do after the scroll ends, you can do it in the next line of code.)

There are also three delegate messages that report zooming:

scrollViewWillBeginZooming:withView:

If the user zooms or you zoom in code, you will receive this message as the zoom begins.

scrollViewDidZoom:

If you zoom in code, even with animation, you will receive this message *once*. If the user zooms, you will receive this message *repeatedly* as the zoom proceeds. (You will probably also receive `scrollViewDidScroll:`, possibly many times, as the zoom proceeds.)

scrollViewDidEndZooming:withView:atScale:

If the user zooms or you zoom in code, you will receive this message after the last `scrollViewDidZoom:`.

In addition, the scroll view has read-only properties reporting its state during a zoom:

zooming

The scroll view is zooming. It is possible for `dragging` to be true at the same time.

zoomBouncing

The scroll view is returning automatically from having been zoomed outside its minimum or maximum limit. As far as I can tell, you'll get only one `scrollView-DidZoom:` while the scroll view is in this state.

Scroll View Touches

Improvements in UIScrollView's internal implementation have eliminated most of the worry once associated with scroll view touches. A scroll view will interpret a drag or a pinch as a command to scroll or zoom, and any other gesture will fall through to the subviews; thus buttons and similar interface objects inside a scroll view work just fine.

You can even put a scroll view inside a scroll view, and this can be quite a useful thing to do, in contexts where you might not think of it at first. Apple's PhotoScroller example, based on principles discussed in a delightful WWDC 2010 video, is an app where a single photo fills the screen: you can page-scroll from one photo to the next, and you can zoom into the current photo with a pinch gesture. This is implemented as a scroll view inside a scroll view: the outer scroll view is for paging between images, and the inner scroll view contains the current image and is for zooming (and for scrolling to different parts of the zoomed-in image). Similarly, a WWDC 2013 video deconstructs the iOS 7 lock screen in terms of scroll views embedded in scroll views.

Gesture recognizers (Chapter 5) have also greatly simplified the task of adding custom gestures to a scroll view. For instance, some older code in Apple's documentation, showing how to implement a double tap to zoom in and a two-finger tap to zoom out, uses old-fashioned touch handling, but this is no longer necessary. Simply attach to your scroll view's scalable subview any gesture recognizers for these sorts of gesture, and they will mediate automatically among the possibilities.

In the past, making something inside a scroll view draggable required setting the scroll view's `canCancelContentTouches` property to `false`. (The reason for the name is that the scroll view, when it realizes that a gesture is a drag or pinch gesture, normally sends `touchesCancelled:forEvent:` to a subview tracking touches, so that the scroll view and not the subview will be affected.) However, unless you're implementing old-fashioned direct touch handling, you probably won't have to concern yourself with this. Regardless of how `canCancelContentTouches` is set, a draggable control, such as a UI-Slider, remains draggable inside a scroll view.

Here's an example of a draggable object inside a scroll view implemented through a gesture recognizer. Suppose we have an image of a map, larger than the screen, and we want the user to be able to scroll it in the normal way to see any part of the map, but we also want the user to be able to drag a flag into a new location on the map. We'll put the map image in an image view and wrap the image view in a scroll view, with the scroll view's `contentSize` the same as the map image view's size. The flag is a small image view; it's another subview of the scroll view, and it has a UIPanGestureRecognizer. The gesture recognizer's action handler allows the flag to be dragged, as described in Chapter 5:

Figure 7-2. A scrollable map with a draggable flag

```
@IBAction func dragging (p : UIPanGestureRecognizer) {
    let v = p.view!
    switch p.state {
    case .Began, .Changed:
        let delta = p.translationInView(v.superview!)
        v.center.x += delta.x
        v.center.y += delta.y
        p.setTranslation(CGPointZero, inView: v.superview)
    }
}
```

The user can now drag the map or the flag (Figure 7-2). Dragging the map brings the flag along with it, but dragging the flag doesn't move the map. The state of the scroll view's canCancelContentTouches is irrelevant, because the flag view isn't tracking the touches manually.

An interesting addition to that example would be to implement *autoscrolling*, meaning that the scroll view scrolls itself when the user drags the flag close to its edge. This, too, is greatly simplified by gesture recognizers; in fact, we can add autoscrolling code directly to the dragging: action handler:

```
@IBAction func dragging (p : UIPanGestureRecognizer) {
    let v = p.view!
    switch p.state {
    case .Began, .Changed:
```

```
            let delta = p.translationInView(v.superview!)
            v.center.x += delta.x
            v.center.y += delta.y
            p.setTranslation(CGPointZero, inView: v.superview)
            if p.state == .Changed {fallthrough}
        case .Changed:
            // autoscroll
            let sv = self.sv
            let loc = p.locationInView(sv)
            let f = sv.bounds
            var off = sv.contentOffset
            let sz = sv.contentSize
            var c = v.center
            // to the right
            if loc.x > CGRectGetMaxX(f) - 30 {
                let margin = sz.width - CGRectGetMaxX(sv.bounds)
                if margin > 6 {
                    off.x += 5
                    sv.contentOffset = off
                    c.x += 5
                    v.center = c
                    self.keepDragging(p)
                }
            }
            // to the left
            if loc.x < f.origin.x + 30 {
                let margin = off.x
                if margin > 6 {
                    // ...
                }
            }
            // to the bottom
            if loc.y > CGRectGetMaxY(f) - 30 {
                let margin = sz.height - CGRectGetMaxY(sv.bounds)
                if margin > 6 {
                    // ...
                }
            }
            // to the top
            if loc.y < f.origin.y + 30 {
                let margin = off.y
                if margin > 6 {
                    // ...
                }
            }
        default: break
        }
}
func keepDragging (p : UIPanGestureRecognizer) {
    let del = 0.1
```

```
        delay(del) {
            self.dragging(p)
        }
    }
```

The `delay` in `keepDragging:` (see Appendix B), combined with the change in offset, determines the speed of autoscrolling. The material marked as omitted in the second, third, and fourth cases is obviously parallel to the first case, and is left as an exercise for the reader.

A scroll view's touch handling is itself based on gesture recognizers attached to the scroll view, and these are available to your code through the scroll view's `panGesture-Recognizer` and `pinchGestureRecognizer` properties. This means that if you want to customize a scroll view's touch handling, it's easy to add more gesture recognizers and have them interact with those already attached to the scroll view.

To illustrate, I'll build on the previous example. Suppose we want the flag to start out offscreen, and we'd like the user to be able to summon it with a rightward swipe. We can attach a UISwipeGestureRecognizer to our scroll view, but it will never recognize its gesture because the scroll view's own pan gesture recognizer will recognize first. But we have access to the scroll view's pan gesture recognizer, so we can compel it to yield to our swipe gesture recognizer by sending it `requireGestureRecognizerToFail::`

```
self.sv.panGestureRecognizer.requireGestureRecognizerToFail(self.swipe)
```

The UISwipeGestureRecognizer will recognize a rightward swipe. In my implementation of its action handler, we position the flag, which has been waiting invisibly offscreen, just off to the top left of the scroll view's visible content, and animate it onto the screen:

```
@IBAction func swiped (g: UISwipeGestureRecognizer) {
    let sv = self.sv
    let p = sv.contentOffset
    self.flag.frame.origin = p
    self.flag.frame.origin.x -= self.flag.bounds.size.width
    self.flag.hidden = false
    UIView.animateWithDuration(0.25, animations:{
        self.flag.frame.origin.x = p.x
        // thanks for the flag, now stop operating altogether
        g.enabled = false
        })
}
```

Floating Scroll View Subviews

A scroll view's subview will appear to "float" over the scroll view if it remains stationary while the rest of the scroll view's content is being scrolled. Before autolayout, this sort of thing was rather tricky to arrange; you had to use a delegate event to respond to every change in the scroll view's bounds origin by shifting the "floating" view's position to compensate, so as to appear to remain fixed. With autolayout, however, all you have to do is set up constraints pinning the subview to something *outside* the scroll view. Here's an example:

```
let iv = UIImageView(image:UIImage(named:"smiley.png"))
iv.setTranslatesAutoresizingMaskIntoConstraints(false)
self.sv.addSubview(iv)
let sup = self.sv.superview!
sup.addConstraint(
    NSLayoutConstraint(item:iv,
        attribute:.Right,
    relatedBy:.Equal,
    toItem:sup, attribute:.Right,
    multiplier:1, constant:-5))
sup.addConstraint(
    NSLayoutConstraint(item:iv, attribute:.Top,
    relatedBy:.Equal,
    toItem:sup, attribute:.Top,
    multiplier:1, constant:25))
```

Scroll View Performance

At several points in earlier chapters I've mentioned performance problems and ways to increase drawing efficiency. Nowhere are you so likely to need these as in connection with a scroll view. As a scroll view scrolls, views must be drawn very rapidly as they appear on the screen. If the view-drawing system can't keep up with the speed of the scroll, the scrolling will visibly stutter.

Performance testing and optimization is a big subject, so I can't tell you exactly what to do if you encounter stuttering while scrolling. But certain general suggestions (mostly extracted from a really great WWDC 2010 video) should come in handy:

- Everything that can be opaque should be opaque: don't force the drawing system to composite transparency, and remember to tell it that an opaque view or layer *is* opaque by setting its opaque property to true. If you really must composite transparency, keep the size of the nonopaque regions to a minimum; for example, if a large layer is transparent at its edges, break it into five layers — the large central layer, which is opaque, and the four edges, which are not.

- If you're drawing shadows, don't make the drawing system calculate the shadow shape for a layer: supply a shadowPath, or use Core Graphics to create the shadow with a drawing. Similarly, avoid making the drawing system composite the shadow as a transparency against another layer; for example, if the background layer is white, your opaque drawing can itself include a shadow already drawn on a white background.

- Don't make the drawing system scale images for you; supply the images at the target size for the correct resolution.

- In a pinch, you can just eliminate massive swatches of the rendering operation by setting a layer's `shouldRasterize` to `true`. You could, for example, do this when scrolling starts and then set it back to `false` when scrolling ends.

Apple's documentation also says that setting a view's `clearsContextBeforeDrawing` to `false` may make a difference. I can't confirm or deny this; it may be true, but I haven't encountered a case that positively proves it.

Xcode provides tools that will help you detect inefficiencies in the drawing system. In the Simulator, the Debug menu shows you blended layers (where transparency is being composited) and images that are being copied, misaligned, or rendered offscreen. On the device, the Core Animation module of Instruments provides the same functionality, plus it tracks the frame rate for you, allowing you to scroll and measure performance objectively where it really counts.

CHAPTER 8

Table Views and Collection Views

I'm gonna ask you the three big questions. — Go ahead. — Who made you? — You did. — Who owns the biggest piece of you? — You do. — What would happen if I dropped you? — I'd go right down the drain.

—Dialogue by Garson Kanin and Ruth Gordon,
Pat and Mike

A table view (UITableView) is a vertically scrolling UIScrollView (Chapter 7) containing a single column of rectangular cells (UITableViewCell, a UIView subclass). It is a keystone of Apple's strategy for making the small iPhone screen useful and powerful, and has three main purposes:

Presentation of information
> The cells typically contain text, which the user can read. The cells are usually quite small, in order to maximize the quantity appearing on the screen at once, so this text is often condensed, truncated, or simplified.

Selection
> A table view can provide the user with a column of choices. The user chooses by tapping a cell, which selects the cell; the app responds appropriately to that choice.

Navigation
> The appropriate response to the user's choosing a cell is often navigation to another interface. This might be done, for example, through a presented view controller or a navigation interface (Chapter 6). An extremely common configuration is a *master–detail interface*, where the master view is a table view within a navigation interface: the user taps a table view cell to navigate to the details about that cell. This is one reason why truncation of text in a table view cell is acceptable: the detail view contains the full information.

Figure 8-1. Four table view variations

In addition to its column of cells, a table view can be extended by a number of other features that make it even more useful and flexible:

- A table can display a header view at the top and a footer view at the bottom.
- The cells can be clumped into sections. Each section can have a header and footer, and these remain visible as long as the section itself occupies the screen, giving the user a clue as to where we are within the table. Moreover, a section index can be provided, in the form of an overlay column of abbreviated section titles, which the user can tap or drag to jump to the start of a section, thus making a long table tractable.
- A table can have a grouped format. This is often used for presenting small numbers of related cells.
- Tables can be editable: the user can be permitted to insert, delete, and reorder cells.

Figure 8-1 illustrates four variations of the table view:

- Apple's Music app lists song titles and artists for a given album in truncated form in a table view within a navigation interface which is itself within a tab bar interface; tapping an album in a table of album titles summons the list of songs within that album, and tapping a song in that list plays it.
- Apple's Settings app uses table view cells in a grouped format with a header, within a navigation interface, to display a switch and a list of Bluetooth devices; tapping a device's name searches for that device or connects to it.
- My Latin vocabulary app lists Latin words and their definitions in alphabetical order, divided into sections by first letter, with section headers and a section index.
- Apple's Music app allows a custom playlist to be edited, with interface for deleting and rearranging cells.

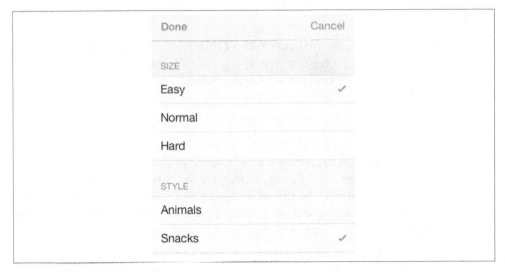

Figure 8-2. A grouped table view as an interface for choosing options

Table view cells, too, can be extremely flexible. Some basic cell formats are provided, such as a text label along with a small image view, but you are free to design your own cell as you would any other view. There are also some standard interface items that are commonly used in a cell, such as a checkmark to indicate selection or a right-pointing chevron to indicate that tapping the cell navigates to a detail view.

It would be difficult to overstate the importance of table views. An iOS app without a table view somewhere in its interface would be a rare thing, especially on the small iPhone screen. I've written apps consisting almost entirely of table views. Indeed, it is not uncommon to use a table view even in situations that have nothing particularly table-like about them, simply because it is so convenient.

For example, in one of my apps I want the user to be able to choose between three levels of difficulty and two sets of images. In a desktop application I'd probably use radio buttons; but there are no radio buttons among the standard iOS interface objects. Instead, I use a grouped table view so small that it doesn't even scroll. This gives me section headers, tappable cells, and a checkmark indicating the current choice (Figure 8-2).

There is a UIViewController subclass, UITableViewController, whose main view is a table view. You never really *need* to use a UITableViewController; it's a convenience, but it doesn't do anything that you couldn't do yourself by other means. Here's some of what using a UITableViewController gives you:

- UITableViewController's `init(style:)` creates the table view with a plain or grouped format.

- The view controller is automatically made the table view's delegate and data source, unless you specify otherwise.

- The table view is made the view controller's `tableView`. It is also, of course, the view controller's `view`, but the `tableView` property is typed as a UITableView, so you can send table view messages to it without typecasting.

Table View Cells

Beginners may be surprised to learn that a table view's structure and contents are generally not configured in advance. Rather, you supply the table view with a data source and a delegate (which will often be the same object), and the table view turns to these in real time, as the app runs, whenever it needs a piece of information about its own structure and contents.

This architecture may sound odd, but in fact it is part of a brilliant strategy to conserve resources. Imagine a long table consisting of thousands of rows. It must appear, therefore, to consist of thousands of cells as the user scrolls. But a cell is a UIView and is memory-intensive; to maintain thousands of cells internally would put a terrible strain on memory. Therefore, the table typically maintains only as many cells as are showing simultaneously at any one moment (about ten, let's say). As the user scrolls to reveal new cells, those cells are created on the spot; meanwhile, the cells that have been scrolled out of view are permitted to die.

This, you may reply, sounds ingenious but a bit wasteful, and possibly time-consuming; wouldn't it be even cleverer if, instead of letting a cell die as it is scrolled *out* of view, it were whisked around to the other side and used again as one of the cells being scrolled *into* view? Yes, and in fact that's exactly what you're supposed to do. You do it by assigning each cell a *reuse identifier*.

As cells with a given reuse identifier are scrolled out of view, the table view maintains a bunch of them in a pile. As cells are scrolled into view, you ask the table view for a cell from that pile, specifying it by means of the reuse identifier. The table view hands an old used cell back to you, and now you can configure it as the cell that is about to be scrolled into view. Cells are thus *reused* to minimize not only the number of actual cells in existence at any one moment, but the number of actual cells *ever created*. A table of 1000 rows might very well never need to create more than a dozen cells over the entire lifetime of the app.

To facilitate this architecture, your code must be prepared, on demand, to supply the table with pieces of requested data. Of these, the most important is the cell to be slotted into a given position. A position in the table is specified by means of an index path (NSIndexPath), a class used here to combine a section number with a row number, and is often referred to simply as a *row* of the table. Your data source object may at any moment be sent the message `tableView:cellForRowAtIndexPath:`, and must respond by returning the UITableViewCell to be displayed at that row of the table. And you must return it *fast*: the user is scrolling *now*, so the table needs the next cell *now*.

In this section, I'll discuss *what* you're going to be supplying — the table view cell. After that, I'll talk about *how* you supply it.

Built-In Cell Styles

The simplest way to obtain a table view cell is to start with one of the four built-in table view cell styles. To create a cell using a built-in style, call `init(style:reuseIdentifier:)`. The `reuseIdentifier:` is what allows cells previously assigned to rows that are no longer showing to be reused for cells that are; it will usually be the same for all cells in a table. Your choices of cell style (UITableViewCellStyle) are:

`.Default`

> The cell has a UILabel (its `textLabel`), with an optional UIImageView (its `imageView`) at the left. If there is no image, the label occupies the entire width of the cell.

`.Value1`

> The cell has two UILabels (its `textLabel` and its `detailTextLabel`) side by side, with an optional UIImageView (its `imageView`) at the left. The first label is left-aligned; the second label is right-aligned. If the first label's text is too long, the second label won't appear.

`.Value2`

> The cell has two UILabels (its `textLabel` and its `detailTextLabel`) side by side. No UIImageView will appear. The first label is right-aligned; the second label is left-aligned. The label sizes are fixed, and the text of either will be truncated if it's too long.

`.Subtitle`

> The cell has two UILabels (its `textLabel` and its `detailTextLabel`), one above the other, with an optional UIImageView (its `imageView`) at the left.

To experiment with the built-in cell styles, do this:

1. Start with an empty application without a storyboard (I explained how to do that at the start of Chapter 1).
2. Choose File → New → File and specify iOS → Source → Cocoa Touch Class. Click Next.
3. Make this class a UITableViewController subclass called RootViewController. The XIB checkbox should be checked; Xcode will create a *.xib* file containing a table view, correctly hooked to our RootViewController class. Click Next.

Hello there! 1

Hello there! 2

Hello there! 3

Hello there! 4

Figure 8-3. The world's simplest table

4. Make sure you're saving into the correct folder and group, and that the app target is checked. Click Create.

To get our table view into the interface, insert this line into AppDelegate's `application:didFinishLaunchingWithOptions:` at the appropriate spot:

```
self.window!.rootViewController = RootViewController(
    nibName: "RootViewController", bundle: nil)
```

Now modify the RootViewController class (which comes with a lot of templated code), as in Example 8-1. Run the app to see the world's simplest table (Figure 8-3).

Example 8-1. The world's simplest table

```
let cellIdentifier = "Cell"
override func numberOfSectionsInTableView(tableView: UITableView)
    -> Int {
        return 1 ❶
}
override func tableView(tableView: UITableView,
    numberOfRowsInSection section: Int) -> Int {
        return 20 ❷
}
override func tableView(tableView: UITableView,
    cellForRowAtIndexPath indexPath: NSIndexPath) -> UITableViewCell {
        var cell =
            tableView.dequeueReusableCellWithIdentifier(
                cellIdentifier) as! UITableViewCell!
        if cell == nil {
            cell = UITableViewCell(
                style:.Default, reuseIdentifier:cellIdentifier) ❸
            cell.textLabel!.textColor = UIColor.redColor() ❹
        }
        cell.textLabel!.text = "Hello there! \(indexPath.row)" ❺
        return cell
}
```

The key parts of the code are:

❶   Our table will have one section.

❷   Our table will consist of 20 rows. Having multiple rows will give us a sense of how our cell looks when placed next to other cells.

❸   This is where you specify the built-in table view cell style you want to experiment with.

❹   At this point in the code you can modify characteristics of the cell (`cell`) that are to be the same for *every* cell of the table. For the moment, I've symbolized this by assuming that every cell's text is to be the same color.

❺   We now have the cell to be used for *this* row of the table, so at this point in the code you can modify characteristics of the cell (`cell`) that are unique to this row. I've symbolized this by appending successive numbers to the text of each row. Of course, in real life the different cells would reflect meaningful data. I'll talk about that later in this chapter.

Now you can experiment with your cell's appearance by tweaking the code and running the app. Feel free to try different built-in cell styles in the place where we are now specifying `.Default`.

The flexibility of each built-in style is based mostly on the flexibility of UILabels. Not everything can be customized, because after you return the cell some further configuration takes place, which may override your settings. For example, the size and position of the cell's subviews are not up to you. (I'll explain, a little later, how to get around that.) But you get a remarkable degree of freedom. Here are a few basic UILabel properties for you to play with now (by customizing `cell.textLabel`), and I'll talk much more about UILabels in Chapter 10:

text
> The string shown in the label.

textColor, highlightedTextColor
> The color of the text. The `highlightedTextColor` applies when the cell is highlighted or selected (tap on a cell to select it).

textAlignment
> How the text is aligned; some possible choices (NSTextAlignment) are `.Left`, `.Center`, and `.Right`.

numberOfLines
> The maximum number of lines of text to appear in the label. Text that is long but permitted to wrap, or that contains explicit linefeed characters, can appear completely in the label if the label is tall enough and the number of permitted lines is sufficient. `0` means there's no maximum; the default is `1`.

font

The label's font. You could reduce the font size as a way of fitting more text into the label. A font name includes its style. For example:

```
cell.textLabel!.font = UIFont(name:"Helvetica-Bold", size:12.0)
```

shadowColor, shadowOffset

The text shadow. Adding a little shadow can increase clarity and emphasis for large text.

You can also assign the image view (cell.imageView) an image. The frame of the image view can't be changed, but you can inset its apparent size by supplying a smaller image and setting the image view's contentMode to .Center. It's probably a good idea in any case, for performance reasons, to supply images at their drawn size and resolution rather than making the drawing system scale them for you (see the last section of Chapter 7). For example:

```
let im = UIImage(named:"moi.png")!
UIGraphicsBeginImageContextWithOptions(CGSizeMake(36,36), true, 0.0)
im.drawInRect(CGRectMake(0,0,36,36))
let im2 = UIGraphicsGetImageFromCurrentImageContext()
UIGraphicsEndImageContext()
cell.imageView!.image = im2
cell.imageView!.contentMode = .Center
```

The cell itself also has some properties you can play with:

accessoryType

A built-in type (UITableViewCellAccessoryType) of accessory view, which appears at the cell's right end. For example:

```
cell.accessoryType = .DisclosureIndicator
```

accessoryView

Your own UIView, which appears at the cell's right end (overriding the accessory-Type). For example:

```
let b = UIButton.buttonWithType(.System) as! UIButton
b.setTitle("Tap Me", forState:.Normal)
b.sizeToFit()
// ... also assign button a target and action ...
cell.accessoryView = b
```

indentationLevel, indentationWidth

These properties give the cell a left margin, useful for suggesting a hierarchy among cells. You can also set a cell's indentation level in real time, with respect to the table row into which it is slotted, by implementing the delegate's table-View:indentationLevelForRowAtIndexPath: method.

separatorInset

A UIEdgeInsets. Only the left and right insets matter. The default is a left inset of 15, though if you don't set it explicitly, the built-in table view cell styles may shift it. This property affects both the drawing of the separator between cells and the indentation of content of the built-in cell styles.

 In iOS 8, the left separator inset in practice is set by default to 16, and an attempt to reduce this value will fail. I regard this as a bug, presumably involving the layout-Margins.

selectionStyle

How the background looks when the cell is selected (UITableViewCellSelection-Style). The default is solid gray (.Default), or you can choose .None.

(The blue and gray gradient backgrounds designated by .Blue and .Gray are left over from iOS 6 and before. They are now abandoned, and are treated as equivalent to .Default.)

backgroundColor
backgroundView
selectedBackgroundView

What's behind everything else drawn in the cell. The selectedBackgroundView is drawn in front of the backgroundView (if any) when the cell is selected, and will appear instead of whatever the selectionStyle dictates. The backgroundColor is behind the backgroundView. (Thus, if both the selectedBackgroundView and the backgroundView have some transparency, both of them and the background-Color can appear composited together when the cell is selected.)

There is no need to set the frame of the backgroundView and selectedBackground-View; they will be resized automatically to fit the cell.

multipleSelectionBackgroundView

If defined (not nil), and if the table's allowsMultipleSelection (or, if editing, allowsMultipleSelectionDuringEditing) is true, used instead of the selected-BackgroundView when the cell is selected.

In this example, we set the cell's backgroundView to display an image with some transparency at the outside edges, so that the backgroundColor shows behind it, and we set the selectedBackgroundView to an almost transparent blue rectangle, to darken that image when the cell is selected (Figure 8-4):

Figure 8-4. A cell with an image background

```
cell.textLabel!.textColor = UIColor.whiteColor()
let v = UIImageView() // no need to set frame
v.contentMode = .ScaleToFill
v.image = UIImage(named:"linen.png")
cell.backgroundView = v
let v2 = UIView() // no need to set frame
v2.backgroundColor = UIColor.blueColor().colorWithAlphaComponent(0.2)
cell.selectedBackgroundView = v2;
cell.backgroundColor = UIColor.redColor()
```

If those features are to be true of every cell ever displayed in the table, then that code should go in the spot numbered 4 in Example 8-1; there's no need to waste time doing the same thing all over again when an existing cell is reused.

Finally, here are a few properties of the table view itself worth playing with:

rowHeight
> The height of a cell. A taller cell may accommodate more information. You can also change this value in the nib editor; the table view's row height appears in the Size inspector. The cell's subviews have their autoresizing set so as to compensate correctly. You can also set a cell's height in real time by implementing the delegate's `tableView:heightForRowAtIndexPath:` method; thus a table's cells may differ from one another in height (more about that later in this chapter).

separatorStyle, separatorColor, separatorInset
> These can also be set in the nib. The table's `separatorInset` is adopted by individual cells that don't have their own explicit `separatorInset`. Separator styles (UITableViewCellSeparatorStyle) are `.None` and `.SingleLine`. (The former `.SingleLine-Etched` style was abandoned in iOS 7, and equates to `.None`.)

backgroundColor, backgroundView
> What's behind all the cells of the table; this may be seen if the cells have transparency, or if the user scrolls the cells beyond their limit. The `backgroundView` is drawn on top of the `backgroundColor`.

`tableHeaderView`, `tableFooterView`

Views to be shown before the first row and after the last row, respectively (as part of the table's scrolling content). Their background color is, by default, the background color of the table, but you can change that. You dictate their heights; their widths will be dynamically resized to fit the table. The user can, if you like, interact with these views (and their subviews); for example, a view can be (or can contain) a UIButton.

You can alter a table header or footer view dynamically during the lifetime of the app; if you change its height, you must set the corresponding table view property afresh to notify the table view of what has happened.

Registering a Cell Class

In `tableView:cellForRowAtIndexPath:`, there are two possible ways to obtain a reusable cell:

- `dequeueReusableCellWithIdentifier:`
- `dequeueReusableCellWithIdentifier:forIndexPath:`

In Example 8-1, I used the first method; but I prefer the second method, which was introduced in iOS 6, and will use it from now on. When I do, I'll always slavishly pass along, as the second parameter, the index path I received to begin with — and so should you. This method has three advantages:

The result is never nil

Unlike `dequeueReusableCellWithIdentifier:`, the value returned by `dequeueReusableCellWithIdentifier:forIndexPath:` is never nil (in Swift, it isn't an Optional). If there is a free reusable cell with the given identifier, it is returned. If there isn't, a new one is created for you. Step 3 of Example 8-1 can thus be eliminated!

The cell size is known earlier

Unlike `dequeueReusableCellWithIdentifier:`, the cell returned by `dequeueReusableCellWithIdentifier:forIndexPath:` has its final bounds. That's possible because you've passed the index path as an argument, so the runtime knows this cell's ultimate destination within the table, and has already consulted the table's `rowHeight` or the delegate's `tableView:heightForRowAtIndexPath:`. This makes laying out the cell's contents much easier.

The identifier is consistent

A danger with `dequeueReusableCellWithIdentifier:` is that you may accidentally pass an incorrect reuse identifier, and end up not reusing cells. With `dequeueReusableCellWithIdentifier:forIndexPath:`, that can't happen.

Before you call `dequeueReusableCellWithIdentifier:forIndexPath:` for the first time, you must *register* with the table itself. You do this by calling `registerClass:for-CellReuseIdentifier:`. This associates a class (which must be UITableViewCell or a subclass thereof) with a string identifier. That's how `dequeueReusableCellWith-Identifier:forIndexPath:` knows what class to instantiate when it creates a new cell for you: you pass an identifier, and you've already told the table what class it signifies. The only cell types you can obtain are those for which you've registered in this way; if you pass a bad identifier, the app will crash (with a helpful log message).

This is a very elegant mechanism. It also raises some new questions:

When should I call `registerClass:forCellReuseIdentifier:`*?*
Call it early, before the table view starts generating cells. `viewDidLoad` is a good place:

```
override func viewDidLoad() {
    super.viewDidLoad()
    self.tableView.registerClass(
        UITableViewCell.self, forCellReuseIdentifier: "Cell")
}
```

How do I specify a built-in table view cell style?
We are no longer calling `init(style:reuseIdentifier:)`, so where do we make our choice of built-in cell style? The default cell style is `.Default`, so if that's what you wanted, the problem is solved. Otherwise, subclass UITableViewCell and override `init(style:reuseIdentifier:)` to substitute the cell style you're after (passing along the reuse identifier you were handed).

For example, let's call our UITableViewCell subclass MyCell. So we now specify `MyCell.self` in our call to `registerClass:forCellReuseIdentifier:`. MyCell's initializer looks like this:

```
override init(style: UITableViewCellStyle, reuseIdentifier: String?) {
    super.init(style:.Subtitle, reuseIdentifier: reuseIdentifier)
}
```

How do I know whether the returned cell is new or reused?
Good question! It's important to know this, because there needs to be a way to distinguish between step 4 of Example 8-1 (configurations to apply once and for all to a *new cell*) and step 5 (configurations that differ for *each row*). The answer is: It's up to you, when performing one-time configuration on a cell, to give that cell some distinguishing mark that you can look for later to determine whether a cell requires one-time configuration.

For example, if every cell is to have a two-line text label, there is no point giving *every* cell returned by `dequeueReusableCellWithIdentifier:forIndexPath:` a two-line text label; the reused cells already have one. Now, however, no cell is nil, and we are never instantiating the cell ourselves. So how will we know which ones need to be given a two-line text label? It's easy: they are the ones *without* a two-line text label:

```
override func tableView(tableView: UITableView,
    cellForRowAtIndexPath indexPath: NSIndexPath) -> UITableViewCell {
        let cell = tableView.dequeueReusableCellWithIdentifier(
            "Cell", forIndexPath:indexPath) as! MyCell
        if cell.textLabel!.numberOfLines != 2 { // never configured
            cell.textLabel!.numberOfLines = 2
            // other one-time configurations here ...
        }
        cell.textLabel!.text = // ...
        // other individual configurations here ...
        return cell
}
```

Custom Cells

The built-in cell styles give the beginner a leg up in getting started with table views, but there is nothing sacred about them, and soon you'll probably want to transcend them, putting yourself in charge of how a table's cells look and what subviews they contain. The thing to remember is that the cell has a contentView property, which is one of its subviews; things like the accessoryView are outside the contentView. All *your* customizations must be confined to subviews of the contentView; this allows the cell to continue working correctly.

I'll illustrate four possible approaches to customizing the contents of a cell:

- Start with a built-in cell style, but supply a UITableViewCell subclass and override layoutSubviews to alter the frames of the built-in subviews.

- In tableView:cellForRowAtIndexPath:, add subviews to each cell's content-View as the cell is created. This approach can be combined with the previous one, or you can ignore the built-in subviews and use your own exclusively.

- Design the cell in a nib, and load that nib in tableView:cellForRowAtIndexPath: each time a cell needs to be created.

- Design the cell in a storyboard.

 What causes the built-in subviews to be present is not the cell style but the fact that you refer to them. As long as you never speak of the cell's textLabel, detailText-Label, or imageView, they are never created or inserted into the cell. Thus, you don't need to remove them if you don't want to use them.

The author of this book, who
would rather be out dirt biking

Figure 8-5. A cell with its label and image view swapped

Overriding a cell's subview layout

You can't directly change the frame of a built-in cell style subview in `tableView:cell-`
`ForRowAtIndexPath:`, because the cell's `layoutSubviews` comes along later and overrides your changes. The workaround is to override the cell's `layoutSubviews`! This is a
straightforward solution if your main objection to a built-in style is the frame of an
existing subview.

To illustrate, let's modify a `.Default` cell so that the image is at the right end instead of
the left end (Figure 8-5). We'll make a UITableViewCell subclass, MyCell, remembering
to register MyCell with the table view, so that `dequeueReusableCellWith-`
`Identifier:forIndexPath:` produces a MyCell instance; here is MyCell's `layout-`
`Subviews`:

```
override func layoutSubviews() {
    super.layoutSubviews()
    let cvb = self.contentView.bounds
    let imf = self.imageView!.frame
    self.imageView!.frame.origin.x = cvb.size.width - imf.size.width - 15
    self.textLabel!.frame.origin.x = 15
}
```

Adding subviews in code

Instead of modifying the existing default subviews, you can add completely new views
to each UITableViewCell's content view. The best place to do this in code is `table-`
`View:cellForRowAtIndexPath:`. Here are some things to keep in mind:

- The new views must be added when we instantiate a new cell, but not when we reuse
  a cell (because a reused cell already has them).

- We must never send `addSubview:` to the cell itself — only to its `contentView` (or
  some subview thereof).

- We should assign the new views an appropriate `autoresizingMask` or constraints,
  because the cell's content view might be resized.

- Each new view should be assigned a tag so that it can be referred to elsewhere.

I'll rewrite the previous example (Figure 8-5) to use this technique. We are no longer
using a UITableViewCell subclass; the registered cell class is UITableViewCell itself. If
this is a new cell, we add the subviews and assign them tags. If this is a reused cell, we

don't add the subviews (the cell already has them), and we use the tags to refer to the subviews:

```
override func tableView(tableView: UITableView,
    cellForRowAtIndexPath indexPath: NSIndexPath) -> UITableViewCell {
        let cell = tableView.dequeueReusableCellWithIdentifier(
            "Cell", forIndexPath:indexPath) as! UITableViewCell
        if cell.viewWithTag(1) == nil { // no subviews! add them
            let iv = UIImageView()
            iv.tag = 1
            cell.contentView.addSubview(iv)
            let lab = UILabel()
            lab.tag = 2
            cell.contentView.addSubview(lab)
            // since we are now adding the views ourselves,
            // we can use autolayout to lay them out
            let d = ["iv":iv, "lab":lab]
            iv.setTranslatesAutoresizingMaskIntoConstraints(false)
            lab.setTranslatesAutoresizingMaskIntoConstraints(false)
            // image view is vertically centered
            cell.contentView.addConstraint(
                NSLayoutConstraint(item:iv, attribute:.CenterY,
                    relatedBy:.Equal, toItem:cell.contentView,
                    attribute:.CenterY, multiplier:1, constant:0))
            // it's a square
            cell.contentView.addConstraint(
                NSLayoutConstraint(item:iv, attribute:.Width,
                    relatedBy:.Equal, toItem:iv,
                    attribute:.Height, multiplier:1, constant:0))
            // label has height pinned to superview
            cell.contentView.addConstraints(
                NSLayoutConstraint.constraintsWithVisualFormat("V:|[lab]|",
                    options:nil, metrics:nil, views:d))
            // horizontal margins
            cell.contentView.addConstraints(
                NSLayoutConstraint.constraintsWithVisualFormat(
                    "H:|-15-[lab]-15-[iv]-15-|",
                    options:nil, metrics:nil, views:d))
        }
        // can refer to subviews by their tags
        let lab = cell.viewWithTag(2) as! UILabel
        let iv = cell.viewWithTag(1) as! UIImageView
        // ...
        return cell
}
```

Using our own cell subviews instead of the built-in cell style subviews has some clear advantages; we no longer have to perform an elaborate dance to escape from the restrictions imposed by the runtime. Still, the verbosity of this code is somewhat overwhelming. We can avoid this by designing the cell in a nib.

Designing a cell in a nib

In designing a cell in a nib, we start by creating a *.xib* file that will consist, in effect, solely of this one cell. In Xcode, create the *.xib* file by specify iOS → User Interface → View. Let's call it *MyCell.xib*. In the nib editor, delete the existing View and replace it with a Table View Cell from the Object library.

The cell's design window shows a standard-sized cell; you can resize it as desired, but the actual size of the cell in the interface will be dictated by the table view's width and its `rowHeight` (or the delegate's response to `tableView:heightForRowAtIndexPath:`). The cell already has a `contentView`, and any subviews you add will be inside that; do not subvert that arrangement.

You can choose a built-in table view cell style in the Style pop-up menu of the Attributes inspector, and this gives you the default subviews, locked in their standard positions; for example, if you choose Basic, the `textLabel` appears, and if you specify an image, the `imageView` appears. If you set the Style pop-up menu to Custom, you start with a blank slate. Let's do that.

We'll implement, from scratch, the same subviews we've already implemented in the preceding two examples: a UILabel on the left side of the cell, and a UIImageView on the right side. Just as when adding subviews in code, we should set each subview's autoresizing behavior or constraints, and *give each subview a tag*, so that later, in `table-View:cellForRowAtIndexPath:`, we'll be able to refer to the label and the image view using `viewWithTag:`, exactly as in the previous example:

```
let lab = cell.viewWithTag(2) as! UILabel
let iv = cell.viewWithTag(1) as! UIImageView
// ...
return cell
```

The only remaining question is how to load the cell from the nib. This is the Really Cool Part. When we register with the table view, which we're currently doing in `viewDid-Load`, instead of calling `registerClass:forCellReuseIdentifier:`, we call a different method: `registerNib:forCellReuseIdentifier:`. To specify the nib, call UINib's class method `nibWithNibName:bundle:`, like this:

```
self.tableView.registerNib(
    UINib(nibName:"MyCell", bundle:nil), forCellReuseIdentifier: "Cell")
```

That's all there is to it! In `tableView:cellForRowAtIndexPath:`, when we call `dequeue-ReusableCellWithIdentifier:forIndexPath:`, if the table has no free reusable cell already in existence, the nib will automatically be loaded and the cell will be instantiated from it and returned to us.

You may wonder how that's possible, when we haven't specified a File's Owner class or added an outlet from the File's Owner to the cell in the nib. The answer is that the nib conforms to a specific format. The UINib instance method `instantiateWith-`

Owner:options: can load a nib with a nil owner; regardless, it returns an array of the nib's instantiated top-level objects. A nib registered with the table view is expected to have exactly one top-level object, and that top-level object is expected to be a UITableViewCell; that being so, the cell can easily be extracted from the resulting array, as it is the array's only element. Our nib meets those expectations!

The advantages of this approach should be immediately obvious. The subviews can now be designed in the nib, and code that was creating *and configuring* each subview can be deleted. For example, suppose we previously had this code:

```
if cell.viewWithTag(1) == nil {
    let iv = UIImageView()
    iv.tag = 1
    cell.contentView.addSubview(iv)
    let lab = UILabel()
    lab.tag = 2
    cell.contentView.addSubview(lab)
    // ... position views ...
    lab.font = UIFont(name:"Helvetica-Bold", size:16)
    lab.lineBreakMode = .ByWordWrapping
    lab.numberOfLines = 2
}
```

All of that can now be eliminated, including setting the label's font, lineBreakMode, and numberOfLines; those configurations are to be applied to the label in *every* cell, so they can be performed in the nib instead.

 The nib *must* conform to the format I've described: it must have exactly one top-level object, a UITableViewCell. This means that some configurations are difficult or impossible in the nib. Consider, for example, the cell's backgroundView. The cell in the nib has a backgroundView outlet, but if we drag a view into the canvas and hook that outlet to it, our app will crash when the nib loads (because there are now two top-level nib objects). The simplest workaround is to add the backgroundView in code.

In tableView:cellForRowAtIndexPath:, we are still referring to the cell's subviews by way of viewWithTag:. There's nothing wrong with that, but perhaps you'd prefer to use names. Now that we're designing the cell in a nib, that's easy. Provide a UITableViewCell subclass with outlet properties, and configure the nib file accordingly:

1. Create a UITableViewCell subclass — let's call it MyCell — and declare two outlet properties:

```
class MyCell : UITableViewCell {
    @IBOutlet var theLabel : UILabel!
    @IBOutlet var theImageView : UIImageView!
}
```

That is the *entirety* of MyCell's code; it exists solely so that we can create these outlets.

2. Edit the table view cell nib *MyCell.xib*. Change the class of the cell to MyCell, and link up the outlets from the cell to the respective subviews.

The result is that in our implementation of `tableView:cellForRowAtIndexPath:`, once we've typed the cell as a MyCell, the compiler will let us use the property names to access the subviews:

```
let cell = tableView.dequeueReusableCellWithIdentifier(
    "Cell", forIndexPath:indexPath) as! MyCell
let lab = cell.theLabel
let iv = cell.theImageView
```

Designing a cell in a storyboard

When your table view comes from a storyboard, it is open to you to employ any of the ways of obtaining and designing its cells that I've already described. There is also an additional option, available only in a UITableViewController scene in the storyboard: you can have the table view obtain the cells from the storyboard itself, and you can also *design* the cell directly in the table view in the storyboard.

To experiment with this way of obtaining and designing a cell, start with a project based on the Single View Application template:

1. In the storyboard, delete the View Controller scene. In the project, delete the View Controller class file.

2. In the project, create a file for a UITableViewController subclass called RootView-Controller, *without* a corresponding *.xib* file.

3. In the storyboard, drag a Table View Controller into the empty canvas, and set its class to RootViewController (and make sure it's the initial view controller).

4. Now comes the Interesting Part. The table view controller in the storyboard comes with a table view. In the storyboard, select that table view, and, in the Attributes inspector, set the Content pop-up menu to Dynamic Prototypes, and set the number of Prototype Cells to 1 (these are the defaults).

The table view now contains a single table view cell with a content view. You can do in this cell exactly what we were doing before when designing a table view cell in a *.xib* file.

So, let's do that. I like being able to refer to my custom cell subviews with property names. Our procedure is just like what we did in the previous example:

1. In the project, add a UITableViewCell subclass — let's call it MyCell — and declare two outlet properties:

```
class MyCell : UITableViewCell {
    @IBOutlet var theLabel : UILabel!
    @IBOutlet var theImageView : UIImageView!
}
```

2. In the storyboard, select the prototype cell and change its class to MyCell.

3. Drag a label and an image view into the prototype cell, position and configure them as desired, and hook up the cell's outlets to them appropriately.

So far, so good; but there is one crucial question I have not yet answered: How will your code tell the table view to get its cells from the storyboard? Clearly, *not* by calling `registerClass:forCellReuseIdentifier:`, and *not* by calling `registerNib:forCell-ReuseIdentifier:`; each of those would do something perfectly valid, but not the thing we want done in this case. The answer is that you *don't register anything with the table view at all!* Instead, when you call `dequeueReusableCellWithIdentifier:forIndex-Path:`, you supply an identifier that matches the prototype cell's *identifier in the storyboard*.

So, return once more to the storyboard:

1. Select the prototype cell.

2. In the Attributes inspector, enter `Cell` in the Identifier field (capitalization counts).

Now RootViewController's `tableView:cellForRowAtIndexPath:` works exactly as it did in the previous example:

```
let cell = tableView.dequeueReusableCellWithIdentifier(
    "Cell", forIndexPath:indexPath) as! MyCell
let lab = cell.theLabel
let iv = cell.theImageView
```

If you call `dequeueReusableCellWithIdentifier:forIndexPath:` with an identifier that you have *not* registered with the table view and that *doesn't* match the identifier of a prototype cell in the storyboard, your app will crash (with a helpful message in the console).

Table View Data

The structure and content of the actual data portrayed in a table view comes from the data source, an object pointed to by the table view's `dataSource` property and adopting the UITableViewDataSource protocol. The data source is thus the heart and soul of the table. What surprises beginners is that the data source operates not by *setting* the table view's structure and content, but by *responding on demand*. The data source, *qua* data source, consists of a set of methods that the table view will call when it needs information; in effect, it will ask your data source some questions. This architecture has important consequences for how you write your code, which can be summarized by these simple guidelines:

Be ready

> Your data source cannot know *when* or *how often* any of these methods will be called, so it must be prepared to answer *any question at any time*.

Be fast

> The table view is asking for data in real time; the user is probably scrolling through the table *right now*. So you mustn't gum up the works; you must be ready to supply responses just as fast as you possibly can. (If you can't supply a piece of data fast enough, you may have to skip it, supply a placeholder, and insert the data into the table later. This may involve you in threading issues that I don't want to get into here. I'll give an example in Chapter 24.)

Be consistent

> There are multiple data source methods, and you cannot know *which* one will be called at a given moment. So you must make sure your responses are mutually consistent at *any* moment. For example, a common beginner error is forgetting to take into account, in your data source methods, the possibility that the data might not yet be ready.

This may sound daunting, but you'll be fine as long as you maintain an unswerving adherence to the principles of model–view–controller. How and when you accumulate the actual data, and how that data is structured, is a *model* concern. Acting as a data source is a *controller* concern. So you can acquire and arrange your data whenever and however you like, just so long as when the table view actually turns to you and asks what to do, you can lay your hands on the relevant data rapidly and consistently. You'll want to design the model in such a way that the controller can access any desired piece of data more or less instantly.

Another source of confusion for beginners is that methods are rather oddly distributed between the data source and the delegate, an object pointed to by the table view's `delegate` property and adopting the UITableViewDelegate protocol; in some cases, one may seem to be doing the job of the other. This is not usually a cause of any real difficulty, because the object serving as data source will probably also be the object serving as delegate. Nevertheless, it is rather inconvenient when you're consulting the documentation; you'll probably want to keep the data source and delegate documentation pages open simultaneously as you work.

 If a table view's contents are known beforehand, you can alternatively design the entire table, *including the contents of individual cells*, in a storyboard. I'll give an example later in this chapter.

The Three Big Questions

Like Katherine Hepburn in *Pat and Mike*, the basis of your success (as a data source) is your ability, at any time, to answer the Three Big Questions. The questions the table view will ask you are a little different from the questions Mike asks Pat, but the principle is the same: know the answers, and be able to recite them at any moment. Here they are:

How many sections does this table have?

> The table will call `numberOfSectionsInTableView:`; respond with an integer. In theory you can sometimes omit this method, as the default response is 1, which is often correct. However, I never omit it; for one thing, returning 0 is a good way to say that the table has no data, and will prevent the table view from asking any other questions.

How many rows does this section have?

> The table will call `tableView:numberOfRowsInSection:`. The table supplies a section number — the first section is numbered 0 — and you respond with an integer. In a table with only one section, of course, there is probably no need to examine the incoming section number.

What cell goes in this row of this section?

> The table will call `tableView:cellForRowAtIndexPath:`. The index path is expressed as an NSIndexPath; this is a sophisticated and powerful class, but you don't actually have to know anything about it, because UITableView provides a category on it that adds two read-only properties — `section` and `row`. Using these, you extract the requested section number and row number, and return a fully configured UITableViewCell, ready for display in the table view. The first row of a section is numbered 0. I have already explained how to obtain the cell in the first place, by calling `dequeueReusableCellWithIdentifier:forIndexPath:`.

I have nothing particular to say about precisely how you're going to fulfill these obligations. It all depends on your data model and what your table is trying to portray. The important thing is to remember that you're going to be receiving an NSIndexPath specifying a section and a row, and you need to be able to lay your hands on the data corresponding to that slot *now* and configure the cell *now*. So construct your model, and your algorithm for consulting it in the Three Big Questions, and your way of configuring the cell, in accordance with that necessity.

For example, suppose our table is to list the names of the Pep Boys. Our data model might be an array of string names (`self.pep`). Our table has only one section. So our code might look like this:

```swift
override func numberOfSectionsInTableView(tableView: UITableView) -> Int {
    if self.pep == nil {
        return 0
    }
}
```

```
        return 1
    }
    override func tableView(tableView: UITableView,
        numberOfRowsInSection section: Int) -> Int {
            return self.pep.count
    }
    override func tableView(tableView: UITableView,
        cellForRowAtIndexPath indexPath: NSIndexPath) -> UITableViewCell {
            let cell = tableView.dequeueReusableCellWithIdentifier(
                "Cell", forIndexPath: indexPath) as! UITableViewCell
            cell.textLabel!.text = pep[indexPath.row]
            return cell
    }
```

At this point you may be feeling some exasperation. You want to object: "But that's trivial!" Exactly so! Your access to the data model *should* be trivial. That's the sign of a data model that's well designed for access by your table view's data source. Your implementation of `tableView:cellForRowAtIndexPath:` might have some interesting work to do in order to configure the *form* of the cell, but accessing the actual *data* should be simple and boring.

Reusing Cells

Another important goal of `tableView:cellForRowAtIndexPath:` should be to conserve resources by reusing cells. As I've already explained, once a cell's row is no longer visible on the screen, that cell can be slotted into a row that *is* visible — with its portrayed data appropriately modified, of course! — so that only a few more than the number of simultaneously visible cells will ever need to be instantiated.

A table view is ready to implement this strategy for you; all you have to do is call `dequeue-ReusableCellWithIdentifier:forIndexPath:`. For any given identifier, you'll be handed either a newly minted cell or a reused cell that previously appeared in the table view but is now no longer needed because it has scrolled out of view.

The table view can maintain more than one cache of reusable cells; this could be useful if your table view contains more than one type of cell (where the meaning of the concept "type of cell" is pretty much up to you). This is why you must *name* each cache, by attaching an identifier string to any cell that can be reused. All the examples in this chapter (and in this book, and in fact in every UITableView I've ever created) use just one cache and just one identifier, but there can be more than one. If you're using a storyboard as a source of cells, there would then need to be more than one prototype cell.

To prove to yourself the efficiency of the cell-caching architecture, do something to differentiate newly instantiated cells from reused cells, and count the newly instantiated cells, like this:

```
override func numberOfSectionsInTableView(tableView: UITableView) -> Int {
    return 1
}
override func tableView(
    tableView: UITableView, numberOfRowsInSection section: Int) -> Int {
        return 1000 // make a lot of rows this time!
}
override func tableView(tableView: UITableView,
    cellForRowAtIndexPath indexPath: NSIndexPath) -> UITableViewCell {
        let cell = tableView.dequeueReusableCellWithIdentifier(
            "Cell", forIndexPath:indexPath) as! MyCell
        let lab = cell.theLabel
        // prove that many rows does not mean many cell objects
        lab.text = "Row \(indexPath.row) of section \(indexPath.section)"
        if lab.tag != 999 {
            lab.tag = 999
            println("New cell \(++self.cells)")
        }
}
```

When we run this code and scroll through the table, every cell is numbered correctly, so there appear to be 1000 cells. But the console messages show that only about a dozen distinct cells are ever actually created.

Be certain that *your* table view code passes that test, and that you are truly reusing cells! Fortunately, one of the benefits of calling dequeueReusableCellWithIdentifier:forIndexPath: is that it forces you to use a valid reuse identifier.

 A common beginner error is to obtain a cell in some other way, such as instantiating it directly every time tableView:cellForRowAtIndexPath: is called. I have even seen beginners call dequeueReusableCellWithIdentifier:forIndexPath:, only to instantiate a fresh cell manually in the *next* line. Don't do that.

When your tableView:cellForRowAtIndexPath: implementation configures *individual* cells (stage 5 in Example 8-1), the cell might be new or reused; at this point in your code, you don't know or care which. Therefore, you should always configure *everything* about the cell that might need configuring. If you fail to do this, and if the cell is reused, you might be surprised when some aspect of the cell is left over from its previous use; similarly, if you fail to do this, and if the cell is new, you might be surprised when some aspect of the cell isn't configured at all.

As usual, I learned that lesson the hard way. In the TidBITS News app, there is a little loudspeaker icon that should appear in a given cell in the master view's table view only if there is a recording associated with this article. So I initially wrote this code:

```
if (item.enclosures != nil) && (item.enclosures.count > 0) {
    cell.speaker.hidden = false
}
```

That turned out to be a mistake, because the cell might be reused. Every reused call *always* had a visible loudspeaker icon if, in a previous usage, that cell had *ever* had a visible loudspeaker icon! The solution was to rewrite the logic to cover all possibilities completely, like this:

```
cell.speaker.hidden =
    !((item.enclosures != nil) && (item.enclosures.count > 0))
```

You do get a sort of second bite of the cherry: there's a delegate method, `tableView:willDisplayCell:forRowAtIndexPath:`, that is called for every cell just before it appears in the table. This is absolutely the last minute to configure a cell. But don't misuse this method. You're functioning as the delegate here, not the data source; you may set the final details of the cell's appearance, but you shouldn't be consulting the data model at this point.

An additional delegate method is `tableView:didEndDisplayingCell:forRowAtIndexPath:`. This tells you that the cell no longer appears in the interface and has become free for reuse. You could take advantage of this to tear down any resource-heavy customization of the cell — I'll give an example in Chapter 24 — or simply to prepare it somehow for subsequent future reuse.

Table View Sections

Your table data may be expressed as divided into sections. You might clump your data into sections for various reasons (and doubtless there are other reasons beyond these):

- You want to supply section headers (or footers, or both).
- You want to make navigation of the table easier by supplying an index down the right side. You can't have an index without sections.
- You want to facilitate programmatic rearrangement of the table. For example, it's very easy to hide or move an entire section at once, possibly with animation.

Section headers and footers

A section header or footer appears between the cells, before the first row of a section or after the last row of a section, respectively. In addition, in a nongrouped table, a section header or footer detaches itself while the user scrolls the table, positioning itself at the top or bottom of the table view and floating over the scrolled rows, so that the user always knows what section is currently being viewed. This can greatly clarify the presentation of your data by giving the user a sense, at every moment, of where we are within the table. Also, a section header or footer can contain custom views, so it's a place where you might put additional information, or even functional interface, such as a button the user can tap.

 Don't confuse the section headers and footers with the header and footer of the table as a whole. The latter are view properties of the table view itself, its table-HeaderView and tableFooterView, discussed earlier in this chapter. The table header appears only when the table is scrolled all the way down; the table footer appears only when the table is scrolled all the way up.

The number of sections is determined by your reply to numberOfSectionsInTable-View:. For each section, the table view will consult your data source and delegate to learn whether this section has a header or a footer, or both, or neither (the default).

The UITableViewHeaderFooterView class is a UIView subclass intended specifically for use as the view of a header or footer; much like a table view cell, it is reusable. It has the following properties:

textLabel
Label (UILabel) for displaying the text of the header or footer.

detailTextLabel
This label, if you set its text, appears only in a grouped style table.

contentView
A subview of the header or footer, to which you can add custom subviews. If you do, you probably should not use the built-in textLabel; the textLabel is not inside the contentView and in a sense doesn't belong to you.

backgroundView
Any view you want to assign. The contentView is in front of the backgroundView. The contentView has a clear background by default, so the backgroundView shows through. An opaque contentView.backgroundColor, on the other hand, would completely obscure the backgroundView.

If the backgroundView is nil (the default), the header or footer view will supply its own background view whose backgroundColor is derived (in some annoyingly unspecified way) from the table's backgroundColor.

backgroundColor
You're not supposed to set the header or footer's backgroundColor; instead, set the backgroundColor of its contentView, or assign a new backgroundView and configure it as you like.

`tintColor`

This property appears to be a kind of dead letter; it exists, and you can set it, but it doesn't do anything. (This feels like a bug; the `tintColor` should affect the color of subviews, such a UIButton's title, but it doesn't.)

You can supply a header or footer in two ways:

Header or footer title string

You implement the data source method `tableView:titleForHeaderInSection:` or `tableView:titleForFooterInSection:` (or both). Return nil to indicate that the given section has no header (or footer). The header or footer view itself is a UITableViewHeaderFooterView, and is reused automatically: there will be only as many as needed for simultaneous display on the screen. The string you supply becomes the view's `textLabel.text`.

(In a grouped style table, the string's capitalization may be changed. To avoid that, use the second way of supplying the header or footer.)

Header or footer view

You implement the delegate method `tableView:viewForHeaderInSection:` or `tableView:viewForFooterInSection:` (or both). The view you supply is used as the entire header or footer and is automatically resized to the table's width and the section header or footer height (I'll discuss how the height is determined in a moment).

You are not required to return a UITableViewHeaderFooterView, but you will probably want to, in order to take advantage of reusability. To do so, the procedure is much like making a cell reusable. You register beforehand with the table view by calling `registerClass:forHeaderFooterViewReuseIdentifier:`. To supply the reusable view, send the table view `dequeueReusableHeaderFooterViewWith-Identifier:`; the result will be either a newly instantiated view or a reused view.

You can then configure this view as desired. For example, you can set its `text-Label.text`, or you can give its `contentView` custom subviews. In the latter case, be sure to set proper autoresizing or constraints, so that the subviews will be positioned and sized appropriately when the view itself is resized.

 The documentation lists a second way of registering a header or footer view for reuse — `registerNib:forHeaderFooterViewReuseIdentifier:`. But the nib editor's Object library doesn't include a UITableViewHeaderFooterView! This makes `registerNib:forHeaderFooterViewReuseIdentifier:` pretty much useless, because there's no way to configure the view correctly in the nib.

In addition, two pairs of delegate methods permit you to perform final configurations on your header or footer views:

`tableView:willDisplayHeaderView:forSection:`
`tableView:willDisplayFooterView:forSection:`

> You can perform further configuration here, if desired. A useful possibility is to generate the default UITableViewHeaderFooterView by implementing `title-For...` and then tweak its form slightly here. These delegate methods are matched by `tableView:didEndDisplayingHeaderView:forSection:` and `tableView:didEndDisplayingFooterView:forSection:`.

`tableView:heightForHeaderInSection:`
`tableView:heightForFooterInSection:`

> The runtime resizes your header or footer before displaying it. Its width will be the table view's width; its height will be the table view's `sectionHeaderHeight` and `sectionFooterHeight` unless you implement one of these methods to say otherwise.

It is possible to implement *both* `viewFor...` and `titleFor....` In that case, `viewFor...` is called first, and if it returns a UITableViewHeaderFooterView, `titleFor...` will set its `textLabel.text`. If you implement both methods and you want `heightFor...` to return the height as set by the table view based on `titleFor...`, return `UITableView-AutomaticDimension`.

> If you implement `tableView:viewForHeaderInSection:` and not `tableView:title-ForHeaderInSection:`, and you *neither* set the table view's `sectionHeaderHeight` *nor* implement `tableView:heightForHeaderInSection:`, *you may or may not see any headers.* (So too, of course, for footers.) The frustrating thing here is that this configuration may seem to work just fine, until one day it doesn't, and you will then waste many hours wondering what went wrong. Can you guess how I know this?

Some lovely effects can be created by making use of the fact that a header or footer view will be further forward than the table's cells. For example, a header with transparency shows the cells as they scroll behind it; a header with a shadow casts that shadow on the adjacent cell.

> When a header or footer view appears in the middle of the table view (between two table cells), there is a transparent gap behind it. If the header or footer view has some transparency, the table view's background is visible through this gap. Be sure to take this into account when planning your color scheme.

Section data

Clearly, a table that is to have sections may require some advance planning in the formation of its data model. The row data must somehow be clumped into sections, because you're going to be asked for a row *with respect to its section*. And, just as with a cell, a section title must be readily available so that it can be supplied quickly in real time. A structure that I commonly use is a pair of parallel arrays: an array of strings containing the section names, and an array of subarrays containing the data for each section.

For example, suppose we intend to display the names of all 50 U.S. states in alphabetical order as the rows of a table view, and that we wish to divide the table into sections according to the first letter of each state's name. Let's say I have the alphabetized list as a text file, which starts like this:

```
Alabama
Alaska
Arizona
Arkansas
California
Colorado
Connecticut
Delaware
...
```

I have properties already initialized as empty arrays, waiting to hold the data model:

```
var sectionNames = [String]()
var sectionData = [[String]]()
```

I'll prepare the data model by loading the text file and walking through it, line by line, creating a new section name and a new subarray when I encounter a new first letter:

```
let s = String(contentsOfFile: NSBundle.mainBundle().pathForResource(
    "states", ofType: "txt")!, encoding: NSUTF8StringEncoding, error: nil)!
let states = s.componentsSeparatedByString("\n")
var previous = ""
for aState in states {
    // get the first letter
    let c = (aState as NSString).substringWithRange(NSMakeRange(0,1))
    // only add a letter to sectionNames when it's a different letter
    if c != previous {
        previous = c
        self.sectionNames.append(c.uppercaseString)
        // and in that case also add new subarray to our array of subarrays
        self.sectionData.append([String]())
    }
    sectionData[sectionData.count-1].append(aState)
}
```

The value of this preparatory dance is evident when we are bombarded with questions from the table view about cells and headers; supplying the answers is trivial, just as it should be:

```
override func numberOfSectionsInTableView(tableView: UITableView) -> Int {
    return self.sectionNames.count
}
override func tableView(tableView: UITableView,
    numberOfRowsInSection section: Int) -> Int {
        return self.sectionData[section].count
}
override func tableView(tableView: UITableView,
    cellForRowAtIndexPath indexPath: NSIndexPath) -> UITableViewCell {
        let cell = tableView.dequeueReusableCellWithIdentifier(
            "Cell", forIndexPath: indexPath) as! UITableViewCell
        let s = self.sectionData[indexPath.section][indexPath.row]
        cell.textLabel!.text = s
        return cell
}
override func tableView(tableView: UITableView,
    titleForHeaderInSection section: Int) -> String? {
        return self.sectionNames[section]
}
```

Let's modify that example to illustrate customization of a header view. I've already registered my header identifier in viewDidLoad:

```
self.tableView.registerClass(UITableViewHeaderFooterView.self,
    forHeaderFooterViewReuseIdentifier: "Header")
```

Now, instead of tableView:titleForHeaderInSection:, I'll implement table-View:viewForHeaderInSection:. For completely new views, I'll place my own label and an image view inside the contentView and give them their basic configuration; then I'll perform individual configuration on all views, new or reused (very much like table-View:cellForRowAtIndexPath:). Note my deliberate misuse of the otherwise useless tintColor property to mark whether a view needs basic configuration:

```
override func tableView(tableView: UITableView,
    viewForHeaderInSection section: Int) -> UIView? {
        let h = tableView.dequeueReusableHeaderFooterViewWithIdentifier(
            "Header") as! UITableViewHeaderFooterView
        if h.tintColor != UIColor.redColor() {
            h.tintColor = UIColor.redColor() // invisible marker, tee-hee
            h.backgroundView = UIView()
            h.backgroundView?.backgroundColor = UIColor.blackColor()
            let lab = UILabel()
            lab.tag = 1
            lab.font = UIFont(name:"Georgia-Bold", size:22)
            lab.textColor = UIColor.greenColor()
            lab.backgroundColor = UIColor.clearColor()
            h.contentView.addSubview(lab)
            let v = UIImageView()
            v.tag = 2
            v.backgroundColor = UIColor.blackColor()
            v.image = UIImage(named:"us_flag_small.gif")
            h.contentView.addSubview(v)
```

```
            lab.setTranslatesAutoresizingMaskIntoConstraints(false)
            v.setTranslatesAutoresizingMaskIntoConstraints(false)
            h.contentView.addConstraints(
                NSLayoutConstraint.constraintsWithVisualFormat(
                    "H:|-5-[lab(25)]-10-[v(40)]",
                    options:nil, metrics:nil, views:["v":v, "lab":lab]))
            h.contentView.addConstraints(
                NSLayoutConstraint.constraintsWithVisualFormat("V:|[v]|",
                    options:nil, metrics:nil, views:["v":v]))
            h.contentView.addConstraints(
                NSLayoutConstraint.constraintsWithVisualFormat("V:|[lab]|",
                    options:nil, metrics:nil, views:["lab":lab]))
        }
        let lab = h.contentView.viewWithTag(1) as! UILabel
        lab.text = self.sectionNames[section]
        return h
    }
```

Section index

If your table view has the plain style, you can add an index down the right side of the table, where the user can tap or drag to jump to the start of a section — helpful for navigating long tables. To generate the index, implement the data source method `sectionIndexTitlesForTableView:`, returning an array of string titles to appear as entries in the index. For our list of state names, that's trivial once again, just as it should be:

```
override func sectionIndexTitlesForTableView(tableView: UITableView)
    -> [AnyObject]! {
        return self.sectionNames
}
```

The index can appear even if there are no section headers. It will appear only if the number of rows exceeds the table view's `sectionIndexMinimumDisplayRowCount` property value; the default is 0, so the index is always displayed by default. You will want the index entries to be short — preferably just one character — because they will be partially obscuring the right edge of the table; plus, each cell's content view will shrink to compensate, so you're sacrificing some cell real estate.

You can modify three properties that affect the index's appearance:

`sectionIndexColor`
    The index text color.

`sectionIndexBackgroundColor`
    The index background color. I advise giving the index some background color, even if it is `clearColor`, because otherwise the index distorts the colors of what's behind it in a distracting way.

`sectionIndexTrackingBackgroundColor`
> The index background color while the user's finger is sliding over it. By default, it's the same as the `sectionIndexBackgroundColor`.

Normally, there will be a one-to-one correspondence between the index entries and the sections; when the user taps an index entry, the table jumps to the start of the corresponding section. However, under certain circumstances you may want to customize this correspondence.

For example, suppose there are 100 sections, but there isn't room to display 100 index entries comfortably on the iPhone. The index will automatically curtail itself, omitting some index entries and inserting bullets to suggest the omission, but you might prefer to take charge of the situation.

To do so, supply a shorter index, and implement the data source method `table-View:sectionForSectionIndexTitle:atIndex:`, returning the number of the section to jump to. You are told both the title and the index number of the section index listing that the user chose, so you can use whichever is convenient.

Apple's documentation elaborates heavily on the details of implementing the model behind a table with an index and suggests that you rely on a class called UILocalized-IndexedCollation. This class is effectively a way of generating an ordered list of letters of the alphabet, with methods for helping to sort an array of strings and separate it into sections. This might be useful if you need your app to be localized, because the notion of the alphabet and its order changes automatically depending on the user's preferred language.

Unfortunately, you can't readily use a UILocalizedIndexCollation to implement your own sort order. For example, UILocalizedIndexCollation was of no use to me in writing my Greek and Latin vocabulary apps, in which the Greek words must be sorted, sectioned, and indexed according to the Greek alphabet, and the Latin words use a reduced version of the English alphabet (no initial J, K, or V through Z). Thus I've never actually bothered to use UILocalizedIndexedCollation.

Refreshing Table View Data

The table view has no direct connection to the underlying data. If you want the table view display to change because the underlying data have changed, you have to cause the table view to refresh itself; basically, you're requesting that the Big Questions be asked all over again. At first blush, this seems inefficient ("regenerate *all* the data??"); but it isn't. Remember, in a table that caches reusable cells, there are no cells of interest other than those actually showing in the table at this moment. Thus, having worked out the layout of the table through the section header and footer heights and row heights, the table has to regenerate only those cells that are actually visible.

You can cause the table data to be refreshed using any of several methods:

reloadData

The table view will ask the Three Big Questions all over again, including heights of rows and section headers and footers, and the index, exactly as it does automatically when the table view first appears.

reloadRowsAtIndexPaths:withRowAnimation:

The table view will ask the Three Big Questions all over again, including heights, but not index entries. Cells are requested only for visible cells among those you specify. The first parameter is an array of index paths; to form an index path, use the initializer init(forRow:inSection:).

reloadSections:withRowAnimation:

The table view will ask the Three Big Questions all over again, including heights of rows and section headers and footers, and the index. Cells, headers, and footers are requested only for visible elements of the sections you specify. The first parameter is an NSIndexSet.

The second two methods can perform animations that cue the user as to what's changing. For the rowAnimation: argument, you'll pass one of the following (UITableViewRow-Animation):

.Fade

The old fades into the new.

.Right, .Left, .Top, .Bottom

The old slides out in the stated direction, and is replaced from the opposite direction.

.None

No animation.

.Middle

Hard to describe; it's a sort of venetian blind effect on each cell individually.

.Automatic

The table view just "does the right thing." This is especially useful for grouped style tables, because if you pick the wrong animation, the display can look very funny as it proceeds.

If all you need to do is to refresh the index, call reloadSectionIndexTitles; this calls the data source's sectionIndexTitlesForTableView:.

If you want the table view to be laid out freshly without reloading *any* cells, send it begin-Updates immediately followed by endUpdates. The section and row structure of the table will be asked for, along with calculation of all heights, but no cells and no headers or footers are requested. This is useful as a way of alerting the table that its measurements have changed. It might be considered a misuse of an updates block (the real use of such a block is discussed later in this chapter); but Apple takes advantage of this trick in the Table View Animations and Gestures example, in which a pinch gesture is used to change a table's row height in real time, so it must be legal.

It is also possible to access and alter a table's individual cells directly. This can be a lightweight approach to refreshing the table, plus you can supply your own animation within the cell as it alters its appearance. It is important to bear in mind, however, that the cells are not the data (view is not model). If you change the content of a cell manually, make sure that you have also changed the model corresponding to it, so that the row will appear correctly if its data is reloaded later.

To do this, you need direct access to the cell you want to change. You'll probably want to make sure the cell is visible within the table view's bounds; nonvisible cells don't really exist (except as potential cells waiting in the reuse cache), and there's no point changing them manually, as they'll be changed when they are scrolled into view, through the usual call to `tableView:cellForRowAtIndexPath:`.

Here are some UITableView methods that mediate between cells, rows, and visibility:

`visibleCells`
An array of the cells actually showing within the table's bounds.

`indexPathsForVisibleRows`
An array of the rows actually showing within the table's bounds.

`cellForRowAtIndexPath:`
Returns a UITableViewCell if the table is maintaining a cell for the given row (typically because this is a visible row); otherwise, returns nil.

`indexPathForCell:`
Given a cell obtained from the table view, returns the row into which it is slotted.

By the same token, you can get access to the views constituting headers and footers, by calling `headerViewForSection:` or `footerViewForSection:`. Thus you could modify a view directly. You should assume that if a section is returned by `indexPathsForVisibleRows`, its header or footer might be visible.

If you want to grant the user some interface for requesting that a table view be refreshed, you might like to use a UIRefreshControl. You aren't required to use this; it's just Apple's attempt to provide a standard interface. It is located behind the top of the scrolling part of the table view. To request a refresh, the user scrolls the table view downward to reveal the refresh control and holds long enough to indicate that this scrolling is deliberate. The refresh control then acknowledges visually that it is refreshing, and remains visible until refreshing is complete.

The refresh control is located *behind the table view's* `backgroundView`. If the table view has an opaque background view, the refresh control will be impossible to see.

To give a table view a refresh control, assign a UIRefreshControl to the table view controller's `refreshControl` property; to do this in the nib editor, set the table view controller's Refreshing pop-up menu to Enabled. A refresh control is a control (UIControl, Chapter 12), and you will want to hook its Value Changed event to an action method; you can do that in the nib editor by making an action connection, or you can do it in code. Here's an example of creating and configuring a refresh control entirely in code:

```
self.refreshControl = UIRefreshControl()
self.refreshControl!.addTarget(
    self, action: "doRefresh", forControlEvents: .ValueChanged)
```

Once a refresh control's action message has fired, the control remains visible and indicates by animation (similar to an activity indicator) that it is refreshing, until you send it the `endRefreshing` message:

```
@IBAction func doRefresh(sender: AnyObject) {
    // ... refresh ...
    (sender as! UIRefreshControl).endRefreshing()
}
```

You can initiate a refresh animation in code with `beginRefreshing`, but this does not fire the action message or display the refresh control; to display it, scroll the table view:

```
self.tableView.setContentOffset(
    CGPointMake(0, -self.refreshControl!.bounds.height), animated:true)
self.refreshControl!.beginRefreshing()
self.doRefresh(self.refreshControl!) // fire action message manually
```

A refresh control also has these properties:

`refreshing` *(read-only)*
Whether the refresh control is refreshing.

`tintColor`
The refresh control's color. It is *not* inherited from the view hierarchy (I regard this as a bug).

`attributedTitle`
Styled text displayed below the refresh control's activity indicator. On attributed strings, see Chapter 10.

`backgroundColor` *(inherited from UIView)*
If you give a table view controller's `refreshControl` a background color, that color completely covers the table view's own background color when the refresh control

is revealed. For some reason, I find the drawing of the `attributedTitle` more reliable if the refresh control has a background color.

Variable Row Heights

Most tables have rows that are all the same height, as set by the table view's `row-Height`. However, the delegate's `tableView:heightForRowAtIndexPath:` can be used to make different rows different heights. You can see an example in the TidBITS News app (Figure 6-1).

Back when I first wrote TidBITS News, variable row heights were possible but virtually unheard-of; I knew of no other app that was using them, and Apple provided no guidance, so I had to invent my own technique by sheer trial-and-error. There were three main challenges:

Measurement
> *What* should the height of a given row be?

Timing
> *When* should the determination of each row's height be made?

Layout
> How should the *subviews* of each cell be configured for its individual height?

Over the years since then, implementing variable row heights has become considerably easier. In iOS 6, with the advent of constraints, both measurement and layout became much simpler. In iOS 7, new table view properties made it possible to improving the timing. And, new in iOS 8, variable row heights can be implemented *automatically*, without your having to worry about any of these problems.

I will briefly describe four different approaches that I have used, in historical order. Perhaps you won't use any of the first three, because iOS 8's new automatic variable row heights feature makes them unnecessary; nevertheless, a basic understanding of them will give you an appreciation of what iOS 8 is doing for you. Besides, in my experience, the new iOS 8 automatic variable row heights feature can be slow; for efficiency and speed, you might want to revert to one of the earlier techniques.

Manual row height measurement

The TidBITS News app, in its earliest implementation, works as follows. Each cell contains two labels. The *measurement* question is, then, given the content that each label will have in a particular cell in a particular row of the table, how tall should the cell be in order to accomodate both labels and their contents?

The cells don't use autolayout, so we have to measure the cells manually. The procedure is simple but somewhat laborious. The NSAttributedString method `boundingRectWith-Size` answers the question, "How tall would this text be if laid out at a fixed width?"

Thus, for each cell, we must answer that question for each label, allow for any vertical spacing above the first label, below the second label, and between the labels, and sum the results.

Then, however, the question of *timing* intrudes. The problem is that the moment when `tableView:heightForRowAtIndexPath:` is called is very different from the moment when `tableView:cellForRowAtIndexPath:` is called. The runtime needs to know the heights of *everything* in the table immediately, before it starts asking for *any* cells. Thus, before we are asked `tableView:cellForRowAtIndexPath:` for even *one* row, we are asked `tableView:heightForRowAtIndexPath:` for *every* row.

In effect, this means we have to gather *all* the data and lay out *all* the cells before we can start showing the data in any *single* row. You can see why this can be problematic. We are being asked up front to measure the entire table, row by row. If that measurement takes a long time, the table view will remain blank during the calculation.

In addition, there is now a danger of duplicating our own work later on, during *layout* (in `tableView:cellForRowAtIndexPath:`, or perhaps in `tableView:willDisplay-Cell:forRowAtIndexPath:`); it appears we will ultimately be laying out every cell *twice*, once when we're asked for all the heights initially, and again later when we're asked for an actual cell.

My solution is to start with an empty array of CGFloat stored in a property, `self.row-Heights`. (A single array is all that's needed, because the table has just one section; the row number can thus serve directly as an index into the array.) Once that array is constructed, it can be used to supply a requested height *instantly*.

Calculating a cell height requires me to lay out that cell in at least a theoretical way. Thus, I have a utility method that lays out a cell for a given row, using the actual data for that row; let's say its name is `setUpCell:forIndexPath:`. It takes a cell and an index path, lays out the cell, and returns the cell's required height as a CGFloat.

When the delegate's `tableView:heightForRowAtIndexPath:` is called, either this is the very first time it's been called or it isn't. Thus, either we've already constructed `self.row-Heights` or we haven't. If we haven't, we construct it, by immediately calling the `setUp-Cell:forIndexPath:` utility method for *every* row and storing each resulting height in `self.rowHeights`. I have no real cells at this point in the story, but I'm using a UITable-ViewCell subclass designed in a nib, so I simply load the nib directly and pull out the cell to use a model. Now I'm ready to answer `tableView:heightForRowAtIndexPath:` for *any* row, *immediately* — all I have to do is return the appropriate value from the `self.rowHeights` array.

Now we come to `tableView:cellForRowAtIndexPath:`. Every time it is called, I call my `setUpCell:forIndexPath:` utility method *again* — but this time, I'm laying out the *real* cell (and ignoring the returned height value).

Measurement and layout with constraints

Constraints assist the process in two ways. Early in the process, in `tableView:height-ForRowAtIndexPath:`, they perform the *measurement* for us. How do they do that? Well, if the cell is designed with constraints that ultimately pin every subview to the `content-View` in such a way as to size the `contentView` unambiguously *from the inside out* — because every subview either is given explicit size constraints or else is the kind of view that has an implicit size based on its contents, like a label or an image view — then we can simply call `systemLayoutSizeFittingSize:` to tell us the resulting height of the cell.

Later in the process, when we come to `tableView:cellForRowAtIndexPath:`, constraints obviously help with *layout* of each cell, because that's what constraints do. Thanks to `dequeueReusableCellWithIdentifier:forIndexPath:`, the cell has the correct height, so the constraints are now determining the size of the subviews *from the outside in*.

 The one danger to watch out for here is that a `.SingleLine` separator eats into the cell height. This can cause the height of the cell in real life to differ very slightly from its height as calculated by `systemLayoutSizeFittingSize:`. If you've overdetermined the subview constraints, this can result in a conflict among constraints. Careful use of lowered constraint priorities can solve this problem nicely if it arises (though it is simpler, in practice, to set the cell separator to `.None`).

I'll show the actual code from another app of mine that uses this technique. My `setUp-Cell:forIndexPath:` no longer needs to return a value; I hand it a reference to a cell, it sets up the cell, and now I can do whatever I like with that cell. If this is the model cell being used for measurement in `tableView:heightForRowAtIndexPath:`, I call `system-LayoutSizeFittingSize:` to get the height; if it's the real cell generated by dequeuing in `tableView:cellForRowAtIndexPath:`, I return it. Thus, `setUpCell:forIndexPath:` is extremely simple: it just configures the cell with actual data from the model:

```
func setUpCell(cell:UITableViewCell, forIndexPath indexPath:NSIndexPath) {
    let row = indexPath.row
    (cell.viewWithTag(1) as! UILabel).text = self.titles[row]
    (cell.viewWithTag(2) as! UILabel).text = self.artists[row]
    (cell.viewWithTag(3) as! UILabel).text = self.composers[row]
}
```

My `self.rowHeights` property is typed as `[CGFloat?]`, and has been initialized to an array the same size as my data model (`self.titles` and so on) with every element set to nil. My implementation of `tableView:heightForRowAtIndexPath::` is called repeatedly (`self.titles.count` times, in fact) before the table is displayed; the *first* time it is called, I calculate *all* the row height values *once* and store them all in `self.rowHeights`:

```
override func tableView(tableView: UITableView,
    heightForRowAtIndexPath indexPath: NSIndexPath) -> CGFloat {
        let ix = indexPath.row
        if self.rowHeights[ix] == nil {
            let objects = UINib(nibName: "TrackCell2", bundle: nil)
                .instantiateWithOwner(nil, options: nil)
            let cell = objects.first as! UITableViewCell
            for ix in 0..<self.rowHeights.count {
                let indexPath = NSIndexPath(forRow: ix, inSection: 0)
                self.setUpCell(cell, forIndexPath: indexPath)
                let v = cell.contentView
                let sz = v.systemLayoutSizeFittingSize(
                    UILayoutFittingCompressedSize)
                self.rowHeights[ix] = sz.height
            }
        }
        return self.rowHeights[ix]!
}
```

My `tableView:cellForRowAtIndexPath:` implementation is trivial, because `setUp-Cell:forIndexPath:` does all the real work:

```
override func tableView(tableView: UITableView,
    cellForRowAtIndexPath indexPath: NSIndexPath) -> UITableViewCell {
        let cell = tableView.dequeueReusableCellWithIdentifier(
            "TrackCell", forIndexPath: indexPath) as! UITableViewCell
        self.setUpCell(cell, forIndexPath:indexPath)
        return cell
}
```

Estimated height

In iOS 7, three new table view properties were introduced:

- `estimatedRowHeight`

- `estimatedSectionHeaderHeight`

- `estimatedSectionFooterHeight`

To accompany those, there are also three table view delegate methods:

- `tableView:estimatedHeightForRowAtIndexPath:`

- `tableView:estimatedHeightForHeaderInSection:`

- `tableView:estimatedHeightForFooterInSection:`

The purpose of these properties and methods is to reduce the amount of time spent calculating row heights at the outset. If you supply an estimated row height, for example, then when `tableView:heightForRowAtIndexPath:` is called repeatedly before the table is displayed, it is called *only for the visible cells* of the table; for the remaining cells, the *estimated* height is used. The runtime thus has enough information to lay out the entire table very quickly: in a table with 300 rows, you don't have to provide the real heights for all 300 rows up front — you only have to provide real heights for, say, the half dozen visible rows. The downside is that this layout is incorrect, and will have to be corrected later: as new rows are scrolled into view, `tableView:heightForRowAtIndexPath:` will be called *again* for those new rows, and the layout of the whole table will be revised accordingly.

Thus, using an estimated height changes the *timing* of when `tableView:heightForRow-AtIndexPath:` is called. To illustrate, I'll revise the previous example to use estimated heights. The estimated height is set in `viewDidLoad`:

```
self.tableView.estimatedRowHeight = 75
```

Now in my `tableView:heightForRowAtIndexPath:` implementation, when I find that a requested height value in `self.rowHeights` is nil, I don't fill in *all* the values of `self.rowHeights` — I fill in *just that one height*. It's simply a matter of removing the for loop:

```
override func tableView(tableView: UITableView,
    heightForRowAtIndexPath indexPath: NSIndexPath) -> CGFloat {
        let ix = indexPath.row
        if self.rowHeights[ix] == nil {
            let objects = UINib(nibName: "TrackCell2", bundle: nil)
                .instantiateWithOwner(nil, options: nil)
            let cell = objects.first as! UITableViewCell
            let indexPath = NSIndexPath(forRow: ix, inSection: 0)
            self.setUpCell(cell, forIndexPath: indexPath)
            let v = cell.contentView
            let sz = v.systemLayoutSizeFittingSize(
                UILayoutFittingCompressedSize)
            self.rowHeights[ix] = sz.height
        }
        return self.rowHeights[ix]!
}
```

Automatic row height

New in iOS 8, a completely automatic calculation of variable row heights is introduced. This, in effect, simply does automatically what I'm already doing in `tableView:height-ForRowAtIndexPath:` in the preceding code: it relies upon autolayout for the calculation of each row's height, and it calculates and caches a row's height the first time it is needed, as it is about to appear on the screen.

To use this mechanism, first configure your cell using autolayout to determine the size of the `contentView` from the inside out. Now all you have to do is to set the table view's `estimatedRowHeight` and *don't* implement `tableView:heightForRowAtIndexPath:` at all!

Thus, to adopt this approach in my app, all I have to do at this point is delete my `table-View:heightForRowAtIndexPath:` implementation entirely.

This approach, however, though obviously easiest, is not necessarily best. You will have to measure performance and decide which approach is most suitable. The four techniques I've outlined here run not only from oldest to newest but also from fastest to slowest. Manual layout is faster than calling `systemLayoutSizeFittingSize:`, and calculating the heights of all rows up front, though it may cause a longer pause initially, makes *scrolling* faster for the user because no row heights have to be calculated while scrolling.

Table View Cell Selection

A table view cell has a normal state, a highlighted state (according to its `highlighted` property), and a selected state (according to its `selected` property). It is possible to change these states directly, possibly with animation, by calling `set-Highlighted:animated:` or `setSelected:animated:` on the cell. But you don't want to act behind the table's back, so you are more likely to manage selection through the table view, letting the table view manage and track the state of its cells.

These two states are closely related. In particular, when a cell is selected, it propagates the highlighted state down through its subviews by setting each subview's `highlighted` property if it has one. That is why a UILabel's `highlightedTextColor` applies when the cell is selected. Similarly, a UIImageView (such as the cell's `imageView`) can have a `highlightedImage` that is shown when the cell is selected, and a UIControl (such as a UIButton) takes on its `highlighted` state when the cell is selected.

One of the chief purposes of your table view is likely to be to let the user select a cell. This will be possible, provided you have not set the value of the table view's `allows-Selection` property to `false`. The user taps a normal cell, and the cell switches to its selected state. By default, this will mean that the cell is redrawn with a gray background view, but you can change this at the individual cell level, as I've already explained: you can set a cell's `selectedBackgroundView` (or `multipleSelectionBackgroundView`), or change its `selectionStyle`. If the user taps an already selected cell, by default it stays selected.

Table views can permit the user to select multiple cells simultaneously. Set the table view's `allowsMultipleSelection` property to `true`. If the user taps an already selected cell, by default it is deselected.

Managing Cell Selection

Your code can learn and manage the selection through these UITableView instance methods:

`indexPathForSelectedRow`
`indexPathsForSelectedRows`

These methods report the currently selected row(s), or nil if there is no selection. Don't accidentally call the wrong one. For example, calling `indexPathForSelected-Row` when the table view allows multiple selection gives a result that will have you scratching your head in confusion. (As usual, I speak from experience.)

`selectRowAtIndexPath:animated:scrollPosition:`

The animation involves fading in the selection, but the user may not see this unless the selected row is already visible. The last parameter dictates whether and how the table view should scroll to reveal the newly selected row; your choices (UITable-ViewScrollPosition) are `.Top`, `.Middle`, `.Bottom`, and `.None`. For the first three options, the table view scrolls (with animation, if the second parameter is `true`) so that the selected row is at the specified position among the visible cells. For `.None`, the table view does not scroll; if the selected row is not already visible, it does not become visible.

`deselectRowAtIndexPath:animated:`

Deselects the given row (if it is selected); the optional animation involves fading out the selection. No automatic scrolling takes place.

To deselect *all* currently selected rows, call `selectRowAtIndexPath:animated:scroll-Position:` with a nil index path. Reloading a cell's data also deselects that cell, and calling `reloadData` deselects all selected rows.

Responding to Cell Selection

Response to user selection is through the table view's delegate:

- `tableView:shouldHighlightRowAtIndexPath:`
- `tableView:didHighlightRowAtIndexPath:`
- `tableView:didUnhighlightRowAtIndexPath:`
- `tableView:willSelectRowAtIndexPath:`
- `tableView:didSelectRowAtIndexPath:`
- `tableView:willDeselectRowAtIndexPath:`
- `tableView:didDeselectRowAtIndexPath:`

Despite their names, the two "will" methods are actually "should" methods and expect a return value:

- Return nil to prevent the selection (or deselection) from taking place.

- Return the index path handed in as argument to permit the selection (or deselection), or a different index path to cause a different cell to be selected (or deselected).

The "highlight" methods are more sensibly named, and they arrive first, so you can return `false` from `tableView:shouldHighlightRowAtIndexPath:` to prevent a cell from being selected.

Let's focus in more detail on the relationship between a cell's highlighted state and its selected state. They are, in fact, two different states. When the user touches a cell, the cell passes through a complete highlight cycle. Then, if the touch turns out to be the beginning of a scroll motion, the cell is unhighlighted immediately, and the cell is not selected. Otherwise, the cell is unhighlighted and selected.

But the user doesn't know the difference between these two states: whether the cell is highlighted or selected, the cell's subviews are highlighted, and the `selectedBackgroundView` appears. Thus, if the user touches and scrolls, what the user sees is the flash of the `selectedBackgroundView` and the highlighted subviews, until the table begins to scroll and the cell returns to normal. If the user touches and lifts the finger, the `selectedBackgroundView` and highlighted subviews appear and remain; there is actually a moment in the sequence where the cell has been highlighted and then unhighlighted and not yet selected, but the user doesn't see any momentary unhighlighting of the cell, because no redraw moment occurs (see Chapter 4).

Here's a summary of the sequence:

1. The user's finger goes down. If `shouldHighlight` permits, the cell highlights, which propagates to its subviews. Then `didHighlight` arrives.
2. There is a redraw moment. Thus, the user will *see* the cell as highlighted (including the appearance of the `selectedBackgroundView`), regardless of what happens next.
3. The user either starts scrolling or lifts the finger. The cell unhighlights, which also propagates to its subviews, and `didUnhighlight` arrives.
   a. If the user starts scrolling, there is a redraw moment, so the user now sees the cell unhighlighted. The sequence ends.
   b. If the user merely lifts the finger, there is no redraw moment, so the cell keeps its highlighted appearance. The sequence continues.
4. If `willSelect` permits, the cell is selected, and `didSelect` arrives. The cell is *not* highlighted, but highlighting is propagated to its subviews.
5. There's another redraw moment. The user still sees the cell as highlighted (including the appearance of the `selectedBackgroundView`).

When `tableView:willSelectRowAtIndexPath:` is called because the user taps a cell, and if this table view permits only single cell selection, `tableView:willDeselectRowAt-IndexPath:` will be called subsequently for any previously selected cells.

Here's an example of implementing `tableView:willSelectRowAtIndexPath:`. The default behavior for `allowsSelection` (not multiple selection) is that the user can select by tapping, and the cell remains selected; if the user taps a selected row, the selection does not change. We can alter this so that tapping a selected row deselects it:

```
override func tableView(tableView: UITableView,
    willSelectRowAtIndexPath indexPath: NSIndexPath) -> NSIndexPath? {
        if tableView.cellForRowAtIndexPath(indexPath)!.selected {
            tableView.deselectRowAtIndexPath(indexPath, animated:false)
            return nil
        }
        return indexPath
}
```

Navigation From a Table View

An extremely common response to user selection is navigation. A master–detail architecture is typical: the table view lists things the user can see in more detail, and a tap displays the detailed view of the selected thing. On the iPhone, very often the table view will be in a navigation interface, and you will respond to user selection by creating the detail view and pushing it onto the navigation controller's stack.

For example, here's the code from my Albumen app that navigates from the list of albums to the list of songs in the album that the user has tapped:

```
override func tableView(tableView: UITableView,
    didSelectRowAtIndexPath indexPath: NSIndexPath) {
        let t = TracksViewController(
            mediaItemCollection: self.albums[indexPath.row])
        self.navigationController!.pushViewController(t, animated: true)
}
```

In a storyboard, when you draw a segue from a UITableViewCell, you are given a choice of two segue triggers: Selection Segue and Accessory Action. If you create a Selection Segue, the segue will be triggered when the user selects a cell. Thus you can readily push or present another view controller in response to cell selection.

If you're using a UITableViewController, then by default, whenever the table view appears, the selection is cleared automatically in `viewWillAppear:`, and the scroll indicators are flashed in `viewDidAppear:`. You can prevent this automatic clearing of the selection by setting the table view controller's `clearsSelectionOnViewWillAppear` to `false`. I sometimes do that, preferring to implement deselection in `viewDidAppear:`; the effect is that when the user returns to the table, the row is still momentarily selected before it deselects itself.

By convention, if selecting a table view cell causes navigation, the cell should be given an `accessoryType` (UITableViewCellAccessory) of `.DisclosureIndicator`. This is a plain gray right-pointing chevron at the right end of the cell. The chevron itself doesn't respond to user interaction; it's not a button, but is just a visual cue that the user can tap the cell to learn more.

Two additional `accessoryType` settings *are* buttons:

`.DetailButton`
> Drawn as a letter "i" in a circle.

`.DetailDisclosureButton`
> Drawn like `.DetailButton`, along with a disclosure indicator chevron to its right.

To respond to the tapping of an accessory button, implement the table view delegate's `tableView:accessoryButtonTappedForRowWithIndexPath:`. Or, in a storyboard, you can Control-drag a connection from a cell and choose an Accessory Action segue.

A common convention is that selecting the cell as a whole does one thing and tapping the detail button does something else. For example, in Apple's Phone app, tapping a contact's listing in the Recents table places a call to that contact, but tapping the detail button navigates to that contact's detail view.

Cell Choice and Static Tables

Another use of cell selection is to implement a choice among cells, where a section of a table effectively functions as an iOS alternative to OS X radio buttons. The table view usually has the grouped format. An `accessoryType` of `.Checkmark` is typically used to indicate the current choice. Implementing radio button behavior is up to you.

As an example, I'll implement the interface shown in Figure 8-2. The table view has the grouped style, with two sections. The first section, with a "Size" header, has three mutually exclusive choices: "Easy," "Normal," and "Hard." The second section, with a "Style" header, has two choices: "Animals" or "Snacks."

This is a *static table*; its contents are known beforehand and won't change. In a case like this, if we're using a UITableViewController subclass instantiated from a storyboard, the nib editor lets us design the entire table, including the headers and the cells *and their content*, directly in the storyboard. Select the table and set its Content pop-up menu in the Attributes inspector to Static Cells to make the table editable in this way (Figure 8-6).

Even though each cell is designed initially in the storyboard, I can still implement `tableView:cellForRowAtIndexPath:` to call `super` and then add further functionality. That's how I'll add the checkmarks. The user defaults are storing the current choice in each of the two categories; there's a `"Size"` preference and a `"Style"` preference, each consisting of a string denoting the title of the chosen cell:

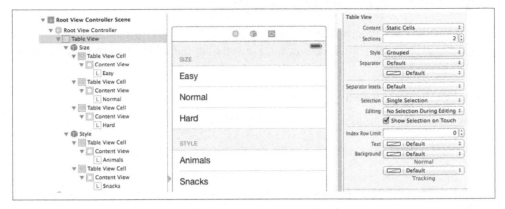

Figure 8-6. Designing a static table in the storyboard editor

```
override func tableView(tv: UITableView,
    cellForRowAtIndexPath indexPath: NSIndexPath) -> UITableViewCell {
        let cell = super.tableView(
            tv, cellForRowAtIndexPath:indexPath) as! UITableViewCell
        let ud = NSUserDefaults.standardUserDefaults()
        cell.accessoryType = .None
        if ud.valueForKey("Style") as? String == cell.textLabel!.text! ||
            ud.valueForKey("Size") as? String == cell.textLabel!.text! {
                cell.accessoryType = .Checkmark
        }
        return cell
}
```

When the user taps a cell, the cell is selected. I want the user to see that selection momentarily, as feedback, but then I want to deselect, adjusting the checkmarks so that that cell is the only one checked in its section. In `tableView:didSelectRowAtIndexPath:`, I set the user defaults, and then I reload the table view's data. This removes the selection and causes `tableView:cellForRowAtIndexPath:` to be called to adjust the checkmarks:

```
override func tableView(tv: UITableView,
    didSelectRowAtIndexPath indexPath: NSIndexPath) {
        let ud = NSUserDefaults.standardUserDefaults()
        let setting = tv.cellForRowAtIndexPath(indexPath)!.textLabel!.text
        let header = self.tableView(
            tv, titleForHeaderInSection:indexPath.section)!
        ud.setValue(setting, forKey:header)
        tv.reloadData()
}
```

Table View Scrolling and Layout

A UITableView is a UIScrollView, so everything you already know about scroll views is applicable (Chapter 7). In addition, a table view supplies two convenience scrolling methods:

- `scrollToRowAtIndexPath:atScrollPosition:animated:`
- `scrollToNearestSelectedRowAtScrollPosition:animated:`

The `scrollPosition` parameter is as for `selectRowAtIndexPath:...`, discussed earlier in this chapter.

The following UITableView methods mediate between the table's bounds coordinates on the one hand and table structure on the other:

- `indexPathForRowAtPoint:`
- `indexPathsForRowsInRect:`
- `rectForSection:`
- `rectForRowAtIndexPath:`
- `rectForFooterInSection:`
- `rectForHeaderInSection:`

The table's own header and footer are direct subviews of the table view, so their positions within the table's bounds are given by their frames.

Table View State Restoration

If a UITableView participates in state saving and restoration (Chapter 6), the restoration mechanism would like to restore the selection and the scroll position. This behavior is automatic; the restoration mechanism knows both what cells should be visible and what cells should be selected, in terms of their index paths. If that's satisfactory, you've no further work to do.

In some apps, however, there is a possibility that when the app is relaunched, the underlying data may have been rearranged somehow. Perhaps what's meaningful in dictating what the user should see in such a case is not the previous *rows* but the previous *data*. The state saving and restoration mechanism doesn't know anything about the relationship between the cells and the underlying data. If you'd like to tell it, adopt the UIDataSourceModelAssociation protocol and implement two methods:

`modelIdentifierForElementAtIndexPath:inView:`
> Based on the index path, you return some string that you will *later* be able to use to identify uniquely this bit of model data.

`indexPathForElementWithModelIdentifier:inView:`
> Based on the unique identifier you provided earlier, you return the index path at which this bit of model data is displayed in the table *now*.

Devising a system of unique identification and incorporating it into your data model is up to you.

Table View Searching

A common need is to make a table view searchable, typically through a search field (a UISearchBar; see Chapter 12). A commonly used interface for presenting the results of such a search is a table view! Thus, in effect, entering characters in the search field appears to filter the original table.

New in iOS 8, this interface is managed through a new UIViewController subclass, UISearchController. (This effectively displaces the UISearchDisplayController class from iOS 7 and before, which is not discussed in this edition.) It is extremely important to understand, before I tell you about UISearchController, that it has nothing to do, *per se*, with table views! A table view is not the only thing you might want to search, and a table view is not the only way you might want to present the results of a search. That, indeed, is exactly *why* UISearchController has been introduced in iOS 8 — it's a way of making the presentation of search results completely agnostic about the form of those results. However, I'm introducing this class in a chapter about table views, so what I'm going to describe is the particular (and common) case of how to use a table view to present the results of searching a table view.

Configuring a Search Controller

Here are the steps for configuring a UISearchController:

1. Create *and retain* a UISearchController instance.

2. As part of the previous step, you'll call the designated initializer, `init(search-ResultsController:)`. The parameter is a view controller — a UIViewController subclass instance that you will have created for this purpose. The search controller will retain this view controller as a child view controller. When the time comes to display search results, the search controller will *present* itself as a presented view controller, with this view controller's view inside its own view; that is where the search results are to be displayed.

3. Assign to the search controller's `searchResultsUpdater` an object to be notified when the search results change. This must be an object adopting the UISearchResultsUpdating protocol, which means that it implements one method: `updateSearchResultsForSearchController:`. Very typically, this will be the same view controller that you passed as the `searchResultsController:` parameter when you initialized the search controller, but no law says that it has to be the same object or even that it has to be a view controller.

4. Acquire the search controller's `searchBar` and put it into the interface.

Thinking about these steps, you can see what the search controller is proposing to do for you — and what it *isn't* going to do for you. It isn't going to display the search results. It isn't going to manage the search results. It isn't even going to do any searching! It owns a search bar, which you have placed into the interface; and it's going to keep an eye on that search bar. When the user taps in that search bar to begin searching, the search controller will respond by presenting itself and managing the view controller you specified. Then, as the user enters characters in the search bar, the search controller will keep calling the search results updater's `updateSearchResultsForSearchController:`. Finally, when the user taps the search bar's Cancel button, the search controller will dismiss itself.

A UISearchController has just a few other properties you might want to configure:

`dimsBackgroundDuringPresentation`
Whether a "dimming view" should appear behind the search controller's own view. Defaults to `true`, but I'll give an example later where it needs to be set to `false`.

`hidesNavigationBarDuringPresentation`
Whether a navigation bar, if present, should be hidden. The default is `true`.

A UISearchController can also be assigned a `delegate` (UISearchControllerDelegate), which is notified before and after presentation and dismissal (and has one more important ability that I'll mention a bit later).

The minimalistic nature of the search controller's behavior is exactly the source of its power and flexibility, because it leaves you the freedom to take care of the details however you please, as I shall now demonstrate.

Using a Search Controller

I'll demonstrate several variations on the theme of using a search controller to make a table view searchable.

Figure 8-7. Searching a table

Minimal search results table

Let's start with what I take to be the simplest possible case. We will have two table view controllers — one managing the original table, the other managing the search results table. The original table can be as elaborate as you please; we'll use the table of U.S. states, with sections and an index, developed earlier in this chapter. The search results table, on the other hand, can be as minimal as you please; I propose to use a rock-bottom table with `.Default` style cells, and each search result will be the text of a cell's `textLabel` (Figure 8-7).

Here's the configuration of the original table's UITableViewController. I have a property, `self.searcher`, waiting to retain the search controller. I also have a second UITable-ViewController subclass, which I have rather boringly called SearchResultsController, whose job will be to obtain and present the search results. In `viewDidLoad`, I instantiate SearchResultsController, create the UISearchController, and put its search bar into the interface as the table view's header view (and scroll to hide that search bar initially, a common convention):

```
let src = SearchResultsController(data: self.sectionData)
let searcher = UISearchController(searchResultsController: src)
self.searcher = searcher
searcher.searchResultsUpdater = src
let b = searcher.searchBar
b.sizeToFit() // crucial, trust me on this one
b.autocapitalizationType = .None
self.tableView.tableHeaderView = b
self.tableView.reloadData()
self.tableView.scrollToRowAtIndexPath(
    NSIndexPath(forRow: 0, inSection: 0),
    atScrollPosition:.Top, animated:false)
```

Adding the search bar as the table view's header view has an odd side effect: it causes the table view's background color to be covered by an ugly gray color, visible above the search bar when the user scrolls down. The official workaround is to assign the table view a backgroundView with the desired color.

Now we turn to SearchResultsController. It is a completely vanilla table view controller, *qua* table view controller. But I've given it two special features:

- It is capable of *receiving the searchable data.* You can see this happening, in fact, in the first line of the preceding code.
- It is capable of *filtering* that data and displaying the filtered data in its table view.

I'm not using sections in the SearchResultsController's table, so it will simplify things if, as I receive the searchable data in the SearchResultsController, I flatten it from an array of arrays to a simple array:

```
init(data:[[String]]) {
    self.originalData = data.reduce([String](),combine:+)
    super.init(nibName: nil, bundle: nil)
}
```

I have stored the flattened data in the self.originalData array, but what I display in the table view is a *different* array, self.filteredData. This is initially empty, because there are no search results until the user starts typing in the search field:

```
override func numberOfSectionsInTableView(tableView: UITableView) -> Int {
    return 1
}
override func tableView(tableView: UITableView,
    numberOfRowsInSection section: Int) -> Int {
        return self.filteredData.count
}
override func tableView(tableView: UITableView,
    cellForRowAtIndexPath indexPath: NSIndexPath) -> UITableViewCell {
        let cell = tableView.dequeueReusableCellWithIdentifier(
            "Cell", forIndexPath: indexPath) as! UITableViewCell
        cell.textLabel!.text = self.filteredData[indexPath.row]
        return cell
}
```

All of that is sheer boilerplate and is perfectly obvious; but how does our search results table go from being empty to displaying any search results? That's the second special feature of SearchResultsController. It adopts UISearchResultsUpdating, so it implements updateSearchResultsForSearchController:. In that implementation, it uses the current text of the search controller's searchBar to filter self.originalData into self.filteredData and reloads the table view:

```
func updateSearchResultsForSearchController(
    searchController: UISearchController) {
        let sb = searchController.searchBar
        let target = sb.text
        self.filteredData = self.originalData.filter {
            s in
            let options = NSStringCompareOptions.CaseInsensitiveSearch
            let found = s.rangeOfString(target, options: options)
            return (found != nil)
        }
        self.tableView.reloadData()
}
```

That's all! Of course, it's an artificially simple example; I'm describing the interface and the use of a UISearchController, not a real app. In real life you would presumably want to allow the user to *do* something with the search results, perhaps by tapping on a cell in the search results table.

Search bar scope buttons

If we wanted our search bar to have scope buttons, we would set its scopeButton-Titles immediately after calling sizeToFit in the preceding code:

```
let b = searcher.searchBar
b.sizeToFit() // crucial, trust me on this one
b.scopeButtonTitles = ["Starts", "Contains"]
```

The scope buttons don't appear in the table header view, but they do appear when the search controller presents itself. However, the search controller does not automatically call us back in updateSearchResultsForSearchController: when the user taps on a scope button. I regard that as a bug, but it's easy to work around it: we must simply make ourselves the search bar's delegate, so as to be notified through the delegate method searchBar:selectedScopeButtonIndexDidChange: — which can then turn right around and call updateSearchResultsForSearchController: (provided it has a reference to the search controller, which is easy to arrange beforehand). Here, I'll make our SearchResultsController respond to the distinction that a state name either starts with or contains the search text:

```
func updateSearchResultsForSearchController(
    searchController: UISearchController) {
        self.searchController = searchController // weak reference
        let sb = searchController.searchBar
        let target = sb.text
        self.filteredData = self.originalData.filter {
            s in
            var options = NSStringCompareOptions.CaseInsensitiveSearch
            // we now have scope buttons; 0 means "starts with"
            if searchController.searchBar.selectedScopeButtonIndex == 0 {
                options = options | .AnchoredSearch
            }
```

```
            let found = s.rangeOfString(target, options: options)
            return (found != nil)
        }
        self.tableView.reloadData()
    }
    func searchBar(searchBar: UISearchBar,
        selectedScopeButtonIndexDidChange selectedScope: Int) {
            self.updateSearchResultsForSearchController(self.searchController!)
    }
```

Customizing the presentation

What should really have you jumping out of your skin with excitement is that the search controller is a presented view controller. This means that the presentation is customizable, as I explained in "Custom Presented View Controller Transition" on page 324. In particular:

- You can customize the presentation *animation* by setting the search controller's `transitioningDelegate`.

- As part of customizing the animation, you can (in fact you must) take charge of *placing the search bar* into the search controller's view; of course you can animate this however you like.

- The search controller's presentation controller is a normal presentation controller, and thus can be adaptive. The significance of this will be clearer when I talk about presenting search results in a popover in Chapter 9.

- If the search controller's delegate implements `presentSearchController:`, the very act of *presenting the search controller* is left up to you. If you don't call `presentViewController:animated:completion:` here, it will be called for you, but this is your chance to perform preparatory customizations, to add a completion handler, to present without animation, and so on.

 I was hoping that it would be possible also to customize the presentation position and chrome by setting the search controller's `modalPresentationStyle` to `.Custom`, but in my tests that didn't work, in the sense that the transitioning delegate's `presentationControllerForPresentedViewController:...` was never called.

In this excerpt from the animation controller's `animateTransition:`, I cause the search bar to appear during the presentation by sliding it down from above:

```
if let v2 = v2 { // presenting, vc2 is the search controller
    con.addSubview(v2) // con is the container view
    v2.frame = r2end
    let sc = vc2 as! UISearchController
    let sb = sc.searchBar
```

```
        sb.removeFromSuperview() // take it out of the original table view
        sb.showsScopeBar = true
        sb.sizeToFit()
        v2.addSubview(sb)
        sb.frame.origin.y = -sb.frame.height
        UIView.animateWithDuration(0.3, animations: {
            sb.frame.origin.y = 0
            }, completion: {
                _ in
                sb.setShowsCancelButton(true, animated: true)
                transitionContext.completeTransition(true)
        })
}
```

No secondary search results view controller

As a final variation, I'll demonstrate how to use a search controller *without* a distinct search results view controller. There will be no SearchResultsController; instead, we'll present the search results *in the original table view*.

To configure our search controller, we pass nil as its `searchResultsController` and set ourselves as the `searchResultsUpdater`. We also set the search controller's `dims-BackgroundDuringPresentation` to `false`; this allows the original table view to remain *visible and touchable* behind the search controller's view:

```
let searcher = UISearchController(searchResultsController:nil)
self.searcher = searcher
searcher.dimsBackgroundDuringPresentation = false
searcher.searchResultsUpdater = self
searcher.delegate = self
```

The implementation is a simple problem in table data source management. We keep an immutable copy of our data model arrays, `self.sectionData` and `self.section-Names` — let's call the copies `self.originalSectionData` and `self.originalSection-Names`. These copies are unused if we're not searching. If we *are* searching, we hear about it through the search controller's delegate methods, and we raise a Bool flag in a property:

```
func willPresentSearchController(searchController: UISearchController) {
    self.searching = true
}
func willDismissSearchController(searchController: UISearchController) {
    self.searching = false
}
```

Any of our table view delegate or data source methods can consult this flag. For example, it might be nice to remove the index while searching is going on:

```
override func sectionIndexTitlesForTableView(tableView: UITableView)
    -> [AnyObject]! {
        return self.searching ? nil : self.sectionNames
}
```

All that remains is to implement updateSearchResultsForSearchController: to filter self.originalSectionData and self.originalSectionNames into the data model arrays self.sectionData and self.sectionNames — or to copy them unfiltered if the search bar's text is empty, which is also the signal that the search controller presentation is over:

```
func updateSearchResultsForSearchController(
    searchController: UISearchController) {
        let sb = searchController.searchBar
        let target = sb.text
        if target == "" {
            self.sectionNames = self.originalSectionNames
            self.sectionData = self.originalSectionData
            self.tableView.reloadData()
            return
        }
        // we have a target string
        self.sectionData = self.originalSectionData.map {
            $0.filter {
                let options = NSStringCompareOptions.CaseInsensitiveSearch
                let found = $0.rangeOfString(target, options: options)
                return (found != nil)
            }
        }.filter {$0.count > 0}
        self.sectionNames = self.sectionData.map {prefix($0[0],1)}
        self.tableView.reloadData()
}
```

Table View Editing

A table view cell has a normal state and an editing state, according to its editing property. The editing state is typically indicated visually by one or more of the following:

Editing controls

> At least one editing control will usually appear, such as a Minus button (for deletion) at the left side.

Shrinkage

> The content of the cell will usually shrink to allow room for an editing control. If there is no editing control, you can prevent a cell shifting its left end rightward in editing mode with the table delegate's tableView:shouldIndentWhileEditingRow-AtIndexPath:. (There is also a cell property shouldIndentWhileEditing, but I find it unreliable.)

Changing accessory view

> The cell's accessory view will change automatically in accordance with its editing-AccessoryType or editingAccessoryView. If you assign neither, so that they are nil, the cell's existing accessory view will vanish when in editing mode.

As with selection, you could set a cell's `editing` property directly (or use `set-Editing:animated:` to get animation), but you are more likely to let the table view manage editability. Table view editability is controlled through the table view's `editing` property, usually by sending the table the `setEditing:animated:` message. The table is then responsible for putting its cells into edit mode.

A cell in edit mode can also be selected by the user if the table view's `allowsSelection-DuringEditing` or `allowsMultipleSelectionDuringEditing` is `true`. But this would be unusual.

Putting the table into edit mode is usually left up to the user. A typical interface would be an Edit button that the user can tap. In a navigation interface, we might have our view controller supply the button as a bar button item in the navigation bar:

```
let b = UIBarButtonItem(
    barButtonSystemItem: .Edit, target: self, action: "doEdit:")
self.navigationItem.rightBarButtonItem = b
```

Our action handler will be responsible for putting the table into edit mode, so in its simplest form it might look like this:

```
func doEdit(sender:AnyObject?) {
    self.tableView.setEditing(true, animated:true)
}
```

But that does not solve the problem of getting *out* of editing mode. The standard solution is to have the Edit button replace itself by a Done button:

```
func doEdit(sender:AnyObject?) {
    var which : UIBarButtonSystemItem
    if !self.tableView.editing {
        self.tableView.setEditing(true, animated:true)
        which = .Done
    } else {
        self.tableView.setEditing(false, animated:true)
        which = .Edit
    }
    let b = UIBarButtonItem(
        barButtonSystemItem: which, target: self, action: "doEdit:")
    self.navigationItem.rightBarButtonItem = b
}
```

However, it turns out that all of that is completely unnecessary! If we want standard behavior, it's already implemented for us. A UIViewController's `editButtonItem` method vends a bar button item that calls the UIViewController's `setEditing:animated:` when tapped, tracks whether we're in edit mode with the UIViewController's `editing` property, and changes its own title accordingly (Edit or Done). Moreover, a UITable-ViewController's implementation of `setEditing:animated:` is to call `set-Editing:animated:` on its table view. Thus, if we're using a UITableViewController, we get all of that behavior for free, just by calling `editButtonItem` and inserting the resulting button into our interface:

```
self.navigationItem.rightBarButtonItem = self.editButtonItem()
```

When the table view enters edit mode, it consults its data source and delegate about the editability of individual rows:

`tableView:canEditRowAtIndexPath:` *to the data source*
 The default is `true`. The data source can return `false` to prevent the given row from entering edit mode.

`tableView:editingStyleForRowAtIndexPath:` *to the delegate*
 Each standard editing style corresponds to a control that will appear in the cell. The choices (UITableViewCellEditingStyle) are:

 `.Delete`
  The cell shows a Minus button at its left end. The user can tap this to summon a Delete button, which the user can then tap to confirm the deletion. This is the default.

 `.Insert`
  The cell shows a Plus button at its left end; this is usually taken to be an insert button.

 `.None`
  No editing control appears.

If the user taps an insert button (the Plus button) or a delete button (the Delete button that appears after the user taps the Minus button), the data source is sent the `table-View:commitEditingStyle:forRowAtIndexPath:` message and is responsible for obeying it. In your response, you will probably want to alter the structure of the table, and UITableView methods for doing this are provided:

- `insertRowsAtIndexPaths:withRowAnimation:`

- `deleteRowsAtIndexPaths:withRowAnimation:`

- `insertSections:withRowAnimation:`

- `deleteSections:withRowAnimation:`

- `moveSection:toSection:`

- `moveRowAtIndexPath:toIndexPath:`

The row animations here are effectively the same ones discussed earlier in connection with refreshing table data; `.Left` for an insertion means to slide in from the left, and for a deletion it means to slide out to the left, and so on. The two "move" methods provide animation with no provision for customizing it.

If you're issuing more than one of these commands, you can combine them by surrounding them with `beginUpdates` and `endUpdates`, forming an *updates block*. An updates block combines not just the animations but the requested changes themselves. This relieves you from having to worry about how a command is affected by earlier commands in the same updates block; indeed, order of commands within an updates block doesn't really matter.

For example, if you delete row 1 of a certain section and then (in a separate command) delete row 2 of the same section, you delete two successive rows, just as you would expect; the notion "2" does not change its meaning because you deleted an earlier row first, because you *didn't* delete an earlier row first — the updates block combines the commands for you, interpreting both index paths with respect to the state of the table before any changes are made. If you perform insertions and deletions together in one animation, the deletions are performed first, regardless of the order of your commands, and the insertion row and section numbers refer to the state of the table after the deletions.

An updates block can also include `reloadRows...` and `reloadSections...` commands (but not `reloadData`).

I need hardly emphasize once again (but I will anyway) that view is not model. It is one thing to rearrange the appearance of the table, another to alter the underlying data. It is up to you to make certain you do both together. Do not, even for a moment, permit the data and the view to get out of synch with each other! If you delete a row, remove from the model the datum that it represents. The runtime will try to help you with error messages if you forget to do this, but in the end the responsibility is yours. I'll give examples as we proceed.

Deleting Cells

Deletion of cells is the default, so there's not much for us to do in order to implement it. If our view controller is a UITableViewController and we've displayed the Edit button in a navigation bar, everything happens automatically: when the user taps the Edit button, the view controller's `setEditing:animated:` is called, the table view's `setEditing:animated:` is called, and the cells all show the Minus button at the left end. The user can then tap a Minus button; a Delete button is shown at the cell's right end. You can customize the Delete button's title with the table view delegate method `tableView:titleForDeleteConfirmationButtonForRowAtIndexPath:`.

What is *not* automatic is the actual response to the Delete button. For that, we need to implement `tableView:commitEditingStyle:forRowAtIndexPath:`. Typically, you'll remove the corresponding entry from the underlying model data, and you'll call `deleteRowsAtIndexPaths:withRowAnimation:` or `deleteSections:withRowAnimation:` to update the appearance of the table. As I said a moment ago, you must delete the row or section in such a way as to keep the table display coordinated with the model's structure. Otherwise, the app may crash (with an extremely helpful error message).

To illustrate, let's suppose once again that the underlying model is a pair of parallel arrays of strings (`self.sectionNames`) and arrays (`self.sectionData`). Our approach will be in two stages:

1. Deal with the model data. We'll delete the datum for the requested row; if this empties the section array, we'll also delete that section array and the corresponding section name.

2. Deal with the table's appearance. If we deleted the section array, we'll call `delete-Sections:withRowAnimation:` (and reload the section index if there is one); otherwise, we'll call `deleteRowsAtIndexPaths:withRowAnimation::`

```
override func tableView(tableView: UITableView,
    commitEditingStyle editingStyle: UITableViewCellEditingStyle,
    forRowAtIndexPath ip: NSIndexPath) {
        switch editingStyle {
        case .Delete:
            if self.sectionData[ip.section].count == 0 {
                self.sectionData.removeAtIndex(ip.section)
                self.sectionNames.removeAtIndex(ip.section)
                tableView.deleteSections(NSIndexSet(index: ip.section),
                    withRowAnimation:.Automatic)
                tableView.reloadSectionIndexTitles()
            } else {
                tableView.deleteRowsAtIndexPaths([ip],
                    withRowAnimation:.Automatic)
            }
        default: break
        }
}
```

The user can also delete a row by sliding it to the left to show its Delete button *without* having explicitly entered edit mode; no other row is editable, and no other editing controls are shown. This feature is implemented "for free" by virtue of our having supplied an implementation of `tableView:commitEditingStyle:forRowAtIndexPath:`. If you're like me, your first response will be: "Thanks for the free functionality, Apple, and now how do I turn this off?" Because the Edit button is already using the UIView-Controller's `editing` property to track edit mode, we can take advantage of this and refuse to let any cells be edited unless the view controller *is* in edit mode:

```
override func tableView(tableView: UITableView,
    editingStyleForRowAtIndexPath indexPath: NSIndexPath)
    -> UITableViewCellEditingStyle {
        return self.editing ? .Delete : .None
}
```

Custom Action Buttons

The table cell is itself inside a little horizontal scroll view; the user who slides a cell to the left is actually scrolling the cell to the left, revealing the Delete button behind it. New in iOS 8, you can customize what buttons will appear when the user slides a cell leftward to enter edit mode, or enters edit mode and taps the Minus button.

To configure the buttons for a row of the table, implement the table view delegate method `tableView:editActionsForRowAtIndexPath:` and return an array of UITableViewRowAction objects in right-to-left order (or nil to get the default Delete button). Create a row action button with its initializer, `init(style:title:handler:)`. The parameters are:

style:
> A UITableViewRowActionStyle, either `.Default` or `.Normal`. By default, `.Default` is a red button signalling a destructive action, like the Delete button, while `.Normal` is a gray button. You can subsequently change the color by setting the button's `backgroundColor`.

title:
> The text of the button.

handler:
> A block (closure) to be called when the button is tapped; it takes two parameters, a reference to the row action and the index path for this cell.

If you want the user to be able to slide the cell to reveal the buttons, you must implement `tableView:commitEditingStyle:forRowAtIndexPath:`, even if your implementation is empty. But even if you *don't* implement this method, the buttons can be revealed by putting the table view into edit mode and tapping the Minus button. Your `handler:` can call `tableView:commitEditingStyle:forRowAtIndexPath:` if appropriate; a custom Delete button, for example, might do so.

In this example, we give our cells a blue Mark button in addition to the default Delete button:

```
override func tableView(tableView: UITableView,
    editActionsForRowAtIndexPath indexPath: NSIndexPath) -> [AnyObject]? {
        let act = UITableViewRowAction(style: .Normal, title: "Mark") {
            action, ip in
            println("Mark") // in real life, do something here
        }
        act.backgroundColor = UIColor.blueColor()
        let act2 = UITableViewRowAction(style: .Default, title: "Delete") {
            action, ip in
            self.tableView(self.tableView, commitEditingStyle:.Delete,
```

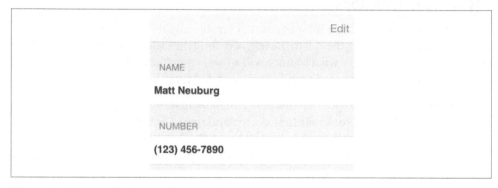

Figure 8-8. A simple phone directory app

```
                forRowAtIndexPath:ip)
        }
        return [act2, act]
    }
```

Configuration of these buttons is disappointingly inflexible — for example, you can't achieve anything like the iOS 8 Mail app's interface — and many developers will prefer to continue rolling their own sliding table cells, as in the past.

Editable Content in Cells

A cell might have content that the user can edit directly, such as a UITextField (Chapter 10). Because the user is working in the view, you need a way to reflect the user's changes into the model. This will probably involve putting yourself in contact with the interface objects where the user does the editing.

To illustrate, I'll implement a table view cell with a text field that is editable when the cell is in editing mode. Imagine an app that maintains a list of names and phone numbers. A name and phone number are displayed as a grouped style table, and they become editable when the user taps the Edit button (Figure 8-8).

We don't need a button at the left end of the cell when it's being edited:

```
override func tableView(tableView: UITableView,
    editingStyleForRowAtIndexPath indexPath: NSIndexPath)
    -> UITableViewCellEditingStyle {
        return .None
}
```

A UITextField is editable if its `enabled` is `true`. To tie this to the cell's `editing` state, it is probably simplest to implement a custom UITableViewCell class. I'll call it MyCell, and I'll design it in the nib, giving it a single UITextField that's pointed to through an outlet property called `textField`. In the code for MyCell, we override `didTransition-ToState:`, as follows:

```
class MyCell : UITableViewCell {
    @IBOutlet weak var textField : UITextField!
    override func didTransitionToState(state: UITableViewCellStateMask) {
        let editing =
            UITableViewCellStateMask.ShowingEditControlMask.rawValue
        if state.rawValue & editing != 0 {
            self.textField.enabled = true
        }
        else {
            self.textField.enabled = false
        }
    }
}
```

In the table view's data source, we make ourselves the text field's delegate when we create and configure the cell:

```
override func tableView(tableView: UITableView,
    cellForRowAtIndexPath indexPath: NSIndexPath) -> UITableViewCell {
        let cell = tableView.dequeueReusableCellWithIdentifier(
            "Cell", forIndexPath:indexPath) as! MyCell
        switch indexPath.section {
        case 0:
            cell.textField.text = self.name
        case 1:
            cell.textField.text = self.numbers[indexPath.row]
            cell.textField.keyboardType = .NumbersAndPunctuation
        default: break
        }
        cell.textField.delegate = self
        return cell
    }
```

We are the UITextField's delegate, so we are responsible for implementing the Return button in the keyboard to dismiss the keyboard (I'll talk more about this in Chapter 10):

```
func textFieldShouldReturn(textField: UITextField) -> Bool {
    textField.endEditing(true)
    return false
}
```

When a text field stops editing, we are its delegate, so we can hear about it in `textField-DidEndEditing:`. We work out which cell this text field belongs to — I like to do this by simply walking up the view hierarchy until I come to a table view cell — and update the model accordingly:

```
func textFieldDidEndEditing(textField: UITextField) {
    // some cell's text field has finished editing; which cell?
    var v : UIView = textField
    do { v = v.superview! } while !(v is UITableViewCell)
```

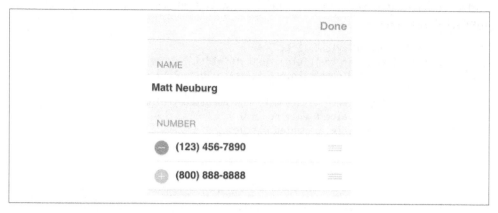

Figure 8-9. Phone directory app in editing mode

```
let cell = v as! MyCell
// update data model to match
let ip = self.tableView.indexPathForCell(cell)!
if ip.section == 1 {
    self.numbers[ip.row] = cell.textField.text
} else if ip.section == 0 {
    self.name = cell.textField.text
}
}
```

Inserting Cells

You are unlikely to attach a Plus (insert) button to every row. A more likely interface is that when a table is edited, every row has a Minus button except the last row, which has a Plus button; this shows the user that a new row can be appended at the end of the list.

Let's implement this for phone numbers in our name-and-phone-number app, allowing the user to give a person any quantity of phone numbers (Figure 8-9):

```
override func tableView(tableView: UITableView,
    editingStyleForRowAtIndexPath indexPath: NSIndexPath)
    -> UITableViewCellEditingStyle {
        if indexPath.section == 1 {
            let ct = self.tableView(
                tableView, numberOfRowsInSection:indexPath.section)
            if ct-1 == indexPath.row {
                return .Insert
            }
            return .Delete;
        }
        return .None
}
```

The person's name has no editing control (a person must have exactly one name), so we prevent it from indenting in edit mode:

```
override func tableView(tableView: UITableView,
    shouldIndentWhileEditingRowAtIndexPath indexPath: NSIndexPath)
    -> Bool {
        if indexPath.section == 1 {
            return true
        }
        return false
}
```

When the user taps an editing control, we must respond. We immediately force our text fields to cease editing: the user have may tapped the editing control while editing, and we want our model to contain the very latest changes, so this is effectively a way of causing our `textFieldDidEndEditing:` to be called. The model for our phone numbers is an array of strings (`self.numbers`). We already know what to do when the tapped control is a delete button; things are similar when it's an insert button, but we've a little more work to do. The new row will be empty, and it will be at the end of the table; so we append an empty string to the `self.numbers` model array, and then we insert a corresponding row at the end of the table view. But now two successive rows have a Plus button; the way to fix that is to reload the first of those rows. Finally, we also show the keyboard for the new, empty phone number, so that the user can start editing it immediately, we do that outside the updates block:

```
override func tableView(tableView: UITableView,
    commitEditingStyle editingStyle: UITableViewCellEditingStyle,
    forRowAtIndexPath indexPath: NSIndexPath) {
        tableView.endEditing(true)
        if editingStyle == .Insert {
            self.numbers += [""]
            let ct = self.numbers.count
            tableView.beginUpdates()
            tableView.insertRowsAtIndexPaths(
                [NSIndexPath(forRow:ct-1, inSection:1)],
                withRowAnimation:.Automatic)
            tableView.reloadRowsAtIndexPaths(
                [NSIndexPath(forRow:ct-2, inSection:1)],
                withRowAnimation:.Automatic)
            tableView.endUpdates()
            // crucial that this next bit be *outside* the update block
            let cell = self.tableView.cellForRowAtIndexPath(
                NSIndexPath(forRow:ct-1, inSection:1))
            (cell as! MyCell).textField.becomeFirstResponder()
        }
        if editingStyle == .Delete {
            self.numbers.removeAtIndex(indexPath.row)
            tableView.beginUpdates()
            tableView.deleteRowsAtIndexPaths(
                [indexPath], withRowAnimation:.Automatic)
```

```
tableView.reloadSections(
    NSIndexSet(index:1), withRowAnimation:.Automatic)
tableView.endUpdates()
    }
}
```

Rearranging Cells

If the data source implements tableView:moveRowAtIndexPath:toIndexPath:, the table displays a reordering control at the right end of each row in editing mode (Figure 8-9), and the user can drag it to rearrange cells. The reordering control can be suppressed for individual cells by implementing tableView:canMoveRowAtIndex-Path:. The user is free to move rows that display a reordering control, but the delegate can limit where a row can be moved to by implementing tableView:targetIndexPath-ForMoveFromRowAtIndexPath:toProposedIndexPath:.

To illustrate, we'll add to our name-and-phone-number app the ability to rearrange phone numbers. There must be multiple phone numbers to rearrange:

```
override func tableView(tableView: UITableView,
    canMoveRowAtIndexPath indexPath: NSIndexPath) -> Bool {
        if indexPath.section == 1 && self.numbers.count > 1 {
            return true
        }
        return false
}
```

A phone number must not be moved out of its section, so we implement the delegate method to prevent this. We also take this opportunity to dismiss the keyboard if it is showing.

```
override func tableView(tableView: UITableView,
    targetIndexPathForMoveFromRowAtIndexPath sourceIndexPath: NSIndexPath,
    toProposedIndexPath proposedDestinationIndexPath: NSIndexPath)
    -> NSIndexPath {
        tableView.endEditing(true)
        if proposedDestinationIndexPath.section == 0 {
            return NSIndexPath(forRow:0, inSection:1)
        }
        return proposedDestinationIndexPath
}
```

After the user moves an item, tableView:moveRowAtIndexPath:toIndexPath: is called, and we trivially update the model to match. We also reload the table, to fix the editing controls:

```
override func tableView(tableView: UITableView,
    moveRowAtIndexPath fromIndexPath: NSIndexPath,
    toIndexPath: NSIndexPath) {
        let s = self.numbers[fromIndexPath.row]
```

```
        self.numbers.removeAtIndex(fromIndexPath.row)
        self.numbers.insert(s, atIndex: toIndexPath.row)
        tableView.reloadData()
    }
```

Dynamic Cells

A table may be rearranged not just in response to the user working in edit mode, but for some other reason entirely. In this way, many interesting and original interfaces are possible.

In this example, we permit the user to double tap on a section header as a way of collapsing or expanding the section — that is, we'll suppress or permit the display of the rows of the section, with a nice animation as the change takes place. (This idea is shamelessly stolen from a WWDC 2010 video.)

One more time, our data model consists of the two arrays, `self.sectionNames` and `self.sectionData`. I've also got an NSMutableSet, `self.hiddenSections`, in which I'll list the sections that aren't displaying their rows. That list is all I'll need, since either a section is showing all its rows or it's showing none of them:

```
override func tableView(tableView: UITableView,
    numberOfRowsInSection section: Int) -> Int {
        if self.hiddenSections.containsObject(section) {
            return 0
        }
        return self.sectionData[section].count
}
```

We need a correspondence between a section header and the number of its section. It's odd that UITableView doesn't give us such a correspondence; it provides `indexPathFor-Cell:`, but there is no `sectionForHeaderFooterView:`. My solution is to subclass UITableViewHeaderFooterView and give my subclass a public property `section`:

```
class MyHeaderView : UITableViewHeaderFooterView {
    var section = 0
}
```

Whenever `tableView:viewForHeaderInSection:` is called, I set the header view's `section` property:

```
override func tableView(tableView: UITableView,
    viewForHeaderInSection section: Int) -> UIView {
        let h = tableView.dequeueReusableHeaderFooterViewWithIdentifier(
            "Header") as! MyHeaderView
        // ...
        h.section = section // *
        return h
}
```

The section headers are a UITableViewHeaderFooterView subclass with user-InteractionEnabled set to true and a UITapGestureRecognizer attached, so we can detect a double tap. When the user double taps a section header, we learn from the header what section this is, we find out from the model how many rows this section has, and we derive the index paths of the rows we're about to insert or remove. Now we look for the section number in our hiddenSections set. If it's there, we're about to display the rows, so we *remove* that section number from hiddenSections, and we *insert* the rows. If it's *not* there, we're about to hide the rows, so we *insert* that section number into hiddenSections, and we *delete* the rows:

```
func tap (g : UIGestureRecognizer) {
    let v = g.view as! MyHeaderView
    let sec = v.section
    let ct = self.sectionData[sec].count
    let arr = Array(0..<ct).map {NSIndexPath(forRow:$0, inSection:sec)}
    if self.hiddenSections.containsObject(sec) {
        self.hiddenSections.removeObject(sec)
        self.tableView.beginUpdates()
        self.tableView.insertRowsAtIndexPaths(arr,
            withRowAnimation:.Automatic)
        self.tableView.endUpdates()
        self.tableView.scrollToRowAtIndexPath(arr[ct-1],
            atScrollPosition:.None,
            animated:true)
    } else {
        self.hiddenSections.addObject(sec)
        self.tableView.beginUpdates()
        self.tableView.deleteRowsAtIndexPaths(arr,
            withRowAnimation:.Automatic)
        self.tableView.endUpdates()
    }
}
```

Table View Menus

A menu, in iOS, is a sort of balloon containing tappable words such as Copy, Cut, and Paste. You can permit the user to display a menu from a table view cell by performing a long press on the cell. The long press followed by display of the menu gives the cell a selected appearance, which goes away when the menu is dismissed.

To allow the user to display a menu from a table view's cells, you implement three delegate methods:

tableView:shouldShowMenuForRowAtIndexPath:
    Return true if the user is to be permitted to summon a menu by performing a long press on this cell.

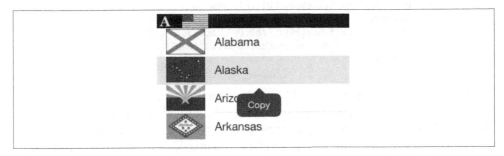

Figure 8-10. A table view cell with a menu

`tableView:canPerformAction:forRowAtIndexPath:withSender:`
> You'll be called repeatedly with selectors for various actions that the system knows about. Returning `true`, regardless, causes the Copy, Cut, and Paste menu items to appear in the menu, corresponding to the `copy:`, `cut:`, and `paste:` actions; return `false` to prevent the menu item for an action from appearing. The menu itself will then appear unless you return `false` to all three actions. The sender is the shared UIMenuController.

`tableView:performAction:forRowAtIndexPath:withSender:`
> The user has tapped one of the menu items; your job is to respond to it somehow.

Here's an example where the user can summon a Copy menu from any cell (Figure 8-10):

```
override func tableView(tableView: UITableView,
    shouldShowMenuForRowAtIndexPath indexPath: NSIndexPath) -> Bool {
        return true
}
override func tableView(tableView: UITableView,
    canPerformAction action: Selector,
    forRowAtIndexPath indexPath: NSIndexPath,
    withSender sender: AnyObject) -> Bool {
        return action == "copy:"
}
override func tableView(tableView: UITableView,
    performAction action: Selector,
    forRowAtIndexPath indexPath: NSIndexPath,
    withSender sender: AnyObject) {
        if action == "copy:" {
            // ... do whatever copying consists of ...
        }
}
```

To add a custom menu item to the menu (other than `copy:`, `cut:`, and `paste:`) is a little more work. First, you must tell the shared UIMenuController to append the menu item to the global menu; the `tableView:shouldShowMenuForRowAtIndexPath:` delegate method is a good place to do this:

```
    override func tableView(tableView: UITableView,
        shouldShowMenuForRowAtIndexPath indexPath: NSIndexPath) -> Bool {
            let mi = UIMenuItem(title: "Abbrev", action: "abbrev:")
            UIMenuController.sharedMenuController().menuItems = [mi]
            return true
    }
```

We have now given the menu an additional menu item whose title is Abbrev, and whose action when the menu item is tapped is abbrev:. (I am imagining here a table of the names of U.S. states, where one can copy a state's two-letter abbreviation to the clipboard.) If we want this menu item to appear in the menu, and if we want to respond to it when the user taps it, we must add that selector to the two performAction: delegate methods:

```
    override func tableView(tableView: UITableView,
        canPerformAction action: Selector,
        forRowAtIndexPath indexPath: NSIndexPath,
        withSender sender: AnyObject) -> Bool {
            return action == "copy:" || action == "abbrev:"
    }
    override func tableView(tableView: UITableView,
        performAction action: Selector,
        forRowAtIndexPath indexPath: NSIndexPath,
        withSender sender: AnyObject) {
            if action == "copy:" {
                // ... do whatever copying consists of ...
            }
            if action == "abbrev:" {
                // ... do whatever abbreviating consists of ...
            }
    }
```

Now comes the tricky part: we must implement our custom selector, abbrev:, *in the cell*. We will therefore need our table to use a custom UITableViewCell subclass. Let's call it MyCell:

```
    class MyCell : UITableViewCell {
        func abbrev(sender:AnyObject!) {
            // ...
        }
    }
```

The Abbrev menu item now appears when the user long-presses a cell of our table, and the cell's abbrev: method is called when the user taps that menu item. We could respond directly to the tap in the cell, but it seems more consistent that our table view delegate should respond. So we work out what table view this cell belongs to and send its delegate the very message it is already expecting:

```
func abbrev(sender:AnyObject!) {
    // find my table view
    var v : UIView = self
    do {v = v.superview!} while !(v is UITableView)
    let tv = v as! UITableView
    // ask it what index path we are
    let ip = tv.indexPathForCell(self)!
    // talk to its delegate
    let action = Selector(__FUNCTION__ + ":") // *
    tv.delegate?.tableView?(
        tv, performAction:action, forRowAtIndexPath:ip, withSender:sender)
}
```

 The starred line calls attention to the fact that Swift's __FUNCTION__ literal does not evaluate to a valid Objective-C selector string; I regard this as a bug.

Collection Views

A collection view (UICollectionView) is a UIScrollView subclass that generalizes the notion of a UITableView. It has many similarities to a table view; indeed, knowing about table views, you know a great deal about collection views already:

- Like a UITableView, you might well manage your UICollectionView through a UIViewController subclass — a subclass of UICollectionViewController.

- Like a UITableView, a collection view has reusable cells. These are UICollection-ViewCell instances, and are extremely minimal.

- Like a UITableView, you'll make the cells reusable by registering a class or nib with the collection view:
  - registerClass:forCellWithReuseIdentifier:
  - registerNib:forCellWithReuseIdentifier:.

  Alternatively, if you've started with a UICollectionViewController in a storyboard, just assign the reuse identifier in the storyboard.

- Like a UITableView, a collection view has a data source (UICollectionViewData-Source) and a delegate (UICollectionViewDelegate), and it's going to ask the data source Three Big Questions:
  - numberOfSectionsInCollectionView:
  - collectionView:numberOfItemsInSection:
  - collectionView:cellForItemAtIndexPath:

- Like a UITableView, to answer the third Big Question, your data source will supply a cell by calling dequeueReusableCellWithReuseIdentifier:forIndexPath:.

- Like a UITableView, a collection view allows the user to select a cell, or multiple cells. The delegate is notified of highlighting and selection just like a table view delegate. Your code can rearrange the cells, inserting, moving, and deleting cells or entire sections. If the delegate permits, the user can long-press a cell to produce a menu.

- A collection view can clump its data into sections, identified by section number.

At this point we come to a slight difference between table views and collection views. With a collection view, a section can have a header and footer, but the collection view itself does not call them that; instead, it generalizes its subview types into cells, on the one hand, and *supplementary views*, on the other. A supplementary view is just a UICollectionReusableView, which happens to be UICollectionViewCell's superclass. A supplementary view is associated with a *kind*, which is just an NSString identifying its type; thus you can have a header as one kind, a footer as another kind, and anything else you can imagine. The similarities then resume:

- As with a UITableView, you can make supplementary views reusable by registering a class with the collection view. The data source method where you are asked for a supplementary view will be:

  - `collectionView:viewForSupplementaryElementOfKind:atIndexPath:`

- As with a UITableView, your data source will then supply a supplementary view by dequeuing it from the collection view.

The *big* difference between a table view and a collection view is *how the collection view lays out its elements* (cells and supplementary views). A table view lays out its cells in just one way: a vertically scrolling column, where the cells are the width of the table view, the height dictated by the table view or the delegate, and touching one another. A collection view doesn't do that. In fact, a collection view doesn't lay out its elements at all! That job is left to another class, a subclass of UICollectionViewLayout.

A UICollectionViewLayout subclass instance is responsible for the overall layout of the collection view that owns it. It does this by answering some Big Questions of its own, posed by the collection view; the most important are these:

collectionViewContentSize
> How big is the entire layout? The collection view needs to know this, because the collection view is a scroll view (Chapter 7), and this will be the content size of the scrollable material that it will display.

layoutAttributesForElementsInRect:
> Where do all the elements go? The layout attributes, as I'll explain in more detail in a moment, are bundles of positional information.

Figure 8-11. A collection view in my Latin flashcard app

To answer these questions, the collection view layout needs to ask the collection view some questions of its own, such as numberOfSections and numberOfItemsIn-Section:. (The collection view, in turn, gets the answers to those questions from its data source.)

The collection view layout can thus assign the elements any positions it likes, and the collection view will faithfully draw them in those positions within its content rectangle. That seems very open-ended, and indeed it is. To get you started, there's a built-in UICollectionViewLayout subclass — UICollectionViewFlowLayout.

UICollectionViewFlowLayout arranges its cells in something like a grid. The grid can be scrolled either horizontally or vertically, so this grid is a series of rows or columns. Through properties and a delegate protocol of its own (UICollectionViewDelegate-FlowLayout), the UICollectionViewFlowLayout instance lets you provide hints about how big the cells are and how they should be spaced out. It defines two supplementary view types, using them to let you give each section a header and a footer.

Figure 8-11 shows a collection view, laid out with a flow layout, from my Latin flashcard app. This interface simply lists the chapters and lessons into which the flashcards themselves are divided, and allows the user to jump to a desired lesson by tapping it. Previously, I was using a table view to present this list; when collection views were introduced (in iOS 6), I adopted one for this interface, and you can see why. Instead of a lesson item like "1a" occupying an entire row that stretches the whole width of a table, it's just a little rectangle; in landscape orientation, the flow layout fits five of these rectangles onto a line for me. So a collection view is a much more compact and appropriate way to present this interface than a table view.

If UICollectionViewFlowLayout doesn't quite meet your needs, you can subclass it, or you can subclass UICollectionViewLayout itself. I'll talk more about that later on.

(In addition to cells and supplementary views, a collection view supports *decoration views*. These are not directly analogous to anything in a table view; they are closest, perhaps, to the section index. They don't represent data; the collection view won't ask the data source about them, and the collection view has no methods about them. They are purely up to the collection view layout; it defines any decoration view types, gives its decoration views actual view content, and states the positions its decoration views are to have. I've never written or used a collection view layout that implemented decoration views, and I'm not going to say any more about them.)

Collection View Classes

Here are the main classes associated with UICollectionView. This is just a conceptual overview; I don't recite all the properties and methods of each class, which you can learn from the documentation:

UICollectionViewController
> A UIViewController subclass. Like a table view controller, UICollectionView-Controller is convenient if a UICollectionView is to be a view controller's view, but is not required. It is the delegate and data source of its `collectionView` by default. The designated initializer requires you to supply a layout instance:

> ```
> let rvc =
>     RootViewController(collectionViewLayout:UICollectionViewFlowLayout())
> ```

> Alternatively, there is a Collection View Controller nib object.

UICollectionView
> A UIScrollView subclass. It has a `backgroundColor` (because it's a view) and optionally a `backgroundView` in front of that. Its designated initializer requires you to supply a layout instance, which will be its `collectionViewLayout`. Alternatively, there is a Collection View nib object, which comes with a Collection View Flow Layout by default; you can change the collection view layout class with the Layout pop-up menu in the Collection View's Attributes inspector.

> A collection view's methods are very much parallel to those of a UITableView, but fewer and simpler:

> - Where a table view speaks of rows, a collection view speaks of *items*. UICollectionView even adds a category to NSIndexPath so that you can refer to its `item` property instead of its `row` property.
> - Where a table view speaks of a header or footer, a collection view speaks of a *supplementary view*.

- A UICollectionView doesn't do layout, so it is not where things like header and cell size are configured.

- A UICollectionView has no notion of editing.

- A UICollectionView has no section index.

- Where a table view batches updates with `beginUpdates` and `endUpdates`, a collection view uses `performBatchUpdates:completion:`, which takes blocks.

- A collection view performs animation when you insert, delete, or move sections or items, but you don't specify an animation type. (The layout can modify the animation.)

Having made those mental adjustments, you can guess correctly all the methods of a UICollectionView, except for a couple whose names begin with `layout-Attributes`.... To understand what they do, you need to know about UICollectionViewLayoutAttributes.

UICollectionViewLayoutAttributes

A UICollectionViewLayoutAttributes object is basically just a glorified struct, tying together an element's `indexPath` with the specifications for how and where it should be drawn — specifications that are remarkably reminiscent of view or layer properties, with names like `frame`, `center`, `size`, `transform`, and so forth. Layout attributes objects function as the mediators between the layout and the collection view; they are what the layout passes to the collection view to tell it where all the elements of the view should go.

UICollectionViewCell

An extremely minimal view class. It has a `highlighted` property and a `selected` property. It has a `contentView`, a `selectedBackgroundView`, a `backgroundView`, and of course (since it's a view) a `backgroundColor`, layered in that order, just like a table view cell; everything else is up to you.

If you start with a collection view controller in a storyboard, you get prototype cells, which you obtain by dequeuing. Otherwise, you obtain cells through registration and dequeuing.

UICollectionReusableView

The superclass of UICollectionViewCell — so it is even more minimal! This is the class of supplementary views such as headers and footers. You obtain reusable views through registration and dequeuing; if you're using a flow layout in a storyboard, you are given a header and footer prototype view.

UICollectionViewLayout

The layout workhorse class for a collection view. A collection view cannot exist without a layout instance! As I've already said, the layout knows how much room all the subviews occupy, and supplies the `collectionViewContentSize` that sets the `contentSize` of the collection view, *qua* scroll view. In addition, the layout must answer questions from the collection view, by supplying a UICollectionViewLayoutAttributes object, or an array of such objects, saying where and how elements should be drawn. These questions come in two categories:

Static attributes

> The collection view wants to know the layout attributes of an item, supplementary view, or decoration view, specified by index path, or of all elements within a given rect.

Dynamic attributes

> The collection view is inserting or removing elements. It asks for the layout attributes that an element, specified by index path, should have before insertion or after removal. The collection view can thus animate between the element's static attributes and these dynamic attributes. For example, if an element's layout attributes `alpha` is `0` after removal, the element will appear to fade away as it is removed.

The collection view also notifies the layout of pending changes through some methods whose names start with `prepare` and `finalize`. This is another way for the layout to participate in animations, or to perform other kinds of preparation and cleanup.

UICollectionViewLayout is an abstract class; to use it, you must subclass it, or start with the built-in subclass, UICollectionViewFlowLayout.

UICollectionViewFlowLayout

> A concrete subclass of UICollectionViewLayout; you can use it as is, or you can subclass it. It lays out items in a grid that can be scrolled either horizontally or vertically, and it defines two supplementary element types to serve as the header and footer of a section. A collection view in the nib editor has a Layout pop-up menu that lets you choose a Flow layout, and you can configure the flow layout in the Size inspector; in a storyboard, you can even add and design a header and a footer.

A flow layout has the following configurations:

- A scroll direction
- A `sectionInset` (the margins for a section)
- An `itemSize`, along with a `minimumInteritemSpacing` and `minimumLineSpacing`
- A `headerReferenceSize` and `footerReferenceSize`

That's all! At a minimum, if you want to see any section headers, you must assign the flow layout a `headerReferenceSize`, because the default is (0.0,0.0). Otherwise, you get initial defaults that will at least allow you to see something immediately, such as an `itemSize` of (50.0,50.0) and reasonable default spacing between items and lines.

UICollectionViewFlowLayout also defines a delegate protocol of its own, UICollectionViewDelegateFlowLayout. The flow layout automatically treats the collection view's delegate as its own delegate. The section margins, item size, item spacing, line spacing, and header and footer size can be set for individual sections, cells, and supplementary views through this delegate.

Using a Collection View

To show that using a collection view is easy, here's how the view shown in Figure 8-11 is created. I have a UICollectionViewController subclass, LessonListController. Every collection view must have a layout, so LessonListController's designated initializer initializes itself with a UICollectionViewFlowLayout:

```
init?(terms data:NSArray) {
    self.terms = data
    let layout = UICollectionViewFlowLayout()
    super.init(collectionViewLayout:layout)
    // ... other self-initializations here ...
}
```

In `viewDidLoad`, we give the flow layout its hints about the sizes of the margins, cells, and headers, as well as registering for cell and header reusability:

```
override func viewDidLoad() {
    super.viewDidLoad()
    let layout = self.collectionView!
        .collectionViewLayout as! UICollectionViewFlowLayout
    layout.sectionInset = UIEdgeInsetsMake(10, 20, 10, 20)
    layout.headerReferenceSize = CGSizeMake(0,40)
    layout.itemSize = CGSizeMake(70,45)
    self.collectionView!.registerNib(
        UINib(nibName:"LessonCell", bundle:nil),
        forCellWithReuseIdentifier: "LessonCell")
    self.collectionView!.registerClass(
        UICollectionReusableView.self,
        forSupplementaryViewOfKind: UICollectionElementKindSectionHeader,
        withReuseIdentifier: "LessonHeader")
    self.collectionView!.backgroundColor = UIColor.myGolden()
    // ...
}
```

The first two of the Three Big Questions to the data source are boring and familiar:

```
override func numberOfSectionsInCollectionView(
    collectionView: UICollectionView) -> Int {
        return self.sectionNames.count
}
override func collectionView(collectionView: UICollectionView,
    numberOfItemsInSection section: Int) -> Int {
        return self.sectionData[section].count
}
```

The third of the Three Big Questions to the data source creates and configures the cells. In a *.xib* file, I've designed the cell with a single subview, a UILabel with tag 1; if the text of that label is still "Label", this is a sign that the cell has come freshly minted from the nib and needs further initial configuration. Among other things, I assign each new cell a selectedBackgroundView and give the label a highlightedTextColor, to get an automatic indication of selection:

```
override func collectionView(collectionView: UICollectionView,
    cellForItemAtIndexPath indexPath: NSIndexPath)
    -> UICollectionViewCell {
        let cell = collectionView.dequeueReusableCellWithReuseIdentifier(
            "LessonCell", forIndexPath: indexPath) as! UICollectionViewCell
        let lab = cell.viewWithTag(1) as! UILabel
        if lab.text == "Label" {
            lab.highlightedTextColor = UIColor.whiteColor()
            cell.backgroundColor = UIColor.myPaler()
            cell.layer.borderColor = UIColor.brownColor().CGColor
            cell.layer.borderWidth = 5
            cell.layer.cornerRadius = 5
            let v = UIView()
            v.backgroundColor =
                UIColor.blueColor().colorWithAlphaComponent(0.8)
            cell.selectedBackgroundView = v
        }
        let term = self.sectionData[indexPath.section][indexPath.item]
        lab.text = term.lesson + term.sectionFirstWord
        return cell
}
```

The fourth data source method asks for the supplementary element views; in my case, these are the section headers. I haven't bothered to design the header in a nib; instead, I configure the entire thing in code. Again I distinguish between newly minted views and reused views; the latter will already have a single subview, a UILabel:

```
override func collectionView(collectionView: UICollectionView,
    viewForSupplementaryElementOfKind kind: String,
    atIndexPath indexPath: NSIndexPath) -> UICollectionReusableView {
        let v = collectionView.dequeueReusableSupplementaryViewOfKind(
            UICollectionElementKindSectionHeader,
            withReuseIdentifier: "LessonHeader",
            forIndexPath: indexPath) as! UICollectionReusableView
        if v.subviews.count == 0 {
```

```
            let lab = UILabel(frame:CGRectMake(10,0,100,40))
            lab.font = UIFont(name:"GillSans-Bold", size:20)
            lab.backgroundColor = UIColor.clearColor()
            v.addSubview(lab)
            v.backgroundColor = UIColor.blackColor()
            lab.textColor = UIColor.myPaler()
        }
        let lab = v.subviews[0] as! UILabel
        lab.text = self.sectionNames[indexPath.section]
        return v
    }
```

As you can see from Figure 8-11, the first section is treated specially — it has no header, and its cell is wider. I take care of that with two UICollectionViewDelegateFlowLayout methods:

```
func collectionView(collectionView: UICollectionView,
    layout collectionViewLayout: UICollectionViewLayout,
    sizeForItemAtIndexPath indexPath: NSIndexPath) -> CGSize {
        var sz =
            (collectionViewLayout as! UICollectionViewFlowLayout)
                .itemSize
        if indexPath.section == 0 {
            sz.width = 150
        }
        return sz
}
func collectionView(collectionView: UICollectionView,
    layout collectionViewLayout: UICollectionViewLayout,
    referenceSizeForHeaderInSection section: Int) -> CGSize {
        var sz =
            (collectionViewLayout as! UICollectionViewFlowLayout)
                .headerReferenceSize
        if section == 0 {
            sz.height = 0
        }
        return sz
}
```

When the user taps a cell, I hear about it through the delegate method `collection-View:didSelectItemAtIndexPath:` and respond accordingly. That is the entire code for managing this collection view!

Here's an example of deleting cells in a collection view. Let's assume that the cells to be deleted have been selected, with multiple selection being possible. If there are selected cells, they are provided as an array of NSIndexPaths. My data model is once again the usual pair of parallel arrays of strings (`sectionNames`) and arrays (`sectionData`); each NSIndexPath gets me directly to the corresponding piece of data in `sectionData`, so I delete each piece of data in reverse order, keeping track of any arrays (sections) that end up empty. Finally, I delete the items from the collection view, and then do the same for the sections:

```
func doDelete(sender:AnyObject) { // button, delete selected cells
    let arr = self.collectionView!.indexPathsForSelectedItems()
        as! [NSIndexPath]
    if arr.count == 0 {
        return
    }
    // sort, reverse
    let arr2 = (arr as NSArray).sortedArrayUsingSelector(
        Selector("compare:")).reverse() as! [NSIndexPath]
    // delete data
    var empties = [Int]() // keep track of what sections get emptied
    for ip in arr2 {
        self.sectionData[ip.section].removeAtIndex(ip.item)
        if self.sectionData[ip.section].count == 0 {
            empties += [ip.section]
        }
    }
    // will need an NSIndexSet version of that empties list
    let emptyset = NSMutableIndexSet()
    for i in empties {
        emptyset.addIndex(i)
    }
    // delete from view, deal with empty sections
    self.collectionView!.performBatchUpdates({
        self.collectionView!.deleteItemsAtIndexPaths(arr2)
        if empties.count > 0 { // delete empty sections
            self.sectionNames.removeAtIndexes(empties)
            self.sectionData.removeAtIndexes(empties)
            self.collectionView!.deleteSections(emptyset)
        }
    }, completion: nil)
}
```

(For the removeAtIndexes: utility, see Appendix B.)

Menu handling is also completely parallel to a table view; if you want additional menu items beyond the standard Copy, Cut, and Paste, the corresponding custom selectors must be implemented in a UICollectionViewCell subclass.

Custom Collection View Layouts

To explore what might be involved in writing your own layout class, let's introduce a simple modification of UICollectionViewFlowLayout.

By default, the flow layout wants to full-justify every row of cells horizontally, spacing the cells evenly between the left and right margins, except for the last row, which is left-aligned. Let's say that this isn't what you want — you'd rather that *every* row be left-

---

aligned, with every cell as far to the left as possible given the size of the preceding cell and the minimum spacing between cells.

To achieve this, you'll need to subclass UICollectionViewFlowLayout and override two methods, `layoutAttributesForElementsInRect:` and `layoutAttributesForItemAt-IndexPath:`. Fortunately, we're starting with a layout, UICollectionViewFlowLayout, whose answers to these questions are almost right. So we call super and make modifications as necessary.

The really important method here is `layoutAttributesForItemAtIndexPath:`, which returns a single UICollectionViewLayoutAttributes object.

If the index path's `item` is 0, we have a degenerate case: the answer we got from super is right. Alternatively, if this cell is at the start of a row — we can find this out by asking whether the left edge of its frame is close to the margin — we have another degenerate case: the answer we got from super is right.

Otherwise, where this cell goes depends on where the previous cell goes, so we obtain the frame of the previous cell recursively; we propose to position our left edge a minimal spacing amount from the right edge of the previous cell. We do that by changing the frame of the UICollectionViewLayoutAttributes object. Then we return that object:

```
override func layoutAttributesForItemAtIndexPath(indexPath: NSIndexPath)
    -> UICollectionViewLayoutAttributes! {
        let atts = super.layoutAttributesForItemAtIndexPath(indexPath)
        if indexPath.item == 0 {
            return atts // degenerate case 1
        }
        if atts.frame.origin.x - 1 <= self.sectionInset.left {
            return atts // degenerate case 2
        }
        let ipPv = NSIndexPath(
            forItem:indexPath.item-1, inSection:indexPath.section)
        let fPv = self.layoutAttributesForItemAtIndexPath(ipPv).frame
        let rightPv =
            fPv.origin.x + fPv.size.width + self.minimumInteritemSpacing
        atts.frame.origin.x = rightPv
        return atts
}
```

The other method, `layoutAttributesForElementsInRect:`, returns an array of UICollectionViewLayoutAttributes objects for all the cells and supplementary views in a rect. Again we call super and modify the resulting array so that if an element is a cell, its UICollectionViewLayoutAttributes is the result of our `layoutAttributesForItem-AtIndexPath:`:

```
override func layoutAttributesForElementsInRect(rect: CGRect)
    -> [AnyObject]? {
        let arr = super.layoutAttributesForElementsInRect(rect)
            as! [UICollectionViewLayoutAttributes]
        return arr.map {
            atts in
            if atts.representedElementKind == nil {
                let ip = atts.indexPath
                atts.frame =
                    self.layoutAttributesForItemAtIndexPath(ip).frame
            }
            return atts
        }
}
```

Apple supplies some further interesting examples of subclassing UICollectionView-FlowLayout. For instance, the LineLayout example (accompanying the WWDC 2012 videos) implements a single row of horizontally scrolling cells, where a cell grows as it approaches the center of the screen and shrinks as it moves away. To do this, it first of all overrides a UICollectionViewLayout method I didn't mention earlier, should-InvalidateLayoutForBoundsChange:; this causes layout to happen repeatedly while the collection view is scrolled. It then overrides layoutAttributesForElementsIn-Rect: to do the same sort of thing I did a moment ago: it calls super and then modifies, as needed, the transform3D property of the UICollectionViewLayoutAttributes for the onscreen cells.

You can also subclass UICollectionViewLayout itself. The WWDC 2012 videos demonstrate a UICollectionViewLayout subclass that arranges its cells in a circle; the WWDC 2013 videos demonstrate a UICollectionViewLayout subclass that piles its cells into a single stack in the center of the collection view, like a deck of cards seen from above.

A collection view layout can be powerful and complex, but getting started writing one from scratch is not difficult. To illustrate, I'll write a collection view layout that ignores sections and presents all cells as a simple grid of squares.

In my UICollectionViewLayout subclass, called MyLayout, the really big questions I need to answer are collectionViewContentSize and layoutAttributesForElements-InRect:. To answer them, I'll calculate the entire layout of my grid beforehand. The prepareLayout method is the perfect place to do this; it is called every time something about the collection view or its data changes. I'll calculate the grid of cells and express their positions as an array of UICollectionViewLayoutAttributes objects; I'll store that array in a property self.atts, and I'll store the size of the grid in a property self.sz:

```
override func prepareLayout() {
    let sections = self.collectionView!.numberOfSections()
    // how many items are there in total?
    let total = Array(0 ..< sections).map {
            self.collectionView!.numberOfItemsInSection($0)
```

```
        }.reduce(0, combine:+)
    // work out cell size based on bounds size
    let sz = self.collectionView!.bounds.size
    let width = sz.width
    let shortside = floor(width/50.0)
    let cellside = width/shortside
    // generate attributes for all cells
    var x = 0
    var y = 0
    var atts = [UICollectionViewLayoutAttributes]()
    for i in 0 ..< sections {
        let jj = self.collectionView!.numberOfItemsInSection(i)
        for j in 0 ..< jj {
            let att = UICollectionViewLayoutAttributes(
                forCellWithIndexPath:
                NSIndexPath(forItem:j, inSection:i))
            att.frame = CGRectMake(
                CGFloat(x)*cellside,CGFloat(y)*cellside,cellside,cellside)
            atts += [att]
            x++
            if CGFloat(x) >= shortside {
                x = 0
                y++
            }
        }
    }
    self.atts = atts
    let fluff = (x == 0) ? 0 : 1
    self.sz = CGSizeMake(width, CGFloat(y+fluff) * cellside)
}
```

collectionViewContentSize and layoutAttributesForElementsInRect: are obvious: I'll just return the sz or atts property, respectively:

```
override func collectionViewContentSize() -> CGSize {
    return self.sz
}
override func layoutAttributesForElementsInRect(rect: CGRect)
    -> [AnyObject]? {
        return self.atts
}
```

layoutAttributesForItemAtIndexPath: is implemented by looking up the corresponding value in my self.atts array:

```
override func layoutAttributesForItemAtIndexPath(indexPath: NSIndexPath)
    -> UICollectionViewLayoutAttributes! {
        for att in self.atts {
            if att.indexPath == indexPath {
                return att
```

```
        }
    }
    return nil // shouldn't happen
}
```

Finally, I want to implement `shouldInvalidateLayoutForBoundsChange:` to return `true`, so that if the interface is rotated, my `prepareLayout` will be called again to recalculate the grid. There's a potential source of inefficiency here, though: the user scrolling the collection view counts as a bounds change as well. Therefore I return `false` unless the bounds width has changed:

```
override func shouldInvalidateLayoutForBoundsChange(newBounds: CGRect)
    -> Bool {
        let ok = newBounds.size.width != self.sz.width
        return ok
}
```

Switching Layouts

An astonishing and delightful feature of a collection view is that its layout object can be swapped out on the fly. You can substitute one layout for another, by calling `set-CollectionViewLayout:animated:completion:`. The data hasn't changed, and the collection view can identify each element uniquely and persistently, so it responds by moving every element from its position according to the old layout to its position according to the new layout — and, if the `animated:` argument is `true`, it does this with animation! Thus the elements are seen to rearrange themselves, as if by magic.

This animated change of layout can even be driven interactively (in response, for example, to a user gesture; compare Chapter 6 on interactive transitions). You call `start-InteractiveTransitionToCollectionViewLayout:completion:` on the collection view, and a special layout object is returned — a UICollectionViewTransitionLayout instance (or a subclass thereof; to make it a subclass, you need to have implemented `collectionView:transitionLayoutForOldLayout:newLayout:` in your collection view delegate). This transition layout is temporarily made the collection view's layout, and your job is then to keep it apprised of the transition's progress (through its `transitionProgress` property) and ultimately to call `finishInteractive-Transition` or `cancelInteractiveTransition` on the collection view.

Furthermore, when one collection view controller is pushed on top of another in a navigation interface, the runtime will do exactly the same thing for you, as a custom view controller transition (again, compare Chapter 6). To arrange this, the first collection view controller's `useLayoutToLayoutNavigationTransitions` property must be `false` and the second collection view controller's `useLayoutToLayoutNavigation-Transitions` property must be `true`. The result is that when the second collection view controller is pushed onto the navigation controller, *the collection view remains in place*, and the layout specified by the second collection view controller is substituted for the collection view's existing layout, with animation.

The effect, as the second collection view controller is pushed onto the navigation stack, is conceptually rather unsettling. Although there are two collection view controllers, and although the second view controller has a view (the collection view), and its `view-DidLoad` and `viewWillAppear:` (as well as the first view controller's `viewWill-Disappear:`) are called as you would expect, the same collection view is also still the *first* view controller's view, and the collection view's data source and delegate are still the *first* view controller. Later, after the transition is complete, the collection view's delegate becomes the *second* view controller, but its data source is *still* the *first* view controller. I find this profoundly weird.

Collection Views and UIKit Dynamics

The UICollectionViewLayoutAttributes class adopts the UIDynamicItem protocol (see Chapter 4). Thus, collection view elements can be animated under UIKit dynamics. The world of the animator here is not a superview but the layout itself; instead of `init(referenceView:)`, you'll create the UIDynamicAnimator with `init(collection-ViewLayout:)`. The layout's `collectionViewContentSize` determines the bounds of this world. Convenience methods are provided so that your code can access an animated collection view item's layout attributes directly from the animator.

You'll need a custom collection view layout subclass, because otherwise you won't be able to see any animation. On every frame of its animation, the UIDynamicAnimator is going to change the layout attributes of some items, but the collection view is still going to draw those items in accordance with the layout's `layoutAttributesFor-ElementsInRect:`. The simplest solution is to override `layoutAttributesForElements-InRect:` so as to obtain those layout attributes from the UIDynamicAnimator. This cooperation will be easiest if the layout itself owns and configures the animator.

In this example, we're in the layout subclass, setting up the animation. The layout subclass has a property to hold the animator, as well as a Bool property to signal when an animation is in progress:

```
let visworld = self.collectionView!.bounds
let anim = UIDynamicAnimator(collectionViewLayout:self)
self.animator = anim
self.animating = true
// ... configure rest of animation
```

Our implementation of `layoutAttributesForElementsInRect:`, if we are animating, substitutes the layout attributes that come from the animator for those we would normally return; the technique I use here relies on the fact that the animator convenience methods `layoutAttributesForCellAtIndexPath:` and so forth return nil if the specified item is not being animated. In this particular example, both cells and supplementary items (headers and footers) can be animated, so the two cases have to be distinguished:

```
override func layoutAttributesForElementsInRect(rect: CGRect)
    -> [AnyObject] {
        let sup = super.layoutAttributesForElementsInRect(rect)
            as! [UICollectionViewLayoutAttributes]
        let arr = sup.map {
            atts -> UICollectionViewLayoutAttributes in
            if atts.representedElementKind == nil {
                let ip = atts.indexPath
                atts.frame =
                    self.layoutAttributesForItemAtIndexPath(ip).frame
            }
            return atts
        }
        if self.animating {
            var marr = [UICollectionViewLayoutAttributes]()
            for atts in arr {
                let path = atts.indexPath
                var atts2 : UICollectionViewLayoutAttributes? = nil
                switch atts.representedElementCategory {
                case .Cell:
                    atts2 = self.animator
                        .layoutAttributesForCellAtIndexPath(path)
                case .SupplementaryView:
                    let kind = atts.representedElementKind
                    atts2 = self.animator
                        .layoutAttributesForSupplementaryViewOfKind(
                            kind, atIndexPath:path)
                default: break
                }
                marr += [atts2 ?? atts]
            }
            return marr
        }
        return arr
}
```

CHAPTER 9

Popovers and Split Views

Popovers and split views are forms of interface designed originally for the iPad. In iOS 7 and before, they existed *only* on the iPad. New in iOS 8, both are available also on the iPhone, where they can either adapt — appearing in an altered form, more appropriate to the smaller screen — or appear just as they do on the iPad.

Popovers

A *popover* is a sort of secondary window or dialog: it displays a view layered on top of the main interface. It is usually associated, through a sort of arrow, with a view in the main interface — usually the button that the user tapped to summon the popover. The popover dims out the rest of the screen, like a `.FormSheet` presented view (see Chapter 6). It might be effectively modal, preventing the user from working in the rest of the interface; alternatively, it might vanish if the user taps outside it.

A popover can bring to the larger iPad the smaller, more lightweight flavor of the iPhone. For example, in my LinkSame app, both the settings view (where the user configures the game) and the help view (which describes how to play the game) are popovers (Figure 9-1). On the iPhone, both these views would occupy the entire screen; for each, we'd need a way to navigate to it, and then the user would have to return to the main interface afterward. But with the larger iPad screen, neither view is large enough, or important enough, to occupy the entire screen exclusively. As popovers, they are characterized as smaller, secondary views which the user summons temporarily and then dismisses.

New in iOS 8, a popover is in fact *a form of presented view controller* — a presented view controller with a `modalPresentationStyle` of `.Popover` (which I didn't tell you about in Chapter 6). This brilliant innovation, which is really how popovers should have worked all along, brings with it some tremendous advantages:

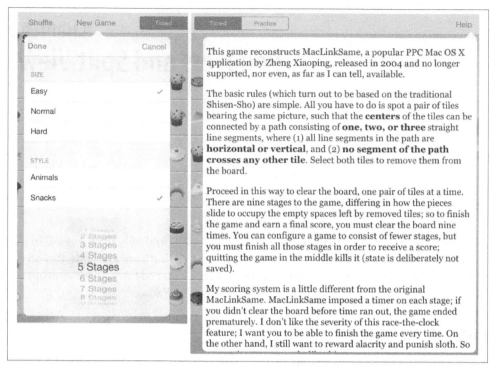

Figure 9-1. Two popovers

Memory management

In iOS 7 and before, it was necessary to create a UIPopoverController and retain it explicitly. A presented view controller, on the other hand, is retained *automatically* by its presenting view controller.

Singularity

In iOS 7 and before, nothing enforced Apple's guideline that a maximum of one popover at a time should be shown. A presented view controller, on the other hand, enforces it *automatically* (a view controller can't have more than one presented view controller at a time).

Adaptibility

In iOS 7 and before, a popover was illegal on the iPhone. Your universal app therefore had to be filled with conditional code: "If we're running on an iPad, show this view controller as a popover; otherwise, make it a presented view controller." Dismissal and cleanup were conditional too, and could be even harder to manage. A presented view controller, on the other hand, can adapt. A `.Popover` presented view controller is *automatically* treated by default as `.FullScreen` on the iPhone (similar to a `.FormSheet` presented view controller). Moreover, if you don't want the default, you don't have to accept it; it is legal for a popover to appear on the iPhone as a popover.

Preparing a Popover

To show a popover, you're going present a view controller. Before that presentation takes place, you'll turn this into a popover presentation by setting the view controller's `modalPresentationStyle` to `.Popover`:

```
let vc = MyViewController()
vc.modalPresentationStyle = .Popover
self.presentViewController(vc, animated: true, completion: nil)
```

This, however, is insufficient; without a little further configuration, that code will crash at runtime when the popover is presented. The additional configuration is performed through the UIPopoverPresentationController (a UIPresentationController subclass) that is responsible for showing this popover. Here's how that UIPopoverPresentationController is created and accessed:

- Setting the view controller's `modalPresentationStyle` to `.Popover` causes its `presentationController` to become a UIPopoverPresentationController.

- After the view controller has been presented, its `popoverPresentationController` points to that UIPopoverPresentationController. Oddly enough, it is perfectly legal (and effective) to finish configuring the popover *after* presenting it.

Arrow source and direction

At a minimum, the UIPopoverPresentationController needs you to set one of the following:

`barButtonItem`
> A bar button item in the interface, with which the popover should be associated. The popover's arrow will point to this bar button item. Typically, this will be the bar button item that was tapped in order to summon the popover (as in Figure 9-1).

`sourceView`, `sourceRect`
> A UIView in the interface, along with the CGRect *in that view's coordinate system*, with which the popover should be associated. The popover's arrow will point to this rect. Typically, the `sourceView` will be the view that was tapped in order to summon the popover, and the `sourceRect` will be its `bounds`.

Thus, here's a minimal popover presentation that actually works; the popover is summoned by tapping a UIButton in the interface, and this is that button's action method:

```
@IBAction func doButton(sender: AnyObject) {
    let vc = MyViewController()
    vc.modalPresentationStyle = .Popover
    self.presentViewController(vc, animated: true, completion: nil)
    if let pop = vc.popoverPresentationController {
        let v = sender as! UIView
        pop.sourceView = v
        pop.sourceRect = v.bounds
    }
}
```

In addition to the arrow source, you can set the desired arrow direction, as the popover presentation controller's `permittedArrowDirections`. This is a bitmask with possible values `.Up`, `.Down`, `.Left`, and `.Right`. The default is `.Any`, comprising all four bitmask values; this is the default and will usually be what you want.

Popover size and position

The presentation of the popover won't fail if you don't supply a size for the popover, but you probably will want to supply one, as the default is unlikely to be desirable. In iOS 8, this information is provided through the presented view controller's `preferred-ContentSize`.

Recall from Chapter 6 that a view controller can use its `preferredContentSize` to communicate to a parent view controller the size that it would like to be. The popover presentation controller is a presentation controller (UIPresentationController), and is therefore also a UIContentContainer; the presentation controller acts as the parent of the presented view controller, and in this situation will consult the presented view controller's wishes and will try to respect them.

I'm deliberately leaving open the question of who will set the presented view controller's `preferredContentSize` and when. The presented view controller might set its own value here; its `viewDidLoad` is a reasonable place, or, if the view controller is instantiated from a nib, the nib editor provides Content Size fields in the Attributes inspector. Alternatively, the presenting view controller might override the will of the presented view controller; in that case, the place where the rest of the configuration is performed will work just fine:

```
if let pop = vc.popoverPresentationController {
    let v = sender as! UIView
    pop.sourceView = v
    pop.sourceRect = v.bounds
    vc.preferredContentSize = CGSizeMake(200,500)
}
```

It is possible to change the presented view controller's `preferredContentSize` while the popover is showing. The popover presentation controller will hear about this (through the mechanism discussed in Chapter 6) and will respond by changing the popover's size, with animation.

If the popover is a navigation controller, the navigation controller will look at its current view controller's `preferredContentSize`, adjust for the presence of the navigation bar, and set its own `preferredContentSize` appropriately. This is delightful, but it is probably unwise to press it too far; subsequently pushing or popping a view controller with a *different* `preferredContentSize` may not work as you expect — to be precise, the popover's *width* will change to match the new preferred width, but the popover's *height* will change only if the new preferred height is *taller*. (It is possible to work around this by resetting the navigation controller's `preferredContentSize` in a navigation controller delegate method.)

 In theory, it should also be possible to set the popover presentation controller's `popoverLayoutMargins` as a way of encouraging the popover to keep a certain distance from the edges of the presenting view controller's view. In fact, however, my experience is that this setting is ignored; I regard this as a bug.

Popover appearance

By default, a popover presentation controller takes charge of the background color of the presented view controller's view, including the arrow, as well the navigation bar in a navigation interface. You can see this in Figure 9-1; the first popover, along with its navigation bar, has automatically adopted a slightly transparent cream color that is apparently derived somehow from the color of what's behind it, and the second popover has the same color on its arrow, causing a mismatch with the background color of the web view displaying the text.

If you don't want this automatic background color and transparency, you can set the popover presentation controller's `backgroundColor`. (In a navigation interface, you can change the navigation bar's color separately, and customize the position and appearance of the navigation bar's bar button items; see Chapter 12.)

You can also customize the outside of the popover — that is, the "frame" surrounding the content, including the arrow. To do so, you set the UIPopoverPresentationController's `popoverBackgroundViewClass` to your own subclass of UIPopoverBackgroundView (a UIView subclass) — at which point you can achieve just about anything you want, including the very silly popover shown in Figure 9-2.

Configuring your UIPopoverBackgroundView subclass is a bit tricky, because this single view is responsible for drawing both the arrow and the frame. Thus, in a complete and correct implementation, you'll have to draw differently depending on the arrow direction, which you can learn from the UIPopoverBackgroundView's `arrowDirection` property.

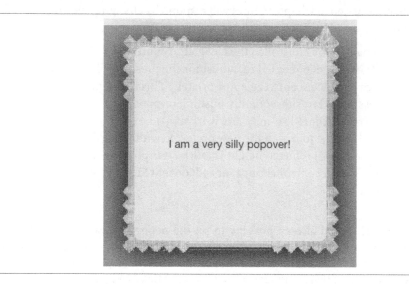

Figure 9-2. A very silly popover

I'll give a simplified example in which I cheat by assuming that the arrow direction will be `.Up`. I start by defining a nested struct to hold two constant values I'm going to need later, the arrow's height and the width of its base:

```
class MyPopoverBackgroundView : UIPopoverBackgroundView {
    struct Arrow {
        static let ARBASE : CGFloat = 20
        static let ARHEIGHT : CGFloat = 20
    }
    // ...
}
```

(I use a nested struct rather than simple constant properties because there are some class functions coming up that will need to access these values: a class function can't access an instance variable, and Swift doesn't have class variables.)

Drawing the frame (`drawRect:`) is easy: here, I divide the view's overall rect into two areas, the arrow area on top and the frame area on the bottom, and I draw the frame into the bottom area as a resizable image (Chapter 2):

```
let linOrig = UIImage(named: "linen.png")!
let capw = linOrig.size.width / 2.0 - 1
let caph = linOrig.size.height / 2.0 - 1
let lin = linOrig.resizableImageWithCapInsets(
    UIEdgeInsetsMake(caph, capw, caph, capw),resizingMode:.Tile)
// ... draw arrow here ...
```

```
var arrow = CGRectZero
var body = CGRectZero
CGRectDivide(rect, &arrow, &body, Arrow.ARHEIGHT, .MinYEdge)
lin.drawInRect(body)
```

I omitted the drawing of the arrow; now let's insert it. The UIPopoverBackgroundView
has arrowHeight and arrowBase class methods that we've overridden to describe the
arrow dimensions to the runtime; here, their values are the two constant static struct
variables, ARHEIGHT and ARBASE:

```
override class func arrowBase() -> CGFloat {
    return Arrow.ARBASE
}
override class func arrowHeight() -> CGFloat {
    return Arrow.ARHEIGHT
}
```

My arrow will consist simply of a texture-filled isosceles triangle, with an excess base
consisting of a rectangle joining it to the frame. The UIPopoverBackgroundView has
an arrowOffset property that the runtime has set to tell you where to draw the arrow:
this offset measures the positive distance between the center of the view's edge and the
center of the arrow. However, the runtime will have no hesitation in setting the arrow-
Offset all the way at the edge of the view, or even beyond its bounds (in which case it
won't be drawn); to prevent this, I provide a maximum offset limit:

```
let con = UIGraphicsGetCurrentContext()
CGContextSaveGState(con)
var propX = self.arrowOffset
let limit : CGFloat = 22.0
let maxX = rect.size.width/2.0 - limit
if propX > maxX {
    propX = maxX
}
if propX < limit {
    propX = limit
}
CGContextTranslateCTM(con, rect.size.width/2.0 + propX - Arrow.ARBASE/2.0, 0)
CGContextMoveToPoint(con, 0, Arrow.ARHEIGHT)
CGContextAddLineToPoint(con, Arrow.ARBASE / 2.0, 0)
CGContextAddLineToPoint(con, Arrow.ARBASE, Arrow.ARHEIGHT)
CGContextClosePath(con)
CGContextAddRect(con, CGRectMake(0,Arrow.ARHEIGHT,Arrow.ARBASE,15))
CGContextClip(con)
lin.drawAtPoint(CGPointMake(-40,-40))
CGContextRestoreGState(con)
```

Finally, the thickness of the four sides of the frame is dictated by implementing the
contentViewInsets class method:

```
override class func contentViewInsets() -> UIEdgeInsets {
    return UIEdgeInsetsMake(20,20,20,20)
}
```

Passthrough views

When you're configuring your popover, you'll want to plan ahead for how the popover is to be dismissed. The base default case is that the user can tap anywhere outside the popover to dismiss it, and this will usually be just what you want. You can, however, modify this behavior in two ways:

UIPopoverPresentationController's `passthroughViews` *property*
> An array of views in the interface behind the popover; the user can interact normally with these views while the popover is showing, and the popover will *not* be dismissed.
>
> What happens if the user taps a view that is *not* listed in the `passthroughViews` array depends on the `modalInPopover` property.

UIViewController's `modalInPopover` *property*
> If this is `true` for the presented view controller (or for its current child view controller, as in a tab bar interface or navigation interface), then if the user taps outside the popover on a view *not* listed in the popover presentation controller's `passthroughViews`, *nothing* happens (the popover is *not* dismissed). The default is `false`.
>
> Clearly, if you've set this property to `true`, you've removed the user's ability to dismiss the popover by tapping outside it. You would then presumably provide some other way of letting the user dismiss the popover — typically, a button *inside* the popover which the user can tap to call `dismissViewController-Animated:completion:`.

 The claim made by the documentation that `modalInPopover` prevents *all* user interaction outside a popover is wrong. The user can still interact with a view listed in the `passthroughViews`, even if `modalInPopover` is true.

Unfortunately — and I can't believe I'm still having to warn about this after all these years — a popover sometimes doesn't conform correctly to the base default case. In particular, if a popover is summoned by the user tapping a UIBarButton item in a toolbar, other UIBarButtonItems in that toolbar are passthrough views! This means that the user can tap any other button in the toolbar — including a button that summons another popover.

Working around this annoying problem is not easy. Setting the popover presentation controller's `passthroughViews` to nil or an empty array just after presenting it doesn't help; your setting is overridden by the runtime. My rather hacky solution is to provide some extra delay, so as to assert my will *after* the runtime:

```
if let pop = vc.popoverPresentationController {
    // ... other configurations go here ...
    delay(0.1) {
        pop.passthroughViews = nil
    }
}
```

Popover Presentation, Dismissal, and Delegate

In iOS 8, because a popover is now just a form of presented view controller, it is shown with `presentViewController:animated:completion:`. If you want to dismiss a popover in code, rather than letting the user dismiss it by tapping outside it, you'll dismiss it with `dismissViewControllerAnimated:completion:`.

Messages to the popover presentation controller's delegate (UIPopoverPresentation-ControllerDelegate) provide further information and control. Typically, you'll set the delegate in the same place you're performing the other configurations:

```
if let pop = vc.popoverPresentationController {
    // ... other configurations go here ...
    pop.delegate = self
}
```

The three most commonly used delegate methods are:

`prepareForPopoverPresentation:`
    The popover is being presented. There is time to perform further initial configurations here (but this method is still called too early for you to work around the `passthroughViews` issue I discussed a moment ago).

`popoverPresentationControllerShouldDismissPopover:`
    The user is dismissing the popover by tapping outside it. Return `false` to prevent dismissal. *Not* called when you dismiss the popover in code.

`popoverPresentationControllerDidDismissPopover:`
    The user has dismissed the popover by tapping outside it. The popover is gone from the screen and dismissal is complete, even though the popover presentation controller still exists. *Not* called when you dismissed the popover in code.

The delegate methods all provide the popover presentation controller as parameter, and if necessary you can probably identify the popover more precisely by querying it further. For example, you can learn what view controller is being presented by examining its `presentedViewController`, or what interface object its arrow is connected to by examining its `sourceView` or `barButtonItem`. Clearly, these delegate methods make up for the fact that, when the user dismisses the popover, you don't have the sort of direct

information and control that you get from calling dismissViewController-
Animated:completion: and setting a completion handler.

If the user can dismiss the popover *either* by tapping outside the popover *or* by tapping
an interface item that calls dismissViewControllerAnimated:completion:, you may
have to duplicate some code in order to cover all cases. For example, consider the first
popover shown in Figure 9-1. It has a Done button and a Cancel button; the idea here
is that the user sets up a desired game configuration and then, while dismissing the
popover, either saves it (Done) or doesn't (Cancel). My approach is to save the user's
configuration (into NSUserDefaults) in real time as the user works within the popover.
But what if the user then cancels? To prepare for that possibility, I copy the relevant user
defaults into a property *before* the popover appears:

```
func prepareForPopoverPresentation(pop: UIPopoverPresentationController) {
    if pop.presentedViewController is UINavigationController {
        self.oldDefs = ud.dictionaryWithValuesForKeys(
            [Default.Style, Default.Size, Default.LastStage])
    }
}
```

If the user taps Done, I dismiss the popover, clear out that property, and proceed to start
a new game:

```
func startNewGame() {
    self.dismissViewControllerAnimated(true, completion: nil)
    self.oldDefs = nil
    self.setUpInterface(nil)
    // ...
}
```

If the user taps Cancel, I dismiss the popover, restore the defaults from the property,
and clear out the property:

```
func cancelNewGame() {
    self.dismissViewControllerAnimated(true, completion: nil)
    if (self.oldDefs != nil) {
        ud.setValuesForKeysWithDictionary(self.oldDefs)
        self.oldDefs = nil
    }
}
```

But what if the user taps outside the popover? I interpret that as cancellation. So I've
implemented the shouldDismiss delegate method to duplicate what I would have done
if the user had tapped Cancel:

```
func popoverPresentationControllerShouldDismissPopover(
    pop: UIPopoverPresentationController) -> Bool {
        if pop.presentedViewController is UINavigationController {
            if (self.oldDefs != nil) {
                ud.setValuesForKeysWithDictionary(self.oldDefs)
                self.oldDefs = nil
```

```
            }
        }
        return true
    }
```

There is one further delegate method:

`popoverPresentationController:willRepositionPopoverToRect:inView:`
>   Called because the popover's `sourceView` is involved in new layout activity. Typically, this is because the interface is rotating. The `rect:` and `view:` parameters are mutable pointers, so you can set their `memory` properties to change the `source-Rect` or `sourceView`, thus changing the attachment of the arrow.

In this (unlikely) example, when the interface rotates, I move the popover's arrow from one button to another:

```
func popoverPresentationController(
    popoverPresentationController: UIPopoverPresentationController,
    willRepositionPopoverToRect rect: UnsafeMutablePointer<CGRect>,
    inView view: AutoreleasingUnsafeMutablePointer<UIView?>) {
        if view.memory == self.button {
            rect.memory = self.button2.bounds
            view.memory - self.button2
        }
}
```

Adaptive Popovers

A popover presentation controller, in iOS 8, is a presentation controller (UIPresentation-Controller), and presentation controllers are adaptive. This means that, by default, in a horizontally compact environment (i.e. on an iPhone), the `.Popover` modal presentation style will be treated as `.FullScreen`. What appears as a popover on the iPad will appear as a fullscreen presented view on the iPhone, completely replacing the interface.

This rescues you from the trouble, so pervasive in iOS 7 and before, of having to code the use of the same view controller twice, conditioned upon the environment. A primary source of inconvenience used to be that the command for showing a presented view controller was not the same as for showing a popover; in addition, memory management of a popover controller was entirely up to you. This pattern (iOS 7, Objective-C) was typical:

```
// iOS 7 code!
if (UI_USER_INTERFACE_IDIOM() == UIUserInterfaceIdiomPhone)
    [self presentViewController:picker animated:YES completion:nil];
else {
    UIPopoverController* pop =
        [[UIPopoverController alloc] initWithContentViewController:picker];
```

```
        [pop presentPopoverFromRect:[sender bounds] inView:sender
            permittedArrowDirections:UIPopoverArrowDirectionAny animated:YES];
        self.currentPop = pop;
    }
```

The same sort of thing could happen on dismissal — because, once again, the command
for dismissing a presented view controller was not the same as for dismissing a popover:

```
    // iOS 7 code!
    -(void)imagePickerController:(UIImagePickerController *)picker
        didFinishPickingMediaWithInfo:(NSDictionary *)info {
            if (self.currentPop && self.currentPop.popoverVisible) {
                [self.currentPop dismissPopoverAnimated:YES];
            } else {
                [self dismissViewControllerAnimated:YES completion:nil];
            }
    }
```

In iOS 8, none of that bifurcation is needed. A popover is simply a form of presented
view controller. You present it and dismiss it, and the right thing happens on both iPad
and iPhone.

Nevertheless, the default behavior might not be quite what you want. A case in point
appears in Figure 9-1. The popover on the right, containing our help info, has no internal
button for dismissal. It doesn't need one, because, on the iPad, the user can dismiss the
popover by tapping outside it. But suppose now that this is a universal app. The same
help info will appear on the iPhone as a fullscreen presented view, and the user will have
no way to dismiss it.

One solution is to design the interface in the nib editor with conditional constraints:
this view controller's view can then have one interface for a .Regular horizontal size
class (iPad) and another interface for a .Compact horizontal size class (iPhone) — and
the difference might involve the presence or absence of a Done button.

Another solution is to take advantage of UIPresentationController delegate methods.
When you set a popover presentation controller's delegate, you set its delegate not only
qua UIPopoverPresentationController (UIPopoverPresentationControllerDelegate)
but also *qua* UIPresentationController (UIAdaptivePresentationControllerDelegate).
You can therefore implement delegate methods to tweak the popover's behavior when
it adapts.

A standard solution in this situation would be to implement `presentation-`
`Controller:viewControllerForAdaptivePresentationStyle:` to substitute a different view controller. Typically, this new view controller might be nothing but the old view
controller wrapped in a UINavigationController! If this view controller has a
`navigationItem` with a working Done button, the problem is now solved: on iPhone,
there's a navigation bar at the top of the interface, and the Done button appears in it.

In order for this trick to work, you must do two additional things:

- Implement the *other* delegate method, `adaptivePresentationStyleFor-PresentationController:` — even if only to return the default, `.FullScreen`.
- Set the presentation controller's delegate *before* calling `presentViewController:animated:completion:`.

If you don't do both of those things, `presentationController:viewControllerForAdaptivePresentationStyle:` won't be called.

Thus, here's a full working example:

```
@IBAction func doButton(sender: AnyObject) {
    let vc = MyViewController()
    vc.preferredContentSize = CGSizeMake(400,500)
    vc.modalPresentationStyle = .Popover
    if let pres = vc.popoverPresentationController {
        pres.delegate = self // must be _before_ presentViewController
    }
    self.presentViewController(vc, animated: true, completion: nil)
    if let pop = vc.popoverPresentationController {
        pop.sourceView = (sender as! UIView)
        pop.sourceRect = (sender as! UIView).bounds
    }
}
func adaptivePresentationStyleForPresentationController(
    controller: UIPresentationController) -> UIModalPresentationStyle {
        return .FullScreen
}
func presentationController(controller: UIPresentationController,
    viewControllerForAdaptivePresentationStyle style:
    UIModalPresentationStyle) -> UIViewController? {
        let vc = controller.presentedViewController
        let nav = UINavigationController(rootViewController: vc)
        return nav
}
```

Another possible override of standard adaptivity behavior is to return `.None`, instead of `.FullScreen`, from `adaptivePresentationStyleForPresentationController:`. If you do, the presented view controller will be treated as a popover *even on iPhone* (Figure 9-3).

Popover Segues

If you're using a storyboard, you can draw (Control-drag) a segue from the button (or view controller) that is to *summon* the popover to the view controller that is to *be* the popover, and specify "popover presentation" as the segue type. The result is a *popover segue*.

This game reconstructs
MacLinkSame, a popular PPC
Mac OS X application by Zheng
Xiaoping, released in 2004 and
no longer supported, nor even,
as far as I can tell, available.

The basic rules (which turn out
to be based on the traditional
Shisen-Sho) are simple. All you
have to do is spot a pair of tiles
bearing the same picture, such
that the **centers** of the tiles can
be connected by a path
consisting of **one, two, or
three** straight line segments,
where (1) all line segments in
the path are **horizontal or
vertical**, and (2) **no segment**

Help

Figure 9-3. A popover appears on an iPhone

A popover segue, when it is triggered, will be an instance of UIStoryboardPopover-PresentationSegue, an undocumented subclass of UIStoryboardSegue. The segue, as it is triggered, configures the presentation just as you would configure it in code. It instantiates and initializes the presented view controller, sets its modal presentation style to `.Popover`, and presents it. You can implement `prepareForSegue:` to perform additional configurations: obtain the segue's `destinationViewController`, get a reference to its `popoverPresentationController`, and configure it. At the time `prepareForSegue:` is called, the presentation has not yet begun, so you can successfully set the popover presentation controller's delegate here as well. You can set its `passthroughViews` too, but you'll still have to provide a delay if your goal is to overcome the default behavior of bar button items:

```
override func prepareForSegue(segue: UIStoryboardSegue, sender: AnyObject?) {
    let dest = segue.destinationViewController as! UIViewController
    if let pop = dest.popoverPresentationController {
        pop.delegate = self
        delay(0.1) {
            pop.passthroughViews = nil
        }
    }
}
```

You'll notice that I didn't set the `sourceView` or `barButtonItem` in that code; that's because those properties can be set in the nib editor (Anchor, in the segue's Attributes inspector). You can also set the passthrough views in the nib editor, but not in such a way as to override the unwanted default bar button item behavior; thus, I've had to do that in code.

The popover version of an unwind segue is dismissal of the popover. Thus, both presentation and dismissal can be managed through the storyboard.

 You *must* be using size classes in your storyboard in order to get the iOS 8 implementation of popovers. Otherwise, the segue type will be "popover," it will be a UIStoryboardPopoverSegue, and the popover will be managed by a UIPopoverController, as in iOS 7 and before.

Popover Presenting a View Controller

A popover can present a view controller internally; you'll specify a `modalPresentationStyle` of `.CurrentContext` or `.OverCurrentContext`, because otherwise the presented view will be fullscreen by default (see Chapter 6). In iOS 7 and before, it was necessary to restrict the modal transition style to `.CoverVertical`; new in iOS 8, that restriction is lifted, with only `.PartialCurl` being forbidden (and I've already suggested that you not use it in any case).

What happens by default when the user taps outside a popover that is displaying a presented view controller's view internally depends rather confusingly on the system version:

iOS 7 and before
> Nothing. The presented view controller's `modalInPopover` is automatically set to `true`, and this means exactly what `modalInPopover` usually means: tapping outside the popover has no effect. Thus, inside the presented view controller's view, you'll need to supply some interface whereby the user can tell you to dismiss the presented view controller by calling `dismissViewControllerAnimated:`.

iOS 8, before iOS 8.3
> The entire popover, including the internal presented view controller, is dismissed.

iOS 8.3
> The internal presented view controller is dismissed, while the popover remains.

In any version of iOS 8, you can restore the iOS 7 behavior by implementing the delegate method `popoverPresentationControllerShouldDismissPopover:` to prevent dismissal if the popover is itself presenting a view controller:

```
func popoverPresentationControllerShouldDismissPopover(
    pop: UIPopoverPresentationController) -> Bool {
        let ok = pop.presentedViewController.presentedViewController == nil
        return ok
}
```

Popover Search Results

As I explained in Chapter 8, in iOS 8 a UISearchController is a UIViewController that presents itself when search results are to be displayed. There is thus no reason why you shouldn't tell the UISearchController to present itself as a popover! Simply set its modal presentation style to `.Popover`.

In this example, my searchable interface belongs to a view controller whose parent is a UINavigationController. Therefore, I add the UISearchController's `searchBar` to the view controller's `navigationItem`, so that it appears in the navigation bar:

```
let src = SearchResultsController(data: self.sectionData)
let searcher = UISearchController(searchResultsController: src)
self.searcher = searcher
searcher.modalPresentationStyle = .Popover // *
searcher.searchResultsUpdater = src
let b = searcher.searchBar
self.navigationItem.titleView = b
searcher.delegate = self
searcher.presentationController?.delegate = self
```

The last two lines allow me to hear about presentation and dismissal of the popover. However, there are some buggy behaviors:

Search controller delegate dismissal methods are not called
> The UISearchControllerDelegate methods `willPresentSearchController:` and `didPresentSearchController:` are called, but the corresponding methods `willDismissSearchController:` and `didDismissSearchController:` are not. I can live with this, because the popover delegate dismissal methods are called instead.

Popover delegate methods are called just once
> The UIPopoverPresentationControllerDelegate methods are called the first time the popover appears and is dismissed, and then never again. I scratched my head over this for a long time until I realized that in fact the popover presentation controller itself was going out of existence after dismissal, and was being replaced by *another* popover presentation controller — whose delegate, of course, had not been set. My workaround is to set the delegate *again*, in the last dismissal method:

```
func popoverPresentationControllerDidDismissPopover(
    pop: UIPopoverPresentationController) {
        self.searcher.presentationController?.delegate = self
}
```

Dismissal doesn't empty the search bar

When the user dismisses the popover, the search bar is not emptied; if it has text in it, that text remains. My workaround is to empty the search bar in code, in the first dismissal method:

```
func popoverPresentationControllerShouldDismissPopover(
    pop: UIPopoverPresentationController) -> Bool {
        self.searcher.searchBar.text = nil
        return true
}
```

Split Views

A *split view* appears in its typical configuration on the iPad as a combination of two views, the first having the width of an iPhone screen in portrait orientation. Under the hood, there is a *split view controller* (UISplitViewController); the two views are the main views of its two child view controllers. The split view controller manages those views differently depending on the orientation of the device:

The iPad is in landscape orientation

The two views appear side by side.

The iPad is in portrait orientation

There are two possibilities:

- Both views continue to appear side by side; the second view is narrower than in landscape orientation, because the screen is narrower. Apple's Settings app is an example.

- Only the second view appears, with an option to summon the first view from the left as an overlay, either by tapping a bar button item or by swiping from left to right. Apple's Mail app is an example (Figure 9-4).

A split view typically expresses a *master–detail architecture*. The smaller, first view is a UITableView where the user is presented with a list (the *master*). The user taps an item of that list to specify what should appear in the larger, second view (the *detail*). We may thus speak of the two children of the split view controller as the *master view controller* and the *detail view controller*. Apple also sometimes calls them the *primary* and *secondary* view controllers. A UIViewController that is a child, at any depth, of a UISplitViewController has a reference to the UISplitViewController through its splitViewController property.

On the smaller iPhone screen, a master–detail interface would usually be expressed as a navigation interface: the user sees the master list, which occupies the entire interface, and taps an item of the list to navigate to the corresponding detail, which again occupies

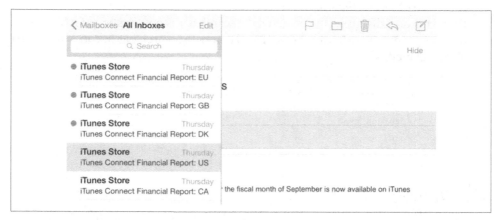

Figure 9-4. A familiar split view interface

the entire interface — because it has been pushed onto the navigation stack. On the larger iPad screen, that interface seems overblown and unnecessary: there is room, especially in landscape orientation, for the master view and the detail view to appear *simultaneously*. That is exactly what the split view does.

In iOS 7 and before, writing a universal app that uses a split view in its iPad incarnation can be challenging. You have to implement two completely different interfaces using two completely different types of view controller — a split view controller on the iPad, but a navigation controller on the iPhone. And over the lifetime of the app, modification of that interface proceeds in two completely different ways: when the user taps an item of the master table view, the iPad version alters the split view controller's detail view controller, whereas the iPhone version pushes a new view controller onto the navigation stack.

New in iOS 8, however, a split view is *adaptive*. This means that UISplitViewController can create and manage the entire architecture on *both* types of device — side by side on iPad, navigation interface on iPhone. And this management is flexible; the iPhone version doesn't *have* to be a navigation interface — in fact, it can even keep the iPad's side by side interface. Also new in iOS 8, the split view controller's interface is structurally flexible; for example, in the side by side arrangement, the width of the views is up to you.

If a split view controller is the top-level view controller, it determines your app's compensatory rotation behavior. To take a hand in that determination without having to subclass UISplitViewController, make one of your objects the split view controller's delegate (UISplitViewControllerDelegate) and implement these methods, as needed:

- `splitViewControllerSupportedInterfaceOrientations:`

- `splitViewControllerPreferredInterfaceOrientationForPresentation:`

 A split view controller does not relegate decisions about the status bar appearance to its children. Thus, for example, to hide the status bar when a split view controller is the root view controller, you will have to subclass UISplitViewController. Alternatively, you might wrap the split view controller in a custom container view controller, as I describe later in this chapter.

Expanded Split View Controller (iPad)

Xcode 6's Master–Detail Application template will give you a complete adaptive UISplit-ViewController with no work on your part, but for pedagogical purposes I'll start by constructing a split view architecture entirely in code, starting from a completely empty app project with no storyboard (see Chapter 1). We'll get it working on the iPad before proceeding to the iPhone version. For reasons that will be clear later, a split view controller on the iPad, by default, is called an *expanded* split view controller. An expanded split view controller has two child view controllers, as I've already described.

Our master view (owned by MasterViewController) will be a table view listing the names of the three Pep boys. Our detail view (owned by DetailViewController) will contain a single label displaying the name of the Pep boy selected in the Master view.

Our first cut at writing MasterViewController merely displays the table view:

```
class MasterViewController: UITableViewController {
    let model = ["Manny", "Moe", "Jack"]
    override func viewDidLoad() {
        super.viewDidLoad()
        self.tableView.registerClass(
            UITableViewCell.self, forCellReuseIdentifier: "Cell")
    }
    override func numberOfSectionsInTableView(
        tableView: UITableView) -> Int {
            return 1
    }
    override func tableView(tableView: UITableView,
        numberOfRowsInSection section: Int) -> Int {
            return model.count
    }
    override func tableView(tableView: UITableView,
        cellForRowAtIndexPath indexPath: NSIndexPath) -> UITableViewCell {
            let cell = tableView.dequeueReusableCellWithIdentifier(
                "Cell", forIndexPath: indexPath) as! UITableViewCell
```

```
            cell.textLabel!.text = model[indexPath.row]
            return cell
        }
    }
```

DetailViewController, in its `viewDidLoad` implementation, puts the label (`self.lab`) into the interface; it also has a public boy string property whose value appears in the label. We are deliberately agnostic about the order of events; our interface works correctly regardless of whether boy is set before or after `viewDidLoad` is called:

```
class DetailViewController: UIViewController {
    var lab : UILabel!
    var boy : String = "" {
        didSet {
            if self.lab != nil {
                self.lab.text = self.boy
            }
        }
    }
    override func viewDidLoad() {
        super.viewDidLoad()
        self.view.backgroundColor = UIColor.whiteColor()
        let lab = UILabel(frame:CGRectMake(100,100,100,30))
        self.view.addSubview(lab)
        self.lab = lab
        self.lab.text = self.boy
    }
}
```

Our app delegate constructs the interface by making a UISplitViewController, giving it its two initial children, and putting its view into the window:

```
func application(application: UIApplication,
    didFinishLaunchingWithOptions launchOptions: [NSObject: AnyObject]?)
    -> Bool {
        self.window = UIWindow(frame:UIScreen.mainScreen().bounds)
        let svc = UISplitViewController()
        svc.addChildViewController(MasterViewController())
        svc.addChildViewController(DetailViewController())
        self.window!.rootViewController = svc
        self.window!.backgroundColor = UIColor.whiteColor()
        self.window!.makeKeyAndVisible()
        return true
}
```

This is already a working split view interface. In landscape orientation, the two views appear side by side. In portrait orientation, only the detail view appears; but the master view can be summoned by swiping from left to right, and can be dismissed by tapping outside it. However, the app itself doesn't yet *do* anything. In particular, when we tap on a Pep boy's name in the master view, the detail view doesn't change. Let's add that code (to MasterViewController):

```
override func tableView(tableView: UITableView,
    didSelectRowAtIndexPath indexPath: NSIndexPath) {
        let detail = DetailViewController()
        detail.boy = model[indexPath.row]
        self.showDetailViewController(detail, sender: self)
}
```

The last line is the surprise. We have not implemented any `showDetailView-Controller:sender:` method; yet we are able to send this message to ourselves, and it works: the new, correctly configured detail view seamlessly replaces the existing detail view, causing the selected Pep boy's name to appear in the interface. How can this be? This method, new in iOS 8, effectively walks up the view controller hierarchy, looking for someone to handle it. (The details are a bit more complicated; I'll discuss them later.) Our DetailViewController can't handle it, but its parent view controller, the UISplit-ViewController, can! It responds by making the specified view controller its second child.

Our app still doesn't quite look like a standard master–detail view interface. The usual thing is for both the master view and the detail view to contain a navigation bar. The detail view in portrait orientation can then display in its navigation bar a left button that summons the master view, so that the user doesn't have to know about the swipe gesture. In iOS 8, this button is vended by the UISplitViewController, through the `displayMode-ButtonItem` method. Thus, we need to change our app delegate code as follows:

```
let svc = UISplitViewController()
let master = MasterViewController()
master.title = "Pep"
let nav1 = UINavigationController(rootViewController:master)
svc.addChildViewController(nav1)
let detail = DetailViewController()
let nav2 = UINavigationController(rootViewController:detail)
svc.addChildViewController(nav2)
self.window!.rootViewController = svc
let b = svc.displayModeButtonItem()
detail.navigationItem.leftBarButtonItem = b
```

But we are still not quite done. Consider what will happen when the user taps a Pep boy name in the master view. At the moment, we are making a new DetailViewController and making it the split view controller's second child. That is now wrong; we must make a new UINavigationController instead, with a new DetailViewController as its child. Moreover, this new DetailViewController doesn't automatically have the `displayMode-ButtonItem` as its `leftBarButtonItem` — we have to set it:

```
override func tableView(tableView: UITableView,
    didSelectRowAtIndexPath indexPath: NSIndexPath) {
        let detail = DetailViewController()
        detail.boy = model[indexPath.row]
        let b = self.splitViewController!.displayModeButtonItem()
        detail.navigationItem.leftBarButtonItem = b
```

```
            detail.navigationItem.leftItemsSupplementBackButton = true
            let nav = UINavigationController(rootViewController: detail)
            self.showDetailViewController(nav, sender: self)
    }
```

Unlike iOS 7 and before, the iOS 8 `displayModeButtonItem` automatically hides itself when the app is in landscape orientation with the two views displayed side by side. Our iPad split view implementation is therefore finished.

Collapsed Split View Controller (iPhone)

Astoundingly, if we now launch our existing app on iPhone, it works almost perfectly. There's a navigation interface. Tapping a Pep boy's name in the master view pushes the new detail view controller onto the navigation stack, with its view displaying that name. The detail view's navigation bar has a back button that pops the detail view controller and returns us to the master view.

The only thing that isn't quite right is that the app launches with the detail view showing, rather than the master view. To fix that, we first modify our app delegate to function as the UISplitViewController's delegate:

```
let svc = UISplitViewController()
svc.delegate = self
// ... the rest as before ...
```

We then implement `splitViewController:collapseSecondaryViewController:ontoPrimaryViewController:` to return `true`:

```
func splitViewController(splitViewController: UISplitViewController,
    collapseSecondaryViewController
    secondaryViewController: UIViewController!,
    ontoPrimaryViewController
    primaryViewController: UIViewController!) -> Bool {
        return true
}
```

That's all! On the iPhone, the app now behaves correctly.

How can this be? To understand what the split view controller is up to, you need to know that it adopts one of two states: it is or it isn't `collapsed`. This distinction corresponds to whether or not the environment's trait collection has a `.Compact` horizontal size class: if so, the split view controller collapses. Thus, the split view controller collapses as it launches on an iPhone.

A collapsed split view controller has only *one* child view controller. This raises the question of how to get from the expanded state to the collapsed state. As the split view controller collapses, it *asks its delegate* how to proceed. In particular, it calls these delegate methods:

`primaryViewControllerForCollapsingSplitViewController:`

> The collapsed split view controller will have only one child view controller. *What* view controller should this be? By default, it will be the current *first* view controller, but you can implement this method to return a different answer.

`splitViewController:collapseSecondaryViewController:ontoPrimaryView-Controller:`

> The collapsing split view controller is going to jettison its *second* view controller. Return `true` to permit this to happen. What happens to the second view controller is now up to you.
>
> If this method returns `false` (the default), the split view controller sends `collapse-SecondaryViewController:forSplitViewController:` to the *first* view controller. What happens to the second view controller is now up to the first view controller.

We are now ready to describe what happens when our app launches on an iPhone:

1. This is a horizontally compact environment, so the split view controller collapses.

2. The split view controller calls its delegate's `primaryViewControllerForCollapsing-SplitViewController:`. We didn't implement this method. The default is to make the first view controller the sole view controller, which is what we want: we want our split view controller to contain the navigation controller containing the Master-ViewController displaying the table view.

3. The split view controller calls its delegate's `splitViewController:collapse-SecondaryViewController:ontoPrimaryViewController:`, which can return `false` or `true`:

   - The default is to return `false`, which causes `collapseSecondaryView-Controller:forSplitViewController:` to be sent to the first view controller. There are two possible outcomes:

     - For a plain vanilla UIViewController, the default implementation of `collapse-SecondaryViewController:forSplitViewController:` does nothing.

     - It happens, however, that our first view controller is a UINavigationController — and UINavigationController implements this method to push the specified view controller (the first parameter) onto its stack!

     We must therefore prevent `collapseSecondaryViewController:forSplitView-Controller:` from being sent to the first view controller if we don't want the app to launch with the second view controller showing.

   - We *do* prevent it, by returning `true` instead! We don't do anything with the second view controller, so it is simply thrown away — which is exactly what we want.

Our app has now launched. Its root view controller is the split view controller. The split view controller has one child — a UINavigationController which, in turn, has one child, namely our MasterViewController. Thus, the table view is visible in a navigation interface. The user taps a row of the table, and our code sends `showDetailView-Controller:sender:` to the MasterViewController. As I mentioned before, the result is a walk up the view controller hierarchy, looking for someone to handle this method. Here's what happens:

1. MasterViewController doesn't handle it, so we proceed to its parent, the UINavigationController.

2. UINavigationController doesn't handle it either! So we proceed to *its* parent, the UISplitViewController.

3. UISplitViewController does handle this message, in one of two ways:

   - If the split view controller is *not* collapsed, it accepts the specified view controller and substitutes it as its own second view controller. The second view controller's view is displayed, so the user now sees it as the detail view. That is what happened when our app ran on the iPad.

   - If the split view controller *is* collapsed, it sends `showViewController:sender:` to its first view controller. The first view controller happens to be a UINavigation-Controller, and we already know (from Chapter 6) how it responds: it pushes the specified view controller onto its stack.

 In our example, the second view controller is a UINavigationController. We are therefore pushing a UINavigationController onto a UINavigationController's stack. This is an odd thing to do, but thanks to some internal voodoo, the parent UINavigationController will do the right thing: in displaying this child's view, it turns to the child UINavigationController's `topViewController` and displays *its* view (and its `navigationItem`), and the child UINavigationController's navigation bar never gets into the interface.

Expanding Split View Controller (iPhone 6 Plus)

The iPhone 6 Plus is an interesting hybrid case: it's horizontally compact in portrait orientation, but *not* in landscape orientation. Thus, in effect, the split view controller thinks it's on an iPhone when the iPhone 6 Plus is in portrait, but it thinks it has been magically moved over to an iPad when the iPhone 6 Plus interface rotates to landscape. Thus, the split view controller *alternates* between `collapsed` being `true` and `false` *on a single device*. In portrait, the split view displays a single navigation interface, with the master view controller at its root, like an iPhone. In landscape, the master and detail views are displayed side by side, like an iPad.

When the app, running on the iPhone 6 Plus, rotates to portrait, or if it launches into portrait, the split view controller goes through the very same procedure I just described for an iPhone. But when it rotates to landscape, it performs the opposite of collapsing — which Apple, not surprisingly, describes as *expanding*. As the split view controller expands, it *asks its delegate* how to proceed:

`primaryViewControllerForExpandingSplitViewController:`
> The collapsed split view controller has just one child. The expanded split view controller will have two children. What view controller should be its *first* child view controller? By default, it will be the *current* child view controller, but you can implement this method to return a different answer.

`splitViewController:separateSecondaryViewControllerFromPrimaryView-Controller:`
> What view controller should be the expanded split view controller's *second* child view controller? Implement this method to provide an answer.
>
> If you don't implement this method, or if you return nil, the split view controller sends `separateSecondaryViewControllerForSplitViewController:` to the *first* view controller. This method returns a view controller, or nil. If it returns a view controller, the split view controller makes that view controller its second view controller.

The default response of a plain vanilla UIViewController to `separateSecondaryView-ControllerForSplitViewController:` is to return nil. A UINavigationController, however, pops its own `topViewController` and returns that view controller. Thus, when our app is rotated from portrait to landscape, exactly the right thing happens: if the navigation controller has pushed a DetailViewController onto its stack, it now pops it and hands it to the split view controller, which displays its view as the detail view.

One other new feature of our app's behavior on the iPhone 6 Plus is that the `display-ModeButtonItem` is present in landscape (whereas it disappears automatically on an iPad in landscape). It takes on a new form: instead of appearing as a "back" chevron, it's an "expand" symbol. When the user taps it, the master view is hidden and the detail view occupies the entire screen — and the `displayModeButtonItem` changes to a chevron. Tapping the chevron toggles back the other way: the master view is shown again.

Customizing a Split View Controller

Properties and delegate methods of a UISplitViewController (mostly new in iOS 8) allow easy customization:

`presentsWithGesture`
> A Bool. If `false`, the left-to-right swipe gesture that shows the master view in portrait orientation on an iPad is disabled. The default is `true`.

preferredDisplayMode

Set this to change the current display mode of an expanded split view controller programmatically. To specify the default mode, use `.Automatic`. To learn the actual display mode being used, ask for the current `displayMode`.

An expanded split view controller has three possible display modes (UISplitView-ControllerDisplayMode) — `.PrimaryHidden`, `.AllVisible`, and `.Primary-Overlay`. The default automatic behaviors are:

iPad in landscape

The `displayModeButtonItem` is hidden and the display mode is `.All-Visible`.

iPad in portrait

The `displayModeButtonItem` is shown, and the display mode toggles between `.PrimaryHidden` and `.PrimaryOverlay`.

iPhone 6 Plus in landscape

The `displayModeButtonItem` is shown, and the display mode toggles between `.PrimaryHidden` and `.AllVisible`.

preferredPrimaryColumnWidthFraction

Sets the master view width in `.AllVisible` and `.PrimaryOverlay` display modes, as a percentage of the whole split view (between 0 and 1). Your setting may have no effect unless you also constrain the width limits absolutely through the `minimum-PrimaryColumnWidth` and `maximumPrimaryColumnWidth` properties. To specify the default width, use `UISplitViewControllerAutomaticDimension`. To learn the actual width being used, ask for the current `primaryColumnWidth`.

You can also track and govern the display mode with these delegate methods:

splitViewController:willChangeToDisplayMode:

The `displayMode` of an expanded split view controller is about to change, meaning that its first view controller's view will be shown or hidden. You might want to alter the interface somehow in response.

targetDisplayModeForActionInSplitViewController:

Called whenever something happens that might affect the display mode. For example:

- The split view controller is showing for the first time.
- The interface is rotating.
- The user summons or dismisses the primary view.

Return a display mode to specify what the user's tapping the `displayModeButton-Item` should subsequently do (and, by extension, how the `displayModeButton-Item` is portrayed), or `.Automatic` to accept what the split view would normally do.

Customizations on a more structural level are performed through the other delegate methods. For example, there might be additional view controllers present, or you might use a split view controller in some completely different way, so that the default collapsed version of a split view controller might not be appropriate. Thus you would implement the delegate methods I described in the preceding two sections to determine how the view controller structure should be rearranged when the split view controller collapses and expands:

- `primaryViewControllerForCollapsingSplitViewController:`
- `splitViewController:collapseSecondaryViewController:ontoPrimaryView-Controller:`
- `primaryViewControllerForExpandingSplitViewController:`
- `splitViewController:separateSecondaryViewControllerFromPrimaryView-Controller:`

Also, your custom view controller can implement `collapseSecondaryView-Controller:forSplitViewController:` and `separateSecondaryViewControllerFor-SplitViewController:`, so that it can take a hand in what happens when it is the primary view controller during collapsing and expanding.

 After collapsing or expanding, a UISplitViewController emits the `UIViewController-ShowDetailTargetDidChangeNotification`.

Setting the Collapsed State

The split view controller can be in a collapsed or an expanded state — its `collapsed` property can be `true` or `false`. But this property is read-only. How, then, would you set the collapsed state? For example, perhaps you want side-by-side display of the two child view controllers' views in landscape *even on an iPhone*. How would you arrange that?

The split view controller decides which state to adopt depending on the environment — in particular, whether the current trait collection's horizontal size class is `.Compact`. The solution, therefore, is to *lie to the split view controller* about its trait collection environment, effectively making it believe, for example, that it's on an iPad even though it's really on an iPhone.

You can do that by interposing your own custom container view controller above the split view controller in the view controller hierarchy — typically, as the split view controller's direct parent. You can then send your container view controller the setOverride-TraitCollection:forChildViewController: message, thus causing it to pass the trait collection of your choosing down the view controller hierarchy to the split view controller.

In this example, our container view controller is the app's root view controller; its child is a split view controller. The split view controller's view completely occupies the container view controller's view (in other words, the container's own view is never seen independently; the container view controller exists *solely* in order to manage the split view controller). Early in the life of the app, the container view controller configures the split view controller and lies to it about the environment. The result is that the split view controller displays both its children's views side by side, both in portrait and landscape, like the Settings app on the iPad, *even on the iPhone*:

```
override func viewWillLayoutSubviews() {
    if !self.didInitialSetup {
        self.didInitialSetup = true
        let svc = self.childViewControllers[0] as! UISplitViewController
        svc.preferredDisplayMode = .AllVisible
        svc.preferredPrimaryColumnWidthFraction = 0.5
        svc.maximumPrimaryColumnWidth = 500
        let traits = UITraitCollection(traitsFromCollections: [
            UITraitCollection(horizontalSizeClass: .Regular)
            ])
        self.setOverrideTraitCollection(traits, forChildViewController: svc)
    }
}
```

Another possibility, based on Apple's AdaptivePhotos sample code, might be to make the iPhone behave like an iPhone 6 Plus, with a .Regular horizontal size class in landscape (the split view controller expands) but a .Compact horizontal size class in portrait (the split view controller collapses):

```
override func viewWillTransitionToSize(size: CGSize,
    withTransitionCoordinator
    coordinator: UIViewControllerTransitionCoordinator) {
        let svc = self.childViewControllers[0] as! UISplitViewController
        if size.width > 320 {
            let traits = UITraitCollection(traitsFromCollections: [
                UITraitCollection(horizontalSizeClass: .Regular)])
            self.setOverrideTraitCollection(
                traits, forChildViewController: svc)
        } else {
            self.setOverrideTraitCollection(
                nil, forChildViewController: svc)
```

```
    }
    super.viewWillTransitionToSize(
        size, withTransitionCoordinator: coordinator)
}
```

Replacing the Child View Controllers

The master–detail architecture that I've been using as an example throughout this discussion uses showDetailViewController:sender: as the standard response to the user tapping an entry in the master list. However, I have not been sending this message directly to the split view controller; instead, I've sent it to self (the master view controller), with an assurance that the message will percolate up to the split view controller. It's now time to talk in more detail about this percolation process.

iOS 8 introduces a new generalized architecture for percolating a message up the view controller hierarchy. The heart of this architecture is the method targetViewControllerForAction:sender:, where the action: parameter is the selector for the method we're inquiring about. This method, using some deep introspective voodoo, looks to see whether the view controller to which the message was sent *overrides the UIViewController implementation* of the method in question. If so, it returns self; if not, it returns the result of calling targetViewControllerForAction:sender: (with the same parameters) on its parent view controller or presenting view controller — or nil if no view controller is ultimately returned to it.

 A view controller subclass that *does* override the method in question but does *not* want to be the target view controller can implement the UIResponder method canPerformAction:withSender: to return false.

The idea is that any UIViewController method can be implemented so as to percolate up the view controller hierarchy in this way, analogously to how the responder chain operates. In particular, two UIViewController methods *are* implemented in this way:

- showViewController:sender:
- showDetailViewController:sender:

These methods are implemented to call targetViewControllerForAction:sender:. If this returns a target, they send themselves to that target. If it *doesn't* return a target, they call presentViewController:animated:completion:.

Thus, what actually happens when I send showDetailViewController:sender: to self (the master view controller) is:

1. The master view controller doesn't implement `showDetailView-Controller:sender:`; it inherits the UIViewController implementation, which is called.

2. The UIViewController implementation of `showDetailViewController:sender:` calls `targetViewControllerForAction:sender:` on `self` (the master view controller) with `"showDetailViewController:sender:"` as its `action:` parameter.

3. `targetViewControllerForAction:sender:` sees that `showDetailViewController:sender:` is not overridden by this view controller (the master view controller), so it calls `targetViewControllerForAction:sender:` on the parent view controller, which is a UINavigationController.

4. `targetViewControllerForAction:sender:` sees that `showDetailViewController:sender:` is not overridden by *this* view controller (the navigation view controller), so it calls `targetViewControllerForAction:sender:` on *its* parent view controller, which is a UISplitViewController.

5. It happens that UISplitViewController *does* override the UIViewController implementation of `showDetailViewController:sender:`. Thus, `targetViewControllerForAction:sender:` in the split view controller returns the split view controller instance, and all the nested calls to `targetViewControllerForAction:sender:` return with the split view controller as the result.

6. We are now back in `showDetailViewController:sender:`, originally sent to the master view controller. From its call to `targetViewControllerForAction:sender:`, it has acquired a target — the split view controller. So it finishes by sending `showDetailViewController:sender:` to the split view controller.

The flexibility illustrated here is what allows these two methods to work *differently* depending on (not the identity, but) the *environment* of the view controller to which they are originally sent — that is, depending upon its *place in the view controller hierarchy*. Two built-in UIViewController subclasses override one or both of these methods, and thus, if they are further up the view controller hierarchy than the view controller on which these methods are called, will affect what happens:

UINavigationController `showViewController:sender:`
> UINavigationController implements `showViewController:sender:` to call `pushViewController:animated:`.

> Thus, if you send `showViewController:sender:` to a view controller whose parent is a UINavigationController, it is the navigation controller's implementation that will be called, meaning that the parameter view controller is *pushed* onto the stack. But if you send `showViewController:sender:` to a view controller *without* a parent that overrides this method, the default implementation is used, meaning that the parameter view is *presented*.

UISplitViewController `showDetailViewController:sender:`

UISplitViewController implements `showDetailViewController:sender:` as follows. First, it calls the delegate method `splitViewController:showDetailViewController:sender:`; if the delegate returns `true`, UISplitViewController does nothing. (In that case, *you* would be responsible for getting the parameter view controller's view into the interface.) Otherwise:

If the split view controller is expanded

It replaces its second child view controller with the parameter view controller.

If the split view controller is collapsed

If its first (and only) child view controller is a UINavigationController, it sends `showViewController:sender:` to it. Otherwise, it calls `presentViewController:animated:completion:`.

UISplitViewController `showViewController:sender:`

UISplitViewController implements `showViewController:sender:` as follows. First, it calls the delegate method `splitViewController:showViewController:sender:`; if the delegate returns `true`, UISplitViewController does nothing. (In that case, *you* would be responsible for getting the parameter view controller's view into the interface.) Otherwise:

If the split view controller is expanded

If the `sender:` is the first view controller, the split view controller replaces the first view controller with the parameter view controller. Otherwise, it replaces its second view controller with the parameter view controller.

If the split view controller is collapsed

It calls `presentViewController:animated:completion:`.

 In general, sending `showViewController:sender:` to a split view controller is buggy and not recommended. In particular, in the case where it replaces the first view controller, the `.PrimaryOverlay` version of the first view controller is *not* replaced.

Now that you understand the percolation mechanism, perhaps you'd like to know whether your own custom methods can participate in it. They can, easily. Extend UIViewController to implement your method such that it calls `targetViewControllerForAction:sender:` on `self` and sends the action method to the target if there is one. For example:

```
extension UIViewController {
    func showHide(sender:AnyObject?) {
        let target =
            self.targetViewControllerForAction("showHide:", sender:sender)
        if target != nil {
```

```
                target!.showHide(self)
            }
        }
    }
```

In that example, I don't know what any particular UIViewController subclass's override of showHide: may do, and I don't care! What matters is that if showHide: is sent to a view controller that *doesn't* override it, it will percolate up the view controller hierarchy until we find a view controller that *does* override it, and it is *that override* that will be called.

Split View Controller in a Storyboard

To see how to configure a split view controller in a storyboard, make a new project from the iPad or Universal version of the Master–Detail Application template and study the storyboard that it provides. This storyboard contains essentially the same configuration I created in code at the start of this section. The split view controller has two relationships, "master view controller" and "detail view controller," specifying its two children. Those two children are both navigation controllers. The first navigation controller has a "root view controller" relationship to a MasterViewController; the second has a "root view controller" relationship to a DetailViewController.

There's one more object in the storyboard, and it's the interesting object: from the prototype table view cell in the Master table view comes a manual segue, triggered by the user selecting the cell — a "show detail" segue whose destination is the Detail navigation controller. It should now be clear what a "show detail" segue does: it calls showDetail-ViewController:sender:. As you know, this means that when the split view controller is expanded, the newly instantiated Detail navigation controller will replace the split view controller's second child view controller; when the split view controller is collapsed, the newly instantiated Detail navigation controller will be pushed onto the Master navigation controller's stack. (The "show detail" segue, new in iOS 8, supersedes the "replace" segue from iOS 7 and before.)

Personally, I prefer to assemble my split view controllers in code. The storyboard version, in my view, is considerably less convenient, because there is so much that remains to be done in code, and it must be done rather clumsily, because the architecture has already been constructed behind your back by the time your code has a chance to run. For example, the app delegate template code configures and adds the displayMode-ButtonItem(); to do this, it must verbosely obtain a reference to the split view controller and to the detail view controller:

```
let splitViewController =
    self.window!.rootViewController as! UISplitViewController
let navigationController = splitViewController.viewControllers[
    splitViewController.viewControllers.count-1] as! UINavigationController
navigationController.topViewController.navigationItem.leftBarButtonItem =
    splitViewController.displayModeButtonItem()
```

Similarly, the master view controller, when the "show detail" segue is triggered, must verbosely get a reference to the Detail view controller:

```
let controller =
    (segue.destinationViewController as! UINavigationController)
        .topViewController as DetailViewController
```

That sort of thing is error-prone and opaque. Code that creates a view controller manually has a direct reference to that view controller, and is clearer and cleaner.

CHAPTER 10

Text

Drawing text into your app's interface is one of the most complex and powerful things that iOS does for you. Fortunately, iOS also shields you from much of that complexity. All you need is some text to draw, and possibly an interface object to draw it for you.

Text to appear in your app's interface will be an NSString or an NSAttributedString. NSAttributedString adds text styling to an NSString, including runs of different character styles, along with paragraph-level features such as alignment, line spacing, and margins.

To make your NSString or NSAttributedString appear in the interface, you can draw it into a graphics context, or hand it to an interface object that knows how to draw it:

Self-drawing text
> Both NSString and NSAttributedString have methods (supplied by the NSString-Drawing category) for drawing themselves into any graphics context.

Text-drawing interface objects
> Interface objects that know how to draw an NSString or NSAttributedString are:

> *UILabel*
>> Displays text, possibly consisting of multiple lines; neither scrollable nor editable.

> *UITextField*
>> Displays a single line of user-editable text; may have a border, a background image, and overlay views at its right and left end.

> *UITextView*
>> Displays scrollable multiline text, possibly user-editable.

Deep under the hood, all text drawing is performed through a low-level technology with a C API called Core Text. Before iOS 7, certain powerful and useful text-drawing features were available *only* by working with Core Text. Now, however, iOS provides Text Kit, a middle-level technology lying on top of Core Text. UITextView is largely just a lightweight drawing wrapper around Text Kit, and Text Kit can also draw directly into a graphics context. By working with Text Kit, you can readily do all sorts of useful text-drawing tricks that previously would have required you to sweat your way through Core Text.

(Another way of drawing text is to use a web view, a scrollable view displaying rendered HTML. A web view can also display various additional document types, such as PDF, RTF, and *.doc*. Web views draw their text using a somewhat different technology, and are discussed in Chapter 11.)

Fonts and Font Descriptors

There are two ways of describing a font: as a UIFont (suitable for use with an NSString or a UIKit interface object) or as a CTFont (suitable for Core Text). Before iOS 7, CTFont and UIFont were unfortunately *not* toll-free bridged to one another, and what you usually started with and wanted to end with was a UIFont; thus, in order to perform font transformations, it was necessary to convert a UIFont to a CTFont manually, work with the CTFont, and then convert back to a UIFont manually — which was by no means trivial. Now, however, UIFont and CTFont *are* toll-free bridged to one another. Moreover, another important Core Text type, CTFontDescriptor, is toll-free bridged to UIFontDescriptor, which can be helpful for performing font transformations.

Fonts

A font (UIFont, toll-free bridged to Core Text's CTFont) is an extremely simple object. You specify a font by its name and size by calling the UIFont initializer `init(name:size:)`, and you can also transform a font of one size to the same font in a different size. UIFont also provides some methods for learning a font's various measurements, such as its `lineHeight` and `capHeight`.

To ask for a font by name, you have to *know* the font's name. Every font variant (bold, italic, and so on) counts as a different font, and font variants are clumped into families. UIFont has class methods that tell you the names of the families and the names of the fonts within them. To learn, in the console, the name of every installed font, you would say:

```
UIFont.familyNames()
    .map{UIFont.fontNamesForFamilyName($0 as! String)}.map(println)
```

You can specify a font by its family name or by its font name (technically, its PostScript name). For example, `"Avenir"` is a family name; the plain font within that family is `"Avenir-Roman"`. Either is legal as the first argument of `init(name:size:)`.

A few fonts can be obtained with reference to their functionality; for example, you can ask for `systemFontOfSize:` to get the font used by default in a UIButton. You should never use the name of such a font for anything, as the details are private and subject to change.

Dynamic Type fonts

The Dynamic Type fonts (introduced in iOS 7) are linked to the slider that the user can adjust in the Settings app, under Display & Brightness → Text Size. The idea is that if you have text for the user to read or edit (as opposed, say, to the static text of a button), you can use a Dynamic Type font; it will be sized and styled for you in accordance with the user's Text Size preference and the role that this text is to play in your layout.

To obtain a Dynamic Type font, call the UIFont class method `preferredFontForTextStyle:`. Possible roles that you can supply as the argument are:

- `UIFontTextStyleHeadline`
- `UIFontTextStyleSubheadline`
- `UIFontTextStyleBody`
- `UIFontTextStyleFootnote`
- `UIFontTextStyleCaption1`
- `UIFontTextStyleCaption2`

You'll probably want to experiment with specifying various roles for your individual pieces of text, to see which looks appropriate in context. For example, in Figure 6-1, the headlines are `UIFontTextStyleSubheadline` and the blurbs are `UIFontTextStyleCaption1`.

Disappointingly, Dynamic Type fonts are *not* actually dynamic; `preferredFontForTextStyle:` will return a font whose size is proportional to the user's Text Size preference only at the moment when it is called. If the user changes that preference, you are expected to call `preferredFontForTextStyle:` again. To hear about such changes, register for `UIContentSizeCategoryDidChangeNotification`. When the notification arrives, you are supposed to set the fonts for your Dynamic Type–savvy text all over again. This, in turn, may have consequences for the physical features of your interface as a whole; autolayout can be a big help here (Chapter 1).

In the nib editor, wherever the Attributes inspector lets you supply a font for an interface object, the Dynamic Type roles are available in a pop-up menu. But you will *still* have to set the font of every such interface object again, in code, when `UIContentSizeCategoryDidChangeNotification` arrives.

In this example, we have a label (`self.lab`) whose font uses Dynamic Type; we have set its font to `UIFontTextStyleHeadline` in the nib editor. We must therefore also update its font manually whenever `UIContentSizeCategoryDidChangeNotification` subsequently arrives:

```
override func viewDidLoad() {
    super.viewDidLoad()
    NSNotificationCenter.defaultCenter().addObserver(
        self, selector: "doDynamicType:",
        name: UIContentSizeCategoryDidChangeNotification, object: nil)
}
func doDynamicType(n:NSNotification) {
    let style = self.lab.font.fontDescriptor()
        .objectForKey(UIFontDescriptorTextStyleAttribute) as! String
    self.lab.font = UIFont.preferredFontForTextStyle(style)
}
```

Needless to say, that kind of thing gets very old very fast — it's enough to put one off using Dynamic Type at all. Fortunately, new in iOS 8, a UITableView whose cells contain labels will watch for `UIContentSizeCategoryDidChangeNotification` for you and will update the label fonts for you automatically. So Dynamic Type in a table view, at least, *is* dynamic.

Adding fonts

You are not limited to fonts installed by default as part of the system. There are two ways to obtain additional fonts:

Include a font in your app bundle
>   A font included at the top level of your app bundle will be loaded at launch time if your *Info.plist* lists it under the "Fonts provided by application" key (`UIAppFonts`).

Download a font in real time
>   All OS X fonts are available for download from Apple's servers; you can obtain and install one while your app is running.

To download a font in real time, you'll have specify the font as a font descriptor (discussed in the next section) and drop down to the level of Core Text (`import Core-Text`) to call `CTFontDescriptorMatchFontDescriptorsWithProgressHandler`. This function takes a block which is called repeatedly at every stage of the download process; the block is called on a background thread, so if you want to use the downloaded font immediately in the interface, you must step out to the main thread (see Chapter 25).

In this example, I'll attempt to use Nanum Brush Script as my UILabel's font; if it isn't installed, I'll attempt to download it and *then* use it as my UILabel's font. I've inserted a lot of unnecessary logging to mark the stages of the download process (using `NSLog` because `println` isn't thread-safe):

```
let name = "NanumBrush"
let size : CGFloat = 24
let f : UIFont! = UIFont(name:name, size:size)
if f != nil {
    self.lab.font = f
    println("already installed")
    return
}
println("attempting to download font")
let desc = UIFontDescriptor(name:name, size:size)
CTFontDescriptorMatchFontDescriptorsWithProgressHandler(
    [desc], nil, {
        (state:CTFontDescriptorMatchingState, prog:CFDictionary!)
            -> Bool in
        switch state {
        case .DidBegin:
            NSLog("%@", "matching did begin")
        case .WillBeginDownloading:
            NSLog("%@", "downloading will begin")
        case .Downloading:
            let d = prog as NSDictionary
            let key = kCTFontDescriptorMatchingPercentage
            let cur : AnyObject? = d[key as NSString]
            if let cur = cur as? NSNumber {
                NSLog("progress: %@%%", cur)
            }
        case .DidFinishDownloading:
            NSLog("%@", "downloading did finish")
        case .DidFailWithError:
            NSLog("%@", "downloading failed")
        case .DidFinish:
            NSLog("%@", "matching did finish")
            dispatch_async(dispatch_get_main_queue(), {
                let f : UIFont! = UIFont(name:name, size:size)
                if f != nil {
                    NSLog("%@", "got the font!")
                    self.lab.font = f
                }
            })
        default:break
        }
        return true
})
```

Font Descriptors

A font descriptor (UIFontDescriptor, toll-free bridged to Core Text's CTFont-Descriptor) is a way of specifying a font, or converting between one font description and another, in terms of its features. For example, given a font descriptor desc, you can ask for a corresponding italic font descriptor like this:

A *wild* and crazy label

Figure 10-1. A Dynamic Type font with an italic variant

```
let desc2 = desc.fontDescriptorWithSymbolicTraits(.TraitItalic)!
```

If `desc` was originally a descriptor for Avenir 15, `desc2` is now a descriptor for Avenir-Oblique 15. However, it is not the *font* Avenir-Oblique 15; a font descriptor is not a font.

To convert from a font to a font descriptor, call its `fontDescriptor` method; to convert from a font descriptor to a font, call the UIFont initializer `init(descriptor:size:)`, typically supplying a size of 0 to signify that the size should not change. Thus, this will be a typical pattern in your code, as you convert from font to font descriptor to perform some transformation, and then back to font:

```
let font = // ...
let desc = font.fontDescriptor()
let desc2 = // font descriptor derived from desc
let font2 = UIFont(descriptor: desc2, size: 0)
```

This same technique is useful for obtaining styled variants of the Dynamic Type fonts. A UIFontDescriptor class method, `preferredFontDescriptorWithTextStyle:`, saves you from having to start with a UIFont. In this example, I prepare to form an NSAttributedString whose font is mostly `UIFontTextStyleBody`, but with one italicized word (Figure 10-1):

```
let body = UIFontDescriptor
    .preferredFontDescriptorWithTextStyle(UIFontTextStyleBody)
if let emphasis = body.fontDescriptorWithSymbolicTraits(.TraitItalic) {
    let fbody = UIFont(descriptor: body, size: 0)
    let femphasis = UIFont(descriptor: emphasis, size: 0)
}
```

 In iOS 8 before iOS 8.3, converting between fonts by calling `fontDescriptorWith-SymbolicTraits:` doesn't work for every font family; instead, you might have to drop down to the level of Core Text. Fortunately, this bug is fixed in iOS 8.3.

You can explore a font's features by way of UIFontDescriptor's `fontAttributes` method, which returns a dictionary of attributes and their values. If you know the name of the attribute whose value you want, you can send `objectForKey:` directly to a UIFont-Descriptor, as I did in an earlier example.

Another use of font descriptors is to access hidden built-in typographical features of individual fonts. In this example, I'll obtain a variant of the Didot font that draws its minuscules as small caps (Figure 10-2):

Figure 10-2. A small caps font variant

```
let desc = UIFontDescriptor(name:"Didot", size:18)
let d = [
    UIFontFeatureTypeIdentifierKey:kLetterCaseType,
    UIFontFeatureSelectorIdentifierKey:kSmallCapsSelector
]
let desc2 = desc.fontDescriptorByAddingAttributes([
    UIFontDescriptorFeatureSettingsAttribute:[d]
])
let f = UIFont(descriptor: desc2, size: 0)
```

Attributed Strings

Styled text — that is, text consisting of multiple style runs, with different font, size, color, and other text features in different parts of the text — is expressed an *attributed string*. Attributed strings (NSAttributedString and its mutable subclass, NSMutableAttributedString) have been around in iOS for a long time, but before iOS 6 they were difficult to use — you had to drop down to the level of Core Text — and they couldn't be used at all in connection with UIKit interface classes such as UILabel and UITextView. Thus, such interface classes couldn't display styled text. In iOS 6, NSAttributedString became a first-class citizen; it can now be used to draw styled text directly, and can be drawn by built-in interface classes.

 In general, interface object methods and properties that accept attributed strings stand side by side with their pre-iOS 6 equivalents; the new ones tend to have "attributed" in their name. Thus, you don't *have* to use attributed strings. If a UILabel, for example, is to display text in a single font, size, color, and alignment, it might be easiest to use the pre-iOS 6 plain-old-NSString features of UILabel. If you do use an attributed string with an interface object, it is best not to mix in any of the pre-iOS 6 settings: let the attributed string do *all* the work of dictating text style features.

An NSAttributedString consists of an NSString (its `string`) plus the attributes, applied in ranges. For example, if the string "one red word" is blue except for the word "red" which is red, and if these are the only changes over the course of the string, then there are three distinct style runs — everything before the word "red," the word "red" itself, and everything after the word "red." However, we can apply the attributes in two steps, first making the whole string blue, and then making the word "red" red, just as you would expect.

Attributed String Attributes

The attributes applied to a range of an attributed string are described in dictionaries. Each possible attribute has a predefined name, used as a key in these dictionaries; here are some of the most important attributes (for the full list, see Apple's *NSAttributedString UIKit Additions Reference*):

NSFontAttributeName
> A UIFont.

NSForegroundColorAttributeName
> The text color, a UIColor.

NSBackgroundColorAttributeName
> The color *behind* the text, a UIColor. You could use this to highlight a word, for example.

NSLigatureAttributeName
> An NSNumber wrapping 0 or 1, expressing whether or not you want ligatures used.

NSKernAttributeName
> An NSNumber wrapping the floating-point amount of kerning. A negative value brings a glyph closer to the following glyph; a positive value adds space between them.

NSStrikethroughStyleAttributeName
NSUnderlineStyleAttributeName
> An NSNumber wrapping one of these values (NSUnderlineStyle) describing the line weight:
>
> - .StyleNone
> - .StyleSingle
> - .StyleDouble
> - .StyleThick

Optionally, you may append (using logical-or) a specification of the line pattern, with names like .PatternDot, .PatternDash, and so on.

Optionally, you may append (using logical-or) .ByWord; if you do not, then if the underline or strikethrough range involves multiple words, the whitespace between the words will be underlined or struck through.

`NSStrikethroughColorAttributeName`
`NSUnderlineColorAttributeName`
> A UIColor. If not defined, the foreground color is used.

`NSStrokeWidthAttributeName`
> An NSNumber wrapping a float. The stroke width is peculiarly coded. If it's positive, then the text glyphs are stroked but not filled, giving an outline effect, and the foreground color is used unless a separate stroke color is defined. If it's negative, then its absolute value is the width of the stroke, and the glyphs are both filled (with the foreground color) and stroked (with the stroke color).

`NSStrokeColorAttributeName`
> The stroke color, a UIColor.

`NSShadowAttributeName`
> An NSShadow object. An NSShadow is just a glorified struct (what Apple calls a "value object"), combining a `shadowOffset`, `shadowColor`, and `shadowBlurRadius`.

`NSTextEffectAttributeName`
> If defined, the only possible value is `NSTextEffectLetterpressStyle`.

`NSAttachmentAttributeName`
> An NSTextAttachment object. A text attachment is basically an inline image. I'll discuss text attachments later on.

`NSLinkAttributeName`
> An NSURL. In a noneditable, selectable UITextView, the link is tappable to go to the URL (depending on your implementation of the UITextViewDelegate method `textView:shouldInteractWithURL:inRange:`). By default, appears as blue without an underline in a UITextView. Appears as blue with an underline in a UILabel, but is not a tappable link there.

`NSBaselineOffsetAttributeName`
`NSObliquenessAttributeName`
`NSExpansionAttributeName`
> An NSNumber wrapping a float.

`NSParagraphStyleAttributeName`
> An NSParagraphStyle object. This is basically just a glorified struct, assembling text features that apply properly to paragraphs as a whole, not merely to characters, even if your string consists only of a single paragraph. Here are its most important properties:

- alignment (NSTextAlignment)
    - .Left
    - .Center
    - .Right
    - .Justified
    - .Natural (left-aligned or right-aligned depending on the writing direction)
- lineBreakMode (NSLineBreakMode)
    - .ByWordWrapping
    - .ByCharWrapping
    - .ByClipping
    - .ByTruncatingHead
    - .ByTruncatingTail
    - .ByTruncatingMiddle
- firstLineHeadIndent, headIndent (left margin), tailIndent (right margin)
- lineHeightMultiple, maximumLineHeight, minimumLineHeight
- lineSpacing
- paragraphSpacing, paragraphSpacingBefore
- hyphenationFactor (0 or 1)
- defaultTabInterval, tabStops (the tab stops are an array of NSTextTab objects)

To construct an NSAttributedString, you can call init(string:attributes:) if the entire string has the same attributes; otherwise, you'll use its mutable subclass NSMutableAttributedString, which lets you set attributes over a range.

To construct an NSParagraphStyle, you'll use its mutable subclass NSMutableParagraphStyle. (The properties of NSParagraphStyle itself are all read-only, for historical reasons.) It is sufficient to apply a paragraph style to the first character of a paragraph; to put it another way, the paragraph style of the first character of a paragraph dictates how the whole paragraph is rendered.

Both NSAttributedString and NSParagraphStyle come with default values for all attributes, so you only have to set the attributes you care about.

Figure 10-3. An attributed string

Making an Attributed String

We now know enough for an example! I'll draw my attributed strings in a disabled (noninteractive) UITextView; its background is white, but its superview's background is gray, so you can see the text view's bounds relative to the text. (Ignore the text's vertical positioning, which is configured by applying a top `contentInset`.)

First, two words of my attributed string are made extra-bold by stroking in a different color. I start by dictating the entire string and the overall style of the text; then I apply the special style to the two stroked words (Figure 10-3):

```
var content : NSMutableAttributedString!
let s1 = "The Gettysburg Address, as delivered on a certain occasion " +
    "(namely Thursday, November 19, 1863) by A. Lincoln"
content = NSMutableAttributedString(string:s1, attributes:[
    NSFontAttributeName: UIFont(name:"Arial-BoldMT", size:15)!,
    NSForegroundColorAttributeName: UIColor(
        red:0.251, green:0.000, blue:0.502, alpha:1)
    ])
let r = (s1 as NSString).rangeOfString("Gettysburg Address")
content.addAttributes([
    NSStrokeColorAttributeName: UIColor.redColor(),
    NSStrokeWidthAttributeName: -2.0
    ], range: r)
self.tv.attributedText = content
```

Carrying on from the previous example, I'll also make the whole paragraph centered and indented from the edges of the text view. To do so, I create a paragraph style and apply it to the first character. Note how the margins are dictated: the `tailIndent` is negative, to bring the right margin leftward, and the `firstLineHeadIndent` must be set separately, as the `headIndent` does not automatically apply to the first line (Figure 10-4):

```
let para = NSMutableParagraphStyle()
para.headIndent = 10
para.firstLineHeadIndent = 10
para.tailIndent = -10
para.lineBreakMode = .ByWordWrapping
```

> The Gettysburg Address, as
> delivered on a certain occasion
> (namely Thursday, November 19,
> 1863) by A. Lincoln

Figure 10-4. An attributed string with a paragraph style

```
para.alignment = .Center
para.paragraphSpacing = 15
content.addAttribute(
    NSParagraphStyleAttributeName,
    value:para, range:NSMakeRange(0,1))
self.tv.attributedText = content
```

When working with a value class, it feels clunky to be forced to instantiate the class and configure the instance *before* using it for the one and only time. So I've written a little Swift generic function, lend (see Appendix B), that lets me do all that in a closure at the point where the value class is used.

In this next example, I'll enlarge the first character of a paragraph. I assign the first character a larger font size, I expand its width slightly, and I reduce its kerning (Figure 10-5):

```
var content2 : NSMutableAttributedString!
let s2 = "Fourscore and seven years ago, our fathers brought forth " +
    "upon this continent a new nation, conceived in liberty and " +
    "dedicated to the proposition that all men are created equal."
content2 = NSMutableAttributedString(string:s2, attributes: [
    NSFontAttributeName: UIFont(name:"HoeflerText-Black", size:16)!
])
content2.addAttributes([
    NSFontAttributeName: UIFont(name:"HoeflerText-Black", size:24)!,
    NSExpansionAttributeName: 0.3,
    NSKernAttributeName: -4
], range:NSMakeRange(0,1))
self.tv.attributedText = content2
```

Carrying on from the previous example, I'll once again construct a paragraph style and add it to the first character. My paragraph style illustrates full justification and automatic hyphenation (Figure 10-6):

Figure 10-5. An attributed string with an expanded first character

Figure 10-6. An attributed string with justification and autohyphenation

```
content2.addAttribute(NSParagraphStyleAttributeName,
    value:lend {
        (para:NSMutableParagraphStyle) in
        para.headIndent = 10
        para.firstLineHeadIndent = 10
        para.tailIndent = -10
        para.lineBreakMode = .ByWordWrapping
        para.alignment = .Justified
        para.lineHeightMultiple = 1.2
        para.hyphenationFactor = 1.0
    }, range:NSMakeRange(0,1))
self.tv.attributedText = content2
```

Now we come to the Really Amazing Part. I can make a *single* attributed string consisting of *both* paragraphs, and a single text view can portray it (Figure 10-7):

```
let end = content.length
content.replaceCharactersInRange(NSMakeRange(end, 0), withString:"\n")
content.appendAttributedString(content2)
self.tv.attributedText = content
```

Tab stops

A tab stop is an NSTextTab, the initializer of which lets you set its location (points from the left edge) and alignment. An options dictionary lets you set the tab stop's column terminator characters; a common use is to create a decimal tab stop, for aligning cur-

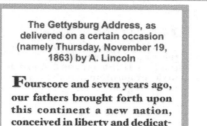

Figure 10-7. A single attributed string comprising differently styled paragraphs

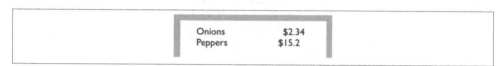

Figure 10-8. Tab stops in an attributed string

rency values at their decimal point. The key, in that case, is NSTabColumnTerminators-
AttributeName; you can obtain a value appropriate to a given NSLocale by calling
NSTextTab's class method columnTerminatorsForLocale:.

Here's an example (Figure 10-8); I have deliberately omitted the "0" from the end of the
second currency value, to prove that the tab stop really is aligning the numbers at their
decimal points:

```
let s = "Onions\t$2.34\nPeppers\t$15.2\n"
let mas = NSMutableAttributedString(string:s, attributes:[
    NSFontAttributeName:UIFont(name:"GillSans", size:15)!,
    NSParagraphStyleAttributeName:lend {
        (p:NSMutableParagraphStyle) in
        var tabs = [NSTextTab]()
        let terms = NSTextTab.columnTerminatorsForLocale(
            NSLocale.currentLocale())
        let tab = NSTextTab(
            textAlignment:.Right, location:170, options:[
                NSTabColumnTerminatorsAttributeName:terms])
        tabs += [tab]
        p.tabStops = tabs
        p.firstLineHeadIndent = 20
    }
])
self.tv.attributedText = mas
```

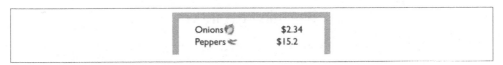

Figure 10-9. Text attachments in an attributed string

Text attachments

A text attachment is basically an inline image. To make one, you need an instance of NSTextAttachment initialized with image data; the easiest way is to start with a UIImage and assign directly to the NSTextAttachment's `image` property. You must also give the NSTextAttachment a nonzero `bounds`; the image will be scaled to the size of the bounds you provide, and a zero origin places the image on the text baseline.

A text attachment is attached to an NSAttributedString using the `NSAttachment-AttributeName` key; the text attachment itself is the value. The range of the string that has this attribute must be a special nonprinting character whose codepoint is `NSAttachmentCharacter` (0xFFFC). The simplest way to arrange that is to call the NSAttributedString initializer `init(attachment:)`; you hand it an NSTextAttachment and it hands you an attributed string consisting of the `NSAttachmentCharacter` with the `NSAttachmentAttributeName` attribute set to that text attachment. You can then insert this attributed string into your own attributed string at the point where you want the image to appear.

To illustrate, I'll add an image of onions and an image of peppers just after the words "Onions" and "Peppers" in the attributed string (`mas`) that I created in the previous example (Figure 10-9):

```
let onions = // ...
let peppers = // ...
let onionatt = NSTextAttachment()
onionatt.image = onions
onionatt.bounds = CGRectMake(0,-5,onions.size.width,onions.size.height)
let onionattchar = NSAttributedString(attachment:onionatt)
let pepperatt = NSTextAttachment()
pepperatt.image = peppers
pepperatt.bounds = CGRectMake(0,-1,peppers.size.width,peppers.size.height)
let pepperattchar = NSAttributedString(attachment:pepperatt)
let r = (mas.string as NSString).rangeOfString("Onions")
mas.insertAttributedString(onionattchar, atIndex:(r.location + r.length))
let r2 = (mas.string as NSString).rangeOfString("Peppers")
mas.insertAttributedString(pepperattchar, atIndex:(r2.location + r2.length))
self.tv.attributedText = mas
```

Underlining is Tricky

Underlining is tricky for two reasons:

- NSUnderlineStyle should be an Int, but Swift wrongly sees it as an enum. Therefore you have to extract the underlying value with `rawValue`.

- In iOS 8, before iOS 8.3, if any of an attributed string has an `NSUnderlineStyle-AttributeName` value, *all* of it must, or you might not see any underlining at all. (This bug is fixed in iOS 8.3.)

So, for example, to create an attributed string "Buy beer" with the word "beer" underlined, in iOS 8 before iOS 8.3, you would underline the whole string with `.StyleNone` before underlining "beer" with `.StyleSingle`:

```
let mas = NSMutableAttributedString(string: "Buy beer", attributes: [
    NSUnderlineStyleAttributeName: NSUnderlineStyle.StyleNone.rawValue
    ])
mas.addAttributes([
    NSUnderlineStyleAttributeName: NSUnderlineStyle.StyleSingle.rawValue
    ], range: NSMakeRange(4, mas.length-4))
```

Other ways to create an attributed string

The nib editor includes an ingenious interface for letting you construct attributed strings wherever built-in interface objects (such as UILabel or UITextView) accept them as a property; it's not perfect, however, and isn't suitable for lengthy or complex text.

It is also possible to import an attributed string from text in some other standard format, such as HTML or RTF. To do so, get the target text into an NSData and call `init(data:options:documentAttributes:error:)`, or start with a file and call `init(fileURL:options:documentAttributes:error:)`. The `options:` allow you to specify the target text's format. For example, here we read an RTF file from the app bundle as an attributed string and show it in a UITextView:

```
let url = NSBundle.mainBundle().URLForResource(
    "test", withExtension: "rtf")!
let opts = [NSDocumentTypeDocumentAttribute:NSRTFTextDocumentType]
let s = NSAttributedString(
    fileURL: url, options: opts, documentAttributes: nil, error: nil)
self.tv.attributedText = s
```

I have not experimented to see how much can get lost in the translation or whether longer strings can cause a delay, but this is certainly an excellent way to generate relatively short, simple strings painlessly. There are also corresponding export methods.

Modifying and Querying an Attributed String

Although attributes are *applied* to ranges, they actually *belong* to each individual character. Thus we can coherently modify just the string part of a mutable attributed string. The key method here is `replaceCharactersInRange:withString:`, which can be used to replace characters with a plain string or, using a zero range length, to insert a plain string at the start, middle, or end of an attributed string. The question is then what attributes will be applied to the inserted string. The rule is:

- If we *replace* characters, the inserted string takes on the attributes of the *first replaced* character.

- If we *insert* characters, the inserted string takes on the attributes of the character *preceding* the insertion — except that, if we insert at the *start*, there is no preceding character, so the inserted string takes on the attributes of the character *following* the insertion.

You can query an attributed string about its attributes one character at a time — asking either about all attributes at once (`attributesAtIndex:effectiveRange:`) or about a particular attribute by name (`attribute:atIndex:effectiveRange:`). In those methods, the `effectiveRange` parameter is a pointer to an NSRange variable, which will be set by indirection to the range over which this same attribute value, or set of attribute values, applies:

```
var range : NSRange = NSMakeRange(0,0)
let d = content.attributesAtIndex(content.length-1, effectiveRange:&range)
```

Because style runs are something of an artifice, the `effectiveRange` might not be what you would think of as the *entire* style run. The methods with `longestEffectiveRange:` in their names do (at the cost of some efficiency) work out the entire style run for you. In practice, however, you typically don't need the entire style run range, because you're cycling through ranges, and speed, even at the cost of *more* iterations, matters more than getting the longest effective range on *every* iteration.

In this example, I start with the combined two-paragraph Gettysburg Address attributed string constructed earlier, and change all the size 15 material to Arial Bold 20. I don't care whether I'm handed longest effective ranges (and my code explicitly says so); I just want to cycle efficiently:

```
let opts : NSAttributedStringEnumerationOptions =
    .LongestEffectiveRangeNotRequired
content.enumerateAttribute(NSFontAttributeName,
    inRange:NSMakeRange(0,content.length),
    options:opts, usingBlock: {
        value, range, stop in
        let font = value as! UIFont
        if font.pointSize == 15 {
            content.addAttribute(NSFontAttributeName,
```

```
                    value:UIFont(name: "Arial-BoldMT", size:20)!,
                    range:range)
            }
        })
```

Custom Attributes

You are permitted to apply your own custom attributes to a stretch of text in an attributed string. Your attributes won't directly affect how the string is drawn, because the text engine doesn't know what to make of them; but it doesn't object to them either. In this way, you can mark a stretch of text invisibly for your own future use.

In this example, I have a UILabel containing some text and a date. Every so often, I want to replace the date by the current date. The problem is that when the moment comes to replace the date, I don't know where it is: I know neither its length nor the length of the text that precedes it. The solution is to use an attributed string, and to mark the date with a secret custom attribute when I first insert it. (My attribute is called "HERE", and I've assigned it a value of 1.) Now I can readily find the date again later, because the text engine will tell me where it is:

```
@IBAction func doUpdateLabel(sender:AnyObject?) {
    let mas =
        self.lab.attributedText.mutableCopy() as! NSMutableAttributedString
    mas.enumerateAttribute(
        "HERE", inRange: NSMakeRange(0, mas.length), options: nil) {
            value, r, stop in
            if let value = value as? Int where value == 1 {
                mas.replaceCharactersInRange(
                    r, withString: NSDate().description)
                stop.memory = true
            }
    }
    self.lab.attributedText = mas
}
```

Drawing and Measuring an Attributed String

You can draw an attributed string directly, without hosting it in a built-in interface object, and sometimes this will prove to be the most reliable approach. An NSString can be drawn into a rect with drawInRect:withAttributes: and related methods; an NSAttributedString can be drawn with drawAtPoint:, drawInRect:, and drawWith-Rect:options:context:.

Here, I draw an attributed string into an image (which might then be displayed by an image view):

```
UIGraphicsBeginImageContextWithOptions(rect.size, true, 0)
UIColor.whiteColor().setFill()
CGContextFillRect(UIGraphicsGetCurrentContext(), rect)
content.drawInRect(rect) // draw attributed string
let im = UIGraphicsGetImageFromCurrentImageContext()
UIGraphicsEndImageContext()
```

Similarly, you can draw an attributed string directly in a UIView's `drawRect:`. For example, imagine that we have a UIView subclass called StringDrawer that has an `attributedText` property. The idea is that we just assign an attributed string to that property and the StringDrawer redraws itself:

```
self.drawer.attributedText = content
```

And here's StringDrawer:

```
class StringDrawer : UIView {
    @NSCopying var attributedText : NSAttributedString! {
        didSet {
            self.setNeedsDisplay()
        }
    }
    override func drawRect(rect: CGRect) {
        let r = rect.rectByOffsetting(dx: 0, dy: 2)
        let opts : NSStringDrawingOptions = .UsesLineFragmentOrigin
        self.attributedText.drawWithRect(r, options: opts, context: nil)
    }
}
```

The use of `.UsesLineFragmentOrigin` is crucial here. Without it, the string is drawn with its *baseline* at the rect origin (so that it appears *above* that rect) and it doesn't wrap. The rule is that `.UsesLineFragmentOrigin` is the implicit default for simple `drawInRect:`, but with `drawWithRect:options:context:` you must specify it explicitly.

NSAttributedString also provides methods to *measure* an attributed string, such as `boundingRectWithSize:options:context:`. Again, the option `.UsesLineFragmentOrigin` is crucial; without it, the measured text doesn't wrap and the returned height will be very small. The documentation warns that the returned height can be fractional and that you should round up with the `ceil` function if the height of a view is going to depend on this result.

The `context:` parameter of methods such as `drawWithRect:options:context:` lets you attach an instance of NSStringDrawingContext, a simple value class whose `totalBounds` property tells you where you just drew.

 Other features of NSStringDrawingContext, such as its `minimumScaleFactor`, appear to be nonfunctional.

Labels

A label (UILabel) is a simple built-in interface object for displaying strings. I listed some of its chief properties in Chapter 8 (in "Built-In Cell Styles" on page 419).

If you're displaying a plain NSString in a label, by way of the label's `text` property, then you are likely also to set its `font`, `textColor`, and `textAlignment` properties, and possibly its `shadowColor` and `shadowOffset` properties. The label's text can have an alternate `highlightedTextColor`, to be used when its `highlighted` property is `true` — as happens, for example, when the label is in a selected cell of a table view.

On the other hand, if you're using an NSAttributedString, then you'll set just the label's `attributedText` property and let the attributes dictate things like color, alignment, and shadow. Those other UILabel properties do mostly still work, but they're going to change the attributes of your *entire* attributed string, in ways that you might not intend. Setting the `text` of a UILabel that has `attributedText` will basically eliminate the attributes. The `highlightedTextColor` property affects the `attributedText` only if the latter is black.

Number of Lines

A UILabel's `numberOfLines` property is extremely important. Together with the label's line breaking behavior and resizing behavior, it determines how much of the text will appear. The default is `1` — a single line — which can come as a surprise. To make a label display more than one line of text, you must explicitly set its `numberOfLines` to a value greater than 1, or to `0` to indicate that there is to be no maximum.

Line break characters in a label's text are honored. Thus, for example, in a single-line label, you won't see whatever follows the first line break character.

Wrapping and Truncation

UILabel line breaking (wrapping) and truncation behavior, which applies to both single-line and multiline labels, is determined by the `lineBreakMode` (of the label or the attributed string). The options (NSLineBreak) are those that I listed earlier in discussing NSParagraphStyle, but their *behavior* within a label needs to be described:

`.ByWordWrapping`
> Lines break at word-end, but if this is a single-line label, indistinguishable from `.ByClipping`.

`.ByClipping`
> Lines break at word-end, but the *last* line can continue past its boundary, even if this leaves a character showing only partially.

`.ByCharWrapping`
> Lines break in mid-word in order to maximize the number of characters in each line.

> (`.ByCharWrapping` was broken in iOS 7: it behaved identically to `.ByWord-Wrapping`. iOS 8 fixes this breakage, restoring the behavior from iOS 6 and before.)

`.ByTruncatingHead`
`.ByTruncatingMiddle`
`.ByTruncatingTail`
> Lines break at word-end; if the text is too long for the label, then the *last* line displays an ellipsis at the start, middle, or end of the line respectively, and text is omitted at the point of the ellipsis.

The default line break mode for a new label is `.ByTruncatingTail`. But the default line break mode for an attributed string's NSParagraphStyle is `.ByWordWrapping`.

 UILabel line break behavior is *not the same* as what happens when an NSAttributedString draws itself — for example, in an image context or a plain UIView, as I described earlier. An NSAttributedString whose NSParagraphStyle's `lineBreakMode` doesn't have "Wrap" in its name *doesn't wrap* when it draws itself — it consists of a single line.

Label Resizing

If a label is too small for its text, the entire text won't show. If a label is too big for its text, the text is vertically centered in the label, with space above and below, which may be undesirable. You might like to shrink or grow a label to fit its text exactly.

If you're not using autolayout, in most simple cases `sizeToFit` will do exactly the right thing; I believe that behind the scenes it is calling `boundingRectWithSize:options:context:`.

 There are cases where UILabel's `sizeToFit` will misbehave. The problem arises particularly with paragraph styles involving margins (`headIndent` and `tailIndent`) — presumably because `boundingRectWithSize:options:context:` ignores the margins.

If you're using autolayout, a label will correctly configure its own `intrinsicContentSize` automatically, based on its contents — and therefore, all other things being equal, will size itself to fit its contents *with no code at all*. Every time you reconfigure the label in a way that affects its contents (setting its text, changing its font, setting its attributed text, and so forth), the label automatically invalidates and recalculates its intrinsic content size. There are two general cases to consider:

Short single-line label

You might give the label no width or height constraints; you'll constrain its position, but you'll let the label's `intrinsicContentSize` provide both the label's width and its height.

Multiline label

In this case, it is more likely that you'll want to dictate the label's width, while letting the label's height change automatically to accommodate its contents. There are two ways to do this:

Set the label's width constraint

This is appropriate particularly when the label's width is to remain fixed ever after.

Set the label's `preferredMaxLayoutWidth`

This property is a hint to help the label's calculation of its `intrinsicContentSize`. It is the width at which the label, as its contents increase, will stop growing horizontally to accommodate those contents, and start growing vertically instead.

If a label's width is to be permitted to vary because of constraints, you can tell it recalculate its height to fit its contents by setting its `preferredMaxLayoutWidth` to its actual width. For example, consider a label whose left and right edges are both pinned to the superview. And imagine that the superview's width can change, thus changing the width of the label. For example, perhaps the superview is a view controller's main view, and is resized as the nib loads; and perhaps the app's interface is permitted to rotate, thus changing the main view's width to match the new orientation of the screen. Nevertheless, if the `preferredMaxLayoutWidth` is adjusted after every such change, the label's height will always perfectly fit its contents.

So how will you ensure that the `preferredMaxLayoutWidth` is adjusted when the label's width changes? Before giving the label constraints and text, set its `preferredMaxLayoutWidth` to 0! This happens to be the default, so there is nothing to do. Now the label will change its `preferredMaxLayoutWidth` *automatically* as its width changes, and will therefore *always* fit its contents, with no further effort on your part. Here's an example of creating such a label in code:

```
let lab = UILabel() // preferredMaxLayoutWidth is 0
lab.numberOfLines = 0
lab.backgroundColor = UIColor.yellowColor()
lab.setTranslatesAutoresizingMaskIntoConstraints(false)
self.view.addSubview(lab)
self.view.addConstraints(
    NSLayoutConstraint.constraintsWithVisualFormat(
```

```
        "H:|-(30)-[v]-(30)-|",
        options: nil, metrics: nil, views: ["v":lab])
)
self.view.addConstraints(
    NSLayoutConstraint.constraintsWithVisualFormat(
        "V:|-(30)-[v]",
        options: nil, metrics: nil, views: ["v":lab])
)
lab.attributedText = // whatever
```

New in iOS 8, you can also perform this configuration in the nib editor: at the top of the Size Inspector, uncheck the Explicit checkbox.

If a situation arises where you need a label to adjust its `preferredMaxLayoutWidth` explicitly in response to being resized, implement `layoutSubviews` in a subclass (this was the standard technique before iOS 7, when automatic adjustment was introduced):

```
class MyLabel : UILabel {
    override func layoutSubviews() {
        super.layoutSubviews()
        self.preferredMaxLayoutWidth = self.bounds.width
    }
}
```

Instead of letting a label grow, you can elect to permit its text font size to shrink if this would allow more of the text to fit. How the text is repositioned when the font size shrinks is determined by the label's `baselineAdjustment` property. The conditions under which this feature operates are:

- The label's `adjustsFontSizeToFitWidth` property must be `true`.
- The label's `minimumScaleFactor` must be less than `1.0`.
- The label's size must be limited.
- *Either* this must be a single-line label (`numberOfLines` is 1) *or* the line break mode (of the label or the attributed string) must *not* have "Wrapping" in its name.

Customized Label Drawing

Methods that you can override in a subclass to modify a label's drawing are `drawTextInRect:` and `textRectForBounds:limitedToNumberOfLines:`.

For example, this is the code for a UILabel subclass that outlines the label with a black rectangle and puts a five-point margin around the label's contents:

```
class BoundedLabel: UILabel {
    override func awakeFromNib() {
        super.awakeFromNib()
        self.backgroundColor = UIColor.myPaler()
        self.layer.borderWidth = 2.0
```

```
            self.layer.cornerRadius = 3.0
        }
        override func drawTextInRect(rect: CGRect) {
            super.drawTextInRect(
                rect.rectByInsetting(dx: 5, dy: 5).integerRect)
        }
    }
```

 A CATextLayer (Chapter 3) is like a lightweight, layer-level version of a UILabel. If the width of the layer is insufficient to display the entire string, we can get truncation behavior with the `truncationMode` property. If the `wrapped` property is set to `true`, the string will wrap. We can also set the alignment with the `alignmentMode` property. And its `string` property can be an NSAttributedString.

Text Fields

A text field (UITextField) portrays just a single line of text; any line break characters in its text are treated as spaces. It has many of the same properties as a label. You can provide it with a plain NSString, setting its `text`, `font`, `textColor`, and `textAlignment`, or provide it with an attributed string, setting its `attributedText`. You can learn a text field's overall text attributes as an attributes dictionary through its `defaultTextAttributes` property. (Under the hood, the text is *always* attributed text, so the displayed text can end up as a combination of, say, the `attributedText` and the `textColor`.)

Under autolayout, a text field's `intrinsicContentSize` will attempt to set its width to fit its contents; if its width is fixed, you can set its `adjustsFontSizeToFitWidth` and `minimumFontSize` properties to allow the text size to shrink somewhat.

Text that is too long for the text field is displayed with an ellipsis at the end. A text field has no `lineBreakMode`, but you can change the position of the ellipsis by assigning the text field an attributed string with different truncation behavior, such as `.ByTruncating-Head`. When long text is being edited, the ellipsis (if any) is removed, and the text shifts horizontally to show the insertion point.

Regardless of whether you originally supplied a plain string or an attributed string, if the text field's `allowsEditingTextAttributes` property is `true`, the user, when editing in the text field, can summon a menu toggling the selected text's bold, italics, or underline features. (Oddly, there's no way to set this property in a nib.)

A text field has a `placeholder` property, which is the text that appears faded within the text field when it has no text (its `text` or `attributedText` has been set to nil, or the user has removed all the text); the idea is that you can use this to suggest to the user what the text field is for. It has a styled text alternative, `attributedPlaceholder`; the runtime will apply an overall light gray color to your attributed string.

If a text field's `clearsOnBeginEditing` property is `true`, it automatically deletes its existing text (and displays the placeholder) when editing begins within it. If a text field's `clearsOnInsertion` property is `true`, then when editing begins within it, the text remains, but is invisibly selected, and will be replaced by the user's typing.

A text field's border drawing is determined by its `borderStyle` property. Your options (UITextFieldBorderStyle) are:

`.None`
No border.

`.Line`
A plain black rectangle.

`.Bezel`
A gray rectangle, where the top and left sides have a very slight, thin shadow.

`.RoundedRect`
A larger rectangle with slightly rounded corners and a flat, faded gray color.

 Calling `sizeToFit` on a text field whose border style is `.RoundedRect` doesn't work properly.

You can supply a background image (`background`); if you combine this with a `borderStyle` of `.None`, or if the image has no transparency, you thus get to supply your own border — unless the `borderStyle` is `.RoundedRect`, in which case the `background` is ignored. The image is automatically resized as needed (and you will probably supply a resizable image). A second image (`disabledBackground`) can be displayed when the text field's `enabled` property, inherited from UIControl, is `false`. The user can't interact with a disabled text field, but without a `disabledBackground` image, the user may lack any visual clue to this fact. You can't set the `disabledBackground` unless you have also set the `background`.

A text field may contain one or two ancillary overlay views, its `leftView` and `rightView`, and possibly a Clear button (a gray circle with a white X). The automatic visibility of each of these is determined by the `leftViewMode`, `rightViewMode`, and `clearViewMode`, respectively. The view mode values (UITextFieldViewMode) are:

`.Never`
The view never appears.

`.WhileEditing`
A Clear button appears if there is text in the field and the user is editing. A left or right view appears if there is *no* text in the field and the user is editing.

`.UnlessEditing`

A Clear button appears if there is text in the field and the user is not editing. A left or right view appears if the user is not editing, or if the user is editing but there is no text in the field.

`.Always`

A Clear button appears if there is text in the field. A left or right view always appears.

Depending on what sort of view you use, your `leftView` and `rightView` may have to be sized manually so as not to overwhelm the text view contents. If a right view and a Clear button appear at the same time, the right view may cover the Clear button unless you reposition it.

The positions and sizes of *any* of the components of the text field can be set in relation to the text field's bounds by overriding the appropriate method in a subclass:

- `clearButtonRectForBounds:`
- `leftViewRectForBounds:`
- `rightViewRectForBounds:`
- `borderRectForBounds:`
- `textRectForBounds:`
- `placeholderRectForBounds:`
- `editingRectForBounds:`

 You should make no assumptions about when or how frequently these methods will be called; the same method might be called several times in quick succession. Also, these methods should all be called with a parameter that is the bounds of the text field, but some are sometimes called with a 100×100 bounds; this feels like a bug.

You can also override in a subclass the methods `drawTextInRect:` and `draw-PlaceholderInRect:`. You should either draw the specified text or call `super` to draw it; if you do neither, the text won't appear. Both these methods are called with a parameter whose size is the dimensions of the text field's text area, but whose origin is (`0.0,0.0`). In effect what you've got is a graphics context for just the text area; any drawing you do outside the given rectangle will be clipped.

Summoning and Dismissing the Keyboard

Making the onscreen simulated keyboard appear when the user taps in a text field is no work at all — it's automatic, as you've probably observed already. Making the keyboard vanish again, on the other hand, can be a bit tricky. (Another problem is that the keyboard can cover the text field that the user just tapped in; I'll talk about that in a moment.)

The presence or absence of the keyboard, and a text field's editing state, are intimately tied to one another, and to the text field's status as the *first responder*:

- When a text field is first responder, it is being edited and the keyboard is present.
- When a text field is no longer first responder, it is no longer being edited, and if no other text field (or text view) becomes first responder, the keyboard is not present. The keyboard is not dismissed if one text field takes over first responder status from another.

Thus, you can programmatically control the presence or absence of the keyboard, together with a text field's editing state, by way of the text field's first responder status:

Becoming first responder
To make the insertion point appear within a text field and to cause the keyboard to appear, you send `becomeFirstResponder` to that text field.

You won't typically have to do that; usually, the user will tap in a text field and it will become first responder automatically. Still, sometimes it's useful to make a text field the first responder programmatically; an example appeared in Chapter 8 ("Inserting Cells" on page 476).

Resigning first responder
To make a text field stop being edited and to cause the keyboard to disappear, you send `resignFirstResponder` to that text field. (Actually, `resignFirstResponder` returns a Bool, because a responder might return `false` to indicate that for some reason it refuses to obey this command.)

Alternatively, send the UIView `endEditing:` method to the first responder *or any superview* (including the window) to ask or compel the first responder to resign first responder status.

 In a view presented in the `.FormSheet` modal presentation style on the iPad (Chapter 6), the keyboard, by default, does *not* disappear when a text field resigns first responder status. This is presumably because a form sheet is intended primarily for text input, so the keyboard is felt as accompanying the form as a whole, not individual text fields. Optionally, you can prevent this exceptional behavior: in your UIViewController subclass, override `disablesAutomaticKeyboardDismissal` to return `false`.

There is no simple way to learn what view is first responder! This is very odd, because a window surely knows what its first responder is — but it won't tell you. There's a method `isFirstResponder`, but you'd have to send it to every view in a window until you find the first responder. One workaround is to store a reference to the first responder yourself, typically in your implementation of the text field delegate's `textFieldDid-BeginEditing:`.

Once the user has tapped in a text field and the keyboard has automatically appeared, how is the user supposed to get rid of it? On the iPad, the keyboard typically contains a special button that dismisses the keyboard. But on the iPhone, this is an oddly tricky issue. You would think that the "return" button in the keyboard would dismiss the keyboard; but, of itself, it doesn't.

One solution is to be the text field's delegate and to implement a text field delegate method, `textFieldShouldReturn:`. When the user taps the Return key in the keyboard, we hear about it through this method, and we tell the text field to resign its first responder status, which dismisses the keyboard:

```
func textFieldShouldReturn(tf: UITextField) -> Bool {
    tf.resignFirstResponder()
    return true
}
```

I'll provide a more automatic solution later in this chapter.

Keyboard Covers Text Field

The keyboard has a position "docked" at the bottom of the screen. This may cover the text field in which the user wants to type, even if it is first responder. On the iPad, this may not be an issue, because the user can "undock" the keyboard (possibly also splitting and shrinking it) and slide it up and down the screen freely. On the iPhone, you'll typically want to do something to reveal the text field.

To help with this, you can register for keyboard-related notifications:

- `UIKeyboardWillShowNotification`
- `UIKeyboardDidShowNotification`
- `UIKeyboardWillHideNotification`
- `UIKeyboardDidHideNotification`

Those notifications all have to do with the *docked* position of the keyboard. On the iPhone, keyboard docking and keyboard visibility are equivalent: the keyboard is visible if and only if it is docked. On the iPad, the keyboard is said to "show" if it is being docked, whether that's because it is appearing from offscreen or because the user is docking it;

and it is said to "hide" if it is undocked, whether that's because it is moving offscreen or because the user is undocking it.

Two additional notifications are sent *both* when the keyboard enters and leaves the screen *and* (on the iPad) when the user drags it, splits or unsplits it, and docks or undocks it:

- `UIKeyboardWillChangeFrameNotification`
- `UIKeyboardDidChangeFrameNotification`

The notification's `userInfo` dictionary contains information about the keyboard describing what it will do or has done, under these keys:

- `UIKeyboardFrameBeginUserInfoKey`
- `UIKeyboardFrameEndUserInfoKey`
- `UIKeyboardAnimationDurationUserInfoKey`
- `UIKeyboardAnimationCurveUserInfoKey`

Thus, to a large extent, you can coordinate your actions with those of the keyboard. In particular, by looking at the `UIKeyboardFrameEndUserInfoKey`, you know what position the keyboard is moving to; you can compare this with the screen bounds to learn whether the keyboard will now be on or off the screen and, if it will now be on the screen, you can see whether it will cover a text field.

Finding a strategy for dealing with the keyboard's presence depends on the needs of your particular app. I'll concentrate on the most universal case, where the keyboard moves into and out of docked position and we detect this with `UIKeyboardWillShow-Notification` and `UIKeyboardWillHideNotification`. What should we do if, when the keyboard appears, it covers the text field being edited?

Sliding the interface

One natural-looking approach is to slide the entire interface upward as the keyboard appears. To make this easy, you might start with a view hierarchy like this: the root view contains a transparent view that's the same size as the root view; everything else is contained in that transparent view. The transparent view's purpose is to host the rest of the interface; if we slide it upward, the whole interface will slide upward.

Here's an implementation involving constraints. The transparent view, which I'll called the *sliding view*, is pinned by constraints at the top and bottom to its superview with a `constant` of `0`, and we have outlets to those constraints. We also have an outlet to the sliding view itself, and we've got a property prepared to hold the first responder:

```
@IBOutlet var topConstraint : NSLayoutConstraint!
@IBOutlet var bottomConstraint : NSLayoutConstraint!
@IBOutlet var slidingView : UIView!
var fr : UIView?
```

In our view controller's `viewDidLoad`, we register for the keyboard notifications:

```
super.viewDidLoad()
NSNotificationCenter.defaultCenter().addObserver(
    self, selector: "keyboardShow:",
    name: UIKeyboardWillShowNotification, object: nil)
NSNotificationCenter.defaultCenter().addObserver(
    self, selector: "keyboardHide:",
    name: UIKeyboardWillHideNotification, object: nil)
```

We are the delegate of the various text fields in our interface. When one of them starts editing, we keep a reference to it as first responder:

```
func textFieldDidBeginEditing(tf: UITextField) {
    self.fr = tf // keep track of first responder
}
```

As I suggested in the previous section, we also dismiss the keyboard by resigning first responder when the user taps the Return button in the keyboard:

```
func textFieldShouldReturn(tf: UITextField) -> Bool {
    tf.resignFirstResponder()
    self.fr = nil
    return true
}
```

As the keyboard threatens to appear, we examine where its top will be. If the keyboard will cover the text field that's about to be edited, we animate the sliding view upward to compensate, by changing the `constant` value of the constraints that pin its top and bottom:

```
func keyboardShow(n:NSNotification) {
    let d = n.userInfo!
    var r = (d[UIKeyboardFrameEndUserInfoKey] as! NSValue).CGRectValue()
    r = self.slidingView.convertRect(r, fromView:nil)
    let f = self.fr!.frame
    let y : CGFloat =
        f.maxY + r.size.height - self.slidingView.bounds.height + 5
    if r.origin.y < f.maxY {
        self.topConstraint.constant = -y
        self.bottomConstraint.constant = y
        self.view.layoutIfNeeded()
    }
}
```

When the keyboard disappears, we put the sliding view back again:

```
func keyboardHide(n:NSNotification) {
    self.topConstraint.constant = 0
    self.bottomConstraint.constant = 0
    self.view.layoutIfNeeded()
}
```

This entire procedure is *much* easier in iOS 8 than in previous systems, because our code is executed inside the keyboard's animation block: our changes to animatable view properties are *automatically* animated together with the keyboard.

Text field in a scroll view

Changing the sliding view's constraints is a way of changing its *frame origin*. Since all we really want is to move the sliding view's subviews, it would be more suitable to change its *bounds origin*. If we're going to do that, we might as well make the sliding view a view that already knows all about shifting its bounds origin — a scroll view! This approach has two notable advantages over the preceding approach:

- We can permit the user to scroll the view within the area not covered by the keyboard. This is a job for `contentInset`, whose purpose, you will recall (Chapter 7), is precisely to make it possible for the user to view all of the scroll view's content even though part of the scroll view is being covered by something.

  (This behavior is in fact implemented automatically by a UITableViewController. When a text field inside a table cell is first responder, the table view controller adjusts the table view's `contentInset` and `scrollIndicatorInsets` to compensate for the keyboard. The result is that the entire table view is available within the space between the top of the table view and the top of the keyboard.)

- A scroll view has some built-in behavior that will help us: it scrolls automatically to reveal the first responder. Furthermore, a UIScrollView has a `keyboardDismissMode`, governing what will happen to the keyboard when the user scrolls.

Let's imitate UITableViewController's behavior with a scroll view containing text fields. In `viewDidLoad`, we register for keyboard notifications, and we are the delegate of any text fields, exactly as in the previous example. When the keyboard appears, we store the current content offset, content inset, and scroll indicator insets; then we alter the insets and allow the scroll view to scroll the first responder into view for us:

```
func keyboardShow(n:NSNotification) {
    self.oldContentInset = self.scrollView.contentInset
    self.oldIndicatorInset = self.scrollView.scrollIndicatorInsets
    self.oldOffset = self.scrollView.contentOffset
    let d = n.userInfo!
    var r = (d[UIKeyboardFrameEndUserInfoKey] as! NSValue).CGRectValue()
```

```
        r = self.scrollView.convertRect(r, fromView:nil)
        self.scrollView.contentInset.bottom = r.size.height
        self.scrollView.scrollIndicatorInsets.bottom = r.size.height
    }
```

When the keyboard disappears, we restore the saved values:

```
func keyboardHide(n:NSNotification) {
    self.scrollView.bounds.origin = self.oldOffset
    self.scrollView.scrollIndicatorInsets = self.oldIndicatorInset
    self.scrollView.contentInset = self.oldContentInset
}
```

UIScrollView's `keyboardDismissMode` provides ways of letting the user dismiss the keyboard. The options (UIScrollViewKeyboardDismissMode) are:

`.None`
The default; we must use code to dismiss the keyboard.

`.Interactive`
The user can dismiss the keyboard by dragging it down.

`.OnDrag`
The keyboard dismisses itself if the user scrolls the scroll view.

Configuring the Keyboard

A UITextField implements the UITextInputTraits protocol, which defines properties on the UITextField that you can set to determine how the keyboard will look and how typing in the text field will behave. (These properties can also be set in the nib.) For example, you can set the `keyboardType` to `.PhonePad` to make the keyboard for this text field consist of digits only. You can set the `returnKeyType` to determine the text of the Return key (if the keyboard is of a type that has one). You can give the keyboard a dark or light shade (`keyboardAppearance`). You can turn off autocapitalization (`autocapitalizationType`) or autocorrection (`autocorrectionType`), make the Return key disable itself if the text field has no content (`enablesReturnKey-Automatically`), and make the text field a password field (`secureTextEntry`). You can even supply your own keyboard or other input mechanism by setting the text field's `inputView`.

 New in iOS 8, your app can supply *other* apps with a keyboard. See the Custom Keyboard chapter of Apple's *App Extension Programming Guide*.

You can attach an accessory view to the top of the keyboard by setting the text field's `inputAccessoryView`. In this example, the accessory view has been loaded from a nib and is available through a property, `self.accessoryView`. When editing starts, we configure the keyboard as we store our reference to the text field:

```
func textFieldDidBeginEditing(tf: UITextField!) {
    self.fr = tf // keep track of first responder
    tf.inputAccessoryView = self.accessoryView
}
```

We have an array property populated with references to all our text fields (this might be an appropriate use of an outlet collection). The accessory view contains a Next button, whose action method is `doNextField:`. When the user taps the button, we move editing to the next text field:

```
func doNextButton(sender:AnyObject) {
    var ix = (self.textFields as NSArray).indexOfObject(self.fr)
    ix = ++ix % self.textFields.count
    let v = self.textFields[ix]
    v.becomeFirstResponder()
}
```

The user can control the localization of the keyboard character set in the Settings app, either through a choice of the system's base language or with General → Keyboard → Keyboards (and possibly Add New Keyboard). In the latter case, the user can switch among keyboard character sets while the keyboard is showing. But, as far as I can tell, your code can't make this choice; you cannot, for example, *force* a certain text field to display the Cyrillic keyboard. You can ask the user to switch keyboards manually, but if you really want a particular keyboard to appear regardless of the user's settings and behavior, you'll have to create it yourself and provide it as the `inputView`.

Text Field Delegate and Control Event Messages

As editing begins and proceeds in a text field, a sequence of messages is sent to the text field's delegate, adopting the UITextFieldDelegate protocol. Some of these messages are also available as notifications. Using them, you can customize the text field's behavior during editing:

`textFieldShouldBeginEditing:`
Return `false` to prevent the text field from becoming first responder.

`textFieldDidBeginEditing:`
`UITextFieldTextDidBeginEditingNotification`
The text field has become first responder.

`textFieldShouldClear:`
Return `false` to prevent the operation of the Clear button or of automatic clearing on entry (`clearsOnBeginEditing`). This event is *not* sent when the text is cleared because `clearsOnInsertion` is `true`, because the user is not clearing the text but rather changing it.

`textFieldShouldReturn:`

The user has tapped the Return button in the keyboard. We have already seen that this can be used as a signal to dismiss the keyboard.

`textField:shouldChangeCharactersInRange:replacementString:`

Sent when the user changes the text in the field by typing or pasting, or by backspacing or cutting (in which case the replacement string will have zero length). Return `false` to prevent the proposed change; you can substitute text by changing the text field's `text` directly (there is no circularity, as this delegate method is not called when you do that).

In this example, the user can enter only lowercase characters:

```
func textField(textField: UITextField,
    shouldChangeCharactersInRange range: NSRange,
    replacementString string: String) -> Bool {
        if string == "\n" {
            return true
        }
        let lc = string.lowercaseString
        textField.text =
            (textField.text as NSString)
                .stringByReplacingCharactersInRange(
                    range, withString:lc)
        return false
}
```

It is common practice to implement `textField:shouldChangeCharactersIn-Range:replacementString:` as a way of learning that the text has been changed, even if you then always return `true`. This method is *not* called when the user changes text styling through the Bold, Italics, or Underline menu items.

`UITextFieldTextDidChangeNotification` corresponds loosely.

`textFieldShouldEndEditing:`

Return `false` to prevent the text field from resigning first responder (even if you just sent `resignFirstResponder` to it). You might do this, for example, because the text is invalid or unacceptable in some way. The user will not know why the text field is refusing to end editing, so the usual thing is to put up an alert (Chapter 13) explaining the problem.

`textFieldDidEndEditing:`
`UITextFieldTextDidEndEditingNotification`

The text field has resigned first responder. See Chapter 8 ("Editable Content in Cells" on page 474) for an example of using `textFieldDidEndEditing:` to fetch the text field's current text and store it in the model.

A text field is also a control (UIControl; see also Chapter 12). This means you can attach a target–action pair to any of the events that it reports in order to receive a message when that event occurs:

- The user can touch and drag, triggering Touch Down and the various Touch Drag events.
- If the user touches in such a way that the text field enters editing mode (and the keyboard appears), Editing Did Begin and Touch Cancel are triggered; if the user causes the text field to enter editing mode in some other way (such as by tabbing into it), Editing Did Begin is triggered without any Touch events.
- As the user edits (including changing attributes), Editing Changed is triggered.
- If the user taps while in editing mode, Touch Down (and possibly Touch Down Repeat) and Touch Cancel are triggered.
- When editing ends, Editing Did End is triggered; if the user stops editing by tapping Return in the keyboard, Did End on Exit is triggered first.

In general, you're more likely to treat a text field as a text field (through its delegate messages) than as a control (through its control events). However, the Did End on Exit event message has an interesting property: it provides an alternative way to dismiss the keyboard when the user taps a text field keyboard's Return button. If there is a Did End on Exit target–action pair for this text field, then if the text field's delegate does not return `false` from `textFieldShouldReturn:`, the keyboard will be dismissed *automatically* when the user taps the Return key. The action handler for Did End on Exit doesn't actually have to *do* anything.

Thus we have a splendid trick for getting automatic keyboard dismissal *with no code at all*. In the nib, edit the First Responder proxy object in the Attributes inspector, adding a new First Responder Action; let's call it `dummy:`. Now hook the Did End on Exit event of the text field to the `dummy:` action of the First Responder proxy object. That's it! Because the text field's Did End on Exit event now has a target–action pair, the text field automatically dismisses its keyboard when the user taps Return; there is no penalty for not finding a handler for a message sent up the responder chain, so the app doesn't crash even though there is no implementation of `dummy:` anywhere.

Alternatively, you can implement the same trick in code:

```
textField.addTarget(
    nil, action:"dummy:", forControlEvents:.EditingDidEndOnExit)
```

A disabled text field emits no delegate messages or control events.

Text Field Menu

When the user double-taps or long-presses in a text field, the menu appears. It contains menu items such as Select, Select All, Paste, Copy, Cut, and Replace; which menu items appear depends on the circumstances. Many of the selectors for these standard menu items are listed in the UIResponderStandardEditActions informal protocol. Commonly used standard actions are:

- `cut:`
- `copy:`
- `select:`
- `selectAll:`
- `paste:`
- `delete:`
- `_promptForReplace:`
- `_define:`
- `_showTextStyleOptions:`
- `toggleBoldface:`
- `toggleItalics:`
- `toggleUnderline:`

The menu can also be customized; just as with a table view cell's menus (Chapter 8), this involves setting the shared UIMenuController object's `menuItems` property to an array of UIMenuItem instances representing the menu items that *may* appear *in addition* to those that the system puts there.

Actions for menu items are nil-targeted, so they percolate up the responder chain. You can thus implement a menu item's action anywhere up the responder chain; if you do this for a standard menu item at a point in the responder chain *before* the system receives it, you can interfere with and customize what it does. You govern the presence or absence of a menu item by implementing the UIResponder method `canPerformAction:withSender:` in the responder chain.

As an example, we'll devise a text field whose menu includes our own menu item, Expand. I'm imagining here, for instance, a text field where the user can select a U.S. state two-letter abbreviation (such as "CA") and can then summon the menu and tap Expand to replace it with the state's full name (such as "California").

I'll implement this in a UITextField subclass, in order to guarantee that the Expand menu item will be available when an instance of this subclass is first responder, but at no other time. My subclass has a property, `self.list`, which has been set to an array of state name abbreviations, each followed by its expanded state name. A utility function looks to see whether a string appears in the list:

```
func stateForAbbrev(abbrev:String) -> String? {
    let ix = find(self.list, abbrev.uppercaseString)
    return ix != nil ? list[ix!+1] : nil
}
```

At some moment before the user taps in an instance of our UITextField subclass (such as `viewDidLoad`), we modify the global menu:

```
let mi = UIMenuItem(title:"Expand", action:"expand:")
let mc = UIMenuController.sharedMenuController()
mc.menuItems = [mi]
```

We implement `canPerformAction:withSender:` to govern the contents of the menu. Let's presume that we want our Expand menu item to be present only if the selection consists of a two-letter state abbreviation. UITextField itself provides no way to learn the selected text, but it conforms to the UITextInput protocol, which does:

```
override func canPerformAction(
    action: Selector, withSender sender: AnyObject?) -> Bool {
        if action == "expand:" {
            if let r = self.selectedTextRange {
                let s = self.textInRange(r)
                return count(s) == 2 && self.stateForAbbrev(s) != nil
            }
        }
        return super.canPerformAction(action, withSender:sender)
}
```

When the user chooses the Expand menu item, the expand: message is sent up the responder chain. We catch it in our UITextField subclass and obey it by replacing the selected text with the corresponding state name:

```
func expand(sender:AnyObject?) {
    if let r = self.selectedTextRange {
        let s = self.textInRange(r)
        if let ss = self.stateForAbbrev(s) {
            self.replaceRange(r, withText:ss)
        }
    }
}
```

We can also implement the selector for, and thus modify the behavior of, any of the standard menu items. For example, I'll implement `copy:` and modify its behavior. First we call `super` to get standard copying behavior; then we modify what's now on the pasteboard:

```
override func copy(sender:AnyObject?) {
    super.copy(sender)
    let pb = UIPasteboard.generalPasteboard()
    if let s = pb.string {
        let ss = // ... alter s here ...
        pb.string = ss
    }
}
```

(Implementing the selectors for toggleBoldface:, toggleItalics:, and toggle-
Underline: is probably the best way to get an event when the user changes these
attributes.)

Text Views

A text view (UITextView) is a scroll view subclass (UIScrollView); it is *not* a control.
Many of its properties are similar to those of a text field:

- A text view has text, font, textColor, and textAlignment properties; it can be
  user-editable or not, according to its editable property.
- A text view has attributedText, allowsEditingTextAttributes, and typing-
  Attributes properties, as well as clearsOnInsertion.
- An editable text view governs its keyboard just as a text field does: when it is first
  responder, it is being edited and shows the keyboard, and it implements the UIText-
  Input protocol and has inputView and inputAccessoryView properties.
- A text view's menu works the same way as a text field's.

A text view provides (official) information about, and control of, its selection: it has a
selectedRange property which you can get and set, along with a scrollRangeTo-
Visible: method so that you can scroll in terms of a range of its text.

A text view's delegate messages (UITextViewDelegate protocol) and notifications, too,
are similar to those of a text field. The following delegate methods (and notifications)
should have a familiar ring:

- textViewShouldBeginEditing:
- textViewDidBeginEditing:, UITextViewTextDidBeginEditingNotification
- textViewShouldEndEditing:
- textViewDidEndEditing:, UITextViewTextDidEndEditingNotification
- textView:shouldChangeTextInRange:replacementText:

Some differences are:

`textViewDidChange:`
`UITextViewTextDidChangeNotification`
> Sent when the user changes text or attributes. A text field has no corresponding delegate method, though the Editing Changed control event and notification are similar.

`textViewDidChangeSelection:`
> In contrast, a text field is officially uninformative about the selection.

A text view's delegate can also decide how to respond when the user taps on a text attachment or a link. The text view must have its `selectable` property set to `true`, and its `editable` property set to `false`:

`textView:shouldInteractWithTextAttachment:inRange:`
> The default is `false`. If you return `true`, the user sees an action sheet offering to copy the image to the clipboard or the photo library.

`textView:shouldInteractWithURL:inRange:`
> The default is `true`: the URL is opened in Safari, or if the user long-presses, an action sheet appears with options Open, Add to Reading List, and Copy.

By returning `false` from either of those methods, you can substitute your own response, effectively treating the image or URL as a button.

A text view also has a `dataDetectorTypes` property; this, too, if the text view is selectable but not editable, allows text of certain types, specified as a bitmask (and presumably located using NSDataDetector), to be treated as tappable links; the types (UIData-DetectorTypes) are:

`.Link`
> The default response is the same as for a link created using `NSLinkAttributeName`.

`.PhoneNumber`
> The default response to a tap is an alert with an option to call the number; the default response to a long press is an action sheet with options Call, Send Message, Add to Contacts, and Copy.

`.Address`
> The default response to a tap is to search for the address in the Maps app; the default response to a long press is an action sheet with options Open in Maps, Add to Contacts, and Copy.

`.CalendarEvent`
> The default response is an action sheet with options Create Event, Show in Calendar, and Copy.

The delegate's implementation of `textView:shouldInteractWithURL:inRange:` catches data detector taps as well, so you can prevent the default behavior and substitute your own. You can distinguish a phone number through the URL's scheme (it will be "tel"), but an address or calendar event will be more or less opaque (the scheme is "x-apple-data-detectors") and returning false probably makes no sense. The delegate method doesn't distinguish a tap from a long press for you.

Text View as Scroll View

A text view is a scroll view, so everything you know about scroll views applies (see Chapter 7). It has, by default, no border, because a scroll view has no border. It can be user-scrollable or not.

A text view's contentSize is maintained for you automatically as the text changes, so as to contain the text exactly; thus, if the text view is scrollable, the user can see any of its text. You can track changes to the content size by tracking changes to the text. A common reason for doing so is to implement a *self-sizing* text view, that is, a text view that adjusts its height automatically to embrace the amount of text it contains. In this example, we have an outlet to the text view's internal height constraint; the rather hacky quality of the code prevents some unfortunate misbehaviors of the text view:

```
func adjustHeight() {
    let sz = self.tv.sizeThatFits(CGSizeMake(self.tv.bounds.width, 10000))
    self.heightConstraint.constant = ceil(sz.height)
}
func textView(textView: UITextView,
    shouldChangeTextInRange range: NSRange,
    replacementText text: String) -> Bool {
        textView.text = (textView.text as NSString)
            .stringByReplacingCharactersInRange(range, withString:text)
        self.adjustHeight()
        return false
}
```

Text View and Keyboard

The fact that a text view is a scroll view comes in handy also when the keyboard partially covers a text view. The text view quite often dominates the screen, or a large portion of the screen, and you can respond to the keyboard partially covering it by adjusting the text view's contentInset, just as we did earlier in this chapter with a scroll view ("Text field in a scroll view" on page 563). As with a scroll view, this is much easier in iOS 8 than it was in iOS 7: we don't have to perform any animation explicitly, and a number of touchy iOS 7 bugs are gone — in particular, once we play our part by setting the contentInset, the text view will scroll as needed to reveal the insertion point.

Now let's talk about what happens when the keyboard is dismissed. First of all, *how* is the keyboard to be dismissed? On the iPad, the virtual keyboard usually contains a button that dismisses the keyboard. But what about the iPhone? The Return key is meaningful for character entry; you aren't likely to want to misuse it as a way of dismissing the keyboard.

On the iPhone, the interface might well consist of a text view and the keyboard, which is *always* showing: instead of dismissing the keyboard, the user dismisses the entire interface. For example, in Apple's Mail app on the iPhone, when the user is composing a message, in what is presumably a presented view controller, the keyboard is present the whole time; the keyboard is dismissed because the user sends or cancels the message and the presented view controller is dismissed.

Alternatively, you can provide interface for dismissing the keyboard explicitly. For example, in Apple's Notes app, a note alternates between being read fullscreen and being edited with the keyboard present; in the latter case, a Done button appears, and the user taps it to dismiss the keyboard. If there's no good place to put a Done button in the interface, you could attach an accessory view to the keyboard itself.

Here's a possible implementation of a Done button's action method, with resulting dismissal of the keyboard:

```
func doDone(sender:AnyObject?) {
    self.view.endEditing(false)
}
func keyboardHide(n:NSNotification) {
    self.tv.contentInset = UIEdgeInsetsZero
    self.tv.scrollIndicatorInsets = UIEdgeInsetsZero
}
```

Text Kit

Text Kit comes originally from OS X, where you may already be more familiar with its use than you realize. For example, much of the text-editing "magic" of Xcode is due to Text Kit. It comprises a small group of classes that are responsible for drawing text; simply put, they turn an NSAttributedString into graphics. You can take advantage of Text Kit to modify text drawing in ways that were once possible (if at all) only by dipping down to the low-level C-based world of Core Text.

A UITextView provides direct access to the underlying Text Kit engine. It has the following Text Kit–related properties:

textContainer
> The text view's text container (an NSTextContainer instance). UITextView's designated initializer is init(frame:textContainer:); the textContainer: can be nil to get a default text container, or you can supply your own custom text container.

textContainerInset

The margins of the text container, designating the area within the `contentSize` rectangle in which the text as a whole is drawn. Changing this value changes the margins immediately, causing the text to be freshly laid out.

layoutManager

The text view's layout manager (an NSLayoutManager instance).

textStorage

The text view's text storage (an NSTextStorage instance).

When you initialize a text view with a custom text container, you hand it the entire "stack" of Text Kit instances: a text container, a layout manager, and a text storage. In the simplest and most common case, a text storage has a layout manager, and a layout manager has a text container, thus forming the "stack." If the text container is a UIText-View's text container, the stack is retained, and the text view is operative. Thus, the simplest case might look like this:

```
let r = // frame for the new text view
let lm = NSLayoutManager()
let ts = NSTextStorage()
ts.addLayoutManager(lm)
let tc = NSTextContainer(size:CGSizeMake(r.width, CGFloat.max))
lm.addTextContainer(tc)
let tv = UITextView(frame:r, textContainer:tc)
```

Here's what the three chief Text Kit classes do:

NSTextStorage

A subclass of NSMutableAttributedString. It is, or holds, the underlying text. It has one or more layout managers, and notifies them when the text changes. By subclassing and delegation (NSTextStorageDelegate), its behavior can be modified so that it applies attributes in a custom fashion.

NSTextContainer

It is owned by a layout manager, and helps that layout manager by defining the region in which the text is to be laid out. It does this in three primary ways:

Size

The text container's top left is the origin for the text layout coordinate system, and the text will be laid out within the text container's rectangle.

Exclusion paths

The `exclusionPaths` property consists of UIBezierPath objects within which no text is to be drawn.

Subclassing

By overriding `lineFragmentRectForProposedRect:atIndex:writing-Direction:remainingRect:`, you can place each chunk of text drawing anywhere at all (except inside an exclusion path).

NSLayoutManager

This is the master text drawing class! It has one or more text containers, and is owned by a text storage — thus forming the Text Kit stack. It draws the text storage's text into the boundaries defined by the text container(s).

A layout manager can have a delegate (NSLayoutManagerDelegate), and can be subclassed. This, as you may well imagine, is a powerful and sophisticated class.

Text Container

An NSTextContainer has a `size`, within which the text will be drawn. By default, as in the preceding code, a text view's text container's width is the width of the text view, while its height is effectively infinite, allowing the drawing of the text to grow vertically but not horizontally beyond the bounds of the text view, and making it possible to scroll the text vertically.

It also has `heightTracksTextView` and `widthTracksTextView` properties, causing the text container to be resized to match changes in the size of the text view — for example, if the text view is resized because of interface rotation. By default, as you might expect, `widthTracksTextView` is `true` (the documentation is wrong about this), while `heightTracksTextView` is `false`: the text fills the width of the text view, and is laid out freshly if the text view's width changes, but its height remains effectively infinite. The text view itself, of course, configures its own `contentSize` so that the user can scroll just to the bottom of the existing text.

When you change a text view's `textContainerInset`, it modifies its text container's size to match, as necessary. In the default configuration, this means that it modifies the text container's width; the top and bottom insets are implemented through the text container's position within the content rect. Within the text container, additional side margins correspond to the text container's `lineFragmentPadding`; the default is 5, but you can change it.

If the text view's `scrollEnabled` is `false`, then by default its text container's `heightTracksTextView` and `widthTracksTextView` are both `true`, and the text container size is adjusted so that the text fills the text view. In that case, you can also set the text container's `lineBreakMode`. This works like the line break mode of a UILabel. For example, if the line break mode is `.ByTruncatingTail`, then the last line has an ellipsis at the end (if the text is too long for the text view). You can also set the text container's

Figure 10-10. A text view with an exclusion path

`maximumNumberOfLines`, which is like a UILabel's `numberOfLines`. In effect, you've turned the text view into a label!

But, of course, a nonscrolling text view isn't *just* a label, because you've got access to the Text Kit stack that backs it. For example, you can apply exclusion paths to the text container. Figure 10-10 shows a case in point. The text wraps in longer and longer lines, and then in shorter and shorter lines, because there's an exclusion path on the right side of the text container that's a rectangle with a large V-shaped indentation.

In Figure 10-10, the text view (`self.tv`) is initially configured in the view controller's `viewDidLoad`:

```
self.tv.attributedText = // ...
self.tv.textContainerInset = UIEdgeInsetsMake(20, 20, 20, 0)
self.tv.scrollEnabled = false
```

The exclusion path is then drawn and applied in `viewDidLayoutSubviews`:

```
override func viewDidLayoutSubviews() {
    let sz = self.tv.textContainer.size
    let p = UIBezierPath()
    p.moveToPoint(CGPointMake(sz.width/4.0,0))
    p.addLineToPoint(CGPointMake(sz.width,0))
    p.addLineToPoint(CGPointMake(sz.width,sz.height))
    p.addLineToPoint(CGPointMake(sz.width/4.0,sz.height))
    p.addLineToPoint(CGPointMake(sz.width,sz.height/2.0))
    p.closePath()
    self.tv.textContainer.exclusionPaths = [p]
}
```

Instead of (or in addition to) an exclusion path, you can subclass NSTextContainer to modify the rectangle in which the layout manager wants to position a piece of text. (Each piece of text is actually a line fragment; I'll explain in the next section what a line fragment is.) In Figure 10-11, the text is inside a circle.

Figure 10-11. A text view with a subclassed text container

To achieve the layout shown in Figure 10-11, I set the attributed string's line break mode to `.ByCharWrapping` (to bring the right edge of each line as close as possible to the circular shape), and constructed the TextKit stack by hand to include an instance of my NSTextContainer subclass:

```
let r = self.tv.frame
let lm = NSLayoutManager()
let ts = NSTextStorage()
ts.addLayoutManager(lm)
let tc = MyTextContainer(size:CGSizeMake(r.width, r.height))
lm.addTextContainer(tc)
let tv = UITextView(frame:r, textContainer:tc)
```

That subclass contains this code, in which I simplemindedly fit each line fragment's horizontal origin and width entirely within a circle:

```
override func lineFragmentRectForProposedRect(
    proposedRect: CGRect, atIndex characterIndex: Int,
    writingDirection baseWritingDirection: NSWritingDirection,
    remainingRect: UnsafeMutablePointer<CGRect>) -> CGRect {
        var result = super.lineFragmentRectForProposedRect(
            proposedRect, atIndex:characterIndex,
            writingDirection:baseWritingDirection,
            remainingRect:remainingRect)
        let r = self.size.height / 2.0
        // convert initial y so that circle is centered at origin
        let y = r - result.origin.y
        let theta = asin(y/r)
        let x = r * cos(theta)
        // convert resulting x from circle centered at origin
        result.origin.x = r-x
        result.size.width = 2*x
        return result
}
```

Figure 10-12. A layout manager with two text containers

Alternative Text Kit Stack Architectures

The default Text Kit stack is one text storage, which has one layout manager, which has one text container. But a text storage can have multiple layout managers, and a layout manager can have multiple text containers. What's that all about?

If a layout manager has multiple text containers, the overflow from each text container is drawn in the next one. For example, in Figure 10-12, there are two text views; the text has filled the first text view, and has then continued by flowing into and filling the second text view. As far as I can tell, the text views can't be made editable in this configuration. But clearly this is a way to achieve a multicolumn or multipage layout, or you could use text views of different sizes for a magazine-style layout.

It is possible to achieve that arrangement by disconnecting the layout managers of existing text views from their text containers and rebuilding the stack from below. However, I think it's probably safer to build the entire stack by hand:

```
let r = // frame
let r2 = // frame
let mas = // content
let ts1 = NSTextStorage(attributedString:mas)
let lm1 = NSLayoutManager()
ts1.addLayoutManager(lm1)
let tc1 = NSTextContainer(size:r.size)
lm1.addTextContainer(tc1)
let tv = UITextView(frame:r, textContainer:tc1)
tv.scrollEnabled = false
let tc2 = NSTextContainer(size:r2.size)
lm1.addTextContainer(tc2)
let tv2 = UITextView(frame:r2, textContainer:tc2)
tv2.scrollEnabled = false
```

Figure 10-13. A text storage with two layout managers

If a text storage has multiple layout managers, then each layout manager is laying out the same text. For example, in Figure 10-13, there are two text views displaying the same text. The remarkable thing is that if you edit one text view, the other changes to match. (That's how Xcode lets you edit the same code file in different windows, tabs, or panes.)

Again, this arrangement is probably best achieved by building the entire text stack by hand:

```
let r = // frame
let r2 = // frame
let mas = // content
let ts1 = NSTextStorage(attributedString:mas)
let lm1 = NSLayoutManager()
ts1.addLayoutManager(lm1)
let lm2 = NSLayoutManager()
ts1.addLayoutManager(lm2)
let tc1 = NSTextContainer(size:r.size)
let tc2 = NSTextContainer(size:r2.size)
lm1.addTextContainer(tc1)
lm2.addTextContainer(tc2)
let tv = UITextView(frame:r, textContainer:tc1)
let tv2 = UITextView(frame:r2, textContainer:tc2)
```

Layout Manager

The first thing to know about a layout manager is the geometry in which it thinks. To envision a layout manager's geometrical world, think in terms of glyphs and line fragments:

Glyph
> The drawn analog of a character. The layout manager's primary job is to get glyphs from a font and draw them.

Line fragment

A rectangle in which glyphs are drawn, one after another. (The reason it's a line *fragment*, and not just a line, is that a line might be interrupted by the text container's exclusion paths.)

A glyph has a location in terms of the line fragment into which it is drawn. A line fragment's coordinates are in terms of the text container. The layout manager can convert between these coordinate systems, and between text and glyphs. Given a range of text in the text storage, it knows where the corresponding glyphs are drawn in the text container. Conversely, given a location in the text container, it knows what glyph is drawn there and what range of text in the text storage that glyph represents.

What's missing from that geometry is what, if anything, the text container corresponds to in the real world. A text container is not, itself, a real rectangle in the real world; it's just a class that tells the layout manager a size to draw into. Making that rectangle meaningful for drawing purposes is up to some other class outside the Text Kit stack. A UITextView, for example, has a text container, which it shares with a layout manager. The text view knows how its own content is scrolled and how the rectangle represented by its text container is inset within that scrolling content. The layout manager, however, doesn't know anything about that; it sees the text container as a purely theoretical rectangular boundary. Only when the layout manager actually draws does it make contact with the real world of some graphics context — and it must be told, on those occasions, how the text container's rectangle is offset within that graphics context.

To illustrate, I'll use a TextKit method to learn the index of the first character visible at the top left of a text view (`self.tv`); I'll then use NSLinguisticTagger to derive the first *word* visible at the top left of the text view. I can ask the layout manager what character or glyph corresponds to a certain point in the text container, but what point should I ask about? Translating from the real world to text container coordinates is up to me; I must take into account both the scroll position of the text view's content and the inset of the text container within that content:

```
let off = self.tv.contentOffset
let top = self.tv.textContainerInset.top
var tctopleft = CGPointMake(0, off.y - top)
```

Now I'm speaking in terms of text container coordinates, which are layout manager coordinates. One possibility is then to ask directly for the index (in the text storage's string) of the corresponding character:

```
var ix = self.tv.layoutManager.characterIndexForPoint(tctopleft,
    inTextContainer:self.tv.textContainer,
    fractionOfDistanceBetweenInsertionPoints:nil)
```

That, however, does not give quite the results one might intuitively expect. If *any* of a word is poking down from above into the visible area of the text view, that is the word whose first character is returned. I think we intuitively expect, if a word isn't fully visible, that the answer should be the word that starts the *next* line, which *is* fully visible. So I'll modify that code in a simpleminded way. I'll obtain the index of the *glyph* at my initial point; from this, I can derive the rect of the line fragment containing it. If that line fragment is not at least three-quarters visible, I'll add one line fragment height to the starting point and derive the glyph index again. Then I'll convert the glyph index to a character index:

```
var ix = self.tv.layoutManager.glyphIndexForPoint(tctopleft,
    inTextContainer:self.tv.textContainer,
    fractionOfDistanceThroughGlyph:nil)
let frag = self.tv.layoutManager.lineFragmentRectForGlyphAtIndex(
    ix, effectiveRange:nil)
if tctopleft.y > frag.origin.y + 0.5*frag.size.height {
    tctopleft.y += frag.size.height
    ix = self.tv.layoutManager.glyphIndexForPoint(tctopleft,
        inTextContainer:self.tv.textContainer,
        fractionOfDistanceThroughGlyph:nil)
}
let charRange = self.tv.layoutManager.characterRangeForGlyphRange(
    NSMakeRange(ix,0), actualGlyphRange:nil)
ix = charRange.location
```

Finally, I'll use NSLinguisticTagger to get the range of the entire word to which this character belongs:

```
let sch = NSLinguisticTagSchemeTokenType
let t = NSLinguisticTagger(tagSchemes:[sch], options:0)
t.string = self.tv.text
var r : NSRange = NSMakeRange(0,0)
let tag = t.tagAtIndex(ix, scheme:sch, tokenRange:&r, sentenceRange:nil)
if tag == NSLinguisticTagWord {
    println((self.tv.text as NSString).substringWithRange(r))
}
```

Clearly, the same sort of technique could be used to formulate a custom response to a tap ("what word did the user just tap on?").

By subclassing NSLayoutManager (and by implementing its delegate), many powerful effects can be achieved. As a simple example, I'll carry on from the preceding code by drawing a rectangular outline around the word we just located. To make this possible, I have an NSLayoutManager subclass, MyLayoutManager, an instance of which is built into the Text Kit stack for this text view. MyLayoutManager has a public NSRange property, wordRange. Having worked out what word I want to outline, I set the layout manager's wordRange and invalidate its drawing of that word, to force a redraw:

```
let lm = self.tv.layoutManager as! MyLayoutManager
lm.wordRange = r
lm.invalidateDisplayForCharacterRange(r)
```

In MyLayoutManager, I've overridden the method that draws the background behind glyphs. At the moment this method is called, there is already a graphics context.

First, I call super. Then, if the range of glyphs to be drawn includes the glyphs for the range of characters in self.wordRange, I ask for the rect of the bounding box of those glyphs, and stroke it to form the rectangle. As I mentioned earlier, the bounding box is in text container coordinates, but now we're drawing in the real world, so I have to compensate by offsetting the drawn rectangle by the same amount that the text container is supposed to be offset in the real world; fortunately, the text view tells us (through the origin: parameter) what that offset is:

```
override func drawBackgroundForGlyphRange(
    glyphsToShow: NSRange, atPoint origin: CGPoint) {
        super.drawBackgroundForGlyphRange(
            glyphsToShow, atPoint:origin)
        if self.wordRange.length == 0 {
            return
        }
        var range = self.glyphRangeForCharacterRange(
            self.wordRange, actualCharacterRange:nil)
        range = NSIntersectionRange(glyphsToShow, range)
        if range.length == 0 {
            return
        }
        if let tc = self.textContainerForGlyphAtIndex(
            range.location, effectiveRange:nil) {
                var r = self.boundingRectForGlyphRange(
                    range, inTextContainer:tc)
                r.origin.x += origin.x
                r.origin.y += origin.y
                let c = UIGraphicsGetCurrentContext()
                CGContextSaveGState(c)
                CGContextSetStrokeColorWithColor(
                    c, UIColor.blackColor().CGColor)
                CGContextSetLineWidth(c, 1.0)
                CGContextStrokeRect(c, r)
                CGContextRestoreGState(c)
        }
    }
```

Text Kit Without a Text View

UITextView is the only built-in iOS class that has a Text Kit stack to which you are given programmatic access. But that doesn't mean it's the only place where you can draw with Text Kit! You can draw with Text Kit *anywhere you can draw* — that is, in any graphics context (Chapter 2). When you do so, you should always call both drawBackgroundFor-GlyphRange:atPoint: (the method I overrode in the previous example) and draw-GlyphsForGlyphRange:atPoint:, in that order. The point: argument is where you consider the text container's origin to be within the current graphics context.

To illustrate, I'll change the implementation of the StringDrawer class that I described earlier in this chapter. Previously, StringDrawer's `drawRect:` implementation told the attributed string (`self.attributedText`) to draw itself:

```
override func drawRect(rect: CGRect) {
    let r = rect.rectByOffsetting(dx: 0, dy: 2)
    let options = NSString.combine(
        .TruncatesLastVisibleLine, with:.UsesLineFragmentOrigin)
    self.attributedText.drawWithRect(r, options: options, context: nil)
}
```

Instead, I'll construct the Text Kit stack and tell its layout manager to draw the text:

```
override func drawRect(rect: CGRect) {
    let lm = NSLayoutManager()
    let ts = NSTextStorage(attributedString:self.attributedText)
    ts.addLayoutManager(lm)
    let tc = NSTextContainer(size:rect.size)
    lm.addTextContainer(tc)
    tc.lineBreakMode = .ByTruncatingTail
    tc.lineFragmentPadding = 0
    let r = lm.glyphRangeForTextContainer(tc)
    lm.drawBackgroundForGlyphRange(r, atPoint:CGPointMake(0,2))
    lm.drawGlyphsForGlyphRange(r, atPoint:CGPointMake(0,2))
}
```

Building the entire Text Kit stack by hand may seem like overkill for that simple example, but imagine what *else* I could do now that I have access to the entire Text Kit stack! I can use properties, subclassing and delegation, and alternative stack architectures to achieve customizations and effects that, before TextKit was migrated to iOS, were difficult or impossible to achieve without dipping down to the level of Core Text.

For example, the two-column display of U.S. state names on the iPad shown in Figure 10-14 was a Core Text example in early editions of this book, requiring 50 or 60 lines of elaborate C code, complicated by the necessity of flipping the context to prevent the text from being drawn upside-down. Nowadays, it can be achieved easily through Text Kit — effectively just by reusing code from earlier examples in this chapter.

Furthermore, the example from previous editions went on to describe how to make the display of state names interactive, with the name of the tapped state briefly outlined with a rectangle (Figure 10-15). With Core Text, this was almost insanely difficult, not least because we had to keep track of all the line fragment rectangles ourselves. But it's easy with Text Kit, because the layout manager knows all the answers.

We have a UIView subclass, StyledText. In its `layoutSubviews`, it creates the Text Kit stack — a layout manager with two text containers, to achieve the two-column layout — and stores the whole stack, along with the rects at which the two text containers are to be drawn, in properties:

Alabama	Montana
Alaska	Nebraska
Arizona	Nevada
Arkansas	New Hampshire
California	New Jersey
Colorado	New Mexico
Connecticut	New York
Delaware	North Carolina
Florida	North Dakota
Georgia	Ohio
Hawaii	Oklahoma
Idaho	Oregon
Illinois	Pennsylvania
Indiana	Rhode Island
Iowa	South Carolina
Kansas	South Dakota
Kentucky	Tennessee
Louisiana	Texas
Maine	Utah
Maryland	Vermont
Massachusetts	Virginia
Michigan	Washington
Minnesota	West Virginia
Mississippi	Wisconsin
Missouri	Wyoming

Figure 10-14. Two-column text in small caps

Arizona
Arkansas
California
Colorado
Connecticut

Figure 10-15. The user has tapped on California

```
override func layoutSubviews() {
    super.layoutSubviews()
    var r1 = self.bounds
    r1.origin.y += 2 // a little top space
    r1.size.width /= 2.0 // column 1
    var r2 = r1
    r2.origin.x += r2.size.width // column 2
    let lm = MyLayoutManager()
    let ts = NSTextStorage(attributedString:self.text)
    ts.addLayoutManager(lm)
    let tc = NSTextContainer(size:r1.size)
    lm.addTextContainer(tc)
    let tc2 = NSTextContainer(size:r2.size)
    lm.addTextContainer(tc2)
    self.lm = lm
    self.ts = ts
```

```
    self.tc = tc
    self.tc2 = tc2
    self.r1 = r1
    self.r2 = r2
}
```

Our `drawRect:` is just like the previous example, except that we have two text containers to draw:

```
override func drawRect(rect: CGRect) {
    let range1 = self.lm.glyphRangeForTextContainer(self.tc)
    self.lm.drawBackgroundForGlyphRange(range1, atPoint: self.r1.origin)
    self.lm.drawGlyphsForGlyphRange(range1, atPoint: self.r1.origin)
    let range2 = self.lm.glyphRangeForTextContainer(self.tc2)
    self.lm.drawBackgroundForGlyphRange(range2, atPoint: self.r2.origin)
    self.lm.drawGlyphsForGlyphRange(range2, atPoint: self.r2.origin)
}
```

So much for drawing the text! Now, when the user taps on our view, a tap gesture recognizer's action handler is called. We are using the same layout manager subclass developed earlier in this chapter: it draws a rectangle around the glyphs corresponding to the characters of its `wordRange` property. Thus, all we have to do in order to make the flashing rectangle around the tapped word is work out what that range is, set the layout manager's `wordRange` and redraw ourselves, and then (after a short delay) set the layout manager's `wordRange` back to a zero range and redraw ourselves again to remove the rectangle.

We start by working out which column the user tapped in; this tells us which text container it is, and what the tapped point is in text container coordinates:

```
var p = g.locationInView(self) // g is the tap gesture recognizer
var tc = self.tc
if !CGRectContainsPoint(self.r1, p) {
    tc = self.tc2
    p.x -= self.r1.size.width
}
```

Now we can ask the layout manager what glyph the user tapped on, and hence the whole range of glyphs within the line fragment the user tapped in. If the user tapped to the left of the first glyph or to the right of the last glyph, no word was tapped, and we return:

```
var f : CGFloat = 0
let ix = self.lm.glyphIndexForPoint(
    p, inTextContainer:tc, fractionOfDistanceThroughGlyph:&f)
var glyphRange : NSRange = NSMakeRange(0,0)
self.lm.lineFragmentRectForGlyphAtIndex(ix, effectiveRange:&glyphRange)
if ix == glyphRange.location && f == 0.0 {
    return
```

```
    }
    if ix == glyphRange.location + glyphRange.length - 1 && f == 1.0 {
        return
    }
```

If the last glyph of the line fragment is a whitespace glyph, we don't want to include it
in our rectangle, so we subtract it from the end of our range. Now we're ready to convert
to a character range, and thus we can learn the name of the state that the user tapped
on:

```
func lastCharIsControl () -> Bool {
    let lastCharRange = glyphRange.location + glyphRange.length - 1
    let property = self.lm.propertyForGlyphAtIndex(lastCharRange)
    let mask1 = property.rawValue
    let mask2 = NSGlyphProperty.ControlCharacter.rawValue
    return mask1 & mask2 != 0
}
while lastCharIsControl() {
    glyphRange.length -= 1
}
let characterRange =
    self.lm.characterRangeForGlyphRange(glyphRange, actualGlyphRange:nil)
let s = (self.text.string as NSString).substringWithRange(characterRange)
```

Finally, we flash the rectangle around the state name by setting and resetting the word-
Range property of the subclassed layout manager:

```
let lm = self.lm as! MyLayoutManager
lm.wordRange = characterRange
self.setNeedsDisplay()
delay(0.3) {
    lm.wordRange = NSMakeRange(0, 0)
    self.setNeedsDisplay()
}
```

CHAPTER 11

Web Views

A web view is a UIView subclass whose primary purpose is to act as a web browser; therefore, it knows how to fetch resources from the Internet, and it understands and can render text in HTML, along with associated information coded as CSS and Java-Script. Thus it is an asynchronous network communication engine on the one hand, and a powerful engine for layout, animation, and media display on the other.

All of that power comes "for free" with a web view. It gives your app a browser interface, comparable to Mobile Safari; you can just stand back and let it do its work. You don't have to know anything about networking. Links and other ancillary resources work automatically. If your web view's HTML refers to an image, the web view will fetch it and display it. If the user taps on a link, the web view will fetch that content and display it; if the link is to some sort of media (a sound or video file), the web view will allow the user to play it.

A web view also knows how to display various other types of content commonly encountered as Internet resources. For example, a web view is an excellent way to display PDF files. It can also display documents in such formats as *.rtf*, Microsoft Word (*.doc* and *.docx*), and Pages. (A Pages file that is actually a bundle must be compressed to form a single *.pages.zip* resource.)

 A web view should also be able to display (compressed) *.rtfd* files, but as of this writing, it can't. Apple suggests that you convert to an attributed string (as I described in Chapter 10; specify a document type of NSRTFDTextDocumentType), or use a QLPreviewController (Chapter 23).

Web view content is loaded *asynchronously* (gradually, in a thread of its own), and it might not be loaded at all (because the user might not be connected to the Internet, the server might not respond properly, and so on). If you're loading a resource directly from disk, loading is quick and nothing is going to go wrong; nevertheless, rendering the content can take time, and even a resource loaded from disk, or content formed directly as an HTML string, might refer to material out on the Internet that takes time to fetch.

Your app's interface, however, is not blocked or frozen while the content is loading. On the contrary, it remains accessible and operative; that's what "asynchronous" means. The web view, in fetching a web page and its linked components, is doing something quite complex, involving both threading and network interaction — I'll have a lot more to say about this in Chapters 24 and 25 — but it shields you from this complexity. Your own interaction with the web view stays on the main thread and is straightforward. You ask the web view to load some content; then you sit back and let it worry about the details.

In iOS 8, there are actually *two* web view objects: UIWebView, which has been around since the earliest days of iOS, and WKWebView, the new kid on the block. The "WK" in WKWebView stands for WebKit; confusingly, both WKWebView and UIWebView use WebKit as their rendering engine, but WebKit is also the name of a framework that is new in iOS 8. The arrival of the WebKit framework allows WKWebKit to perform some cool tricks that UIWebKit can't do.

Unfortunately, the new kid is having some teething pains; thus, depending on your use case, you may not be able to take advantage of WKWebView's cool new features. The most obvious limitation is that, as of this writing, a URL pointing to resource on disk — including inside your app's bundle — will fail with a WKWebView. This is a pity, because that's a great use of a web view. For example, in my Latin flashcard app and my Zotz! game, I present the Help documentation in a UIWebView just because it's so convenient for laying out styled text with pictures; the documentation comes from my app bundle, so I can't substitute a WKWebView. Another shortcoming of WKWebView is that it can't be instantiated from a nib.

Therefore, since you might be using either WKWebView or UIWebView, I will describe both of them.

 It is possible to design an entire app that is effectively nothing but a web view — especially if you have control of the server with which the user is interacting. Indeed, before the advent of iOS, an iPhone app *was* a web application. There are still iOS apps that work this way, but such an approach to app design is outside the scope of this book.

WKWebView

WKWebView is part of the WebKit framework; to use it, you'll need to `import Web-Kit` and create the web view in code. The designated initializer for WKWebView is init(frame:configuration:), where the configuration: is a WKWebView-Configuration. You can create a configuration beforehand:

```
let config = WKWebViewConfiguration()
// ... configure config here ...
let wv = WKWebView(frame: CGRectZero, configuration:config)
```

Alternatively, you can initialize your web view with init(frame:) to get a default configuration and modify it through the web view's configuration property later:

```
let wv = WKWebView(frame: CGRectZero)
// ... configure wv.configuration here ...
```

Either way, you'll probably want to perform configurations before the web view has a chance to load any content, because some settings will affect *how* it loads or renders that content.

Here are some of the more important WKWebViewConfiguration properties:

suppressesIncrementalRendering
> If true, the web view's visible content doesn't change until all linked renderable resources (such as images) have finished loading. The default is false.

allowsInlineMediaPlayback
> If true, linked media are played inside the web page. The default is false (the fullscreen player is used).

mediaPlaybackRequiresUserAction
> If false, linked media are played automatically. The default is true.

preferences
> A WKPreferences object. This is a simple value class (a glorified struct) embodying three properties:
>
> - minimumFontSize
> - javaScriptEnabled
> - javaScriptCanOpenWindowsAutomatically

userContentController
> A WKUserContentController object. This is how you can inject JavaScript into a web page and communicate between your code and the web page's content. I'll give an example later.

Having created your web view, you'll place it in your interface and, if necessary, size and position it:

```
self.view.addSubview(wv)
wv.setTranslatesAutoresizingMaskIntoConstraints(false)
self.view.addConstraints(
    NSLayoutConstraint.constraintsWithVisualFormat(
        "H:|[wv]|", options: nil, metrics: nil, views: ["wv":wv])
)
self.view.addConstraints(
    NSLayoutConstraint.constraintsWithVisualFormat(
        "V:|[wv]|", options: nil, metrics: nil, views: ["wv":wv])
)
```

A WKWebView is not a scroll view, but it *has* a scroll view (scrollView). You can use this to scroll the web view's content programatically; you can also get references to its gesture recognizers, and add gesture recognizers of your own (see Chapter 7).

WKWebView Content

You can supply a web view with content in one of two forms:

An NSURLRequest
> Formed with an NSURL, using init(URL:). (Recall that local file URLs are currently *not* working for WKWebView!) Optionally, you can add a cache policy and a timeout interface, using init(URL:cachePolicy:timeoutInterval:). For additional configuration, start with an NSMutableURLRequest; now you can set such properties as allowsCellularAccess. When ready, call loadRequest:.

An HTML string
> Prepare a string consisting of valid HTML, and call loadHTMLString:baseURL:. (The baseURL: specifies how partial URLs in your HTML are to be resolved.)

For example, starting with a URL:

```
let url = NSURL(string: "http://www.apple.com")!
self.wv.loadRequest(NSURLRequest(URL:url))
```

Starting with an HTML string is useful particularly when you want to construct your HTML programmatically or make changes to it before handing it to the web view. In this example, I have a template file in my app bundle containing placeholders to be filled in depending on the circumstances at runtime:

```
let templatepath = NSBundle.mainBundle().pathForResource(
    "htmlTemplate", ofType:"txt")!
let base = NSURL.fileURLWithPath(templatepath)!
var s = String(contentsOfFile:templatepath,
    encoding:NSUTF8StringEncoding, error:nil)!
let ss = // actual body content for this page
s = s.stringByReplacingOccurrencesOfString("<content>", withString:ss)
// ... additional modifications go here ...
self.wv.loadHTMLString(s, baseURL:base)
```

Tracking Changes in a WKWebView

A WKWebView has properties that can be tracked with key–value observing, such as:

- `loading`
- `estimatedProgress`
- `URL`
- `title`

You can observe these properties to be notified as a web page loads or changes. For example, as preparation to give the user feedback while a page is loading, I'll put an activity indicator (Chapter 12) in the center of my web view, keep a reference to it, and observe the web view's `loading` property:

```
let act = UIActivityIndicatorView(activityIndicatorStyle:.WhiteLarge)
act.backgroundColor = UIColor(white:0.1, alpha:0.5)
self.activity = act
wv.addSubview(act)
act.setTranslatesAutoresizingMaskIntoConstraints(false)
self.view.addConstraint(
    NSLayoutConstraint(
        item: act, attribute: .CenterX, relatedBy: .Equal,
        toItem: wv, attribute: .CenterX, multiplier: 1, constant: 0)
)
self.view.addConstraint(
    NSLayoutConstraint(
        item: act, attribute: .CenterY, relatedBy: .Equal,
        toItem: wv, attribute: .CenterY, multiplier: 1, constant: 0)
)
wv.addObserver(self, forKeyPath: "loading", options: .New, context: nil)
```

When the web view starts loading or stops loading, I'm notified, so I can show or hide the activity view:

```
override func observeValueForKeyPath(keyPath: String,
    ofObject object: AnyObject, change: [NSObject : AnyObject],
    context: UnsafeMutablePointer<()>) {
        if let wv = object as? WKWebView {
            switch keyPath {
            case "loading":
                if let val:AnyObject = change[NSKeyValueChangeNewKey] {
                    if let val = val as? Bool {
                        if val {
                            self.activity.startAnimating()
                        } else {
                            self.activity.stopAnimating()
                        }
                    }
                }
            }
        }
```

```
            default:break
            }
        }
    }
```

Do not forget to remove yourself as an observer as you go out of existence. If, as is usually the case, this means also that the web view itself is going out of existence, I like to stop any loading that it may be doing at that moment as well:

```
deinit {
    self.wv.removeObserver(self, forKeyPath: "loading")
    self.wv.stopLoading()
}
```

WKWebView Navigation

A WKWebView maintains a back and forward list of the URLs to which the user has navigated. The list is its `backForwardList`, a WKBackForwardList, which is a collection of read-only properties (and one method) such as:

- `currentItem`
- `backItem`
- `forwardItem`
- `itemAtIndex:`

Each item in the list is a WKBackForwardItem, a simple value class basically consisting of a `URL` and a `title`.

The WKWebView itself responds to `goBack`, `goForward` and `goToBackForwardList-Item:`, so you can tell it in code to navigate the list. Its properties `canGoBack` and `canGoForward` are key–value observable; typically you would use that fact to enable or disable a Back and Forward button in your interface in response to the list changing.

A WKWebView also has one settable property, `allowsBackForwardNavigation-Gestures`. The default is `false`; if `true`, the user can supposedly swipe sideways to go back and forward in the list, but I have not in fact been able to make this gesture.

To prevent or reroute navigation that the user tries to perform by tapping links, set yourself as the WKWebView's `navigationDelegate` (WKNavigationDelegate) and implement `webView:decidePolicyForNavigationAction:decisionHandler:`. You are handed a `decisionHandler` closure which you must call, handing it a WKNavigation-ActionPolicy — either `.Cancel` or `.Allow`. You can examine the incoming `navigation-Action` (a WKNavigationAction) to help make your decision. It has a `request` which is the NSURLRequest we are proposing to perform — and you can look at its `URL` to see where we proposing to go — along with a navigationType which will be one of the following (WKNavigationType):

- .LinkActivated
- .BackForward
- .Reload
- .FormSubmitted
- .FormResubmitted
- .Other

In this example, I permit navigation in the most general case — otherwise nothing would ever appear in my web view! — but if the user taps a link, I forbid it and show that URL in Mobile Safari instead:

```
func webView(webView: WKWebView,
    decidePolicyForNavigationAction navigationAction: WKNavigationAction,
    decisionHandler: ((WKNavigationActionPolicy) -> Void)) {
        if navigationAction.navigationType == .LinkActivated {
            let url = navigationAction.request.URL
            UIApplication.sharedApplication().openURL(url!)
            decisionHandler(.Cancel)
            return
        }
        decisionHandler(.Allow)
}
```

Several other WKNavigationDelegate methods can notify you as a page loads (or fails to load). Under normal circumstances, you'll receive them in this order:

- webView:didStartProvisionalNavigation:
- webView:didCommitNavigation:
- webView:didFinishNavigation:

Those delegate methods, and all navigation commands, supply a WKNavigation object. This object is completely opaque and has no properties, but you can use it in an equality comparison to determine whether the navigations referred to in different methods are the same navigation (roughly speaking, the same page-loading operation).

Communicating With a WKWebView Web Page

Your code can get messages into and out of a WKWebView's web page, thus allowing you to change the page's contents or respond to changes within it, even while it is being displayed.

To send a message into an already loaded WKWebView web page, call `evaluateJava-Script:completionHandler:`. Your JavaScript runs within the context of the web page.

In this example, the user is able to decrease the size of the text in the web page. We have prepared some JavaScript that generates a `<style>` element containing CSS that sets the `font-size` for the page's `<body>` in accordance with a property, `self.fontsize`:

```
var fontsize = 18
var cssrule : String {
get {
    var s = "var s = document.createElement('style');\n"
    s += "s.textContent = '"
    s += "body { font-size: \(self.fontsize)px; }"
    s += "';\n"
    s += "document.documentElement.appendChild(s);\n"
    return s
}
}
```

When the user taps a button, we decrement `self.fontsize`, construct that JavaScript, and send it to the web page:

```
func doDecreaseSize (sender:AnyObject) {
    self.fontsize -= 1
    let s = self.cssrule
    self.wv.evaluateJavaScript(s, completionHandler: nil)
}
```

That's clever, but we have not done anything about setting the web page's *initial* `font-size`. A WKWebView allows us to inject JavaScript into the web page at the time it is loaded. To do so, we use the `userContentController` of the WKWebView's `configuration`. We create a WKUserScript, specifying the JavaScript it contains, along with an `injectionTime` which can be either before (`.DocumentStart`) or after (`.DocumentEnd`) a page's content has loaded. In this case, we want it to be before; otherwise, the user will see the font size change suddenly:

```
let s = self.cssrule
let script = WKUserScript(
    source: s, injectionTime: .AtDocumentStart, forMainFrameOnly: true)
self.wv.configuration.userContentController.addUserScript(script)
```

To communicate out of a web page, you need first to install a message handler to receive the communication. Again, this involves the `userContentController`. You call `add-ScriptMessageHandler:name:`, where the first argument is an object that must implement the WKScriptMessageHandler protocol, so that its `userContentController:did-ReceiveScriptMessage:` method can be called later:

```
self.wv.configuration.userContentController.addScriptMessageHandler(
    self, name: "playbutton")
```

We have now installed a playbutton message handler. This means that the DOM for our web page now contains an element, among its window.webkit.messageHandlers, called playbutton. A message handler sends its message when it receives a post-Message() function call. Thus, to sum up, self will get a call to its userContent-Controller:didReceiveScriptMessage: method if JavaScript inside the web page calls window.webkit.messageHandlers.playbutton.postMessage().

To make that actually happen, I've put an <img> tag into my web page's HTML, specifying an image that will act as a tappable button:

```
<img src=\"listen.png\"
onclick=\"window.webkit.messageHandlers.playbutton.postMessage('play')\">
```

When the user taps that image, the message is posted, and so my code runs and I can respond:

```
func userContentController(
    userContentController: WKUserContentController,
    didReceiveScriptMessage message: WKScriptMessage) {
        if message.name == "playbutton" {
            if let body = message.body as? String {
                if body == "play" {
                    // ... do stuff here! ...
                }
            }
        }
}
```

There's just one little problem: that code causes a retain cycle. The reason is that a WKUserContentController leaks, and it retains the WKScriptMessageHandler, which in this case is self — and so self will never be deallocated. My solution is to create an intermediate trampoline object that can be harmlessly retained, and that has a weak reference to self:

```
class MyMessageHandler : NSObject, WKScriptMessageHandler {
    weak var delegate : WKScriptMessageHandler?
    init(delegate:WKScriptMessageHandler) {
        self.delegate = delegate
        super.init()
    }
    func userContentController(
        userContentController: WKUserContentController,
        didReceiveScriptMessage message: WKScriptMessage) {
            delegate?.userContentController(
                userContentController, didReceiveScriptMessage: message)
    }
}
```

Now when I add myself as a script message handler, I do it by way of the trampoline object:

```
self.wv.configuration.userContentController.addScriptMessageHandler(
    MyMessageHandler(delegate:self), name: "playbutton")
```

The trampoline object leaks, but it's an extremely lightweight object so it doesn't matter much. However, I can do even better; now that I've broken the retain cycle, my own `deinit` is called, and I can release the offending objects:

```
deinit {
    self.wv.removeObserver(self, forKeyPath: "loading")
    self.wv.stopLoading()
    // break all retains
    self.wv.configuration.userContentController
        .removeAllUserScripts()
    self.wv.configuration.userContentController
        .removeScriptMessageHandlerForName("playbutton")
}
```

UIWebView

Despite the advent of WKWebView, you may find that you prefer to stay with UIWeb-View for now. It has some automatic features that WKWebView lacks; it can load content using a file URL, including from inside your app bundle; and it works in connection with view controller state restoration.

UIWebView's back and forward list is much simpler than WKWebView's; two properties, `canGoBack` and `canGoForward`, and two methods, `goBack` and `goForward`, let you interact with the list.

Like WKWebView, a UIWebView has a `scrollView` property.

A UIWebView is zoomable if its `scalesToFit` property is `true`. In that case, it initially scales its content to fit, and the user can zoom the content; this includes use of the gesture, familiar from Mobile Safari, whereby double-tapping part of a web page zooms to that region of the page.

Like a text view (Chapter 10), a UIWebView's `dataDetectorTypes` property lets you set certain types of data to be automatically converted to tappable links.

The `suppressesIncrementalRendering` property is just like that of a WKWebView-Configuration.

UIWebView Content

Providing a UIWebView with content is much like providing a WKWebView with content. You will need one of three things:

An NSURLRequest
    Construct an NSURLRequest and call `loadRequest:`.

An HTML string

Construct a string consisting of valid HTML and call `loadHTMLString:baseURL:`.

Data and a MIME type

Obtain an NSData object and call `loadData:MIMEType:textEncodingName:base-URL:`.

UIWebView Navigation

A UIWebView's delegate (UIWebViewDelegate) gets three messages that notify you of the start and end of the loading process:

- `webViewDidStartLoad:`
- `webViewDidFinishLoad:`
- `webView:didFailLoadWithError:`

A web view's `loading` property tells you whether it is in the process of loading a request. If, at the time a web view is to be destroyed, its `loading` is YES, it is up to you to cancel the request by sending it the `stopLoading` message first; actually, it does no harm to send the web view `stopLoading` in any case. In addition, UIWebView is one of those weird classes whose memory management behavior is odd: Apple's documentation warns that if you assign a UIWebView a delegate, you must nilify its `delegate` property before releasing the web view. Thus, in a view controller class whose view contains a web view, I do an extra little dance in `deinit`:

```
deinit {
    self.wv.stopLoading()
    self.wv.delegate = nil
}
```

A related problem is that a web view will sometimes leak memory. I've never understood what causes this, but the workaround appears to be to load the empty string into the web view:

```
override func viewWillDisappear(animated: Bool) {
    if self.isMovingFromParentViewController() {
        self.wv.loadHTMLString("", baseURL:nil)
    }
}
```

To customize what happens when content is about to load, implement the delegate method `webView:shouldStartLoadWithRequest:navigationType:`. This is roughly parallel to WKWebView's `webView:decidePolicyForNavigationAction:decision-Handler:`. If you return `false`, the content won't load. The second parameter is an NSURLRequest, whose URL property you can examine. The third parameter is a constant describing the type of navigation involved, whose value (UIWebViewNavigationType) will be one of the following:

- `.LinkClicked`
- `.BackForward`
- `.Reload`
- `.FormSubmitted`
- `.FormResubmitted`
- `.Other`

This is the UIWebView equivalent of the WKWebView code I showed earlier:

```
func webView(webView: UIWebView,
    shouldStartLoadWithRequest r: NSURLRequest,
    navigationType nt: UIWebViewNavigationType) -> Bool {
        if nt == .LinkClicked { // disable link-clicking
            UIApplication.sharedApplication().openURL(r.URL!)
            return false
        }
        return true
}
```

Communicating with a UIWebView

Communication from your code into a UIWebView's content is similar to a WKWeb-View: you construct some JavaScript and call `stringByEvaluatingJavaScriptFrom-String:`.

There is no provision for communication in the other direction, from the UIWebView's content to your code. What I do is misuse `webView:shouldStartLoadWith-Request:navigationType:`. Recall my WKWebView example of a tappable image, where my code is to be notified when the image is tapped. With UIWebView, I add an `onclick` handler that uses a custom scheme:

```
document.location='play:me'
```

When the user taps the image, the web view delegate's `webView:shouldStartLoadWith-Request:navigationType:` gets an NSURLRequest `play:me`. That's the signal telling me that the user has tapped the Listen image:

```
func webView(webView: UIWebView,
    shouldStartLoadWithRequest r: NSURLRequest,
    navigationType nt: UIWebViewNavigationType) -> Bool {
        if let scheme = r.URL?.scheme where scheme == "play" {
            // ... do something ...
            return false
```

```
        }
        // ...
        return true
    }
```

Paginated Web Views

A UIWebView can break its content into pages, allowing the user to browse that content in chunks by scrolling horizontally or vertically. This may seem an unaccustomed way of viewing web pages, but as I mentioned earlier, a web view is good for content that is not obviously a web page.

Configuration can be as simple as setting the web view's `paginationMode` property:

```
self.wv.paginationMode = .LeftToRight
```

The result of that code is that the web view's content is rendered into columns; instead of scrolling down in one long single column to read the content, the user scrolls left or right to see one screenful at a time. Scrolling does not automatically snap to pages, but you can enable that through the web view's `scrollView`:

```
self.wv.paginationMode = .LeftToRight
self.wv.scrollView.pagingEnabled = true
```

You can set the page size (`pageLength`, the same as the viewport size by default) and the gap between pages (`gapBetweenPages`, 0 by default).

UIWebView State Restoration

If you provided an HTML string to your web view, then restoring its state when the app is relaunched is up to you; you can use the built-in state saving and restoration to help you, but you'll have to do all the work yourself. The web view has a `scrollView` which has a `contentOffset`, so it's easy to save the scroll position in `encodeRestorableState-WithCoder:`, and restore it in `decodeRestorableStateWithCoder:`. In this example, I use a property (`self.oldOffset`) which is an NSValue wrapping a CGPoint:

```
override func encodeRestorableStateWithCoder(coder: NSCoder) {
    super.encodeRestorableStateWithCoder(coder)
    let off = self.wv.scrollView.contentOffset
    coder.encodeObject(NSValue(CGPoint:off), forKey:"oldOffset")
}
override func decodeRestorableStateWithCoder(coder: NSCoder) {
    super.decodeRestorableStateWithCoder(coder)
    self.oldOffset = coder.decodeObjectForKey("oldOffset") as? NSValue
}
```

Observe that I have not yet set the `contentOffset` of the UIWebView's `scrollView`. That's because we don't yet have any content! In `viewDidAppear:`, we load the content manually; when the content has loaded, we set its scroll position:

```
func webViewDidFinishLoad(wv: UIWebView) {
    if self.oldOffset != nil {
        wv.scrollView.contentOffset = self.oldOffset!.CGPointValue()
    }
    self.oldOffset = nil
}
```

If, however, the web view had a URL request (not an HTML string) when the user left the app, then the state restoration mechanism will *automatically* restore that request, in the web view's `request` property, along with its Back and Forward lists. To restore the web view's actual content, simply send it the `reload` message. The web view will then restore its old contents and its old scroll position! A good place to do this is `applicationFinishedRestoringState`:

```
override func applicationFinishedRestoringState() {
    if self.wv.request != nil {
        self.wv.reload()
    }
}
```

I have not discovered any evidence that WKWebView participates in state restoration — and you can't readily hack your way around this, because a WKWebView's `back-ForwardList` is not writable — so this could be a good reason for preferring to stick with UIWebView.

Developing Web View Content

Before designing the HTML to be displayed in a web view, you might want to read up on the brand of HTML native to the mobile WebKit rendering engine. There are certain limitations; for example, mobile WebKit notoriously doesn't use plug-ins, such as Flash, and it imposes limits on the size of resources (such as images) that it can display. On the plus side, WebKit is in the forefront of the march toward HTML 5 and CSS 3, and has many special capabilities suited for display on a mobile device. For documentation and other resources, see Apple's Safari Dev Center.

A good place to start is the *Safari Web Content Guide*. It contains links to other relevant documentation, such as the *Safari CSS Visual Effects Guide*, which describes some things you can do with WebKit's implementation of CSS3 (like animations), and the *Safari HTML5 Audio and Video Guide*, which describes WebKit's audio and video player support.

If nothing else, you'll want to be aware of one important aspect of web page content — the *viewport*. This is typically set through a `<meta>` tag in the `<head>` area. For example:

```
<meta name="viewport" content="initial-scale=1.0, user-scalable=no">
```

Without that line, or something similar, a web page may be laid out incorrectly when it is rendered. This is noticeable especially if the web view changes size (perhaps because

Figure 11-1. The Web Inspector inspects an app running in the Simulator

the app's interface rotates): in one orientation or the other, the page will be too wide for the web view, and the user has to scroll horizontally to read it. The *Safari Web Content Guide* explains why: if no viewport is specified, the viewport can change when the app rotates. Setting the `initial-scale` causes the viewport size to adopt correct values in both orientations.

Another important section of the *Safari Web Content Guide* describes how you can use a `media` attribute in the `<link>` tag that loads your CSS to load *different* CSS depending on what kind of device your app is running on. For example, you might have one CSS file that lays out your web view's content on an iPhone, and another that lays it out on an iPad.

Inspecting, debugging, and experimenting with web view content is greatly eased by the Web Inspector, built into Safari on the desktop. It can see a web view in your app running in the Simulator, and lets you analyze every aspect of how it works. For example, in Figure 11-1, I'm examining an image to see how it is sized and scaled.

Moreover, the Web Inspector lets you change your web view's content in real time, with many helpful features such as CSS autocompletion; this can be a better way to discover WebKit CSS features than the documentation, which isn't always kept up to date. For example, your web view can display Dynamic Type fonts, as discussed in Chapter 10, by setting the `font` CSS property to `-apple-system-body` and so forth; but, as of this writing, the only way to discover that is apparently through the Web Inspector's auto-completion.

JavaScript and the document object model (*DOM*) are also extremely powerful. Event listeners allow JavaScript code to respond directly to touch and gesture events, so that the user can interact with elements of a web page much as if they were touchable views; it can also take advantage of Core Location and Core Motion facilities to respond to where the user is on earth and how the device is positioned (Chapter 22). Additional helpful documentation includes Apple's *WebKit DOM Programming Topics* and *Safari DOM Additions Reference*.

CHAPTER 12

Controls and Other Views

This chapter discusses all UIView subclasses provided by UIKit that haven't been discussed already. It's remarkable how few of them there are; UIKit exhibits a notable economy of means in this regard.

Additional UIView subclasses, as well as UIViewController subclasses that create interface, are provided by other frameworks. There will be lots of examples in Part III. For example, the Map Kit framework provides the MKMapView (Chapter 21); and the MessageUI framework provides MFMailComposeViewController, which supplies a user interface for composing and sending a mail message (Chapter 20).

UIActivityIndicatorView

An activity indicator (UIActivityIndicatorView) appears as the spokes of a small wheel. You set the spokes spinning with `startAnimating`, giving the user a sense that some time-consuming process is taking place. You stop the spinning with `stopAnimating`. If the activity indicator's `hidesWhenStopped` is `true` (the default), it is visible only while spinning.

An activity indicator comes in a style, its `activityIndicatorViewStyle`; if it is created in code, you'll set its style with `init(activityIndicatorStyle:)`. Your choices (UIActivityIndicatorViewStyle) are:

- `.WhiteLarge`
- `.White`
- `.Gray`

An activity indicator has a standard size, which depends on its style. Changing its size in code changes the size of the view, but not the size of the spokes. For bigger spokes, you can resort to a scale transform.

Figure 12-1. A large activity indicator

You can assign an activity indicator a `color`; this overrides the color assigned through the style. An activity indicator is a UIView, so you can set its `backgroundColor`; a nice effect is to give an activity indicator a contrasting background color and to round its corners by way of the view's layer (Figure 12-1).

Here's some code from a UITableViewCell subclass in one of my apps. In this app, it takes some time, after the user taps a cell to select it, for me to construct the next view and navigate to it; to cover the delay, I show a spinning activity indicator in the center of the cell while it's selected:

```
override func setSelected(selected: Bool, animated: Bool) {
    super.setSelected(selected, animated: animated)
    if selected {
        let v = UIActivityIndicatorView(activityIndicatorStyle: .WhiteLarge)
        v.color = UIColor.yellowColor()
        dispatch_async(dispatch_get_main_queue()) {
            v.backgroundColor = UIColor(white:0.2, alpha:0.6)
        }
        v.layer.cornerRadius = 10
        v.frame = v.frame.rectByInsetting(dx: -10, dy: -10)
        let cf = self.contentView.convertRect(self.bounds, fromView:self)
        v.center = CGPointMake(cf.midX, cf.midY);
        v.tag = 1001
        self.contentView.addSubview(v)
        v.startAnimating()
    } else {
        if let v = self.viewWithTag(1001) {
            v.removeFromSuperview()
        }
    }
}
```

If activity involves the network, you might want to set UIApplication's `networkActivity-IndicatorVisible` to `true`. This displays a small spinning activity indicator in the status bar. The indicator is not reflecting actual network activity; if it's visible, it's spinning. Be sure to set it back to `false` when the activity is over.

An activity indicator is simple and standard, but you can't change the way it's drawn. One obvious alternative would be a UIImageView with an animated image, as described in Chapter 4.

Figure 12-2. A progress view

UIProgressView

A progress view (UIProgressView) is a "thermometer," graphically displaying a percentage. It is often used to represent a time-consuming process whose percentage of completion is known (if the percentage of completion is unknown, you're more likely to use an activity indicator). But it's good for static percentages too. In one of my apps, I use a progress view to show the current position within the song being played by the built-in music player; in another app, which is a card game, I use a progress view to show how many cards are left in the deck.

A progress view comes in a style, its progressViewStyle; if the progress view is created in code, you'll set its style with init(progressViewStyle:). Your choices (UIProgress-ViewStyle) are:

- .Default
- .Bar

A .Bar progress view is intended for use in a UIBarButtonItem, as the title view of a navigation item, and so on. Both styles by default draw the thermometer extremely thin — just 2 pixels and 3 pixels, respectively. (Figure 12-2 shows a .Default progress view.) Changing a progress view's frame height directly has no visible effect on how the thermometer is drawn. Under autolayout, to make a thicker thermometer, supply a height constraint with a larger value (thus overriding the intrinsic content height). Alternatively, subclass UIProgressView and override sizeThatFits:.

The fullness of the thermometer is the progress view's progress property. This is a value between 0 and 1, inclusive; you'll usually need to do some elementary arithmetic in order to convert from the actual value you're reflecting to a value within that range. (It is also a Float; in Swift, you may have to cast explicitly.) For example, to reflect the number of cards remaining in a deck of 52 cards:

```
let r = self.deck.cards().count
self.prog.progress = Float(r) / 52
```

A change in progress value can be animated by calling setProgress:animated:.

The default color of the filled portion of a progress view is the tintColor (which may be inherited from higher up the view hierarchy). The default color for the unfilled portion is gray for a .Default progress view and transparent for a .Bar progress view. You

Figure 12-3. A thicker progress view using a custom progress image

can customize the colors; set the progress view's `progressTintColor` and `trackTint-Color`, respectively. This can also be done in the nib.

In theory, you should alternatively be able to customize the image used to draw the filled portion of the progress view, its `progressImage`, along with the image used to draw the unfilled portion, the `trackImage`. This can also be done in the nib. Each image must be stretched to the length of the filled or unfilled area, so you'll want to use a resizable image.

Here's a simple example from one of my apps (Figure 12-3):

```
self.prog.backgroundColor = UIColor.blackColor()
self.prog.trackTintColor = UIColor.blackColor()
UIGraphicsBeginImageContextWithOptions(CGSizeMake(10,10), true, 0)
let con = UIGraphicsGetCurrentContext()
CGContextSetFillColorWithColor(con, UIColor.yellowColor().CGColor)
CGContextFillRect(con, CGRectMake(0, 0, 10, 10))
let r = CGRectInset(CGContextGetClipBoundingBox(con),1,1)
CGContextSetLineWidth(con, 2)
CGContextSetStrokeColorWithColor(con, UIColor.blackColor().CGColor)
CGContextStrokeRect(con, r)
CGContextStrokeEllipseInRect(con, r)
let im =
    UIGraphicsGetImageFromCurrentImageContext()
        .resizableImageWithCapInsets(
            UIEdgeInsetsMake(4, 4, 4, 4), resizingMode:.Stretch)
UIGraphicsEndImageContext()
self.prog.progressImage = im
```

I say "in theory" because that code, which worked for years up through iOS 7.0, broke in iOS 7.1 and hasn't worked since then. Of course I regard this as a huge bug. A possible workaround, which is extremely fragile and hacky, is to try to find the UIImageView that is intended to hold the UIProgressView's `progressImage` and set its `image` directly:

```
let ims = self.prog2.subviews.filter {$0 is UIImageView} as! [UIImageView]
ims[1].image = im // progressImage
```

For maximum flexibility, you can design your own UIView subclass that draws something similar to a thermometer. Figure 12-4 shows a simple custom thermometer view; it has a `value` property, and you set this to something between 0 and 1 and call `setNeeds-Display` to make the view redraw itself. Here's its `drawRect:` code:

Figure 12-4. A custom progress view

```
override func drawRect(rect: CGRect) {
    let c = UIGraphicsGetCurrentContext()
    UIColor.whiteColor().set()
    let ins : CGFloat = 2.0
    let r = self.bounds.rectByInsetting(dx: ins, dy: ins)
    let radius : CGFloat = r.size.height / 2.0
    let mpi = CGFloat(M_PI)
    let path = CGPathCreateMutable()
    CGPathMoveToPoint(path, nil, r.maxX - radius, ins)
    CGPathAddArc(path, nil,
        radius+ins, radius+ins, radius, -mpi/2.0, mpi/2.0, true)
    CGPathAddArc(path, nil,
        r.maxX - radius, radius+ins, radius, mpi/2.0, -mpi/2.0, true)
    CGPathCloseSubpath(path)
    CGContextAddPath(c, path)
    CGContextSetLineWidth(c, 2)
    CGContextStrokePath(c)
    CGContextAddPath(c, path)
    CGContextClip(c)
    CGContextFillRect(c, CGRectMake(
        r.origin.x, r.origin.y, r.size.width * self.value, r.size.height))
}
```

UIPickerView

A picker view (UIPickerView) displays selectable choices using a rotating drum metaphor. It has a standard legal range of possible heights, which is undocumented but seems to be between 162 and 180; its width is largely up to you. Each drum, or column, is called a *component*.

Your code configures the UIPickerView's content through its data source (UIPickerViewDataSource) and delegate (UIPickerViewDelegate), which are usually the same object. Your data source and delegate must answer questions similar to those posed by a UITableView (Chapter 8):

`numberOfComponentsInPickerView:` *(data source)*
How many components (drums) does this picker view have?

`pickerView:numberOfRowsInComponent:` *(data source)*
How many rows does this component have? The first component is numbered 0.

`pickerView:titleForRow:forComponent:`
`pickerView:attributedTitleForRow:forComponent:`
`pickerView:viewForRow:forComponent:reusingView:` *(delegate)*

What should this row of this component display? The first row is numbered 0. You can supply a simple string, an attributed string (Chapter 10), or an entire view such as a UILabel; but you should supply every row of every component the same way. The `reusingView:` parameter, if not nil, is supposed to be a view that you supplied for a row now no longer visible, giving you a chance to reuse it, much as cells are reused in a table view.

 In actual fact, the `reusingView:` parameter is *always* nil; views are not reused. They don't leak — they go out of existence in good order when they are no longer visible — but they aren't reused either. I regard this as a bug.

Here's the code for a UIPickerView (Figure 12-5) that displays the names of the 50 U.S. states, stored in an array. We implement `pickerView:viewForRow:for-Component:reusingView:` just because it's the most interesting case; as our views, we supply UILabel instances. The state names appear centered because the labels are centered within the picker view:

```
func numberOfComponentsInPickerView(pickerView: UIPickerView) -> Int {
    return 1
}
func pickerView(pickerView: UIPickerView,
    numberOfRowsInComponent component: Int) -> Int {
        return 50
}
func pickerView(pickerView: UIPickerView, viewForRow row: Int,
    forComponent component: Int, reusingView view: UIView!) -> UIView {
        var lab : UILabel
        if let label = view as? UILabel { // never happens
            lab = label
        } else {
            lab = UILabel()
        }
        lab.text = self.states[row]
        lab.backgroundColor = UIColor.clearColor()
        lab.sizeToFit()
        return lab
}
```

The delegate may further configure the UIPickerView's physical appearance by means of these methods:

Figure 12-5. A picker view

- `pickerView:rowHeightForComponent:`

- `pickerView:widthForComponent:`

The delegate may implement `pickerView:didSelectRow:inComponent:` to be notified each time the user spins a drum to a new position. You can also query the picker view directly by sending it `selectedRowInComponent:`.

You can set the value to which any drum is turned using `selectRow:in-Component:animated:`. Other handy picker view methods allow you to request that the data be reloaded, and there are properties and methods to query the picker view's contents (though of course they do not relieve you of responsibility for knowing the data model from which the picker view's contents are supplied):

- `reloadComponent:`

- `reloadAllComponents`

- `numberOfComponents`

- `numberOfRowsInComponent:`

- `viewForRow:forComponent:`

By implementing `pickerView:didSelectRow:inComponent:` and using `reload-Component:`, you can make a picker view where the values displayed by one drum depend dynamically on what is selected in another. For example, one can imagine expanding our U.S. states example to include a second drum listing major cities in each state; when the user switches to a different state in the first drum, a different set of major cities appears in the second drum.

UISearchBar

A search bar (UISearchBar) is essentially a wrapper for a text field; it has a text field as one of its subviews, though there is no official access to it. It is displayed by default as a rounded rectangle containing a magnifying glass icon, where the user can enter text

Figure 12-6. A search bar with a search results button

(Figure 12-6). It does not, of itself, do any searching or display the results of a search; a common interface involves displaying the results of a search as a table, and the UI-SearchController class makes this easy to do (see Chapter 8).

A search bar's current text is its `text` property. It can have a `placeholder`, which appears when there is no text. A `prompt` can be displayed above the search bar to explain its purpose. Delegate methods (UISearchBarDelegate) notify you of editing events; for their use, compare the text field and text view delegate methods discussed in Chapter 10:

- `searchBarShouldBeginEditing:`
- `searchBarTextDidBeginEditing:`
- `searchBar:textDidChange:`
- `searchBar:shouldChangeTextInRange:replacementText:`
- `searchBarShouldEndEditing:`
- `searchBarTextDidEndEditing:`

A search bar has a `barStyle`, for which your choices and their default appearances are (UIBarStyle):

- `.Default`, a flat light gray background and a white search field
- `.Black`, a black background and a black search field

In addition, there's a `searchBarStyle` property (UISearchBarStyle):

- `.Default`, as already described
- `.Prominent`, identical to `.Default`
- `.Minimal`, transparent background and dark transparent search field

Alternatively, you can set a search bar's `barTintColor` to change its background color; if the bar style is `.Black`, the `barTintColor` will also tint the search field itself. An opaque `barTintColor` is a way to make a search bar opaque. The `tintColor` property, meanwhile, whose value may be inherited from higher up the view hierarchy, governs the color of search bar components such as the Cancel button title and the flashing insertion cursor.

A search bar can also have a custom `backgroundImage`; this will be treated as a resizable image. The full setter method is `setBackgroundImage:forBarPosition:bar-Metrics:`; I'll talk later about what bar position and bar metrics are. The `background-Image` overrides all other ways of determining the background, and the search bar's `backgroundColor`, if any, appears behind it — though under some circumstances, if the search bar's `translucent` is `false`, the `barTintColor` may appear behind it instead.

The search field area where the user enters text can be offset with respect to its background, using the `searchFieldBackgroundPositionAdjustment` property; you might do this, for example, if you had enlarged the search bar's height and wanted to position the search field within that height. The text can be offset within the search field with the `searchTextPositionAdjustment` property.

You can also replace the image of the search field itself; this is the image that is normally a rounded rectangle. To do so, call `setSearchFieldBackgroundImage:forState:`. According to the documentation, the possible `state:` values are `.Normal` and `.Disabled`; but the API provides no way to disable a search field, so what does Apple have in mind here? The only way I've found is to cycle through the search bar's subviews, find the text field, and disable that:

```
for v in (self.sb.subviews[0] as! UIView).subviews as! [UIView] {
    if let tf = v as? UITextField {
        tf.enabled = false
        break
    }
}
```

The search field image will be drawn vertically centered in front of the background and behind the contents of the search field (such as the text); its width will be adjusted for you, but it is up to you choose an appropriate height, and to ensure an appropriate color in the middle so the user can read the text.

A search bar displays an internal cancel button automatically (normally an X in a circle) if there is text in the search field. Internally, at its right end, a search bar may display a search results button (`showsSearchResultsButton`), which may be selected or not (`searchResultsButtonSelected`), or a bookmark button (`showsBookmarkButton`); if you ask to display both, you'll get the search results button. These buttons vanish if text is entered in the search bar so that the cancel button can be displayed. There is also an option to display a Cancel button externally (`showsCancelButton`, or call `setShows-CancelButton:animated:`). The internal cancel button works automatically to remove whatever text is in the field; the other buttons do nothing, but delegate methods notify you when they are tapped:

- `searchBarResultsListButtonClicked:`
- `searchBarBookmarkButtonClicked:`

- `searchBarCancelButtonClicked:`

You can customize the images used for the search icon (a magnifying glass, by default) and any of the internal right icons (the internal cancel button, the search results button, and the bookmark button) with `setImage:forSearchBarIcon:state:`. The images will be resized for you, except for the internal cancel button, for which about 20×20 seems to be a good size. The icons are specified with constants (UISearchBarIcon):

- `.Search`
- `.Clear` (the internal cancel button)
- `.Bookmark`
- `.ResultsList`

The documentation says that the possible `state:` values are `.Normal` and `.Disabled`, but this is wrong; the choices are `.Normal` and `.Highlighted`. The highlighted image appears while the user taps on the icon (except for the search icon, which isn't a button). If you don't supply a normal image, the default image is used; if you supply a normal image but no highlighted image, the normal image is used for both. Setting `search-ResultsButtonSelected` to `true` reverses the search results button's behavior: it displays the highlighted image, but when the user taps it, it displays the normal image.

The position of an icon can be adjusted with `setPositionAdjustment:forSearchBar-Icon:`.

A search bar may also display scope buttons (see the example in Chapter 8). These are intended to let the user alter the meaning of the search; precisely how you use them is up to you. To make the scope buttons appear, use the `showsScopeBar` property; the button titles are the `scopeButtonTitles` property, and the currently selected scope button is the `selectedScopeButtonIndex` property. The delegate is notified when the user taps a different scope button:

- `searchBar:selectedScopeButtonIndexDidChange:`

The overall look of the scope bar can be heavily customized. Its background is the `scope-BarBackgroundImage`, which will be stretched or tiled as needed. To set the background of the smaller area constituting the actual buttons, call `setScopeBarButtonBackground-Image:forState:`; the states are `.Normal` and `.Selected`. If you don't supply a separate selected image, a darkened version of the normal image is used. If you don't supply a resizable image, the image will be made resizable for you; the runtime decides what region of the image will be stretched behind each button.

The dividers between the buttons are normally vertical lines, but you can customize them as well: call `setScopeBarButtonDividerImage:forLeftSegmentState:right-`

Figure 12-7. A horrible search bar

`SegmentState:`. A full complement of dividers consists of three images, one when the buttons on both sides of the divider are normal (unselected) and one each when a button on one side or the other is selected; if you supply an image for just one state combination, it is used for the other two state combinations. The height of the divider image is adjusted for you, but the width is not; you'll normally use an image just a few pixels wide.

The font attributes of the titles of the scope buttons can customized by calling `setScope-BarButtonTitleTextAttributes:forState:`. The `attributes:` argument is an NSAttributedString attributes dictionary.

 It may appear that there is no way to customize the external Cancel button, but in fact, although you've no official direct access to it through the search bar, the Cancel button is a UIBarButtonItem and you can customize it using the UIBarButtonItem appearance proxy, discussed later in this chapter.

By combining the various customization possibilities, a completely unrecognizable search bar of inconceivable ugliness can easily be achieved (Figure 12-7). Let's be careful out there.

The problem of allowing the keyboard to appear without hiding the search bar is exactly as for a text field (Chapter 10). Text input properties of the search bar configure its keyboard and typing behavior like a text field as well:

- `keyboardType`
- `autocapitalizationType`
- `autocorrectionType`
- `spellCheckingType`
- `inputAccessoryView`

When the user taps the Search key in the keyboard, the delegate is notified, and it is then up to you to dismiss the keyboard (`resignFirstResponder`) and perform the search:

- `searchBarSearchButtonClicked:`

A common interface is a search bar at the top of the screen. On the iPad, a search bar can be embedded as a bar button item's view in a toolbar at the top of the screen. On the iPhone, a search bar can be a navigation item's `titleView`. In Chapter 9, I gave an example of a search bar in a navigation bar. A search bar used in this way, however, has some limitations: for example, there may be no room for a prompt, scope buttons, or an external Cancel button, and you might not be able to assign it a background image or change its `barTintColor`.

Alternatively, a UISearchBar can itself function as a top bar, *like* a navigation bar without being *in* a navigation bar. If you use a search bar in this way, you'll want its height to be extended automatically under the status bar; I'll explain later in this chapter how to arrange that.

UIControl

UIControl is a subclass of UIView whose chief purpose is to be the superclass of several further built-in classes (controls) and to endow them with common behavior.

The most important thing that controls have in common is that they automatically track and analyze touch events (Chapter 5) and report them to your code as significant control events by way of action messages. Each control implements some subset of the possible control events. The full set of control events is listed under UIControlEvents in the Constants section of the UIControl class documentation:

- `.TouchDown`
- `.TouchDownRepeat`
- `.TouchDragInside`
- `.TouchDragOutside`
- `.TouchDragEnter`
- `.TouchDragExit`
- `.TouchUpInside`
- `.TouchUpOutside`
- `.TouchCancel`
- `.ValueChanged`
- `.EditingDidBegin`
- `.EditingChanged`
- `.EditingDidEnd`

- `.EditingDidEndOnExit`
- `.AllTouchEvents`
- `.AllEditingEvents`
- `.AllEvents`

The control events also have informal names that are visible in the Connections inspector when you're editing a nib. I'll mostly use the informal names in the next couple of paragraphs.

Control events fall roughly into three groups: the user has touched the screen (Touch Down, Touch Drag Inside, Touch Up Inside, etc.), edited text (Editing Did Begin, Editing Changed, etc.), or changed the control's value (Value Changed).

Apple's documentation is rather coy about which controls normally emit actions for which control events, so here's a list obtained through experimentation (but keep in mind that Apple's silence on this matter may mean that the details are subject to change):

UIButton
All "Touch" events.

UIDatePicker
Value Changed.

UIPageControl
All "Touch" events, Value Changed.

UIRefreshControl
Value Changed.

UISegmentedControl
Value Changed.

UISlider
All "Touch" events, Value Changed.

UISwitch
All "Touch" events, Value Changed.

UIStepper
All "Touch" events, Value Changed.

UITextField
All "Touch" events except the "Up" events, and all "Editing" events (see Chapter 10 for details).

UIControl (generic)
All "Touch" events.

For each control event that you want to hear about automatically, you attach to the control one or more target–action pairs. You can do this in the nib or in code.

For any given control, each control event and its target–action pairs form a dispatch table. The following methods permit you to manipulate and query the dispatch table:

- `addTarget:action:forControlEvents:`
- `removeTarget:action:forControlEvents:`
- `actionsForTarget:forControlEvent:`
- `allTargets`
- `allControlEvents` (a bitmask of control events to which a target–action pair is attached)

An action method (the method that will be called on the target when the control event occurs) may adopt any of three signatures, whose parameters are:

- The control and the UIEvent
- The control only
- No parameters

The second signature is by far the most common. It's unlikely that you'd want to dispense altogether with the parameter telling you which control sent the control event. On the other hand, it's equally unlikely that you'd want to examine the original UIEvent that triggered this control event, since control events deliberately shield you from dealing with the nitty-gritty of touches. (I suppose you might, on rare occasions, have some reason to examine the UIEvent's `timestamp`.)

When a control event occurs, the control consults its dispatch table, finds all the target–action pairs associated with that control event, and reports the control event by sending each action message to the corresponding target.

 The action messaging mechanism is actually more complex than I've just stated. The UIControl does not really send the action message directly; rather, it tells the shared application to send it. When a control wants to send an action message reporting a control event, it calls its own `sendAction:to:forEvent:` method. This in turn calls the shared application instance's `sendAction:to:from:forEvent:`, which actually sends the specified action message to the specified target. In theory, you could call or override either of these methods to customize this aspect of the message-sending architecture, but it is extremely unlikely that you would do so.

To make a control emit its action message(s) corresponding to a particular control event right now, in code, call its `sendActionsForControlEvents:` method (which is never called automatically by the runtime). For example, suppose you tell a UISwitch programmatically to change its setting from Off to On. This doesn't cause the switch to report a control event, as it would if the *user* had slid the switch from Off to On; if you wanted it to do so, you could use `sendActionsForControlEvents:`, like this:

```
self.sw.setOn(true, animated: true)
self.sw.sendActionsForControlEvents(.ValueChanged)
```

You might also use `sendActionsForControlEvents:` in a subclass to customize the circumstances under which a control reports control events. I'll give an example later in this chapter.

A control has `enabled`, `selected`, and `highlighted` properties; any of these can be `true` or `false` independently of the others. Together, they correspond to the control's `state`, which is reported as a bitmask of three possible values (UIControlState):

- `.Highlighted`
- `.Disabled`
- `.Selected`

Figure 12-8. A switch

A fourth state, .Normal, corresponds to a zero state bitmask, and means that enabled is true and selected, and highlighted are false.

A control that is not enabled does not respond to user interaction. Whether the control also portrays itself differently, to cue the user to this fact, depends upon the control. For example, a disabled UISwitch is faded; but a rounded rect text field gives the user no cue that it is disabled. The visual nature of control selection and highlighting, too, depends on the control. Neither highlighting nor selection make any difference to the appearance of a UISwitch, but a highlighted UIButton usually looks quite different from a nonhighlighted UIButton.

A control has contentHorizontalAlignment and contentVerticalAlignment properties. These matter only if the control has content that can be aligned. You are most likely to use them in connection with a UIButton to position its title and internal image.

A text field (UITextField) is a control; see Chapter 10. A refresh control (UIRefresh-Control) is a control; see Chapter 8. The remaining controls are covered here, and then I'll give a simple example of writing your own custom control.

UISwitch

A switch (UISwitch, Figure 12-8) portrays a Bool value: it looks like a sliding switch, and its on property is either true or false. The user can slide or tap to toggle the switch's position. When the user changes the switch's position, the switch reports a Value Changed control event. To change the on property's value with accompanying animation, call setOn:animated:.

A switch has only one size (51×31); any attempt to set its size will be ignored.

You can customize a switch's appearance by setting these properties:

onTintColor
    The color of the track when the switch is in the On position.

thumbTintColor
    The color of the slidable button.

tintColor
    The color of the outline when the switch is in the Off position.

Figure 12-9. A stepper

A switch's track when the switch is in the Off position is transparent, and can't be customized. I regard this as a bug. (Changing the switch's backgroundColor is not a successful workaround, because the background color shows outside the switch's outline.)

 The UISwitch properties onImage and offImage, added in iOS 6 after much clamoring (and hacking) by developers, were unfortunately withdrawn in iOS 7, making a UISwitch once again almost impossible to customize to any appreciable degree. I regard this as a bug.

UIStepper

A stepper (UIStepper, Figure 12-9) lets the user increase or decrease a numeric value: it looks like two buttons side by side, one labeled (by default) with a minus sign, the other with a plus sign. The user can tap or hold a button, and can slide a finger from one button to the other as part of the same interaction with the stepper. It has only one size (apparently 94×29). It maintains a numeric value, which is its value. Each time the user increments or decrements the value, it changes by the stepper's stepValue. If the minimumValue or maximumValue is reached, the user can go no further in that direction, and to show this, the corresponding button is disabled — unless the stepper's wraps property is true, in which case the value goes beyond the maximum by starting again at the minimum, and *vice versa*.

As the user changes the stepper's value, a Value Changed control event is reported. Portraying the numeric value itself is up to you; you might, for example, use a label or (as here) a progress view:

```
@IBAction func doStep(sender:AnyObject!) {
    let step = sender as! UIStepper
    self.prog.setProgress(
        Float(step.value / (step.maximumValue - step.minimumValue)),
        animated:true)
}
```

If a stepper's continuous is true (the default), a long touch on one of the buttons will update the value repeatedly; the updates start slowly and get faster. If the stepper's autorepeat is false, the updated value is not reported as a Value Changed control event until the entire interaction with the stepper ends; the default is true.

Figure 12-10. A customized stepper

The appearance of a stepper can be customized. The color of the outline and the button captions is the stepper's `tintColor`, which may be inherited from further up the view hierarchy. You can also dictate the images that constitute the stepper's structure with these methods:

- `setDecrementImageForState:`
- `setIncrementImageForState:`
- `setDividerImage:forLeftSegmentState:rightSegmentState:`
- `setBackgroundImage:forState:`

The images work similarly to a search bar's scope bar (described earlier in this chapter). The background images should probably be resizable. They are stretched behind both buttons, half the image being seen as the background of each button. If the button is disabled (because we've reached the value's limit in that direction), it displays the `.Disabled` background image; otherwise, it displays the `.Normal` background image, except that it displays the `.Highlighted` background image while the user is tapping it. You'll probably want to provide all three background images if you're going to provide any; the default is used if a state's background image is nil. You'll probably want to provide three divider images as well, to cover the three combinations normal-left and normal-right, highlighted-left and normal-right, and normal-left and highlighted-right. The increment and decrement images, replacing the default minus and plus signs, are composited on top of the background image; they are treated as template images, colored by the `tintColor`, unless you explicitly provide an `.AlwaysOriginal` image. If you provide only a `.Normal` image, it will be adjusted automatically for the other two states. Figure 12-9 shows a customized stepper.

UIPageControl

A page control (UIPageControl) is a row of dots; each dot is called a *page*, because it is intended to be used in conjunction with some other interface that portrays something analogous to pages, such as a UIScrollView with its `pagingEnabled` set to `true`. Coordinating the page control with this other interface is usually up to you; see Chapter 7 for an example. A UIPageViewController in scroll style can optionally display a page control that's automatically coordinated with its content (Chapter 6).

The number of dots is the page control's `numberOfPages`. To learn the minimum size required for a given number of pages, call `sizeForNumberOfPages:`. You can make the page control wider than the dots to increase the target region on which the user can tap. The user can tap to one side or the other of the current page's dot to increment or decrement the current page; the page control then reports a Value Changed control event. It is possible to set a page control's `backgroundColor` to show the user the tappable area, but that isn't commonly done: the background is usually transparent.

The dot colors differentiate the current page, the page control's `currentPage`, from the others; by default, the current page is portrayed as a solid dot, while the others are slightly transparent. You can customize a page control's `pageIndicatorTintColor` (the color of the dots in general) and `currentPageIndicatorTintColor` (the color of the current page's dot); you will almost certainly want to do this, as the default dot color is white, which under normal circumstances may be impossible to see.

If a page control's `hidesForSinglePage` is `true`, the page control becomes invisible when its `numberOfPages` changes to 1.

If a page control's `defersCurrentPageDisplay` is `true`, then when the user taps to increment or decrement the page control's value, the display of the current page is not changed. A Value Changed control event is reported, but it is up to your code to handle this action and call `updateCurrentPageDisplay`. A case in point might be if the user's changing the current page triggers an animation, and you don't want the current page dot to change until the animation ends.

UIDatePicker

A date picker (UIDatePicker) looks like a UIPickerView (discussed earlier in this chapter), but it is not a UIPickerView subclass; it uses a UIPickerView to draw itself, but it provides no official access to that picker view. Its purpose is to express the notion of a date and time, taking care of the calendrical and numerical complexities so that you don't have to. When the user changes its setting, the date picker reports a Value Changed control event.

A UIDatePicker has one of four modes (`datePickerMode`), determining how it is drawn (UIDatePickerMode):

.Time
> The date picker displays a time; for example, it has an hour component and a minutes component.

.Date
> The date picker displays a date; for example, it has a month component, a day component, and a year component.

`.DateAndTime`

    The date picker displays a date and time; for example, it has a component showing day of the week, month, and day, plus an hour component and a minutes component.

`.CountDownTimer`

    The date picker displays a number of hours and minutes; for example, it has an hours component and a minutes component.

Exactly what components a date picker displays, and what values they contain, depends by default upon the user's preferences in the Settings app (General → Language & Region → Region). For example, a U.S. time displays an hour numbered 1 through 12 plus minutes and AM or PM, but a British time displays an hour numbered 1 through 24 plus minutes. If the user changes the region format in the Settings app, the date picker's display will change immediately.

A date picker has `calendar` and `timeZone` properties, respectively an NSCalendar and an NSTimeZone; these are nil by default, meaning that the date picker responds to the user's system-level settings. You can also change these values manually; for example, if you live in California and you set a date picker's `timeZone` to GMT, the displayed time is shifted forward by 8 hours, so that 11 AM is displayed as 7 PM (if it is winter).

 Don't change the `timeZone` of a `.CountDownTimer` date picker; if you do, the displayed value will be shifted, and you will confuse the heck out of yourself (and your users).

The minutes component, if there is one, defaults to showing every minute, but you can change this with the `minuteInterval` property. The maximum value is `30`, in which case the minutes component values are 0 and 30. An attempt to set the `minuteInterval` to a value that doesn't divide evenly into 60 will be silently ignored.

The date represented by a date picker (unless its mode is `.CountDownTimer`) is its `date` property, an NSDate. The default date is now, at the time the date picker is instantiated. For a `.Date` date picker, the time by default is 12 AM (midnight), local time; for a `.Time` date picker, the date by default is today. The internal value is reckoned in the local time zone, so it may be different from the displayed value, if you have changed the date picker's `timeZone`.

The maximum and minimum values enabled in the date picker are determined by its `maximumDate` and `minimumDate` properties. Values outside this range may appear disabled. There isn't really any practical limit on the range that a date picker can display, because the "drums" representing its components are not physical, and values are added dynamically as the user spins them. In this example, we set the initial minimum and maximum dates of a date picker (dp) to the beginning and end of 1954. We also set the actual date, so that the date picker will be set initially to a value within the minimum–maximum range:

```
dp.datePickerMode = .Date
let dc = NSDateComponents()
dc.year = 1954
dc.month = 1
dc.day = 1
let c = NSCalendar(calendarIdentifier:NSCalendarIdentifierGregorian)!
let d1 = c.dateFromComponents(dc)!
dp.minimumDate = d1
dp.date = d1
dc.year = 1955
let d2 = c.dateFromComponents(dc)!
dp.maximumDate = d2
```

 Don't set the maximumDate and minimumDate properties values for a .CountDown-Timer date picker; if you do, you might cause a crash with an out-of-range exception.

To convert between an NSDate and a string, you'll need an NSDateFormatter (see Apple's *Date and Time Programming Guide*):

```
func dateChanged(sender:AnyObject) {
    let dp = sender as! UIDatePicker
    let d = dp.date
    let df = NSDateFormatter()
    df.timeStyle = .FullStyle
    df.dateStyle = .FullStyle
    println(df.stringFromDate(d))
    // Tuesday, August 10, 1954 at 3:16:00 AM GMT-07:00
}
```

The value displayed in a .CountDownTimer date picker is its countDownDuration; this is an NSTimeInterval, which is a double representing a number of seconds, even though the minimum interval displayed is a minute. A .CountDownTimer date picker does not actually do any counting down! You are expected to use some other interface to display the countdown. The Timer tab of Apple's Clock app shows a typical interface; the user configures the date picker to set the countDownDuration initially, but once the counting starts, the date picker is hidden and a label displays the remaining time.

Converting the countDownDuration from an NSTimeInterval to hours and minutes is up to you; if your purpose is to display a string, you could use NSDateComponents-Formatter (new in iOS 8):

```
let t = dp.countDownDuration
let f = NSDateComponentsFormatter()
f.allowedUnits = .CalendarUnitHour | .CalendarUnitMinute
f.unitsStyle = .Abbreviated
if let s = f.stringFromTimeInterval(t) {
    println(s) // "1h 12m"
}
```

 A nasty bug makes the Value Changed event from a .CountDownTimer date picker unreliable (especially just after the app launches, and whenever the user has tried to set the timer to zero). The workaround is not to rely on the Value Changed event; for example, provide a button in the interface that the user can tap to make your code read the date picker's countDownDuration.

UISlider

A slider (UISlider) is an expression of a continuously settable value (its value, a Float) between some minimum and maximum (its minimumValue and maximumValue; they are 0 and 1 by default). It is portrayed as an object, the *thumb*, positioned along a *track*. As the user changes the thumb's position, the slider reports a Value Changed control event; it may do this continuously as the user presses and drags the thumb (if the slider's continuous is true, the default) or only when the user releases the thumb (if its continuous is false). While the user is pressing on the thumb, the slider is in the highlighted state.

 According to the documentation, you should be able to change a slider's value with animation by calling setValue:animated:. But this broke in iOS 7 — there is no animation — and has not been fixed in iOS 8.

A commonly expressed desire is to modify a slider's behavior so that if the user taps on its track, the slider moves to the spot where the user tapped. Unfortunately, a slider does not, of itself, respond to taps on its track; such a tap doesn't even cause it to report a Touch Up Inside control event. However, with a gesture recognizer, most things are possible; here's the action handler for a UITapGestureRecognizer attached to a UISlider:

```
func tapped(g:UIGestureRecognizer) {
    let s = g.view as! UISlider
    if s.highlighted {
        return // tap on thumb, let slider deal with it
    }
    let pt = g.locationInView(s)
    let track = s.trackRectForBounds(s.bounds)
    if !CGRectContainsPoint(CGRectInset(track, 0, -10), pt) {
        return // not on track, forget it
    }
```

Figure 12-11. Repositioning a slider's images and track

```
    let percentage = Float(pt.x / s.bounds.size.width)
    let delta = percentage * (s.maximumValue - s.minimumValue)
    let value = s.minimumValue + delta
    s.setValue(value, animated:true) // but animation is broken
}
```

A slider's `tintColor` (which may be inherited from further up the view hierarchy) determines the color of the track to the left of the thumb. You can change the color of the two parts of the track with the `minimumTrackTintColor` and `maximumTrackTintColor` properties.

To go further, you can provide your own thumb image and your own track image, along with images to appear at each end of the track, and you can override in a subclass the methods that position these.

The images at the ends of the track are the slider's `minimumValueImage` and `maximumValueImage`, and they are nil by default. If you set them to actual images (which can also be done in the nib), the slider will attempt to position them within its own bounds, shrinking the drawing of the track to compensate.

You can change that behavior by overriding `minimumValueImageRectForBounds:`, `maximumValueImageRectForBounds:`, and `trackRectForBounds:` in a subclass. The bounds passed in are the slider's bounds. In this example (Figure 12-11), we expand the track width to the full width of the slider, and draw the images outside the slider's bounds. The images are still visible, because the slider does not clip its subviews to its bounds. In the figure, I've given the slider a background color so you can see how the track and images are related to its bounds:

```
override func maximumValueImageRectForBounds(bounds: CGRect) -> CGRect {
    return super.maximumValueImageRectForBounds(bounds)
        .rectByOffsetting(dx: 31, dy: 0)
}
override func minimumValueImageRectForBounds(bounds: CGRect) -> CGRect {
    return super.minimumValueImageRectForBounds(bounds)
        .rectByOffsetting(dx: -31, dy: 0)
}
override func trackRectForBounds(bounds: CGRect) -> CGRect {
    var result = super.trackRectForBounds(bounds)
    result.origin.x = 0
    result.size.width = bounds.size.width
    return result
}
```

Figure 12-12. Replacing a slider's thumb

The thumb is also an image, and you set it with `setThumbImage:forState:`. There are two chiefly relevant states, `.Normal` and `.Highlighted`. If you supply images for both, the thumb will change automatically while the user is dragging it. By default, the image will be centered in the track at the point represented by the slider's current value; you can shift this position by overriding `thumbRectForBounds:trackRect:value:` in a subclass. In this example, the image is repositioned upward slightly (Figure 12-12):

```
override func thumbRectForBounds(
    bounds: CGRect, trackRect rect: CGRect, value: Float) -> CGRect {
        return super.thumbRectForBounds(
            bounds, trackRect: rect, value: value)
                .rectByOffsetting(dx: 0, dy: -7)
}
```

Enlarging or offsetting a slider's thumb can mislead the user as to the area on which it can be touched to drag it. The slider, not the thumb, is the touchable UIControl; only the part of the thumb that intersects the slider's bounds will be draggable. The user may try to drag the part of the thumb that is drawn outside the slider's bounds, and will fail (and be confused). A solution is to increase the slider's height; if you're using autolayout, you can add an explicit height constraint in the nib, or override `intrinsicContent-Size` in code (Chapter 1).

The track is two images, one appearing to the left of the thumb, the other to its right. They are set with `setMinimumTrackImage:forState:` and `setMaximumTrackImage:for-State:`. If you supply images both for `.Normal` state and for `.Highlighted` state, the images will change while the user is dragging the thumb.

The images should be resizable, because that's how the slider cleverly makes it look like the user is dragging the thumb along a single static track. In reality, there are two images; as the user drags the thumb, one image grows horizontally and the other shrinks horizontally. For the left track image, the right end cap inset will be partially or entirely hidden under the thumb; for the right track image, the left end cap inset will be partially or entirely hidden under the thumb. Figure 12-13 shows a track derived from a single 15×15 image of a circular object (a coin):

```
let coinEnd = UIImage(named:"coin.png")!.resizableImageWithCapInsets(
    UIEdgeInsetsMake(0,7,0,7), resizingMode: .Stretch)
self.setMinimumTrackImage(coinEnd, forState: .Normal)
self.setMaximumTrackImage(coinEnd, forState: .Normal)
```

Figure 12-13. Replacing a slider's track

Figure 12-14. A segmented control

 The thumbTintColor property does nothing. It stopped working in iOS 7 and doesn't work in iOS 8 either.

UISegmentedControl

A segmented control (UISegmentedControl, Figure 12-14) is a row of tappable segments; a segment is rather like a button. The user is thus choosing among options. By default (momentary is false), the most recently tapped segment remains selected. Alternatively (momentary is true), the tapped segment is shown as highlighted momentarily (by default, highlighted is indistinguishable from selected, but you can change that); afterward, no segment selection is displayed, though internally the tapped segment remains the selected segment.

The selected segment can be set and retrieved with the selectedSegmentIndex property; when you set it in code, the selected segment remains visibly selected, even for a momentary segmented control. A selectedSegmentIndex value of UISegmented-ControlNoSegment means no segment is selected. When the user taps a segment that isn't already visibly selected, the segmented control reports a Value Changed event.

A segment can be separately enabled or disabled with setEnabled:forSegmentAt-Index:, and its enabled state can be retrieved with isEnabledForSegmentAtIndex:. A disabled segment, by default, is drawn faded; the user can't tap it, but it can still be selected in code.

A segment has either a title or an image; when one is set, the other becomes nil. An image is treated as a template image, colored by the tintColor, unless you explicitly provide an .AlwaysOriginal image. The methods for setting and fetching the title and image for existing segments are:

- setTitle:forSegmentAtIndex:, titleForSegmentAtIndex:

- setImage:forSegmentAtIndex:, imageForSegmentAtIndex:

You will also want to set the title or image when creating the segment. You can do this in code if you're creating the segmented control from scratch, with init(items:), which takes an array each item of which is either a string or an image:

```
let seg = UISegmentedControl(
    items: [
        UIImage(named:"one.png")!.imageWithRenderingMode(.AlwaysOriginal),
        "Two"
    ])
seg.frame.origin = CGPointMake(30,30)
self.view.addSubview(seg)
```

Methods for managing segments dynamically are:

- insertSegmentWithTitle:atIndex:animated:

- insertSegmentWithImage:atIndex:animated:

- removeSegmentAtIndex:animated:

- removeAllSegments

The number of segments can be retrieved with the read-only numberOfSegments property.

A segmented control has a standard height; if you're using autolayout, you can change the height through constraints or by overriding intrinsicContentSize — or by setting its background image, as I'll describe in a moment.

If you're using autolayout, the widths of all segments and the intrinsicContentSize width of the entire segmented control are adjusted automatically whenever you set a segment's title or image. If the segmented control's apportionsSegmentWidthsBy-Content property is false, segment sizes will be made equal to one another; if it is true, each segment will be sized individually to fit its content. Alternatively, you can set a segment's width explicitly with setWidth:forSegmentAtIndex: (and retrieve it with widthForSegmentAtIndex:); setting a width of 0 means that this segment is to be sized automatically.

To change the position of the content (title or image) within a segment, call setContent-Offset:forSegmentAtIndex: (and retrieve it with contentOffsetForSegmentAt-Index:).

The color of a segmented control's outline, title text, and selection are dictated by its tintColor, which may be inherited from further up the view hierarchy.

Figure 12-15. A segmented control, customized

Further methods for customizing a segmented control's appearance are parallel to those for setting the look of a stepper or the scope bar portion of a search bar, both described earlier in this chapter. You can set the overall background, the divider image, the text attributes for the segment titles, and the position of segment contents:

- `setBackgroundImage:forState:barMetrics:`
- `setDividerImage:forLeftSegmentState:rightSegmentState:barMetrics:`
- `setTitleTextAttributes:forState:`
- `setContentPositionAdjustment:forSegmentType:barMetrics:`

You don't have to customize for every state, as the segmented control will use the `.Normal` state setting for the states you don't specify. As I mentioned a moment ago, setting a background image changes the segmented control's height.

Here's the code that achieved Figure 12-15. Selecting a segment automatically darkens the background image for us (similar to a button's `adjustsImageWhenHighlighted`, described in the next section), so there's no need to specify a separate selected image; for `imageOfSize:`, see Appendix B:

```
// background, set desired height but make width resizable
// sufficient to set for Normal only
let sz = CGSizeMake(100,60)
let im = imageOfSize(sz) {
    UIImage(named:"linen.png")!
        .drawInRect(CGRect(origin: CGPoint(), size: sz))
    }.resizableImageWithCapInsets(
        UIEdgeInsetsMake(0,10,0,10), resizingMode: .Stretch)
self.seg.setBackgroundImage(im, forState: .Normal, barMetrics: .Default)
// segment images, redraw at final size
let pep = ["manny", "moe", "jack"].map {$0 + ".jpg"}
for (i, boy) in enumerate(pep) {
    let sz = CGSizeMake(30,30)
    let im = imageOfSize(sz) {
        UIImage(named:boy)!
            .drawInRect(CGRect(origin: CGPoint(), size: sz))
        }.imageWithRenderingMode(.AlwaysOriginal)
    self.seg.setImage(im, forSegmentAtIndex: i)
    self.seg.setWidth(80, forSegmentAtIndex: i)
}
// divider, set at desired width, sufficient to set for Normal only
```

```
let sz2 = CGSizeMake(2,10)
let div = imageOfSize(sz2) {
    UIColor.whiteColor().set()
    CGContextFillRect(UIGraphicsGetCurrentContext(),
        CGRect(origin: CGPoint(), size: sz2))
}
self.seg.setDividerImage(div,
    forLeftSegmentState: .Normal, rightSegmentState: .Normal,
    barMetrics: .Default)
```

The `segmentType:` parameter in `setContentPositionAdjustment:forSegmentType:barMetrics:` is needed because, by default, the segments at the two extremes have rounded ends (and, if a segment is the lone segment, both its ends are rounded). The argument (UISegmentedControlSegment) allows you distinguish between the various possibilities:

- `.Any`
- `.Left`
- `.Center`
- `.Right`
- `.Alone`

The `barMetrics:` parameter will be ignored unless its value is `.Default`.

UIButton

A button (UIButton) is a fundamental tappable control, which may contain a title, an image, and a background image (and may have a `backgroundColor`). A button has a type, and the code creation method is a class method, `buttonWithType:` (which, maddeningly, returns an AnyObject, which means that in Swift you'll have to cast explicitly to UIButton). The types (UIButtonType) are:

`.System`
> The title text appears in the button's `tintColor`, which may be inherited from further up the view hierarchy; when the button is tapped, the title text color momentarily changes to a color derived from what's behind it (which might be the button's `backgroundColor`). The image is treated as a template image, colored by the `tintColor`, unless you explicitly provide an `.AlwaysOriginal` image; when the button is tapped, the image (even if it isn't a template image) is momentarily tinted to a color derived from what's behind it.

`.DetailDisclosure`
`.InfoLight`

`.InfoDark`

`.ContactAdd`

Basically, these are all `.System` buttons whose image is set automatically to standard button images. The first three are an "i" in a circle, and the last is a Plus in a circle; the two `Info` types are identical, and they differ from the `DetailDisclosure` type only in that their `showsTouchWhenHighlighted` is `true` by default.

`.Custom`

Similar to `.System`, except that there's no automatic coloring of the title or image by the `tintColor` or the color of what's behind the button, and the image is a normal image by default.

There is no built-in button type with an outline (border), comparable to the Rounded Rect style of iOS 6 and before. You can add an outline — by adding a background image, for example, or by manipulating the button's layer — but the default look of a button is the text or image alone. In one of my apps, I make a button stand out a bit more entirely through settings made in the nib:

- In the Attributes inspector, I give the button a background color.
- In the Identity inspector, I use the User Defined Runtime Attributes to set the button's `layer.borderWidth` to 2 and its `layer.cornerRadius` to 5.

A button has a title, a title color, and a title shadow color — or you can supply an attributed title, thus dictating these features and more in a single value through an NSAttributedString (Chapter 10).

Distinguish a button's image, which is an internal image, from its background image. The background image, if any, is stretched, if necessary, to fill the button's bounds (technically, its `backgroundRectForBounds:`). The internal image, on the other hand, if smaller than the button, is not resized. The button can have both a title and an image, if the image is small enough; in that case, the image is shown to the left of the title by default.

These six features (title, title color, title shadow color, attributed title, image, and background image) can all be made to vary depending on the button's current state: `.Highlighted`, `.Selected`, `.Disabled`, and `.Normal`. The button can be in more than one state at once, except for `.Normal` which means "none of the other states." A state change, whether automatic (the button is highlighted while the user is tapping it) or programmatically imposed, will thus in and of itself alter a button's appearance. The methods for setting these button features, therefore, all involve specifying a corresponding state — or multiple states, using a bitmask:

- `setTitle:forState:`
- `setTitleColor:forState:`

- `setTitleShadowColor:forState:`
- `setAttributedTitle:forState:`
- `setImage:forState:`
- `setBackgroundImage:forState:`

Similarly, when getting these button features, you must either specify a single state you're interested in or ask about the feature as currently displayed:

- `titleForState:`, `currentTitle`
- `titleColorForState:`, `currentTitleColor`
- `titleShadowColorForState:`, `currentTitleShadowColor`
- `attributedTitleForState:`, `currentAttributedTitle`
- `imageForState:`, `currentImage`
- `backgroundImageForState:`, `currentBackgroundImage`

If you don't specify a feature for a particular state, or if the button adopts more than one state at once, an internal heuristic is used to determine what to display. I can't describe all possible combinations, but here are some general observations:

- If you specify a feature for a particular state (highlighted, selected, or disabled), and the button is in *only* that state, that feature will be used.
- If you *don't* specify a feature for a particular state (highlighted, selected, or disabled), and the button is in *only* that state, the normal version of that feature will be used as fallback. (That's why many examples earlier in this book have assigned a title for `.Normal` only; this is sufficient to give the button a title in every state.)
- Combinations of states often cause the button to fall back on the feature for normal state. For example, if a button is both highlighted and selected, the button will display its normal title, even if it has a highlighted title, a selected title, or both.

A `.System` button with an attributed normal title will tint the title to the `tintColor` if you don't give the attributed string a color, and will tint the title while highlighted to the color derived from what's behind the button if you haven't supplied a highlighted title with its own color. But a `.Custom` button will not do any of that; it leaves control of the title color for each state completely up to you.

In addition, a UIButton has some properties determining how it draws itself in various states, which can save you the trouble of specifying different images for different states:

`showsTouchWhenHighlighted`
> If `true`, then the button projects a circular white glow when highlighted. If the button has an internal image, the glow is centered behind it. Thus, this feature is

suitable particularly if the button image is small and circular; for example, it's the default behavior for a `.InfoLight` or `.InfoDark` button. If the button has no internal image, the glow is centered at the button's center. The glow is drawn on top of the background image or color, if any.

`adjustsImageWhenHighlighted`

In a `.Custom` button, if this property is `true` (the default), then if there is no separate highlighted image (and if `showsTouchWhenHighlighted` is `false`), the normal image is darkened when the button is highlighted. This applies equally to the internal image and the background image. (A `.System` button is already tinting its highlighted image, so this property doesn't apply.)

`adjustsImageWhenDisabled`

If `true`, then if there is no separate disabled image, the normal image is shaded when the button is disabled. This applies equally to the internal image and the background image. The default is `true` for a `.Custom` button and `false` for a `.System` button.

A button has a natural size in relation to its contents. If you're using autolayout, the button can adopt that size automatically as its `intrinsicContentSize`, and you can modify the way it does this by overriding `intrinsicContentSize` in a subclass or by applying explicit constraints. If you're not using autolayout and you create a button in code, send it `sizeToFit` or give it an explicit size — otherwise, the button will have a zero size and you'll be left wondering why your button hasn't appeared in the interface.

The title is a UILabel (Chapter 10), and the label features of the title can be accessed through the button's `titleLabel`. Its properties may be set, provided they do not conflict with existing UIButton features. For example, you can set the title's `font` and `shadowOffset` by way of the label, but the title's text, color, and shadow color should be set using the appropriate button methods. If the title is given a shadow in this way, then the button's `reversesTitleShadowWhenHighlighted` property also applies: if `true`, the `shadowOffset` values are replaced with their additive inverses when the button is highlighted. Similarly, you can manipulate the label's wrapping behavior to make the button's title consist of multiple lines. The modern way, however, is to manipulate all these features using attributed strings.

The internal image is drawn by a UIImageView (Chapter 2), whose features can be accessed through the button's `imageView`. Thus, for example, you can change the internal image view's `alpha` to make the image more transparent.

The internal position of the image and title as a whole are governed by the button's `contentVerticalAlignment` and `contentHorizontalAlignment` (inherited from UIControl). You can also tweak the position of the image and title, together or separately, by setting the button's `contentEdgeInsets`, `titleEdgeInsets`, or `imageEdgeInsets`.

Increasing an inset component increases that margin; thus, for example, a positive top component makes the distance between that object and the top of the button larger than normal (where "normal" is where the object would be according to the alignment settings). The titleEdgeInsets or imageEdgeInsets values are added to the overall contentEdgeInsets values. So, for example, if you really wanted to, you could make the internal image appear to the right of the title by decreasing the left titleEdgeInsets and increasing the left imageEdgeInsets.

Four methods also provide access to the button's positioning of its elements:

- titleRectForContentRect:
- imageRectForContentRect:
- contentRectForBounds:
- backgroundRectForBounds:

These methods are called whenever the button is redrawn, including every time it changes state. The content rect is the area in which the title and image are placed. By default, contentRectForBounds: and backgroundRectForBounds: yield the same result. You can override these methods in a subclass to change the way the button's elements are positioned.

Here's an example of a customized button. In a UIButton subclass, we increase the button's intrinsicContentSize to give it larger margins around its content, and we override backgroundRectForBounds to shrink the button slightly when highlighted as a way of providing feedback; for sizeByDelta, see Appendix B:

```
override func backgroundRectForBounds(bounds: CGRect) -> CGRect {
    var result = super.backgroundRectForBounds(bounds)
    if self.highlighted {
        result.inset(dx: 3, dy: 3)
    }
    return result
}
override func intrinsicContentSize() -> CGSize {
    return super.intrinsicContentSize().sizeByDelta(dw:25, dh: 20)
}
```

The button, which is a .Custom button, is assigned an internal image and a background image from the same resizable image, along with attributed titles for the .Normal and .Highlighted states. The internal image glows when highlighted, thanks to adjustsImageWhenHighlighted (Figure 12-16).

Figure 12-16. A custom button

Custom Controls

If you create your own UIControl subclass, you automatically get the built-in "Touch" events; in addition, there are several methods that you can override in order to customize touch tracking, along with properties that tell you whether touch tracking is going on:

- `beginTrackingWithTouch:withEvent:`
- `continueTrackingWithTouch:withEvent:`
- `endTrackingWithTouch:withEvent:`
- `cancelTrackingWithEvent:`
- `tracking` (property)
- `touchInside` (property)

With the advent of gesture recognizers (Chapter 5), such direct involvement with touch tracking is probably less needed than it used to be, especially if your purpose is to modify the behavior of a built-in UIControl subclass. So, to illustrate their use, I'll give a simple example of creating a custom control. The main reason for doing this (rather than using, say, a UIView and gesture recognizers) would probably be to obtain the convenience of control events. Also, the touch-tracking methods, though not as high-level as gesture recognizers, are at least a level up from the UIResponder `touches...` methods (Chapter 5): they track a single touch, and both `beginTracking...` and `continueTracking...` return a Bool, giving you a chance to stop tracking the current touch.

We'll build a simplified knob control (Figure 12-17). The control starts life at its minimum position, with an internal angle value of 0; it can be rotated clockwise with a single finger as far as its maximum position, with an internal angle value of 5 (radians). To keep things simple, the words "Min" and "Max" appearing in the interface are actually labels; the control just draws the knob, and to rotate it we'll apply a rotation transform.

Our control is a UIControl subclass, MyKnob. It has a public CGFloat `angle` property, and a private CGFloat property `self.initialAngle` that we'll use internally during rotation. Because a UIControl is a UIView, it can draw itself, which it does with an image file included in our app bundle:

Figure 12-17. A custom control

```
override func drawRect(rect: CGRect) {
    UIImage(named:"knob.png")!.drawInRect(rect)
}
```

We'll need a utility function for transforming a touch's Cartesian coordinates into polar coordinates, giving us the angle to be applied as a rotation to the view:

```
func pToA (touch:UITouch) -> CGFloat {
    let loc = touch.locationInView(self)
    let c = CGPointMake(self.bounds.midX, self.bounds.midY)
    return atan2(loc.y - c.y, loc.x - c.x)
}
```

Now we're ready to override the tracking methods. `beginTrackingWithTouch:with-Event:` simply notes down the angle of the initial touch location. `continueTracking-WithTouch:withEvent:` uses the difference between the current touch location's angle and the initial touch location's angle to apply a transform to the view, and updates the `angle` property. `endTrackingWithTouch:withEvent:` triggers the Value Changed control event. So our first draft looks like this:

```
override func beginTrackingWithTouch(
    touch: UITouch, withEvent event: UIEvent) -> Bool {
        self.initialAngle = pToA(touch)
        return true
}
override func continueTrackingWithTouch(
    touch: UITouch, withEvent event: UIEvent) -> Bool {
        let ang = pToA(touch) - self.initialAngle
        let absoluteAngle = self.angle + ang
        self.transform = CGAffineTransformRotate(self.transform, ang)
        self.angle = absoluteAngle
        return true
}
override func endTrackingWithTouch(
    touch: UITouch, withEvent event: UIEvent) {
        self.sendActionsForControlEvents(.ValueChanged)
}
```

This works: we can put a MyKnob into the interface and hook up its Value Changed control event (this can be done in the nib editor), and sure enough, when we run the app, we can rotate the knob and, when our finger lifts from the knob, the Value Changed action handler is called.

However, our class needs modification. When the `angle` is set programmatically, we should respond by rotating the knob; at the same time, we need to peg the incoming value at the allowable minimum or maximum:

```
var angle : CGFloat = 0 {
    didSet {
        if self.angle < 0 {
            self.angle = 0
        }
        if self.angle > 5 {
            self.angle = 5
        }
        self.transform = CGAffineTransformMakeRotation(self.angle)
    }
}
```

Now we should revise `continueTrackingWithTouch:withEvent:`. We no longer need to perform the rotation, since setting the `angle` will do that for us. On the other hand, we do need to peg the gesture when the minimum or maximum rotation is exceeded. My solution is simply to stop tracking; in that case, `endTracking...` will never be called, so we also need to trigger the Value Changed control event. Also, it might be nice to give the programmer the option to have the Value Changed control event reported continuously as `continueTracking...` is called repeatedly; so we'll add a public continuous Bool property and obey it. Here, then, is our revised `continueTracking...` implementation:

```
override func continueTrackingWithTouch(
    touch: UITouch, withEvent event: UIEvent) -> Bool {
        let ang = pToA(touch) - self.initialAngle
        let absoluteAngle = self.angle + ang
        switch absoluteAngle {
        case let ang where ang < 0:
            self.angle = 0
            self.sendActionsForControlEvents(.ValueChanged)
            return false
        case let ang where ang > 5:
            self.angle = 5
            self.sendActionsForControlEvents(.ValueChanged)
            return false
        default:
            self.angle = absoluteAngle
            if self.continuous {
                self.sendActionsForControlEvents(.ValueChanged)
```

```
            }
            return true
        }
    }
```

Bars

There are three bar types: navigation bar (UINavigationBar), toolbar (UIToolbar), and tab bar (UITabBar). They are often used in conjunction with a built-in view controller (Chapter 6):

- A UINavigationController has a UINavigationBar.
- A UINavigationController has a UIToolbar.
- A UITabBarController has a UITabBar.

You can also use these bar types independently. You are most likely to do that with a UIToolbar, which is often used as an independent bottom bar. On the iPad, it can also be used as a top bar, adopting a role analogous to a menu bar on the desktop.

This section summarizes the facts about the three bar types (along with UISearchBar, which can act as a top bar), and about the items that populate them.

Bar Position and Bar Metrics

If a bar is to occupy the top of the screen, its height should be increased to underlap the transparent status bar. To make this possible, iOS provides the notion of a *bar position*. The UIBarPositioning protocol, adopted by UINavigationBar, UIToolbar, and UISearchbar — the bars that can go at the top of the screen — defines one property, barPosition, whose possible values (UIBarPosition) are:

- .Any
- .Bottom
- .Top
- .TopAttached

But barPosition is read-only, so how are you supposed to set it? Use the bar's delegate! The delegate protocols UINavigationBarDelegate, UIToolbarDelegate, and UISearchBarDelegate all conform to UIBarPositioningDelegate. The UIBarPositioningDelegate protocol defines one method, positionForBar:. This provides a way for a bar's delegate to dictate the bar's barPosition.

The rule is that the bar's height will be extended upward, so that its top can go behind the status bar, if the bar's delegate returns `.TopAttached` from its implementation of `positionForBar:`. To get the final position right, the bar's top should also have a zero-length constraint to the view controller's top layout guide. (If you're not using autolayout, then the bar's top should have a y value of 20.)

A bar's height is reflected also by its *bar metrics*. This refers to a change in the standard height of the bar in reponse to a change in the orientation of the app. This change is performed automatically by a UINavigationController on its own navigation bar or toolbar. The standard heights are 44 (portrait) and 32 (landscape) — plus 20 if the bar also underlaps the status bar, but this is *not* reported as part of the bounds height. Possible bar metrics values are (UIBarMetrics):

- `.Default`
- `.Compact`
- `.DefaultPrompt`
- `.CompactPrompt`

The "Compact" metrics apply in a vertically compact environment, such as an iPhone app in landscape orientation. The "Prompt" metrics apply to a bar whose height is extended downward to accommodate prompt text (and to a search bar whose scope buttons are showing).

 The older names for the "Compact" values, containing the word "Landscape," are deprecated in iOS 8, which emphasizes size classes over orientation.

When you're customizing a feature of a bar, you may find yourself calling a method that takes a bar metrics parameter, and possibly a bar position parameter as well. The idea is that you can customize that feature differently depending on the bar metrics and the bar position. You don't have to set that value for *every* possible combination of bar position and bar metrics! In general (though, unfortunately, the details are a little inconsistent from class to class), `UIBarPosition.Any` and `UIBarMetrics.Default` are treated as defaults that encompass any positions and metrics you don't specify.

The interface object classes and their features that participate in this system are:

UISearchBar
   A search bar can function as a top bar and can have a prompt. You can set its background image.

UINavigationBar

> A navigation bar can function as a top bar, it can have a prompt, and its height in a navigation interface is changed automatically on the iPhone depending on the app's orientation. You can set its background image. In addition, the vertical offset of its title can depend on the bar metrics.

UIToolbar

> A toolbar can function as a top bar or a bottom bar, and its height in a navigation interface is changed automatically on the iPhone depending on the app's orientation. You can set its background image. In addition, its shadow can depend on its bar position.

UIBarButtonItem

> You can set a bar button item's image, image inset, background image, title offset, and background offset, so as to depend upon the bar metrics of the containing bar, either a UINavigationBar or a UIToolbar (and the bar position is irrelevant).

Bar Appearance

The overall look of the three bar types is identical by default. A bar can be styled at three levels:

`barStyle, translucent`

> The `barStyle` options are (UIBarStyle):
>
> - `.Default`
> - `.Black`
>
> The bar styles are flat white and flat black respectively. The `translucent` property turns on or off the characteristic blurry translucency.

`barTintColor`

> This property tints the bar with a solid color. If you set the `barTintColor` and you want translucency, then supplying a color with a low `alpha` component is up to you. However, if you set the bar's `translucent` to `false`, then the `barTintColor` is treated as opaque.

`backgroundImage`

> This, as I've just explained, can vary depending on the bar position and bar metrics (`setBackgroundImage:forBarPosition:barMetrics:`). The transparency of the image is obeyed, but if you set the bar's `translucent` to `false`, then the `barTint-Color` will appear opaque behind the image. If the image is too large, it is sized down to fit; if it is too small, it is tiled by default, but you can change that behavior by supplying a resizable image.

If you assign a bar a background image, you can also customize its shadow, which is cast from the bottom of the bar (if the bar is at the top) or the top of the bar (if the bar is at the bottom) on whatever is behind it. The setter is usually the shadowImage property, but a toolbar can be either at the top or the bottom, so its setter is setShadowImage:for-ToolbarPosition:, and the barPosition is used to decide whether the shadow should appear at the top or the bottom of the toolbar.

You'll want a shadow image to be very small and very transparent; the image will be tiled horizontally. Here's an example for a navigation bar:

```
let sz = CGSizeMake(4,4)
self.navbar.shadowImage = imageOfSize(sz) {
    UIColor.grayColor().colorWithAlphaComponent(0.3).setFill()
    CGContextFillRect(UIGraphicsGetCurrentContext(), CGRectMake(0,0,4,2))
    UIColor.grayColor().colorWithAlphaComponent(0.15).setFill()
    CGContextFillRect(UIGraphicsGetCurrentContext(), CGRectMake(0,2,4,2))
}
```

 In a UINavigationController, there is a reason why you might set the navigation bar's barStyle even if you are configuring the bar's appearance in some other way — namely, because the navigation controller will pass this setting along in its implementation of preferredStatusBarStyle. In other words, you set the navigation controller's navigation bar's bar style as a way of setting the *status bar's* bar style.

UIBarButtonItem

The only things that can appear inside a navigation bar or a toolbar — aside from a navigation bar's title and prompt — are bar button items (UIBarButtonItem, a subclass of UIBarItem). This is not much of a limitation, however, because a bar button item can contain a custom view, which can be any type of UIView at all. A bar button item itself, however, is not a UIView subclass.

A bar button item may be instantiated with any of five methods:

- init(barButtonSystemItem:target:action:)
- init(title:style:target:action:)
- init(image:style:target:action:)
- init(image:landscapeImagePhone:style:target:action:)
- init(customView:)

A bar button item's image is treated by default as a template image, unless you explicitly provide an .AlwaysOriginal image.

The style: options are (UIBarButtonItemStyle):

- `.Plain`

- `.Done` (the title text is bold)

As I mentioned a moment ago, many aspects of a bar button item can be made dependent upon the bar metrics of the containing bar. Thus, you can initialize a bar button item with both an `image` and a `landscapeImagePhone`, the latter to be used when the bar metrics has "Compact" in its name. (Ironically, iOS 8 has caused a naming mismatch by deprecating the "Landscape" terminology in the bar metrics names.) A bar button item inherits from UIBarItem the ability to adjust the image position with `image-Insets` (and `landscapeImagePhoneInsets`), plus the `enabled` and `tag` properties. Recall from Chapter 6 that you can also set a bar button item's `possibleTitles` and `width` properties, to determine its width.

A bar button item's `tintColor` property tints the title text or template image of the button; it is inherited from the `tintColor` of the bar, or you can override it for an individual bar button item.

You can apply an attributes dictionary to a bar button item's title, and you can give it a background image:

- `setTitleTextAttributes:forState:` (inherited from UIBarItem)

- `setTitlePositionAdjustment:forBarMetrics:`

- `setBackgroundImage:forState:barMetrics:`

- `setBackgroundImage:forState:style:barMetrics:`

- `setBackgroundVerticalPositionAdjustment:forBarMetrics:`

In addition, these methods apply only if the bar button item is being used as a back button item in a navigation bar (as I'll describe in the next section):

- `setBackButtonTitlePositionAdjustment:forBarMetrics:`

- `setBackButtonBackgroundImage:forState:barMetrics:`

- `setBackButtonBackgroundVerticalPositionAdjustment:forBarMetrics:`

 In a bar button item with a custom view, the background vertical position adjustment doesn't apply (because the custom view is the button's content, not its background). To shift the apparent position of a custom view, construct the custom view as a subview within a superview, and shift the position of the subview. This technique can cause the subview to appear outside the containing bar, so be careful.

Figure 12-18. A bar button item with a border

No bar button item style supplies an outline (border); the default look of a button is just the text or image. (The pre–iOS 7 bar button item style `.Bordered` is now deprecated, and its appearance is identical to `.Plain`.) If you want an outline, you have to supply it yourself by way of the background image. Here's how I create the background image for the left bar button item in the settings view of my Zotz! app (Figure 12-18):

```
b.setBackgroundImage(imageOfSize(CGSizeMake(15,15)) {
    let grad = CAGradientLayer()
    grad.frame = CGRectMake(0,0,15,15)
    grad.colors = [
        UIColor(red: 1, green: 1, blue: 0, alpha: 0.8).CGColor,
        UIColor(red: 0.7, green: 0.7, blue: 0.3, alpha: 0.8).CGColor]
    let p = UIBezierPath(
        roundedRect: CGRectMake(0,0,15,15), cornerRadius: 8)
    p.addClip()
    grad.renderInContext(UIGraphicsGetCurrentContext())
    UIColor.blackColor().setStroke()
    p.lineWidth = 2
    p.stroke()
}.resizableImageWithCapInsets(
    UIEdgeInsetsMake(7,7,7,7), resizingMode: .Stretch),
    forState: .Normal)
```

UINavigationBar

A navigation bar (UINavigationBar) is populated by navigation items (UINavigation-Item). The UINavigationBar maintains a stack; UINavigationItems are pushed onto and popped off of this stack. Whatever UINavigationItem is currently topmost in the stack (the UINavigationBar's `topItem`), in combination with the UINavigationItem just beneath it in the stack (the UINavigationBar's `backItem`), determines what appears in the navigation bar:

`title`, `titleView`

> The `title` (string) or `titleView` (UIView) of the `topItem` appears in the center of the navigation bar.

`prompt`

> The `prompt` (string) of the `topItem` appears at the top of the navigation bar, whose height increases to accommodate it.

Figure 12-19. A back button animating to the left

rightBarButtonItem, leftBarButtonItem

> The rightBarButtonItem and leftBarButtonItem appear at the right and left ends of the navigation bar. A UINavigationItem can have multiple right bar button items and multiple left bar button items; its rightBarButtonItems and leftBarButton-Items properties are arrays (of bar button items). The bar button items are displayed from the outside in: that is, the first item in the leftBarButtonItems is leftmost, while the first item in the rightBarButtonItems is rightmost. If there are multiple buttons on a side, the rightBarButtonItem is the first item of the rightBarButton-Items array, and the leftBarButtonItem is the first item of the leftBarButton-Items array.

backBarButtonItem

> The backBarButtonItem *of the backItem* appears at the left end of the navigation bar. It is automatically configured so that, when tapped, the topItem is popped off the stack. If the backItem has *no* backBarButtonItem, then there is *still* a back button at the left end of the navigation bar, taking its title from the title of the backItem. However, if the topItem has its hidesBackButton set to true, the back button is suppressed. Also, unless the topItem has its leftItemsSupplementBack-Button set to true, the back button is suppressed if the topItem has a leftBar-ButtonItem.

The indication that the back button *is* a back button is supplied by the navigation bar's backIndicatorImage, which by default is a left-pointing chevron appearing to the left of the back button. You can customize this image; the image that you supply is treated as a template image by default. If you set the backIndicatorImage, you must also supply a backIndicatorTransitionMaskImage. The purpose of the mask image is to indicate the region where the back button should disappear as it slides out to the left when a new navigation item is pushed onto the stack. For example, in Figure 12-19, the back button title, which is sliding out to the left, is visible to the right of the chevron but not to the left of the chevron; that's because on the left side of the chevron it is masked out.

In this example, I replace the chevron with a vertical bar. The vertical bar is not the entire image; the image is actually a wider rectangle, with the vertical bar at its right side. The mask is the entire wider rectangle, and is completely transparent; thus, the back button disappears as it passes behind the bar and stays invisible as it continues on to the left:

```
self.navbar.backIndicatorImage =
    imageOfSize(CGSizeMake(10,20)) {
        CGContextFillRect(
            UIGraphicsGetCurrentContext(), CGRectMake(6,0,4,20))
self.navbar.backIndicatorTransitionMaskImage =
    imageOfSize(CGSizeMake(10,20)) {}
```

Changes to the navigation bar's buttons can be animated by sending its `topItem` any of these messages:

- `setRightBarButtonItem:animated:`

- `setLeftBarButtonItem:animated:`

- `setRightBarButtonItems:animated:`

- `setLeftBarButtonItems:animated:`

- `setHidesBackButton:animated:`

UINavigationItems are pushed and popped with `pushNavigationItem:animated:` and `popNavigationItemAnimated:`, or you can set all items on the stack at once with `setItems:animated:`.

You can set the title's attributes dictionary (`titleTextAttributes`), and you can shift the title's vertical position by calling `setTitleVerticalPositionAdjustment:forBarMetrics:`.

When you use a UINavigationBar implicitly as part of a UINavigationController interface, the navigation controller is the navigation bar's delegate. If you were to use a UINavigationBar on its own, you might want to supply your own delegate. The delegate methods are:

- `navigationBar:shouldPushItem:`

- `navigationBar:didPushItem:`

- `navigationBar:shouldPopItem:`

- `navigationBar:didPopItem:`

This simple (and silly) example of a standalone UINavigationBar implements the legendary baseball combination trio of Tinker to Evers to Chance; see the relevant Wikipedia article if you don't know about them (Figure 12-20, which also shows the custom back indicator and shadow I described earlier):

```
override func viewDidLoad() {
    super.viewDidLoad()
    let ni = UINavigationItem(title: "Tinker")
    let b = UIBarButtonItem(
        title: "Evers", style: .Plain, target: self, action: "pushNext:")
```

Figure 12-20. A navigation bar

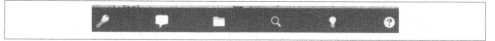

Figure 12-21. A toolbar

```
    ni.rightBarButtonItem = b
    self.navbar.items = [ni]
}
func pushNext(sender:AnyObject) {
    let oldb = sender as! UIBarButtonItem
    let s = oldb.title
    let ni = UINavigationItem(title:s)
    if s == "Evers" {
        let b = UIBarButtonItem(title:"Chance",
            style: .Plain, target:self, action:"pushNext:")
        ni.rightBarButtonItem = b
    }
    self.navbar.pushNavigationItem(ni, animated:true)
}
```

UIToolbar

A toolbar (UIToolbar, Figure 12-21) is intended to appear at the bottom of the screen; on the iPad, it may appear at the top. It displays a row of UIBarButtonItems, which are its `items`. The items are displayed from left to right in the order in which they appear in the `items` array. You can set the items with animation by calling `set-Items:animated:`. The items within the toolbar are positioned automatically; you can intervene in this positioning by using the system bar button items `.FlexibleSpace` and `.FixedSpace`, along with the UIBarButtonItem `width` property.

UITabBar

A tab bar (UITabBar) displays tab bar items (UITabBarItem), its `items`, each consisting of an image and a name. To change the items in an animated fashion, call `set-Items:animated:`.

The tab bar maintains a current selection among its items, its `selectedItem`, which is a UITabBarItem, not an index number; you can set it in code, or the user can set it by tapping on a tab bar item. To hear about the user changing the selection, implement `tabBar:didSelectItem:` in the delegate (UITabBarDelegate).

You get some control over how the tab bar items are laid out:

`itemPositioning`
> There are three possible values (UITabBarItemPositioning):
>
> `.Centered`
>> The items are crowded together at the center.
>
> `.Fill`
>> The items are spaced out evenly.
>
> `.Automatic`
>> On the iPad, the same as `.Centered`; on the iPhone, the same as `.Fill`.

`itemSpacing`
> The space between items, if the positioning is `.Centered`. For the default space, specify 0.

`itemWidth`
> The width of items, if the positioning is `.Centered`. For the default width, specify 0.

You can set the image drawn behind the selected tab bar item to indicate that it's selected, the `selectionIndicatorImage`.

A UITabBarItem is created with one of these two methods:

- `init(tabBarSystemItem:tag:)`
- `init(title:image:tag:)`

UITabBarItem is a subclass of UIBarItem, so in addition to its `title` and `image` it inherits the ability to adjust the image position with `imageInsets`, plus the `enabled` and `tag` properties.

A bar item title text and template image are tinted, by default, with the tab bar's `tintColor` *when selected*; there's no way to set the deselected tint color (this was possible before iOS 7, so I regard the change as a bug).

A tab bar item's image is treated as a template image, but you can override that by supplying an `.AlwaysOriginal` image. Similarly, you can customize a tab bar item's title (including its color) with an attributes dictionary (`setTitleTextAttributes:forState:`, inherited from UIBarItem), and you can adjust the title's position with the `titlePositionAdjustment` property.

Figure 12-22. A tab bar

Figure 12-22 is an example of a customized tab bar; I've set the selection indicator image (the checkmark), the tint color, and the text attributes (including the color, when selected) of the tab bar items.

The user can be permitted to alter the contents of the tab bar, setting its tab bar items from among a larger repertory of tab bar items. To summon the interface that lets the user do this, call beginCustomizingItems:, passing an array of UITabBarItems that may or may not appear in the tab bar. (To prevent the user from removing an item from the tab bar, include it in the tab bar's items and *don't* include it in the argument passed to beginCustomizingItems:.) A presented view with a Done button appears, behind the tab bar but in front of everything else, displaying the customizable items. The user can then drag an item into the tab bar, replacing an item that's already there. To hear about the customizing view appearing and disappearing, implement delegate methods:

- tabBar:willBeginCustomizingItems:

- tabBar:didBeginCustomizingItems:

- tabBar:willEndCustomizingItems:changed:

- tabBar:didEndCustomizingItems:changed:

A UITabBar on its own (outside a UITabBarController) does not provide any automatic access to the user customization interface; it's up to you. In this (silly) example, we populate a UITabBar with four system tab bar items and a More item; we also populate an instance variable array with those same four system tab bar items, plus three more. When the user taps the More item, we show the user customization interface with all seven tab bar items:

```
var items : [UITabBarItem] = {
    Array(1..<8).map {
        UITabBarItem(
            tabBarSystemItem:UITabBarSystemItem(rawValue:$0)!, tag:$0)
    }
}()
override func viewDidLoad() {
    super.viewDidLoad()
    self.tabbar.items = Array(self.items[0..<4]) +
        [UITabBarItem(tabBarSystemItem: .More, tag: 0)]
    self.tabbar.selectedItem = self.tabbar.items![0] as? UITabBarItem
}
func tabBar(tabBar: UITabBar, didSelectItem item: UITabBarItem!) {
```

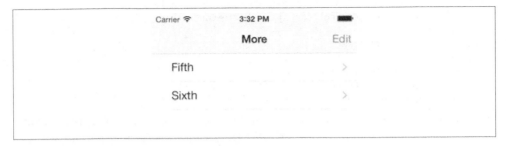

Figure 12-23. Automatically generated More list

```
if item.tag == 0 {
    // More button
    tabBar.selectedItem = nil
    tabBar.beginCustomizingItems(self.items)
}
}
func tabBar(tabBar: UITabBar, didEndCustomizingItems items: [AnyObject],
    changed: Bool) {
        self.tabbar.selectedItem = self.tabbar.items![0] as? UITabBarItem
}
```

When used in conjunction with a UITabBarController, the customization interface is provided automatically, in an elaborate way. If there are a lot of items, a More item is automatically present, and can be used to access the remaining items in a table view. Here, the user can select any of the excess items, navigating to the corresponding view. Or, the user can switch to the customization interface by tapping the Edit button. (See the iPhone Music app for a familiar example.) Figure 12-23 shows how a More list looks by default.

The way this works is that the automatically provided More item corresponds to a UINavigationController with a root view controller (UIViewController) whose view is a UITableView. Thus, a navigation interface containing this UITableView appears through the tabbed interface when the user taps the More button. When the user selects an item in the table, the corresponding UIViewController is pushed onto the UINavigationController's stack.

You can access this UINavigationController: it is the UITabBarController's more-NavigationController. Through it, you can access the root view controller: it is the first item in the UINavigationController's viewControllers array. And through that, you can access the table view: it is the root view controller's view. This means you can customize what appears when the user taps the More button! For example, let's make the navigation bar red with white button titles, and let's remove the word More from its title:

```
let more = self.tabBarController.moreNavigationController
let list = more.viewControllers[0] as! UIViewController
list.title = ""
let b = UIBarButtonItem()
b.title = "Back"
list.navigationItem.backBarButtonItem = b
more.navigationBar.barTintColor = UIColor.redColor()
more.navigationBar.tintColor = UIColor.whiteColor()
```

We can go even further by supplementing the table view's data source with a data source of our own, thus proceeding to customize the table itself. This is tricky because we have no internal access to the actual data source, and we mustn't accidentally disable it from populating the table. Still, it can be done. I'll start by replacing the table view's data source with an instance of my own MyDataSource, initializing it with a reference to the *original* data source object:

```
let tv = list.view as! UITableView
let mds = MyDataSource(originalDataSource: tv.dataSource!)
self.myDataSource = mds
tv.dataSource = mds
```

In MyDataSource, I'll use message forwarding (see Apple's *Objective-C Runtime Programming Guide*) so that MyDataSource acts as a front end for originalDataSource. MyDataSource will magically appear to respond to any message that originalData-Source responds to, and any message that arrives that MyDataSource can't handle will be magically forwarded to originalDataSource. This way, the insertion of the My-DataSource instance as data source doesn't break whatever the original data source does:

```
override func forwardingTargetForSelector(aSelector: Selector)
    -> AnyObject? {
        if self.originalDataSource.respondsToSelector(aSelector) {
            return self.originalDataSource
        }
        return super.forwardingTargetForSelector(aSelector)
}
```

Finally, we'll implement the two Big Questions required by the UITableViewDataSource protocol, to quiet the compiler. In both cases, we first pass the message along to original-DataSource (somewhat analogous to calling super); then we add our own customizations as desired. Here, just as a proof of concept, I'll change each cell's text font (Figure 12-24):

```
func tableView(tv: UITableView, numberOfRowsInSection sec: Int) -> Int {
    return self.originalDataSource.tableView(
        tv, numberOfRowsInSection: sec)
}
func tableView(tv: UITableView, cellForRowAtIndexPath ip: NSIndexPath)
    -> UITableViewCell {
        let cell = self.originalDataSource.tableView(
```

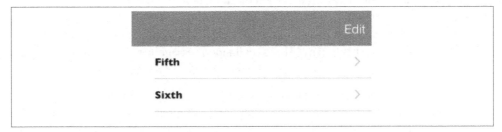

Figure 12-24. Customized More list

```
        tv, cellForRowAtIndexPath: ip)
    cell.textLabel!.font = UIFont(name: "GillSans-Bold", size: 14)!
    return cell
}
```

Tint Color

The UIView and UIBarButtonItem tintColor property has a remarkable built-in feature: its value, if not set explicitly (or if set to nil), is inherited from its superview. The idea is to simplify the task of giving your app a consistent overall appearance.

This works exactly the way you would expect. You can set the tintColor of your UI-Window instance, and its value will be inherited by every view that ever appears. Any built-in interface object whose details are colored by the tintColor will display this same color. For example, if you set your window's tintColor to red, then every .System button that appears anywhere in your interface will have red title text by default.

Moreover, the inherited tintColor can be overridden by setting a view's tintColor explicitly. In other words, you can set the tintColor of a view partway down the view hierarchy so that it and all its subviews have a *different* tintColor from the rest of the interface. In this way, you might subtly suggest that the user has entered a different world.

If you change the tintColor of a view, the change immediately propagates down the hierarchy of its subviews — except, of course, that a view whose tintColor has been explicitly set to a color of its own is unaffected, along with its subviews.

When you ask a view for its tintColor, what you get is the tintColor of the view itself, if its own tintColor has been explicitly set to a color, or else the tintColor inherited from up the view hierarchy. In this way, you can always learn what the *effective* tint color of a view is.

Whenever a view's `tintColor` changes, including when its `tintColor` is initially set at launch time, *it and all its affected subviews* are sent the `tintColorDidChange` message. A subview whose `tintColor` has previously been explicitly set to a color of its own isn't affected, so it is *not* sent the `tintColorDidChange` message merely because its super-view's `tintColor` changes — the subview's own `tintColor` *didn't* change.

A UIView also has a `tintAdjustmentMode`. Under certain circumstances, such as the summoning of an alert (Chapter 13) or a popover (Chapter 9), the system will set the `tintAdjustmentMode` of the view at the top of the view hierarchy to `.Dimmed`. This causes the `tintColor` to change to a variety of gray. The idea is that the tinting of the background should become monochrome, thus emphasizing the primacy of the view that occupies the foreground (the alert or popover). This change in the `tintAdjustmentMode` propagates all the way down the view hierarchy, changing *all* `tintAdjustmentMode` values and *all* `tintColor` values — and sending *all* subviews the `tintColorDidChange` message. When the foreground view goes away, the system will set the topmost view's `tintAdjustmentMode` to `.Normal`, and that change will propagate down the hierarchy.

The default `tintAdjustmentMode` value is `.Automatic`, meaning that you want this view's `tintAdjustmentMode` to adopt its superview's `tintAdjustmentMode` automatically. When you ask for such a view's `tintAdjustmentMode`, what you get is just like what you get for `tintColor` — you're told the *effective* tint adjustment mode (`.Normal` or `.Dimmed`) inherited from up the view hierarchy.

If, on the other hand, you set a view's `tintAdjustmentMode` *explicitly* to `.Normal` or `.Dimmed`, this tells the system that you want to be left in charge of the `tintAdjustmentMode` for this part of the hierarchy; the automatic propagation of the `tintAdjustmentMode` down the view hierarchy is prevented. To turn automatic propagation back on, set the `tintAdjustmentMode` back to `.Automatic`. (See "Custom Presented View Controller Transition" on page 324 for an example of setting the interface's `tintAdjustmentMode` to `.Dimmed`.)

You can take advantage of `tintColorDidChange` to make your custom UIView subclass behave like a built-in UIView subclass. For example, a `.Custom` UIButton might not automatically dim the title text color. But the button's `tintColor` is still being dimmed, even though that color isn't being applied to the visible interface; thus, to imitate a `.System` UIButton, you can apply the `tintColor` yourself.

 Don't set the `tintColor` from within `tintColorDidChange` without taking precautions against an infinite recursion.

Appearance Proxy

When you want to customize the look of an interface object, instead of sending a message to the object itself, you can send that message to an *appearance proxy* for that object's class. The appearance proxy then passes that same message along to the actual *future* instances of that class. You'll usually configure your appearance proxies very early in the lifetime of the app, and never again. The app delegate's `application:didFinish-LaunchingWithOptions:`, before the app's window has been displayed, is the most obvious and common location.

Like the `tintColor` that I discussed in the previous section, this architecture helps you give your app a consistent appearance, as well as saving you from having to write a lot of code. For example, instead of having to send `setTitleTextAttributes:forState:` to *every* UIBarButtonItem your app *ever* instantiates, you send it *once* to the appearance proxy, and it is sent to all future UIBarButtonItems for you:

```
UIBarButtonItem.appearance()
    .setTitleTextAttributes(
        [NSFontAttributeName: UIFont(name:"GillSans-Bold", size:16)!],
        forState: .Normal)
```

Also, the appearance proxy sometimes provides access to interface objects that might otherwise be difficult to refer to. For example, you don't get direct access to a search bar's external Cancel button, but it is a UIBarButtonItem and you can customize it through the UIBarButtonItem appearance proxy.

There are four class methods for obtaining an appearance proxy:

appearance
> Returns a general appearance proxy for the receiver class.

appearanceForTraitCollection:
> Returns an appearance proxy applicable to situations where the environment matches the specified trait collection. This method is new in iOS 8.

appearanceWhenContainedIn:
> The argument is a nil-terminated comma-separated list (not an array!) of classes, arranged in order of containment from inner to outer. The method you send to the appearance proxy returned from this call will be passed on only to instances of the receiver class that are actually contained in the way you describe. The notion of what "contained" means is deliberately left vague; basically, it works the way you intuitively expect it to work.

appearanceForTraitCollection:whenContainedIn:
> A combination of the preceding two: returns an appearance proxy applicable when both the specified trait collection and the specified containment hierarchy are matched.

The whenContainedIn: parameter can't be expressed in Swift. You'll have to use Objective-C code to call those two methods.

When configuring appearance proxy objects, *specificity trumps generality*. Thus, you could call appearance to say what should happen for *most* instances of some class, and call appearanceForTraitCollection: or appearanceWhenContainedIn: to say what should happen *instead* for *certain* instances of that class. Similarly, longer appearance-WhenContainedIn: chains are more specific than shorter ones.

For example, here's some code from my Latin flashcard app (myGolden and myPaler are methods defined by a category on UIColor; the code is in Objective-C, because I need to call appearanceWhenContainedIn:):

```
[[UIBarButtonItem appearance]
    setTintColor: [UIColor myGolden]]; ❶
[[UIBarButtonItem appearanceWhenContainedIn:
    [UIToolbar class], nil]
        setTintColor: [UIColor myPaler]]; ❷
[[UIBarButtonItem appearanceWhenContainedIn:
    [UIToolbar class], [DrillViewController class], nil]
        setTintColor: [UIColor myGolden]]; ❸
```

That means:

❶ In general, bar button items should be tinted golden.

❷ But bar button items in a toolbar are an exception: they should be tinted paler.

❸ But bar button items in a toolbar in DrillViewController's view are an exception to the exception: they should be tinted golden.

(If you're looking at this book's figures in color, you can see this difference made manifest in Figures 6-3 and 6-5.)

Sometimes, in order to express sufficient specificity, I find myself defining subclasses for no other purpose than to refer to them when obtaining an appearance proxy. For example, here's some more code from my Latin flashcard app:

```
[[UINavigationBar appearance] setBackgroundImage:marble2
                                forBarMetrics:UIBarMetricsDefault];
// counteract the above for the black navigation bar
[[BlackNavigationBar appearance] setBackgroundImage:nil
                                forBarMetrics:UIBarMetricsDefault];
```

In that code, BlackNavigationBar is a UINavigationBar subclass that does nothing whatever. Its sole purpose is to tag one navigation bar in my interface so that I can refer to it in that code! Thus, I'm able to say, in effect, "All navigation bars in this app should have `marble2` as their background image, unless they are instances of BlackNavigation-Bar."

The ultimate in specificity is, of course, to customize the look of an instance directly. Thus, for example, if you set one particular UIBarButtonItem's `tintColor` property, then setting the tint color by way of a UIBarButtonItem appearance proxy will have no effect on that particular bar button item.

Be warned, however, that not every message that can be sent to an instance of a class can be sent to that class's appearance proxy. Unfortunately, the compiler can't help you here; illegal code like this will compile, but will crash at runtime:

```
UIBarButtonItem.appearance().action = "crashme" // thanks, I will
```

When in doubt, look at the class documentation; there should be a section that lists the properties and methods applicable to the appearance proxy for this class. For example, the UINavigationBar class documentation has a section called "Customizing the Bar Appearance," the UIBarButtonItem class documentation has a section called "Customizing Appearance," and so forth.

 The headers and other documentation may appear to warn that `tintColor` is not a legal appearance proxy message. Don't worry; it *is* legal. However, it is also true that the *normal* `tintColor` property can conflict with appearance proxy settings. For example, setting an object's `tintColor` directly can undo a UIBarButtonItem's title font set previously through the appearance proxy's title text attributes.

CHAPTER 13

Modal Dialogs

A modal dialog demands attention; while it is present, the user can do nothing other than work within it or dismiss it. You might need to put up a simple modal dialog in order to give the user some information or to ask the user how to proceed. iOS provides two types of rudimentary modal dialog — alerts and action sheets.

A local notification is an alert that the system presents at a predetermined time on your app's behalf when your app isn't frontmost. I discuss local notifications in this chapter as well. I'll also talk about today extensions, a mechanism whereby your app can present interface on the Today side of the notification center.

An activity view is a modal dialog displaying icons representing possible courses of action, and intended in certain circumstances to replace the action sheet. For example, Mobile Safari presents an activity view from its Action button; the icons represent external modes of sharing a URL such as Mail, Message, and Twitter, as well as internal actions such as Bookmark and Add to Reading List. I'll describe how to present an activity view and how to provide your own activities, either privately within your app or publicly as an action extension.

Alerts and Action Sheets

New in iOS 8, alerts and action sheets are both forms of presented view controller. They are managed through the UIAlertController class, a UIViewController subclass. (This architecture replaces that of iOS 7 and before, where alerts and action sheets were windows interposed in front of your app by the system, and were configured through the UIAlertView and UIActionSheet classes.)

To show an alert or an action sheet is a three-step process:

1. Instantiate UIAlertController by calling `init(title:message:preferred-Style:)`. The `title:` and `message:` are large and small descriptive text to appear

at the top of the dialog. The `preferredStyle:` (UIAlertControllerStyle) will be either `.Alert` or `.ActionSheet`.

2. Configure the dialog by calling `addAction:` on the UIAlertController as many times as needed. An action is a UIAlertAction, which basically means it's a button to appear in the dialog, along with a closure to be executed when the button is tapped; to create one, call `init(title:style:handler:)`. (This closure-based architecture is much clearer and more self-contained than the old delegate-based architecture of iOS 7 and before.) Possible `style:` values are (UIAlertActionStyle):

   - `.Default`
   - `.Cancel`
   - `.Destructive`

   An alert may also have text fields (I'll talk about that in a moment).

3. Call `presentViewController:animated:completion:` to present the UIAlert-Controller.

The dialog is automatically dismissed when the user taps any button.

Alerts

An alert (UIAlertController style `.Alert`) pops up unexpectedly in the middle of the screen, with an elaborate animation, and may be thought of as an attention-getting interruption. It contains a title, a message, and some number of buttons, one of which may be the cancel button, meaning that it does nothing but dismiss the alert. In addition, an alert may contain one or two text fields.

Alerts are minimal, but intentionally so; they are intended for simple, quick interaction or display of information. Often there is only a cancel button, the primary purpose of the alert being to show the user the message ("You won the game"); additional buttons may be used to give the user a choice of how to proceed ("You won the game; would you like to play another?" "Yes," "No," "Replay"). Text fields might allow the user to supply login credentials.

Figure 13-1 shows a basic alert, illustrating the title, the message, and the three button styles: `.Destructive`, `.Default`, and `.Cancel` respectively. Here's the code that generated it:

```
let alert = UIAlertController(title: "Not So Fast!",
    message: "Do you really want to do this " +
        "tremendously destructive thing?",
    preferredStyle: .Alert)
func handler(act:UIAlertAction!) {
    println("User tapped \(act.title)")
```

Figure 13-1. An alert

```
    }
alert.addAction(UIAlertAction(
    title: "No", style: .Cancel, handler: handler))
alert.addAction(UIAlertAction(
    title: "Yes", style: .Destructive, handler: handler))
alert.addAction(UIAlertAction(
    title: "Maybe", style: .Default, handler: handler))
self.presentViewController(alert, animated: true, completion: nil)
```

In Figure 13-1, observe that the `.Destructive` button appears first and the `.Cancel` button appears last, without regard to the order in which they are defined. The `.Default` button order of definition, on the other hand, will be the order of the buttons themselves. If no `.Cancel` button is defined, the last `.Default` button will be displayed as a `.Cancel` button.

As I've already mentioned, the dialog is dismissed automatically when the user taps a button. If you don't want to respond to the tap of a particular button, you can assign a nil `handler:` argument. In the preceding code, I've provided a minimal `handler:` function for each button, just to show what one looks like. As the example demonstrates, the function receives the original UIAlertAction as a parameter, and can examine it as desired. The function can also access the alert controller itself, if necessary, provided the alert controller is in scope at the point where the handler function is defined (which will usually be the case). My example code assigns the same function to all three buttons, but more often you'll give each button its own individual handler.

Now let's talk about adding text fields to an alert. Because space is limited on the smaller iPhone screen, especially when the keyboard is present, an alert that is to contain a text field should probably should have at most two buttons, with short titles such as "OK" and "Cancel," and at most two text fields. To add a text field to an alert, call `addText-FieldWithConfigurationHandler:`. The handler will receive the text field as a parameter; it is called before the alert appears, and can be used to configure the text field. Other handlers, such as the handler of a button, can access the text field through the alert's `textFields` property, which is an array. In this example, the user is invited to enter a number in the text field; if the alert is dismissed with the OK button, its handler reads the text from the text field:

```
let alert = UIAlertController(
    title: "Enter a number:", message: nil, preferredStyle: .Alert)
alert.addTextFieldWithConfigurationHandler {
    (tf:UITextField!) in
    tf.keyboardType = .NumberPad
}
func handler(act:UIAlertAction!) {
    let tf = alert.textFields![0] as! UITextField
    let s = tf.text // ... and now do something with the text ...
}
alert.addAction(UIAlertAction(
    title: "Cancel", style: .Cancel, handler: nil))
alert.addAction(UIAlertAction(
    title: "OK", style: .Default, handler: handler))
self.presentViewController(alert, animated: true, completion: nil)
```

A puzzle arises as to how to prevent the user from dismissing the alert if the text fields are not acceptably filled in. The alert will be dismissed if the user taps a button, and no button handler can prevent this. The solution is to disable the relevant buttons until the text fields are satisfactory. A UIAlertAction has an **enabled** property for this very purpose. I'll modify the preceding example so that the OK button can't initially be tapped:

```
alert.addAction(
    UIAlertAction(title: "Cancel", style: .Cancel, handler: nil))
alert.addAction(
    UIAlertAction(title: "OK", style: .Default, handler: handler))
(alert.actions[1] as! UIAlertAction).enabled = false
self.presentViewController(alert, animated: true, completion: nil)
```

But this raises a new puzzle: how will the OK button be enabled? The text field can have a delegate or a control event target–action pair, and so we can hear about the user typing in it. I'll modify the example again so that I'm notified as the user edits in the text field:

```
alert.addTextFieldWithConfigurationHandler {
    (tf:UITextField!) in
    tf.keyboardType = .NumberPad
    tf.addTarget(self,
        action: "textChanged:", forControlEvents: .EditingChanged)
}
```

Our `textChanged:` method will now be called when the user edits, but this raises one final puzzle: how will this method, which receives a reference to the text field, get a reference to the OK button in the alert in order to enable it? My approach is to work my way up the responder chain from the text field to the alert controller. Here, I enable the OK button if and only if the text field contains some text:

```
func textChanged(sender:AnyObject) {
    let tf = sender as! UITextField
    var resp : UIResponder! = tf
    while !(resp is UIAlertController) { resp = resp.nextResponder() }
    let alert = resp as! UIAlertController
    (alert.actions[1] as! UIAlertAction).enabled = (tf.text != "")
}
```

Action Sheets

An action sheet (UIAlertController style .ActionSheet) may be considered the iOS equivalent of a menu; it consists primarily of buttons. On the iPhone, it slides up from the bottom of the screen; on the iPad, it appears as a popover.

Where an alert is an interruption, an action sheet is a logical branching of what the user is already doing: it typically divides a single piece of interface into multiple possible courses of action. For example, in Apple's Mail app, a single Action button summons an action sheet that lets the user reply to the current message, forward it, or print it (or cancel and do nothing).

Figure 13-2 shows a basic action sheet on the iPhone. Here's the code that constructed it:

```
let action = UIAlertController(
    title: "Choose New Layout", message: nil, preferredStyle: .ActionSheet)
action.addAction(UIAlertAction(
    title: "Cancel", style: .Cancel, handler: nil))
func handler(act:UIAlertAction!) {
    let s = act.title // ... and do something with that info here ...
}
for s in ["3 by 3", "4 by 3", "4 by 4", "5 by 4", "5 by 5"] {
    action.addAction(
        UIAlertAction(title: s, style: .Default, handler: handler))
}
self.presentViewController(action, animated: true, completion: nil)
```

On the iPad, the action sheet wants to be a popover. This means that a UIPopover-PresentationController will take charge of it. It will thus be incumbent upon you to provide something for the popover's arrow to point to; otherwise, you'll crash at runtime. Recall (from Chapter 9) that the way to deal with this situation is to test for a popoverPresentationController *after* presenting the action sheet; that way, the same code will work equally well on an iPhone and on an iPad:

Figure 13-2. An action sheet on the iPhone

```
self.presentViewController(action, animated: true, completion: nil)
if let pop = action.popoverPresentationController {
    let v = sender as! UIView
    pop.sourceView = v
    pop.sourceRect = v.bounds
}
```

In that code, we're assuming that the sender (whatever was tapped in order to summon the action sheet) is a UIView. If it's a UIBarButtonItem, then obviously you'll set the popover presentation controller's barButtonItem, and you may want to do the little dance I demonstrated in Chapter 9 to set its passthroughViews to nil.

The Cancel button for a popover action sheet is suppressed, because the user can dismiss the popover by tapping outside it.

An action sheet can also be presented *inside* a popover. In that case, the containing popover is treated as an iPhone: the action sheet slides up from the bottom of the popover, and the Cancel button is *not* suppressed. The action sheet's modal presentation style defaults to .OverCurrentContext, which is exactly what we want, so there is no need to set it. You are then presenting a view controller inside a popover; see "Popover Presenting a View Controller" on page 513 for the considerations that apply.

Dialog Alternatives

Alerts and action sheets are limited, inflexible, and inappropriate to any but the simplest cases. Their interface can contain title text, buttons, and (for an alert) one or two text fields, and that's all. What if you wanted more interface than that?

Figure 13-3. A presented view behaving like an alert

Some developers have hacked into their alerts or action sheets in an attempt to force them to be more customizable. *This is wrong*, and in any case there is no need for such extremes. These are just presented view controllers, after all, and if you don't like what they contain, you can make your own presented view controller with its own customized view. As I have already shown ("Custom Presented View Controller Transition" on page 324), it is easy to create a small presented view that looks and behaves quite like an alert or action sheet, floating in front of the main interface and darkening everything behind it — the difference being that this is an ordinary view controller's view, belonging entirely to you, and capable of being populated with any interface you like (Figure 13-3). You can even add a UIMotionEffect to your presented view, giving it the same parallax as a real alert.

More generally, it is worthwhile asking yourself whether an alert or action sheet is even needed. On the iPhone, for example, it is always possible to navigate to a new screenful of interface, whether by way of a navigation interface or by using a presented view (Chapter 6). The color picker in my Zotz! app (Figure 13-4) has the same lightweight, temporary quality that an alert offers, and on the desktop would probably be presented as part of a secondary Preferences window; it happens that, on the iPhone, it occupies the entire screen, but it is still effectively a modal dialog.

On the iPad, a popover is virtually a secondary window, and can be truly modal. The popovers in Figure 9-1, for example, are effectively modal dialogs. A popover can internally display a secondary presented view or even an action sheet, as we've already seen. Also on the iPad, a presented view can use the `UIModalPresentationFormSheet` presentation style, which is effectively a dialog window smaller than the screen; and even a smaller presented view, such as the one shown in Figure 13-3, works just as well on the iPad as on the iPhone.

Local Notifications

A *local notification* is an alert to the user that can appear even if your app is not running. Where it may appear depends upon the user's preferences in the Settings app, either under Notification Center or under your app's own listing which, new in iOS 8, is created

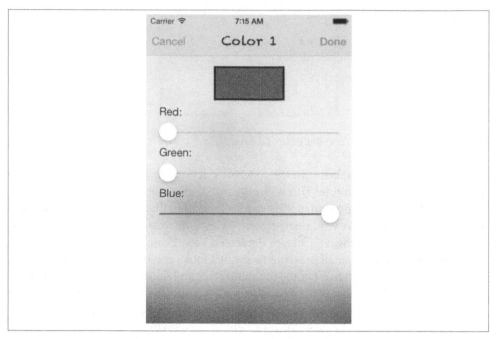

Figure 13-4. A presented view functioning as a modal dialog

automatically for this purpose. In addition to optionally producing a sound, a local notification's interface possibilities are (Figure 13-5, clockwise from the top left):

- A modal alert, similar to a UIAlertController's alert
- A momentary banner at the top of the screen, which vanishes automatically if the user does nothing; this interface is mutually exclusive with the modal alert interface
- A row on the lock screen
- A row in the notification center

 This use of the term *notification* has nothing to do with NSNotification; the ambiguity is unfortunate.

Your app does not present a local notification; the system does. You hand the system instructions for when the local notification is to *fire*, and then you just stand back and let the system deal with it. That's why the local notification can appear even if your app isn't frontmost or isn't even running. Indeed, if your app *is* frontmost, the local notification's alert or banner does *not* automatically appear when it fires; instead, your app is

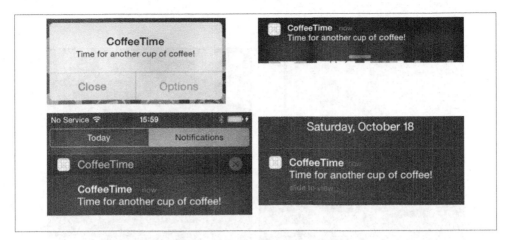

Figure 13-5. Local notification interface possibilities

Figure 13-6. The user will see this only once

notified, and you can notify the user if you like. The only local notification alert that can appear when your app is frontmost is some *other* app's local notification (and in that case, your app will become inactive; see Appendix A).

The user, in the Settings app, can veto any of your local notification's interface options, or turn off your app's local notifications entirely. Thus, your local notification can be effectively suppressed; you can still create a local notification, but when it fires, only your app will hear about it, and only if it is frontmost. New in iOS 8, moreover, the system will suppress your local notifications by default unless the user approves first. Thus, in contrast to iOS 7 and before, where your local notification might appear for the first time, and then the user who preferred to suppress it would opt *out* in the Settings app, in iOS 8 the user must deliberately opt *in* if your notification is ever to appear in any form. Figure 13-6 shows the alert that the system will show your user, once, offering the initial opportunity to opt in to your local notifications.

Figure 13-7. Local notifications with custom actions

The interface whereby a notification presents itself provides a way for the user to summon your app in response, bringing it to the front if it is backgrounded, and launching it if it isn't running. In iOS 7 and before, a notification could also have an action button, in at least some of its forms; new in iOS 8, an action button can appear in *any* of a notification's forms, you can customize it, you can have more than one, and an action button can communicate with your app without bringing it to the front. Thus, from a presented notification, the user can elect to open your app or to tap an action button; either way, your app will know what happened, as I'll explain in a moment.

Figure 13-7 shows how two custom action buttons appear in each of a local notification's interface possibilities. In the alert (top left), the user has tapped the Options button in the first alert from Figure 13-5; in the banner, the user has pulled down; in the lock screen and notification center, the user has slid the row to the left.

I'll treat the creation of a local notification in iOS 8 as involving three steps:

1. Your app must *register* for notifications. This is new in iOS 8. Registration states what sorts of interface your notifications will want to use, and ensures that the user has seen the opt-in dialog (Figure 13-6). This is also the moment when you provide action buttons. You may register as many times as you like (the opt-in dialog won't be repeated); each registration cancels the previous registration settings and replaces them with new ones.

2. Your app creates and schedules a local notification.

3. Your app is prepared to hear about the user responding to the notification.

Registering a Notification

When should registration be performed? Apple has not provided clear guidance; they say only "during your launch cycle." This would seem to suggest `application:did-FinishLaunchingWithOptions:` as a possible location. But this, as my test reveals, has a fatal flaw in the following scenario:

1. You register in `application:didFinishLaunchingWithOptions:`.

2. The user sees the dialog and refuses to allow your app to present local notifications.

3. Some time later, the user goes to the Settings app and enables local notifications for your app.

4. You present a local notification — and your custom actions are missing. This is because you registered only once, and the user declined on that occasion, so your custom actions were never registered.

To work around this scenario (which I regard as a bug), I recommend also registering in `applicationWillEnterForeground:`. You'll be registering every time your app comes to the front, which is wasteful but mostly harmless, and at least you are guaranteed of registering your custom actions if the user has visited the Settings app in the meantime.

To register, you must supply two things:

Interface types
> Interface types (UIUserNotificationType) are `.Alert` (meaning alerts and banners), `.Sound`, and `.Badge`, forming a bitmask. Omit any that your app will never use, and that type will be omitted from Settings for your app; regardless of your registered interface types, the user will always see the options to show your notifications in the notification center and the lock screen.

Categories
> A category (UIUserNotificationCategory, along with its mutable subclass) is a value class comprising a string identifier along with any custom action buttons. When you create and schedule a local notification, you will associate it with a category by using the string identifier, thus determining what custom action buttons will be present.

An action button (UIUserNotificationAction, along with its mutable subclass) has the following properties:

identifier

A private string identifier; this is how your app will know what button was tapped.

title

The visible title of the button. Keep it short!

destructive

If `true`, the button will be shown in red.

activationMode

A UIUserNotificationActivationMode, either `.Foreground` or `.Background`. In the latter case, your app will not be brought to the front when the user taps this button; instead, your app will be permitted to run briefly in the background.

authenticationRequired

If `true`, *and if this is a* `.Background` *button,* then if the user's device requires a passcode to go beyond the lock screen, tapping this button in the lock screen will also require a passcode. The idea is to prevent performance of a dangerous action without authentication directly from the lock screen.

We now know enough for an example! Here's the code that registers the notification shown in Figure 13-7:

```
let types : UIUserNotificationType = .Alert | .Sound
let category = UIMutableUserNotificationCategory()
category.identifier = "coffee"
let action1 = UIMutableUserNotificationAction()
action1.identifier = "yum"
action1.title = "Yum" // user will see this
action1.activationMode = .Foreground
let action2 = UIMutableUserNotificationAction()
action2.identifier = "ohno"
action2.title = "Oh, No!" // user will see this
action2.activationMode = .Background
category.setActions([action1, action2], forContext: .Default)
let settings = UIUserNotificationSettings(
    forTypes: types, categories: Set([category]))
application.registerUserNotificationSettings(settings)
```

In `setActions:forContext:`, the possible contexts are `.Default` and `.Minimal`. A `.Default` context, a full-fledged alert, can have a maximum of four buttons; the other forms of interface can have a maximum of two. Thus, if you had more than two buttons for the `.Default` context, you would use an additional call to `setActions:forContext:` to say which buttons should appear in the `.Minimal` context.

Your code can subsequently discover whether the user has granted permissions for the notification types you requested. For example:

```
let settings = UIApplication.sharedApplication()
    .currentUserNotificationSettings()
if settings.types.rawValue & UIUserNotificationType.Alert.rawValue != 0 {
    // alerts are enabled
}
```

It is difficult, however, to see how this information is useful, as there is unfortunately no way to learn whether the user has completely turned off notifications for your app. Thus, although Apple claims you might call `currentUserNotificationSettings` in order to save yourself the trouble of preparing a certain notification, I don't think you would *ever* not send one, as there is always a chance that, even if alerts are turned off, your notification might appear in the notification center or the lock screen.

After you call `registerUserNotificationSettings:`, your app delegate will receive `application:didRegisterUserNotificationSettings:`. I don't understand why this is useful either, since you know perfectly well that you just registered, and if you want to know what the notification settings are you can always call `currentUser-NotificationSettings`.

Scheduling a Notification

We are now ready for the second step — creating and scheduling a notification. To create a local notification, you configure a UILocalNotification object and hand it to the shared UIApplication instance by calling `scheduleLocalNotification:`. The UILocal-Notification object has properties as follows:

`category`
> The identifier of a category you provided when you registered (new in iOS 8). If your category has actions, this also tells the runtime to provide them. (The `has-Action` and `alertAction` properties from iOS 7 and before are thus superseded.)

`alertBody`
> The message to be displayed in the notification.

`soundName`
> The name of a sound file at the top level of your app bundle, to be played when the alert appears. This should be an uncompressed sound (AIFF or WAV). Alternatively, you can specify the default sound, `UILocalNotificationDefaultSound-Name`. If you don't set this property, there won't be a sound (and of course the user can prevent your app's notifications from emitting any sound).

`userInfo`
> An optional dictionary whose contents are up to you. Your app can retrieve this dictionary later on, if it receives the notification after the notification fires.

`fireDate, timeZone`
> When you want the local notification to fire. The `fireDate` is an NSDate. If you don't include a `timeZone`, the date is measured against universal time; if you do include a `timeZone`, the date is measured against the user's local time zone, and thus it keeps working correctly if that time zone changes (because the user travels, for instance).

`repeatInterval, repeatCalendar`
> If set, the local notification will recur. The `repeatInterval` (an NSCalendarUnit) must be a minute or longer; setting it to `.CalendarUnitSecond` will result in a value of `.CalendarUnitMinute`. Recurrence survives a restart of the device.

Additional UIApplication methods let you manipulate the list of local notifications you've already scheduled. You can cancel one or all scheduled local notifications (`cancelLocalNotification:`, `cancelAllLocalNotifications:`); you can also manipulate the list directly by setting UIApplication's `scheduledLocalNotifications`, an array property.

 Canceling a recurring local notification is up to your code; if you don't provide a way of doing that, and if the user wants to prevent the notification from recurring, the user's only recourse will be to delete your app.

Here's the code for creating and scheduling the local notification that results in Figure 13-5:

```
let ln = UILocalNotification()
ln.category = "coffee" // causes action buttons to spring to life
ln.alertBody = "Time for another cup of coffee!"
ln.fireDate = NSDate(timeIntervalSinceNow:15)
ln.soundName = UILocalNotificationDefaultSoundName
UIApplication.sharedApplication().scheduleLocalNotification(ln)
```

Hearing About a Local Notification

Now let's talk about what happens when one of your scheduled local notifications fires. There are three possibilities, depending on the state of your app at that moment:

Your app is frontmost
> The user won't be informed by the system that the notification has fired; there won't be any sound, alert, or banner. Your notification *will* be listed in the notification center if the user has granted permission.

> Your app delegate will receive `application:didReceiveLocalNotification:`, where the second parameter is the UILocalNotification, and your application's `applicationState` will be `.Active`.

Your app is suspended or not running

What happens depends on what the user does in response to the firing of the alert:

The user summons your app

If the user taps the top of the banner or the Open button in the alert, or taps your notification in the notification center, or slides your notification in the lock screen to the right, your app is brought to the front, and:

- If your app was *suspended*, your app delegate will receive `application:did-ReceiveLocalNotification:`, where the second parameter is the UILocal-Notification, and your application's `applicationState` will be `.Inactive`.

- If your app was *not running*, your app delegate will receive `application:didFinishLaunchingWithOptions:`, with a dictionary parameter that includes the `UIApplicationLaunchOptionsLocal-NotificationKey`, whose value is the UILocalNotification.

The user taps an action button

If the user taps an action button, then your app delegate will receive `application:handleActionWithIdentifier:forLocalNotification:completionHandler:`. You *must* call the completion handler at the end of your implementation!

If this is a `.Foreground` button and your app wasn't running, your app delegate will of course also receive `application:didFinishLaunchingWithOptions:`, but the options dictionary will be nil.

If this is a `.Background` button, your app is now running in the background. You have very little time before being suspended, so respond quickly.

Nothing (or close)

If the user does nothing, or closes the banner, or taps Close in the alert, that's the end of the matter; your app will never be informed that the notification fired.

Here's a minimal implementation of `application:handleActionWithIdentifier:for-LocalNotification:completionHandler::`

```
func application(application: UIApplication,
    handleActionWithIdentifier id: String?,
    forLocalNotification n: UILocalNotification,
    completionHandler: () -> Void) {
        // ... examine id and n as desired ...
        completionHandler() // crucial!
}
```

Thus, to cover all possible cases, you should implement all three app delegate methods:

`application:didFinishLaunchingWithOptions:`
> Check its second parameter to see whether we are launching in response to a local notification.

`application:didReceiveLocalNotification:`
> Check the UIApplication's `applicationState` and the notification as desired.

`application:handleActionWithIdentifier:forLocalNotification:completion-Handler:`
> Check the identifier and notification as desired, and remember to call the completion handler.

It is a pity that your app, when coming to the front, can't learn that a notification fired while it was suspended or not running, if the user *doesn't* use the notification interface to bring the app to the front and *doesn't* tap an action button. If your app's logic is about firing notifications at certain times, you'll need to implement your own model to keep track of those times and look to see, when you come the front, whether those times have passed.

If your app wasn't frontmost and the user summons it from a notification, you may want to show the user, immediately, some interface appropriate to this local notification. However, as your app appears, the user will first see either your default launch image (if the app is launched from scratch) or the screenshot image taken by the system when your app was suspended (if the app is activated from the background). To prevent a mismatch between that image and what the user will see when your app's interface actually appears, you can include in the original UILocalNotification an `alertLaunch-Image` that more closely matches your app's interface.

Under some special circumstances (addressed, for example, in Chapters 14 and 22), your app might be running, *not* suspended, in the background, when your notification fires. In this case, the situation is similar to what happens when your app *is* suspended: the user may be notified, and can summon your app to the front. Your running-in-the-background app can even schedule a notification to fire immediately with the convenience method `presentLocalNotificationNow:`.

 New in iOS 8, a local notification can fire in response to the user's location rather than in reponse to the arrival of a certain time. I'll talk about that in Chapter 21.

Today Extensions

New in iOS 8, your app can obtain a bit of real estate on the other side of the notification center — the Today side, as opposed to the Notifications side. To do so, you add to your

Figure 13-8. A today extension

app a *today extension*. Your app vends the extension, and the user has the option of adding it to the Today side of the notification center (Figure 13-8).

To add a today extension to your app, create a new target and specify iOS → Application Extension → Today Extension. The template gives you a good start on your extension. You have a storyboard with a single scene, and the code for a corresponding view controller that adopts the NCWidgetProviding protocol. You might need to edit the extension's *Info.plist* and set the "Bundle display name" entry — this is the title that will appear above your extension in the notification center.

Design your extension's interface in the storyboard provided. Use autolayout to position your views, and provide sufficient constraints to determine the full height of your extension's interface from the inside out. (Apple says that you can alternatively determine your extension's height by setting your view controller's preferredContentSize, but in my experimentation, autolayout proved more reliable.) If you want to add a UIVisual-EffectView with vibrancy, do so in code, initializing the view's effect by calling UIVibrancyView's class method notificationCenterVibrancyEffect:

```
let v = UIVisualEffectView(
    effect: UIVibrancyEffect.notificationCenterVibrancyEffect())
```

Your interface will appear aligned to the notification center's margins, which by default involve a large left margin. To counteract that, implement the NCWidgetProviding protocol method widgetMarginInsetsForProposedMarginInsets:. For example:

```
func widgetMarginInsetsForProposedMarginInsets(
    defaultMarginInsets: UIEdgeInsets) -> UIEdgeInsets {
        return UIEdgeInsetsMake(0,16,0,16)
}
```

Each time your today extension's interface is about to appear, your code is given an opportunity to update its interface, through its implementation of widgetPerform-UpdateWithCompletionHandler:. Be sure to finish up by calling the completion-Handler, handing it an NCUpdateResult, which will be .NewData, .NoData, or .Failed. Time-consuming work should be performed off the main thread (see Chapter 25):

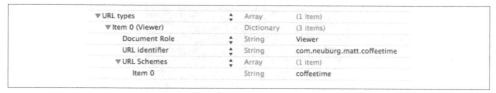

▼ URL types		Array	(1 item)
▼ Item 0 (Viewer)		Dictionary	(3 items)
Document Role		String	Viewer
URL identifier		String	com.neuburg.matt.coffeetime
▼ URL Schemes		Array	(1 item)
Item 0		String	coffeetime

Figure 13-9. A custom URL declaration

```
func widgetPerformUpdateWithCompletionHandler(
    completionHandler: ((NCUpdateResult) -> Void)!) {
        // ... do stuff off the main thread here ...
        // ... then get back on the main thread and call:
        completionHandler(NCUpdateResult.NewData)
}
```

That's basically all there is to a today extension, but be sure to read the NCWidget-Providing protocol header and the "Today" chapter of Apple's *App Extension Programming Guide*. Also, look at the "Handling Common Scenarios" section to understand how to communicate data and messages between your app and the extension. The extension is not running within your app, but is being hosted by some other app; thus, there are some calls you can't make — for example, there is no shared application object — and communication can be a bit tricky. In Figure 13-8, two buttons invite the user to set up a reminder; I've implemented these to open our CoffeeTime app by calling openURL:completionHandler: — a method of the automatically provided extension-Context, not the shared application:

```
@IBAction func doButton(sender: AnyObject) {
    let v = sender as! UIView
    let t = v.tag // tag is number of minutes
    if let url = NSURL(string:"coffeetime://\(String(t))") {
        self.extensionContext?.openURL(url, completionHandler: nil)
    }
}
```

The CoffeeTime app receives this message because I've given it two things:

A custom URL scheme

The coffeetime scheme is declared in the app's *Info.plist* (Figure 13-9).

An implementation of application:handleOpenURL:

In the app delegate, I've implemented application:handleOpenURL: to analyze the URL when it arrives. I've coded the original URL so that the "host" is actually the number of minutes announced in the tapped button; thus, I can respond appropriately (presumably by scheduling a local notification for that number of minutes from now):

```
func application(
    application: UIApplication, handleOpenURL url: NSURL) -> Bool {
        let scheme = url.scheme
        let host = url.host
        if scheme == "coffeetime" {
            if let min = host?.toInt() {
                // ... do something here ...
                return true
            }
        }
        return false
}
```

Activity Views

An activity view is the view belonging to a UIActivityViewController. You start with one or more pieces of data, such as a string, that you want the user to have the option of sharing or working with in your app. The activity view contains an icon for every activity (UIActivity) that can work with this type of data. The user may tap an icon in the activity view, and is then perhaps shown additional interface, belonging to the provider of the chosen activity.

 Don't confuse UIActivityViewController, UIActivity, UIActivityItemProvider, and UIActivityItemSource, on the one hand, with UIActivityIndicatorView (Chapter 12) on the other. The similarity of the names is unfortunate.

There are 14 built-in activities, and your app can provide more activities that are available only within your app. Figure 13-10 shows an example, from Mobile Safari:

In Figure 13-10, the top row of the activity view lists some applicable built-in system-wide activites; the bottom row shows some activities provided internally by Safari itself. New in iOS 8, an app can provide system-wide activities that are available in *any* app. Such activities come in two forms:

Share extensions
A *share extension* is shown in the *upper* row of an activity view. Share extensions are for situations where you run some kind of server and are offering to give the user interface for posting information to it — similar to the activities that appear there by default, such as Twitter and Facebook.

Action extensions
An *action extension* is shown in the *lower* row of an activity view. Action extensions offer to perform some kind of manipulation on the data provided by the host app, and can even hand back data in reply.

Figure 13-10. An activity view

I'll describe how to present an activity view and how to construct an activity that's private to your app. Then I'll give an example of writing an action extension. (Share extensions require a custom server and are beyond the scope of this book.)

Presenting an Activity View

To present an activity view:

1. Instantiate UIActivityViewController. The initializer you'll be calling is `init(activityItems:applicationActivities:)`, where the first argument is an array of objects to be shared or operated on, such as string or image objects. Presumably these are objects associated somehow with the interface the user is looking at right now.

2. Set the controller's `completionWithItemsHandler` (superseding the `completionHandler` from iOS 7 and before) to a closure that will be called when the user's interaction with the activity interface ends.

3. Present the controller, as a presented view controller; on the iPad, it will be a popover, so you'll also configure the popover presentation controller if there is one. The presented view or popover will be dismissed automatically when the user cancels or chooses an activity.

So, for example:

```
let url = NSBundle.mainBundle().URLForResource(
    "sunglasses", withExtension:"png")!
let things = ["This is cool", url] // a string and an image file URL
let avc = UIActivityViewController(
```

```
        activityItems:things, applicationActivities:nil)
    avc.completionWithItemsHandler = {
        (s: String!, ok: Bool, items: [AnyObject]!, err:NSError!) -> Void in
        // ... optionally do something here; only the ok parameter matters ...
    }
    self.presentViewController(avc, animated:true, completion:nil)
    if let pop = avc.popoverPresentationController {
        let v = sender as! UIView
        pop.sourceView = v
        pop.sourceRect = v.bounds
    }
```

There is no Cancel button in the popover presentation of the activity view; the user cancels by tapping outside the popover. Actually, the user can cancel by tapping outside the activity view even on the iPhone.

The activity view is populated automatically with known system-wide activities that can handle any of the types of data you provided as the activityItems: argument. These activities represent UIActivity types, and are designated by string constants:

- UIActivityTypePostToFacebook
- UIActivityTypePostToTwitter
- UIActivityTypePostToWeibo
- UIActivityTypeMessage
- UIActivityTypeMail
- UIActivityTypePrint
- UIActivityTypeCopyToPasteboard
- UIActivityTypeAssignToContact
- UIActivityTypeSaveToCameraRoll
- UIActivityTypeAddToReadingList
- UIActivityTypePostToFlickr
- UIActivityTypePostToVimeo
- UIActivityTypePostToTencentWeibo
- UIActivityTypeAirDrop

Consult the UIActivity class documentation to learn what types of activity item each of these activities can handle. For example, the UIActivityTypeMail activity will accept a string, an image, or a file on disk (such as an image file) designated by an NSURL; it will present a mail composition interface with the activity item(s) in the body of the email.

Since the default is to include all the system-wide activities that can handle the provided data, if you *don't* want a certain system-wide activity included in the activity view, you must exclude it explicitly. You do this by setting the UIActivityViewController's excludedActivityTypes property to an array of activity type constants.

 The UIActivityItemSource protocol and the UIActivityItemProvider class give you a way to supply an activity item whose real value differs from its surface value, or whose real data takes time to obtain. I'm not going to describe them here.

Custom Activities

The purpose of the `applicationActivities:` parameter of `init(activity-Items:applicationActivities:)` is for you to list any additional activities implemented internally by your own app, so that their icons will appear as choices in the activity view as well. Each activity will be an instance of one of your own UIActivity subclasses.

To illustrate, I'll create a minimal (and nonsensical) activity called Be Cool that accepts string activity items. It is a UIActivity subclass called MyCoolActivity. So, to include Be Cool among the choices presented to the user by a UIActivityViewController, I'd say:

```
let avc = UIActivityViewController(
    activityItems:things, applicationActivities:[MyCoolActivity()])
```

Now let's implement MyCoolActivity. It has an array property called `items`, for reasons that will be apparent in a moment. We need to arm ourselves with an image to represent this activity in the activity view; this will be treated as a template image. It should be no larger than 60×60 (76×76 on iPad); it can be smaller, and looks better if it is, because the system will draw a rounded rectangle around it, and the image should be somewhat inset from this. It needn't be square, as it will be centered in the rounded rectangle automatically.

Here's the preparatory part of the implementation of MyCoolActivity:

```
override class func activityCategory() -> UIActivityCategory {
    return .Action // the default
}
override func activityType() -> String? {
    return "com.neuburg.matt.coolActivity"
}
override func activityTitle() -> String? {
    return "Be Cool"
}
override func activityImage() -> UIImage? {
    return self.image // prepared beforehand
}
override func canPerformWithActivityItems(
```

```
        activityItems: [AnyObject]) -> Bool {
            for obj in activityItems {
                if obj is String {
                    return true
                }
            }
            return false
    }
    override func prepareWithActivityItems(activityItems: [AnyObject]) {
        self.items = activityItems
    }
```

If we return `true` from `canPerformWithActivityItems:`, then an icon for this activity, labeled Be Cool and displaying our `activityImage`, will appear in the activity view. If the user taps our icon, `prepareWithActivityItems:` will be called. We retain the `activityItems` into a property, because they won't be arriving again when we are actually told to perform the activity.

To perform the activity, we implement one of two methods:

`performActivity`
> We simply perform the activity directly, using the activity items we've already retained. If the activity is time-consuming, the activity should be performed on a background thread (Chapter 25) so that we can return immediately; the activity view interface will be taken down and the user will be able to go on interacting with the app.

`activityViewController`
> We have further interface that we'd like to show the user as part of the activity, so we return a UIViewController subclass. The activity view mechanism will present this UIViewController for us; it is not our job to present or dismiss it. (We may, however, present or dismiss dependent interface. For example, if our UIViewController is a navigation controller with a custom root view controller, we might push another view controller onto its stack while the user is working on the activity.)

No matter which of these two methods we implement, we *must* eventually call this activity instance's `activityDidFinish:`. This is the signal to the activity view mechanism that the activity is over. If the activity view mechanism is still presenting any interface, it will be taken down, and the argument we supply here, a Bool signifying whether the activity completed successfully, will be passed into the block we supplied earlier as the activity view controller's `completionWithItemsHandler`. So, for example:

```
    override func performActivity() {
        // ... do something with self.items here ...
        self.activityDidFinish(true)
    }
```

If your UIActivity is returning a view controller from `activityViewController`, it will want to hand that view controller a reference to `self` before returning it, so that the view controller can call its `activityDidFinish:` when the time comes.

For example, suppose our activity involves letting the user draw a mustache on a photo of someone. Our view controller will provide interface for doing that, including some way of letting the user signal completion, such as a Cancel button and a Done button. When the user taps either of those, we'll do whatever else is necessary (such as saving the altered photo somewhere if the user tapped Done) and then call `activityDid-Finish:`. Thus, we could implement `activityViewController` like this:

```
override func activityViewController() -> UIViewController? {
    let mvc = MustacheViewController(activity: self, items: self.items!)
    return evc
}
```

And then MustacheViewController would have code like this:

```
weak var activity : UIActivity?
var items: [AnyObject]
init(activity:UIActivity, items:[AnyObject]) {
    self.activity = activity
    self.items = items
    super.init(nibName: "MustacheViewController", bundle: nil)
}
// ... other stuff ...
@IBAction func doCancel(sender:AnyObject) {
    self.activity?.activityDidFinish(false)
}
@IBAction func doDone(sender:AnyObject) {
    self.activity?.activityDidFinish(true)
}
```

Note that MustacheViewController's reference to the UIActivity (`self.activity`) is weak; otherwise, a retain cycle ensues.

Action Extensions

To provide a system-wide activity, you can write an action extension (new in iOS 8). As with today extensions, start with the appropriate target template, iOS → Application Extension → Action Extension. There are two kinds of action extension, with or without an interface; you'll make your choice in the second pane as your create the target.

Preparation of the *Info.plist* is a bit more elaborate than for a today extension. In addition to setting the bundle name, which will appear below the activity's icon in the activity view, you'll use the *Info.plist* to specify what types of data this activity accepts as its operands. In the `NSExtensionActivationRule` dictionary, you'll provide one or more keys, such as:

▼ NSExtension		Dictionary	(3 items)
▼ NSExtensionAttributes		Dictionary	(3 items)
▼ NSExtensionActivationRule		Dictionary	(1 item)
NSExtensionActivationSupportsText		Boolean	YES
NSExtensionPointName		String	com.apple.ui-services
NSExtensionPointVersion		String	1.0
NSExtensionMainStoryboard		String	MainInterface
NSExtensionPointIdentifier		String	com.apple.ui-services

Figure 13-11. An activity view

- `NSExtensionActivationSupportsFileWithMaxCount`

- `NSExtensionActivationSupportsImageWithMaxCount`

- `NSExtensionActivationSupportsMovieWithMaxCount`

- `NSExtensionActivationSupportsText`

- `NSExtensionActivationSupportsWebURLWithMaxCount`

(For the full list, see the "Action Extension Keys" section of Apple's *Information Property List Key Reference*.) Figure 13-11 shows the relevant part of the *Info.plist* for an action extension that accepts one text object.

Your app will provide your action extension to the system, and it will appear in an activity view for any app that provides the appropriate type(s) of data. There is, however, one huge difference between an action extension and a custom UIActivity: an action extension can return data to the calling app. The transport mechanism for this data is rather elaborate.

 There is much more to action extensions than this chapter has room to discuss. My example will get you started with a conceptual understanding, but you'll want to study the relevant documentation and WWDC 2014 videos.

Action extension without an interface

I'll start by giving an example of an action extension that has no interface. This extension takes a string object and returns a string. In particular, it accepts a string that might be the two-letter abbreviation of one of the U.S. states, and if it is, it returns the name of the actual state. The class provided by the template, ActionRequestHandler, is an NSObject subclass. To prepare, we provide some properties:

```
let list : [String] = {
    let path = NSBundle.mainBundle().URLForResource(
        "abbreviations", withExtension:"txt")!
    let s = String(
        contentsOfURL:path, encoding:NSUTF8StringEncoding, error:nil)!
```

```
        return s.componentsSeparatedByString("\n")
    }()
var extensionContext: NSExtensionContext?
let desiredType = kUTTypePlainText as String // import MobileCoreServices
```

`self.list` is a string alternating abbreviations with state names; observe that we are permitted to read a text file out of our extension's bundle. `self.extensionContext` is a place to store the NSExtensionContext that will be provided to us. `self.desired-Type` is just a convenient constant expressing the acceptable data type.

There is just one entry point into our extension's code — `beginRequestWithExtension-Context:`. Here we must store a reference to the incoming NSExtensionContext, retrieve the data, process the data, and return the result. You will probably want to factor the processing of the data out into a separate function; I've called mine `processItem:`. Here's a sketch of my `beginRequestWithExtensionContext:` implementation:

```
func beginRequestWithExtensionContext(context: NSExtensionContext!) {
    self.extensionContext = context
    let items = self.extensionContext!.inputItems
    //  ... retrieve the data ...
    // if there is data, call self.processItem on the main thread
    // if we get here, there is no data
    self.processItem(nil)
}
```

As you can see, I've omitted retrieval of the data from `items` for now. Our code contains two possible calls to `self.processItem:`, one passing the string retrieved from `items` (and then returning), the other passing nil.

Now let's implement the retrieval of the data. Think of this as a series of envelopes (or nested matryoshka dolls) that we must examine and open:

- Our local `items` variable is an array, presumably containing NSExtensionItem objects.

- An NSExtensionItem may have an `attachments` array, presumably containing NSItemProvider objects.

- An NSItemProvider vends items; in particular:

  - We can ask whether an NSItemProvider has an item of a particular type, by calling `hasItemConformingToTypeIdentifier:`.

  - We can retrieve the item of a particular type, by calling `loadItemForType-Identifier:options:completionHandler:`. The item may take time to prepare and provide, so we proceed in the `completionHandler:` to receive the item and do something with it.

Fortunately, we are expecting only one item, so it will be provided by the first NSItem-Provider inside the first NSExtensionItem. Here, then, is the code that I omitted from `beginRequestWithExtensionContext`:

```
if let extensionItem = items[0] as? NSExtensionItem {
    if let provider = extensionItem.attachments?[0] as? NSItemProvider {
        if provider.hasItemConformingToTypeIdentifier(self.desiredType) {
            provider.loadItemForTypeIdentifier(
                self.desiredType, options:nil) {
                    (item:NSSecureCoding!, err:NSError!) -> () in
                        dispatch_async(dispatch_get_main_queue()) {
                            self.processItem(item as? String)
                        }
                }
        }
        return
    }
}
```

Now we're ready for `processItem:`. It must do two things: it should call the NSExtension-Context's `completeRequestReturningItems:completionHandler:` to hand back the data, and it should release the NSExtensionContext by setting our retaining property to nil.

I'll start with the simplest case: we didn't get any data. In that case, the returned value is nil:

```
func processItem(item:String?) {
    if (item == nil) {
        self.extensionContext?.completeRequestReturningItems(
            nil, completionHandler: nil)
    } else {
        // hmmm....
    }
    self.extensionContext = nil
}
```

That was easy, because we cleverly omitted the only case where we have any work to do. Now let's implement that case. We have received a string in the `item` parameter. The first question is: is it the abbreviation of a state? To answer that question, I've implemented a utility function:

```
func stateForAbbrev(abbrev:String) -> String? {
    let ix = find(list, abbrev.uppercaseString)
    return ix != nil ? list[ix!+1] : nil
}
```

If we call that method with our `item` string and the answer comes back nil, we simply proceed just as before — we return nil:

```
    if let abbrev = self.stateForAbbrev(item!) {
        // hmmm....
    } else {
        self.extensionContext?.completeRequestReturningItems(
            nil, completionHandler: nil)
    }
```

We come at last to the dreaded moment that I have been tantalizingly postponing all this time. What if we get an abbreviation? In that case, we must reverse the earlier process of opening envelopes: we must put envelopes within envelopes and hand back an array of NSExtensionItems. We have only one result, so this will be an array of one NSExtensionItem, whose `attachments` is an array of one NSItemProvider, whose `item` is the string and whose `typeIdentifier` is the type of that string. Confused? Here, I've written a little utility function that should clarify:

```
func stuffThatEnvelope(item:String) -> [NSExtensionItem] {
    let extensionItem = NSExtensionItem()
    let itemProvider = NSItemProvider(
        item: item, typeIdentifier: self.desiredType)
    extensionItem.attachments = [itemProvider]
    return [extensionItem]
}
```

We can now write the full implementation of `processItem:`, and our action extension is finished:

```
func processItem(item:String?) {
    if (item == nil) {
        self.extensionContext?.completeRequestReturningItems(
            nil, completionHandler: nil)
    } else {
        if let abbrev = self.stateForAbbrev(item!) {
            self.extensionContext?.completeRequestReturningItems(
                self.stuffThatEnvelope(abbrev), completionHandler: nil)
        } else {
            self.extensionContext?.completeRequestReturningItems(
                nil, completionHandler: nil)
        }
    }
    self.extensionContext = nil
}
```

Action extension with an interface

If an action extension has an interface, then the template provides a storyboard with one scene, along with the code for a corresponding UIViewController class. The code is actually simpler, because:

- A view controller already has an `extensionContext` property and it is automatically set for us.

- There are no special entry points to our code. This is a UIViewController, and everything happens just as you would expect.

So, in my implementation, I use `viewDidLoad` to open the data envelope from `self.extensionContext`, get the abbreviation if there is one (storing it in a property, `self.abbrev`), *and stop.* The interface contains a Done button and a Cancel button. The action handlers for those buttons are where I hand the result back to the `extensionContext`:

```
@IBAction func cancel(sender: AnyObject) {
    self.extensionContext?.completeRequestReturningItems(
        nil, completionHandler: nil)
}
@IBAction func done(sender: AnyObject) {
    self.extensionContext?.completeRequestReturningItems(
        self.stuffThatEnvelope(self.abbrev!), completionHandler: nil)
}
```

The runtime responds by dismissing the interface in good order.

Receiving data from an action extension

Recall the earlier discussion of how your app presents a UIActivityViewController. In a world containing action extensions, presenting the UIActivityViewController is no different; but retrieving the returned data is. In my earlier implementation, I avoided this issue by pretending that action extensions didn't exist. Here's a sketch for a more complete implementation:

```
let avc = UIActivityViewController(
    activityItems:things, applicationActivities:nil)
avc.completionWithItemsHandler = {
    (s: String!, ok: Bool, items: [AnyObject]!, err:NSError!) -> Void in
    if ok {
        if items == nil || items.count == 0 {
            return // nothing returned, nothing to do
        }
        // ... open the envelopes! ....
    }
}
self.presentViewController(avc, animated:true, completion:nil)
```

If what the user interacted with in the activity view is one of the built-in UIActivity types, or is one of our own internal custom UIActivity subclasses, then only the `ok` parameter matters. It will be either `true` or `false`, but even if it is `true`, the other parameters will be empty. No data value has been returned.

But if the user interacted with an action extension, then it is up to us to open the `items` envelopes. The structure here is exactly the same as the `items` of an NSExtension-Context: `items` is an array, each element of which is presumably an NSExtensionItem, whose `attachments` is presumably an array of NSItemProvider objects, each of which can be queried for its data.

In the case where we know in advance that we are expecting a single string, therefore, the code is effectively just the same as the envelope-opening code from earlier in this chapter. In the more general case, however, you would presumably need to be more exploratory. Unfortunately, Apple has not demonstrated how you're supposed to do this, and it seems to me that there is insufficient API for your UIActivityViewController to determine what action extensions the user may have loaded into it, how their returned data is structured, and whether that data is something your app even wants to receive and do something with.

PART III

Some Frameworks

Cocoa supplies numerous specialized optional frameworks. This part of the book explains the basics of some of these frameworks, showing you how to get started, and training you to understand and explore these and related frameworks independently if your app requires a further level of depth and detail.

- Chapter 14 introduces the various iOS means for playing sound files, including audio sessions and playing sounds in the background.
- Chapter 15 describes some basic ways of playing video (movies), along with an introduction to the powerful AV Foundation framework.
- Chapter 16 is about how an app can access the user's music library.
- Chapter 17 is about how an app can access the user's photo library, along with the ability to take photos and capture movies.
- Chapter 18 discusses how an app can access the user's address book.
- Chapter 19 talks about how an app can access the user's calendar data.
- Chapter 20 describes how an app can allow the user to compose and send email and SMS messages and social media posts.
- Chapter 21 explains how an app can display a map, along with custom annotations and overlays. It also talks about how a map can display the user's current location and how to convert between a location and an address.
- Chapter 22 is about how an app can learn where the device is located, how it is moving, and how it is oriented.

Audio

iOS provides various means and technologies for allowing your app to produce, record, and process sound. The topic is a large one, so this chapter can only introduce it; I'll concentrate on basic sound production. You'll want to read Apple's *Multimedia Programming Guide* and *Core Audio Overview*.

None of the classes discussed in this chapter provides any user interface within your application for allowing the user to stop and start playback of sound. You can create your own such interface, and I'll discuss how you can associate the "remote control" buttons with your application. Also, a web view (Chapter 11) supports the HTML 5 <audio> tag; this can be a simple, lightweight way to play audio and to allow the user to control playback. (By default, a web view even allows use of AirPlay.) Alternatively, you could treat the sound as a movie and use the classes discussed in Chapter 15; this can also be a good way to play a sound file located remotely over the Internet.

System Sounds

The simplest form of sound is *system sound*, which is the iOS equivalent of the basic computer "beep." This is implemented through System Sound Services, part of the Audio Toolbox framework; you'll need to `import AudioToolbox`. You'll be calling one of two C functions, which behave very similarly to one another:

AudioServicesPlayAlertSound
> On an iPhone, may also vibrate the device, depending on the user's settings.

AudioServicesPlaySystemSound
> On an iPhone, there won't be an accompanying vibration, but you can specifically elect to have this "sound" *be* a device vibration (by passing kSystemSound-ID_Vibrate as the name of the "sound").

The sound file to be played needs to be an uncompressed AIFF or WAV file (or an Apple CAF file wrapping one of these). To hand the sound to these functions, you'll need a SystemSoundID, which you obtain by calling `AudioServicesCreateSystemSoundID` with an NSURL that points to a sound file. In this example, the sound file is in our app bundle:

```
let sndurl = NSBundle.mainBundle().URLForResource(
    "test", withExtension: "aif")
var snd : SystemSoundID = 0
AudioServicesCreateSystemSoundID(sndurl, &snd)
AudioServicesPlaySystemSound(snd)
```

However, there's a problem with that code: we have failed to exercise proper memory management. We need to call `AudioServicesDisposeSystemSoundID` to release our SystemSoundID. But when shall we do this? `AudioServicesPlaySystemSound` executes asynchronously. So the solution can't be to call `AudioServicesDisposeSystemSoundID` in the next line of the same snippet, because this would release our sound just as it is about to start playing, resulting in silence.

The solution is to implement a sound completion handler, a function that is called when the sound has finished playing. The sound completion handler is specified by calling `AudioServicesAddSystemSoundCompletion`. Unfortunately, this function requires that the actual sound completion handler be supplied as a C function address — which can't be obtained in Swift. The simplest approach is to write a small Objective-C helper class that implements the sound completion handler along with a method returning its address. I call mine SystemSoundHelper:

```
// SystemSoundHelper.h:
#import <UIKit/UIKit.h>
@import AudioToolbox;
@interface SystemSoundHelper : NSObject
- (AudioServicesSystemSoundCompletionProc) completionHandler;
@end
// SystemSoundHelper.m:
@implementation SystemSoundHelper
void soundFinished (SystemSoundID snd, void* context) {
    AudioServicesRemoveSystemSoundCompletion(snd);
    AudioServicesDisposeSystemSoundID(snd);
}
- (AudioServicesSystemSoundCompletionProc) completionHandler {
    return soundFinished;
}
@end
```

Note that in `soundFinished`, when we are about to release the sound, we first release the sound completion handler information applied to it.

Back in Swift, we add a SystemSoundHelper property:

```
let helper = SystemSoundHelper()
```

And our sound-playing code now looks like this:

```
let sndurl = NSBundle.mainBundle().URLForResource(
    "test", withExtension: "aif")
var snd : SystemSoundID = 0
AudioServicesCreateSystemSoundID(sndurl, &snd)
AudioServicesAddSystemSoundCompletion(
    snd, nil, nil, self.helper.completionHandler(), nil)
AudioServicesPlaySystemSound(snd)
```

Audio Session

If your app is going to use a more sophisticated way of producing sound, such as an audio player (discussed in the next section), it must specify a *policy* regarding that sound. This policy will answer such questions as:

- Should sound stop when the screen is locked?
- Should sound interrupt existing sound (being played, for example, by the Music app) or should it be layered on top of it?

Your policy is declared in an *audio session*, which is a singleton AVAudioSession instance created automatically as your app launches. This is part of the AV Foundation framework; you'll need to import AVFoundation. You'll refer to your app's AVAudioSession by way of the class method sharedInstance. This shared audio session instance is actually your pipeline to the part of the system that mediates *all* audio belonging to *all* apps and processes, the *media services daemon*; this daemon must juggle many demands, which is why your app's audio can be affected and even overruled by other apps and external factors.

To declare your audio session's policy, you'll set its *category*, by calling setCategory:withOptions:error:. The basic policies for audio playback are:

Ambient (AVAudioSessionCategoryAmbient)
Your app's audio plays even while Music app music or other background audio is playing, and is silenced by the phone's Silent switch and screen locking.

Solo Ambient (AVAudioSessionCategorySoloAmbient, *the default*)
Your app stops Music app music or other background audio from playing, and is silenced by the phone's Silent switch and screen locking.

Playback (AVAudioSessionCategoryPlayback)
Your app stops Music app music or other background audio from playing, and is *not* silenced by the Silent switch. It is silenced by screen locking, unless it is also configured to play in the background (as explained later in this chapter).

Audio session category options, supplied as the `withOptions:` parameter of `set-Category:withOptions:error:`, allow you to modify the playback policies to some extent (AVAudioSessionCategoryOptions):

Mixable audio

> You can override the Playback policy so as to allow Music app music or other background audio to play (`.MixWithOthers`). Your sound is then said to be *mixable*. If you don't make your sound mixable, then mixable background audio will still be able to play, but non-mixable background audio won't be able to play.

Ducking audio

> You can override a policy that allows Music app music or other background audio to play, so as to *duck* (diminish the volume of) that background audio (`.Duck-Others`). Ducking does *not* depend automatically on whether your app is actively producing any sound; rather, it starts as soon as you turn this override on and remains in place until your audio session is deactivated.

It is common practice to declare your app's initial audio session policy very early in the life of the app, possibly as early as `application:didFinishLaunchingWithOptions:`. You can later, if necessary, change your audio session policy as your app runs.

Your audio session policy is not in effect, however, unless your audio session is also *active*. By default, it isn't. Thus, asserting your audio session policy is done by a combination of configuring the audio session and activating the audio session. To activate (or deactivate) your audio session, you call `setActive:withOptions:error:`.

The question then is *when* to call `setActive:withOptions:error:`. This is a little tricky because of multitasking. Your audio session can be deactivated automatically if your app is no longer active. So if you want your policy to be obeyed under all circumstances, you must explicitly activate your audio session each time your app becomes active. The best place to do this is in `applicationDidBecomeActive:`, as this is the only method guaranteed to be called every time your app is reactivated under circumstances where your audio session might have been deactivated in the background (see Appendix A).

 Apple suggests that you might want to register for AVAudioSessionMediaServices-WereResetNotification. If this notification arrives, the media services daemon was somehow hosed, and your whole audio session has probably been blown away as well. Thus you should activate your audio session in response, as well as resetting and recreating any audio-related objects. See Apple's *Technical Q&A QA1749*.

The first parameter to `setActive:withOptions:error:` is a Bool saying whether we want to activate or deactivate our audio session. There are various reasons why you might deactivate (and perhaps reactivate) your audio session over the lifetime of your app.

One such reason is that you no longer need to hog the device's audio, and you want to yield to other apps to play music in the background. The second parameter to `set-Active:withOptions:error:` lets you supply a single `AVAudioSessionSetActive-Options` option, `.OptionNotifyOthersOnDeactivation` (only when the first parameter is `false`). I'll give an example later in this chapter.

Another reason for deactivating (and reactivating) your audio session is to bring a change of audio policy into effect. A good example is *ducking*. Let's say that, in general, we don't play any sounds, and we want background sound, such as Music app sound, to continue playing while our app runs. So we configure our audio session to use the Ambient policy in `application:didFinishLaunchingWithOptions:`, as follows:

```
AVAudioSession.sharedInstance().setCategory(
    AVAudioSessionCategoryAmbient, withOptions: nil, error: nil)
```

We aren't interrupting any other audio with our Ambient policy, so it does no harm to activate our audio session every time our app becomes active, no matter how, in `applicationDidBecomeActive:`, like this:

```
AVAudioSession.sharedInstance().setActive(
    true, withOptions: nil, error: nil)
```

That's all it takes to set and enforce your app's overall audio session policy. Now let's say we do *sometimes* play a sound, but it's brief and doesn't require background sound to stop entirely; it suffices for background audio to be quieter momentarily while we're playing our sound. That's ducking! So, just before we play our sound, we duck any background sound by changing the options on our Ambient category:

```
AVAudioSession.sharedInstance().setCategory(
    AVAudioSessionCategoryAmbient, withOptions: .DuckOthers, error: nil)
```

When we finish playing our sound, we turn off ducking. This is the tricky part. Not only must we remove the ducking property from our audio session policy, but we must also *deactivate our audio session* to make the change take effect immediately and bring the background sound back to its original level; there is then no harm in reactivating our audio session:

```
let sess = AVAudioSession.sharedInstance()
sess.setActive(false, withOptions: nil, error: nil)
sess.setCategory(
    AVAudioSessionCategoryAmbient, withOptions: nil, error: nil)
sess.setActive(true, withOptions: nil, error: nil)
```

Interruptions

Your audio session can be *interrupted*. This could mean that some other app deactivates it: for example, on an iPhone a phone call can arrive or an alarm can go off. In the multitasking world, it could mean that another app asserts its audio session over yours.

To learn of interruptions, register for AVAudioSessionInterruptionNotification.

To learn whether the interruption began or ended, examine the AVAudioSession-InterruptionTypeKey entry in the notification's userInfo dictionary; this will be a UInt equating to an AVAudioSessionInterruptionType, either .Began or .Ended. So, for example:

```
NSNotificationCenter.defaultCenter().addObserverForName(
    AVAudioSessionInterruptionNotification, object: nil,
    queue: NSOperationQueue.mainQueue(), usingBlock: {
        (note:NSNotification!) in
        let why : AnyObject? =
            note.userInfo?[AVAudioSessionInterruptionTypeKey]
        if let why = why as? UInt {
            if let why = AVAudioSessionInterruptionType(rawValue: why) {
                if why == .Began {
                    // began
                } else {
                    // ended
                }
            }
        }
})
```

When an interruption ends, the userInfo dictionary may also contain an AVAudio-SessionInterruptionOptionKey entry. If so, it will be a UInt whose value, as an AVAudio-SessionInterruptionOptions, may be .OptionShouldResume:

```
let opt : AnyObject? = note.userInfo![AVAudioSessionInterruptionOptionKey]
if let opt = opt as? UInt {
    let opts = AVAudioSessionInterruptionOptions(opt)
    if opts == .OptionShouldResume {
        // ...
    }
}
```

.OptionShouldResume is the flip side of .OptionNotifyOthersOnDeactivation, which I mentioned earlier: some other app that interrupted you has now deactivated its audio session, and is telling you to feel free to resume your audio.

Interruptions are not as intrusive as you might suppose. When your audio session is interrupted, your audio has already stopped and your audio session has been deactivated; you might respond by altering something about your app's user interface to reflect the fact that your audio isn't playing, but apart from this there's no particular work for you to do. When the interruption ends, on the other hand, activating your audio session and possibly resuming playback of your audio might be up to you.

In the multitasking world, when your app switches to the background, your audio is paused (unless your app plays audio in the background, as discussed later in this chapter). Various things can happen when your app comes back to the front:

- If you were playing audio with an audio player (AVAudioPlayer, discussed in the next section), it's possible that the AVAudioPlayer will handle the entire situation: it will automatically reactivate your audio session and resume playing, and *you won't get any interruption notifications*.

- If you're *not* using an AVAudioPlayer, it is likely that being moved into the background will count as an interruption of your audio session. You don't get any notifications while you're suspended in the background, so everything happens at once when your app comes back to the front: at that time, you'll be notified that the interruption began, then notified that it ended, and then your `applicationDid-BecomeActive:` will be called, all in quick succession (and in that order). Make sure that your responses to these events, arriving in a sudden cluster, don't step on each other's toes.

Secondary Audio

When your app is frontmost and the user brings up the control center and uses the Play button to resume the current Music app song, you may get a notification that an interruption began; when the user dismisses the control center, you get `applicationDid-BecomeActive:`, but — even if the user has stopped play of the Music app from the control center — you do *not* get any notification that the interruption has ended (and an AVAudioPlayer does not automatically resume playing).

In previous editions of this book I complained that this seems incoherent. New in iOS 8, however, is another notification that takes care of the situation nicely — `AVAudio-SessionSilenceSecondaryAudioHintNotification`.

This notification, corresponding to a new AVAudioSession Bool property `secondary-AudioShouldBeSilencedHint`, expresses a fine-grained distinction between primary and secondary audio. Apple's example is a game app, where intermittent sound effects are the primary audio, while an ongoing underlying soundtrack is the secondary audio. The idea is that the user might start playing a song from the Music app, and that your app would therefore pause its secondary audio while continuing to produce its primary audio — because the user's chosen Music track will do just as well as a background soundtrack behind your game's sound effects. You'll receive this notification only while your app is *in the foreground* — for example, during exactly the sort of control center–based Music app manipulation I described a moment ago.

To respond to this notification, examine the `AVAudioSessionSilenceSecondaryAudio-HintTypeKey` entry in the notification's `userInfo` dictionary; this will be a UInt equating to an AVAudioSessionSilenceSecondaryAudioHintType, either `.Begin` or `.End`. So, for example:

```
NSNotificationCenter.defaultCenter().addObserverForName(
    AVAudioSessionSilenceSecondaryAudioHintNotification, object: nil,
    queue: NSOperationQueue.mainQueue(), usingBlock: {
        (note:NSNotification!) in
        let why : AnyObject? =
            note.userInfo?[AVAudioSessionSilenceSecondaryAudioHintTypeKey]
        if let why = why as? UInt {
            if let why = AVAudioSessionSilenceSecondaryAudioHintType(
                rawValue:why) {
                    if why == .Begin {
                        // silence secondary audio
                    } else {
                        // resume secondary audio
                    }
            }
        }
    }
})
```

Routing Changes

Your audio is routed through a particular output (and input). The user can make changes in this routing — for example, by plugging headphones into the device, which causes sound to stop coming out of the speaker and to come out of the headphones instead. By default, your audio continues uninterrupted if any is playing, but your code might like to be notified when routing is changed. You can register for AVAudioSessionRoute-ChangeNotification to hear about routing changes.

The notification's userInfo dictionary is chock full of useful information about what just happened. Here's the console display of the dictionary that results when I detach headphones from the device:

```
AVAudioSessionRouteChangeReasonKey: 2,
AVAudioSessionRouteChangePreviousRouteKey:
<AVAudioSessionRouteDescription: 0x17d8e910,
    inputs = (null);
    outputs = (
        "<AVAudioSessionPortDescription: 0x17d76e20,
            type = Headphones;
            name = Headphones;
            UID = Wired Headphones;
            selectedDataSource = (null)>"
    )>
```

Upon receipt of this notification, I can find out what the audio route is now, by calling AVAudioSession's currentRoute method:

```
<AVAudioSessionRouteDescription: 0x17d74ea0,
    inputs = (null);
    outputs = (
        "<AVAudioSessionPortDescription: 0x17d828b0,
            type = Speaker;
```

```
        name = Speaker;
        UID = Built-In Speaker;
        selectedDataSource = (null)>"
    )>
```

The classes mentioned here — AVAudioSessionRouteDescription and AVAudioSession-PortDescription — are value classes (glorified structs). The AVAudioSessionRoute-ChangeReasonKey encodes an AVAudioSessionRouteChangeReason; the value here, 2, is .OldDeviceUnavailable — we stopped using the headphones because there are no headphones any longer.

A routing change may not of itself interrupt your sound, but Apple suggests that in this particular situation you might like to respond by stopping your audio deliberately, because otherwise sound may now suddenly be coming out of the speaker in a public place.

Audio Player

An *audio player* (AVAudioPlayer) is the easiest way to play sounds with any degree of sophistication. A wide range of sound types is acceptable, including MP3, AAC, and ALAC, as well as AIFF and WAV. You can set a sound's volume and stereo pan features, loop a sound, synchronize the playing of multiple sounds simultaneously, change the playing rate, and set playback to begin somewhere in the middle of a sound.

AVAudioPlayer is part of the AV Foundation framework; you'll need to `import AVFoundation`. An audio player should always be used in conjunction with an audio session.

An audio player can possess and play only one sound, but it can play that sound repeatedly, and you can have multiple audio players, possibly playing simultaneously. An audio player is initialized with its sound, using a local file URL or NSData; optionally, the initializer can also state the expected sound file format. To play the sound, first tell the audio player to `prepareToPlay`, causing it to load buffers and initialize hardware; then tell it to `play`. The audio player's delegate (AVAudioPlayerDelegate) is notified when the sound finishes playing (`audioPlayerDidFinishPlaying:successfully:`); do *not* repeatedly check the audio player's `playing` property to learn its state. Other useful methods include `pause` and `stop`; the chief difference between them is that `pause` doesn't release the buffers and hardware set up by `prepareToPlay`, but `stop` does, so you'd want to call `prepareToPlay` again before resuming play. Neither `pause` nor `stop` changes the playhead position, the point in the sound where playback will start if `play` is sent again; for that, use the `currentTime` property.

Devising a strategy for instantiating, retaining, and releasing your audio players is up to you. In one of my apps, I define a class called Player, which implements a `playFile-AtPath:` method expecting a string path to a sound file. This method creates a new AVAudioPlayer, stores it as a property, and tells it to play the sound file; it also sets itself up as that audio player's delegate, and notifies its own delegate when the sound finishes playing (by way of a PlayerDelegate protocol that I also define). In this way, by maintaining a single Player instance, I can play different sounds in succession:

```
var player : AVAudioPlayer!
weak var delegate : PlayerDelegate?
func playFileAtPath(path:String) {
    self.player?.delegate = nil
    self.player?.stop()
    let fileURL = NSURL(fileURLWithPath: path)
    self.player = AVAudioPlayer(contentsOfURL: fileURL, error: nil)
    self.player.prepareToPlay()
    self.player.delegate = self
    self.player.play()
}
func audioPlayerDidFinishPlaying(AVAudioPlayer!, successfully: Bool) {
    self.delegate?.soundFinished(self)
}
```

Here are some useful audio player properties:

pan, volume
> Stereo positioning and loudness, respectively.

numberOfLoops
> How many times the sound should repeat after it finishes playing; 0 (the default) means it doesn't repeat. A negative value causes the sound to repeat indefinitely (until told to stop).

duration
> The length of the sound (read-only).

currentTime
> The playhead position within the sound. If the sound is paused or stopped, play will start at the currentTime. You can set this in order to "seek" to a playback position within the sound.

enableRate, rate
> These properties allow the sound to be played at anywhere from half speed (0.5) to double speed (2.0). Set enableRate to true *before* calling prepareToPlay; you are then free to set the rate.

meteringEnabled
> If true (the default is false), you can call updateMeters followed by averagePowerForChannel: and/or peakPowerForChannel:, periodically, to track how loud the sound is. Presumably this would be so you could provide some sort of graphical representation of this value in your interface.

Figure 14-1. The software remote controls in the control center

settings
> A read-only dictionary describing features of the sound, such as its bit rate (AVEncoderBitRateKey), its sample rate (AVSampleRateKey), and its data format (AVFormatIDKey).

The playAtTime: method allows playing to be scheduled to start at a certain time. The time should be described in terms of the audio player's deviceCurrentTime property.

As I mentioned in the previous section, an audio player handles interruptions seamlessly; in particular, it resumes playing when your app comes to the front if it was playing and was forced to stop playing when your app was moved to the background.

 Delegate methods audioPlayerBeginInterruption: and audioPlayerEnd-Interruption:withOptions: from iOS 7 and before are deprecated in iOS 8. If you need to hear about interruptions, use the AVAudioSession notifications instead.

Remote Control of Your Sound

Various sorts of signal constitute *remote control*. There is hardware remote control; the user might be using earbuds with buttons, for example. There is also software remote control — for example, the playback controls that you see in the control center (Figure 14-1) and in the lock screen (Figure 14-2).

Your app can arrange to be targeted by *remote control events* reporting that the user has tapped a remote control. Your sound-playing app can respond to the remote play/pause button, for example, by playing or pausing its sound.

Remote control events are a form of UIEvent, and they are sent initially to the first responder. To arrange to be a recipient of remote control events:

Figure 14-2. The software remote controls on the locked screen

- Your app must contain a UIResponder in its responder chain that returns `true` from `canBecomeFirstResponder`, and that responder must actually be first responder.

- Some UIResponder in the responder chain, at or above the first responder, must implement `remoteControlReceivedWithEvent:`.

- Your app must call the UIApplication instance method `beginReceivingRemoteControlEvents`.

- Your app's audio session policy must be Playback.

- Your app must emit some sound. The rule is that the running app that is capable of receiving remote control events and that last actually produced sound is the target of remote events. The remote control event target defaults to the Music app if no other app takes precedence by this rule.

A typical place to put all of this is in your view controller, which is, after all, a UIResponder:

```
override func canBecomeFirstResponder() -> Bool {
    return true
}
override func viewDidAppear(animated: Bool) {
    super.viewDidAppear(animated)
    self.becomeFirstResponder()
    UIApplication.sharedApplication().beginReceivingRemoteControlEvents()
}
override func remoteControlReceivedWithEvent(event: UIEvent) {
    // ...
}
```

The question is then how to implement `remoteControlReceivedWithEvent:`. Your implementation will examine the `subtype` of the incoming UIEvent to decide what to do. There are various possible `subtype` values (UIEventSubtype). Earbuds with a central button will probably send `.RemoteControlTogglePlayPause`. In iOS 6 and before, the software remote control play/pause button *used* to send `.RemoteControlTogglePlayPause` as well; starting with iOS 7, however, it now sends `.RemoteControlPlay` or `.RemoteControlPause`. So your code needs to cover all three possibilities at a minimum. Here's an example in an app where sound is produced by an AVAudioPlayer:

```
override func remoteControlReceivedWithEvent(event: UIEvent) {
    let rc = event.subtype
    let p = // our AVAudioPlayer
    switch rc {
    case .RemoteControlTogglePlayPause:
        if p.playing { p.pause() } else { p.play() }
    case .RemoteControlPlay:
        p.play()
    case .RemoteControlPause:
        p.pause()
    default:break
    }
}
```

You can also influence what information the user will see, in the remote control interface, about what's being played. For that, you'll use MPNowPlayingInfoCenter, from the Media Player framework; you'll need to `import MediaPlayer`. Call the class method `defaultCenter` and set the resulting instance's `nowPlayingInfo` property to a dictionary. The relevant keys are listed in the class documentation; they will make more sense after you've read Chapter 16, which discusses the Media Player framework. Here's some example code from my TidBITS News app:

```
let mpic = MPNowPlayingInfoCenter.defaultCenter()
mpic.nowPlayingInfo = [
    MPMediaItemPropertyTitle: self.titleLabel.text,
    MPMediaItemPropertyArtist: self.authorLabel.text
]
```

Playing Sound in the Background

In the multitasking world, when the user switches away from your app to another app, by default, your app is suspended and stops producing sound. But if the business of your app is to play sound, you might like your app to continue playing sound in the background. In earlier sections of this chapter, I've spoken about how your app, in the foreground, relates its sound production to background sound such as the Music app. Now we're talking about how your app can *be* the source of that background sound, possibly playing sound while some other app is in the foreground.

To play sound in the background, your app must do these things:

- In your *Info.plist*, you must include the "Required background modes" key (UIBackgroundModes) with a value that includes "App plays audio" (audio). The simplest way to arrange this is through the checkbox in the Capabilities tab of the target editor (Figure 14-3).

- Your audio session's policy must be active and must be Playback.

Figure 14-3. Using Capabilities to enable background audio

If those things are true, then the sound that your app is playing, when the user clicks the Home button and dismisses your app or switches to another app, will go right on playing. Also, when the screen is locked, your app can continue to play sound only if it is capable of playing sound in the background.

Moreover, your app may be able to start playing in the background even if it was *not* playing previously — namely, if it is mixable (`.MixWithOthers`, see earlier in this chapter), or if it is capable of being the remote control target. Indeed, an extremely cool feature of playing sound in the background is that remote control events continue to work. Even if your app was *not* actively playing at the time it was put into the background, it may nevertheless be the remote control target (because it *was* playing sound earlier, as explained in the preceding section). In that case, if the user causes a remote control event to be sent, your app, if suspended in the background, will be woken up (still in the background) in order to receive the remote control event and can begin playing sound. However, the rules for interruptions still apply; another app can interrupt your app's audio session while your app is in the background, and if that app receives remote control events, then your app is no longer the remote control target.

If your app is the remote control target in the background, then another app can interrupt your app's audio, play some audio of its own, and then deactivate its own audio session with the option telling your app to resume playing. I'll give a minimal example of how this works with an AVAudioPlayer.

Let's call the two apps BackgroundPlayer and Interrupter. Suppose Interrupter has an audio session policy of Ambient. This means that when Interrupter comes to the front, background audio doesn't stop. But now Interrupter wants to play a brief sound of its own, temporarily stopping background audio. To pause the background audio, it sets its own audio session policy to Playback before telling its AVAudioPlayer to play:

```
AVAudioSession.sharedInstance().setCategory(
    AVAudioSessionCategoryPlayback, withOptions: nil, error: nil)
AVAudioSession.sharedInstance().setActive(
    true, withOptions: nil, error: nil)
self.player.prepareToPlay()
self.player.delegate = self
self.player.play()
```

When Interrupter's sound finishes playing, its AVAudioPlayer's delegate is notified. In response, Interrupter deactivates its audio session with the `.OptionNotifyOthersOn-Deactivation` option; then it's fine for it to switch its audio session policy back to Ambient and activate it once again:

```
func audioPlayerDidFinishPlaying(AVAudioPlayer!, successfully: Bool) {
    let sess = AVAudioSession.sharedInstance()
    sess.setActive(
        false, withOptions: .OptionNotifyOthersOnDeactivation, error: nil)
    sess.setCategory(
        AVAudioSessionCategoryAmbient, withOptions: nil, error: nil)
    sess.setActive(true, withOptions: nil, error: nil)
}
```

So much for Interrupter. Now let's turn to BackgroundPlayer, which was playing in the background when Interrupter came along:

When Interrupter changes its audio session policy to Playback
> BackgroundPlayer receives `AVAudioSessionInterruptionNotification` (if registered for it) with `AVAudioSessionInterruptionTypeKey` set to `.Began` — and BackgroundPlayer's AVAudioPlayer *automatically* stops playing.

When Interrupter deactivates its audio session
> BackgroundPlayer receives `AVAudioSessionInterruptionNotification` (if registered for it) with `AVAudioSessionInterruptionTypeKey` set to `.Ended` — but its AVAudioPlayer does *not* automatically resume.

Thus, it is up to BackgroundPlayer to notice that the interruption has ended, and to resume its AVAudioPlayer manually. For example:

```
self.observer = NSNotificationCenter.defaultCenter().addObserverForName(
    AVAudioSessionInterruptionNotification,
    object: nil, queue: NSOperationQueue.mainQueue(), usingBlock: {
        [weak self](n:NSNotification!) in
        let why : AnyObject? =
            n.userInfo?[AVAudioSessionInterruptionTypeKey]
        if let why = why as? UInt {
            if let why = AVAudioSessionInterruptionType(rawValue: why) {
                if why == .Ended {
                    let opt : AnyObject? =
                        n.userInfo![AVAudioSessionInterruptionOptionKey]
                    if let opt = opt as? UInt {
                        let opts = AVAudioSessionInterruptionOptions(opt)
```

```
                    if opts == .OptionShouldResume {
                        self?.player.prepareToPlay()
                        self?.player.play()
                    }
                }
            }
        }
    }
})
```

In that code, when the interruption ends, I examine the secondary `AVAudioSession-InterruptionOptionKey` to see whether it is `.OptionShouldResume`. In this case, it is — because Interrupter deactivated its audio session with the `.OptionNotifyOthersOn-Deactivation` option. Thus, everyone in this story is a good citizen.

An interesting byproduct of your app being capable of playing sound in the background is that while it *is* playing sound, an NSTimer can fire. The timer must have been created and scheduled in the foreground, but after that, it will fire even while your app is in the background, unless your app is currently not playing any sound. This is remarkable, because many other sorts of activity are forbidden when your app is running in the background.

Another byproduct of your app playing sound in the background has to do with app delegate events (see Appendix A). Typically, your app delegate will probably never receive the `applicationWillTerminate:` message, because by the time the app terminates, it will already have been suspended and incapable of receiving any events. However, an app that is playing sound in the background is *not* suspended, even though it is in the background. If it is terminated while playing sound in the background, it will receive `applicationDidEnterBackground:`, even though it has *already* received this event previously when it was moved into the background, and then it *will* receive `applicationWillTerminate:`. This is one of the few situations in which `application-WillTerminate:` is sent to an app in the modern multitasking world.

AVAudioEngine

New in iOS 8 is AVAudioEngine, which is modeled after a mixer board. You can construct and manipulate a graph of sound-producing objects in real time, varying their relative volumes and other attributes, mixing them down to a single sound (which can optionally be recorded into a file as it plays). This is a deep topic; I'll just provide an introductory overview.

The key classes are:

AVAudioEngine
> The overall engine object, representing the world in which everything else happens. You'll probably make and retain just one. Its chief jobs are:

- To connect and disconnect *nodes* (AVAudioNode), analogous to patch cords on a mixer board. The engine has three built-in nodes: its `inputNode`, its `outputNode`, and its `mixerNode`.

- To start and stop the production of sound.

AVAudioNode

An abstract class embracing the various types of object for producing, processing, and receiving sound in the mixer. An audio node has inputs and outputs, and may optionally be given a *tap*, a buffer through which the node's sound can be analyzed and recorded. Some subclasses are:

AVAudioMixerNode

A node with an output volume; it mixes its inputs down to a single output. The AVAudioEngine's built-in `mixerNode` is an AVAudioMixerNode.

AVAudioIONode

A node that patches through to the system's (device's) own input (AVAudio-InputNode) or output (AVAudioOutputNode). The AVAudioEngine's built-in `inputNode` and `outputNode` are AVAudioIONodes.

AVAudioPlayerNode

A node that produces sound, analogous to an AVAudioPlayer. It can play from a file or from a buffer.

AVAudioUnit

A node that processes its input with special effects before passing it to the output. Built-in subclasses include:

AVAudioUnitTimePitch

Independently changes the pitch and rate of the input.

AVAudioUnitVarispeed

Changes the pitch and rate of the input together.

AVAudioUnitDelay

Adds to the input a delayed version of itself.

AVAudioUnitDistortion

Adds distortion to the input.

AVAudioUnitEQ

Constructs an equalizer, for processing different frequency bands separately.

AVAudioUnitReverb

Adds a reverb effect to the input.

Just to give an idea of what working with AVAudioEngine looks like, I'll start by simply playing a file. We need an AVAudioPlayerNode and an AVAudioFile. We hand the AVAudioPlayerNode to the engine and patch it to the engine's built-in mixer node. (In this simple case, we could have patched the player node to the engine's output node; but the engine's mixer node is already patched to the output node, so it makes no difference.) We associate the file with the player node and start the engine running. Finally, we tell the player node to play:

```
let player = AVAudioPlayerNode()
let url = NSBundle.mainBundle().URLForResource(
    "aboutTiagol", withExtension: "m4a")
let f = AVAudioFile(forReading: url, error: nil)
let mixer = engine.mainMixerNode
engine.attachNode(player)
engine.connect(player, to: mixer, format: f.processingFormat)
player.scheduleFile(f, atTime: nil, completionHandler:nil)
engine.prepare()
engine.startAndReturnError(nil)
player.play()
```

You can also play sound from a buffer. This is a little more involved, but not much. Here, I'll start with an AVAudioFile again, but this time I'll feed it into a buffer; this allows me to do a little trickery, such as cutting out everything but the first third of the file:

```
let url2 = NSBundle.mainBundle().URLForResource(
    "Hooded", withExtension: "mp3")
let f2 = AVAudioFile(forReading: url2, error: nil)
let buffer = AVAudioPCMBuffer(
    PCMFormat: f2.processingFormat, frameCapacity: UInt32(f2.length/3))
f2.readIntoBuffer(buffer, error: nil)
let player2 = AVAudioPlayerNode()
engine.attachNode(player2)
let mixer = engine.mainMixerNode
engine.connect(player2, to: mixer, format: f2.processingFormat)
player2.scheduleBuffer(
    buffer, atTime: nil, options: nil, completionHandler: nil)
engine.prepare()
engine.startAndReturnError(nil)
player2.play()
```

So far, we've done virtually nothing that we couldn't have done with an AVAudioPlayer. But now let's start patching some more nodes into the graph. I'll play both files simultaneously; I'll pass the first sound through a time-pitch effect node and then through a reverb effect node; I'll loop the second sound; and I'll set the volumes and pan positions of the sounds:

```
// first sound
let player = AVAudioPlayerNode()
let url = NSBundle.mainBundle().URLForResource(
    "aboutTiagol", withExtension: "m4a")
let f = AVAudioFile(forReading: url, error: nil)
```

```
engine.attachNode(player)
// add some effect nodes to the chain
let effect = AVAudioUnitTimePitch()
effect.rate = 0.9
effect.pitch = -300
engine.attachNode(effect)
engine.connect(player, to: effect, format: f.processingFormat)
let effect2 = AVAudioUnitReverb()
effect2.loadFactoryPreset(.Cathedral)
effect2.wetDryMix = 40
engine.attachNode(effect2)
engine.connect(effect, to: effect2, format: f.processingFormat)
// patch last node into engine mixer and start playing first sound
let mixer = engine.mainMixerNode
engine.connect(effect2, to: mixer, format: f.processingFormat)
player.scheduleFile(f, atTime: nil, completionHandler:nil)
engine.prepare()
engine.startAndReturnError(nil)
player.play()
// second sound; loop it this time
let url2 = NSBundle.mainBundle().URLForResource(
    "Hooded", withExtension: "mp3")
let f2 = AVAudioFile(forReading: url2, error: nil)
let buffer = AVAudioPCMBuffer(
    PCMFormat: f2.processingFormat, frameCapacity: UInt32(f2.length/3))
f2.readIntoBuffer(buffer, error: nil)
let player2 = AVAudioPlayerNode()
engine.attachNode(player2)
engine.connect(player2, to: mixer, format: f2.processingFormat)
player2.scheduleBuffer(
    buffer, atTime: nil, options: .Loops, completionHandler: nil)
// mix down a little, start playing second sound
player.pan = -0.5
player2.volume = 0.5
player2.pan = 0.5
player2.play()
```

Finally, I'll demonstrate how to patch the sound produced from one file into a new file. This is done by installing a tap on a node to collect its sound into a buffer and writing the buffer into a file. When I started writing this example, I was hoping that the processing would be done rapidly in the background, but that's not how AVAudioEngine works: you have to play the sound in real time.

So, I'll pass a sound file through a reverb effect and patch the output into a new file. The most interesting challenge in this example turned out to be knowing when to stop! You can't just stop when the original input file buffer empties, because the reverb effect has yet to finish fading away. To know when that happens, I watch for the last output buffer value to become very small:

```
let url2 = NSBundle.mainBundle().URLForResource(
    "Hooded", withExtension: "mp3")
let f2 = AVAudioFile(forReading: url2, error: nil)
let buffer = AVAudioPCMBuffer(
    PCMFormat: f2.processingFormat, frameCapacity: UInt32(f2.length/3))
f2.readIntoBuffer(buffer, error: nil)
let player2 = AVAudioPlayerNode()
engine.attachNode(player2)
let effect = AVAudioUnitReverb()
effect.loadFactoryPreset(.Cathedral)
effect.wetDryMix = 40
engine.attachNode(effect)
engine.connect(player2, to: effect, format: f2.processingFormat)
let mixer = engine.mainMixerNode
engine.connect(effect, to: mixer, format: f2.processingFormat)
// create the output file
let fm = NSFileManager.defaultManager()
let doc = fm.URLForDirectory(
    .DocumentDirectory, inDomain: .UserDomainMask,
    appropriateForURL: nil, create: true, error: nil)
let outurl = doc!.URLByAppendingPathComponent("myfile.aac")
var err : NSError?
let outfile = AVAudioFile(forWriting: outurl, settings: [
    AVFormatIDKey : kAudioFormatMPEG4AAC,
    AVNumberOfChannelsKey : 1,
    AVSampleRateKey : 22050,
    AVEncoderBitRatePerChannelKey : 16
    ], error: &err)
// install a tap on the reverb effect node
var done = false // flag: don't stop until input buffer is empty!
effect.installTapOnBus(0, bufferSize: 4096,
    format: outfile.processingFormat, block: {
        (buffer : AVAudioPCMBuffer!, time : AVAudioTime!) in
        let dataptrptr = buffer.floatChannelData
        let dataptr = dataptrptr.memory
        let datum = dataptr[Int(buffer.frameLength) - 1]
        // stop when input is empty and sound is very quiet
        if done && fabs(datum) < 0.000001 {
            self.engine.stop()
            return
        }
        var err : NSError?
        let ok = outfile.writeFromBuffer(buffer, error:&err)
        if !ok {
            println(err)
        }
    })
player2.scheduleBuffer(buffer, atTime: nil, options: nil,
    completionHandler: {
        done = true // raise flag: input buffer is empty!
```

```
})
engine.prepare()
engine.startAndReturnError(nil)
player2.play()
```

As I've said, there's much more to know about AVAudioEngine, but that should suffice to suggest some of the possibilities.

Speech Synthesis

Text can be transformed into synthesized speech. This can be extremely easy to do, using the AVSpeechUtterance and AVSpeechSynthesizer classes. In this example, I also use the AVSpeechSynthesisVoice class to make sure the device speaks the text in English, regardless of the user's language settings:

```
let utter = AVSpeechUtterance(string:"Polly, want a cracker?")
let v = AVSpeechSynthesisVoice(language: "en-US")
utter.voice = v
self.talker.delegate = self
self.talker.speakUtterance(utter)
```

You can also set the speech rate. The delegate (AVSpeechSynthesizerDelegate) is told when the speech starts, when it comes to a new range of text (usually a word), and when it finishes.

Further Topics in Sound

iOS is a powerful milieu for production and processing of sound; its sound-related technologies are extensive. This is a big topic, and an entire book could be written about it (in fact, such books do exist). I'll talk in Chapter 16 about accessing sound files in the user's music library. But here are some further topics that there is no room to discuss here:

Other audio session policies

If your app accepts sound input or does audio processing, you'll want to look into additional audio session policies I didn't talk about earlier — Record, Play and Record, and Audio Processing. In addition, if you're using Record or Play and Record, there are modes — voice chat, video recording, and measurement (of the sound being input) — that optimize how sound is routed (for example, what microphone is used) and how it is modified.

Your app must obtain the user's permission to use the microphone. This permission will be requested on your behalf when you adopt a Record audio session policy. You can modify the body of the system alert by setting the "Privacy — Microphone Usage Description" key (NSMicrophoneUsageDescription) in your app's *Info.plist*. New in iOS 8, you can learn whether permission has been granted by calling the audio session's recordPermission method.

Recording sound
> To record sound simply, use AVAudioRecorder. Your audio session policy will need to adopt a Record policy before recording begins.

Audio queues
> Audio queues implement sound playing and recording through a C API with more granularity than the Objective-C AVAudioPlayer and AVAudioRecorder (though it is still regarded as a high-level API), giving you access to the buffers used to move chunks of sound data between a storage format (a sound file) and sound hardware.

Extended Audio File Services
> A C API for reading and writing sound files in chunks. It is useful in connection with technologies such as audio queues.

Audio Converter Services
> A C API for converting sound files between formats.

Streaming audio
> Audio streamed in real time over the network, such as an Internet radio station, can be played with Audio File Stream Services, in connection with audio queues.

OpenAL
> An advanced technology for playing sound with fine control over its stereo stage and directionality.

Audio units
> Plug-ins that filter and modify the nature and quality of a sound as it passes through them. See the *Audio Unit Hosting Guide for iOS*.

MIDI
> The CoreMIDI framework allows interaction with MIDI devices. The Audio Toolbox framework allows you to play a MIDI file, possibly passing it through an AU-Graph that uses the AUSampler audio unit to produce synthesized sound.

Sound sharing
> Sound generated or processed by one app can be streamed to and recorded by another app.

CHAPTER 15

Video

Video playback is performed using classes such as AVPlayer provided by the AV Foundation framework (`import AVFoundation`). An AVPlayer is not a view; rather, an AVPlayer's content is made visible through a CALayer subclass, AVPlayerLayer, which can be added to your app's interface.

New in iOS 8, an AV Foundation video playback interface can be wrapped in a simple view controller, AVPlayerViewController, provided by the AVKit framework (`import AVKit`): you provide an AVPlayer, and the AVPlayerViewController *automatically* hosts an associated AVPlayerLayer in its own main view, providing standard playback transport controls so that the user can start and stop play, seek to a different frame, and so forth.

AVPlayerViewController effectively supersedes the Media Player framework's MPMoviePlayerController and MPMoviePlayerViewController, which are not discussed in this edition.

A simple interface for letting the user trim video (UIVideoEditorController) is also supplied. Sophisticated video editing can be performed through the AV Foundation framework, as I'll demonstrate later in this chapter.

If an AVPlayer produces sound, you may need to concern yourself with your application's audio session; see Chapter 14. AVPlayer deals gracefully with the app being sent into the background: it will pause when your app is backgrounded and resume when your app returns to the foreground.

A movie file can be in a standard movie format, such as *.mov* or *.mp4*, but it can also be a sound file. An AVPlayerViewController is thus an easy way to play a sound file, including a sound file obtained in real time over the Internet, along with standard controls for pausing the sound and moving the playhead — unlike AVAudioPlayer, which, as I pointed out in Chapter 14, lacks a user interface.

A mobile device does not have unlimited power for decoding and presenting video in real time. A video that plays on your computer might not play at all on an iOS device. See the "Media Layer" chapter of Apple's *iOS Technology Overview* for a list of specifications and limits within which video is eligible for playing.

A web view (Chapter 11) supports the HTML 5 <video> tag. This can be a simple lightweight way to present video and to allow the user to control playback. Both web view video and AVPlayer support AirPlay.

AVPlayerViewController

An AVPlayerViewController, new in iOS 8, is a view controller; thus, you already know how to display its view. There are two main approaches:

Fullscreen AVPlayerViewController
> Create an AVPlayerViewController and add it to your view controller hierarchy, typically as a presented view controller or pushed onto a navigation controller's stack.

Embedded AVPlayerViewController
> Structure your own view controller as a custom container view controller, make an AVPlayerViewController its child view controller, and place the AVPlayerViewController's view manually into your own view controller's view.

 You can instantiate an AVPlayerViewController from a storyboard; look for the AVKit Player View Controller object in the Object library. However, you will then need to link your target manually to the AVKit framework: edit the target and add *AVKit.framework* under Linked Frameworks and Libraries in the General tab.

Fullscreen AVPlayerViewController

The absolute rock-bottom simplest way to display video is to use an AVPlayerViewController as a presented view controller. All you need to know is that an AVPlayerViewController must be assigned a player, which is an AVPlayer, and that an AVPlayer can be initialized directly from the URL of the video it is to play, with init(URL:). In this example, I present a video from the app bundle:

```
let av = AVPlayerViewController()
let url = NSBundle.mainBundle().URLForResource(
    "ElMirage", withExtension: "mp4")
let player = AVPlayer(URL: url)
av.player = player
self.presentViewController(av, animated: true, completion: nil)
```

Figure 15-1. A presented AVPlayerViewController

The resulting view is intelligently adapted to its environment. It knows that it's being shown as a presented view controller's view, so it provides fullscreen video controls, including a Done button which *automatically dismisses the presented view controller.* Thus, there is literally no further work for you to do.

Figure 15-1 shows a presented AVPlayerViewController. Exactly what controls you'll see depends on the circumstances; in my case, at the top there's the Done button, the current playhead position slider, and the expand/contract button, and at the bottom there are the three standard transport buttons and a volume slider. (If my network were more interesting, we would also see an AirPlay button.) The user can hide or show the controls by tapping the video, and can expand or contract the video by double-tapping it.

The black color of the background is the `backgroundColor` of the AVPlayerView-Controller's view, which you are free to change.

If the movie file is in fact a sound file, the central region is replaced by a QuickTime symbol, and the controls can't be hidden (Figure 15-2).

Instead of presenting an AVPlayerViewController, you might push it onto a navigation controller's stack. Again, the AVPlayerViewController behaves intelligently. There is now no Done button. Instead, the lower controls include a fullscreen button. Tapping the fullscreen button results in almost exactly the same interface shown in Figure 15-1: the view is displayed fullscreen, and its controls then include a Done button which exits fullscreen mode.

Figure 15-2. A presented AVPlayerViewController with a sound file

Embedded AVPlayerViewController

If you want the convenience and the control interface that come from using an AV-PlayerViewController, while displaying its view as a *subview* of your own view controller's view, make your view controller a parent view controller and add the AVPlayer-ViewController's view in good order:

```
let url = NSBundle.mainBundle().URLForResource(
    "ElMirage", withExtension:"mp4")
let player = AVPlayer(URL:url)
let av = AVPlayerViewController()
av.player = player
av.view.frame = CGRectMake(10,10,300,200)
self.addChildViewController(av)
self.view.addSubview(av.view)
av.didMoveToParentViewController(self)
```

Once again, the AVPlayerViewController behaves intelligently, reducing its controls to a minimum to adapt to the reduced size of its view. On my device, at the given view size, there is room for a play button, a playhead position slider, a full-screen button, and nothing else (Figure 15-3). However, the user can enter full-screen mode, either by tapping the full-screen button or by pinching outwards on the video view, and now the full complement of controls is present.

Other AVPlayerViewController Properties

An AVPlayerViewController has very few properties:

Figure 15-3. An embedded AVPlayerViewController's view

`player`

The view controller's AVPlayer, whose AVPlayerLayer will be hosted in the view controller's view. You can set the `player` while the view is visible, to change what video it displays (though you are more likely to keep the `player` and tell *it* to change the video). It is legal to assign an AVQueuePlayer, an AVPlayer subclass; an AVQueuePlayer has multiple items, and the AVPlayerViewController will treat these as chapters of the video. (I'll give an example of using an AVQueuePlayer in Chapter 16.)

`showsPlaybackControls`

If `false`, the controls are hidden. This could be useful, for example, if you want to display a video for decorative purposes, or if you are substituting your own controls.

`contentOverlayView`

A UIView to which you are free to add subviews. These subviews will appear overlaid in front of the video but behind the playback controls.

`videoGravity`

How the video should be positioned within the view. Possible values are:

- `AVLayerVideoGravityResizeAspect` (the default)
- `AVLayerVideoGravityResizeAspectFill`
- `AVLayerVideoGravityResize` (fills the view, possibly distorting the video)

`videoBounds`
`readyForDisplay`

The video position within the view, and the ability of the video to display its first frame and start playing, respectively. If the video is not ready for display, we probably don't yet know its bounds either. In any case, `readyForDisplay` will initially be `false` and the `videoBounds` will initially be reported as `CGRectZero`. This is because, with video, things take time to prepare. I'll discuss this further in a moment.

Everything else there is to know about an AVPlayerViewController comes from its player, an AVPlayer. Thus, it is now time to turn to AVPlayer and some related basic AV Foundation classes.

Introducing AV Foundation

The video display performed by AVPlayerViewController is supplied by classes from the AV Foundation framework. This is a big framework with a lot of classes; the *AV Foundation Framework Reference* lists about 130 classes and 20 protocols. This may seem daunting, but there's a good reason for it: video has a lot of structure and can be manipulated in many ways, and AV Foundation very carefully and correctly draws all the distinctions needed for good object-oriented encapsulation.

Because AV Foundation is so big, all I can do here is introduce it. I'll point out some of the principal classes, features, and techniques associated with video. Further AV Foundation examples will appear in Chapters 16 and 17. Eventually you'll want to read Apple's *AV Foundation Programming Guide* for a full overview.

Some AV Foundation Classes

The heart of AV Foundation video playback is AVPlayer. It is not a UIView; rather, it is the locus of video transport (and the actual video, if shown, appears in an AVPlayerLayer associated with the AVPlayer). For example, AVPlayerViewController provides a play button, but what if you wanted to start video playback in code? You'd tell the AVPlayer-ViewController's player (an AVPlayer) to play.

An AVPlayer's video is its currentItem, an AVPlayerItem. This may come as a surprise, because in the examples earlier in this chapter we initialized an AVPlayer directly from a URL, with no reference to any AVPlayerItem. That, however, was just a shortcut. AVPlayer's *real* initializer is init(playerItem:); when we called init(URL:), the AVPlayerItem was created for us.

An AVPlayerItem, too, can be initialized from a URL with init(URL:), but again, this is just a shortcut. AVPlayerItem's *real* initalizer is init(asset:), which takes an AVAsset. An AVAsset is an actual video resource, and comes in one of two subclasses:

AVURLAsset
  An asset specified through an NSURL.

AVComposition
  An asset constructed by editing video in code. I'll give an example later in this chapter.

Thus, to configure an AVPlayer using the complete "stack" of objects that constitute it, you could say something like this:

```
let url = NSBundle.mainBundle().URLForResource(
    "ElMirage", withExtension:"mp4")
let asset = AVURLAsset(URL:url, options:nil)
let item = AVPlayerItem(asset:asset)
let player = AVPlayer(playerItem:item)
```

Once an AVPlayer exists and has an AVPlayerItem, that player item's tracks, as seen from the player's perspective, are AVPlayerItemTrack objects, which can be individually enabled or disabled. That's different from an AVAssetTrack, which is a fact about an AVAsset. This distinction is a good example of what I said earlier about how AV Foundation encapsulates its objects correctly: an AVAssetTrack is a hard and fast reality, but an AVPlayerItemTrack lets a track be manipulated for purposes of playback on a particular occasion.

Another important use of an AVPlayerItem is as the locus of information about the arrival and playback of an AVAsset from across the network. Properties such as playbackLikelyToKeepUp and accessLog, along with notifications such as AVPlayer-ItemPlaybackStalledNotification, can be helpful in keeping you abreast of any issues.

Things Take Time

Working with video is time-consuming. Just because you give an AVPlayer a command or set a property doesn't mean that reaction time is immediate. All sorts of operations, from reading a video file and learning its metadata to transcoding and saving a video file, take a significant amount of time. The user interface must not freeze while a video task is in progress, so AV Foundation relies heavily on threading (Chapter 25). In this way, AV Foundation covers the complex and time-consuming nature of its operations; but your code must cooperate. You'll frequently use key–value observing and callbacks to run your code at the right moment.

Here's a simple example. There's an elementary interface flaw in the code presented earlier for displaying an embedded video:

```
let url = NSBundle.mainBundle().URLForResource(
    "ElMirage", withExtension:"mp4")
let player = AVPlayer(URL:url)
let av = AVPlayerViewController()
av.player = player
av.view.frame = CGRectMake(10,10,300,200)
self.addChildViewController(av)
self.view.addSubview(av.view)
av.didMoveToParentViewController(self)
```

The problem is that the AVPlayerViewController's view is appearing in the interface when the video is not yet ready for display — resulting in a visible, rather nasty flash when the video *is* ready for display. To prevent this flash, let's start with the AVPlayer-ViewController's view hidden and not show it until readyForDisplay is true.

But how will we know when that is? *Not* by repeatedly polling the `readyForDisplay` property! That sort of behavior is absolutely wrong. Rather, we will use KVO to register as an observer of this property:

```
av.view.frame = CGRectMake(10,10,300,200)
av.view.hidden = true // *
self.addChildViewController(av)
self.view.addSubview(av.view)
av.didMoveToParentViewController(self)
av.addObserver(
    self, forKeyPath: "readyForDisplay", options: nil, context: nil) // *
```

Sooner or later, `readyForDisplay` will become `true`, and we'll be notified. Now we can unregister from KVO and show the AVPlayerViewController's view:

```
override func observeValueForKeyPath(
    keyPath: String, ofObject object: AnyObject,
    change: [NSObject : AnyObject], context: UnsafeMutablePointer<()>) {
        if keyPath == "readyForDisplay",
            let obj = object as? AVPlayerViewController,
            ok = change[NSKeyValueChangeNewKey] as? Bool where ok {
                dispatch_async(dispatch_get_main_queue(), {
                    self.finishConstructingInterface(obj)
                })
        }
    }
}
func finishConstructingInterface (vc:AVPlayerViewController) {
    vc.removeObserver(self, forKeyPath:"readyForDisplay")
    vc.view.hidden = false
}
```

Note that, in that code, I make no assumptions about what thread KVO calls me back on: I intend to operate on the interface, so I step out to the main thread.

In the same way, you can observe an embedded AVPlayerViewController's `video-Bounds` property as a way of learning when the user toggles it into fullscreen mode.

For the sake of efficiency, many AV Foundation object properties are *never* evaluated unless you specifically ask for them. AV Foundation objects that behave this way conform to the AVAsynchronousKeyValueLoading protocol. You call `loadValues-AsynchronouslyForKeys:completionHandler:` for any properties you're going to be interested in. When your `completionHandler:` is called, you check the status of a key and, if its status is `.Loaded`, you are now free to access it.

Here's a rather overblown example (deliberately so, because I want to illustrate asynchronous key loading). In the preceding code, I've been assigning the AVPlayerViewController's view an arbitrary size, thus causing some letterboxing above and below the actual video when it appears. Let's say that I'd like to learn the video's actual size and give the AVPlayerViewController's view the same aspect ratio. An AVAsset has `tracks` (AVAssetTrack); in particular, an AVAsset representing a video has a video track. A video track has a `naturalSize`. Both AVAsset's `tracks` and AVAssetTrack's `naturalSize` are properties that we can load asynchronously.

I'll start by creating the AVAsset and then stop, waiting to hear that its `tracks` property is ready:

```
let url = NSBundle.mainBundle().URLForResource(
    "ElMirage", withExtension:"mp4")
let asset = AVURLAsset(URL:url, options:nil)
asset.loadValuesAsynchronouslyForKeys(["tracks"], completionHandler: {
    let status = asset.statusOfValueForKey("tracks", error: nil)
    if status == .Loaded {
        dispatch_async(dispatch_get_main_queue(), {
            self.getVideoTrack(asset)
        })
    }
})
```

When the `tracks` property is ready, my `getVideoTrack` method is called. I obtain the video track and stop once again, waiting to hear when the video track's `naturalSize` property is ready:

```
func getVideoTrack(asset:AVAsset) {
    let vtrack = asset.tracksWithMediaCharacteristic(
        AVMediaCharacteristicVisual)[0] as! AVAssetTrack
    vtrack.loadValuesAsynchronouslyForKeys(
        ["naturalSize"], completionHandler: {
            let status =
                vtrack.statusOfValueForKey("naturalSize", error: nil)
            if status == .Loaded {
                dispatch_async(dispatch_get_main_queue(), {
                    self.getNaturalSize(vtrack, asset)
                })
            }
        })
}
```

When the `naturalSize` property is ready, my `getNaturalSize` method is called. I get the natural size and use it to finish constructing the AVPlayer and to set AVPlayer-Controller's frame — and the rest is as before:

```
func getNaturalSize(vtrack:AVAssetTrack, _ asset:AVAsset) {
    let sz = vtrack.naturalSize
    let item = AVPlayerItem(asset:asset)
    let player = AVPlayer(playerItem:item)
    let av = AVPlayerViewController()
    av.view.frame = AVMakeRectWithAspectRatioInsideRect(
        sz, CGRectMake(10,10,300,200))
    av.player = player
    // ...
}
```

AVPlayerItem provides another way of loading an asset's properties: initialize it with `init(asset:automaticallyLoadedAssetKeys:)` and observe its `status` using KVO. When that `status` is `.ReadyToPlay`, you are guaranteed that the player item's `asset` has attempted to load those keys, and you can query them just as you would in `loadValues-AsynchronouslyForKeys:completionHandler:`.

Time is Measured Oddly

Another peculiarity of AV Foundation is that time is measured in an unfamiliar way. This is necessary because calculations using an ordinary built-in numeric class such as CGFloat will always have slight rounding errors that quickly begin to matter when you're trying to specify a time within a large piece of media.

Therefore, the Core Media framework (`import CoreMedia`) provides the CMTime class, which under the hood is a pair of integers; they are called the `value` and the `timescale`, but they are simply the numerator and denominator of a rational number. The denominator represents the degree of granularity; a typical value is 600, sufficient to specify individual frames in common video formats.

In the convenience function `CMTimeMakeWithSeconds`, however, the two arguments are *not* the numerator and denominator; they are the time's equivalent in seconds and the denominator. For example, `CMTimeMakeWithSeconds(2.5,600)` yields the CMTime `(1500,600)`.

Constructing Media

AV Foundation allows you to construct your own media asset in code as an AVComposition, an AVAsset subclass, using *its* subclass, AVMutableComposition. An AVMutableComposition is an AVAsset, so given an AVMutableComposition `comp` we could make an AVPlayerItem from it and hand it over to an AVPlayerViewController's player:

```
let item = AVPlayerItem(asset:comp)
let vc = self.childViewControllers[0] as! AVPlayerViewController
let p = vc.player
p.replaceCurrentItemWithPlayerItem(item)
```

Let's try it! In this example, I start with an AVAsset (a video file) and assemble its first 5 seconds of video and its last 5 seconds of video into a new AVAsset:

```
let oldAsset = p.currentItem.asset
let type = AVMediaTypeVideo
let arr = oldAsset.tracksWithMediaType(type)
let track = arr.last as! AVAssetTrack
let duration : CMTime = track.timeRange.duration
let comp = AVMutableComposition()
let comptrack = comp.addMutableTrackWithMediaType(type,
```

```
        preferredTrackID: Int32(kCMPersistentTrackID_Invalid))
comptrack.insertTimeRange(
    CMTimeRangeMake(
        CMTimeMakeWithSeconds(0,600),
        CMTimeMakeWithSeconds(5,600)),
    ofTrack:track, atTime:CMTimeMakeWithSeconds(0,600), error:nil)
comptrack.insertTimeRange(
    CMTimeRangeMake(
        CMTimeSubtract(duration, CMTimeMakeWithSeconds(5,600)),
        CMTimeMakeWithSeconds(5,600)),
    ofTrack:track, atTime:CMTimeMakeWithSeconds(5,600), error:nil)
```

This works perfectly. We are not very good video editors, however, as we have forgotten the corresponding soundtrack. Let's go back and get it and add it to our AVMutableComposition (comp):

```
let type2 = AVMediaTypeAudio
let arr2 = oldAsset.tracksWithMediaType(type2)
let track2 = arr2.last as! AVAssetTrack
let comptrack2 = comp.addMutableTrackWithMediaType(type2,
    preferredTrackID:Int32(kCMPersistentTrackID_Invalid))
comptrack2.insertTimeRange(
    CMTimeRangeMake(
        CMTimeMakeWithSeconds(0,600),
        CMTimeMakeWithSeconds(5,600)),
    ofTrack:track2, atTime:CMTimeMakeWithSeconds(0,600), error:nil)
comptrack2.insertTimeRange(
    CMTimeRangeMake(
        CMTimeSubtract(duration, CMTimeMakeWithSeconds(5,600)),
        CMTimeMakeWithSeconds(5,600)),
    ofTrack:track2, atTime:CMTimeMakeWithSeconds(5,600), error:nil)
```

But wait! Now let's overlay *another* audio track; this might be, for example, some additional narration:

```
let type3 = AVMediaTypeAudio
let s = NSBundle.mainBundle().URLForResource(
    "aboutTiagol", withExtension:"m4a")
let asset = AVURLAsset(URL:s, options:nil)
let arr3 = asset.tracksWithMediaType(type3)
let track3 = arr3.last as! AVAssetTrack
let comptrack3 = comp.addMutableTrackWithMediaType(type3,
    preferredTrackID:Int32(kCMPersistentTrackID_Invalid))
comptrack3.insertTimeRange(
    CMTimeRangeMake(
        CMTimeMakeWithSeconds(0,600),
        CMTimeMakeWithSeconds(10,600)),
    ofTrack:track3, atTime:CMTimeMakeWithSeconds(0,600), error:nil)
```

You can also apply audio volume changes and video opacity and transform changes to the playback of individual tracks. I'll continue from the previous example, applying a fadeout to the last three seconds of the narration track (comptrack3) by creating an AVAudioMix:

```
let params = AVMutableAudioMixInputParameters(track:comptrack3)
params.setVolume(1, atTime:CMTimeMakeWithSeconds(0,600))
params.setVolumeRampFromStartVolume(
    1, toEndVolume:0,
    timeRange:CMTimeRangeMake(
        CMTimeMakeWithSeconds(7,600),
        CMTimeMakeWithSeconds(3,600)))
let mix = AVMutableAudioMix()
mix.inputParameters = [params]
```

The audio mix must be applied to a playback milieu, such as an AVPlayerItem. So when we make an AVPlayerItem out of our AVComposition (comp), as I showed at the start of this section, we can set its audioMix property to mix.

Synchronizing Animation With Video

An intriguing feature of AV Foundation is AVSynchronizedLayer, a CALayer subclass that effectively crosses the bridge between video time (the CMTime within the progress of a movie) and Core Animation time (the time within the progress of an animation). This means that you can coordinate animation in your interface (Chapter 4) with the playback of a movie. You attach an animation to a layer in more or less the usual way, but the animation takes place in movie playback time: if the movie is stopped, the animation is stopped; if the movie is run at double rate, the animation runs at double rate; and the current "frame" of the animation always corresponds to the current frame, within its entire duration, of the video.

The synchronization is performed with respect to an AVPlayer's AVPlayerItem. To demonstrate, I'll draw a long thin gray rectangle containing a little black square; the horizontal position of the black square within the gray rectangle will be synchronized to the movie playhead position:

```
let vc = self.childViewControllers[0] as! AVPlayerViewController
let p = vc.player
let item = p.currentItem
let syncLayer = AVSynchronizedLayer(playerItem:item)
// put synch layer into the interface
syncLayer.frame = CGRectMake(10,220,300,10)
syncLayer.backgroundColor = UIColor.lightGrayColor().CGColor
self.view.layer.addSublayer(syncLayer)
// give synch layer a sublayer
let subLayer = CALayer()
subLayer.backgroundColor = UIColor.blackColor().CGColor
subLayer.frame = CGRectMake(0,0,10,10)
syncLayer.addSublayer(subLayer)
// animate the sublayer
let anim = CABasicAnimation(keyPath:"position")
```

Figure 15-4. The black square's position is synchronized to the movie

```
anim.fromValue = NSValue(CGPoint: subLayer.position)
anim.toValue = NSValue(CGPoint: CGPointMake(295,5))
anim.removedOnCompletion = false
anim.beginTime = AVCoreAnimationBeginTimeAtZero // important trick
anim.duration = CMTimeGetSeconds(item.asset.duration)
subLayer.addAnimation(anim, forKey:nil)
```

The result is shown in Figure 15-4. The gray rectangle is the AVSynchronizedLayer, tied to our movie. The little black square inside it is its sublayer; when we animate the black square, that animation will be synchronized to the movie, changing its position from the left end of the gray rectangle to the right end, starting at the beginning of the movie and with the same duration as the movie. Thus, although we attach this animation to the black square layer in the usual way, that animation is frozen: the black square *doesn't move* until we start the movie playing. Moreover, if we pause the movie, the black square stops. The black square is thus *automatically* representing the current play position within the movie. This may seem a silly example, but if you were to suppress the video controls it could prove downright useful.

AVPlayerLayer

An AVPlayer is not an interface object. The corresponding interface object — an AV-Player made visible, as it were — is an AVPlayerLayer (a CALayer subclass). It has no controls for letting the user play and pause a movie and visualize its progress; it just shows the movie, acting as a bridge between the AV Foundation world of media and the CALayer world of things the user can see.

AVKit and AVPlayerViewController host an AVPlayerLayer for you automatically; otherwise you would not see any video in the AVPlayerViewController's view. But there may certainly be situations where you find AVPlayerViewController too heavyweight, where you don't need the standard transport controls, where you don't want the video to be expandable or to have a fullscreen mode — you just want the simple direct power that can be obtained only by putting an AVPlayerLayer into the interface yourself. And you are free to do so!

Here, I'll display the same movie as before, but without an AVPlayerViewController:

```
let m = NSBundle.mainBundle().URLForResource(
    "ElMirage", withExtension:"mp4")
let asset = AVURLAsset(URL:m, options:nil)
let item = AVPlayerItem(asset:asset)
let p = AVPlayer(playerItem:item)
self.player = p // might need a reference later
let lay = AVPlayerLayer(player:p) // *
lay.frame = CGRectMake(10,10,300,200)
self.view.layer.addSublayer(lay) // *
```

As before, if we want to prevent a flash when the video becomes ready for display, we can postpone adding the AVPlayerLayer to our interface until its readyForDisplay property becomes true — which we can learn through KVO.

The movie is now visible in the interface, but it isn't doing anything. We haven't told our AVPlayer to play, and there are no transport controls, so the user can't tell the video to play either. This is why I kept a reference to the AVPlayer in a property! We can start play either by calling play or by setting the AVPlayer's rate. Here, I imagine that we've provided a simple play/pause button that toggles the playing status of the movie by changing its rate:

```
@IBAction func doButton (sender:AnyObject!) {
    let rate = self.player.rate
    if rate < 0.01 {
        self.player.rate = 1
    } else {
        self.player.rate = 0
    }
}
```

Without trying to replicate the transport controls, we might also like to give the user a way to jump the playhead back to the start of the movie. The playhead position is a feature, not of an AVPlayer, but of an AVPlayerItem:

```
@IBAction func restart (sender:AnyObject!) {
    let item = self.player.currentItem
    item.seekToTime(CMTimeMake(0, 1))
}
```

Further Exploration of AV Foundation

Here are some other things you can do with AV Foundation:

- Extract single images ("thumbnails") from a movie (AVAssetImageGenerator).

- Export a movie in a different format (AVAssetExportSession), or read/write raw uncompressed data through a buffer to or from a track (AVAssetReader, AVAsset-ReaderOutput, AVAssetWriter, AVAssetWriterInput, and so on).

- Capture audio, video, and stills through the device's hardware (AVCaptureSession and so on). I'll say more about this in Chapter 17.

- Tap into video and audio being captured or played, including capturing video frames as still images (AVPlayerItemVideoOutput, AVCaptureVideoDataOutput, and so on; and see Apple's *Technical Q&A QA1702*).

UIVideoEditorController

UIVideoEditorController is a view controller that presents an interface where the user can trim video. Its view and internal behavior are outside your control, and you're not supposed to subclass it. You are expected to treat the view controller as a presented view controller on the iPhone or as a popover on the iPad, and respond by way of its delegate.

 UIVideoEditorController is one of the creakiest pieces of interface in iOS. It dates back to iOS 3.1, and hasn't been revised since its inception — and it looks and feels like it. It has *never* worked properly on the iPad, and still doesn't. I'm going to show how to use it, but I'm not going to explore its bugginess in any depth or we'd be here all day.

Before summoning a UIVideoEditorController, be sure to call its class method canEdit-VideoAtPath:. (This call can take some noticeable time to return.) If this call returns false, don't instantiate UIVideoEditorController to edit the given file. Not every video format is editable, and not every device supports video editing. You must also set the UIVideoEditorController instance's delegate and videoPath before presenting it; the delegate should adopt both UINavigationControllerDelegate and UIVideoEditor-ControllerDelegate. Setting the UIVideoEditorController's modalPresentationStyle to .Popover on the iPad is up to you (a good instance of the creakiness I was just referring to):

```
let path = NSBundle.mainBundle().pathForResource(
    "ElMirage", ofType: "mp4")!
let can = UIVideoEditorController.canEditVideoAtPath(path)
if !can {
    println("can't edit this video")
    return
}
let vc = UIVideoEditorController()
vc.delegate = self
```

```
    vc.videoPath = path
    if UIDevice.currentDevice().userInterfaceIdiom == .Pad {
        vc.modalPresentationStyle = .Popover
    }
    self.presentViewController(vc, animated: true, completion: nil)
    if let pop = vc.popoverPresentationController {
        let v = sender as! UIView
        pop.sourceView = v
        pop.sourceRect = v.bounds
        pop.delegate = self
    }
```

The view's interface (on the iPhone) contains Cancel and Save buttons, a trimming box displaying thumbnails from the movie, a play/pause button, and the movie itself. The user slides the ends of the trimming box to set the beginning and end of the saved movie. The Cancel and Save buttons do *not* dismiss the presented view; you must do that in your implementation of the delegate methods. There are three of them, and you should implement all three and dismiss the presented view in all of them:

- `videoEditorController:didSaveEditedVideoToPath:`

- `videoEditorControllerDidCancel:`

- `videoEditorController:didFailWithError:`

Implementing the second two delegate methods is straightforward:

```
func videoEditorControllerDidCancel(editor: UIVideoEditorController) {
    self.dismissViewControllerAnimated(true, completion: nil)
}
func videoEditorController(editor: UIVideoEditorController,
    didFailWithError error: NSError) {
        println("error: \(error.localizedDescription)")
        self.dismissViewControllerAnimated(true, completion: nil)
}
```

Saving the trimmed video is more involved. Like everything else about a movie, it takes time. When the user taps Save, there's a progress view while the video is trimmed and compressed. By the time the delegate method `videoEditorController:didSaveEdited-VideoToPath:` is called, the trimmed video has *already* been saved to a file in your app's temporary directory (the same directory returned from a call to `NSTemporary-Directory`).

Doing something useful with the saved file at this point is up to you; if you merely leave it in the temporary directory, you can't rely on it to persist. In this example, I copy the edited movie into the user's photo library. That takes time too, so when I call `UISave-VideoAtPathToSavedPhotosAlbum`, I configure a callback to a method that dismisses the editor *after* the saving is over:

```
func videoEditorController(editor: UIVideoEditorController,
    didSaveEditedVideoToPath editedVideoPath: String) {
        if UIVideoAtPathIsCompatibleWithSavedPhotosAlbum(
            editedVideoPath) {
                UISaveVideoAtPathToSavedPhotosAlbum(
                    editedVideoPath, self,
                    "video:savedWithError:ci:", nil)
        } else {
            // need to think of something else to do with it
        }
}
```

In our callback method (here, `video:savedWithError:ci:`), it's important to check for errors, because things can still go wrong. In particular, the user could deny us access to the photo library (see Chapter 17 for more about that). If that's the case, we'll get an NSError whose domain is `ALAssetsLibraryErrorDomain`:

```
func video(video:NSString!, savedWithError error:NSError!,
    ci:UnsafeMutablePointer<()>) {
        if error != nil {
            println("did save, error:\(error)")
        }
        self.dismissViewControllerAnimated(true, completion: nil)
}
```

CHAPTER 16

Music Library

An iOS device can be used for the same purpose as the original iPod — to hold and play music, podcasts, and audiobooks. These items constitute the device's music library. (The relevant guide in Apple's documentation, *iPod Library Access Programming Guide*, preserves a more archaic name.) iOS provides the programmer with various forms of access to the device's music library; you can:

- Explore the music library.
- Play an item from the music library.
- Learn and control what the Music app's music player is doing.
- Present a standard interface for allowing the user to select a music library item.

These abilities are provided by the Media Player framework; you'll need to `import MediaPlayer`.

Exploring the Music Library

Everything in the music library, as seen by your code, is an MPMediaEntity. This is an abstract class that endows its subclasses with the ability to describe themselves through key–value pairs called *properties*.

The property keys have names like `MPMediaItemPropertyTitle`. To fetch a property's value, call `valueForProperty:` with its key. You can fetch multiple properties with `enumerateValuesForProperties:usingBlock:`. Thus, the use of the word "properties" here has nothing to do with object properties; these properties are more like entries in an NSDictionary. However, starting in iOS 7, an MPMediaEntity is endowed with some object properties whose names correspond to the property names. Thus, for example, you can say either `myItem.valueForProperty(MPMediaItemPropertyTitle)` or `myItem.title`.

MPMediaEntity has two concrete subclasses, MPMediaItem and MPMediaCollection. An MPMediaItem is a single item (a "song"). An MPMediaCollection is an ordered list of MPMediaItems, rather like an array; it has a count, and its items property *is* an array.

An MPMediaItem has a type, according to the value of its MPMediaItemPropertyMedia-Type: it might, for example, be music, a podcast, an audiobook, or a video. A media item's properties will be intuitively familiar from your use of iTunes: it has a title, an album title, a track number, an artist, a composer, and so on. Different types of item have slightly different properties; for example, a podcast, in addition to its normal title, has a podcast title.

A playlist is an MPMediaPlaylist, a subclass of MPMediaCollection. Its properties include a title, a flag indicating whether it is a "smart" playlist, and so on.

An item's artwork image is an instance of the MPMediaItemArtwork class, from which you are supposed to be able to get the image itself scaled to a specified size by calling imageWithSize:; my experience is that in reality you'll receive an image of any old size the system cares to give you, so you may have to scale it further yourself. This, for example, is what my Albumen app does:

```
let art : MPMediaItemArtwork = // ...
var im = art.imageWithSize(CGSizeMake(36,36))
if im != nil {
    // it probably *isn't* 36 by 36; scale it so that it is
    let r = AVMakeRectWithAspectRatioInsideRect(
        im.size, CGRectMake(0,0,36,36))
    UIGraphicsBeginImageContextWithOptions(r.size, false, 0)
    im.drawInRect(r)
    im = UIGraphicsGetImageFromCurrentImageContext()
    UIGraphicsEndImageContext()
}
```

Querying the Music Library

Obtaining actual information from the music library requires a *query*, an MPMedia-Query. First, you *form* the query. There are three main ways to do this:

Without limits

> Create a simple MPMediaQuery by calling init. The result is an unlimited query; it asks for everything in the music library.

With a convenience constructor

> MPMediaQuery provides several class methods that form a query ready to ask the music library for a limited subset of its contents — all of its songs, or all of its podcasts, and so on. Here's the complete list:

- songsQuery
- podcastsQuery

- audiobooksQuery

- playlistsQuery

- albumsQuery

- artistsQuery

- composersQuery

- genresQuery

- compilationsQuery

With filter predicates

You can limit a query more precisely by attaching to the query one or more MPMediaPropertyPredicate instances. These predicates filter the music library according to criteria you specify; to be included in the result, a media item must successfully pass through all the filters (in other words, the predicates are combined using logical-and). A predicate is a simple comparison. It has three aspects:

A property

The key to the property you want to compare against. Not every property can be used in a filter predicate; the documentation makes the distinction clear (and you can get additional help from an MPMediaEntity class method, canFilter-ByProperty:).

A value

The value that the property must have in order to pass through the filter.

A comparison type (optional)

An MPMediaPredicateComparison. In order to pass through the filter, a media item's property value can either *match* the value you provide (.EqualTo, the default) or *contain* the value you provide (.Contains).

The two ways of forming a limited query are actually the same; a convenience constructor is just a quick way of obtaining a query already endowed with a filter predicate.

A query also *groups* its results, according to its groupingType (MPMediaGrouping). Your choices are:

- .Title

- .Album

- .Artist

- .AlbumArtist

- .Composer

- .Genre

- `.Playlist`

- `.PodcastTitle`

The query convenience constructors all supply a `groupingType` in addition to a filter predicate. Indeed, the grouping is often the salient aspect of the query. For example, an `albumsQuery` is in fact merely a `songsQuery` with the added feature that its results are grouped by album.

The groups resulting from a query are *collections*; that is, each is an MPMediaItem-Collection. This class, you will recall, is an MPMediaEntity subclass, so a collection has properties. In addition, it has `items` and a `count`. It also has a `representativeItem` property, which gives you just one item from the collection. The reason you need this is that properties of a collection are often embodied in its items rather than in the collection itself. For example, an album has no title; rather, its items have album titles that are all the same. So to learn the title of an album, you ask for the album title of a representative item.

After you form the query, you *perform* the query. You do this simply by asking for the query's results. You can ask either for its `collections` (if you care about the groups returned from the query) or for its `items`. Here, I'll discover the titles of all the albums:

```
let query = MPMediaQuery.albumsQuery()
let result = query.collections as! [MPMediaItemCollection]
// prove we've performed the query, by logging the album titles
for album in result {
    println(album.representativeItem.albumTitle)
}
/*
Output starts like this on my device:
Beethoven Canons
Beethoven Dances
Beethoven Piano Duet
Beethoven Piano Other
Brahms Lieder
...
*/
```

Now let's make our query more elaborate; we'll get the titles of all the albums whose name contains "Beethoven." Observe that what we really do is to ask for all songs whose album title contains "Beethoven" grouped by album; then we learn the album title of a representative item from each resulting collection:

```
let query = MPMediaQuery.albumsQuery()
let hasBeethoven = MPMediaPropertyPredicate(value:"Beethoven",
    forProperty:MPMediaItemPropertyAlbumTitle,
    comparisonType:.Contains)
query.addFilterPredicate(hasBeethoven)
let result = query.collections as! [MPMediaItemCollection]
for album in result {
```

```
    println(album.representativeItem.albumTitle)
}
/*
Output on my device:
Beethoven Canons
Beethoven Dances
Beethoven Piano Duet
Beethoven Piano Other
*/
```

Similarly, we can get the titles of all the albums containing any songs whose name contains "Sonata." To do so, we ask for all songs whose title contains "Sonata" grouped by album; then, as before, we learn the album title of a representative item from each resulting collection:

```
let query = MPMediaQuery.albumsQuery()
let hasSonata = MPMediaPropertyPredicate(value:"Sonata",
    forProperty:MPMediaItemPropertyTitle,
    comparisonType:.Contains)
query.addFilterPredicate(hasSonata)
let result = query.collections as! [MPMediaItemCollection]
for album in result {
    println(album.representativeItem.albumTitle)
}
/*
Output on my device:
Beethoven Piano Duet
Beethoven Piano Other
Scarlatti Complete Sonatas, Vol. I
*/
```

An interesting complication is that the Scarlatti album listed in the results of that example is not actually present on my device. The user's music library can include purchases and iTunes Match songs that are actually off in "the cloud." The user can prevent such songs from appearing in the Music app (in the Settings app, Music → Show All Music → Off), but they are still present in the library, and therefore in the results of our queries.

I'll modify the previous example to list only albums containing "Sonata" songs that are also present on the device. The concept "present on the device" is embodied by MPMediaItemPropertyIsCloudItem. All we have to do is add a second predicate:

```
let query = MPMediaQuery.albumsQuery()
let hasSonata = MPMediaPropertyPredicate(value:"Sonata",
    forProperty:MPMediaItemPropertyTitle,
    comparisonType:.Contains)
query.addFilterPredicate(hasSonata)
let isPresent = MPMediaPropertyPredicate(value:false,
    forProperty:MPMediaItemPropertyIsCloudItem,
    comparisonType:.EqualTo)
query.addFilterPredicate(isPresent)
```

```
let result = query.collections as! [MPMediaItemCollection]
for album in result {
    println(album.representativeItem.albumTitle)
}
/*
Output on my device:
Beethoven Piano Duet
Beethoven Piano Other
*/
```

The results of an `albumsQuery` are actually songs (MPMediaItems). That means we can immediately access any song in any of those albums. Let's modify the output from our previous query to print the titles of all the matching songs in the first album returned, which happens to be the Beethoven Piano Duet album. We don't have to change our query, so I'll start at the point where we perform it; `result` is the array of collections returned from our query:

```
// ... same as before ...
let album = result[0]
for song in album.items as! [MPMediaItem] {
    println(song.title)
}
/*
Output on my device:
Sonata for piano 4-hands in D major Op. 6 - 1. Allegro molto
Sonata for piano 4-hands in D major Op. 6 - 2. Rondo
*/
```

Persistence and Change in the Music Library

One of the properties of an MPMediaEntity is its *persistent ID*, which uniquely identifies this song (MPMediaItemPropertyPersistentID) or playlist (`MPMediaPlaylist-PropertyPersistentID`). No other means of identification is guaranteed unique; two songs or two playlists can have the same title, for example. Using the persistent ID, you can retrieve again at a later time the same song or playlist you retrieved earlier, even across launches of your app. All sorts of things have persistent IDs — entities in general (`MPMediaEntityPropertyPersistentID`), albums, artists, composers, and more.

While you are maintaining the results of a search, the contents of the music library may themselves change. For example, the user might connect the device to a computer and add or delete music with iTunes. This can put your results out of date. For this reason, the library's own modified date is available through the MPMediaLibrary class. Call the class method `defaultMediaLibrary` to get the actual library instance; now you can ask it for its `lastModifiedDate`. You can also register to receive a notification, `MPMedia-LibraryDidChangeNotification`, when the music library is modified. This notification is not emitted unless you first send the library `beginGeneratingLibraryChange-`

Notifications; you should eventually balance this with `endGeneratingLibrary-ChangeNotifications`.

 The library's notion of what constitutes a change can be somewhat incoherent with regard to cloud-based items. For example, the user can explicitly download a cloud song; this can cause `MPMediaLibraryDidChangeNotification` to be triggered numerous times in quick succession.

Music Player

The Media Player framework class for playing an MPMediaItem is MPMusicPlayerController. It comes in two flavors, depending on which class method you use to get an instance:

`systemMusicPlayer`

The global music player — the very same player used by the Music app. This might already be playing an item, or might be paused with a current item, at any time while your app runs; you can learn or change what item this is. The global music player continues playing independently of the state of your app, and the user, by way of the Music app, can at any time alter what it is doing. (The name `systemMusic-Player`, new in iOS 8, supersedes the name `iPodMusicPlayer` from iOS 7 and before, which is deprecated.)

`applicationMusicPlayer`

Plays an MPMediaItem from the music library within your application. The song being played by the `applicationMusicPlayer` can be different from the Music app's current song. This player stops when your app is not in the foreground.

An `applicationMusicPlayer` MPMusicPlayerController is not really inside your app. It is actually the global music player behaving differently. It has its own audio session. You cannot play its audio when your app is in the background. You cannot make it the target of remote control events. If these limitations prove troublesome, use the `systemMusicPlayer` (or some other means of playing the song, as discussed later in this chapter).

A music player doesn't merely play an item; it plays from a *queue* of items. This behavior is familiar from iTunes and the Music app. For example, in iTunes, when you switch to a playlist and double-click the first song to start playing, when iTunes comes to the end of that song, it proceeds by default to the next song in the playlist. So at that moment, its queue is the totality of songs in the playlist. The music player behaves the same way; when it reaches the end of a song, it proceeds to the next song in its queue.

Your methods for controlling playback also reflect this queue-based orientation. In addition to the expected `play`, `pause`, and `stop` commands, there's a `skipToNextItem` and skipToPreviousItem command. Anyone who has ever used iTunes or the Music app (or, for that matter, an old-fashioned iPod) will have an intuitive grasp of this and everything else a music player does. For example, you can also set a music player's repeat-Mode and shuffleMode, just as in iTunes.

You provide a music player with its queue in one of two ways:

With a query
> You hand the music player an MPMediaQuery. The query's items are the items of the queue.

With a collection
> You hand the music player an MPMediaItemCollection. This might be obtained from a query you performed, but you can also assemble your own collection of MPMediaItems in any way you like, putting them into an array and calling init(items:).

In this example, we collect all songs actually present in the library shorter than 30 seconds into a queue and set the queue playing in random order using the application-internal music player:

```
let query = MPMediaQuery.songsQuery()
let isPresent = MPMediaPropertyPredicate(value:false,
    forProperty:MPMediaItemPropertyIsCloudItem,
    comparisonType:.EqualTo)
query.addFilterPredicate(isPresent)
let shorties = (query.items as! [MPMediaItem]).filter {
    let dur = $0.playbackDuration
    return dur < 30
}
if shorties.count == 0 {
    println("no songs that short!")
    return
}
let queue = MPMediaItemCollection(items:shorties)
let player = MPMusicPlayerController.applicationMusicPlayer()
player.setQueueWithItemCollection(queue)
player.shuffleMode = .Songs
player.play()
```

If a music player is currently playing, setting its queue will stop it; restarting play is up to you.

You can ask a music player for its nowPlayingItem, and since this is an MPMediaItem, you can learn all about it through its properties. Unfortunately, you can't query a music player as to its queue, but you can keep your own pointer to the MPMediaItemCollection constituting the queue when you hand it to the music player, and you can ask the music player which song within the queue is currently playing (indexOfNowPlayingItem). The user can completely change the queue of the `systemMusicPlayer`, so if control over the queue is important to you, use the `applicationMusicPlayer`.

A music player has a `playbackState` that you can query to learn what it's doing (whether it is playing, paused, stopped, or seeking). It also emits notifications so you can hear about changes in its state:

- `MPMusicPlayerControllerPlaybackStateDidChangeNotification`
- `MPMusicPlayerControllerNowPlayingItemDidChangeNotification`
- `MPMusicPlayerControllerVolumeDidChangeNotification`

These notifications are not emitted until you tell the music player to `beginGenerating-PlaybackNotifications`. This is an instance method, so you can arrange to receive notifications from just one of the two possible music players. If you do receive notifications from both, you can distinguish them by examining the NSNotification's `object` and comparing it to each player. You should eventually balance this call with `end-GeneratingPlaybackNotifications`.

To illustrate, I'll extend the previous example to set the text of a UILabel in our interface (`self.label`) every time a different song starts playing. Before we start the player playing, we insert these lines to generate the notifications:

```
player.beginGeneratingPlaybackNotifications()
NSNotificationCenter.defaultCenter().addObserver(
    self, selector: "changed:",
    name: MPMusicPlayerControllerNowPlayingItemDidChangeNotification,
    object: player)
self.q = queue // retain a pointer to the queue
```

And here's how we respond to those notifications:

```
func changed(n:NSNotification) {
    self.label.text = ""
    let player = MPMusicPlayerController.applicationMusicPlayer()
    if n.object === player { // just playing safe
        if let title : AnyObject = player.nowPlayingItem?.title {
            if let title = title as? String {
                let ix = player.indexOfNowPlayingItem
                if ix != NSNotFound {
                    self.label.text =
                        "\(ix+1) of \(self.q.count): \(title)"
                }
            }
        }
    }
}
```

There's no periodic notification as a song plays and the current playhead position advances. To get this information, you'll have to resort to polling. This is not objectionable as long as your polling interval is reasonably sparse; your display may occasionally fall a little behind reality, but this won't usually matter. To illustrate, let's add to our existing example a UIProgressView (`self.prog`) showing the current percentage of the current song being played by the music player. I'll use an NSTimer to poll the state of the player every second:

```
self.timer = NSTimer.scheduledTimerWithTimeInterval(
    1, target: self, selector: "timerFired:",
    userInfo: nil, repeats: true)
self.timer.tolerance = 0.1
```

When the timer fires, the progress view displays the state of the currently playing item:

```
func timerFired(_:AnyObject) {
    let player = MPMusicPlayerController.applicationMusicPlayer()
    let item = player.nowPlayingItem
    if item == nil || player.playbackState == .Stopped {
        self.prog.hidden = true
        return
    }
    self.prog.hidden = false
    let current = player.currentPlaybackTime
    let total = item.playbackDuration
    self.prog.progress = Float(current / total)
}
```

The `applicationMusicPlayer` has no user interface, unless you count the remote playback controls (Figure 14-1); if you want the user to have controls for playing and stopping a song, you'll have to create them yourself. The `systemMusicPlayer` has its own natural interface — the Music app.

MPVolumeView

The Media Player framework offers a slider for letting the user set the system output volume, along with an AirPlay route button if appropriate; this is an MPVolumeView. An MPVolumeView works only on a device — not in the Simulator. It is customizable similarly to a UISlider (Chapter 12); you can set the images for the two halves of the track, the thumb, and even the AirPlay route button, for both the normal and the highlighted state (while the user is touching the thumb). You can also customize the image (`volumeWarningSliderImage`) that flashes in the right half of the track when the user tries to exceed the volume limit (set in the Settings app, Music → Volume Limit).

 In my testing, the orange warning flash never appears unless the EU Volume Limit setting is also switched to On (Developer → EU Volume Limit in the Settings app). Presumably this feature works on devices destined for the European Union market, but on my device, the MPVolumeView ignores the Volume Limit from the Settings app.

For further customization, you can subclass MPVolumeView and override `volume-SliderRectForBounds:`. (An additional overridable method is documented, `volume-ThumbRectForBounds:volumeSliderRect:value:`, but in my testing it is never called; I regard this as a bug.)

You can register for notifications when a wireless route (Bluetooth or AirPlay) appears or disappears (`MPVolumeViewWirelessRoutesAvailableDidChangeNotification`) and when a wireless route becomes active or inactive (`MPVolumeViewWirelessRoute-ActiveDidChangeNotification`).

Playing Songs With AV Foundation

MPMusicPlayerController is convenient and simple, but it's also simpleminded. Its audio session isn't your audio session; the music player doesn't really belong to you. An MPMediaItem, however, has an `MPMediaItemPropertyAssetURL` key whose value is a URL. Now everything from Chapters 14 and 15 comes into play.

So, for example, having obtained an MPMediaItem's `MPMediaItemPropertyAssetURL`, you could use that URL to initialize an AVAudioPlayer, an AVPlayer, or an AVAsset. Each of these ways of playing an MPMediaItem has its advantages. For example, an AVAudioPlayer is easy to use, and lets you loop a sound, poll the power value of its channels, and so forth. An AVPlayer assigned to an AVPlayerViewController gives you a built-in play/pause button and playhead slider. An AVAsset gives you the full power of the AV Foundation framework, letting you edit the sound, assemble multiple sounds, perform a fadeout effect, and even attach the sound to a video (and then play it with an AVPlayer).

In this example, I'll use an AVQueuePlayer (an AVPlayer subclass) to play a sequence of MPMediaItems, just as MPMusicPlayerController does:

```
let arr = // array of MPMediaItem
let assets = arr.map {
    let url = $0.assetURL
    let asset = AVAsset.assetWithURL(url) as! AVAsset
    return AVPlayerItem(asset: asset)
}
self.qp = AVQueuePlayer(items:assets)
self.qp.play()
```

That works, but I have the impression, based on something said in one of the WWDC 2011 videos, that instead of adding a whole batch of AVPlayerItems to an AVQueue-Player all at once, you're supposed to add just a few AVPlayerItems to start with and then add each additional AVPlayerItem when an item finishes playing. So I'll start out by adding just three AVPlayerItems, and use key–value observing to watch for changes in the AVQueuePlayer's `currentItem`:

```
let arr = // array of MPMediaItem
self.assets = arr.map {
    let url = $0.assetURL
    let asset = AVAsset.assetWithURL(url) as! AVAsset
    return AVPlayerItem(
        asset: asset, automaticallyLoadedAssetKeys: ["duration"])
    // duration needed later
}
self.total = self.assets.count
let seed = min(3,self.assets.count)
self.qp = AVQueuePlayer(items:Array(self.assets[0..<0+seed]))
self.assets = Array(self.assets[seed..<self.assets.count])
// use .Initial option so that we get an observation for the first item
self.qp.addObserver(
    self, forKeyPath:"currentItem", options:.Initial, context:nil)
self.qp.play()
```

In observeValueForKeyPath:..., we pull an AVPlayerItem off the front of our assets mutable array and add it to the end of the AVQueuePlayer's queue. The AVQueuePlayer itself deletes an item from the start of its queue after playing it, so in this way the queue never exceeds three items in length:

```
let item = self.qp.currentItem
if self.assets.count == 0 {
    return
}
let newItem = self.assets.removeAtIndex(0)
self.qp.insertItem(
    newItem, afterItem:self.qp.items().last as! AVPlayerItem)
```

As long as observeValueForKeyPath:... is notifying us each time a new song starts playing, let's insert some code to update a label's text with the title of each successive song. This will demonstrate how to extract metadata from an AVAsset by way of an AVMetadataItem; in this case, we fetch the AVMetadataCommonKeyTitle and get its value property, as the equivalent of fetching an MPMediaItem's MPMediaItemProperty-Title in our earlier code:

```
self.curnum++
var arr = item.asset.commonMetadata
arr = AVMetadataItem.metadataItemsFromArray(arr,
    withKey:AVMetadataCommonKeyTitle,
    keySpace:AVMetadataKeySpaceCommon)
let met = arr[0] as! AVMetadataItem
met.loadValuesAsynchronouslyForKeys(["value"]) {
    if met.statusOfValueForKey("value", error: nil) == .Loaded {
        dispatch_async(dispatch_get_main_queue()) {
            self.label.text =
                "\(self.curnum) of \(self.total): \(met.value)"
        }
    }
}
```

We can also update a progress view in response to the firing of a timer to reflect the current item's current time and duration. I created the AVPlayerItem with `init(asset:automaticallyLoadedAssetKeys:)` to guarantee that the `duration` property would have attempted to load by now, but it is still necessary to check that it *has* loaded:

```
func timerFired(sender:AnyObject) {
    if let item = self.qp.currentItem {
        let asset = item.asset
        if asset.statusOfValueForKey("duration", error: nil) == .Loaded {
            let cur = self.qp.currentTime()
            let dur = asset.duration
            self.prog.progress =
                Float(CMTimeGetSeconds(cur)/CMTimeGetSeconds(dur))
            self.prog.hidden = false
        }
    } else { // finished!
        self.label.text = ""
        self.prog.hidden = true
        self.timer.invalidate()
    }
}
```

Media Picker

The media picker (MPMediaPickerController), supplied by the Media Player framework, is a view controller whose view is a self-contained interface in which the user can select a media item from the music library, similar to the Music app. You are expected to present the view controller (`presentViewController:animated:completion:`).

You can limit the type of media items displayed by creating the media picker using `init(mediaTypes:)`. You can make a prompt appear at the top of the navigation bar (`prompt`). And you can govern whether the user can choose multiple media items or just one, with the `allowsPickingMultipleItems` property. You can filter out items stored in the cloud by setting `showsCloudItems` to `false`.

While the view is showing, you learn what the user is doing through two delegate methods (MPMediaPickerControllerDelegate); the presented view controller is not automatically dismissed, so it is up to you dismiss it in these delegate methods:

- `mediaPicker:didPickMediaItems:`
- `mediaPickerDidCancel:`

The behavior of the delegate methods depends on the value of the controller's allows-PickingMultipleItems:

The controller's allowsPickingMultipleItems *is* false *(the default)*
> There's a Cancel button. When the user taps a media item, your mediaPicker:did-PickMediaItems: is called, handing you an MPMediaItemCollection consisting of that item; you are likely to dismiss the presented view controller at this point. When the user taps Cancel, your mediaPickerDidCancel: is called.

The controller's allowsPickingMultipleItems *is* true
> There's a Done button. Every time the user taps a media item, it is disabled to indicate that it has been selected. When the user taps Done, mediaPicker:didPick-MediaItems: is called, handing you an MPMediaItemCollection consisting of all items the user tapped. Your mediaPickerDidCancel: is *never* called.

In this example, we put up the media picker; we then play the user's chosen media item(s) with the application's music player. The example works equally well whether allows-PickingMultipleItems is true or false:

```
func presentPicker (sender:AnyObject) {
    let picker = MPMediaPickerController(mediaTypes:.Music)
    picker.delegate = self
    // picker.allowsPickingMultipleItems = true
    self.presentViewController(picker, animated: true, completion: nil)
}
func mediaPicker(mediaPicker: MPMediaPickerController!,
    didPickMediaItems mediaItemCollection: MPMediaItemCollection!) {
        let player = MPMusicPlayerController.applicationMusicPlayer()
        player.setQueueWithItemCollection(mediaItemCollection)
        player.play()
        self.dismissViewControllerAnimated(true, completion: nil)
}
func mediaPickerDidCancel(mediaPicker: MPMediaPickerController!) {
    self.dismissViewControllerAnimated(true, completion: nil)
}
```

On the iPad, the media picker can be displayed as a presented view, and I think it looks best that way. But it also works reasonably well in a popover, especially if we increase its preferredContentSize. This code presents as fullscreen on an iPhone and as a reasonably-sized popover on an iPad:

```
func presentPicker (sender:AnyObject) {
    let picker = MPMediaPickerController(mediaTypes:.Music)
    picker.delegate = self
    picker.allowsPickingMultipleItems = true
    picker.modalPresentationStyle = .Popover
    picker.preferredContentSize = CGSizeMake(500,600)
    self.presentViewController(picker, animated: true, completion: nil)
    if let pop = picker.popoverPresentationController {
        if let b = sender as? UIBarButtonItem {
            pop.barButtonItem = b
        }
    }
}
```

CHAPTER 17

Photo Library and Image Capture

The photos and videos accessed by the user through the Photos app constitute the device's photo library. Your app can give the user an interface for exploring this library through the UIImagePickerController class.

In addition, the Photos framework lets you access the photo library and its contents programmatically — including the ability to modify a photo's image. You'll need to import Photos.

The UIImagePickerController class can also be used to give the user an interface similar to the Camera app, letting the user take photos and videos on devices with the necessary hardware. At a deeper level, the AV Foundation framework (Chapter 15) provides direct control over the camera hardware. You'll need to import AVFoundation (and probably CoreMedia).

Constants such as kUTTypeImage, referred to in this chapter, are provided by the Mobile Core Services framework; you'll need to import MobileCoreServices.

Photo Library Authorization

Access to the photo library requires user authorization. You can use UIImagePicker-Controller without prior authorization, as authorization will be requested for you automatically and the interface works coherently if authorization has been refused. Nevertheless, it is probably good policy for any app that's going to need photo library access to ascertain authorization status at launch time, and to try to obtain authorization if needed. My strategy is to check the authorization status every time the root view controller appears and whenever the app is brought to the foreground:

```
override func viewDidAppear(animated: Bool) {
    super.viewDidAppear(animated)
    self.determineStatus()
    NSNotificationCenter.defaultCenter().addObserver(self,
```

```
            selector: "determineStatus",
            name: UIApplicationWillEnterForegroundNotification,
            object: nil)
    }
```

My `determineStatus` method returns a Bool, even though I'm disregarding the returned value in the preceding code; that way, I can also learn authorization status at *any* time while the app runs. In `determineStatus`, I first ask what our authorization status is. That's done by way of the Photos framework, by calling `PHPhotoLibrary.authorizationStatus()`. There are four possible status responses:

Not determined

Authorization has never been requested. In that case, I explicitly request it by calling `PHPhotoLibrary.requestAuthorization()`, which causes the runtime to present an authorization request alert on our behalf. It is possible to supply a completion handler here, which will be called when the user dismisses the alert; but there is nothing of any particular importance to be learned at this point, since I can always check the status again later, so I don't use a completion handler.

Authorized

There is nothing do; we're already authorized.

Restricted

This means that we have been denied authorization and that the user may not have the power to authorize us. There's no point harassing the user about this, so I do nothing.

Denied

This means that we have been denied authorization. I could do nothing, but it is also reasonable to put up an alert begging for authorization. New in iOS 8, you can now take the user directly to the spot in the Settings app where the user can provide authorization, so I offer to do that.

Here's my `determineStatus` method for the photo library:

```
func determineStatus() -> Bool {
    let status = PHPhotoLibrary.authorizationStatus()
    switch status {
    case .Authorized:
        return true
    case .NotDetermined:
        PHPhotoLibrary.requestAuthorization(nil)
        return false
    case .Restricted:
        return false
    case .Denied:
        let alert = UIAlertController(
            title: "Need Authorization",
            message: "Wouldn't you like to authorize this app " +
```

Figure 17-1. The system prompts for photo library access

```
            "to use your Photo library?",
        preferredStyle: .Alert)
    alert.addAction(UIAlertAction(
        title: "No", style: .Cancel, handler: nil))
    alert.addAction(UIAlertAction(
        title: "OK", style: .Default, handler: {
        _ in
        let url = NSURL(string:UIApplicationOpenSettingsURLString)!
        UIApplication.sharedApplication().openURL(url)
    }))
    self.presentViewController(alert, animated:true, completion:nil)
    return false
    }
}
```

One final bit of preparation is needed: The *Info.plist* should contain some text that the system authorization request alert can use to explain why your app wants access. For the photo library, the relevant key is "Privacy — Photo Library Usage Description" (NSPhotoLibraryUsageDescription). Figure 17-1 shows the authorization request alert containing my (rather bland) usage description:

 To retest the system authorization request alert and other access-related behaviors, go to the Settings app and choose General → Reset → Reset Location & Privacy. This, unfortunately, causes the system to revert to its default settings for *everything* in the Privacy section of Settings: Location Services and all System Services will be On, and all permissions lists will be empty.

Choosing From the Photo Library

UIImagePickerController is a view controller providing an interface in which the user can choose an item from the photo library, similar to the Photos app. You are expected treat the UIImagePickerController as a presented view controller (by calling present-ViewController:animated:completion:). You can use a popover on the iPad, but it looks good as a fullscreen presented view.

The documentation claims that a fullscreen presented view is forbidden on the iPad; this is not true (though it was true in early versions of iOS).

To let the user choose an item from the photo library, instantiate UIImagePicker-Controller and assign its `sourceType` one of these values (UIImagePickerController-SourceType):

`.PhotoLibrary`
> The user is shown a table of all albums, and can navigate into any of them.

`.SavedPhotosAlbum`
> In theory, the user is confined to the contents of the Camera Roll album. In reality, in iOS 8, the interface is called Moments and all photos are shown (I regard this as an atrocious bug).

You should call the class method `isSourceTypeAvailable:` beforehand; if it doesn't return `true`, don't present the controller with that source type.

You'll probably want to specify an array of `mediaTypes` you're interested in. This array will usually contain `kUTTypeImage`, `kUTTypeMovie`, or both; or you can specify all available types by calling the class method `availableMediaTypesForSourceType:`.

After doing all of that, and having supplied a delegate (adopting UIImagePicker-ControllerDelegate and UINavigationControllerDelegate), present the UIImagePicker-Controller:

```
let src = UIImagePickerControllerSourceType.SavedPhotosAlbum
let ok = UIImagePickerController.isSourceTypeAvailable(src)
if !ok {
    println("alas")
    return
}
let arr = UIImagePickerController.availableMediaTypesForSourceType(src)
if arr == nil {
    println("no available types")
    return
}
let picker = UIImagePickerController()
picker.sourceType = src
picker.mediaTypes = arr!
picker.delegate = self
self.presentViewController(picker, animated: true, completion: nil)
```

If authorization has not been granted, the UIImagePickerController is presented, but it will be empty (with a reminder that the user has denied your app access to the photo library) and the user won't be able to do anything but cancel (Figure 17-2). Thus, your code is unaffected.

Figure 17-2. The image picker, when the user has denied access

The delegate will receive one of these messages:

- `imagePickerController:didFinishPickingMediaWithInfo:`
- `imagePickerControllerDidCancel:`

If a UIImagePickerControllerDelegate method is not implemented, the view controller is dismissed automatically at the point where that method would be called; but rather than relying on this, you should probably implement both delegate methods and dismiss the view controller yourself in each.

The `didFinish...` method is handed a dictionary of information about the chosen item. The keys in this dictionary depend on the media type:

An image
The keys are:

`UIImagePickerControllerMediaType`
A UTI; probably `"public.image"`, which is the same as `kUTTypeImage`.

`UIImagePickerControllerReferenceURL`
An asset URL pointing to the *original* image file in the library.

`UIImagePickerControllerOriginalImage`
A UIImage. This is the output you are expected to use. For example, you might display it in a UIImageView.

A movie
The keys are:

`UIImagePickerControllerMediaType`
A UTI; probably `"public.movie"`, which is the same as `kUTTypeMovie`.

UIImagePickerControllerReferenceURL

An asset URL pointing to the *original* movie file in the library.

UIImagePickerControllerMediaURL

A file URL to a copy of the movie saved into a temporary directory. This is the output you are expected to use. For example, you might display it in an AV-PlayerViewController's view or an AVPlayerLayer (Chapter 15).

Optionally, you can set the view controller's allowsEditing to true. In the case of an image, the interface then allows the user to scale the image up and to move it so as to be cropped by a preset rectangle; the dictionary will include two additional keys:

UIImagePickerControllerCropRect

An NSValue wrapping a CGRect.

UIImagePickerControllerEditedImage

A UIImage. This becomes the image you are expected to use.

In the case of a movie, if the view controller's allowsEditing is true, the user can trim the movie just as with a UIVideoEditorController (Chapter 15). The dictionary keys are the same as before.

Here's an example implementation of imagePickerController:didFinishPicking-MediaWithInfo: that covers the fundamental cases:

```
func imagePickerController(picker: UIImagePickerController,
    didFinishPickingMediaWithInfo info: [NSObject : AnyObject]) {
        let url = info[UIImagePickerControllerMediaURL] as? NSURL
        var im = info[UIImagePickerControllerOriginalImage] as? UIImage
        let edim = info[UIImagePickerControllerEditedImage] as? UIImage
        if edim != nil {
            im = edim
        }
        self.dismissViewControllerAnimated(true) {
            let type = info[UIImagePickerControllerMediaType] as? String
            if type != nil {
                switch type! {
                case kUTTypeImage as! String:
                    if im != nil {
                        self.showImage(im!)
                    }
                case kUTTypeMovie as! String:
                    if url != nil {
                        self.showMovie(url!)
                    }
                default:break
                }
            }
        }
}
```

UIImagePickerController provides no way to govern its supported interface orientations (rotation). The delegate method `navigationControllerSupported-InterfaceOrientations:` is ineffective. My solution is to subclass.

Photos Framework

The Photos framework, also known as *Photo Kit*, does for the photo library roughly what the Media Player framework does for the music library (Chapter 16), letting your code explore the library's contents — and then some. You can manipulate albums, and can even perform edits on the user's photos.

 The Photos framework is new in iOS 8, and supersedes the Assets Library framework from iOS 7 and before. The Assets Library framework is not discussed in this edition.

The photo library itself is represented by the PHPhotoLibrary class — which I used earlier in this chapter to authorize access — and by its shared instance, which you can obtain through the `sharedPhotoLibrary` method. You will not often need to use this class, however, and you do not need to retain the shared photo library instance. More important are the classes representing the kinds of things that inhabit the library (the *photo entities*):

PHAsset
> A single photo or video file.

PHCollection
> An abstract class representing collections of all kinds. Its concrete subclasses are:
>
> PHAssetCollection
> > A collection of photos; albums and moments are PHAssetCollections.
>
> PHCollectionList
> > A collection of asset collections. For example, a year of moments is a collection list; a folder of albums is a collection list.

Finer typological distinctions are drawn, not through subclasses, but through a system of types and subtypes. For example, a PHAsset might have a `mediaType` of `.Image` and a `mediaSubtypes` of `.PhotoPanorama`; a PHAssetCollection might have an `assetCollectionType` of `.Album` and an `assetCollectionSubtype` of `.AlbumRegular`; and so on.

The photo entity classes are actually all subclasses of PHObject, an abstract class that endows them all with a `localIdentifier` property that functions as a persistent unique identifier.

Querying the Photo Library

The photo entity classes supply class methods whose names begin with fetch.... These are the methods you'll call in order to probe the photo library. Many of them have options that help to limit and define the search. In addition, you can supply a PHFetch-Options object letting you refine the results even further: you can set its predicate to limit your request results, and its sortDescriptors to determine the results order.

The result of calling a fetch... method is a PHFetchResult, a collection object that behaves very like an array: you can ask for its count, obtain the object at a given index (including the use of subscripting), look for an object within the collection, and enumerate the collection with an enumerate... method. The objects within the collection are of the class you started with — the one you said fetch... to originally. To put it another way: the photo entity class you start with is the class of object you want to fetch a collection of.

For example, let's say we want to know how moments are divided into years. A year's worth of moments is a PHCollectionList, so the relevant class is PHCollectionList. This code is a fairly standard template for any sort of information fetching:

```
let opts = PHFetchOptions()
let desc = NSSortDescriptor(key: "startDate", ascending: true)
opts.sortDescriptors = [desc]
let result = PHCollectionList.fetchCollectionListsWithType(
    .MomentList, subtype: .MomentListYear, options: opts)
result.enumerateObjectsUsingBlock {
    (obj:AnyObject!, ix:Int, stop:UnsafeMutablePointer<ObjCBool>) in
    let list = obj as! PHCollectionList
    let f = NSDateFormatter()
    f.dateFormat = "yyyy"
    println(f.stringFromDate(list.startDate))
}
/*
output on my device:
1987
1988
1989
1990
...
*/
```

Each resulting list object in the preceding code is a new PHCollectionList comprising a list of moments. Let's dive into that object to see how those moments are clumped into clusters. A cluster of moments is a PHAssetCollection, so the relevant class is PHAssetCollection:

```
let result = PHAssetCollection.fetchMomentsInMomentList(
    list, options: nil)
result.enumerateObjectsUsingBlock {
    (obj:AnyObject!, ix:Int, stop:UnsafeMutablePointer<ObjCBool>) in
    let coll = obj as! PHAssetCollection
    if ix == 0 {
        println("======= \(result.count) clusters")
    }
    f.dateFormat = ("yyyy-MM-dd")
    println("starting \(f.stringFromDate(coll.startDate)): " +
        "\(coll.estimatedAssetCount)")
}
/*
output on my device:
======= 12 clusters
starting 1987-05-15: 2
starting 1987-05-16: 6
starting 1987-05-17: 2
starting 1987-05-20: 4
....
*/
```

Observe that in that code we can learn how many actual moments are in each cluster only as its `estimatedAssetCount`. This is probably the right answer, but to obtain the real count, we'd have to dive one level deeper and fetch the cluster's actual moments.

Next, let's list all albums that have been synced onto the device from iPhoto. An album is a PHAssetCollection, so the relevant class is PHAssetCollection:

```
let result = PHAssetCollection.fetchAssetCollectionsWithType(
    .Album, subtype: .AlbumSyncedAlbum, options: nil)
result.enumerateObjectsUsingBlock {
    (obj:AnyObject!, ix:Int, stop:UnsafeMutablePointer<ObjCBool>) in
    let album = obj as! PHAssetCollection
    println("\(album.localizedTitle)")
}
```

Again, let's dive further: given an album, let's fetch its photos (assets). A photo is a PHAsset, so the relevant class is PHAsset:

```
let result = PHAsset.fetchAssetsInAssetCollection(album, options: nil)
result.enumerateObjectsUsingBlock {
    (obj:AnyObject!, ix:Int, stop:UnsafeMutablePointer<ObjCBool>) in
    let asset = obj as! PHAsset
    println(asset)
}
```

There are many more `fetch...` methods, and thus many other ways to fetch information from the photo library. You can fetch PHAssets by identifier, by URL, by media type; you can fetch PHAssetCollections by identifier, by URL, by whether they contain a given PHAsset; you can fetch PHCollectionLists by identifier, by whether they contain given a PHAssetCollection; and more.

Modifying the Library

Structural modifications to the photo library are performed through a change request class corresponding to the class of photo entity we wish to modify. Thus:

- For PHAsset, there's the PHAssetChangeRequest class.
- For PHAssetCollection, there's the PHAssetCollectionChangeRequest class.
- For PHCollectionList, there's the PHCollectionListChangeRequest class.

A change request is usable only with a `performChanges:` block sent to the shared photo library. Typically, the method in question will be `performChanges:completionHandler:`, which takes two closures: the first is where you specify the changes you want performed; the second is called back after the changes have been performed.

The reason for this peculiar structure is that the photo library is a live database. While we are working, the photo library can change. Therefore, a `performChanges:` block is used to batch our desired changes and send them off as a single transaction to the photo library, which responds when the outcome of the entire batch is known.

For example, let's create an album called "Test Album." An album is a PHAsset-Collection, so we start with the PHAssetCollectionChangeRequest class and call its creation method in the `performChanges:` block:

```
PHPhotoLibrary.sharedPhotoLibrary().performChanges({
    let t = "TestAlbum"
    let creat = PHAssetCollectionChangeRequest
        .creationRequestForAssetCollectionWithTitle(t)
    }, completionHandler: {
        (ok:Bool, err:NSError!) in
        println("created TestAlbum: \(ok)")
})
```

It may appear, in that code, that we didn't actually do anything — we asked for a creation request, but we didn't tell it to do any creating. Nevertheless, that code is sufficient; generating the creation request for a new asset collection in the `performChanges:` block constitutes an instruction to create an asset collection.

It is also possible to obtain a change request for an *existing* asset collection, by calling `changeRequestForAssetCollection:`. This does not, of itself, cause any changes to be performed. Rather, both `creationRequestForAssetCollectionWithTitle:` and `changeRequestForAssetCollection:` return a PHAssetCollectionChangeRequest instance that can *then* be used to perform changes to the asset collection it refers to. For example, to add an asset to an asset collection, we would send `addAssets:` to a PHAsset-CollectionChangeRequest returned by either of those methods.

In this example, I'll create an album and immediately add to it the first asset from the Recently Added smart album. I start by fetching the Recently Added smart album; then

I fetch its first asset; finally, I create a batch request to create the new album and add the asset to it:

```
let result = PHAssetCollection.fetchAssetCollectionsWithType(
    .SmartAlbum, subtype: .SmartAlbumRecentlyAdded, options: nil)
let rec = result.firstObject as! PHAssetCollection!
if rec == nil {
    return // no album
}
let result2 = PHAsset.fetchAssetsInAssetCollection(rec, options: nil)
let ph = result2.firstObject as! PHAsset!
if ph == nil {
    return // no asset
}
PHPhotoLibrary.sharedPhotoLibrary().performChanges({
    let t = "My Cool Album"
    let creat = PHAssetCollectionChangeRequest
        .creationRequestForAssetCollectionWithTitle(t)
    creat.addAssets([ph])
    }, completionHandler: {
        (ok:Bool, err:NSError!) in
        println("created My Cool Album: \(ok)")
})
```

In addition to addAssets:, there are change request instance methods for operations such as inserting an asset at a certain position, replacing one asset with another, moving an asset from one position to another, and removing an asset.

In that example, we created an asset collection and added something to it, all in one batch request. But what if we created an asset collection and wanted to add *it* to something (presumably to a PHCollectionList), all in one batch request? Requesting the creation of an asset collection gives us a PHAssetCollectionChangeRequest; you can't add *that* to a collection. And the requested PHAssetCollection itself hasn't been created yet! The solution is to call the change request instance method placeholderForCreated-AssetCollection; this yields a PHObjectPlaceholder object, which has the remarkable feature that it can be used instead of a "real" object in the parameter of calls such as add-ChildCollections: (because it is a PHObject subclass).

Everything that I've just said about PHAssetCollection and PHAssetCollectionChange-Request is equally true of PHCollectionList and PHCollectionListChangeRequest. The third group, PHAsset and PHAssetChangeRequest, is obviously slightly different, because a PHAsset isn't a collection, but it isn't that different: you can create an asset, delete an asset, or generate a change request from which you can alter such features as the asset's creation date or its associated geographical location.

When the library is modified, either by your code or by some other means while your app is running, any information you've collected about the library — information which you may even be displaying in your interface at that very moment — may become out-of-date. To cope with this possibility, you should, early in the life of your app, register a change observer (adopting the PHPhotoLibraryChangeObserver protocol) with the photo library:

```
PHPhotoLibrary.sharedPhotoLibrary().registerChangeObserver(self)
```

The outcome is that, whenever the library changes, the observer is sent the photo-LibraryDidChange: method, with a PHChange object encapsulating a description of the change. The observer can then probe the PHChange object, using one (or both) of these methods:

changeDetailsForObject:
> The parameter is a single PHAsset, PHAssetCollection, or PHCollectionList you're interested in. The result is a PHObjectChangeDetails object, with properties like objectBeforeChanges, objectAfterChanges, and objectWasDeleted.

changeDetailsForFetchResult:
> The parameter is a previously obtained PHFetchResult. The result is a PHFetch-ResultChangeDetails object, with properties like fetchResultBeforeChanges, fetchResultAfterChanges, removedObjects, insertedObjects, and many others.

For example, suppose my interface is displaying a list of album names, which I obtained originally through a fetch request like this:

```
self.albums = PHAssetCollection.fetchAssetCollectionsWithType(
    .Album, subtype: .AlbumRegular, options: nil)
```

The key move here is that I retain, in a property, a reference to the fetch result. Thus, if my photoLibraryDidChange: method is called, I can find out whether any albums were added or removed, update the fetch result, and change my interface accordingly:

```
func photoLibraryDidChange(changeInfo: PHChange!) {
    if self.albums !== nil {
        if let details =
            changeInfo.changeDetailsForFetchResult(self.albums) {
                dispatch_async(dispatch_get_main_queue()) {
                    if details.insertedObjects != nil {
                        self.albums = details.fetchResultAfterChanges
                        // adjust interface here ...
                    }
                }
        }
    }
}
```

One word of caution: merely performing a fetch request can generate a PHChange report. If you don't want that, supply to the fetch request a PHFetchOptions object whose wantsIncrementalChangeDetails is false.

Displaying Images

Up to this point, we've been gathering and changing structural information about the contents of the photo library, but we haven't yet used that information to display any photos.

Actual PHAsset data is retrieved through the PHImageManager `defaultManager` object. For example, to obtain a UIImage from a photo asset, you would call `requestImageForAsset:targetSize:contentMode:options:resultHandler:`. The process of obtaining an image can be time-consuming, and information about the image may increase in accuracy and detail as it proceeds — with the curious consequence that your `resultHandler:` is not only called asynchronously but may be called multiple times.

In this example, I have a view controller called DataViewController, good for viewing one photo. It has an image view outlet (`self.iv`). It also has a PHAsset property, `self.dataObject`, which is assumed to have been set when this DataViewController instance was created. In `viewWillAppear:`, I call my `setUpInterface` utility method to populate the interface:

```
func setUpInterface() {
    if self.dataObject == nil {
        return
    }
    PHImageManager.defaultManager().requestImageForAsset(
        self.dataObject, targetSize: CGSizeMake(300,300),
        contentMode: .AspectFit, options: nil) {
            (im:UIImage!, info:[NSObject : AnyObject]!) in
            self.iv.image = im
        }
}
```

This may result in the image view's `image` being set multiple times as the requested image's quality improves, but there is nothing wrong with that.

Now imagine an app whose interface is a UIPageViewController permitting the user to view each individual image in an album. Let's say, for example, that the album is the user's Camera Roll. I'll start by obtaining a fetch result collecting all the image assets in the Camera Roll:

```
let result = PHAssetCollection.fetchAssetCollectionsWithType(
    .SmartAlbum, subtype: .SmartAlbumUserLibrary, options: nil)
let rec = result.firstObject as! PHAssetCollection!
if rec == nil {
    return
}
let options = PHFetchOptions() // photos only, please
let pred = NSPredicate(format: "mediaType = %@", NSNumber(
```

```
            integer:PHAssetMediaType.Image.rawValue))
options.predicate = pred
let result2 = PHAsset.fetchAssetsInAssetCollection(rec, options: options)
self.photos = result2
```

The fetch result, `self.photos`, is now our model object. Given an index number, I can provide a DataViewController displaying the corresponding photo:

```
func viewControllerAtIndex(index: Int, storyboard: UIStoryboard)
    -> DataViewController? {
        if self.photos == nil ||
        self.photos.count == 0 ||
        index >= self.photos.count {
            return nil
        }
        let dvc = storyboard.instantiateViewControllerWithIdentifier(
            "DataViewController") as! DataViewController
        dvc.dataObject = self.photos[index] as! PHAsset
        return dvc
    }
```

I can also find the index of any DataViewController's corresponding `dataObject` in `self.photos`:

```
func indexOfViewController(dvc: DataViewController) -> Int {
    let asset = dvc.dataObject
    let ix = self.photos.indexOfObject(asset)
    return ix
}
```

Writing the UIPageViewControllerDataSource methods is now trivial (and is left as an exercise for the reader). For a more elaborate example displaying photos in a UICollectionView, look at Apple's SamplePhotosApp sample code.

The `info` parameter in an image request's result handler is a dictionary whose elements may be useful in a variety of circumstances; for example:

`PHImageResultRequestIDKey`
> Uniquely identifies a single image request for which this result handler is being called multiple times. You can also use this identifier to call `cancelImageRequest:` if it turns out that you don't need this image after all.

`PHImageResultIsInCloudKey`
> Warns that the image is in the cloud and that your request must be resubmitted with explicit permission to use the network.

`PHImageCancelledKey`
> Reports that an attempt to cancel an image request with `cancelImageRequest:` succeeded.

If you imagine that your interface is a table view or collection view, you can see why the asynchronous, time-consuming nature of image fetching can be of importance. As the user scrolls, a cell comes into view and you request the corresponding image. But as the user keeps scrolling, that cell goes out of view, and now the requested image, if it hasn't arrived, is no longer needed, so you cancel the request. (I'll tackle the same sort of problem with regard to Internet-based images in a table view in Chapter 24.)

Editing Images

Astonishingly, Photo Kit allows you to *change* an image in the user's photo library. Why is this even legal? There are two reasons:

- The user will have to give permission every time your app proposes to modify a photo in the library.
- Changes to library photos are undoable, because the original image remains in the database along with the changed image that the user sees.

To change a photo is a three-step process:

1. You send a PHAsset the `requestContentEditingInputWithOptions:completion-Handler:` message. Your `completionHandler:` is called, and is handed a PHContent-EditingInput object. This object wraps some image data which you can display to the user (`displaySizeImage`), along with a pointer to the real image data on disk (`fullSizeImageURL`).

2. You create a PHContentEditingOutput object by calling `init(contentEditing-Input:)`, handing it the PHContentEditingInput object. This PHContentEditing-Output object has a `renderedContentURL` property, which is an NSURL representing a URL on disk. Your mission is to *write the edited photo image data to that URL*. Typically what you'll do is to fetch the image data from the PHContentEditing-Input's `fullSizeImageURL`, process it, and write it to the PHContentEditing-Output object's `renderedContentURL`.

3. You notify the photo library that it should pick up the edited version of the photo. To do so, you call `performChanges:completionHandler:` and, inside the `perform-Changes:` block, create a PHAssetChangeRequest and *set its contentEditing-Output property to the PHContentEditingOutput object*. This is when the user will be shown the alert requesting permission to modify this photo; your `completion-Handler:` is then called, with a first parameter of `false` if the user refuses.

However, if you do only what I have just described, your attempt to modify the photo will fail silently. The reason is that I have omitted something: before the third step, you *must* set the PHContentEditingOutput object's `adjustmentData` property to a newly instantiated PHAdjustmentData object. The initializer is `init(format-`

Identifier:formatVersion:data:). What goes into these parameters is completely up to you, and it is perfectly legal for the data: to be nil. The idea, however, is to send a message to your future self in case you are called upon to edit the same photo again later.

Here's how the adjustmentData works. It, too, works in three steps, interwoven with the three steps I already outlined:

1. When you call requestContentEditingInputWithOptions:completionHandler:, the options: argument should be a PHContentEditingInputRequestOptions object. You are to create this object and set its canHandleAdjustmentData property to a closure that takes a PHAdjustmentData and returns a Bool. This Bool should be based simply on whether you recognize this PHAdjustmentData as yours — typically because you recognize its formatIdentifier. That determines what image you'll get when you receive your PHContentEditingInput object:

   Your closure returns false
   The image you'll be editing is the edited image displayed in the Photos app.

   Your closure returns true
   The image you'll be editing is the *original* image, stripped of your edits. This is because, by returning true, you are asserting that you can recreate the content of your edits based on what's in the PHAdjustmentData's data.

2. When your completionHandler: is called and you receive your PHContentEditingInput object, it has (you guessed it) an adjustmentData property! If this is not nil, it is a PHAdjustmentData object; in that case, you know that the PHContentEditingInput object's image is the original unedited image, and that the PHAdjustmentData object's data is the data you put in the last time you edited this image. You are expected to extract this data and use it to recreate the edited state of the image.

3. When you prepare the PHContentEditingOutput, you give it a new PHAdjustmentData object, as I already explained. If you are performing edits, the data of this new PHAdjustmentData object can be a summary of the edited state of the photo from your point of view — and so the whole cycle can start again if the same photo is to be edited again later.

This may sound confusing or complicated, but in fact an actual implementation is quite straightforward and almost pure boilerplate. The details will vary only in regard to the actual editing of the photo and the actual data by which you'll summarize that editing — so, in constructing an example, I'll keep that part very simple. Recall, from Chapter 2 ("CIFilter and CIImage" on page 85), my example of a custom "vignette" CIFilter called MyVignetteFilter. I'll provide an interface whereby the user can apply that filter to a photo. My interface will include a slider that allows the user to set the *degree* of vignetting that should be applied (MyVignetteFilter's inputPercentage). Moreover, my interface will include a button that lets the user remove *all* vignetting from the photo — even if that vignetting was applied in a previous editing session — thanks to the PHAdjustmentData.

First, I'll plan the structure of the PHAdjustmentData. The `formatIdentifier` can be any unique string; I'll use `"com.neuburg.matt.PhotoKitImages.vignette"`, a constant that I'll store in a property (`self.myidentifier`). The `formatVersion` is likewise arbitrary; I'll use `"1.0"`. Finally, the `data` will express the only thing about my editing that is adjustable — the `inputPercentage`. The `data` will wrap an NSNumber which itself wraps a Double whose value is the `inputPercentage`.

As editing begins, I construct the PHContentEditingInputRequestOptions object that expresses whether a photo's most recent editing belongs to me. I then obtain the photo that is to be edited (a PHAsset) and ask for the PHContentEditingInput object:

```
let options = PHContentEditingInputRequestOptions()
options.canHandleAdjustmentData = {
    (adjustmentData : PHAdjustmentData!) in
    return adjustmentData.formatIdentifier == self.myidentifier
}
let asset = self.dataObject
asset.requestContentEditingInputWithOptions(options, completionHandler: {
    // ...
})
```

Inside the `completionHandler:`, I receive my PHContentEditingInput object. I'm going to need this object later when editing ends, so I immediately store it in a property. I then unwrap its `adjustmentData` and construct the editing interface; in this case, that happens to be a presented view controller, but the details are irrelevant and omitted here:

```
(input:PHContentEditingInput!, info:[NSObject : AnyObject]!) in
self.input = input
let im = input.displaySizeImage // show this to the user during editing
if let adj = input.adjustmentData {
    if adj.formatIdentifier == self.myidentifier && adj.data != nil {
        if let vigAmount =
            NSKeyedUnarchiver.unarchiveObjectWithData(
                adj.data) as? Double {
                    // ... store vigAmount ...
                }
    }
}
// ... present editing interface ...
```

The idea is that if we were able to extract a `vigAmount` from the `adjustmentData`, then the `displaySizeImage` is the *original, unvignetted image* and the editing interface itself initially applies the `vigAmount` of vignetting to it — thus *reconstructing the vignetted state of the photo* as shown in the Photos app, while allowing the user to *change* the amount of vignetting, or even to remove all vignetting entirely.

(If we *weren't* able to extract a `vigAmount` from the `adjustmentData`, then there is nothing to reconstruct; the `displaySizeImage` is just the photo image from the Photos app, and we will apply vignetting to it directly.)

Editing now ends. If the user cancelled, that's all; the user doesn't want to modify the photo after all. Otherwise, the user either asked to apply a certain amount of vignetting or asked to remove *all* vignetting from the *original* image. In the latter case, I use an arbitrary vignetting value of -1 as a signal. If that's the case, the output image consists of the input image — because the input image *is* the original, unvignetted image! So I simply copy the input image to the output image URL, and the PHAdjustmentData's `data` is nil:

```
let vignetteAmount = // -1, or a positive NSNumber between 0 and 1
let input = self.input
let inurl = input.fullSizeImageURL
let output = PHContentEditingOutput(contentEditingInput: input)
let outurl = output.renderedContentURL
if vignette < 0 {
    output.adjustmentData = PHAdjustmentData(
        formatIdentifier: myidentifier, formatVersion: "1.0", data: nil)
    let fm = NSFileManager.defaultManager()
    fm.copyItemAtURL(inurl, toURL: outurl, error: nil)
} else {
    // ... something goes here ... *
}
```

If the desired vignetting value is a positive number, then it represents the amount of vignetting to be applied to the photo. We have been working all this time, in the editing interface, with the PHContentEditingInput's `displaySizeImage`. Now, however, we must apply this amount of vignetting to the *real* photo image, which has been sitting waiting for us all this time, untouched, at the PHContentEditingInput's `fullSizeImage-URL`. This is a *much* bigger image, which will take significant time to load, to alter, and to save — which is why we haven't been working with it live in the editing interface. Now, however, is the moment! This is the code that replaces the starred comment line in the previous code. We read the image from the `fullSizeImageURL`, apply the vignetting, and save to the PHContentEditingOutput's `renderedContentURL` — and we set the PHAdjustmentData's `data` to the vignetting amount:

```
let outcgimage = {
    () -> CGImage in
    let ci = CIImage(contentsOfURL: inurl)
    let vig = MyVignetteFilter()
    vig.setValue(ci, forKey: "inputImage")
    vig.setValue(vignetteAmount, forKey: "inputPercentage")
    let outim = vig.outputImage
    // this next line is time-consuming!
    let outimcg =
        CIContext(options: nil).createCGImage(
```

```
            outim, fromRect: outim.extent())
        return outimcg
    }()
let data = NSKeyedArchiver.archivedDataWithRootObject(vignetteAmount)
output.adjustmentData = PHAdjustmentData(
    formatIdentifier: self.myidentifier, formatVersion: "1.0", data: data)
let dest = CGImageDestinationCreateWithURL(outurl, kUTTypeJPEG, 1, nil)
CGImageDestinationAddImage(
    dest, outcgimage,
    [kCGImageDestinationLossyCompressionQuality as String:1])
CGImageDestinationFinalize(dest)
```

(The image that we save at the renderedContentURL must be a maximum-quality JPEG. I achieve that by using the ImageIO framework, discussed in Chapter 23.)

One way or another, the finished image is now sitting at the renderedContentURL, and we tell the photo library to retrieve it:

```
PHPhotoLibrary.sharedPhotoLibrary().performChanges({
    let asset = self.dataObject
    let req = PHAssetChangeRequest(forAsset: asset)
    req.contentEditingOutput = output
    }, completionHandler: {
        (ok:Bool, err:NSError!) in
        if ok {
            // image changed! adjust interface
        } else {
            println(err)
        }
})
```

Photo Editing Extension

In the preceding section I described how you can modify a photo in the user's photo library from *within your app*. A photo editing extension is photo-modifying code supplied by your app that is effectively *injected into the Photos app*. When the user edits a photo from *within the Photos app*, your extension appears as an option and can modify the photo being edited.

To make a photo editing extension, create a new target in your app, specifying iOS → Application Extension → Photo Editing Extension. The template supplies a storyboard containing one scene, along with the code file for a corresponding UIViewController subclass. This file imports not only the Photos framework but also the PhotosUI framework, which supplies the PHContentEditingController protocol, to which the view controller conforms. This protocol specifies the methods through which the runtime will communicate with your extension's code.

A photo editing extension works almost exactly the same way as modifying photo library assets in general, as I described in the preceding section. The chief differences are:

- You don't put a Done or a Cancel button into your editing interface. The Photos app will wrap your editing interface in its own interface, which supplies them when it presents your view.

- You must situate the pieces of your code in such a way that those pieces respond to the calls that will come through the PHContentEditingController methods.

The PHContentEditingController methods are as follows:

`canHandleAdjustmentData:`
You will not be instantiating PHContentEditingInput; the runtime will do it for you. Therefore, instead of configuring a PHContentEditingInputRequestOptions object and setting its `canHandleAdjustmentData`, you implement this method to return a Bool.

`startContentEditingWithInput:placeholderImage:`
The runtime has obtained the PHContentEditingInput object for you. Now it supplies that object to you, along with a very temporary initial version of the image to be displayed in your interface; you are expected to replace this with the PHContentEditingInput object's `displaySizeImage`. Just as in the previous section's code, you should retain the PHContentEditingInput object in a property, as you will need it again later.

`cancelContentEditing`
The user tapped Cancel. You may well have nothing to do here.

`finishContentEditingWithCompletionHandler:`
The user tapped Done. In your implementation, you get onto a background thread (the template configures this for you) and do *exactly* the same thing you would do if this were not a photo editing extension — get the PHContentEditingOutput object and set its `adjustmentData`; get the photo from the PHContentEditingInput object's `fullSizeImageURL`, modify it, and save the modified image as a full-quality JPEG at the PHContentEditingOutput object's `renderedContentURL`. When you're done, *don't* notify the PHPhotoLibrary; instead, call the `completionHandler` that arrived as a parameter, handing it the PHContentEditingOutput object.

So, for example, here's the structure of my implementation of a photo editing extension based on the vignetting example from the preceding section:

```
func canHandleAdjustmentData(adjustmentData: PHAdjustmentData?) -> Bool {
    return adjustmentData?.formatIdentifier == myidentifier
}
func startContentEditingWithInput(
    contentEditingInput: PHContentEditingInput?,
    placeholderImage: UIImage) {
        self.input = contentEditingInput!
        self.displayImage = self.input.displaySizeImage
```

```
                if let adj = input.adjustmentData {
                    if adj.formatIdentifier == myidentifier && adj.data != nil {
                        if let vigAmount =
                            NSKeyedUnarchiver.unarchiveObjectWithData(
                                adj.data) as? Double {
                                    // ...
                            }
                    }
                }
                // ... finish configuring initial interface ...
        }
        func cancelContentEditing() {} // nothing to do
        func finishContentEditingWithCompletionHandler(
            completionHandler: ((PHContentEditingOutput!) -> Void)!) {
                dispatch_async(
                    dispatch_get_global_queue(
                        DISPATCH_QUEUE_PRIORITY_DEFAULT, 0)) {
                            let output = PHContentEditingOutput(
                                contentEditingInput: self.input)
                            // ... the rest exactly as before! Then:
                            completionHandler?(output)
                    }
        }
```

Using the Camera

The simplest way to prompt the user to take a photo or video is to use our old friend UIImagePickerController, which provides an interface similar to the Camera app. I'll describe this approach first, and then proceed to talk about controlling the camera directly through the AV Foundation framework.

Camera Authorization

New in iOS 8, use of the camera requires explicit authorization from the user. (In iOS 7, this was true only for devices destined for certain regional markets. In iOS 8, it is true universally.) The system will present the access request dialog; you should modify the body of this dialog by setting the "Privacy — Camera Usage Description" key (NSCamera-UsageDescription) in your app's *Info.plist*.

Using the UIImagePickerController to control the camera for the first time will cause the system to present the authorization dialog on your behalf, but if you'd like to ascertain the authorization status beforehand and summon the authorization dialog, you can. The relevant calls are completely parallel to the photo library authorization code I presented at the start of this chapter; the difference is that you'll be talking to the AVCaptureDevice class (you'll need to import AVFoundation). Here's how to learn the current authorization status for use of the camera:

```
let status =
    AVCaptureDevice.authorizationStatusForMediaType(AVMediaTypeVideo)
```

If the status is `.NotDetermined` and you'd like to summon the authorization dialog explicitly:

```
AVCaptureDevice.requestAccessForMediaType(
    AVMediaTypeVideo, completionHandler: nil)
```

If your app will let the user capture video, you will also need to obtain permission from the user to access the microphone. You should modify the body of the authorization alert by setting the "Privacy — Microphone Usage Description" key (`NSMicrophone-UsageDescription`) in your app's *Info.plist*. The relevant authorization methods are AVAudioSession's `recordPermission` and `requestRecordPermission:` (Chapter 14).

Using the Camera with UIImagePickerController

To use UIImagePickerController to control the camera, first check `isSourceType-Available:` for `.Camera`; it will be `false` if the user's device has no camera or the camera is unavailable. If it is `true`, call `availableMediaTypesForSourceType:` to learn whether the user can take a still photo (`kUTTypeImage`), a video (`kUTTypeMovie`), or both. Now instantiate UIImagePickerController, set its source type to `.Camera`, and set its `media-Types` in accordance with which types you just learned are available; if your setting is an array of both `kUTTypeImage` and `kUTTypeMovie`, the user will see a Camera-like interface allowing a choice of either one. Finally, set a delegate (adopting UINavigation-ControllerDelegate and UIImagePickerControllerDelegate), and present the UIImage-PickerController.

So, for example:

```
let ok = UIImagePickerController.isSourceTypeAvailable(.Camera)
if (!ok) {
    println("no camera")
    return
}
let arr = UIImagePickerController
    .availableMediaTypesForSourceType(.Camera) as! [String]
let desiredType = kUTTypeImage as! String
if find(arr, desiredType) == nil {
    println("no stills")
    return
}
let picker = UIImagePickerController()
picker.sourceType = .Camera
picker.mediaTypes = [desiredType]
picker.delegate = self
self.presentViewController(picker, animated: true, completion: nil)
```

For video, you can also specify the videoQuality and videoMaximumDuration. Moreover, these additional properties and class methods allow you to discover the camera capabilities:

isCameraDeviceAvailable:
: Checks to see whether the front or rear camera is available, using one of these values as argument (UIImagePickerControllerCameraDevice):

  - .Front
  - .Rear

cameraDevice
: Lets you learn and set which camera is being used.

availableCaptureModesForCameraDevice:
: Checks whether the given camera can capture still images, video, or both. You specify the front or rear camera; returns an array of integers. Possible modes are (UIImagePickerControllerCameraCaptureMode):

  - .Photo
  - .Video

cameraCaptureMode
: Lets you learn and set the capture mode (still or video).

isFlashAvailableForCameraDevice:
: Checks whether flash is available.

cameraFlashMode
: Lets you learn and set the flash mode (or, for a movie, toggles the LED "torch"). Your choices are (UIImagePickerControllerCameraFlashMode):

  - .Off
  - .Auto
  - .On

 Setting camera-related properties such as cameraDevice when there is no camera or when the UIImagePickerController is not set to .Camera mode can crash your app.

When the view controller's view appears, the user will see the interface for taking a picture, familiar from the Camera app, possibly including flash options, camera selection button, digital zoom (if the hardware supports it), photo/video option (if your mediaTypes setting allows both), and Cancel and shutter buttons. If the user takes a picture, the presented view offers an opportunity to use the picture or to retake it.

Allowing the user to edit the captured image or movie (allowsEditing), and handling the outcome with the delegate messages, is the same as I described earlier for dealing with an image or movie selected from the photo library. There won't be any UIImage-PickerControllerReferenceURL key in the dictionary delivered to the delegate, because the image isn't in the photo library. A still image might report a UIImagePicker-ControllerMediaMetadata key containing the metadata for the photo. The photo library was not involved in the process of media capture, so no user permission to access the photo library is needed; of course, if you *now* propose to save the media into the photo library, you *will* need permission.

Customizing the Image Capture Interface

You can customize the UIImagePickerController interface. If you need to do that, you should probably consider dispensing with UIImagePickerController altogether and designing your own image capture interface from scratch, based around AV Foundation and AVCaptureSession, which I'll introduce in the next section. Still, it may be that a modified UIImagePickerController is all you need.

In the image capture interface, you can hide the standard controls by setting shows-CameraControls to false, replacing them with your own overlay view, which you supply as the value of the cameraOverlayView. In this case, you're probably going to want some means in your overlay view to allow the user to take a picture! You can do that through these methods:

- takePicture
- startVideoCapture
- stopVideoCapture

In this example, I'll remove all the default controls and use a gesture recognizer on the cameraOverlayView to permit the user to double-tap the image in order to take a picture:

```
picker.showsCameraControls = false
let f = self.view.window!.bounds
let v = UIView(frame:f)
let t = UITapGestureRecognizer(target:self, action:"tap:")
t.numberOfTapsRequired = 2
v.addGestureRecognizer(t)
picker.cameraOverlayView = v
self.picker = picker // we'll need this later
```

Our tap: gesture recognizer action handler simply calls takePicture:

```
func tap (g:UIGestureRecognizer) {
    self.picker?.takePicture()
}
```

It would be nice, however, to *tell* the user to double-tap to take a picture; we also need to give the user a way to dismiss the image capture interface. We could put a button and a label into the cameraOverlayView, but here, I'll take advantage of the fact that the UIImagePickerController is a UINavigationController. Thus, it has a toolbar that we can bend to our own purposes. Moreover, we are the UIImagePickerController's delegate, meaning that we are not only its UIImagePickerControllerDelegate but also its UINavigationControllerDelegate; I'll use a delegate method to populate the toolbar:

```
func navigationController(nc: UINavigationController,
    didShowViewController vc: UIViewController, animated: Bool) {
        nc.toolbarHidden = false
        let sz = CGSizeMake(10,10)
        let im = imageOfSize(sz) {
            UIColor.blackColor().colorWithAlphaComponent(0.1).setFill()
            CGContextFillRect(
                UIGraphicsGetCurrentContext(),
                CGRect(origin: CGPoint(), size: sz))
        }
        nc.toolbar.setBackgroundImage(
            im, forToolbarPosition: .Any, barMetrics: .Default)
        nc.toolbar.translucent = true
        let b = UIBarButtonItem(
            title: "Cancel", style: .Plain,
            target: self, action: "doCancel:")
        let lab = UILabel()
        lab.text = "Double tap to take a picture"
        lab.textColor = UIColor.whiteColor()
        lab.backgroundColor = UIColor.clearColor()
        lab.sizeToFit()
        let b2 = UIBarButtonItem(customView: lab)
        nc.topViewController.toolbarItems = [b,b2]
}
```

When the user double-taps to take a picture, our imagePickerController:didFinish-PickingMediaWithInfo: delegate method is called, just as before. We don't automatically get the secondary interface where the user is shown the resulting image and offered an opportunity to use it or retake the image. But we can provide such an interface ourselves, by pushing another view controller onto the navigation controller:

```
func imagePickerController(picker: UIImagePickerController,
    didFinishPickingMediaWithInfo info: [NSObject : AnyObject]) {
        var im = info[UIImagePickerControllerOriginalImage] as? UIImage
        if im == nil {
            return
```

```
    }
    let svc = SecondViewController(image:im)
    picker.pushViewController(svc, animated: true)
}
```

(Designing the SecondViewController class is left as an exercise for the reader.)

Image Capture With AV Foundation

Instead of using UIImagePickerController, you can control the camera and capture images directly using the AV Foundation framework (Chapter 15). You get no help with interface (except for displaying in your interface what the camera "sees"), but you get vastly more detailed control than UIImagePickerController can give you; for example, for stills, you can control focus and exposure directly and independently, and for video, you can determine the quality, size, and frame rate of the resulting movie.

The heart of all AV Foundation capture operations is an AVCaptureSession object. You configure this and provide it as desired with inputs (such as a camera) and outputs (such as a file); then you call `startRunning` to begin the actual capture. You can reconfigure an AVCaptureSession, possibly adding or removing an input or output, while it is running — indeed, doing so is far more efficient than stopping the session and starting it again — but you should wrap your configuration changes in `beginConfiguration` and `commitConfiguration`.

As a rock-bottom example, let's start by displaying in our interface, in real time, what the camera sees. This requires an AVCaptureVideoPreviewLayer, a CALayer subclass. This layer is not an AVCaptureSession output; rather, the layer receives its imagery by *owning* the AVCaptureSession. Our AVCaptureSession's input is the default video camera. We have no intention, as yet, of doing anything with the captured video other than displaying it in the interface, so our AVCaptureSession doesn't need an output:

```
self.sess = AVCaptureSession()
let cam = AVCaptureDevice.defaultDeviceWithMediaType(AVMediaTypeVideo)
let input = AVCaptureDeviceInput(device:cam, error:nil)
self.sess.addInput(input)
let lay = AVCaptureVideoPreviewLayer(session:self.sess)
lay.frame = self.previewRect
self.view.layer.addSublayer(lay)
self.previewLayer = lay // keep a ref
self.sess.startRunning()
```

Presto! Our interface now contains a window on the world, so to speak.

Expanding on that example, let's permit the user to snap a still photo, which our interface will then display. Now we *do* need an output for our AVCaptureSession; since all we want is a still image, this will be an AVCaptureStillImageOutput, and we'll set its output-Settings to specify the quality of the JPEG image we're after. We also need to configure the quality of image that the camera is to capture; the simplest and most common way

---

is to apply a `sessionPreset` to the AVCaptureSession. In this case, since this image is to go directly into our interface, we won't need the vast multimegapixel image size of which the camera is capable; so we'll configure our AVCaptureSession's `session-Preset` to ask for a much smaller image:

```
self.sess = AVCaptureSession()
self.sess.sessionPreset = AVCaptureSessionPreset640x480
self.snapper = AVCaptureStillImageOutput()
self.snapper.outputSettings = [
    AVVideoCodecKey: AVVideoCodecJPEG,
    AVVideoQualityKey: 0.6
]
self.sess.addOutput(self.snapper)
// ... and the rest is as before ...
```

When the user asks to snap a picture, we send `captureStillImageAsynchronouslyFrom-Connection:completionHandler:` to our AVCaptureStillImageOutput object. The first argument is an AVCaptureConnection; to obtain it, we ask the output for its connection that is currently inputting video. The second argument is the block that will be called, possibly on a background thread, when the image data is ready; in the block, we capture the data into a UIImage and, stepping out to the main thread (Chapter 25), we remove the AVCaptureVideoPreviewLayer and stop the AVCaptureSession (and at that point we can do something with the UIImage, such as displaying it in the interface):

```
if self.sess == nil || !self.sess.running {
    return
}
let vc = self.snapper.connectionWithMediaType(AVMediaTypeVideo)
self.snapper.captureStillImageAsynchronouslyFromConnection(vc) {
    (buf:CMSampleBuffer!, err:NSError!) in
    let data = AVCaptureStillImageOutput
        .jpegStillImageNSDataRepresentation(buf)
    let im = UIImage(data:data)
    dispatch_async(dispatch_get_main_queue()) {
        self.previewLayer.removeFromSuperlayer()
        self.sess.stopRunning()
        self.sess = nil
        // ... do something with im here ...
    }
}
```

My favorite part of that example is that capturing the image emits, automatically, the built-in "shutter" sound!

Our code has not illustrated setting the focus, changing the flash settings, and so forth; doing so is not difficult (see the class documentation on AVCaptureDevice), but note that you should wrap such changes in calls to `lockForConfiguration:` and `unlockFor-Configuration`. Also, always call the corresponding `is...Supported:` method before setting any feature of an AVCaptureDevice; for example, before setting the `flashMode`, call `isFlashModeSupported:` for that mode. New in iOS 8, you get direct hardware-level control over the camera focus, manual exposure, and white balance; for a good introduction, watch the WWDC 2014 video on camera capture, and look at the AVCam-Manual sample code. Also, the new BracketStripes example shows how to capture multiple bracketed images.

You can stop the flow of video data by setting the AVCaptureConnection's `enabled` to `false`, and there are some other interesting AVCaptureConnection features, mostly involving stabilization of the video image (not relevant to the example, because a preview layer's video isn't stabilized). Plus, AVCaptureVideoPreviewLayer provides methods for converting between layer coordinates and capture device coordinates; without such methods, this can be a very difficult problem to solve. You can also scan bar codes, shoot video at 60 frames per second (on some devices), and more. You can turn on the LED "torch" by setting the back camera's `torchMode` to `AVCaptureTorchModeOn`, even if no AVCaptureSession is running.

AV Foundation's control over the camera, and its ability to process incoming data — especially video data — goes far deeper than there is room to discuss here, so consult the documentation; in particular, see the "Media Capture" chapter of the *AV Foundation Programming Guide*. There are also excellent WWDC videos on AV Foundation, and some fine sample code; I found Apple's AVCam example very helpful while preparing this discussion.

CHAPTER 18

Address Book

The user's address book, which the user sees through the Contacts app, is effectively a database that your code can access programmatically through the Address Book framework. You'll need to `import AddressBook`. This is, unfortunately, an archaic C API without memory management information, so you're going to be intervening constantly to help manage memory.

A user interface for interacting with the address book is provided by the Address Book UI framework. You'll need to `import AddressBookUI`.

Address Book Database

The address book is an ABAddressBook object obtained by calling `ABAddressBook-CreateWithOptions`. There are in fact no options to pass. You're probably going to need a single persistent reference to the address book, so it is tempting to assign this reference to a property as its default value:

```
var adbk : ABAddressBook =
    ABAddressBookCreateWithOptions(nil, nil).takeRetainedValue()
```

However, there's a serious problem with that approach. Access to the address book database requires user authorization. If the authorization status is `.NotDetermined`, the preceding code does a very bad thing: it fails silently, yielding a non-nil result and not reporting an error. You thus end up with an ABAddressBook reference that is completely invalid and useless — and you have no way of finding out that this has happened. It is crucial, therefore, to verify authorization status independently, as I shall now describe.

Address Book Authorization

Address book authorization is parallel to the authorization verification that I described at the start of Chapter 17. To learn the authorization status, call `ABAddressBookGet-`

AuthorizationStatus. To request authorization if the status is .NotDetermined, call ABAddressBookRequestAccessWithCompletion. Your *Info.plist* should contain some text that the system authorization request alert can use to explain why your app wants access. For the address book library, the relevant key is "Privacy — Contacts Usage Description" (NSContactsUsageDescription).

The problem is to combine authorization with the need to maintain a single global persistent reference to the ABAddressBook. Here's my suggested strategy. I maintain an ABAddressBook property typed as an implicitly unwrapped Optional ABAddressBook:

```
var adbk : ABAddressBook!
```

The assumption is that self.adbk will be non-nil only if it also valid. Now we need to enforce that assumption. I have a utility method, createAddressBook, that attempts to create a valid self.adbk — but only if it hasn't been created already:

```
func createAddressBook() -> Bool {
    if self.adbk != nil {
        return true
    }
    var err : Unmanaged<CFError>? = nil
    let adbk : ABAddressBook? =
        ABAddressBookCreateWithOptions(nil, &err).takeRetainedValue()
    if adbk == nil {
        println(err)
        self.adbk = nil
        return false
    }
    self.adbk = adbk
    return true
}
```

My createAddressBook method is called only by my determineStatus method. The latter is very similar to determineStatus in Chapter 17, but with this difference: if we learn that we have no authorization, we set self.adbk to nil:

```
func determineStatus() -> Bool {
    let status = ABAddressBookGetAuthorizationStatus()
    switch status {
    case .Authorized:
        return self.createAddressBook()
    case .NotDetermined:
        var ok = false
        ABAddressBookRequestAccessWithCompletion(nil) {
            (granted:Bool, err:CFError!) in
            dispatch_async(dispatch_get_main_queue()) {
                if granted {
                    ok = self.createAddressBook()
                }
            }
        }
```

```
            if ok == true {
                return true
            }
            self.adbk = nil
            return false
        case .Restricted:
            self.adbk = nil
            return false
        case .Denied:
            // ... could put up alert begging for authorization here ...
            self.adbk = nil
            return false
        }
    }
```

Finally, as in Chapter 17, I call `determineStatus` when my root view appears, when the app comes to the foreground, and just before doing anything that depends upon access to the address book:

```
override func viewDidAppear(animated: Bool) {
    super.viewDidAppear(animated)
    self.determineStatus()
    NSNotificationCenter.defaultCenter().addObserver(
        self, selector: "determineStatus",
        name: UIApplicationWillEnterForegroundNotification,
        object: nil)
}
```

The outcome is that our `self.adbk` property is kept up to date. If we had authorization and we discover that we have lost it, we set `self.adbk` to nil. If we did not have authorization and we discover that we have obtained it, we call `ABAddressBookCreateWith-Options` to set `self.adbk` to a valid `ABAddressBook`. If we already have authorization, it does no harm to check for authorization, because the existing `self.adbk` will be nonnil and valid and we won't needlessly call `ABAddressBookCreateWithOptions` again.

 To retest the system authorization request alert and other access-related behaviors, go to the Settings app and choose General → Reset → Reset Location & Privacy. This, unfortunately, causes the system to revert to its default settings for *everything* in the Privacy section of Settings: Location Services and all System Services will be On, and all permissions lists will be empty.

Address Book Changes

The address book's data starts out exactly the same as the user's Contacts data. If you make any changes to the data, they are not written through to the user's real address book until you call `ABAddressBookSave`.

The user's real address book can change behind your back while your app is running (the user might edit with the Calendar app, or changes might percolate in from the network), which can put your information out of date. To learn of such changes, you need to register, early in the life of your app, for a notification. Call `ABAddressBook-RegisterExternalChangeCallback`, passing it the address of a function to be called when there's a change; this function must take three parameters: an ABAddressBook, a CFDictionary, and a pointer-to-void. Unfortunately, you can't get the address of a C function in Swift, so both the callback function and the taking of its address must be performed in an Objective-C helper class (as I described in Chapter 14 for the system sound completion handler).

When your change callback function is called, what should you do? Apple recommends that, if you don't have (or can afford to lose) any unsaved changes, you should simply call `ABAddressBookRevert`, causing your reference to the address book information to be updated.

Persons and Addresses

The primary constituent record of the address book database is the ABPerson. You'll typically extract persons from the address book by using these functions:

- `ABAddressBookGetPersonCount`
- `ABAddressBookGetPersonWithRecordID`
- `ABAddressBookCopyPeopleWithName`
- `ABAddressBookCopyArrayOfAllPeople`

An ABPerson doesn't formally exist as a type; it is actually an ABRecord, and by virtue of this has an ID, a type, and properties with values. To fetch the value of a property, you'll call `ABRecordCopyValue`, supplying a property identifier to specify the property that interests you. ABPerson properties, as you might expect, include things like first name, last name, and email.

Working with a property value is a little tricky, because the way you treat it depends on what type of value it is. You can learn a property value's type dynamically by calling `ABPersonGetTypeOfProperty`, but usually you'll know in advance. Some values are simple, but some are not. For example, a last name is a string, which is straightforward. But a person can have more than one email, so an email value is a "multistring." To work with it, you'll treat it as an ABMultiValue. This is like an array of values where each value also has a label and an identifier. The label categorizes — for example, a Home email as opposed to a Work email — but is not a unique specifier (because a person might have, say, two or more Work emails); the identifier is the unique specifier.

A person's address is even more involved because not only is it an ABMultiValue (a person can have more than one address), but also a particular address is itself a dictionary (a CFDictionary). Each dictionary may have a key for street, city, state, country, and so on.

There is more to parsing address book information, but that's enough to get started with; we are now ready for an example! I'll fetch my own record out of the address book database on my device and detect that I've got two email addresses:

```
if !self.determineStatus() {
    println("not authorized")
    return
}
var moi : ABRecord! = nil
let matts = ABAddressBookCopyPeopleWithName(
    self.adbk, "Matt").takeRetainedValue() as [AnyObject]
for matt in matts {
    if let last = ABRecordCopyValue(
        matt, kABPersonLastNameProperty).takeRetainedValue() as? String {
            if last == "Neuburg" {
                moi = matt
                break
            }
    }
}
if moi == nil {
    println("couldn't find myself")
    return
}
// parse my emails
let emails:ABMultiValue = ABRecordCopyValue(
    moi, kABPersonEmailProperty).takeRetainedValue()
for ix in 0 ..< ABMultiValueGetCount(emails) {
    let label = ABMultiValueCopyLabelAtIndex(
        emails,ix).takeRetainedValue() as String
    let value = ABMultiValueCopyValueAtIndex(
        emails,ix).takeRetainedValue() as! String
    println("I have a \(label) address: \(value)")
}
/*
output:
I have a _$!<Home>!$_ address: matt@tidbits.com
I have a _$!<Work>!$_ address: matt@tidbits.com
*/
```

You can also modify an existing record, add a new record (ABAddressBookAddRecord), and delete a record (ABAddressBookRemoveRecord). In this example, I'll create a person called Snidely Whiplash with a Home email snidely@villains.com, add him to the database, and save the database:

Figure 18-1. A contact created programmatically

```
if !self.determineStatus() {
    println("not authorized")
    return
}
let snidely:ABRecord = ABPersonCreate().takeRetainedValue()
ABRecordSetValue(snidely, kABPersonFirstNameProperty, "Snidely", nil)
ABRecordSetValue(snidely, kABPersonLastNameProperty, "Whiplash", nil)
let addr:ABMutableMultiValue = ABMultiValueCreateMutable(
    ABPropertyType(kABStringPropertyType)).takeRetainedValue()
ABMultiValueAddValueAndLabel(
    addr, "snidely@villains.com", kABHomeLabel, nil)
ABRecordSetValue(snidely, kABPersonEmailProperty, addr, nil)
ABAddressBookAddRecord(self.adbk, snidely, nil)
ABAddressBookSave(self.adbk, nil)
```

Sure enough, if we then check the state of the database through the Contacts app, the new person exists (Figure 18-1).

There are also groups (ABGroup); a group, like a person, is a record (ABRecord), so you can add a new group, delete an existing group, add a person to a group, and remove a person from a group (which is more than the Contacts app allows the user to do!). A group doesn't own a person, nor a person a group; they are independent, and a person can be associated with multiple groups just as a group is associated with multiple persons. At an even higher level, there are sources (yet another kind of ABRecord): a person or group might be on the device or might come from an Exchange server or a CardDAV server. The source really does, in a sense, own the group or person; a person can't belong to two sources. A complicating factor, however, is that the same *real* person might appear in two different sources as two different ABPersons; to deal with this, it is possible for multiple persons to be linked, indicating that they are the same person. For a practical introduction to groups and sources, see Apple's ABUIGroups sample code.

Address Book Interface

The Address Book UI framework puts a user interface, similar to the Contacts app, in front of common tasks involving the address book database. This is a great help, because designing your own interface to do the same thing would be tedious and involved. The framework provides four UIViewController subclasses:

ABPeoplePickerNavigationController
> Presents a navigation interface, effectively the same as the Contacts app but without an Edit button: it lists the people in the database and allows the user to pick one and view the details.

ABPersonViewController
> Presents an interface showing the properties of a specific person in the database, possibly editable.

ABNewPersonViewController
> Presents an interface showing the editable properties of a new person.

ABUnknownPersonViewController
> Presents an interface showing a proposed person with a partial set of noneditable properties.

These view controllers operate coherently with respect to the question of whether your app has access to the address book. ABPeoplePickerNavigationController can operate without access (new in iOS 8). ABNewPersonViewController will lack interface for saving into the database if your app has been denied access, and the user's only option will be to back out of the view controller. On the other hand, you can't even get started usefully with ABPersonViewController if you don't already have access, so if you lack access, you'll discover that fact beforehand.

ABPeoplePickerNavigationController

An ABPeoplePickerNavigationController is a UINavigationController. With it, the user can survey all contacts, and can also see a list of groups, along with the names of all persons in each group. Presenting it can be as simple as instantiating it, assigning it a delegate, and showing it as a presented view controller; on the iPad, you might elect to use a popover, but you don't have to:

```
let picker = ABPeoplePickerNavigationController()
picker.peoplePickerDelegate = self
self.presentViewController(picker, animated:true, completion:nil)
```

Note that I didn't check whether we have address book authorization. New in iOS 8, ABPeoplePickerNavigationController operates even if there is no authorization — even if authorization has been denied! This is possible because, in the absence of authorization, it fetches a copy of the data; the user can view the address book information, but can't modify it.

New in iOS 8, three NSPredicate properties determine whether a given person is enabled or selectable and whether a given property is selectable. Persons can be picked out by their properties; properties are picked out using constants such as `ABPersonFamilyName-Property` and `ABPersonEmailAddressesProperty`:

`predicateForEnablingPerson`

> If the predicate returns `false`, that person's name is visible in the list but is dimmed (and tapping it does nothing). In this example, only people named Neuburg are enabled:

```
picker.predicateForEnablingPerson = NSPredicate(
    format: "%K like %@", ABPersonFamilyNameProperty, "Neuburg")
```

`predicateForSelectionOfPerson`

> If the predicate returns `true`, tapping a person's name is the end of the story: the person has been selected, the delegate method `peoplePickerNavigation-Controller:didSelectPerson:` reports this fact, and the presented view controller is dismissed. If it returns `false`, tapping a person's name pushes a new view controller onto the navigation stack, displaying details about that person.

`predicateForSelectionOfProperty`

> Relevant only if the details view controller was pushed onto the navigation stack. If the predicate returns `true`, tapping a property is the end of the story: the property has been selected, the delegate method `peoplePickerNavigationController:did-SelectPerson:property:identifier:` reports this fact, and the presented view controller is dismissed. If it returns `false`, tapping a property may cause that property to be handled by some other app; for example, tapping an email address will switch to the Mail app and create a new outgoing message with that address (and the presented view controller is not dismissed and no delegate methods are called).

If the details view controller is to be pushed onto the navigation stack, you can limit what properties appear by setting the ABPeoplePickerNavigationController's `displayedProperties` to an array of ABPropertyID values, such as `kABPersonEmail-Property`. These are *not* the same as the property name constants used in NSPredicates (such as `ABPersonEmailAddressesProperty`)! You'll have to coerce each ABPropertyID to an Int, because Swift won't convert an array of ABPropertyID to an Objective-C array for you:

```
picker.displayedProperties = [Int(kABPersonEmailProperty)]
```

The delegate is *not* the controller's `delegate` property! It is the controller's `peoplePicker-Delegate` property. You should implement both delegate methods:

`peoplePickerNavigationController:didSelectPerson:`

> A person was selected; the selected person arrives as the second parameter. The presented view controller will be dismissed automatically if you don't dismiss it explicitly.

`peoplePickerNavigationController:didSelectPerson:property:identifier:`

> A person's property was selected; the person arrives as the second parameter, and the property is identified by the third and possibly (for an ABMultiValue) by the fourth parameter, but the *value* of the property is not supplied! Fetching it is up to you. In this example, the `displayedProperties` has enabled emails only:

```
func peoplePickerNavigationController(
    peoplePicker: ABPeoplePickerNavigationController!,
    didSelectPerson person: ABRecordRef!,
    property: ABPropertyID,
    identifier: ABMultiValueIdentifier) {
        if property != kABPersonEmailProperty {
            return // shouldn't happen
        }
        let emails:ABMultiValue = ABRecordCopyValue(
            person, property).takeRetainedValue()
        let ix = ABMultiValueGetIndexForIdentifier(
            emails, identifier)
        let email = ABMultiValueCopyValueAtIndex(
            emails, ix).takeRetainedValue() as! String
        // ... do something with the email here ...
}
```

 These delegate methods are new in iOS 8, superseding the three older delegate methods which are now deprecated. Unfortunately, the other Address Book UI view controllers have not been updated to match.

ABPersonViewController

An ABPersonViewController is a UIViewController. To use it, instantiate it, set its `displayedPerson` and `personViewDelegate` (*not* `delegate`); you must also explicitly pass a reference to the address book into the ABPersonViewController's `addressBook` property. Then push the ABPersonViewController onto an existing navigation controller's stack. The user's only way out of the resulting interface will be through the back button. For example:

```
if !self.determineStatus() {
    println("not authorized")
    return
}
let snides = ABAddressBookCopyPeopleWithName(
    self.adbk, "Snidely Whiplash").takeRetainedValue() as [AnyObject]
if snides.count == 0 {
```

```
        println("no Snidely")
        return
    }
    let snidely : ABRecord = snides[0]
    let pvc = ABPersonViewController()
    pvc.addressBook = self.adbk
    pvc.displayedPerson = snidely
    pvc.personViewDelegate = self
    self.showViewController(pvc, sender:self) // push onto nav controller
```

You can limit the properties to be displayed, as with ABPeoplePickerNavigation-
Controller, by setting the displayedProperties. You can highlight a property with set-
HighlightedItemForProperty:withIdentifier:.

The delegate is notified when the user taps a property, by calling this method:

- personViewController:shouldPerformDefaultActionFor-
  Person:property:identifier:

Return true to allow some other app, such as Maps or Mail, to open the tapped property
value; return false to prevent this.

If ABPersonViewController's allowsActions is true (the default), then buttons such
as Send Message, FaceTime, Share Contact, and Add to Favorites appear in the interface.
(Exactly what buttons appear depends on what categories of information are displayed.)

If ABPersonViewController's allowsEditing is true (the default), the right bar button
is an Edit button. If the user taps this, the interface is transformed into the same sort of
editing interface as ABNewPersonViewController. The user can tap Done or Cancel; if
Done, the edits are automatically saved into the database. Either way, the user returns
to the original display of the person's properties. Your code is not notified that the user
has edited the person.

ABNewPersonViewController

An ABNewPersonController is a UIViewController. To use it, instantiate it, set its new-
PersonViewDelegate (*not* delegate), instantiate a UINavigationController with the
ABNewPersonController as its root view controller, and present the navigation con-
troller:

```
let npvc = ABNewPersonViewController()
npvc.newPersonViewDelegate = self
let nc = UINavigationController(rootViewController:npvc)
self.presentViewController(nc, animated:true, completion:nil)
```

The interface allows the user to fill in all properties of a new contact. You cannot limit
the properties displayed. You can provide properties with default values by creating a

fresh ABRecord representing an ABPerson with `ABPersonCreate`, giving it any property values you like, and assigning it to the `displayedPerson` property.

The delegate has one method, `newPersonViewController:didCompleteWithNewPerson:`, which is responsible for dismissing the presented view controller. If the new person is nil, the user tapped Cancel. Otherwise, the user tapped Done; the new person is an ABRecord *and has already been saved into the database*.

But what if you don't want the new person saved into the database? What if you were presenting this interface merely because it's such a convenient way of letting the user fill in the property values of an ABPerson? Then simply remove the newly created person from the database, like this:

```
func newPersonViewController(
    newPersonView: ABNewPersonViewController!,
    didCompleteWithNewPerson person: ABRecord!) {
        if person != nil {
            ABAddressBookRemoveRecord(self.adbk, person, nil)
            ABAddressBookSave(self.adbk, nil)
            // ... do something with new person ...
        }
        self.dismissViewControllerAnimated(true, completion:nil)
}
```

ABUnknownPersonViewController

An ABUnknownPersonViewController is a UIViewController. It presents, as it were, a proposed partial person. You can set the name displayed as the controller's `alternateName` property, and the text below this as the controller's `message` property. You can add actual person property values just as for an ABNewPersonViewController, namely, by creating a fresh ABRecord representing an ABPerson with `ABPersonCreate`, giving it some property values, and assigning it to the `displayedPerson` property.

To use ABUnknownPersonViewController, instantiate it, set the properties listed in the foregoing paragraph, set its `unknownPersonViewDelegate` (*not* `delegate`), and push it onto the stack of an existing navigation controller. The user's only way out of the resulting interface will be through the back button. For example:

```
let unk = ABUnknownPersonViewController()
unk.message = "Person who really knows trees"
unk.allowsAddingToAddressBook = true
unk.allowsActions = true
let person:ABRecord = ABPersonCreate().takeRetainedValue()
ABRecordSetValue(person, kABPersonFirstNameProperty, "Johnny", nil)
ABRecordSetValue(person, kABPersonLastNameProperty, "Appleseed", nil)
let addr:ABMutableMultiValue = ABMultiValueCreateMutable(
    ABPropertyType(kABStringPropertyType)).takeRetainedValue()
ABMultiValueAddValueAndLabel(addr, "johnny@seeds.com", kABHomeLabel, nil)
```

```
ABRecordSetValue(person, kABPersonEmailProperty, addr, nil)
unk.displayedPerson = person
unk.unknownPersonViewDelegate = self
self.showViewController(unk, sender:self) // push onto nav controller
```

What the user can do here depends on two other properties:

allowsAddingToAddressBook

> If true (the default), and if your app has access to the address book, a Create New Contact button and an Add to Existing Contact button appear:

> *The user taps Create New Contact*
>> The editing interface appears (as in ABNewPersonViewController and an editable ABPersonViewController). It is filled in with the property values of the displayedPerson. If the user taps Done, the person is saved into the database.

> *The user taps Add to Existing Contact*
>> A list of all contacts appears (as in the first screen of ABPersonViewController). The user can Cancel or tap a person. If the user taps a person, the properties from the displayedPerson are merged into that person's record.

allowsActions

> If true (the default), buttons such as Send Message, FaceTime, and Share Contact appear. (Exactly what buttons appear depends on what categories of information are displayed.)

The delegate has two methods, the first of which is required:

unknownPersonViewController:didResolveToPerson:

> Called if allowsAddingToAddressBook is true and the user finishes working in a presented editing view. The editing view has already been dismissed and the user has either cancelled (the second parameter is nil) or has tapped Done (the second parameter is the ABPerson already saved into the database).

unknownPersonViewController:shouldPerformDefaultActionForPerson:property:
identifier:

> Return false to prevent a tap on a property value from navigating to another app, such as Maps or Mail.

CHAPTER 19

Calendar

The user's calendar information, which the user sees through the Calendar app, is effectively a database of calendar events. The calendar database also includes reminders, which the user sees through the Reminders app. This database can be accessed directly through the Event Kit framework. You'll need to `import EventKit`.

 Type names in the Event Kit framework have not been abbreviated for Swift. For example the EKEntityType names are `EKEntityTypeEvent` and `EKEntityType-Reminder`, not `.Event` and `.Reminder`.

A user interface for interacting with the calendar is also provided, through the Event Kit UI framework. You'll need to `import EventKitUI`.

Calendar Database

The calendar database is accessed as an instance of the EKEventStore class. This instance is expensive to obtain but lightweight to maintain, so your usual strategy will be to instantiate and retain one EKEventStore instance. Fortunately, a calendar database instance, unlike an address book database instance (see Chapter 18), cannot be faulty; thus there is no harm whatever in initializing a property as an EKEventStore instance and keeping that reference for the rest of the app's lifetime:

```
var database = EKEventStore()
```

In the examples in this chapter, my EKEventStore instance is called `self.database` throughout.

Calendar Database Authorization

Calendar database authorization is parallel to the authorization verification that I described at the start of Chapter 18. The chief difference is that, although there is one database, access to calendar events and access to reminders are considered two separate forms of access and require separate authorizations. To learn authorization status, call the EKEventStore *class* method authorizationStatusForEntityType: with either EKEntityTypeEvent (for access to calendar events) or EKEntityTypeReminder (for access to reminders). To request authorization if the status is .NotDetermined, call the EKEventStore *instance* method requestAccessToEntityType:completion:. You should supply the body of the authorization request alert by setting the "Privacy — Calendars Usage Description" key (NSCalendarsUsageDescription) or the "Privacy — Reminders Usage Description" key (NSRemindersUsageDescription) in your app's *Info.plist*.

A possible strategy is thus completely parallel to the code at the start of Chapter 17 for access to the photo library:

```
func determineStatus() -> Bool {
    let type = EKEntityTypeEvent
    let stat = EKEventStore.authorizationStatusForEntityType(type)
    switch stat {
    case .Authorized:
        return true
    case .NotDetermined:
        self.database.requestAccessToEntityType(type, completion:{_,_ in})
        return false
    case .Restricted:
        return false
    case .Denied:
        // ... possible alert offering to go to Settings app ...
        return false
    }
}
```

In that code, the completion handler is empty (if it is nil, your app will crash). If you supply a real completion handler, it may be run on a background thread; you'll want to step out to the main thread before doing anything further (Chapter 25).

 To retest the system authorization request alert and other access-related behaviors, go to the Settings app and choose General → Reset → Reset Location & Privacy. This, unfortunately, causes the system to revert to its default settings for *everything* in the Privacy section of Settings: Location Services and all System Services will be On, and all permissions lists will be empty.

Calendar Database Contents

Starting with an EKEventStore instance, you can obtain two kinds of object — a calendar or a calendar item.

Calendars

A calendar represents a named (`title`) collection of calendar items, meaning events or reminders. It is an instance of EKCalendar. Curiously, however, an EKCalendar instance doesn't contain or link to its calendar items; to obtain and create calendar items, you work directly with the EKEventStore itself. A calendar's `allowedEntityTypes`, despite the plural, will probably return just one entity type; you can't create a calendar that allows both.

Calendars have various types (`type`), reflecting the nature of their origin: a calendar can be created and maintained by the user locally (`EKCalendarTypeLocal`), but it might also live remotely on the network (`EKCalendarTypeCalDAV`, `EKCalendarTypeExchange`), possibly being updated by subscription (`EKCalendarTypeSubscription`); the Birthday calendar (`EKCalendarTypeBirthday`) is generated automatically from information in the address book.

The `type` is supplemented and embraced by the calendar's `source`, an EKSource whose `sourceType` can be `EKSourceTypeLocal`, `EKSourceTypeExchange`, `EKSourceTypeCal-DAV` (which includes iCloud), and so forth; a source can also have a `title`, and it has a unique identifier (`sourceIdentifier`). You can get an array of all `sources` known to the EKEventStore, or specify a source by its identifier. You'll probably use the `source` exclusively and ignore the calendar's `type` property.

There are three ways of requesting a calendar:

All calendars

Fetch all calendars permitting a particular calendar item type (`EKEntityType-Event` or `EKEntityTypeReminder`) by calling `calendarsForEntityType:`. You can send this message either to the EKEventStore or to an EKSource.

Particular calendar

Fetch an individual calendar by means of a previously obtained `calendar-Identifier` by calling `calendarWithIdentifier:`.

Default calendar

Fetch the default calendar for a particular calendar item type through the `default-CalendarForNewEvents` property or the `defaultCalendarForNewReminders` property; this is appropriate particularly if your intention is to create a new calendar item.

You can also create a calendar, by calling `calendarForEntityType:eventStore:`. At that point, you can specify the source to which the calendar belongs.

Depending on the source, a calendar will be modifiable in various ways. The calendar might be `subscribed`. If the calendar is `immutable`, you can't delete the calendar or change its attributes; but its `allowsContentModifications` might still be `true`, in which case you can add, remove, and alter its events. You can update your copy of the calendar from any remote sources by calling `refreshSourcesIfNecessary`.

Calendar items

A calendar item (EKCalendarItem) is either a calendar event (EKEvent) or a reminder (EKReminder). Think of it as a memorandum describing when something happens. As I mentioned a moment ago, you don't get calendar items from a calendar; rather, a calendar item *has* a `calendar`, but you get it from the EKEventStore as a whole. There are two chief ways of doing so:

By predicate
   Fetch all events or reminders according to a predicate:

   * `eventsMatchingPredicate:`

   * `enumerateEventsMatchingPredicate:`

   * `fetchRemindersMatchingPredicate:completion:`

   Methods starting with `predicate...` allow you to form the predicate. The predicate specifies things like the calendar(s) the item is to come from and the item's date range.

By identifier
   Fetch an individual calendar item by means of a previously obtained `calendarItem-Identifier` by calling `calendarItemWithIdentifier:`.

Calendar Database Changes

Changes to the database can be atomic. There are two prongs to the implementation of this feature:

* The methods for saving and removing calendar items and calendars have a `commit:` parameter. If you pass `false` as the argument, the changes that you're ordering are batched; later, you can call `commit:` (or `reset` if you change your mind). If you pass `false` and fail to call `commit:` later, your changes will never happen.

* An abstract class, EKObject, functions as the superclass for all the other persistent object types, such as EKCalendar, EKCalendarItem, EKSource, and so on. It endows

those classes with methods `isNew` and `hasChanges`, along with `refresh`, `rollback`, and `reset`.

The calendar database is an odd sort of database, because calendars can be maintained in so many ways and places. A calendar can change while your app is running (the user might sync, or the user might edit with the Calendar app), which can put your information out of date. You can register for a single EKEventStore notification, `EKEvent-StoreChangedNotification`; if you receive it, you should assume that any calendar-related instances you're holding are invalid. This situation is made relatively painless, though, by the fact that every calendar-related instance can be refreshed with `refresh`. Keep in mind that `refresh` returns a Boolean; if it returns `false`, this object is *really* invalid and you should stop working with it entirely (it may have been deleted from the database).

Creating Calendars and Events

Let's start by creating an events calendar. We need to assign a source; we'll choose `EKSourceTypeLocal`, meaning that the calendar will be created on the device itself. We can't ask the database for the local source directly, so we have to cycle through all sources looking for it. When we find it, we make a new calendar called "CoolCal":

```
if !self.determineStatus() { // not authorized
    return
}
var src : EKSource! = nil
for source in self.database.sources() as! [EKSource] {
    if source.sourceType.value == EKSourceTypeLocal.value {
        src = source
        break
    }
}
if src == nil { // failed to find local source
    return
}
let cal = EKCalendar(forEntityType:EKEntityTypeEvent,
    eventStore:self.database)
cal.source = src
cal.title = "CoolCal"
var err : NSError?
let ok = self.database.saveCalendar(cal, commit:true, error:&err)
if !ok {
    println("save calendar error: \(err!.localizedDescription)")
    return
}
```

If a device's calendar is subscribed to a remote source (such as iCloud), `EKCalendar-TypeLocal` calendars are inaccessible. The examples in this chapter use a local calendar (because I don't want to risk damaging your online calendars); to test them, you'll have to unsubscribe from iCloud.

Now let's create an event. EKEvent is a subclass of EKCalendarItem, from which it inherits some of its important properties. If you've ever used the Calendar app in iOS or OS X, you already have a sense for how an EKEvent can be configured. It has a `title` and optional `notes`. It is associated with a `calendar`, as I've already said. It can have one or more alarms and one or more recurrence rules; I'll talk about both of those in a moment. All of that is inherited from EKCalendarItem. EKEvent itself adds the all-important `startDate` and `endDate` properties; these are NSDates and involve both date and time. If the event's `allDay` property is `true`, the time aspect of its dates is ignored; the event is associated with a day or a stretch of days as a whole. If the event's `allDay` property is `false`, the time aspect of its dates matters; a typical event will then usually be bounded by two times on the same day.

Making an event is simple, if tedious. You *must* provide a `startDate` and an `endDate`! The simplest way to construct dates is with NSDateComponents. I'll create an event and add it to our new calendar. First, I need a way to locate the new calendar. I'll locate it by its title. I really should be using the `calendarIdentifier`; the title isn't reliable, since the user might change it, and since multiple calendars can have the same title. However, it's only an example:

```
func calendarWithName( name:String ) -> EKCalendar? {
    let calendars =
        self.database.calendarsForEntityType(
            EKEntityTypeEvent) as! [EKCalendar]
    for cal in calendars {
        if cal.title == name {
            return cal
        }
    }
    return nil
}
```

Now I'll create an event, configure it, and add it to our CoolCal calendar:

```
if !self.determineStatus() { // not authorized
    return
}
let cal : EKCalendar! = self.calendarWithName("CoolCal")
if cal == nil { // no calendar
    return
}
let greg = NSCalendar(calendarIdentifier:NSCalendarIdentifierGregorian)!
let comp = NSDateComponents()
```

```
comp.year = 2015
comp.month = 8
comp.day = 10
comp.hour = 15
let d1 = greg.dateFromComponents(comp)
comp.hour = comp.hour + 1
let d2 = greg.dateFromComponents(comp)
let ev = EKEvent(eventStore:self.database)
ev.title = "Take a nap"
ev.notes = "You deserve it!"
ev.calendar = cal
ev.startDate = d1
ev.endDate = d2
var err : NSError?
let ok = self.database.saveEvent(
    ev, span:EKSpanThisEvent, commit:true, error:&err)
if !ok {
    println("save simple event \(err!.localizedDescription)")
    return
}
```

An alarm is an EKAlarm, a very simple class; it can be set to fire either at an absolute date or at a relative offset from the event time. On an iOS device, an alarm fires through a local notification (Chapter 13). We could easily have added an alarm to our event as we were configuring it:

```
let alarm = EKAlarm(relativeOffset:-3600) // one hour before
ev.addAlarm(alarm)
```

Recurrence

Recurrence is embodied in a recurrence rule (EKRecurrenceRule); a calendar item can have multiple recurrence rules, which you manipulate through its `recurrenceRules` property, along with methods `addRecurrenceRule:` and `removeRecurrenceRule:`. A simple EKRecurrenceRule is described by three properties:

Frequency
By day, by week, by month, or by year.

Interval
Fine-tunes the notion "by" in the frequency. A value of 1 means "every." A value of 2 means "every other." And so on.

End
Optional, because the event might recur forever. It is an EKRecurrenceEnd instance, describing the limit of the event's recurrence either as an end date or as a maximum number of occurrences.

The options for describing a more complex EKRecurrenceRule are best summarized by its initializer:

```
init!(recurrenceWithFrequency type: EKRecurrenceFrequency,
             interval interval: Int,
           daysOfTheWeek days: [AnyObject]!,
         daysOfTheMonth monthDays: [AnyObject]!,
       monthsOfTheYear months: [AnyObject]!,
         weeksOfTheYear weeksOfTheYear: [AnyObject]!,
           daysOfTheYear daysOfTheYear: [AnyObject]!,
             setPositions setPositions: [AnyObject]!,
                 end end: EKRecurrenceEnd!)
```

The meanings of all these parameters are mostly obvious from their names. The arrays are of Int, except for daysOfTheWeek, which is an array of EKRecurrenceDayOfWeek, a class that allows specification of a week number as well as a day number so that you can say things like "the fourth Thursday of the month." Many of these values can be negative to indicate counting backward from the last one. Numbers are all 1-based, not 0-based. The setPositions parameter is an array of Int filtering the occurrences defined by the rest of the specification against the interval; for example, if daysOfTheWeek is Sunday, -1 means the final Sunday. You can use any valid combination of parameters; the penalty for an invalid combination is a return value of nil.

An EKRecurrenceRule is intended to embody the RRULE event component in the iCalendar standard specification (originally published as RFC 2445 and recently superseded by RFC 5545, *http://datatracker.ietf.org/doc/rfc5545*); in fact, the documentation tells you how each EKRecurrenceRule property corresponds to an RRULE attribute, and if you log an EKRecurrenceRule, what you're shown *is* the underlying RRULE. RRULE can describe some amazingly sophisticated recurrence rules, such as this one:

```
RRULE:FREQ=YEARLY;INTERVAL=2;BYMONTH=1;BYDAY=SU
```

That means "every Sunday in January, every other year." Let's form this rule. Observe that we should attach it to an event whose startDate and endDate make sense as an example of the rule — that is, on a Sunday in January. Fortunately, NSDateComponents makes that easy:

```
// ... make sure we have authorization ...
// ... obtain our calendar (cal) ...
// form the rule
let everySunday = EKRecurrenceDayOfWeek(1)
let january = 1
let recur = EKRecurrenceRule(
    recurrenceWithFrequency:EKRecurrenceFrequencyYearly, // every year
    interval:2, // no, every *two* years
    daysOfTheWeek:[everySunday],
    daysOfTheMonth:nil,
    monthsOfTheYear:[january],
    weeksOfTheYear:nil,
    daysOfTheYear:nil,
    setPositions: nil,
```

Figure 19-1. The user specifies a span

```
     end:nil)
let ev = EKEvent(eventStore:self.database)
ev.title = "Mysterious biennial Sunday-in-January morning ritual"
ev.addRecurrenceRule(recur)
ev.calendar = cal
// need a start date and end date
let greg = NSCalendar(calendarIdentifier:NSCalendarIdentifierGregorian)!
let comp = NSDateComponents()
comp.year = 2015
comp.month = 1
comp.weekday = 1 // Sunday
comp.weekdayOrdinal = 1 // *first* Sunday
comp.hour = 10
ev.startDate = greg.dateFromComponents(comp)
comp.hour = 11
ev.endDate = greg.dateFromComponents(comp)
var err : NSError?
let ok = self.database.saveEvent(
    ev, span:EKSpanFutureEvents, commit:true, error:&err)
if !ok {
    println("save recurring event \(err!.localizedDescription)")
    return
}
```

In that code, the event we save into the database is a recurring event. When we save or delete a recurring event, we must specify a `span:` argument. This is either `EKSpanThis-Event` or `EKSpanFutureEvents`, and corresponds exactly to the two buttons the user sees in the Calendar interface when saving or deleting a recurring event (Figure 19-1). The buttons and the span types reflect their meaning exactly: the change affects either this event alone, or this event plus all *future* (not past) recurrences. This choice determines not only how this and future recurrences of the event are affected now, but also how they relate to one another from now on.

Fetching Events

Now let's talk about how to extract an event from the database. One way, as I mentioned earlier, is by its unique identifier (`calendarItemIdentifier`). Not only is this identifier a fast and unique way to obtain an event, but also it's just a string, which means that it persists even if the EKEventStore subsequently goes out of existence. Remember to obtain it, though, while the EKEventStore *is* still in existence; an EKEvent drawn from the database loses its meaning and its usability if the EKEventStore instance is destroyed. (Even this unique identifier *might* not survive changes in a calendar between launches of your app.)

You can also extract events from the database by matching a predicate (NSPredicate). To form this predicate, you specify a start and end date and an array of eligible calendars, and call the EKEventStore method `predicateForEventsWithStartDate:end-Date:calendars:`. That's the only kind of predicate you can use, so any further filtering of events is then up to you. In this example, I'll gather all events from our "CoolCal" calendar; because I have to specify a date range, I ask for events occurring over the next year. Because `enumerateEventsMatchingPredicate:` can be time-consuming, it's best to run it on a background thread (Chapter 25):

```
// ... make sure we have authorization ...
// ... obtain our calendar (cal) ...
let d1 = NSDate() // today
let greg = NSCalendar(calendarIdentifier:NSCalendarIdentifierGregorian)!
let comp = NSDateComponents()
comp.year = 1 // we're going to add 1 to the year
let d2 = greg.dateByAddingComponents(comp, toDate:d1, options:nil)
let pred = self.database.predicateForEventsWithStartDate(
    d1, endDate:d2, calendars:[cal])
var events = [EKEvent]()
dispatch_async(dispatch_get_global_queue(0, 0)) {
    self.database.enumerateEventsMatchingPredicate(pred) {
        (event:EKEvent!, stop:UnsafeMutablePointer<ObjCBool>) in
            events += [event]
            if (event.title as NSString)
                .rangeOfString("nap").location != NSNotFound {
                    self.napid = event.calendarItemIdentifier
                }
    }
    sort(&events) {
        return $0.compareStartDateWithEvent($1) == .OrderedAscending}
    // ... do something with results here ...
}
```

That example shows you what I mean about further filtering of events. I obtain the "nap" event and the "mysterious biennial Sunday-in-January morning ritual" events, but the "nap" event is the one I really want, so I filter further to find it in the block. (In real life, if I weren't also testing this call by collecting all returned events into an array, I would then set `stop.memory` to `true` to end the enumeration.) The events are enumerated in no particular order; the convenience method `compareStartDateWithEvent:` is provided as a sort selector to put them in order by start date.

When you extract events from the database, event recurrences are treated as separate events (as happened in the preceding example). Recurrences of the same event will have different start and end dates but the same identifier. When you fetch an event by identifier, you get the *earliest* event with that identifier. This makes sense, because if you're going to make a change affecting this and future recurrences of the event, you need the option to start with the earliest possible recurrence (so that "future" means "all").

Reminders

A reminder (EKReminder) is very parallel to an event (EKEvent); they both inherit from EKCalendarItem, so a reminder has a calendar (which the Reminders app refers to as a "list"), a title, notes, alarms, recurrence rules, and attendees. Instead of a start date and an end date, it has a start date, a due date, a completion date, and a `completed` property. The start date and due date are expressed directly as NSDateComponents, so you can supply as much detail as you wish: if you don't include any time components, it's an all-day reminder.

To illustrate, I'll make an all-day reminder for today:

```
if !self.determineStatus() { // no authorization
    return
}
let cal = self.database.defaultCalendarForNewReminders()
if cal == nil { // no default calendar
    return
}
let rem = EKReminder(eventStore:self.database)
rem.title = "Get bread"
rem.calendar = cal
let today = NSDate()
let greg = NSCalendar(calendarIdentifier:NSCalendarIdentifierGregorian)!
let comps : NSCalendarUnit =
    .CalendarUnitYear | .CalendarUnitMonth | .CalendarUnitDay
rem.dueDateComponents = greg.components(comps, fromDate:today)
var err : NSError?
let ok = self.database.saveReminder(rem, commit:true, error:&err)
if !ok {
    println("save calendar \(err!.localizedDescription)")
    return
}
```

When you call `fetchRemindersMatchingPredicate:completion:`, the possible predicates let you fetch all reminders in given calendars, incomplete reminders, or completed reminders.

Proximity Alarms

A proximity alarm is triggered by the user's approaching or leaving a certain location (also known as *geofencing*). This is appropriate particularly for reminders: one might wish to be reminded of something when approaching the place where that thing can be accomplished. To form the location, you'll need to use the CLLocation class (see Chapter 22). Here, I'll attach a proximity alarm to a reminder (rem); the alarm will fire when I'm near my local Trader Joe's:

```
let alarm = EKAlarm()
let loc = EKStructuredLocation(title:"Trader Joe's")
loc.geoLocation = CLLocation(latitude:34.271848, longitude:-119.247714)
loc.radius = 10*1000 // metres
alarm.structuredLocation = loc
alarm.proximity = EKAlarmProximityEnter // alarm when *arriving*
rem.addAlarm(alarm)
```

Use of a proximity alarm requires authorization, but that's of no concern here, because the app that needs this authorization is not our app but the Reminders app! Now that we've placed a reminder with a proximity alarm into the database, the Reminders app will request authorization, if needed, the next time the user brings it frontmost. If you add a proximity alarm to the event database and the Reminders app can't perform background geofencing, the alarm will not fire (unless the Reminders app is frontmost).

 New in iOS 8, you can fire a local notification based on geofencing without involving reminders or the Reminders app. See Chapter 22.

Calendar Interface

The Event Kit UI framework provides three view controller classes that manage views for letting the user work with events and calendars:

EKEventViewController
> Shows the description of a single event, possibly editable.

EKEventEditViewController
> Allows the user to create or edit an event.

EKCalendarChooser
> Allows the user to pick a calendar.

These view controllers automatically listen for changes in the database and, if needed, will automatically call refresh on the information being edited, updating their display to match. If a view controller is displaying an event in the database and the event is

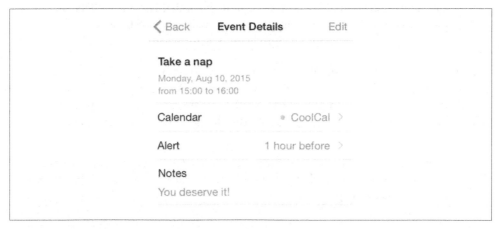

Figure 19-2. The event interface

deleted while the user is viewing it, the delegate will get the same notification as if the user had deleted it.

EKEventViewController

EKEventViewController shows the event display listing the event's title, date and time, calendar, alert, and notes, familiar from the Calendar app (Figure 19-2). To use EKEventViewController, instantiate it, give it an event in the database, assign it a delegate (EKEventViewDelegate), make it the root view controller of a UINavigation-Controller, and present the navigation controller. It looks best on the iPad as a popover. This code gives a good result on both iPhone and iPad:

```
let evc = EKEventViewController()
evc.event = ev
evc.delegate = self
let nav = UINavigationController(rootViewController: evc)
nav.modalPresentationStyle = .Popover
self.presentViewController(nav, animated: true, completion: nil)
if let pop = nav.popoverPresentationController {
    if let v = sender as? UIView {
        pop.sourceView = v
        pop.sourceRect = v.bounds
    }
}
```

The delegate method, `eventViewController:didCompleteWithAction:`, is called when the user taps Done; dismissing the presented view controller is up to you. This method is called also if the user deletes an event or accepts an invitation.

Do *not* use EKEventViewController for an event that isn't in the database, or at a time when the database isn't open! It won't function correctly if you do.

If `allowsEditing` is `true` (the default), an Edit button appears in the navigation bar, and by tapping this, the user can edit the various aspects of an event in the same interface as the Calendar app, including the Delete button at the bottom. If the user ultimately deletes the event, or edits it and taps Done, the change is saved into the database.

 Even if `allowsEditing` is `false`, the user can change what calendar this event belongs to, can change an alert's firing time if there is one, and can delete the event. I regard this as a bug.

EKEventEditViewController

EKEventEditViewController (a UINavigationController) presents the interface for editing an event. To use it, set its `eventStore` and `editViewDelegate` (EKEventEditViewDelegate, *not* `delegate`), and optionally its `event`, and present it as a presented view controller (which looks best on the iPad as a popover). The event can be nil for a completely empty new event; it can be an event you've just created (and possibly partially configured) and not stored in the database, or it can be an existing event from the database. If access to the database has been denied, the interface will be empty and the user will simply cancel.

The delegate method `eventEditViewControllerDefaultCalendarForNewEvents:` may be implemented to specify what calendar a completely new event should be assigned to. If you're partially constructing a new event, you can assign it a calendar then, and of course an event from the database already has a calendar.

You must implement the delegate method `eventEditViewController:didCompleteWithAction:` so that you can dismiss the presented view controller. Possible actions are that the user cancelled, saved the edited event into the database, or deleted an already existing event from the database. You can get a reference to the edited event as the EKEventEditViewController's `event`.

EKCalendarChooser

EKCalendarChooser displays a list of calendars, choosable by tapping; a chosen calendar displays a checkmark. To use it, instantiate it with `init(selectionStyle:displayStyle:entityType:eventStore:)`, set a `delegate` (EKCalendarChooserDelegate), make it the root view controller of a UINavigationController, and show the navigation controller as a presented view controller (which looks best as a popover on the iPad). The `selectionStyle` dictates whether the user can pick one or multiple calendars; the `displayStyle` states whether all calendars or only writable calendars will be displayed. If access to the database has been denied, the interface will be empty and the user will simply cancel.

Two properties, `showsCancelButton` and `showsDoneButton`, determine whether these buttons will appear in the navigation bar. In a fullscreen presented view controller, you'll certainly show at least one and probably both, because otherwise the user has no way to dismiss the presented view controller!

There are three delegate methods, all of them required:

- `calendarChooserSelectionDidChange:`
- `calendarChooserDidFinish:` (the user tapped Done)
- `calendarChooserDidCancel:`

In the Finish and Cancel methods, you should dismiss the presented view controller.

In this example, we implement a potentially destructive action: we offer to delete the selected calendar. Because this is potentially destructive, we pass through an action sheet for confirmation:

```
@IBAction func deleteCalendar (sender:AnyObject!) {
    let choo = EKCalendarChooser(
        selectionStyle:EKCalendarChooserSelectionStyleSingle,
        displayStyle:EKCalendarChooserDisplayAllCalendars,
        entityType:EKEntityTypeEvent,
        eventStore:self.database)
    choo.showsDoneButton = true
    choo.showsCancelButton = true
    choo.delegate = self
    let nav = UINavigationController(rootViewController: choo)
    nav.modalPresentationStyle = .Popover
    self.presentViewController(nav, animated: true, completion: nil)
    if let pop = nav.popoverPresentationController {
        if let v = sender as? UIView {
            pop.sourceView = v
            pop.sourceRect = v.bounds
        }
    }
}
func calendarChooserDidCancel(calendarChooser: EKCalendarChooser!) {
    self.dismissViewControllerAnimated(true, completion: nil)
}
func calendarChooserDidFinish(calendarChooser: EKCalendarChooser!) {
    let cals = calendarChooser.selectedCalendars as! Set<EKCalendar>!
        if cals != nil && cals.count > 0 {
            let calsToDelete = map(cals!) {$0.calendarIdentifier}
            let alert = UIAlertController(
                title: "Delete selected calendar?", message: nil,
```

```
                  preferredStyle: .ActionSheet)
        alert.addAction(UIAlertAction(
            title: "Cancel", style: .Cancel, handler: nil))
        alert.addAction(UIAlertAction(
            title: "Delete", style: .Destructive, handler: {
            _ in
            for ident in calsToDelete {
                if let cal = self.database.calendarWithIdentifier(
                    ident as String) {
                        self.database.removeCalendar(
                            cal, commit: true, error: nil)
                }
            }
            // dismiss *everything*
            self.dismissViewControllerAnimated(true, completion: nil)
        }))
        // alert sheet inside presented-or-popover
        calendarChooser.presentViewController(
            alert, animated: true, completion: nil)
        return
    }
    self.dismissViewControllerAnimated(true, completion:nil)
}
```

That code, by the way, is vastly simpler than the corresponding code in previous editions of this book, because in iOS 8 a popover is a presented view controller and an action sheet's button handlers are closures.

CHAPTER 20

Mail and Messages

Your app can present an interface allowing the user to edit and send a mail message or an SMS message. Two view controller classes are provided by the Message UI framework; you'll need to import MessageUI. In addition, the Social framework lets you post to Twitter or Facebook on the user's behalf. You'll need to import Social. The classes are:

MFMailComposeViewController
    Allows composition and sending of a mail message.

MFMessageComposeViewController
    Allows composition and sending of an SMS message.

SLComposeViewController
    Allows composition and sending of a Twitter or Facebook post. Alternatively, you can prepare and post a message directly using SLRequest.

UIActivityViewController (Chapter 13) also provides a unified interface for permitting the user to choose any of the built-in messaging milieus and to send a message through it. However, the Message UI framework and the Social framework remain important, because the user can be presented with a message form without having to pass through an activity view, and because you can fill in fields, such as the To field in a mail composition form, that UIActivityViewController doesn't let you fill in.

 New in iOS 8, you write your own share extension to appear in the top row of a UIActivityViewController in any app. This book doesn't discuss how to write a share extension.

Mail Message

The MFMailComposeViewController class, a UINavigationController, allows the user to edit a mail message. The user can attempt to send the message there and then, or can cancel but save a draft, or can cancel completely. Before using this class to present a view, call `canSendMail`; if the result is `false`, go no further, as a negative result means that the device is not configured for sending mail. A positive result does not mean that the device is connected to the network and can send mail right now, only that sending mail is generally possible with this device; actually sending the mail (or storing it as a draft) will be up to the device's internal processes.

To use MFMailComposeViewController, instantiate it, provide a `mailCompose-Delegate` (*not* `delegate`), and configure the message to any desired extent. Configuration methods are:

- `setSubject:`
- `setToRecipients:`
- `setCcRecipients:`
- `setBccRecipients:`
- `setMessageBody:isHTML:`
- `addAttachmentData:mimeType:fileName:`

Typically, you'll show the MFMailComposeViewController as a presented view controller. (On the iPad, a `.FormSheet` presentation feels less overwhelming.) The user can later alter your preset configurations, at which time the message details will be out of your hands.

The delegate (MFMailComposeViewControllerDelegate) will receive the message `mail-ComposeController:didFinishWithResult:error:` describing the user's final action, which might be any of these:

- `MFMailComposeResultCancelled`
- `MFMailComposeResultSaved`
- `MFMailComposeResultSent`
- `MFMailComposeResultFailed`

Dismissing the presented view controller is up to you, in the delegate method. Here's a minimal example:

```
@IBAction func doMail (sender:AnyObject!) {
    let ok = MFMailComposeViewController.canSendMail()
    if !ok {
        return
    }
    let vc = MFMailComposeViewController()
    vc.mailComposeDelegate = self
    self.presentViewController(vc, animated:true, completion:nil)
}
func mailComposeController(
    controller: MFMailComposeViewController!,
    didFinishWithResult result: MFMailComposeResult,
    error: NSError!) {
        // can do something with result here
        self.dismissViewControllerAnimated(true, completion: nil)
}
```

Text Message

The MFMessageComposeViewController class is a UINavigationController subclass. Before using this class to present a view, call `canSendText`; if the result is `false`, go no further. The user has no option to save an SMS message as a draft, so even if this device sometimes *can* send text, there's no point proceeding if the device can't send text *now*. However, you can register for the `MFMessageComposeViewControllerTextMessage-AvailabilityDidChangeNotification` in the hope that the device might later be able to send text; if the notification arrives, examine its `MFMessageComposeViewController-TextMessageAvailabilityKey`.

To use MFMessageComposeViewController, instantiate the class, give it a `message-ComposeDelegate` (*not* `delegate`), and configure it as desired through the `recipients` (phone number strings) and body properties. You can also configure the message subject and provide attachments. For the subject, call the class method `canSendSubject`, and if it returns `true`, you can set the `subject`. For attachments, call the class method `can-SendAttachments`, and if it returns `true`, you may want to call `isSupportedAttachment-UTI:` to see if a particular file type can be sent as an attachment; finally, call `add-AttachmentURL:withAlternateFilename:` (if you have a file URL) or `addAttachment-Data:typeIdentifier:filename:`.

When you've finished configuring the MFMessageComposeViewController, show it as a presented view controller. The user can later alter your preset configurations, at which time the message details will be out of your hands.

The delegate (MFMessageComposeViewControllerDelegate) will receive the message `messageComposeViewController:didFinishWithResult:` with a description of the user's final action, which might be any of these:

- `MessageComposeResultCancelled`

- `MessageComposeResultSent`

- `MessageComposeResultFailed`

Dismissing the presented view controller is up to you, in the delegate method. Here's a minimal example:

```
@IBAction func doMessage (sender:AnyObject!) {
    let ok = MFMessageComposeViewController.canSendText()
    if !ok {
        return
    }
    let vc = MFMessageComposeViewController()
    vc.messageComposeDelegate = self
    self.presentViewController(vc, animated:true, completion:nil)
}
func messageComposeViewController(
    controller: MFMessageComposeViewController!,
    didFinishWithResult result: MessageComposeResult) {
        // can do something with result here
        self.dismissViewControllerAnimated(true, completion: nil)
}
```

Twitter Post

The interface for letting the user construct a Twitter post is SLComposeViewController, part of the Social framework. Twitter, together with Facebook (and Weibo), are represented by constant strings. You'll use the class method `isAvailableForServiceType:` to learn whether the desired service is available; if it is, you can instantiate SLCompose-ViewController for that service and present it as a presented view controller. Instead of a delegate, SLComposeViewController has a `completionHandler`. Set it to a closure taking one parameter, an SLComposeViewControllerResult. In the closure, dismiss the view controller. The result will be one of these:

- `SLComposeViewControllerResultCancelled`

- `SLComposeViewControllerResultDone`

Here's a minimal example:

```
@IBAction func doTwitter (sender:AnyObject!) {
    let ok = SLComposeViewController
        .isAvailableForServiceType(SLServiceTypeTwitter)
    if !ok {
        return
    }
    let vc : SLComposeViewController! =
        SLComposeViewController(forServiceType:SLServiceTypeTwitter)
```

```
        if vc == nil {
            return
        }
        vc.completionHandler = {
            (result:SLComposeViewControllerResult) in
            // can do something with result here
            self.dismissViewControllerAnimated(true, completion:nil)
        };
        self.presentViewController(vc, animated:true, completion:nil)
    }
```

You can also, with the user's permission, gain secure access to the user's account information through the ACAccountStore class (part of the Accounts framework). Using this, along with the SLRequest class, your app can construct and post a message *directly*, without passing through the message composition interface. The ACAccountStore class can manipulate accounts in other ways as well.

CHAPTER 21

Maps

Your app can imitate the Maps app, displaying a map interface and placing annotations and overlays on the map. The relevant classes are provided by the Map Kit framework. You'll need to `import MapKit`. The classes used to describe locations in terms of latitude and longitude, whose names start with "CL," come from the Core Location framework, but you won't need to import it explicitly.

Displaying a Map

A map is displayed through a UIView subclass, an MKMapView.

 You can instantiate an MKMapView from a nib. However, you will then need to link your target manually to the MapKit framework: edit the target and add *Map-Kit.framework* under Linked Frameworks and Libraries in the General tab.

A map has a `type`, which is one of the following (MKMapType):

- `.Standard`
- `.Satellite`
- `.Hybrid`

The area displayed on the map is its `region`, an MKCoordinateRegion. This is a struct comprising a location (a CLLocationCoordinate2D), describing the latitude and longitude of the point at the center of the region (the map's `centerCoordinate`), along with a span (an MKCoordinateSpan), describing the quantity of latitude and longitude embraced by the region and hence the scale of the map. Convenience functions help you construct an MKCoordinateRegion.

Figure 21-1. A map view showing a happy place

In this example, I'll initialize the display of an MKMapView (`self.map`) to show a place where I like to go dirt biking (Figure 21-1):

```
let loc = CLLocationCoordinate2DMake(34.927752,-120.217608)
let span = MKCoordinateSpanMake(0.015, 0.015)
let reg = MKCoordinateRegionMake(loc, span)
self.map.region = reg
```

An MKCoordinateSpan is described in degrees of latitude and longitude. It may be, however, that what you know is the region's proposed dimensions in meters. To convert, call `MKCoordinateRegionMakeWithDistance`. The ability to perform this conversion is important, because an MKMapView shows the world through a Mercator projection, where longitude lines are parallel and equidistant, and scale increases at higher latitudes.

I happen to know that the area I want to display is about 1200 meters on a side. Hence, this is another way of displaying roughly the same region:

```
let loc = CLLocationCoordinate2DMake(34.927752,-120.217608)
let reg = MKCoordinateRegionMakeWithDistance(loc, 1200, 1200)
self.map.region = reg
```

Yet another way of describing a map region is with an MKMapRect, a struct built up from MKMapPoint and MKMapSize. The earth has already been projected onto the map for us, and now we are describing a rectangle of that map, in terms of the units in which the map is drawn. The exact relationship between an MKMapPoint and the corresponding latitude/longitude coordinates is arbitrary and of no interest; what matters is that you can ask for the conversion, along with the ratio of points to meters (which will vary with latitude):

- `MKMapPointForCoordinate`

- `MKCoordinateForMapPoint`

- `MKMetersPerMapPointAtLatitude`

- `MKMapPointsPerMeterAtLatitude`

- `MKMetersBetweenMapPoints`

To determine what the map view is showing in MKMapRect terms, use its `visibleMap-Rect` property. Thus, this is another way of displaying approximately the same region:

```
let loc = CLLocationCoordinate2DMake(34.927752,-120.217608)
let pt = MKMapPointForCoordinate(loc)
let w = MKMapPointsPerMeterAtLatitude(loc.latitude) * 1200
self.map.visibleMapRect = MKMapRectMake(pt.x - w/2.0, pt.y - w/2.0, w, w)
```

In none of those examples did I bother with the question of the actual dimensions of the map view itself. I simply threw a proposed region at the map view, and it decided how best to portray the corresponding area. Values you assign to the map's `region` and `visibleMapRect` are unlikely to be the exact values the map adopts in any case; that's because the map view will optimize for display without distorting the map's scale. You can perform this same optimization in code by calling these methods:

- `regionThatFits:`

- `mapRectThatFits:`

- `mapRectThatFits:edgePadding:`

By default, the user can zoom and scroll the map with the usual gestures; you can turn this off by setting the map view's `zoomEnabled` and `scrollEnabled` to `false`. Usually you will set them both to `true` or both to `false`. For further customization of an MKMapView's response to touches, use a UIGestureRecognizer (Chapter 5).

You can change programmatically the region displayed, optionally with animation, by calling these methods:

- `setRegion:animated:`

- `setCenterCoordinate:animated:`

- `setVisibleMapRect:animated:`

- `setVisibleMapRect:edgePadding:animated:`

The map view's delegate (MKMapViewDelegate) is notified as the map loads and as the region changes (including changes triggered programmatically):

- `mapViewWillStartLoadingMap:`

- `mapViewDidFinishLoadingMap:`

- `mapViewDidFailLoadingMap:withError:`
- `mapView:regionWillChangeAnimated:`
- `mapView:regionDidChangeAnimated:`

You can also enable 3D viewing of the map (`pitchEnabled`), and there's a large and powerful API putting control of 3D viewing in your hands. Discussion of 3D map viewing is beyond the scope of this chapter; an excellent WWDC 2013 video surveys the topic.

 Data types such as MKCoordinateSpan are documented in the *Map Kit Data Types Reference*, but convenience functions such as `MKCoordinateSpanMake` are documented in the *Map Kit Functions Reference* — and there are some useful constants in the *Map Kit Constants Reference*. For a better overview, refer to the *MKGeometry.h* header.

Annotations

An annotation is a marker associated with a location on a map. To make an annotation appear on a map, two objects are needed:

The object attached to the MKMapView
> The annotation itself is attached to the MKMapView. It consists of any instance whose class adopts the MKAnnotation protocol, which specifies a `coordinate`, a `title`, and a `subtitle` for the annotation. You might have reason to define your own class to handle this task, or you can use the simple built-in MKPointAnnotation class. The annotation's coordinate is crucial; it says where on earth the annotation should be drawn. The title and subtitle are optional, to be displayed in a callout.

The object that draws the annotation
> An annotation is drawn by an MKAnnotationView, a UIView subclass. This can be extremely simple. In fact, even a nil MKAnnotationView might be perfectly satisfactory: it draws a red pin. If red is not your favorite color, a built-in MKAnnotation-View subclass, MKPinAnnotationView, displays a pin in red, green, or purple; by convention you are supposed to use these colors for different specific purposes — destination points, starting points, and user-specified points, respectively. For more flexibility, you can provide your own UIImage as the MKAnnotationView's `image` property. And for even *more* flexibility, you can take over the drawing of an MKAnnotationView by overriding `drawRect:` in a subclass.

Not only does an annotation require two separate objects, but in fact those objects do not initially exist together. An annotation object has no pointer to the annotation view object that will draw it. Rather, it is up to you to supply the annotation view object in

Figure 21-2. A simple annotation

real time, on demand, in the MKMapView's delegate. This architecture may sound confusing, but in fact it's a very clever way of reducing the amount of resources needed at any given moment. An annotation itself is merely a lightweight object that a map can always possess; the corresponding annotation view is a heavyweight object that is needed only so long as that annotation's coordinates are within the visible portion of the map.

Let's add the simplest possible annotation to our map. The point where the annotation is to go has been stored in an instance variable:

```
self.annloc = CLLocationCoordinate2DMake(34.923964,-120.219558)
```

We create the annotation, configure its properties, and add it to the MKMapView:

```
let ann = MKPointAnnotation()
ann.coordinate = self.annloc
ann.title = "Park here"
ann.subtitle = "Fun awaits down the road!"
self.map.addAnnotation(ann)
```

That code is sufficient to produce Figure 21-2. I didn't implement any MKMapView delegate methods, so the MKAnnotationView is nil. But a nil MKAnnotationView, as I've already said, produces a red pin. I've also tapped the annotation, to display its callout, containing the annotation's title and subtitle.

Custom Annotation View

The location marked by our annotation is the starting point of a suggested dirt bike ride, so by convention the pin should be green. We can easily create a green pin using MKPinAnnotationView, which has a `pinColor` property. To supply the annotation view, we must give the map view a delegate (MKMapViewDelegate) and implement `map-View:viewForAnnotation:`.

The structure of `mapView:viewForAnnotation:` is rather similar to the structure of `tableView:cellForRowAtIndexPath:` (Chapter 8), which is not surprising, considering that they both do the same sort of thing. Recall that the goal of `tableView:cellForRow-AtIndexPath:` is to allow the table view to reuse cells, so that at any given moment only as many cells are needed as are *visible* in the table view, regardless of how many rows the table as a whole may consist of. The same thing holds for a map and its annotation views. The map may have a huge number of annotations, but it needs to display annotation views for only those annotations that are within its current `region`. Any extra annotation views that have been scrolled out of view can thus be reused and are held for us by the map view in a cache for exactly this purpose.

So, in `mapView:viewForAnnotation:`, we start by calling `dequeueReusableAnnotation-ViewWithIdentifier:` to see whether there's an already existing annotation view that's not currently being displayed and that we might be able to reuse. If there isn't, we create one, attaching to it an appropriate reuse identifier.

Here's our implementation of `mapView:viewForAnnotation:`. Observe that in creating our green pin, we explicitly set its `canShowCallout` to `true`, as this is not the default:

```
func mapView(mapView: MKMapView!,
    viewForAnnotation annotation: MKAnnotation!) -> MKAnnotationView! {
        var v : MKAnnotationView! = nil
        if annotation.title == "Park here" { ❶
            let ident = "greenPin" ❷
            v = mapView.dequeueReusableAnnotationViewWithIdentifier(ident)
            if v == nil {
                v = MKPinAnnotationView(
                    annotation:annotation, reuseIdentifier:ident)
                (v as! MKPinAnnotationView).pinColor = .Green
                v.canShowCallout = true
            }
            v.annotation = annotation ❸
        }
        return v
}
```

The structure of this implementation of `mapView:viewForAnnotation:` is typical (though it seems pointlessly elaborate when we have only one annotation in our map):

❶ We might have more than one reusable type of annotation view, so we must somehow distinguish the possible cases, based on *something about the incoming annotation*. Here, I use the annotation's title as a distinguishing mark; later in this chapter, I'll suggest a much better approach.

❷ For each reusable type, we proceed much as with table view cells. We have an identifier that categorizes this sort of reusable view. We try to dequeue an unused annotation view of the appropriate type, and if we can't, we create one and configure it.

❸ Even if we *can* dequeue an unused annotation view, and even if we have no other configuration to perform, we must associate the annotation view with the incoming annotation by assigning the annotation to this annotation view's annotation property.

MKAnnotationView has one more option of which we might avail ourselves: when it draws the annotation view (the pin), it can animate it into place, dropping it in the manner familiar from the Maps app. All we have to do is add one line of code:

```
(v as! MKPinAnnotationView).animatesDrop = true
```

Now let's go further. Instead of a green pin, we'll substitute our own artwork. I'll revise the code at the heart of my mapView:viewForAnnotation: implementation, such that instead of creating an MKPinAnnotationView, I create an instance of its superclass, MKAnnotationView, and give it a custom image showing a dirt bike. The image is too large, so I shrink the view's bounds before returning it; I also move the view up a bit, so that the bottom of the image is at the coordinates on the map (Figure 21-3):

```
func mapView(mapView: MKMapView!,
    viewForAnnotation annotation: MKAnnotation!) -> MKAnnotationView! {
        var v : MKAnnotationView! = nil
        if annotation.title == "Park here" {
            let ident = "bike"
            v = mapView.dequeueReusableAnnotationViewWithIdentifier(ident)
            if v == nil {
                v = MKAnnotationView(
                    annotation:annotation, reuseIdentifier:ident)
                v.image = UIImage(named:"clipartdirtbike.gif")
                v.bounds.size.height /= 3.0
                v.bounds.size.width /= 3.0
                v.centerOffset = CGPointMake(0,-20)
                v.canShowCallout = true
            }
            v.annotation = annotation
        }
        return v
}
```

For more flexibility, we can create our own MKAnnotationView subclass and endow it with the ability to draw itself. At a minimum, such a subclass should override the initializer and assign itself a frame, and should implement drawRect:. Here's the implementation for a class MyAnnotationView that draws a dirt bike:

```
class MyAnnotationView : MKAnnotationView {
    override init(annotation:MKAnnotation, reuseIdentifier:String) {
        super.init(
            annotation: annotation, reuseIdentifier: reuseIdentifier)
        let im = UIImage(named:"clipartdirtbike.gif")!
        self.frame = CGRectMake(
            0, 0, im.size.width / 3.0 + 5, im.size.height / 3.0 + 5)
```

Figure 21-3. A custom annotation image

```
        self.centerOffset = CGPointMake(0,-20)
        self.opaque = false
    }
    override init(frame: CGRect) {
        super.init(frame:frame)
    }
    required init(coder: NSCoder) {
        fatalError("NSCoding not supported")
    }
    override func drawRect(rect: CGRect) {
        let im = UIImage(named:"clipartdirtbike.gif")!
        im.drawInRect(self.bounds.rectByInsetting(dx: 5, dy: 5))
    }
}
```

The corresponding implementation of `mapView:viewForAnnotation:` now has much less work to do:

```
func mapView(mapView: MKMapView!,
    viewForAnnotation annotation: MKAnnotation!) -> MKAnnotationView! {
        var v : MKAnnotationView! = nil
        if annotation.title == "Park here" {
            let ident = "bike"
            v = mapView.dequeueReusableAnnotationViewWithIdentifier(ident)
            if v == nil {
                v = MyAnnotationView(
                    annotation:annotation, reuseIdentifier:ident)
                v.canShowCallout = true
            }
            v.annotation = annotation
        }
        return v
}
```

Custom Annotation Class

For ultimate flexibility, we can provide our own annotation class as well! A minimal annotation class will look like this:

```
class MyAnnotation : NSObject, MKAnnotation {
    dynamic var coordinate: CLLocationCoordinate2D
    var title: String!
    var subtitle: String!
    init(location coord:CLLocationCoordinate2D) {
        self.coordinate = coord
        super.init()
    }
}
```

Now when we create our annotation and add it to our map, our code looks like this:

```
let ann = MyAnnotation(location:self.annloc)
ann.title = "Park here"
ann.subtitle = "Fun awaits down the road!"
self.map.addAnnotation(ann)
```

A major advantage of this change appears in our implementation of `mapView:viewForAnnotation:`, where we test for the annotation type. Formerly, it wasn't easy to distinguish those annotations that needed to be drawn as a dirt bike; we were rather artificially examining the title:

```
if annotation.title == "Park here" {
```

Now, however, we can just look at the class:

```
if annotation is MyAnnotation {
```

A further advantage of supplying our own annotation class is that this approach gives our implementation room to grow. For example, at the moment, every MyAnnotation is drawn as a bike, but we could now add another property to MyAnnotation that tells us what drawing to use. We could also give MyAnnotation further properties saying such things as which way the bike should face, what angle it should be drawn at, and so on. Each instance of MyAnnotationView will end up with a reference to the corresponding MyAnnotation instance (as its `annotation` property), so it would be able to read those MyAnnotation properties and draw itself appropriately.

Other Annotation Features

To add our own animation to an annotation view as it appears on the map, analogous to the built-in MKPinAnnotationView pin-drop animation, we implement the map view delegate method `mapView:didAddAnnotationViews:`. The key fact here is that at the moment this method is called, the annotation view has been added but the redraw moment has not yet arrived (Chapter 4). So if we animate the view, that animation will be performed at the moment the view appears onscreen. Here, I'll animate the opacity of the view so that it fades in, while growing the view from a point to its full size; I identify the view type through its `reuseIdentifier`:

```
func mapView(mapView: MKMapView!,
    didAddAnnotationViews views: [AnyObject]!) {
        for aView in views as! [MKAnnotationView] {
            if aView.reuseIdentifier == "bike" {
                aView.transform = CGAffineTransformMakeScale(0, 0)
                aView.alpha = 0
                UIView.animateWithDuration(0.8) {
                    aView.alpha = 1
                    aView.transform = CGAffineTransformIdentity
                }
            }
        }
}
```

The callout is visible in Figures 21-2 and 21-3 because before taking the screenshot, I tapped on the annotation, thus *selecting* it. MKMapView has methods allowing annotations to be selected or deselected programmatically, thus (by default) causing their callouts to appear or disappear. The delegate has methods notifying you when the user selects or deselects an annotation, and you are free to override your custom MKAnnotationView's `setSelected:animated:` if you want to change what happens when the user taps an annotation. For example, you could show and hide a custom view instead of, or in addition to, the built-in callout.

A callout can contain left and right accessory views; these are the MKAnnotationView's `leftCalloutAccessoryView` and `rightCalloutAccessoryView`. They are UIViews, and should be small (less than 32 pixels in height). The map view's `tintColor` (see Chapter 12) affects such accessory view elements as template images and button titles. You can respond to taps on these views as you would any view or control; as a convenience, a delegate method `mapView:annotationView:calloutAccessoryControl-Tapped:` is called when the user taps an accessory view, provided it is a UIControl.

An MKAnnotationView can optionally be draggable by the user; set its `draggable` property to `true` and implement the map view delegate's `mapView:annotationView:did-ChangeDragState:fromOldState:`. A minimal implementation must update the MKAnnotationView's `dragState`, like this:

```
func mapView(mapView: MKMapView!, annotationView view: MKAnnotationView!,
    didChangeDragState newState: MKAnnotationViewDragState,
    fromOldState oldState: MKAnnotationViewDragState) {
        switch (newState) {
        case .Starting:
            view.dragState = .Dragging
        case .Ending, .Canceling:
            view.dragState = .None
        default: break
        }
}
```

(You can also customize changes to the appearance of the view as it is dragged, by implementing your annotation view class's `setDragState:animated:` method.) If you're using a custom annotation class, its `coordinate` property must also be settable; in our custom annotation class, MyAnnotation, the `coordinate` property is explicitly declared as a read-write property (`var`), as opposed to the `coordinate` property in the MKAnnotation protocol which is read-only.

Certain annotation properties and annotation view properties are automatically animatable through view animation, provided you've implemented them in a KVO compliant way. For example, in MyAnnotation, the `coordinate` property is KVO compliant (because we declared it `dynamic`); therefore, we are able to animate shifting the annotation's position:

```
UIView.animateWithDuration(0.25) {
    var loc = ann.coordinate
    loc.latitude = loc.latitude + 0.0005
    loc.longitude = loc.longitude + 0.001
    ann.coordinate = loc
}
```

MKMapView has extensive support for adding and removing annotations. Also, given a bunch of annotations, you can ask your MKMapView to zoom in such a way that all of them are showing (`showAnnotations:animated:`).

Annotation views don't change size as the map is zoomed in and out, so if there are several annotations and they are brought close together by the user zooming out, the display can become crowded. Moreover, if too many annotations are being drawn simultaneously in a map view, scroll and zoom performance can degrade. The only way to prevent this is to respond to changes in the map's visible region (for example, in the delegate method `mapView:regionDidChangeAnimated:`) by removing and adding annotations dynamically. This is a tricky problem; MKMapView's `annotationsInMapRect:` efficiently lists the annotations within a given MKMapRect, but deciding which ones to eliminate or restore, and when, is still up to you.

Overlays

An overlay differs from an annotation in being drawn entirely with respect to points on the surface of the earth. Thus, whereas an annotation's size is always the same, an overlay's size is tied to the zoom of the map view.

Overlays are implemented much like annotations. You provide an object that adopts the MKOverlay protocol (which itself conforms to the MKAnnotation protocol) and add it to the map view. When the map view delegate method `mapView:viewForOverlay:` is called, you provide an MKOverlayRenderer and hand it the overlay object; the overlay renderer then draws the overlay on demand. As with annotations, this architecture

Figure 21-4. An overlay

means that the overlay itself is a lightweight object, and the overlay is drawn only if the part of the earth that the overlay covers is actually being displayed in the map view. An MKOverlayRenderer has no reuse identifier.

Some built-in MKShape subclasses adopt the MKOverlay protocol: MKCircle, MKPolygon, and MKPolyline. In parallel to those, MKOverlayRenderer has built-in subclasses MKCircleRenderer, MKPolygonRenderer, and MKPolylineRenderer, ready to draw the corresponding shapes. Thus, as with annotations, you can base your overlay entirely on the power of existing classes.

In this example, I'll use MKPolygonRenderer to draw an overlay triangle pointing up the road from the parking place annotated in our earlier examples (Figure 21-4). We add the MKPolygon as an overlay to our map view, and derive the MKPolygonRenderer from it in our implementation of `mapView:viewForOverlay:`. First, the MKPolygon overlay:

```
let lat = self.annloc.latitude
let metersPerPoint = MKMetersPerMapPointAtLatitude(lat)
var c = MKMapPointForCoordinate(self.annloc)
c.x += 150/metersPerPoint
c.y -= 50/metersPerPoint
var p1 = MKMapPointMake(c.x, c.y)
p1.y -= 100/metersPerPoint
var p2 = MKMapPointMake(c.x, c.y)
p2.x += 100/metersPerPoint
var p3 = MKMapPointMake(c.x, c.y)
p3.x += 300/metersPerPoint
p3.y -= 400/metersPerPoint
var pts = [
    p1, p2, p3
]
let tri = MKPolygon(points:&pts, count:3)
self.map.addOverlay(tri)
```

Second, the delegate method, where we provide the MKPolygonRenderer:

```
func mapView(mapView: MKMapView!,
    rendererForOverlay overlay: MKOverlay!) -> MKOverlayRenderer! {
        var v : MKPolygonRenderer! = nil
        if let overlay = overlay as? MKPolygon {
            v = MKPolygonRenderer(polygon:overlay)
            v.fillColor = UIColor.redColor().colorWithAlphaComponent(0.1)
            v.strokeColor = UIColor.redColor().colorWithAlphaComponent(0.8)
            v.lineWidth = 2
        }
        return v
}
```

Custom Overlay Class

The triangle in Figure 21-4 is rather crude; I could draw a better arrow shape using a CGPath (Chapter 2). The built-in MKOverlayRenderer subclass that lets me do that is MKOverlayPathRenderer. To structure my use of MKOverlayRenderer similarly to the preceding example, I'll supply the CGPath when I add the overlay instance to the map view. No built-in class lets me do that, so I'll use a custom class, MyOverlay, that implements the MKOverlay protocol.

A minimal overlay class looks like this:

```
class MyOverlay : NSObject, MKOverlay {
    var coordinate : CLLocationCoordinate2D {
        get {
            let pt = MKMapPointMake(
                MKMapRectGetMidX(self.boundingMapRect),
                MKMapRectGetMidY(self.boundingMapRect))
            return MKCoordinateForMapPoint(pt)
        }
    }
    var boundingMapRect : MKMapRect
    init(rect:MKMapRect) {
        self.boundingMapRect = rect
        super.init()
    }
}
```

Our actual MyOverlay class will also have a `path` property; this will be a UIBezierPath that holds our CGPath and supplies it to the MKOverlayRenderer.

Just as the `coordinate` property of an annotation tells the map view where on earth the annotation is to be drawn, the `boundingMapRect` property of an overlay tells the map view where on earth the overlay is to be drawn. Whenever any part of the `boundingMap-Rect` is displayed within the map view's bounds, the map view will have to concern itself with drawing the overlay. With MKPolygon, we supplied the points of the polygon in earth coordinates and the `boundingMapRect` was calculated for us. With our custom overlay class, we must supply or calculate it ourselves.

At first it may appear that there is a typological impedance mismatch: the boundingMap-Rect is an MKMapRect, whereas a CGPath is defined by CGPoints. However, it turns out that these units are interchangeable: the CGPoints of our CGPath will be translated for us directly into MKMapPoints on the same scale — that is, the *distance* between any two CGPoints will be the distance between the two corresponding MKMapPoints. However, the *origins* are different: the CGPath must be described relative to the top-left corner of the boundingMapRect — to put it another way, the boundingMapRect is described in earth coordinates, but the top-left corner of the boundingMapRect is {0,0} as far as the CGPath is concerned. (You might think of this difference as analogous to the difference between a UIView's frame and its bounds.)

To make life simple, I'll think in meters; actually, I'll think in chunks of 75 meters, because this turns out to be a good unit for positioning and laying out the arrow. Thus, a line one unit long would in fact be 75 meters long if I were to arrive at this actual spot on the earth and discover the overlay literally drawn on the ground. Having derived this chunk (unit), I use it to lay out the boundingMapRect, four units on a side and positioned slightly east and north of the annotation point (because that's where the road is). Then I simply construct the arrow shape within the 4×4-unit square, rotating it so that it points in roughly the same direction as the road:

```
// start with our position and derive a nice unit for drawing
let lat = self.annloc.latitude
let metersPerPoint = MKMetersPerMapPointAtLatitude(lat)
let c = MKMapPointForCoordinate(self.annloc)
let unit = CGFloat(75.0/metersPerPoint)
// size and position the overlay bounds on the earth
let sz = CGSizeMake(4*unit, 4*unit)
let mr = MKMapRectMake(
    c.x + 2*Double(unit), c.y - 4.5*Double(unit),
    Double(sz.width), Double(sz.height))
// describe the arrow as a CGPath
let p = CGPathCreateMutable()
let start = CGPointMake(0, unit*1.5)
let p1 = CGPointMake(start.x+2*unit, start.y)
let p2 = CGPointMake(p1.x, p1.y-unit)
let p3 = CGPointMake(p2.x+unit*2, p2.y+unit*1.5)
let p4 = CGPointMake(p2.x, p2.y+unit*3)
let p5 = CGPointMake(p4.x, p4.y-unit)
let p6 = CGPointMake(p5.x-2*unit, p5.y)
var points = [
    start, p1, p2, p3, p4, p5, p6
]
// rotate the arrow around its center
let t1 = CGAffineTransformMakeTranslation(unit*2, unit*2)
let t2 = CGAffineTransformRotate(t1, CGFloat(-M_PI)/3.5)
var t3 = CGAffineTransformTranslate(t2, -unit*2, -unit*2)
CGPathAddLines(p, &t3, &points, 7)
CGPathCloseSubpath(p)
// create the overlay and give it the path
```

Figure 21-5. A nicer overlay

```
let over = MyOverlay(rect:mr)
over.path = UIBezierPath(CGPath:p)
// add the overlay to the map
self.map.addOverlay(over)
```

The delegate method, where we provide the MKOverlayPathRenderer, is simple. We pull the CGPath out of the MyOverlay instance and hand it to the MKOverlayPathRenderer, also telling the MKOverlayPathRenderer how to stroke and fill that path:

```
func mapView(mapView: MKMapView!,
    rendererForOverlay overlay: MKOverlay!) -> MKOverlayRenderer! {
        var v : MKOverlayPathRenderer! = nil
        if let overlay = overlay as? MyOverlay {
            v = MKOverlayPathRenderer(overlay:overlay)
            v.path = overlay.path.CGPath
            v.fillColor = UIColor.redColor().colorWithAlphaComponent(0.2)
            v.strokeColor = UIColor.blackColor()
            v.lineWidth = 2
        }
        return v
}
```

The result is a much nicer arrow (Figure 21-5), and of course this technique can be generalized to draw an overlay from any CGPath we like.

Custom Overlay Renderer

For full generality, you could define your own MKOverlayRenderer subclass; your subclass must override and implement drawMapRect:zoomScale:inContext:. The incoming mapRect: parameter describes a tile of the visible map (not the size and position of the overlay). The overlay itself is available through the inherited overlay property, and conversion methods such as rectForMapRect: are provided for converting between the map's mapRect: coordinates and the overlay renderer's graphics context coordinates.

In our example, we can move the entire functionality for drawing the arrow into an MKOverlayRenderer subclass, which I'll call MyOverlayRenderer. Its initializer takes an angle: parameter, with which I'll set its angle property; now our arrow can point in any direction. Another nice benefit of this architectural change is that we can use the zoomScale: parameter to determine the stroke width. For simplicity, our implementation of drawMapRect:zoomScale:inContext: ignores the incoming mapRect value and just draws the entire arrow every time it is called:

```
var angle : CGFloat
init(overlay:MKOverlay!, angle:CGFloat) {
    self.angle = angle
    super.init(overlay:overlay)
}
override func drawMapRect(
    mapRect: MKMapRect, zoomScale: MKZoomScale,
    inContext context: CGContext!) {
        CGContextSetStrokeColorWithColor(
            context, UIColor.blackColor().CGColor)
        CGContextSetFillColorWithColor(context,
        UIColor.redColor().colorWithAlphaComponent(0.2).CGColor)
        CGContextSetLineWidth(context, 1.2/zoomScale)
        let unit =
            CGFloat(MKMapRectGetWidth(self.overlay.boundingMapRect)/4.0)
        let p = CGPathCreateMutable()
        let start = CGPointMake(0, unit*1.5)
        let p1 = CGPointMake(start.x+2*unit, start.y)
        let p2 = CGPointMake(p1.x, p1.y-unit)
        let p3 = CGPointMake(p2.x+unit*2, p2.y+unit*1.5)
        let p4 = CGPointMake(p2.x, p2.y+unit*3)
        let p5 = CGPointMake(p4.x, p4.y-unit)
        let p6 = CGPointMake(p5.x-2*unit, p5.y)
        let points = [
            start, p1, p2, p3, p4, p5, p6
        ]
        // rotate the arrow around its center
        let t1 = CGAffineTransformMakeTranslation(unit*2, unit*2)
        let t2 = CGAffineTransformRotate(t1, self.angle)
        var t3 = CGAffineTransformTranslate(t2, -unit*2, -unit*2)
        CGPathAddLines(p, &t3, points, 7)
        CGPathCloseSubpath(p)
        CGContextAddPath(context, p)
        CGContextDrawPath(context, kCGPathFillStroke)
}
```

To add the overlay to our map, we still must determine its MKMapRect:

```
let lat = self.annloc.latitude
let metersPerPoint = MKMetersPerMapPointAtLatitude(lat)
let c = MKMapPointForCoordinate(self.annloc)
let unit = 75.0/metersPerPoint
// size and position the overlay bounds on the earth
let sz = CGSizeMake(4*CGFloat(unit), 4*CGFloat(unit))
let mr = MKMapRectMake(
```

```
        c.x + 2*unit, c.y - 4.5*unit,
        Double(sz.width), Double(sz.height))
    let over = MyOverlay(rect:mr)
    self.map.addOverlay(over)
```

The delegate, providing the overlay renderer, now has very little work to do; in our implementation, it must supply an angle for the arrow:

```
func mapView(mapView: MKMapView!,
    rendererForOverlay overlay: MKOverlay!) -> MKOverlayRenderer! {
        var v : MKOverlayRenderer! = nil
        if overlay is MyOverlay {
            v = MyOverlayRenderer(
                overlay:overlay, angle: -CGFloat(M_PI)/3.5)
        }
        return v
}
```

Other Overlay Features

Our MyOverlay class, adopting the MKOverlay protocol, also implements the coordinate getter method to return the center of the boundingMapRect. This is crude, but it's a good minimal implementation. The purpose of the MKOverlay coordinate property is to specify the position where you would add an annotation describing the overlay. For example:

```
// ... create overlay and assign it a path as before ...
self.map.addOverlay(over)
let annot = MKPointAnnotation()
annot.coordinate = over.coordinate
annot.title = "This way!"
self.map.addAnnotation(annot)
```

The MKOverlay protocol also lets you provide an implementation of intersectsMap-Rect: to refine your overlay's definition of what constitutes an intersection with itself; the default is to use the boundingMapRect, but if your overlay is drawn in some non-rectangular shape, you might want to use its actual shape as the basis for determining intersection.

Overlays are maintained by the map view as an array and are drawn from back to front starting at the beginning of the array. MKMapView has extensive support for adding and removing overlays, and for managing their layering order. When you add the overlay to the map, you can say where you want it drawn among the map view's sublayers; methods for adding and inserting overlays have a level: parameter (for example, add-Overlay:level:). The levels are (MKOverlayLevel):

- `.AboveRoads` (and below labels)
- `.AboveLabels`

The MKOverlayTile class, adopting the MKOverlay protocol, lets you superimpose, or even substitute (`canReplaceMapContent`), a map view's drawing of the map itself. It works much like CATiledLayer (Chapter 7): you provide a set of tiles at multiple sizes to match multiple zoom levels, and the map view fetches and draws the tiles needed for the current `region` and degree of zoom. In this way, for example, you could integrate your own topo map into an MKMapView's display. It takes a lot of tiles to draw an area of any size, so MKOverlayTile starts with a URL, which can be a remote URL for tiles to be fetched across the Internet.

Map Kit and Current Location

A device may have sensors that can determine its current location (Chapter 22). Map Kit provides simple integration with these facilities. Keep in mind that the user can turn off these sensors or can refuse your app access to them (in the Settings app, under Privacy → Location Services), so trying to use these features may fail. Also, determining the device's location can take time.

You can ask an MKMapView in your app to display the device's location just by setting its `showsUserLocation` property to `true`; the map will then automatically put an annotation at that location. New in iOS 8, however, you must obtain authorization first. You'll need a CLLocationManager instance — the usual thing is to retain it in a property — and you'll request authorization through the instance method `requestWhenInUse-Authorization`. Also, you *must* have an NSLocationWhenInUseUsageDescription entry in your app's *Info.plist*. (I'll talk more about location authorization in Chapter 22.)

The `userLocation` property of the map view is an MKUserLocation, adopting the MKAnnotation protocol. It has a `location` property, a CLLocation, whose `coordinate` is a CLLocationCoordinate2D; if the map view's `showsUserLocation` is `true` and the map view has actually worked out the user's location, the `coordinate` describes that location. It also has `title` and `subtitle` properties, plus you can check whether it is currently `updating`. The default annotation appearance comes from the map view's `tintColor`. You are free to supply your own annotation view to be displayed for this annotation, just as for any annotation.

Displaying the appropriate region of the map — that is, actually *showing* the part of the world where the user is located — is a separate task. The simplest way is to take advantage of the MKMapView's `userTrackingMode` property, which determines how the user's real-world location should be tracked *automatically* by the map display; your options are (MKUserTrackingMode):

`.None`
> If `showsUserLocation` is `true`, the map gets an annotation at the user's location, but that's all; the map's `region` is unchanged. You could set it manually by responding to the delegate method `mapView:didUpdateUserLocation:`.

`.Follow`
> Setting this mode sets `showsUserLocation` to `true`. The map automatically centers the user's location and scales appropriately. When the map is in this mode, you should *not* set the map's `region` manually, as you'll be struggling against the tracking mode's attempts to do the same thing.

`.FollowWithHeading`
> Like `.Follow`, but the map is also rotated so that the direction the user is facing is up. In this case, the `userLocation` annotation also has a `heading` property, a CLHeading; I'll talk more about headings in Chapter 22.

So, presume we have CLLocationManager property:

```
let locman = CLLocationManager()
```

Then this code is sufficient to start displaying the user's location:

```
self.locman.requestWhenInUseAuthorization()
self.map.userTrackingMode = .Follow // sets showsUserLocation to true
```

When the `userTrackingMode` is one of the `Follow` modes, if the user is left free to zoom and scroll the map, and if the user scrolls in such a way that the user location annotation is no longer visible, the `userTrackingMode` may be automatically changed back to `.None` (and the user location annotation may be removed). You'll probably want to provide a way to let the user turn tracking back on again, or to toggle among the three tracking modes.

One way to do that is with an MKUserTrackingBarButtonItem, a UIBarButtonItem subclass. You initialize MKUserTrackingBarButtonItem with a map view, and its behavior is automatic from then on: when the user taps it, it switches the map view to the next tracking mode, and its icon reflects the current tracking mode. This is the same bar button item that appears at the far left in the toolbar of the Maps app.

You can ask the map view whether the user's location, if known, is in the visible region of the map (`isUserLocationVisible`).

It is also possible to ask the Maps app to display the device's current location, as I'll describe in the next section.

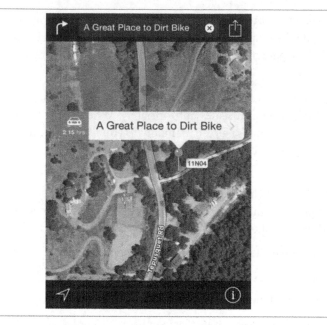

Figure 21-6. The Maps app displays our point of interest

Communicating With the Maps App

Your app can communicate with the Maps app. For example, instead of displaying a point of interest in a map view in our own app, we can ask the Maps app to display it. The user could then bookmark or share the location. The channel of communication between your app and the Maps app is the MKMapItem class.

Here, I'll ask the Maps app to display the same point marked by the annotation in our earlier examples, on a hybrid map portraying the same region of the earth (Figure 21-6):

```
let p = MKPlacemark(coordinate:self.annloc, addressDictionary:nil)
let mi = MKMapItem(placemark: p)
mi.name = "A Great Place to Dirt Bike" // label to appear in Maps app
let opts = [
    MKLaunchOptionsMapTypeKey: MKMapType.Hybrid.rawValue
]
mi.openInMapsWithLaunchOptions(opts)
```

 In theory it should be possible to set the zoom level of the Maps app display with the MKLaunchOptionsMapSpanKey key, but in my experimentation this has no effect. I regard that as a bug.

If you start with an MKMapItem returned by the class method `mapItemForCurrent-Location`, you're asking the Maps app to display the device's current location. This call doesn't attempt to determine the device's location, nor does it contain any location information; it merely generates an MKMapItem which, when sent to the Maps app, will cause *it* to attempt to determine (and display) the device's location:

```
let mi = MKMapItem.mapItemForCurrentLocation()
mi.openInMapsWithLaunchOptions(
    [MKLaunchOptionsMapTypeKey: MKMapType.Standard.rawValue])
```

Geocoding, Searching, and Directions

Map Kit provides your app with three services that involve performing queries over the network. These services take time and might not succeed at all, as they depend upon network and server availability; moreover, results may be more or less uncertain. Therefore, they involve a completion handler that is called back asynchronously on the main thread. The three services are:

Geocoding
> Translation of a street address to a coordinate and *vice versa*. For example, what address am I at right now? Or conversely, what are the coordinates of my home address?

Searching
> Lookup of possible matches for a natural language search. For example, what are some Thai restaurants near me?

Directions
> Lookup of turn-by-turn instructions and route mapping from a source location to a destination location.

The completion handler is called, in every case, with a single response object plus an NSError. If the response object is nil, the NSError tells you what the problem was.

Geocoding

Geocoding functionality is encapsulated in the CLGeocoder class. The response, if things went well, is an array of CLPlacemark objects, a series of guesses from best to worst; if things went *really* well, the array will contain exactly one CLPlacemark.

A CLPlacemark can be used to initialize an MKPlacemark, a CLPlacemark subclass that adopts the MKAnnotation protocol, and is therefore suitable to be handed directly over to an MKMapView for display.

Here is an (unbelievably simpleminded) example that allows the user to enter an address in a UISearchBar (Chapter 12) to be displayed in an MKMapView:

```
let s = searchBar.text
let geo = CLGeocoder()
geo.geocodeAddressString(s) {
    (placemarks : [AnyObject]!, error : NSError!) in
    if nil == placemarks {
        println(error.localizedDescription)
        return
    }
    let p = placemarks[0] as! CLPlacemark
    let mp = MKPlacemark(placemark:p)
    self.map.removeAnnotations(self.map.annotations)
    self.map.addAnnotation(mp)
    self.map.setRegion(
        MKCoordinateRegionMakeWithDistance(mp.coordinate, 1000, 1000),
        animated: true)
}
```

By default, the resulting annotation's callout `title` contains a nicely formatted string describing the address.

That example illustrates *forward geocoding*, the conversion of an address to a coordinate. Instead of a string, you can provide a dictionary. By an amazing coincidence, the keys of this dictionary are exactly the keys you would get by extracting an address from the user's address book (Chapter 18); thus, you can go quite directly from an address book contact to a coordinate.

The converse operation is *reverse geocoding*: you start with a coordinate — actually a CLLocation, which you'll obtain from elsewhere, or construct from a coordinate using `init(latitude:longitude:)` — and call `reverseGeocodeLocation:completion-Handler:` in order to obtain an address. The address is expressed through the CLPlacemark `addressDictionary` property, which is an address in address book format; you can translate it to a string with `ABCreateStringWithAddressDictionary` (you'll need to `import AddressBookUI`). Alternatively, you can consult directly various CLPlacemark properties, such as `subthoroughfare` (a house number), `thoroughfare` (a street name), `locality` (a town), and `administrativeArea` (a state).

 Those properties are present in a placemark resulting from forward geocoding as well; thus, one nice byproduct of forward geocoding is that it can format and complete an address, including adding a zip code (`postalCode`) to the address.

In this example of reverse geocoding, we have an MKMapView that is already tracking the user, and so we have the user's location as the map's `userLocation`; we ask for the corresponding address:

```
let loc = self.map.userLocation.location
let geo = CLGeocoder()
geo.reverseGeocodeLocation(loc) {
    (placemarks : [AnyObject]!, error : NSError!) in
    if placemarks != nil {
        let p = placemarks[0] as! CLPlacemark
        let s = ABCreateStringWithAddressDictionary(
            p.addressDictionary, false)
        println("you are at:\n\(s)")
    }
}
```

Searching

The MKLocalSearch class, along with MKLocalSearchRequest and MKLocalSearch-Response, lets you ask the server to perform a natural language search for you. This is less formal than forward geocoding, described in the previous section; instead of searching for an address, you can search for a point of interest by name or description. It can be useful, for some types of search, to constrain the area of interest by setting the MKLocalSearchRequest's `region`. In this example, I'll do a natural language search for a Thai restaurant near the user location currently displayed in the map, and I'll display it with an annotation in our map view:

```
let userLoc = self.map.userLocation
let loc = userLoc.location
let req = MKLocalSearchRequest()
req.naturalLanguageQuery = "Thai restaurant"
req.region = MKCoordinateRegionMake(
    loc.coordinate, MKCoordinateSpanMake(1,1))
let search = MKLocalSearch(request:req)
search.startWithCompletionHandler() {
    (response : MKLocalSearchResponse!, error : NSError!) in
    if response == nil {
        println(error)
        return
    }
    self.map.showsUserLocation = false
    let mi = response.mapItems[0] as! MKMapItem // I'm feeling lucky
    let place = mi.placemark
    let loc = place.location.coordinate
    let reg = MKCoordinateRegionMakeWithDistance(loc, 1200, 1200)
    self.map.setRegion(reg, animated:true)
    let ann = MKPointAnnotation()
    ann.title = mi.name
    ann.subtitle = mi.phoneNumber
    ann.coordinate = loc
    self.map.addAnnotation(ann)
}
```

Directions

The MKDirections class, along with MKDirectionsRequest and MKDirections-Response, looks up walking or driving directions between two locations expressed as MKMapItem objects. The resulting MKDirectionsResponse includes an array of MKRoute objects; each MKRoute includes an MKPolyline suitable for display as an overlay in your map, as well as an array of MKRouteStep objects, each of which provides its own MKPolyline plus instructions and distances. The MKDirectionsResponse also has its own source and destination MKMapItems, which may be different from what we started with.

To illustrate, I'll continue from the Thai food example in the previous section, starting at the point where we obtained the Thai restaurant's MKMapItem:

```
// ... same as before up to this point ...
let mi = response.mapItems[0] as! MKMapItem // I'm still feeling lucky
let req = MKDirectionsRequest()
req.setSource(MKMapItem.mapItemForCurrentLocation())
req.setDestination(mi)
let dir = MKDirections(request:req)
dir.calculateDirectionsWithCompletionHandler() {
    (response:MKDirectionsResponse!, error:NSError!) in
    if response == nil {
        println(error)
        return
    }
    println("got directions")
    let route = response.routes[0] as! MKRoute // I'm feeling really lucky
    let poly = route.polyline
    self.map.addOverlay(poly)
    for step in route.steps {
        println("After \(step.distance) metres: \(step.instructions)")
    }
}
```

The step-by-step instructions appear in the console; in real life, of course, we would presumably display these in our app's interface. The route is drawn in our map view, provided we have an appropriate implementation of mapView:rendererForOverlay:, such as this:

```
func mapView(mapView: MKMapView!,
    rendererForOverlay overlay: MKOverlay!) -> MKOverlayRenderer! {
        var v : MKPolylineRenderer! = nil
        if let overlay = overlay as? MKPolyline {
            v = MKPolylineRenderer(polyline:overlay)
            v.strokeColor =
                UIColor.blueColor().colorWithAlphaComponent(0.8)
            v.lineWidth = 2
        }
        return v
}
```

CHAPTER 22

Sensors

A device may contain hardware for sensing the world around itself — where it is located, how it is oriented, how it is moving.

Information about the device's current location and how that location is changing over time, using its Wi-Fi, cellular networking, and GPS capabilities, along with information about the device's orientation relative to north, using its magnetometer, is provided through the Core Location framework. You'll need to `import CoreLocation`.

Information about the device's change in speed and attitude using its accelerometer is provided through the UIEvent class (for device shake) and the Core Motion framework, which provides increased accuracy by incorporating the device's gyroscope, if it has one, as well as the magnetometer; you'll need to `import CoreMotion`.

One of the major challenges associated with writing code that takes advantage of the sensors is that different devices have different hardware. If you don't want to impose stringent restrictions on what devices your app will run on in the first place (`UIRequired-DeviceCapabilities` in the *Info.plist*), your code must be prepared to fail gracefully and possibly provide a subset of its full capabilities when it discovers that the current device lacks certain features.

Moreover, certain sensors may experience momentary inadequacy; for example, Core Location might not be able to get a fix on the device's position because it can't see cell towers, GPS satellites, or both. And some sensors take time to "warm up," so that the values you'll get from them initially will be invalid. You'll want to respond to such changes in the external circumstances, in order to give the user a decent experience of your application regardless.

In addition, all sensor usage means battery usage, to a lesser or greater degree — sometimes to a *considerably* greater degree. There's a compromise to be made here: you want to please the user with your app's convenience and usefulness without disagreeably surprising and annoying the user through the device's rapid depletion of its battery charge.

These are all topics to which I'll be returning often throughout the course of this chapter.

Core Location

The Core Location framework provides facilities for the device to determine and report its location (*location services*). It takes advantage of three sensors:

Wi-Fi
> The device, if Wi-Fi is turned on, may scan for nearby Wi-Fi devices and compare these against an online database.

Cell
> The device, if it has cell capabilities and they are not turned off, may compare nearby telephone cell towers against an online database.

GPS
> The device's GPS, if it has one, may be able to obtain a position fix from GPS satellites. The GPS is obviously the most accurate location sensor, but it takes the longest to get a fix, and in some situations it will fail — indoors, for example, or in a city of tall buildings, where the device can't "see" enough of the sky.

Core Location will automatically use whatever facilities the device has available; all *you* have to do is ask for the device's location. Core Location allows you to specify how accurate a position fix you want; more accurate fixes may require more time.

Use of Core Location requires a *location manager* object, an instance of CLLocation-Manager. There is no reason not to create this object early and maintain it as a property:

```
var locman = CLLocationManager()
```

The notion of a location is encapsulated by the CLLocation class and its properties, which include:

coordinate
> A CLLocationCoordinate2D, a struct consisting of two doubles representing latitude and longitude.

altitude
> A CLLocationDistance, which is a double representing a number of meters.

speed
> A CLLocationSpeed, which is a double representing meters per second.

course
> A CLLocationDirection, which is a double representing degrees (*not* radians) clockwise from north.

`horizontalAccuracy`
> A CLLocationAccuracy, which is a double representing meters.

`timestamp`
> An NSDate.

Behavior of your app may depend on the device's physical location. To help you test, Xcode lets you pretend that the device is at a particular location on earth. The Simulator's Debug → Location menu lets you enter a location; the Scheme editor lets you set a default location (under Options); and the Debug → Simulate Location menu lets you switch among locations. You can set a built-in location or supply a standard GPX file containing a waypoint. You can also set the location to None; it's important to test for what happens when no location information is available.

Core Location Authorization

New in iOS 8, use of Core Location requires that you explicitly request authorization from the user. Moreover, there are now two types of authorization:

When in use
> When In Use authorization allows your app to perform basic location determination and no more. Background modes, and in particular modes where the system tracks the device's location on your behalf and notifies your app even if your app isn't running, are unavailable. Your app, tracking location in the foreground, can continue tracking location if the user backgrounds it, but the device will make the user aware that this is happening through a double-height status bar (similar to the in-call status bar).

Always
> Always authorization gives your app use of all Core Location modes and features. Even after you are granted authorization, if your app does in fact track location in the background, the system will periodically present the authorization dialog again, every few days, to remind the user of the situation.

 An app from iOS 7 and before that hasn't been recompiled against iOS 8 will need Always authorization in order to use Core Location at all.

The purpose of this authorization policy is evidently to make the user as mindful as possible of how apps are using Core Location. Core Location usage, as I've already said, can constitute a major battery drain; moreover, users are particularly sensitive to the notion that their location may be tracked without their knowledge. The two levels of authorization, along with their concomitant notifications to the user, provide a measure of reassurance that secret or inadvertent location tracking is unlikely to take place.

Authorization methods are follows. At the broadest level, the CLLocationManager class method `locationServicesEnabled` reports whether location services as a whole are switched off; if you now proceed to try to use Core Location, the system may put up an alert on your behalf offering to switch to the Settings app so that the user can switch location services on. The class method `authorizationStatus` reports the authorization status; two possible results correspond to the two types of authorization, `.Authorized-WhenInUse` and `.AuthorizedAlways`. To request authorization if the status is `.Not-Determined`, call one of two instance methods, either `requestWhenInUse-Authorization` or `requestAlwaysAuthorization`; you *must* also have a corresponding entry in your app's *Info.plist*, either `NSLocationWhenInUseUsageDescription` or `NSLocationAlwaysUsageDescription`, providing the body of the authorization request alert.

The two `request` methods have no completion handler. They are not run synchronously — your code continues even after the request dialog appears — but there is no penalty for trying to obtain the device's location while the request dialog is present: the location manager itself will pause and wait for the user to deal with the dialog. Therefore, my approach to requesting authorization is a just-in-time strategy; I don't call my `determine-Status` method until I'm ready to start actively using location services:

```
@IBAction func doFindMe (sender:AnyObject!) {
    if !self.determineStatus() {
        println("not authorized")
        return
    }
    // ...
}
```

Here's my `determineStatus` method; the starred lines call attention to differences from the approach used in previous chapters:

```
func determineStatus() -> Bool {
    let ok = CLLocationManager.locationServicesEnabled() // *
    if !ok {
        return true // *
    }
    let status = CLLocationManager.authorizationStatus()
    switch status {
    case .AuthorizedAlways, .AuthorizedWhenInUse:
        return true
    case .NotDetermined:
        self.locman.requestWhenInUseAuthorization()
        return true // *
    case .Restricted:
        return false
    case .Denied:
```

```
            // ... can offer to switch to Settings here ...
            return false
        }
    }
```

We return `true` under two circumstances where we don't have authorization but we might get it. That way, if the caller proceeds to attempt to use location services anyway, either the system dialog will appear and we might even obtain authorization and use of location services will succeed, or we can fail gracefully at that time (as I'll demonstrate in the next section).

 To retest the system authorization request alert and other access-related behaviors, go to the Settings app and choose General → Reset → Reset Location & Privacy. This, unfortunately, causes the system to revert to its default settings for *everything* in the Privacy section of Settings: Location Services and all System Services will be On, and all permissions lists will be empty.

Basic Location Determination

To ask where the device is:

1. Set yourself as the location manager's delegate (CLLocationManagerDelegate).

2. Configure the location manager. I'll talk more about this in a moment.

3. Tell the location manager to begin generating information. For basic location information, that means calling `startUpdatingLocation`. The location manager, in turn, will begin calling the appropriate delegate method repeatedly; in the case of `startUpdatingLocation`, it's `locationManager:didUpdateLocations:`. Your delegate will also always implement `locationManager:didFailWithError:` to receive error messages. You'll deal with each delegate method call in turn. Remember to call the corresponding `stop...` method when you no longer need location services.

Here are some location manager configuration properties that are useful to set:

`desiredAccuracy`
Your choices are:

- `kCLLocationAccuracyBestForNavigation`

- `kCLLocationAccuracyBest`

- `kCLLocationAccuracyNearestTenMeters`

- `kCLLocationAccuracyHundredMeters`

- `kCLLocationAccuracyKilometer`

- kCLLocationAccuracyThreeKilometers

It might be sufficient for your purposes to know very quickly but very roughly the device's location. Highest accuracy may also cause the highest battery drain; indeed, kCLLocationAccuracyBestForNavigation is supposed to be used only when the device is connected to external power. The accuracy setting is not a filter: the location manager will send you whatever location information it has, even if it isn't as accurate as you asked for, and checking a location's horizontalAccuracy is then up to you.

distanceFilter
Perhaps you don't need a location report unless the device has moved a certain distance since the previous report. This property can help keep you from being bombarded with events you don't need.

activityType
Your choices are (CLActivityType):

- .Fitness
- .AutomotiveNavigation
- .OtherNavigation
- .Other

This affects how persistently and frequently updates will be sent, based on the movement of the device. With .AutomotiveNavigation, updates can cease temporarily if the device is not moving significantly. With .Fitness, on the other hand, the user is assumed to be on foot, so updates may arrive even if the device is stationary.

As a simple example, we'll use location services just long enough to see if we can determine our position; a Bool property, self.trying, acts as a flag stating whether we are in the middle of this attempt, and an Optional NSDate property, self.startTime, tracks how long this attempt has been going on:

```
if !self.determineStatus() {
    println("not authorized")
    return
}
if self.trying { return }
self.trying = true
self.locman.delegate = self
self.locman.desiredAccuracy = kCLLocationAccuracyBest
self.locman.activityType = .Fitness
self.startTime = nil
self.locman.startUpdatingLocation()
```

We have a utility method for turning off updates and resetting our properties:

```
func stopTrying () {
    self.locman.stopUpdatingLocation()
    self.startTime = nil
    self.trying = false
}
```

If something goes wrong, we'll just turn updates back off. This handles the situation where we don't have authorization and determineStatus returns true; we might obtain authorization at this point, but if we don't, we now fail gracefully:

```
func locationManager(manager: CLLocationManager!,
    didFailWithError error: NSError!) {
        println("failed: \(error)")
        self.stopTrying()
}
```

If things go well, we'll be handed our location as soon as it is determined, in location-Manager:didUpdateLocations:. For purposes of this example, I'm going to insist on a fairly high level of accuracy; if I don't get it, I wait for the next update. But I don't want to wait too long, either, so on the very first pass I record the current time, so that I can compare the location's timestamp on subsequent calls. (Observe that I also return immediately from the first update, as I find that it contains spurious information.) If I get the desired accuracy within the desired time, I turn off updates and am ready to use the location information:

```
let REQ_ACC : CLLocationAccuracy = 10
let REQ_TIME : NSTimeInterval = 10
func locationManager(manager: CLLocationManager!,
    didUpdateLocations locations: [AnyObject]!) {
        print("did update location ")
        let loc = locations.last as! CLLocation
        let acc = loc.horizontalAccuracy
        let time = loc.timestamp
        let coord = loc.coordinate
        if self.startTime == nil {
            self.startTime = NSDate()
            return // ignore first attempt
        }
        println(acc)
        let elapsed = time.timeIntervalSinceDate(self.startTime)
        if elapsed > REQ_TIME {
            println("This is taking too long")
            self.stopTrying()
            return
        }
        if acc < 0 || acc > REQ_ACC {
            return // wait for the next one
        }
```

```
            // got it
            println("You are at \(coord.latitude) \(coord.longitude)")
            self.stopTrying()
    }
```

Feel free to experiment with different values for the required accuracy and the required time. On my device, it was clearly worth waiting a few cycles to get better accuracy; you can see the accuracy improving as the sensors warm up:

```
did update location 1285.19869645162
did update location 1285.19869645172
did update location 1285.19869645173
did update location 65.0
did update location 65.0
did update location 30.0
did update location 30.0
did update location 30.0
did update location 10.0
You are at ...
```

Heading

For appropriately equipped devices, Core Location supports use of the magnetometer to determine which way the device is facing (its *heading*). Although this information is accessed through a location manager, you do *not* need location services to be turned on merely to use the magnetometer to report the device's orientation with respect to *magnetic* north; but you do need location services to be turned on in order to report *true* north, as this depends on the device's location.

As with location, you'll first check that the desired feature is available (`heading-Available`); then you'll instantiate and configure the location manager, and call `start-UpdatingHeading`. The delegate will be sent `locationManager:didUpdateHeading:` (or `locationManager:didFailWithError:`). A heading object is a CLHeading instance; its `magneticHeading` and `trueHeading` properties are CLLocationDirection values, which report degrees (*not* radians) clockwise from the reference direction (magnetic or true north, respectively). If the `trueHeading` is not available, it will be reported as `-1`. The `trueHeading` will *not* be available unless both of the following are true in the Settings app:

- Location services are turned on (Privacy → Location Services).
- Compass calibration is turned on (Privacy → Location Services → System Services).

Beyond that, explicit user authorization is *not* needed in order to get the device's heading with respect to true north.

In this example, I'll use the device as a compass. The `headingFilter` setting is to prevent us from being bombarded constantly with readings. For best results, the device should probably be held level (like a tabletop, or a compass); we are setting the heading-Orientation so that the reported heading will be the direction in which the top of the device (the end away from the Home button) is pointing:

```
if !CLLocationManager.headingAvailable() {return}
if self.updating {return}
self.locman.delegate = self
self.locman.headingFilter = 5
self.locman.headingOrientation = .Portrait
self.updating = true
self.locman.startUpdatingHeading()
```

In the delegate, I'll display our heading as a rough cardinal direction in a label in the interface (self.lab). If we have a trueHeading, I'll use it; otherwise I'll use the magnetic-Heading:

```
func locationManager(manager: CLLocationManager!,
    didUpdateHeading newHeading: CLHeading!) {
        var h = newHeading.magneticHeading
        let h2 = newHeading.trueHeading
        if h2 >= 0 {
            h = h2
        }
        let cards = ["N", "NE", "E", "SE", "S", "SW", "W", "NW"]
        var dir = "N"
        for (ix, card) in enumerate(cards) {
            if h < 45.0/2.0 + 45.0*Double(ix) {
                dir = card
                break
            }
        }
        if self.lab.text != dir {
            self.lab.text = dir
        }
    }
```

Background Location

You can use Core Location when your app is not in the foreground. There are two quite different ways to do this:

Continuous background location

> This is an extension of what we did earlier. You tell the location manager to start-UpdatingLocation, and updates are permitted to continue even if the app goes into the background. Your app runs in the background in order to receive these updates (except during periods when you elect to receive deferred updates, if the hardware supports it).

Location monitoring

Your app does *not* run in the background! Rather, the system monitors location for you. If a significant location event occurs, your app may be awakened in the background (or launched in the background, if it is not running) and notified.

 The General → Background App Refresh setting, introduced in iOS 7, does not affect background use of location services in iOS 8. (The two things should never have been intertwined in the first place.) Use of background location services is now based on location authorization.

Continuous background location

Use of Core Location to perform continuous background updates is very similar to production of sound in the background (Chapter 14). In your app's *Info.plist*, the "Required background modes" key (`UIBackgroundModes`) should include `location`; you can set this up easily by checking "Location updates" under Background Modes in the Capabilities tab when editing the target. The result is that if you have a location manager to which you have sent `startUpdatingLocation` and the user sends your app into the background, your app is not suspended: the use of location services continues, and your delegate keeps receiving Core Location events. If your app has When In Use authorization, the blue double-height status bar will be present as long as your app is in the background and is actively updating the device's location (and the user can tap it to summon your app to the front).

Background use of location services can cause a power drain, but if you want your app to function as a positional data logger, for instance, it may be the only way; you can also help conserve power by making judicious choices, such as setting a coarse `distanceFilter` value, by not requiring overly high accuracy, and by being correct about the `activityType`.

Core Location may be able to operate in deferred mode (`allowDeferredLocationUpdatesUntilTraveled:timeout:`) so that your background app doesn't receive updates until the user has moved a specified amount or until a fixed time interval has elapsed; this, too, can help conserve power, especially if the user locks the screen, as the device may be able to power down some of its sensors temporarily, and your app can be allowed to stop running in the background. This feature is dependent on hardware capabilities; use it only if the class method `deferredLocationUpdatesAvailable` returns `true`. For this feature to work, the location manager's `desiredAccuracy` must be `kCLLocationAccuracyBest` or `kCLLocationAccuracyBestForNavigation`, and its `distanceFilter` must be `kCLDistanceFilterNone` (the default).

Deferred mode doesn't mean that location updates are fewer or filtered; it affects only the *delivery* of those updates. Updates are accumulated and then delivered all at once after the specified distance or time: the delegate is sent these messages:

- `locationManager:didFinishDeferredUpdatesWithError:`
- `locationManager:didUpdateLocations:`

The `locations:` parameter of `locationManager:didUpdateLocations:` in this situation is an array of *all the accumulated updates*. At this point, deferred updating has ceased; asking for the next set of updates to be deferred is up to you, by calling `allow-Deferred...` again. If the user brings your app to the foreground, any undelivered accumulated updates are delivered then and there, so that your interface can present the most recent information.

Location monitoring

Using Core Location to perform location monitoring without being in the foreground *doesn't* require your app to run in the background, and you do *not* have to set the `UIBackgroundModes` of your *Info.plist*. That's because the system is going to do all the work on your behalf. Your app still needs the appropriate authorization, however (because the system is doing this work on *your* behalf).

Some forms of location monitoring involve use of a CLRegion, which basically expresses a *geofence*, an area that triggers a notification when the user enters or leaves it (or both). This class was broken up in iOS 7 into two classes, CLBeaconRegion and CLCircular-Region. CLBeaconRegion is used in connection with iBeacon monitoring; I'm not going to discuss iBeacon in this book, so that leaves us with CLCircularRegion. The initializer is `init(center:radius:identifier:)`, where the `center:` is a CLLocation-Coordinate2D; the `identifier` serves as a unique key. You should also set the region's `notifyOnEntry` or `notifyOnExit` to `false` if you're interested in just one type of event.

There are four distinct forms of location monitoring:

Geofenced local notifications (new in iOS 8)
> This is a local notification (UILocalNotification, Chapter 13) that is triggered, not by the arrival of a certain time, but by the user's crossing a geofence. You will need a location manager and When In Use authorization. Create the local notification and set its `region` to a CLRegion. The notification's `regionTriggersOnce` is `true` by default; if `false`, the notification will be triggered *every* time the region is entered or exited (in accordance with the `notifyOnEntry` and `notifyOnExit` settings). Apart from this, the local notification is a standard local notification.

Significant location monitoring

If the class method `significantLocationChangeMonitoringAvailable` returns `true`, you can call `startMonitoringSignificantLocationChanges`. You will need a location manager and Always authorization. The delegate's `locationManager:did-UpdateLocations:` will be called when the device's location has changed significantly.

Visit monitoring (new in iOS 8)

By tracking significant changes in your location along with the *pauses* between those changes, the system decides that the user is visiting a spot. You will need a location manager and Always authorization. Call `startMonitoringVisits`. The delegate's `locationManager:didVisit:` will be called when the user's location pauses in a way that suggests a visit is beginning, and again when a visit ends. The second parameter is a CLVisit, a simple value class wrapping visit data; in addition to `coordinate` and `horizontalAccuracy`, you get an `arrivalDate` and `departureDate`. If this is an arrival, the `departureDate` will be `NSDate.distantFuture()`. If this is a departure and we were not monitoring visits when the user arrived, the `arrivalDate` will be `NSDate.distantPast()`.

Visit monitoring is basically a form of significant location monitoring, but requires even less power and notifies you less often, because locations that don't involve pauses are filtered out. (I presume, although the documentation does not say this, that you should check `significantLocationChangeMonitoringAvailable` before monitoring visits.)

Region monitoring

If the class method `isMonitoringAvailableForClass:` with an argument of `CLCircularRegion.Type` returns `true`, then you can call `startMonitoringFor-Region:` for each region in which you are interested. You will need a location manager and Always authorization. Regions are collected as a Set, which is the location manager's `monitoredRegions`. A region's `identifier` serves as a unique key, so that if you start monitoring for a region whose identifier matches that of a region already in the `monitoredRegions` set, the latter will be ejected from the set. The following delegate methods may be called:

- `locationManager:didEnterRegion:`
- `locationManager:didExitRegion:`
- `locationManager:monitoringDidFailForRegion:withError:`

Location monitoring is much less battery-intensive than full-fledged constant location updating. That's because it relies on cell tower position to estimate the device's location. Since the cell is probably working anyway — for example, the device is a phone, so the cell is always on and is always concerned with what cell towers are available — little or no additional power is required. Apple says that the system will also take advantage of other clues (requiring no extra battery drain) to decide that there may have been a change in location: for example, the device may observe a change in the available Wi-Fi networks, strongly suggesting that the device has moved.

Notifications for location monitoring can arrive even if your app isn't in the foreground. In that case, there are two possible states in which your app might find itself when an event arrives:

Your app is suspended in the background
> Your app is woken up (remaining in the background) long enough to receive the normal delegate event and do something with it.

Your app is not running at all
> Your app is relaunched (remaining in the background), and your app delegate will be sent `application:didFinishLaunchingWithOptions:` with an NSDictionary containing `UIApplicationLaunchOptionsLocationKey`, thus allowing it to discern the special nature of the situation. At this point you probably have no location manager — your app has just launched from scratch. So you should get yourself a location manager and start up location services for long enough to receive the normal delegate event.

Acceleration and Attitude

Acceleration results from the application of a force to the device, and is detected through the device's accelerometer, supplemented by the gyroscope if it has one. Gravity is a force, so the accelerometer always has something to measure, even if the user isn't consciously applying a force to the device; thus the device can report its attitude relative to the vertical.

Acceleration information can arrive in two ways:

As a prepackaged UIEvent
> You can receive a UIEvent notifying you of a predefined gesture performed by accelerating the device. At present, the only such gesture is the user shaking the device.

With the Core Motion framework
> You instantiate CMMotionManager and then obtain information of a desired type. You can ask for accelerometer information, gyroscope information, or device motion information (and you can also use Core Motion to get magnetometer information); device motion combines the gyroscope data with data from the other sensors to give you the best possible description of the device's attitude in space.

Shake Events

A shake event is a UIEvent (Chapter 5). Receiving shake events is rather like receiving remote events (Chapter 14), involving the notion of the first responder. To receive shake events, your app must contain a UIResponder which:

- Returns true from canBecomeFirstResponder
- Is in fact first responder

This responder, or a UIResponder further up the responder chain, should implement some or all of these methods:

motionBegan:withEvent:
> Something has started to happen that might or might not turn out to be a shake.

motionEnded:withEvent:
> The motion reported in motionBegan:withEvent: is over and has turned out to be a shake.

motionCancelled:withEvent:
> The motion reported in motionBegan:withEvent: wasn't a shake after all.

It might be sufficient to implement motionEnded:withEvent:, because this arrives if and only if the user performs a shake gesture. The first parameter will be the event subtype, but at present this is guaranteed to be .MotionShake, so testing it is pointless.

The view controller in charge of the current view is a good candidate to receive shake events. Thus, a minimal implementation might look like this:

```
override func canBecomeFirstResponder() -> Bool {
    return true
}
override func viewDidAppear(animated: Bool) {
    super.viewDidAppear(animated)
    self.becomeFirstResponder()
}
override func motionEnded(
    motion: UIEventSubtype, withEvent event: UIEvent) {
        println("hey, you shook me!")
}
```

By default, if some other object is first responder, and is of a type that supports undo (such as a UITextField), and if motionBegan:withEvent: is sent up the responder chain, and if you have not set the shared UIApplication's applicationSupportsShakeToEdit property to false, a shake will be handled through an Undo or Redo alert. Your view controller might not want to rob any responders in its view of this capability. A simple way to prevent this is to test whether the view controller is itself the first responder; if it isn't, we call super to pass the event on up the responder chain:

```
override func motionEnded(
    motion: UIEventSubtype, withEvent event: UIEvent) {
        if self.isFirstResponder() {
            println("hey, you shook me!")
        } else {
            super.motionEnded(motion, withEvent: event)
        }
}
```

Raw Acceleration

If the device has an accelerometer but no gyroscope, you can learn about the forces being applied to it, but some compromises will be necessary. The chief problem is that, even if the device is completely motionless, its acceleration values will constitute a normalized vector pointing toward the center of the earth, popularly known as *gravity*. The accelerometer is thus constantly reporting a combination of gravity and user-induced acceleration. This is good and bad. It's good because it means that, with certain restrictions, you can use the accelerometer to detect the device's attitude in space. It's bad because gravity values and user-induced acceleration values are mixed together. Fortunately, there are ways to separate these values mathematically:

With a low-pass filter
  A low-pass filter will damp out user acceleration so as to report gravity only.

With a high-pass filter
  A high-pass filter will damp out the effect of gravity so as to detect user acceleration only, reporting a motionless device as having zero acceleration.

In some situations, it is desirable to apply both a low-pass filter and a high-pass filter, so as to learn both the gravity values and the user acceleration values. A common additional technique is to run the output of the high-pass filter itself through a low-pass filter to reduce noise and small twitches. Apple provides some nice sample code for implementing a low-pass or a high-pass filter; see especially the AccelerometerGraph example, which is also very helpful for exploring how the accelerometer behaves.

The technique of applying filters to the accelerometer output has some serious downsides, which are inevitable in a device that lacks a gyroscope:

- It's up to you to apply the filters; you have to implement boilerplate code and hope that you don't make a mistake.
- Filters mean *latency*. Your response to the accelerometer values will lag behind what the device is actually doing; this lag may be noticeable.

Reading raw accelerometer values with Core Motion is really a subset of how you read *any* values with Core Motion; in some ways it is similar to how you use Core Location:

1. You start by instantiating CMMotionManager; retain the instance somewhere, typically as a property. There is no reason not to initialize the property directly:

   ```
   let motman = CMMotionManager()
   ```

2. Confirm that the desired hardware is available.

3. Set the interval at which you wish the motion manager to update itself with new sensor readings.

4. Call the appropriate `start...` method.

5. Poll the motion manager whenever you want data, asking for the appropriate `data` property. This step is surprising; you probably expected that the motion manager would call into a delegate, but in fact a motion manager has no delegate. The polling interval doesn't have to be the same as the motion manager's update interval; when you poll, you'll obtain the motion manager's *current* data — that is, the data generated by its most recent update, whenever that was.

   Alternatively, if your app's purpose is to collect all the data, then instead of calling a `start...` method, you can call a `start...UpdatesToQueue:withHandler:` method and receive callbacks in a block, possibly on a background thread, managed by an NSOperationQueue (Chapter 25).

6. Don't forget to call the corresponding `stop...` method when you no longer need data.

In this example, I will simply report whether the device is lying flat on its back. I start by configuring my motion manager; then I launch a repeating timer to trigger polling:

```
if !self.motman.accelerometerAvailable {
    println("Oh, well")
    return
}
self.motman.accelerometerUpdateInterval = 1.0 / 30.0
self.motman.startAccelerometerUpdates()
self.timer = NSTimer.scheduledTimerWithTimeInterval(
    self.motman.accelerometerUpdateInterval,
    target: self, selector: "pollAccel:",
    userInfo: nil, repeats: true)
```

My `pollAccel:` method is now being called repeatedly. In `pollAccel:`, I ask the motion manager for its accelerometer data. This arrives as a CMAccelerometerData object, which is a timestamp plus a CMAcceleration; a CMAcceleration is simply a struct of three values, one for each axis of the device, measured in Gs. The positive x-axis points to the right of the device. The positive y-axis points toward the top of the device, away from the Home button. The positive z-axis points out the front of the screen.

The two axes orthogonal to gravity, which are the x- and y-axes when the device is lying more or less on its back, are much more accurate and sensitive to small variation than the axis pointing toward or away from gravity. So our approach is to ask first whether the x and y values are close to zero; only then do we use the z value to learn whether the device is on its back or on its face. To keep from updating our interface constantly, we implement a crude state machine; the state property (`self.state`) starts out at `-1`, and then switches between `0` (device on its back) and `1` (device not on its back), and we update the interface only when there is a state change:

```
let dat = self.motman.accelerometerData
let acc = dat.acceleration
let x = acc.x
let y = acc.y
let z = acc.z
let accu = 0.08
if abs(x) < accu && abs(y) < accu && z < -0.5 {
    if self.state == -1 || self.state == 1 {
        self.state = 0
        self.label.text = "I'm lying on my back... ahhh..."
    }
} else {
    if self.state == -1 || self.state == 0 {
        self.state = 1
        self.label.text = "Hey, put me back down on the table!"
    }
}
```

This works, but it's sensitive to small motions of the device on the table. To damp this sensitivity, we can run our input through a low-pass filter. The low-pass filter code comes straight from Apple's own examples, and involves maintaining the previously filtered reading as a set of properties:

```
func addAcceleration(accel:CMAcceleration) {
    let alpha = 0.1
    self.oldX = accel.x * alpha + self.oldX * (1.0 - alpha)
    self.oldY = accel.y * alpha + self.oldY * (1.0 - alpha)
    self.oldZ = accel.z * alpha + self.oldZ * (1.0 - alpha)
}
```

Our polling code now starts out by passing the data through the filter:

```
let dat = self.motman.accelerometerData
self.addAcceleration(dat.acceleration)
let x = self.oldX
let y = self.oldY
let z = self.oldZ
// ... and the rest is as before ...
```

As I mentioned earlier, instead of polling, you can receive callbacks in a block. This approach is useful particularly if your goal is to receive every update or to receive updates on a background thread (or both). To illustrate, I'll rewrite the previous example to use this technique; to keep things simple, I'll ask for my callbacks on the main thread (the documentation advises against this, but Apple's own sample code does it). We now start our accelerometer updates like this:

```
self.motman.startAccelerometerUpdatesToQueue(
    NSOperationQueue.mainQueue(), withHandler: {
        (accelerometerData:CMAccelerometerData!, error:NSError!) in
        if error != nil {
            println(error)
            self.stopAccelerometer()
            return
        }
        self.receiveAccel(accelerometerData)
})
```

`receiveAccel:` is just like our earlier `pollAccel:`, except that we already have the accelerometer data:

```
func receiveAccel (dat:CMAccelerometerData) {
    self.addAcceleration(dat.acceleration)
    // ... and the rest is as before ...
}
```

In this next example, the user is allowed to slap the side of the device into an open hand — perhaps as a way of telling it to go to the next or previous image or whatever it is we're displaying. We pass the acceleration input through a high-pass filter to eliminate gravity (again, the filter code comes straight from Apple's examples):

```
func addAcceleration(accel:CMAcceleration) {
    let alpha = 0.1
    self.oldX = accel.x - ((accel.x * alpha) + (self.oldX * (1.0 - alpha)))
    self.oldY = accel.y - ((accel.y * alpha) + (self.oldY * (1.0 - alpha)))
    self.oldZ = accel.z - ((accel.z * alpha) + (self.oldZ * (1.0 - alpha)))
}
```

What we're looking for, in our polling routine, is a high positive or negative x value. A single slap is likely to consist of several consecutive readings above our threshold, but we want to report each slap only once, so we take advantage of the timestamp attached to a CMAccelerometerData, maintaining the timestamp of our previous high reading as a property and ignoring readings that are too close to one another in time. Another problem is that a sudden jerk involves both an acceleration (as the user starts the device moving) and a deceleration (as the device stops moving); thus a left slap might be preceded by a high value in the opposite direction, which we might interpret wrongly as a right slap. We can compensate crudely, at the expense of some latency, with delayed performance; for the CancelableTimer object stored at `self.canceltimer`, see Appendix B:

```
func pollAccel(_:AnyObject!) {
    let dat = self.motman.accelerometerData
    if dat == nil { return }
    self.addAcceleration(dat.acceleration)
    let x = self.oldX
```

```
    let thresh = 1.0
    if x < -thresh {
        if dat.timestamp - self.oldTime > 0.5 || self.lastSlap == 1 {
            self.oldTime = dat.timestamp
            self.lastSlap = -1
            self.canceltimer?.cancel()
            self.canceltimer = CancelableTimer(once: true) {
                println("left")
            }
            self.canceltimer.startWithInterval(0.5)
        }
    } else if x > thresh {
        if dat.timestamp - self.oldTime > 0.5 || self.lastSlap == -1 {
            self.oldTime = dat.timestamp
            self.lastSlap = 1
            self.canceltimer?.cancel()
            self.canceltimer = CancelableTimer(once: true) {
                println("right")
            }
            self.canceltimer.startWithInterval(0.5)
        }
    }
}
```

The gesture we're detecting is a little tricky to make: the user must slap the device into an open hand *and hold it there*; if the device jumps out of the open hand, that movement may be detected as the last in the series, resulting in the wrong report (left instead of right, or *vice versa*). And the latency of our gesture detection is very high.

Of course we might try tweaking some of the magic numbers in this code to improve accuracy and performance, but a more sophisticated analysis would probably involve storing a stream of all the most recent CMAccelerometerData objects and studying the entire stream to work out the overall trend.

Gyroscope

The inclusion of an electronic gyroscope in the panoply of onboard hardware in some devices has made a huge difference in the accuracy and speed of gravity and attitude reporting. A gyroscope has the property that its attitude in space remains constant; thus it can detect any change in the attitude of the containing device. This has two important consequences for accelerometer measurements:

- The accelerometer can be supplemented by the gyroscope to detect quickly the difference between gravity and user-induced acceleration.

- The gyroscope can observe pure rotation, where little or no acceleration is involved and so the accelerometer would not have been helpful. The extreme case is constant attitudinal rotation around the gravity axis, which the accelerometer alone would be completely unable to detect (because there is no user-induced force, and gravity remains constant).

It is possible to track the raw gyroscope data: make sure the device has a gyroscope (`gyroAvailable`), and then call `startGyroUpdates`. What we get from the motion manager is a CMGyroData object, which combines a timestamp with a CMRotationRate that reports the *rate of rotation* around each axis, measured in radians per second, where a positive value is *counterclockwise* as seen by someone whose eye is pointed to by the positive axis. (This is the opposite of the direction graphed in Figure 3-9.) The problem, however, is that the gyroscope values are *scaled* and *biased*. This means that the values are based on an arbitrary scale and are increasing (or decreasing) at a roughly constant rate. Thus there is very little merit in the exercise of dealing with the raw gyroscope data.

What you are likely to be interested in is a combination of at least the gyroscope and the accelerometer. The mathematics required to combine the data from these sensors can be daunting. Fortunately, there's no need to know anything about that. Core Motion will happily package up the calculated combination of data as a CMDeviceMotion instance, with the effects of the sensors' internal bias and scaling already factored out. CMDeviceMotion consists of the following properties, all of which provide a triple of values corresponding to the device's natural 3D frame (x increasing to the right, y increasing to the top, z increasing out the front):

gravity
> A CMAcceleration expressing a vector with value 1 pointing to the center of the earth, measured in Gs.

userAcceleration
> A CMAcceleration describing user-induced acceleration, with no gravity component, measured in Gs.

rotationRate
> A CMRotationRate describing how the device is rotating around its own center. This is essentially the CMGyroData `rotationRate` with scale and bias accounted for.

magneticField
> A CMCalibratedMagneticField describing (in its `field`, a CMMagneticField) the magnetic forces acting on the device, measured in microteslas. The sensor's internal bias has already been factored out. The `accuracy` is one of the following:
>
> - CMMagneticFieldCalibrationAccuracyUncalibrated
> - CMMagneticFieldCalibrationAccuracyLow
> - CMMagneticFieldCalibrationAccuracyMedium

- CMMagneticFieldCalibrationAccuracyHigh

attitude
>   A CMAttitude, descriptive of the device's instantaneous attitude in space. When you ask the motion manager to start generating updates, you can specify a reference frame for the attitude (having first called the class method availableAttitude-ReferenceFrames to ascertain that the desired reference frame is available on this device). In every case, the negative z-axis points at the center of the earth:

CMAttitudeReferenceFrameXArbitraryZVertical
>   The x-axis and y-axis, though orthogonal to the other axes, could be pointing anywhere.

CMAttitudeReferenceFrameXArbitraryCorrectedZVertical
>   The same as in the previous option, but the magnetometer is used to maintain accuracy (preventing drift of the reference frame over time).

CMAttitudeReferenceFrameXMagneticNorthZVertical
>   The x-axis points toward magnetic north.

CMAttitudeReferenceFrameXTrueNorthZVertical
>   The x-axis points toward true north. This value will be inaccurate unless you are also using Core Location to obtain the device's location.

The attitude value's numbers can be accessed through various CMAttitude properties corresponding to three different systems, each being convenient for a different purpose:

pitch, roll, yaw
>   The device's angle of offset from the reference frame, in radians, around the device's natural x-axis, y-axis, and z-axis respectively.

rotationMatrix
>   A CMRotationMatrix struct embodying a 3×3 matrix expressing a rotation in the reference frame.

quaternion
>   A CMQuaternion describing an attitude. (Quaternions are commonly used in OpenGL.)

In this example, we turn the device into a simple compass/clinometer, merely by asking for its attitude with reference to magnetic north and taking its pitch, roll, and yaw. We begin by making the usual preparations; notice the use of the showsDeviceMovement-Display property, intended to allow the runtime to prompt the user if the magnetometer needs calibration:

```
if !self.motman.deviceMotionAvailable {
    println("Oh, well")
    return
}
let ref = CMAttitudeReferenceFrame.XMagneticNorthZVertical
let avail = CMMotionManager.availableAttitudeReferenceFrames()
if avail.rawValue & ref.rawValue == 0 {
    println("darn")
    return
}
self.motman.showsDeviceMovementDisplay = true
self.motman.deviceMotionUpdateInterval = 1.0 / 30.0
self.motman.startDeviceMotionUpdatesUsingReferenceFrame(ref)
let t = self.motman.deviceMotionUpdateInterval * 10
self.timer = NSTimer.scheduledTimerWithTimeInterval(t, target:self,
    selector:"pollAttitude:",userInfo:nil, repeats:true)
```

In `pollAttitude:`, we wait until the magnetometer is ready, and then we start taking attitude readings (converted to degrees):

```
let mot = self.motman.deviceMotion
if mot == nil {return}
let acc = mot.magneticField.accuracy.value
if acc <= CMMagneticFieldCalibrationAccuracyLow.value {
    return // not ready yet
}
let att = mot.attitude
let to_deg = 180.0 / M_PI
println("\(att.pitch * to_deg), \(att.roll * to_deg), \(att.yaw * to_deg)")
```

The values are all close to zero when the device is level with its x-axis pointing to magnetic north, and each value increases as the device is rotated *counterclockwise* with respect to an eye that has the corresponding positive axis pointing at it. So, for example, a device held upright (top pointing at the sky) has a `pitch` approaching 90; a device lying on its right edge has a `roll` approaching 90; and a device lying on its back with its top pointing north has a `yaw` approaching -90.

There are some quirks in the way Euler angles operate mathematically:

- `roll` and `yaw` increase with counterclockwise rotation from 0 to π (180 degrees) and then jump to -π (-180 degrees) and continue to increase to 0 as the rotation completes a circle; but `pitch` increases to $\pi/2$ (90 degrees) and then decreases to 0, then decreases to -$\pi/2$ (-90 degrees) and increases to 0. This means that `attitude` alone, if we are exploring it through `pitch`, `roll`, and `yaw`, is insufficient to describe the device's attitude, since a `pitch` value of, say, $\pi/4$ (45 degrees) could mean two different things. To distinguish those two things, we can supplement `attitude` with the z-component of `gravity`:

```
let g = mot.gravity
let whichway = g.z > 0 ? "forward" : "back"
println("pitch is tilted \(whichway)")
```

- Values become inaccurate in certain orientations. In particular, when `pitch` is ±90 degrees (the device is upright or inverted), `roll` and `yaw` become erratic. (You may see this effect referred to as "the singularity" or as "gimbal lock.") I believe that, depending on what you are trying to accomplish, you can solve this by using a different expression of the attitude, such as the `rotationMatrix`, which does not suffer from this limitation.

This next (simple and very silly) example illustrates a use of CMAttitude's `rotation-Matrix` property. Our goal is to make a CALayer rotate in response to the current attitude of the device. We start as before, except that our reference frame is `CMAttitude-ReferenceFrameXArbitraryZVertical`; we are interested in how the device moves from its initial attitude, without reference to any particular fixed external direction such as magnetic north. In `pollAttitude`, our first step is to store the device's current attitude in a CMAttitude property, `self.ref`:

```
let mot = self.motman.deviceMotion
if mot == nil {return}
let att = mot.attitude
if self.ref == nil {
    self.ref = att
    return
}
```

That code works correctly because on the first few polls, as the attitude-detection hardware warms up, `att` is nil, so we don't get past the `return` call until we have a valid initial attitude. Our next step is highly characteristic of how CMAttitude is used: we call the CMAttitude instance method `multiplyByInverseOfAttitude:`, which transforms our attitude so that it is relative *to the stored initial attitude*:

```
att.multiplyByInverseOfAttitude(self.ref)
```

Finally, we apply the attitude's rotation matrix directly to a layer in our interface as a transform. Well, not quite directly: a rotation matrix is a 3×3 matrix, whereas a CA-Transform3D, which is what we need in order to set a layer's `transform`, is a 4×4 matrix. However, it happens that the top left nine entries in a CATransform3D's 4×4 matrix constitute its rotation component, so we start with an identity matrix and set those entries directly:

```
let r = att.rotationMatrix
var t = CATransform3DIdentity
t.m11 = CGFloat(r.m11)
t.m12 = CGFloat(r.m12)
t.m13 = CGFloat(r.m13)
t.m21 = CGFloat(r.m21)
```

```
t.m22 = CGFloat(r.m22)
t.m23 = CGFloat(r.m23)
t.m31 = CGFloat(r.m31)
t.m32 = CGFloat(r.m32)
t.m33 = CGFloat(r.m33)
let lay = // whatever
CATransaction.setAnimationDuration(1.0/10.0)
lay.transform = t
```

The result is that the layer apparently tries to hold itself still as the device rotates. The example is rather crude because we aren't using OpenGL to draw a three-dimensional object, but it illustrates the principle well enough.

There is a quirk to be aware of in this case as well: over time, the transform has a tendency to drift. Thus, even if we leave the device stationary, the layer will gradually rotate. That is the sort of effect that `CMAttitudeReferenceFrameXArbitraryCorrectedZVertical` is designed to help mitigate, by bringing the magnetometer into play.

Here are some additional considerations to be aware of when using Core Motion:

- The documentation warns that your app should create only one CMMotion-Manager instance. This is not a terribly onerous restriction, but it's rather odd that, if this is important, the API doesn't provide a shared singleton instance accessed through a class method.

- Use of Core Motion is legal while your app is running in the background. To take advantage of this, your app would need to be running in the background for some *other* reason; there is no Core Motion `UIBackgroundModes` setting in an *Info.plist*. For example, you might run in the background because you're using Core Location, and take advantage of this to employ Core Motion as well.

- Core Motion requires that various sensors be turned on, such as the magnetometer and the gyroscope. This can result in some increased battery drain, so try not to use any sensors you don't have to, and remember to stop generating updates as soon as you no longer need them.

 The iPhone 6 and iPhone 6 Plus have a barometer! You can get altitude information using the CMAltimeter and CMAltitudeData classes.

Motion Activity

Some devices have a motion coprocessor chip with the ability to detect, analyze, and keep a record of device motion even while the device is asleep and with very little drain on power. This is *not* a form of location determination; it is an analysis of the device's physical motion and attitude in order to draw conclusions about what the user has been doing while carrying or wearing the device. You can learn that the user is walking, or walked for an hour, but not where the user was walking.motion activity

Interaction with the motion coprocessor is through a CMMotionActivityManager instance. There is no reason not to initialize a property with this instance:

```
let actman = CMMotionActivityManager()
```

The device must actually *have* a motion coprocessor; call the class method isActivity-Available. The user must also grant authorization, and, having granted it, can later deny it (in the Settings app, under Privacy → Motion Activity). There are no authorization methods; the technique is to "tickle" the activity manager by trying to query it and seeing if you get an error. In this example, I have a Bool property, self.authorized, which I set based on the outcome of trying to query the activity manager:

```
let now = NSDate()
self.actman.queryActivityStartingFromDate(now,
    toDate:now, toQueue:NSOperationQueue.mainQueue()) {
        (arr:[AnyObject]!, err:NSError!) in
        let notauth = Int(CMErrorMotionActivityNotAuthorized.value)
        if err != nil && err.code == notauth {
            self.authorized = false
        } else {
            self.authorized = true
        }
}
```

On the first run of that code, the system puts up the authorization request alert. The completion handler is not called until the user deals with the alert, so the outcome tells you what the user decided. On subsequent runs, that code reports the current authorization status.

There are two approaches to querying the activity manager:

Real-time updates
> This is similar to getting motion manager updates with a handler. You call start-ActivityUpdatesToQueue:withHandler:, and the handler is called periodically. When you no longer need updates, call stopActivityUpdates.

Historical data
> The motion coprocessor records about a week's-worth of data. You ask for a chunk of that recorded data by calling queryActivityStartingFromDate:toDate:to-Queue:withHandler:.

I'll illustrate querying for historical data. In this example, I fetch the data for the past 24 hours. I have prepared an NSOperationQueue property, self.queue:

```
    let now = NSDate()
    let yester = now.dateByAddingTimeInterval(-60*60*24)
    self.actman.queryActivityStartingFromDate(yester, toDate: now,
        toQueue: NSOperationQueue.mainQueue()) {
            (arr:[AnyObject]!, err:NSError!) -> Void in
            var acts = arr as! [CMMotionActivity]
            // ...
    }
```

We now have an array of CMMotionActivity objects representing every *change* in the device's activity status. This is a value class. It has a `startDate`, a `confidence` (a CMMotionActivityConfidence, `.Low`, `.Medium`, or `.High`) describing how sure the activity manager is in its analysis of what the user was doing, and a bunch of Bool properties categorizing the activity:

- `stationary`
- `walking`
- `running`
- `automotive`
- `cycling` (new in iOS 8)
- `unknown`

A common first response to the flood of data is to pare it down. To help with this, I've extended CMMotionActivity with a utility method that summarizes its Bool properties as a string:

```
extension CMMotionActivity {
    private func tf(b:Bool) -> String {
        return b ? "t" : "f"
    }
    func overallAct() -> String {
        let s = tf(self.stationary)
        let w = tf(self.walking)
        let r = tf(self.running)
        let a = tf(self.automotive)
        let u = tf(self.unknown)
        return "\(s) \(w) \(r) \(a) \(u)"
    }
}
```

So, as a straightforward way of paring down the data, I walk backwards through the data, removing every CMMotionActivity with no definite activity, with a low degree of confidence, or whose activity is the same as its predecessor. Then I set a property, and my data are ready for use:

```
for i in stride(from: acts.count-1, through: 0, by: -1) {
    if acts[i].overallAct() == "f f f f f" {
        acts.removeAtIndex(i)
    }
}
for i in stride(from: acts.count-1, through: 0, by: -1) {
    if acts[i].confidence.rawValue < 2 {
        acts.removeAtIndex(i)
    }
}
for i in stride(from: acts.count-1, through: 1, by: -1) {
    if acts[i].overallAct() == acts[i-1].overallAct() {
        acts.removeAtIndex(i)
    }
}
dispatch_async(dispatch_get_main_queue()) {
    self.data = acts
}
```

New in iOS 8, there is also a CMPedometer class; before using it, check the `isStep-CountingAvailable` class method. Some devices can deduce the size of the user's stride and compute distance (`isDistanceAvailable`); some devices can use barometric data to estimate what floor of a building the user is on (`isFloorCountingAvailable`). Pedometer data is queried just like motion activity data; data arrives as a CMPedometerData object. (I believe that CMPedometer supersedes CMStepCounter from iOS 7.)

PART IV

Final Topics

This part of the book is a miscellany of topics.

- Chapter 23 is about files. It explains how your app can store data on disk to be retrieved the next time the app runs (including both standalone files and user defaults). It also discusses sharing files with the user through iTunes and with other apps, plus the document architecture and iCloud, and concludes with a survey of how iOS can work with some common file formats (XML, SQLite, Core Data, and image files).

- Chapter 24 introduces networking, with an emphasis on HTTP downloading of data. It also introduces in-app purchasing (a specialized form of networking) and Bonjour.

- Chapter 25 is about threads. Making your code multithreaded can introduce great complexity and is not a beginner topic, but you still might need to understand the basic concepts of multithreading, either in order to prevent a lengthy task from blocking user interaction with your app, or because some framework explicitly relies on it. Particular attention is paid to the advantages of NSOperation and (especially) Grand Central Dispatch.

- Chapter 26 describes how iOS supports Undo in your app.

CHAPTER 23

Persistent Storage

The device on which your app runs contains flash memory that functions as the equivalent of a hard disk, holding files that survive between runs of your app, even if the device is powered down. This chapter is about how and where files are saved and retrieved, and about some of the additional ways in which files can be manipulated: for example, apps can define document types in which they specialize and can hand such documents to one another, and can share documents into the cloud (iCloud), so that multiple copies of the same app can retrieve them on different devices. The chapter also explains how user preferences are maintained in NSUserDefaults, and describes some specialized file formats and ways of working with their data, such as XML, SQLite, Core Data, and images.

The Sandbox

The hard disk as a whole is not open to your app's view. A limited portion of the hard disk is dedicated to your app alone: this is your app's *sandbox*. The idea is that every app, seeing only its own sandbox, is hindered from spying or impinging on the files belonging to other apps, and in turn is protected from having its own files spied or impinged on by other apps. Your app's sandbox is thus a safe place for you to store your data. Your sandbox, and hence your data, will be deleted if the user deletes your app; otherwise, it should reliably persist.

Standard Directories

The sandbox contains some standard directories, and there are built-in methods for referring to them. For example, suppose you want a reference to the Documents directory. Here's one way to access it:

```
let docs = NSSearchPathForDirectoriesInDomains(
    .DocumentDirectory, .UserDomainMask, true).last as! String
```

That code returns a path string for the Documents directory. The preferred way to refer to a file or directory, however, is with a URL. You can obtain this from an NSFileManager instance:

```
let fm = NSFileManager()
var err : NSError?
if let docsurl = fm.URLForDirectory(
    .DocumentDirectory, inDomain: .UserDomainMask,
    appropriateForURL: nil, create: true, error: &err) {
        // use docsurl here
    } else {
        // error, examine err here
    }
```

A question that will immediately occur to you is: *where* should I put files and folders that I want to save now and read later? The Documents directory can be a good place. But if your app supports file sharing (discussed later in this chapter), the user can see and modify your app's Documents directory through iTunes, so you might not want to put things there that the user isn't supposed to see and change.

Personally, I favor the Application Support directory for most purposes. In OS X, this directory is shared by multiple applications, each of which must confine itself to an individual subfolder, but on iOS each app has its own private Application Support directory in its own sandbox, so you can safely put files anywhere within it. This directory may not exist initially, so you can obtain it and create it at the same time:

```
let fm = NSFileManager()
var err : NSError?
if let suppurl = fm.URLForDirectory(
    .ApplicationSupportDirectory, inDomain: .UserDomainMask,
    appropriateForURL: nil, create: true, error: &err) {
        // use suppurl here
    } else {
        // error, examine err here
    }
```

Temporary files, whose loss you are willing to accept (because their contents can be recreated), can be written into the Caches directory (`NSCachesDirectory`) or the Temporary directory (`NSTemporaryDirectory`). You can write temporary files into the Application Support folder, but by default this means they can be backed up by the user through iTunes or iCloud; to prevent that, exclude such a file from backup by way of its file URL:

```
myDocumentURL.setResourceValue(
    true, forKey: NSURLIsExcludedFromBackupKey, error: &err)
```

Although URLs are the favored way of referring to files and folders, they are a more recent innovation than path strings, and you may encounter file operations that still require a string. To derive a path string from an NSURL, send it the `path` message.

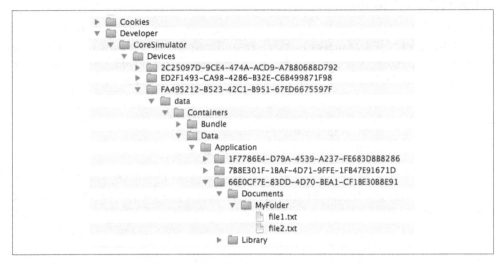

Figure 23-1. An app's sandbox in the Simulator

Visually Inspecting the Sandbox

The Simulator's sandbox is a folder on your Mac that you can inspect visually. This is more difficult with Xcode 6 than in previous versions, because the sandbox folder layout has changed in iOS 8. In your user *~/Library/Developer/CoreSimulator/Devices* folder, you'll find mysteriously named folders representing the different simulators. The *device.plist* file inside each folder can help you identify which simulator a folder represents; so can xcrun simctl list at the command line. Inside a simulator's *data/Containers/Data/Application* folder are more mysteriously named folders representing apps on that simulator. I don't know how to identify the different apps, but one of them is the app you're interested in, and inside it is that app's sandox.

In Figure 23-1, I've drilled down from my user *Library* to an app that I've run in the Simulator. My app's Documents folder is visible, and I've opened it to show a folder and a couple of files that I've created programmatically (the code that created that folder and files will appear later in this chapter). Also visible is the app's *Library* folder; the app's *Application Support* folder is inside it.

You can also view the file structure of the sandbox on the device; indeed, you may find this simpler than identifying the Simulator sandbox. When the device is connected and no app is being run from Xcode, choose Window → Devices. Select your device on the left; on the right, under Installed Apps, select your app. Click the Gear icon and choose Show Container to view your app's sandbox hierarchy in a modal sheet. Alternatively, choose Download Container to copy your app's sandbox to your computer; the sandbox arrives on your computer as an *.xcappdata* package, and you can open it in the Finder with Show Package Contents.

Basic File Operations

Let's say we intend to create a folder *MyFolder* inside the Documents directory. Assume that we have an NSFileManager instance `fm` and an NSURL `docsurl` pointing at the Documents directory. We can then generate a reference to *MyFolder*, from which we can ask our NSFileManager instance to create the folder if it doesn't exist already:

```
var err : NSError?
let myfolder = docsurl.URLByAppendingPathComponent("MyFolder")
var ok = fm.createDirectoryAtURL(
    myfolder, withIntermediateDirectories: true,
    attributes: nil, error: &err)
// ... error-checking omitted
```

To learn what files and folders exist within a directory, you can ask for an array of the directory's contents:

```
var err : NSError?
let arr = fm.contentsOfDirectoryAtURL(docsurl,
    includingPropertiesForKeys: nil, options: nil, error: &err)
// ... error-checking omitted
(arr as! [NSURL]).map{$0.lastPathComponent!}.map(println)
/*
MyFolder
*/
```

The array resulting from `contentsOfDirectoryAtURL:...` lists full URLs of the directory's *immediate* contents; it is shallow. For a deep array, which might be very big, you can enumerate the directory, so that you are handed only one file reference at a time:

```
let dir = fm.enumeratorAtURL(docsurl, includingPropertiesForKeys: nil,
    options: nil, errorHandler: nil)!
while let f = dir.nextObject() as? NSURL {
    if f.pathExtension == "txt" {
        println(f.lastPathComponent!)
    }
}
/*
file1.txt
file2.txt
*/
```

A directory enumerator also permits you to decline to dive into a particular subdirectory (`skipDescendants`), so you can make your traversal even more efficient.

Consult the NSFileManager class documentation for more about what you can do with files, and see also Apple's *File System Programming Guide*.

Saving and Reading Files

To save or read a simple file, you are likely to use one of the convenience methods for the class appropriate to the file's contents. NSString, NSData, NSArray, and NSDictionary provide methods `writeToURL:...` (for writing) and `init(contentsOfURL:...)` (for reading).

NSString and NSData objects map directly between their own contents and the contents of the file. Here, I'll generate a text file directly from a string:

```
var err : NSError?
ok = "howdy".writeToURL(myfolder.URLByAppendingPathComponent("file1.txt"),
    atomically: true, encoding: NSUTF8StringEncoding, error: &err)
// ... error-checking omitted
```

 You can also read and write an attributed string using a file in a standard format, as I mentioned in Chapter 10.

NSArray and NSDictionary files are actually property lists, and will work only if all the contents of the array or dictionary are property list types (NSString, NSData, NSDate, NSNumber, NSArray, and NSDictionary).

So how do you save to a file an object of some other class? Well, if an object's class adopts the NSCoding protocol, you can convert it to an NSData and back again using NSKeyedArchiver and NSKeyedUnarchiver; the problem is then solved, because an NSData can be saved as a file or in a property list.

You can make your own class adopt the NSCoding protocol. This can become somewhat complicated because an object can refer (through a property) to another object, which may also adopt the NSCoding protocol, and thus you can end up saving an entire graph of interconnected objects if you wish. However, I'll confine myself to illustrating a simple case (and you can read Apple's *Archives and Serializations Programming Guide* for more information).

Let's say, then, that we have a simple Person class with a `firstName` property and a `lastName` property. We'll declare that it adopts the NSCoding protocol:

```
class Person: NSObject, NSCoding {
    var firstName : String
    var lastName : String
    override var description : String {
        return self.firstName + " " + self.lastName
    }
    init(firstName:String, lastName:String) {
        self.firstName = firstName
```

```
            self.lastName = lastName
            super.init()
        }
    }
```

To make this class actually conform to NSCoding, we must implement encodeWith-
Coder: to archive the object, and init(coder:) to unarchive the object. In encodeWith-
Coder:, we must first call super if the superclass adopts NSCoding — in this case, it
doesn't — and then call the appropriate encode... method for each property we want
preserved:

```
    func encodeWithCoder(coder: NSCoder) {
        // do not call super in this case
        coder.encodeObject(self.lastName, forKey: "last")
        coder.encodeObject(self.firstName, forKey: "first")
    }
```

In init(coder:), we call the appropriate decode... method for each property stored
earlier, thus restoring the state of our object. We must also call super, using either
init(coder:) if the superclass adopts the NSCoding protocol or the designated initializer if not:

```
    required init(coder: NSCoder) {
        self.lastName = coder.decodeObjectForKey("last") as! String
        self.firstName = coder.decodeObjectForKey("first") as! String
        // do not call super init(coder:) in this case
        super.init()
    }
```

We can test our code by creating, configuring, and saving a Person instance as a file:

```
    let moi = Person(firstName: "Matt", lastName: "Neuburg")
    let moidata = NSKeyedArchiver.archivedDataWithRootObject(moi)
    let moifile = docsurl.URLByAppendingPathComponent("moi.txt")
    moidata.writeToURL(moifile, atomically: true)
```

We can retrieve the saved Person at a later time:

```
    let persondata = NSData(contentsOfURL: moifile)!
    let person =
        NSKeyedUnarchiver.unarchiveObjectWithData(persondata) as! Person
    println(person) // Matt Neuburg
```

If the NSData object is itself the entire content of the file, as here, then instead of using
archivedDataWithRootObject: and unarchiveObjectWithData:, you can skip the intermediate NSData object and use archiveRootObject:toFile: and unarchiveObject-
WithFile:.

Saving a single Person as an archive may seem like overkill; why didn't we just make a
text file consisting of the first and last names? But imagine that a Person has a lot more
properties, or that we have an array of hundreds of Persons, or an array of hundreds of

dictionaries where one value in each dictionary is a Person; now the power of an archivable Person is evident. Even though Person now adopts the NSCoding protocol, an NSArray containing a Person object still cannot be written to disk using NSArray's writeToFile... or writeToURL..., because Person is still not a property list type. But the array can be archived and written to disk with NSKeyedArchiver.

File Coordinators

New in iOS 8, you can expose a file owned by your app to reading and writing by other apps. In this situation, there needs to be a coherent way for your app to read and write to that file without interference from other apps. The solution is to use an NSFile-Coordinator.

To read or write through an NSFileCoordinator, instantiate NSFileCoordinator along with an NSFileAccessIntent appropriate for reading or writing, to which you have handed the URL of your target file. Then call a coordinate... method. I'll demonstrate the use of coordinateAccessWithIntents(intents:queue:byAccessor:). The accessor: is a closure where you do your actual reading or writing in the normal way, except that the URL for reading or writing now comes from the NSFileAccessIntent object.

So, to write a Person out to a file under the auspices of an NSFileCoordinator:

```
let fc = NSFileCoordinator()
let intent = NSFileAccessIntent.writingIntentWithURL(moifile, options: nil)
fc.coordinateAccessWithIntents(
    [intent], queue: NSOperationQueue.mainQueue()) {
        (err:NSError!) in
        let ok = moidata.writeToURL(intent.URL, atomically: true)
}
```

And to read a Person from a file using an NSFileCoordinator:

```
let fc = NSFileCoordinator()
let intent = NSFileAccessIntent.readingIntentWithURL(moifile, options: nil)
fc.coordinateAccessWithIntents(
    [intent], queue: NSOperationQueue.mainQueue()) {
        (err:NSError!) in
        let persondata = NSData(contentsOfURL: intent.URL)!
        let person =
            NSKeyedUnarchiver.unarchiveObjectWithData(persondata) as! Person
}
```

User Defaults

User defaults (NSUserDefaults) are intended as the persistent storage of the user's preferences. They are little more, really, than a special case of an NSDictionary property list file. You talk to the NSUserDefaults standardUserDefaults object much as if it were a dictionary; it has keys and values. And the only legal values are property list values; thus, for example, to store a Person in user defaults, you'd have to archive it first to an NSData object. Unlike NSDictionary, NSUserDefaults provides convenience methods for converting between a simple data type such as a Float or a Bool and the object that is stored in the defaults (setFloat:forKey:, floatForKey:, and so forth). But the defaults themselves are still a dictionary.

Meanwhile, somewhere on disk, this dictionary is being saved for you automatically as a property list file — though you don't concern yourself with that. You simply set or retrieve values from the dictionary by way of their keys, secure in the knowledge that the file is being read into memory or written to disk as needed. Your chief concern is to make sure that you've written everything needful into user defaults before your app terminates; in the multitasking world (Appendix A), this will usually mean when the app delegate receives applicationDidEnterBackground: at the latest. If you're worried that your app might crash, you can tell the standardUserDefaults object to synchronize as a way of forcing it to save right now, but this is rarely necessary.

To provide the value for a key before the user has had a chance to do so — the default default, as it were — use registerDefaults:. What you're supplying here is a dictionary whose key–value pairs will each be written into the user defaults, but only if there is no such key already. For example:

```
NSUserDefaults.standardUserDefaults().registerDefaults([
    "cardMatrixRows" : 4,
    "cardMatrixColumns" : 3
])
```

The idea is that we call registerDefaults: extremely early as the app launches. Either the app has run at some time previously and the user has set these preferences, in which case this call has no effect and does no harm, or not, in which case we now have initial values for these preferences with which to get started. So, in the game app from which that code comes, we start out with a 4×3 game layout, but the user can change this at any time.

This leaves only the question of how the user is to interact with the defaults. One way is that your app provides some kind of interface. For example, the game app from which the previous code comes has a tab bar interface; the second tab is where the user sets preferences (Figure 23-2).

Alternatively, you can provide a *settings bundle*, consisting mostly of one or more property list files describing an interface and the corresponding user default keys and their initial values; the Settings app is then responsible for translating your instructions into an actual interface, and for presenting it to the user.

Using a settings bundle has some obvious disadvantages: the user has to leave your app to access preferences, and you don't get the kind of control over the interface that you

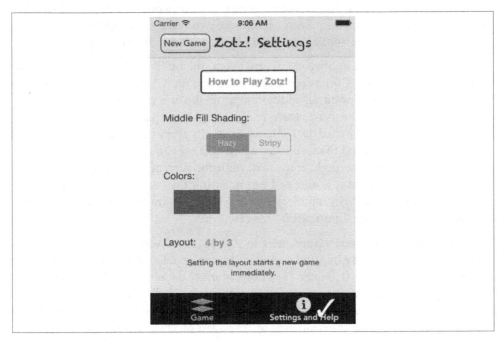

Figure 23-2 An app's preferences interface

have within your own app. Also, the user can set your preferences while your app is backgrounded or not running; you'll need to register for NSUserDefaultsDidChange-Notification in order to hear about this.

In some situations, though, a settings bundle has some clear advantages. Keeping the preferences interface out of your app can make your app's own interface cleaner and simpler. You don't have to write any of the "glue" code that coordinates the preferences interface with the user default values. And it may be appropriate for the user to be able to set at least certain preferences for your app when your app isn't running.

In iOS 7 and before, another objection to a settings bundle was that the user might not think to look in the Settings app for your preferences. New in iOS 8, however, this is less of an issue, because you can transport your user directly from your app to your app's preferences in the Settings app:

```
let url = NSURL(string:UIApplicationOpenSettingsURLString)!
UIApplication.sharedApplication().openURL(url)
```

Writing a settings bundle is described in Apple's *Preferences and Settings Programming Guide*.

It is common practice to misuse NSUserDefaults ever so slightly for various purposes. For example, every method in your app can access the standardUserDefaults object, so it often serves as a global "drop" where one instance can deposit a piece of information for another instance to pick up later, when those two instances might not have ready communication with one another or might not even exist simultaneously.

NSUserDefaults is also a lightweight alternative to the built-in view controller–based state saving and restoration mechanism discussed in Chapter 6. My Zotz! app (Figure 23-2) is a case in point. In addition to using the user defaults to store the user's actual preferences, it also misuses them to store state information: it records the state of the game board and the card deck into user defaults every time these change, so that if the app is terminated and then launched again later, we can restore the game as it was when the user left off. One might argue that, while the current card layout may be state, the card deck itself is data — and so I am misusing the user defaults to store data. However, while purists may grumble, it's a very small amount of data and I don't think the distinction is terribly significant in this case.

Yet another use of NSUserDefaults, new in iOS 8, is as a way to communicate data between your app and an extension provided by your app. For example, let's say you've written a today extension (Chapter 13) whose interface details depend upon some data belonging to your app. After configuring your extension and your app to constitute an app group, both the extension and the app can access the NSUserDefaults associated with the app group (call `init(suiteName:)` instead of `standardUserDefaults`). For more information, see the "Handling Common Scenarios" chapter of Apple's *App Extension Programming Guide*.

Simple Sharing and Previewing of Files

iOS provides some simple and safe passageways by which a file can pass in and out of your sandbox. File sharing lets the user manipulate the contents of your app's Documents directory. UIDocumentInteractionController allows the user to tell another app to hand your app a copy of a document, or to tell your app to hand a copy of a document to another app. UIDocumentInteractionController also permits previewing a document, provided it is compatible with Quick Look.

 New in iOS 8 is an elaborate mechanism for allowing one app to share an area of its sandbox directly with other apps — document provider extensions, along with related classes such as UIDocumentMenuViewController and UIDocumentPick-erViewController. This edition does *not* discuss this topic; see the "Document Provider" chapter of Apple's *App Extension Programming Guide*.

File Sharing

If your app supports file sharing, its Documents directory becomes available to the user through iTunes (Figure 23-3). The user can add files to your app's Documents directory,

Figure 23-3. The iTunes file sharing interface

and can save files and folders from your app's Documents directory to the computer, as well as renaming and deleting files and folders. This could be appropriate, for example, if your app works with common types of file that the user might obtain elsewhere, such as PDFs or JPEGs.

To support file sharing, set the *Info.plist* key "Application supports iTunes file sharing" (`UIFileSharingEnabled`).

Once your entire Documents directory is exposed to the user this way, you are unlikely to use the Documents directory to store private files. As I mentioned earlier, I like to use the Application Support directory instead.

Your app doesn't get any automatic notification when the user has altered the contents of the Documents directory. Noticing that the situation has changed and responding appropriately is entirely up to you; Apple's DocInteraction sample code demonstrates one approaching using the kernel-level `kqueue` mechanism.

Document Types and Receiving a Document

Your app can declare itself willing to open documents of a certain type. In this way, if another app obtains a document of this type, it can propose to hand a copy of the document over to your app. For example, the user might download the document with Mobile Safari, or receive it in a mail message with the Mail app; now we need a way to get it from Safari or Mail to you.

To let the system know that your app is a candidate for receiving a certain kind of document, you will configure the "Document types" (`CFBundleDocumentTypes`) key in your *Info.plist*. This is an array, where each entry will be a dictionary specifying a document type by using keys such as "Document Content Type UTIs" (`LSItemContentTypes`), "Document Type Name" (`CFBundleTypeName`), `CFBundleTypeIconFiles`, and

Figure 23-4. Creating a document type

LSHandlerRank. Far and away the simplest method for configuring the *Info.plist* is through the interface available in the Info tab when you edit the target.

For example, suppose I want to declare that my app opens PDFs and text files. In my target's Info tab in Xcode, I would edit the Document Types section to look like Figure 23-4.

The result is that my *Info.plist* contains this entry:

```
<key>CFBundleDocumentTypes</key>
<array>
    <dict>
        <key>CFBundleTypeIconFiles</key>
        <array/>
        <key>CFBundleTypeName</key>
        <string>PDF</string>
        <key>LSItemContentTypes</key>
        <array>
            <string>com.adobe.pdf</string>
        </array>
    </dict>
    <dict>
        <key>CFBundleTypeIconFiles</key>
        <array/>
        <key>CFBundleTypeName</key>
        <string>TEXT</string>
        <key>LSItemContentTypes</key>
```

Figure 23-5. The Mail app offers to hand off a PDF

```
        <array>
            <string>public.plain-text</string>
        </array>
    </dict>
</array>
```

Now suppose the user receives a PDF in an email message. The Mail app can display this PDF, but the user can also bring up an activity view offering, among other things, to open the file in some other app. The interface will resemble Figure 23-5; various apps that can deal with a PDF are listed here, and my app is among them.

So far, so good. But what if the user actually *taps* the button that sends the PDF over to my app? For this to work, my app delegate must implement `application:open-URL:sourceApplication:annotation:`. When that method is called, my app has been brought to the front, either by launching it from scratch or by reviving it from background suspension; its job is now to handle the opening of the document whose URL has arrived as the second parameter. The system has already copied the document into my app's Inbox directory, which it has created in my Documents folder for exactly this purpose.

 The Inbox directory is created in your Documents folder. Thus, if your app implements file sharing, the user can see the Inbox folder; you may wish to delete the Inbox folder, therefore, as soon as you're done retrieving files from it.

In this simple example, my app has just one view controller, which has an outlet to a UIWebView where we will display any PDFs that arrive in this fashion. So my app delegate contains this code:

```
func application(application: UIApplication, openURL url: NSURL,
    sourceApplication: String?, annotation: AnyObject?) -> Bool {
        let vc = self.window!.rootViewController as! ViewController
        vc.displayDoc(url)
        return true
}
```

And my view controller contains this code:

```
func displayDoc (url:NSURL) {
    let req = NSURLRequest(URL: url)
    self.wv.loadRequest(req)
}
```

In real life, things might be more complicated. Our implementation of `application:openURL:...` might check to see whether this really *is* a PDF, and return `false` if it isn't. Also, our app might be in the middle of something else, possibly displaying a completely different view controller's view; because `application:openURL:...` can arrive at any time, we may have to be prepared to drop whatever we were doing and display the incoming document instead.

If our app is launched from scratch by the arrival of this URL, `application:didFinishLaunchingWithOptions:` will be sent to our app delegate as usual. The options dictionary (the second parameter) will contain the `UIApplicationLaunchOptionsURLKey`, and we can take into account, if we like, the fact that we are being launched specifically to open a document. We can also return `false` to refuse to open the document. If we return `true` as usual, `application:openURL:...` will arrive in good order after our interface has been set up.

The example I've been discussing assumes that the UTI for the document type is standard and well-known. It is also possible that your app will operate on a new document type, that is, a type of document that the app itself defines. In that case, you'll also want to add this UTI to your app's list of Exported UTIs in the *Info.plist*. I'll give an example later in this chapter.

Handing Over a Document

The converse of the situation discussed in the previous section is this: your app has somehow acquired a document and wants to let the user hand over a copy of it to some other app to deal with it. This is done through the UIDocumentInteractionController class. This class operates asynchronously, so retaining an instance of it is up to you; typically, you'll store it in a property, and there is no reason not to initialize this property directly:

```
let dic = UIDocumentInteractionController()
```

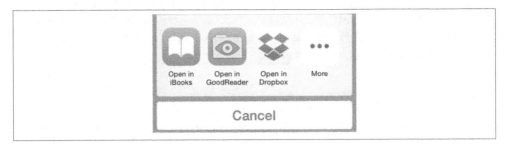

Figure 23-6. The document Open In activity view

For example, assuming we have a file URL `url` pointing to a document on disk, presenting the interface for handing the document over to some other application (Figure 23-6) could be as simple as this (`sender` is a button that the user has just tapped):

```
self.dic.URL = url
let v = sender as! UIView
let ok = self.dic.presentOpenInMenuFromRect(
    v.bounds, inView: v, animated: true)
```

This interface is an activity view (Chapter 13). There are actually two activity views available:

`presentOpenInMenuFromRect:inView:animated:`
`presentOpenInMenuFromBarButtonItem:animated:`
> Presents an activity view listing apps in which the document can be opened (like Figure 23-6).

`presentOptionsMenuFromRect:inView:animated:`
`presentOptionsMenuFromBarButtonItem:animated:`
> Presents an activity view listing apps in which the document can be opened, along with other possible actions, such as Print, Copy, and Mail (like Figure 23-5).

 Your app can't learn *which* other applications are capable of accepting the document! Indeed, it can't even learn in advance whether *any* other applications are capable of accepting the document; your only clue is that the returned Bool value afterward will be `false` if the UIDocumentInteractionController couldn't present the requested interface.

Previewing a Document

A UIDocumentInteractionController can be used for an entirely different purpose: it can present a preview of the document, if the document is of a type for which preview is enabled, by calling `presentPreviewAnimated:`. You must give the UIDocument-

InteractionController a delegate (UIDocumentInteractionControllerDelegate), and the delegate must implement `documentInteractionControllerViewControllerFor-Preview:`, returning an existing view controller that will contain the preview's view controller. So, here we ask for the preview:

```
self.dic.URL = url
self.dic.delegate = self
self.dic.presentPreviewAnimated(true)
```

In the delegate, we supply the view controller; it happens that, in my code, this delegate *is* a view controller, so it simply returns `self`:

```
func documentInteractionControllerViewControllerForPreview(
    controller: UIDocumentInteractionController) -> UIViewController {
        return self
}
```

If the view controller returned were a UINavigationController, the preview's view controller would be pushed onto it. In this case it isn't, so the preview's view controller is a presented view controller with a Done button. The preview interface also contains an Action button that lets the user summon the Options activity view. In fact, this preview interface is exactly the same interface already familiar from the Mail app.

 New in iOS 8, you cannot preview a document in your app's Inbox folder. Copy the document to a different location in your sandbox, such as the Documents folder, before trying to preview it.

Delegate methods allow you to track what's happening in the interface presented by the UIDocumentInteractionController. Probably most important are those that inform you that key stages of the interaction are ending:

- `documentInteractionControllerDidDismissOptionsMenu:`
- `documentInteractionControllerDidDismissOpenInMenu:`
- `documentInteractionControllerDidEndPreview:`
- `documentInteractionController:didEndSendingToApplication:`

Previews are actually provided through the Quick Look framework, and you can skip the UIDocumentInteractionController and present the preview yourself through a QLPreviewController; you'll need to `import QuickLook`. It's a view controller, so to display the preview you show it as a presented view controller or push it onto a navigation controller's stack, just as UIDocumentInteractionController would have done. A nice feature of QLPreviewController is that you can give it more than one document to preview; the user can move between these, within the preview, by paging sideways or using a table of contents summoned by a button at the bottom of the interface. Apart from this, the interface looks like the interface presented by the UIDocument-InteractionController.

In this example, I may have in my Documents directory one or more PDF or text documents. I acquire a list of their URLs and present a preview for them (`self.exts` has been initialized to `["pdf", "txt"]`):

```
self.docs = [NSURL]()
let fm = NSFileManager()
var err : NSError?
let docsurl = fm.URLForDirectory(.DocumentDirectory,
    inDomain: .UserDomainMask, appropriateForURL: nil,
    create: true, error: &err)
let dir = fm.enumeratorAtURL(
    docsurl!, includingPropertiesForKeys: nil,
    options: nil, errorHandler: nil)
while let f = dir?.nextObject() as? NSURL {
    if find(self.exts, f.pathExtension!) != nil {
        if QLPreviewController.canPreviewItem(f) {
            self.docs.append(f)
        }
    }
}
if self.docs.count == 0 {return}
let preview = QLPreviewController()
preview.dataSource = self
preview.currentPreviewItemIndex = 0
self.presentViewController(preview, animated: true, completion: nil)
```

You'll notice that I haven't told the QLPreviewController what documents to preview. That is the job of QLPreviewController's data source. In my code, I (`self`) am also the data source. I simply fetch the requested information from the list of URLs, which I previously saved into `self.docs`:

```
func numberOfPreviewItemsInPreviewController(
    controller: QLPreviewController!) -> Int {
        return self.docs.count
}
func previewController(controller: QLPreviewController!,
    previewItemAtIndex index: Int) -> QLPreviewItem! {
        return self.docs[index]
}
```

The second data source method requires us to return an object that adopts the QLPreviewItem protocol. By a wildly improbable coincidence, NSURL *does* adopt this protocol, so the example works.

Document Architecture

If your app opens and saves documents of a type peculiar to itself, you may want to take advantage of the *document architecture*. This architecture revolves around a class, UIDocument, that takes care of a number of pesky issues, such as the fact that loading or writing your data might take some time. Plus, UIDocument provides autosaving behavior, so that your data is written out automatically whenever it changes. Moreover, UIDocument is your gateway to allowing your documents to participate in iCloud; with iCloud, your app's documents on one of the user's devices can automatically be mirrored onto another of the user's devices.

Getting started with UIDocument is not difficult. You'll start with a UIDocument subclass, and you'll override two methods:

loadFromContents:ofType:error:
> Called when it's time to open a document from disk. You are expected to convert the contents value into a model object that your app can use, store that model object, and return true. (If there was a problem, you'll set the error: by indirection and return false.)

contentsForType:error:
> Called when it's time to save a document to disk. You are expected to convert the app's model object into an NSData instance (or, if your document is a package, an NSFileWrapper) and return it. (If there was a problem, you'll set the error: by indirection and return nil.)

Your UIDocument subclass will need a place to store and retrieve the data model object. Obviously, this can be a property of the UIDocument subclass itself. At the same time, keep in mind that your UIDocument instance will probably be partnered in some way with a view controller instance, which will also need access to the same data.

To instantiate a UIDocument, call its designated initializer, init(fileURL:). This sets the UIDocument's fileURL property, and associates the UIDocument with this file on disk, typically for the remainder of its lifetime.

In my description of the two key UIDocument methods that your subclass will override, I used the phrase, "when it's time" (to open or save the document). This raises the question of how your UIDocument instance will know when to open and save a document. There are three circumstances to distinguish:

Make a new document
> The fileURL: points to a nonexistent file. Immediately after instantiating the UIDocument, you send it saveToURL:forSaveOperation:completionHandler:, where the second argument (a UIDocumentSaveOperation) is .ForCreating. (The first argument will be the UIDocument's own fileURL.) This in turn causes contentsForType:error: to be called, and the contents of an empty document are

saved out to disk. This implies that your UIDocument subclass should know of some default value that represents the model data when there is no data.

Open an existing document

Send the UIDocument instance `openWithCompletionHandler:`. This in turn causes `loadFromContents:ofType:error:` to be called.

Save an existing document

There are two approaches to saving an existing document:

Autosave

Usually, you'll mark the document as "dirty" by calling `updateChangeCount:`. From time to time, the UIDocument will notice this situation and will save the document to disk, calling `contentsForType:error:` in the process.

Manual save

On certain occasions, waiting for autosave won't be appropriate. We've already seen an example of such an occasion — when the file itself needs to be created on the spot. Another is when the app is going into the background; we will want to preserve our document there and then, in case the app is terminated. You'll call `saveToURL:forSaveOperation:completionHandler:`; if the file is not being created for the first time, the second argument will be `.ForOverwriting`. Alternatively, if you know you're finished with the document (perhaps the interface displaying the document is about to be torn down) you can call `closeWithCompletionHandler:`.

The `open...`, `close...`, and `saveTo...` methods have a `completionHandler:` argument. This is UIDocument's solution to the fact that reading and saving may take time. The file operations themselves take place on a background thread; the `completionHandler:` block is then called on the main thread.

We now know enough for an example! I'll reuse my Person class from earlier in this chapter. Imagine a document effectively consisting of multiple Person instances; I'll call each such document a *people group*. Our app, People Groups, will list all people groups in the user's Documents folder; it will also open any people group from disk and display its contents, allowing the user to edit any Person's `firstName` or `lastName` (Figure 23-7).

My first step is to define a custom UTI in my app's *Info.plist*, associating a file type `com.neuburg.pplgrp` with a file extension `"pplgrp"`. I then also define a document type that uses this UTI, as shown earlier in this chapter (Figure 23-8).

A document consists of multiple Persons, so a natural model implementation is an array of Persons. Moreover, as I mentioned earlier, since Person implements NSCoding, an NSArray of Persons can be archived directly into an NSData. Thus, our UIDocument subclass (which I'll call PeopleDocument) has a public array `people` property, and can be implemented very simply: we initialize our `people` property to an empty Person array,

Figure 23-7. The People Groups interface

Figure 23-8. Defining a custom UTI

so that we have something to save into a new empty document, and to mediate between our model and the data on disk, we use NSKeyedUnarchiver and NSKeyedArchiver exactly as in our earlier examples:

```
class PeopleDocument: UIDocument {
    var people = [Person]()
    override func loadFromContents(contents: AnyObject,
        ofType typeName: String,
        error outError: NSErrorPointer) -> Bool {
            if let contents = contents as? NSData {
                let arr =
                    NSKeyedUnarchiver.unarchiveObjectWithData(
                        contents) as! [Person]
                self.people = arr
                return true
            }
            return false
    }
    override func contentsForType(typeName: String,
        error outError: NSErrorPointer) -> AnyObject? {
            let data =
                NSKeyedArchiver.archivedDataWithRootObject(self.people)
            return data
    }

}
```

The remaining questions are architectural: when should a PeopleDocument be initialized, where should it be stored, and what should be the nature of communications with it?

The first view controller, DocumentLister, merely lists documents by name, and provides an interface for letting the user create a new group; only the second view controller, PeopleLister, the one that displays the first and last names of the people in the group, actually needs to work with PeopleDocument.

PeopleLister's designated initializer therefore requires that it be given a fileURL: argument, with which it sets its own fileURL property. In its viewDidLoad implementation, PeopleLister instantiates a PeopleDocument with that same fileURL, and retains it through a PeopleDocument property (self.doc); PeopleLister's own people property will be nothing but a front for this PeopleDocument's people property. If fileURL points to a nonexistent file, PeopleLister requests that it be created by calling saveToURL:forSaveOperation:completionHandler:; otherwise, it requests that the document be read, by calling openWithCompletionHandler:. Either way, the completion handler refreshes the interface:

```
let fileURL : NSURL
var doc : PeopleDocument!
var people : [Person] { // front end for the document's model object
    get {
        return self.doc.people
    }
    set (val) {
        self.doc.people = val
    }
}
init(fileURL:NSURL) {
    self.fileURL = fileURL
    super.init(nibName: "PeopleLister", bundle: nil)
}
required init(coder: NSCoder) {
    fatalError("NSCoding not supported")
}
override func viewDidLoad() {
    super.viewDidLoad()
    self.title =
        self.fileURL.lastPathComponent!.stringByDeletingPathExtension
    // ...
    let fm = NSFileManager()
    self.doc = PeopleDocument(fileURL:self.fileURL)
    func listPeople(success:Bool) {
        if success {
            self.tableView.reloadData()
        }
    }
    if !fm.fileExistsAtPath(self.fileURL.path!) {
        self.doc.saveToURL(self.doc.fileURL,
            forSaveOperation: .ForCreating,
            completionHandler: listPeople)
    } else {
        self.doc.openWithCompletionHandler(listPeople)
    }
}
```

When the user performs a significant editing maneuver, such as creating or deleting a person or editing a person's first or last name, PeopleLister tells its PeopleDocument that the document is dirty, and allows autosaving to take it from there:

```
self.doc.updateChangeCount(.Done)
```

When the app is about to go into the background, or when PeopleLister's own view is disappearing, PeopleLister forces PeopleDocument to save immediately:

```
func forceSave(_:AnyObject?) {
    self.tableView.endEditing(true)
    self.doc.saveToURL(self.doc.fileURL,
        forSaveOperation:.ForOverwriting, completionHandler:nil)
}
```

That's all it takes; adding UIDocument support to your app is easy, because UIDocument is merely acting as a supplier and preserver of your app's data model object. UIDocument presents itself in the documentation as a large and complex class, but that's chiefly because it is so heavily customizable both at high and low levels; for the most part, you won't need any of that heavy customization, and use of UIDocument really will be as simple as what I've shown here. You might go further in order to give your UIDocument a more sophisticated understanding of what constitutes a significant change in your data by working with its undo manager; I'll talk about undo managers in Chapter 26. For further details, see Apple's *Document-based App Programming Guide for iOS*.

iCloud

Once your app is operating through UIDocument, basic iCloud compatibility effectively falls right into your lap. You have just two steps to perform:

Obtain iCloud entitlements

> Edit the target and, in the Capabilities tab, set the iCloud switch to On. This causes a transaction to take place between Xcode and the Member Center; automatically, your app gets a Ubiquity Container, and an appropriately configured entitlements file is added to the project.

Obtain an iCloud-compatible directory

> Early in your app's lifetime, call NSFileManager's `URLForUbiquityContainer-Identifier:` (typically passing nil as the argument), on a background thread, to obtain the URL of the cloud-shared directory. Any documents your app puts here by way of a UIDocument subclass will be automatically shared into the cloud.

Thus, having switched on iCloud support, I can make my People Groups example app iCloud-compatible with just two code changes. In the app delegate, as my app launches, I step out to a background thread (Chapter 25), obtain the cloud-shared directory's URL, and then step back to the main thread and retain the URL through a property, `self.ubiq`:

```
dispatch_async(dispatch_get_global_queue(0, 0)) {
    let fm = NSFileManager()
    let ubiq = fm.URLForUbiquityContainerIdentifier(nil)
    dispatch_async(dispatch_get_main_queue()) {
        self.ubiq = ubiq
    }
}
```

When I specify where to seek and save people groups, I continue using the user's Documents folder if `ubiq` is nil, but otherwise I use `ubiq` itself:

```
var docsurl : NSURL {
    get {
        let del = UIApplication.sharedApplication().delegate
        if let ubiq = (del as! AppDelegate).ubiq {
            return ubiq
        } else {
            let fm = NSFileManager()
            return fm.URLForDirectory(
                .DocumentDirectory, inDomain: .UserDomainMask,
                appropriateForURL: nil, create: true, error: nil)!
        }
    }
}
```

To test, I run the app on a device (with iCloud → Documents & Data switched to On in the Settings app) and create a people group with some people in it. I then switch to a different device (also with iCloud → Documents & Data switched to On) and run the app there, and tap the Refresh button, which looks through the docsurl directory for pplgrp files:

```
let fm = NSFileManager()
self.files = fm.contentsOfDirectoryAtURL(
    self.docsurl,
    includingPropertiesForKeys: nil, options: nil, error: nil)!
        .filter { ($0 as! NSURL).pathExtension == "pplgrp" } as! [NSURL]
self.tableView.reloadData()
```

Presto, the app now displays my people group containing my people! It's quite thrilling.

There are a few further refinements that my app probably needs in order to be a good iCloud citizen. For example, my app is not automatically aware that a new document has appeared in the cloud (that's why I had to tap Refresh to discover an existing people group). To be notified of that, I'd want to run an NSMetadataQuery. The usual strategy is: instantiate NSMetadataQuery, configure the search, register for notifications such as NSMetadataQueryDidFinishGatheringNotification and NSMetadataQueryDid-UpdateNotification, start the search, and retain the NSMetadataQuery instance with the search continuing to run for the entire lifetime of the app.

Another concern is that my app should be notified when the currently open document changes on disk because a new version of it was downloaded from the cloud (that is, someone edited the document while I had it open). For that, register for UIDocument-StateChangedNotification. To learn the document's state, consult its document-State property (UIDocumentState). A big issue is likely to be what should happen if the document state is .InConflict. You'll want to resolve the conflict in coordination with the NSFileVersion class; for details and example code, see the "Resolving Document Version Conflicts" chapter of Apple's *Document-based App Programming Guide for iOS.*

Yet another issue is the question of what should happen if the availability of iCloud changes in the course of our app's career. The problem here is that the data is stored in two different places — the Documents directory or the cloud-shared directory. Suppose, for example, that our app starts life without iCloud — because the user hasn't registered for it, or has it turned off for our app — and then suddenly iCloud is available. We could then call NSFileManager's `setUbiquitous:itemAtURL:destinationURL:error:` to transfer the document to our ubiquity container directory. However, it is not so obvious what to do if iCloud is switched from On to Off, as it is now too late to access the ubiquity container directory to rescue the document; in effect, the cloud-based data is lost (until the user logs back into that iCloud account).

Along the same lines, as my app launches, before I even ask for the ubiquity container, I should probably call NSFileManager's `ubiquityIdentityToken`. If the result is nil, iCloud isn't available, or this user hasn't registered for iCloud, and we might as well omit any subsequent attempt to work with iCloud. If it *isn't* nil, it identifies the user's iCloud account; this can be useful, for example, to detect when the user has logged into a different account.

Instead of, or in addition to, storing full-fledged documents in the cloud, your app might like to store some key–value pairs, similar to a sort of online NSUserDefaults. To do so, check the "Use key–value store" checkbox when you configure your entitlements in the Capabilities tab, and then use the NSUbiquitousKeyValueStore class; get the `default-Store` shared object and talk to it much as you would talk to NSUserDefaults. The `NSUbiquitousKeyValueStoreDidChangeExternallyNotification` tells you when data is changed in the cloud. Material that you store in the cloud through NSUbiquitous-KeyValueStore does *not* count against the user's iCloud storage limit, but it needs to be kept short and simple.

New in iOS 8, a UIDocument-based app that supports iCloud can also support Handoff, allowing the user who switches to a different device to see the same data *in the same state* as on the previous device. Handoff is outside the scope of this edition; see the "Supporting User Activities" section of the UIDocument class reference.

Further iCloud details are outside the scope of this discussion; see Apple's *iCloud Design Guide*. Getting started is easy; making your app a good iCloud citizen, capable of dealing with the complexities that iCloud may entail, is not.

 iOS 8 introduces iCloud Drive, a Dropbox-like cloud-based storage mechanism that can share documents from any app; iCloud Drive is not covered in this edition.

XML

XML is a highly flexible and widely used general-purpose text file format for storage and retrieval of structured data. You might use it yourself to store data that you'll need to retrieve later, or you could encounter it when obtaining information from elsewhere, such as the Internet.

OS X Cocoa provides a set of classes (NSXMLDocument and so forth) for reading, parsing, maintaining, searching, and modifying XML data in a completely general way, but iOS does *not* include these. I think the reason must be that their tree-based approach is too memory-intensive. Instead, iOS provides NSXMLParser, a much simpler class that walks through an XML document, sending delegate messages as it encounters elements. With this, you can parse an XML document once, but what you do with the pieces as you encounter them is up to you. The general assumption here is that you know in advance the structure of the particular XML data you intend to read and that you have provided classes for storage of the same data in object form and for transforming the XML pieces into that storage.

To illustrate, let's return once more to our Person class with a `firstName` and a `lastName` property. Imagine that as our app starts up, we would like to populate it with Person objects, and that we've stored the data describing these objects as an XML file in our app bundle, like this:

```
<?xml version="1.0" encoding="utf-8"?>
<people>
    <person>
        <firstName>Matt</firstName>
        <lastName>Neuburg</lastName>
    </person>
    <person>
        <firstName>Snidely</firstName>
        <lastName>Whiplash</lastName>
    </person>
    <person>
        <firstName>Dudley</firstName>
        <lastName>Doright</lastName>
    </person>
</people>
```

This data could be mapped to an array of Person objects, each with its `firstName` and `lastName` properties appropriately set. (This is a deliberately easy example, of course; not all XML is so readily expressed as objects.) Let's consider how we might do that.

Using NSXMLParser is not difficult in theory. You create the NSXMLParser, handing it the URL of a local XML file (or an NSData, perhaps downloaded from the Internet), set its delegate, and tell it to `parse`. The delegate starts receiving delegate messages. For simple XML like ours, there are only three delegate messages of interest:

`parser:didStartElement:namespaceURI:qualifiedName:attributes:`
   The parser has encountered an opening element tag. In our document, this would be `<people>`, `<person>`, `<firstName>`, or `<lastName>`.

`parser:didEndElement:namespaceURI:qualifiedName:`
: The parser has encountered the corresponding closing element tag. In our document this would be `</people>`, `</person>`, `</firstName>`, or `</lastName>`.

`parser:foundCharacters:`
: The parser has encountered some text between the starting and closing tags for the current element. In our document this would be, for example, `Matt` or `Neuburg` and so on.

In practice, responding to these delegate messages poses challenges of maintaining state. If there is just one delegate, it will have to bear in mind at every moment what element it is currently encountering; this could make for a lot of properties and a lot of if-statements in the implementation of the delegate methods. To aggravate the issue, `parser:foundCharacters:` can arrive multiple times for a single stretch of text; that is, the text may arrive in pieces, so we have to accumulate it into a property.

An elegant way to meet these challenges is by resetting the NSXMLParser's delegate to different objects at different stages of the parsing process. We make each delegate responsible for parsing one element; when a child of that element is encountered, we make a new object and make *it* the delegate. The child element delegate is then responsible for making the parent the delegate once again when it finishes parsing its own element. This is slightly counterintuitive because it means `parser:didStartElement...` and `parser:didEndElement...` for the same element are arriving at *two different objects*. Imagine, for example, what the job of our `<people>` parser will be:

- When `parser:didStartElement...` arrives, the `<people>` parser looks to see if this is a `<person>`. If so, it creates an object that knows how to deal with a `<person>` (a `<person>` parser), handing that object a reference to itself (the `<people>` parser), and makes it the delegate.

- Delegate messages now arrive at this newly created `<person>` parser. If any text is encountered, `parser:foundCharacters:` will be called, and the text must be accumulated into a property.

- Eventually, `parser:didEndElement...` arrives. The `<person>` parser now uses its reference to make the `<people>` parser the delegate once again. Thus, the `<people>` parser is in charge once again, ready if another `<person>` element is encountered (and the old `<person>` parser might now go quietly out of existence).

With this in mind, we can design a simple all-purpose base class for parsing an element (simple especially because we are taking no account of namespaces, attributes, and other complications). I'll show you the design and explain its architecture before I fill in the blanks with actual code:

```
class MyXMLParserDelegate : NSObject {
    var name : String!
    var text = ""
    weak var parent : MyXMLParserDelegate?
    var child : MyXMLParserDelegate!
    required init(name:String, parent:MyXMLParserDelegate?) {}
    func makeChild(klass:MyXMLParserDelegate.Type,
        elementName:String,
        parser:NSXMLParser) {}
    func finishedChild(s:String) {}
}
```

Here's how these properties and methods are intended to work:

`name`
> The name of the element we are parsing now.

`text`
> A place for any characters to accumulate as we parse our element.

`parent`
> A reference to the MyXMLParserDelegate who created us and whose child we are.

`child`
> If we encounter a child element, we'll create a MyXMLParserDelegate and retain it here, making it the delegate and making ourselves its `parent`.

`makeChild:elementName:parser:`
> If we encounter a child element, there's a standard dance to do: instantiate some subclass of MyXMLParserDelegate, make ourself its `parent`, make it our `child`, and make it the parser's delegate. This is a utility method that embodies that dance.

`finishedChild:`
> When a child receives `parser:didEndElement...`, it should send this message to its parent before making its parent the delegate. The parameter is the `text`, but the parent can use this signal to obtain any information it expects from the child before the child goes out of existence.

Now we can sketch in the default implementations for the methods I just described:

```
required init(name:String, parent:MyXMLParserDelegate?) {
    self.name = name
    self.parent = parent
    super.init()
}
func makeChild(klass:MyXMLParserDelegate.Type,
    elementName:String,
    parser:NSXMLParser) {
        let del = klass(name:elementName, parent:self)
        self.child = del
        parser.delegate = del
```

```
    }
    func finishedChild(s:String) { // subclasses must override!
        fatalError("Subclass must implement finishedChild:!")
    }
```

But that's only half the story. MyXMLParserDelegate is also an NSXMLParserDelegate — that's the point! Thus, I now extend MyXMLParserDelegate to adopt NSXMLParser-Delegate:

```
extension MyXMLParserDelegate : NSXMLParserDelegate {
    func parser(parser: NSXMLParser, foundCharacters string: String?) {
        self.text = self.text + string!
    }
    func parser(parser: NSXMLParser, didEndElement elementName: String,
        namespaceURI: String?, qualifiedName qName: String?) {
            if self.parent != nil {
                self.parent!.finishedChild(self.text)
                parser.delegate = self.parent
            }
    }
}
```

That completes the picture, and we can now proceed to create specialized subclasses of MyXMLParserDelegate, one for each kind of element we expect to parse. Each subclass has very little work to do:

- In parser:didStartElement..., if a child element is encountered, it should call the utility method makeChild:elementName:parser: to create the appropriate child parser.

- The reverse process is already built into the default implementation of parser:did-EndElement...: we call the parent's finishedChild: and make the parent the delegate. Each subclass should implement finishedChild: in order to receive whatever data the child hands back.

We can now parse our sample XML into an array of Person objects very easily. We start by obtaining the URL of the XML file, handing it to an NSXMLParser, creating our first delegate parser and making it the delegate, and telling the NSXMLParser to start parsing:

```
if let url = NSBundle.mainBundle().URLForResource(
    "folks", withExtension: "xml") {
        if let parser = NSXMLParser(contentsOfURL: url) {
            let people = MyPeopleParser(name:"", parent:nil)
            parser.delegate = people
            parser.parse()
            // all done! do something with people.people here
        }
}
```

MyPeopleParser is the top-level parser. It has a `people` property that starts out as an empty Person array; as it encounters a `<person>` element, its creates a `<person>` parser (MyPersonParser), and its `finishedChild:` implementation expects that MyPerson-Parser's `person` to supply a Person object, which it will put into its own `people` property:

```
var people = [Person]()
func parser(parser: NSXMLParser, didStartElement elementName: String,
    namespaceURI: String?, qualifiedName qName: String?,
    attributes attributeDict: [NSObject : AnyObject]!) {
        if elementName == "person" {
            self.makeChild(
                MyPersonParser.self, elementName: elementName,
                parser: parser)
        }
}
override func finishedChild(s: String) {
    self.people.append((self.child as! MyPersonParser).person)
}
```

MyPersonParser does the same child-making dance when it encounters a `<firstName>` or a `<lastName>` element; it uses a plain vanilla MyXMLParserDelegate to parse these children, because the built-in ability to accumulate text and hand it back is all that's needed. In `finishedChild:`, key–value coding is elegantly used to match the name of the element with the name of the Person property to be set:

```
var person = Person(firstName: "", lastName: "")
func parser(parser: NSXMLParser, didStartElement elementName: String,
    namespaceURI: String?, qualifiedName qName: String?,
    attributes attributeDict: [NSObject : AnyObject]!) {
        self.makeChild(MyXMLParserDelegate.self,
            elementName: elementName, parser: parser)
}
override func finishedChild(s: String) {
    self.person.setValue(s, forKey:self.child.name)
}
```

This may seem like a lot of work to parse such a simple bit of XML, but it is neatly object-oriented and requires very little new code once we've established the MyXMLParser-Delegate superclass, which is of course reusable in many other situations.

A foundation class for constructing and parsing JSON strings is also provided — NSJSONSerialization. It's a very simple class: all its methods are class methods, and eligible structures are required to be an array or dictionary (corresponding to what JSON calls an *object*) whose elements must be a string, number, array, dictionary, or null. NSData is used as the medium of exchange; you'll archive or unarchive as appropriate. JSON arises often as a lightweight way of communicating structured data across the network; for more information, see *http://www.json.org/*.

SQLite

SQLite (*http://www.sqlite.org/docs.html*) is a lightweight, full-featured relational database that you can talk to using SQL, the universal language of databases. This can be an appropriate storage format when your data comes in rows and columns (records and fields) and needs to be rapidly searchable. Also, the database as a whole is never loaded into memory; the data is accessed only as needed. This is valuable in an environment like an iOS device, where memory is at a premium.

To use SQLite, link to *libsqlite3.dylib* (and import <sqlite3.h>). Talking to sqlite3 involves an elaborate C interface which may prove annoying; there are, however, a number of lightweight Objective-C front ends. In this example, I use fmdb (*https://github.com/ccgus/fmdb*) to read the names of people out of a previously created database:

```
let docsdir = NSSearchPathForDirectoriesInDomains(
    .DocumentDirectory, .UserDomainMask, true).last as! String
let dbpath = docsdir.stringByAppendingPathComponent("people.db")
let db = FMDatabase(path:self.dbpath)
if !db.open() {
    return
}
let rs = db.executeQuery("select * from people", withArgumentsInArray:nil)
while rs.next() {
    print(rs["firstname"]); print(" "); println(rs["lastname"])
}
db.close()
/*
Matt Neuburg
Snidely Whiplash
Dudley Doright
*/
```

You can include a previously constructed SQLite file in your app bundle, but you can't write to it there; the solution is to copy it from your app bundle into another location, such as the Documents directory, before you start working with it.

Core Data

The Core Data framework provides a generalized way of expressing objects and properties that form a relational graph; moreover, it has built-in facilities for persisting those objects to disk — typically using SQLite as a storage format — and reading them from disk only when they are needed, thus making efficient use of memory. For example, a person might have not only multiple addresses but also multiple friends who are also persons; expressing persons and addresses as explicit object types, working out how to link them and how to translate between objects in memory and data in storage, and tracking the effects of changes, such as when a person is deleted from the data, can be tedious. Core Data can help.

It is important to stress, however, that Core Data is *not* a beginner-level technology. It is difficult to use and extremely difficult to debug. It expresses itself in a highly verbose, rigid, arcane way. It has its own elaborate way of doing things — everything you already know about how to create, access, alter, or delete an object within an object collection becomes completely irrelevant! — and trying to bend it to your particular needs can be tricky and can have unintended side effects. Nor should Core Data be seen as a substitute for a true relational database.

Therefore, I have no intention of explaining Core Data; that would require an entire book. Indeed, such books exist, and if Core Data interests you, you should read some of them. See also Apple's *Core Data Programming Guide* and the other resources referred to there. I will, however, illustrate what it's like to work with Core Data.

I will rewrite the People Groups example from earlier in this chapter as a Core Data app. We will no longer have multiple documents, each representing a single group of people; instead, we will now have a single document, maintained for us by Core Data, containing all of our groups and all of their people.

A Core Data project must `import CoreData`. To construct a Core Data project from scratch, it is simplest to specify the Master–Detail Application template (or the Single View Application template) and check Use Core Data in the second screen. This gives you the necessary linkage to the Core Data framework, along with template code in the app delegate implementation file for constructing the Core Data *persistence stack*, a set of objects that work together to fetch and save your data; in most cases there will no reason to alter this template code, and I have not done so for this example.

The app delegate template code gives the app delegate three properties representing the important singleton objects constituting the persistence stack: `managedObject-Context`, `managedObjectModel`, and `persistentStoreCoordinator`. It also supplies `lazy` initializers to give these properties their values when first needed. Of these, the `managedObjectContext` is the most important for other classes to have access to. The managed object context is the world in which your data objects live and move and have their being: to obtain an object, you fetch it from the managed object context; to create an object, you insert it into the managed object context; to save your data, you save the managed object context.

The Master–Detail Application template also gives the Master view controller a `managed-ObjectContext` property, and the app delegate sets its value. My Master view controller is called GroupLister, so the app delegate's `application:didFinishLaunchingWith-Options:` contains these lines:

```
let navigationController =
    self.window!.rootViewController as! UINavigationController
let controller = navigationController.topViewController as! GroupLister
controller.managedObjectContext = self.managedObjectContext
```

Figure 23-9. The Core Data model for the People Groups app

To describe the structure and relationships of the objects constituting your data model, you design an object graph in a data model document. Our object graph is very simple: a Group can have multiple Persons (Figure 23-9). The attributes, analogous to object properties, are all strings, except for the timestamps which are dates; the timestamps will be used for determining the sort order in which groups and people will be displayed in the interface — the display order is the order of creation.

Core Data attributes are not quite object properties. Group and Person are not classes; they are entity names. All Core Data model objects are instances of NSManagedObject, and therefore they do not, of themselves, have a name property, a firstName property, a lastName property, and so on. Instead, Core Data model objects make themselves dynamically KVC compliant for attribute names. For example, Core Data knows, thanks to our object graph, that a Person entity is to have a firstName attribute, so you can set a Person's firstName attribute using KVC (setValue:forKey:). I find this maddening, so, at the very least, I like to give NSManagedObject the necessary properties through a category (in Objective-C, because you can't define a stored property in a Swift extension):

```
// NSManagedObject+GroupAndPerson.h:
#import <CoreData/CoreData.h>
@interface NSManagedObject (GroupAndPerson)
@property (nonatomic) NSString *firstName, *lastName;
@property (nonatomic) NSString *name, *uuid;
@property (nonatomic) NSDate* timestamp;
@property (nonatomic) NSManagedObject* group;
@end
// NSManagedObject+GroupAndPerson.m:
```

```
#import "NSManagedObject+GroupAndPerson.h"
@implementation NSManagedObject (GroupAndPerson)
@dynamic firstName, lastName, name, uuid, timestamp, group;
@end
```

Now we'll be able to use `name` and `firstName` and the rest as properties, and CoreData will generate the corresponding accessors for us.

Now let's talk about the first view controller, GroupLister. Its job is to list groups and to allow the user to create a new group (Figure 23-7). The way you ask Core Data for a model object is with a fetch request. In iOS, where Core Data model objects are often the data source for a UITableView, fetch requests are conveniently managed through an NSFetchedResultsController. The template code gives us an NSFetchedResults-Controller private property with a corresponding public computed property that generates an NSFetchedResultsController if the private property is nil; this seems over-blown, and in my implementation I've replaced it with a single `lazy` NSFetchedResults property, which I've called `frc`. My entity name is Group and my cache name is Groups; apart from that, and some shortened variable names, this is pure template code:

```
lazy var frc : NSFetchedResultsController = {
    let req = NSFetchRequest()
    let entity = NSEntityDescription.entityForName(
        "Group", inManagedObjectContext:self.managedObjectContext)
    req.entity = entity
    req.fetchBatchSize = 20
    let sortDescriptor = NSSortDescriptor(key:"timestamp", ascending:true)
    req.sortDescriptors = [sortDescriptor]
    let afrc = NSFetchedResultsController(fetchRequest:req,
        managedObjectContext:self.managedObjectContext,
        sectionNameKeyPath:nil,
        cacheName:"Groups")
    afrc.delegate = self
    var error : NSError? = nil
    if !afrc.performFetch(&error) {
        println("Unresolved error \(error!) \(error!.userInfo)")
        fatalError("Aborting with unresolved error")
    }
    return afrc
}()
```

The result is that `self.frc` is the data model, analogous to an array of Group objects. The implementation of the table view's Three Big Questions to the data source, all pretty much straight from the template code, looks like this:

```
override func numberOfSectionsInTableView(tableView: UITableView) -> Int {
    return self.frc.sections!.count
}
override func tableView(tableView: UITableView,
    numberOfRowsInSection section: Int) -> Int {
        let sectionInfo =
            self.frc.sections![section] as! NSFetchedResultsSectionInfo
```

```
            return sectionInfo.numberOfObjects
    }
    override func tableView(tableView: UITableView,
        cellForRowAtIndexPath indexPath: NSIndexPath) -> UITableViewCell {
            let cell = tableView.dequeueReusableCellWithIdentifier(
                "Cell", forIndexPath:indexPath) as! UITableViewCell
            cell.accessoryType = .DisclosureIndicator
            let object = self.frc.objectAtIndexPath(indexPath) as! NSManagedObject
            cell.textLabel!.text = object.name
            return cell
    }
```

Now let's talk about object creation. GroupLister's table is initially empty because our app starts life with no data. When the user asks to create a group, I put up an alert asking for the name of the new group. In the handler for its OK button, if the user provides a valid name, I create a new Group entity and save the managed object context. Again, this is almost boilerplate code, copied from the template's `insertNewObject:` method:

```
av.addAction(UIAlertAction(title: "OK", style: .Default) {
    _ in
    let name = (av.textFields![0] as! UITextField).text
    if name == nil || name == "" {return}
    let context = self.frc.managedObjectContext
    let entity = self.frc.fetchRequest.entity!
    let mo = NSEntityDescription.insertNewObjectForEntityForName(
        entity.name!, inManagedObjectContext: context) as! NSManagedObject
    mo.name = name
    mo.uuid = NSUUID().UUIDString
    mo.timestamp = NSDate()
    var error : NSError? = nil
    let ok = context.save(&error)
    if !ok {
        println(error!)
        return
    }
    let pl = PeopleLister(groupManagedObject: mo)
    self.navigationController!.pushViewController(pl, animated: true)
})
```

The second view controller class is PeopleLister (Figure 23-7). It lists all the people in a particular Group, so I don't want PeopleLister to be instantiated without a Group; therefore, its designated initializer is `init(groupManagedObject:)`. To navigate from the GroupLister view to the PeopleLister view, I instantiate PeopleLister and push it onto the navigation controller's stack, as the preceding code shows; I do the same sort of thing when the user taps an existing Group name in the GroupLister table view:

```
override func tableView(tableView: UITableView,
    didSelectRowAtIndexPath indexPath: NSIndexPath) {
        let pl = PeopleLister(
            groupManagedObject:
                self.frc.objectAtIndexPath(indexPath) as! NSManagedObject)
        self.navigationController!.pushViewController(pl, animated: true)
}
```

PeopleLister, too, has an `frc` property, along with a `lazy` initializer that is almost identical to the template code for generating an NSFetchedResultsController — almost, but not quite. In the case of GroupLister, we wanted *every* group; but a PeopleLister instance should list only the People belonging to *one particular group*, which has been stored as the `groupObject` property. So PeopleLister's implementation of the `frc` initializer contains these lines:

```
let pred = NSPredicate(format:"group = %@", self.groupObject)
req.predicate = pred // req is the fetch request we're configuring
```

As you can see from Figure 23-7, the PeopleLister interface consists of a table of text fields. Populating the table is easy enough:

```
override func tableView(tableView: UITableView,
    cellForRowAtIndexPath indexPath: NSIndexPath) -> UITableViewCell {
        let cell = tableView.dequeueReusableCellWithIdentifier(
            "Person", forIndexPath:indexPath) as! UITableViewCell
        let object =
            self.frc.objectAtIndexPath(indexPath) as! NSManagedObject
        let first = cell.viewWithTag(1) as! UITextField
        let last = cell.viewWithTag(2) as! UITextField
        first.text = object.firstName
        last.text = object.lastName
        first.delegate = self; last.delegate = self
        return cell
}
```

When the user edits a text field (the first or last name of a Person), I update the data model and save the managed object context; the first part of this code should be familiar from Chapter 8:

```
func textFieldDidEndEditing(textField: UITextField) {
    println("did end editing")
    var v = textField.superview!
    while !(v is UITableViewCell) {v = v.superview!}
    let cell = v as! UITableViewCell
    let ip = self.tableView.indexPathForCell(cell)!
    let object = self.frc.objectAtIndexPath(ip) as! NSManagedObject
    object.setValue(textField.text,
        forKey: ((textField.tag == 1) ? "firstName" : "lastName"))
    var error : NSError? = nil
    let ok = object.managedObjectContext!.save(&error)
    if !ok {
```

```
        println(error!)
        return
    }
}
```

The trickiest part is what happens when the user asks to make a new Person. It starts out analogously to making a new Group: I make a new Person entity, configure its attributes with an empty first name and last name, and save the context. But we must also make this empty Person appear in the table! To do so, we act as the NSFetched-ResultsController's delegate (NSFetchedResultsControllerDelegate); the delegate methods are triggered by the change in the managed object context:

```
func doAdd(_:AnyObject) {
    self.tableView.endEditing(true)
    let context = self.frc.managedObjectContext
    let entity = self.frc.fetchRequest.entity!
    let mo = NSEntityDescription.insertNewObjectForEntityForName(
        entity.name!, inManagedObjectContext:context) as! NSManagedObject
    mo.group = self.groupObject
    mo.lastName = ""
    mo.firstName = ""
    mo.timestamp = NSDate()
    var error : NSError? = nil
    let ok = context.save(&error)
    if !ok {
        println(error!)
        return
    }
}
// ================= delegate methods =======================
func controllerWillChangeContent(controller: NSFetchedResultsController) {
    self.tableView.beginUpdates()
}
func controllerDidChangeContent(controller: NSFetchedResultsController) {
    self.tableView.endUpdates()
}
func controller(controller: NSFetchedResultsController,
    didChangeObject anObject: AnyObject,
    atIndexPath indexPath: NSIndexPath?,
    forChangeType type: NSFetchedResultsChangeType,
    newIndexPath: NSIndexPath?) {
        if type == .Insert {
            self.tableView.insertRowsAtIndexPaths(
                [newIndexPath!], withRowAnimation: .Automatic)
            dispatch_async(dispatch_get_main_queue()) {
                let cell =
                    self.tableView.cellForRowAtIndexPath(newIndexPath!)!
                let tf = cell.viewWithTag(1) as! UITextField
                tf.becomeFirstResponder()
            }
        }
    }
}
```

Image File Formats

The Image I/O framework provides a simple, unified way to open image files (from disk or downloaded from the network, as described in Chapter 24), to save image files, to convert between image file formats, and to read metadata from standard image file formats, including EXIF and GPS information from a digital camera. You'll need to `import ImageIO`.

Obviously, such features were not entirely missing from iOS before the Image I/O framework was introduced (starting in iOS 4). UIImage can read the data from most standard image formats, and you can convert formats with functions such as `UIImage-JPEGRepresentation` and `UIImagePNGRepresentation`. But you could not, for example, save an image as a TIFF without the Image I/O framework.

The Image I/O framework introduces the notion of an *image source* (CGImageSource). This can be created from the URL of a file on disk or from an NSData object (actually CFData, to which NSData is toll-free bridged). You can use this to obtain a CGImage of the source's image (or, if the source format contains multiple images, a particular image). But you can also obtain metadata from the source *without* transforming the source into a CGImage, thus conserving memory. For example:

```
let url = NSBundle.mainBundle().URLForResource(
    "colson", withExtension: "jpg")
let src = CGImageSourceCreateWithURL(url, nil)
let result =
    CGImageSourceCopyPropertiesAtIndex(src, 0, nil) as [NSObject:AnyObject]
// ... do something with result ...
```

Without having opened the image file as an image, we now have a dictionary full of information about it, including its pixel dimensions (`kCGImagePropertyPixelWidth` and `kCGImagePropertyPixelHeight`), its resolution, its color model, its color depth, and its orientation — plus, because this picture originally comes from a digital camera, the EXIF data such as the aperture and exposure at which it was taken, plus the make and model of the camera.

We can obtain the image as a CGImage, with `CGImageSourceCreateImageAtIndex`. Alternatively, we can request a thumbnail version of the image. This is a very useful thing to do, and the name "thumbnail" doesn't really do justice to its importance and power. If your purpose in opening this image is to display it in your interface, you don't care about the original image data; a thumbnail is *precisely* what you want, especially because you can specify any size for this "thumbnail" all the way up to the original size of the image! This is tremendously convenient, because to assign a small UIImageView a large image wastes all the memory reflected by the size difference.

To generate a thumbnail at a given size, you start with a dictionary specifying the size along with other instructions, and pass that, together with the image source, to `CGImage-`

`SourceCreateThumbnailAtIndex`. The only pitfall is that, because we are working with a CGImage and specifying actual pixels, we must remember to take account of the scale of our device's screen. So, for example, let's say we want to scale our image so that its largest dimension is no larger than the width of the UIImageView (`self.iv`) into which we intend to place it:

```
let url = NSBundle.mainBundle().URLForResource(
    "colson", withExtension: "jpg")
let src = CGImageSourceCreateWithURL(url, nil)
let scale = UIScreen.mainScreen().scale
let w = self.iv.bounds.width * scale
let d : [NSObject:AnyObject] = [
    kCGImageSourceShouldAllowFloat : true,
    kCGImageSourceCreateThumbnailWithTransform : true,
    kCGImageSourceCreateThumbnailFromImageAlways : true,
    kCGImageSourceThumbnailMaxPixelSize : w
]
let imref = CGImageSourceCreateThumbnailAtIndex(src, 0, d)
let im = UIImage(CGImage: imref, scale: scale, orientation: .Up)!
self.iv.image = im
```

The Image I/O framework also introduces the notion of an *image destination*, used for saving an image into a specified file format. As a final example, I'll show how to save our image as a TIFF. We never open the image as an image! We save directly from the image source to the image destination:

```
let url = NSBundle.mainBundle().URLForResource(
    "colson", withExtension: "jpg")
let src = CGImageSourceCreateWithURL(url, nil)
let fm = NSFileManager()
let suppurl = fm.URLForDirectory(.ApplicationSupportDirectory,
    inDomain: .UserDomainMask, appropriateForURL: nil,
    create: true, error: nil)!
let tiff = suppurl.URLByAppendingPathComponent("mytiff.tiff")
let dest = CGImageDestinationCreateWithURL(tiff, kUTTypeTIFF, 1, nil)
CGImageDestinationAddImageFromSource(dest, src, 0, nil)
let ok = CGImageDestinationFinalize(dest)
```

CHAPTER 24

Basic Networking

Networking is difficult and complicated, chiefly because it's ultimately out of your control. My motto with regard to the network is, "There's many a slip 'twixt the cup and the lip." You can ask for a resource from across the network, but at that point anything can happen: the resource might not be found (the server is down, perhaps), it might take a while to arrive, it might never arrive, the network itself might vanish after the resource has partially arrived. iOS, however, makes at least the *basics* of networking very easy, so that's what this chapter will deal with.

To go further into networking than this chapter takes you, start with Apple's *URL Loading System Programming Guide*. To go even deeper under the hood, see the *CFNetwork Programming Guide*. Apple also provides a generous amount of sample code. See in particular SimpleURLConnections, AdvancedURLConnections, SimpleNetworkStreams, SimpleFTPSample, and MVCNetworking.

Many earlier chapters have described interface and frameworks that network for you automatically. Put a web view in your interface (Chapter 11) and poof, you're networking; the web view does all the grunt work, and it does it a lot better than you'd be likely to do it from scratch. The same is true of AVPlayer (Chapter 15), MFMailComposeViewController (Chapter 20), and MKMapView (Chapter 24).

HTTP Requests

An HTTP request is made through an NSURLSession object. An NSURLSession is a kind of grand overarching environment in which network-related tasks are to take place. You will often need only one NSURLSession object:

- For very simple, occasional use, this object might be the singleton `shared-Session` object.

- More generally, you'll create your own NSURLSession by calling `init(configuration:)` or `init(configuration:delegate:delegateQueue:)`, handing it an NSURLSessionConfiguration object describing the desired environment.

To use the NSURLSession object to perform a request across the network, you ask it for a new NSURLSessionTask object. This is the object that actually performs (and represents) one upload or download process. NSURLSessionTask is an abstract superclass, embodying various properties, such as:

- A `taskDescription` and `taskIdentifier`; the former is up to you, while the latter is a unique identifier within the NSURLSession

- The `originalRequest` and `currentRequest` (the request can change because there might be a redirect)

- An initial `response` from the server

- Various `countOfBytes...` properties allowing you to track progress

- A `state`, which might be (NSURLSessionTaskState):
    - `.Running`
    - `.Suspended`
    - `.Canceling`
    - `.Completed`

- An `error` if the task failed

In addition, you can tell a task to `resume`, `suspend`, or `cancel`. A task is born suspended, and does not start until it is told to `resume` for the first time.

New in iOS 8, you can also set an NSURLSessionTask's `priority` to a Float between 0 and 1; this is just a hint to the system, and may be used to rank the relative importance of your tasks. For convenience, three constant values are also provided:

- `NSURLSessionTaskPriorityLow` (0.25)

- `NSURLSessionTaskPriorityDefault` (0.5)

- `NSURLSessionTaskPriorityHigh` (0.75)

There are three kinds of actual session task:

NSURLSessionDataTask

> An NSURLSessionTask subclass. With a data task, the data is provided incrementally to your app as it arrives across the network.

NSURLSessionDownloadTask

> An NSURLSessionTask subclass. With a download task, the data is stored as a file, and the saved file URL is handed to you at the end of the process. The file is outside your sandbox and will be destroyed, so preserving it (or its contents) is up to you.

NSURLSessionUploadTask

> An NSURLSessionDataTask subclass. With an upload task, you can provide a file to be uploaded and stand back, though you can also hear about the upload progress if you wish.

Once you've obtained a new session task from the NSURLSession, you can keep a reference to it if you wish, but you don't have to; the NSURLSession retains it. The NSURL-Session will provide you with a list of its tasks in progress; call `getTasksWithCompletion-Handler:`. The completion handler is handed three arrays, one for each type of task. The NSURLSession releases a task after it is cancelled or completed. Thus, if an NSURL-Session has no running or suspended tasks, the three arrays are empty.

There are two ways to ask your NSURLSession for a new NSURLSessionTask:

Call a convenience method

> The convenience methods all take a `completionHandler:` parameter. This completion handler is called when the task process ends.

Call a delegate-based method

> You give the NSURLSession a delegate when you create it, and the delegate is called back at various stages of a task's progress.

The two ways of asking for an NSURLSessionTask entail two different ways of working with it. I'll demonstrate both.

Simple HTTP Request

I'll start by illustrating the utmost in simplicity:

- We use the shared NSURLSession.
- We obtain a download task, handing it a URL and a completion handler.
- We call `resume` to start the task.

Our code then finishes. Meanwhile, the download proceeds asynchronously on a background thread; thus, the interface is not blocked, and the user can tap buttons and so forth. When the download finishes, the completion handler is called. We must make no assumptions about when the completion handler will be called or what thread it will be called on; indeed, unless we take steps to the contrary, it will be a background thread. In this particular example, the URL is that of an image that I intend to display in my interface; therefore, I step out to the main thread (Chapter 25) in order to talk to the interface:

```
let s = "http://www.someserver.com/somefolder/someimage.jpg"
let url = NSURL(string:s)!
let session = NSURLSession.sharedSession()
let task = session.downloadTaskWithURL(url) {
    (loc:NSURL!, response:NSURLResponse!, error:NSError!) in
    let d = NSData(contentsOfURL:loc)!
    let im = UIImage(data:d)
    dispatch_async(dispatch_get_main_queue()) {
        self.iv.image = im
    }
}
task.resume()
```

There's many a slip, as I've already mentioned, so in real life I would probably hedge my bets a little more by checking for errors along the way; but the skeleton of the structure remains exactly the same:

```
let s = "http://www.someserver.com/somefolder/someimage.jpg"
let url = NSURL(string:s)!
let session = NSURLSession.sharedSession()
let task = session.downloadTaskWithURL(url) {
    (loc:NSURL!, response:NSURLResponse!, error:NSError!) in
    if error != nil {
        println(error)
        return
    }
    let status = (response as! NSHTTPURLResponse).statusCode
    if status != 200 {
        println("response status: \(status)")
        return
    }
    let d = NSData(contentsOfURL:loc)!
    let im = UIImage(data:d)
    dispatch_async(dispatch_get_main_queue()) {
        self.iv.image = im
    }
}
task.resume()
```

Formal HTTP Request

Now let's go to the other extreme and be very formal:

- We'll create and retain our own NSURLSession.
- We'll configure the NSURLSession with an NSURLSessionConfiguration object.

- We'll give the session a delegate.
- Instead of a mere URL, we'll start with an NSURLRequest.

The NSURLSession initializers permit us to supply an NSURLSessionConfiguration object dictating various options to be applied to the session. Possible options include:

- Whether to permit cell data use, or to require Wi-Fi
- The maximum number of simultaneous connections to the remote server
- Timeout values:

  `timeoutIntervalForRequest`
  > The maximum time you're willing to wait *between* pieces of data.

  `timeoutIntervalForResource`
  > The maximum time for the *entire* download to arrive.

- Cookie, caching, and credential policies

We're going to call `init(configuration:delegate:delegateQueue:)`, so we'll also specify a delegate, as well as stating the queue (roughly, the thread — see Chapter 25) on which the delegate methods are to be called. For each type of task, there's a delegate protocol, which is itself often a composite of multiple protocols.

For example, for a data task, we would want a data delegate — an object conforming to the NSURLSessionDataDelegate protocol, which itself conforms to the NSURLSession-TaskDelegate protocol, which in turn conforms to the NSURLSessionDelegate protocol, resulting in about a dozen delegate methods we could implement, though only a few are crucial:

`URLSession:dataTask:didReceiveData:`
> Some data has arrived, as an NSData object. The data will arrive piecemeal, so this method may be called many times during the download process, supplying new data each time. Our job is to accumulate all those chunks of data; this involves maintaining state between calls.

`URLSession:task:didCompleteWithError:`
> If there is an error, we'll find out about it here. If there's no error, this is our signal that the download is over; we can now do something with the accumulated data.

Similarly, for a download task, we need a download delegate, conforming to NSURL-SessionDownloadDelegate, which conforms to NSURLSessionTaskDelegate, which conforms to NSURLSessionDelegate. Here are some useful delegate methods:

`URLSession:downloadTask:didResumeAtOffset:expectedTotalBytes:`
> This method is of interest only in the case of a resumable download that has in fact been paused and resumed.

URLSession:downloadTask:didWriteData:totalBytesWritten:totalBytes-
ExpectedToWrite:
> Called periodically, to keep us apprised of the download's progress.

URLSession:downloadTask:didFinishDownloadingToURL:
> Called at the end of the process; we must grab the downloaded file immediately, as it will be destroyed. This is the only required delegate method.

It's also a good idea to implement URLSession:task:didCompleteWithError:; if there was a communication problem, the error: parameter will tell you about it.

Here, then, is my recasting of the same image file download as in the previous example. I'm going to keep a reference both to the NSURLSession (self.session) and to the current download task (self.task). In this particular example, I'll perform just one task at a time, so I can use the task instance variable as a flag to indicate that the task is in progress. Since one NSURLSession can perform multiple tasks, there will typically be just one NSURLSession; so I'll make a lazy initializer that creates and configures it:

```
var task : NSURLSessionTask!
lazy var session : NSURLSession = {
    let config = NSURLSessionConfiguration.ephemeralSessionConfiguration()
    config.allowsCellularAccess = false
    let session = NSURLSession(configuration: config,
        delegate: self, delegateQueue: NSOperationQueue.mainQueue())
    return session
}()
```

I've specified, for purposes of the example, that no caching is to take place and that data downloading via cell is forbidden; you could configure the NSURLSession much more heavily and meaningfully, of course. I have specified self as the delegate, and I have requested delegate callbacks on the main thread.

Here we go. I blank out the image view, to make the progress of the task more obvious for test purposes, and I create, retain, and start the download task:

```
let s = "http://www.someserver.com/somefolder/someimage.jpg"
let url = NSURL(string:s)!
let req = NSMutableURLRequest(URL:url)
let task = self.session.downloadTaskWithRequest(req)
self.task = task
self.iv.image = nil
task.resume()
```

In this particular example, there is very little merit in using an NSURLRequest instead of an NSURL to form our task. Still, an NSURLRequest can come in handy (as I'll demonstrate later in this chapter), and an upload task requires one.

Do *not* use the NSURLRequest to configure properties of the request that are configurable through the NSURLSession. (Those properties are left over from the era before NSURLSession existed.) For example, there is no point setting the NSURLRequest's `timeoutInterval`, as it is the NSURLSession's timeout properties that are significant.

Here are some delegate methods for responding to the download:

```
func URLSession(session: NSURLSession,
    downloadTask: NSURLSessionDownloadTask,
    didWriteData bytesWritten: Int64,
    totalBytesWritten writ: Int64,
    totalBytesExpectedToWrite exp: Int64) {
        println("downloaded \(100*writ/exp)%")
}
func URLSession(session: NSURLSession,
    task: NSURLSessionTask,
    didCompleteWithError error: NSError?) {
        println("completed: error: \(error)")
}
func URLSession(session: NSURLSession,
    downloadTask: NSURLSessionDownloadTask,
    didFinishDownloadingToURL location: NSURL) {
        self.task = nil
        let response = downloadTask.response as! NSHTTPURLResponse
        let stat = response.statusCode
        println("status \(stat)")
        if stat != 200 {
            return
        }
        let d = NSData(contentsOfURL:location)!
        let im = UIImage(data:d)
        dispatch_async(dispatch_get_main_queue()) {
            self.iv.image = im
        }
}
```

That was a download task; now I'll describe a data task. A data task is a little more elaborate than a download task, but not much; the chief difference is that it's up to you to accumulate the data as it arrives in chunks. For this purpose, you'll want to keep an NSMutableData object on hand; I'll use a property:

```
var data = NSMutableData()
```

When I create the data task, I am careful to prepare `self.data` (by setting its `length` to 0):

```
let s = "http://www.someserver.com/somefolder/someimage.jpg"
let url = NSURL(string:s)!
let req = NSMutableURLRequest(URL:url)
let task = self.session.dataTaskWithRequest(req) // *
```

```
    self.task = task
    self.iv.image = nil
    self.data.length = 0 // *
    task.resume()
```

As the chunks of data arrive, I keep appending them to `self.data`. When all the data
has arrived, it is ready for use:

```
func URLSession(session: NSURLSession,
    dataTask: NSURLSessionDataTask,
    didReceiveData data: NSData) {
        self.data.appendData(data)
}
func URLSession(session: NSURLSession,
    task: NSURLSessionTask,
    didCompleteWithError error: NSError?) {
        self.task = nil
        if error == nil {
            self.iv.image = UIImage(data:self.data)
        }
}
```

Some delegate methods provide a `completionHandler:` parameter. These are delegate
methods that require a response from you. For example, in the case of a data task,
`URLSession:dataTask:didReceiveResponse:completionHandler:` arrives when we
first connect to the server. Here, we could check the status code of the initial
NSHTTPURLResponse. We must also return a response saying whether or not to proceed (or whether to convert the data task to a download task, which could certainly
come in handy). But because of the multithreaded nature of networking, we do this, not
by returning a value directly, but by calling the `completionHandler:` that we're handed
as a parameter and passing our response into it. Several of the delegate methods are
constructed in this way.

There is one final and extremely important consideration when using NSURLSession
with a delegate — memory management. The NSURLSession *retains its delegate*. This
is understandable, as it would be disastrous if the delegate could simply vanish out from
the middle of an asynchronous time-consuming process; but it is also unusual, and
requires special measures on our part. In the examples I've been describing in this section, we have a retain cycle! We have an NSURLSession instance variable
`self.session`, but that NSURLSession is retaining `self` as its delegate.

As with an NSTimer, the solution is to invalidate the NSURLSession at some appropriate
moment. There are two ways to do this:

`finishTasksAndInvalidate`
    Allows any existing tasks to run to completion. Afterward, the NSURLSession re-
    leases the delegate and cannot be used for anything further.

`invalidateAndCancel`
> Interrupts any existing tasks immediately. The NSURLSession releases the delegate and cannot be used for anything further.

Let's suppose that `self` is a view controller. Then `viewWillDisappear:` could be a good place to invalidate the NSURLSession. (We cannot use `deinit`, because `deinit` won't be called until *after* we have invalidated the NSURLSession; that's what it means to have a retain cycle.) So, for example:

```
override func viewWillDisappear(animated: Bool) {
    super.viewWillDisappear(animated)
    self.session.finishTasksAndInvalidate()
}
```

Encapsulating the Session, Task, and Delegate

The little memory-management dance at the end of the preceding section reveals a weakness in our architecture. I've been implementing all this code directly in a view controller subclass: the NSURLSession is a property of the view controller, and the view controller is the NSURLSession's delegate. This is a misuse of a view controller. Things would be better if we had an instance of some *separate class* whose job is to hold the NSURLSession in a property and to serve as its delegate. There would still be a retain cycle until the NSURLSession was invalidated, but at least the management of this object's memory would not be entangled with that of a view controller.

To illustrate, I'll design a class MyDownloader, which holds an NSURLSession and serves as its delegate, and which has a public method `cancelAllTasks`. I imagine that our view controller will then create and maintain an instance of MyDownloader early in its lifetime, and can invalidate it in `deinit`:

```
lazy var downloader : MyDownloader = {
    let d : MyDownloader = // ??
    return d
}()
deinit {
    self.downloader.cancelAllTasks()
}
```

In that code, I omitted the initialization of MyDownloader. How should this work? The MyDownloader object will create its own NSURLSession, but I think the client should be allowed to configure the session; fortunately, that's extremely convenient, because the NSURLSessionConfiguration is a separate object! So the missing initialization should look like this:

```
let config : NSURLSessionConfiguration = // ...
let d : MyDownloader = MyDownloader(configuration:config)
```

Now let's decide how a client will communicate with a MyDownloader object. The client will presumably hand a MyDownloader a URL string; the MyDownloader will generate the NSURLSessionDownloadTask and tell it to resume. Acting as the NSURLSession's delegate, the MyDownloader will be told when the download is over. At that point, the MyDownloader has a file URL for the downloaded object, which it needs to hand back to the client immediately. How should *this* work?

One solution might be for MyDownloader to define a delegate protocol; the client would then be the delegate, and the MyDownloader could call the client back using a method defined by the protocol. But that's far too rigid and restrictive. One NSURLSession can have many simultaneous tasks; I want a MyDownloader to be able to serve as a central locus for lots of downloading activity. I'm imagining, for example, that a MyDownloader might have multiple clients, or that a single client might initiate multiple downloads from various different contexts. All that downloading takes place asynchronously, and perhaps simultaneously. When the MyDownloader hands a downloaded file's URL to a client, how is that client to know which download request this file URL corresponds to?

My solution, which I think is rather elegant, is that the client, when it hands the My-Downloader object a URL string to initiate a download, should also hand the My-Downloader *a completion handler*. To return the file URL at the end of a download, the MyDownloader calls that handler, handing it the URL as a parameter. I can even define a `typealias` naming my completion handler type:

```
typealias MyDownloaderCompletion = (NSURL!) -> ()
```

From the client's point of view, then, the process will look something like this:

```
let s = "http://www.someserver.com/somefolder/someimage.jpg"
self.downloader.download(s) {
    url in
    if url == nil {
        return
    }
    if let d = NSData(contentsOfURL: url) {
        let im = UIImage(data:d)
        dispatch_async(dispatch_get_main_queue()) {
            self.iv.image = im
        }
    }
}
```

That looks excellent, so now let's implement this architecture within MyDownloader. We have posited a method `download:completionHandler:`. When that method is called, MyDownloader stores the completion handler; it then asks for a new download task and sets it going:

```
func download(s:String,
    completionHandler ch : MyDownloaderCompletion)
    -> NSURLSessionTask {
        let url = NSURL(string:s)!
        let req = NSMutableURLRequest(URL:url)
        // ... store the completion handler somehow ...
        let task = self.session.downloadTaskWithRequest(req)
        task.resume()
        return task
}
```

(I return to the client a reference to the task, so that the client can cancel the task later if need be. I'll give an example later.)

When the download finishes, the MyDownloader hears about it (as session delegate) and calls the completion handler:

```
func URLSession(session: NSURLSession,
    downloadTask: NSURLSessionDownloadTask,
    didFinishDownloadingToURL location: NSURL) {
        let response = downloadTask.response as! NSHTTPURLResponse
        let stat = response.statusCode
        var url : NSURL! = nil
        if stat == 200 {
            url = location
        }
        let ch = // ... retrieve the completion handler somehow ...
        ch(url)
}
```

In my carefree speculative coding design, I have repeatedly postponed grappling with the heart of the matter. It is now time to face the problem (signified by the word "somehow" in the preceding two code snippets). Actually, there are two related problems:

- The completion handler arrives in one method (`download:completionHandler:`) but is called in another (`URLSession:downloadTask:didFinishDownloadingTo-URL:`). The completion handler clearly needs to be stored, in the first method, in such a way that it can be retrieved, in the second method.

- You might respond: So put it in a property. But a simple property won't do here. In my design, there can be *multiple* download tasks — and each one has a *different* completion handler associated with it. Thus we need a way to implement this association.

Clearly, we want to store each completion handler *together with* its download task. But wait! We are guaranteed that the *same* download task instance makes its appearance in *both* methods, because the download task we create in the first method is handed back to the delegate in the second method. Thus, it would be truly ideal if we could store the completion handler *in* its download task!

At first glance, it appears that this is impossible, because we can't subclass NSURLSession-DownloadTask (and even if we could, we can't ask NSURLSession to generate an instance of our subclass). But there is, in fact, a way to do this. It turns out that we are allowed to *attach an arbitrary property* to an NSURLRequest, as long as we start with its mutable subclass, NSMutableURLRequest. The mechanism for doing this is a little weird — we actually call an NSURLProtocol class method — but that doesn't matter. The NSURLRequest is attached to the download task as its originalRequest, and we can retrieve it, and hence the arbitrary property, at the end of the download.

Doing this in Swift is a bit tricky. The methods for attaching a property to an NSMutable-URLRequest and retrieving it again later are:

- setProperty:forKey:inRequest:
- propertyForKey:inRequest:

The property: in the first method, and the result returned by the second method, is an AnyObject. But a Swift closure is *not* an AnyObject. One simple solution (see also Appendix B) is a generic wrapper class:

```
class Wrapper<T> {
    let p:T
    init(_ p:T){self.p = p}
}
```

We can hand anything to a Wrapper, which will store it in its p property; and a Wrapper *is* an AnyObject, so it can travel anywhere.

At long last we are ready to write MyDownloader for real. Here it is:

```
let config : NSURLSessionConfiguration
lazy var session : NSURLSession = {
    let queue = NSOperationQueue.mainQueue()
    return NSURLSession(configuration:self.config,
        delegate:self, delegateQueue:queue)
}()
init(configuration config:NSURLSessionConfiguration) {
    self.config = config
    super.init()
}
func download(s:String, completionHandler ch : MyDownloaderCompletion)
    -> NSURLSessionTask {
        let url = NSURL(string:s)!
        let req = NSMutableURLRequest(URL:url)
        NSURLProtocol.setProperty(Wrapper(ch), forKey:"ch", inRequest:req)
        let task = self.session.downloadTaskWithRequest(req)
        task.resume()
        return task
}
func URLSession(session: NSURLSession,
```

```
        downloadTask: NSURLSessionDownloadTask,
        didFinishDownloadingToURL location: NSURL) {
            let req = downloadTask.originalRequest
            let ch : AnyObject =
                NSURLProtocol.propertyForKey("ch", inRequest:req)!
            let response = downloadTask.response as! NSHTTPURLResponse
            let stat = response.statusCode
            var url : NSURL! = nil
            if stat == 200 {
                url = location
            }
            let ch2 = (ch as! Wrapper).p as MyDownloaderCompletion
            ch2(url)
    }
    func cancelAllTasks() {
        self.session.invalidateAndCancel()
    }
```

(As written, MyDownloader's delegate methods are being called on the main thread. It may be preferable to run that code on a background thread. I'll describe in Chapter 25 how to do that.)

Multiple Tasks

To exercise MyDownloader, I'll show how to solve a pesky problem that arises quite often in real life: we have a UITableView where each cell displays text and a picture, and the picture needs to be downloaded in real time. The idea is to supply each picture lazily, on demand, downloading a picture only when its cell becomes visible.

The model could be an array of dictionaries, but it is better to design a dedicated model object, even if it is nothing but a value class (a bundle of properties):

```
class Model {
    var text : String!
    var im : UIImage!
    var picurl : String!
}
```

Our model is now an array of Model:

```
array
    Model
        text: @"Manny"
        im: initially nil
        picurl: String URL for a downloadable image of Manny
    Model
        text: @"Moe"
        im: initially nil
        picurl: String URL for a downloadable image of Moe
    Model
```

```
text: @"Jack"
im: initially nil
picurl: String URL for a downloadable image of Jack
....
```

When the table turns to the data source for a cell (`tableView:cellForRowAtIndex-Path:`), the data source will turn to the model and consult the Model object corresponding to the requested row, asking for its `im` property, which is supposed to be its image. Initially, this will be nil. In that case, the data source will display no image in this cell — and will turn to the downloader and ask for the image to be downloaded from this Model object's `picurl`.

When the downloader succeeds in downloading an image, it calls the table's data source back through the completion block. Here we come to the *Insanely Cool Part* (pat. pend.). This completion block has captured the contextual environment from inside `table-View:cellForRowAtIndexPath:`, where it was defined. In effect, therefore, we are back in the very same call to `tableView:cellForRowAtIndexPath:`, accessing the very same Model object as before! We can thus set that Model object's `im` property, and tell the table to reload this row. The table thus calls `tableView:cellForRowAtIndexPath:` *again*, for the very same row, and the data source turns to the same Model object and asks for its `im` property *again* — and finds it, and displays the image in the cell:

```
override func tableView(tableView: UITableView,
    cellForRowAtIndexPath indexPath: NSIndexPath) -> UITableViewCell {
    let cell = tableView.dequeueReusableCellWithIdentifier(
        "Cell", forIndexPath:indexPath) as! UITableViewCell
    let m = self.model[indexPath.row]
    cell.textLabel!.text = m.text
    // have we got a picture?
    if let im = m.im {
        cell.imageView!.image = im
    } else {
        cell.imageView!.image = nil
        self.downloader.download(m.picurl) {
            url in
            if url == nil {
                return
            }
            let data = NSData(contentsOfURL: url)!
            let im = UIImage(data:data)
            m.im = im
            dispatch_async(dispatch_get_main_queue()) {
                self.tableView.reloadRowsAtIndexPaths(
                    [indexPath], withRowAnimation: .None)
            }
        }
    }
    return cell
}
```

A further refinement is to make it possible to cancel a download. Recall that My-Downloader's `download:completionHandler:` returns a reference to the download task exactly so that this will be possible. Why would we want to do this? Well, consider what happens when the user scrolls quickly through the entire table, possibly passing through hundreds of rows. The downloads for all of those rows, if they do not already have their pictures, will be initiated. If a row is scrolled out of sight before it has its picture, it doesn't *need* its picture after all. So to continue to download the picture is wasteful.

To prevent such waste, we can implement `tableView:didEndDisplayingCell:forRow-AtIndexPath:` to send `cancel` to the NSURLSessionTask. To make that possible, we need to capture the task when calling the downloader's `download:completionHandler:` and store it somewhere. Obviously, the place to store it is in the Model object for this row, which now looks like this:

```
class Model {
    var text : String!
    var im : UIImage!
    var picurl : String!
    var task : NSURLSessionTask!
}
```

Our `tableView:cellForRowAtIndexPath:` is now a little more complicated. We store in our Model object's `task` property the value returned from `download:completion-Handler:`, but we should also set that `task` property to nil as soon as we no longer need it. Moreover, each `task` is retaining a closure that refers to `self`; that's a potential retain cycle, which we break through a `weak` reference to `self`:

```
override func tableView(tableView: UITableView,
    cellForRowAtIndexPath indexPath: NSIndexPath) -> UITableViewCell {
        let cell = tableView.dequeueReusableCellWithIdentifier(
            "Cell", forIndexPath:indexPath) as! UITableViewCell
        let m = self.model[indexPath.row]
        cell.textLabel!.text = m.text
        // have we got a picture?
        if let im = m.im {
            cell.imageView!.image = im
        } else {
            if m.task == nil { // no task? start one!
                cell.imageView!.image = nil
                m.task = self.downloader.download(m.picurl) { // *
                    [weak self] url in // *
                    m.task == nil // *
                    if url == nil {
                        return
                    }
                    let data = NSData(contentsOfURL: url)!
                    let im = UIImage(data:data)
                    m.im = im
                    dispatch_async(dispatch_get_main_queue()) {
```

```
                    self!.tableView.reloadRowsAtIndexPaths(
                        [indexPath], withRowAnimation: .None)
                }
            }
        }
    }
    return cell
}
```

Now when a row scrolls out of view its download task can be cancelled:

```
override func tableView(tableView: UITableView,
    didEndDisplayingCell cell: UITableViewCell,
    forRowAtIndexPath indexPath: NSIndexPath) {
        let m = self.model[indexPath.row]
        if let task = m.task {
            if task.state == .Running {
                task.cancel()
                m.task = nil
            }
        }
}
```

Another question is what should happen when a picture download fails. If you believe that the download might succeed later, you will want to try again later, rather than letting the row sit there devoid of an image forever. If the user scrolls the failed cell out of view and later scrolls it back into view, the table will ask the data source for that cell and the downloader will try again to download its image. But that won't happen for a failed cell that's *never* scrolled out of view. How you deal with this is up to you; it's a matter of providing the best user experience without having an undue impact upon performance, battery, and so forth. In this instance, because these images are fairly unimportant, I might arrange that when an NSTimer with a fairly large interval fires (every 60 seconds, say), we reload the visible rows; this will cause any visible row without an image to try again to download its image.

Finally, I have avoided a rather tricky problem by implementing MyDownloader to perform an NSURLSessionDownloadTask. If there are multiple downloads, the runtime keeps their data separate and gives each completed download its own file URL. But suppose we were to perform an NSURLSessionDataTask instead. Now we must maintain the accumulated data ourselves — and in a world where multiple downloads can happen simultaneously, that's not going to be simple. A single NSMutableData property won't do: different data tasks must not share the same NSMutableData! One possible solution is to make our property a dictionary of NSMutableData buffers, keyed by the data task's unique identifier (`taskIdentifier`).

Background Downloads

If your app goes into the background while in the middle of a download, the download might be completed coherently, or it might not. To ensure that an NSURLSession-DownloadTask (or an NSURLSessionUploadTask) is carried out regardless, even if your app isn't frontmost — indeed, even if your app isn't running! — make your NSURL-SessionConfiguration a background configuration (call `backgroundSession-ConfigurationWithIdentifier:` to create it).

A background configuration hands the work of downloading over to the system. Your app is not actually involved. You still need an NSURLSession, but this serves primarily as a gateway for putting your app in touch with the download process; in particular, you need to operate as the NSURLSession's delegate.

The argument that you pass to `backgroundSessionConfigurationWithIdentifier:` is a string identifier. It is arbitrary, but it will distinguish your background session from all the other background sessions that other apps have requested from the system. Therefore, it should be unique to your app; a good approach is to use your app's bundle ID as its basis.

You may also want to set your configuration's `discretionary` to `true`. This will permit the system to postpone network communications to some moment that will conserve bandwidth and battery — for example, when Wi-Fi is available, and the device is plugged into a power socket. Of course, that might be days from now! But this is part of the beauty of background downloads.

There are three possibilities for how a background download will conclude, depending on the state of your app at that moment:

Your app is frontmost
> If your app is frontmost during any part of a background download, the download is treated normally: your session delegate will get `URLSession:downloadTask:did-WriteData...` and `URLSession:downloadTask:didFinishDownloadingToURL:` messages, just as you expect.

Your app is suspended in the background
> Your app is awakened, still in the background, long enough to receive `URLSession:downloadTask:didFinishDownloadingToURL:` and deal with it.

Your app is not running
> Your app is launched in the background. You have no NSURLSession, because your app has just launched from scratch. You will need to create one, calling `background-SessionConfigurationWithIdentifier:` with the *same identifier* as before; you will then be able to receive delegate messages, including `URLSession:download-Task:didFinishDownloadingToURL:`.

As with location monitoring (Chapter 22), your app does not formally run in the background, so you do *not* have to set the `UIBackgroundModes` of your *Info.plist*.

You do have to implement two extra methods, to be called if your app is not frontmost at the time the download is completed:

`application:handleEventsForBackgroundURLSession:completionHandler:`
:   This message is sent *to the app delegate*. The `session:` parameter is the string identifier you handed earlier to the configuration object; you might use this to identify the session, or even as a prompt to create and configure the session if you haven't done so already. The app delegate must store the `completionHandler:` parameter as a property, because it will be needed later.

`URLSessionDidFinishEventsForBackgroundURLSession:`
:   This message is sent *to the session delegate*. The session delegate must call the previously stored completion handler. This is how the system knows that your app has finished updating its interface. The system will thereupon take a new snapshot of your app's interface, still in the background, to serve as your app's thumbnail in the app switcher interface — and your app will then be suspended.

All of this is much easier if the app delegate and the session delegate are one and the same object. In this example, the app delegate holds the NSURLSession property, as well as the completion handler property that will be needed if the download completes when we are not frontmost:

```
lazy var session : NSURLSession = {
    let config =
        NSURLSessionConfiguration
            .backgroundSessionConfigurationWithIdentifier(
                "com.neuburg.matt.ch37backgroundDownload")
    config.allowsCellularAccess = false
    // could set config.discretionary here
    let sess = NSURLSession(
        configuration: config, delegate: self,
        delegateQueue: NSOperationQueue.mainQueue())
    return sess
}()
var ch : (() -> ())!
```

The NSURLSessionDownloadDelegate methods are exactly as before. Finally, we have the two extra methods that come into play only if the download completes when we are not frontmost:

```
func application(application: UIApplication,
    handleEventsForBackgroundURLSession identifier: String,
    completionHandler: () -> Void) {
        self.ch = completionHandler
}
func URLSessionDidFinishEventsForBackgroundURLSession(
    session: NSURLSession) {
```

```
            if self.ch != nil {
                self.ch()
            }
    }
```

 If the user kills your app in the background by way of the app switcher interface, pending background downloads will *not* be completed. The system assumes that the user doesn't want your app coming magically back to life in the background.

Background App Refresh

The idea of background app refresh is that if your app has a periodic network download to perform — because, for example, it is a news app — you can ask the system to wake or launch your app in the background from time to time so that it can perform that download in the background. That way, the next time the user brings your app to the front, it has already been refreshed with recent downloaded content.

 The user can disable your app's ability to use background app refresh, in the Settings app, under General → Background App Refresh.

This feature is a background mode; in the Capabilities tab for your app target, switch on Background Modes and check "Background fetch." Your code must also set the shared application's `minimumBackgroundFetchInterval` property; you can supply an actual number here, but in most cases you'll want to use `UIApplicationBackground-FetchIntervalMinimum`, which lets the system work out the best moments for your app to refresh its content, based on the user's behavior.

When it's time to perform a background fetch, the app delegate will be sent `application:performFetchWithCompletionHandler:`. At that moment, a clock starts counting down; your job is to do whatever needs doing, just as fast as possible, and then call the `completionHandler:` parameter to stop the clock, passing in one of these values (UIBackgroundFetchResult):

- `.NewData`
- `.NoData`
- `.Failed`

If you don't do that fast enough, the clock will time out and your app will be suspended; and the longer you take, the less willing the system will be to send you `application:performFetchWithCompletionHandler:` in the first place. If the value

Figure 24-1. Interface for an in-app purchase

you return is `.NewData`, a new snapshot will be taken, still with your app in the background, so that the thumbnail in the app switcher matches your updated app.

In-App Purchases

An in-app purchase is a specialized form of network communication: your app communicates with the App Store to permit the user to buy something there, or to confirm that something has already been bought there. For example, your app might be free, but the user could then be offered the opportunity to pay to unlock additional functionality. In-app purchases are made possible through the Store Kit framework; you'll need to `import StoreKit`.

There are various kinds of in-app purchase; you'll want to read the relevant chapter in Apple's *iTunes Connect Developer Guide* and the *In-App Purchase Programming Guide*, along with the PDF *Getting Started* guide available at *https://developer.apple.com/in-app-purchase/In-App-Purchase-Guidelines.pdf*.

I'll describe the simplest possible in-app purchase: my app offers a single one-time purchase, which unlocks additional functionality, allowing the user to choose a photo from the photo library (Chapter 17). (This is what Apple calls a *non-consumable* purchase.) When the user taps the Choose button, if the in-app purchase has not been made, a pair of dialogs appear, offering and describing the purchase (Figure 24-1); if the in-app purchase *has* been made, a UIImagePickerController's view appears instead.

To configure an in-app purchase, you need first to use iTunes Connect to create, in connection with your app, something that the user can purchase; this is easiest to do if your app is already available through the App Store. For a simple non-consumable purchase like mine, you are associating your app's bundle ID with a name and arbitrary product ID representing your in-app purchase, along with a price. You'll also want to create a special Apple ID for testing purposes; you can't test your in-app purchase interface without such a test Apple ID. (If you accidentally perform the in-app purchase later when logged into the App Store with your *real* Apple ID, you'll be charged for the purchase and you won't be able to get your money back. Can you guess how I know that?)

Let's skip merrily past all that and proceed to your app's interface and inner workings. For a non-consumable in-app purchase, your app must provide the following interface (all of which is visible in Figure 24-1):

- A place where the in-app purchase is described. I say "a place" rather than "a description" because you do not hard-code the description into your app; rather, it is downloaded in real time from the App Store, using the Display Name and Description (and price) that you entered at iTunes Connect.

- A button that launches the purchase process.

- A button that *restores* an existing purchase. The idea here is that the user has performed the purchase, but is now on a different device or has deleted and reinstalled your app, so that the NSUserDefaults entry stating that the purchase has been performed is missing. The user needs to be able to contact the App Store to get your app to recognize that the purchase has been performed and turn on the purchased functionality.

Both the purchase process and the restore process are performed through dialogs presented by the system; the purpose of the interface shown in Figure 24-1 is to give the user a way to initiate those processes.

In my app, the purchase process proceeds in two stages. When the user taps the Learn More button (StoreViewController), I first confirm that the user has not been restricted from making purchases, and I then create an SKProductsRequest, which will attempt to download an SKProductsResponse object embodying the in-app purchase corresponding to my single product ID:

```
if !SKPaymentQueue.canMakePayments() {
    // ... put up alert saying we can't do it ...
    return
}
let req = SKProductsRequest(
    productIdentifiers: Set(["DiabelliChoose"]))
req.delegate = self
req.start()
```

This kicks off some network activity, and eventually the delegate of this SKProducts-Request, namely self (conforming to SKProductsRequestDelegate), is called back with one of two delegate messages. If we get request:didFailWithError:, I put up an apologetic alert, and that's the end. But if we get productsRequest:didReceiveResponse:, the request has succeeded, and we can proceed to the second stage.

The response from the App Store arrives as an SKProductsResponse object containing an SKProduct representing the proposed purchase. I create the second view controller, give it a reference to the SKProduct, and present it:

```
func productsRequest(request: SKProductsRequest!,
    didReceiveResponse response: SKProductsResponse!) {
        let p = response.products[0] as! SKProduct
        let s = StoreViewController2(product:p)
        // and on to the next view controller
        if let presenter = self.presentingViewController {
            self.dismissViewControllerAnimated(true, completion: {
                presenter.presentViewController(
                    s, animated: true, completion: nil)
            })
        }
}
```

We are now in my second view controller (StoreViewController2). It has a product property, and in its viewDidLoad it populates its interface based on the information that the product contains:

```
self.titleLabel.text = self.product.localizedTitle
self.descriptionLabel.text = self.product.localizedDescription
let numberFormatter = NSNumberFormatter()
numberFormatter.formatterBehavior = .Behavior10_4
numberFormatter.numberStyle = .CurrencyStyle
numberFormatter.locale = self.product.priceLocale
self.priceLabel.text =
    numberFormatter.stringFromNumber(self.product.price)
```

If the user taps the Purchase button, I dismiss the presented view controller, load the SKProduct into the default SKPaymentQueue, and stand back:

```
self.dismissViewControllerAnimated(true, completion: {
    let p = SKPayment(product:self.product)
    let q = SKPaymentQueue.defaultQueue()
    q.addPayment(p)
})
```

The system is now in charge of presenting a sequence of dialogs, confirming the purchase, asking for the user's App Store password, and so forth. My app knows nothing about that. If the user performs the purchase, however, my transaction observer will be sent paymentQueue:updatedTransactions:. I'll return in a moment to the implementation of this method.

Now let's talk about what happens when the user taps the Restore button (back in the first view controller, StoreViewController). It's very simple; I just tell the default SKPaymentQueue to restore any existing purchases:

```
self.dismissViewControllerAnimated(true, completion: {
    _ in
    SKPaymentQueue.defaultQueue().restoreCompletedTransactions()
})
```

Again, what happens now in the interface is out of my hands; the system will present the necessary dialogs. If the purchase is restored, however, my transaction observer will be sent paymentQueue:updatedTransactions:.

All the rest of the action, then, takes place in my transaction observer. But how does the runtime know who that is? When my app launches, it must *register a transaction observer*, that is, some object whose job it will be to receive transactions from the payment queue:

```
func application(application: UIApplication,
    didFinishLaunchingWithOptions launchOptions: [NSObject : AnyObject]?)
    -> Bool {
        // ...
        SKPaymentQueue.defaultQueue().addTransactionObserver(
            self.window!.rootViewController as! ViewController)
        return true
}
```

As you can see, I've made my root view controller the transaction observer. It adopts the SKPaymentTransactionObserver protocol. There is only one required method — paymentQueue:updatedTransactions:. This arrives with a reference to the payment queue and an array of SKPaymentTransaction objects. My job is to cycle through these transactions and, for each one, do whatever it requires, and then (*this is crucial*) send finishTransaction: to the payment queue.

My implementation is extremely simple, because I have only one purchasable product, and because I'm not maintaining any separate record of receipts. For each transaction, I check its transactionState (SKPaymentTransactionState). If this is .Purchased or .Restored, I pull out its payment, confirm that the payment's productIdentifier is my product identifier (it had darned well better be, since I have only the one product), and, if so, I throw the NSUserDefaults switch that indicates to my app that the user has performed the purchase. Otherwise, I do nothing, but I *always* call finish-Transaction:, no matter what:

```
func paymentQueue(queue: SKPaymentQueue!,
    updatedTransactions transactions: [AnyObject]!) {
        for t in transactions as! [SKPaymentTransaction] {
            switch t.transactionState {
            case .Purchased, .Restored:
                let p = t.payment
                if p.productIdentifier == "DiabelliChoose" {
                    NSUserDefaults.standardUserDefaults().setBool(
                        true, forKey: "choose")
                    queue.finishTransaction(t)
```

```
        }
    default:
        queue.finishTransaction(t)
    }
  }
}
```

Bonjour

Bonjour is the ingenious technology, originated at Apple and now becoming a universal standard, for allowing network devices to advertise services they provide and to discover dynamically other devices offering such services. Once an appropriate service is detected, a client device can resolve it to get a network address and can then begin communicating with the server device. Communicating itself is outside the scope of this book, but device discovery via Bonjour is easy.

In this example, we'll look to see whether any device, such as a Mac, is running iTunes with library sharing turned on. (This is not Home Sharing in the iTunes File menu; it's the "Share my library on my local network" checkbox in the iTunes Sharing preferences.) We can search for domains or for a particular service; here, we'll pass the empty string as the domain to signify "any domain," and concentrate on the service, which is "_daap._tcp". We maintain two properties, the NSNetServiceBrowser that will look for devices, and an NSNetService array in which to store any services it discovers:

```
self.services.removeAll()
self.nsb = NSNetServiceBrowser()
self.nsb.delegate = self
self.nsb.searchForServicesOfType("_daap._tcp", inDomain: "")
```

The NSNetServiceBrowser is now searching for devices advertising iTunes sharing and will keep doing so until we destroy it or tell it to stop. It is common to leave the service browser running, because devices can come and go very readily. As they do, the service browser's delegate (NSNetServiceBrowserDelegate) will be informed. For purposes of this example, I'll simply maintain a list of services, and update the app's interface when the situation changes:

```
func netServiceBrowser(aNetServiceBrowser: NSNetServiceBrowser,
    didFindService aNetService: NSNetService, moreComing: Bool) {
        self.services.append(aNetService)
        if !moreComing {
            self.updateInterface()
        }
}
func netServiceBrowser(aNetServiceBrowser: NSNetServiceBrowser,
    didRemoveService aNetService: NSNetService, moreComing: Bool) {
        if let ix = find(self.services, aNetService) {
            self.services.removeAtIndex(ix)
            if !moreComing {
```

```
                self.updateInterface()
            }
        }
    }
```

The delegate messages very kindly tell me whether they have finished listing a series of changes, so I can wait to update the interface until after a full batch of changes has ended. In this example, I don't really have any interface to update; I'll just log the list of services, each of which is an NSNetService instance:

```
func updateInterface () {
    for service in self.services {
        if service.port == -1 {
            println("service \(service.name) of type \(service.type)" +
                " not yet resolved")
        }
    }
}
```

To connect to a service, we would first need to *resolve* it, thus obtaining an address and other useful information. An unresolved service has port -1, as shown in the previous code. To resolve a service, you tell it to resolve (resolveWithTimeout:); you will probably also set a delegate on the service (NSNetServiceDelegate), so as to be notified when the resolution succeeds (or fails). Here, I'll have the delegate call my update-Interface method again if a resolution succeeds, and I'll extend updateInterface to show the port number for any resolved services:

```
func updateInterface () {
    for service in self.services {
        if service.port == -1 {
            println("service \(service.name) of type \(service.type)" +
                " not yet resolved")
            service.delegate = self
            service.resolveWithTimeout(10)
        } else {
            println("service \(service.name) of type \(service.type)," +
                "port \(service.port), addresses \(service.addresses)")
        }
    }
}
func netServiceDidResolveAddress(sender: NSNetService) {
    self.updateInterface()
}
```

The addresses of a resolved service constitute an array of NSData. Logging an address like this is largely pointless, as it is not human-readable, but it's useful for handing to a CFSocket. In general you'll call the service's getInputStream:outputStream: to start talking over the connection; that's outside the scope of this discussion. See Apple's WiTap example for more.

CHAPTER 25

Threads

A *thread* is, simply put, a subprocess of your app that can execute even while other subprocesses are also executing. Such simultaneous execution is called *concurrency*. The iOS frameworks use threads all the time; if they didn't, your app would be less responsive to the user — perhaps even completely unresponsive. The genius of the frameworks, though, is that, for the most part, they use threads precisely so that you don't have to.

For example, suppose your app is downloading something from the network (Chapter 24). This download doesn't happen all by itself; somewhere, someone is running code that interacts with the network and obtains data. Similarly, how does Core Motion work (Chapter 22)? The data from the sensors is being gathered and processed constantly, with extra calculations to separate gravity from user-induced acceleration and to account for bias and scaling in the gyroscope. Yet none of that interferes with your code, or prevents the user from tapping and swiping things in your interface. That's concurrency in action.

This chapter discusses concurrency that involves *your* code in deliberate use of threading. It would have been nice to dispense with this topic altogether. Threads can be difficult and are always potentially dangerous, and should be avoided if possible. But sometimes that *isn't* possible. So this chapter introduces threads, along with a warning: threads entail complications and subtle pitfalls, and can make your code hard to debug. There is much more to threading, and especially to making your threaded code safe, than this chapter can possibly touch on. For detailed information about the topics introduced in this chapter, read Apple's *Concurrency Programming Guide* and *Threading Programming Guide*.

Main Thread

You are always using *some* thread. All your code must run somewhere; "somewhere" means a thread. When code calls a method, that method normally runs on the same thread as the code that called it. Your code is called through events; those events normally call your code on the *main thread*. The main thread has certain special properties:

The main thread automatically has a run loop.

A *run loop* is a recipient of events. It is how your code is notified that something is happening; without a run loop, a thread can't receive events. Cocoa events normally arrive on the main thread's run loop; that's why your code, called by those events, executes on the main thread.

The main thread is the interface thread.

When the *user* interacts with the interface, those interactions are reported as events — on the main thread. When *your code* interacts with the interface, it too must do so on the main thread. Of course that will normally happen automatically, because your code normally runs on the main thread.

The main thread thus has a very great deal of work to do. Here's how life goes in your app:

1. An event arrives on the main thread; the user has tapped a button, for example, and this is reported to your app as a UIEvent and to the button through the touch delivery mechanism (Chapter 5) — on the main thread.

2. The control event causes your code (the action handler) to be called — on the main thread. Your code now runs — on the main thread. *While your code runs, nothing else can happen on the main thread.* Your code might command some changes in the interface; this is safe, because your code is running on the main thread.

3. Your code finishes. The main thread's run loop is now free to report more events, and the user is free to interact with the interface once again.

The bottleneck here is obviously step 2, the running of your code. Your code runs on the main thread. That means the main thread can't do anything else while your code is running. No events can arrive while your code is running. The user can't interact with the interface while your code is running. But this is usually no problem, because:

- Your code executes really fast. It's true that the user can't interact with the interface while your code runs, but this is such a tiny interval of time that the user will probably never even notice.

- Your code, as it runs, blocks the user from interacting with the interface. But that's not bad: it's good! Your code, in response to what the user does, might update the interface; it would be insane if the user could do something else in the interface while you're in the middle of updating it.

On the other hand, as I've already mentioned, the frameworks operate in secondary threads all the time. The reason this doesn't affect you is that they usually talk to *your* code on the *main* thread. You have seen many examples of this in the preceding chapters:

- During an animation (Chapter 4), the interface remains responsive to the user, and it is possible for your code to run. The Core Animation framework is running the animation and updating the presentation layer on a background thread. But your delegate methods or completion blocks are called on the main thread.

- A web view's fetching and loading of its content is asynchronous (Chapter 11); that means the work is done in a background thread. But your delegate methods are called on the main thread.

- Sounds are played asynchronously (Chapters 14 and 16). But your delegate methods are called on the main thread. Similarly, loading, preparation, and playing of movies happens asynchronously (Chapter 15). But your delegate methods are called on the main thread.

- Saving a movie file takes time (Chapters 15 and 17). So the saving takes place on a background thread. Similarly, UIDocument saves and reads on a background thread (Chapter 23). But your delegate methods or completion blocks are called on the main thread.

Thus, you can (and should) usually ignore threads and just keep plugging away on the main thread. However, there are two kinds of situation in which your code will need to be explicitly aware of threading issues:

Your code is called back, but not on the main thread.

Some frameworks explicitly inform you in their documentation that callbacks are not guaranteed to take place on the main thread. For example, the documentation on CATiledLayer (Chapter 7) warns that `drawLayer:inContext:` is called in a background thread. By implication, our `drawRect:` code, triggered by CATiled-Layer to update tiles, is running in a background thread. (Fortunately, drawing into the current context is thread-safe.)

Similarly, the documentation on AV Foundation (Chapters 15 and 17) warns that its blocks and notifications can arrive on a background thread. So if you intend to update the user interface, or use a value that might also be used by your main-thread code, you'll need to be thread-conscious.

Your code takes significant time.

If your code takes significant time to run, you might need to run that code on a background thread, rather than letting it block the main thread and prevent anything else from happening there. For example:

During startup

You want your app to launch as quickly as possible. In Chapter 23, I called `URLForUbiquityContainerIdentifier:` during app launch. The documentation told me to call this method on a background thread, because it can take some time to return; we don't want to block the main thread waiting for it, because the app is trying to launch on the main thread, and the user won't see our interface until the launch process is over.

When the user can see or interact with the app

In Chapter 19, I called `enumerateEventsMatchingPredicate:` on a background thread in order to prevent the user interface from freezing up in case the enumeration took a long time. If I hadn't done this, then when the user taps the button that triggers this call, the button will stay highlighted for a significant amount of time, during which the interface will be completely frozen.

Similarly, when your app is in the process of being suspended into the background, or resumed from the background, your app should not block the main thread for too long; it must act quickly and get out of the way.

Moving time-consuming code off the main thread, so that the main thread is not blocked, isn't just a matter of aesthetics or politeness: the system "watchdog" will summarily *kill your app* if it discovers that the main thread is blocked for too long.

Why Threading Is Hard

The one certain thing about computer code is that it just clunks along the path of execution, one statement at a time. Lines of code, in effect, are performed in the order in which they appear. With threading, that certainty goes right out the window. If you have code that can be performed on a background thread, then you don't know when it will be performed in relation to the code being performed on any other thread. Any line of your background-thread code could be interleaved between any two lines of your main-thread code.

You also might not know *how many times* a piece of your background-thread code might be running simultaneously. Unless you take steps to prevent it, the same code could be spawned off as a thread even while it's already running in a thread. So any line of your background-thread code could be interleaved between any two lines of *itself*. (I'll discuss later in this chapter a situation in which this very thing does happen.)

This situation is particularly threatening with regard to *shared data*. Suppose two threads were to get hold of the same object and change it. Who knows what horrors might result? Objects in general have state, adding up to the state of your app as a whole. If multiple threads are permitted to access your objects, they and your entire app can be put into an indeterminate or nonsensical state.

This problem cannot be solved by simple logic. For example, suppose you try to make data access safe with a condition, as in this pseudocode:

```
if no other thread is touching this data {
    ... do something to the data ...
}
```

Such logic is utterly specious. Suppose the condition succeeds: no other thread is touching this data. But between the time when that condition is evaluated and the time when the next line executes and you start to do something to the data, another thread can still come along and start touching the data!

It is possible to request assistance at a deeper level to ensure that a section of code is not run by two threads simultaneously. For example, you can implement a *lock* around a section of code. But locks generate an entirely new level of potential pitfalls. In general, a lock is an invitation to forget to use the lock, or to forget to remove the lock after you've set it. And threads can end up contending for a lock in a way that permits neither thread to proceed.

Another problem is that the lifetime of a thread is independent of the lifetimes of other objects in your app. When an object is about to go out of existence and its `deinit` has been called and executed, you are guaranteed that none of your code in that object will ever run again. But a thread might still be running, and might try to talk to your object, even after your object has gone out of existence.

Not only is threaded code hard to get right; it's also hard to test and hard to debug. It introduces indeterminacy, so you can easily make a mistake that never appears in your testing, but that does appear for some user. The real danger is that the user's experience will consist only of distant consequences of your mistake, long after the point where you made it, making the true cause of the problem extraordinarily difficult to track down.

Perhaps you think I'm trying to scare you away from using threads. You're right! For an excellent (and suitably frightening) account of some of the dangers and considerations that threading involves, see Apple's *Technical Note TN2109*. If terms like *race condition* and *deadlock* don't strike fear into your veins, look them up on Wikipedia.

 Xcode's Debug navigator distinguishes threads; new in Xcode 6, you can even see pending blocks and learn when a block was enqueued. Also, when you call `NSLog` in your multithreaded code, the output in the console displays a number (in square brackets, after the colon) identifying the thread on which it was called — a simple but unbelievably helpful way of distinguishing threads.

Blocking the Main Thread

To illustrate making your code multithreaded, I need some code that is worth making multithreaded. I'll use as my example an app that draws the Mandelbrot set. (This code is adapted from a small open source project I downloaded from the Internet.) All it does is draw the basic Mandelbrot set in black and white, but that's a sufficiently elaborate calculation to introduce a significant delay, especially on an older, slower device. The idea is then to see how we can safely get that delay off the main thread.

The app contains a UIView subclass, MyMandelbrotView, which has one property, a CGContext called `bitmapContext`. Here's the structure of MyMandelbrotView's implementation:

```
let MANDELBROT_STEPS = 200 // determines how long the calculation takes
var bitmapContext: CGContext!
// jumping-off point: draw the Mandelbrot set
func drawThatPuppy () {
    self.makeBitmapContext(self.bounds.size)
    let center = CGPointMake(self.bounds.midX, self.bounds.midY)
    self.drawAtCenter(center, zoom:1)
    self.setNeedsDisplay()
}
// create bitmap context
func makeBitmapContext(size:CGSize) {
    var bitmapBytesPerRow = Int(size.width * 4)
    bitmapBytesPerRow += (16 - (bitmapBytesPerRow % 16)) % 16
    let colorSpace = CGColorSpaceCreateDeviceRGB()
    let prem = CGBitmapInfo(CGImageAlphaInfo.PremultipliedLast.rawValue)
    let context = CGBitmapContextCreate(
        nil, Int(size.width), Int(size.height), 8,
        bitmapBytesPerRow, colorSpace, prem)
    self.bitmapContext = context
}
// draw pixels of bitmap context
func drawAtCenter(center:CGPoint, zoom:CGFloat) {
    func isInMandelbrotSet(re:Float, im:Float) -> Bool {
        var fl = true
        var (x:Float, y:Float, nx:Float, ny:Float) = (0,0,0,0)
        for _ in 0 ..< MANDELBROT_STEPS {
            nx = x*x - y*y + re
            ny = 2*x*y + im
            if nx*nx + ny*ny > 4 {
                fl = false
                break
            }
            x = nx
            y = ny
        }
        return fl
    }
    CGContextSetAllowsAntialiasing(self.bitmapContext, false)
    CGContextSetRGBFillColor(self.bitmapContext, 0, 0, 0, 1)
    var re : CGFloat
    var im : CGFloat
    let maxi = Int(self.bounds.size.width)
    let maxj = Int(self.bounds.size.height)
    for i in 0 ..< maxi {
        for j in 0 ..< maxj {
            re = (CGFloat(i) - 1.33 * center.x) / 160
            im = (CGFloat(j) - 1.0 * center.y) / 160
            re /= zoom
```

```
        im /= zoom
        if (isInMandelbrotSet(Float(re), Float(im))) {
            CGContextFillRect (
                self.bitmapContext, CGRectMake(CGFloat(i),
                CGFloat(j), 1.0, 1.0))
        }
      }
    }
  }
  // turn pixels of bitmap context into CGImage, draw into ourselves
  override func drawRect(rect: CGRect) {
      if self.bitmapContext != nil {
          let context = UIGraphicsGetCurrentContext()
          let im = CGBitmapContextCreateImage(self.bitmapContext)
          CGContextDrawImage(context, self.bounds, im)
      }
  }
}
```

The `drawAtCenter:zoom:` method, which calculates the pixels of `self.bitmap-Context`, is time-consuming, and we can see this by running the app on a device. If the entire process is kicked off by tapping a button whose action handler calls `drawThat-Puppy`, there is a significant delay before the Mandelbrot graphic appears in the interface, during which time *the button remains highlighted*. That is a sure sign that we are blocking the main thread.

We need to move the calculation-intensive part of this code onto a background thread, so that the main thread is not blocked by the calculation. In doing so, we have two chief concerns:

Synchronization of threads

  The button is tapped, and `drawThatPuppy` is called, on the main thread. Thus, `set-NeedsDisplay` is called on the main thread — and rightly so, since this affects the interface. Therefore, `drawRect:` is called on the main thread. In between, however, the calculation-intensive `drawAtCenter:zoom:` is to be called on a background thread. Yet these three methods must still be called in order: `drawThatPuppy`, then `drawAtCenter:zoom:`, then `drawRect:`. How is this going to work? Clearly it can't work as we have things structured now; if `drawThatPuppy` calls `drawAt-Center:zoom:` and immediately calls `setNeedsDisplay`, the former on a background thread and the latter on the main thread, the view will be redrawn too soon, before `drawAtCenter:zoom:` has had a chance to update the bitmap.

Shared data

  The property `self.bitmapContext` is referred to in three different methods — in `makeBitmapContext:`, which is called by `drawThatPuppy`; in `drawAtCenter:zoom:`; and in `drawRect:`. But we have just said that those three methods involve two different threads; they must not be permitted to touch the same property in a way that might conflict or clash. A further danger is that `drawAtCenter:zoom:` is run on a background thread, and we have no way of knowing how many such background threads there may be; the user might tap the button several times in quick succession, kicking off several simultaneous calculations. The access to `self.bitmap-Context` by `drawAtCenter:zoom:` must thus not be permitted to conflict or clash *with itself.* (This problem, mercifully, does not arise in connection with the main thread; there is only one main thread, so it *can't* conflict with itself.)

NSOperation

The essence of NSOperation is that it encapsulates a task, not a thread. The operation described by an NSOperation object may be performed on a background thread, but you don't have to concern yourself with that directly. You describe the operation and add the NSOperation to an NSOperationQueue to set it going. You arrange to be notified when the operation ends, typically by the NSOperation posting a notification. You can query both the queue and its operations from outside with regard to their state.

We'll rewrite MyMandelbrotView to use NSOperation. We need a property, an NSOperationQueue; we'll call it `queue`, and we'll create and configure it in its initializer:

```
let queue : NSOperationQueue = {
    let q = NSOperationQueue()
    // ... further configurations can go here ...
    return q
}()
```

We also have a new class, MyMandelbrotOperation, an NSOperation subclass. (It is possible to take advantage of a built-in NSOperation subclass such as NSBlockOperation, but I'm deliberately illustrating the more general case by subclassing NSOperation itself.) Our implementation of `drawThatPuppy` thus creates an instance of MyMandelbrotOperation, configures it, registers for its notification, and adds it to the queue:

```
func drawThatPuppy () {
    let center = CGPointMake(self.bounds.midX, self.bounds.midY)
    let op = MyMandelbrotOperation(
        size: self.bounds.size, center: center, zoom: 1)
    NSNotificationCenter.defaultCenter().addObserver(
        self, selector: "operationFinished:",
        name: "MyMandelbrotOperationFinished", object: op)
    self.queue.addOperation(op)
}
```

Our time-consuming calculations are performed by MyMandelbrotOperation. An NSOperation subclass, such as MyMandelbrotOperation, will typically have at least two methods:

A designated initializer

The NSOperation may need some configuration data. Once the NSOperation is added to a queue, it's too late to talk to it, so you'll usually hand it this configuration data as you create it, in its designated initializer.

A `main` *method*

This method will be called (with no parameters) automatically by the NSOperation-Queue when it's time for the NSOperation to start.

MyMandelbrotOperation has three private properties for configuration (`size`, `center`, and `zoom`), to be set in its initializer; it must be told MyMandelbrotView's geometry explicitly because it is completely separate from MyMandelbrotView. MyMandelbrotOperation also has its own CGContext property, `bitmapContext`; it must be publicly gettable so that MyMandelbrotView can retrieve a reference to this graphics context when the operation has finished. Note that this is different from MyMandelbrotView's `bitmapContext`, thus helping to solve the problem of sharing data promiscuously between threads:

```
private let size : CGSize
private let center : CGPoint
private let zoom : CGFloat
private(set) var bitmapContext : CGContext!
init(size sz:CGSize, center c:CGPoint, zoom z:CGFloat) {
    self.size = sz
    self.center = c
    self.zoom = z
    super.init()
}
```

All the calculation work has been transferred from MyMandelbrotView to MyMandelbrotOperation without change; the only difference is that `self.bitmap-Context` now means MyMandelbrotOperation's property. The only method of real interest is `main`. First, we call the NSOperation method `isCancelled` to make sure we haven't been cancelled while sitting in the queue; this is good practice. Then, we do exactly what `drawThatPuppy` used to do, initializing our graphics context and drawing into its pixels:

```
let MANDELBROT_STEPS = 200
// create instance variable
func makeBitmapContext(size:CGSize) {
    // ... same as before
}
func drawAtCenter(center:CGPoint, zoom:CGFloat) {
    // ... same as before
}
override func main() {
    if self.cancelled {
        return
    }
```

```
    self.makeBitmapContext(self.size)
    self.drawAtCenter(self.center, zoom: self.zoom)
    if !self.cancelled {
        NSNotificationCenter.defaultCenter().postNotificationName(
            "MyMandelbrotOperationFinished", object: self)
    }
}
```

The last line of main is our signal to MyMandelbrotView that the calculation is over and it's time to come and fetch our data. There are two ways to do this; either main can post a notification through the NSNotificationCenter, or MyMandelbrotView can use key-value observing to be notified when our isFinished property changes. We've chosen the former approach; observe that we check one more time to make sure we haven't been cancelled.

Now we are back in MyMandelbrotView, hearing through the notification that My-MandelbrotOperation has finished. We must immediately pick up any required data, because the NSOperationQueue is about to release this NSOperation. However, we must be careful; the notification may have been posted on a background thread, in which case our method for responding to it will also be called on a background thread. We are about to set our own graphics context and tell ourselves to redraw; those are things we want to do on the main thread. So we immediately step out to the main thread (using Grand Central Dispatch, described more fully in the next section). We remove ourselves as notification observer for this operation instance, copy the operation's bitmapContext into our own bitmapContext, and now we're ready for the last step, drawing ourselves:

```
// warning! called on background thread
func operationFinished(n:NSNotification) {
    if let op = n.object as? MyMandelbrotOperation {
        dispatch_async(dispatch_get_main_queue()) {
            NSNotificationCenter.defaultCenter().removeObserver(
                self, name: "MyMandelbrotOperationFinished", object: op)
            self.bitmapContext = op.bitmapContext
            self.setNeedsDisplay()
        }
    }
}
```

Adapting our code to use NSOperation involves some work, but the result has many advantages that help to ensure that our use of multiple threads is coherent and safe:

The operation is encapsulated.
    Because MyMandelbrotOperation is an object, we've been able to move all the code having to do with drawing the pixels of the Mandelbrot set into it. The *only* My-MandelbrotView method that can be called in the background is operation-Finished:, and that's a method we'd never call explicitly ourselves, so we won't misuse it accidentally — and it immediately steps out to the main thread in any case.

The data sharing is rationalized.

Because MyMandelbrotOperation is an object, it has its own `bitmapContext` property. The only moment of data sharing comes in `operationFinished:`, when we must set MyMandelbrotView's `bitmapContext` to MyMandelbrotOperation's `bitmapContext`. Even if multiple MyMandelbrotOperation objects are added to the queue, the moments when we set MyMandelbrotView's `bitmapContext` and then redraw ourselves using that bitmap context all occur on the main thread, so they cannot conflict with one another.

The threads are synchronized.

The calculation-intensive operation doesn't start until MyMandelbrotView tells it to start (`self.queue.addOperation(op)`). MyMandelbrotView then takes its hands off the steering wheel and makes *no* attempt to draw itself. If `drawRect:` is called by the runtime, `self.bitmapContext` will be nil (or will contain the results of an earlier calculation operation) and no harm done. Nothing else happens until the operation ends and the notification arrives (`operationFinished:`); then and only then does MyMandelbrotView update the interface — on the main thread.

If we are concerned with the possibility that more than one instance of MyMandelbrot-Operation might be added to the queue and executed concurrently, we have a further line of defense — we can set the NSOperationQueue's maximum concurrency level to 1:

```
let q = NSOperationQueue()
q.maxConcurrentOperationCount = 1
return q
```

This turns the NSOperationQueue into a true serial queue; every operation on the queue must be completely executed before the next can begin. This might cause an operation added to the queue to take longer to execute, if it must wait for another operation to finish before it can even get started; however, this delay might not be important. What *is* important is that by executing the operations on this queue separately from one another, we guarantee that only one operation at a time can do any data sharing. A serial queue is thus a form of data locking.

Because MyMandelbrotView can be destroyed (if, for example, its view controller is destroyed), there is still a risk that it will create an operation that will outlive it and will try to access it after it has been destroyed. We can reduce that risk by canceling all operations in our queue before releasing it:

```
deinit {
    self.queue.cancelAllOperations()
}
```

Operation queues are good to know about for other reasons as well. A number of useful methods mentioned earlier in this book expect an NSOperationQueue argument; see, for example, Chapter 22 (`startDeviceMotionUpdatesToQueue:withHandler:`, and similarly for the other sensors) and Chapter 24 (`sessionWithConfiguration:delegate:delegateQueue:`).

Grand Central Dispatch

Grand Central Dispatch, or *GCD*, is a sort of low-level analogue to NSOperation and NSOperationQueue (in fact, NSOperationQueue uses GCD under the hood). When I say GCD is low-level, I'm not kidding; it is effectively baked into the operating system kernel. Thus it can be used by any code whatsoever and is tremendously efficient.

GCD is like NSOperationQueue in that it uses queues: you express a task and add it to a queue, and the task is executed on a thread as needed. Moreover, by default these queues are serial queues, with each task on a queue finishing before the next is started, which, as I've already said, is a form of data locking. However, it has the advantage over NSOperationQueue that there is no need to create any extra objects; GCD uses closures (blocks), so all your code to be executed on different threads can appear in the same place. Also, GCD is about much more than threading, as I'll discuss at the end of this section.

We'll rewrite MyMandelbrotView to use GCD. The structure of its interface is very slightly changed from the original, nonthreaded version. We have a new property to hold our queue, which is a *dispatch queue*; a dispatch queue is a lightweight opaque pseudo-object consisting essentially of a list of blocks to be executed. I want my dispatch queue to have a name (its `label`); this must be a C string, so I do a little dance in some top-level variables to create it:

```
let qvalString = "com.neuburg.mandeldraw" as NSString
var QVAL = qvalString.UTF8String
class MyMandelbrotView : UIView {
    let MANDELBROT_STEPS = 200
    var bitmapContext: CGContext!
    let draw_queue : dispatch_queue_t = {
        let q = dispatch_queue_create(QVAL, nil)
        return q
    }()
    // ...
}
```

(A call to `dispatch_queue_create` must be balanced by a call to `dispatch_release`. However, Swift memory management understands GCD pseudo-objects and will take care of this for us — in fact, calling `dispatch_release` explicitly is forbidden.)

Our `makeBitmapContext:` method now returns a graphics context rather than setting a property directly:

```
func makeBitmapContext(size:CGSize) -> CGContext {
    // ... as before ...
    let context = CGBitmapContextCreate(
        nil, Int(size.width), Int(size.height), 8,
        bitmapBytesPerRow, colorSpace, prem)
    return context
}
```

Also, our `drawAtCenter:zoom:` method now takes an additional parameter, the graphics context to draw into:

```
func drawAtCenter(center:CGPoint, zoom:CGFloat, context:CGContext) {
    // ... as before, but we refer to local context, not self.context
}
```

Now for the implementation of `drawThatPuppy`. This is where all the action is! Here it is:

```
func drawThatPuppy () {
    let center = CGPointMake(self.bounds.midX, self.bounds.midY) ❶
    dispatch_async(self.draw_queue) { ❷
        let bitmap = self.makeBitmapContext(self.bounds.size)
        self.drawAtCenter(center, zoom:1, context:bitmap)
        dispatch_async(dispatch_get_main_queue()) { ❸
            self.bitmapContext = bitmap
            self.setNeedsDisplay()
            UIApplication.sharedApplication().endBackgroundTask(bti)
        }
    }
}
```

That's all there is to it: *all* our app's multithreading is contained in those few lines. There are no notifications, no sharing of data between threads; and the entire sequential synchronization of our threads is completely handled and expressed with startling clarity. Here's how `drawThatPuppy` works:

❶   We begin by calculating our `center`, as before. This value will be visible within the blocks, because blocks can see their surrounding context.

❷   Now comes our task to be performed in a background thread on our queue, `self.draw_queue`. We specify this task with the `dispatch_async` function. GCD has a lot of functions, but this is the one you'll use 99 percent of the time; it's the most important thing you need to know about GCD. We specify a queue and we provide a block saying what we'd like to do. In the block, we begin by declaring `bitmap` as a variable *local to the block*. We then call `makeBitmapContext:` to create the graphics context `bitmap`, and `drawAtCenter:zoom:context:` to set its pixels. Bear in mind that those calls are made on a background thread, because `self.draw_queue` is a background queue.

❸ Now we need to step back out to the main thread. How do we do that? With dispatch_async again! We specify the main queue (which is effectively the main thread) with a function provided for this purpose and describe what we want to do in *another* block. This second block is nested inside the first, so it isn't performed until the preceding commands in the first block have finished; moreover, because the first block is part of the second block's surrounding context, the second block can see our block-local bitmap variable! We set our bitmapContext property and call setNeedsDisplay — on the main thread! — and we're done.

The benefits and elegance of GCD as a form of concurrency management are simply stunning. There is no data sharing, because the bitmap variable is not shared; it is local to each specific call to drawThatPuppy. The threads are synchronized, because the nested blocks are executed in succession, so any instance of bitmap must be completely filled with pixels before being used to set the bitmapContext property. Moreover, the *entire* operation is performed on a serial queue, and bitmapContext is touched only from code running on the main thread; thus there is no possibility of conflict. Our code is also highly maintainable, because the entire task on all threads is expressed within the single drawThatPuppy method, thanks to the use of blocks; indeed, the code is only very slightly modified from the original, nonthreaded version.

You might object that we still have methods makeBitmapContext: and drawAt-Center:zoom:context: hanging around MyMandelbrotView, and that we must therefore still be careful not to call them on the main thread, or indeed from anywhere except from within drawThatPuppy. If that were true, we could at this point destroy makeBitmap-Context: and drawAtCenter:zoom:context: and move their functionality completely into drawThatPuppy. But it *isn't* true, because these methods are now *thread-safe*: they are self-contained utilities that touch no properties or persistent objects, so it doesn't matter what thread they are called on. Still, I'll demonstrate in a moment how we can intercept an accidental attempt to call a method on the wrong thread.

The two most important GCD functions are:

dispatch_async
> Push a block onto the end of a queue for later execution, and proceed immediately with our own code. Thus, we can finish our own execution without waiting for the block to execute.
>
> Examples of using dispatch_async to execute code in a background thread (dispatch_get_global_queue(0,0)) appeared in Chapters 19 and 23. Examples of using dispatch_async as a way of stepping back onto the main thread (dispatch_get_main_queue) in order to talk to the interface from inside code that might be executed on a background thread appeared in Chapters 10, 15, 16, 17, and 24 (and elsewhere).

Also, it can be useful to call `dispatch_async` to step out to the main thread even though you're *already* on the main thread, as a way of waiting for the run loop to complete and for the interface to settle down — a minimal form of delayed performance. I used that technique in Chapters 12 and 23.

`dispatch_sync`
Push a block onto the end of a queue for later execution, and wait until the block has executed before proceeding with our own code — because, for example, you intend to use a result that the block is to provide. The purpose of the queue would be, once again, as a lightweight, reliable version of a lock, mediating access to a shared resource. Here's a case in point, adapted from Apple's own code:

```
func asset() -> AVAsset? {
    var theAsset : AVAsset!
    dispatch_sync(self.assetQueue) {
        theAsset = self.getAssetInternal().copy() as! AVAsset
    }
    return theAsset
}
```

Any thread might call the `asset` method; to avoid problems with shared data, we require that only blocks that are executed from a particular queue (`self.asset-Queue`) may touch an AVAsset. But we need the result that this block returns; hence the call to `dispatch_sync`.

In Chapter 7 I encountered a problem where I discovered that the runtime was calling my CATiledLayer's `drawRect:` simultaneously on multiple threads — a rare example of Apple's code involving me unawares and unwillingly in complications of threading. To close the door to this sort of behavior, it suffices to wrap the interior of my `drawRect:` implementation in a call to `dispatch_sync`. This is a safe and reliable mode of locking: once any thread has started to run my `drawRect:`, no other thread can start to run it until the first thread has finished with it. Thus my `drawRect:`, though it can be (and will be) run on a background thread, is immune to being run on *multiple* background threads. I have defined a property to hold a dedicated serial queue:

```
let drawQueue = dispatch_queue_create(nil, DISPATCH_QUEUE_SERIAL)
```

And here's how `drawRect:` is structured:

```
override func drawRect(r: CGRect) {
    dispatch_sync(drawQueue, {
        // ... draw here ...
    })
}
```

An interesting and useful exercise is to revise the MyDownloader class from Chapter 24 so that the delegate methods are run on a background thread, thus taking some strain off the main thread (and hence the user interface) while these messages are flying around behind the scenes. This looks like a reasonable and safe thing to do, because the NSURL-Session and the delegate methods are all packaged inside the MyDownloader object, isolated from our view controller.

To do so, the first step is to declare our completion handler `typealias` using the undocumented `@objc_block` attribute; otherwise, we won't get proper memory management of our stored handler:

```
typealias MyDownloaderCompletion = @objc_block (NSURL!) -> ()
```

We'll also need our own background NSOperationQueue, which we can maintain as a property:

```
let q = NSOperationQueue()
```

Our session is now configured and created using this background queue:

```
lazy var session : NSURLSession = {
    let queue = self.q
    return NSURLSession(configuration:self.config,
        delegate:self, delegateQueue:queue)
}()
```

We must now give some thought to what will happen in `URLSession:downloadTask:did-FinishDownloadingToURL:` when we call back into the client through the completion handler that we received in `download:completionHandler:`. It would not be very nice to involve the client in threading issues; our entire goal is to isolate such issues within MyDownloader itself. Therefore we must step out to the main thread as we call the completion handler. But we cannot do this by calling `dispatch_async`:

```
dispatch_async(dispatch_get_main_queue()) {
    ch2(url)
}
```

The reason is that the downloaded file is slated to be destroyed as soon as we return from `URLSession:downloadTask:didFinishDownloadingToURL:` — and if we call `dispatch_async`, we will return *immediately*. Thus the downloaded file *will* be destroyed, and `url` will end up pointing at nothing by the time the client receives it. The solution is to use `dispatch_sync` instead:

```
dispatch_sync(dispatch_get_main_queue()) {
    ch2(url)
}
```

That code steps out to the main thread and also postpones returning from `URLSession:downloadTask:didFinishDownloadingToURL:` until the client has had an opportunity to do something with the file pointed to by `url`. We are blocking our background NSOperationQueue, but only very briefly. Again, our real purpose in using `dispatch_sync` is to lock down some shared data — in this case, the downloaded file.

It is also good to know about the GCD function `dispatch_after`; many examples in this book have made use of it, by way of my utility method `delay` (see Appendix B) — see, for instance, Chapters 2, 7, and 10.

Another useful GCD function is `dispatch_once`, a thread-safe way of ensuring that code is run only once; I probably could have used this instead of the Bool property flags scattered throughout my example code (such as `self.viewInitializationDone` in Chapter 6). Your call to this function must be accompanied by a reference to an already defined variable which serves as a *token* (a `dispatch_once_t`); the scope of the notion "once" is determined by the scope and lifetime at which this token is declared. Thus, in the following example, the code in question will run just once *per instance of this class*, because the token is declared as a property, at the level of the instance:

```
class SomeClass {
    var once_token : dispatch_once_t = 0
    func test() {
        dispatch_once(&once_token) {
            // this code will run just once in the life of this object
        }
    }
}
```

In Objective-C, `dispatch_once` is often used to vend a singleton; in Swift, however, you are more likely to use the built-in lazy initialization feature.

Besides serial dispatch queues, there are also *concurrent* dispatch queues. A concurrent queue's blocks are started in the order in which they were submitted to the queue, but a block is allowed to start while another block is still executing. Obviously, you wouldn't want to submit to a concurrent queue a task that touches a shared resource — that would be throwing away the entire point of serial queues. The advantage of concurrent queues is a possible speed boost when you don't care about the order in which multiple tasks are finished — for example, when you want to do something with regard to every element of an array.

The built-in global queues (available by calling `dispatch_get_global_queue`) are concurrent; you can also create a concurrent queue by passing `DISPATCH_QUEUE_CONCURRENT` as the second argument to `dispatch_queue_create`.

A frequent use of concurrent queues is with `dispatch_apply`. This function is like `dispatch_sync` (the caller pauses until the block has finished executing), but the block is called multiple times with an iterator argument. Thus, `dispatch_apply` on a concurrent queue is like a for loop whose iterations are multithreaded; on a device with multiple cores, this could result in a speed improvement. (Of course, this technique is applicable only if the iterations do not depend on one another.)

Arbitrary context data can be attached to a queue in the form of key–value pairs (dispatch_queue_set_specific) and retrieved by key. There are two ways to retrieve the context data:

dispatch_queue_get_specific
    Retrieves a key's value for a queue to which we already have a valid reference.

dispatch_get_specific
    Retrieves a key's value for the *current* queue, the one in whose thread we are actually running. In fact, dispatch_get_specific is the *only* valid way to identify the current queue. (dispatch_get_current_queue, a function formerly used for this purpose, has been shown to be potentially unsafe and is now deprecated.)

We can use this technique, for example, to make certain that a method is called only on the correct queue. Recall that in our Mandelbrot-drawing example, we may be concerned that a method such as makeBitmapContext: might be called on some other queue than the background queue that we created for this purpose. If this is really a worry, we can attach an identifying key–value pair to that queue when we create it. The value should be a pointer; that's why I created a C string variable at the top level of the file, and now I'll add a second variable to act as the key:

```
let qkeyString = "label" as NSString
var QKEY = qkeyString.UTF8String
let qvalString = "com.neuburg.mandeldraw" as NSString
var QVAL = qvalString.UTF8String
```

We then create and configure the queue like this:

```
let q = dispatch_queue_create(QVAL, nil)
dispatch_queue_set_specific(q, QKEY, &QVAL, nil)
```

Later, we can examine that identifying key–value pair for the queue on which a particular method is called:

```
func assertOnBackgroundThread() {
    let s = dispatch_get_specific(QKEY)
    assert(s == &QVAL)
}
```

Threads and App Backgrounding

When your app is backgrounded and suspended, a problem arises if your code is running. The system doesn't want to stop your code while it's executing; on the other hand, some other app may need to be given the bulk of the device's resources now. So as your app goes into the background, the system waits a very short time for your app to finish doing whatever it may be doing, and it then suspends your app.

This shouldn't be a problem from your main thread's point of view, because your app shouldn't have any time-consuming code on the main thread in the first place; you now know that you can avoid this by using a background thread. On the other hand, it could be a problem for lengthy background operations, including asynchronous tasks performed by the frameworks. You can request extra time to complete a lengthy task (or at to least abort it yourself, coherently) in case your app is backgrounded, by wrapping it in calls to UIApplication's beginBackgroundTaskWithExpirationHandler: and endBackgroundTask:. Here's how you do it:

- You call beginBackgroundTaskWithExpirationHandler: to announce that a lengthy task is beginning; it returns an identification number. This tells the system that if your app is backgrounded, you'd like to be woken from suspension in the background now and then in order to complete the task.

- At the end of your lengthy task, you call endBackgroundTask:, passing in the same identification number that you got from your call to beginBackgroundTaskWithExpirationHandler:. This tells the system that your lengthy task is over and that there is no need to grant you any more background time.

The argument to beginBackgroundTaskWithExpirationHandler: is a block, but this block does *not* express the lengthy task. It expresses what you will do *if your extra time expires* before you finish your lengthy task. At the very least, your expiration handler must call endBackgroundTask:! Otherwise, the runtime won't know that you've run your expiration handler, and your app may be killed, as a punishment for trying to use too much background time. If your expiration handler block *is* called, you should make no assumptions about what thread it is running on.

Let's use MyMandelbrotView as an example. Let's say that if drawThatPuppy is started, we'd like it to be allowed to finish, even if the app is suspended in the middle of it, so that our bitmapContext property is updated as requested. To try to ensure this, we call beginBackgroundTaskWithExpirationHandler: beforehand and call endBackgroundTask: at the end of the innermost block:

```
func drawThatPuppy () {
    let center = CGPointMake(self.bounds.midX, self.bounds.midY)
    // === configure background task
    var bti : UIBackgroundTaskIdentifier = 0
    bti = UIApplication.sharedApplication()
        .beginBackgroundTaskWithExpirationHandler({
            UIApplication.sharedApplication().endBackgroundTask(bti)
        })
    if bti == UIBackgroundTaskInvalid {
        return
    }
    // ===
    dispatch_async(self.draw_queue) {
        let bitmap = self.makeBitmapContext(self.bounds.size)
        self.drawAtCenter(center, zoom:1, context:bitmap)
        dispatch_async(dispatch_get_main_queue()) {
```

```
                    self.bitmapContext = bitmap
                    self.setNeedsDisplay()
                    UIApplication.sharedApplication().endBackgroundTask(bti) // *
                }
            }
        }
```

If our app is backgrounded while drawThatPuppy is in progress, it will (we hope) be given enough background time to run that it can eventually proceed all the way to the end. Thus, the property bitmapContext will be updated, and setNeedsDisplay will be called, while we are still in the background. Our drawRect: will not be called until our app is brought back to the front, but there's nothing wrong with that.

Declaring bti in a separate line before calling beginBackgroundTaskWithExpiration-Handler: to set bti to its real value allows us to access, inside the block, the value that bti *will* have when the call to beginBackgroundTaskWithExpirationHandler: returns. The check against UIBackgroundTaskInvalid can do no harm, and there may be situations or devices where our request to complete this task in the background will be denied.

It's good policy to use a similar technique when you're notified that your app is being backgrounded. You might respond to the app delegate message applicationDid-EnterBackground: (or the corresponding UIApplicationDidEnterBackground-Notification) by saving data and reducing memory usage, but this can take time, whereas you'd like to return from applicationDidEnterBackground: as quickly as possible. A reasonable solution is to implement applicationDidEnterBackground: very much like drawThatPuppy in the example I just gave: call beginBackgroundTask-WithExpirationHandler: and then call dispatch_async to get off the main thread, and do your saving and so forth in its block.

CHAPTER 26

Undo

The ability to undo the most recent action is familiar from OS X. The idea is that, provided the user realizes soon enough that a mistake has been made, that mistake can be reversed. Typically, a Mac application will maintain an internal stack of undoable actions; choosing Edit → Undo or pressing Command-Z will reverse the action at the top of the stack, and will also make that action available for Redo.

Some iOS apps, too, may benefit from at least a limited Undo facility, and this is not difficult to implement. Some built-in views — in particular, those that involve text entry, UITextField and UITextView (Chapter 10) — implement Undo already. And you can add it in other areas of your app.

Undo is provided through an instance of NSUndoManager, which basically just maintains a stack of undoable actions, along with a secondary stack of redoable actions. The goal in general is to work with the NSUndoManager so as to handle both Undo and Redo in the standard manner: when the user chooses to undo the most recent action, the action at the top of the Undo stack is popped off and reversed and is pushed onto the top of the Redo stack.

In this chapter, I'll illustrate a simple NSUndoManager for a simple app that has just one kind of undoable action. More complicated apps, obviously, will be more complicated! On the other hand, iOS apps, unlike OS X apps, do not generally need deep or pervasive Undo functionality. For more about the NSUndoManager class and how to use it, read Apple's *Undo Architecture* as well as the documentation for the class itself. Also, UIDocument (see Chapter 23) has an undo manager (its undoManager property), which automatically and appropriately updates the document's "dirty" state for you.

Undo Manager

In our artificially simple app, the user can drag a small square around the screen. We'll start with an instance of a UIView subclass, MyView, to which has been attached a

UIPanGestureRecognizer to make it draggable, as described in Chapter 5. The gesture recognizer's action target is the MyView instance itself:

```
func dragging (p : UIPanGestureRecognizer) {
    switch p.state {
    case .Began, .Changed:
        let delta = p.translationInView(self.superview!)
        var c = self.center
        c.x += delta.x; c.y += delta.y
        p.setTranslation(CGPointZero, inView: self.superview!)
    default:break
    }
}
```

To make dragging of this view undoable, we need an NSUndoManager instance. Let's store this in a property of MyView itself, self.undoer:

```
let undoer = NSUndoManager()
```

Target–Action Undo

There are two ways to register an action as undoable. I'll start with the NSUndoManager method registerUndoWithTarget:selector:object:. This method uses a target–action architecture: you provide a target, a selector for a method that takes one parameter, and the object value to be passed as argument when the method is called. Then, later, if the NSUndoManager is sent the undo message, it simply sends that action to that target with that argument. The job of the action method is to undo whatever it is that needs undoing.

What we want to undo here is the setting of our center property. This can't expressed directly using a target–action architecture, because the parameter of setCenter: needs to be a CGPoint; we can't use a CGPoint as the object: in registerUndoWith-Target:selector:object:, because it isn't an Objective-C object (Swift will complain that it doesn't conform to AnyObject). Therefore we're going to have to provide, as our action method, a secondary method that *does* take an object parameter. This is neither bad nor unusual; it is quite common for actions to have a special representation just for the purpose of making them undoable.

So, in our dragging: method, instead of setting self.center to c directly, we now call a secondary method (let's call it setCenterUndoably:):

```
var c = self.center
c.x += delta.x; c.y += delta.y
self.setCenterUndoably(NSValue(CGPoint:c))
```

At a minimum, setCenterUndoably: should do the job that setting self.center used to do:

```
func setCenterUndoably (newCenter:NSValue) {
    self.center = newCenter.CGPointValue()
}
```

This works in the sense that the view is draggable exactly as before, but we have not yet made this action undoable. To do so, we must ask ourselves what message the NSUndo-Manager would need to send in order to undo the action we are about to perform. We would want the NSUndoManager to set self.center back to the value it has *now*, before we change it as we are about to do. And what method would NSUndoManager call in order to do that? It would call setCenterUndoably:, the very method we are implementing now! So:

```
func setCenterUndoably (newCenter:NSValue) {
    self.undoer.registerUndoWithTarget(
        self, selector: "setCenterUndoably:",
        object: NSValue(CGPoint:self.center))
    self.center = newCenter.CGPointValue()
}
```

That code has a remarkable effect: it makes our action not only undoable but also redoable. The reason is that NSUndoManager has an internal state, and responds differently to registerUndoWithTarget:selector:object: depending on its state. If the NSUndoManager is sent registerUndoWithTarget:selector:object: *while it is undoing*, it puts the target–action information on the Redo stack instead of the Undo stack (because Redo *is* the Undo of an Undo, if you see what I mean).

Here's how our code works to Undo and then Redo an action:

1. We perform an action by way of setCenterUndoably:, which calls registerUndo-WithTarget:selector:object: with the *old* value of self.center. The NSUndo-Manager adds this to its Undo stack.

2. Now suppose we want to undo that action. We send undo to the NSUndoManager.

3. The NSUndoManager calls setCenterUndoably: with the old value that we passed in earlier when we called registerUndoWithTarget:selector:object:. Thus, we are going to set the center back to that old value. But before we do that, we send registerUndoWithTarget:selector:object: to the NSUndoManager with the *current* value of self.center. The NSUndoManager knows that it is currently undoing, so it understands this registration as something to be added to its Redo stack.

4. Now suppose we want to redo that Undo. We send redo to the NSUndoManager, and sure enough, the NSUndoManager calls setCenterUndoably: with the value that we previously undid. (And, once again, we call registerUndoWith-Target:selector:object: with an action that goes onto the NSUndoManager's Undo stack.)

Undo Grouping

So far, so good. But our implementation of Undo is very annoying, because we are adding a single object to the Undo stack every time `dragging:` is called — and it is called many times during the course of a single drag. Thus, undoing merely undoes the tiny increment corresponding to one individual `dragging:` call. What we'd like, surely, is for undoing to undo an *entire* dragging gesture. We can implement this through *undo grouping*. As the gesture begins, we start a group; when the gesture ends, we end the group:

```
func dragging (p : UIPanGestureRecognizer) {
    switch p.state {
    case .Began:
        self.undoer.beginUndoGrouping()
        fallthrough
    case .Began, .Changed:
        let delta = p.translationInView(self.superview!)
        var c = self.center
        c.x += delta.x; c.y += delta.y
        self.setCenterUndoably(NSValue(CGPoint:c))
        p.setTranslation(CGPointZero, inView: self.superview!)
    case .Ended, .Cancelled:
        self.undoer.endUndoGrouping()
    default:break
    }
}
```

This works: each complete gesture of dragging MyView, from the time the user's finger contacts the view to the time it leaves, is now undoable (and then redoable) as a single unit.

A further refinement would be to animate the "drag" that the NSUndoManager performs when it undoes or redoes a user drag gesture. To do so, we take advantage of the fact that we, too, can examine the NSUndoManager's state by way of its `isUndoing` and `isRedoing` properties; we animate the `center` change when the NSUndoManager is "dragging," but not when the user is dragging:

```
func setCenterUndoably (newCenter:NSValue) {
    self.undoer.registerUndoWithTarget(
        self, selector: "setCenterUndoably:",
        object: NSValue(CGPoint:self.center))
    if self.undoer.undoing || self.undoer.redoing {
        UIView.animateWithDuration(
            0.4, delay: 0.1, options: nil, animations: {
                self.center = newCenter.CGPointValue()
            }, completion: nil)
    } else {
```

```
        // just do it
        self.center = newCenter.CGPointValue()
    }
}
```

Invocation Undo

Earlier I said that `registerUndoWithTarget:selector:object:` was one of two ways to register an action as undoable. The other is `prepareWithInvocationTarget:`. In general, the advantage of `prepareWithInvocationTarget:` is that it lets you specify a method with any number of parameters, and those parameters needn't be objects. You provide the target and, *in the same line of code*, send to the object returned from this call the message and arguments you want sent when the NSUndoManager is sent `undo` or `redo`. So, in our example, instead of this line:

```
self.undoer.registerUndoWithTarget(
    self, selector: "setCenterUndoably:",
    object: NSValue(CGPoint:self.center))
```

You'd say this:

```
self.undoer.prepareWithInvocationTarget(self)
    .setCenterUndoably(self.center)
```

That code seems impossible: how can we send `setCenterUndoably:` without *calling* `set-CenterUndoably:`? Either we are sending it to `self`, in which case it should actually be called at this moment, or we are sending it to some other object that doesn't implement `setCenterUndoably:`, in which case our app should crash. However, under the hood, the NSUndoManager is cleverly using dynamism (similarly to the message-forwarding example in Chapter 12) to capture this call as an NSInvocation object, which it can use later to send the same message with the same arguments to the specified target.

If we're going to use `prepareWithInvocationTarget:`, there's no need to wrap the CGPoint value representing the old and new `center` of our view as an NSValue. So our complete implementation now looks like this:

```
func setCenterUndoably (newCenter:CGPoint) { // *
    self.undoer.prepareWithInvocationTarget(self)
        .setCenterUndoably(self.center) // *
    if self.undoer.undoing || self.undoer.redoing {
        UIView.animateWithDuration(
            0.4, delay: 0.1, options: nil, animations: {
                self.center = newCenter // *
            }, completion: nil)
    } else {
        // just do it
        self.center = newCenter // *
    }
}
func dragging (p : UIPanGestureRecognizer) {
```

```
        switch p.state {
        case .Began:
            self.undoer.beginUndoGrouping()
            fallthrough
        case .Began, .Changed:
            let delta = p.translationInView(self.superview!)
            var c = self.center
            c.x += delta.x; c.y += delta.y
            self.setCenterUndoably(c) // *
            p.setTranslation(CGPointZero, inView: self.superview!)
        case .Ended, .Cancelled:
            self.undoer.endUndoGrouping()
        default:break
        }
    }
```

Undo Interface

We must also decide how to let the user *request* Undo and Redo. In developing the code from the preceding section, I used two buttons: an Undo button that sent undo to the NSUndoManager, and a Redo button that sent redo to the NSUndoManager. This can be a perfectly reasonable interface, but let's talk about some others.

Shake-To-Edit

By default, your app supports *shake-to-edit*. This means the user can shake the device to bring up an undo/redo interface. We discussed this briefly in Chapter 22. If you don't turn off this feature by setting the shared UIApplication's applicationSupportsShake-ToEdit property to false, then when the user shakes the device, the runtime walks up the responder chain, starting with the first responder, looking for a responder whose inherited undoManager property returns an actual NSUndoManager instance. If it finds one, it puts up an undo/redo interface, allowing the user to communicate with that NSUndoManager.

You will recall what it takes for a UIResponder to be first responder in this sense: it must return true from canBecomeFirstResponder, and it must actually be made first responder through a call to becomeFirstResponder. Let's make MyView satisfy these requirements. For example, we might call becomeFirstResponder at the end of dragging:, like this:

```
override func canBecomeFirstResponder() -> Bool {
    return true
}
func dragging (p : UIPanGestureRecognizer) {
    switch p.state {
    // ... the rest as before ...
    case .Ended, .Cancelled:
        self.undoer.endUndoGrouping()
```

Figure 26-1. The shake-to-edit undo/redo interface

```
        self.becomeFirstResponder()
    default:break
    }
}
```

Then, to make shake-to-edit work, we have only to provide a getter for the `undo-Manager` property that returns our undo manager, `self.undoer`:

```
let undoer = NSUndoManager()
override var undoManager : NSUndoManager {
    get {
        return self.undoer
    }
}
```

This works: shaking the device now brings up the undo/redo interface, and its buttons work correctly. However, I don't like the way the buttons are labeled; they just say Undo and Redo. To make this interface more expressive, we should provide a string describing each undoable action by calling `setActionName:`. We can appropriately and conveniently do this in `setCenterUndoably:`, as follows:

```
self.undoer.prepareWithInvocationTarget(self)
    .setCenterUndoably(self.center)
self.undoer.setActionName("Move")
// ... and so on ...
```

Now the undo/redo interface has more informative labels, as shown in Figure 26-1.

Undo Menu

Another possible interface is through a menu (Figure 26-2). Personally, I prefer this approach, as I am not fond of shake-to-edit (it seems both violent and unreliable). This is the same menu used by a UITextField or UITextView for displaying the Copy and Paste menu items (Chapter 10). The requirements for summoning this menu are effectively the same as those for shake-to-edit: we need a responder chain with a first

Figure 26-2. The shared menu as an undo/redo interface

responder at the bottom of it. So the code we've just supplied for making MyView first responder remains applicable.

We can make a menu appear, for example, in response to a long press on our MyView instance. So let's attach another gesture recognizer to MyView. This will be a UILong-PressGestureRecognizer, whose action handler is called `longPress:`. Recall from Chapter 10 how to implement the menu: we get the singleton global UIMenuController object and specify an array of custom UIMenuItems as its `menuItems` property. We can make the menu appear by sending the UIMenuController the `setMenuVisible:animated:` message. But a particular menu item will appear in the menu only if we also return `true` from `canPerformAction:withSender:` for that menu item's action. Delightfully, the NSUndoManager's `canUndo` and `canRedo` methods tell us what value `canPerform-Action:withSender:` should return. We can also get the titles for our custom menu items from the NSUndoManager itself, by calling `undoMenuItemTitle:`

```
func longPress (g : UIGestureRecognizer) {
    if g.state == .Began {
        let m = UIMenuController.sharedMenuController()
        m.setTargetRect(self.bounds, inView: self)
        let mi1 = UIMenuItem(
            title: self.undoer.undoMenuItemTitle, action: "undo:")
        let mi2 = UIMenuItem(
            title: self.undoer.redoMenuItemTitle, action: "redo:")
        m.menuItems = [mi1, mi2]
        m.setMenuVisible(true, animated:true)
    }
}
override func canPerformAction(
    action: Selector, withSender sender: AnyObject!) -> Bool {
        if action == Selector("undo:") {
            return self.undoer.canUndo
        }
        if action == Selector("redo:") {
            return self.undoer.canRedo
        }
        return super.canPerformAction(action, withSender: sender)
```

```
}
func undo(_:AnyObject?) {
    self.undoer.undo()
}
func redo(_:AnyObject?) {
    self.undoer.redo()
}
```

Application Lifetime Events

Your app's one and only application object (a UIApplication instance, or on rare occasions a UIApplication subclass instance) is created for you as the shared application object by UIApplicationMain, along with its delegate; in the Xcode project templates, this is an instance of the AppDelegate class. The application reports lifetime events through method calls to its delegate; other instances can also register to receive most of these events as notifications.

What application lifetime events you can receive depends on whether or not your app participates in *multitasking*. It almost certainly will. In the old days, before iOS 4, there was no multitasking. If the user pressed the Home button while running your app, your app was terminated. The next time the user launched your app by tapping its icon, your app launched from scratch. Even today, your app can opt out of multitasking and behave like a pre–iOS 4 app, if you set the "Application does not run in background" key (UIApplicationExitsOnSuspend) in your *Info.plist*. For some apps, such as certain games, this might be a reasonable thing to do.

In the multitasking world, however, the Home button doesn't terminate your app; it *backgrounds and suspends* it. This means that your app is essentially freeze-dried in the background; its process still exists, but it isn't actively running, and it isn't getting any events — though notifications can be stored by the system for later delivery if your app comes to the front once again. If your app is terminated, it's not because the user switches away from it, but because the system has killed it while it was suspended — for example, because it needed to reclaim the memory your suspended app was using, or because the user switched off the device.

(A backgrounded app can, however, continue to run certain specialized activities, such as playing music, and a backgrounded app can be woken periodically in order to update its data via the network. See Chapters 14, 22, and 24. So a backgrounded app isn't always necessarily completely suspended. But in general, most backgrounded apps are suspended most of the time.)

The suite of basic application lifetime events in the multitasking world is quite limited; indeed, in my opinion, the information your app is given is unfortunately rather too coarse-grained. The events are as follows:

`application:didFinishLaunchingWithOptions:`
> The app has started up. You'll typically perform initializations here. If an app doesn't have a main storyboard, this code must also create the app's window and show it.
>
> (Another event, `application:willFinishLaunchingWithOptions:`, arrives even earlier. Its purpose is to allow your app to participate in the state saving and restoration mechanism discussed in Chapter 6.)

`applicationDidBecomeActive:`
> Received after `application:didFinishLaunchingWithOptions:`. Also received after the end of the situation that caused the app delegate to receive `applicationWillResignActive:`.

`applicationWillResignActive:`
> One possibility is that something has blocked the app's interface — for example, the screen has been locked. A local notification alert or an incoming phone call could also cause this event. When this situation ends, the app delegate will receive `applicationDidBecomeActive:`.
>
> Alternatively, the app may be about to go into the background (and will then be suspended); in that case, the next event will be `applicationDidEnterBackground:`.

`applicationDidEnterBackground:`
> The application has been backgrounded (and is probably about to be suspended). Always preceded by `applicationWillResignActive:`.

`applicationWillEnterForeground:`
> The application was backgrounded, and is now coming back to the front. Always followed by `applicationDidBecomeActive:`. Note that this message is *not* sent on launch, because the app wasn't previously in the background.

An additional event, `applicationWillTerminate:`, was your last signal in the non-multitasking world to preserve state and perform other final cleanup tasks. In the multitasking world, however, you'll probably *never* get `applicationWillTerminate:`, because by the time your app is terminated by the system, it was already suspended and incapable of receiving events. (I'll mention an exception, though, in a moment; and see Chapter 14 for another.)

The application lifetime events are best understood through some typical scenarios:

The app launches freshly
> Your app delegate receives these messages:

- `application:didFinishLaunchingWithOptions:`
- `applicationDidBecomeActive:`

The user clicks the Home button
Your app delegate receives these messages:

- `applicationWillResignActive:`
- `applicationDidEnterBackground:`

Your app will then probably be suspended; before that happens, you have a little time to finish up last-minute tasks, such as relinquishing unneeded memory (see Chapter 6), and if you need more time for a lengthy task, you can ask for it (see Chapter 25).

The user summons your backgrounded app to the front
Your app delegate receives these messages:

- `applicationWillEnterForeground:`
- `applicationDidBecomeActive:`

If the user summons your backgrounded app to the front indirectly, another delegate message may be sent between these two calls. For example, if the user asks another app to hand a file over to your app (Chapter 23), your app receives `application:handleOpenURL:` between `applicationWillEnterForeground:` and `applicationDidBecomeActive:`.

The user double-clicks the Home button
The user can now work in the app switcher interface. If your app is frontmost, your app delegate receives this message:

- `applicationWillResignActive:`

The user, in the app switcher, chooses another app
If your app was frontmost, your app delegate receives this message:

- `applicationDidEnterBackground:`

The user, in the app switcher, chooses your app
If your app was the most recently frontmost app, then it was never backgrounded, so your app delegate receives this message:

- `applicationDidBecomeActive:`

The user summons the control center or notification center
If your app is frontmost, your app delegate receives this message:

- `applicationWillResignActive:`

The user dismisses the control center or notification center
If your app is frontmost, your app delegate receives this message:

- `applicationDidBecomeActive:`

A local notification alert from another app appears
If your app is frontmost, your app delegate receives this message:

- `applicationWillResignActive:`

From a local notification alert, the user launches the other app
Your app delegate receives this message:

- `applicationDidEnterBackground:`

The screen is locked
If your app is frontmost, your app delegate receives these messages:

- `applicationWillResignActive:`
- `applicationDidEnterBackground:`

The screen is unlocked
If your app is frontmost, your app delegate receives these messages:

- `applicationWillEnterForeground:`
- `applicationDidBecomeActive:`

The user holds the screen-lock button down
The device offers to shut itself down. If your app is frontmost, your app delegate receives this message:

- `applicationWillResignActive:`

The user, as the device offers to shut itself down, cancels
If your app is frontmost, your app delegate receives this message:

- `applicationDidBecomeActive:`

The user, as the device offers to shut itself down, accepts
If your app is frontmost, the app delegate receives these messages:

- `applicationDidEnterBackground:`
- `applicationWillTerminate:` (probably the only way a normal app will receive this message in a multitasking world)

Unfortunately, you can't make any assumptions about the *timing* of the app delegate messages with respect to lifetime events received by other objects. They may well be interwoven in surprising ways. For example, the root view controller may receive its initial lifetime events, such as `viewDidLoad:` and `viewWillAppear:`, before `application:didFinishLaunchingWithOptions:` has even finished running.

New in iOS 8, the app delegate receives `applicationDidBecomeActive:` *after* the root view controller's interface has appeared and the root view controller has received `viewDidAppear:`. This change has been a disaster for many of my apps. I very typically register for `UIApplicationDidBecomeActiveNotification` in the view controller's `viewDidAppear:` in order to be notified of *subsequent* activations of the app; in iOS 8, however, that notification now arrives *immediately*.

Some Useful Utility Functions

As you work with iOS and Swift, you'll doubtless develop a personal library of frequently used convenience functions. Here are some that have come in handy in my own life, to which I've referred in the course of this book.

Delayed Performance

Delayed performance is of paramount importance in iOS programming, where it is often the case that the interface must be given a moment to settle down before we proceed to the next command in a sequence. Calling `dispatch_after` is particularly tedious in Swift, because its strict numeric typing necessitates a lot of casting, so here's a utility function:

```
func delay(delay:Double, closure:()->()) {
    dispatch_after(
        dispatch_time(
            DISPATCH_TIME_NOW,
            Int64(delay * Double(NSEC_PER_SEC))
        ),
        dispatch_get_main_queue(), closure)
}
```

And call it like this:

```
delay(0.4) {
    // do something here
}
```

In my world, this is far and away the most important utility function; I use it in every single app.

Center of a CGRect

One so frequently wants the center point of a CGRect that even the Swift shorthand `CGPointMake(rect.midX, rect.midY)` becomes tedious. You can extend CGRect to do the work for you:

```
extension CGRect {
    var center : CGPoint {
        return CGPointMake(self.midX, self.midY)
    }
}
```

Adjust a CGSize

There's a CGRect `inset` (or `rectByInsetting`), but there's no comparable method for changing an existing CGSize by a width delta and a height delta. Let's make one:

```
extension CGSize {
    func sizeByDelta(#dw:CGFloat, dh:CGFloat) -> CGSize {
        return CGSizeMake(self.width + dw, self.height + dh)
    }
}
```

Dictionary of Views

There are no Swift macros (because there's no Swift preprocessor), so you can't write the equivalent of Objective-C's `NSDictionaryOfVariableBindings`, which turns a literal list of view names into a dictionary of string names and view references for use in connection with NSLayoutConstraint's `constraintsWithVisualFormat`. You can, however, generate such a dictionary with fixed string names, like this:

```
func dictionaryOfNames(arr:UIView...) -> [String:UIView] {
    var d = [String:UIView]()
    for (ix,v) in enumerate(arr) {
        d["v\(ix+1)"] = v
    }
    return d
}
```

This utility function takes a list of views and simply makes up new string names for them, of the form `"v1"`, `"v2"`, and so on, in order. Knowing the rule by which the string names are generated, you then use those string names in your visual format strings. For example, if you generate the dictionary by calling `dictionaryOfNames(mainView, myLabel)`, then in any visual format string that uses this dictionary, you will refer to `mainView` by the name `v1` and `myLabel` by the name `v2`.

Constraint Issues

These are NSLayoutConstraint class methods, added in an extension, aimed at helping to detect and analyze constraint issues (referred to in Chapter 1):

```
extension NSLayoutConstraint {
    class func reportAmbiguity (var v:UIView?) {
        if v == nil {
            v = UIApplication.sharedApplication().keyWindow
        }
        for vv in v!.subviews as! [UIView] {
            println("\(vv) \(vv.hasAmbiguousLayout())")
            if vv.subviews.count > 0 {
                self.reportAmbiguity(vv)
            }
        }
    }
    class func listConstraints (var v:UIView?) {
        if v == nil {
            v = UIApplication.sharedApplication().keyWindow
        }
        for vv in v!.subviews as! [UIView] {
            let arr1 = vv.constraintsAffectingLayoutForAxis(.Horizontal)
            let arr2 = vv.constraintsAffectingLayoutForAxis(.Vertical)
            NSLog("\n\n%@\nH: %@\nV:%@", vv, arr1, arr2);
            if vv.subviews.count > 0 {
                self.listConstraints(vv)
            }
        }
    }
}
```

Drawing Into an Image Context

Our goal here is to encapsulate the boring, repetitive, clunky, imperative-programming dance of beginning a UIGraphics image context, drawing into it, extracting the image, and ending the context. This utility function expresses everything but the drawing; you hand the function a closure describing the drawing, and the function returns an image:

```
func imageOfSize(size:CGSize, opaque:Bool = false, closure:() -> ())
    -> UIImage {
        UIGraphicsBeginImageContextWithOptions(size, opaque, 0)
        closure()
        let result = UIGraphicsGetImageFromCurrentImageContext()
        UIGraphicsEndImageContext()
        return result
}
```

You call it like this:

```
let im = imageOfSize(CGSizeMake(100,100)) {
    let con = UIGraphicsGetCurrentContext()
    CGContextAddEllipseInRect(con, CGRectMake(0,0,100,100))
    CGContextSetFillColorWithColor(con, UIColor.blueColor().CGColor)
    CGContextFillPath(con)
}
```

Finite Repetition of an Animation

This is a generalized version of the tail-recursion example in Chapter 4 showing how to repeat a view animation a small fixed number of times. Because of Swift's limitations against a local function recursing while capturing the environment, it is simplest to implement this as two class functions, a wrapper function that provides the API to the caller and a recursing helper function that does the actual work:

```
extension UIView {
    class func animateWithTimes(times:Int, duration: NSTimeInterval,
        delay: NSTimeInterval, options: UIViewAnimationOptions,
        animations: () -> Void, completion: ((Bool) -> Void)?) {
            self.animHelper(
                times-1, duration, delay, options, animations, completion)
    }
    class func animHelper(t:Int, _ dur: NSTimeInterval, _ del: NSTimeInterval,
        _ opt: UIViewAnimationOptions,
        _ anim: () -> Void, _ com: ((Bool) -> Void)?) {
            UIView.animateWithDuration(dur, delay: del, options: opt,
                animations: anim, completion: {
                    done in
                    if com != nil {
                        com!(done)
                    }
                    if t > 0 {
                        self.animHelper(t-1, dur, del, opt, anim, com)
                    }
            })
    }
}
```

The calling syntax is exactly like ordering a UIView animation in its full form, except that there's an initial **times** parameter:

```
let opts = UIViewAnimationOptions.Autoreverse
let xorig = self.v.center.x
UIView.animateWithTimes(3, duration:1, delay:0, options:opts, animations:{
    self.v.center.x += 100
    }, completion:{
        _ in
        self.v.center.x = xorig
})
```

Remove Multiple Indexes From Array

It is often convenient to collect the indexes of items to be deleted from an array, and then to delete those items. An Array extension can be helpful here. We must be careful to sort the indexes in decreasing numeric order first, because array indexes will be off by one after an item at a lower index is removed:

```
extension Array {
    mutating func removeAtIndexes (ixs:[Int]) -> () {
        for i in ixs.sorted(>) {
            self.removeAtIndex(i)
        }
    }
}
```

Configure a Value Class At the Point of Use

A recurring pattern in Cocoa is that a value class is instantiated and that instance is configured beforehand for a one-time use:

```
let para = NSMutableParagraphStyle()
para.headIndent = 10
para.firstLineHeadIndent = 10
para.tailIndent = -10
para.lineBreakMode = .ByWordWrapping
para.alignment = .Center
para.paragraphSpacing = 15
content.addAttribute(
    NSParagraphStyleAttributeName,
    value:para, range:NSMakeRange(0,1))
```

This has a clunky, procedural feel. It would clearer and more functional, as well as reflecting the natural order of thought, if all of that could happen at the actual point of use. Here's a generic function that permits us to do that:

```
func lend<T where T:NSObject> (closure:(T)->()) -> T {
    let orig = T()
    closure(orig)
    return orig
}
```

Now we can express ourselves like this:

```
content.addAttribute(NSParagraphStyleAttributeName,
    value:lend {
        (para:NSMutableParagraphStyle) in
        para.headIndent = 10
        para.firstLineHeadIndent = 10
        para.tailIndent = -10
```

```
            para.lineBreakMode = .ByWordWrapping
            para.alignment = .Center
            para.paragraphSpacing = 15
    }, range:NSMakeRange(0,1))
```

Cancelable Closure-Based Timer

The Objective-C methods performSelector:withObject:afterDelay: and cancel-
PreviousPerformRequestsWithTarget: are unavailable in Swift, so it would be nice to
have an alternative. My replacement is a class, CancelableTimer; it is basically a combination of a Swift closure and a GCD timer dispatch source. The initializer is
init(once:handler:). The handler: is called when the timer fires. If once: is false,
this will be a repeating timer. It obeys two methods, startWithInterval: and cancel:

```
class CancelableTimer: NSObject {
    private var q = dispatch_queue_create("timer",nil)
    private var timer : dispatch_source_t!
    private var firsttime = true
    private var once : Bool
    private var handler : () -> ()
    init(once:Bool, handler:()->()) {
        self.once = once
        self.handler = handler
        super.init()
    }
    func startWithInterval(interval:Double) {
        self.firsttime = true
        self.cancel()
        self.timer = dispatch_source_create(
            DISPATCH_SOURCE_TYPE_TIMER,
            0, 0, self.q)
        dispatch_source_set_timer(self.timer,
            dispatch_walltime(nil, 0),
            UInt64(interval * Double(NSEC_PER_SEC)),
            UInt64(0.05 * Double(NSEC_PER_SEC)))
        dispatch_source_set_event_handler(self.timer, {
            if self.firsttime {
                self.firsttime = false
                return
            }
            self.handler()
            if self.once {
                self.cancel()
            }
        })
        dispatch_resume(self.timer)
    }
    func cancel() {
        if self.timer != nil {
```

```
            dispatch_source_cancel(timer)
        }
    }
}
```

Generic Wrapper

This is the generic wrapper class used in Chapter 24. I didn't think of this; the idea comes from a Stack Overflow post (*http://stackoverflow.com/a/24760061/341994*):

```
class Wrapper<T> {
    let p:T
    init(_ p:T){self.p = p}
}
```

This is useful because it is an AnyObject and can therefore be passed into an Objective-C API wherever an AnyObject is expected. Making a Wrapper object is easy:

```
let w = Wrapper(anything)
```

Retrieving the `anything` when a Wrapper returns to you as an AnyObject requires that you discover, or know in advance, the type of its p and that you cast to that type:

```
let thing : AnyObject = // some kind of Wrapper
let realthing = (thing as! Wrapper).p as SomeType
```

Index

We'd like to hear your suggestions for improving our indexes. Send email to index@oreilly.com.

About the Author

Matt Neuburg has a PhD in Classics and has taught at many universities and colleges. He has been programming computers since 1968. He has written applications for OS X and iOS, is a former editor of *MacTech Magazine*, and is a long-standing contributing editor for TidBITS. His previous O'Reilly books are *Frontier: The Definitive Guide*, *REALbasic: The Definitive Guide*, and *AppleScript: The Definitive Guide*. He makes a living writing books, articles, and software documentation, as well as by programming, consulting, and training.

Colophon

The animal on the cover of *Programming iOS 8* is a kingbird, one of the 13 species of North American songbirds making up the genus *Tyrannus*. A group of kingbirds is called a "coronation," a "court," or a "tyranny."

Kingbirds eat insects, which they often catch in flight, swooping from a perch to grab the insect midair. They may also supplement their diets with berries and fruits. They have long, pointed wings, and males perform elaborate aerial courtship displays.

Both the genus name (meaning "tyrant" or "despot") and the common name ("king bird") refer to these birds' aggressive defense of their territories, breeding areas, and mates. They have been documented attacking red-tailed hawks (which are more than twenty times their size), knocking bluejays out of trees, and driving away crows and ravens. (For its habit of standing up to much larger birds, the gray kingbird has been adopted as a Puerto Rican nationalist symbol.)

"Kingbird" most often refers to the Eastern kingbird (*T. tyrannus*), an average-size kingbird (7.5–9 inches long, wingspan 13–15 inches) found all across North America. This common and widespread bird has a dark head and back, with a white throat, chest, and belly. Its red crown patch is rarely seen. Its high-pitched, buzzing, stuttering sounds have been described as resembling "sparks jumping between wires" or an electric fence.

The cover image is from *Cassell's Natural History*. The cover fonts are URW Typewriter and Guardian Sans. The text font is Adobe Minion Pro; the heading font is Adobe Myriad Condensed; and the code font is Dalton Maag's Ubuntu Mono.

Have it your way.

Get even more for your money.